DON'T THROW THIS CARD AWAY!
THIS MAY BE REQUIRED FOR YOUR COURSE!

THOMSON ONE Business School Edition

Congratulations!

Your purchase of this NEW textbook includes complimentary access to THOMSON ONE – Business School Edition for Accounting. THOMSON ONE – Business School Edition is a Web-based portal product that provides integrated access to Thomson Financial content for the purpose of financial analysis. This is an educational version of the same financial resources used by Wall Street analysts on a daily basis!

For hundreds of companies, this online resource provides seamless access to:

- **Current and Past Company Data:** Worldscope which includes company profiles, financials and accounting results, market per-share data, annual information, and monthly prices going back to 1980.

- **Financial Analyst Data and Forecasts:** I/B/E/S Consensus Estimates which provides consensus estimates, analyst-by-analyst earnings coverage, and analysts' forecasts.

- **SEC Disclosure Statements:** Disclosure SEC Database which includes company profiles, annual and quarterly company financials, pricing information, and earnings.

- **And More!**

THOMSON ONE Business School Edition

ACCESS CODE

PP21QV6PPLMJP6

HOW TO REGISTER YOUR ACCESS CODE

1. Launch a web browser and go to **http://tabseacct.swlearning.com**

2. Click the "Register" button to enter your access code.

3. Enter your access code **exactly** as it appears here and create a unique User ID, or enter an existing User ID if you have previously registered for a different South-Western product via an access code.

4. When prompted, create a password (or enter an existing password, if you have previously registered for a different product via an access code.) Submit the necessary information when prompted. **Record your User ID and password in a secure location.**

5. Once registered, return to the URL above and select the "Enter" button; have your User ID and password handy.

NOTE: The duration of your access to the product begins when registration is complete.

For technical support, contact 1-800-423-0563 or email **tl.support@thomson.com**

Clyde P. Stickney   Roman L. Weil
Dartmouth College   University of Chicago

Financial Accounting
11th Edition

An Introduction to
Concepts, Methods, and Uses

THOMSON
SOUTH-WESTERN

Australia · Canada · Mexico · Singapore · Spain · United Kingdom · United States

THOMSON

SOUTH-WESTERN

Financial Accounting: An Introduction to Concepts, Methods, and Uses, 11e
Clyde P. Stickney, Roman L. Weil

VP/Editorial Director:
Jack W. Calhoun

Publisher:
Rob Dewey

Acquisitions Editor:
Julie Moulton

Developmental Editor:
Carol Bennett

Production Editor:
Heather Mann

Manufacturing Coordinator:
Doug Wilke

Technology Project Editor:
Robin Browning

Web Coordinator:
Kelly Reid

Art Director:
Chris Miller

Production House:
Navta Associates, Inc.

Cover Designer:
Beckmeyer Design

Cover Image:
© Corbis

Internal Designer:
Beckmeyer Design

Printer:
RR Donnelley
Willard, OH

For

Baillie, Charlie Parker, Greta, Isabella, and Lily

For

Kathy and Katherine

With Thanks

For Our Students

Whatever be the detail with which you cram your students, the chance of their meeting in after-life exactly that detail is infinitesimal; and if they do meet it, they will probably have forgotten what you taught them about it. The really useful training yields a comprehension of a few general principles with a thorough grounding in the way they apply to a variety of concrete details. In subsequent practice the students will have forgotten your particular details; but they will remember by an unconscious common sense how to apply principles to immediate circumstances.

Alfred North Whitehead
The Aims of Education and Other Essays

WARNING: Study of this book is known to cause thinking, occasionally deep thinking. Typical side effects include mild temporary anxiety followed by profound long-term understanding and satisfaction.

Preface

*O*ver the years, we have come to refer to our book's title by the acronym FACMU—Financial Accounting: An Introduction to Concepts, Methods, and Uses. We take concepts, methods, and uses to be the central elements in learning and teaching about financial accounting.

Although it incorporates changes large and small throughout its chapters, the eleventh edition of *FACMU* has the same principal objectives as the previous editions.

- To help students develop a sufficient understanding of the basic concepts underlying financial statements so that they can apply the concepts to new and different situations.
- To train students in accounting terminology and methods so that they can interpret, analyze, and evaluate financial statements currently published in corporate annual reports.

Most introductory financial accounting textbooks state these, or similar, objectives. Textbooks differ in their relative emphasis on concepts, methods, and uses.

1. **Concepts**   This book emphasizes the rationale for, and implications of, important accounting concepts. To learn accounting, students must develop the ability to conceptualize the transactions that accounting summarizes and the process of summarization. Without such concepts, students will have difficulty focusing on the relevant issues in new and different situations.

   Each chapter begins by identifying important accounting concepts. Several numerical examples illustrating their application then follow. The end-of-chapter material includes numerous short exercises and longer problems to check students' ability to apply the concepts to different situations.

2. **Methods**   We place sufficient emphasis on accounting procedures so students can interpret, analyze, and evaluate published financial statements. The text does not emphasize procedures to such an extent that students bog down in detail. All writers of accounting textbooks must decide just how much accounting procedure to include. We believe students will learn most effectively by working exercises and problems. Too much emphasis on accounting procedures lulls students into the security of thinking they understand accounting concepts when they do not. For many years we have used the mixture of concepts and procedures in this book and have found it effective in the classroom.

   Understanding the accounting implications of an event requires that students construct the journal entry for that event. Throughout this book we use journal entries in describing the nature of accounting events. Moreover, most chapters contain exercises and problems that require the analysis of transactions with debits and credits. Do not conclude by a glance at this text that it is primarily procedural. We want students to learn concepts, and believe that the procedures enhance the learning of concepts.

3. **Uses**   This book attempts to bridge the gap between the preparation of financial statements and their use in various decisions. The chapters consider the effects of alternative accounting principles on the measurement of earnings and financial position and the appropriate interpretations of them. Numerous problems based on financial statement data of actual companies appear at the end of most chapters.

Changes in this Edition

The most important changes made in this revision are as follows:

1. **Replace T-accounts with Microsoft Excel spreadsheet for recording transactions.**   We have found our students increasingly use an Excel spreadsheet when they prepare solutions to assigned problems that require them to record transactions and generate balance sheets and income statements. We have substituted a spreadsheet for T-accounts for the recording transactions in **Chapters 2** and **3**. The web site for the book contains a transactions spreadsheet template for students' use in preparing solutions to problems (see **Exhibit 2.2** on page **54**). We continue to use journal entries in these chapters and in the remainder of the book to illustrate the effects of transactions on the financial statements. The web site for the book provides a description of the use of T-accounts for instructors to distribute to their students if the instructor prefers their students to use T-accounts instead of a spreadsheet.

2. **Increased emphasis on the direct method of computing cash flow from operations.** Our students encounter difficulty with the indirect method of computing cash flow from operations when they initially study the statement of cash flows in **Chapter 4.** We have found that introducing the direct method initially helps them to understand the adjustments required to convert net income to cash flow from operations under the indirect method. Chapter 4 therefore places increased emphasis on the direct method, for which the FASB has expressed a preference, without deleting material on the indirect method commonly found in practice. Consistent with substituting an Excel spreadsheet for T-accounts in **Chapters 2** and **3**, we delete the T-account work sheet used in previous editions for preparing the statement of cash flows and instead use a columnar work sheet.

3. **Increased emphasis on ethical considerations in financial reporting.** We have been reluctant in previous editions to include material on ethical considerations in financial reporting, in part because we find some of our students bristle at our trying to impart our value systems to them. The events of recent years convince us that we should at least attempt to increase students' sensitivity to ethical issues and encourage them to think carefully and systematically about how they would deal with such situations. We include a new section on identifying and reflecting on ethical concerns in **Chapter 1.** Subsequent chapters include problems and questions that address ethical issues.

4. **Increased use of the financial statements of Wal-Mart Stores.** **Chapter 1** of the previous edition used Wal-Mart Stores (Wal-Mart) to illustrate the form and content of the principal financial statements. This edition uses Wal-Mart more extensively in subsequent chapters to illustrate various topics. **Chapter 5** uses Wal-Mart to illustrate the calculation and interpretation of financial statement ratios.

5. **Increased use of real world examples.** Enron, Global Crossing, Qwest Communications, Xerox, and others provide rich examples of financial reporting choices that firms have made. We incorporate these into the text and problems at the end of the chapters.

6. **Shift of more complex topics to the website.** The previous edition moved complex material on deferred taxes, foreign currency translation, pension plans, and others to the web site. We continue this practice by placing material on accounting for derivatives, and consolidated financial statement preparation on the web site. We have also placed material on the statement of cash flows (**Chapter 13** of the previous edition) and synthesis of GAAP (**Chapter 14** of the previous edition) on the web site.

7. **Inclusion of more short exercises.** Each chapter now includes seven to ten short exercises, in addition to the longer exercises used in previous editions. Exercises generally focus on a single concept. The short exercises permit students to grasp quickly the important concepts discussed in the chapters as a prelude to working longer exercises and problems

8. **Inclusion of new or revised end-of-chapter materials.** We have revised or replaced approximately 30 percent of the end-of-chapter questions, exercises, problems, and cases.

Organization

This book comprises three major parts:

- Part One: "Overview of Financial Statements," consisting of **Chapter 1**.
- Part Two: "Accounting Concepts and Methods," **Chapters 2** through **5**.
- Part Three: "Measuring and Reporting Assets and Equities," **Chapters 6** through **12**.

In our view, the three parts are steps in the learning process. **Part One** presents a general overview of the principal financial statements. **Part Two** discusses the basic accounting model accountants use to generate the principal financial statements. **Part Three** considers the specific accounting principles or methods used in preparing the financial statements. This organization reflects the view that learning takes place most effectively when students begin with a broad picture, then break up that broad picture into smaller pieces until achieving the desired depth.

Chapter 1 presents a brief description of the principal activities of a business firm (goal setting and strategy formulation, investing, financing, and operating) and shows how the three principal financial statements—the balance sheet, the income statement, and the statement of cash flows—report the results of these activities. We use the business activities and the financial statements of Wal-Mart to illustrate the important concepts. Chapter 1 also provides an overview of the financial reporting environment. Many students feel deluged with the multitude of new terms and concepts after reading Chapter 1. Most of these same students admit later that the broad overview helped piece material together as they later explored individual topics at greater length.

Chapters 2 through **4** present the basic accounting model that generates the three principal financial statements. In each case, the discussion begins with a description of the important concepts underlying each statement. The chapter then describes and illustrates procedures accountants use to generate the financial statements. Each chapter uses the balance sheet equation or changes in the balance sheet equation to motivate understanding of the preparation procedures. Although these chapters emphasize debit/credit procedures, instructors can use the balance sheet equation approach to communicate the basics of statement preparation. **Chapters 2** and **3** use an Excel spreadsheet based on the balance sheet equation as a tool for recording transactions. Each of these chapters includes one or more simple problems that students can work using the balance sheet approach to prepare the principal financial statements. Unlike treatments in other texts, **Chapter 3** integrates the accounting entries for transactions during a period with the related adjusting entries at the end of the period. When textbooks discuss these two types of entries in separate chapters, students often lose sight of the fact that measurement of net income and financial position requires both kinds of entries.

We continue to put coverage of the statement of cash flows early in the text (**Chapter 4**). This placement serves two purposes. First, it elevates the statement to its rightful place among the three principal financial statements. Students can thereby integrate the concepts of profitability and cash flow more effectively and begin to understand that one does not necessarily accompany the other. Covering this statement at the end of the course (in many cases, when time is running out) can lead students to think the cash flow statement less important. Placing this chapter early in the book forces the student to cement understanding of the basic accounting model from **Chapters 2** and **3**. Preparing the statement of cash flows requires the student to work backward from the balance sheet and income statement to reconstruct the transactions that took place. As the previous section discussed, we place increased emphasis on the direct method of computing cash flow from operations, without detracting from the importance of understanding the indirect method.

Chapters 2, **3**, and **4** each conclude with a section on analyzing and interpreting financial statements, serving as a prelude to the integrated analysis of profitability and risk in **Chapter 5**.

Chapter 5 describes and illustrates tools for analyzing the financial statements, using the financial statements of Wal-Mart. The discussion structures the various financial statement ratios in a multi-level format that students have found minimizes the need to memorize formulas. Instructors who incorporate annual reports of actual companies throughout their course will find that analysis of the financial statements of such companies provides effective synthesis at this point. An appendix to Chapter 5 illustrates procedures for preparing pro forma financial statements. This topic helps cement understanding of the relation among the three principal financial statements.

Chapters 6 through **12** discuss the various generally accepted accounting principles that accountants use in generating the financial statements. Each chapter not only describes and illustrates the application of the various accounting methods but also considers their effects on the financial statements. This approach reflects the view that students should be able to interpret and analyze published financial statements and to understand the effect of alternative accounting methods on such assessments. The quality of earnings issue appears throughout these chapters.

An appendix to the book describes compound interest and present value computations.

The end of the book includes a comprehensive **glossary** of accounting terms. It serves as a useful reference tool for accounting and other business terms and provides additional descriptions of a few topics, such as accounting changes and inventory profit, considered only briefly in the text.

The web site for the book (http://facmu.swlearning.com) includes interactive quizzes, additional cases, and expanded discussion of topics in the text, including income taxes, retirement benefits, derivatives, consolidation, foreign currency translation, and general price-level accounting.

Related Materials Accompanying the Textbook

The following supplementary materials augment the textbook.

Instructor's Manual   The instructor's manual presents suggested outlines for courses of varying lengths, a list of chapter objectives, helpful teaching hints, and detailed lecture and discussion outlines, including the numbers of particularly relevant questions, exercises, problems, and cases. The instructor's manual also presents a listing showing the correspondence between problem material in this and the previous (tenth) edition.

Solutions Manual   The solutions manual provides full solutions for all end-of-chapter assignment items, including questions, exercises, problems, and cases. Computations show how we reach a particular answer.

Study Guide   This study guide, by LeBrone C. Harris and James E. Moon, lists highlights from each chapter and provides numerous short true/false, matching, multiple-choice questions, and exercises, with answers.

Test Bank   Prepared by Peter Ben Ezra of George Washington University, the test bank includes multiple-choice items, matching questions, short essay questions, and problems.

ExamView Computerized Testing Software   All items in the test bank are available in ExamView, computerized testing software format for Microsoft Windows. This supplement allows instructors to add or edit questions, instructions, and answers by previewing them onscreen. They can also create and administer quizzes online—whether over the internet, a local area network (LAN), or wide area network (WAN).

Lecture Presentation Software in PowerPoint   Sample lectures, created by Michael Blue of Bloomburg, aid in lecture preparation by those using this text. Software is available by download on the book's Web site.

 Spreadsheet Template Software   At least three problems per chapter indicated in the margin have a corresponding template where basic problem data appear on a Microsoft Excel Spreadsheet to reduce tedium in solving problems and increase student awareness of basic software applications. Software is available by download on the book's Web site.

Solutions Transparencies   A package of solutions acetates contains all numerical end-of-chapter exercises, problems, and cases and some key exhibits from the text.

WebTutor Toolbox on WebCT and Blackboard   WebTutor allows instructors to easily teach their course online and provides students with online learning features that make learning financial accounting easier and more portable.

Instructors can contact their Thomson Business and Professional Publishing/South-Western sales representative for information and samples of these items.

Acknowledgments

We gratefully acknowledge the helpful criticisms and suggestions of the following people who used the previous edition or reviewed the manuscript for this edition:

Andrew W. Alford
Matthew J. Anderson Michigan State University
Joseph H. Anthony Michigan State University
Gary C. Biddle Hong Kong University of Science and Technology
Peggy Bishop University of Pennsylvania
Germain B. Boer Vanderbilt University
Paul R. Brown New York University
Robert M. Bushman University of North Carolina
Jake Cohen Harvard Business School
Kevin M. Devine Xavier University
Elizabeth Demers University of Rochester
Gordon L. Duke University of Minnesota

Kirsten M. Ely Georgia Institute of Technology
Merle M. Erickson University of Chicago
Kathleen Fitzgerald University of Chicago
Suresh Govindaraj Rutgers University
Parveen P. Gupta Lehigh University
Doug Hanna Southern Methodist University
Sheila Handy Lafayette College
Bertrand N. Horwitz SUNY Binghamton
Jennifer J. Jones Duke University
A. Ronald Kucic University of Denver
Bob Hartman University of Iowa
James A. Largay III Lehigh University
Laureen A. Maines Indiana University
Edward L. Maydew University of North Carolina
Alan P. Mayer-Sommer Georgetown University
Michael G. McMillan Johns Hopkins University
Janette Moody The Citadel
Patricia C. O'Brien University of Waterloo
Steve Orpurt Southern Methodist University
Eugene Orza Major League Baseball Players' Association
Glen E. Owen
Glenn Pfeiffer Chapman College
George Plesko MIT/Sloan
Gordon S. Potter Cornell University
Grace Pownall Emory University
Alan Reinstein Wayne State University
Anne J. Rich Quinnipiac College
Susan Riffe Southern Methodist University
Katherine Schipper Financial Accounting Standards Board
Catherine M. Schrand University of Pennsylvania
Chandra Seethamraju Washington University
Stephan E. Sefcik University of Washington
Thomas I. Selling American Graduate School of International Management
Galen R. Sevcik Georgia State University
Lawrence G. Singleton George Washington University
Virginia E. Soybel Babson College
Brett Trueman University of California, Berkeley
Bob Virgil Edward Jones and Co.
Ira Weiss Columbia Business School
Peter R. Wilson Duke University
J. Scott Whisenant University of Houston
Teri Yohn Georgetown University
Stephen A. Zeff Rice University

Thomas Horton and Daughters, Inc., permits us to reproduce material from *Accounting: The Language of Business*. **Problems 37** to **39** in **Chapter 3** derive from ones prepared by George H. Sorter. These problems involve working backward from one financial statement to another, and we have found them useful in cementing understanding. Steve Zeff provided us with many thought-provoking problems, which we have used or adapted for this edition.

We thank Katherine Xenophon-Rybowiak for helping us to prepare the manuscript for this edition and Cherie Weil for preparing the index.

We thank the following at Thomson Learning : Julie Moulton, acquisitions editor; Carol Bennett, developmental editor; Heather Mann, production editor, and Chris Miller, art director, for coordinating the production of the book, as well as Nikki Wise and the compositors at Navta Associates for their excellent work on page-makeup.

Finally, Sidney Davidson. What can we say? For over thirty-one years he has taught us and guided us and wrote with us. Thank you.

Brief Contents

Contents

Part One

Overview of Financial Statements

1

FACMU11

chapter 1

Introduction to Business Activities and Overview of Financial Statements and the Reporting Process

Learning Objectives

1. Develop an understanding of four principal activities of business firms: (a) establishing goals and strategies, (b) obtaining financing, (c) making investments, and (d) conducting operations.

2. Develop an understanding of the purpose and content of the three principal financial statements that business firms prepare to measure and report the results of their business activities: (a) balance sheet, (b) income statement, and (c) statement of cash flows.

3. Develop a sensitivity to financial reporting issues, including the following: (a) the potential conflict of interest between management's self-interest for job security and career enhancement with its responsibility to shareholders, (b) the alternative approaches to establishing accounting measurement and reporting standards, and (c) the role of the independent audit of a firm's financial statements.

4. Develop a sensitivity to ethical issues in financial reporting using a framework for thinking about ethical questions.

$\mathcal{E}$nron. Global Crossing. WorldCom. Qwest Communication. Adelphia. Freddie Mac. The list seems to go on and on of companies accused of issuing fraudulent or misleading financial statements in recent years. Yet, the proper allocation of resources in an economy depends on reliable and relevant information about the profitability and risk of firms. How does one know if a firm has "cooked its books" in an effort to mislead users of its financial statements? What safeguards exist to minimize the risk of such financial shenanigans?

You are about to embark on a study of financial accounting. You will learn the important concepts underlying financial statements, the accounting principles firms use to measure the results of their business activities, and some tools for analyzing financial statements. You will consider the judgments that firms make in measuring and reporting business activities and the opportunity such judgments provide for biasing the reported amounts. Our perspective throughout this study is that of a user of financial statements. We presume that you will not become an accountant, or even an expert at detecting misleading financial reports. Our aim is to equip you with sufficient understanding of the concepts, methods, and uses of financial statements so that you can use accounting data effectively. We also describe recent legislated efforts to enhance the quality of financial information and reduce the risk of financial reporting abuses.

This chapter overviews the whole book. We begin by studying how a typical firm carries out its business activities. We next see how the firm measures the results of these business activities and reports them in the financial statements. We then raise several issues about the financial reporting process. This chapter introduces material that later chapters will cover in greater depth. At this point in your study of financial accounting, you will not fully understand all of the concepts and terms discussed in this chapter. As the chapter title suggests, we introduce the big picture of the concepts, methods, and uses to be discussed later.

Overview of Business Activities

Firms prepare financial statements for various external users: owners, lenders, regulators, and employees. The financial statements attempt to present meaningful information about a firm's business activities. Understanding these financial statements requires an understanding of the business activities that they attempt to portray.

Example 1 Wal-Mart Stores, Inc. (Wal-Mart) is the largest retailing firm in the world. It emphasizes an everyday-low-price strategy and operates through three principal store concepts:

Wal-Mart Stores: discount department stores that offer clothing, housewares, electronic equipment, pharmaceuticals, health and beauty products, sporting goods, and similar items.

Wal-Mart Supercenters: full-line supermarkets offering grocery products combined with Wal-Mart's traditional discount stores.

Sam's Clubs: members-only warehouse stores that offer food, household, automotive, electronic, sporting, and other products in unusually large quantities (for example, toothpaste by the quart) or containers at wholesale prices.

The following sections describe some of the more important business activities that the management of firms such as Wal-Mart must understand.

Establishing Corporate Goals and Strategies

A firm's **goals** state the targets, or end results, toward which the firm directs its energies. A firm's **strategies** state the means for achieving these goals. The firm sets goals and strategies in light of the economic, institutional, and cultural environment in which it intends to operate. For example, a firm might set goals to

- maximize the return to the owners of the firm;
- provide a stimulating and stable lifetime working environment for employees; and
- contribute to and integrate with national goals and policies.

Management sets strategies for a firm as a whole. For example, a firm might choose to operate in one industry or several industries. It might integrate backward into production of raw materials or forward into distribution of products to customers. It might operate in the United States only or in other countries too.

Management also sets strategies for each business unit or product. For example, a firm might attempt to find a niche for each of its products. Such a strategy might permit the firm to obtain favorable selling prices for its products relative to competitors so that it can pass along cost increases to its customers. Common business terminology refers to this as a *product differentiation strategy.* Alternatively, the firm might choose primarily to emphasize cost control and might strive to be the low-cost producer in its industry. Such a strategy might permit it to charge aggressively low prices and generate high volumes. Terminology refers to this as a *low-cost leadership strategy,* which Wal-Mart follows. Some products lend themselves more naturally to one strategy or the other, whereas the firm might pursue either or both strategies for other products.

When establishing goals and strategies, the firm must consider external environmental factors, such as the following:

1. Who are the firm's competitors, and what goals and strategies do they pursue?
2. What barriers, such as patents or large investments in buildings and equipment, might preclude new firms from entering the industry? Or, are entry barriers low?
3. Is the demand for products within the industry increasing rapidly, such as for Internet software and biotechnology products, or is the demand relatively stable, such as the demand for groceries?
4. Is the industry subject to government regulation, such as for food and pharmaceutical products, or is it unregulated, such as for clothes and paper towels?

Wal-Mart and other publicly traded firms have a common goal—to increase the value of the firm and the wealth of its owners. Wal-Mart likely pursues other goals, such as providing for employees' ongoing development and welfare as well as contributing to the needs in the community. Its annual report to shareholders suggests that Wal-Mart's strategies to accomplish these goals include the following:

1. Wal-Mart will continue to convert existing discount stores into supercenters and open new supercenters to capitalize on one-stop shopping by customers and to gain efficiencies in product distribution, stocking, and advertising.
2. Wal-Mart will expand into other countries by acquiring existing retail chains instead of opening new stores on its own. Wal-Mart will then install its information, purchasing, and distribution systems into these retail chains in an effort to add value by reducing costs.
3. Wal-Mart will open smaller grocery stores in neighborhoods too thinly populated to justify a supercenter.

Obtaining Financing

Before Wal-Mart can implement these growth and expansion strategies, it must obtain the necessary financing. **Financing activities** involve obtaining funds from two principal sources: owners and creditors.

Owners Owners provide funds to a firm and in return receive some evidence of their ownership. For a corporation, shares of common stock provide evidence of ownership, and the owners are called *shareholders* or *stockholders*.[1] The firm need not repay the owners at a particular future date. Instead, the owners receive distributions, called **dividends**, from the firm only when the firm decides to pay them. The owners also have a claim on all the firm's increases in value resulting from future profitable operations.

Creditors Creditors provide funds but, unlike owners, require that the firm repay the funds, usually with interest, in specific amounts at specific dates. The length of time that elapses until final repayment varies.

Long-term creditors may provide funds and not require repayment for 20 years or more. A bond usually evidences such borrowings. In a bond agreement, the borrowing company promises to make payments to the creditors at specific dates in the future, some of which represents interest on the amounts borrowed and some represents repayments of the amount borrowed.

Banks usually lend for periods between several months and several years. A note, in which the borrowing company promises to repay the amount borrowed plus interest at some future date, provides evidence of bank borrowings.

Suppliers of raw materials or merchandise do not always view themselves as supplying funds to a firm. Yet when they sell raw materials or merchandise but do not require payment for 30 days, they implicitly provide funds—the firm gets raw materials or merchandise now but need not pay cash until later. Likewise, employees paid weekly or monthly, and governmental units requiring only monthly or quarterly tax payments, provide funds by not demanding payment hourly or daily.

Each firm will make its own financing decisions, choosing the proportion of funds it will obtain from owners, long-term creditors, and short-term creditors. Corporate finance courses cover such financing decisions.

Making Investments

Once a firm has obtained funds, it usually invests them to carry out its business activities. Such **investing activities** involve acquiring some of the following:

1. **Land, buildings, and equipment.** These investments, which provide a firm with a capacity to manufacture and sell its products, usually take years to provide all of the potential services for which the firm acquired them.
2. **Patents, licenses, and other contractual rights.** These investments provide a firm with the legal right to use certain property or processes in pursuing its business activities.
3. **Common shares or bonds of other firms.** A firm might purchase shares or bonds of another firm (thereby becoming one of its owners or creditors). A firm might acquire these holdings for a few months with temporarily excess cash or might invest for longer-term purposes, such as to secure a source for critical raw materials or gain entrance into an emerging technology.
4. **Inventories.** To satisfy the needs of customers as they arise, firms must maintain an inventory of products to sell. A firm does not usually invest in specific inventory items for long because it will soon sell the items to customers. Because firms must have at least small amounts of inventory on hand, however, they must always invest some of their funds in inventory items.
5. **Accounts receivable from customers.** When a firm sells its products but does not require customers to pay immediately, the firm provides funds to its customers in the sense that it saves its customers from having to raise funds immediately to pay for purchases. Carrying some amount of accounts receivable may be in the best interest of the firm if, by doing so, the firm increases its sales and earnings. In extending credit to customers, the firm forgoes collecting its cash right away, but if it did not extend the credit, it might not make the sale

---

[1]When a firm operates as a partnership, its owners are partners. When a firm operates as a sole proprietorship, its owner is a sole proprietor. This book focuses on the corporate form of legal entity.

in the first place. Insofar as the firm delays the collection of needed cash from its customers, it must obtain funds elsewhere. Carrying accounts receivable, therefore, implies that as the firm needs cash, it must raise funds elsewhere. In this sense, carrying accounts receivable uses funds.

6. **Cash.** Most firms will leave a portion of their funds as cash in checking accounts so that they can pay their current bills. Sophisticated cash management systems can keep these amounts small.

Managerial accounting and corporate finance courses cover the techniques that firms use to make investment decisions.

Carrying Out Operations

A firm obtains financing and invests the funds in various resources to generate earnings. The **operating activities** of the firm comprise the following:

1. **Purchasing.** The purchasing department of a merchandising firm acquires products needed by its retail stores. The purchasing department of a manufacturing firm acquires raw materials needed for production.
2. **Production.** The production department in a manufacturing firm combines raw materials, labor services, and other manufacturing inputs to produce the products, or outputs, of a firm. A firm that offers services combines labor services with other inputs in creating its product.
3. **Marketing.** The marketing department oversees selling and distributing a firm's products to customers.
4. **Administration.** The administrative activity of a firm supports purchasing, production, marketing, and other operating departments. Administrative activities include data processing, legal services, research and development, and other support services.

Managerial accounting, marketing, and production courses cover the appropriate bases for making operating decisions.

Summary of Business Activities

Figure 1.1 summarizes the principal business activities discussed in this section. These business activities appear as interconnected cogwheels that must move in concert with each other if a firm is to succeed. Figure 1.1 also shows the relation of these business activities to the three principal financial statements, a topic discussed in the next section.

Principal Financial Statements

Firms typically communicate the results of their business activities through the **annual report to shareholders**. (See the annual report of Wal-Mart at www.wal-mart.com). The annual report usually begins with a letter from the chairperson of the firm's board of directors and from its chief executive officer summarizing the activities of the past year and assessing the firm's prospects for the coming year. Descriptions and pictures of the firm's products, facilities, and employees usually follow. An important section of the annual report is the **Management Discussion and Analysis,** called the **MD&A,** in which a firm's management discusses reasons for changes in profitability and risk during the past year. The final section of the annual report includes the firm's financial statements and supplementary information, including the following:

1. Balance sheet
2. Income statement
3. Statement of cash flows
4. Notes to the financial statements, including various supporting schedules, and
5. Opinion of the independent certified public accountant.

The following sections of this chapter briefly discuss each of these five items.

FIGURE 1.1	Overview of Business Activities

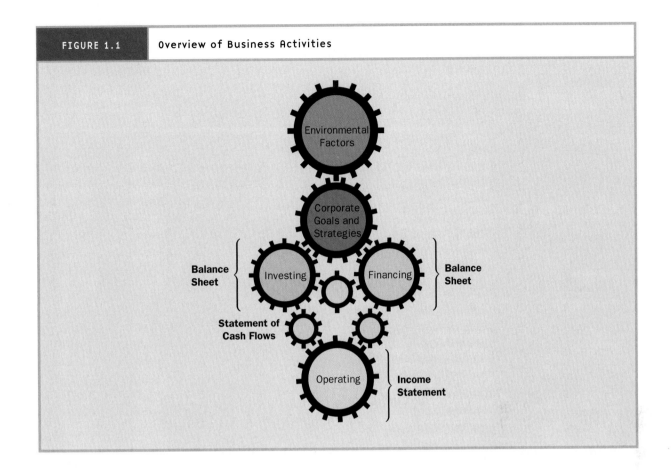

Balance Sheet

One question that a user of financial statements might ask is: *"What is the financial position, or financial health, of a firm?"* The **balance sheet** attempts to answer this question by presenting a snapshot at a moment in time of the results of the firm's investing and financing activities. **Exhibit 1.1** presents a comparative balance sheet for Wal-Mart as of January 31, Year 13, and January 31, Year 14. Firms typically present balance sheets as of the beginning and end of their most recent year. Note several aspects of the balance sheet.

Snapshot at a Moment in Time
The balance sheet presents a firm's investments and financing on a particular date (January 31, Year 13, and January 31, Year 14, for Wal-Mart). A snapshot permits the user to compare the types of investments made with the manner in which the firm financed those investments at that moment. The user must recognize, however, that the financial position of the firm at other times during the year can differ substantially from that depicted in this particular snapshot.

Concepts of Assets, Liabilities, and Shareholders' Equity
The balance sheet presents a listing of a firm's assets, liabilities, and shareholders' equity.

Assets are economic resources with the ability or potential to provide future benefits to a firm. For example, Wal-Mart can use cash to purchase inventory, new stores, and equipment. The firm can sell inventory to customers for an amount it hopes will provide positive earnings. Wal-Mart can use equipment to transport inventory from its warehouses to its retail stores.

Liabilities are creditors' claims on the assets of a firm and show some of the sources of the funds the firm uses to acquire the assets.

- Wal-Mart has purchased merchandise inventories from its suppliers but has not paid for a portion of the purchases. As a result, these creditors have provided funds to the firm and have a claim on its assets. Wal-Mart includes its obligations to suppliers in Accounts Payable.

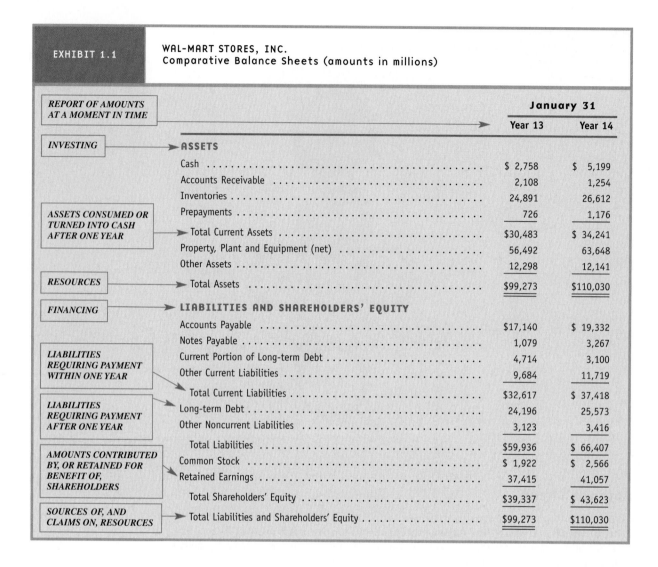

EXHIBIT 1.1

WAL-MART STORES, INC.
Comparative Balance Sheets (amounts in millions)

REPORT OF AMOUNTS AT A MOMENT IN TIME		January 31	
		Year 13	Year 14
INVESTING → ASSETS			
Cash		$ 2,758	$ 5,199
Accounts Receivable		2,108	1,254
Inventories		24,891	26,612
Prepayments		726	1,176
ASSETS CONSUMED OR TURNED INTO CASH AFTER ONE YEAR → Total Current Assets		$30,483	$ 34,241
Property, Plant and Equipment (net)		56,492	63,648
Other Assets		12,298	12,141
RESOURCES → Total Assets		$99,273	$110,030
FINANCING → **LIABILITIES AND SHAREHOLDERS' EQUITY**			
Accounts Payable		$17,140	$ 19,332
Notes Payable		1,079	3,267
LIABILITIES REQUIRING PAYMENT WITHIN ONE YEAR Current Portion of Long-term Debt		4,714	3,100
Other Current Liabilities		9,684	11,719
Total Current Liabilities		$32,617	$ 37,418
LIABILITIES REQUIRING PAYMENT AFTER ONE YEAR Long-term Debt		24,196	25,573
Other Noncurrent Liabilities		3,123	3,416
Total Liabilities		$59,936	$ 66,407
AMOUNTS CONTRIBUTED BY, OR RETAINED FOR BENEFIT OF, SHAREHOLDERS Common Stock		$ 1,922	$ 2,566
Retained Earnings		37,415	41,057
Total Shareholders' Equity		$39,337	$ 43,623
SOURCES OF, AND CLAIMS ON, RESOURCES → Total Liabilities and Shareholders' Equity		$99,273	$110,030

- Employees have provided labor services for which Wal-Mart has not made payment as of January 31, Year 13 and Year 14. These employees likewise have provided funds to the firm and have a claim on its assets. Wal-Mart includes its obligation to employees in Other Current Liabilities.

Creditors' claims, or liabilities, result from a firm's having previously received benefits (cash, inventories, labor services) for which the firm must pay a specified amount on a specified date.

Shareholders' equity shows the amounts of funds owners have provided and, in parallel, their claims on the assets of a firm. Unlike creditors, the owners have only a residual interest; that is, owners have a claim on all assets in excess of those required to meet creditors' claims. The shareholders' equity generally comprises two parts: contributed capital and retained earnings. **Contributed capital** reflects the funds invested by shareholders for an ownership interest. By January 31, Year 14, the owners have contributed $2,566 million for shares of Wal-Mart's common stock.

Retained earnings represent the source of funds a firm derives from its earnings that exceed the dividends it has distributed to shareholders since its formation. When a firm has earnings, it generates new assets. It can distribute those assets to owners as dividends. To the extent it keeps the new assets in the firm, it has retained earnings. The Retained Earnings designation in share-holders' equity shows the source of the funding for assets reinvested by management for the benefit of shareholders and the shareholders' claims on those assets. Management attempts to direct the use of a firm's assets so that over time it generates positive earnings, that is, it receives more assets than it consumes in operations. This increase in assets, after any claims of creditors, belongs to the firm's owners. As of January 31, Year 14, Wal-Mart's cumulative earnings exceed its cumulative dividends by $41,057 million. An amount of assets equal to retained earnings does not appear on any single line in Wal-Mart's balance sheet. Instead, Wal-Mart has used the cash generated by the retention of earnings to acquire inventories, new stores, equipment, and other assets. Almost all successful firms use a large percentage of the assets they generate by earnings to replace assets and to grow, rather than to pay dividends.

Equality of Assets and Liabilities Plus Shareholders' Equity As the balance sheet for Wal-Mart shows, assets equal liabilities plus shareholders' equity.

$$\text{Assets} = \text{Liabilities} + \text{Shareholders' Equity}$$

A firm invests every dollar of resources it obtains from financing. The balance sheet views the same resources from two angles: in a list of the assets the firm currently holds, having acquired them with its funds, and in a list of the parties (creditors and owners) who provided the funds and so have a claim on those assets. Thus,

$$\text{Assets} = \text{Liabilities} + \text{Shareholders' Equity,}$$

or

$$\text{Investing} = \text{Financing}$$
$$\text{Resources} = \text{Sources of Resources}$$
$$\text{Resources} = \text{Claims on Resources}$$

The *asset mix* (that is, the proportions of total assets represented by accounts receivable, inventories, equipment, and other assets, respectively) reflects a firm's investment decisions, and the mix of liabilities plus shareholders' equity reflects a firm's financing decisions, each measured at a moment in time.

Balance Sheet Classification The balance sheet classifies assets and liabilities as being either current or noncurrent.

Current assets include cash and assets that a firm expects to turn into cash, sell, or consume within approximately one year from the date of the balance sheet. Cash, temporary investments in securities, accounts receivable from customers, and inventories are the most common current assets. Current liabilities represent obligations a firm expects to pay within one year. Examples are notes payable to banks, accounts payable to suppliers, salaries payable to employees, and taxes payable to governments.

Noncurrent assets, typically held and used for several years, include land, buildings, equipment, patents, and long-term investments in securities. Noncurrent liabilities and shareholders' equity are a firm's longer-term sources of funds.

Balance Sheet Valuation Assets, liabilities, and shareholders' equity items appear on the balance sheet at monetary amounts. Accountants measure the amounts using one of two conceptual bases: (1) a **historical valuation,** which reflects the acquisition cost of assets or the amounts of funds originally obtained from creditors or owners, or (2) a **current valuation,** which reflects the current cost of acquiring assets or the current market value of creditors' and shareholders' claims on a firm. As Chapter 2 discusses, accountants can more easily verify historical valuations and will disagree less often as to their amounts, whereas financial statement users probably find current valuations more relevant for decision making. Ascertaining current valuations requires, however, greater subjectivity than does ascertaining historical costs.

The balance sheet reports cash as the amount of cash on hand or in the bank (a current valuation). Accounts receivable appear at the amount of cash the firm expects to collect from customers (often, approximating a current valuation). Liabilities generally appear at present value of the cash required to pay liabilities.

The remaining assets appear either at acquisition cost or at acquisition cost net of accumulated depreciation or amortization (a historical valuation). For example, inventories and land usually appear at the amount of cash or other resources that the firm originally sacrificed to acquire those assets. Buildings, equipment, and patents appear at acquisition cost, adjusted downward to reflect the portion of the assets' services that the firm has used since acquisition.[2]

---

[2] Sometimes, balance sheet amounts for inventories, buildings, land, equipment, and patents will reflect amounts lower than historical cost when these items decline in value after the firm acquires them. Later chapters discuss these exceptions, called *impairments*.

Common stock appears at the amount invested by owners when the firm first issued common stock (a historical valuation). Retained earnings shows the sum of all prior years' earnings in excess of dividends (a combination of historical and current valuations). **Chapters 3** and **12** discuss further the valuation, or measurement, of retained earnings.

Analysis of the Balance Sheet   Firms typically finance current assets with current liabilities and finance noncurrent assets with noncurrent liabilities and shareholders' equity. Current liabilities require payment within one year. Current assets generally convert into cash within one year. Firms can use this near-term cash flow to pay current liabilities. Long-term liabilities require payment over some number of future years. Noncurrent assets, such as buildings and equipment, generate cash flows over longer periods. Firms can use these more extended cash inflows to repay the noncurrent liabilities as they come due. Firms generally should not finance noncurrent assets with current liabilities. Noncurrent assets do not generate cash quickly enough to repay debt within one year. The balance sheet of Wal-Mart on January 31, Year 14 reveals the following:

Current Assets	$ 34,241	Current Liabilities	$ 37,418
		Noncurrent Liabilities and	
Noncurrent Assets	75,789	Shareholders' Equity	72,612
Total	$110,030	Total	$110,030

Thus, Wal-Mart used short-term financing to raise funds approximately equal to its current assets and it uses long-term financing to raise an amount of funds approximately equal to the cost of its noncurrent assets. Current liabilities exceed current assets, an unusual relation. **Chapters 2** and **5** discuss more fully the analysis of a firm's financial health using the balance sheet.

Income Statement

Another question that a user of financial statements might ask is: *"How profitable is the firm?"* The second principal financial statement, the **income statement**, attempts to answer this question. **Exhibit 1.2** shows the income statement for Wal-Mart for the years ending January 31, Year 12, Year 13, and Year 14. The income statement indicates the **net income** or **earnings** for those time periods. Net income is revenues minus expenses. An analysis of revenues and expenses permits the user to understand why a firm's profitability changes over time and how it differs from that of other firms. Note several aspects of the income statement.

Report of Amounts for a Period of Time   We noted earlier that the balance sheet reports amounts at a moment in time. The income statement, on the other hand, reports amounts for a period of time. Most firms use the calendar year as their reporting period. Wal-Mart uses an accounting period ending on January 31 each year, after the end of the busy holiday shopping season.

Concepts of Net Income, Revenue, and Expense   The terms *net income* and *earnings* are synonyms used interchangeably in corporate annual reports and throughout this text. Most business firms aim to generate earnings from operating activities. The income statement reports a firm's success in achieving this goal for a given time span. The income statement reports the sources and amounts of a firm's revenues and the nature and amount of a firm's expenses. The excess of revenues over expenses equals the earnings for the period.

Revenues measure the inflows of assets (or reductions in liabilities) from selling goods and providing services to customers. During Years 12 to 14, Wal-Mart generated almost all of its revenues from the sale of merchandise. It generated a minor amount of revenue from other sources, primarily interest revenue on its bank accounts. From its customers, Wal-Mart received either cash or promises that it would receive cash in the future, called Accounts Receivable. Both are assets. Thus the firm generated revenues and increased assets. A firm cannot generate revenues without simultaneously generating net assets.

Expenses measure the outflow of assets (or increases in liabilities) used in generating revenues. Cost of Goods Sold (an expense) measures the cost of inventories sold to customers. Selling and administrative expenses measure the cash paid or the liabilities incurred to make future cash payments for selling and administrative services received during the period. For each dollar of expense, either an asset decreases or a liability increases.

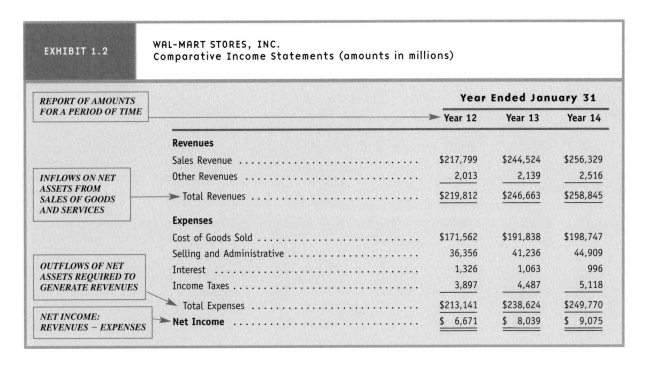

EXHIBIT 1.2	WAL-MART STORES, INC. Comparative Income Statements (amounts in millions)		

REPORT OF AMOUNTS FOR A PERIOD OF TIME		**Year Ended January 31**		
		Year 12	**Year 13**	**Year 14**
	Revenues			
	Sales Revenue	$217,799	$244,524	$256,329
INFLOWS ON NET ASSETS FROM SALES OF GOODS AND SERVICES	Other Revenues	2,013	2,139	2,516
	Total Revenues	$219,812	$246,663	$258,845
	Expenses			
	Cost of Goods Sold	$171,562	$191,838	$198,747
	Selling and Administrative	36,356	41,236	44,909
OUTFLOWS OF NET ASSETS REQUIRED TO GENERATE REVENUES	Interest	1,326	1,063	996
	Income Taxes	3,897	4,487	5,118
	Total Expenses	$213,141	$238,624	$249,770
NET INCOME: REVENUES − EXPENSES	**Net Income**	$ 6,671	$ 8,039	$ 9,075

A firm strives to generate an excess of net asset inflows from revenues over net asset outflows from expenses required to generate the revenues. Net income indicates a firm's accomplishments (revenues) relative to the efforts required (expenses) in pursuing its operating activities. When expenses for a period exceed revenues, a firm incurs a **net loss**.

Classification of Revenues and Expenses The income statement for Wal-Mart classifies some expenses by the department that carried out the firm's operating activities (retailing, selling, administration) and some expenses by their nature (interest, income taxes). Alternatively, the firm might classify all expenses by their nature (for example, salaries, depreciation, utilities). Firms classify revenues and expenses in their income statements in different ways.

Relation to Balance Sheet The income statement links the balance sheet at the beginning of the period with the balance sheet at the end of the period. The balance sheet amount for retained earnings represents the sum of all prior earnings of a firm in excess of dividends. The amount of net income for the current period helps explain the change in retained earnings between the beginning and the end of the period. During Year 14, Wal-Mart had net income of $9,075 million. It declared and paid dividends of $1,569 million. Wal-Mart also repurchased shares of its common stock and retired them, reducing retained earnings by $3,864 during Year 14 (**Chapter 12** discusses the accounting for common stock repurchases). Retained earnings during Year 14, therefore, increased by $3,642 as follows:

Retained Earnings, January 31, Year 13	$37,415
Add Net Income for Year 14	9,075
Subtract Dividends Declared and Paid during Year 14	(1,569)
Subtract Amounts Related to Repurchase of Wal-Mart Common Stock	(3,864)
Retained Earnings, January 31, Year 14	$41,057

Analysis of the Income Statement A percentage comparison of net income to revenues indicates how much of each dollar of revenues remains to benefit the common shareholders after the firm covers all expenses. The net income to revenues, or *profit margin*, percentages for Wal-Mart are as follows:

Year 12: $6,671/$219,812 = 3.0%

Year 13: $8,039/$246,663 = 3.3%

Year 14: $9,075/$258,845 = 3.5%

The profit margin percentage increased during the three-year period. By calculating expenses to revenues percentages for each expense item, we can identify the reason for any changes in the profit margin. **Chapter 5** further examines the reasons for the increasing profit margin for Wal-Mart.

Statement of Cash Flows

Another question that users of financial statements might ask is: *"Is the firm generating sufficient cash flows from its customers to finance operations and to acquire buildings and equipment? Or, must it seek new funds from lenders or owners?"* The third principal financial statement, the **statement of cash flows**, attempts to answer this question. **Exhibit 1.3** presents the statement of cash flows for Wal-Mart for the years ending January 31, Year 12, Year 13, and Year 14. This statement reports the net cash flows derived from (or used by) operating, investing, and financing activities for those time periods. Of what significance is a statement explaining or analyzing the change in cash during a period of time? The following example illustrates the usefulness.

Example 2 Diversified Technologies Corporation began business four years ago. In its first four

EXHIBIT 1.3	WAL-MART STORES, INC. Comparative Statements of Cash Flows (amounts in millions)			

REPORT AMOUNTS FOR A PERIOD OF TIME		Year Ended January 31		
		Year 12	Year 13	Year 14
	Operations			
	Net Income	$ 6,671	$ 8,039	$ 9,075
	Depreciation	3,290	3,432	3,852
	(Increase) Decrease in Accounts Receivable	(210)	(101)	373
	(Increase) in Inventories	(1,235)	(2,236)	(1,973)
	(Increase) Decrease in Prepayments	(180)	745	(450)
	Increase in Accounts Payable	368	1,447	2,803
	Increase in Other Current Liabilities	1,556	1,206	2,411
NET CASH INFLOW FROM SALES TO CUSTOMERS	Cash Flow from Operations	$10,260	$12,532	$ 16,091
	Investing			
	Acquisition of Property, Plant, and Equipment	$ (8,383)	$ (9,355)	$(10,308)
NET CASH OUTFLOW FROM INVESTMENT IN RETAILING CAPACITY	Other	1,237	(354)	2,046
	Cash Flow from Investing	$ (7,146)	$ (9,709)	$ (8,262)
	Financing			
	Increase (Decrease) in Short-Term Borrowing	$ (1,533)	$ 1,836	$ 688
	Increase in Long-term Borrowing	4,591	2,044	4,099
	Decrease in Long-term Borrowing	(3,686)	(1,479)	(3,541)
NET CASH OUTFLOW FROM SHORT- AND LONG-TERM CREDITORS AND OWNERS	Acquisition of Common Stock	(1,214)	(3,232)	(5,182)
	Dividends	(1,249)	(1,328)	(1,569)
	Other	84	(67)	117
	Cash Flow from Financing	$ (3,007)	$ (2,226)	$ (5,388)
CHANGE IN CASH = NET CASH FLOW FROM OPERATING, INVESTING, AND FINANCING	Change in Cash	$ 107	$ 597	$ 2,441
AMOUNTS FOR CASH ON THE BALANCE SHEET	Cash, Beginning of Year	2,054	2,161	2,758
	Cash, End of Year	$ 2,161	$ 2,758	$ 5,199

years, it generated net income of $100,000, $300,000, $800,000, and $1,500,000, respectively. The company retained all of the assets generated by its earnings for growth (reflected on the balance sheet as increases in both net assets and retained earnings). Early in the fifth year, the company learned that, despite paying no dividends, it was running out of cash. Analysis revealed the company was expanding accounts receivable, inventories, buildings, and equipment so fast that operations and external financing were not generating cash quickly enough to keep pace with the growth.

This example illustrates a common phenomenon for business firms. A firm might not generate cash in sufficient amounts or at the proper times to finance all ongoing or growing operations. If a firm is to continue operating successfully, it must generate more cash than it spends. In some cases it can borrow from creditors to replenish its cash, but future operations must generate cash to repay these loans. Often a growing business finds that it can't collect cash from customers fast enough to pay its own bills even though the customers owe the firm more cash than the firm owes to its suppliers. A simple example of this occurs when a firm must pay its own suppliers faster, say, in 20 days, than it collects from its own customers, say, in 30 days.

Report of Amounts for a Period of Time The statement of cash flows reports cash inflows and outflows for a period of time. This financial statement, like the income statement and unlike the balance sheet, shows amounts over time.

Classification of Items in the Statement of Cash Flows Exhibit 1.3, a standard format for the statement of cash flows, classifies cash flows for Wal-Mart using the three-way classification of the principal business activities described earlier in the chapter: operations, investing, and financing. **Figure 1.2** depicts these various sources and uses of cash.

1. **Operations.** Most firms expect their primary source of cash to result from the excess of cash they receive from customers over the amount of cash they pay to suppliers, employees, and others in carrying out the firms' operating activities. Wal-Mart generated positive cash flow from operations in amounts larger than annual net income in each of the three years. Chapter 4 discusses the adjustments required to convert net income to cash flow from operations.

2. **Investing.** Firms that expect either to maintain current operating levels or to grow must continually acquire buildings, equipment, and other noncurrent assets. Just to keep productive capacity constant requires cash to replace assets used up. To grow requires even more. A firm can obtain some of the cash needed from selling existing land, buildings, and equipment. The firm's cash needs, however, usually exceed the cash proceeds of such disposals. Wal-Mart increased its cash outflows for the acquisition of property, plant, and equipment during the last three years as it built new superstores.

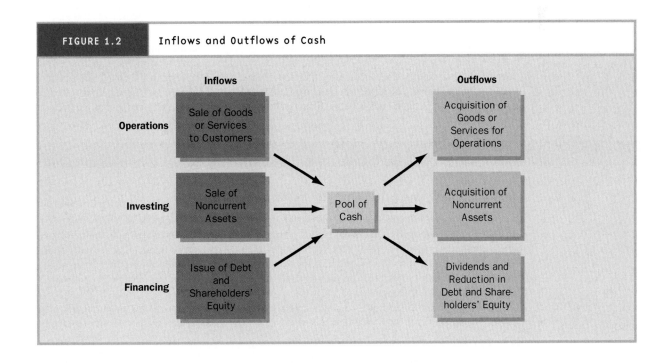

FIGURE 1.2   **Inflows and Outflows of Cash**

3. **Financing.** Firms obtain additional financing to support operating and investing activities by issuing bonds or common stock. The firm uses cash to pay dividends and to retire old financing, such as repaying long-term debt when it comes due. Wal-Mart generated more than sufficient cash flow from operations during Year 12 to Year 14 to finance expenditures on property, plant, and equipment. It used this excess cash flow and the cash received from issuing long-term debt in excess of that needed to retire long-term liabilities to pay dividends to shareholders and acquire shares of its common stock.

Relation to Balance Sheet and Income Statement The statement of cash flows explains the change in cash between the beginning and the end of the period. Note on the bottom of the statement of cash flows for Wal-Mart that the amount of cash on the balance sheet was $2,758 million on January 31, Year 13, and $5,199 million on January 31, Year 14. The statement of cash flows shows the reasons for this $2,441 million increase in cash, as the following analysis shows:

Cash on the Balance Sheet, January 31, Year 13	$ 2,758
Cash Flow from Operations during Year 14	16,091
Cash Flow for Investing during Year 14	(8,262)
Cash Flow for Financing during Year 14	$(5,388)
Cash on the Balance Sheet, January 31 Year 13	$ 5,199

The statement of cash flows also shows the relation between net income and cash flow from operations. Cash flow from operations exceeds net income each year for Wal-Mart. **Chapter 4** discusses the reasons for this excess.

Summary of Principal Financial Statements

Refer again to **Figure 1.1** on page 7, which depicts the principal business activities as interconnected cogwheels. Note that the balance sheet reports the results of investing and financing activities at a moment in time. The income statement reports the success of a firm in using assets to generate earnings for a period of time. The statement of cash flows reports the net cash inflow or outflow from operating, investing, and financing activities for the same period of time. The financial statements seek to measure the success of a firm's business activities by providing information about a firm's:

Financial position (balance sheet)

Profitability (income statement)

Cash-generating ability (statement of cash flows)

Figure 1.3 depicts the relation between the three principal financial statements over time. The balance sheet reports the assets, liabilities, and shareholders' equity at a moment in time. The income statement reports net income for a period of time and helps explain the change in retained earnings on the balance sheet between the beginning and end of the period. The statement of cash flows explains the change in cash on the balance sheet between the beginning and end of the period.

Other Items in Annual Reports

Supporting Schedules and Notes

The balance sheet, income statement, and statement of cash flows present information condensed to ease comprehension by the typical reader. Some readers desire additional details omitted from these condensed versions. Firms therefore usually include with their financial statements additional schedules that provide more detail for some of the items reported in the three main statements. For example, most firms present separate schedules to explain the change in contributed capital and retained earnings.

Every set of published financial statements also contains explanatory notes as an integral part of the statements. As later chapters make clear, a firm must select the accounting methods

Problem 1.1 for Self-Study

Preparing a balance sheet and an income statement. The accounting records of Gateway, a manufacturer and direct marketer of personal computers, reveal the following (all dollar amounts in thousands):

	December 31	
	Year 3	**Year 4**
Balance Sheet Items		
Accounts Payable	$411,788	$ 488,717
Accounts Receivable	449,723	510,679
Buildings and Equipment (net of accumulated depreciation)	227,477	315,038
Cash	447,718	593,601
Common Stock	290,829	295,535
Computer Software Development Cost (net of accumulated amortization)	31,873	39,998
Goodwill from Corporate Acquisitions	35,631	118,121
Inventories	278,043	249,224
Land	14,888	21,431
Long-term Debt	7,244	7,240
Notes Payable	15,041	13,969
Other Current Assets	74,216	152,531
Other Current Liabilities	207,336	315,292
Other Noncurrent Liabilities	50,857	98,081
Retained Earnings	410,870	634,509
Royalties Payable	125,270	159,418
Short-term Cash Investments	0	38,648
Taxes Payable	40,334	26,510
Income Statement Items		
Cost of Goods Sold		$5,217,239
Income Tax Expense		93,823
Interest Expense		1,740
Interest Revenue		28,929
Sales		6,293,680
Selling and Administrative Expenses		786,168

a. Prepare a comparative balance sheet for Gateway as of December 31, Year 3 and Year 4. Classify the balance sheet items into the following categories: current assets, noncurrent assets, current liabilities, noncurrent liabilities, and shareholders' equity. Refer to the Glossary at the back of the book if you have difficulty with any of the accounts.

b. Prepare an income statement for Gateway for the year ending December 31, Year 4. Classify income statement items into revenues and expenses.

c. Calculate the amount of dividends declared and paid to common shareholders during the year ending December 31, Year 4.

d. Did the increase in cash between December 31, Year 3, and December 31, Year 4, primarily result from operating activities, investing activities, or financing activities? Explain. Solutions to self-study problems appear at the end of the chapter.

followed in preparing its financial statements from a set of generally accepted methods. The notes indicate the actual accounting methods the firm uses and also disclose additional information that elaborates on items presented in the three principal statements. To understand fully a

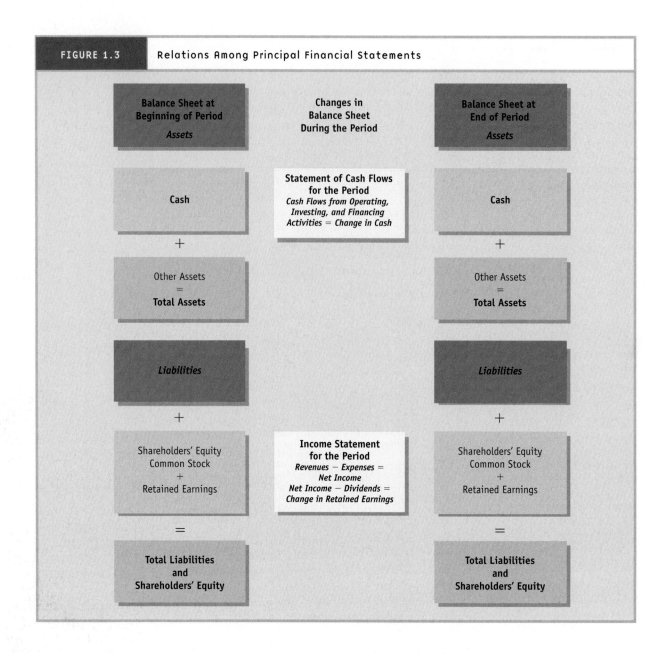

FIGURE 1.3   Relations Among Principal Financial Statements

firm's balance sheet, income statement, and statement of cash flows requires understanding the notes. No such notes appear here for the financial statements of Wal-Mart because they would not mean much at this stage. Do not let this omission lead you to conclude that the notes are unimportant.

Auditor's Opinion

Regulatory bodies generally require firms whose shares of common stock publicly trade in the capital markets to obtain an audit of their financial statements by an independent auditor. The annual report to the shareholders contains the opinion of the independent auditor, or certified public accountant, on the financial statements, supporting schedules, and notes.

The auditor's opinion generally follows a standard format, with some variations to meet specific circumstances. The auditor's opinion on the financial statements of Wal-Mart reads as follows:

We have audited the accompanying consolidated balance sheet of Wal-Mart Stores, Inc. as of January 31, Year 13 and Year 14, and the related consolidated statements of net income and cash flows for each of the three years ended January 31, Year 14. These financial statements are the responsibility of the Company's management. Our responsibility is to express an opinion on these financial statements based on our audits.

We conducted our audit in accordance with the standards of the Public Company Accounting Oversight Board (United States). Those standards require that we plan and perform the audit to obtain reasonable assurance about whether the financial statements are free of material misstatement. An audit includes examining, on a test basis, evidence supporting the amounts and disclosures in the financial statements. An audit also includes assessing the accounting principles used and significant estimates made by management, as well as evaluating the overall financial statement presentation. We believe that our audit provides a reasonable basis for our opinion.

In our opinion, the financial statements referred to above present fairly, in all material respects, the consolidated financial position of Wal-Mart Stores, Inc. at January 31, Year 13 and Year 14, and the consolidated results of their operations and their cash flows for each of the three years ended January 31, Year 14, in conformity with generally accepted accounting principles in the United States.

Ernst & Young LLP Tulsa, Oklahoma

March 19, Year 14.

The opinion usually contains three paragraphs. The first paragraph indicates the financial presentations covered by the opinion and indicates that the responsibility for the financial statements rests with management. The second paragraph affirms that the auditor has followed auditing standards and practices generally accepted by the accounting profession unless otherwise noted and described. Exceptions to the statement that the auditor conducted the examination "in accordance with the standards of the Public Company Accounting Oversight Board." are rare. There are occasional references to the auditor having relied on financial statements examined by other auditors, particularly for subsidiaries or for data from prior periods.

The auditor's opinion expressed in the third paragraph is the heart of the report. It may be an **unqualified** or a **qualified opinion**. Most opinions are unqualified; that is, the auditor describes no exceptions or qualifications to its opinion that the statements "present fairly . . . the financial position . . . and the results of its operations and its cash flows . . . in conformity with generally accepted accounting principles." Qualifications to the opinion result primarily from material uncertainties regarding realization or valuation of assets, outstanding litigation or tax liabilities, or accounting inconsistencies between periods caused by changes in the application of accounting principles.

A qualification so material that the auditor cannot express an opinion as to the fairness of the financial statements as a whole must result in either a **disclaimer of opinion** or an **adverse opinion**. Disclaimers of opinion and adverse opinions rarely appear in published annual reports.

Financial Reporting Issues

The financial reporting process involves activities of four principal participants:

1. Business firms and their managers
2. Accounting standard setting and regulatory bodies
3. Independent auditors
4. Security analysts and other users of financial statements

This section discusses the role of each of these participants and issues raised for the financial reporting process by the sometimes-conflicting goals or interests of each.

Business Firms and Their Managers

Business firms receive funds from owners with the expectation that managers will use the funds to increase the value of the firm and the wealth of its owners. From a legal perspective, managers are agents of the shareholders, and are responsible for safeguarding and properly using the firm's resources. Managers establish internal control procedures to ensure the proper recording of business transactions and the appropriate measurement and reporting of the results of those transactions. Management thereby carries out its stewardship, or fiduciary, responsibility to owners.

Managers also have a self-interest in promoting job security, high salaries, and bonuses as well as professional career enhancement. The self-interest of management and management's responsibility to shareholders sometimes conflict. For example, a firm might experience a period of weak profitability that could negatively affect stock prices and the shareholders' assessment of management. In an effort to improve reported results in the short term, management might sell strategically important assets at a gain or accelerate the recording of sales of a subsequent period in order to turn a weak profitability record into a seemingly stronger one in an attempt to keep shareholders happy. Shareholders need to know quickly, however, if management does not perform well.

One approach to dealing with management's potential conflict of interest is to design compensation systems that encourage management to act in the best interests of shareholders. Providing bonuses or awarding stock options to management if the firm meets certain earnings or stock price targets are means of aligning management and stockholder interests. Ideally, these compensation plans should reward management for real economic value enhancement and not simply short-term gaming by managers to protect their jobs.

Accounting Standard Setting and Regulatory Bodies

Firms use various accounting standards, or methods, in preparing their financial statements. One issue is who should decide which alternative accounting measurement and reporting standards firms can use and which they cannot use. For example, should a governmental body, practicing accountants, financial statement users, or the reporting firms make these decisions?

A governmental body might set such accounting standards and use the legislative power of the government to enforce them. With this approach to standard setting, one would worry that government employees might represent neither preparer nor user perspectives and thereby might specify accounting standards that were either impracticable to apply or irrelevant to user needs. One would also worry that a government body could encounter political pressures in **establishing acceptable accounting standards** that both meet the information needs of financial statement users and permit the government to collect tax payments from taxpayers.

A private-sector body lacks legal enforcement power for its accounting standards but can more likely incorporate viewpoints of various preparer and user groups. Placing the standard-setting process in the private sector does not, however, eliminate political pressures. Firms reporting about themselves sometimes prefer to report less accounting information when it is costly to prepare or when it provides competitors with otherwise secret information. Users desire more accounting information because they do not bear the cost of preparing the additional information and can ignore information that turns out to be unhelpful. The standard-setting body must deal with these conflicting viewpoints in gaining acceptance for its pronouncements.

A second issue concerns the desired degree of **uniformity in selecting accounting methods** across firms. Should standard-setters require all firms to follow the same accounting method for similar transactions? Such an approach might cause less confusion for financial statement users than if standard-setting bodies permitted firms a choice of several alternative methods. Requiring uniformity also reduces a firm's flexibility to manage reported earnings through its selection of accounting methods. An opposing argument is that because the economic characteristics of firms differ, management should be free, within certain prescribed limits, to select those accounting methods that best capture the firm's particular economics. This view suggests greater **flexibility in selecting accounting methods.**

A third issue concerns the type of accounting standards that standard-setting bodies should adopt. One approach is to specify **general principles** for a particular reporting topic and permit firms and their independent auditors to make judgments as to the application of those general principles to the particular circumstances. At the opposite extreme is a detailed **rules-based approach** in which standard-setting bodies attempt to anticipate the various games firms will play to work around the particular reporting requirements. The appeals of the general principles approach are the likely greater consistency of reporting standards with the broad concepts and principles of financial reporting and the greater opportunity for independent accountants to make professional judgments. The concern with the general principles approach is that it gives managers more "wiggle room" to avoid reporting in ways viewed as undesirable by management. The detailed rules approach attempts to constrain such opportunistic actions by management by closing perceived loopholes in reporting standards. This approach, however, can result in lengthy and complex reporting standards. It can also lead to a mentality of "show me where it says I can't report the way I want to," causing management to fine-tune transactions to skirt the rules put into effect to achieve uniformity.

Independent Auditors

An audit of a firm's financial statements involves (1) an assessment of the capability of a firm's accounting system to accumulate, measure, and synthesize transactional data properly, and (2) an assessment of the operational effectiveness of this accounting system. The auditor obtains evidence for the first assessment by studying the procedures and internal controls built into the accounting system. The auditor obtains evidence for the second assessment by examining a sample of actual transactions.

Employees of a firm might conduct such audits (called **internal audits**). The employees' knowledge and familiarity with the activities of their firm probably enhance the quality of the audit work and increase the likelihood that the audit will generate suggestions for improving operations. Because internal auditors work for the firm, their audits do not add as much credibility to the firm's financial statements as an **external, independent audit** provides. Because the managers of a firm have incentives to report as favorable a picture as possible in the financial statements, an external audit by independent auditors acts to control, but not always successfully, management's optimistic inclinations.

To serve effectively as a control on management's actions, the auditors must maintain independence from the firm. Yet, business firms hire and compensate their auditors, thereby putting pressure on the client-auditor relationship and potentially compromising the auditor's independence. To maintain the integrity of the audit, auditors must have access to all information that might impact the financial statements. In cases where confrontations with management arise, auditors must have access to members of the firm's board of directors who are not managers or employees of the firm. The auditor works for the Audit Committee of the Board of Directors, whose members are themselves independent of management. Auditors need access to a higher-level body, such as an administrative agency of the government, to adjudicate conflicts that arise in the audit.

Security Analysts and Other Users of Financial Statements

Financial statements should serve as reliable signals of value changes of firms so that investors, security analysts, and other users can make wise, economic decisions. Minimizing intentional management bias through appropriately applied accounting standards and effective, independent audits enhances the reliability of the financial statements.

Yet, security analysts may exhibit conflicts of interests when using accounting information. Security analysts often work for securities firms that invest in the business firms for which analysts make investment recommendations. Also, securities firms often compensate their analysts for short-term performance, providing security analysts with the same incentives as management to hide poor performance in a particular year.

Ethical Issues in the Financial Reporting Process

Recent financial reporting abuses have raised ethical issues for the various participants in the financial reporting process. Consider the following examples for financial reporting choices made by three firms.

Example 3. Centennial Technologies, a designer, manufacturer, and marketer of PC cards for computers, printers, and other software-based equipment, engaged in various actions to inflate its earnings, including recording fictitious sales, accelerating revenues from a later year into an earlier one, and manipulating the count of inventories at year end.

Example 4. Enron Corporation set up various entities to which Enron sold some of its securities and derivatives at a gain, increasing earnings. If these entities were independent of Enron, then recognition of the gain was appropriate. If these entities were not independent of Enron, then Enron should have consolidated its financial statements with those of these other entities and delayed recognition of any gain until these other entities sold the securities and derivatives to outsiders. Enron did not disclose sufficient information in its financial statements for users to decide if the entities were independent.

Example 5. Delta Air Lines uses the straight-line method to depreciate its aircraft, even though an accelerated depreciation method better reflects the economic decline in the value of the aircraft. Generally accepted accounting principles (GAAP) allow firms to choose between these two depreciation methods.

Does an ethical issue arise in each of these situations? The response depends on an individual's value system. The actions of Centennial Technologies were clearly intended to mislead users of the financial statements and were therefore fraudulent. The proper functioning of the capital system requires reliable financial information. Society, through its elected representatives, has judged that fraudulent actions are not in the best interest of society and has ruled them illegal. Does the legality of an action make it ethical?

Consider next the actions of Enron. Whether one entity is independent of another is a matter of degree and requires judgment. Enron, desiring to recognize the gains on sales to these entities, sought to structure the entities so that they were sufficiently, but not totally, independent of Enron. Enron consulted with its auditor, Arthur Andersen, as it set up these entities to ensure that Arthur Anderson concurred with Enron's treatment of these entities as "independent." These consultations led to certain changes in the structure of these entities until Arthur Andersen concurred with Enron's treatment of the entities as independent. Is it ethical for supposedly independent auditors to be so closely involved in decisions and actions made by management? Assume now that the evidence provided by Enron to Arthur Andersen was sufficient to justify not consolidating these entities. Was it ethical not to disclose sufficient information about these entities for users of the financial statements to make their own judgments about independence? Is a legal action, accompanied by full disclosure, sufficient to constitute ethical behavior?

Finally, consider the choice of depreciation method made by Delta Air Lines. GAAP allow various accounting methods for certain items without prescribing the specific conditions firms should use to choose between them. Delta's choice of the straight-line depreciation method permits it to report larger cumulative earnings at any time prior to sale or disposal of the aircraft. Delta's depreciation method is also consistent with that used by its principal competitors. Is it ethical for Delta to use a depreciation method allowed by GAAP even though another depreciation method more closely reflects the decline in the services of aircraft? Does ethical behavior require legality, adequate disclosure, and selection of accounting methods that best reflect economic reality?

These three examples illustrate the difficulties managers and accountants often encounter in identifying ethical issues and ethical behavior. A person whose value system says that any action that is legal is also ethical would not view Delta's reporting choice as involving ethical concerns. If GAAP allow a choice, then any choice is appropriate and therefore an ethical issue does not arise. A person whose value system places heavy weight on legality and adequate disclosure so that users can make their own judgments would judge Enron's actions as unethical because of its inadequate disclosure. However, if Enron had made fuller disclosure, such a person would view Enron as satisfying its ethical responsibility. A person whose value system requires that financial statements reflect economic reality in as reliable a manner as possible would argue that Delta has not satisfied its ethical responsibility.

Ethical issues arise for other participants in the financial reporting process. Consider briefly the following questions:

1. Is it ethical for a member of the family of the independent auditor to hold shares of common stock in a client of the independent auditing firm?
2. Is it ethical for the independent auditing firm of Delta Air Lines in **Example 5** to express an unqualified audit opinion even though it judges that an accelerated depreciation method better reflects the earnings and financial position of Delta?
3. Is it ethical for a standard-setting body to issue an accounting standard requiring an accounting method preferred by reporting firms or legislators even though it concludes that another accounting method better reflects the economics of the transaction?
4. Is it ethical for security analysts of an investment-banking firm to make investment recommendations on a particular firm's securities when the investment-banking firm is also selling those securities?

For some of the ethical issues raised in this section, either laws or pronouncements from professional bodies have defined ethical behavior. An individual, however, may choose a higher standard of ethical behavior than that legislated. In practice, employees who demand standards of behavior beyond those of a particular corporation's culture will often lose their jobs. External pressure to conform coupled with personal standards can place employees in an uncomfortable position. We do not attempt in this book to impose our value systems on you. Our purpose in raising ethical concerns is to increase your sensitivity to situations where ethical judgments likely arise and encourage you to apply your value system in a thoughtful and directed manner.

The Financial Reporting Process in the United States

The **Securities and Exchange Commission (SEC)**, an agency of the federal government, has the legal authority to set acceptable accounting methods, or standards, in the United States. The SEC looks to the **Financial Accounting Standards Board (FASB)**, a private-sector body, for leadership in establishing such standards. The seven-member FASB contains various combinations of financial statement users, practicing accountants, and representatives from business firms, academia, and the government. Board members work full-time for the FASB and sever all relations with their previous employers. Thus, a private-sector body containing representatives from a broad set of constituencies establishes acceptable accounting standards.[3]

Common terminology includes the pronouncements of the FASB (and its predecessors) in the compilation of accounting rules, procedures, and practices known as **generally accepted accounting principles (GAAP)**. GAAP (a plural noun) include, as well, writings of the SEC, the Emerging Issues Task Force (a committee jointly sponsored by the FASB and the SEC), the AICPA, and scholarly writings. The FASB issues its major pronouncements in the form of *Statements of Financial Accounting Standards.* The FASB has issued more than 150 statements since it began operating in 1973. For some financial reporting topics, the FASB requires the use of a uniform accounting method by all firms. In other cases, firms enjoy some freedom to select from a limited set of alternative methods. Thus, the current standard-setting approach lies somewhere between uniformity and flexibility, tilting toward uniformity.

With the exception of one method of accounting for inventories and cost of goods sold (discussed in **Chapter 7**), the accounting methods that firms use for financial reporting can differ from the methods used in calculating taxable income. Permitting different methods recognizes that the goal of providing useful information to financial statement users may require accounting rules that differ from those that aid the taxation authorities in their attempt to efficiently raise revenues.

As the FASB contemplates a reporting issue, its due-process procedure ensures that it receives input from various preparer and user groups. Involving these constituencies in the deliberations also identifies concerns and increases the likelihood of acceptance of the final reporting standards.

The FASB recognizes that it needs some theoretical structure to guide its deliberations. The Board has developed a conceptual framework to use, not as a rigorous deductive scheme but as a guiding mechanism for setting accounting standards. The conceptual framework contains guidance about the following:

1. Objectives of financial reporting
2. Qualitative characteristics of accounting information
3. Elements of financial statements
4. Recognition and measurement principles

The FASB reports the components of its conceptual framework in *Statements of Financial Accounting Concepts.* **Figure 1.4** summarizes the **financial reporting objectives** established by the FASB and their relation to the principal financial statements.

1. **Financial reporting should provide information useful for making rational investment and credit decisions.** This general-purpose objective simply states that financial reporting should aim primarily at investors and creditors and should help these individuals in their decision making.
2. **Financial reporting should provide information to help investors and creditors assess the amount, timing, and uncertainty of future cash flows.** This objective flows from the first by defining "useful information" more fully. It states that investors and creditors primarily want to know about the cash they will receive from investing in a firm. The ability of the firm to generate cash flows affects the amount of cash that will likely flow to investors and creditors.
3. **Financial reporting should provide information about the economic resources of a firm and the claims on those resources.** The balance sheet attempts to accomplish this objective.
4. **Financial reporting should provide information about a firm's operating performance during a period.** The income statement attempts to accomplish this objective.

---

[3]You may want to visit the web site of the Financial Accounting Standards Board at http://www.fasb.org to learn more about the purpose, procedures, and pronouncements of the FASB.

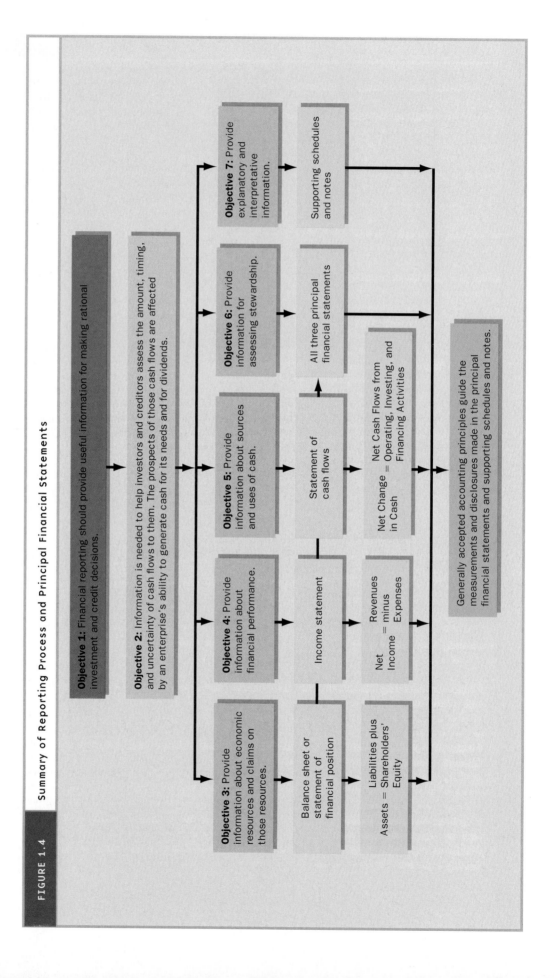

FIGURE 1.4   Summary of Reporting Process and Principal Financial Statements

5. **Financial reporting should provide information about how an enterprise obtains and uses cash.** The statement of cash flows accomplishes this objective.
6. **Financial reporting should provide information about how management has discharged its stewardship responsibility to owners.** Stewardship refers to the prudent use of resources entrusted to a firm. No single statement helps in assessing stewardship. Rather, owners assess stewardship using information from all three financial statements and the notes.
7. **Financial reporting should include explanations and interpretations to help users understand the financial information provided.** Supporting schedules and notes to the financial statements attempt to satisfy this objective.

Concerns over the quality of financial reporting have led, and continue to lead, to government initiatives to deal with the problems. The Congress passed the **Sarbanes-Oxley Act** in 2002. The Act set up the **Public Company Accounting Oversight Board (PCAOB)**, which has responsibility for monitoring the quality of audits and the financial reporting process. The Act requires the PCAOB to register firms conducting independent audits, establish or adopt acceptable auditing, quality control, and independence standards, and provide for periodic "audits" of the auditors. Initiatives to improve the quality of security analysts' services and the operations of mutual funds are also underway.

An International Perspective

The processes for setting accounting principles in countries other than the United States vary. In some countries, the measurement rules followed in preparing the financial statements match those followed in computing taxable income. Thus, the legislative branch of the government sets acceptable accounting principles. In other countries, an agency of the government sets acceptable accounting principles, but the measurement rules differ from those used in computing taxable income. In still other countries, the accounting profession, through its various boards and committees, plays a major role in setting accounting principles. Not surprisingly, the differing objectives of these standard-setting bodies (for example, taxation, accomplishment of government policy objectives, fair reporting to investors) result in diverse sets of accounting principles across countries.

The globalization of capital markets has increased the need for comparable and understandable financial statements across countries. To address this need, the **International Accounting Standards Board (IASB)**, an independent entity comprised of 14 members and full-time professional staff, has played an increasingly important role in developing acceptable accounting principles worldwide. Although the IASB has no legal authority, it encourages its members to exert influence on the standard-setting process within their own countries to reduce diversity. Stock exchanges in many countries now allow foreign firms to list their securities on the exchanges as long as the financial statements of these firms reflect pronouncements of the IASB. Standard-setting boards in several countries now accept IASB pronouncements as allowable accounting principles within their countries. The European Commission has ruled that firms within member countries must conform their financial statements to the reporting standards of the IASB by 2005.[4]

Summary

This chapter shows how a business's activities relate to the principal financial statements included in its annual reports to shareholders. The chapter raises questions that it does not fully answer. It provides you with a broad overview of the various financial statements before you examine the concepts and procedures underlying each statement.

Chapters 2 through **4** discuss and illustrate the concepts and procedures of the balance sheet, income statement, and statement of cash flows, respectively. **Chapter 5** considers techniques for analyzing and interpreting these financial statements. **Chapters 6** through **12** explore more fully the principles of accounting for individual assets, liabilities, and shareholders' equities. The web

---

[4] You may want to visit the web site of the International Accounting Standards Board at http://www.iasb.org to learn more about the purpose, procedures, and pronouncements of the IASB. The Big 4 accounting firm, Deloitte, has a web site full of useful information about international accounting developments: http://www.iasplus.com.

site for this book contains additional information on particular topics not covered fully in this book (go to: http://facmu.swlearning.com).

Now we turn to the study of financial accounting. To comprehend the concepts and procedures in the book, you should study the numerical examples presented in each chapter and prepare solutions to several problems, including the self-study problems. You may find the glossary of terms at the back of the book useful.

Solution to Self-Study Problem

SUGGESTED SOLUTION TO PROBLEM 1.1 FOR SELF-STUDY

(Gateway: preparing a balance sheet and an income statement)
a. See Exhibit 1.4.

EXHIBIT 1.4	**GATEWAY** **Comparative Balance Sheet December 31, Year 3 and Year 4** **(Problem 1.1 for Self-Study)**

	December 31	
	Year 3	**Year 4**
ASSETS		
Current Assets		
Cash	$ 447,718	$ 593,601
Short-term Cash Investments	0	38,648
Accounts Receivable	449,723	510,679
Inventories	278,043	249,224
Other Current Assets	74,216	152,531
Total Current Assets	$1,249,700	$1,544,683
Noncurrent Assets		
Land	$ 14,888	$ 21,431
Buildings and Equipment (net of accumulated depreciation)	227,477	315,038
Computer Software Development Cost (net of accumulated amortization)	31,873	39,998
Goodwill from Corporate Acquisitions	35,631	118,121
Total Noncurrent Assets	$ 309,869	$ 494,588
Total Assets	$1,559,569	$2,039,271
LIABILITIES AND SHAREHOLDERS' EQUITY		
Current Liabilities		
Accounts Payable	$ 411,788	$ 488,717
Notes Payable	15,041	13,969
Royalties Payable	125,270	159,418
Taxes Payable	40,334	26,510
Other Current Liabilities	207,336	315,292
Total Current Liabilities	$ 799,769	$1,003,906
Noncurrent Liabilities		
Long-term Debt	$ 7,244	$ 7,240
Other Noncurrent Liabilities	50,857	98,081
Total Noncurrent Liabilities	$ 58,101	$ 105,321
Total Liabilities	$ 857,870	$1,109,227
Shareholders' Equity		
Common Stock	$ 290,829	$ 295,535
Retained Earnings	410,870	634,509
Total Shareholders' Equity	$ 701,699	$ 930,044
Total Liabilities and Shareholders' Equity	$1,559,569	$2,039,271

b. See Exhibit 1.5.

EXHIBIT 1.5	GATEWAY Income Statement for the Year Ended December 31, Year 4 (Problem 1.1 for Self-Study)

Revenues	
Sales	$6,293,680
Interest Revenue	28,929
Total Revenues	$6,322,609
Expenses	
Cost of Goods Sold	$5,217,239
Selling and Administrative Expenses	786,168
Interest Expense	1,740
Income Tax Expense	93,823
Total Expenses	$6,098,970
Net Income	$ 223,639

c. Gateway did not declare or pay a dividend to the common shareholders during Year 4 because the change in retained earnings equals net income, as the following analysis shows (amounts in thousands):

Retained Earnings, December 31, Year 3	$410,870
Plus Net Income for Year 4	223,639
Less Dividend Declared	0
Retained Earnings, December 31, Year 4	$634,509

d. Gateway experienced only minor changes in accounts related to financing activities (notes payable, long-term debt, common stock). The firm experienced increases in accounts related to investing activities (land, buildings and equipment, computer software development costs, goodwill from acquisitions), which would likely have reduced cash. Thus, the increase in cash primarily resulted from profitable operations. Note, though, that the increase in cash and short-term investments of cash of $184,531 [= ($593,601 + $38,648) − $447,718] is less than net income for the year of $223,639.

Key Terms and Concepts

Goals contrasted with strategies
Financing activities
Dividends
Investing activities
Operating activities
Annual report to shareholders
Management Discussion and Analysis
    (MD&A)
Balance sheet
Assets
Liabilities
Shareholders' equity
Contributed capital
Retained earnings
Historical valuation
Current valuation
Income statement
Net income, earnings

Revenues
Expenses
Net loss
Statement of cash flows
Unqualified, qualified opinion
Disclaimer of opinion
Adverse opinion
Establishing acceptable accounting standards
Uniformity versus flexibility in selecting
    accounting methods
General principles versus rule-based approach
    to establishing accounting standards
Internal audits versus external audits
Securities and Exchange Commission (SEC)
Financial Accounting Standards Board
    (FASB)
Generally accepted accounting principles
    (GAAP)

Statements of Financial Accounting Standards
Statements of Financial Accounting Concepts
Financial reporting objectives
Sarbanes-Oxley Act

Public Company Accounting Oversight Board
  (PCAOB)
International Accounting Standards Board
  (IASB)

Questions, Short Exercises, Exercises, Problems, and Cases

For additional student
resources, content, and
interactive quizzes for
this chapter visit the
FACMU website:
http://facmu.swlearning.com

QUESTIONS

1. Review the meaning of the terms and concepts listed in Key Terms and Concepts.
2. The chapter describes four activities common to all entities: setting goals and strategies, financing activities, investing activities, and operating activities. How would these four activities likely differ for a charitable organization versus a business firm?
3. "The photographic analogy for the balance sheet is a snapshot, and for the income statement and statement of cash flows, it is a motion picture." Explain.
4. "Asset valuation and income measurement are closely related." Explain.
5. A student states, "It is inconceivable to me that a firm could report increasing net income yet run out of cash." Clarify this seeming contradiction.
6. Does an unqualified, or "clean," opinion of an independent auditor indicate that the financial statements are free of errors and misrepresentations? Explain.
7. Suggest reasons why the format and content of financial accounting reports tend to be more standardized than the format and content of accounting reports that firms prepare for their internal decision-making, planning, and control purposes.
8. In some countries, governmental entities establish acceptable accounting standards and generally require conformity between financial reporting and tax reporting. Describe the advantages and disadvantages of this approach to standard setting.
9. "Prescribing a single method of accounting for a particular financial statement item will result in uniform reporting across firms." Do you agree? Why or why not?
10. "Politics is inherent to the accounting standard-setting process." Explain.
11. "Research on the efficiency of capital markets suggests that market prices adjust quickly and in an unbiased manner to new information about a firm. The efficiency of capital markets therefore eliminates the need for financial accounting reports." Do you agree? Why or why not?

SHORT EXERCISES

12. **Balance sheet relations.** The balance sheet of Harley-Davidson Company, a manufacturer of motorcycles, showed current assets of $2,067 million, current liabilities of $990 million, shareholders' equity of $2,233 million, and noncurrent assets of $1,794 million at the end of Year 12. Net income for Year 12 was $580 million. Compute the amount of noncurrent liabilities on the balance sheet at the end of Year 12.
13. **Balance sheet relations.** The balance sheet of Mattel, a creator and manufacturer of toys and games, showed noncurrent assets of $2,071 million, noncurrent liabilities of $832 million, shareholders' equity of $1,979 million, and current liabilities of $1,649 million at the end of Year 12. Net loss for Year 12 was $22 million. Compute the amount of current assets on the balance sheet at the end of Year 12.
14. **Retained earnings relations.** The balance sheet of Reebok, a designer and manufacturer of athletic shoes, showed retained earnings of $411 million at the end of Year 11 and $446 million at the end of Year 12. The income statement for Year 12 showed net income of $52 million. Compute the amount of dividends declared during Year 12.
15. **Retained earnings relations.** The balance sheet of Ruby Tuesday, a restaurant chain, showed retained earnings of $326 million at the end of Year 12. Net income for Year 12 was $58 million and dividends declared and paid during Year 12 totaled $3 million. Compute the amount in retained earnings at the end of Year 11.
16. **Cash flow relations.** The statement of cash flows for Yahoo, Inc., an Internet service provider, showed a net cash inflow from operations of $303 million, a net cash outflow for investing of $346 million, and a net cash outflow for financing of $19 million for Year 12. The balance sheet at the end of Year 11 showed a balance in cash of $373 million. Compute the amount of cash on the balance sheet at the end of Year 12.

17. **Cash flow relations.** The statement of cash flows for Nike, a designer and manufacturer of athletic shoes, showed a net cash inflow from operations of $917.4 million and a net cash outflow for financing of $643.3 million for Year 12. The comparative balance sheets showed a balance in cash of $575.5 million at the end of Year 11 and $634.0 million at the end of Year 12. Net income for Year 12 was $474.0 million. Compute the net amount of cash provided or used for investing activities for Year 12.

EXERCISES

18. **Preparing a personal balance sheet.** Prepare a balance sheet of your personal assets, liabilities, and owner's equity. How does the presentation of owner's equity on your balance sheet differ from that in **Exhibit 1.1**?

19. **Classifying financial statement accounts.** The balance sheet or income statement classifies various items in one of the following ways:

    CA—Current assets
    NA —Noncurrent assets
    CL—Current liabilities
    NL—Noncurrent liabilities
    CC—Contributed capital
    RE—Retained earnings
    NI—Income statement item (revenue or expense)
    X—Item generally not appearing on a balance sheet or an income statement

    Using the letters, indicate the classification of each of the following items:
    a. Factory
    b. Interest revenue
    c. Common stock issued by a corporation
    d. Goodwill developed by a firm (see Glossary)
    e. Automobiles used by sales staff
    f. Cash on hand
    g. Unsettled damage suit against a firm
    h. Commissions earned by sales staff
    i. Supplies inventory
    j. Note payable, due in three months
    k. Increase in market value of land held
    l. Dividends declared
    m. Employee payroll taxes payable
    n. Note payable, due in six years

20. **Balance sheet relations.** Selected balance sheet amounts for Lowe's, a retailer of home construction and repair supplies, for four recent years appear below (amounts in millions):

	Year 9	Year 10	Year 11	Year 12
Noncurrent Assets	$3,759	$5,302	$ 7,201	?
Shareholders' Equity	?	4,695	5,495	$ 6,674
Total Assets	?	?	11,376	?
Current Liabilities	1,765	2,386	?[a]	?[b]
Current Assets	2,586	?	?[a]	?[b]
Noncurrent Liabilities	1,444	?	?	4,045
Total Liabilities and Shareholders' Equity	?	9,012	?	13,736

[a] Current Assets — Current Liabilities = $1,246.
[b] Current Assets — Current Liabilities = $1,903.

    a. Compute the missing balance sheet amounts for each of the four years.
    b. How did the mix of total assets (that is, the proportion of current versus noncurrent assets) change over the four-year period? What might account for such a change?
    c. How did the mix of current liabilities, noncurrent liabilities, and shareholders' equity change over the four-year period? What might account for such a change?

21. **Balance sheet relations.** Selected balance sheet amounts for PepsiCo, a manufacturer of soft drinks and snacks, for four recent years appear below (amounts in millions):

	Year 8	Year 9	Year 10	Year 11
Total Assets	$22,660	?	?	$21,695
Noncurrent Liabilities	8,345	$ 6,882	?	8,023
Noncurrent Assets	?	13,378	$13,735	?
Total Liabilities and Shareholders' Equity	?	17,551	?	?
Current Liabilities	7,914	?	3,935	4,998
Shareholders' Equity	?	6,881	7,249	?
Current Assets	4,362	?	4,604	5,853

    a. Compute the missing balance sheet amounts for each of the four years.

    b. How did the mix of total assets (that is, the proportion of current versus noncurrent assets) change over the four-year period? What might account for such a change?

    c. How did the mix of current liabilities, noncurrent liabilities, and shareholders' equity change over the four-year period? What might account for such a change?

22. **Balance sheet relations.** Selected balance sheet amounts for Johnson & Johnson, a consumer products company, for four recent years appear below (amounts in millions):

	Year 8	Year 9	Year 10	Year 11
Current Assets	$11,132	?[a]	$15,450	$18,473
Noncurrent Assets	?	?	15,871	?
Total Assets	?	$29,163	?	?
Current Liabilities	8,162	7,454	7,140	?[c]
Noncurrent Liabilities	4,459	?	5,373	?
Contributed Capital	?	458	?	1,727
Retained Earnings	13,556	15,755	?[b]	?[d]
Total Liabilities and Shareholders' Equity	26,211	?	?	34,488

[a] Current Assets − Current Liabilities = $5,746.
[b] Net income for Year 10 is $4,276 and dividends are $1,724.
[c] Current Assets − Current Liabilities = $10,429.
[d] Net income for Year 11 is $6,246 and dividends are $2,047.

    a. Compute the missing balance sheet amounts for each of the four years.

    b. How did the mix of total assets (that is, the proportion of current versus noncurrent assets) change over the four-year period? What might account for such a change?

    c. How did the mix of current liabilities, noncurrent liabilities, and shareholders' equity change over the four-year period? What might account for such a change?

23. **Balance sheet relations.** Selected balance sheet amounts for Intel, a developer and manufacturer of semiconductors, for four recent years appear below (amounts in millions):

	Year 9	Year 10	Year 11	Year 12
Current Assets	?	$21,150	$17,633	?
Noncurrent Assets	$26,030	?	26,762	?
Total Assets	?	47,945	?	?
Current Liabilities	7,099	?	6,570	$6,595
Noncurrent Liabilities	4,095	?	1,995	2,161
Contributed Capital	?	8,389	?	7,578
Retained Earnings	25,349	28,933	?[a]	?[b]
Total Liabilities and Shareholders' Equity	43,849	?	?	?
Current Assets/Current Liabilities	?	2,445	?	2,870

[a] Net loss for Year 11 was $1,220 and dividends were $538.
[b] Net income for Year 12 was $1,248 and dividends were $533.

    a. Compute the missing amounts for each of the four years.

b. Identify changes in the mix of total assets (that is, the proportion of current versus non-current assets) and in the mix of total liabilities versus shareholders' equity over the four years above. Suggest the events or transactions that might explain these changes.

24. **Retained earnings relations.** Hewlett-Packard Corporation develops and manufactures a diversified line of computer products. Its sales tend to vary with changes in the business cycle. Selected data from its financial statements for four recent years appear below (amounts in millions):

	Year 9	Year 10	Year 11	Year 12
Retained Earnings, Beginning of Year	$16,909	?	$14,097	$13,693
Net Income	2,026	$ 3,697	?	?
Dividends Declared and Paid	650	?	621	801
Retained Earnings, End of Year	?	14,097	13,693	11,973

a. Compute the missing amounts for each year.
b. What is the likely reason for the variations in net income and net loss?
c. Why might explain the unusual pattern of dividends over the four-year period?

25. **Retained earnings relations.** Selected data affecting retained earnings for Ford Motor Company, an automobile manufacturer, for four recent years appear below (amounts in millions):

	Year 9	Year 10	Year 11	Year 12
Retained Earnings, January 1	$12,221	?	?	$10,502
Net Income	7,237	$ 3,467	?	?
Dividends Declared and Paid	2,290	?	1,929	743
Retained Earnings, December 31	?	17,884	10,502	8,659

a. Compute the missing amounts for each of the four years.
b. What is the likely reason for the pattern of net income and net loss over the four-year period?
c. What is the likely reason for the pattern of dividends over the four-year period?

26. **Relating net income to balance sheet changes.** The comparative balance sheets for Target Corporation, a discount retailer, as of January 31, Year 11; January 31, Year 12; and January 31, Year 13, appear below (amounts in millions):

TARGET CORPORATION
Comparative Balance Sheet
January 31, Year 11, Year 12, and Year 13

	January 31		
	Year 11	Year 12	Year 13
Total Assets	$19,490	$24,154	$28,603
Liabilities	$12,971	$16,294	$19,160
Common Stock	977	1,173	1,336
Retained Earnings	5,542	6,687	8,107
Total Liabilities and Shareholders' Equity	$19,490	$24,154	$28,603

Target Corporation declared and paid dividends of $203 million during fiscal Year 12 and $218 million during fiscal Year 13.
a. Compute net income for fiscal Year 12 and Year 13 by analyzing the change in retained earnings.
b. Demonstrate that the following relation holds:

$$\text{Net Income} = \text{Increase in Assets} - \text{Increase in Liabilities}$$
$$- \text{Increase in Contributed Capital} + \text{Dividends}$$

27. **Income statement relations.** Selected income statement information for Dell Computer, a manufacturer of personal computers, for three recent years appears below (amounts in millions):

	Year 10	Year 11	Year 12
Sales	$31,888	?	$35,404
Cost of Goods Sold	25,445	25,661	?
Selling and Administrative Expenses	3,193	2,784	3,050
Research and Development Expense	482	452	455
Income Tax Expense	830	636	846
Net Income	?	1,635	1,998

   a. Compute the missing amounts for each of the three years.

   b. Prepare a common-size income statement for each year, in which sales is equal to 100 percent and each expense and net income are expressed as a percentage of sales. What factors appear to explain the change in the ratio of net income to sales?

28. **Income statement relations.** Selected income statement information for Pfizer, a pharmaceutical company, for three recent years appears below (amounts in millions):

	Year 10	Year 11	Year 12
Sales	$26,045	?	$32,373
Cost of Goods Sold	3,755	$3,823	?
Selling and Administrative Expenses	9,566	9,717	10,846
Research and Development Expense	4,374	4,776	5,176
Income Tax Expense	3,074	2,720	2,830
Net Income	?	7,988	9,476

   a. Compute the missing amounts for each of the three years.

   b. Prepare a common-size income statement for each year, in which sales equals 100 percent and each expense and net income are expressed as a percentage of sales. What factors appear to explain the change in the ratio of net income to sales?

29. **Statement of cash flows relations.** Selected data from the statement of cash flows for Amazon.com, an on-line retailer, for Year 10, Year 11, and Year 12 appear below (amounts in thousands):

	Year 10	Year 11	Year 12
Inflows of Cash			
Increase in Short-term Debt	$ 0	$ 0	$ 0
Issue of Long-term Debt	681,499	10,000	0
Issue of Common Stock	44,697	116,456	121,689
Revenues from Operations Increasing Cash	2,753,398	3,143,165	3,892,988
Sale of Marketable Securities (net)	361,269	0	0
Other Financing Activities	0	0	38,471
Outflows of Cash			
Acquisition of Property and Equipment	134,758	50,321	39,163
Purchase of Marketable Securities (net)	0	196,775	82,521
Decrease in Long-term Debt	33,049	19,575	14,795
Acquisition of Investments in Other Companies	62,533	6,198	0
Expenses for Operations Decreasing Cash	2,883,840	3,262,947	3,718,697
Other Financing Activities	37,557	15,958	0
Increase (Decrease) in Cash	689,126	(282,153)	197,972

   a. Prepare a statement of cash flows for Amazon.com for the three years using the format in Exhibit 1.3. Set cash flow from operations equal to revenues providing cash minus expenses using cash. The balance in cash at the beginning of Year 10 was $133,309. Changes in marketable securities are investing activities.

b. Comment on the relation among cash flows from operating, investing, and financing activities during the three years.

30. **Statement of cash flows relations.** Selected data from the statement of cash flows for AMR Corporation, the parent company of American Airlines, for three recent years appear below (amounts in millions):

	Year 10	Year 11	Year 12
Inflows of Cash			
Proceeds from Long-term Borrowings	$ 836	$ 5,096	$ 3,190
Revenues from Operations Increasing Cash	19,536	19,083	17,233
Issue of Common Stock	67	37	3
Sale of Property, Plant, and Equipment	332	401	220
Other Investing Transactions	71	0	268
Total Inflows	$20,842	$24,617	$20,914
Outflows of Cash			
Acquisition of Property, Plant, and Equipment	$ 3,678	$ 3,640	$ 1,881
Expenses for Operations Decreasing Cash	16,394	18,541	18,344
Repayments of Long-term Debt	766	922	687
Other Investing Activities	0	1,501	0
Total Outflows	$20,838	$24,604	$20,912
Increase (Decrease) in Cash	$ 4	$ 13	$ 2

a. Prepare a statement of cash flows for AMR for each of the three years using the format in **Exhibit 1.3**. Set cash flow from operations equal to revenues providing cash minus expenses using cash. The balance in cash at the beginning of Year 10 was $85 million.

b. Comment on the relation among cash flows from operating, investing, and financing activities during the three years.

31. **Relations between financial statements.** Compute the missing information in each of the following four independent cases. The letters in parentheses refer to the following:

BS—Balance sheet
IS—Income statement
SCF—Statement of cash flows

a.	Accounts Receivable, Jan. 1, Year 2 (BS)	$ 630
	Sales on Account for Year 2 (IS)	3,290
	Collections from Customers on Account during Year 2 (SCF)	2,780
	Accounts Receivable, Dec. 31, Year 2 (BS)	?
b.	Income Taxes Payable, Jan. 1, Year 2 (BS)	$ 1,240
	Income Tax Expense for Year 2 (IS)	?
	Payments to Governments during Year 2 (SCF)	8,290
	Income Taxes Payable, Dec. 31, Year 2 (BS)	1,410
c.	Building (net of depreciation), Jan. 1, Year 2 (BS)	$ 89,000
	Depreciation Expense for Year 2 (IS)	?
	Purchase of Building during Year 2 (SCF)	17,600
	Building (net of depreciation), Dec. 31, Year 2 (BS)	102,150
d.	Retained Earnings, Jan. 1, Year 2 (BS)	$ 76,200
	Net Income for Year 2 (IS)	14,200
	Dividends Declared and Paid during Year 2 (SCF)	?
	Retained Earnings, Dec. 31, Year 2 (BS)	83,300

PROBLEMS AND CASES

32. Preparing a balance sheet and income statement. The accounting records of eBay appear below (amounts in thousands).

	December 31	
Balance Sheet Items	**Year 11**	**Year 12**
Cash	$ 723,419	$1,199,033
Accounts Receivable	101,703	131,453
Other Current Assets	58,683	138,002
Property, Plant, and Equipment (net of depreciation)	142,349	218,028
Investment in Securities (noncurrent)	416,612	604,871
Goodwill and Other Intangibles	198,639	1,735,489
Other Noncurrent Assets	37,124	97,598
Accounts Payable to Suppliers	33,235	47,424
Other Current Liabilities	146,904	338,800
Long-term Debt	12,008	13,798
Other Noncurrent Liabilities	57,244	167,949
Common Stock	1,275,517	3,108,754
Retained Earnings	153,621	447,719

Income statement items	**For Year 12**
Net Operating Revenues	$1,214,100
Interest and Other Revenues	96,352
Cost of Net Operating Revenues	213,876
Product Development Expenses	104,636
Selling Expenses	349,650
Administrative Expenses	171,785
Other Operating Expenses	28,969
Interest Expense	1,492
Income Taxes	145,946

Dividend Information	
Dividends Declared and Paid	$ 0

a. Prepare an income statement for eBay for the year ending December 31, Year 12. Refer to **Exhibit 1.2** for help in designing the format of the statement.

b. Prepare a comparative balance sheet for eBay on December 31, Year 11, and December 31, Year 12. Refer to **Exhibit 1.1** for help in designing the format of the statement.

c. Prepare an analysis of the change in retained earnings during the year ending December 31, Year 12.

33. Preparing a balance sheet and income statement. The accounting records of The GAP, a retail clothing store, reveal the following for a recent year (amounts in thousands):

	January 31	
Balance Sheet Items	**Year 9**	**Year 10**
Accounts Payable	$ 684,130	$ 805,945
Cash	565,253	450,352
Common Stock	354,719	135,034
Merchandise Inventory	1,056,444	1,462,045
Notes Payable to Banks (due within one year)	90,690	168,961
Long-term Debt	496,455	784,925
Other Current Assets	250,127	285,393
Other Current Liabilities	778,283	777,973

(continued)

Other Noncurrent Assets	215,725	275,651
Other Noncurrent Liabilities	340,682	417,907
Property, Plant, and Equipment (net)	1,876,370	2,715,315
Retained Earnings	1,218,960	2,098,011

Income Statement Items	For the Year Ended January 31, Year 10
Administrative Expenses	$ 803,995
Cost of Goods Sold	6,775,262
Income Tax Expense	657,884
Interest Expense	31,755
Sales Revenue	11,635,398
Selling Expenses	2,239,437

a. Prepare a comparative balance sheet for The GAP as of January 31, Year 9 and Year 10. Classify each balance sheet item into one of the following categories: current assets, noncurrent assets, current liabilities, noncurrent liabilities, and shareholders' equity.

b. Prepare an income statement for The GAP for the year ended January 31, Year 10. Separate income items into revenues and expenses.

c. Prepare a schedule explaining the change in retained earnings between January 31, Year 9 and January 31, Year 10.

d. Compare the amounts on The GAP's balance sheet on January 31, Year 9 and January 31, Year 10. Identify the major changes and suggest possible explanations for these changes.

34. **Preparing a balance sheet and income statement.** The accounting records of Southwest Airlines reveal the following for a recent year (amounts in thousands):

Balance Sheet Items	December 31	
	Year 8	Year 9
Accounts Payable	$ 157,415	$ 156,755
Accounts Receivable	88,799	73,448
Cash	378,511	418,819
Common Stock	352,943	449,934
Current Maturities of Long-term Debt	11,996	7,873
Inventories	50,035	65,152
Long-term Debt	623,309	871,717
Other Current Assets	56,810	73,586
Other Current Liabilities	681,242	795,838
Other Noncurrent Assets	4,231	12,942
Other Noncurrent Liabilities	844,116	984,142
Property, Plant, and Equipment (net)	4,137,610	5,008,166
Retained Earnings	2,044,975	2,385,854

Income Statement Items	For the Year Ended December 31, Year 9
Fuel Expense	$ 492,415
Income Tax Expense	299,233
Interest Expense	22,883
Interest Revenue	14,918
Maintenance Expense	367,606
Other Operating Expenses	1,638,753
Sales Revenue	4,735,587
Salaries and Benefits Expense	1,455,237

a. Prepare a comparative balance sheet for Southwest Airlines as of December 31, Year 8 and Year 9. Classify each balance sheet item into one of the following categories: current assets, noncurrent assets, current liabilities, noncurrent liabilities, and shareholders' equity.

    b. Prepare an income statement for Southwest Airlines for the year ended December 31, Year 9. Separate income items into revenues and expenses.

    c. Prepare a schedule explaining the change in retained earnings between December 31, Year 8 and December 31, Year 9.

    d. Compare the amounts on Southwest Airlines' balance sheet on December 31, Year 8 and December 31, Year 9. Identify the major changes and suggest possible explanations for the changes.

35. Relations between net income and cash flows. The ABC Company starts the year in fine shape. The firm makes widgets—just what the customer wants. It makes them for $0.75 each and sells them for $1.00. The ABC Company keeps an inventory equal to shipments of the past 30 days, pays its bills promptly, and collects cash from customers within 30 days after the sale. The sales manager predicts a steady increase in sales of 500 widgets each month beginning in February. It looks like a great year, and it begins that way.

January 1	Cash, $875; receivables, $1,000; inventory, $750
January	In January the firm sells, on account for $1,000, 1,000 widgets costing $750. Net income for the month is $250. The firm collects receivables outstanding at the beginning of the month. Production equals 1,000 units at a total cost of $750. The books at the end of January show the following:
February 1	Cash, $1,125; receivables, $1,000; inventory, $750
February	This month's sales jump, as predicted, to 1,500 units. With a corresponding step-up in production to maintain the 30-day inventory, ABC Company makes 2,000 units at a cost of $1,500. All receivables from January sales are collected. Net income so far is $625. Now the books look like this:
March 1	Cash, $625; receivables, $1,500; inventory, $1,125
March	March sales are even better, increasing to 2,000 units. Collections are on time. Production, to adhere to the inventory policy, is 2,500 units. Operating results for the month show net income of $500. Net income to date is $1,125. The books show the following:
April 1	Cash, $250; receivables, $2,000; inventory, $1,500
April	In April, sales jump another 500 units to 2,500, and the manager of ABC Company shakes the sales manager's hand. Customers are paying right on time. Production is pushed to 3,000 units, and the month's business nets $625 for a net income to date of $1,750. The manager of ABC Company takes off for Miami before the accountant's report is issued. Suddenly a phone call comes from the treasurer: "Come home! We need money!"
May 1	Cash, $0; receivables, $2,500; inventory, $1,875

    a. Prepare an analysis that explains what happened to ABC Company. (*Hint:* Compute the amount of cash receipts and cash disbursements for each month during the period January 1 to May 1.)

    b. How can a firm show increasing net income but a decreasing amount of cash?

    c. What insights are provided by the problem about the need for all three financial statements—balance sheet, income statement, and statement of cash flows?

    d. What actions would you suggest that ABC Company take to deal with its cash flow problem?

36. Balance sheet and income statement relations. (Prepared by Professor Wesley T. Andrews Jr. and reproduced, with adaptation, by permission.)[5]

Once upon a time many, many years ago, a feudal landlord lived in a small province of central Europe. The landlord, called the Red-Bearded Baron, lived in a castle high on a hill. This benevolent fellow took responsibility for the well-being of many peasants who occupied the lands surrounding his castle. Each spring, as the snow began to melt, the Baron would decide how to provide for all his serf dependents during the coming year.

One spring, the Baron was thinking about the wheat crop of the coming growing season. "I believe that 30 acres of my land, being worth five bushels of wheat per acre, will produce enough wheat for next winter," he mused, "but who should do the farming? I believe I'll give Ivan the Indefatigable and Igor the Immutable the task of growing the wheat." Whereupon he

---

[5]*Accounting Review* (April 1974). Reproduced by permission of the American Accounting Association.

summoned Ivan and Igor, two gentry noted for their hard work and not overly active minds, for an audience.

"Ivan, you will farm on the 20-acre plot of ground, and Igor will farm the 10-acre plot," the Baron began. "I will give Ivan 20 bushels of wheat for seed and 20 pounds of fertilizer. (Twenty pounds fertilizer are worth two bushels of wheat.) Igor will get 10 bushels of wheat for seed and 10 pounds of fertilizer. I will give each of you an ox to pull a plow, but you will have to make arrangements with Feyador, the Plowmaker, for a plow. The oxen, incidentally, are only three years old and have never been used for farming, so they should have a good 10 years of farming ahead of them. Take good care of them, because an ox is worth 40 bushels of wheat. Come back next fall and return the oxen and the plows along with your harvest." Ivan and Igor bowed and withdrew from the Great Hall, taking with them the things provided by the Baron.

The summer came and went. After the harvest Ivan and Igor returned to the Great Hall to account to their master for the things given them in the spring. Ivan, pouring 223 bushels of wheat onto the floor, said, "My Lord, I present you with a slightly used ox, a plow broken beyond repair, and 223 bushels of wheat. I, unfortunately, owe Feyador, the Plowmaker, three bushels of wheat for the plow I got from him last spring. And, as you might expect, I used all the fertilizer and seed you gave me last spring. You will also remember, my Lord, that you took 20 bushels of my harvest for your own personal use."

Igor, who had been given 10 acres of land, 10 bushels of wheat, and 10 pounds of fertilizer, spoke next. "Here, my Lord, is a partially used-up ox, the plow for which I gave Feyador, the Plowmaker, three bushels of wheat from my harvest, and 105 bushels of wheat. I, too, used all my seed and fertilizer last spring. Also, my Lord, you took 30 bushels of wheat several days ago for your own table. I believe the plow is good for two more seasons."

"Knaves, you did well," said the Red-Bearded Baron. Blessed with this benediction, the two serfs departed. After the servants had taken their leave, the Red-Bearded Baron, watching the two hungry oxen slowly eating the wheat piled on the floor, began to contemplate what had happened. "Yes," he thought, "they did well, but I wonder which one did better?"

a. What measuring unit should the Red-Bearded Baron use to measure financial position and operating performance?

b. Prepare a balance sheet for Ivan and for Igor at both the beginning and the end of the period.

c. Prepare an income statement for Ivan and for Igor for the period.

d. Prepare a schedule reconciling the change in owner's equity between the beginning and the end of the period.

e. Did Ivan or Igor perform better during the period? Explain.

37. Ethical issues in financial reporting. A multinational computer equipment manufacturer reported the following amounts for two recent years (in millions).

	Year 9	Year 10
Revenues	$87,548	$88,396
Expenses	(75,791)	(76,862)
Income Before Income Taxes	$11,757	$11,534
Income Tax Expense	(4,045)	(3,441)
Net Income	$ 7,712	$ 8,093

a. Compute the ratio of net income divided by revenues for each year.

b. Compute the ratio of income before taxes divided by revenues for each year.

c. Compute the ratio of income tax expense divided by income before taxes, a ratio called the *effective tax rate*.

d. What do these ratios suggest as to the principal reason for the change in profitability between Year 9 and Year 10?

e. This firm reported increased revenues, net income, and profit margin between Year 9 and Year 10, despite weak conditions in technology industries. The explanation for the increased net income and profit margins was a reduction in the firm's effective tax rate.

To understand the reason for the reduced effective tax rate, the user of the financial statements would need to read the note to the financial statements on income taxes. Generally accepted accounting principles require firms to show the reasons why their effective tax rate differs from the statutory tax rate of 35 percent. The income tax note for this firm showed that the decreased effective tax rate was due to lower foreign taxes, the result of shifting certain foreign operations to countries with lower income tax rates. Understanding the income tax note requires knowledge of accounting and taxes usually attained by security analysts but not typically by the average investor.

Identify any ethical issues that this scenario raises and express your view as to whether this firm reported in an ethical manner.

Part Two

Accounting Concepts *and* Methods

2

FACMU11

chapter 2

Balance Sheet: Presenting the Investments and Financing of a Firm

Learning Objectives

1. Understand the accounting concepts of assets, liabilities, and shareholders' equity, including the conditions when firms recognize such items (recognition issues), their amounts (valuation issues), and where these items appear on the balance sheet (classification issues).

2. Understand the dual-entry recording framework and learn to use it to record a series of transactions, ending with the balance sheet.

3. Develop skills to analyze a balance sheet, focusing on the relations between assets, liabilities, and shareholders' equity that one would expect for financially healthy firms in different industries.

he user of the financial statements might raise questions such as the following with respect to items on the balance sheet:

1. Why does the stock market value Wal-Mart's common stock at $210.1 billion when the balance sheet reports total shareholders' equity of only $43.6 billion?
2. Why do current liabilities comprise 60 percent of total financing ($=$ total liabilities plus shareholders' equity) of Interpublic Group, a marketing services firm, whereas they comprise only 24 percent of total financing of American Airlines?
3. Why does long-term debt comprise 41 percent of total financing of American Airlines, whereas it comprises only 10 percent of total financing for Merck, a pharmaceutical company?
4. Why can savings and loan associations (S&L) face financial difficulties when their assets comprise loans receivable for residential housing and their financing included savings accounts and certificates of deposit?

Understanding the balance sheet permits the user to answer these and other questions about the financial position of a firm. This chapter discusses concepts underlying the balance sheet, illustrates procedures for preparing the balance sheet, and demonstrates relations the user should look for when analyzing the balance sheets of healthy firms in different industries. This chapter and the book take the perspective of a financial statement user. An understanding of the principal concepts underlying the balance sheet aids the user in analyzing and interpreting published balance sheets. Mastery of the concepts requires some understanding of the accounting methods (or procedures) that accountants follow in preparing the balance sheet.

Underlying Concepts

Chapter 1 introduced the balance sheet, one of the three principal financial statements. Common terminology in some countries refers to this financial statement as a *statement of financial position*. The balance sheet presents a snapshot of the investments of a firm (assets) and the financing of those investments (liabilities and shareholders' equity) as of a specific time. The balance sheet shows the following balance, or equality:

$$\text{Assets} = \text{Liabilities} + \text{Shareholders' Equity}$$

This equation states that a firm's assets balance with the sources of funds (the financing) provided by creditors and owners that the firm used to acquire those assets. The balance sheet presents resources from two angles: a listing of the specific forms in which a firm holds them (for example, cash, inventory, equipment), and a listing of the people or entities (for example, suppliers, employees, governments, shareholders) who have a claim on the assets because they provided the financing. Accountants often refer to the sum of liabilities plus shareholders' equity as *total equities* or *total financing*. You can think of the sum as total *sources of financing,* if that helps you to understand. The introduction to the balance sheet in **Chapter 1** left several questions unanswered:

1. Which resources does a firm recognize as assets?
2. What valuations does it place on these assets, that is, what number appears on the balance sheet for the asset?
3. How does it classify, or group, assets within the balance sheet?
4. Which claims against a firm's assets appear on the balance sheet as liabilities?
5. What valuations does a firm place on these liabilities?
6. How does a firm classify liabilities within the balance sheet?
7. What valuation does a firm place on shareholders' equity?
8. How does it disclose the shareholders' equity within the balance sheet and what is the economic significance, if any, of the differences among the various components of shareholders' equity?

The following discussion not only provides a background for understanding the balance sheet as currently prepared but also permits the reader to assess alternative methods for measuring financial position.

Asset Recognition

An asset is a resource that has the potential for providing a firm with a future economic benefit—the ability to generate future cash inflows or to reduce future cash outflows. A firm will recognize a resource as an asset only if (1) the firm has acquired rights to its use in the future as a result of a past transaction or exchange, and (2) the firm can measure or quantify the future benefits with a reasonable degree of precision.[1] All assets are future benefits; however, not all future benefits are assets.

Example 1 Miller Corporation sold merchandise and received a note from the customer, who agreed to pay $2,000 within four months. This note receivable is an asset of Miller Corporation because Miller has a right to receive a definite amount of cash in the future as a result of the previous sale of merchandise.

Example 2 Miller Corporation acquired manufacturing equipment costing $40,000 and agreed to pay the seller over three years. After the final payment, but not until then, the seller will transfer legal title to the equipment to Miller Corporation. Even though Miller Corporation will not have legal title for three years, the equipment is Miller's asset because Miller has the rights, responsibilities, rewards, and risks of ownership and can maintain those rights as long as it makes payments on schedule. The seller exchanged the use of the equipment in return for cash and rights to receive cash in the future.

Example 3 Miller Corporation has developed a well-known brand name for its products. Management expects this brand name to provide benefits to the firm in future sales of its products to customers. A brand name developed by a firm, however, is generally not an accounting asset. Although Miller Corporation has made various expenditures in the past to develop the brand name, accounting U.S. judges the future benefits too difficult to quantify with sufficient precision to allow Miller to recognize the name brand as an asset.

Example 4 Miller Corporation makes research and development expenditures each year to develop new technologies and create new products. Accounting views the future benefits of this research to be too uncertain to justify recognition of an asset.

As **Examples 3** and **4** illustrate, accountants sometimes encounter difficulty in quantifying future benefits with sufficient precision to justify recognizing an asset. Let's extend **Examples 3** and **4** by assuming that Miller Corporation plans to acquire another firm with recognizable brand names and proved technologies. Miller Corporation hires a valuation appraisal firm to value these brand names and proved technologies and assist Miller Corporation in deciding how much to pay for the other firm. Accounting requires Miller to allocate portions of the purchase price to the brand names and proved technologies and report them as assets because the independent appraisal

---

[1] Financial Accounting Standards Board, *Statement of Financial Accounting Concepts No. 6*, "Elements of Financial Statements," 1985, par. 25. See the glossary for the Board's actual definition of an asset.

and the negotiation between an independent buyer and seller as to the purchase price establish the existence and value of the future benefits.

Example 5   Miller Corporation plans to acquire a fleet of new trucks next year to replace those that are wearing out. These new trucks are not assets now because Miller Corporation has made no exchange with a supplier and, therefore, has not established a right to the future use of the trucks.

Another difficulty that accountants encounter in deciding which items to recognize as assets relates to mutually unexecuted contracts, sometimes called **executory contracts**. An executory contract involves a contractual exchange of promises to perform in the future but neither party has yet performed. In **Example 5**, suppose that Miller Corporation entered into a contract with a local truck dealer to acquire the trucks next year at a cash price of $80,000. Miller Corporation has acquired rights to future benefits, but the contract remains unexecuted by both the truck dealer (who must deliver the trucks) and Miller Corporation (who must pay the agreed cash price). Accounting does not generally recognize executory contracts, a *mere exchange of promises,* as assets. Miller Corporation will recognize an asset for the trucks when it receives them next year.

To take the illustration one step further, assume that Miller Corporation advances the truck dealer $15,000 of the purchase price at the time it signs the contract. Miller Corporation has acquired rights to future benefits and has exchanged cash. Thus, the contract is partially executed. Current accounting practice treats the $15,000 advance on the purchase of equipment as an asset reported under a title such as Advances to Suppliers. The trucks would not be assets at this time, however, because Miller Corporation has not yet received sufficient future rights to the services of the trucks to justify their inclusion in the balance sheet. Similar asset-recognition questions arise when a firm leases buildings and equipment for its own use under long-term leases or when a firm contracts with a transport company to deliver all of the firm's products to customers for some period of years. Later chapters discuss these issues more fully.

Asset Valuation

Accounting must assign a monetary amount to each asset in the balance sheet. The accountant might use several methods of computing this amount.

Acquisition or Historical Cost
The amount of cash paid (or the cash equivalent value of other forms of payment) in acquiring an asset is the **acquisition (historical) cost** of the asset. The accountant can typically ascertain this amount by referring to contracts, invoices, and canceled checks related to the acquisition of the asset. Nothing compels a firm to acquire a given asset, so accountants assume that the firm expects the future benefits from an acquired asset to be at least as large as the acquisition cost. At the time of acquisition, historical cost sets the lower limit on the value of the asset's future benefits to the firm.

Current Replacement Cost
Each asset might appear on the balance sheet at the current cost of replacing it. Because the firm has to pay this amount to gain entry to use the asset and enjoy its future benefits, accountants sometimes refer to **current replacement cost** as an **entry value**.

For assets purchased frequently, such as merchandise inventory, the accountant can often calculate current replacement cost by consulting suppliers' catalogs or price lists. But accountants have difficulty in measuring the replacement costs of assets purchased less frequently—assets such as land, buildings, and equipment. A major obstacle to using current replacement cost as the valuation basis is the absence of well-organized secondhand markets for many used assets. When a firm cannot easily find similar used assets for sale, ascertaining current replacement cost requires finding the cost of a similar new asset and then adjusting that amount downward for the services of the asset already used. Difficulties can arise, however, in finding a similar asset. With technological improvements and other quality changes, equipment purchased currently will likely differ from equipment that a firm acquired 10 years earlier but still uses. Consider, for example, the difficulties in ascertaining the current replacement cost of a five-year-old computer, computer software package, or cellular phone—you just can't find a new item with the same (limited) features of the old one. An accountant who cannot find the replacement cost of the specific old one might substitute the current replacement cost of an asset capable of rendering equivalent services. This approach, however, requires subjectivity in identifying assets with equivalent service potential.

Current Net Realizable Value   The net amount of cash (selling price less selling costs) that a firm would receive currently if it sold an asset is its **current net realizable value**. Because the firm would receive this amount if it exited ownership, accountants refer to net realizable value as an **exit value**. In measuring net realizable value, one generally assumes that the firm sells the asset as a willing seller, in an orderly fashion, rather than through a forced sale at some distress price.

Measuring net realizable value entails difficulties similar to those encountered in measuring current replacement cost. Without well-organized secondhand markets for used equipment, the accountant cannot readily measure net realizable value, particularly for equipment specially designed for a firm's needs. In this case, the future benefits to the firm from using the asset (value in use) will generally exceed the current selling price of the asset (value in exchange).

Present Value of Future Net Cash Flows   An asset provides a future benefit. This future benefit results from the asset's ability either to generate future net cash receipts or to reduce future cash expenditures. Accounting could measure the net **present value** of the expected cash flows and use that amount for the valuation. For example, accounts receivable from customers will lead directly to future cash receipts. The firm can sell merchandise inventory for cash or promises to pay cash. The firm can use equipment to manufacture products that it can sell for cash. A building that the firm owns reduces future cash outflows for rental payments. Because these cash flows represent the future services, or benefits, of assets, the accountant might base asset valuations on them.

Because cash can earn interest over time, today's value of a stream of future cash flows, called its *present value*, is less than the sum of the future cash amounts that a firm will receive or save over time. The balance sheet shows asset valuations measured as of a current date. If valuation of an asset as of a current date reflects its future cash flows, then the accountant must discount the future net cash flows to find their present value as of the date of the balance sheet. **Chapters 9** and **10** and the **Appendix** discuss the discounting methodology. The following example presents the general approach.

Example 6   Miller Corporation sold merchandise to a reliable customer, General Models Company, who promised to pay $10,000 one year after the date of sale. General Models Company signed a promissory note to that effect and gave the note to Miller Corporation. Miller Corporation judges that the current borrowing rate of General Models Company is 10 percent per year. That is, if Miller Corporation voluntarily made a loan to General Models Company, the loan would carry an interest rate of 10 percent. Miller Corporation will receive $10,000 one year from today. The $10,000 includes both the amount lent initially plus interest on that amount for one year. Today's value of the $10,000 to be received in one year is not $10,000 but about $9,091; that is, $9,091 plus 10 percent interest on $9,091 equals $10,000 (= 1.10 × $9,091). Hence, the present value of $10,000 to be received one year from today is $9,091. (Miller Corporation is indifferent between receiving approximately $9,091 today and a promise from General Models Company for $10,000 due one year from today.) The asset represented by General Models Company's promissory note has a present value of $9,091. If the balance sheet states the note at the present value of the future cash flows, it would appear at approximately $9,091 on the date of sale.

Using discounted cash flows to value individual assets requires solving several problems. First: one must deal with the uncertainty of the amounts of future cash flows. The amounts a firm will receive can depend on whether competitors introduce new products, the rate of inflation, and other factors. Second: one must decide how to allocate the cash receipts from the sale of a single item of merchandise inventory to all of the assets involved in its production and distribution (for example, equipment, buildings, sales staff's automobiles). Third: one must decide how to select the appropriate rate to use to discount the future cash flows to the present. Shall the interest rate be the firm's borrowing rate? Or should the firm use the rate at which it could invest excess cash? Or, should the firm use its cost of capital (a concept introduced in managerial accounting and finance courses)? In the **Example 6** above, the facts make General Models's borrowing rate the right one.

Selecting the Appropriate Valuation Basis

The valuation basis selected depends on the purpose of the financial report.

Example 7   Miller Corporation prepares its income tax return for the current year. The Internal Revenue Code and Regulations specify that firms must use acquisition or adjusted acquisition cost valuations in most instances.

Example 8   A fire recently destroyed the manufacturing plant, equipment, and inventory of Miller Corporation. The firm's fire insurance policy provides coverage in an amount equal to the cost of replacing the assets destroyed. Thus, current replacement cost at the time of the fire provides the appropriate support for the insurance claim.

Example 9   Miller Corporation plans to dispose of a manufacturing division that has operated unprofitably. In deciding on the lowest price to accept for the division as a unit, the firm considers the net realizable value of each asset, which it will sum to estimate a lower bound on the acceptable selling price for the division.

Example 10   Brown Corporation considers purchasing Miller Corporation. The highest price that Brown Corporation should pay is the present value of the future net cash flows it can realize from owning Miller Corporation.

Example 11   Miller Corporation discovers that the demand for land it owns has declined so much that the original cost of the land exceeds the sum of all expected rental receipts for the indefinite future. Generally accepted accounting principles (GAAP) require Miller Corporation to show the land on the balance sheet at the net present value of the expected cash flows, discounted using a rate adjusted for the risk of the expected cash flows—the more certain the cash flows, the lower the discount rate.[2]

Generally Accepted Accounting Asset Valuation Bases

The asset valuation basis appropriate for financial statements issued to shareholders and other investors is not so obvious. The financial statements currently prepared by publicly held firms use two valuation bases for assets that have not declined substantially in value since the firm acquired them, one basis for monetary assets and a different basis for nonmonetary assets.

Monetary assets include cash and claims to specified amounts of cash to be received in the future, such as accounts receivable. Monetary assets generally appear on the balance sheet at their net present value—their current cash, or cash equivalent, value. Cash appears at the amount of cash on hand or in the bank. Accounts receivable from customers appear at the amount of cash the firm expects to collect in the future. If the time until a firm collects a receivable spans more than one year, the firm discounts the expected future cash inflow to a present value. Most firms, however, collect their accounts receivable within one to three months. The amount of future cash flows (undiscounted) approximately equals the present (discounted) value of these flows; thus accounting ignores the discounting process on the basis of a lack of materiality.

Nonmonetary assets will generate unknown, rather than specified, amounts of cash in the future and include merchandise inventory, land, buildings, and equipment. Nonmonetary assets generally appear at acquisition costs, in some cases adjusted downward to reflect that the firm has consumed some of the assets' services and, in others, to recognize some declines in market value. **Chapters 3, 7**, and **8** discuss these adjustments, called *depreciation* when the firm has used some of the services from the asset, and called *holding losses* or *impairments* when market value has declined even more than the amount of the depreciation. Some nonmonetary assets, such as holdings of marketable securities, appear on the balance sheet at current market value.

The acquisition cost of an asset includes more than its invoice price. Acquisition cost includes all expenditures made or obligations incurred to prepare an asset for its intended use by a firm. Transportation costs, installation costs, handling charges, and any other necessary and reasonable costs incurred until the firm puts the asset into service are part of the total cost assigned to the asset. For example, the accountant might calculate the cost of an item of equipment as follows:

---

[2] Financial Accounting Standards Board, *Statement of Financial Accounting Standards No. 121*, "Accounting for the Impairment of Long-Lived Assets and for Long-Lived Assets to Be Disposed Of," 1995.

Invoice Price of Equipment	$120,000
Less: 2 Percent Discount for Prompt Cash Payment	(2,400)
Net Invoice Price	$117,600
Transportation Cost	3,260
Installation Costs	7,350
Total Cost of Equipment	$128,210

The accountant records the acquisition cost of this equipment as $128,210.

Instead of disbursing cash or incurring a liability, the firm might give (or swap or barter) other forms of consideration (for example, common stock, merchandise inventory, or land) in acquiring an asset. In these cases, acquisition cost will reflect the market value of the consideration the firm gives or the market value of the asset it receives, whichever market value the firm can more reliably measure.

Example 12   Miller Corporation issued 1,000 shares of its common stock to the former owner in acquiring a used machine. The common stock of Miller Corporation traded on a stock exchange for $15 per share on the day of the exchange. The firm records the machine on the books of Miller Corporation for $15,000.

Foundations for Acquisition Cost   Accounting's use of acquisition cost valuations for nonmonetary assets rests on three important concepts or conventions.

First, accounting assumes that a firm is a **going concern**. In other words, accounting assumes a firm will remain in operation long enough to carry out all of its current plans. The firm will realize any increases in the market value of assets held in the normal course of business when the firm receives higher prices for its products. Imagine a furniture maker who purchased several years ago now-rare Honduran mahogany. The mahogany has increased in value, but the furniture maker will not recognize that increase until later when a customer purchases, say, a table made from that mahogany. Accounting generally assumes that the current values of the individual assets have little relevance for users.

Second, acquisition cost valuations provide more reliable information than do the other valuation methods. **Reliability** in accounting refers to the ability of a measure, such as acquisition cost, to faithfully represent what it purports to measure (that is, the economic value sacrificed to acquire an asset). Reliability also encompasses the ability to verify, or audit, the measured amount. Different accountants will likely agree on the acquisition cost of an asset. Differences among observers can arise in ascertaining an asset's current replacement cost, current net realizable value, and present value of future cash flows.

Third, acquisition cost generally provides more conservative (that is, lower) valuations of assets (and measures of earnings) than do the other valuation methods. Many accountants believe that financial statements will less likely mislead users if balance sheets report assets at lower rather than higher amounts. Thus, **conservatism** has evolved as a convention to justify acquisition cost valuations (and subsequent downward, but generally not upward, adjustments to acquisition cost valuations).

The general acceptance of these valuation bases does not justify them. Research has not provided guidance as to the valuation basis—chosen from acquisition cost, current replacement cost, current net realizable value, and present value of future net cash flows—that has most relevance to financial statement users. Many preparers of financial statements prefer acquisition cost valuations to those based on market values because market valuations cause reported income to be more volatile than do acquisition cost valuations.

Asset Classification

The classification of assets within the balance sheet varies in published annual reports. The following discussion gives the principal asset categories.

Current Assets   Cash and other assets that a firm expects to turn into cash or to sell or consume during the normal operating cycle of the business are **current assets**. The operating cycle refers to the period of time during which a given firm converts cash into salable goods and services, sells those goods and services to customers, and receives cash from customers in payment for their purchases. The operating cycle for most manufacturing, retailing, and service firms spans one to three months, whereas for firms in some industries, such as building construction or liquor distilling, the operating cycle may span several years. Except for firms that have an operating cycle longer than one year, conventional accounting practice uses one year as the dividing line between current assets and noncurrent assets. Current assets include the following: cash; marketable securities held for the short term; accounts and notes receivable; inventories of merchandise, raw materials, supplies, work in process, and finished goods; and prepaid operating costs, such as insurance and rent paid for in advance. Prepaid costs, or prepayments, are current assets because if the firm did not pay for them in advance, it would use current assets within the next operating cycle to acquire those services.

Investments   A second section of the balance sheet, labeled *Investments*, includes long-term (noncurrent) investments in securities of other firms. For example, a firm might purchase shares of common stock of a supplier to help ensure continued availability of raw materials. Or, it might acquire shares of common stock of a firm in another area of business activity to permit the acquiring firm to diversify its operations. When one corporation (the parent) owns more than 50 percent of the voting stock in another corporation (the subsidiary), it usually prepares a single set of consolidated financial statements; that is, the firm merges, or consolidates, the specific assets, liabilities, revenues, and expenses of the subsidiary with its own in the financial statements. The securities shown in the Investments section of the balance sheet therefore represent investments in firms whose assets and liabilities the parent or investor firm has not consolidated with its own. **Chapter 11** discusses consolidated financial statements and other methods of accounting for inter-corporate investments.

Property, Plant, and Equipment   The phrase *property, plant, and equipment* (sometimes called **plant,** or **fixed, assets**) designates the tangible, long-lived assets used in a firm's operations over a period of years and generally not acquired for resale. This category includes land, buildings, machinery, automobiles, furniture, fixtures, computers, and other equipment. The balance sheet shows these items (except land) at acquisition cost reduced by the cumulative (or *accumulated,* to use common accounting terminology) depreciation since the firm acquired the assets. (**Chapter 8** discusses additional downward adjustments if the assets have declined in value, beyond that indicated by depreciation calculations.) Frequently, only the net balance, or book value, appears on the balance sheet. Land usually appears at acquisition cost.

Intangible Assets   Such items as patents, trademarks, franchises, and goodwill are **intangible assets**. Accountants generally do not recognize as assets those expenditures that a firm makes in developing intangibles because of the difficulty of ascertaining the existence and value of future benefits. Consider, for example, the difficulty of identifying whether future benefits exist when a firm expends cash to research new technologies or advertise its products. Accountants do, however, recognize as assets those specifically identifiable intangibles that firms acquire in market exchanges with other entities—intangibles such as a patent or brand name acquired from its holder. Accounting's recognition of an asset in the latter case presumes that a firm would not purchase a patent, brand name, or other intangible from another entity unless the firm expected future benefits. The exchange between an independent purchaser and seller provides reliable evidence of the value of the future benefits. **Chapter 8** discusses more fully the accounting used for internally developed intangibles versus that used for externally purchased intangibles, a topic that remains controversial.

Problem 2.1 for Self-Study

Asset recognition and valuation.   The transactions listed below relate to Coca-Cola Company. Indicate whether or not each transaction immediately gives rise to an asset of the company under GAAP. If accounting recognizes an asset, state the account title and amount.

a. The company spends $10 million to develop a new soft drink. No commercially feasible product has yet evolved, but the company hopes that such a product will evolve in the near future.
b. The company signs a contract with United Can Corporation for the purchase of $4 million of soft drink cans. It makes a deposit of $400,000 on signing the contract.

(continued)

Problem 2.1 for Self-Study *(continued)*

c. The company spends $2 million for advertisements that appeared during the past month: $500,000 to advertise the Coca-Cola name and $1,500,000 for specific brand advertisements, such as those for Diet Coke.

d. The company issues 50,000 shares of its common stock, valued on the market at $2.5 million, in the acquisition of all the outstanding stock of Corning Glass Company, a supplier of soft-drink bottles.

e. The company spends $800,000 on educational-assistance programs for its middle-level managers to obtain MBAs. Historically, 80 percent of the employees involved in the program receive their MBAs and remain with the company 10 years or more.

f. The company acquires and occupies land and a building near Atlanta by signing a mortgage payable for $75 million. Because the company has not yet paid the mortgage, the title document for the land and building remains in the vault of the bank, the holder of the mortgage note.

Solutions to self-study problems appear at the end of the chapter.

Liability Recognition

A liability arises when a firm receives benefits or services and in exchange promises to pay the provider of those goods or services a reasonably definite amount at a reasonably definite future time. The firm usually pays cash but may give goods or services.[3] All liabilities are obligations; however, not all obligations are accounting liabilities.

Example 13 Miller Corporation purchased merchandise inventory and agreed to pay the supplier $8,000 within 30 days. This obligation is a liability because Miller Corporation received the goods and must pay a definite amount at a reasonably definite future time.

Example 14 Miller Corporation borrowed $4 million by issuing long-term bonds. On December 31 of each year it must make annual interest payments of 10 percent of the amount borrowed, and it must repay the $4 million principal in 20 years. This obligation is a liability because Miller Corporation received the cash and must repay the debt in definite amounts at definite future times.

Example 15 Miller Corporation received an advance of $600 from a customer for products that Miller Corporation will manufacture next year. The cash advance creates a liability of $600. Miller Corporation must manufacture and deliver the products next year or return the cash advance. (In some transactions of this sort, the manufacturer does not have the option to return the cash. If it does not provide the goods as promised it may find itself liable for court-awarded damages.)

Example 16 Miller Corporation provides a three-year warranty on its products. The obligation to maintain the products under warranty plans creates a liability. The selling price for its products includes a charge for future warranty services even when the price tag or invoice does not explicitly show a separate charge for the promise. As customers pay the selling price, Miller Corporation receives a benefit (that is, the cash collected). Past experience provides a basis for estimating the amount of the liability. Miller Corporation can estimate the proportion of customers who will seek services under the warranty agreement and the expected cost of providing the warranty services. Thus, Miller Corporation can measure the amount of the obligation with a reasonable degree of accuracy and will show it as a liability.

Example 17 A customer has sued Miller Corporation, claiming damages of $10 million from faulty products manufactured by Miller Corporation. The case has not yet gone to trial. Accounting

---

[3] *SFAC No. 6*, par. 35. See the **Glossary** for the Board's actual definition of a liability.

typically does not recognize unsettled lawsuits as liabilities because of uncertainty regarding both the need to pay and the amount, as well as the timing, of any payment. Miller will disclose in notes to its financial statements the fact of the lawsuit and the potential for future payments.

Example 18   Miller Corporation has guaranteed the payment of a personal loan from a local bank by its chief executive officer (CEO) if the CEO cannot make payment as the loan agreement requires. Accounting does not recognize loan guarantees as liabilities because of the uncertainty regarding the need to pay.

One of the troublesome questions of liability recognition relates to **contingent obligations**. Contingent obligations require some future event to occur before accounting can establish the existence and amount of a liability. The unsettled lawsuit in **Example 17** and the loan guarantee in **Example 18** are contingent obligations. GAAP requires the recognition of a liability only when the payment is probable. As **Chapter 9** discusses, most accountants interpret *probable* to mean greater than 80 or 85 percent. The obligation under the warranty plan in **Example 16** meets this probable criterion because past experience shows that a predictable percentage of customers will make claims of an estimated amount.

Example 19   Miller Corporation signed an agreement with its employees' labor union, promising to increase wages by 6 percent and to provide for medical and life insurance. Although this agreement creates an obligation, it does not immediately create an accounting liability. Employees have not yet provided labor services that would require the firm to pay wages and insurance. As employees work, a liability arises.

A second troublesome question of liability recognition relates to obligations under mutually unexecuted contracts. The labor union agreement in **Example 19** is a mutually unexecuted contract. Other examples include some leases, purchase order commitments, and employment contracts. Accounting does not usually recognize as liabilities the obligations created by mutually unexecuted contracts. As **Example 5** illustrates, accounting likewise does not recognize assets related to mutually unexecuted contracts. **Chapter 10** discusses the accounting treatment of these off-balance-sheet financing arrangements.

Liability Valuation

Most liabilities are monetary, requiring payments of specific amounts of cash. Those due within one year or less appear at the amount of cash the firm expects to pay to discharge the obligation. If the payment dates extend more than one year into the future (for example, as in the case of the bonds in **Example 14**), the liability appears at the present value of the future cash outflows.

A liability that requires delivering goods or rendering services, rather than paying cash, is nonmonetary. The warranty liability in **Example 16** is nonmonetary and appears on the balance sheet at the estimated cost of providing the warranty services. The cash advance in **Example 15** is also nonmonetary but appears on the balance sheet at the amount of cash received. The seemingly inconsistent valuation of these two nonmonetary liabilities results from accounting's view that the warranty liability relates to products that the firm has already sold, whereas the cash advance relates to products that the firm will manufacture and deliver to customers next year. Other examples of nonmonetary liabilities arising from cash advances include amounts received by magazine publishers for future magazine subscriptions, by theatrical and sports teams for future performances or games, and by landlords for future rental services. The title frequently used for liabilities of this type is Advances from Customers.

Liability Classification

The balance sheet typically classifies liabilities in one of the following categories.

Current Liabilities   Obligations that a firm expects to pay or discharge during the normal operating cycle of the firm, usually one year, are **current liabilities**. In general, the firm uses current assets to pay current liabilities. This category includes liabilities to merchandise suppliers, employees, and governmental units. It also includes notes and bonds payable to the extent that they will require the use of current assets within the next year.

Long-Term Debt   Obligations arising from borrowings having due dates, or maturities, more than one year after the balance sheet date are long-term debt. Long-term debt includes bonds, mortgages, and similar debts, as well as some obligations under long-term leases.

Other Long-Term Liabilities   Obligations not properly considered as current liabilities or long-term debt appear as other long-term liabilities, which include items such as deferred income taxes and some retirement obligations.

Problem 2.2 for Self-Study

Liability recognition and valuation.   The transactions listed below relate to the New York Times Company. Indicate whether or not each transaction immediately gives rise to a liability of the company under GAAP. If the company recognizes a liability, state the account title and amount.

a. The company receives $10 million for newspaper subscriptions covering the one-year period beginning next month.
b. The company receives an invoice for $4 million from its advertising agency for television advertisements that appeared last month promoting the New York Times.
c. The company signs a one-year lease for rental of new delivery vehicles it will use in Brooklyn. It pays $50,000 of the annual rental of $80,000 at the signing.
d. Attorneys have notified the company that a New York City resident, seriously injured by one of the company's delivery vehicles in lower Manhattan, has sued the company for $10 million. Company lawyers have predicted that the court is likely to find the company liable in the lawsuit, but the company carries sufficient insurance to cover any losses.
e. Refer to part **d** above. Assume now that the company carries no insurance against such losses.
f. A two-week strike by employees has closed down newspaper publishing operations. As a result, the company could not deliver subscriptions totaling $2 million.

Shareholders' Equity Valuation and Disclosure

The shareholders' equity in a firm is a residual interest or claim[4]—that is, the owners have a claim on all assets not required to meet the claims of creditors.[5] The valuation of the assets and liabilities included in the balance sheet therefore determines the valuation of total shareholders' equity.

Accounting distinguishes between capital contributed by owners and earnings retained by a firm. The balance sheet for a corporation generally separates the amount that shareholders contribute directly for an interest in the firm (that is, common stock) from earnings the firm subsequently realizes in excess of dividends declared (that is, retained earnings).

In addition, the balance sheet usually further disaggregates the amount received from shareholders into the **par** or **stated value** of the shares and the amounts contributed in excess of par value or stated value. The par or stated value of a share of stock is an amount assigned to comply with the corporation laws of each state and rarely equals the market price of the shares at the time the firm issues them.

The distinctions between common stock and retained earnings, and between the par or stated value and the amounts received in excess of par or stated value, sometimes have legal implications but not economic significance. Shareholders have a claim of all assets in excess of all liabilities, which equals total shareholders' equity. (**Chapter 12** discusses details of accounting for shareholders' equity.)

Example 20   Stephens Corporation legally incorporated on January 1, Year 1. It issued 15,000 shares of $10 par value common stock for $10 cash per share. During Year 1, Stephens Corporation generated net income of $30,000 and paid dividends of $10,000 to shareholders.

---

[4] Although shareholders' equity is equal to assets minus liabilities, accounting provides an independent method for computing the amount. This and the next chapter present this method.

[5] *SFAC No. 6,* par. 49.

The shareholders' equity section of the balance sheet of Stephens Corporation on December 31, Year 1, is as follows:

Common Stock (par value of $10 per share, 15,000 shares issued and outstanding)	$150,000
Retained Earnings	20,000
Total Shareholders' Equity	$170,000

Example 21 Instead of issuing $10 par value common stock as in **Example 20**, Stephens Corporation issued 15,000 shares of $1 par value common stock for $10 cash per share. (The market price of a share of common stock depends on the economic value of the firm, not on the par value of the shares.) The shareholders' equity section of the balance sheet of Stephens Corporation on December 31, Year 1, is as follows:

Common Stock (par value of $1 per share, 15,000 shares issued and outstanding)	$ 15,000
Additional Paid-in Capital (or Capital Contributed in Excess of Par Value)	135,000
Retained Earnings	20,000
Total Shareholders' Equity	$170,000

Firms legally organized as partnerships or sole proprietorships, instead of as corporations, do not make a distinction between contributed capital and retained earnings in their balance sheets. Rather, the owners' equity section of the balance sheet combines each owner's share of capital contributions and each owner's share of earnings in excess of distributions.

Example 22 Refer to **Examples 20** and **21**. Assume that William Kinsey and Brenda Stephens organized this business firm as a partnership, with Kinsey and Stephens as equal partners. The owners' equity section of the firm's balance sheet on December 31, Year 1, is as follows:

William Kinsey, Capital	$ 85,000
Brenda Stephens, Capital	85,000
Total Owners' Equity	$170,000

A sole proprietorship would, by definition, have only one owner.

Accounting Procedures for Preparing the Balance Sheet

Keeping in mind the concepts underlying assets, liabilities, and shareholders' equity, we can now consider how accounting applies these concepts in preparing the balance sheet. A user of the financial statements does not need to understand the record-keeping procedures that accountants follow to prepare a balance sheet. However, the user needs some type of analytical framework to understand how various transactions or events affect a firm's financial position, profitability, and cash flows. This chapter introduces an analytical framework based on the balance sheet equation and applies it to the preparation of the balance sheet. **Chapter 3** extends the analytical framework to include income transactions. **Chapter 4** extends the analytical framework to the statement of cash flows.

Our presentation of the analytical framework proceeds in three steps:

1. Demonstrate that all transactions and events have a dual effect on the balance sheet equation.
2. Illustrate the use of a spreadsheet for accumulating information about the dual effects of transactions and events in order to prepare a balance sheet.
3. Illustrate the use of journal entries for summarizing the dual effects of any particular transaction or event.

Dual Effects of Transactions on the Balance Sheet Equation

Firms engage in various transactions, or exchanges, with other entities or individuals during a period. For example, firms acquire merchandise from suppliers, pay employees for labor services received, sell merchandise to customers, pay taxes to governments, and so on. Other events occur during the period, which do not necessarily involve an exchange with another entity during that period. For example, firms consume the services of buildings and equipment as they use them in operations and incur an obligation to pay interest on outstanding loans. These transactions and events are the initial building blocks for the financial statements. Accountants record the effects of *each* of these transactions and events as they occur during the period and then *accumulate* the effects of all transactions and events for presentation in the financial statements. Thus,

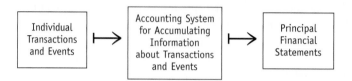

The analytical framework that we use throughout this book for understanding the effects of trans-actions and events on the financial statements relies on the balance sheet equation as its structural base. As this and subsequent chapters illustrate, the balance sheet equation provides a rich struc-tural base for the analytical framework because it incorporates investing, financing, and operating transactions—three key activities of business firms. As we apply the analytical framework to successively more complex transactions in later chapters, you will want to recall that the basic balance sheet equation underlies the recording of all business transactions and events.

The balance sheet equation shows the equality of assets with liabilities plus shareholders' equity. The balance sheet equation maintains this equality by reporting the effects of each trans-action in a dual manner. Any single transaction will have one of the following four effects or some combination of these effects:

1. It increases an asset and increases either a liability or shareholders' equity (an increase in investments and financing).
2. It decreases an asset and decreases either a liability or shareholders' equity (a decrease in investments and financing).
3. It increases one asset and decreases another asset (a change in the mix of investments).
4. It increases one liability or shareholders' equity and decreases another liability or sharehold-ers' equity (a change in the mix of financing).

To understand the dual effects of various transactions on the balance sheet equation, consider the following transactions for Miller Corporation during January as it prepares to open for busi-ness on February 1:

(1) On January 1, the firm issues 10,000 shares of $10 par value common stock for $100,000 cash.
(2) On January 5, it pays $60,000 cash to purchase equipment.
(3) On January 15, Miller Corporation purchases merchandise inventory costing $15,000 from a supplier, agreeing to pay later.
(4) On January 21, it pays the supplier in (3) $8,000 of the amount due.
(5) On January 25, the supplier in (3) accepts 700 shares of common stock at par value in settle-ment of the $7,000 amount still owed.
(6) On January 31, the firm pays $600 cash for a one-year insurance premium for coverage beginning February 1.
(7) On January 31, Miller Corporation receives $3,000 from a customer for merchandise to be delivered during February.

Exhibit 2.1 illustrates the dual effects of these transactions on the balance sheet equation. Note that after each transaction, assets equal liabilities plus shareholders' equity.

Each transaction has two effects—an outflow and an inflow. For example, the firm issues common stock to shareholders and receives cash. The firm makes a cash expenditure and receives equipment. The firm promises to make a future cash payment to a supplier and receives merchandise inventory. Most transactions and events recorded in the accounting

	EXHIBIT 2.1	MILLER CORPORATION Illustration of Dual Effects of Transactions on Balance Sheet Equation					

Transaction		Assets	=	Liabilities	+	Shareholders' Equity
(1)	On January 1, Miller Corporation issues 10,000 shares of $10 par value common stock for $100,000 cash (an increase in an asset and a shareholders' equity).	+$100,000	=	$ 0	+	$100,000
	Subtotal	$100,000	=	$ 0	+	$100,000
(2)	On January 5, the firm pays $60,000 cash to purchase equipment (an increase in one asset and a decrease in another asset).	− 60,000 + 60,000				
	Subtotal	$100,000	=	$ 0	+	$100,000
(3)	On January 15, the firm purchases merchandise inventory costing $15,000 from a supplier on account (an increase in an asset and a liability).	+ 15,000		+15,000		
	Subtotal	$115,000	=	$ 15,000	+	$100,000
(4)	On January 21, the firm pays the supplier in (3) $8,000 of the amount due (a decrease in an asset and a liability).	− 8,000		− 8,000		
	Subtotal	$107,000	=	$ 7,000	+	$100,000
(5)	On January 25, the supplier in (3) accepts 700 shares of common stock in settlement of the $7,000 still owed (an increase in a shareholders' equity and a decrease in a liability).			− 7,000	+	7,000
	Subtotal	$107,000	=	$ 0		$107,000
(6)	On January 31, the firm pays $600 cash for a one-year insurance premium for coverage beginning February 1 (an increase in one asset and a decrease in another asset).	+ 600 − 600				
	Subtotal	$107,000	=	$ 0	+	$107,000
(7)	On January 31, the firm receives $3,000 from a customer for merchandise to be delivered during February (an increase in an asset and a liability).	+ 3,000		+ 3,000		
	Total—January 31	$110,000	=	$ 3,000	+	$107,000

system result from exchanges. The accounting records reflect the inflows and outflows arising from these exchanges.

At this early stage in your study of accounting, we cannot overemphasize the importance of identifying the dual effects of every transaction on the balance sheet equation. You will not fully understand the business transaction or event unless you can identify these dual effects.

Although **Exhibit 2.1** illustrates the dual effects of individual transactions, it does not provide a useful framework for preparing a balance sheet at the end of a period. We cannot easily know how much of the total assets of $110,000 represents cash, how much represents inventory, how much represents equipment, and so on. We need to move to an additional level of disaggregation of assets, liabilities, and shareholders' equity to obtain the needed amounts for a balance sheet. To do this, we move next in our development of the analytical framework to the use of a spreadsheet for accumulating information about individual transactions and events during a period.

Problem 2.3 for Self-Study

Dual effects of transactions on balance sheet equation. Using the format in **Exhibit 2.1**, indicate the effects of each of the following transactions of Gaines Corporation on the balance sheet equation.

1. The firm issues 20,000 shares of $10 par value common stock for $12 cash per share.
2. The firm issues $100,000 principal amount of bonds for $100,000 cash.

(continued)

Problem 2.3 for Self-Study *(continued)*

3. The firm acquires, with $220,000 in cash, land costing $40,000 and a building costing $180,000.
4. The firm acquires, on account, equipment costing $25,000 and merchandise inventory costing $12,000.
5. The firm signs an agreement to rent equipment from its owner and pays $1,500 rental in advance.
6. The firm pays $28,000 to the suppliers in **4**.

Spreadsheet Analysis of Business Transactions

Exhibit 2.1 presents the balance sheet equation horizontally. That is,

$$\text{Assets} = \text{Liabilities} + \text{Shareholders' Equity}$$

Recall though that the balance sheet reports amounts at a moment in time. Picture now the balance sheet equation presented vertically at the beginning and end of a period. Thus,

This vertical arrangement of the balance sheet equation corresponds with the depiction in **Figure 1.3** in **Chapter 1** of the relation between the balance sheet, income statement, and statement of cash flows for a period of time. We use this vertical arrangement to design a spreadsheet for recording the dual effects of transactions on the balance sheet equation.

Exhibit 2.2 presents the spreadsheet template, which you can download from the web site for this book at http://facmu.swlearning.com. The column, Balance: Beginning of Period, reports amounts on the balance sheet at the beginning of a period and the column, Balance: End of Period, reports amounts on the balance sheet at the end of the period. The rows of the spreadsheet show the various categories of assets (current and noncurrent), liabilities (current and noncurrent), and shareholders' equity. We leave space to add individual accounts, such as for cash, accounts payable, and common stock. The amounts showing dashes represent various subtotals and totals. The columns labeled Transactions by Number and Description refer to transactions during a period that transform the balance sheet at the beginning of the period to the balance sheet at the end of the period. We use this spreadsheet to show the dual effects of a firm's transactions, entering the appropriate account titles in the rows in the first column. The next to last row of the spreadsheet, labeled *Imbalance, if Any,* serves as an arithmetical check to ensure that the user records each transaction in a dual manner to maintain the balance sheet equation. You can ignore the row labeled Income Statement Accounts, which we discuss in **Chapter 3**.[6]

We illustrate the use of this spreadsheet template using the seven transactions for Miller Corporation for the month of January as it prepares to open for business on February 1. We indicate whether each account is an asset (A), liability (L), or shareholders' equity (SE) account. **Exhibit 2.3** shows the completed spreadsheet incorporating the seven transactions.

Transaction 1: On January 1, Miller Corporation issues 10,000 shares of $10 par value common stock for $100,000 cash. This transaction increases cash by $100,000 and common stock, a shareholders' equity account, by an equal amount. Thus,

---

[6] The transactions template follows the usual procedures for the use of an Excel spreadsheet. If a particular problem has more than eight transactions, the Insert Column command allows for additional columns. The Insert Row command allows for additional rows for more accounts than the space provided. Insert columns and rows as indicated on the transactions template to ensure that summation formulas include the effects of additional rows and columns. The Edit Delete Row or Edit Delete Column commands allow for the deletion of rows and columns not needed for a particular problem.

```
(A) Cash . . . . . . . . . . . . . . . . . . . . . . . . . . .    +100,000
(SE) Common Stock . . . . . . . . . . . . . . . . . . .         +100,000
```

We enter the account title, Cash, on the first row under Current Assets and the account title, Common Stock, on the first row under Shareholders' Equity and place 100,000 in each of these accounts under the Transaction 1 column. A non-zero amount in the Imbalance, if Any row would indicate an incorrect recording of the transaction, which we must correct before moving to the next transaction.

Transaction 2: On January 5, Miller Corporate pays $60,000 cash to purchase equipment. This transaction decreases cash by $60,000 and increases equipment, a noncurrent asset, by $60,000. Thus,

```
(A) Cash . . . . . . . . . . . . . . . . . . . . . . . . . . .    −  60,000
(A) Equipment  . . . . . . . . . . . . . . . . . . . . . .      +  60,000
```

Transaction 3: On January 15, the firm purchases merchandise costing $15,000 from a supplier on account, agreeing to pay later. This transaction increases inventory by $15,000 and accounts payable, a current liability, by $15,000. Thus,

```
(A) Inventory . . . . . . . . . . . . . . . . . . . . . . . .    +  15,000
(L) Accounts Payable  . . . . . . . . . . . . . . . . .         +  15,000
```

Transaction 4: On January 21, the firm pays the supplier in Transaction 3 above $8,000 of the amount due. This transaction reduces cash and accounts payable by $8,000. Thus,

```
(A) Cash . . . . . . . . . . . . . . . . . . . . . . . . . . .    −   8,000
(L) Accounts Payable  . . . . . . . . . . . . . . . . .         −   8,000
```

Transaction 5: On January 25, the supplier in Transaction 3 above accepts 700 shares of common stock in settlement of the $7,000 still owed. This transaction reduces accounts payable and increases common stock by $7,000. Thus,

```
(L) Accounts Payable  . . . . . . . . . . . . . . . . .         −   7,000
(SE) Common Stock . . . . . . . . . . . . . . . . . . .         +   7,000
```

Transaction 6: On January 31, the firm pays $600 cash for a one-year insurance premium for coverage beginning February 1. This transaction reduces cash by $600 and increases Prepaid Insurance, a current asset, for the future benefits of insurance coverage. Thus,

```
(A) Cash . . . . . . . . . . . . . . . . . . . . . . . . . . .    −     600
(A) Prepaid Insurance  . . . . . . . . . . . . . . . . .        +     600
```

Transaction 7: On January 31, the firm receives $3,000 from a customer for merchandise to be delivered during February. This transaction increases cash and increases Advances from Customers, a current liability, by $3,000. Thus,

```
(A) Cash . . . . . . . . . . . . . . . . . . . . . . . . . . .    +   3,000
(L) Advances from Customer . . . . . . . . . . . . .           +   3,000
```

The last column on the right shows the amounts for the balance sheet on January 31. The amounts result from summing the amounts from the balance sheet at the beginning of the period (zero in this case) and the amounts for each transaction during the period. We can then use the amounts in the spreadsheet to prepare a balance sheet. **Exhibit 2.4** presents the balance sheet for Miller Corporation on January 31.

Analysis of Business Transactions Using Journal Entries

The spreadsheet illustrated in the preceding section works well when we want to aggregate the effects of many transactions during a period and then prepare a balance sheet (or income statement). We use the spreadsheet throughout **Chapters 2** and **3** for this purpose. In many settings, however, we want to observe the effect of a single transaction, or a small number of related transactions, on the financial statements. For example, consider the effect on the balance sheet of a firm issuing long-term debt and common stock in the acquisition of land, buildings, and equipment. Or, consider a more complicated transaction from **Chapter 10**: a lessee or tenant makes a payment to a lessor or landlord and must recognize the amount of the payment, the use of the asset, the amount of interest,

EXHIBIT 2.2

Transactions Spreadsheet Template

Balance Sheet Accounts

Transactions, By Number and Description

	Balance: Beginning of Period	Describe Transaction Here	1	2	3	4	5	6	7	Balance: End of Period

ASSETS

Current Assets:

Total Current Assets
Noncurrent Assets:

Total Noncurrent Assets
Total Assets

LIABILITIES AND SHAREHOLDERS' EQUITY

Current Liabilities:

Total Current Liabilities
Noncurrent Liabilities:

Total Noncurrent Liabilities
Total Liabilities
Shareholders' Equity:

Total Shareholders' Equity
Total Liabilities and Shareholders' Equity

Imbalance, *if Any*

Income Statement Accounts

EXHIBIT 2.3

Transactions Spreadsheet for Miller Corporation

Transactions, By Number and Description

Balance Sheet Accounts	Balance: Beginning of Period	Issue Common Stock for Cash	Purchase Equip. for Cash	Purchase Inv. On Account	Pay Cash to Supplier	Give Common Stock to Supplier	Prepay Insurance	Receives Advance from Customer	Balance: End of Period
		1	2	3	4	5	6	7	
ASSETS									
Current Assets:									
Cash		100,000	260,000		28,000	-7,000	2600	3,000	34,400
Inventory				15,000					15,000
Prepaid Insurance							600		600
Total Current Assets									50,000
Noncurrent Assets:									
Equipment			60,000						60,000
Total Noncurrent Assets									60,000
Total Assets									110,000
LIABILITIES AND SHAREHOLDERS' EQUITY									
Current Liabilities:									
Accounts Payable				15,000	28,000	-7,000			3,000
Advance from Customer								3,000	3,000
Total Current Liabilities									3,000
Noncurrent Liabilities:									
Total Noncurrent Liabilities									
Total Liabilities									3,000
Shareholders' Equity:									
Common Stock		100,000				7,000			107,000
Total Shareholders' Equity									107,000
Total Liabilities and Shareholders' Equity									110,000
Imbalance, if Any									
Income Statement Accounts									

EXHIBIT 2.4	MILLER CORPORATION Balance Sheet, January 31

ASSETS

Current Assets

Cash	$ 34,400
Merchandise Inventory	15,000
Prepaid Insurance	600
Total Current Assets	$ 50,000

Property, Plant, and Equipment

Equipment	60,000
Total Assets	$110,000

LIABILITIES AND SHAREHOLDERS' EQUITY

Current Liabilities

Advance from Customer	$ 3,000

Shareholders' Equity

Common Stock	107,000
Total Liabilities and Shareholders' Equity	$110,000

Problem 2.4 for Self-Study

Spreadsheet analysis of business transactions. Design a spreadsheet similar to that in **Exhibit 2.2** or use the transactions spreadsheet template available with this text at http://facmu.swlearning.com. Enter each of the transactions in **Problem 2.3 for Self-Study** and derive the amounts for the balance sheet after the six transactions.

---

and the amount of debt repaid. Setting up a spreadsheet for these single, although complex, transactions is unnecessarily time consuming and detracts from your thinking about the transaction itself and its effect on the financial statements. For this and similar purposes, we summarize the effects of the transaction on the financial statements using **journal entries**. Journal entries:

- Rely on the concept that every transaction or event has a dual effect on the balance sheet equation (as illustrated in **Exhibit 2.1**).
- Require knowledge of the accounts on the financial statements that a particular transaction affects and whether those accounts increase or decrease (as illustrated in **Exhibit 2.3**).

Journal entries add to these two building blocks already discussed a standard format for summarizing the effects of a particular business transaction. The standard format is as follows:

Account Title . . . . Amount	
Account Title	Amount

The journal entry indicates the dual effects of a transaction as to both accounts and amounts. Accountants refer to the first line of the journal entry as the **debit** line and the second line of the journal as the **credit** line. Thus,

Account Debited . . . . Amount Debited	
Account Credited	Amount Credited

Accountants follow these rules for increases and decreases in asset, liability, and shareholders' equity accounts:

1. Debits (a) increase in an asset account, or (b) decrease a liability or shareholders' equity account.
2. Credits (a) decrease an asset account, or (b) increase a liability or shareholders' equity account.

These rules have an element of logic. Assets appear on the left of the equal sign in the balance sheet equation. Increases in assets appear as debits. Liabilities and shareholders' equity appear on the right of the equal sign in the balance sheet equation. Increases in liabilities and shareholders' equity appear as credits. Thus,

Asset Increases and Liability or Shareholders' Equity Decreases	Amount Debited
Asset Decreases and Liability or Shareholders' Equity Increase	Amount Credited

The journal entries for the seven transactions of Miller Corporation appear next. We include the date of the transaction to the left of the entry and a description of the transaction below the entry. We also indicate in parentheses whether the debits and credits increase or decrease the asset, liability, or shareholders' equity account.

(1) Jan. 1	Cash (Asset Increase)	100,000	
	Common Stock (Shareholders' Equity Increase)		100,000
	Issue 10,000 shares of $10-par value common stock for cash.		
(2) Jan. 5	Equipment (Asset Increase)	60,000	
	Cash (Asset Decrease)		60,000
	Purchase equipment costing $60,000 in cash.		
(3) Jan. 15	Merchandise Inventory (Asset Increase)	15,000	
	Accounts Payable (Liability Increase)		15,000
	Purchase merchandise inventory costing $15,000 on account.		
(4) Jan. 21	Accounts Payable (Liability Decrease)	8,000	
	Cash (Asset Decrease)		8,000
	Pay liabilities of $8,000 with cash.		
(5) Jan. 25	Accounts Payable (Liability Decrease)	7,000	
	Common Stock (Shareholders' Equity Increase)		7,000
	Issue 700 shares of $10-par value common stock in settlement of $7,000 account payable.		
(6) Jan. 31	Prepaid Insurance (Asset Increase)	600	
	Cash (Asset Decrease)		600
	Pay one-year fire insurance premium of $600 in advance.		
(7) Jan. 31	Cash (Asset Increase)	3,000	
	Advance from Customer (Liability Increase)		3,000
	Receive $3,000 from customer for merchandise to be delivered in February.		

Problem 2.5 for Self-Study

Journal entries for business transactions. Prepare journal entries for each of the six transactions in **Problem 2.3 for Self-Study**.

Balance Sheet Account Titles

This section describes the balance sheet account titles commonly used. The descriptions should help you understand the nature of various assets, liabilities, and shareholders' equities as well as select appropriate account names to use when you solve problems. You can use alternative account titles. The list does not show all the account titles we use in this book or that appear in the financial statements of publicly held firms. Many beginning students become overly concerned about precise wording for account titles. We require of our students only that the titles be descriptive and unambiguous and that students use the identical (or similar) account titles for identical (or similar) items. Later chapters discuss more fully the use of some of the account titles described below.

Assets

Cash: coins and currency and items such as bank checks and money orders (the latter items are merely claims against individuals or institutions but by custom are called cash), bank deposits against which the firm can draw checks, and time deposits, usually savings accounts and certificates of deposit.

Marketable Securities: government bonds or corporate stocks and bonds that the firm plans to hold for a relatively short time. The word marketable implies that the firm can buy and sell them readily through a security exchange such as the New York Stock Exchange.

Accounts Receivable: amounts due from customers of a business from the sale of goods or services. The collection of cash occurs sometime after the sale. These accounts are also known as "charge accounts" or "open accounts." The general term Accounts Receivable used in the balance sheet describes the figure representing the total amount receivable from all customers. The firm, of course, keeps a separate record for each customer.

Notes Receivable: amounts due from customers or from others to whom a firm has made loans or extended credit. The customer or other borrower puts the claim into writing in the form of a formal note (which distinguishes the claim from an open account receivable).

Interest Receivable: interest—on assets such as promissory notes or bonds—that has accrued (or come into existence) through the passing of time but that the firm has not yet collected as of the date of the balance sheet.

Merchandise Inventory: goods on hand purchased for resale, such as canned goods on the shelves of a grocery store or suits on the racks of a clothing store.

Raw Materials Inventory: materials as yet unused for manufacturing products.

Supplies Inventory: lubricants, abrasives, and other incidental materials used in manufacturing operations; stationery, computer drives, flash memory cards, pens, and other office supplies; bags, twine, boxes, and other packaging supplies; gasoline, oil, spare parts, and other delivery supplies.

Work-in-Process Inventory: partially completed manufactured products.

Finished Goods Inventory: completed, but unsold, manufactured products.

Advances to Suppliers: payments made in advance for goods or services that a firm will receive at a later date. If the firm does not make a cash expenditure when it places an order, it does not recognize an asset until it receives the goods or services ordered.

Prepaid Rent: rent paid in advance for the future use of land, buildings, or equipment. Beginning accounting students sometimes get confused with the title Prepaid Rent because it could mean the asset on the balance sheet of the tenant or the liability on the balance sheet of the landlord. Using the title Advances to Landlord for the asset and Advances from Tenants for the liability avoids this confusion.

Prepaid Insurance: insurance premiums paid for future coverage. One could call this Advances to Insurance Company.

Investment in Securities: bonds or shares of common or preferred stock that the firm plans to hold for a relatively long time, typically longer than one year.

Land: land used in operations or occupied by buildings used in operations.

Buildings: factory buildings, store buildings, garages, warehouses, and so forth.

Equipment: lathes, ovens, machine tools, boilers, computers, bins, cranes, conveyors, automobiles, and so forth.

Furniture and Fixtures: desks, tables, chairs, counters, showcases, scales, and other selling and office equipment.

Accumulated Depreciation: the cumulative amount of the acquisition cost of long-term assets (such as buildings and equipment) allocated to the costs of production or to current and prior periods in measuring net income. The amount in this account reduces the acquisition cost of the long-term asset to which it relates when measuring the net book value of the asset shown in the balance sheet.

Leasehold: the right to use property owned by someone else.

Organization Costs: amounts paid for legal and incorporation fees, for printing the certificates for shares of stock, and for accounting and other costs incurred in organizing a business so that it can function. GAAP require firms to expense organization costs in the year incurred.[7]

Patents: rights granted for up to 20 years by the federal government to exclude others from manufacturing, using, or selling certain processes or devices. Under current GAAP, the firm must expense research and development costs in the year incurred rather than recognize them as assets

---

[7] American Institute of Certified Public Accountants, *Statement of Position 98-5,* "Reporting the Cost of Start-up Activities," 1998.

with future benefits.[8] As a result, a firm that develops a patent will not normally show it as an asset. On the other hand, a firm that purchases a patent from another firm or from an individual will recognize the patent as an asset. **Chapter 8** discusses this inconsistent treatment of internally developed and externally purchased patents.

Goodwill: When one firm acquires another firm, it allocates the purchase price to individual identifiable assets acquired and liabilities assumed, using their current market values. When the purchase price exceeds the amounts assigned to identifiable assets and liabilities, accounting assumes that the excess relates to intangibles that the acquiring firm cannot separately identify, such as customer goodwill or a well-trained labor force, and calls the excess goodwill. Accounting generally does not recognize as assets the good reputation and other desirable attributes that a firm creates or develops for itself. However, when one firm acquires another firm, accounting recognizes these desirable attributes as assets insofar as they cause the amount paid for the acquired firm to exceed the sum of the values assigned to all the other assets, less liabilities, identified in the acquisition.

Liabilities

Accounts Payable: amounts owed for goods or services acquired under an informal credit agreement. The firm must pay these accounts fairly soon after the balance sheet date, usually within one or two months, although amounts due as much as 12 months later are current liabilities. The same items appear as Accounts Receivable on the creditor's books.

Notes Payable: the face amount of promissory notes given in connection with loans from a bank or with the purchase of goods or services. The same items appear as Notes Receivable on the creditor's (lender's) books. Most Accounts Payable, Accounts Receivable, Notes Payable, and Notes Receivable are current items, due within a year of the balance sheet date. Similar items due more than one year after the balance sheet date could have the same account titles, but would appear in the noncurrent section of the balance sheet.

Interest Payable: interest—on obligations—that has accrued or accumulated with the passage of time but that the firm has not yet paid as of the date of the balance sheet. The liability for interest customarily appears separately from the face amount of the obligation. The same items appear as Interest Receivable on the creditor's books.

Income Taxes Payable: the estimated liability for income taxes, accumulated and unpaid, based on the taxable income of the business from the beginning of the taxable year to the date of the balance sheet.

Advances from Customers: the general name used to indicate the obligation incurred when the firm receives payments in advance for goods or services it will furnish to customers in the future; a nonmonetary liability. The firm has an obligation to deliver goods or services, not return the cash. Even so, the firm records this liability at the amount of cash it receives. If the firm does not receive cash when a customer places an order, it does not record a liability; such a contract is mutually unexecuted and called *executory*.

Advances from Tenants, or Rent Received in Advance: another example of a nonmonetary liability. For example, a firm owns a building that it rents to a tenant. The tenant prepays the rental charge for several months in advance. The firm cannot include the amount applicable to future months as a component of income until the firm renders a rental service as time passes. Meanwhile the advance payment results in a liability payable in services (that is, in the use of the building). On the records of the tenant, the same amount appears as an asset, Prepaid Rent (or Advances to Landlord).

Mortgage Payable: long-term promissory notes that the borrower has protected by pledging specific pieces of property as security for payment. If the borrower does not pay the loan or interest according to the agreement, the lender can require the sale of the property to generate funds to repay the loan.

Bonds Payable: amounts borrowed by a business for a relatively long period of time under a formal written contract called an *indenture*. The borrower usually raises the funds from a number of lenders, all of whom receive written evidence of their share of the loan.

Convertible Bonds: bonds payable that the holder can convert into, or trade in for, shares of common stock. The bond indenture specifies the number of shares the lenders will receive when they convert their bonds into stock, the dates when conversion can occur, and other details.

---

[8] Financial Accounting Standards Board, *Statement of Financial Accounting Standards No. 2*, "Accounting for Research and Development Costs," 1974.

Capitalized Lease Obligations: the present value of the commitment to make future cash payments in return for the right to use property owned by someone else. **Chapter 10** discusses the conditions under which a firm recognizes lease obligations as liabilities.

Deferred Income Taxes: particular income tax amounts that are delayed beyond the current accounting period. **Chapter 10** discusses this item, which appears on the balance sheet of most U.S. corporations.

Shareholders' Equity

Common Stock: amounts received equal to the par or stated value of a firm's principal class of voting stock.

Preferred Stock: amounts received for the par value of a class of a firm's stock that has some preference relative to the common stock, usually in the area of dividends and assets in the event of corporate liquidation. Sometimes preferred shareholders may convert the stock into common stock.

Additional Paid-in Capital: in the issuance of common or preferred stock, the amounts received in excess of par value or stated value. Some firms use for this account the alternative title "Capital Contributed in Excess of Par (or Stated) Value." Accountants and analysts often refer to the sum of the amounts in this account and the two accounts above as *contributed capital.*

Retained Earnings: since the time a business began operations, net assets (= all assets − all liabilities) increase as the firm generates earnings in excess of cash (or other net assets) distributed by dividend declarations. Retained Earnings is the account title for the account with a credit balance, which indicates that the owners provided (are the source of) those net assets and have claims on them. Retained earnings provide financing just as amounts explicitly contributed by owners do. When a firm declares dividends, net assets decrease (liability for dividends payable increases), and retained earnings decrease by an equal amount. As **Chapters 4** and **12** discuss, a firm does not generally hold net assets generated from retained earnings as cash. A common misconception of beginning students confuses Retained Earnings, an account with a credit balance, with Cash, an account with a debit balance.

Accumulated Other Comprehensive Income: An account summarizing gains and losses on some assets that the firm has not yet reported as part of income, so these gains and losses do not appear in Retained Earnings. We delay discussion of accumulated other comprehensive income until **Chapter 12**.

Treasury Shares: the cost of shares of stock that a firm originally issued but subsequently reacquires. Treasury shares do not receive dividends, and accountants do not identify them as outstanding shares. The cost of treasury shares almost always appears on the balance sheet as a deduction from the total of the other shareholders' equity accounts. **Chapter 12** discusses the accounting for treasury shares.

Problem 2.6 for Self-Study

Journal entries, transaction spreadsheet template, and balance sheet preparation. Electronics Appliance Corporation begins operations on September 1. The firm engages in the following transactions during the month of September:

(1) September 1: Issues 4,000 shares of $10 par value common stock for $12 cash per share.
(2) September 2: Gives 600 shares of $10 par value common stock to acquire a patent from another firm. The two entities agree on a price of $7,200 for the patent.
(3) September 5: Pays $10,000 as two months' rent in advance on a factory building that is leased for the three years beginning October 1. Monthly rental payments are $5,000.
(4) September 12: Purchases raw materials on account for $6,100.
(5) September 15: Receives a check for $900 from a customer as a deposit on a special order for equipment that Electronics plans to manufacture. The contract price is $4,800.
(6) September 20: Acquires office equipment with a list price of $950. After deducting a discount of $25 in return for prompt payment, it issues a check in full payment.

(continued)

Problem 2.6 for Self-Study *(continued)*

(7) September 28: Issues a cash advance totaling $200 to three new employees who will begin work on October 1.

(8) September 30: Purchases factory equipment costing $27,500. It issues a check for $5,000 and assumes a long-term mortgage liability for the balance.

(9) September 30: Pays $450 for the labor costs of installing the new equipment in (8).

    a. Prepare journal entries for each of the nine transactions.

    b. Using the transactions spreadsheet template available with this book, enter each of the nine transactions. Note that the amounts for the balance sheet at the beginning of September are zero.

    c. Prepare a balance sheet for Electronics Appliance Corporation as of September 30.

Analysis of the Balance Sheet

Later chapters will caution you not to analyze the balance sheet in isolation from the income statement, the statement of cash flows, and other information about a firm. The balance sheet does provide, however, useful insights about the nature and mix of assets as well as the nature and mix of financing for those assets. A careful user should also be alert to asset and liability recognition and valuation questions that impact the interpretation of the balance sheet.

Analysts often use a **common-size balance sheet** to study the nature and mix of assets and their financing. In a common-size balance sheet, the analyst expresses each balance sheet item as a percentage of total assets or total liabilities plus shareholders' equity. **Exhibit 2.5** presents common-size balance sheets for Wal-Mart Stores (discount stores, superstores, and warehouse clubs), American Airlines (airline services), Merck (pharmaceuticals), Interpublic Group (advertising services), and Citigroup (financial institution). **Exhibit 2.5** also shows the market-to-book-value ratio for each firm at the end of a recent year. The market-to-book-value ratio compares the market value of each firm's common shares with the book value of shareholders' equity as reported on the balance sheet.

Assessing the Nature and Mix of Financing

The balance sheet reflects the effects of a firm's investing and financing decisions. One question the user of the balance sheet should ask is: Does the firm have the right mix of financing for its assets? Two principles guide decisions about financing:

1. Firms generally use short-term financing for assets that a firm expects to turn into cash soon, such as accounts receivable and inventories, and long-term financing (debt or shareholders' equity) for assets that a firm expects to turn into cash over a longer period, such as property, plant, and equipment.

2. The mix of long-term financing depends on the nature of long-term assets and the amount of operating risk in the business. Firms with tangible long-term assets and predictable cash flows, such as electric utilities, tend to use a high proportion of long-term debt. The property, plant, and equipment serve as collateral for the borrowing (that is, the lender can repossess or confiscate the assets if the firm fails to make debt payments on time). The predictable cash flows reduce the risk that the firm will not have sufficient cash to make interest and principal payments when due. Firms with tangible long-term assets but less predictable cash flows, such as auto manufacturers and steel companies, whose sales vary with changes in economic conditions, tend to use a more balanced mix of long-term debt and shareholders' equity financing. The property, plant, and equipment serve as collateral for the borrowing, but the more uncertain cash flows suggest a lower proportion of long-term debt in the capital structure. Firms with high proportions of intangibles, whether recognized as assets on the balance sheet or not, tend to use low proportions of long-term debt. Lacking collateral, lenders must rely on cash flows from operations to service the debt. The less predictable these cash flows, the smaller is the proportion of long-term debt.

EXHIBIT 2.5	Common-Size Balance Sheets for Selected Companies				
	Wal-Mart Stores	**American Airlines**	**Merck**	**Interpublic Group**	**Citigroup**
ASSETS					
Cash	2.8%	6.4%	10.5%	7.9%	3.1%
Accounts Receivable	2.1	4.9	11.4	38.3	82.2
Inventories	25.1	2.1	7.2	—	—
Prepayments	0.7	2.9	2.1	7.4	—
Total Current Assets	30.7%	16.3%	31.2%	53.6%	a
Investments in Securities	—	—	15.3	3.0	—
Property, Plant, and Equipment	56.9	62.5	29.8	7.0	2.1
Intangible Assets	8.9	4.3	15.2	29.3	3.2
Other Assets	3.5	16.9	8.5	7.1	9.4
Total Assets	100.0%	100.0%	100.0%	100.0%	100.0%
LIABILITIES AND SHAREHOLDERS' EQUITY					
Accounts Payable	17.3%	4.0%	5.1%	43.5%	68.5%
Notes Payable	1.1	2.9	7.7	1.8	—
Other Current Liabilities	14.5	17.0	13.2	14.8	21.3
Total Current Liabilities	32.9%	23.9%	26.0%	60.1%	a
Long-term Debt	24.4	40.7	10.3	15.4	—
Other Noncurrent Liabilities	3.1	32.2	15.1	6.1	2.3
Total Liabilities	60.4%	96.8%	51.4%	81.6%	92.1%
Shareholders' Equity	39.6	3.2	48.6	18.4	7.9
Total Liabilities and Shareholders' Equity	100.0%	100.0%	100.0%	100.0%	100.0%
Market-value-to-book-value Ratio	4.4	0.4	7.1	2.6	2.2

[a] Financial institutions typically do not distinguish current and noncurrent assets and liabilities.

The underlying rationale for these generalizations about the nature and mix of financing relates to lenders' and investors' assessments of the overall risk profile of a business. Firms incur risk both from the asset, or operating, side and from the financing side of their business. Risks on the operating side include variability in sales from changing economic conditions (cyclicality risk) or from short product life cycles (because of technological change or changes in consumer taste, for example) and variability of earnings from having a high proportion of fixed costs that do not change as sales change, such as depreciation expense on capital-intensive manufacturing facilities. When firms incur substantial risk on the operating side, they tend not to take on still higher risk on the financing side in the form of long-term debt. The firm must make principal and interest payments on the debt. The more variable the cash flows from operating activities, the more risk the firm will not have sufficient cash to service its debt. The less risk on the operating side, the more the firm will borrow for the long term.

Refer to the data in **Exhibit 2.5**. Wal-Mart Stores maintains a large percentage of its assets in merchandise inventories, which it expects to sell within a period of one to two months. It matches these investments in inventories with a similar proportion of short-term financing that appears in current liabilities. Wal-Mart also maintains a high percentage of its assets in property, plant, and equipment. It uses approximately 40 percent debt and 60 percent shareholders' equity financing for these long-term assets. Wal-Mart generates relatively predictable cash flows from its stores. With the stores serving as collateral, Wal-Mart appears able to manage a higher proportion of long-term debt than **Exhibit 2.5** shows. Although Wal-Mart uses long-term debt to finance much of its growth in new stores, the retention of earnings has caused shareholders' equity to increase to an unusually high percentage of long-term financing.

American Airlines invests a large percentage of its assets in property, plant, and equipment. It finances these assets with long-term sources of financing (long-term debt plus shareholders' equity). Airlines tend to use more long-term debt than shareholders' equity to finance the acquisition of equipment because (1) the equipment serves as collateral for the borrowing, and (2) long-term debt usually has a lower economic cost to the firm than do funds provided by shareholders. Economic conditions, however, impact the demand for air travel and cause sales to vary over time. With the high proportion of fixed costs from depreciation and, to a lesser extent, compensation, airlines tend not to want to add too much long-term debt with its fixed interest costs to their capital structures. Varying sales combined with high fixed costs increase the probability of bankruptcy. Thus, although airlines rely heavily on long-term debt, they include more shareholders' equity funds than if their sales were more predictable and less variable. The proportion of long-term financing provided by shareholders appears low in this case because American Airlines operated at a net loss for several years, lowering its retained earnings.

Merck also invests a high proportion of its balance sheet assets in property, plant, and equipment. It has substantial investments in the drug patents it has developed within the firm, but these patents do not appear on the balance sheet. Pharmaceutical companies tend to maintain capital-intensive, automated manufacturing facilities to ensure quality control of their products. Unlike airlines, however, pharmaceutical companies tend not to carry much long-term debt. One reason for not using debt results from the nature of the resources of a pharmaceutical company. Key resources include its research scientists, who could leave the firm at any time, and its patents on pharmaceutical products, which competitors could render worthless at any moment by developing new, superior products. Given the risk inherent in these resources, which do not appear on the balance sheet, pharmaceutical firms tend not to add risk on the financing side of their balance sheets by taking on debt, which requires fixed interest and principal payments.

Interpublic Group provides advertising services for clients. It purchases time or space in various media (television, newspapers, magazines), for which it incurs an obligation (reported as Accounts Payable). It develops advertising copy for clients and sells them media time or space to promote their products, resulting in a receivable from the clients (Accounts Receivable). Thus, current receivables dominate the asset side of the balance sheet and current payables dominate the financing side of the balance sheet. Service firms such as Interpublic Group have few assets other than their employees, which accounting does not recognize as assets. Interpublic Group made several acquisitions of other marketing services firms and allocated a portion of the purchase price to goodwill and other intangibles. Thus, intangibles comprise a larger portion of Interpublic Group's total assets.

Citigroup, like most financial institutions, does not distinguish current from noncurrent assets and liabilities. Loans to customers for houses dominate the asset side of the balance sheet. These loans have maturities up to 25 years. Deposits by customers, denoting the source of funds that the customers may withdraw at any time, dominate the financing side. The use of short-term financing to support acquisition of long-term assets got S&Ls in trouble in the late 1980s; customers, fearing the bankruptcy of the S&Ls because many of the S&Ls' investments lost market value, began withdrawing their deposits. The S&Ls were not able to turn their long-term loans into cash quickly enough to satisfy deposit withdrawals. Although the balance sheets of S&Ls still contain their inherent imbalance, government guarantees of deposits up to certain limits and stronger oversight of the financial condition of S&Ls by regulators have reinstated confidence in them.

Assessing the Impact of Asset and Liability Recognition and Valuation Issues

This chapter indicates that the balance sheet does not always provide data useful for analysts because, as a result of following GAAP,

- Not all resources of a firm appear on the balance sheet as assets,
- Assets on the balance sheet do not typically reflect current market valuations,
- Not all obligations of a firm appear on the balance sheet as liabilities,
- Liabilities on the balance sheet do not necessarily reflect current market valuations.

The analyst should recognize these weaknesses of the balance sheet when attempting to assess the financial condition of a firm. The market sets the price of a firm's common stock unconstrained by GAAP. The market price will likely increase when a pharmaceutical firm discovers a new drug, even though GAAP does not permit the firm to show it as an asset on the balance sheet. We can compare the market-to-book-value ratios for each of the firms in **Exhibit 2.5** to identify possible asset and liability recognition and valuation issues for these firms. Note that the competitive position of each of these firms and their growth potential will also impact the market-to-book-value ratio. We do not consider these factors in the discussion below.

Wal-Mart has a market-to-book-value ratio of 4.4. One reason for this ratio exceeding 1.0 is that the property, plant, and equipment of Wal-Mart appear on the balance sheet at acquisition cost adjusted downward for depreciation to date. The current market values of fixed assets likely exceed their book values, particularly for the land underlying stores. Wal-Mart also has several intangibles that do not appear on its balance sheet, including its brand name, its buying power with suppliers due to its size, its information systems that tie stores worldwide to each other and to suppliers, and its efficient distribution system from regional warehouses.

American Airlines has a market-to-book-value ratio less than 1.0. Its property, plant, and equipment appear at acquisition cost adjusted downward for depreciation. Airlines in recent years have increased the depreciable lives of their equipment, reducing the rate at which they write down equipment, perhaps resulting in an overvaluation of its fixed assets. American Airlines also has an obligation under its frequent flier program that appears on the balance sheet at the estimated incremental cost of providing free flights. Perhaps the market values this liability at a higher amount than the liability appears on the balance sheet. American Airlines also operated at a net loss for several years, increasing the proportion of liabilities on the balance sheet and increasing the probability of bankruptcy. The market recognized this risk and reduced its valuation of the common stock of American Airlines.

Merck has a market-to-book-value ratio of 7.1. This large ratio reflects GAAP's requirement that firms cannot recognize the value of internally developed patents and other technologies as assets on the balance sheet. The market incorporates estimates of the values of these technologies in setting Merck's market price. Merck recognizes the value of patents when it acquires other firms, which it reports in intangible assets. Unsettled lawsuits against the firm that Merck does not recognize as liabilities until the cash outflows to settle a claim are probable and likely reduce the market value of Merck's shares and depress the market-to-book-value ratio.

Interpublic Group has a market-to-book-value ratio of 2.6. The key resource of Interpublic Group is the creative talent of its employees. GAAP do not permit firms to recognize this resource as an asset on the balance sheet. The various marketing service agencies that comprise Interpublic Group also have recognized brand names, such as Foote, Cone, and Belding, and loyal corporate customers that enhance the market value of the firm even though not appearing on the balance sheet as an asset. Interpublic Group has acquired several marketing services firms in recent years. A large portion of the price paid for these firms is for their brand names and creative talent, which Interpublic Group includes in Goodwill, an intangible asset.

Citigroup trades at a market-to-book-value ratio of 2.2. The assets of financial institutions include primarily investments in securities and loans receivable, which appear on the balance sheet at amounts close to market value. One would therefore expect financial institutions to have a market-to-book-value ratio close to 1.0. The larger ratio for Citigroup likely reflects the value of the firm's brand name, its dominating presence in most of the markets it serves, and the value of its skilled workforce.

These asset and liability recognition and valuation concerns might tempt a user of the financial statements to ignore the balance sheet entirely when evaluating a firm. Although the user should keep these limitations in mind, keep also in mind that GAAP govern the preparation of the balance sheet across firms and across time. Thus, firms prepare their balance sheets on a consistent basis. By incorporating the known biases injected by GAAP into their assessments, users can gain insight about the nature and mix of assets and their related financing.

An International Perspective

The format of the balance sheet in some countries differs from that discussed in this chapter. In Germany, France, and some other European countries, property, plant, and equipment and other noncurrent assets appear first, followed by current assets. On the equities side, shareholders' equity appears first, followed by noncurrent liabilities, and then current liabilities. **Exhibit 2.6** presents the balance sheet of BMW, the German automobile manufacturer, for two recent years. Note that this balance sheet maintains the equality of investments and financing. Note also that some terms differ from those commonly used in the United States.

EXHIBIT 2.6	BMW Comparative Balance Sheet (in millions of Euros)		

		December 31	
		Year 11	Year 12
ASSETS			
Intangible Assets		€ 2,419	€ 2,741
Property, Plant, and Equipment		7,355	8,578
Financial Assets		786	498
Leased Products		7,908	7,012
Total Noncurrent Assets		€18,468	€18,829
Inventories		€ 4,501	€ 5,197
Trade Receivables		2,135	1,818
Receivables from Sales Financing		17,398	19,493
Other Receivables		4,208	6,056
Marketable Securities		907	1,105
Cash and Cash Equivalents		2,437	2,333
Total Current Assets		€31,586	€36,002
Prepayment and Other Assets		€ 1,205	€ 680
Total Assets		€51,259	€55,511
SHAREHOLDERS' EQUITY AND LIABILITIES			
Subscribed Capital		€ 673	€ 674
Capital Reserve		1,937	1,954
Revenue Reserves		9,405	11,075
Accumulated Other Equity		(1,245)	168
Total Shareholders' Equity		€10,770	€13,871
Provisions		6,824	7,666
Debt		25,665	26,262
Trade Payables		3,015	3,069
Other Liabilities		4,985	4,643
Total Liabilities		€40,489	€41,640
Total Shareholders' Equity and Liabilities		€51,259	€55,511

Term Used in Exhibit 2.6	Common Term Used in the United States
Financial Assets	Investment in Securities
Trade Receivables	Accounts Receivable
Subscribed Capital	Common Stock
Capital Reserve	Additional Paid-in Capital
Revenue Reserves	Retained Earnings
Accumulated Other Equity	Accumulated Other Comprehensive Income
Provisions	Other Liabilities
Debt	Bonds Payable
Trade Payables	Accounts Payable

In the United Kingdom, the balance sheet presents the following form of the balance sheet equation.

$$\text{Noncurrent Assets} + \left(\text{Current Assets} - \text{Current Liabilities} \right) - \text{Noncurrent Liabilities} = \text{Shareholders' Equity}$$

EXHIBIT 2.7	ROLLS-ROYCE Comparative Balance Sheet in U.K. Format and Terminology (in millions of pounds)

	August 31	
	Year 11	Year 12
FIXED ASSETS		
Intangible Assets	£ 823	£ 868
Tangible Assets	1,732	1,876
Investments	234	266
Total Fixed Assets	£ 2,789	£ 3,010
CURRENT ASSETS		
Stocks	£ 1,222	£ 1,158
Debtors	2,450	2,413
Short-Term Deposits and Investments	301	84
Cash at Bank and In Hand	578	634
Creditors Due within One Year		
Borrowings	(276)	(275)
Other Creditors	(2,720)	(2,727)
Net Current Assets	£ 1,555	£ 1,287
Total Assets Less Current Liabilities	£ 4,344	£ 4,297
Creditors Due after More Than One Year		
Borrowings	(1,104)	(1,038)
Other Creditors	(288)	(450)
Provisions for Liabilities	(882)	(772)
Total Assets Less Total Liabilities	£ 2,070	£ 2,037
Capital and Reserves		
Called-up Share Capital	£ 320	£ 323
Share Premium Account	636	634
Revaluation Reserve	103	100
Other Reserves	189	195
Profit and Loss Account	820	783
Minority Interests	2	2
Total Shareholders' Equity	£ 2,070	£ 2,037

   Exhibit 2.7 presents a balance sheet for Rolls Royce, a British manufacturer of engines for aircraft, ships, and other large equipment, for two recent years. This form of balance sheet does not permit a direct comparison of investments with financing. The analyst must rearrange such balance sheets to obtain the desired information. A balance sheet for Rolls Royce in the format discussed in this chapter and using terminology typically found in the United States appears in **Exhibit 2.8**. Terms used in the balance sheet in **Exhibit 2.7** that differ from those discussed in this chapter appear below.

Term Used in Exhibit 2.7	Common Term Used in the United States
Tangible Assets	Property, Plant, and Equipment
Stocks	Inventories
Debtors	Accounts Receivable
Borrowings	Notes Payable, Bonds Payable
Called-up Share Capital	Common Stock
Share Premium Account	Additional Paid-in Capital
Profit and Loss Account	Retained Earnings

EXHIBIT 2.8	ROLLS-ROYCE Comparative Balance Sheet in U.S. Format and Terminology (in millions of pounds)		

		August 31	
		Year 11	Year 12
ASSETS			
Cash		£ 578	£ 634
Marketable Securities		301	84
Accounts Receivable		2,450	2,413
Inventories		1,222	1,158
Total Current Assets		£4,551	£4,289
Investments		234	266
Property, Plant, and Equipment		1,732	1,876
Intangible Assets		823	868
Total Assets		£7,340	£7,299
LIABILITIES AND SHAREHOLDERS' EQUITY			
Notes Payable		£ 276	£ 275
Other Current Liabilities		2,720	2,727
Total Current Liabilities		£2,996	£3,002
Long-Term Debt		1,104	1,038
Other Noncurrent Liabilities		1,170	1,222
Total Liabilities		£5,270	£5,262
SHAREHOLDERS' EQUITY			
Common Stock		£ 320	£ 323
Additional Paid-in Capital		636	634
Retained Earnings		820	783
Revaluation Reserve		103	100
Other Reserves		189	195
Minority Interest		2	2
Total Shareholders' Equity		£2,070	£2,037
Total Liabilities and Shareholders' Equity		£7,340	£7,299

One account reported in **Exhibit 2.7** seldom appears on balance sheets in the United States and most other countries: Revaluation Reserve. Common practice in most countries reports nonmonetary assets (for example, inventories and property, plant, and equipment) at acquisition, or historical, cost. Accounting standards in the United Kingdom and in a few other countries permit the periodic revaluation of property, plant, and equipment to current market values. Firms obtain appraisals of the market values of their tangible fixed assets and intangibles such as brand names at periodic intervals (every three to five years). They then reflect the revaluation in the accounts with a journal entry such as the following:

Tangible Fixed Assets (Asset Increase)	Amount
Revaluation Reserve (Shareholders' Equity Increase)	Amount
To revalue tangible assets to current market value.	

At the end of Year 11, Rolls-Royce reports a balance in the Revaluation Reserve account of £103 million, suggesting that the current market values of its property, plant, and equipment and some intangibles, such as brand names exceed acquisition cost by £103 million. The Revaluation Reserve decreased to £100 at the end of Year 12. The journal entry to record a decrease in market values subtracts £3 from Tangible Fixed Assets and from Revaluation Reserve during Year 12.

An analyst wanting to convert the balance sheets of Rolls Royce to U.S. accounting standards would make the following restatements.

End of Year 11:

Revaluation Reserve (Shareholders' Equity Decrease)   103

    Tangible Fixed Assets (Asset Decrease)   103

To convert tangible fixed assets from current market values to historical costs.

End of Year 12:

Revaluation Reserve (Shareholders' Equity Decrease)   100

    Tangible Fixed Assets (Asset Decrease)   100

To convert tangible fixed assets from current market values to historical costs.

You will likely find the discussion of different balance sheet formats, terminology, and restatement entries discussed in this section somewhat difficult to follow at this early stage in your study of financial accounting.

The message delivered here is that a solid grasp of important balance sheet concepts, as discussed throughout most of this chapter, will permit you to apply those concepts to balance sheets for firms around the world.

Summary

The balance sheet comprises three major classes of items: assets, liabilities, and shareholders' equity.

Resources become accounting assets when a firm has acquired the rights to their future use as a result of a past transaction or exchange, and when it can measure the value of the future benefits with a reasonable degree of precision. Monetary assets appear, in general, at their current cash, or cash equivalent, values. Nonmonetary assets appear at acquisition cost, in some cases adjusted downward either for the cost of services that a firm has consumed or for the effects of technological or other obsolescence. Liabilities represent obligations of a firm to make payments of a reasonably definite amount at a reasonably definite future time for benefits already received. Shareholders' equity, the difference between total assets and total liabilities, for corporations typically comprises contributed capital and retained earnings.

Recording the effects of each transaction in a dual manner in the accounts maintains the equality of total assets and total liabilities plus shareholders' equity. The accountant initially records the dual effects of each transaction using the following format:

Debit Account (Asset Increases and Liability
    or Shareholders' Equity Decreases) . . . .   Debit Amount

    Credit Account (Asset Decreases and Liability
        or Shareholders' Equity Increases) . . . .   Credit Amount

When analyzing a balance sheet, one looks for a reasonable match between the nature and mix of assets and the nature and mix of liabilities plus shareholders' equity. The proportion of short-term versus long-term financing should match the proportion of current assets versus noncurrent assets. The mix of long-term debt versus shareholders' equity should reflect the degree of operating risk in the business. The larger is the operating risk from cyclical sales, short product life cycles, high proportions of fixed costs, and similar factors, the more shareholders' equity capital as opposed to long-term debt one should look for on the balance sheet. The user, however, must recognize biases injected into the balance sheet as a result of applying GAAP in its preparation.

SUGGESTED SOLUTION TO PROBLEM 2.1 FOR SELF-STUDY

(Coca-Cola Company; asset recognition and valuation)

a. GAAP do not recognize research and development expenditures as assets because of the uncertainty of future benefits that a firm can measure with reasonable precision.

b. Deposit on Containers, $400,000. This is a partially executed contract, which accountants recognize as an asset to the extent of the partial performance.

c. GAAP do not allow firms to capitalize advertising expenditures as assets because of the uncertainty of future benefits which firms can measure with reasonable precision.

d. Investment in Common Stock, $2.5 million.

e. GAAP do not recognize an asset for the same reasons as in part **a** above.

f. Land and Building, $75 million. The accountant must allocate the aggregate purchase price between the land and the building because the building is depreciable and the land is not. Legal passage of title is not necessary to justify recognition of an asset. Coca-Cola has acquired the rights to use the land and building and can sustain those rights as long as it makes the required payments on the mortgage obligation.

SUGGESTED SOLUTION TO PROBLEM 2.2 FOR SELF-STUDY

(New York Times Company; liability recognition and valuation)

a. Subscription Fees Received in Advance, $10 million.

b. Accounts Payable, $4 million. Other account titles are also acceptable.

c. GAAP do not recognize a liability in this case because the life of the vehicles substantially exceeds the one-year rental period. **Chapter 10** discusses the criteria for recognition of leases as liabilities.

d. GAAP do not recognize a liability because of the low probability, given the insurance coverage, that the firm will make a future cash payment.

e. GAAP require the recognition of a liability when a cash payment is "probable." GAAP provide no specific guidelines as to how high the probability needs to be to recognize a liability. Anecdotal evidence suggests that practicing accountants use 80 to 85 percent.

f. The firm likely previously recorded the $2 million in the account Subscription Fees Received in Advance. The strike will probably extend the subscription period by two weeks. Thus, the firm has already recognized a liability.

SUGGESTED SOLUTION TO PROBLEM 2.3 FOR SELF-STUDY

(Gaines Corporation; dual effects of transactions on balance sheet equation)

Transaction		Assets	Liabilities	Shareholders' Equity
1.	The firm issues 20,000 shares of $10 par value common stock for $12 cash per share.	+ $240,000	0	+ $240,000
2.	The firm issues $100,000 principal amount of bonds for $100,000 cash	+ 100,000	+ $100,000	0
3.	The firm acquires, with $220,000 cash, land costing $40,000 and a building costing $180,000	+ 220,000 − 220,000	0	0
4.	The firm acquires, on account, equipment costing $25,000 and merchandise inventory costing $12,000 . .	+ 37,000	+ 37,000	0
5.	The firm signs an agreement to rent equipment from its owner and pays $1,500 rental in advance.	+ 1,500 − 1,500	0	0
6.	The firm pays $28,000 to the suppliers in **4**	− 28,000	− 28,000	
	Totals.	$349,000	$109,000	$240,000

SUGGESTED SOLUTION TO PROBLEM 2.4 FOR SELF-STUDY

(Gaines Corporation; spreadsheet analysis of business transactions.) See **Exhibit 2.9.**

EXHIBIT 2.9   Transactions Spreadsheet for Gaines Corporation (Problem 2.4 for Self-Study)

Balance Sheet Accounts

Transactions, By Number and Description

	Balance: Beginning of Period	Issue Common Stock for Cash	Issue Bond for Cash	Acquire Land and Building for Cash	Acquire Equip. and Inventory on Account	Pay Rental in Advance	Pay Supplier	Balance: End of Period
		1	**2**	**3**	**4**	**5**	**6**	
ASSETS								
Current Assets:								
Cash		240,000	100,000	−220,000		−1,500	−28,000	90,500
Merchandise Inventory					12,000			12,000
Prepaid Rent						1,500		1,500
Total Current Assets								104,000
Noncurrent Assets:								
Land				40,000				40,000
Building				180,000				180,000
Equipment					25,000			25,000
Total Noncurrent Assets								245,000
Total Assets								349,000
LIABILITIES AND SHAREHOLDERS' EQUITY								
Current Liabilities:								
Accounts Payable					37,000		−28,000	9,000
Total Current Liabilities								9,000
Noncurrent Liabilities:								
Bonds Payable			100,000					100,000
Total Noncurrent Liabilities								100,000
Total Liabilities								109,000
Shareholders' Equity:								
Common Stock		200,000						200,000
Additional Paid-in Capital		40,000						40,000
Total Shareholders' Equity								240,000
Total Liabilities and Shareholders' Equity								349,000
Imbalance, *if Any*								
Income Statement Accounts								

SUGGESTED SOLUTION TO PROBLEM 2.5 FOR SELF-STUDY

(Gaines Corporation; journal entries for business transactions.)

(1)	Cash (Asset Increase)	240,000	
	Common Stock (Shareholders' Equity Increase).............		200,000
	Additional Paid-in Capital (Shareholders' Equity Increase)		40,000
	Issues 20,000 shares of $10 par value common stock for $12 cash per share.		
(2)	Cash (Asset Increase)	100,000	
	Bonds Payable (Liability Increase).		100,000
	Issues $100,000 principal amount of bonds for $100,000 cash.		
(3)	Land (Asset Increase)	40,000	
	Building (Asset Increase)	180,000	
	Cash (Asset Decrease)		220,000
	Acquires for $220,000 cash land costing $40,000 and a building costing $180,000.		
(4)	Equipment (Asset Increase)	25,000	
	Merchandise Inventory (Asset Increase)	12,000	
	Accounts Payable (Liability Increase)		37,000
	Purchases equipment costing $25,000 and merchandise inventory costing $12,000 on account.		
(5)	Prepaid Rent (Asset Increase)	1,500	
	Cash (Asset Decrease)		1,500
	Paid $1,500 as advance rental on equipment.		
(6)	Accounts Payable (Liability Decrease)	28,000	
	Cash (Asset Decrease)		28,000
	Pays $28,000 to the suppliers in **(4)**.		

SUGGESTED SOLUTION TO PROBLEM 2.6 FOR SELF-STUDY

(Electronics Appliance Corporation; journal entries, transactions spreadsheet, and balance sheet preparation)

a. Journal entries for the nine transactions follow:

(1) Sept. 1	Cash (Asset Increase)	48,000	
	Common Stock (Shareholders' Equity Increase)		40,000
	Additional Paid-in Capital (Shareholders' Equity Increase)		8,000
	Issue 4,000 shares of $10 par value common stock for $12 cash per share.		
(2) Sept. 2	Patent (Asset Increase)	7,200	
	Common Stock (Shareholders' Equity Increase)		6,000
	Additional Paid-in Capital (Shareholders' Equity Increase)		1,200
	Issue 600 shares of $10 par value common stock in the acquisition of a patent.		
(3) Sept. 5	Prepaid Rent or Advances to Landlord (Asset Increase)	10,000	
	Cash (Asset Decrease)		10,000
	Prepay rent for October and November on factory building.		
(4) Sept. 12	Raw Materials Inventory (Asset Increase)	6,100	
	Accounts Payable (Liability Increase)		6,100
	Purchase raw materials costing $6,100 on account.		
(5) Sept. 15	Cash (Asset Increase)	900	
	Advances from Customers (Liability Increase)		900
	Receive an advance of $900 from a customer as a deposit on equipment to be manufactured in the future.		
(6) Sept. 20	Equipment (Asset Increase)	925	
	Cash (Asset Decrease)		925
	Acquire equipment with a list price of $950 for $925 after taking a discount for prompt payment.		
(7) Sept. 28	Advances to Employees (Asset Increase)	200	
	Cash (Asset Decrease)		200
	Give cash advances of $200 to employees beginning work on Oct. 1.		

EXHIBIT 2.10

Transaction Spreadsheet for Electronics Appliance Corporation (Problem 2.6 for Self-Study)

Transactions, By Number and Description

Balance Sheet Accounts	Balance: Beginning of Period	Issue Common Stock for Cash	Issue Common Stock for a Patent	Pay Two Months Rent in Advance	Purchase Raw Materials on Account	Receive Deposit from Customer	Acquire Equipment for Cash	Make Cash Advance to Employee	Purchase Equip. for Cash and Mortgage	Pay to Install Equipment	Balance: End of Period
		1	2	3	4	5	6	7	8	9	
ASSETS											
Current Assets:											
Cash		48,000		−10,000		900	−925	−200	−5,000	−450	32,325
Advances to Employees								200			200
Raw Materials Inventory					6,100						6,100
Prepaid Rent				10,000							10,000
Total Current Assets											48,625
Noncurrent Assets:											
Equipment							925		27,500	450	28,875
Patent			7,200								7,200
Total Noncurrent Assets											36,025
Total Assets											84,700
LIABILITIES AND SHAREHOLDERS' EQUITY											
Current Liabilities:											
Accounts Payable					6,100						6,100
Advances from Customers						900					900
Total Current Liabilities											7,000
Noncurrent Liabilities:											
Mortgage Payable									22,500		22,500
Total Noncurrent Liabilities											22,500
Total Liabilities											29,500
Shareholders' Equity:											
Common Stock		40,000	6,000								46,000
Additional Paid-in Capital		8,000	1,200								9,200
Total Shareholders' Equity											55,200
Total Liabilities and Shareholders' Equity											84,700
Imbalance, *if Any*											
Income Statement Accounts											

(8) Sept. 30 Equipment (Asset Increase) 27,500
               Cash (Asset Decrease)   5,000
               Mortgage Payable (Liability Increase)   22,500
               Acquire equipment for $5,000 cash and assume a $22,500
               mortgage for the balance of the purchase price.

(9) Sept. 30 Equipment (Asset Increase) 450
               Cash (Asset Decrease)   450
               Pay installation cost of $450 on equipment acquired
               in **(8)**.

b. **Exhibit 2.10** presents the transactions spreadsheet for Electronics Appliance Corporation.
c. **Exhibit 2.11** presents a balance sheet as of September 30.

EXHIBIT 2.11	ELECTRONICS APPLIANCE CORPORATION Balance Sheet, September 30 (Problem 2.6 for Self-Study)

ASSETS			LIABILITIES AND SHAREHOLDERS' EQUITY		
Current Assets			**Current Liabilities**		
Cash	$32,325		Accounts Payable	$ 6,100	
Advances to Employees	200		Advances from Customers	900	
Raw Materials Inventory	6,100		Total Current Liabilities		$ 7,000
Prepaid Rent	10,000				
			Long-Term Debt		
Total Current Assets		$48,625	Mortgage Payable		22,500
			Total Liabilities		$29,500
Property, Plant, and Equipment					
Equipment		28,875	**Shareholders' Equity**		
			Common Stock, $10 Par Value	$46,000	
Intangibles			Additional Paid-in Capital	9,200	
Patent		7,200			
			Total Shareholders' Equity		55,200
			Total Liabilities and Shareholders' Equity		$84,700
Total Assets		$84,700			

Key Terms and Concepts

Executory contract
Acquisition (historical) cost
Current replacement cost (entry value)
Current net realizable value (exit value)
Present value
Monetary assets
Nonmonetary assets
Going concern assumption
Reliability
Conservatism

Current assets
Plant, or fixed, assets
Intangible assets
Contingent obligations
Current liabilities
Par or stated value
Journal entry
Debit
Credit
Common-size balance sheet

Questions, Short Exercises, Exercises, Problems, and Cases

QUESTIONS

1. Review the meaning of the terms and concepts listed above in Key Terms and Concepts.
2. Conservatism is generally regarded as a convention in accounting. Indicate whom this might hurt.
3. One of the criteria for the recognition of an asset or a liability is that there be an exchange. What justification can you see for this requirement?

For additional student resources, content, and interactive quizzes for this chapter visit the FACMU website:

http://facmu.swlearning.com

4. Accounting typically does not recognize either assets or liabilities for mutually unexecuted contracts. What justification can you see for this treatment?

5. Accounting treats cash discounts taken on the purchase of merchandise or equipment as a reduction in the amount recorded for the assets acquired. What justification can you see for this treatment?

6. A group of investors owns an office building that it rents unfurnished to tenants. It purchased the building five years previously from a construction company. At that time, it expected the building to have a useful life of 40 years. Indicate the procedures you might follow to ascertain the valuation amount for this building under each of the following valuation methods:
   a. Acquisition cost
   b. Adjusted acquisition cost (reduced for services already consumed)
   c. Current replacement cost
   d. Current net realizable value
   e. Present value of future net cash flows

7. Some of the assets of one firm correspond to the liabilities of another firm. For example, an account receivable on the seller's balance sheet is an account payable on the buyer's balance sheet. For each of the following items, indicate whether it is an asset or a liability and give the corresponding account title on the balance sheet of the other party to the transaction:
   a. Advances by Customers
   b. Bonds Payable
   c. Interest Receivable
   d. Prepaid Insurance
   e. Rental Fees Received in Advance

SHORT EXERCISES

8. **Asset and liability recognition and valuation.** The San Francisco Giants sign Barry Bonds to a five-year contract beginning next year. The contract calls for payments of $50 million each year for next five years, beginning next year. Assume that these payments have a present value of $200 million. The contract also provides that the San Francisco Giants give Barry Bonds an Italian sports car valued at $250,000 at the time of signing the contract. Indicate the treatment of this contract at the time of signing.

9. **Asset recognition and valuation.** Citigroup, a financial services firm, provides tuition support for employees who pursue an MBA degree in the evenings. Employees receiving the support must continue working for Citigroup for five years or repay a ratable portion of the benefit. During the current year, Citigroup paid $10 million in tuition support to various employees. Citigroup estimates, based on experience, that the MBA education enhances employees' skills by $15 million. Indicate Citigroup's treatment of the $10 million.

10. **Liability recognition and valuation.** Delta Air Lines offers frequent flyer benefits to customers that reach specified levels of miles flown. The present value of the future loss in revenues due to customers earning free flights during the current year is $200 million. The present value of the estimated cost of providing the free flights is $25 million. Indicate the amount, if any, that Delta Air Lines should recognize as a liability for its frequent flyer program for the current year.

11. **Asset valuation.** Pizza Hut purchased a used van from Domino's Pizza to deliver pizzas. Pizza Hut paid $14,500 for the van. It paid $1,200 to have the Domino's Pizza name removed from the van and repainted with the Pizza Hut colors and name. It paid $75 for the license fee and $680 for insurance for the first year of use, which begins next month. How much should Pizza Hut record as the acquisition cost of this van? Describe the treatment of any of the above amounts that you did not include in the acquisition cost of the van.

12. **Dual effects on balance sheet equation.** Target Stores engaged in the following three transactions: (1) purchased and received merchandise costing $25 million on account from various suppliers, (2) returned merchandise costing $1.5 million because of damage or incorrect shipments, (3) paid the suppliers the amount due from purchases on account. Indicate the effects of each of these three transactions on the balance sheet equation.

13. **Journal entry for acquisition.** Leonard Corporation gave $10 million cash and shares of its common stock valued at $60 million for all of the assets of Newsom Corporation. The assets received consisted of inventory valued at $20 million and land, buildings and equipment valued at $40 million. Leonard Corporation also assumed responsibility for $25 of liabilities of Newsom Corporation. Give the journal entry to record this transaction.

EXERCISES

14. **Asset recognition and valuation.** The following transactions relate to IBM Corporation, a manufacturer of electronic equipment and provider of computer services. Indicate whether or not each transaction immediately gives rise to an asset of the company under GAAP. If accounting recognizes an asset, state the account title, the amount, and the classification of the asset on the balance sheet as either a current asset or a noncurrent asset.
    a. The firm invests $8,000,000 in a government bond. The bond has a maturity value of $10,000,000 in three years, and IBM intends to hold the bond to maturity.
    b. The firm sends a check for $600,000 to a landlord for two months' rent in advance on warehouse facilities. The rental period begins next month.
    c. The firm writes a check for $1,000,000 to obtain an option to purchase a tract of land. The price of the land is $10,000,000.
    d. The firm signs a four-year employment agreement with its president for $30,000,000 per year. The contract period begins next month.
    e. The firm purchases a patent on a laser printer from its creator for $8,500,000.
    f. The firm receives a patent on a new computer processor that it developed. The firm spent $3,200,000 to develop the patented invention.
    g. The firm received notice that a supplier had shipped by freight memory chips billed at $12,000,000, with payment due in 30 days. The seller retains title to the memory chips until received by the buyer.

15. **Asset recognition and valuation.** The transactions listed below relate to Delta Air Lines, a provider of airline services. Indicate whether or not each transaction immediately gives rise to an asset of Delta Air Lines under GAAP. If accounting recognizes an asset, give the account title, the amount, and the classification of the asset on the balance sheet as either a current asset or a noncurrent asset.
    a. The firm places an order with Boeing for 10 Boeing 767 airplanes, costing $80 million each.
    b. Delta writes a check for a total of $5 million as a deposit on the aircraft it ordered in part **a**.
    c. The firm spends $4 million to obtain landing rights for the next five years at Boston's Logan Airport.
    d. The firm writes a check for $1.5 million and assumes a mortgage from its bank for $8.5 million to purchase new ground equipment costing $10 million.
    e. The firm signs a four-year employment agreement with its president for $15 million per year. The contract period begins next month.
    f. The firm issues common stock with a market value of $60 million to acquire used aircraft from a bankrupt regional airline. The equipment had a book value on the bankrupt airline's books of $75 million.
    g. The firm spends $2 million to advertise flights to the Bahamas that it intends to add to its flight schedule next month.
    h. The firm invests $4 million in a government bond. The bond has a maturity value of $5 million in 3 years, and Delta intends to hold the bond to maturity.

16. **Asset recognition and valuation.** The transactions listed below relate to McDonald's, a fast food chain. Indicate whether or not each transaction immediately gives rise to an asset under GAAP. If accounting recognizes an asset, state the account title, the amount, and classification of the asset on the balance sheet as a current asset or a noncurrent asset.
    a. The firm spends $2,500,000 to develop and test-market a new dinner meal. It intends to launch the new product nationally next month.
    b. The firm spends $3,900,000 to acquire rights to prepare and sell a new sugar-free dessert bar.
    c. The firm spends $2,800,000 to obtain options to purchase land as future sites for its McDonald's restaurants.
    d. The firm spends $920,000 for television advertisements that appeared last month.
    e. The firm issues shares of its common stock currently selling on the market for $20,000,000 for 40 percent of the shares of Philadelphia Markets, another restaurant chain. Recent appraisals suggest that a 40 percent share of Philadelphia Markets is worth between $18,000,000 and $22,000,000. McDonald's intends to hold these shares as a long-term investment.
    f. The firm acquires land and a building costing $5,000,000 by paying $1,200,000 in cash and signing a promissory note for the remaining $3,800,000 of the purchase price. McDonald's expends $80,000 for a title search and other legal fees, $6,000 in recording fees with the state of Illinois, and $180,000 to destroy the building. McDonald's intends to use the land for a parking lot.

17. **Asset recognition and valuation.** The transactions below relate to Office Depot, an office supply retailer. Indicate whether or not each transaction immediately gives rise to an asset under GAAP. If accounting recognizes an asset, state the account title, the amount, and the classification of the asset on the balance sheet as either a current asset or a noncurrent asset.

   a. The firm rents retail space in a local shopping center for the five-year period beginning next month. Office Depot pays $255,000, which includes $125,000 as rent for the first year and $130,000 as a security deposit against future damages and unpaid rent. The firm commits to paying $500,000 later, for the last four years of the lease.

   b. The firm spends $10,000 to install partitions between administrative and retail space, $6,500 to paint the walls colors that are consistent with other Office Depot stores, and $20,000 to install carpeting.

   c. The firm purchases display counters with a list price of $30,000. It pays for the display counters in time to take a 2 percent discount for prompt payment. Costs to transport the display counters to the new location total $1,200, and costs to install them total $800.

   d. The firm hires a store manager at an annual salary of $60,000.

   e. The firm spends $1,500 in newspaper and television advertisements that appeared this month.

   f. The firm purchases inventory with an invoice price of $160,000. It pays for merchandise with an original invoice price of $120,000 in time to take a 2 percent discount for prompt payment. It has not yet paid for the remainder of the merchandise purchased. The firm treats cash discounts taken as a reduction in the acquisition cost of merchandise. An inspection of the merchandise reveals that merchandise with an original invoice price of $12,000 is defective. Office Depot returns this merchandise to the supplier, having not yet paid for it.

18. **Liability recognition and valuation.** Indicate whether or not each of the following events immediately gives rise to a liability under GAAP. If accounting recognizes a liability, state the account title, the amount, and the classification of the liability on the balance sheet as either a current liability or a noncurrent liability.

   a. A landscaper agrees to improve land owned by a firm during the next year. The agreed price for the work is $7,500. Consider from the standpoint of the firm owning the land.

   b. A magazine publisher receives a check for $72 for a 1-year subscription to a magazine. The subscription period begins next month. Consider from the standpoint of the publisher.

   c. A construction company agrees to build a bridge for $10 million. It receives a down payment of $2 million upon signing the contract; it is entitled to the remainder when it completes the bridge, which is expected to be in three years.

   d. A firm issues additional common stock with a par value of $3,000,000 for $7,600,000.

   e. A firm receives a 60-day, 6-percent loan of $100,000 from a local bank. Consider from the standpoint of the firm receiving the loan.

   f. A firm signs a contract to purchase at least $60,000 of merchandise from a particular supplier during the next year. Consider from the standpoint of the purchaser of the merchandise.

   g. Refer to part f. The firm places an order for $15,000 of merchandise with the supplier.

19. **Liability recognition and valuation.** The transactions below relate to Kansas City Royals, Inc., owner of a professional baseball team and Kauffman Stadium. Indicate whether or not each of the following transactions immediately gives rise to a liability of the firm under GAAP. If accounting recognizes a liability, state the account title, the amount, and the classification of the liability on the balance sheet as either a current liability or a noncurrent liability.

   a. The firm signs a five-year contract with Joe Superstar for $7,400,000 per year. The contract period begins on February 1 of next year.

   b. The firm receives $2,700,000 from sales of season tickets for the baseball season starting April 1 of next year.

   c. The firm issues bonds in the principal amount of $8,000,000 for $8,400,000. The bonds mature in 20 years and bear interest at 8 percent per year. The firm intends to use the proceeds to expand Kauffman Stadium.

   d. The firm receives a bill for utility services received last month totaling $3,400.

   e. The firm receives notice that a former player has filed suit against Kansas City Royals, Inc., alleging nonperformance of contractual terms. The player claims $10,000,000 in damages.

   f. The firm orders new uniforms for the team for the baseball season beginning next spring. The contract calls for a $10,000 deposit upon signing the contract and a $15,000 payment on delivery of the uniforms in February of next year. The firm signs the contract and sends a check for $10,000.

20. **Liability recognition and valuation.** The transactions below relate to the activities of a local college. Indicate whether or not each of the following transactions immediately gives rise to a liability under GAAP. If accounting recognizes a liability, state the account title, the amount, and the classification of the liability on the balance sheet as either a current liability or a non-current liability.

    a. The college issues bonds with a principal amount and issue price of $10,000,000. The college must pay interest at a rate of 7 percent of the principal amount each year and repay the principal in 15 years. The college intends to use the proceeds to construct a new dormitory.

    b. The college contracts with a construction company to build the dormitory in part **a** for a contract price of $12,000,000. The college pays $2,000,000 at the time of signing the contract and must pay the remainder as construction progresses. Construction begins next month and should take three years to complete.

    c. The college institutes a guaranteed tuition plan for students entering next fall. The tuition for the academic year beginning next fall is $15,000 per year. Although the college expects tuition to increase each year, any entering student who pays $45,000 in advance will receive rights to a four-year undergraduate education without additional tuition payments. The college receives $1,800,000 from students who are entering next fall and who signed up for the guaranteed tuition plan.

    d. The college bookstore receives textbooks for the coming academic year with an invoice price of $170,000.

    e. The college owes employees $280,000 in compensation for the last pay period. The college is also responsible for payment of payroll taxes of 6 percent of compensation.

    f. The college receives a grant from the Carnegie Foundation for $1,500,000 to enhance undergraduate teaching. The college intends to disburse the funds to faculty members to develop new teaching materials.

21. **Liability recognition and valuation.** The events below relate to the Chicago Symphony Orchestra. Indicate whether or not each of the following events immediately gives rise to a liability under GAAP. If accounting recognizes a liability, state the account title, the amount, and the classification of the liability on the balance sheet as either a current liability or a non-current liability.

    a. The firm receives $340,000 for season tickets sold for next season.

    b. The firm places an order with a printer company totaling $85,000 for symphony performance programs for next season.

    c. The firm receives the programs ordered in part **b**, along with an invoice for $85,000.

    d. The firm receives notice from its attorneys that a loyal customer attending a concert last season and sitting in the first row of the symphony hall has sued the Chicago Symphony Orchestra for $10 million claiming hearing loss. The customer normally sits further back but was asked to move forward for this particular concert because of damage to the regular seat.

    e. The firm signs a three-year contract with its first violinist at a salary of $140,000 per year.

    f. For $225,000, the firm issues additional common stock with a par value of $200,000.

    g. The firm receives a 90-day, 8-percent loan of $40,000 from a local bank.

22. **Balance sheet classification.** GAAP classify items on the balance sheet in one of the following ways:

    (1) Asset

    (2) Liability

    (3) Shareholders' equity

    (4) Item that would not appear on the balance sheet as conventionally prepared under GAAP.

    Using these numbers, indicate the appropriate classification of each of the following items:

    a. Salaries payable

    b. Retained earnings

    c. Notes receivable

    d. Unfilled customers' orders

    e. Land

    f. Interest payable

    g. Work-in-process inventory

    h. Mortgage payable

    i. Organization costs

    j. Advances by customers

    k. Advances to employees
    l. Patents
   m. Good credit standing
    n. Common stock

23. **Balance sheet classification.** GAAP classify items on the balance sheet in one of the following ways:
   (1) Asset
   (2) Liability
   (3) Shareholders' equity
   (4) Item that would not appear on the balance sheet as conventionally prepared under GAAP.

   Using these numbers, indicate the appropriate classification of each of the following items:
   a. Preferred stock
   b. Furniture and fixtures
   c. Potential liability under lawsuit (case has not yet gone to trial)
   d. Prepaid rent
   e. Capital contributed in excess of par value
   f. Cash on hand
   g. Goodwill
   h. Estimated liability under warranty contract
   i. Raw materials inventory
   j. Rental fees received in advance
   k. Bonds payable
   l. Prepaid insurance
   m. Income taxes payable
   n. Treasury stock

PROBLEMS AND CASES

24. **Dual effects of transactions on balance sheet equation and journal entries.** A firm engages in the following six transactions.
   (1) The firm issues 5,000 shares of $10 par value common stock for $60,000 cash.
   (2) It purchases merchandise costing $29,200 on account.
   (3) The firm acquires store equipment costing $32,700. It issues a check for $5,000, with the balance payable over three years under an installment contract.
   (4) The firm issues a check for $4,500 covering two months' rent in advance.
   (5) Refer to transaction **(3)**. The firm issues 2,000 shares of its $10-par value common stock with a market value of $27,700 in full settlement of the installment contract.
   (6) The firm pays the merchandise supplier in transaction **(2)** the amount due.

   a. Indicate the effects of these six transactions on the balance sheet equation using this format:

Transaction Number	Assets	=	Liabilities	+	Shareholders' Equity
(1)	+$60,000		$0		+$60,000
Subtotal	$60,000	=	$0	+	$60,000

   b. Give the journal entry for each of the six transactions.

25. **Dual effects of transactions on balance sheet equation and journal entries.** A firm engages in the following six transactions.
   (1) The firm issues 12,000 shares of $1 par value common stock for $12 cash per share.
   (2) The firm acquires land costing $50,000 and a building costing $900,000. It gives $110,000 in cash and 70,000 shares of its $1 par value common stock valued at $840,000 to acquire the land and building.
   (3) The firm pays $6,000 cash for a one-year insurance policy on the land and building. The policy period commences next month.
   (4) The firm acquires merchandise inventory costing $150,000 on account from various suppliers.
   (5) The firm pays $147,000 in cash to the suppliers in transaction **(4)** for its previous purchases on account. The $3,000 difference between the original inventory cost and the amount paid represents a discount for prompt payment, which the firm treats as a reduction in the cost of the merchandise.

(6) The firm received $1,300 from a customer as an advance on inventory that the firm will deliver to the customer next month.

a. Indicate the effects of these six transactions on the balance sheet equation using this format:

Transaction Number	Assets	=	Liabilities	+	Shareholders' Equity
(1)	+$144,000		$0	+	$144,000
Subtotal	$144,000	=	$0	+	$144,000

b. Give the journal entry for each of the six transactions.

26. **Journal entries for various transactions.** Present journal entries for each of the following transactions of Kirkland Corporation. You may omit dates and explanations for the journal entries.

(1) Issues 10,000 shares of $10 par value common stock in the acquisition of the assets of Ragsdale Corporation. The common shares given in the exchange have a market value of $250,000 on the New York Stock Exchange. The identifiable assets received and their market values are: inventories, $30,000; land, $15,000; buildings, $125,000; equipment, $60,000.

(2) Orders merchandise costing $36,000, paying $5,000 in advance to the supplier.

(3) Receives the merchandise ordered in (2) and an invoice for the $31,000 due.

(4) Inspects the merchandise and discovers that merchandise costing $3,500 is damaged and returns it to the supplier. The account has not yet been paid.

(5) Pays the amount due to the supplier in transactions (2), (3), and (4) after subtracting a 2-percent discount for prompt payment. The discount applies to the full amount of purchases ($36,000) net of returns ($3,500). Kirkland Corporation treats cash discounts taken as a reduction in the acquisition cost of merchandise.

(6) Receives an order from a customer for $8,000 of merchandise to be delivered next month. The customer sends an $800 check with the order as a deposit on the purchase.

(7) Acquires an automobile costing $18,000 by paying $2,000 in cash and signing a note payable for the balance. The note bears interest at 8 percent per year and is due in 12 months.

(8) Pays $24,000 for property and liability insurance for the one-year period beginning next month.

27. **Journal entries for various transactions.** Express the following transactions of Winkle Grocery Store, Inc., in journal entry form. If an entry is not required, indicate the reason. You may omit explanations for the journal entries.

(1) Receives $30,000 from John Winkle in return for 1,000 shares of the firm's $30 par value common stock.

(2) Gives a 60-day, 8-percent note to a bank and receives $5,000 cash from the bank.

(3) Rents a building and pays the annual rental of $12,000 in advance.

(4) Acquires display equipment costing $8,000 and issues a check in full payment.

(5) Acquires merchandise inventory costing $25,000. The firm issues a check for $12,000, with the remainder payable in 30 days.

(6) Signs a contract with a nearby restaurant under which the restaurant agrees to purchase $2,000 of groceries each week. The firm receives a check for the first two weeks' orders in advance.

(7) Obtains a fire insurance policy providing $50,000 coverage beginning next month. It pays the one-year premium of $1,200.

(8) Pays $600 for advertisements that will appear in newspapers next month.

(9) Places an order with suppliers for $35,000 of merchandise to be delivered next month.

28. **Journal entries for various transactions.** The transactions below relate to Wendy's International, Inc., a restaurant chain. Express each transaction in journal entry form. If an entry is not required, indicate the reason. You may omit explanations for the journal entries.

(1) The firm places an order for restaurant supplies totaling $1,600,000 to be delivered next month.

(2) The firm receives the supplies ordered in transaction (1) on open account.

(3) The firm discovers supplies received in transaction (2) costing $40,000 are defective and returns them to the supplier for full credit.

(4) The firm pays for some of the purchases in transactions (1) and (2) originally invoiced for $1,400,000 in time to take advantage of 2-percent discounts for prompt payment. The firm treats discounts taken as a reduction in the cost of supplies.

(5) The firm pays for the remaining purchases—see transactions (1) through (4).

(6) The firm places an order, totaling $900,000, for refrigerated salad bars for its restaurants. It pays $200,000 at the time of signing the contract and agrees to pay the remainder at delivery.

D/e

(7) The firm receives the salad bars ordered in transaction (6) and pays the amount due.

(8) The firm pays $27,000 to install the salad bars in its restaurants.

(9) The firm discovers that salad bars costing $22,000 are defective and returns them to the supplier, expecting a cash refund.

(10) The firm receives a check for $22,000 from the supplier in transaction (9).

29. **Preparation of transactions spreadsheet and balance sheet.** Moulton Corporation engaged in the following seven transactions during December, Year 12 in preparation for opening the business on January 1, Year 13.

(1) Issued for cash 80,000 shares of $10 par value at par.

(2) Acquired for cash land costing $50,000 and a building costing $450,000. The building has an expected useful life of 25 years beginning on January 1, Year 13.

(3) Purchased merchandise inventory costing $280,000 on account from various suppliers.

(4) Paid for inventory purchased in (3) with an original invoice price of $250,000 in time to take advantage of a 2-percent discount for prompt payment. The firm treats discounts taken as a reduction in the cost of inventories. The firm has not yet paid for the remaining $30,000 of purchases on account.

(5) Paid $12,000 for a one-year insurance policy on the land and building. The insurance coverage begins January 1.

(6) Borrowed $300,000 from a bank on December 31, Year 12. The loan bears interest at an annual rate of 8 percent and is due in five years. The interest is payable on January 1 of each year, beginning January 1, Year 14, and the $300,000 amount borrowed is due on December 31, Year 17.

(7) Acquired equipment on December 31 costing $80,000 and signed a 6-percent note payable to the supplier. The note is due on June 30, Year 13. The equipment has an estimated useful life of 5 years.

a. Prepare a transactions spreadsheet for the seven transactions. You may wish to use the transactions spreadsheet template available with this book.

b. Prepare a balance sheet for Moulton Corporation as of December 31.

Note: Problem 3.32 extends the problem to income transactions for January.

30. **Preparation of transactions spreadsheet and balance sheet.** Veronica Regaldo creates a new business firm in Mexico on January 2, Year 8, to operate a retail store. Transactions of Regaldo Department Stores during January in preparation for opening its first retail store in February appear below:

(1) January 2: Receives Ps500,000 from Veronica Regaldo for all of the common stock of Regaldo Department Stores. The stock has no par or stated value.

(2) January 5: Pays another firm Ps20,000 for a patent and pays the Mexican government Ps4,000 to register the patent.

(3) January 10: Orders merchandise from various suppliers at a cost of Ps200,000. See transactions (5), (6), and (7) below for later information regarding these merchandise orders.

(4) January 15: Signs a lease to rent land and a building for Ps30,000 a month. The rental period begins February 1. Regaldo pays Ps60,000 for the first two months' rent in advance.

(5) January 20: Receives the merchandise ordered on January 10. Regaldo delays payment for the merchandise until it receives an invoice from the supplier—see transaction (7) below.

(6) January 21: Discovers that merchandise costing Ps8,000 is defective and returns the items to the supplier.

(7) January 25: Receives invoices for Ps160,000 of the merchandise received on January 20. After subtracting an allowed discount of 2 percent of the invoice for paying promptly, Regaldo pays the suppliers the amount due of Ps156,800 (0.98 × Ps160,000). The firm treats cash discounts taken as a reduction in the acquisition cost of the merchandise.

(8) January 30: Obtains fire and liability insurance coverage from Windwards Islands Insurance Company for the period beginning February 1, Year 8. It pays the one-year insurance premium of Ps12,000.

a. Prepare a transactions spreadsheet for the eight transactions. You may wish to use the transactions spreadsheet template available with this book.

b. Prepare a balance sheet for Regaldo Department Stores on January 31, Year 8.

Note: Problem 3.33 extends this problem to income transactions for February.

31. **Preparation of transactions spreadsheet and balance sheet.** Patterson Corporation begins operations on January 1, Year 13. See the assumptions given at the end of the list. The firm engages in the following transactions during January:

(1) Issues 15,000 shares of $10 par value common stock for $210,000 in cash.

(2) Issues 28,000 shares of common stock in exchange for land, building, and equipment.

The land appears at $80,000, the building at $220,000, and the equipment at $92,000 on the balance sheet.

(3) Issues 2,000 shares of common stock to another firm to acquire a patent.

(4) Acquires merchandise inventories with a list price of $75,000 on account from suppliers.

(5) Acquires equipment with a list price of $6,000. It deducts a $600 discount and pays the net amount in cash. The firm treats cash discounts as a reduction in the acquisition cost of equipment.

(6) Pays freight charges of $350 for delivery of the equipment in **(5)**.

(7) Discovers that merchandise inventories with a list price of $800 are defective and returns them to the supplier for full credit. The merchandise inventories had been purchased on account—see **(4)**—and no payment had been made as of the time that the goods were returned.

(8) Signs a contract for the rental of a fleet of automobiles beginning February 1. Pays the $1,400 rental for February in advance.

(9) Pays invoices for merchandise inventories purchased in **(4)** with an original list price of $60,000, after deducting a discount of 3 percent for prompt payment. The firm treats cash discounts as a reduction in the acquisition cost of merchandise inventories.

(10) Obtains fire and liability insurance coverage from Southwest Insurance Company. The two-year policy, beginning February 1, carries a $2,400 premium that has not yet been paid.

(11) Signs a contract with a customer for $20,000 of merchandise that Patterson plans to deliver in the future. The customer advances $4,500 toward the contract price.

(12) Acquires a warehouse costing $60,000 on January 31. The firm makes a down payment of $7,000 and assumes a 20-year, 6-percent mortgage for the balance. Interest is payable on January 31 each year.

(13) Discovers that merchandise inventories with an original list price of $1,500 are defective and returns them to the supplier. This inventory was paid for in **(9)**. The returned merchandise inventories are the only items purchased from this particular supplier during January. A cash refund has not yet been received from the supplier.

(14) On January 31, the firm purchases 6,000 shares of $10 par value common stock of the General Cereal Corporation for $95,000. This purchase is a short-term use of excess cash. The shares of General Cereal Corporation trade on the New York Stock Exchange.

The following assumptions will help you resolve certain accounting uncertainties:

- transactions **(2)** and **(3)** occur on the same day as transaction **(1)**; and
- the invoices paid in **(9)** are the only purchases for which suppliers made discounts available to the purchaser.

a. Prepare a transactions spreadsheet and enter the 14 transactions. You may wish to use the transactions spreadsheet available with this book.

b. Prepare a balance sheet as of January 31, Year 13.

Note: Problem 3.34 extends this problem to income transactions for February.

32. Preparation of transactions spreadsheet and balance sheet. Whitley Products Corporation begins operations on April 1. The firm engages in the following transactions during April:

(1) Issues 25,000 shares of $10 par value common stock for $15 per share in cash.

(2) Acquires land costing $25,000 and a building costing $275,000 by paying $50,000 in cash and signing a note payable to a local bank for the remainder of the purchase price. The note bears interest at 8 percent per year and matures in three years.

(3) Acquires equipment costing $125,000 for cash.

(4) Pays $2,800 to transport the equipment to the office of Whitley Products Corporation.

(5) Pays $3,200 to install and test the equipment.

(6) Pays the one-year premium of $12,000 for property and liability insurance on the building and equipment for coverage beginning May 1.

(7) Agrees to manufacture custom order merchandise for a particular customer beginning in May at a selling price of $15,000. The customer advances $1,500 of the selling price with the order.

(8) Orders raw materials costing $60,000 from various suppliers.

(9) Receives notification from the suppliers that the raw materials ordered in transaction **(8)** were shipped. The merchandise belongs to the suppliers until received by Whitley Products Corporation.

(10) Receives the raw materials shipped in transaction **(9)**.

(11) Discovers that raw materials costing $8,000 are damaged, and returns them to the supplier. The firm has not yet paid the supplier.

(12) Pays the raw materials suppliers in transactions **(8)**, **(9)**, **(10)**, and **(11)** the amounts due, after subtracting 2 percent for prompt payment. The firm treats cash discounts as a reduction in the acquisition cost of the raw materials.

    a. Prepare a transactions spreadsheet and enter the twelve transactions. You may wish to use the transactions spreadsheet template available with this book.

    b. Prepare a balance sheet for Whitley Products Corporation as of April 30.

33. **Effect of recording errors on the balance sheet equation.** Using the notation O/S (overstated), U/S (understated), or No (no effect), indicate the effects on assets, liabilities, and shareholders' equity *of failing to record or recording incorrectly* each of the following transactions or events. For example, a failure to record the issuance of common stock for $10,000 cash would be shown as follows:

- Assets—U/S $10,000
- Liabilities—No
- Shareholders' equity—U/S $10,000

    (1) A firm ordered $23,000 of merchandise from a supplier but did not record anything in its accounts.

    (2) The firm received the merchandise in transaction **(1)** and recorded it by debiting Merchandise Inventory and crediting Accounts Payable for $32,000.

    (3) The firm acquired an automobile costing $20,000 by paying $2,000 in cash and signing a note payable for the remainder of the purchase price. It recorded the acquisition by debiting Automobile for $20,000, crediting Cash for $18,000, and crediting Note Payable for $2,000.

    (4) The firm paid the $1,800 annual insurance premium on the automobile in transaction **(3)** by debiting Automobile and crediting Cash for $1,800. The insurance period begins next month.

    (5) The firm received an order from a customer for $5,500 of merchandise that the firm will deliver next month. The customer included a check for $1,500. The firm made no entry for this transaction.

    (6) The firm issued 2,000 shares of its $10 par value common stock having a market value of $32,000 in exchange for land. It recorded the transaction by debiting Land and crediting Common Stock for $20,000.

    (7) The firm signed a three-year employment agreement with its chief executive officer at an annual salary of $275,000. The employment period begins next month. The firm did not record anything in its accounts related to this agreement.

34. **Effect of recording errors on the balance sheet equation.** A firm recorded various transactions with the journal entries shown below. Using the notation O/S (overstated), U/S (understated), or No (no effect), indicate the effects on assets, liabilities, and shareholders' equity of any errors in recording each of these transactions. For example, if a firm recorded the issue of $10,000 of common stock by debiting Cash and crediting Bonds Payable, the effects of the error are shown as follows:

- Assets—No
- Liabilities—O/S $10,000
- Shareholders' equity—U/S $10,000

(1) Equipment (Asset Increase)	10,000	
Cash (Asset Decrease)		2,000
Note Receivable (Asset Decrease)		8,000
To record acquisition of equipment for $2,000 cash and signing of an $8,000 promissory note for the balance.		
(2) Equipment (Asset Increase)	4,000	
Cash (Asset Decrease)		1,000
Note Payable (Liability Increase)		3,000
To record the placing of an order for equipment to be delivered next month. The firm made a $1,000 deposit with the order.		
(3) Cash (Asset Increase)	800	
Accounts Receivable (Asset Decrease)		800
To record an advance from a customer on merchandise to be shipped next month. The customer did not owe the firm any amounts at the time of this transaction.		
(4) Prepaid Rent (Asset Increase)	1,000	
Rent Payable (Liability Increase)		1,000
To record the signing of a rental agreement for warehouse space for a one-year period beginning next month. The monthly rental fee of $1,000 is due on the first day of each month.		

(5) Patent (Asset Increase)	2,500	
Cash (Asset Decrease)		2,500
To record the issuance of common stock in the acquisition of a patent.		
(6) Merchandise Inventories (Asset Increase)	4,900	
Cash (Asset Decrease)		4,900
To record the acquisition of office equipment for cash.		

35. **Balance sheet format, terminology, and accounting methods. Exhibit 2.12** presents a balance sheet for Marks and Spencer, PLC, a department store chain headquartered in the United Kingdom. This balance sheet appears in the format and uses terminology and accounting methods commonly found in the United Kingdom.

   a. Prepare a balance sheet for Marks and Spencer on March 30, Year 4, and March 30, Year 5, following the format, terminology, and accounting methods commonly found in the United States. Use the category Other Noncurrent Assets for assets that do not fit any typical U.S. grouping.

   b. Comment on the term structure of Marks and Spencer's assets relative to its financing.

36. **Balance sheet format, terminology, and accounting methods. Exhibit 2.13** presents a balance sheet for United Breweries Group, a Danish brewing company. This balance sheet appears in the format and uses the terminology and accounting methods commonly found in Denmark.

   a. Prepare a balance sheet for United Breweries Group on September 30, Year 8, and September 30, Year 9, following the format, terminology, and accounting methods commonly found in the United States.

   b. Comment on the term structure of United Breweries Group's investments relative to its financing.

37. **Interpreting balance sheet changes. Exhibit 2.14** presents a common-size balance sheet for Outback Steakhouse, a restaurant chain, for two recent years.

   a. Identify the ways in which the structure of Outback Steakhouse's assets and the structure of its financing correspond to what one would expect of a restaurant chain. What aspects of the structure of its assets and the structure of its financing are not what one would expect?

   b. Identify the major changes in the nature and mix of assets and the nature and mix of financing between the two year-ends and suggest possible reasons for the changes.

   c. "An increase in the common-size balance sheet percentage between two year-ends for a particular balance sheet item (for example, cash) does not necessarily mean that its dollar amount increased." Explain.

38. **Interpreting balance sheet changes. Exhibit 2.15** presents a common-size balance sheet for Pacific Gas and Electric (PG&E), an electric and gas utility, for two recent years.

   a. In what ways is the common-size balance sheet of PG&E on January 31, Year 9, typical of an electric and gas utility?

   b. Identify the major changes in the nature and mix of assets and the nature and mix of financing between the two year-ends and suggest possible reasons for the changes.

39. **Relating market value to book value of shareholders' equity.** Firms prepare their balance sheets using GAAP for the recognition and valuation of assets and liabilities. Accountants refer to the total common shareholders' equity appearing on the balance sheet as the *book value of shareholders' equity*. The *market value of shareholders' equity* equals the number of shares of common stock outstanding times the market price per share. Financial analysts frequently examine the ratio of the market value of shareholders' equity to the book value of shareholders' equity, referred to as the *market-to-book-value ratio,* in assessing current market prices. Theoretical and empirical research suggests that the size of the market-to-book-value ratio is related to (1) a firm's ability to generate higher rates of profitability than its competitors, (2) its rate of growth, and (3) its use of GAAP in measuring assets and liabilities, which net to the book value of shareholders' equity.

   Exhibit 2.16 presents balance sheet information for five firms at the end of a recent year. It also shows their market-to-book-value ratios. Additional information regarding the five companies follows:

   (1) *Coca-Cola (Coke):* Coke markets soft drinks worldwide. It has grown primarily by internal expansion rather than by acquiring other soft-drink firms. Coke maintains less than 50 percent ownership in a large number of its bottlers.

   (2) *Bristol-Myers Squibb (Bristol):* Bristol generates approximately 75 percent of its revenues from prescription drugs and medical devices and 25 percent from nonprescription health products, toiletries, and beauty aids.

EXHIBIT 2.12	MARKS AND SPENCER Balance Sheet (in millions of pounds) (Problem 35)		
		March 30	
		Year 4	**Year 5**
Fixed Assets			
Land and Buildings		£2,094	£2,193
Fixtures, Fittings, and Equipment		375	419
Total Fixed Assets		£2,469	£2,612
Current Assets			
Stocks		£ 374	£ 351
Debtors (Note 1)		538	618
Investments		28	29
Cash at Bank and in Hand		266	293
Total Current Assets		£1,206	£1,291
Current Liabilities			
Creditor Amounts Falling Due within One Year (Note 2)		(925)	(897)
Net Current Assets		£ 281	£ 394
Total Assets Less Current Liabilities		£2,750	£3,006
Creditor Amounts Falling Due within One Year		(565)	(550)
Other Noncurrent Liabilities and Provisions		(4)	(19)
Net Assets		£2,181	£2,437
Capital and Reserve			
Called-Up Share Capital		£ 675	£ 680
Share Premium Account		50	69
Revaluation Reserve (Note 3)		458	460
Profit and Loss Account		998	1,228
Total Capital Employed		£2,181	£2,437

Note 1: Debtors include the following:

Amounts Falling Due within One Year:			
Accounts Receivable		£ 192	£ 212
Prepayments		134	142
Amounts Falling Due after One Year:			
Accounts Receivable		174	217
Prepayments		38	47
		£ 538	£ 618

Note 2: Creditor amounts falling due within one year include the following:

Accounts Payable		£ 187	£ 168
Bank Loans		100	107
Other		638	622
		£ 925	£ 897

Note 3: The revaluation reserve arises from the restatement of land and buildings to current market value. None of the restatement affected net income.

(3) *Bankers Trust (Bankers):* Bankers obtains funds primarily from depositors (reported on the Accounts Payable line in **Exhibit 2.16**) and invests them in short-term liquid assets or lends them to businesses and consumers. It also engages in investment activities on its own account.

(4) *International Paper (IP):* IP has the largest holdings of forest lands of any nongovernmental entity in the United States. It processes timber into wood products for the

EXHIBIT 2.13	UNITED BREWERIES Balance Sheet (in millions of kronor) (Problem 36)		

		December 31	
		Year 11	**Year 12**
ASSETS			
Fixed Assets			
Tangible Fixed Assets		Kr 3,934	Kr 4,106
Investments in Securities		422	573
Total Fixed Assets		Kr 4,356	Kr 4,679
Current Assets			
Stocks		Kr 1,290	Kr 1,393
Trade Debtors		1,413	1,444
Prepayments		317	285
Securities		3,018	3,460
Cash at Bank and in Hand		810	1,224
Total Current Assets		Kr 6,848	Kr 7,806
Total Assets		Kr 11,204	Kr 12,485
LIABILITIES			
Capital and Reserves			
Share Capital		Kr 976	Kr 976
Revaluation Reserves (Note 1)		416	561
Other Reserves (Note 2)		3,169	3,672
Total Capital and Reserves		Kr 4,561	Kr 5,209
Provisions (Note 3)		Kr 1,149	Kr 1,425
Long-Term Debt		Kr 1,805	Kr 1,723
Short-Term Debt			
Bank Debt		Kr 619	Kr 986
Trade Creditors		913	902
Other		2,157	2,240
Total Short-Term Debt		Kr 3,689	Kr 4,128
Total Capital and Liabilities		Kr 11,204	Kr 12,485

Note 1: The Revaluation Reserves result from restating tangible fixed assets to current market values.

Note 2: Other Reserves represent cumulative net income in excess of dividends.

Note 3: Provisions represent noncurrent liabilities for income taxes and miscellaneous obligations.

construction industry and processes pulp from the timber into various types of commodity and specialty papers.

(5) *Walt Disney (Disney):* Disney produces motion picture films and operates theme parks.

a. The market-to-book-value ratios differ from 1.0 in part because the rates of profitability and growth of these five firms differ from those of their competitors. This problem does not provide you with sufficient information to assess the impact of these two factors on the market-to-book-value ratio. The ratios also differ from 1.0 because of the use of GAAP for assets and liabilities, which this chapter discussed. Identify the GAAP that most likely explain the market-to-book-value ratios for each of the five firms (that is, identify which accounting principles cause the book values of assets and liabilities to differ from the market value of shareholders' equity).

b. Discuss the likely rationale for the nature and mix of assets and the nature and mix of financing for each of the five firms.

40. **Relating market value to book value of shareholders' equity.** Firms prepare their balance sheets using GAAP for the recognition and valuation of assets and liabilities. Accountants refer

EXHIBIT 2.14	OUTBACK STEAKHOUSE Common-Size Balance Sheet (Problem 37)		
		December 31	
		Year 11	**Year 12**
ASSETS			
Cash		7.6%	12.3%
Accounts Receivable		0.9	0.9
Inventories		3.3	2.6
Other Current Assets		1.7	1.5
Total Current Assets		13.5%	17.3%
Property, Plant, and Equipment		68.1	67.9
Other Assets		18.4	14.8
Total Assets		100.0%	100.0%
LIABILITIES AND SHAREHOLDERS' EQUITY			
Current Liabilities			
Accounts Payable		4.0%	4.0%
Notes Payable		1.1	1.3
Other Current Liabilities		10.8	12.4
Total Current Liabilities		15.9%	17.7%
Noncurrent Liabilities			
Bonds Payable		1.2%	1.1%
Other Noncurrent Liabilities		3.9	3.1
Total Noncurrent Liabilities		5.1%	4.2%
Total Liabilities		21.0%	21.9%
Shareholders' Equity			
Common Stock		15.1%	11.1%
Retained Earnings		63.9	67.0
Total Shareholders' Equity		79.0%	78.1%
Total Liabilities and Shareholders' Equity		100.0%	100.0%

to the total common shareholders' equity appearing on the balance sheet as the *book value of shareholders' equity.* The *market value of shareholders' equity* equals the number of shares of common stock outstanding times the market price per share. Financial analysts frequently examine the ratio of the market value of shareholders' equity to the book value of shareholders' equity, referred to as the *market-to-book-value ratio,* in assessing current market prices. Theoretical and empirical research suggests that the size of the market-to-book-value ratio is related to (1) a firm's ability to generate higher rates of profitability than its competitors, (2) its rate of growth, and (3) its use of GAAP in measuring assets and liabilities, which net to the book value of shareholders' equity.

Exhibit 2.17 presents balance sheet information for six firms at the end of a recent year. It also shows their market-to-book-value ratios.

Additional information regarding the six companies follows:

(1) Pfizer is a pharmaceutical company headquartered in the United States.

(2) Nestlé is a consumer products company headquartered in Switzerland. In addition to its chocolate products, it manufactures and distributes beverages (Nestea, Poulin Springs mineral water), frozen foods (Stouffer's), milk products (infant formulas), and pet foods (Alpo).

(3) Promodes is a French company that operates chains of supermarkets (Champion), hypermarkets (Continent, Continente), convenience stores (Promocash, Punt&Cash), and restaurant supply stores (Prodirest).

(4) Deutsche Bank is a German commercial bank that provides both traditional commercial

EXHIBIT 2.15	PACIFIC GAS AND ELECTRIC COMPANY Common-Size Balance Sheet (Problem 38)		

		December 31	
		Year 9	**Year 10**
ASSETS			
Current Assets			
Cash		1.6%	7.2%
Accounts Receivable		5.0	9.6
Inventories		1.5	1.1
Prepayments		4.0	13.7
Total Current Assets		12.1%	31.6%
Property, Plant, and Equipment		67.0	57.1
Other Assets		20.9	11.3
Total Assets		100.0%	100.0%
LIABILITIES AND SHAREHOLDERS' EQUITY			
Current Liabilities			
Accounts Payable		2.4%	10.7%
Note Payable		8.0	20.4
Other Current Liabilities		10.2	17.9
Total Current Liabilities		20.6%	49.0%
Noncurrent Liabilities			
Bonds Payable		49.6%	38.3%
Other Noncurrent Liabilities		3.8	1.5
Total Noncurrent Liabilities		53.4%	39.8%
Total Liabilities		74.0%	88.8%
Shareholders' Equity			
Preferred Stock		1.6%	1.4%
Common Stock		17.7	15.0
Retained Earnings		6.7	(5.2)
Total Shareholders' Equity		26.0%	11.2%
Total Liabilities and Shareholders' Equity		100.0%	100.0%

banking services (deposit taking, loan making) and investment banking services (investment management, financial consulting).

(5) British Airways is headquartered in the United Kingdom and provides air transportation services.

(6) New Oji Paper Co. is a Japanese forest-products company. It purchases wood pulp from Canada and the United States and processes it into various papers for sale in Japan.

a. The market-to-book-value ratios differ from 1.0 in part because the rates of profitability and growth of these six firms differ from those of their competitors. This problem does not provide you with sufficient information to assess the impact of these two factors on the market-to-book-value ratio. The ratios also differ from 1.0 because of the use of GAAP for assets and liabilities, which this chapter discussed. Identify the GAAP that most likely explain the market-to-book-value ratios for each of the six firms (that is, identify which accounting principles cause the book values of assets and liabilities to differ from the market value of shareholders' equity).

b. Discuss the likely rationale for the nature and mix of assets and the nature and mix of financing for each of the six firms.

41. Identifying industries using common-size balance sheet percentages. Exhibit 2.18 presents common-size balance sheets for five firms. The firms and a description of their activities follow:

(1) Commonwealth Edison: Generates and sells electricity to businesses and households.

(2) Hewlett-Packard: Develops, assembles, and sells computer hardware and printers. The firm outsources many of its computer and printer components.

EXHIBIT 2.16	Balance Sheets for Selected Companies (all dollar amounts in millions) (Problem 39)				
	Coca-Cola	**Bristol-Myers Squibb**	**Bankers Trust**	**International Paper**	**Walt Disney**
ASSETS					
Cash and Marketable Securities	$ 1,531	$ 2,423	$79,048	$ 270	$ 1,510
Accounts and Notes Receivable	1,525	2,043	11,249	2,241	1,671
Inventories	1,047	1,397	—	2,075	2,264
Other Current Assets	1,102	847	—	244	—
Total Current Assets	$ 5,205	$ 6,710	$90,297	$ 4,830	$ 5,445
Investments in Securities	3,928	—	—	1,032	630
Property, Plant, and Equipment	4,080	3,666	915	9,941	5,814
Other Noncurrent Assets	660	2,534	5,804	2,033	937
Total Assets	$13,873	$12,910	$97,016	$17,836	$12,826
LIABILITIES AND SHAREHOLDERS' EQUITY					
Accounts Payable	$ 2,564	$ 693	$24,939	$ 1,204	$ 2,475
Short-term Borrowing	2,083	725	55,166	2,083	—
Other Current Liabilities	1,530	2,856	5,502	747	967
Total Current Liabilities	$ 6,177	$ 4,274	$85,607	$ 4,034	$ 3,442
Long-term Debt	1,426	644	6,455	4,464	2,937
Other Noncurrent Liabilities	1,035	2,288	—	2,824	939
Total Liabilities	$ 8,638	$ 7,206	$92,062	$11,322	$ 7,318
Preferred Stock	—	—	$ 645	—	—
Common Stock	$ 1,600	$ 451	1,401	$ 1,914	$ 945
Retained Earnings	10,708	7,299	3,324	4,711	5,849
Treasury Stock	(7,073)	(2,046)	(416)	(111)	(1,286)
Total Shareholders' Equity	$ 5,235	$ 5,704	$ 4,954	$ 6,514	$ 5,508
Total Liabilities and Shareholders' Equity	$13,873	$12,910	$97,016	$17,836	$12,826
Market Value/Book Value Ratio	12.6	5.2	1.0	1.3	4.4

(3) Household International: Lends money to consumers for periods ranging from several months to several years.

(4) May Department Stores: Operates department store chains and offers its own credit card.

(5) Newmont Mining: Mines for gold and other minerals, utilizing heavy equipment.

Use whatever clues that you can to match up the companies listed above with the firms listed in **Exhibit 2.18**. Describe your reasoning.

42. **Ethical issues in asset revaluations.** GAAP in the United Kingdom permit firms to report property, plant and equipment on the balance sheet either at acquisition cost (net of depreciation) or current replacement cost. Firms choosing to revalue property, plant and equipment must revalue all assets of the same class, defined as those with a similar nature, function, or use. Firms must revalue such assets periodically, but not necessarily every year.

Unilever PLC is a consumer foods company headquartered in the United Kingdom. Its balance sheet for Year 12 reports total assets of £43,318 million, total liabilities of £39,689 million, and total shareholders' equity of £3,629 million. Total assets on this date include property, plant and equipment of £9,240 million, which Unilever reports at acquisition cost net of depreciation. The firm discloses in notes to the financial statements that the current replacement cost of this property, plant and equipment is £10,529 million. Unilever has reported the acquisition cost and current replacement cost of its property, plant and equipment in notes to its financial statements for many years.

a. Lenders to a firm often calculate the ratio of total liabilities to total assets to assess the risk of bankruptcy. Calculate this ratio for Unilever using the amounts reported on its balance sheet.

				Deutsche Bank	British Airways	New Oji Paper Co.
EXHIBIT 2.17 — Common-Size Balance Sheets for Selected Companies (Problem 40)						
	Pfizer	**Nestlé**	**Promodes**	**Deutsche Bank**	**British Airways**	**New Oji Paper Co.**
ASSETS						
Cash and Marketable Securities	20.5%	11.5%	12.9%	44.2%	6.5%	2.1%
Accounts and Notes Receivable	16.4	18.9	22.6	50.4	13.5	19.8
Inventories	8.1	13.4	18.4	—	0.7	8.5
Other Current Assets	6.3	1.4	—	—	—	1.5
Total Current Assets	51.3%	45.2%	53.9%	94.6%	20.7%	31.9%
Investments in Securities	7.5	7.1	8.7	2.7	6.6	24.5
Property, Plant, and Equipment	28.2	43.7	28.3	1.2	72.7	43.6
Other Noncurrent Assets	13.0	4.0	9.1	1.5	—	—
Total Assets	100.0%	100.0%	100.0%	100.0%	100.0%	100.0%
LIABILITIES AND SHAREHOLDERS' EQUITY						
Accounts Payable	5.1%	11.2%	44.3%	66.5%	9.4%	10.2%
Short-term Borrowing	12.8	18.1	3.3	16.0	5.3	16.2
Other Current Liabilities	17.8	9.6	12.6	4.9	15.6	10.7
Total Current Liabilities	35.7%	38.9%	60.2%	87.4%	30.3%	37.1%
Long-term Debt	3.4	6.7	7.7	1.2	36.8	16.9
Other Noncurrent Liabilities	12.9	9.2	4.1	8.0	4.0	4.8
Total Liabilities	52.0%	54.8%	72.0%	96.6%	71.1%	58.8%
Common Stock	27.5%	3.0%	0.8%	1.7%	8.1%	17.3%
Retained Earnings	43.9	42.7	27.2	1.7	20.8	23.9
Treasury Stock	(23.4)	(0.5)	—	—	—	—
Total Shareholders' Equity	48.0%	45.2%	28.0%	3.4%	28.9%	41.2%
Total Liabilities and Shareholders' Equity	100.0%	100.0%	100.0%	100.0%	100.0%	100.0%
Market Value/Book Value Ratio	8.2	3.3	4.6	1.7	2.4	1.4

b. Compute this ratio assuming that Unilever chose to revalue its property, plant and equipment to current replacement cost.

c. Assume that Unilever has a restriction in its borrowing agreements that stipulates that major borrowings become immediately due if the total liabilities to total assets ratio exceeds 90 percent at any time. Before issuing financial statements for Year 12 with the amounts shown above, Unilever contemplates changing the accounting for its property, plant, and equipment from acquisition cost (net of depreciation) to current replacement cost. Identify any ethical issues that you think Unilever should consider in this decision. What advice would you give to the firm?

EXHIBIT 2.18	Common-Size Balance Sheets for Five Companies (Problem 41)				

	(1)	(2)	(3)	(4)	(5)
Cash and Marketable Securities	8.5%	0.1%	9.5%	12.1%	1.1%
Receivables	81.9	2.8	1.4	25.7	24.1
Inventories	—	2.0	9.0	23.2	23.6
Property, Plant, and Equipment (net)	1.2	74.3	62.6	20.0	41.4
Other Assets	8.4	20.8	17.5	19.0	9.8
Total Assets	100.0%	100.0%	100.0%	100.0%	100.0%
Current Liabilities	38.8%	8.4%	10.8%	38.3%	29.1%
Long-term Debt	50.0	47.7	28.1	9.3	28.3
Other Noncurrent Liabilities	—	13.9	6.7	3.9	6.2
Shareholders' Equity	11.2	30.0	54.4	48.5	36.4
Total Liabilities and Shareholders' Equity	100.0%	100.0%	100.0%	100.0%	100.0%

Income Statement: Reporting the Results of Operating Activities

Learning Objectives

1. Understand the accrual basis of accounting and why accountants believe that the accrual basis provides measures of operating performance usually superior to those provided by the cash basis of accounting.

2. Deepen your understanding of the accrual basis of accounting by examining when firms recognize revenues and expenses and how they measure these two components of net income.

3. Build on your skills in recording transactions and other events in the accounts by extending the dual-entry recording framework studied in Chapter 2 to include income statement items.

4. Develop skills to analyze the income statement, focusing on the relations between revenues, expenses, and net income for various types of businesses.

Users of financial statements often look at the relation between net income and revenues, referred to as the **profit margin percentage**, when evaluating the profitability of a firm. Consider the following firms and their profit margin percentages for a recent year:

- AK Steel (steel manufacturing): 1.4%
- Kellogg (branded food processing): 8.7%
- Omnicom Group (marketing services): 9.4%
- Pfizer (pharmaceuticals): 27.5%
- Wal-Mart Stores (discount retailing): 3.3%

Did AK Steel and Wal-Mart Stores perform more poorly and did Pfizer perform better than Kellogg and Omnicom Group? Do these different profit margins signal differences in operating performance and do they have economic or strategic explanations? Answering these questions requires a deeper understanding of the income statement than the overview that **Chapter 1** provides. Recall that the income statement reports **net income**, or earnings, for a particular period of time. Net income equals revenues minus expenses. **Revenues** measure the net assets (assets less liabilities) that flow into a firm when it sells goods or renders services. **Expenses** measure the net assets that a firm consumes in the process of generating revenues. As a measure of operating performance, revenues reflect the services rendered by a firm, and expenses indicate the efforts required.

This chapter considers the measurement principles and accounting procedures that underlie the income statement and the insights it provides about the operating performance of a firm. We begin by considering the concept of an accounting period, the span of time over which accountants measure operating performance. Next, the chapter describes and illustrates two common approaches to measuring operating performance, the cash basis and the accrual basis. It then illustrates the accounting procedures used in applying the accrual basis of accounting for a merchandising firm. Finally, the chapter discusses relations between revenues, expenses, and net income for different types of businesses.

The Accounting Period Convention

The income statement reports operating performance for a specific time period. Years ago, the length of this period varied among firms. Firms prepared income statements at the completion of some activity, such as after the completion of a construction project.

The operating activities of most modern firms do not divide so easily into distinguishable projects. Instead, the income-generating activity occurs continually. For example, a firm acquires a plant and uses it in manufacturing products for a period of 40 years or more. A firm purchases delivery equipment and uses it in transporting merchandise to customers for four, five, or more years. If preparing the income statement awaited the completion of all operating activities, the firm might prepare the report only when it ceased to exist and the report would be too late to help a reader appraise operating performance. An **accounting period** of uniform length facilitates timely comparisons and analyses among firms. One might think of an accounting period as the time elapsing between balance sheet dates. Balance sheets prepared at the end of the day on December 31 of one year and at the end of the day on December 31 of the next year bound a calendar-year accounting period. Balance sheets prepared at the end of the day on November 30 and at the end of the day on December 31 bound a one-month accounting period—the month of December.

An accounting period of one year underlies the principal financial statements distributed to shareholders and potential investors. Most firms prepare their annual reports using the calendar year as the accounting period. Many firms, however, use **a natural business year** or **fiscal period** to attempt to measure performance at a time when they have concluded most operating activities for the period. The ending date of a natural business year varies from one firm to another and usually occurs when inventories are at their lowest level during the year. For example, JCPenney, a retailer, uses a natural business year ending near the end of January, which comes after the Christmas shopping season and before the start of the Easter season. Winnebago Industries, a manufacturer of recreational vehicles, uses a year ending in late August, the end of its model year.

Firms frequently prepare reports of performance for periods shorter than a year to indicate progress during the year. These are known as *interim reports* or *reports for interim periods*. Preparing interim reports does not eliminate the need to prepare an annual report.

Accounting Methods for Measuring Performance

Figure 3.1 depicts the operating process for the acquisition and sale of merchandise. A retailing firm, such as Wal-Mart, purchases merchandise and then holds the merchandise in inventory until a customer purchases it. At the time of sale, the inventory changes hands. The firm need not, however, receive cash right away. Thus, a second period may commence before the firm collects cash from sales made during the first period.

Some operating activities both start and finish within a given accounting period. For example, operating process B in **Figure 3.1** occurs entirely in Year 2. These cases present few difficulties in measuring operating performance. The difference between the cash received from customers and the cash disbursed to acquire, hold, sell, and deliver the merchandise represents earnings from this series of transactions.

Many operating activities, however, start in one accounting period and finish in another. Operating process A in **Figure 3.1** begins during Year 1 and finishes in Year 2. The firm pays for the merchandise and other operating costs in Year 1 but receives cash from customers in Year 2. Operating process C begins in Year 2 and finishes in Year 3. The firm pays out cash in Year 2 to purchase, hold, and sell the merchandise but receives cash from customers in Year 3. To measure performance for a specific accounting period, such as Year 2 in **Figure 3.1**, requires measuring

FIGURE 3.1	Operating Process for a Firm's Acquisition and Sale of Merchandise

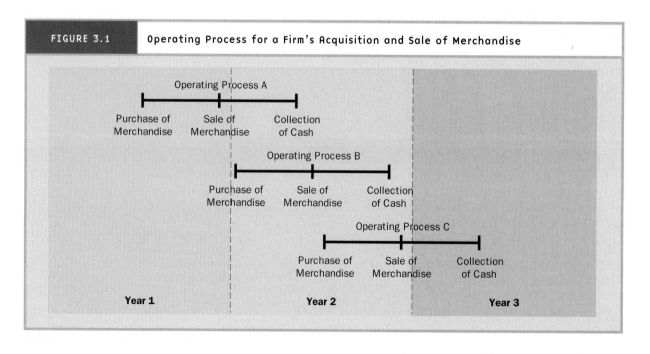

the amount of revenues and expenses from operating activities already begun by the beginning of the period and other activities not yet complete at the end of the period.

Figure 3.1 oversimplifies the problem in measuring operating performance for discrete accounting periods. For example, a firm may acquire a building in one period and use it for 30 or more years. Thus, the length of the operating process line may extend over many periods. Firms may purchase merchandise in one accounting period, pay for it in a second, sell it during a third, and collect cash from customers in a fourth. Moreover, the events need not occur in that order. Cash payments can precede the acquisition of merchandise, such as for the acquisition of buildings to store and display the merchandise, or follow it, such as payments to sell and deliver the merchandise and provide warranty services. Cash collection can precede the sale of merchandise, as occurs when customers make advance payments, or follow it, as occurs with sales on account. To measure performance for a specific accounting period requires measuring the amount of revenues and expenses from operating activities that span more than that one accounting period. Two approaches to measuring operating performance are (1) the cash basis of accounting and (2) the accrual basis of accounting.

Cash Basis of Accounting

Under the **cash basis of accounting**, a firm measures performance from selling goods and providing services as it receives cash from customers and makes cash expenditures to providers of goods and services. To understand the measurement of performance under the cash basis of accounting, consider the following information.

Donald and Joanne Allens open a hardware store on January 1, Year 1. The firm receives $20,000 in cash from the Allens and borrows $12,000 from a local bank. It must repay the loan on June 30, Year 1, with interest charged at the rate of 8 percent per year. The firm rents a store building on January 1 and pays two months' rent of $4,000 in advance. On January 1, it also pays the premium of $2,400 for property and liability insurance coverage for the year ending December 31, Year 1. During January it acquires merchandise costing $40,000, of which it purchases $26,000 for cash and $14,000 on account for payment in February. Sales to customers during January total $50,000, of which $34,000 is for cash and $16,000 is on account for collection in February and March. The firm paid $32,000 for the merchandise sold during January and $5,000 in salaries to various employees.

Example 1 **Exhibit 3.1** presents an income statement for Allens' Hardware Store for the month of January, Year 1, using the cash basis of accounting. Cash receipts of $34,000 from sales of merchandise represent the portion of the total January sales, $50,000, that the firm collects during January. Whereas the firm acquires merchandise costing $40,000 during January, it disburses only $26,000 cash to suppliers and therefore subtracts only this amount in measuring performance under the cash basis. The firm also subtracts the amounts of cash expenditures made during January for salaries, rent, and insurance, without regard to whether the firm fully consumes the services by the end of the month. Cash expenditures for merchandise and services exceeded cash receipts from customers during January by $3,400. Note that under the cash basis, the income statement does not include cash received from owners or from borrowing, both of which are financing transactions.

As a basis for measuring performance for a particular accounting period (here, January, Year 1, for Allens' Hardware Store), the cash basis of accounting has three weaknesses.

Inadequately Matches Inflows and Outflows First, the cash basis does not adequately match the cost of the efforts required in generating inflows with the inflows themselves. The cash outflows of one period can relate to operating activities whose cash inflows occur in preceding or succeeding periods. The store rental payment of $4,000 provides rental services for both January and February, but the cash basis subtracts the full amount in measuring performance during January, but none for February. As a result, February's performance could look better than January's for no reason other than the happenstance of timing of cash payments. Likewise, the annual insurance premium paid in January provides coverage for the full year, whereas the cash basis of accounting subtracts none of this insurance cost in measuring performance during February through December.

The longer the period over which a firm receives future benefits, the more deficient becomes the cash basis for reporting. Consider, for example, a capital-intensive firm's investments in buildings and equipment that it will use for 20 or more years. The length of time between the purchase of these assets and the collection of cash for goods produced and sold can span many years and

EXHIBIT 3.1	ALLENS' HARDWARE STORE Income Statement for the Month of January, Year 1 Cash Basis of Accounting		
Cash Receipts from Sales of Merchandise			$34,000
Less Cash Expenditures for Merchandise and Services:			
Merchandise		$26,000	
Salaries		5,000	
Rent.		4,000	
Insurance		2,400	
Total Cash Expenditures.			37,400
Excess of Cash Expenditures over Cash Receipts.			$ (3,400)

distort the measurement of performance during both the period of the cash expenditure and subsequent periods. The longer the accounting period, however, the less the cash basis suffers from mismatching through time.

Unnecessarily Delays the Recognition of Revenues
Second, the cash basis of accounting unnecessarily postpones the time when the firm recognizes revenue. A firm should recognize revenue when it has delivered goods or services and finished the parts of the operating process that are difficult to control and predict. To complete the operating process involves the following actions by the seller:

- Acquiring goods and labor
- If a manufacturing firm, converting the goods and labor into sellable products
- Persuading the customer to buy the goods or services
- Delivering the goods or services to the customer
- Collecting cash from the customer
- Waiting, in the case of sales of goods, until the period of warranty (or right to return) expires

The most difficult parts of the operating process for manufacturing and retailing firms are persuading the customer to buy the goods and delivering the goods. The most difficult parts for service firms are persuading the customer to use the services and then rendering the services. Most firms have little difficulty in predicting the amounts and timing

- of cash collections or returns from customers, and
- of expenditures to fulfill warranty promises.

In these cases, awaiting the measurement of performance until the firm collects cash often results in reporting the effects of operating activities one or more periods after the critical revenue-generating activity—having the customer purchase the goods—has occurred. For example, sales to customers during January by Allens' Hardware Store totaled $50,000. Under the cash basis of accounting, the firm will not recognize $16,000 of this amount until it collects the cash during February or later. If the firm checks the creditworthiness of customers before making the sales on account, it will probably collect the cash, or at least a predictable fraction of the cash, and therefore need not postpone recognition of the revenue until the time it actually collects the cash.

Provides Opportunities to Distort the Measurement of Operating Performance
A third criticism of the cash basis is it provides an opportunity for firms to distort the measurement of operating performance by timing their cash expenditures. Firms might delay cash expenditures near the end of the accounting period in an effort to increase earnings and appear more profitable. Firms might accelerate cash expenditures to appear less profitable and perhaps discourage competitors from entering the industry or labor unions from negotiating higher wages for employees.

Who uses the cash basis of accounting? Lawyers, accountants, and other professionals, who have relatively small investments in inventories and multi-period assets, such as buildings and

EXHIBIT 3.2	ALLENS' HARDWARE STORE Income Statement for the Month of January, Year 1 Accrual Basis of Accounting		
Sales Revenue.			$50,000
Less Expenses:			
Cost of Goods Sold.		$32,000	
Salaries Expense		5,000	
Rent Expense		2,000	
Insurance Expense		200	
Interest Expense		80	
Total Expenses.			39,280
Net Income			$10,720

equipment, and usually collect cash from clients soon after they render services, are the most frequent users of the cash basis. Most of these firms actually use a modified cash basis of accounting, under which they treat the costs of buildings, equipment, and similar items as assets when purchased. They then recognize a portion of the acquisition cost as an expense when they consume services of these assets. Except for the treatment of these long-lived assets, such firms measure performance at the times they receive and disburse cash.

Most individuals use the cash basis of accounting for the purpose of computing personal income and personal income taxes. When a firm, such as one in merchandising or manufacturing, uses inventories as an important factor in generating revenues, the Internal Revenue Code prohibits the firm from using the cash basis of accounting in its income tax returns.

Accrual Basis of Accounting

The **accrual basis of accounting** typically recognizes revenue when a firm sells goods (manufacturing and retailing firms) or renders services (service firms). At these points the firm has usually identified a customer, agreed upon a price, and delivered the good or service. At these points the firm also knows the costs of assets already used in producing revenues (such as the acquisition cost of merchandise sold) and can estimate any future costs it will incur (such as for warranties) in connection with the good or service sold. The firm recognizes these costs as expenses in the period when the firm recognizes the revenues that the costs helped produce. Thus accrual accounting attempts to match expenses with associated revenues. When the usage of an asset's future benefits does not match with particular revenues, the firm recognizes the costs of these assets as expenses of the period during which the firm uses the benefits provided by the assets.

Example 2 Exhibit 3.2 presents an income statement for Allens' Hardware Store for January of Year 1 using the accrual basis of accounting. The firm recognizes the entire $50,000 of sales during January as revenue, even though it has received only $34,000 in cash by the end of January. The firm will probably collect the remaining accounts receivable of $16,000 in February or later periods. Therefore, the sale of the goods, rather than the collection of cash from customers, triggers the recognition of revenue.[1] The merchandise sold during January cost $32,000. Recognizing this amount as an expense (cost of goods sold) matches the cost of the merchandise sold with revenue from sales of those goods. Of the advance rental payment of $4,000, only $2,000 applies to the cost of benefits consumed during January. The remaining rental of $2,000 purchases benefits for the month of February and will therefore appear on the balance sheet on January 31 as an asset. Likewise, only $200 of the $2,400 insurance premium represents the cost of coverage used up during January. The remaining $2,200 of the insurance premium provides coverage for February through December and will become an expense during those months. In the meantime, it appears

---

[1] This example assumes that the firm collects all its receivables from sales. Later, we relax this assumption and assume merely that the firm collects a predictable proportion of its sales on account. When the firm collects a predictable proportion of its sales on account, we can still say that the sale triggers revenue recognition, but the amount of the revenue results from calculations about expected cash collections.

as an asset on the balance sheet on January 31. The interest expense of $80 represents one month's interest on the $12,000 bank loan at an annual rate of 8 percent (= $12,000 $\times$ 0.08 $\times$ 1/12).[2] Although the firm will not pay this interest until the loan comes due (technically, matures) on June 30, Year 1, the firm benefited from using the funds during January; it should therefore recognize one month of the total interest cost on the loan as an expense of January. The firm reports its obligation to pay the $80 as a liability on the balance sheet on January 31. The salaries, rent, insurance, and interest expenses, unlike the cost of merchandise sold, do not directly match revenues recognized during the period. These costs therefore become expenses of January to the extent that the firm consumed services during the month.

An important concept for understanding accrual accounting is the *matching principle*. The data for Allens' Hardware Store helps in understanding the subtleties of the matching principle. In January, sales were $50,000, of which the store collected $34,000 in cash and expected to collect the rest later. The cost of the goods sold to customers was $32,000, of which the store paid $26,000 in cash and expected to pay the rest later. First, consider comparing the $50,000 they have or will collect for those goods delivered in January to the $32,000 cost of goods put into the hands of customers in January. Next, consider comparing the $34,000 cash the store received in January from customers to the $26,000 it paid in January to suppliers. Which comparison provides a more useful measure of January's operating activities? If you can see that the comparison of the expected total collections to the expected total costs of those goods provides more useful information about operating performance than does comparing the $34,000 cash collected during the month to the $26,000 cash paid to suppliers during the month, then you understand the matching principle That principle suggests that the *eventual total* cash inflows and outflows for operations of a period provide information more useful for assessing performance of that period than does comparing the actual cash inflows and outflows that occurred during the period.

More advanced applications of the matching principle relate all the costs of carrying out a specific set of activities (for example, salaries, interest, taxes) to all the benefits from performing those activities, no matter when the firm paid cash or when it collects cash. Cash flows for a period provide useful information, as **Chapter 4** shows, but they do not measure operating performance for short time periods as well as do the results of applying the matching principle in accrual accounting.

Thus, the accrual basis of accounting provides a better measure of operating performance for Allens' Hardware Store for the month of January than does the cash basis for two reasons:

1. Revenues more accurately reflect the results of sales activity during January than does cash received from customers during that period.
2. Expenses more closely match reported revenues than expenditures match receipts.

Likewise, the accrual basis will provide a superior measure of performance for future periods because activities of those periods will bear their share of the costs of rental, insurance, and other services the firm will consume. Thus the accrual basis focuses on inflows of net assets from operations (revenues) and the use of net assets in operations (expenses), independent of whether the firm has collected cash for those inflows and spent cash for the outflows of net assets.

Many accountants argue that the accrual basis provides fewer opportunities than the cash basis to distort the measurement of earnings. The matching of expenses with associated revenues serves as a guiding principle that constrains a firm's efforts to time the recognition of expenses to suit its particular reporting objectives. As later chapters make clear, however, timing revenue recognition and measuring related expenses under the accrual basis both often involve judgment. Thus, even the accrual basis provides opportunities for earnings management.

Most business firms, particularly those involved in merchandising and manufacturing activities, use the accrual basis of accounting. From this point on in the book, all discussions assume use of the accrual basis of accounting. We introduced the cash basis of accounting in this section primarily to demonstrate the deficiencies of the cash basis and the related rationale for the accrual basis. The next section examines the measurement principles of accrual accounting.

---

[2] By convention in business practice, interest rates on loans almost always refer to annual interest rates. Also, to simplify the calculation of interest, convention assumes a year equal to 12 months of 30 days each, or 360 days.

Problem 3.1 for Self-Study

Cash versus accrual basis of accounting.   Thompson Hardware Store commences operations on January 1, Year 5. J. Thompson invests $10,000, and the firm borrows $8,000 from a local bank. The firm must repay the loan on June 30, Year 5, with interest at the rate of 6 percent per year.

The firm rents a building on January 1 and pays two months' rent in advance in the amount of $2,000. On January 1, it also pays the $1,200 premium for property and liability insurance coverage for the year ending December 31, Year 5.

The firm purchases $28,000 of merchandise inventory on account on January 2 and pays $10,000 of this amount on January 25. A physical inventory indicates that the cost of merchandise on hand on January 31 is $15,000.

During January, the firm makes cash sales to customers totaling $20,000 and sales on account totaling $9,000. The firm collects $2,000 from these credit sales by the end of January.

The firm pays other costs during January as follows: utilities, $400; salaries, $650; and taxes, $350.

a. Prepare an income statement for January, assuming that Thompson uses the accrual basis of accounting and recognizes revenue at the time goods are sold (delivered).
b. Prepare an income statement for January, assuming that Thompson uses the cash basis of accounting.
c. Which basis of accounting do you believe provides a better indication of the operating performance of the firm during January? Why?

Solutions to the self-study problems appear at the end of the chapter.

Measurement Principles of Accrual Accounting

Under the accrual basis of accounting, one must consider when a firm recognizes revenues and expenses (timing questions) and how much it recognizes (measurement questions).

Timing of Revenue Recognition

Refer again to **Figure 3.1**. A firm could conceivably recognize revenue, a measure of the increase in net assets from selling goods or providing services, at the time of purchase of merchandise, at the time of sale to customers, at the time of cash collection from customers, at some point(s) between these events, or even continually. Answering the timing question requires a set of criteria for revenue recognition.

Criteria for Revenue Recognition The accrual basis of accounting recognizes revenue when both of the following events have occurred:

1. A firm has performed all, or most of, the services it expects to provide.
2. The firm has received cash or some other asset such as a receivable, whose cash-equivalent value it can measure with reasonable precision.

Accrual accounting requires matching expenses with related revenues, which requires that the firm either know or can estimate the expenses it will incur in generating revenues. Delaying revenue recognition until the firm has substantially completed performance increases the likelihood that it can measure expenses, and thereby net income, accurately. Thus, the first criterion for revenue recognition provides that firms must meet a minimum threshold for measuring expenses before they can justify recognizing revenues. Most firms involved in selling goods and services recognize revenue at the time of sale (delivery). The firm has transferred the goods to a buyer or has performed the services. The firm can estimate with reasonable precision the cost of future services, such as for warranties and the amounts it will have to give back because customers return goods.

The second criterion for revenue recognition focuses on measuring accurately the amount of cash the firm will ultimately receive. The exchange between an independent buyer and seller provides a reliable initial measure of the amount of revenue. If the firm makes the sale on account, past experience and an assessment of credit standings of customers provide a basis for predicting the amount and timing of the initial selling price the firm will collect in cash.

Thus, the time of sale usually meets the criteria for revenue recognition. In general, the firm will recognize revenue when it has no further significant uncertainty about the amount and timing of cash inflows and outflows from the sales transaction.

Understand the importance of these criteria by considering an example of a firm that should not recognize revenue at the time of sale, such as a software developer shipping a new product, where the customers have a right of return. The developer can estimate neither how many of the customers will return the product nor the cost of debugging the software once customers start to use it. Hence, that developer cannot estimate with reasonable precision the eventual cash inflows (that is, revenues) and cash outflows (that is, expenses).

Measurement of Revenue

A firm measures the amount of revenue by the cash or cash-equivalent value of other assets it receives from customers. As a starting point, this amount is the agreed-upon price between buyer and seller at the time of sale. If a firm recognizes revenue in a period before it collects the cash, however, it will likely need to make adjustments to the agreed-upon price in measuring revenue to recognize the effects of the time delay.

Uncollectible Accounts If a firm expects not to collect some portion of the sales for a period, it must adjust the amount of revenue recognized during that period for estimated uncollectible accounts arising from those sales. This adjustment of revenue occurs in the period when the firm recognizes revenue and not in the later period when it identifies specific customers' accounts as uncollectible. If the firm postpones the adjustment, earlier decisions to extend credit to customers will affect income of subsequent periods. A failure to recognize anticipated uncollectibles at the time of sale incorrectly measures the performance of the firm for both the period of sale and the period when the firm judges the account uncollectible. **Chapter 6** considers these problems further.

Sales Discounts and Allowances Customers may take advantage of discounts for prompt payment, and the seller may grant allowances for unsatisfactory merchandise. In these cases, the firm will eventually receive cash in a smaller amount than the stated selling price. The firm must estimate these amounts and make appropriate reductions, in the period of the sale, in measuring the amount of revenue it recognizes.

Sales Returns Customers may return goods. If so, the firm will eventually receive cash in an amount smaller than the original sales price. The firm must estimate the expected returns and make appropriate reductions in revenue measured at the time of sale.

Timing of Expense Recognition

Assets provide future benefits to a firm. Expenses measure the assets consumed in generating revenue. Assets are **unexpired costs**, and expenses are **expired costs** or "gone assets." We focus on *when* the asset expiration takes place. The critical question is, "When do the benefits of an asset expire, leaving the balance sheet, and become expenses, entering the income statement as reductions in retained earnings, a shareholders' equity account?"

Balance Sheet	Income Statement
Assets or Unexpired Costs ⟶	Expenses or Expired Costs (which reduce retained earnings on the balance sheet)

Criteria for Expense Recognition Accountants recognize expenses as follows:

1. If the event triggering an asset expiration relates to the recognition of a particular revenue, that expiration becomes an expense in the period when the firm recognizes the revenue. For example, the sale of merchandise usually results in the seller's recognizing revenue and the immediate disappearance, as cost of goods sold, of the firm's benefits of having held the merchandise inventory. This treatment—the **matching principle**—matches cost expirations with revenues.

2. If the event triggering an asset expiration does not relate to a particular revenue, that expiration becomes an expense of the period when the firm consumes the benefits of that asset in operations.

Product Costs The matching principle most clearly applies to the cost of goods sold because the firm can easily associate the asset expiration with the revenue from selling the goods. At the time of sale, the asset physically changes hands. The firm recognizes sales revenue, and the cost of the goods sold becomes an expense.

A merchandising firm purchases inventory and later sells it without changing its physical form. The inventory appears initially as an asset stated at acquisition cost on the balance sheet. Later, when the firm sells the inventory, the same amount of acquisition cost appears as an expense (cost of goods sold) on the income statement.

A manufacturing firm, on the other hand, incurs various costs as it changes the physical form of the goods it produces. These costs are not yet expenses—gone assets—but represent the transformation of one form of asset into another. A firm incurs three types of costs in manufacturing: (1) direct material costs, (2) direct labor costs, and (3) manufacturing overhead costs (sometimes called "indirect manufacturing costs"). A firm incurs direct material and direct labor costs because it manufactures particular products, so the firm can associate those costs with the particular products manufactured. Manufacturing overhead includes a mixture of costs that provides a firm with a capacity to produce. Examples of manufacturing overhead costs are expenditures for supervisors' salaries, utilities, property taxes, and insurance on the factory, as well as depreciation on manufacturing plant and equipment. The firm uses the services of each of these items during a period when it creates new assets—the inventory of goods it works on or holds for sale. Accountants call these costs *indirect* because they jointly benefit all goods produced during the period, not any one particular item.

The manufacturing process transfers the benefits from direct material, direct labor, and manufacturing overhead to the asset represented by units of inventory. Because the firm shows the inventory items as assets until it sells them to customers, the various direct material, direct labor, and manufacturing overhead costs incurred in producing the goods remain as assets on the balance sheet in the manufacturing inventory under the titles Work-in-Process Inventory and Finished Goods Inventory. Such costs, called **product costs,** are assets transformed from one form to another. They remain on the balance sheet as assets until the firm sells the goods that they embody; then, they become expenses. **Chapter 7** discusses more fully the accounting for manufacturing costs.

Marketing Costs The costs a firm incurs in marketing or selling its products during a period relate primarily to the units it sells during the period. In generating current revenue, a firm incurs costs for salaries and commissions of the sales staff, for sales literature used, and for advertising. Because these marketing costs associate with the revenues of the period, accounting reports them as expenses in the period when the firm uses their services. One might argue that some marketing costs, such as advertising and other sales promotion, provide future-period benefits for a firm and that therefore the firm should continue to treat them as assets. Accountants cannot readily distinguish the portion of the cost relating to the current period (an expense) from the portion relating to future periods (an asset). They therefore treat most marketing activity costs as expenses of the period when the firm uses the services. Even when such costs enhance the future marketability of a firm's products, accounting treats these marketing costs as **period expenses** rather than assets—an expedient practice, not one derived from fundamental concepts.

Administrative Costs The cost of administering the activities of a firm include the president's salary, accounting and information systems costs, and the costs of conducting various supportive activities such as legal services, employee training, and corporate planning. These costs do not relate directly to particular units produced or sold, so accounting treats administrative costs, like marketing costs, as period expenses.

Measurement of Expenses

Expenses result from the firm's consuming assets during the period, so the amount of an expense equals the portion of the asset's cost consumed. The basis for expense measurement is the same as for asset measurement. Because accounting reports assets primarily at acquisition cost on the balance sheet, it measures expenses by the acquisition cost of the assets sold or used during the period.

Classification of Expenses

Firms vary in the classification of expenses in the income statement. Some firms classify expenses by the function within the firm: cost of goods sold for the merchandise or manufacturing function, selling expenses for marketing activities, and administrative expenses for administrative activities. Other firms classify their expenses by the nature of the expense, such as salary expense, depreciation expense, and so on. Most firms use a mixture of classifications, but maintain those classifications over time. **Chapters 6** and **12** discuss income statement classification more fully.

Summary

Over sufficiently long time periods, the amount of net income equals cash inflows minus cash outflows from operating, investing, and debt servicing activities; that is, the amount of net income equals the difference between the cash received from customers and the amount of cash paid to suppliers, employees, and other providers of goods and services.[3] Users of financial statements, however, desire information about a firm's operating performance for short time periods, such as a year or less. Thus, accountants slice up this total amount of net income and allocate a portion to each period. Using the timing of cash flows to dictate the allocation of this total income usually provides a poor measure of operating performance. Cash receipts from customers do not always occur in the same accounting period as the related cash expenditures to the providers of goods and services. The accrual basis allocates net income so that outflows of net assets more closely match inflows of net assets of the period, independent of whether the net assets are currently in the form of cash.

The accrual basis determines the timing of income recognition. The accrual basis typically recognizes revenue at the time of sale (delivery). Costs that associate directly with particular revenues become expenses in the period when a firm recognizes the revenues. A firm treats the cost of acquiring or manufacturing inventory items in this manner. Costs that do not closely associate with particular revenue streams become expenses of the period when a firm consumes the goods or services in operations. Most marketing and administrative costs receive this treatment.

The next section considers the preparation of the income statement.

Problem 3.2 for Self-Study

Revenue and expense recognition.   A firm uses the accrual basis of accounting and recognizes revenues at the time it sells goods or renders services. Indicate the amount of revenue or expense that the firm recognizes during April in each of the following transactions:

a. Collects $4,970 cash from customers during April for merchandise sold and delivered in March.
b. Sells merchandise to customers during April for $14,980 cash.
c. Sells to customers during April merchandise totaling $5,820 that the firm expects to collect in cash during May.
d. Pays suppliers $2,610 during April for merchandise received by the firm and sold to customers during March.
e. Pays suppliers $5,440 during April for merchandise received and sold to customers during April.
f. Receives from suppliers and sells to customers during April merchandise that cost $2,010 and that the firm expects to pay for during May.
g. Receives from suppliers during April merchandise that cost $1,570 and that the firm expects to pay and sell to customers during May.

Accounting Procedures for Preparing the Income Statement

As we discussed in connection with the balance sheet in **Chapter 2**, you need not be able to prepare an income statement in order to use it in assessing a firm's operating performance. To

---

[3] Sometimes we state this fundamental principle of accrual accounting more succinctly: Over long enough time periods, net income equals cash-in less cash-out, other than transactions with owners. (Consider, for example, shareholders paying for shares of stock or receiving dividends, which do not affect net income.)

assess a firm's performance, you must understand how various business transactions affect a firm's net income for a period and its financial position at the end of the period. We extend the analytical framework discussed in **Chapter 2** to include income transactions. We use both the transaction spreadsheet template and journal entries. Recall that this analytical framework relies on the balance sheet equation as its building block.

Relation between Balance Sheet and Income Statement

Refer to **Exhibit 1.3**, which shows the relation between the balance sheet at the beginning and end of a period and the income statement and statement of cash flows for the period. Note the following relations:

Balance Sheet at Beginning of Period	Changes in Balance Sheet During the Period	Balance Sheet at End of Period
Assets		Assets
=		=
Liabilities		Liabilities
+		+
Common Stock		Common Stock
+		+
Retained Earnings $\longrightarrow$	Net Income Minus Dividends $\longrightarrow$	Retained Earnings

Retained earnings change between the beginning and end of a period by the amount of net income for the period in excess of dividends declared to shareholders. The income statement shows the amount of net income for the period, but this is not its principal purpose. The purpose of the income statement is to help users understand *why* net income was what it was. A user desiring to assess a firm's past operating performance, project its likely future profitability, and make comparisons of performance across companies will need to know not just the amount of net income, but the revenues and expenses that net to this net income amount. Thus, preparing the income statement requires that we accumulate information about the various types of revenues (sales, interest) and the various types of expenses (cost of good sold, selling and administrative expenses, interest expense, income tax expense). We can therefore expand the Retained Earnings line above as follows:

$$\text{Retained Earnings at Beginning of Period} + \text{Revenues (various types)} - \text{Expenses (various types)} - \text{Dividends} = \text{Retained Earnings at End of Period}$$

Although we accumulate information about particular revenues and expenses during a period, revenues and expenses are elements of the Retained Earnings account. Dividends also reduce retained earnings. Their arithmetic effect on retained earnings is the same as expenses. However, accounting views **dividends** as a distribution of net assets generated by operating activities and not as a cost of generating revenues. Thus, dividends do not appear as expenses on the income statement.

Recall from **Chapter 2** that every transaction or event has a dual effect on the balance sheet equation. Revenues increase retained earnings and must also either increase an asset or reduce a liability. The sale of goods or services increases retained earnings and either increases Cash (an asset) or Accounts Receivables (an asset) or reduces Advances from Customers (a liability). Expenses decrease retained earnings and must also either decrease an asset or increase a liability. Compensation expense for employees reduces retained earnings and either reduces Cash (an asset) or increases Compensation Payable (a liability). We illustrate the recording of income transactions in the next section.

Illustration of the Recording of Income Transactions

Chapter 2 illustrated the transactions of Miller Corporation for the month of January as it prepared to open for business on February 1. None of the transactions during January involve income statement accounts. The first column of **Exhibit 3.3** shows a transaction spreadsheet for Miller Corporation as it opens for business on February 1. The first column shows the balance sheet as of January 31, taken from the last column of **Exhibit 2.3**. Note that retained earnings show a balance of zero on this date. The firm has not yet generated revenues, nor incurred expenses, nor declared a dividend. **Exhibit 3.3** also shows the effects of the transactions described next for the month of February. We show both the effect on the spreadsheet and the related journal entry.

EXHIBIT 3.3   Transactions Spreadsheet for Miller Corporation for February

Balance Sheet Accounts	Balance: Beginning of Period	1 Purchase Inventory On Account	2 Sell Merchandise To Customers	3 Recognize Cost of Goods Sold	4 Pay S&A Expense	5 Collect Cash from Customer	6 Pay Cash to Suppliers	7 Recognize Depreciation On Equipment	8 Recognize Insurance Expense	9 Recognize Inc. Tax Expense	10 Declare and Pay Dividend	Balance: End of Period
ASSETS												
Current Assets:												
Cash	34,400				-14,500	35,000	-20,000				-1,000	33,900
Accounts Receivable			47,000			-35,000						12,000
Inventory	15,000	25,000		-30,000								10,000
Prepaid Insurance	600								-50			550
Total Current Assets	50,000											56,450
Noncurrent Assets:												
Equipment	60,000											60,000
Accumulated Depreciation								-1,000				(1,000)
Total Noncurrent Assets	60,000											59,000
Total Assets	110,000											115,450
LIABILITIES AND SHAREHOLDERS' EQUITY												
Current Liabilities:												
Accounts Payable		25,000					-20,000					5,000
Advance from Customer	3,000		-3,000									–
Income Tax Payable										1,780		1,780
Total Current Liabilities	3,000											6,780
Noncurrent Liabilities:												
Total Noncurrent Liabilities	–											–
Total Liabilities	3,000											6,780
Shareholders' Equity:												
Common Stock	107,000											107,000
Retained Earnings			50,000	-30,000	-14,500			-1,000	-50	-1,780	-1,000	1,670
Total Shareholders' Equity	107,000											108,670
Total Liabilities and Shareholders' Equity	110,000											115,450
Imbalance, if Any	–		–	–	–	–	–			–	–	–
Income Statement Accounts			Sales Rev	COGS	S&A Exp			S&A Exp	Insur Exp	S&A Exp		

Transaction 1: On February 5, Miller Corporation purchases an additional $25,000 of merchandise on account. This transaction increases inventory and accounts payable. Thus,

Spreadsheet Entry

(A) Inventory		+25,000
(L) Accounts Payable		+25,000

Journal Entry

Inventory (Asset Increase)	25,000	
Accounts Payable (Liability Increase)		25,000

Transaction 2: During the month of February, Miller Corporation sells merchandise to customers for $50,000. Of this amount, $3,000 represents sales to customers who paid $3,000 to Miller Corporation on January 31, which we recorded at the end of January as Advances from Customers. Miller Corporation makes the remaining $47,000 of sales on account. Retail firms typically recognize revenue at the time of delivery of merchandise to customers, regardless of whether or not they have yet received cash from the customers. The entries to record these sales are:

Spreadsheet Entry

(L) Advances from Customers		− 3,000
(A) Accounts Receivable		+47,000
(SE) Retained Earnings (Sales Revenue)		+50,000

Journal Entry

Advances from Customers (Liability Decrease)	3,000	
Accounts Receivable (Asset Increase)	47,000	
Retained Earnings (Sales Revenue) (Shareholders' Equity Increase)		50,000

Assets minus liabilities, or net assets, increase by $50,000 [= $47,000 − (−$3,000)] and retained earnings, a shareholders' equity account, increases by $50,000. We enter Sales Rev in the Income Statement Accounts row of the spreadsheet to designate the name of the income account affected by this transaction.

Transactions 3: The historical, or acquisition, cost of the merchandise sold to customers in Transaction 2 is $30,000. Because Miller no longer holds this merchandise in inventory, it is no longer an asset. We must reduce the inventory account and recognize the cost of the inventory as an expense to match against the sales revenue in Transaction 2. Thus,

Spreadsheet Entry

(A) Inventory		−30,000
(SE) Retained Earnings (Cost of Goods Sold)		−30,000

Journal Entry

Retained Earnings (Cost of Goods Sold) (Shareholders' Equity Decrease)	30,000	
Inventory (Asset Decrease)		30,000

Firms generally use the account, Cost of Goods Sold, for the cost of items sold and do not include the word "Expense" in the account title, although the account is an expense. Note that expenses reduce retained earnings and shareholders' equity. Thus, the minus sign on the amount for Cost of Goods Sold does not mean that the expense decreases, but that retained earnings and shareholders' equity decrease. We enter COGS in the Income Statement Accounts row of the spreadsheet to remind ourselves of the account title when we are ready to prepare the income statement for February.

Transaction 4: Miller Corporation incurs and pays selling and administrative expenses in the aggregate of $14,500 during February. We record this transaction as follows:

Spreadsheet Entry

(A) Cash		−14,500
(SE) Retained Earnings (Selling and Administrative Expense)		−14,500

Journal Entry

Retained Earnings (Selling and Administrative Expense)		
(Shareholders' Equity Decrease)	14,500	
Cash (Asset Decrease)		14,500

Miller Corporation presumably received all of the benefits of these selling and administrative services during February. Thus, the full amount is an expense for the month, which we match against revenues. None of the expenditure results in an asset that would appear on the balance sheet at the end of February.

Transaction 5: Miller Corporation collects $35,000 from customers for sales previously made on account. The firm recognized revenue from these sales at the time of sale (see Transaction 2 for February). The collection of the cash increases cash and decreases accounts receivable. Thus,

Spreadsheet Entry

(A) Cash		+35,000
(A) Accounts Receivable		−35,000

Journal Entry

Cash (Asset Increase)	35,000	
Accounts Receivable (Asset Decrease)		35,000

Transaction 6: The firm pays $20,000 to suppliers for merchandise previously purchased on account. We record this transaction as follows:

Spreadsheet Entry

(A) Cash		−20,000
(L) Accounts Payable		−20,000

Journal Entry

Accounts Payable (Liability Decrease)	20,000	
Cash (Asset Decrease)		20,000

Transactions 1 to 6 involved transactions, or exchanges, with other entities during the month of February. The transaction triggers the making of an entry in the accounts. The passage of time may also trigger the need to make entries. For example, interest expense on borrowing accrues as time passes. Most firms do not make entries related to the passage of time during the accounting period, but instead wait until the end of the period.[4] Miller Corporation makes the next three entries at the end of February.

Transaction 7: The firm recognizes depreciation on the $60,000 of equipment purchased during January. Miller Corporation purchased the equipment during January and recorded it as an asset. It did not begin consuming the services of the equipment until it started using it on February 1. Miller Corporation estimates that the equipment has a five-year life and zero salvage at the end of five years. It will depreciate, or write off, the equipment straight line over the useful life. Thus, depreciation each month is $1,000 (= $60,000/60 months). Miller Corporation includes depreciation of equipment as part of selling and administrative expenses. The firm could record depreciation by reducing the equipment account by $1,000 and reducing retaining earnings by $1,000. Instead of reducing the equipment account directly, firms typically use an account called Accumulated Depreciation to record the writedown in the cost of the equipment for services used during the period. The Accumulated Depreciation account appears on the balance sheet as a subtraction from the acquisition cost of the

---

[4]Accountants refer to these end-of-the-period entries as *adjusting entries* because they adjust the amounts of various accounts to properly reflect net income for the period and the balance sheet at the end of the period.

equipment. Accountants refer to accounts such as Accumulated Depreciation as *contra accounts*, because they appear as subtractions from the amounts in other related accounts. Thus:

Spreadsheet Entry

(A) Accumulated Depreciation	−1,000	
(SE) Retained Earnings (Selling and Administrative Expense)	−1,000	

Journal Entry

Retained Earnings (Selling and Administrative Expense)		
(Shareholders' Equity Decrease)	1,000	
Accumulated Depreciation (Asset Decrease)		1,000

Note that the minus sign on the Accumulated Deprecation account in the spreadsheet entry indicates the effect on assets, not on accumulated depreciation. Likewise, the minus sign on Selling and Administrative Expense indicates the effect on retained earnings and shareholders' equity, not on depreciation expense.

Transaction 8: Miller Corporation records the portion of the cost of the prepaid insurance of $600 attributable to insurance services received during February. The firm paid the one-year insurance premium on January 31 for insurance coverage from February 1 of this year through January 31 of next year. Assuming the allocation of an equal amount of this insurance premium to each month of the year, $50 (= $600/12) applies to February. Miller Corporation includes the cost of insurance in selling and administrative expenses. The entries are:

Spreadsheet Entry

(A) Prepaid Insurance	−50	
(SE) Retained Earnings (Selling and Administrative Expense)	−50	

Journal Entry

Retained Earnings (Selling and Administrative Expense)		
(Shareholders' Equity Decrease)	50	
Prepaid Insurance (Asset Decrease)		50

The remaining $550 of prepaid insurance becomes an expense during the next eleven months. Note that firms typically reduce the Prepaid Insurance account directly, instead of using an account similar to accumulated depreciation for equipment.

Transaction 9: Miller Corporation recognizes income tax expense on the net income before income taxes for February. Assume an income tax rate of 40 percent. Net income before income taxes for February equals $4,450 (= $50,000 − $30,000 − $14,500 − $1,000 − $50). Income tax expense is therefore $1,780 (= 0.40 × $4,450). Firms pay their income taxes quarterly. Thus, the income taxes remain unpaid at the end of February. Even though the income taxes are not yet payable, they represent an expense that Miller Corporation must match against the net income before taxes for February under the accrual basis of accounting. The entries are:

Spreadsheet Entry

(L) Income Tax Payable	+1,780	
(SE) Retained Earnings (Income Tax Expense) ..	−1,780	

Journal Entry

Retained Earnings (Income Tax Expense) (Shareholders' Equity		
Decrease)	1,780	
Income Tax Payable (Liability Increase)		1,780

Transaction 10: Miller Corporation declares and pays a dividend to shareholders of $1,000. The entries to record the dividend are:

Spreadsheet Entry

(A) Cash	−1,000	
(SE) Retained Earnings (Dividend)	−1,000	

Journal Entry

Retained Earnings (Dividend) (Shareholders' Equity Decrease)	1,000	
Cash (Asset Decrease)		1,000

Note that the effect of a dividend on retained earnings is the same as an expense. Dividends, however, do not appear on the income statement as an expense in measuring net income.

The final column on the right shows the amounts for the balance sheet at the end of February. The amounts on the retained earnings row show the revenues, expenses, and dividends that net to the change in retained earnings for the month. Using the account titles on the Income Statement Accounts row and the corresponding amounts for revenues and expenses on the retained earnings row, we can prepare an income statement for the month of February. **Exhibit 3.4** shows the income statement for February and **Exhibit 3.5** shows a comparative balance sheet for January 31 and February 28.

EXHIBIT 3.4	Income Statement for Miller Corporation For the Month of February

Sales Revenue	$ 50,000
Cost of Goods Sold	(30,000)
Selling and Administrative Expenses	(15,550)
Income before Income Taxes	$ 4,450
Income Tax Expense	(1,780)
Net Income	$ 2,670

EXHIBIT 3.5	Comparative Balance Sheet for Miller Corporation

	January 31	February 28
ASSETS		
Cash	$ 34,400	$ 33,900
Accounts Receivable	—	12,000
Inventory	15,000	10,000
Prepaid Insurance	600	550
Total Current Assets	$ 50,000	$ 56,450
Equipment (at acquisition cost)	$ 60,000	$ 60,000
Less Accumulated Depreciation	—	(1,000)
Equipment-Net	$ 60,000	$ 59,000
Total Assets	$110,000	$115,450
LIABILITIES AND SHAREHOLDERS' EQUITY		
Accounts Payable	$ —	$ 5,000
Advance from Customer	3,000	—
Income Tax Payable	—	1,780
Total Current Liabilities	$ 3,000	$ 6,780
Noncurrent Liabilities	—	—
Total Liabilities	$ 3,000	$ 6,780
Common Stock	$107,000	$107,000
Retained Earnings	—	1,670
Total Shareholders' Equity	$107,000	$108,670
Total Liabilities and Shareholders' Equity	$110,000	$115,450

Note that retained earnings increases for the month by $1,670, from zero at the end of January to $1,670 at the end of February. The change in retained earnings equals net income of $2,670 minus dividends of $1,000. Retained earnings begins the month of March with a balance of $1,670. Net income minus dividends for the month of March added to $1,670 will yield the balance in retained earnings at the end of March, assuming that Miller declares a dividend. Thus, the retained earnings account, as with all other balance sheet accounts, reflects the *cumulative* effect of transactions affecting that account.

Problem 3.3 for Self-Study

Journal Entries, Transactions Spreadsheet, Income Statement and Balance Sheet Preparation.   The balance sheet of Rybowiak's Building Supplies on June 30, Year 12, appears in **Exhibit 3.6**.

EXHIBIT 3.6	RYBOWIAK'S BUILDING SUPPLIES Balance Sheet June 30, Year 12	
Assets		
Cash		$ 44,200
Accounts Receivable		27,250
Merchandise Inventory		68,150
Prepaid Insurance		400
Total Current Assets		$140,000
Equipment (at cost)		$210,000
Less Accumulated Depreciation		(84,000)
Equipment-Net		$126,000
Total Assets		$266,000
Liabilities and Shareholders' Equity		
Accounts Payable		$ 33,100
Note Payable		5,000
Salaries Payable		1,250
Total Current Liabilities		$ 39,350
Common Stock		$150,000
Retained Earnings		76,650
Total Shareholders' Equity		$226,650
Total Liabilities and Shareholders' Equity		$266,000

The following transactions occurred during the month of July.

(1) Sold merchandise on account for a total selling price of $85,000.
(2) Purchased merchandise inventory on account from various suppliers for $46,300.
(3) Paid rent for the month of July of $11,750.
(4) Paid salaries to employees during July of $20,600.
(5) Collected accounts receivable of $34,150.
(6) Paid accounts payable of $38,950.
(7) The firm paid the premium on a one-year insurance policy on March 1, Year 12, with coverage beginning on that date. This is the only insurance policy in force on June 30, Year 12.
(8) The firm depreciates its equipment over a 10-year life. Estimated salvage value of the equipment is negligible.
(9) Employees earned salaries of $1,600 during the last two days of July but were not paid. These are the only unpaid salaries at the end of July.

(continued)

Problem 3.3 for Self-Study *(continued)*

(10) The note payable is a 90-day, 6-percent note issued on June 30, Year 12.

(11) Merchandise inventory on hand on July 31, Year 12, totals $77,950. The cost of goods sold for July equals merchandise inventory on June 30, Year 12, plus purchases of merchandise during July minus merchandise inventory on July 31, Year 12.

    a. Prepare journal entries to reflect the transactions and other events during July. The firm classifies expenses by their nature (that is, insurance, depreciation). Revenues and expenses should appear in the Retained Earnings account but with an indication of the specific revenue or expense account debited or credited. Be sure to indicate whether each entry increases or decreases assets, liabilities, or shareholders' equity.

    b. Using the transaction spreadsheet template available with this book, enter the amounts from the June 30, Year 12 balance sheet and the effects of the transactions during July in the spreadsheet to derive the balance sheet on July 31, Year 12.

    c. Prepare an income statement for the month of July. Ignore income taxes.

    d. Prepare a comparative balance sheet as of June 30, and July 31, Year 12.

Interpreting and Analyzing the Income Statement

The income statement provides information for assessing the operating profitability of a firm. One tool for analysis, a **common-size income statement**, expresses each expense and net income as a percentage of revenues. A common-size income statement permits an analysis of changes or differences in the relations between revenues, expenses, and net income and identifies relations that the analyst should explore further.

Time Series Analysis

Exhibit 3.7 presents a common-size income statement for Bed Bath & Beyond, a retailing firm specializing in home furnishings, for a recent five-year period. The changes in sales from the preceding year were as follows: Year 10, 34.4 percent; Year 11, 29.0 percent; Year 12, 22.2 percent; Year 13, 25.2 percent.

    Bed Bath & Beyond experienced a steadily increasing profit margin percentage (= net income divided by sales) during this five-year period. The increasing profit margin results primarily from a decreasing selling-and-administrative-expense-to-sales percentage. The cost-of-goods-sold-to-sales percentage remained relatively stable, suggesting that the firm priced its products at a

EXHIBIT 3.7	BED BATH & BEYOND Common-Size Income Statement				
	Year 9	**Year 10**	**Year 11**	**Year 12**	**Year 13**
Sales	100.0%	100.0%	100.0%	100.0%	100.0%
Cost of Goods Sold	(58.3)	(58.7)	(58.8)	(58.8)	(58.6)
Selling and Administrative Expenses	(30.3)	(30.0)	(29.8)	(29.4)	(28.3)
Net Interest Revenue (Expense)	0.3	0.3	0.4	0.4	0.3
Income Tax Expense	(4.7)	(4.5)	(4.6)	(4.7)	(5.2)
Net Income	7.0%	7.1%	7.2%	7.5%	8.2%

	AK Steel	Kellogg	Omnicom Group	Pfizer	Wal-Mart Stores
EXHIBIT 3.8	Common-Size Income Statements for Five Firms				
Sales	100.0%	100.0%	100.0%	100.0%	100.0%
Other Revenues	—	0.3	0.2	1.2	0.9
Cost of Goods or Services Sold	(88.3)	(55.0)	(65.7)	(12.5)	(78.5)
Selling and Administrative Expenses	(6.3)	(26.8)	(19.6)	(33.5)	(16.9)
Research and Development Expense	—	—	—	(16.0)	—
Interest Expense	(3.0)	(4.7)	(0.4)	(0.8)	(0.4)
Income Tax Expense	(1.0)	(5.1)	(5.1)	(10.9)	(1.8)
Net Income	1.4%	8.7%	9.4%	27.5%	3.3%

relatively constant markup on the cost of purchasing the merchandise. Sales increased significantly each year. Many selling and administrative expenses do not increase proportionally with sales. Individual stores need not add employees at the same rate as the increases in sales, for example, if employees are working at less than capacity. The cost of information systems and accounting and legal costs need not increase proportionally with sales. Thus, the rapid sales increases coupled with less than proportional increases in selling and administrative expenses led to a decline in this expense percentage.

Cross-Section Analysis

A common-size income statement also provides information about differences in the economic characteristics and business strategies of firms. **Exhibit 3.8** presents common-size income statements for AK Steel (steel manufacturing), Kellogg (branded food processing), Omnicom Group (marketing services), Pfizer (pharmaceuticals), and Wal-Mart (discount retailing).

Pfizer has the highest profit margin of the five firms. Pharmaceutical products enjoy patent protection for a 20-year period, which gives pharmaceutical companies a monopoly on a particular prescription drug until another firm discovers a superior product. Customers needing the drug view it as a necessity. Medical insurance often pays for all or most of the cost of the drug. Thus, demand for prescription drugs is relatively price inelastic so that changes in selling prices do not have a significant effect on demand. Pfizer also incurs research and development costs up front before obtaining approval to sell the drug. A significant portion of research and development costs does not result in viable products. Pharmaceutical companies argue that they need the large profit margins to induce them to take the risks inherent in incurring high costs researching new drugs without promise of payback. Thus, the need to make up-front expenditures on research and development with an uncertain outcome requires a higher profit rate than do less risky businesses to induce investors to provide financing. Note that the cost of manufacturing pharmaceutical products is a relatively small percentage of the selling price, 12.5 percent for Pfizer. The cost of marketing the product to physicians using a sales force and to consumers through advertising and administrative costs represents the largest single expense item. The cost of researching and developing new profitable drugs is larger in this year than the manufacturing costs of the drugs sold. Note that interest expense is a relatively small percentage of sales revenue, suggesting that Pfizer does not borrow extensively. Its most important assets are its employees, who can leave the firm at any time, and its patents, which can become obsolete quickly. Thus, Pfizer and most other pharmaceutical companies do not have significant assets that can serve as collateral for borrowing. In addition, profitable pharmaceutical firms do not likely need to engage in extensive borrowing.

Omnicom Group has the next largest profit margin percentage. It differentiates its product (marketing services) by the quality of the creative talent it employs. The individual agencies that comprise Omnicom Group have maintained a reputation for developing innovative and effective advertising campaigns. Its customers return and willingly pay for their services, which provide a profit margin larger than earned by companies without such reputations. Note that interest expense is a relatively small percentage of revenues, similar to Pfizer. The most important asset of marketing services firms is their employees, who cannot serve as desirable collateral for borrowing.

Kellogg has the next highest profit margin percentage, almost as large as that of Omnicom Group. Whereas a pharmaceutical company enjoys patent protection and a marketing service firm enjoys a reputation for creative employees, Kellogg enjoys trademark protection for its brand names, which provides a degree of monopoly power. Although close substitutes for most branded food products exist, advertising, experience in using the product, and other factors create the impression of a differentiated product and keep customers coming back. Those loyal customers provide Kellogg with a higher profit rate than earned by similar companies with less well-known brands. Branded products provide predictable cash flows and permit consumer products companies to borrow extensively for new product development and corporate acquisitions.

Wal-Mart and AK Steel both have relatively small profit margin percentages. Neither company sells a differentiated product. Customers can obtain virtually identical products from competitors. Business terminology refers to their products as *commodities*. Demand is relatively price elastic. If either firm raised its prices, customers would likely switch to a competitor. The strategy of both firms is to keep their costs as low as possible and attempt to price their products lower than competitors. They strive to make up for the low profit margins by selling higher volumes of products. High profit margins would induce new competitors, who need only retail space and inventory, to enter. Thus competition, both actual and potential, is intense. The manufacturing facilities for steel production are capital-intensive. The need to use the fixed manufacturing facilities as fully as possible induces steel firms to price low in an effort to gain market share. When excess manufacturing capacity exists in the industry, as was the case in this year, competition is intense and profit margins decline. Note the differences in the selling and administrative expense percentages for Wal-Mart and AK Steel. Wal-Mart spends a higher percentage of its sales on marketing and administration, primarily in promoting its stores to consumers. AK Steel spends less on attempting to create demand and relies on its sales force primarily to take customers' orders. The capital-intensive nature of steel manufacturing results in a high expense percentage for interest to finance the manufacturing facilities, which serve as collateral for the borrowing.

Exhibit 3.9 summarizes the factors that tend to differentiate firms and industries with low profit margins from those with high profit margins.

EXHIBIT 3.9	Economic Characteristics of Firms with Low and High Profit	
Characteristic	**Low Profit Margins**	**High Profit Margins**
Nature of Product	Undifferentiated	Differentiated
Barriers to Competition	Low	High
Extent of Competition	Highly Competitive	More Monopolistic
Price Elasticity of Demand	Relatively Elastic	Relatively Inelastic

We explore interpretation and analysis of the income statement more fully in **Chapters 5** and **6**.

Summary

Net income for a period is the difference between revenues from selling goods and services and the expenses incurred to generate those revenues. In an effort to match expenses with associated revenues, firms typically measure net income using the accrual basis of accounting. Under the accrual basis, firms recognize revenue when they can predict with reasonable assurance the amount of cash they will ultimately receive from customers and the amount of cash they will ultimately expend to make and sell the good or service. They then attempt to match associated expenses with the revenues, to the extent possible, or with the period when they consume assets in operations.

Measurement of net income for a period directly affects financial position at the end of a period. Revenues result in increases in assets or decreases in liabilities. Expenses decrease assets or increase liabilities. Because revenues represent increases in retained earnings, revenue transactions result in credits (increases) to shareholders' equity and in debits either to assets (an increase) or to liabilities (a decrease). Expenses represent decreases in retained earnings and result in debits (decreases) to shareholders' equity and credits either to assets (decreases) or to liabilities (increases).

Some events will not enter the regular day-to-day recording process during the period because no explicit transaction between the firm and some external party (such as a customer, creditor, or governmental unit) has taken place to require a journal entry. Such events require adjusting entries at the end of the period so that the firm's periodic income and its financial position properly appear in the financial statements reported on an accrual basis.

The accrual basis of accounting uses information about the amount of cash received and expended to measure revenues and expenses. However, the accrual basis does not use the receipt or expenditure of cash to trigger the recognition of revenue or expense. **Exhibit 3.10** summarizes the relation between cash inflows/outflows and the recognition of revenues/expenses.

EXHIBIT 3.10	Relation of Cash Flows (Receipts and Expenditures) to Recognition of Revenues and Expenses

	Journal Entry Each Year		
Transaction	**Year 1**	**Year 2**	**Year 3**
1. Cash received from customer in Year 1 for services to be performed in Year 2	(T)[a] Cash . . . . . X Liability X	(A)[b] Liability . . . . X Revenue X	
2. Cash received from customer in Year 2 for services to be performed in Year 2		(T) Cash . . . . X Revenue X	
3. Services performed in Year 2 for which cash will not be received until Year 3		(A) Accounts Receivable . . X Revenue X	(T) Cash . . . . . . X Accounts Receivable X
4. Cash expended in Year 1 for services consumed in Year 2	(T) Asset . . . . . X Cash X	(A) Expense . . . . X Asset X	
5. Cash expended in Year 2 for services consumed in Year 2		(T) Expense . . . . X Cash X	
6. Services consumed in Year 2 for which cash will not be expended until Year 3		(A) Expense . . . . X Liability X	(T) Liability . . . . X Cash X

[a](T) is a transaction entry made during the period.
[b](A) is an adjusting entry made at the end of a period.

Interpreting the income statement involves studying the relation between revenues, expenses, and net income both over time and across firms. Changes in economic conditions, technologies, government policies, competitive conditions, and similar factors can affect relations between these items over time. Differences in profit margins across firms and industries relate to the degree of product differentiation, barriers to competition, the extent of competition, and the price elasticity of demand.

Solutions to Self-Study Problems

SUGGESTED SOLUTION TO PROBLEM 3.1 FOR SELF-STUDY

(J. Thompson; cash versus accrual basis of accounting.)
a. and **b.**

	a. Accrual Basis	b. Cash Basis
Sales Revenue	$29,000	$22,000
Less Expenses:		
Cost of Merchandise Sold	$13,000	—
Payments on Merchandise Purchased	—	$10,000
Rental Expense	1,000	2,000
Insurance Expense	100	1,200
Interest Expense	40	—
Utilities Expense	400	400
Salaries Expense	650	650
Taxes Expense	350	350
Total Expenses	$15,540	$14,600
Net Income	$13,460	$ 7,400

c. The accrual basis gives a better measure of operating performance because it matches revenue generated during January with costs incurred in generating that revenue. The cash basis emphasizes cash inflows and outflows, regardless of whether inflows and outflows relate to the same goods or services sold. Note that the capital contributed by Thompson and the bank loan do not give rise to revenue under either basis of accounting because they are financing, not operating, activities.

SUGGESTED SOLUTION TO PROBLEM 3.2 FOR SELF-STUDY

(Revenue and expense recognition.)
a. None
b. $14,980
c. $5,820
d. None
e. $5,440
f. $2,010
g. None

SUGGESTED SOLUTION TO PROBLEM 3.3 FOR SELF-STUDY

(Rybowiak Building Supplies; journal entries, transactions spreadsheet, income statement and balance sheet preparation.)
a.

(1)	Accounts Receivable (Asset Increase)		85,000	
	Retained Earnings (Sales Revenue) (Shareholders' Equity Increase)			85,000
	Sale of merchandise on account.			
(2)	Merchandise Inventory (Asset Increase)		46,300	
	Accounts Payable (Liability Increase)			46,300
	Purchase of merchandise inventory on account.			
(3)	Retained Earnings (Rent Expense) (Shareholders' Equity Decrease)		11,750	
	Cash (Asset Decrease)			11,750
	Paid rent for July.			
(4)	Salaries Payable (Liability Decrease)		1,250	
	Retained Earnings (Salary Expense) (Shareholders' Equity Decrease)		19,350	
	Cash (Asset Decrease)			20,600
	Paid salaries for July.			
(5)	Cash (Asset Increase)		34,150	
	Accounts Receivable (Asset Decrease)			34,150
	Collected accounts receivable.			
(6)	Accounts Payable (Liability Decrease)		38,950	
	Cash (Asset Decrease)			38,950
	Paid accounts payable..			

| (7) | Retained Earnings (Insurance Expense) (Shareholders' Equity Decrease) .... | 50 | |
| | Prepaid Insurance (Asset Decrease) .... | | 50 |

Recognize insurance expense for July: $50 = $400/8. The Prepaid Insurance account has a balance of $400 on June 30, Year 12. Because the firm paid the one-year insurance premium on March 1, Year 12, we know that the policy has eight remaining months on June 30, Year 12.

| (8) | Retained Earnings (Depreciation Expense) (Shareholders' Equity Decrease) .... | 1,750 | |
| | Accumulated Depreciation (Asset Decrease) .... | | 1,750 |

Recognize depreciation for July: $1,750 = $210,000/120.

| (9) | Retained Earnings (Salary Expense) (Shareholders' Equity Decrease) .... | 1,600 | |
| | Salaries Payable (Liability Increase) .... | | 1,600 |

Recognize unpaid salaries for July.

| (10) | Retained Earnings (Interest Expense) (Shareholders' Equity Decrease) .... | 25 | |
| | Interest Payable (Liability Increase) .... | | 25 |

Recognize unpaid interest for July: $5,000 \times .06 \times 30/360$.

| (11) | Retained Earnings (Cost of Goods Sold) (Shareholders' Equity Decrease) .... | 36,500 | |
| | Merchandise Inventory (Asset Decrease) .... | | 36,500 |

To recognize cost of goods sold for July: $36,500 = $68,150 + $46,300 − $77,950.

b. Exhibit 3.11 presents transactions spreadsheet for Rybowiak Building Supplies.

c.

RYBOWIAK'S BUILDING SUPPLIES
Income Statement
For the Month of July, Year 12

Sales Revenue		$85,000
Less Expenses:		
Cost of Goods Sold	$36,500	
Salaries Expense ($19,350 + $1,600)	20,950	
Rent Expense	11,750	
Depreciation Expense	1,750	
Insurance Expense	50	
Interest Expense	25	(71,025)
Net Income		$ 13,975

d.

RYBOWIAK'S BUILDING SUPPLIES
Balance Sheet
June 30 and July 31, Year 12

Assets	June 30	July 31
Current Assets:		
Cash	$44,200	$7,050
Accounts Receivable	27,250	78,100
Merchandise Inventory	68,150	77,950
Prepaid Insurance	400	350
Total Current Assets	$140,000	$163,450
Noncurrent Assets:		
Equipment—at Cost	$210,000	$210,000
Less Accumulated Depreciation	(84,000)	(85,750)
Total Noncurrent Assets	126,000	$124,250
Total Assets	$266,000	$287,700

(continued)

EXHIBIT 3.11

Transactions Spreadsheet for Rybowiak Building Supplies for July (Problem 3.3 for Self-Study)

Transactions, By Number and Description

Balance Sheet Accounts	Balance: Beginning of Period	Sell Merchandise On Account (1)	Purchase Merchandise On Account (2)	Pay July Rent (3)	Pay Salaries During July (4)	Collect Accounts Receivable (5)	Pay Accounts Payment (6)	Recognize Insurance For July (7)	Recognize Depreciation For July (8)	Recognize Unpaid Sal. For July (9)	Recognize Interest For July (9)	Recognize COGS For July (10)	Balance: End of Period
ASSETS													
Current Assets:													
Cash	44,200			−11,750	−20,600	34,150	−38,950						7,050
Accounts Receivable	27,250	85,000				−34,150							78,100
Merchandise Inventory	68,150		46,300									−36,500	77,950
Prepaid Insurance	400							−50					350
Total Current Assets	140,000												163,450
Noncurrent Assets:													
Equipment	210,000												210,000
Accumulated Depreciation	−84,000								−1,750				(85,750)
Total Noncurrent Assets	126,000												124,250
Total Assets	266,000												287,700
LIABILITIES AND SHAREHOLDERS' EQUITY													
Current Liabilities:													
Accounts Payable	33,100		46,300				−38,950						40,450
Notes Payable	5,000												5,000
Salaries Payable	1,250				−1,250					1,600			1,600
Interest Payable											25		25
Total Current Liabilities	39,350												47,075
Noncurrent Liabilities:													
Total Noncurrent Liabilities	–												–
Total Liabilities	39,350												47,075
Shareholders' Equity:													
Common Stock	150,000												150,000
Retained Earnings	76,650	85,000		−11,750	−19,350			−50	−1,750	−1,600	−25	−36,500	90,625
Total Shareholders' Equity	226,650												240,625
Total Liabilities and Shareholders' Equity	266,000												287,700
Imbalance, if Any	–	–	–	–	–	–	–	–	–	–	–	–	
Income Statement Accounts		Sales Rev		Rent Exp	Salary Exp			Insurance Exp	Depre. Exp	Salary Exp	Interest Exp	COGS	

LIABILITIES AND SHAREHOLDERS' EQUITY

Current Liabilities:

Accounts Payable	$ 33,100	$ 40,450
Note Payable	5,000	5,000
Salaries Payable	1,250	1,600
Interest Payable	—	25
Total Current Liabilities	$ 39,350	$ 47,075

Shareholders' Equity:

Common Stock	$150,000	$150,000
Retained Earnings	76,650	90,625
Total Shareholders' Equity	$226,650	$240,625
Total Liabilities and Shareholders' Equity	$266,000	$287,700

Key Terms and Concepts

Profit margin percentage
Net income or net loss
Revenues
Expenses
Accounting period
Natural business year or fiscal period
Cash basis of accounting
Accrual basis of accounting
Unexpired costs

Expired costs
Matching principle
Product costs
Period expenses
Dividends
Common-size income statement
Times Series Analysis
Cross Section Analysis

Questions, Short Exercises, Exercises, Problems, and Cases

QUESTIONS

1. Review the meaning of the terms and concepts listed above in Key Terms and Concepts.
2. "If the accounting period were long enough, the distinction between the cash and accrual basis of accounting would disappear." Do you agree? Why or why not?
3. "Cash flows determine the amount of revenue and expense but not the timing of their recognition." Explain.
4. "The valuation of assets and liabilities relates closely to the measurement of revenues and expenses." Explain.
5. Distinguish between a cost and an expense.
6. "The key term for understanding the accrual basis of accounting is matching." Explain.
7. Both interest expense on borrowing and dividends on common stock reduce net assets and reduce shareholders' equity. Yet, accountants treat interest as an expense in measuring net income but do not treat dividends on common stock as an expense. Explain the rationale for this apparent inconsistency.
8. What is the purpose of using contra accounts? What is the alternative to using them?

For additional student resources, content, and interactive quizzes for this chapter visit the FACMU website:
http://facmu.swlearning.com

SHORT EXERCISES

9. **Analyzing changes in accounts receivable.** Microsoft Corporation reported a balance of $5,129 million in accounts receivable at the beginning of Year 13 and $5,196 million at the end of Year 13. Its income statement reported sales revenue of $32,120 million for Year 13. Assuming that Microsoft Corporation makes all sales on account, compute the amount of cash collected from customers during Year 13.
10. **Analyzing changes in inventory.** General Electric Company reported a balance of $8,565 million in inventory at the beginning Year 12 and $9,247 million at the end of Year 12. Its income statement reported cost of goods sold of $63,072 million for Year 12. Compute the cost of inventory either purchased or manufactured during Year 12.

11. **Analyzing changes in inventory and accounts payable.** Ann Taylor Stores reported a balance in inventories of $180.1 million at the beginning of Year 13 and $185.5 million at the end of Year 13. It reported a balance in accounts payable for merchandise purchases of $52.0 million at the beginning of Year 13 and $57.1 million at the end of Year 13. Its income statement showed cost of goods sold of $633.5 million for Year 13. Compute the amount of cash paid to suppliers of inventory during Year 13 for purchases made on account.

12. **Analyzing changes in salaries payable.** AMR, the parent company of American Airlines, reported a balance in salaries payable of $721 million at the beginning of Year 12 and $705 million at the end of Year 12. Its income statement reported salary expense of $8,392 million for Year 12. Compute the amount of cash paid to employees for salaries during Year 12.

13. **Analyzing changes in retained earnings.** Johnson & Johnson, a pharmaceutical and medical products company, reported a balance in retained earnings of $23,066 million at the beginning of Year 12 and $26,571 million at the end of Year 12. It reported dividends declared and paid of $3,092 million for Year 12. Compute the amount of net income for Year 12.

14. **Computing interest expense.** Gillette borrowed $250 million on October 1, Year 12. The debt carries an annual interest rate of 6 percent and is payable in two installments, on April 1 and October 1 of each year. The debt matures on October 1, Year 32. Gillette's accounting period ends on December 31 of each year. Compute the amount of interest expense for Year 12 assuming that Gillette uses the accrual basis of accounting.

15. **Computing income tax expense and income taxes paid.** Radio Shack reported a balance in Income Taxes Payable of $78.1 million at the beginning of Year 13 and $60.1 million at the end of Year 13. Net income before income taxes for Year 13 totaled $424.9 million. The firm is subject to an income tax rate of 38 percent. Compute the amount of cash payments made for income taxes during Year 13.

16. **Journal entry for prepaid rent.** A firm reported a balance in its Prepaid Rent account of $1,200 on January 1, Year 12. On February 1, Year 12, the firm paid $18,000 as the annual rental for the period from February 1, Year 12 to January 31, Year 13. It recorded this rental payment by debiting Retained Earnings (rent expense) and crediting Cash for $18,000. This is the only entry made in the accounting records during Year 12 related to rent. The firm uses the calendar year as its reporting period. Give the journal entry that this firm must make on December 31, Year 12, to correctly report Prepaid Rent and Rent Expense in its accounts.

17. **Journal entry to correct recording error.** A firm acquired equipment on January 1, Year 12 for $20,000. The equipment has an expected useful life of 5 years and zero salvage value. The firm recorded the acquisition by debiting Retained Earnings (Equipment Expense) and crediting Cash for $20,000. Give the journal entries that the firm must make on December 31, Year 12 to correct its initial recording error and any related effects (ignore income tax effects).

EXERCISES

18. **Revenue recognition.** Neiman Marcus uses the accrual basis of accounting and recognizes revenue at the time it sells merchandise or renders services. Indicate the amount of revenue (if any) the firm recognizes during the months of February, March, and April in each of the following transactions. The firm does the following:

   a. Collects $800 cash from a customer during March for a custom-made suit that the firm will make and deliver to the customer in April.

   b. Collects $2,160 cash from customers for meals served in the firm's restaurant during March.

   c. Collects $39,200 cash from customers during March for merchandise sold and delivered in February.

   d. Sells merchandise to customers during March on account, for which the firm will collect $59,400 cash from customers during April.

   e. Rents space in its store to a travel agency for $9,000 a month, effective March 1. Receives $18,000 cash on March 1 for two months' rent.

   f. Same as part **e**, except that it receives the check for the March and April rent on April 1.

19. **Revenue recognition.** Indicate which of the following transactions or events immediately gives rise to the recognition of revenue under the accrual basis of accounting.

   a. A custom T-shirt manufacturer completes production of an order for an upcoming rock concert. It has not yet delivered the T-shirts to the purchaser or received any cash.

   b. The publisher of *Business Week* ships magazines that subscribers paid for in advance.

   c. The Miami Marlins, a professional baseball team, sells season tickets for next year's games.

    d. General Mills earns interest on a bond issued by Ford Motor Company. Ford will pay the interest next year.

    e. Sears collects cash from customers for sales made on account last year.

    f. Interpublic Group performs advertising services for clients on account. The advertisements will appear in three months.

20. Expense recognition. Sun Microsystems uses the accrual basis of accounting and recognizes revenue at the time its sells goods or renders services. Indicate the amount of expenses (if any) the firm recognizes during the months of June, July, and August in each of the following transactions. The firm does the following:

    a. Pays rent of $180,000 on July 1 for one year's rent on a warehouse beginning on that date.

    b. Receives a utility bill on July 2 totaling $4,560 for services received during June. It pays the utility bill during July.

    c. Purchases office supplies on account costing $12,600 during July. It pays $5,500 for these purchases during July and the remainder during August. Office supplies on hand on July 1 cost $2,400, on July 31 cost $9,200, and on August 31 cost $2,900.

    d. Pays $7,200 on July 15 for property taxes on office facilities for the current calendar year.

    e. Pays $2,000 on July 15 as a deposit on a custom-made delivery van that the manufacturer will deliver in September.

    f. Pays $4,500 on July 25 as an advance on the August salary of an employee.

    g. Pays $6,600 on July 25 for advertisements that appeared in computer journals during June.

21. Expense recognition. Kroger Stores uses the accrual basis of accounting and recognizes revenue at the time its sells goods or renders services. Indicate the amount of expense recognized during October (if any) from each of the following transactions or events:

    a. Pays $4,670 on October 5 for advertisements that appeared in local newspapers during September.

    b. Pays $12,000 on October 6 for refrigerators delivered to its stores on September 30. The firm expects the refrigerators to last for five years and have no salvage value.

    c. Pays $24,000 on October 10 for property taxes for the period October 1 of this year to September 30 of next year.

    d. Pays $12,900 on October 15 for cleaning supplies purchased on October 10. Cleaning supplies on hand on October 1 cost $2,900 and on October 31 cost $3,500.

    e. Pays $1,200 on October 20 for repairs done to a forklift truck on October 1. The truck had a remaining useful life of five years on October 1.

    f. Pays $10,000 on October 25 as a deposit on land Kroger plans to purchase for a new store.

    g. Pays $20,000 on October 31 as rent on a warehouse for October and November.

22. Journal entries for notes receivable and notes payable. Corner Grocery Store borrows $100,000 from Citizen's Bank on December 1, Year 12, using a 90-day note as evidence of the loan. The note bears interest at an annual rate of 6 percent and is due on March 1, Year 13. Both firms use the calendar year as their reporting period.

    a. Present journal entries for the Corner Grocery Store from December 1, Year 12, through payment at maturity. Assume each calendar month contains 30 days.

    b. Present journal entries for Citizen's Bank from December 1, Year 12, through repayment at maturity.

23. Journal entries for inventories. On January 1, Year 12, the Merchandise Inventories account of Dollar General had a balance of $1,131 million. During the Year 12, Dollar General purchased inventories on account for $4,368 million. On December 31, Year 12, it finds that merchandise inventory still on hand amounts to $1,123 million. The Accounts Payable account had a balance of $322 million on January 1, Year 12, and $341 million on December 31, Year 12. Present journal entries to account for all changes in the Merchandise Inventories and Accounts Payable accounts during Year 12.

24. Journal entries for insurance. Eason Corporation commenced business on September 1, Year 12. It paid the one-year insurance premium of $3,600 for property and liability protection on this date and debited Prepaid Insurance. On September 1, Year 13, it renewed the insurance policy and paid the $4,800 one-year insurance premium, again debiting Prepaid Insurance. Eason Corporation uses the calendar year as its reporting period. Give the journal entries that Eason Corporation would make on September 1, Year 12, December 31, Year 12, September 1, Year 13, and December 31, Year 13.

25. Effect of errors on financial statements. Using the notation O/S (overstated), U/S (understated), and NO (no effect), indicate the effects (direction and amount) on assets, liabilities, and shareholders' equity as of December 31, Year 5, of the following independent errors or omissions. Ignore income tax implications.

a. On December 1, Year 5, a firm paid $12,000 for rental of a building for December, Year 5 and January, Year 6. The firm debited Retained Earnings (Rent Expense) and credited Cash on December 1 and made no further entries with respect to this rental during December or January.

b. On December 15, Year 5, a firm received $1,200 from a customer as a deposit on merchandise the firm expects to deliver to the customer in January, Year 6. The firm debited Cash and credited Retained Earnings (Sales Revenue) on December 15 and made no further entries with respect to this deposit during December or January.

c. On December 1, a firm acquired a used forklift truck costing $4,800. The truck was expected to have a two-year life and zero salvage value. The firm recorded the transaction by debiting Retained Earnings (Repair Expense) and crediting Cash for $4,800 and made no further entries during December with respect to the acquisition.

d. On December 15, a firm purchased office supplies costing $8,600. It recorded the purchase by debiting Retained Earnings (Office Supplies Expense) and crediting Cash. The Office Supplies Inventory account on December 1 had a balance of $2,700. The firm took a physical inventory of office supplies on December 31 and found that office supplies costing $2,450 were on hand. The firm made no entries in its accounts with respect to office supplies on December 31.

e. A firm incurs expense for interest of $1,500 for the month of December on a 45-day loan obtained on December 1. The firm properly recorded the loan on its books on December 1 but made no entry to record interest on December 31. The loan is payable with interest on January 15, Year 5.

f. A firm purchased merchandise on account costing $11,600 on December 23, Year 5, debiting Merchandise Inventory and crediting Accounts Payable. The firm paid for this purchase on December 28, Year 5, debiting Retained Earnings (Cost of Goods Sold) and crediting Cash. The merchandise had not been sold as of December 31, Year 6.

26. **Effect of recording errors on financial statements.** Forgetful Corporation neglected to make various adjusting entries on December 31, Year 8, the end of its accounting period. Indicate the effects on assets, liabilities, and shareholders' equity on December 31, Year 8, of failing to adjust for the following independent items as appropriate, using the notation O/S (overstated), U/S (understated), and NO (no effect). Also, give the amount of the effect. Ignore income tax implications.

a. On December 15, Year 8, Forgetful Corporation received a $1,400 advance from a customer for products to be manufactured and delivered in January, Year 9. The firm recorded the advance by debiting Cash and crediting Retained Earnings (Sales Revenue) and has made no adjusting entry as of December 31, Year 8.

b. On July 1, Year 8, Forgetful Corporation acquired a machine for $5,000 and recorded the acquisition by debiting Retained Earnings (Cost of Goods Sold) and crediting Cash. The machine has a five-year useful life and zero estimated salvage value.

c. On November 1, Year 8, Forgetful Corporation received a $2,000 note receivable from a customer in settlement of an accounts receivable. It debited Notes Receivable and credited Accounts Receivable on receipt of the note. The note is a six-month note due April 30, Year 9, and bears interest at an annual rate of 12 percent. Forgetful Corporation made no other entries related to this note during Year 8.

d. Forgetful Corporation paid its annual insurance premium of $1,200 on October 1, Year 8, the first day of the year of coverage. It debited Prepaid Insurance $900, debited Retained Earnings (Insurance Expense) $300, and credited Cash for $1,200. It made no other entries related to this insurance during Year 8.

e. The Board of Directors of Forgetful Corporation declared a dividend of $1,500 on December 31, Year 8. The dividend will be paid on January 15, Year 9. Forgetful Corporation neglected to record the dividend declaration.

f. On December 1, Year 8, Forgetful Corporation purchased a machine on account for $50,000, debiting Machinery and crediting Accounts Payable for $50,000. Ten days later, the account was paid, and the company took the allowed 2 percent discount. Cash was credited $49,000, Retained Earnings (Miscellaneous Revenue) was credited $1,000, and Accounts Payable was debited $50,000. It is the policy of Forgetful Corporation to record cash discounts taken as a reduction in the cost of assets. On December 28, Year 8, the machine was installed for $4,000 in cash; Retained Earnings (Maintenance Expense) was debited and Cash was credited for $4,000. The machine started operation on January 1, Year 9. Since the machine was not placed into operation until January 1, Year 9, as appropriate, no depreciation was recorded for Year 8.

PROBLEMS AND CASES

27. Cash versus accrual basis of accounting. Ailawadi Corporation began operations on January 1, Year 6. The firm's cash account revealed the following transactions for the month of January.

Date	Transaction	Amount
Cash Receipts		
Jan. 1	Investment by Praveen Ailawadi for 100 percent of Ailawadi Corporation's Common Stock	$ 75,000
Jan. 1	Loan from Upper Valley Bank, due June 30, Year 6, with interest at 6 percent per year	40,000
Jan. 15	Advance from a customer for merchandise scheduled for delivery in February, Year 6	1,200
Jan. 1–31	Sales to customers	60,000
Cash Disbursements		
Jan. 1	Rental of retail space at a monthly rental of $3,000	(6,000)
Jan. 1	Purchase of display equipment (three-year life, zero salvage value)	(36,000)
Jan. 1	Premium on property and liability insurance for coverage from January 1 to December 31, Year 6	(1,200)
Jan. 15	Payment of utility bills	(750)
Jan. 16	Payment of salaries	(3,500)
Jan. 1–31	Purchase of merchandise	(44,800)
	Balance, January 31, Year 6	$ 83,950

The following information relates to Ailawadi Corporation as of January 31, Year 6:

    (1) Customers owe the firm $9,500 from sales made during January.

    (2) The firm owes suppliers $3,900 for merchandise purchased during January.

    (3) Unpaid utility bills total $260, and unpaid salaries total $1,260.

    (4) Merchandise inventory on hand totals $5,500.

    a. Prepare an income statement for January, assuming that Ailawadi Corporation uses the accrual basis of accounting and recognizes revenue at the time it sells goods to customers.

    b. Prepare an income statement for January, assuming that Ailawadi Corporation uses a cash basis of accounting.

    c. Which basis of accounting do you believe provides a better indication of the operating performance of the firm during January? Why?

28. Cash versus accrual basis of accounting. McKindly Consultants, Inc., opens a consulting business on July 1, Year 2. Dick Gray and Paula Mosenthal each contribute $50,000 cash for shares of the firm's common stock. The corporation borrows $60,000 from a local bank on August 1, Year 2. The loan is repayable on July 31, Year 3, with interest at the rate of 8 percent per year.

    The firm rents office space on August 1, paying two months' rent in advance. It pays the remaining monthly rental fees of $1,500 per month on the first of each month, beginning October 1. The firm purchases office equipment with a five-year life for cash on August 1 for $24,000.

The firm renders consulting services for clients between August 1 and December 31, Year 2, totaling $135,000. It collects $109,000 of this amount by year-end.

    It incurs and pays other costs by the end of the year as follows: utilities, $3,460; salaries, $98,500; supplies, $2,790. It has unpaid bills at year-end as follows: utilities, $580; salaries, $11,300; supplies, $840. The firm used all the supplies it had acquired.

    a. Prepare an income statement for the five months ended December 31, Year 2, assuming that the corporation uses the accrual basis of accounting and recognizes revenue at the time it renders services.

    b. Prepare an income statement for the five months ended December 31, Year 2, assuming that the corporation uses the cash basis of accounting.

    c. Which basis of accounting do you believe provides a better indication of the operating performance of the consulting firm for the period? Why?

29. Preparing income statement and balance sheet using accrual basis. Bob Hansen opens a retail store on January 1, Year 8. Hansen invests $50,000 for all of the common stock of the firm. The store borrows $40,000 from a local bank. The store must repay the loan with interest for both Year 8 and Year 9 on December 31, Year 9. The interest rate is 10 percent per year. The store purchases a building for $60,000 cash for use as a retail store. The building has a 30-year life, zero estimated salvage value, and is to be depreciated using the straight-line method.

The store purchases $125,000 of merchandise on account during Year 8 and pays $97,400 of the amount by the end of Year 8. A physical inventory taken on December 31, Year 8 indicates $15,400 of merchandise is still on hand.

During Year 8, the store makes cash sales to customers totaling $52,900 and sales on account totaling $116,100. Of the sales on account, the store collects $54,800 by December 31, Year 8.

The store incurs and pays other costs as follows: salaries, $34,200; utilities, $2,600. It has unpaid bills at the end of Year 8 as follows: salaries, $2,400; utilities, $180. The firm is subject to an income tax rate of 40 percent. Income taxes for Year 8 are payable on March 15, Year 9.

a. Prepare an income statement for Hansen Retail Store for Year 8, assuming that the retail store uses the accrual basis of accounting and recognizes revenue at the time of sale. Show supporting computations for each revenue and expense.

b. Prepare a balance sheet for Hansen Retail Store as of December 31, Year 8. Show supporting computations for each balance sheet item.

30. **Miscellaneous transactions and adjusting entries.** Give the journal entry to record (1) each of the following transactions as well as (2) any necessary adjusting entries on December 31, Year 6, assuming that the firm uses a calendar-year accounting period. You may omit explanations for the journal entries.

a. Sung Corporation gives a 60-day note to a supplier on December 2, Year 6. The note in the face amount of $6,000 replaces an open account payable of the same amount. The note is due on January 30, Year 7, with interest at 10 percent per year.

b. Allstate Insurance Company sells a two-year insurance policy on September 1, Year 6, receiving the two-year premium of $18,000 in advance. It credits a liability account.

c. Blaydon Company acquires a machine on October 1, Year 6, for $40,000 cash. It expects the machine to have a $4,000 salvage value and a four-year life.

d. Pyke Electronics Company acquires an automobile on July 1, Year 6, for $24,000 cash. It expects the automobile to have a $3,000 salvage value and a three-year life.

e. Devine Company rents needed office space for the three-month period beginning December 1, Year 6. It pays the three months' total rent of $12,000 on this date, debiting an asset account.

f. Hall Corporation begins business on November 1, Year 6. It acquires office supplies costing $7,000 on account, debiting an asset account. Of this amount, it pays $5,000 by year-end. A physical inventory indicates that office supplies costing $1,500 are on hand on December 31, Year 6.

31. **Miscellaneous transactions and adjusting entries.** Give the journal entry to record (1) each of the following transactions as well as (2) any necessary adjusting entries on December 31, Year 3, assuming that the firm uses a calendar-year accounting period. You may omit explanations for the journal entries.

a. Gale Company rents out excess office space on October 1, Year 3. It receives on that date the annual rental of $48,000 for the period from October 1, Year 3, to September 30, Year 4, and credits a liability account.

b. Whitley Company receives a $10,000, two-month, 6-percent note on December 1, Year 3, in full payment of an open account receivable.

c. The balance in the Prepaid Insurance account of Pierce Company on January 1, Year 3, was $500. On March 1, Year 3, the company renews its only insurance policy for another two years, beginning on that date, by paying the $6,600 two-year premium. It debits an asset account for the payment.

d. The Repair Parts Inventory account of Kelly Company showed a balance of $4,000 on January 1, Year 3. During Year 3, the firm purchases parts costing $14,900 and charges them to Retained Earnings (Repair Expense). An inventory of repair parts at the end of December reveals parts costing $3,800 on hand.

e. Roberts Company acquires with cash an office machine on July 1, Year 3, costing $200,000. It estimates that the machine will have a 10-year life and a $20,000 residual value. It uses the straight-line depreciation method.

f. Lovejoy Company pays its property taxes for the year ending December 31, Year 3, of $12,000 on September 1, Year 3. It debits Retained Earnings (Property Tax Expense) at the time of the payment.

32. Spreadsheet analysis of transactions and preparation of income statement and balance sheet. Refer to the information for Moulton Corporation as of December 31, Year 12 in **Problem 29** of **Chapter 2**. Moulton Corporation opened for business on January 1, Year 13. It uses the accrual basis of accounting. Transactions and events during Year 13 were as follows:

(1) During Year 13: Purchased inventory on account costing $1,100,000 from various suppliers.

(2) During Year 13: Sold merchandise to customers for $2,000,000 on account.

(3) During Year 13: The cost of merchandise sold to customers totaled $1,200,000.

(4) During Year 13: Collected $1,400,000 from customers for sales made previously on account.

(5) During Year 13: Paid merchandise suppliers $950,000 for purchases made previously on account.

(6) During Year 13: Paid various suppliers of selling and administrative services $625,000. The firm consumed all of the benefits of these services during Year 13.

(7) June 30, Year 13: Repaid the note payable to a supplier with interest (see transaction (7) in **Problem 2.29**).

(8) December 31, Year 13: Recognized interest on the long-term bank loan (see transaction (6) in **Problem 2.29**).

(9) December 31, Year 13: Recognized insurance expense for Year 13 (see transaction (5) in **Problem 2.29**).

(10) December 31, Year 13: Recognized depreciation expense for Year 13 (see transactions (2) and (7) of **Problem 2.29**).

(11) December 31, Year 13: Recognize income tax expense and income tax payable for Year 13. The income tax rate is 40 percent. Assume that income taxes for Year 13 are payable by March 15, Year 14.

a. Using the transactions spreadsheet template available with this book, enter the balances in balance sheet accounts on January 1, Year 13 (see **Problem 29** in **Chapter 2**) and the effects of the 11 transactions above. Be sure that you enter the dual effects of each transaction so that you maintain the balance sheet equality of assets with liabilities and shareholders' equity.

b. Prepare an income statement for Year 13.

c. Prepare a comparative balance sheet as of December 31, Year 12, and December 31, Year 13.

33. Spreadsheet analysis of transactions and preparation of income statement and balance sheet. Refer to the information for Regaldo Department Stores as of January 31, Year 8 in **Problem 30** of **Chapter 2**. Regaldo Department Stores opened for business during February, Year 8. It uses the accrual basis of accounting. Transactions and events during February were as follows.

(1) February 1: Purchased display counters and computer equipment for Ps90,000. The firm borrowed Ps90,000 from a local bank to finance the purchases. The bank loan bears interest at a rate of 12 percent each year and is repayable with interest on February 1, Year 9.

(2) During February: Purchased merchandise on account totaling Ps217,900.

(3) During February: Sold merchandise costing Ps162,400 to various customers for Ps62,900 cash and Ps194,600 on account. *Hint:* Enter the sales transaction and the recognition of the cost of goods sold in separate columns on the spreadsheet.

(4) During February: Paid to employees compensation totaling Ps32,400 for services rendered during the month.

(5) During February: Paid utility (electric, water, gas) bills totaling Ps2,700 for services received during February.

(6) During February: Collected Ps84,600 from customers from sales on account (see transaction (3) above).

(7) During February: Paid invoices from suppliers of merchandise (see transaction (2) above) with an original purchase price of Ps210,000 in time to receive a 2-percent discount for prompt payment and Ps29,000 to other suppliers after the discount period had elapsed. The firm treats discounts taken as a reduction in the acquisition cost of merchandise. *Hint:* Enter the payment of accounts payable within the discount period and after the discount period in separate columns on the spreadsheet.

(8) February 28: Compensation that employees earned during the last several days in February and that the firm will pay early in March totaled Ps6,700.

(9) February 28: Utility services that the firm used during February and that the firm will not pay until March totaled Ps800.

(10) February 28: The display counters and computer equipment purchased in transaction (1) have an expected useful life of five years and zero salvage value at the end of the five years. The firm depreciates such equipment on a straight-line basis over the expected life and uses an Accumulated Depreciation account.

(11) February 28: The firm recognizes an appropriate portion of the prepaid rent as of January 31 (see **Problem 30** in **Chapter 2**).

(12) February 28: The firm recognizes an appropriate portion of the prepaid insurance as of January 31 (see **Problem 30** in **Chapter 2**).

(13) February 28: The firm amortizes (that is, recognizes as an expense) the patent over 60 months (see **Problem 30** in **Chapter 2**). The firm does not use a separate Accumulated Amortization account for the patent.

(14) February 28: The firm recognizes an appropriate amount of interest expense on the loan in transaction (1) above.

(15) February 28: The firm is subject to an income tax rate of 30 percent of net income before income taxes. The income tax law requires firms to pay income taxes on the fifteenth day of the month after the end of each quarter (that is, April 15, July 15, October 15, and January 15).

   a. Using the transactions spreadsheet template available with this book, enter the balances in balance sheet accounts on February 1, Year 8 (see **Problem 30** in **Chapter 2**) and the effects of the 15 transactions above. Be sure that you enter the dual effects of each transaction so that you maintain the balance sheet equality of assets with liabilities and shareholders' equity.

   b. Prepare an income statement for the month of February, Year 8.

   c. Prepare a comparative balance sheet as of January 31 and February 28, Year 8.

34. **Spreadsheet analysis of transactions and preparation of income statement and balance sheet.** Refer to the information for Patterson Corporation for January, Year 13, in **Problem 31** in **Chapter 2**. The following transactions occur during February.

   (1) February 1: The firm pays the two-year insurance premium of $2,400 for fire and liability coverage beginning February 1.

   (2) February 5: Acquires merchandise costing $1,050,000. Of this amount, $1,455 is from suppliers to whom Patterson returned defective merchandise during January but for which the firm had not yet received a refund for amounts paid. Patterson Corporation acquired the remaining purchases on account.

   (3) During February: Sells merchandise to customers totaling $1,500,000. Of this amount, $4,500 was to customers who had advanced Patterson Corporation cash during January. Patterson Corporation makes the remaining sales on account.

   (4) During February: The cost of the goods sold in transaction (3) was $950,000.

   (5) During February: Pays in cash selling and administrative expenses of $235,000.

   (6) During February: Collects $1,206,000 from customer for sales previously made on account.

   (7) During February: Pays $710,000 to suppliers of merchandise for purchases previously made on account.

   (8) February 28: Recognizes rent expense for February.

   (9) February 28: Recognizes depreciation expense of $2,500 for February. Patterson Corporation uses an Accumulated Depreciation account.

   (10) February 28: Recognizes amortization expense of $450 on the patent. Patterson Corporation does not use an Accumulated Amortization account for patents.

   (11) February 28: Recognizes an appropriate amount of insurance expense for February.

   (12) February 28: Recognizes interest expense on the mortgage payable (see **Problem 31** in **Chapter 2**).

   (13) February 28: Recognizes income tax expense for February. The income tax rate is 40 percent. Income taxes for February are payable by April 15.

   a. Using the transactions spreadsheet template available with this book, enter the balances in balance sheet accounts on February 1, Year 13 (see **Problem 31** in **Chapter 2**), and the effects of the 12 transactions above. Be sure that you enter the dual effects of each transaction so that you maintain the balance sheet equality of assets with liabilities and shareholders' equity.

   b. Prepare an income statement for the month of February, Year 13.

   c. Prepare a comparative balance sheet as January 31 and February 28, Year 13.

35. **Spreadsheet analysis of transactions and preparation of income statement and balance sheet.** Zealock Bookstore opened a bookstore near a college campus on July 1, Year 10.

Transactions and events of Zealock Bookstore during Year 10 appear below. The firm uses the calendar year as its reporting period.

(1) July 1: Receives $25,000 from Quinn Zealock for 25,000 shares of the bookstore's $1 par value common stock.

(2) July 1: Obtains a $30,000 loan from a local bank for working capital needs. The loan bears interest at 6 percent per year. The loan is repayable with interest on June 30, Year 11.

(3) July 1: Signs a rental agreement for three years at an annual rental of $20,000. Pays the first year's rent in advance.

(4) July 1: Acquires bookshelves for $4,000 cash. The bookshelves have an estimated useful life of 5 years and zero salvage value.

(5) July 1: Acquires computers for $10,000 cash. The computers have an estimated useful life of 3 years and $1,000 salvage value.

(6) July 1: Makes security deposits with various book distributors totaling $8,000. The deposits are refundable on June 30, Year 11 if the bookstore pays on time all amounts due for books purchased from the distributors between July 1, Year 10 and June 30, Year 11.

(7) During Year 10: Purchases books on account from various distributors costing $160,000.

(8) During Year 10: Sells books costing $140,000 for $172,800. Of the total sales, $24,600 is for cash and $148,200 is on account. *Hint:* Enter the sales transaction in a separate column in the spreadsheet than the recognition of the cost of goods sold.

(9) During Year 10: Returns unsold books and books ordered in error costing $14,600. The firm had not yet paid for these books.

(10) During Year 10: Collects $142,400 from sales on account.

(11) During Year 10: Pays employees compensation of $16,700.

(12) During Year 10: Pays book distributors $139,800 of the amounts due for purchases on account.

(13) December 28, Year 10: Receives advances from customers of $850 for special order books that the bookstore will order and expects to receive during Year 11.

(14) December 31, Year 10: Records an appropriate amount of interest expense on the loan in **(2)** for Year 10.

(15) December 31, Year 10: Records an appropriate amount of rent expense for Year 10.

(16) December 31, Year 10: Records an appropriate amount of depreciation expense on the bookshelves in **(4)**.

(17) December 31, Year 10: Records an appropriate amount of depreciation expense on the computers in **(5)**.

(18) December 31, Year 10: Records an appropriate amount of deposit expense from **(6)**.

(19) December 31, Year 10: Records an appropriate amount of income tax expense for Year 10. The income tax rate is 40 percent. The taxes are payable on March 15, Year 11.

  a. Using the transactions spreadsheet template available with this book, enter the 19 transactions and events above.

  b. Prepare an income statement for Year 10.

  c. Prepare a balance sheet on December 31, Year 10. Classify assets and liabilities as current and noncurrent.

  d. Evaluate the operating performance for Year 10 and financial health of Zealock Bookstore at the end of Year 10.

36. Spreadsheet analysis of transactions and preparation of comparative income statements and balance sheets. Refer to the information for Zealock Bookstore in problem 35. The following transactions relate to Year 11.

  (1) March 15: Pays income taxes for Year 10.

  (2) June 30: Repays the bank loan with interest.

  (3) July 1: Obtains a new bank loan for $75,000. The loan is repayable on June 30, Year 12, with interest due at maturity of 8 percent.

  (4) July 1: Receives the security deposit back from the book distributors.

  (5) July 1: Pays the rent due for the period July 1, Year 11, to June 30, Year 12.

  (6) During Year 11: Purchases books on account costing $310,000.

  (7) During Year 11: Sells books costing $286,400 for $353,700. Of the total sales, $24,900 is for cash, $850 is from special orders received during December Year 10, and $327,950 is on account.

  (8) During Year 11: Returns unsold books costing $22,700. The firm had not yet paid for these books.

  (9) During Year 11: Collects $320,600 from sales on account.

  (10) During Year 11: Pays employees compensation of $29,400.

(11) During Year 11: Pays book distributors $281,100 for purchases of books on account.

(12) December 31, Year 11: Declares and pays a dividend of $4,000.

  a. Using the transactions spreadsheet template available with this book, enter the amounts for the balance sheet on December 31, Year 10, from **Problem 35**, the effects of the 12 transaction above, and any required entries on December 31, Year 11, to properly measure net income for Year 11 and financial position on December 31, Year 11.

  b. Prepare a comparative income statement for Year 10 and Year 11.

  c. Prepare a comparative balance sheet for December 31, Year 10, and December 31, Year 11.

  d. Evaluate the operating performance and financial health of Zealock Bookstore.

37. **Working backward to the balance sheet at the beginning of the period. (Problems 37** through **39** derive from problems by George H. Sorter.) The following data relate to the Prima Company.

  (1) Exhibit 3.12: Balance sheet at December 31, Year 2

  (2) Exhibit 3.13: Statement of net income and retained earnings for Year 2.

  (3) Exhibit 3.14: Statement of cash receipts and disbursements for Year 2

  Purchases of merchandise during the period, all on account, were $127,000. All "Other Operating Expenses" were credited to Prepayments.

  Prepare a balance sheet for January 1, Year 2. (*Hint:* Using the transactions spreadsheet template available with this book, set up row labels for each of the accounts in the balance sheet and enter the December 31, Year 2 amounts from the balance sheet in the last column of the spreadsheet. Using the information in the income statement and statement of cash receipts and disbursements, reconstruct the transactions that took place during the year and enter the amounts in the appropriate rows and columns of the spreadsheet. Finally, program the cells under the January 1, Year 2, column to compute the amounts in balance sheet accounts on January 1, Year 2).

38. **Working backward to cash receipts and disbursements. Exhibit 3.15** presents the comparative balance sheet of The Secunda Company as of the beginning and end of Year 2. **Exhibit 3.16** presents the income statement for Year 2. The company makes all sales on account and purchases all goods and services on account. The Other Operating Expenses account includes

EXHIBIT 3.12	PRIMA COMPANY Balance Sheet December 31, Year 2 (Problem 37)

Assets

Cash	$ 10,000
Marketable Securities	20,000
Accounts Receivable	25,000
Merchandise Inventory	30,000
Prepayments for Miscellaneous Services	3,000
Total Current Assets	$ 88,000
Land, Buildings, and Equipment (at cost)	40,000
Less Accumulated Depreciation	(16,000)
Land, Buildings, and Equipment (net)	$ 24,000
Total Assets	$112,000

Liabilities and Shareholders' Equity

Accounts Payable (for merchandise)	$ 25,000
Interest Payable	300
Taxes Payable	4,000
Total Current Liabilities	$ 29,300
Note Payable (6 percent, long-term)	20,000
Total Liabilities	$ 49,300
Common Stock	50,000
Retained Earnings	12,700
Total Shareholders' Equity	$ 62,700
Total Liabilities and Shareholders' Equity	$112,000

EXHIBIT 3.13	**PRIMA COMPANY** **Statement of Net Income and Retained Earnings** **for Year 2** **(Problem 37)**		
Sales...			$200,000
Less Expenses:			
Cost of Goods Sold	$130,000		
Depreciation Expense.....................................	4,000		
Taxes Expense...	8,000		
Other Operating Expenses.................................	47,700		
Interest Expense...	1,200		
Total Expenses		190,900	
Net Income		$ 9,100	
Less Dividends		5,000	
Increase in Retained Earnings.............................		$ 4,100	

EXHIBIT 3.14	**PRIMA COMPANY** **Statement of Cash Receipts and Disbursements** **for Year 2** **(Problem 37)**		
Cash Receipts			
Cash Sales	$ 47,000		
Collection from Credit Customers.........................	150,000		
Total Receipts		$197,000	
Cash Disbursements			
Payment to Suppliers of Merchandise......................	$128,000		
Payment to Suppliers of Miscellaneous Services.............	49,000		
Payment of Taxes	7,500		
Payment of Interest......................................	1,200		
Payment of Dividends	5,000		
Purchase of Marketable Securities	8,000		
Total Disbursements...................................		198,700	
Excess of Disbursements over Receipts.....................		$ 1,700	

depreciation charges and expirations of prepayments. The company debits dividends declared during the year to Retained Earnings.

Prepare a schedule showing all cash transactions for Year 2. (*Hint:* Using the transactions spreadsheet template available with this book, set up accounts for each of the accounts in the balance sheet and enter the amounts shown as of January 1, Year 2, and December 31, Year 2. Starting with the revenue and expense accounts, reconstruct the transactions that took place during the year, and enter the amounts in the appropriate columns and rows of the spreadsheet. The Retained Earnings account in the balance sheet on December 31, Year 2, reflects the effects of earnings and dividends activities during Year 2.)

39. **Working backward to the income statement.** Tertia Company presents balance sheets at the beginning and end of Year 2 (**Exhibit 3.17**), as well as a statement of cash receipts and disbursements (**Exhibit 3.18**). Prepare a combined statement of income and retained earnings for Year 2. (*Hint:* Using the transactions spreadsheet template available with this book, set up accounts for each of the balance sheet accounts and enter the amounts shown as of January 1, Year 2, and December 31, Year 2. Starting with the cash receipts and disbursements for the year, reconstruct the transactions that took place during the year, and enter them in the appropriate rows and columns of the spreadsheet. The Retained Earnings account reflects the effect of earnings activities and dividends for Year 2.)

40. **Reconstructing the income statement and balance sheet.** (Adapted from a problem by Stephen A. Zeff.) Portobello Co., a firm that sells merchandise to retail customers, is in its

EXHIBIT 3.15	THE SECUNDA COMPANY Balance Sheet January 1 and December 31, Year 2 (Problem 38)		

	1/1/Year 2	12/31/Year 2
Assets		
Cash	$ 20,000	$ 9,000
Accounts Receivable	36,000	51,000
Merchandise Inventory.	45,000	60,000
Prepayments.	2,000	1,000
Total Current Assets	$103,000	$121,000
Land, Buildings, and Equipment (at cost).	$ 40,000	$ 40,000
Less Accumulated Depreciation	(16,000)	(18,000)
Land, Buildings, and Equipment (net)	$ 24,000	$ 22,000
Total Assets	$127,000	$143,000
Liabilities and Shareholders' Equity		
Interest Payable	$ 1,000	$ 2,000
Accounts Payable	30,000	40,000
Total Current Liabilities	$ 31,000	$ 42,000
Mortgage Payable	20,000	17,000
Total Liabilities	$ 51,000	$ 59,000
Common Stock	$ 50,000	$ 50,000
Retained Earnings	26,000	34,000
Total Shareholders' Equity	$ 76,000	$ 84,000
Total Liabilities and Shareholders' Equity	$127,000	$143,000

EXHIBIT 3.16	THE SECUNDA COMPANY Income Statement For Year 2 (Problem 38)		

Sales Revenue.		$100,000
Less Expenses:		
Cost of Goods Sold	$50,000	
Interest Expense.	3,000	
Other Operating Expenses.	29,000	
Total Expenses.		82,000
Net Income		$ 18,000

tenth year of operation. On December 28, Year 10, three days before the close of its fiscal year, a flash flood devastated the company's administrative office and destroyed almost all of its accounting records. The company was able to save the balance sheet on December 31, Year 9 (see **Exhibit 3.19**), the checkbook, the bank statements, and some soggy remains of the specific accounts receivable and accounts payable balances. Based on a review of the surviving documents and a series of interviews with company employees, you obtain the following information.

(1) The company's insurance agency advises that a four-year insurance policy has six months to run as of December 31, Year 10. The policy cost $12,000 when the company paid the four-year premium during Year 7.

(2) During Year 10, the company's board of directors declared $6,000 of dividends, of which the firm paid $3,000 in cash to shareholders during Year 10 and will pay the remainder during Year 11. Early in Year 10, the company also paid dividends of $1,800 cash that the board of directors had declared during Year 9.

EXHIBIT 3.17	TERTIA COMPANY Balance Sheets January 1 and December 31, Year 2 (Problem 39)		

	1/1/Year 2	12/31/Year 2
Assets		
Cash	$ 40,000	$ 67,800
Accounts and Notes Receivable	36,000	41,000
Merchandise Inventory	55,000	49,500
Interest Receivable	1,000	700
Prepaid Miscellaneous Services	4,000	5,200
Building, Machinery, and Equipment	47,000	47,000
Accumulated Depreciation	(10,000)	(12,000)
Total Assets	$173,000	$199,200
Liabilities and Shareholders' Equity		
Accounts Payable (miscellaneous services)	$ 2,000	$ 2,500
Accounts Payable (merchandise purchases)	34,000	41,000
Property Taxes Payable	1,000	1,500
Mortgage Payable	35,000	30,000
Total Liabilities	$ 72,000	$ 75,000
Common Stock	$ 25,000	$ 25,000
Retained Earnings	76,000	99,200
Total Shareholders Equity	$101,000	$124,200
Total Liabilities and Shareholders' Equity	$173,000	$199,200

EXHIBIT 3.18	TERTIA COMPANY Statement of Cash Receipts and Disbursements For Year 2 (Problem 39)	

	Year 2
Cash Receipts	
1. Collection from Credit Customers	$144,000
2. Cash Sales	63,000
3. Collection of Interest	1,000
Total Cash Receipts	$208,000
Less Cash Disbursements	
4. Payment to Suppliers of Merchandise	$114,000
5. Repayment on Mortgage	5,000
6. Payment of Interest	500
7. Prepayment to Suppliers of Miscellaneous Services	57,500
8. Payment of Property Taxes	1,200
9. Payment of Dividends	2,000
Total Cash Disbursements	$180,200
Increase in Cash Balance for Year 2	$ 27,800

(3) On April 1, Year 10, the company received from Appleton Co. $10,900 cash, which included principal of $10,000 and interest, in full settlement of Appleton's nine-month note dated July 1, Year 9. According to the terms of the note, Appleton paid all interest at maturity on April 1, Year 10.

(4) The amount owed by the company to merchandise suppliers on December 31, Year 10, was $20,000 less than the amount owed on December 31, Year 9. During Year 10, the

	PORTOBELLO CO.
EXHIBIT 3.19	Balance Sheet December 31, Year 9 (Problem 40)

Assets

Cash	$ 18,600
Accounts Receivable	33,000
Notes Receivable	10,000
Interest Receivable	600
Merchandise Inventories	22,000
Prepaid Insurance	4,500
Total Current Assets	$ 88,700
Computer System:	
At Cost	$ 78,000
Less Accumulated Depreciation	(26,000)
Net	$ 52,000
Total Assets	$140,700

Liabilities and Shareholders' Equity

Accounts Payable for Merchandise	$ 36,000
Dividend Payable	1,800
Salaries Payable	6,500
Taxes Payable	10,000
Advances from Customers	600
Total Liabilities	$ 54,900
Common Stock	$ 40,000
Retained Earnings	45,800
Total Shareholders' Equity	$ 85,800
Total Liabilities and Shareholders' Equity	$140,700

company paid $115,000 to merchandise suppliers. The cost of merchandise inventory on December 31, Year 10, based on a physical count, was $18,000 larger than the balance in the Merchandise Inventory account on the December 31, Year 9, balance sheet. On December 8, Year 10, the company exchanged shares of its common stock for merchandise inventory costing $11,000. The company's policy is to purchase all merchandise on account.

(5) The company purchased delivery trucks on March 1, Year 10, for $60,000. To finance the acquisition, it gave the seller a $60,000 four-year note that bears interest at 10 percent per year. The company must pay interest on the note each six months, beginning September 1, Year 10. The company made the required payment on this date. The delivery trucks have an expected useful life of 10 years and an estimated salvage value of $6,000. The company uses the straight-line depreciation method.

(6) The company's computer system has a six-year total expected life and zero expected salvage value.

(7) The company makes all sales on account and recognizes revenue at the time of shipment to customers. During Year 10, the company received $210,000 cash from its customers. The company's accountant reconstructed the Accounts Receivable subsidiary ledger, the detailed record of the amount owed to the company by each customer. It showed that customers owed the company $51,000 on December 31, Year 10. A close examination revealed that $1,400 of the cash received from customers during Year 10 applies to merchandise that the company will not ship until Year 11. Also, $600 of the cash received from customers during Year 9 applies to merchandise not shipped to customers until Year 10.

(8) The company paid $85,000 in cash to employees during Year 10. Of this amount, $6,500 relates to services that employees performed during Year 9, and $4,000 relates to services that employees will perform during Year 11. Employees performed the remainder

of the services during Year 10. On December 31, Year 10, the company owes employees $1,300 for services performed during the last several days of Year 10.

(9) The company paid $27,000 in cash for property and income taxes during Year 10. Of this amount, $10,000 relates to income taxes applicable to Year 9, and $3,000 relates to property taxes applicable to Year 11. The company owes $4,000 in income taxes on December 31, Year 10.

(10) The company entered into a contract with a management consulting firm for consulting services. The total contract price is $48,000. The contract requires the company to pay the first installment of $12,000 cash on January 1, Year 11, and the company intends to do so. The consulting firm had performed 10 percent of the estimated total consulting services under the contract by December 31, Year 10.

Prepare an income statement for Year 10 and a balance sheet on December 31, Year 10. (*Hint:* Using the transactions spreadsheet available with this book, set up accounts for each of the accounts on the December 31, Year 9, balance sheet, and enter the appropriate amounts at that time. Next, enter the information for each of the 10 items, listed above, in the T-accounts, adding income statement and additional balance sheet accounts as needed.)

41. Reconstructing the income statement and balance sheet. Computer Needs, Inc., operates a retail store that sells computer hardware and software. It began operations on January 2, Year 8, and operated successfully during its first year, generating net income of $8,710 and ending the year with $15,600 in its bank account. **Exhibit 3.20** presents an income statement for Year 8, and **Exhibit 3.21** presents a balance sheet as of the end of Year 8.

As Year 9 progressed, the owners and managers of Computer Needs, Inc., felt that they were doing even better. Sales seemed to be running ahead of Year 8, and customers were always in the store. Unfortunately, a freak lightning storm hit the store on December 31, Year 9, and completely destroyed the computer on which Computer Needs, Inc., kept its records. It now faces the dilemma of figuring how much income it generated during Year 9 in order to assess its operating performance and figure out how much income taxes it owes for the year.

You are asked to prepare an income statement for Year 9 and a balance sheet at the end of Year 9. To assist in this effort, you obtain the following information.

(1) The bank at which Computer Needs, Inc., maintains its account provided a summary of the transactions during Year 9, as shown in **Exhibit 3.22**.

(2) Collections received during January, Year 10, from third-party credit card companies and from customers for sales made during Year 9 totaled $40,300. This is your best estimate of accounts receivable outstanding on December 31, Year 9.

(3) A physical inventory of merchandise was taken on January 1, Year 10. Using current catalogs from suppliers, you estimate that the merchandise has an approximate cost of $60,700.

(4) Computer Needs, Inc., had paid its annual insurance premium on October 1, Year 9 (included in the amounts in **Exhibit 3.22**). You learn that $1,800 of the insurance premium applies to coverage during Year 10.

(5) Based on depreciation claimed during Year 8 and new equipment purchased during Year 9, you approximate that depreciation expense for Year 9 was $3,300.

(6) Bills received from merchandise suppliers during January, Year 10, totaled $45,300. This is your best estimate of accounts payable outstanding to these suppliers on December 31, Year 9.

EXHIBIT 3.20	COMPUTER NEEDS, INC. Income Statement For the Year Ended December 31, Year 8 (Problem 41)

Sales	$152,700
Cost of Goods Sold	(116,400)
Selling and Administrative Expenses	(17,400)
Depreciation	(2,800)
Interest	(4,000)
Income Taxes	(3,388)
Net Income	$ 8,712

	COMPUTER NEEDS, INC. Balance Sheet December 31, Year 8 (Problem 41)
EXHIBIT 3.21	

Assets

Cash	$ 15,600
Accounts Receivable	32,100
Inventories	46,700
Prepayments	1,500
Total Current Assets	$ 95,900
Property, Plant, and Equipment:	
At Cost	$ 59,700
Less Accumulated Depreciation	(2,800)
Net	$ 56,900
Total Assets	$152,800

Liabilities and Shareholders' Equity

Accounts Payable—Merchandise Suppliers	$ 37,800
Income Tax Payable	3,388
Other Current Liabilities	2,900
Total Current Liabilities	$ 44,088
Mortgage Payable	50,000
Total Liabilities	$ 94,088
Common Stock	$ 50,000
Retained Earnings	8,712
Total Shareholders' Equity	$ 58,712
Total Liabilities and Shareholders' Equity	$152,800

	COMPUTER NEEDS, INC. Analysis of Changes in Bank Accounts For the Year Ended December 31, Year 9 (Problem 41)
EXHIBIT 3.22	

Balance, January 1, Year 9	$ 15,600
Receipts:	
Cash from Cash Sales	37,500
Checks Received from Third-Party Credit Cards and Customers ...	151,500
Disbursements:	
To Merchandise Supplier	(164,600)
To Employees and Other Providers of Selling and Administrative Activities	(21,000)
To U.S. Government for Income Taxes for Year 8	(3,388)
To Bank for Interest ($4,000) and Principal on Mortgage ($800) ..	(4,800)
To Supplier of Equipment	(6,000)
Balance, December 31, Year 9	$ 4,812

(7) Other Current Liabilities represent amounts payable to employees and other providers of selling and administrative services. Other Current Liabilities as of December 31, Year 9, total $1,200.

a. Prepare an income statement for Computer Needs, Inc., for Year 9 and a balance sheet on December 31, Year 9. The income tax rate is 28 percent. (*Hint:* Using the transactions spreadsheet template available with this book, set up accounts for each of the balance sheet accounts on December 31, Year 8, and enter the balances in these accounts on that date. Then enter the information in items (**1**) to (**7**) above to derive the income statement amounts for Year 9.)

b. How well did Computer Needs, Inc., perform during Year 9?

42. **Interpreting common-size income statements. Exhibit 3.23** presents common-size income statements for The GAP and Limited Brands, two apparel retailing firms, for three recent years. In addition to the cost of merchandise sold, both firms include occupancy expense for their stores (rent, utilities, depreciation) in cost of goods sold. The GAP tends to rely on print advertising to create demand, whereas Limited Brands relies more heavily on in-store promotions (2-for-1 discounts and special daily price reductions). The GAP recently expanded into other countries, whereas Limited Brands operates almost exclusively in the United States.

EXHIBIT 3.23	Common-Size Income Statements for The GAP and Limited Brands (Problem 42)					
	The GAP			**Limited Brands**		
	Year 8	Year 9	Year 10	Year 8	Year 9	Year 10
Sales	100.0%	100.0%	100.0%	100.0%	100.0%	100.0%
Other Revenues	0.2	0.1	1.2	0.4	0.6	0.5
Cost of Goods Sold or Services Sold	(59.0)	(56.8)	(56.0)	(66.2)	(64.1)	(62.8)
Selling and Administrative Expenses	(25.8)	(26.5)	(26.7)	(23.1)	(24.6)	(25.3)
Interest Expense	(3.0)	(2.2)	(2.2)	(5.3)	(5.4)	(5.5)
Income Tax Expense	(4.2)	(5.5)	(6.6)	(2.0)	(2.3)	(2.4)
Net Income/Sales	8.2%	9.1%	9.7%	3.8%	4.2%	4.5%

   a. Suggest possible reasons for the decreasing cost of goods sold to sales percentages for the two firms during the three-year period.
   b. Suggest possible reasons why the cost of goods sold to sales percentages for The GAP are less than that for Limited Brands.
   c. Suggest possible reasons for the increasing selling and administrative expenses to sales percentages for the two firms for the three-year period.
   d. Suggest possible reasons why the selling and administrative expenses to sales percentages for Limited Brands are less than that for The GAP.
   e. Suggest possible reasons for the different pattern of changes in the interest expense to sales percentages for the two firms during the three-year period.
   f. Suggest possible reasons for the increasing income tax expense to sales percentages for the two firms during the three-year period.
   g. Are the profit margin percentages of The GAP or those of Limited Brands closer to the level you would expect for a specialty apparel retailer? Explain your reasoning. You may wish to refer to the data for the five firms in **Exhibit 3.8** in responding to this question.

43. **Interpreting common-size income statements.** The Coca-Cola Company (Coke) and PepsiCo dominate the non-alcoholic beverage segment in the United States. Most beverage manufacturing involves adding water to a previously prepared syrup. This mixing process usually occurs at the stage just prior to bottling the beverage. Coke relies on independent companies to conduct the mixing, bottling, and distribution operations, with Coke selling the syrup to the bottlers. PepsiCo relies more heavily on owning its bottlers and thereby remains involved in both manufacturing and distribution. **Exhibit 3.24** present common-size income statements for Coke and PepsiCo for three recent years.
   a. Suggest possible reasons why the cost of goods sold to sales percentages for Coke are significantly lower than those of PepsiCo.
   b. Suggest reasons why the selling and administrative expense to sales percentages steadily increased for Coke but steadily decreased for PepsiCo.
   c. Suggest possible reasons for the decreasing interest expense to sales percentages for both firms.
   d. Coke's income tax expense to sales percentages are larger than those for PepsiCo, suggesting that Coke has a higher income tax burden. For a different perspective, compute the ratio of income tax expense to net income before income taxes for each firm. For

EXHIBIT 3.24	Common-Size Income Statements for Coke and PepsiCo (Problem 43)					
	Coke			**PepsiCo**		
	Year 10	**Year 11**	**Year 12**	**Year 10**	**Year 11**	**Year 12**
Sales	100.0%	100.0%	100.0%	100.0%	100.0%	100.0%
Other Revenues	0.9	3.3	1.2	0.8	0.9	1.3
Cost of Goods Sold	(35.7)	(34.4)	(36.3)	(45.8)	(45.7)	(45.8)
Selling and Administrative Expenses	(34.7)	(35.0)	(35.8)	(36.3)	(35.5)	(34.5)
Interest Expense	(2.6)	(1.6)	(1.0)	(1.2)	(0.9)	(0.7)
Income Tax Expense	(10.0)	(9.6)	(7.8)	(5.6)	(6.4)	(6.5)
Net Income	17.9%	22.7%	20.3%	11.9%	12.4%	13.8%
Sales Growth	1.8%	6.5%	8.2%	−2.7%	5.3%	6.8%

example, this percentage for Coke for Year 10 is 35.8 percent [= 10.0%/(17.9% + 10.0%)]. What insight does this measure provide regarding the income tax burden of Coke versus PepsiCo?

e. Compare the net income to sales percentages for Coke and PepsiCo with those of the five firms in **Exhibit 3.8**. Suggest reasons for the levels of the profit margins of Coke and PepsiCo relative to these other five firms.

44. **Interpreting common-size income statements.** Nokia has a 28 percent worldwide market share in cellular phones, the largest share of any company. Its sales have grown approximately 50 percent annually in recent years. Nokia's cellular phones use digital technology, which permits them to interact with computers and the Internet. **Exhibit 3.25** presents common-size income statements for Nokia for three recent years. Discuss the likely reasons for the increasing profit margin for Nokia over the three-year period.

45. **Interpreting common-size income statements.** McDonald's is the largest fast food restaurant chain in the United States. This segment of the restaurant market has experienced increased competition in recent years with aggressive actions from existing firms and the entry of new restaurant concepts. **Exhibit 3.26** presents common-size income statements for McDonald's for three recent years. Discuss the likely reasons for the decreasing profit margin for McDonald's over the three-year period.

46. **Identifying industries using common-size income statement percentages. Exhibit 3.27** presents common-size income statements for six firms. The six firms and a description of their operations follow.

a. Commonwealth Edison: generates and sells electricity to businesses and households in capital-intensive plants.

b. Delta Airlines: provides airline transportation services.

EXHIBIT 3.25	Common-Size Income Statements for Nokia (Problem 44)		
	Year 7	**Year 8**	**Year 9**
Sales	100.0%	100.0%	100.0%
Other Revenues	1.6	1.2	0.5
Cost of Goods Sold	(64.6)	(62.3)	(61.8)
Selling and Administrative Expenses	(10.4)	(10.3)	(9.5)
Research and Development Expense	(9.0)	(8.8)	(9.1)
Interest Expense	(1.9)	(1.5)	(1.2)
Income Tax Expense	(4.0)	(5.7)	(6.1)
Net Income/Sales	11.7%	12.6%	12.8%

EXHIBIT 3.26	Common-Size Income Statements for McDonald's (Problem 45)		

	Year 10	Year 11	Year 12
Sales	100.0%	100.0%	100.0%
Other Revenues	0.6	1.4	0.0
Cost of Goods Sold	(64.6)	(66.9)	(69.0)
Selling and Administrative Expenses	(11.1)	(11.1)	(11.2)
Interest Expense	(3.1)	(3.1)	(3.1)
Income Tax Expense	(7.1)	(6.4)	(5.0)
Net Income/Sales	14.7%	13.9%	11.7%

EXHIBIT 3.27	Common-Size Income Statements for Six Firms (Problem 46)					

	(1)	(2)	(3)	(4)	(5)	(6)
Sales	100.0%	100.0%	100.0%	100.0%	100.0%	100.0%
Other Revenues	—	—	0.5	0.9	—	—
Cost of Goods and Services Sold	(73.6)	(81.4)	(60.6)	(63.0)	(61.3)	(34.4)
Selling and Administrative Expenses	(19.9)	(14.1)	(17.9)	(24.0)	(5.0)	(40.9)
Depreciation	(2.1)	(0.8)	(5.1)	(3.4)	(8.7)	(3.9)
Interest	(1.4)	—	(8.0)	(0.9)	(7.3)	(0.8)
Income Taxes	(1.4)	(1.5)	(3.3)	(2.9)	(6.7)	(7.4)
Net Income	1.6%	2.2%	5.6%	6.7%	11.0%	12.6%

   c. Gillette: manufactures and sells a variety of branded consumer personal care and household products.

   d. Hewlett-Packard: manufactures and sells computers, printers, and other hardware.

   e. Kroger Stores: operates a chain of grocery stores nationwide.

   f. Kelly Services: provides temporary office services to businesses and other firms. Sales revenue represents amounts billed to customers for temporary help services and cost of goods and services sold includes amounts paid to Kelly temporary help employees.

     Use whatever clues you can to match the companies in **Exhibit 3.27** with the six firms listed above. Explain your reasoning.

47. Preparing adjusting entries. To achieve efficient recording of day-to-day cash receipts and disbursements relating to operations, a firm may credit all cash receipts to revenue accounts and debit all cash disbursements to expense accounts. The efficiency stems from treating all receipts in the same way and all disbursements in the same way. The firm can program its computer to automatically record operating cash receipts and disbursements in this way. In the day-to-day recording of transactions, the computer program need not be concerned with whether a specific cash transaction reflects settlement of a past accrual, a revenue or expense correctly assigned to the current period, or a prepayment relating to a future period. At the end of the period, accountants analyze the existing account balances and construct the adjusting entries required to correct them. This process results in temporarily incorrect balances in some balance sheet and income statement accounts during the accounting period.

     Construct the adjusting entry required for each of the following scenarios.

   a. On September 1, Year 2, a tenant paid $24,000 rent for the one-year period starting at that time. The tenant debited the entire amount to Rent Expense and credited Cash. The tenant made no adjusting entries for rent between September 1 and December 31. Construct the adjusting entry to be made on December 31, Year 2, to recognize the proper balances in the Prepaid Rent and Rent Expense accounts. What is the amount of Rent Expense for Year 2?

b. Refer to part **a**. The tenant's books for December 31, Year 2, after adjusting entries, show a balance in the Prepaid Rent account of $16,000. This amount represents rent for the period January 1 through August 31, Year 3. On September 1, Year 3, the tenant paid $30,000 for rent for the one-year period starting September 1, Year 3. The tenant debited this amount to Rent Expense and credited Cash but made no adjusting entries for rent during Year 3. Construct the adjusting entry required on December 31, Year 3. What is Rent Expense for Year 3?

c. Refer to part **b**. The tenant's books for December 31, Year 3, after adjusting entries, show a balance in the Prepaid Rent account of $20,000. This amount represents rent for the period January 1 through August 31, Year 4. On September 1, Year 4, the tenant paid $18,000 for rent for the six-month period starting September 1, Year 4. The tenant debited this amount to Rent Expense and credited Cash but made no adjusting entries during Year 4. Construct the adjusting entry required on December 31, Year 4. What is Rent Expense for Year 4?

d. Whenever the firm makes payments for wages, it debits Wage Expense. At the start of April, the Wages Payable account had a balance of $5,000, representing wages earned but not paid during the last few days of March. During April, the firm paid $30,000 in wages, debiting the entire amount to Wage Expense. At the end of April, analysis of amounts earned since the last payday indicates that employees have earned wages of $4,000 that they have not received. These are the only unpaid wages at the end of April. Construct the required adjusting entry. What is Wage Expense for April?

e. A firm purchased an insurance policy providing one year's coverage from May 1, Year 1, and debited the entire amount to Insurance Expense. After the firm made adjusting entries, the balance sheet on December 31, Year 1, correctly showed Prepaid Insurance of $3,000. Construct the adjusting entry that the firm must make on January 31, Year 2, if the firm closes its books monthly and prepares a balance sheet for January 31, Year 2.

f. The record-keeping system for an apartment building instructs the bookkeeper always to credit rent revenue when the firm collects a payment from tenants. At the beginning of Year 3, the liability account Advances from Tenants had a credit balance of $25,000, representing collections from tenants for rental services to be rendered during Year 3. During Year 3, the firm collected $250,000 from tenants; it debited Cash and credited Rent Revenue. It made no adjusting entries during Year 3. At the end of Year 3, analysis of the individual accounts indicates that of the amounts already collected, $30,000 represents collections for rental services to be provided to tenants during Year 4. Present the required adjusting entry. What is Rent Revenue for Year 3?

g. When the firm acquired new equipment costing $10,000 on January 1, Year 1, the bookkeeper debited Depreciation Expense and credited Cash for $10,000 but made no further entries for this equipment during Year 1. The equipment has an expected service life of five years and an estimated salvage value of zero. Construct the adjusting entry required before the accountant can prepare a balance sheet for December 31, Year 1.

48. Ethical issues in accounting choices. Firms must make various choices in applying generally accepted accounting principles under the accrual basis of accounting (for example, depreciable lives for buildings and equipment, estimated uncollectibles for accounts receivable, estimated warranty costs). Selected data from the financial statements of AMR (parent company of American Airlines), Delta Air Lines, and UAL (parent company of United Airlines) appear below (in millions):

	AMR	Delta	UAL
(1) Average Assets Subject to Depreciation and Amortization	$29,826.5	$24,919.5	$22,835.5
(2) Depreciation and Amortization Expense	$1,336.0	$1,181.0	$970.0
(3) Average Depreciation and Amortization Life: (3) = (1)/(2)	21.8 years	21.1 years	23.5 years
(4) Estimated Uncollectible Accounts as a Percentage of Accounts Receivable	7.1%	10.2%	3.5%

These firms provide similar types of airline services with similar types of assets. They each received unqualified opinions from their independent auditors. Yet, UAL appears to apply its accounting principles more aggressively in income-enhancing ways relative to AMR and Delta. Discuss any ethical issues suggested by the above data.

chapter 4

Statement of Cash Flows: Reporting the Effects of Operating, Investing, and Financing Activities on Cash Flows

Learning Objectives

1. Understand why using the accrual basis of accounting to prepare the balance sheet and income statement creates the need for a statement of cash flows.

2. Understand the types of transactions that result in cash flows from operating, investing, and financing activities.

3. Develop an ability to prepare a statement of cash flows from a comparative balance sheet and income statement.

4. Distinguish between the direct and indirect methods of reporting and analyzing cash flows from operations.

5. Develop an ability to analyze the statement of cash flows, including the relation among cash flows from operating, investing, and financing activities for businesses in various stages of their growth.

4

What do General Cinema, United Air Lines, and MCI have in common? Each of these firms filed for bankruptcy during the late 1900s and early 2000s. Yet each of these firms operated profitably for most of the years preceding its bankruptcy filing. The bankruptcies occurred because these firms were unable to generate sufficient cash to cover operating costs, debt service costs, and capital expenditures. This chapter discusses the statement of cash flows, which reports the impact of a firm's operating, investing, and financing activities on cash flows during an accounting period.

Need for a Statement of Cash Flows

How can a profitable firm run out of cash? Two explanations, at least, suggest answers.

1. **Net income for a particular period does not equal cash flow from operations. Chapter 3** points out that most firms use the accrual basis of accounting in measuring operating performance. Firms typically recognize revenue at the time of sale, even though they may receive cash from customers prior to, or coincident with, or after the time of sale. Thus, revenues on the income statement for any period will not likely equal cash received from customers. Likewise, firms match expenses either with associated revenues or with the period they consume goods or services in operations. The cash outflow for the expense may occur prior to, or coincident with, or subsequent to the recognition of the expense. Thus, expenses on the income statement will not likely equal cash paid to suppliers of goods and services each period. Firms typically make most of the cash outflows for expenses prior to or coincident with the sale of the good or service, whereas they usually receive cash after the sale. This lag between cash outflows and cash inflows can lead to cash shortfalls, particularly for a growing firm. Consider the typical firm where cash disbursements to employees and suppliers precede cash collections from customers. The faster such a firm grows, the shorter of cash it will find itself, until it takes steps to provide the funds necessary to pay suppliers while it awaits cash collections from its own customers. The use of the accrual basis of accounting in measuring net income creates the need for a separate financial statement that reports the impact of operations on cash flows so the reader can judge a firm's cash flow needs and how it has dealt with them.

2. **Firms receive cash inflows and disburse outflows because of investing and financing activities, which the income statement does not report directly, although it provides hints of such activities.** Firms building their productive capacity generally use cash to acquire property, plant, and equipment. Short- and long-term borrowing comes due, requiring cash. Firms that pay dividends regularly to shareholders are reluctant to curtail the dividends when cash is tight. Thus, a profitable firm may generate positive cash flow from operations and still have cash shortages.

The balance sheet reports the balance in cash at the beginning and end of the year, but does not explain how it changed during the period. The income statement measures the value added from selling goods and services for more than their costs. Although a primary goal of business firms is to generate a profit, firms need adequate cash to carry out this goal. The statement of cash flows explains how a firm obtains and uses cash.

Overview of the Statement of Cash Flows

Exhibit 4.1, which is similar to **Exhibit 1.3** discussed briefly in **Chapter 1**, presents a statement of cash flows for Wal-Mart Stores for three recent years. Note the following aspects of this statement.

EXHIBIT 4.1	WAL-MART STORES, INC. Comparative Statement of Cash Flows with Reconciliation of Net Income to Cash Flow from Operations ($ amounts in millions)

	Year 12	Change	Year 13	Change	Year 14
Cash Provided by Operating Activities					
Sources of Cash					
Cash Received from Customers	$ 219,602	$ 26,960	$ 246,562	$12,656	$ 259,218
Uses of Cash					
Cash Paid for Goods Available for Sale	(172,429)	(20,198)	(192,627)	(5,290)	(197,917)
Cash Paid for Selling and Administrative Items	(31,690)	(4,163)	(35,853)	(3,243)	(39,096)
Cash Paid for Interest	(1,326)	263	(1,063)	67	(996)
Cash Paid for Income Taxes	(3,897)	(590)	(4,487)	(631)	(5,118)
Net Cash Provided by Operating Activities	$ 10,260	$ 2,272	$ 12,532	$ 3,559	$ 16,091
Reconciliation of Net Income to Cash Provided **by Operating Activities**					
Net Income	$ 6,671	$ 1,368	$ 8,039	$ 1,036	$ 9,075
Adjustments to Reconcile Net Income to Net Cash Provided					
Depreciation	3,290	142	3,432	420	3,852
(Increase) Decrease in Accounts Receivable	(210)	109	(101)	474	373
(Increase) Decrease in Inventories	(1,235)	(1,001)	(2,236)	263	(1,973)
(Increase) Decrease in Prepayments	(180)	925	745	(1,195)	(450)
Increase in Accounts payable	368	1,079	1,447	1,356	2,803
Increase in Other Current Liabilities	1,556	(350)	1,206	1,205	2,411
Net Cash Provided by Operating Activities	$ 10,260	$ 2,272	$ 12,532	$ 3,559	$ 16,091
Investing					
Acquisition of Property, Plant, and Equipment	$ (8,383)		$ (9,355)		$ (10,308)
Other	1,237		(354)		2,046
Cash Flow from Investing	$ (7,146)		$ (9,709)		$ (8,262)
Financing					
Increase (Decrease) in Short-term Borrowing	$ (1,533)		$ 1,836		$ 688
Increase in Long-term Borrowing	4,591		2,044		4,099
Increase in Common Stock	0		0		0
Decrease in Long-term Borrowing	(3,686)		(1,479)		(3,541)
Acquisition of Common Stock	(1,214)		(3,232)		(5,182)
Dividends	(1,249)		(1,328)		(1,569)
Other	84		(67)		117
Cash Flow from Financing	$ (3,007)		$ (2,226)		$ (5,388)
Change in Cash	$ 107		$ 597		$ 2,441
Cash, Beginning of Year	2,054		2,161		2,758
Cash, End of Year	$ 2,161		$ 2,758		$ 5,199

Year Ended January 31

The Statement Explains the Reasons for the Change in Cash between Balance Sheet Dates

The last two lines of the statement of cash flows report the amount of cash on Wal-Mart's balance sheet at the beginning and the end of each year. The FASB requires that the statement of cash flows explain changes in cash and cash equivalents. Cash equivalents represent short-term, highly liquid investments in which a firm has temporarily placed excess cash. Throughout this text, we use the term *cash flows* to refer to flows of cash and cash equivalents.[1] The remaining lines show the inflows and outflows of cash during the year, which explain the net change between the two balance sheet dates. Thus, the statements of cash flows reports flows, or changes over time, whereas the balance sheet reports amounts at a moment in time.

The Statement Classifies the Reasons for the Change in Cash as an Operating, or Investing, or Financing Activity

Various inflows and outflows of cash during the year appear in the statement of cash flows in one of three categories: operating, investing, and financing. **Figure 4.1** presents the three major types of cash flows, which the following sections describe.

Operations   Selling goods and providing services are the most important ways for a financially healthy company to generate cash. Assessed over several years, the cash flow from operations indicates the extent to which operating activities generate more cash than they use. A firm can use the excess **cash flow from operations** to acquire buildings and equipment, pay dividends, retire long-term debt, and conduct other investing and financing activities.

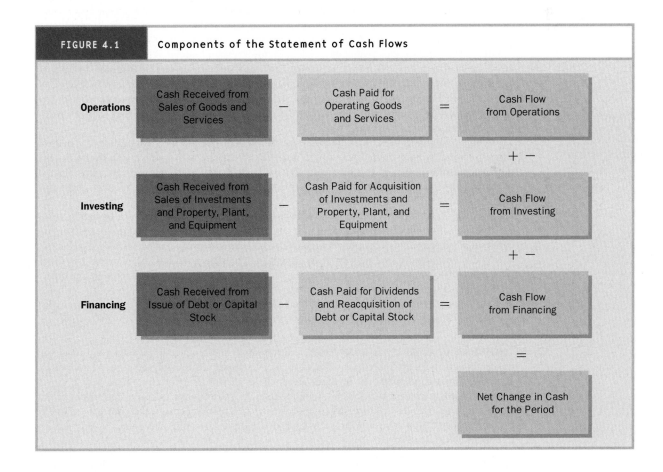

| FIGURE 4.1 | Components of the Statement of Cash Flows |

---

[1] See Financial Accounting Standards Board (FASB), *Statement of Financial Accounting Standards No. 95,* "Statement of Cash Flows," 1987.

Investing   The second section of the statement of cash flows shows the amount of **cash flow from investing activities**. The acquisition of non-current assets, particularly property, plant, and equipment, usually represents a major ongoing use of cash. A firm must replace such assets as they wear out, and it must acquire additional non-current assets if it is to grow. A firm obtains part of the cash needed to acquire non-current assets from sales of existing non-current assets. Such cash inflows seldom, however, cover the entire cost of new acquisitions. Firms not experiencing rapid growth can usually finance capital expenditures with cash flow from operations. Firms growing rapidly must often borrow funds or issue common stock to finance their acquisitions of non-current assets.

Financing   Third, a firm obtains cash from short- and long-term borrowing and from issues of common or preferred stock. It uses cash to pay dividends to shareholders, to repay short- or long-term borrowing, and to reacquire shares of outstanding common or preferred stock. These amounts appear as **cash flow from financing activitie**s in the statement of cash flows.

Refer to **Exhibit 4.1**. Wal-Mart reported positive cash flow from operations in each of the three years. Cash flow from operations exceeded the cash outflow needed to acquire additional property, plant, and equipment each year. Business terminology refers to an excess of cash flow from operations over cash flow for investing as *free cash flow*. Firms can use free cash flow to repay borrowing, pay a dividend, repurchase common stock, and add to cash on the balance sheet. Wal-Mart used the free cash flow, plus the cash received from additional borrowing in excess of the cash used to repay old borrowing, to pay dividends and reacquire shares of its common stock. **Chapter 5** explores more fully why Wal-Mart uses its excess cash, in particular, to reacquire its common stock.

Ambiguities in Classifying Cash Flows   Cash flows do not always fit unambiguously into only one of these three categories of cash flows. For example, you might think of cash received from interest and dividend revenues generated by investments in securities as coming from operating activities. The logic for this treatment is that interest and dividends appear as revenues in the income statement, the financial statement that reports the results of a firm's operations. Alternatively, cash received from interest and dividends might appear as coming from investing activities. The logic for this treatment is that cash flows related to the purchase and sale of investments in securities, other than trading securities (a distinction discussed in **Chapter 11**) appear as investing activities. The Financial Accounting Standards Board's *Statement of Financial Accounting Standards No. 95* requires firms to classify the receipt of cash from interest and dividend revenues as an operating activity but the cash related to the purchase and sale of investments in securities as an investing activity.[2]

Similar ambiguities arise with interest expense on debt. Should the cash outflow for interest expense appear as an operating activity (to achieve consistency with its inclusion in the income statement as an expense) or as a financing activity (to achieve consistency with the classification of debt issues and retirements as a financing activity)? FASB *SFAS No. 95* requires that firms classify interest expense as an operating activity but the issue or redemption of debt as a financing activity.[3] Dividends that a firm pays to its shareholders appear, however, as a financing activity.[4] The classification of interest expense on debt as an operating activity and dividends paid on common or preferred stock as a financing activity appears inconsistent. The FASB's likely rationale is that accountants treat interest as an expense in computing net income, whereas dividends represent a distribution of assets generated by net income, not an expense reducing net income.

Similar ambiguities arise in classifying purchases and sales of marketable securities (treated as investing, not operating, activities) and increases and decreases in short-term bank borrowings (treated as financing, not operating, activities). Later chapters discuss these items more fully.

Treatment of Noncash Transactions   Firms sometimes engage in investing and financing transactions that do not directly involve cash. For example, a firm may acquire a building by assuming a mortgage obligation or might exchange a tract of land for equipment. Holders of a firm's debt might convert the debt into common stock. These transactions do not appear in the statement of cash flows as either investing or financing activities because they are not factors in explaining the change in cash. Firms must disclose noncash investing and financing activities in a separate schedule or note.[5]

---

[2] Ibid., para 16, 17, 22.

[3] Ibid., para 19, 20, 23.

[4] Ibid., para 20.

[5] Ibid., para 32.

The Statement Reconciles Net Income with Cash Flow from Operations

The first section of the statement of cash flows derives cash flow from operations. FASB *Statement No. 95* permits firms to report cash flow from operations in either of two ways:

1. **Direct Method** The direct method reports the amounts of cash received from customers less cash disbursed to various suppliers, employees, lenders for interest payments, and taxing authorities. The top panel of **Exhibit 4.1** illustrates the direct method. The FASB has said that it prefers this method, but most firms use the alternative, described next.
2. **Indirect Method** The indirect method begins with net income for a period and then shows adjustments to net income to convert revenues to cash received from customers and to convert expenses to cash disbursed to various suppliers of goods and services. The boxed section of **Exhibit 4.1** illustrates the indirect method of reporting cash flow from operations.

Statement No. 95 permits firms to report cash flow from operations using either the direct or the indirect method. A firm that presents the preferred, but less often used, direct method must show a reconciliation (see the boxed section of **Exhibit 4.1**) between net income and cash flow from operations either at the bottom of the statement of cash flows or in a separate note.

The majority of firms report cash flow from operations using the indirect method because, before the FASB expressed a preference for the direct method in 1987, most firms used the indirect method, so both preparers and users had become familiar with it. Experienced financial analysts who have used the statement of cash flows generally understand the adjustments required to convert net income to cash flow from operations. Our experience in teaching the statement of cash flows indicates, however, that students have difficulty on their initial exposure to the statement of cash flows understanding these adjustments, whereas they find the direct method easier to comprehend. We therefore illustrate the computation of cash flow from operations using both the direct and indirect methods.

Overview of Adjustments to Net Income to Compute Cash Flow from Operations Under the Indirect Method
This section presents an overview of the types of required adjustments to net income to compute cash flow from operations. Later sections of the chapter illustrate these adjustments more fully. The reconciliation of net income to cash flow from operations that a firm using the direct method must provide is essentially the indirect method. In this chapter, you will usually see a boxed Reconciliation in the statement of cash flows, which is, even though not explicitly described as such, the indirect method.

Refer to the reconciliation of net income to cash flow from operations in the boxed section of **Exhibit 4.1**. The first line in the reconciliation shows the amount of net income for each year from the income statement. Accountants use the accrual basis of accounting to compute net income. The reconciliation shows the adjustments required to convert net income, measured on an accrual basis, to the amount of net cash flow generated from operations during the period.

Wal-Mart shows an addition to net income each year for depreciation. To understand the reconciliation's adjustment, first examine the top section deriving net cash flow as the excess of receipts over disbursements. Depreciation has no place in that section because it uses no cash this period. Wal-Mart used cash in some earlier period to acquire a store building or equipment, and in that period reported the use of cash as an investing activity. Depreciation appears as an expense on the income statement because operating retail stores requires using a portion of the service potential of buildings and equipment. The events causing the firm to recognize depreciation expense, however, consume not cash but other assets (buildings, equipment). Each year, Wal-Mart recognizes Depreciation Expense, decreasing shareholders' equity, and Accumulated Depreciation, decreasing total assets. The reconciliation starts with net income, which had a subtraction for depreciation expense. Because depreciation reduces net income but does not use cash, the reconciliation adds back the amount to derive cash flow from operations. Subtracting depreciation expense in arriving at the amount of net income on the first line of the reconciliation and then adding the same amount on the second line results in a zero net effect on cash flow from operations. Thus, the reconciliation's adjustment for depreciation removes the amount of a noncash expense.

Conceptual Note. Once you understand the preceding paragraph and its implications, you will have mastered most of the difficulty that financial statement readers have with the indirect method of computing cash flow from operations. Perhaps this will help your understanding: Imagine a firm whose only activity for a period was the recording of depreciation expense of

$100—nothing else. That firm would show negative net income, a loss, of $100, but it would have had no change in cash. Cash flow from operations is zero. So, the reconciliation must start with the −$100 for net income, then add back the $100 depreciation expense, in order to reconcile net income of −$100 with the zero cash flow from operations.

The Reconciliation for Wal-Mart shows a subtraction for the change (increase) in accounts receivable. How would you derive the amount of cash Wal-Mart collected from its customers during a particular period? Wal-Mart has made sales in periods before this one as well as in this one. (For now, assume Wal-Mart does not receive cash from customers in the current period as an advance on goods it will deliver in future periods.) Wal-Mart received cash this period from customers who purchased before this period where the revenue appeared in an earlier period's income statement. This resulted in an increase in Wal-Mart's accounts receivable in the earlier period, with a decrease this period when the firm collected cash. Wal-Mart received cash also from customers who both purchased and paid this period, resulting in no change in accounts receivable. Finally, Wal-Mart made sales this period, which it will collect in future periods, resulting in an increase in accounts receivable this period. So the amount of cash Wal-Mart received from customers in a period equals the amount of sales for that period, reduced by the increase in accounts receivable during the period or increased by the decrease in accounts receivable during the period.

Exercises to Cement Understanding. Look at the data in **Exhibits 1.2** and **1.3**. Copy down the amount of total revenues for Year 13 from **Exhibit 1.2**, $246,663. Note the amount by which Accounts Receivable increased between Year 12 and Year 13 in **Exhibit 1.3**, $101. Subtract that $101 from total revenues of $246,663. Note this difference, $246,562, equals the Cash Received from Customers in **Exhibit 4.1**. Now, repeat this exercise for Year 14: Copy down the total revenues for Year 14 from **Exhibit 1.2**. Note the amount by which Accounts Receivable *decreased* between Years 13 and 14.[6] *Add* the amount of the decrease to total revenues and see that the sum equals Cash Received from Customers in **Exhibit 4.1**. When Accounts Receivable decrease, the firm has collected an amount of cash greater than its sales on account for the year.

Problem 4.1 for Self-Study

Classifying cash flows by type of activity. Indicate whether each of the following transactions of the current period would appear as an operating, investing, or financing activity in the statement of cash flows. If any transaction would not appear in the statement of cash flows, suggest the reason.

a. Disbursement of $96,900 to merchandise suppliers.

b. Receipt of $200,000 from issuing common stock.

c. Receipt of $49,200 from customers for sales made this period.

d. Receipt of $22,700 from customers this period for sales made last period.

e. Receipt of $1,800 from a customer for goods the firm will deliver next period.

f. Disbursement of $16,000 for interest expense on debt.

g. Disbursement of $40,000 to acquire land.

h. Issue of common stock with market value of $60,000 to acquire land.

i. Disbursement of $25,300 as compensation to employees for services rendered this period.

(continued)

---

[6]A more advanced issue: if you were to look at the Wal-Mart balance sheet in Exhibit 1.1, you would see that the amounts for Accounts Receivable reported there for Year 14 decreased by $854, from $2,108 to $1,254, while the Statement of Cash Flows in **Exhibit 1.3** shows a decrease of only $373. These numbers might differ because Wal-Mart sold some receivables during the year in financing transactions or as part of a dis-investing transaction. **Chapter 6** discusses the raising of cash by selling, or otherwise using, accounts receivable. Sometimes a comparison of the balance sheet and statement of cash flows amounts for changes in accounts receivable shows a larger balance sheet increase than does the statement of cash flows. This difference likely results from the company's buying an entire business during the year and acquiring all the acquired company's assets, including its accounts receivable.

Problem 4.1 for Self-Study *(continued)*

j. Disbursement of $7,900 to employees for services rendered last period but not paid for last period.

k. Disbursement of $53,800 for a patent purchased from its inventor.

l. Acquisition of a building by issuing a note payable to a bank.

m. Disbursement of $19,300 as a dividend to shareholders.

n. Receipt of $12,000 from the sale of equipment that originally cost $20,000 and had $8,000 of accumulated depreciation at the time of sale.

o. Disbursement of $100,000 to redeem bonds at maturity.

p. Disbursement of $40,000 to acquire shares of IBM common stock.

q. Receipt of $200 in dividends from IBM relating to the shares of common stock acquired in transaction **p** above.

Income includes all sales, even if cash collections for those sales did not occur this period. So, the reconciliation, which starts with net income, including all sales, must have a subtraction for the increase in accounts receivable, and cash will come in a later period. This chapter discusses these and other adjustments to reconcile net income with cash flow from operations.

Preparing the Statement of Cash Flows

Firms could prepare their statement of cash flows directly from entries in their cash account. To do so would require them to classify each transaction affecting cash as an operating, or investing, or financing activity. As the number of transactions affecting cash increases, however, this approach becomes cumbersome. Most firms design their accounting systems to accumulate the information needed to prepare income statements and balance sheets. They then use a work sheet at the end of the period to transform information from the income statement and balance sheet into a statement of cash flows.

We present a columnar work sheet for preparing the statement of cash flows. The work sheet computes cash flow from operations using both the direct and the indirect methods.

Algebraic Formulation

Fundamental to the preparation of a statement of cash flows is an understanding of how changes in cash relate to changes in noncash accounts. Reexamine the accounting equation, using the following notation:

C — cash

$N\$A$ — noncash assets

L — liabilities

SE — shareholders' equity

Δ — the change in an item; it may be positive (an increase) or negative (a decrease) from the beginning of a period to the end of the period.

The accounting equation states:

Assets $=$ Liabilities $+$ Shareholders' Equity

$C + N\$A = \quad L \quad + \quad SE$ Equation (1), Balance Sheet Equation

Furthermore, this equation must be true for balance sheets constructed at both the start of the period and the end of the period. If the start-of-the-period and end-of-the-period balance sheets maintain the accounting equation, then the following equation must also be valid:

$$\Delta C + \Delta N\$A = \Delta L + \Delta SE \qquad \text{Equation (2), Balance Sheet Change Equation}$$

Rearranging terms in this equation, we obtain the equation for changes in cash:

$$\Delta C = \Delta L + \Delta SE - \Delta N\$A \qquad \text{Equation (3), Cash Change Equation}$$

The left-hand side of the **Cash Change Equation** (3) represents the change in cash. The right-hand side of the equation, reflecting changes in all noncash accounts, must also net to the change in cash. The equation states that the changes in cash (left-hand side) equal the changes in liabilities plus the changes in shareholders' equity less the changes in noncash assets (right-hand side). For example, a loan from a bank or another lender increases cash and increases a liability. The issue of common stock increases cash and increases shareholders' equity. The purchase of equipment decreases cash and increases noncash assets. Increases in noncash assets carry a negative sign on the right-hand side of the equation. *Thus, we can identify the causes of the change in cash by studying the changes in noncash accounts and classifying those changes as operating, investing, and financing activities.* Focus on the preceding italicized sentence. It provides the overview, the big picture, of the procedures that underlie the columnar work sheet for the statement of cash flows.

Data for Illustrations

To illustrate the preparation of the statement of cash flows in this chapter, we use information for Solinger Electric Corporation for Year 4. **Exhibit 4.2** presents the balance sheet at the beginning and end of Year 4. **Exhibit 4.3** presents the income statement for Year 4. Solinger Electric Corporation declared and paid $6,000 in dividends during Year 4.

Illustration of Columnar Work Sheet

Exhibit 4.4 presents a **columnar work sheet** for the preparation of the statement of cash flows for Solinger Electric Company. The upper panel shows the computation of cash flow from operations using the indirect method. The lower panel illustrates the computation of cash flow from operations using the indirect and the direct methods. This work sheet involves the following steps.

Step 1   Compute the change in each balance sheet account between the beginning and the end of the year. Enter the changes in the noncash balance sheet accounts in the first column of the upper panel of the work sheet using the following rules regarding signs, which follow from the cash change equation:

- Increases in noncash assets reduce cash and therefore appear with negative signs. [The equation shows that if a noncash asset increases, cash decreases.]
- Decreases in noncash assets increase cash and therefore appear with positive signs.
- Increases in liability and shareholders' equity accounts increase cash and appear with positive signs.
- Decreases in liability and shareholders' equity accounts decrease cash and appear with negative signs.

Enter the net change in cash on the last line of the top panel of the work sheet. As the cash change equation above shows, the net change in noncash accounts (right-hand side of the equation) should equal the change in cash. The net change in noncash balance sheet accounts of a negative $24,000 equals the decrease in cash of $24,000 for the year.

In addition, enter the amounts of revenues and expenses for the period in the first column of the lower panel of the work sheet. We use information in this lower panel to compute cash flow from operations under the direct method.

Step 2   Classify the change in each balance sheet account in the upper panel of the work sheet as an operating, or investing, or financing activity and enter it in the appropriate column of the work sheet using the same sign as in the first column. Most of the changes in noncash accounts presented to this point in the book affect only one of these three categories of activities. Here, however, Retained Earnings increased for net income (an operating activity) and decreased for dividends (a financing activity), so the total change, split into two pieces, appears in two columns.

Repeated for convenience:

$$\Delta C = \Delta L + \Delta SE - \Delta N\$A \qquad \text{Equation (3), Cash Change Equation}$$

In addition, enter the change in each balance sheet account that relates to an operating activity (for example, accounts receivable, merchandise inventories, accounts payable) on the revenue or expense line in the lower panel to which it relates. For example, changes in accounts receivable relate to sales revenue. Changes in inventory and accounts payable for inventory relate to cost of goods sold.

We discuss below the treatment of each line of the columnar work sheet.

Line (11)   We begin with line **(11)**, the change in retained earnings, because we think you will find the remaining adjustments in the work sheet easier to understand if you remember that the calculation of cash from operations under the indirect method begins with net income and then derives the amounts of cash received from customers and cash disbursed to various suppliers of goods and services. Retained earnings increased by $13,000 during Year 4. **Exhibit 4.3** indicates that Solinger Electric Corporation generated net income of $19,000. It declared and paid dividends of $6,000. We enter the increase in retained earnings from net income of $19,000 in the Operations column as a positive amount. The initial assumption is that cash flow from operations increased by the amount of net income for the period. We know that cash flow from operations seldom equals net income. Thus, we must adjust net income to compute cash from operations, which we discuss below. We also enter the dividend of $6,000 in the Financing column as a negative amount. The increase of $19,000 in the Operations column and the decrease of $6,000 in the Financing column net to the $13,000 increase in retained earnings.

Line (1)   The income statement in the lower panel reports sales revenues, which increase shareholders' equity and increase either cash or accounts receivable. Revenues that simultaneously increase cash require no adjustment when converting revenues to cash received from customers. Revenues that do not immediately increase cash, however, require an adjustment. To understand the adjustment, recall that accounts receivable increase each year for sales made on account and decrease for collections from customers. To derive the cash receipts from customers, we subtract the amount of an increase in receivables from revenues. When accounts receivable increase during a period, the firm collects less cash than sales made on account. Refer to the amounts for Solinger Electric Corporation. Accounts receivable increased by $35,000 during the year. This firm recognized revenues of $125,000, but did not collect this amount in cash. Its cash collections from customers were only $90,000 (= revenues of $125,000 less the increase in accounts receivable of $35,000). We show the conversion of sales revenue to cash receipts from customers on the Revenues line in the lower panel of the work sheet. We also show a subtraction of $35,000 on the Accounts Receivable line in the Operations column of the upper panel of the work sheet to adjust the amount of net income on line **(11)** to the amount of cash received from customers.

If accounts receivable decrease during a period, the firm collects more cash than the amount of sales revenue. The work sheet shows an addition to revenues in the lower panel to indicate that the firm collected more cash from customers than its sales revenue for the period. The work sheet also shows an addition on the Accounts Receivable line in the upper panel for this excess of cash received over the amount of sales revenue included in net income on line **(11)**.

Line (2)   Merchandise inventories increase each year for purchases of inventories and decrease for the cost of goods sold. Whereas the income statement reports the cost of the inventory sold as Cost of Goods Sold, the statement of cash flows reports the cash payments for inventory, whether sold or kept in inventory. Computing this cash outflow requires knowing the amounts payable to suppliers of inventory, which we can find by understanding (1) how much inventory the firm purchased this period, and (2) how much the firm paid for purchases this period. Inventories for Solinger Electric Corporation increased by $10,000, indicating that the firm acquired more inventory than it sold. The lower panel of the work sheet shows a subtraction of $10,000 on the Cost of Goods Sold line to indicate that the firm purchased more inventory than it sold. Total purchases during the period were $70,000 (= $60,000 + $10,000). We also enter this $10,000 negative amount on the Merchandise Inventories line in the Operations column in the upper panel, indicating that the firm purchased more inventory than the amount of cost of goods sold subtracted when computing net income on line **(11)** of the work sheet. Later, on line **(5)** in the analysis of accounts payable for inventory, we shall find out how much the firm paid for inventory this period. If accounts payable for inventory did not change, the firm must have paid cash for all its inventory acquisitions. If payables increased, then the firm paid less cash than the amount it acquired. If payables decreased, then the firm paid more cash than the amount it acquired.

EXHIBIT 4.2	SOLINGER ELECTRIC CORPORATION Comparative Balance Sheet for December 31, Year 3 and 4		

| | | December 31 | |
		Year 3	Year
ASSETS			
Current Assets			
Cash		$ 30,000	$ 6,0
Accounts Receivable		20,000	55,0
Merchandise Inventory		40,000	50,0
Total Current Assets		$ 90,000	$111,0
Noncurrent Assets			
Buildings and Equipment (Cost)		$100,000	$225,0
Accumulated Depreciation		(30,000)	(40,0
Total Noncurrent Assets		$ 70,000	$185,0
Total Assets		$160,000	$296,0
LIABILITIES AND SHAREHOLDERS' EQUITY			
Current Liabilities			
Accounts Payable—Merchandise Suppliers		$ 24,000	$ 47,0
Accounts Payable—Other Suppliers		10,000	12,0
Salaries Payable		5,000	6,0
Interest Payable		6,000	3,0
Total Current Liabilities		$ 45,000	$ 68,0
Noncurrent Liabilities			
Bonds Payable		$ 0	$100,0
Shareholders' Equity			
Common Stock		$100,000	$100,0
Retained Earnings		15,000	28,0
Total Shareholders' Equity		$115,000	$128,0
Total Liabilities and Shareholders' Equity		$160,000	$296,0

EXHIBIT 4.3	SOLINGER ELECTRIC CORPORATION Income Statement For Year 4

Sales Revenue	$125,000
Cost of Goods Sold	(60,000)
Depreciation Expense	(10,000)
Salary Expense	(20,000)
Interest Expense	(5,000)
Other Expenses	(11,000)
Net Income	$ 19,000

> *Repeated for convenience:*
>
> $$\Delta C = \Delta L + \Delta SE - \Delta N\$A \qquad \text{Equation (3), Cash Change Equation}$$

Line (3)   The building and equipment account (at cost) increased $125,000 during the year. This account increases for new buildings and equipment acquired and decreases for old buildings and equipment sold. The accounting records of Solinger Electric Corporation will provide detailed information about the increases and decreases during the year. We have no indication that the firm sold buildings and equipment during Year 4. One such indication would be the disclosure of a gain or loss on sale of buildings and equipment in the income statement, which does not appear in the Year 4 income statement. We therefore assume that the firm must have purchased new buildings and equipment costing $125,000. We enter this amount as a cash outflow in the Investing column.

EXHIBIT 4.4	SOLINGER ELECTRIC CORPORATION Work Sheet for Preparing the Statement of Cash Flows and Reconciliation of Net Income to Cash Flows from Operating Activities For Year 4

CLASSIFICATION OF BALANCE SHEET CHANGES

	Account		Classification by Kind of Activity for Source or Use of Cash				
Balance Sheet Accounts	Changes	=	Operations	+	Investing	+	Financing
(Increase) Decrease in Assets							
[1] Accounts Receivable	$ (35,000)		$(35,000) [1]				
[2] Merchandise Inventories	(10,000)		(10,000) [2]				
[3] Buildings and Equipment	(125,000)				(125,000) [3]		
[4] Accumulated Depreciation	10,000		10,000 [4]				
Increase (Decrease) in Liabilities and Shareholders' Equity							
[5] Accounts Payable—Merchandise Suppliers	23,000		23,000 [5]				
[6] Accounts Payable—Other Suppliers	2,000		2,000 [6]				
[7] Salaries Payable	1,000		1,000 [7]				
[8] Interest Payable	(3,000)		(3,000) [8]				
[9] Bonds Payable	100,000						$100,000 [9]
[10] Common Stock							
[11] Retained Earnings	13,000		19,000 [11]				(6,000) [11]
[12] Increase (Decrease) in Cash	$ (24,000)	=	$ 7,000	+	$(125,000)	+	$ 94,000 [12]

	Income Statement	Indirect Method for Cash Flows from Operations Income Plus Changes in Balance Sheet Operating Accounts	=	Direct Method for Cash Flows from Operations			
				Cash Receipts	+	Cash Payments	=	Net Cash Inflow (Outflow)
Net Income		$ 19,000					
Revenues	$125,000	$(35,000) [1]		$90,000			= $90,000
Less: Cost of Goods Sold	(60,000)	(10,000) [2] 23,000 [5]				$(47,000)	= (47,000)
Depreciation Expense	(10,000)	10,000 [4]					
Salary Expense	(20,000)	1,000 [7]				(19,000)	= (19,000)
Other Expenses	(11,000)	2,000 [6]				(9,000)	= (9,000)
Interest Expense	(5,000)	(3,000) [8]				(8,000)	= (8,000)
Net Income	$ 19,000						
Cash Flow from Operations		$ 7,000		$90,000	+	$(83,000)	= $ 7,000

Line (4) The accumulated depreciation account increased $10,000 during the year. Recall that this account shows the cumulative depreciation recognized to date on buildings and equipment still in use. This account increases for depreciation recognized during the current period on buildings and equipment in service. It decreases for the accumulated depreciation on any buildings and equipment sold during the year and therefore removed from the accounting records. The discussion for line **(3)** suggests that Solinger Electric Corporation did not sell buildings and equipment during Year 4. The increase in the accumulated depreciation account must therefore represent depreciation for the year. The income statement in the lower panel reports depreciation expense of $10,000. The lower panel of the work sheet shows an addition of $10,000 on the Depreciation Expense line in the second column to offset the negative $10,000 in the first column, in effect zeroing out the depreciation expense in the computation of cash expenditures for expenses. We also enter this amount as an addition on the Accumulated Depreciation line in the Operations column of the upper panel. As an earlier section discusses, depreciation does not use cash during the current period. The firm used cash when it acquired the buildings and equipment. When it did so, it entered the cash outflow in the Investing column (as we did on line **(3)** above for acquisition during Year 4).

Line (5) Accounts payable to merchandise suppliers increases each period for new purchases on account and decreases for cash payments made to merchandise suppliers. Insofar as suppliers do not require cash payment in the period when a customer acquires inventory, the amount for purchases of inventory exceeds the cash payments for inventory. The discussion for line **(2)** indicates that the firm purchased $70,000 of inventory during the period. The increase in accounts payable of $23,000 for Year 4 indicates that the firm did not pay for the full amount of inventory purchased. That is, the total amount purchased exceeded the cash used for purchases by the $23,000 amount that the Accounts Payable account increased. We enter the increase in accounts payable as a positive amount on the Cost of Goods Sold line in the lower panel, resulting in a cash disbursement of $47,000 (= −$70,000 + $23,000) for inventory. We also enter the $23,000 as a positive amount on the Accounts Payable to Merchandise Suppliers line in the Operations column in the upper panel. The following summarizes the cash payments for merchandise, appearing in the bottom panel:

Cost of Goods Sold (from the Income Statement)	$(60,000)
Less Increase in Merchandise Inventories	(10,000)
= Purchases of Merchandise Inventories	$(70,000)
Plus Increase in Accounts Payable for Merchandise	23,000
= Cash Payments Made for Purchases of Merchandise Inventories	$(47,000)

Line (6) Accounts Payable to Other Suppliers increases for goods (other than merchandise) and services received on account and decreases for cash payments made. The income statement in the lower panel of **Exhibit 4.3** indicates that Other Expenses totaled $11,000 during Year 4. Solinger did not pay for all those goods and services in cash during the year, as you can see from the $2,000 increase in the account for Accounts Payable to Other Suppliers. Solinger Electric Corporation used $2,000 less cash in paying for goods and services than the cost of the goods and services it purchased from these suppliers. Thus, cash payments to other suppliers totaled $9,000 (= $11,000 − $2,000). We enter the $2,000 increase in Accounts Payable to Other Suppliers as a positive amount on the Other Expenses line in the lower panel and on the Accounts Payable to Other Suppliers line in the Operations column of the upper panel.

Line (7) Salaries Payable increased by $1,000, indicating that Solinger Electric Corporation paid to those who earned the salaries $1,000 less in cash than the amount earned. The lower panel reports Salary Expense of $20,000 for Year 4. Because Salaries Payable increased by $1,000, we know that the firm paid only $19,000 to employees during the year. We add $1,000 on the Salary Expense line in the lower panel and $1,000 on the Salaries Payable line in the Operations column of the upper panel.

Line (8) Interest Payable increases when the firm records interest expense and decreases when the firm makes payments. The FASB classifies payments for interest as an operating use of cash. Solinger Electric Corporation reports interest expense of $5,000 for the year. The decrease in interest payable of $3,000 means that the firm paid $3,000 more in cash than the amount of interest expense. We show the additional cash used as a subtraction on the Interest Expense line in the lower

---

Repeated for convenience:

$$\Delta C = \Delta L + \Delta SE - \Delta N\$A \qquad \text{Equation (3), Cash Change Equation}$$

---

panel to compute the $8,000 (= -$5,000 - $3,000) the firm paid for interest. We also show the $3,000 as a subtraction on the Interest Payable line in the Operations column in the upper panel.

Line (9) The Bonds Payable account increases for new bonds issued and decreases for outstanding bonds redeemed. We have no evidence that Solinger Electric Corporation redeemed bonds during Year 4. Thus, we assume that it issued new bonds for $100,000. We enter the $100,000 in the Financing column.

Line (10) The Common Stock account did not change during the year. If there were transactions affecting this account, they had zero net effect. Lacking information regarding any such transactions, we assume that Solinger Electric Corporation made no entries in this account during the year.

Students often notice that the changes in accounts on published balance sheets, such as inventories or accounts payable, sometimes differ from the amounts that appear in the statements of cash flows. The usual explanation is that the firm acquired another entity during the year and appropriately classified the cash used to make the acquisition as an investing activity. Part of the change in the balance sheet accounts, say for inventories, results from the firm's operating activities, and part relates to inventories acquired in the acquisition. Firms have the necessary information internally to distinguish the portion of the change in each balance sheet account that relates to operating, investing, and financing activities. The problems in this book will provide the necessary information if part of the change in a balance sheet account relates to an acquisition.

Step 3 The final step in preparing the work sheet is to sum the entries in the Operations, Investing, and Financing columns and net the three sums to ensure that they equal the net change in cash. The test is as follows:

Cash Flow from Operations	$ 7,000
Cash Flow from Investing	(125,000)
Cash Flow from Financing	94,000
Net Change in Cash	$ (24,000)

We also sum the amounts in each of the columns in the lower panel and check to ensure that net income plus changes in operating balance sheet accounts equals cash received from customers minus cash disbursed to suppliers of various goods and services, which in turns equals cash flow from operations.

The work sheet provides the information needed to prepare the statement of cash flows using either the direct method or the indirect method of computing cash flow from operations. **Exhibit 4.5** shows the statement of cash flows for Solinger Electric Corporation for Year 4 using the indirect method based on information from the upper panel of the work sheet. **Exhibit 4.6** shows the statement of cash flows using the direct method based on information from the lower panel of the work sheet for cash flow from operations and from the upper panel of the work sheet for investing and financing activities. Note that the only difference between the two cash flow statements is in the computation of cash flow from operation. **Exhibit 4.6** also shows the reconciliation between net income of $19,000 and cash flow from operations of $7,000, a required disclosure when firms report cash flow from operations using the direct method. The information for this reconciliation appears in the Operations column of the upper panel of the work sheet and in the second column ("Income plus Changes . . .") of the lower panel.

Net income of $19,000 exceeds cash flow from operations of $7,000 primarily because sales revenue exceeded cash collections from customers during the year. When a growing firm allows its customers to delay payment, it will often find that revenues exceed collections from customers, which implies that net income exceeds cash flow from operations. Cash flow from operations fell short of the amount the firm needed to finance the acquisition of buildings and equipment, so it incurred long-term debt to finance these capital expenditures. As the discussion in **Chapter 2** makes clear, firms tend to use long-term financing when acquiring long-term assets.

EXHIBIT 4.5	SOLINGER ELECTRIC CORPORATION Statement of Cash Flows for Year 4 (Direct Method with Reconciliation of Net Income to Cash Flow from Operations)

OPERATING ACTIVITIES

Sources of Cash

Cash Received from Customers	$ 90,000	

Uses of Cash

Payments to Suppliers of Merchandise	(47,000)	
Payments for Employee Compensation	(19,000)	
Payments to Other Suppliers	(9,000)	
Payments for Interest	(8,000)	
Cash Flow from Operations		$ 7,000

RECONCILIATION OF NET INCOME TO CASH PROVIDED BY OPERATING ACTIVITIES

Net Income	$ 19,000	
Adjustments to Reconcile Net Income to Net Cash Provided		
Depreciation	10,000	
(Increase) in Accounts Receivable	(35,000)	
(Increase) in Inventories	(10,000)	
Increase in Accounts Payable for Merchandise	23,000	
(Increase) in Payables to Other Suppliers	2,000	
Increase in Salaries Payable	1,000	
Decrease in Interest Payable	(3,000)	
Net Cash Provided by Operating Activities	$ 7,000	

INVESTING

Cash Used for Acquisition of Building and Equipment		(125,000)

FINANCING

Cash Used for Dividends	$ (6,000)	
Proceeds for Long-term Bond Issued	100,000	
Cash Flow from Financing		94,000
Net Change in Cash for Year		$ (24,000)
Cash, January 1, Year 4		30,000
Cash, December 31, Year 4		$ 6,000

Problem 4.2 for Self-Study

Preparing a columnar work sheet for a statement of cash flows. **Exhibit 4.7** presents an income statement for Year 2. During Year 2 the firm sold no plant and equipment. It declared and paid dividends of $2,000. **Exhibit 4.8** presents a comparative balance sheet for Robbie Corporation as of December 31, Year 1 and Year 2. Using the format shown in the upper panel of **Exhibit 4.4**, compute the change in each balance sheet account and classify it as an operating, investing, or financing activity.

Repeated for convenience:

$$\Delta C = \Delta L + \Delta SE - \Delta N\$A \quad \text{Equation (3), Cash Change Equation}$$

EXHIBIT 4.6	SOLINGER ELECTRIC CORPORATION Statement of Cash Flows for Year 4 (Indirect Method)

Operating Activities

Net Income	$ 19,000	
Adjustments to Reconcile Net Income to Net Cash Provided		
Depreciation	10,000	
(Increase) in Accounts Receivable	(35,000)	
(Increase) in Inventories	(10,000)	
Increase in Accounts Payable for Merchandise	23,000	
(Increase) in Payable to Other Suppliers	2,000	
Increase in Salaries Payable	1,000	
Decrease in Interest Payable	(3,000)	
Net Cash Provided by Operating Activities		$ 7,000
Investing		
Cash Used for Acquisition of Building and Equipment		(125,000)
Financing		
Cash Used for Dividends	$ (6,000)	
Proceeds for Long-term Bond Issued	100,000	
Cash Flow from Financing		94,000
Net Change in Cash for Year		$ (24,000)
Cash, January 1, Year 4		30,000
Cash, December 31, Year 4		$ 6,000

EXHIBIT 4.7	ROBBIE CORPORATION Income Statement for Year 2 (all dollar amounts in thousands Problem 4.2 for Self Study)

Sales Revenue	$ 180
Cost of Goods Sold	(140)
Selling and Administrative Expenses	(25)
Depreciation Expense	(6)
Interest Expense	(2)
Net Income	$ 7

Problem 4.3 for Self-Study

Computing cash flow from operations, both direct and indirect, from the columnar work sheet. Refer to **Problem 4.2 for Self-Study**. **Exhibit 4.7** presents an income statement for Robbie Corporation for Year 2. **Exhibit 4.8** presents a comparative balance sheet for Robbie Corporation as of December 31, Year 1 and Year 2. Compute the amount of cash flow from operations using the format shown in the lower panel of **Exhibit 4.4**.

EXHIBIT 4.8	ROBBIE CORPORATION Comparative Balance Sheet December 31, Year 1 and Year 2 (all dollar amounts in thousands Problem 4.2 for Self-Study)		

	December 31	
	Year 1	**Year 2**
ASSETS		
Current Assets		
Cash	$ 10	$ 25
Accounts Receivable	15	22
Merchandise Inventories	20	18
Total Current Assets	$ 45	$ 65
NONCURRENT ASSETS		
Property, Plant, and Equipment	$ 50	$ 66
Less Accumulated Depreciation	(25)	(31)
Total Property, Plant, and Equipment	$ 25	$ 35
Total Assets	$ 70	$100
LIABILITIES AND SHAREHOLDERS' EQUITY		
Current Liabilities		
Accounts Payable	$ 30	$ 37
Total Current Liabilities	$ 30	$ 37
LONG-TERM DEBT		
Bonds Payable	10	18
Total Liabilities	$ 40	$ 55
SHAREHOLDERS' EQUITY		
Common Stock	$ 10	$ 20
Retained Earnings	20	25
Total Shareholders' Equity	$ 30	$ 45
Total Liabilities and Shareholder's Equity	$ 70	$100

An International Perspective

Standard No. 7 of the International Accounting Standards Committee recommends the preparation of a statement of cash flows that reports cash flows from operating, investing, and financing activities.[7] Standard-setting bodies in most countries have adopted this standard, so that firms in these countries prepare a statement of cash flows following the format illustrated in this chapter.

Problem 4.4 for Self-Study

Preparing a statement of cash flows. **Exhibit 4.9** presents a comparative balance sheet for Gordon Corporation as of December 31, Year 1 and Year 2. **Exhibit 4.10** shows the income statement for Year 2.

a. Prepare a columnar work sheet for a statement of cash flows and a reconciliation of net income to cash flows from operations. Gordon Corporations shows Buildings and Equipment net on the balance sheet, so you will have to compute the change in the accounts for Buildings and Equipment [at Cost] and Accumulated Depreciation.

b. Prepare a formal statement of cash flows using the direct method, which always must include a reconciliation of net income to cash flow from operations as when using the indirect method.

---

[7]International Accounting Standards Committee, *International Accounting Standard No. 7*, "Cash Flow Statements," 1994.

Repeated for convenience:

$$\Delta C = \Delta L + \Delta SE - \Delta N\$A \qquad \text{Equation (3), Cash Change Equation}$$

EXHIBIT 4.9	GORDON CORPORATION Comparative Balance Sheet December 31, Year 1 and Year 2 (all dollar amounts in thousands) (Problem 4.4 for Self-Study)

	December 31 Year 1	December 31 Year 2
ASSETS		
Current Assets		
Cash	$ 70	$ 40
Accounts Receivable	320	420
Merchandise Inventories	360	470
Prepayments	50	70
Total Current Assets	$ 800	$1,000
Property, Plant, and Equipment		
Land	$ 200	$ 250
Buildings and Equipment (net of accumulated depreciation of $800 and $840)	1,000	1,150
Total Property, Plant, and Equipment	$1,200	$1,400
Total Assets	$2,000	$2,400
LIABILITIES AND SHAREHOLDERS' EQUITY		
Current Liabilities		
Accounts Payable	$ 320	$ 440
Income Taxes Payable	60	90
Other Current Liabilities	170	350
Total Current Liabilities	$ 550	$ 880
Noncurrent Liabilities		
Bonds Payable	250	200
Total Liabilities	$ 800	$1,080
Shareholders' Equity		
Common Stock	$ 500	$ 540
Retained Earnings	700	780
Total Shareholders' Equity	$1,200	$1,320
Total Liabilities and Shareholders' Equity	$2,000	$2,400

Problem 4.5 for Self-Study

Solinger Electric Company, revised to derive Statement of Cash Flows with disposition of noncurrent assets at book value. Refer to the data for Solinger Electric Company presented in Exhibits 4.2 through 4.6. Assume that, in addition to the data given earlier, Solinger Electric Company disposed of buildings and equipment that had originally cost $5,000 and, at the disposition, had accumulated depreciation of $4,000. Solinger Electric Company received $1,000 cash for the used equipment, an amount exactly equal to its book value at the time of disposition. The text does not explain how to deal with this transaction. You can use this problem and its answer to see how to handle disposition of plant assets.

a. Prepare a columnar work sheet to derive the statement of cash flows for Solinger Electric Company, using the additional information about the disposition of buildings and equipment.

b. Prepare a statement of cash flows using the direct method for Solinger Electric Company, using the additional information about the disposition of buildings and equipment.

EXHIBIT 4.10	GORDON CORPORATION Income Statement for Year 2 (all dollar amounts in thousands) (Problem 4.4 for Self-Study)

Revenues	$1,600
Less:	
Cost of Goods Sold	(900)
Depreciation Expense	(40)
Selling and Administrative Expense	(300)
Interest Expense	(30)
Income Tax Expense	(130)
Net Income	$ 200

Using Information in the Statement of Cash Flows

The statement of cash flows provides information that helps the reader in (1) assessing the impact of operations on liquidity and (2) assessing the relations among cash flows from operating, investing, and financing activities.

Impact of Operations on Liquidity

Perhaps the most important factor not reported on either the balance sheet or the income statement is how the operations of a period affected cash flows. Increased earnings do not always generate increased cash flow from operations. When increased earnings result from expanding operations (that is, more units of sales in contrast to mere increases in selling price or reductions in cost), the firm usually has decreased cash flow from operations. A growing, successful firm—such as Wal-Mart, discussed in connection with **Exhibit 4.1**—may have increasing amounts for accounts receivable and inventories, resulting in a lag between earnings and cash flows. The need to await the collection of accounts receivable but to acquire and pay for inventory in anticipation of larger sales in the future can cause cash shortages from operations. Successful, growing businesses will need permanent financing from long-term debt issues or common stock issues to cover short-term cash needs. Some successful firms find themselves constantly short of cash because they have not adequately obtained long-term financing to cover perpetual short-term needs. Financial managers need to anticipate that the more successful the firm becomes, the more long-term sources of funds it will need to finance operations.

On the other hand, increased cash flow can accompany reduced earnings. Consider, for example, a firm that is experiencing operating problems and reduces the scope of its activities. Such a firm likely will report reduced net income or even losses. However, it might experience positive cash flow from operations because it collects accounts receivable from prior periods but does not replace inventories, thus saving cash.

Relations among Cash Flows from Operating, Investing, and Financing Activities

The relations among the cash flows from each of the three principal business activities likely differ depending on the characteristics of the firm's products and the maturity of its industry. Consider each of the four following patterns of cash flows.

Cash Flows from:	A	B	C	D
Operations	$ (3)	$ 7	$15	$ 8
Investing	(15)	(12)	(8)	(2)
Financing	18	5	(7)	(6)
Net Cash Flow	$ 0	$ 0	$ 0	$ 0

Repeated for convenience:

$$\Delta C = \Delta L + \Delta SE - \Delta N\$A \qquad \text{Equation (3), Cash Change Equation}$$

Case A illustrates a typical new, rapidly growing firm. It does not yet operate profitably, and it experiences buildups of its accounts receivable and inventories. Thus, it has negative cash flow from operations. To sustain its rapid growth, the firm must invest heavily in plant and equipment. During this stage, the firm must rely on external sources of cash to finance both its operating and its investing activities.

Case B illustrates a somewhat more seasoned firm than the one in **Case A**, but one that is still growing. It operates profitably, but because its rapid growth has begun to slow, it generates positive cash flow from operations. However, this cash flow from operations falls short of the amount the firm needs to finance acquisitions of plant and equipment. The firm therefore requires external financing.

Case C illustrates the cash flow pattern of a mature, stable firm. It generates a healthy cash flow from operations—more than enough to acquire new plant and equipment. It uses the excess cash flow to repay financing from earlier periods and, perhaps, to pay dividends.

Case D illustrates a firm in the early stages of decline. Its cash from operations has begun to decrease but remains positive because of decreases in accounts receivable and inventories. In the later stages of decline, its cash flow from operations may even turn negative as it finds itself unable to sell its products at a positive net cash flow. It cuts back significantly on capital expenditures because it is in a declining industry. It uses some of its excess cash flow to repay outstanding financing, and it has the remainder available for investment in new products or other industries.

Refer to the statements of cash flows for the four firms for a recent year in **Exhibit 4.11**. You will find the statement of cash flows more informative when you study cash flows for several years. These single-year statements illustrate some important relations for firms in different stages of growth.

EXHIBIT 4.11	Excerpts from Statements of Cash Flows for Four Firms (all dollar amounts in millions)			
	Amazon.com	**Discount Auto Parts**	**Anheuser-Busch**	**Levitz Furniture**
OPERATIONS				
Cash Flow from Operations	$(130)	$ 28	$ 2,258	$ (14)
INVESTING				
Sale of Fixed Assets.................................	$ —	$ —	$ —	$ 12
Acquisition of Fixed Assets	(135)	(69)	(1,075)	(6)
Sale of Marketable Securities	299	—	—	—
Other Investing Transactions........................	—	5	(43)	—
Cash Flow from Investing	$ 164	$(64)	$(1,118)	$ 6
FINANCING				
Increase in Short-term Borrowing	$ —	$ —	$ —	$ 670
Increase in Long-term Borrowing	648	40	804	—
Increase in Capital Stock	45	—	135	—
Decrease in Short-term Borrowing	—	—	—	(659)
Decrease in Long-term Borrowing	—	—	(514)	(2)
Decrease in Capital Stock	—	—	(986)	—
Dividends	—	—	(571)	—
Other Financing Transactions	(38)	—	—	—
Cash Flow from Financing	$ 655	$ 40	$(1,132)	$ 9
Change in Cash	$ 689	$ 4	$ 8	$ 1
Cash, Beginning of Year	133	8	152	5
Cash, End of Year	$ 822	$ 12	$ 160	$ 6

Amazon.com depicts typical cash flows of a new, rapidly growing firm. It operated at a net loss for the year and its operations consumed cash—it generated negative cash flow from operations. The firm also made expenditures on additional property, plant, and equipment to maintain its growth. It financed the negative cash flow from operations and capital expenditures by selling marketable securities and issuing additional long-term debt. The firm had issued common stock in an earlier year and invested the cash temporarily in marketable securities. It needed the cash this year and therefore sold a portion of its marketable securities. The proceeds of the new borrowing increased its cash balance on the balance sheet.

Discount Auto Parts depicts typical cash flows for a firm in the rapid growth phase, but somewhat more seasoned than Amazon.com. It posted a positive net income for the year and generated positive cash flow from operations. This cash flow from operations still fell short of the amounts it needed to finance acquisitions of property, plant, and equipment. Discount Auto Parts financed the shortfall with additional long-term borrowing, appropriate financing for noncurrent assets.

Anheuser-Busch depicts a cash flow pattern typical of a mature firm. It reports positive net income and positive cash flow from operations. Cash flow from operations exceeds the amounts the firm needs to finance investments in new property, plant, and equipment. The firm used the excess net cash flow from operating and investing activities to pay dividends and repurchase shares of its common stock.

The cash flows for Levitz Furniture are for a period just prior to its filing for bankruptcy and therefore in the late stage of the decline phase. It operated at a net loss and generated negative cash flow from operations. The investing section indicates the cash inflows from selling property, plant, and equipment. Given its poor financial condition, Levitz Furniture had to rely on short-term financing. Lenders required the firm to repay financing within one year and replace it with new financing.

These four cases do not, of course, cover all of the patterns of cash flows found in corporate annual reports. They illustrate, however, how the characteristics of a firm's products and industry can affect the interpretation of information in the statement of cash flows.

Ethical Issues and the Statement of Cash Flows

Many analysts focus attention on cash flow from operations, thinking it as important, or more so, than net income. A common misconception believes that the management has little opportunity to manipulate transactions affecting the statement of cash flows. After all, goes the logic: cash is cash; how can you fake a cash flow? The manipulation possibilities arise, not from the amounts of cash flows, which indeed management cannot easily fudge, but with either (1) their timing, or (2) their classification and disclosure in the statement and related notes.

Timing of Operating Cash Flows

Firms have some choice as to when they disburse cash. Firms that delay making payments to suppliers, employees, and others during the last several days of an accounting period conserve cash and thereby increase cash flow from operations for that period. When these firms make the cash payments during the early part of the next period, cash flow from operations declines. Thus, the firm increases cash flow from operations during the first period but decreases cash flow from operations during the second period. The firm, however, can delay making payments at the end of the second period to offset the negative cash flow effects of the payments made early in that period. As long as the firm continues to grow, it reports larger cash flow from operations each period than if it had not delayed making the cash payments at the end of each period.

Unless contracts or other agreements preclude the firm from delaying payments each period, the firm does not appear to engage in illegal activity. The ethical issues concern whether the firm portrays a misleading picture of its operating cash flows and whether it discloses sufficient information for the user to assess how much manipulation has occurred.

Classification and Disclosure of Transactions

Firms have also contrived to improve the appearance of operating cash flow by manipulating borrowing with an asset as collateral—a financing transaction—into a sale of an operating asset, which appears as an operating source of cash.

> *Repeated for convenience:*
>
> $$\Delta C = \Delta L + \Delta SE - \Delta N\$A \qquad \text{Equation (3), Cash Change Equation}$$

Example. Enron raised funds by borrowing from Merrill Lynch using barges anchored off the coast of Nigeria as collateral. Rather than execute a note and raise cash with an explicit borrowing, Enron arranged to sell the barges to Merrill Lynch for cash with an unwritten understanding that Enron would repurchase the barges later at a price equal to the original sale plus an amount equivalent to the interest on the borrowed funds for the term of the loan. Enron treated the barges as operating assets, so it showed the proceeds from Merrill Lynch as operating cash inflows, rather than as financing cash inflows.

If there had been no commitment by Enron to repurchase, then treatment of the sale of the barges as operating cash flow is consistent with GAAP: Enron sold some of its operating assets, just as another company might sell its inventory. [Even so, one might argue such a sale is a disposition of a long-term asset, hence a (dis-)investing source of cash.] When, as actually happened, Enron has a firm commitment to repurchase the barges, the economic substance is a borrowing and GAAP requires the firm to account for it as such. The ethical issue here is whether the managers of Enron willingly disclosed the repurchase commitment to its auditors or simply waited for the auditors to ask if such a repurchase agreement exists. A related ethical issue is whether Enron disclosed sufficient information about this transaction for the user of the financial statement to assess if the accounting was appropriate.

Summary

The statement of cash flows reports the effects of a firm's operating, investing, and financing activities on cash flows. Information in the statement helps in understanding

1. how operations affect the liquidity of a firm,
2. the level of capital expenditures needed to support ongoing and growing levels of activity, and
3. the major changes in the financing of a firm.

To prepare the statement of cash flows requires analyzing changes in balance sheet accounts during the accounting period, as represented by the Cash Change Equation (3). As a by-product of correct double-entry recording of all transactions, the net change in cash will equal the net change in all noncash accounts.

The statement of cash flows usually presents cash flow from operations in the indirect format, beginning with net income for the period. The statement then adjusts for revenues not providing cash, for expenses not using cash, and for changes in operating working capital accounts. The result is cash flow from operations. Some firms follow a more direct approach to calculating cash flow from operations by listing all revenues that provide cash and subtracting all expenses that use cash. Such firms present a reconciliation of net income to cash flow from operations. The cash flows from investing activities and financing activities appear after cash flow from operations.

Interpreting a statement of cash flows requires an understanding of the economic characteristics of the industries in which a firm conducts its activities, including capital intensity, growth characteristics, and similar factors.

Problem 4.6 for Self-Study

Effect of transactions on the statement of cash flows. **Exhibit 4.12** shows a simplified statement of cash flows for a period. Numbers appear on eleven of the lines in the statement. Other lines are various subtotals and grand totals; ignore these in the remainder of the problem. Assume that the accounting cycle is complete for the period and that the firm has prepared all of the financial statements. It then discovers that it has overlooked a transaction. It records that transaction in the accounts and corrects all of the financial statements. For each of the following transactions, indicate which of the numbered lines of the statement of cash flows change, and

(continued)

Problem 4.6 for Self-Study *(continued)*

state the amount and direction of the change. If net income, line (1), changes, be sure to indicate whether it decreases or increases. Ignore income tax effects. *(Hint:* First, construct the entry the firm would make in its accounts to record the transaction. Then, for each line of the journal entry, identify the line of **Exhibit 4.12** affected.)

a. Depreciation expense of $2,000 on an office computer
b. Purchase of machinery for $10,000 cash
c. Declaration of a cash dividend of $6,500 on common stock; the firm paid the dividend by the end of the fiscal year
d. Issue of common stock for $12,000 cash
e. Proceeds of the sale of a common stock investment, a noncurrent asset, for $15,000 cash; the firm sold the investment for its book value of $15,000

EXHIBIT 4.12	Simplified Statement of Cash Flows (Problem 4.6 for Self-Study)

Operations

Cash Receipts from Customers	[1]
Less: Cash Payments to Suppliers, Employees, and Others	−[2]
Cash Flow from Operations [= (1) − (2)]	S1

Reconciliation of Net Income to Cash Flow from Operations

Net Income	[3]
Additions to Net Income to Compute Cash Flow from Operations	+[4]
Subtractions from Net Income to Compute Cash Flow from Operations	−[5]
Cash Flow from Operations [= (3) + (4) − (5)]	S1

Investing

Proceeds from Dispositions of "Investing" Assets	+[6]
Cash Used to Acquire "Investing" Assets	−[7]
Cash Flow from Investing [= (6) − (7)]	S2

Financing

Cash Provided by Increases in Debt or Capital Stock	+[8]
Cash Used to Reduce Debt or Capital Stock	−[9]
Cash Used for Dividends	−[10]
Cash Flow from Financing [= (8) − (9) − (10)]	S3
Net Change in Cash [= S1 + S2 + S3]	[11]
Cash, Beginning of the Period	S4
Cash, End of the Period [= (11) + S4]	S5

Solutions to Self-Study Problems

SUGGESTED SOLUTION TO PROBLEM 4.1 FOR SELF-STUDY

(Classifying cash flows by type of activity.)

a. Operating
b. Financing
c. Operating
d. Operating
e. Operating
f. Operating
g. Investing

h. Item does not affect cash flows during the current period and would therefore not appear in the statement of cash flows. The firm must disclose this transaction in a separate schedule or a note to the financial statements.

i. Operating

j. Operating

k. Investing

l. Item does not affect cash flows during the current period and would therefore not appear in the statement of cash flows. The firm must disclose this transaction in a separate schedule or note to the financial statements.

m. Financing

n. Investing

o. Financing

p. Investing

q. Operating

SUGGESTED SOLUTION TO PROBLEM 4.2 FOR SELF-STUDY

(Robbie Corporation; preparing a columnar work sheet for a statement of cash flows.) **Exhibit 4.13** presents a completed columnar work sheet for Robbie Corporation.

EXHIBIT 4.13	ROBBIE CORPORATION Work Sheet for Preparing the Statement of Cash Flows For Year 2

CLASSIFICATION OF BALANCE SHEET CHANGES

Balance Sheet Accounts	Account Changes	=	Operations	+	Investing	+	Financing	
(Increase) Decrease in Assets								
[1] Accounts Receivable	$ (7)		$ (7) [1]					
[2] Merchandise Inventories	2		2 [2]					
[3] Buildings and Equipment	(16)				$(16) [3]			
[4] Accumulated Depreciation	6		6 [4]					
Increase (Decrease) in Liabilities and Shareholders' Equity								
[5] Accounts Payable—Merchandise Suppliers	7		7 [5]					
[6] Bonds Payable	8						$ 8	[6]
[7] Common Shares	10						10	[7]
[8] Retained Earnings	5		7 [8]				(2)	[8]
[9] Increase (Decrease) in Cash	$ 15	=	$15	+	$(16)	+	$16	[9]

SUGGESTED SOLUTION TO PROBLEM 4.3 FOR SELF-STUDY

(Robbie Corporation; computing cash flow from operations, both direct and indirect, from the columnar work sheet.) **Exhibit 4.14** presents a completed work sheet for cash flow from operations using both direct and indirect methods for Robbie Corporation.

SUGGESTED SOLUTION TO PROBLEM 4.4 FOR SELF-STUDY

(Gordon Corporation; preparing a statement of cash flows.) **Exhibit 4.15** presents a completed columnar work sheet for Gordon Corporation. **Exhibit 4.16** presents a formal statement of cash flows.

SUGGESTED SOLUTION TO PROBLEM 4.5 FOR SELF-STUDY

(Solinger Electric Company, revised to derive Statement of Cash Flows with disposition of noncurrent assets at book value.)

EXHIBIT 4.14	ROBBIE CORPORATION Work Sheet for Preparing both Indirect and Direct Methods for the Statement of Cash Flows For Year 2

	Income Statement	**Indirect Method for Cash Flows from Operations** Income Plus Changes in Balance Sheet Operating Accounts =	**Direct Method for Cash Flows from Operations**		
			Cash Receipts +	Cash Payments =	Net Cash Inflow (Outflow)
Net Income		$ 7			
Revenues	$ 180	$ (7) **[1]**	$173	=	$ 173
Less:					
Cost of Goods Sold	(140)	2 **[2]**			
		7 **[5]**		$(131) =	(131)
Depreciation Expense	(6)	6 **[4]**		—	—
Selling and Administrative	(25)	—		(25) =	(25)
				=	—
Interest Expense	(2)	—		(2) =	(2)
Net Income	$ 7				
Cash Flow From Operations		$15	$173 +	$(158) =	$ 15

SUGGESTED SOLUTION TO PROBLEM 4.6 FOR SELF-STUDY

(Effect of transactions on the statement of cash flows.) Preparing the journal entry for each transaction aids in understanding the effect on the eleven numbered lines in **Exhibit 4.12**.

a. Retained Earnings (Depreciation Expense)(Shareholders' Equity Decrease)   2,000
        Accumulated Depreciation (Asset Decrease)   2,000

$$\Delta C \quad = \quad \Delta L \quad + \quad \Delta SE \quad - \quad \Delta N\$A$$
$$0 \quad = \quad 0 \quad + \quad -2{,}000 \quad - \quad -2{,}000$$

This entry has no impact on operating cash flows, so no effect on lines **(1)** and **(2)**. It involves a debit to an income statement account, so line **(3)** decreases by $2,000. Depreciation expense reduces net income but does not affect cash line **(11)**. Thus, line **(4)** must increase by $2,000 for the addback of depreciation expense to net income. This addback eliminates the effect of depreciation on both cash flow from operations and cash.

b. Machinery (Asset Increase)   10,000
        Cash (Asset Decrease)   10,000

$$\Delta C \quad = \quad \Delta L \quad + \quad \Delta SE \quad - \quad \Delta N\$A$$
$$-10{,}000 \quad = \quad 0 \quad + \quad 0 \quad - \quad 10{,}000$$

This entry does not involve receipts from customers nor payments to suppliers, so does not affect lines **(1)** and **(2)**. It involves a credit to Cash, so line **(11)** decreases by $10,000. Because line **(11)** is the net change in cash for the period, some other line must change as well. Acquisitions of equipment represent Investing activities, so line **(7)** increases by $10,000. Note that line **(7)** has a negative sign, so this means an increase to an amount subtracted; increasing this line reduces cash.

c. Retained Earnings (Shareholders' Equity Decrease)   6,500
        Cash (Asset Decrease)   6,500

$$\Delta C \quad = \quad \Delta L \quad + \quad \Delta SE \quad - \quad \Delta N\$A$$
$$-6{,}500 \quad = \quad 0 \quad + \quad -6{,}500 \quad - \quad 0$$

EXHIBIT 4.15

GORDON CORPORATION
Work Sheet for Preparing the Statement of Cash Flows and Reconciliation
of Net Income to Cash Flows from Operating Activities
For Year 2

CLASSIFICATION OF BALANCE SHEET CHANGES

Balance Sheet Accounts	Account Changes	=	Operations	+	Investing	+	Financing
			Classification by Kind of Activity for Source or Use of Cash				
(Increase) Decrease in Assets							
[1] Accounts Receivable	$(100)		$(100) [1]				
[2] Merchandise Inventories	(110)		(110) [2]				
[3] Prepayments	(20)		(20) [3]				
[4] Land	(50)				$ (50) [4]		
[5] Building and Equipment	(190) [a]				$(190) [5]		
[6] Accumulated Depreciation	40		40 [6]				
Increase (Decrease) in Liabilities and Shareholders' Equity							
[7] Accounts Payable	120		120 [7]				
[8] Income Taxes Payable	30		30 [8]				
[9] Other Current Liabilities	180		180 [9]				
[10] Bonds Payable	(50)						$ (50) [10]
[11] Common Shares	40						40 [11]
[12] Retained Earnings	80		200 [12]				(120) [12]
[13] Increase (Decrease) in Cash	$ (30)	=	$ 340	+	$(240)	+	$(130) [13]

	Income Statement		Indirect Method for Cash Flows from Operations — Income Plus Changes in Balance Sheet Operating Accounts =	Direct Method for Cash Flows from Operations — Cash Receipts +	(Cash Payments) =	Net Cash Inflow (Outflow)
Net Income			$ 228			
Revenues	$1,600		$(100) [1]	$1,500		= $1,500
Less:						
Cost of Goods Sold	(900)		(110) [2] 120 [7]		$ (890) =	(890)
Depreciation Expense	(40)		40 [6]		—	—
Selling and Administrative	(300)		180 [9] (20) [3]		(140) =	(140)
Interest Expense	(2)		—		(2) =	(2)
Income Tax Expense	(130)		30 [8]		(100) =	(100)
Net Income	$ 228					
Cash Flow from Operations			$ 368	$1,500 +	$(1,132) =	$ 368

[a] Buildings and Equipment at Cost at the beginning of the year was
$1,800 = $800 + $1,000; at the end of the year was $1,990 = $840 + $1,150

This entry involves a credit to Cash, so line **(11)** decreases by $6,500. Dividends are a financing activity, so line **(10)** increases by $6,500.

d. Cash (Asset Increase)	12,000	
Common Stock (Shareholders' Equity Increase)		12,000

$$\Delta C \quad = \quad \Delta L \quad + \quad \Delta SE \quad - \quad \Delta N\$A$$
$$12{,}000 \quad = \quad 0 \quad + \quad 12{,}000 \quad - \quad 0$$

The debit to Cash means that line **(11)** increases by $12,000. Issuing stock is a financing transaction, so line **(8)** increases by $12,000.

EXHIBIT 4.16	**GORDON CORPORATION** **Statement of Cash Flows for Year 2** **(all dollar amounts in thousands) (Problem 4.4 for Self-Study)**

OPERATIONS

Receipts from Customers		$1,500
Payments to Suppliers of Merchandise		(890)
Paid for Selling and Administrative Expenses		(140)
Payments to Lenders for Interest		(30)
Payments for Income Taxes		(100)
Cash Flow from Operating Activities		$ 340

RECONCILIATION OF NET INCOME TO CASH PROVIDED BY OPERATIONS

Net Income	$ 200	
Additions:		
Depreciation Expense	40	
Increase in Accounts Payable	120	
Increase in Income Taxes Payable	30	
Increase in Other Current Liabilities	180	
Subtractions:		
Increase in Accounts Receivable	(100)	
Increase in Merchandise Inventories	(110)	
Increase in Prepayments	(20)	
Cash Flow from Operations	$ 340	

INVESTING

Acquisition of Land	$ (50)	
Acquisition of Buildings and Equipment	(190)	
Cash Used for Investing		(240)

FINANCING

Common Stock Issued	$ 40	
Dividends Paid	(120)	
Repayment of Bonds	(50)	
Cash Used for Financing		(130)
Net Decrease in Cash		$ (30)
Cash, Beginning of Year 2		70
Cash, End of Year 2		$ (40)

e.	Cash (Asset Increase)	15,000	
	Investment in Securities (Asset Decrease)		15,000

$$\Delta C \quad = \quad \Delta L \quad + \quad \Delta SE \quad - \quad \Delta N\$A$$
$$15,000 \quad = \quad 0 \quad + \quad 0 \quad - \quad -15,000$$

The debit to Cash means that line **(11)** increases by $15,000. Selling investments in securities is an investing activity, so line **(6)** increases by $15,000.

EXHIBIT 4.17	SOLINGER ELECTRIC CORPORATION Work Sheet for Preparing the Revised Statement of Cash Flows and Reconciliation of Net Income to Cash Flows from Operating Activities For Year 4

Statement Revised to Incorporate Sale of Buildings and Equipment for $1,000
Original Cost of $5,000, with Accumulated Depreciation of $4,000
Numbers affected by revision appear in **color**.

CLASSIFICATION OF BALANCE SHEET CHANGES

Balance Sheet Accounts	Account Changes	=	Operations	+	Investing	+	Financing	
(Increase) Decrease in Assets								
[1] Accounts Receivable	$ (35,000)		$(35,000) [1]					
[2] Merchandise Inventories	(10,000)		(10,000) [2]					
[3] Buildings and Equipment	(125,000)							
Sold B&E Costing $5,000 for $1,000	5,000				1,000	[3]		
Purchased new Buildings and Equipment	(130,000)				(130,000)	[3]		
[4] Accumulated Depreciation	6,000							
Depreciation Expense for Year . .	10,000		10,000 [4]					
Sold B&E with Accumulated Depreciation of	(4,000)							
Increase (Decrease) in Liabilities and Shareholders' Equity								
[5] Accounts Payable—Merchandise Suppliers .	23,000		23,000 [5]					
[6] Accounts Payable—Other Suppliers	2,000		2,000 [6]					
[7] Salaries Payable	1,000		1,000 [7]					
[8] Interest Payable	(3,000)		(3,000) [8]					
[9] Bonds Payable	100,000						$100,000	[9]
[10] Common Shares	—							
[11] Retained Earnings	13,000		19,000 [11]				(6,000)	[11]
[12] Increase (Decrease) in Cash	(28,000)	=	$ 7,000	+	(129,000)	+	$ 94,000	[12]

		Indirect Method for Cash Flows from Operations	Direct Method for Cash Flows from Operations			
	Income Statement	Income Plus Changes in Balance Sheet Operating Accounts =	Cash Receipts +	(Cash Payments) =	Net Cash Inflow (Outflow)	
Net Income		$ 19,000				
Revenues	$125,000	$(35,000) [1]	$90,000		= $ 90,000	
Less:						
Cost of Goods Sold	(60,000)	(10,000) [2]				
		23,000 [5]		$(47,000) =	(47,000)	
Depreciation Expense	(10,000)	10,000 [4]		—	—	
Salary Expense	(20,000)	1,000 [7]		(19,000) =	(19,000)	
Other Expenses	(11,000)	2,000 [6]		(9,000) =	(9,000)	
Interest Expense	(5,000)	(3,000) [8]		(8,000) =	(8,000)	
Net Income	$ 19,000					
Cash Flow From Operations		$ 7,000	$90,000 +	$(83,000) =	$ 7,000	

EXHIBIT 4.18	SOLINGER ELECTRIC CORPORATION, Revised Statement of Cash Flows for Year 4 (Direct Method with Reconciliation of Net Income to Cash Flow from Operations)

Statement Revised to Incorporate Sale of Buildings and Equipment for $1,000
Original Cost of $5,000, with Accumulated Depreciation of $4,000
Numbers Differing from Original Exhibit Appear in **Color**

OPERATING ACTIVITIES

Sources of Cash

Cash Received from Customers	$ 90,000	
Uses of Cash		
Payments to Suppliers of Merchandise	(47,000)	
Payments for Employee Compensation	(19,000)	
Payments to Other Suppliers	(9,000)	
Payments for Interest	(8,000)	
Cash Flow from Operations		$ 7,000

RECONCILIATION OF NET INCOME TO CASH PROVIDED BY OPERATING ACTIVITIES

Net Income	$ 19,000	
Adjustments to Reconcile Net Income to Net Cash Provided		
Depreciation	10,000	
(Increase) in Accounts Receivable	(35,000)	
(Increase) in Inventories	(10,000)	
Increase in Accounts Payable for Merchandise	23,000	
(Increase) in Payables to Other Suppliers	2,000	
Increase in Salaries Payable	1,000	
Decrease in Interest Payable	(3,000)	
Net Cash Provided by Operating Activities	$ 7,000	

Investing

Cash Used for Acquisition of Buildings and Equipment	(130,000)	
Proceeds from Sale of Buildings and Equipment	1,000	
Cash Flow from Investing		(129,000)

Financing

Cash Used for Dividends	$ (6,000)	
Proceeds for Long-term Bond Issued	100,000	
Cash Flow from Financing		94,000
Net Change in Cash for Year		$ (28,000)
Cash, January 1, Year 4		30,000
Cash, December 31, Year 4		$ 2,000

Key Terms and Concepts

Cash flow from operations
Cash flow from investing activities
Cash flow from financing activities
Direct method

Indirect method
Cash Change Equation
Columnar work sheet

Questions, Short Exercises, Exercises, Problems, and Cases

QUESTIONS

1. Review the meaning of the terms and concepts listed above in Key Terms and Concepts.

2. "One can most easily accomplish the reporting objective of the income statement under the accrual basis of accounting and the reporting objective of the statement of cash flows by issuing a single income statement using the cash basis of accounting." Evaluate this proposal.

3. "The accrual basis of accounting creates the need for a statement of cash flows." Explain.

4. "The statement of cash flows provides information about changes in the structure of a firm's assets and equities." Explain.

5. A student remarked: "The direct method of computing cash flow from operations is easier to understand than the indirect method. Why do the vast majority of firms follow the indirect method in preparing their statements of cash flows?" Respond to this student.

6. The statement of cash flows classifies cash expenditures for interest expense as an operating activity but classifies cash expenditures to redeem debt as a financing activity. Explain this apparent paradox.

7. The statement of cash flows classifies cash expenditures for interest on debt as an operating activity but classifies cash expenditures for dividends to shareholders as a financing activity. Explain this apparent paradox.

8. The statement of cash flows classifies changes in accounts payable as an operating activity but classifies changes in short-term bank borrowing as a financing activity. Explain this apparent paradox.

9. The acquisition of equipment by assuming a mortgage is a transaction that firms cannot report in their statement of cash flows but must report in a supplemental schedule or note. Of what value is information about this type of transaction? What is the reason for its exclusion from the statement of cash flows?

10. One writer stated, "Depreciation expense is a firm's chief source of cash for growth." A reader criticized this statement by replying: "The fact remains that if companies had elected, in any year, to charge off $10 million more depreciation than they did charge off, they would not thereby have added one dime to the total of their cash available for expanding plants or for increasing inventories or receivables. Therefore, to speak of depreciation expense as a source of cash is incorrect and misleading." Comment on these statements, taking into account income tax effects.

11. A firm generated net income for the current year, but cash flow from operations was negative. How can this happen?

12. A firm operated at a net loss for the current year, but cash flow from operations was positive. How can this happen?

13. The sale of equipment for an amount of cash greater than the book value of the equipment results in a cash receipt equal to the book value of the equipment plus the gain on the sale, which appears in income. How might the accountant treat this transaction in the statement of cash flows? Consider both the direct and indirect methods.

For additional student resources, content, and interactive quizzes for this chapter visit the FACMU website: **http://facmu.swlearning.com**

SHORT EXERCISES

14. **Derive sales revenue from data in the statement of cash flows and balance sheet.** Microsoft Corporation reported a balance of $5,196 million in accounts receivable at the beginning of Year 14 and $5,334 million at the end of Year 14. Its statement of cash flows using the direct method reported cash collections from customers of $33,551 million for Year 14. Assuming that Microsoft Corporation makes all sales on account, compute the amount of sales during Year 14.

15. **Derive cost of goods sold from data in the statement of cash flows.** The section showing cash flow from operations, using the indirect method, for General Electric Company reported an increase in inventories during Year 13 of $1,753 million and no change in accounts payable for inventories. The direct method would show cash payments for inventory, purchased and manufactured, totaling $64,713 million. Compute the cost of goods sold for Year 13.

16. **Derive cost of goods sold from data in the statement of cash flows.** The section showing cash flow from operations, using the indirect method, for Ann Taylor Stores reported an increase in inventories of $5.7 million during Year 13. It reported also that the balance in accounts payable for inventories increased by $5.9 million. The direct method would show cash payments for merchandise inventory purchased of $646.9 million. Compute the cost of goods sold for Year 13.

17. **Derive wages and salaries expense from data in the statement of cash flows.** AMR, the parent company of American Airlines, reported in its reconciliation of net income to cash flow from operations a decrease in wages and salaries payable of $21 million during Year 13. It provided data showing that cash payments for wages and salaries to employees for Year 13 were $8,853 million. Compute the amount of wages and salaries expense for Year 13.

18. **Derive cash disbursements for dividends.** Johnson & Johnson, a pharmaceutical and medical products company, reported a balance in retained earnings of $26,571 million at the beginning of Year 13 and $28,132 million at the end of Year 13. Its dividends payable account increased

by $233 million during Year 13. It reported net income for Year 13 of $5,030 million. How much cash did Johnson & Johnson disburse for dividends during Year 13? Indicate where this information would appear in the simplified statement of cash flows in **Exhibit 4.12**.

19. **Effect of borrowing and interest on statement of cash flows.** Gillette borrowed $250 million on October 1, Year 12. The debt carries an annual interest rate of 6 percent and is payable in two installments, on April 1 and October 1 of each year. The debt matures on October 1, Year 32. Gillette's accounting period ends on December 31 of each year. Using the format of **Exhibit 4.12**, indicate the effects of all these transactions on Gillette's statement of cash flows for Year 12.

20. **Effect of income taxes on statement of cash flows.** Radio Shack reported a balance in Income Taxes Payable of $78.1 million at the beginning of Year 13, $60.1 million at the end of Year 13, and income tax expense for the year of $161.5 million. Using the format of **Exhibit 4.12**, indicate the effects of all these transactions on Radio Shack's statement of cash flows for Year 13.

21. **Effect of rent transactions on statement of cash flows.** A firm reported a balance in its Prepaid Rent (Advances to Landlords) account of $1,200 on January 1, Year 12, for use of the building for the month of January, Year 12. On February 1, Year 12, the firm paid $18,000 as the annual rental for the period from February 1, Year 12 to January 31, Year 13. It recorded this rental payment by debiting Prepaid Rent (Advances to Landlord) and crediting Cash for $18,000. At the end of Year 12, the firm made all proper adjusting entries to correctly report balance sheet and income statement amounts. Using the format of **Exhibit 4.12**, indicate the effects of all these transactions on the firm's statement of cash flows for Year 12.

22. **Calculating components of cash flow from operations. Exhibit 4.19** provides items from the financial statements of Information Technologies, a systems engineering firm, for Year 2. How much cash did Information Technologies collect from its customers during Year 2?

EXHIBIT 4.19	Information Technologies Data from Income Statement for Year 2 (Problem 22) (All amounts in thousands)

Sales	$ 14,508
Cost of Goods Sold	(11,596)
Depreciation Expense	(114)
Other Expenses, Including Salaries and Wages Expense	(2,276)
Income Taxes	(210)
Net Income	$ 312

Data from Beginning of Year 2 and End of Year 2 Balance Sheets

Accounts Receivable	$782	Decrease
Inventories	66	Decrease
Prepayments for Other Costs	102	Decrease
Accounts Payable for Inventories	90	Increase
Current Liabilities for Wages and Salaries Payable	240	Decrease

23. **Calculating components of cash flow from operations.** Refer to **Exhibit 4.19**, which provides items from the financial statements of Information Technologies. How much cash did Information Technologies pay during Year 2 to its suppliers of goods?

24. **Calculating components of cash flow from operations.** Refer to **Exhibit 4.19**, which provides items from the financial statements of Information Technologies. How much cash did Information Technologies pay during Year 2 to its employees and suppliers of other services?

25. **Working backward from changes in the Buildings and Equipment account.** The comparative balance sheets of American Airlines show a balance in the Buildings and Equipment account at cost on December 31, Year 4, of $17,369 million; at December 31, Year 3, the balance was $16,825 million. The Accumulated Depreciation account shows a balance of $5,465 million at December 31, Year 4, and of $4,914 million at December 31, Year 3. The statement of cash flows reports that expenditures for buildings and equipment during Year 4 totaled $1,314 million. The income statement indicates a depreciation charge of $1,253 million during Year 4. The firm sold buildings and equipment during the year at their book value.

Calculate the acquisition cost and accumulated depreciation of the buildings and equipment that were retired during the year and the proceeds from the disposition.

EXERCISES

26. Calculating and interpreting cash flows. Amazon.com sells books over the Internet. The changes in its balance sheet accounts for two recent years appear below (amounts in thousands):

	Year 4	Year 5
Cash	$5,252 Increase	$103,561 Increase
Marketable Securities	—	15,256 Increase
Inventories	554 Increase	8,400 Increase
Prepayments	307 Increase	2,977 Increase
Property, Plant, and Equipment (at cost)	1,360 Increase	15,283 Increase
Accumulated Depreciation	286 Increase	4,742 Increase
Accounts Payable—Merchandise Suppliers	2,753 Increase	29,845 Increase
Other Current Liabilities	2,010 Increase	7,603 Increase
Long-term Debt	—	78,202 Increase
Common Stock	8,201 Increase	52,675 Increase
Retained Earnings	5,777 Decrease	27,590 Decrease

  a. Prepare columnar work sheets for the statement of cash flows for Year 4 and Year 5 using the format in the upper panel of **Exhibit 4.4**. Amazon.com did not declare or pay dividends during either year.
  b. Prepare a statement of cash flows for Year 4 and Year 5 using the indirect method of computing cash flow from operations. The balance in cash was $6,248 at the end of Year 4, and $109,809 at the end of Year 5.
  c. Discuss the relation between net income and cash flow from operations and the relation between cash flow from operating, investing, and financing activities during the two years.

27. Calculating and interpreting cash flows. Yahoo, Inc., is an Internet service provider. The changes in its balance sheet accounts for two recent years appear below (amounts in thousands):

	Year 8	Year 9
Cash	$ 28,250 Increase	$28,991 Increase
Marketable Securities (current asset)	60,689 Increase	32,917 Decrease
Accounts Receivable	4,267 Increase	5,904 Increase
Prepayments	384 Increase	5,509 Increase
Property, Plant, and Equipment (at cost)	3,155 Increase	14,930 Increase
Accumulated Depreciation	552 Increase	2,554 Increase
Investments in Securities (noncurrent asset)	10,477 Increase	9,053 Increase
Accounts Payable	1,086 Increase	3,605 Increase
Other Current Liabilities	6,447 Increase	11,598 Increase
Common Stock	103,796 Increase	36,980 Increase
Retained Earnings	4,659 Decrease	23,267 Decrease

  a. Prepare columnar work sheets for the statement of cash flows for Year 8 and Year 9 using the format in the upper panel of **Exhibit 4.4**. Yahoo, Inc., did not declare or pay dividends during either year. It sold marketable securities during Year 9 at no gain or loss.
  b. Prepare a statement of cash flows for Year 8 and Year 9 using the indirect method of computing cash flow from operations. The balance in cash was $33,547 at the end of Year 8 and $62,538 at the end of Year 9.
  c. Discuss the relation between net income and cash flow from operations and the relation between cash flow from operating, investing, and financing activities during the two years.

28. Preparing a columnar work sheet for a statement of cash flows from changes in balance sheet accounts. The balance sheets of Green Mountain Coffee Roasters allow the following computation of changes in account balances for a year (amounts in thousands):

Change	Amount	Direction
Cash	$ 74[a]	Increase
Accounts Receivable	2,231	Increase
Inventories	59	Decrease
Prepayments	475	Decrease
Property, Plant, and Equipment (at cost)	2,129[b]	Increase
Accumulated Depreciation	1,038[b]	Increase
Other Noncurrent Assets	434	Increase
Accounts Payable	1,574	Increase
Other Current Liabilities	560	Increase
Bonds Payable	$2,827[c]	Increase
Common Stock	5,878	Decrease
Retained Earnings	4,213[d]	Increase

[a] Cash was $415 thousand at the beginning of the year and $489 thousand at the end of the year.
[b] The firm sold for $538 thousand during the year equipment costing $2,468 thousand, with accumulated depreciation of $1,930 thousand.
[c] The firm retired during the year bonds with a face value and book value of $2,740 thousand, at no gain or loss.
[d] The firm did not declare or pay dividends during the year.

a. Prepare a columnar work sheet for the statement of cash flows for the current year using the format in the upper panel of **Exhibit 4.4**.

b. Comment on the most important reasons for the change in cash during the year.

29. Calculating and interpreting cash flow from operations. Selected data for Nokia, a Finnish cellular phone manufacturer, appear below (amounts in millions of Euros):

	Year 8	Year 9	Year 10	Year 11
Net Income (Loss)	€1,032	€1,689	€2,542	€3,847
Depreciation Expense	465	509	665	1,009
Increase (Decrease) in:				
Accounts Receivable	272	1,573	982	2,304
Inventories	121	103	362	422
Prepayments	(77)	17	33	(49)
Accounts Payable	90	140	312	458
Other Current Liabilities	450	1,049	867	923

a. Compute the amount of cash flow from operations for each of the four years using the indirect method.

b. Discuss briefly the most important reasons why cash flow from operations differs from net income or net loss for each year.

30. Calculating and interpreting cash flows. Omnicom Group is a marketing services firm. Omnicom Group creates advertising copy for clients and places the advertising in television, magazines, and other media. Accounts receivable represent amounts owed by clients and accounts payable represent amounts payable to various media. Omnicom Group has purchased other marketing services firms in recent years. Selected data for Omnicom Group for three recent years appear below (amounts in millions):

	Year 3	Year 4	Year 5
Net Income	$279	$363	$499
Depreciation and Amortization Expense	164	196	226
Increase (Decrease) in Accounts Receivable	238	648	514
Increase (Decrease) in Inventories	35	13	98
Increase (Decrease) in Prepayments	64	(10)	125

(continued)

(continued)	Year 3	Year 4	Year 5
Increase (Decrease) in Accounts Payable	330	786	277
Increase (Decrease) in Other Current Liabilities . . .	70	278	420
Acquisition of Property, Plant, and Equipment	115	130	150
Acquisition of Investments in Securities (noncurrent)	469	643	885
Dividends Paid	88	104	122
Long-term Debt Issued	208	83	599
Common Stock Issued (Reacquired)	42	(252)	(187)

a. Prepare a comparative statement of cash flows for Omnicom Group for the three years. Use the indirect method of computing cash flow from operations.

b. Discuss the relation between net income and cash flow from operations and the pattern of cash flow from operating, investing, and financing activities during the three years.

31. **Effects of gains and losses from sales of equipment on cash flows.** The text does not present material that shows how to answer these questions. You will need to think the answers through for yourself. **Exhibit 4.20** presents an abbreviated statement of cash flows for Largay Corporation for the current year (amounts in thousands). After preparing this statement of cash flows for the current year, you discover that the firm sold an item of equipment on the last day of the year but failed to record it in the accounts or to deposit the check received from the purchaser. The equipment originally cost $50,000 and had accumulated depreciation of $40,000 at the time of sale. Recast the statement of cash flows in the exhibit, assuming that Largay Corporation sold the equipment for cash in the following amounts (ignore income taxes):

a. $10,000

b. $12,000

c. $8,000

EXHIBIT 4.20	**LARGAY CORPORATION** **Statement of Cash Flows for the Current Year** **(Exercise 31) (all dollar amounts in thousands)**

OPERATIONS	
Net Income	$100
Depreciation Expense	15
Changes in Working Capital Accounts	(40)
Cash Flow from Operations	$ 75
INVESTING	
Acquisition of Buildings and Equipment	(30)
FINANCING	
Repayment of Long-term Debt	(40)
Change in Cash	$ 5
Cash, Beginning of Year	27
Cash, End of Year	$ 32

32. **Effect of various transactions on the statement of cash flows. Exhibit 4.12** shows a simplified statement of cash flows for a period. Numbers appear on eleven of the lines in the statement. Other lines are various subtotals and grand totals; ignore these in the remainder of the problem. Assume that the accounting cycle is complete for the period and that the firm has prepared all of the financial statements. It then discovers that it has overlooked a transaction. It records that transaction in the accounts and corrects all of the financial statements. For each of the following transactions, indicate which of the numbered lines of the statement of cash flows change, and state the amount and direction of the change. If net income, line **(3)**, changes, be sure to indicate whether it decreases or increases. Ignore income tax effects. (*Hint:* First, construct the entry the firm would enter in the accounts to record the transaction in the accounts.

Then, for each line of the journal entry, identify the line of **Exhibit 4.12** affected.)

a. Amortization of a patent, treated as an expense, $600

b. Acquisition of a factory site financed by issuing capital stock with a market value of $50,000 in exchange

c. Purchase of inventory on account for $7,500; assume inventory had increased for the year before the firm recorded this overlooked transaction.

d. Purchase of inventory for cash of $6,000; assume inventory had increased for the year before the firm recorded this overlooked transaction.

e. Uninsured fire loss of merchandise inventory totaling $1,500; assume inventory had increased for the year before the firm recorded this overlooked transaction.

f. Collection of an account receivable totaling $1,450; assume accounts receivable had increased for the year before the firm recorded this overlooked transaction.

g. Issue of bonds for $10,000 cash

h. Sale of equipment for cash at its book value of $4,500

PROBLEMS AND CASES

33. Preparing and interpreting the statement of cash flows using a columnar work sheet. The accounting records of The GAP, a clothing retailer, for Year 6 and Year 7 indicate the following changes in its balance sheet accounts (amounts in millions):

	Year 6	Year 7
Cash	$ 94 Decrease	$428 Increase
Marketable Securities (current asset)	46 Increase	46 Decrease
Merchandise Inventories	96 Increase	154 Increase
Prepayments	1 Increase	56 Increase
Property, Plant, and Equipment (at cost)	372 Increase	466 Increase
Accumulated Depreciation	215 Increase	270 Increase
Other Noncurrent Assets	51 Increase	15 Increase
Accounts Payable—Merchandise Suppliers	114 Increase	134 Increase
Notes Payable to Banks (current liability)	18 Increase	45 Increase
Income Taxes Payable	26 Increase	7 Decrease
Other Current Liabilities	90 Increase	123 Increase
Bonds Payable	—	577 Increase
Common Stock	360 Decrease	524 Decrease
Retained Earnings	369 Increase	455 Increase

Income statement data for The GAP appear below:

	Year 6	Year 7
Sales	$ 5,284	$ 6,508
Cost of Goods Sold	(3,285)	(4,022)
Selling and Administrative Expenses	(1,250)	(1,632)
Income Tax Expense	(296)	(320)
Net Income	$ 453	$ 534

a. Prepare a columnar work sheet for the statement of cash flows for Year 6 and Year 7 (see the upper panel of **Exhibit 4.4** for the desired format). The GAP sold marketable securities during Year 7 at their book value (that is, at no gain or loss). The firm did not sell property, plant, and equipment during either year. Treat changes in other noncurrent assets as an investing activity.

b. Prepare a statement of cash flows for Year 6 and Year 7 using the indirect method for computing cash flow from operations. The balance in cash was $486 at the end of Year 6 and $914 at the end of Year 7.

c. Compute cash flow from operations for Year 6 and Year 7 using the direct method (see the lower panel of **Exhibit 4.4** for the desired format). The GAP includes depreciation in selling and administrative expenses. Your analysis should show how much cash The GAP collected from customers and how much cash The GAP paid to merchandise suppliers, to governments for income taxes, and to other providers of goods and services.

d. Comment on the pattern of cash flows from operating, investing, and financing activities.

34. Preparing and interpreting the statement of cash flows using a columnar work sheet. The accounting records of Circuit City for Year 7 and Year 8 indicate the following changes in balance sheet accounts (amounts in millions):

	Year 7	Year 8
Cash	$159 Increase	$ 86 Decrease
Accounts Receivable	208 Increase	66 Increase
Merchandise Inventories	69 Increase	19 Increase
Prepayments	8 Decrease	15 Decrease
Property, Plant, and Equipment (at cost)	209 Increase	291 Increase
Accumulated Depreciation	99 Increase	116 Increase
Accounts Payable—Merchandise Suppliers	117 Increase	44 Increase
Notes Payable to Banks (current asset)	92 Decrease	27 Increase
Other Current Liabilities	71 Decrease	9 Decrease
Bonds Payable	31 Increase	19 Decrease
Common Stock	428 Increase	25 Increase
Retained Earnings	125 Increase	91 Increase

Income statement data appear below:

	Year 7	Year 8
Sales	$ 7,664	$ 8,871
Cost of Goods Sold	(5,903)	(6,827)
Selling and Administrative Expenses	(1,511)	(1,849)
Interest Expense	(30)	(27)
Income Tax Expense	(84)	(64)
Net Income	$ 136	$ 104

a. Prepare a columnar work sheet for the statement of cash flows for Circuit City for Year 7 and Year 8 (see the upper panel of **Exhibit 4.4** for the desired format). The firm did not sell property, plant, and equipment during either year. It includes depreciation in selling and administrative expenses. It retired bonds during Year 8 at their book value.

b. Prepare a statement of cash flows for Circuit City for Year 7 and Year 8 using the indirect method of computing cash flow from operations. The balance in cash was $203 at the end of Year 7 and $117 at the end of Year 8.

c. Calculate the amount of cash collected from customers each year.

d. Calculate the amount of cash paid to suppliers of merchandise each year.

e. Calculate the amount of cash paid to suppliers of selling and administrative services during each year.

f. Comment on the pattern of cash flows from operating, investing, and financing activities each year.

35. Inferring cash flows from trial balance data. Exhibit 4.21 presents data from the financial statements for Heidi's Hide-Out, a bar and video-game club, with private rooms for rent for parties. Heidi's deals with

- many employees, to some of whom it has made advances on wages and to some of whom it owes wages for past work;
- many landlords, to some of whom it has made advance payments and to some of whom it owes rent for past months;
- many customers, some of whom have paid for special parties not yet held and some of whom have not yet paid for parties they have held; and
- many suppliers of goods, including food and beverages, some of whom Heidi's has paid for orders not yet received and some of whom have delivered goods for which Heidi's has not yet paid.

EXHIBIT 4.21	HEIDI'S HIDE-OUT Selected Detail from Financial Statements For the Current Year (Problem 35)		
		Beginning of Year	**End of Year**
BALANCE SHEETS			
Cash		$22,000	$ 10,000
Accounts Receivable from Retail Customers		8,000	8,900
Inventory of Retail Merchandise		11,000	10,000
Advances to Employees		1,000	1,500
Advances to Landlords (Prepaid Rent)		5,000	5,600
Advances to Suppliers of Retail Merchandise		10,000	10,500
Total Assets		$57,000	$ 46,500
Accounts Payable to Suppliers of Retail Merchandise		$ 8,000	$ 7,700
Advances from Retail Customers		9,000	10,000
Rent Payable to Landlords		6,000	5,300
Wages Payable to Employees		2,000	1,800
Owners' Equity		32,000	21,700
Total Liabilities and Owners' Equity		$57,000	$ 46,500
INCOME STATEMENT FOR THE YEAR			
Sales Revenue from Retail Customers			$ 120,000
Cost of Retail Merchandise Sold		$90,000	
Rent Expense		33,000	
Wage Expense		20,000	
Less: Total Expenses			(143,000)
Net Income			$ (23,000)

Heidi's and its customers, suppliers, and employees settle all transactions with cash, never with noncash assets.

a. Calculate the amount of cash received from retail customers during the current year.

b. Calculate the amount of cash Heidi's paid landlords during the current year for the rental of space.

c. Calculate the amount of cash Heidi's paid employees during the current year.

d. Calculate the amount of cash Heidi's paid suppliers of retail merchandise, which includes food and beverages it sells to retail customers, during the current year.

36. **Inferring cash flows from balance sheet and income statement data.** (Based on a problem prepared by Stephen A. Zeff.) You work for the Plains State Bank in Miles City, Montana, as an analyst specializing in the financial statements of small businesses seeking loans from the bank. Digit Retail Enterprises, Inc., provides you with its balance sheet on December 31, Year 4 and Year 5 (**Exhibit 4.22**), and its income statement for Year 5 (**Exhibit 4.23**). The firm's independent accountant has audited these financial statements and found them to be in conformity with generally accepted accounting principles. Digit Retail Enterprises acquired no new property, plant, and equipment during the year.

a. Calculate the amount of cash received from customers during the year.

b. Calculate the acquisition cost of merchandise purchased during the year.

c. Calculate the amount of cash paid to suppliers of merchandise during the year.

d. Calculate the amount of cash paid to salaried employees during the year.

e. Calculate the amount of cash paid to insurance companies during the year.

f. Calculate the amount of cash paid to landlords for rental of space during the year.

g. Calculate the amount of dividends paid during the year.

h. Calculate the amount of cash received when property, plant, and equipment were sold during the year.

EXHIBIT 4.22	DIGIT RETAIL ENTERPRISES, INC. Balance Sheet (Problem 36)

	December 31, Year 4	December 31 Year 5
ASSETS		
Current Assets		
Cash	$ 36,000	$ 50,000
Accounts Receivable	23,000	38,000
Notes Receivable	7,500	—
Interest Receivable	100	—
Merchandise Inventory	48,000	65,000
Prepaid Insurance	9,000	12,000
Prepaid Rent	2,000	—
Total Current Assets	$125,600	$165,000
Property, Plant, and Equipment		
At Cost	$100,000	$ 90,000
Less Accumulated Depreciation	(20,000)	(35,000)
Net	$ 80,000	$ 55,000
Total Assets	$205,600	$220,000
LIABILITIES AND SHAREHOLDERS' EQUITY		
Current Liabilities		
Accounts Payable—Merchandise Suppliers	$ 18,000	$ 20,000
Salaries Payable	2,100	2,800
Rent Payable	—	3,000
Advances from Customers	8,500	6,100
Note Payable	—	5,500
Dividends Payable	4,200	2,600
Other Current Liabilities	1,300	3,700
Total Current Liabilities	$ 34,100	$ 43,700
Shareholders' Equity		
Common Stock	$160,000	$164,500
Retained Earnings	11,500	11,800
Total Shareholders' Equity	$171,500	$176,300
Total Liabilities and Shareholders' Equity	$205,600	$220,000

EXHIBIT 4.23	DIGIT RETAIL ENTERPRISES, INC. Income Statement For Year 5 (Problem 36)

Sales Revenue	$270,000
Gain on Sale of Property, Plant, and Equipment	3,200
Interest Revenue	200
Total Revenues	$273,400
Less Expenses:	
Cost of Goods Sold	$145,000
Salaries Expense	68,000
Rent Expense	12,000
Insurance Expense	5,000
Depreciation Expense	20,000
Other Expenses	13,800
Total Expenses	$263,800
Net Income	$ 9,600

37. **Preparing and interpreting a statement of cash flows using a columnar work sheet.** **Exhibit 4.24** presents a comparative balance sheet for Swan Corporation as of the beginning and the end of the current year. The firm made no dispositions of property, plant, and equipment during the year, nor did it declare or pay dividends.

  a. Prepare a columnar work sheet for the statement of cash flows for Swan Corporation for the current year (see the upper panel of **Exhibit 4.4** for the desired format).

  b. Prepare a statement of cash flows for the current year using the indirect method of computing cash flow from operations.

  c. Comment on the pattern of cash flows from operating, investing, and financing activities.

EXHIBIT 4.24	SWAN CORPORATION Comparative Balance Sheet (Problem 37)		
		January 1	**December 31**
ASSETS			
Current Assets			
Cash		$ 12,000	$ 15,000
Accounts Receivable		144,000	156,000
Merchandise Inventories		190,000	210,000
Total Current Assets		$ 346,000	$ 381,000
Property, Plant, and Equipment		$ 700,000	$ 775,000
Less Accumulated Depreciation		(246,000)	(325,000)
Total Property, Plant, and Equipment		$ 454,000	$ 450,000
Total Assets		$ 800,000	$ 831,000
LIABILITIES AND SHAREHOLDERS' EQUITY			
Current Liabilities			
Accounts Payable		$ 190,000	$ 165,000
Income Taxes Payable		20,000	25,000
Total Current Liabilities		$ 210,000	$ 190,000
Long-term Debt			
Bonds Payable		100,000	96,000
Total Liabilities		$ 310,000	$ 286,000
Shareholders' Equity			
Common Stock		$ 210,000	$ 215,000
Retained Earnings		280,000	330,000
Total Shareholders' Equity		$ 490,000	$ 545,000
Total Liabilities and Shareholders' Equity		$ 800,000	$ 831,000

38. **Preparing a statement of cash flows with disposal of long-term assets.** Condensed financial statement data for Hale Company for the current year appear in **Exhibits 4.25** and **4.26**. During the current year, the firm sold for $5,000 equipment costing $15,000 with $10,000 of accumulated depreciation. The text does not treat this transaction, but see **Problem 4.5 for Self-Study**, which illustrates how to deal with it.

  a. Prepare statements of cash flows for Hale Company for the year using the indirect and direct methods of computing cash flow from operations. Support the statements with a columnar work sheet.

  b. Calculate the amount of cash received from customers during the year.

  c. Calculate the amount of cash paid to suppliers of inventory during the year.

  d. Calculate the amount of cash paid to lenders for interest during the year.

  e. Comment on the pattern of cash flows from operations, investing, and financing activities.

39. **Preparing and interpreting a statement of cash flows using a columnar work sheet.** GTI, Inc. manufactures parts, components, and processing equipment for electronics and semiconductor applications in the communication, computer, automotive, and appliance industries. Its

EXHIBIT 4.25	HALE COMPANY Comparative Balance Sheet (Problem 38)		
		January 1	**December 31**
Assets			
Cash		$ 52,000	$ 58,000
Accounts Receivable		93,000	106,000
Inventory		151,000	162,000
Land		30,000	30,000
Buildings and Equipment (cost)		790,000	830,000
Less Accumulated Depreciation		(460,000)	(504,000)
Total Assets		$ 656,000	$ 682,000
Liabilities and Shareholders' Equity			
Accounts Payable for Inventory		$ 136,000	$ 141,000
Interest Payable		10,000	8,000
Mortgage Payable		120,000	109,000
Common Stock		250,000	250,000
Retained Earnings		140,000	174,000
Total Liabilities and Shareholders' Equity		$ 656,000	$ 682,000

EXHIBIT 4.26	HALE COMPANY Statement of Income and Retained Earnings for the Current Year (Problem 38)	
Sales Revenues		$1,200,000
Expenses		
Cost of Goods Sold	$788,000	
Wages and Salaries	280,000	
Depreciation	54,000	
Interest	12,000	
Income Taxes	22,000	
Total		$1,156,000
Net Income		$ 44,000
Dividends on Common Stock		(10,000)
Addition to Retained Earnings for Year		$ 34,000
Retained Earnings, January 1		140,000
Retained Earnings, December 31		$ 174,000

sales tend to vary with changes in the business cycle since the sales of most of its customers are cyclical. **Exhibit 4.27** presents balance sheets for GTI as of December 31, Year 7 through Year 9, and **Exhibit 4.28** presents income statements for Year 8 and Year 9.

  a. Prepare a columnar work sheet for the preparation of a statement of cash flows for GTI, Inc. for Year 8 and Year 9. Notes to the firm's financial statements reveal the following (amounts in thousands):

    (1) Depreciation expense was $641 in Year 8 and $625 in Year 9.

    (2) Other Noncurrent Assets represent patents. Patent amortization was $25 in Year 8 and $40 in Year 9.

    (3) Changes in Other Noncurrent Liabilities are operating transactions.

  b. Prepare a statement of cash flows, using both the direct and indirect methods for cash flow from operations, for GTI, Inc. for Year 8 and Year 9.

  c. Discuss the relation between net income and cash flow from operations and the pattern of cash flows from operating, investing, and financing activities.

EXHIBIT 4.27	GTI, INC. Balance Sheets (all dollar amounts in thousands) (Problem 39)			

		December 31		
		Year 7	Year 8	Year 9
ASSETS				
Cash		$ 430	$ 475	$ 367
Accounts Receivable		3,768	3,936	2,545
Inventories		2,334	2,966	2,094
Prepayments		116	270	122
Total Current Assets		$ 6,648	$ 7,647	$ 5,128
Property, Plant, and Equipment (net)		3,806	4,598	4,027
Other Noncurrent Assets		193	559	456
Total Assets		$10,647	$12,804	$ 9,611
LIABILITIES AND SHAREHOLDERS' EQUITY				
Accounts Payable		$ 1,578	$ 809	$ 796
Notes Payable to Banks		11	231	2,413
Other Current Liabilities		1,076	777	695
Total Current Liabilities		$ 2,665	$ 1,817	$ 3,904
Long-term Debt		2,353	4,692	2,084
Other Noncurrent Liabilities		126	89	113
Total Liabilities		$ 5,144	$ 6,598	$ 6,101
Preferred Stock		$ —	$ 289	$ 289
Common Stock		83	85	86
Additional Paid-in Capital on Common Stock		4,385	4,392	4,394
Retained Earnings		1,035	1,440	(1,259)
Total Shareholders' Equity		$ 5,503	$ 6,206	$ 3,510
Total Liabilities and Shareholders' Equity		$10,647	$12,804	$ 9,611

EXHIBIT 4.28	GTI, INC. Income Statements (all dollar amounts in thousands) (Problem 39)		

		Year 8	Year 9
Sales		$ 22,833	$ 11,960
Cost of Goods Sold		$(16,518)	$(11,031)
Selling and Administrative Expenses		(4,849)	(3,496)
Interest Expense		(459)	(452)
Income Tax Expense		(590)	328
Net Income		$ 417	$ (2,691)
Dividends on Preferred Stock		(12)	(8)
Net Income Available to Common		$ 405	$ (2,699)

40. **Working backward through the statement of cash flows.** Quinta Company presents the balance sheet shown in **Exhibit 4.29** and the statement of cash flows shown in **Exhibit 4.30** for Year 5. The firm sold investments, equipment, and land for cash at their net book value. The accumulated depreciation of the equipment sold was $20,000.

    Prepare a balance sheet for the beginning of the year, January 1, Year 5.

41. **Analog for direct and indirect methods for preparing the statement of cash flows.** John earns $1,000 and spends $700. Mary earns $1,200 and spends $650. The following statement shows earnings, expenditures by individuals, and total family savings.

EXHIBIT 4.29	QUINTA COMPANY All Balance Sheet Accounts on December 31, Year 5 (Problem 40)

ASSETS

Cash	$ 25,000
Accounts Receivable	220,000
Merchandise Inventories	320,000
Land	40,000
Buildings and Equipment (at cost)	500,000
Less: Accumulated Depreciation	(200,000)
Investments (noncurrent)	100,000
Total Assets	$1,005,000

LIABILITIES AND SHAREHOLDERS' EQUITY

Accounts Payable	$ 280,000
Other Current Liabilities	85,000
Bonds Payable	100,000
Common Stock	200,000
Retained Earnings	340,000
Total Liabilities and Shareholders' Equity	$1,005,000

EXHIBIT 4.30	QUINTA COMPANY Statement of Cash Flows for Year 5 (Problem 40)

OPERATIONS

Net Income	$ 200,000	
Additions:		
Depreciation Expense	60,000	
Increase in Accounts Payable	25,000	
Subtractions:		
Increase in Accounts Receivable	(30,000)	
Increase in Merchandise Inventories	(40,000)	
Decrease in Other Current Liabilities	(45,000)	
Cash Flow from Operations		$ 170,000
Investing		
Sale of Investments	$ 40,000	
Sale of Buildings and Equipment	15,000	
Sale of Land	10,000	
Acquisition of Buildings and Equipment	$(130,000)	
Cash Flow from Investing		(65,000)
Financing		
Common Stock Issued	$ 60,000	
Bonds Issued	40,000	
Dividends Paid	(200,000)	
Cash Flow from Financing		$(100,000)
Net Change in Cash		$ 5,000

EXHIBIT 4.31	NIKE, INC. Statement of Cash Flows (all dollar amounts in millions) (Problem 42)			

	Year 7	Year 8	Year 9
OPERATIONS			
Net Income	$ 167	$ 243	$ 287
Depreciation and Amortization	15	17	34
Other Addbacks and Subtractions	(5)	5	3
Working Capital Provided by Operations	$ 177	$ 265	$ 324
(Increase) Decrease in Accounts Receivable	(38)	(105)	(120)
(Increase) Decrease in Inventories	(25)	(86)	(275)
(Increase) Decrease in Other Operating Current Assets	(2)	(5)	(6)
Increase (Decrease) in Accounts Payable	21	36	59
Increase (Decrease) in Other Current Operating Liabilities	36	22	32
Cash Flow from Operations	$ 169	$ 127	$ 14
Investing			
Sale of Property, Plant, and Equipment	$ 3	$ 1	$ 2
Acquisition of Property, Plant, and Equipment	(42)	(87)	(165)
Acquisition of Investment	(1)	(3)	(48)
Cash Flow from Investing	$ (40)	$ (89)	$(211)
Financing			
Increase in Short-term Debt	—	—	$ 269
Increase in Long-term Debt	—	$ 1	5
Issue of Common Stock	$ 3	2	3
Decrease in Short-term Debt	(96)	(8)	—
Decrease in Long-term Debt	(4)	(2)	(10)
Dividends	(22)	(26)	(41)
Cash Flow from Financing	$(119)	$ (33)	$ 226
Change in Cash	$ 10	$ 5	$ 29
Cash, Beginning of Year	74	84	89
Cash, End of Year	$ 84	$ 89	$ 118

John's Earnings	$1,000
Mary's Earnings	1,200
John's Expenditures	(700)
Mary's Expenditures	(650)
Family Savings	$ 850

a. What does Mary contribute to family savings?

b. Repeat part **a** starting with total family savings and making suitable adjustments for John's earnings not affecting Mary's savings, and for John's expenditures not affecting Mary's savings.

42. **Interpreting the statement of cash flows. Exhibit 4.31** presents a statement of cash flows for Nike, Inc., maker of athletic shoes, for three recent years.

    a. Why did Nike experience increasing net income but decreasing cash flow from operations during this three-year period?

    b. What is the likely explanation for the changes in Nike's cash flow from investing during the three-year period?

    c. How did Nike finance its investing activities during the three-year period?

    d. Evaluate the appropriateness of Nike's use of short-term borrowing during Year 9.

43. **Interpreting the statement of cash flows. Exhibit 4.32** presents a statement of cash flows for Boise Cascade Corporation, a forest products company, for three recent years.

   a. Boise Cascade operated at a net loss each year but generated positive cash flow from operations. Explain.
   b. What is the likely explanation for the changes in Boise Cascade's cash flow from investing activities during the three-year period?
   c. What is the likely explanation for the changes in long-term financing during Year 5 and Year 6?

EXHIBIT 4.32	**BOISE CASCADE CORPORATION** **Statement of Cash Flows** **(all dollar amounts in millions) (Problem 43)**		
		Year 5	**Year 6**	**Year 7**

	Year 5	Year 6	Year 7
OPERATIONS			
Net Income (Loss)	$(154)	$ (77)	$ (63)
Depreciation	266	268	236
Other Addbacks (Subtractions)	(56)	(43)	41
(Increase) Decrease in Accounts Receivable	(46)	—	(68)
(Increase) Decrease in Inventories	(3)	(31)	6
Increase (Decrease) in Accounts Payable	9	15	55
Increase (Decrease) in Other Current Liabilities	50	(1)	9
Cash Flow from Operations	$ 66	$ 131	$ 216
Investing			
Sale of Property, Plant, and Equipment	$ 202	$ 24	$ 171
Acquisition of Property, Plant, and Equipment	(283)	(222)	(271)
Other Investing Transactions	(31)	9	(75)
Cash Flow from Investing	$(112)	$(189)	$(175)
Financing			
Increase (Decrease) in Short-term Borrowing	$ (54)	$ 27	$ 25
Increase in Long-term Debt	131	84	139
Increase in Preferred Stock	191	287	—
Decrease in Long-term Debt	(164)	(269)	(116)
Dividends	(55)	(67)	(84)
Other Financing Transactions	(5)	(2)	2
Cash Flow from Financing	$ 44	$ 60	$ (34)
Change in Cash	$ (2)	$ 2	$ 7
Cash, Beginning of Year	22	20	22
Cash, End of Year	$ 20	$ 22	$ 29

44. **Interpreting the statement of cash flow relations. Exhibit 4.33** presents statements of cash flow for eight companies for a recent year:
   a. American Airlines (airline transportation)
   b. American Home Products (pharmaceuticals)
   c. Interpublic Group (advertising and other marketing services)
   d. Procter & Gamble (consumer products)
   e. Reebok (athletic shoes)
   f. Texas Instruments (electronics)
   g. Limited Brands (specialty retailing)
   h. Upjohn (pharmaceuticals)

   Discuss the relation between net income and cash flow from operations, and the pattern of cash flows from operating, investing, and financing activities for each firm.

45. **Northrop Grumman Corporation; interpreting direct and indirect methods.**
   a. Refer to **Exhibit 4.34** for Northrop Grumman, which shows excerpts from its Statements of Cash Flows, with cash flow from operations presented with the indirect method, for

EXHIBIT 4.33

Statements of Cash Flows for Selected Companies
(all dollar amounts in millions) (Problem 44)

	American Airlines	American Home Products	Interpublic Group	Procter & Gamble	Reebok	Texas Instruments	Limited Brands	Upjohn
OPERATIONS								
Net Income (Loss)	$ (110)	$ 1,528	$ 125	$ 2,211	$ 254	$ 691	$ 455	$ 491
Depreciation	1,223	306	61	1,134	37	665	247	175
Other Addbacks (Subtractions)	166	71	23	196	(4)	(9)	—	7
(Increase) Decrease in Receivables	37	14	(66)	40	(65)	(197)	(102)	6
(Increase) Decrease in Inventories	(27)	(157)	16	25	(82)	(60)	(74)	(21)
Increase (Decrease) in Payables	34	325	59	98	35	330	118	63
Increase (Decrease) in Other Current Liabilities	54	(185)	(15)	(55)	(2)	112	110	(11)
Cash Flow from Operations	$ 1,377	$ 1,902	$ 203	$ 3,649	$ 173	$ 1,532	$ 754	$ 710
Investing								
Capital Expenditures (net)	$(2,080)	$ (473)	$ (79)	$(1,841)	$ (62)	$(1,076)	$(430)	$(224)
Sale (Acquisition) of Marketable Securities	290	24	3	23	—	(47)	—	(287)
Sale (Acquisition) of Other Businesses	—	(9,161)	—	(295)	—	—	(60)	308
Other Investing	36	(5)	(85)	105	(4)	—	—	(1)
Cash Flow from Investing	$(1,754)	$(9,615)	$(161)	$(2,008)	$ (66)	$(1,123)	$(490)	$(204)
Financing								
Increase (Decrease) in Short-term Borrowing	$ (380)	$ 8,640	$ 35	$ (281)	$ 37	$ (1)	$(322)	$ 5
Increase in Long-term Debt	730		42	414	—	1	150	15
Increase in Capital Stock	1,081	38	19	36	13	110	17	—
Decrease in Long-term Debt	(1,069)		(15)	(797)	(3)	(88)	—	(46)
Acquisition of Treasury Stock	—	(314)	(37)	(14)	(112)	—	—	(32)
Dividends	(49)	(903)	(36)	(949)	(25)	(79)	(102)	(264)
Other Financing	82	11	(14)	1	(12)	4	—	37
Cash Flow from Financing	$ 395	$ 7,472	$ (6)	$(1,590)	$(102)	$ (53)	$(257)	$(285)
Change in Cash	$ 18	$ (241)	$ 36	$ 51	$ 5	$ 356	$ 7	$ 221
Cash, Beginning of Year	45	1,937	256	2,322	79	404	34	281
Cash, End of Year	$ 63	$ 1,696	$ 292	$ 2,373	$ 84	$ 760	$ 41	$ 502

three recent years. Write a short (no more than 50 words) explanation of why Northrop Grumman's cash flow from operations declined by about 20 percent per year between Years 7 and 8 and then again between Years 8 and 9. If you cannot explain, then explain why that might be.

b. Refer to **Exhibit 4.35** for Northrop Grumman, which shows excerpts from its Statements of Cash Flows, with cash flow from operations presented with the direct method, for three recent years, the same years as in part **a**. Write a short (no more than 50 words) explanation of why Northrop Grumman's cash flow from operations declined by about 20 percent per year between Years 7 and 8 and then again between Years 8 and 9. If you cannot explain, then explain why that might be.

c. Which method of presenting cash flow from operations do you find easier to interpret?

EXHIBIT 4.34	NORTHROP GRUMMAN CORPORATION Data Taken from Consolidated Statements of Cash Flows (Shaded Columns Showing Changes Do Not Appear in Original) (all dollar amounts in millions) (Problem 45)					

Indirect Method

Years ended December 31	Year 7	Change	Year 8	Change	Year 9
Cash Provided by Operating Activities					
Net income	$ 467	*141*	$ 608	*(181)*	$ 427
Adjustments to reconcile net income to net cash provided					
by operations:					
Depreciation	193	*(18)*	175	*91*	266
Amortization of intangible assets	196	*10*	206	*173*	379
Common stock issued to employees	2	*6*	8	*38*	46
Loss on disposal of discontinued operations	—	*56*	56	*(56)*	—
Loss(gain) on disposals of property, plant, and equipment	21	*(8)*	13	*(20)*	(7)
Retiree benefits income	(249)	*(243)*	(492)	*223*	(269)
Decrease(increase) in					
Accounts receivable	170	*(849)*	(679)	*1,952*	1,273
Inventoried costs	172	*(95)*	77	*(105)*	(28)
Prepaid expenses and other current assets	45	*(73)*	(28)	*45*	17
Increase (decrease) in					
Advances from customers on long-term contracts	21	*645*	666	*(1,314)*	(648)
Accounts payable and accruals	(2)	*89*	87	*(783)*	(696)
Provisions for contract losses	(8)	*28*	20	*(85)*	(65)
Deferred income taxes	230	*115*	345	*(171)*	174
Income taxes payable	58	*(30)*	28	*(41)*	(13)
Retiree benefits	(129)	*37*	(92)	*17*	(75)
Other noncash transaction	20	*(8)*	12	*24*	36
Net cash provided by operating activities	$1,207	*(197)*	$1,010	*(193)*	$ 817

46. Ethical issues in manipulating cash flows from operations. Top financial management wants to increase cash flow from operations. It asks you to implement the following strategies. Which of these, if implemented, will increase cash flow from operations contrasted to the amount if you do not implement the strategy for the firm? Comment on the wisdom and ethics of these strategies.

a. The firm delays maintaining equipment until after the start of the next period.

b. The firm delays purchasing new equipment until after the start of the next period.

c. The firm sells $1 million of accounts receivable for $980,000 cash to a financial institution, but agrees to reimburse the purchaser for the amount by which uncollectible accounts exceed $20,000.

d. The firm delays paying for its employees' insurance premiums until after the start of the next period.

EXHIBIT 4.35	NORTHROP GRUMMAN CORPORATION Data Taken from Consolidated Statements of Cash Flows (Shaded Columns Showing Changes do Not Appear in Original) (all dollar amounts in millions) (Problem 45)

Direct Method (without Reconciliation of Net Income to Cash Flow from Operations)
(Shaded Columns Showing Changes Do Not Appear in Original)

Years ended December 31	Year 7	Change	Year 8	Change	Year 9
Cash Provided by Operating Activities					
Sources of Cash					
Cash received from customers					
Collections from customers on long-term contracts	$ 1,691	*(253)*	$ 1,438	*1,664*	$ 3,102
Other collections	7,450	*(447)*	7,003	*4,145*	11,148
Less: Cash paid to suppliers and employees	(7,715)	*465*	(7,250)	*(6,001)*	(13,251)
Net cash margin	$ 1,426	*(235)*	$ 1,191	*(192)*	$ 999
Cash Contribution Margin Percentage	15.6%		14.1%		7.0%
Proceeds from litigation settlement	—	—	—	*220*	220
Interest received	18	*(1)*	17	*—*	17
Income tax refunds received	75	*(60)*	15	*8*	23
Other cash receipts	7	*3*	10	*14*	24
Cash provided by operating activities	$ 1,526	*(293)*	$ 1,233	*50*	$ 1,283
Other Operating Uses of Cash					
Interest paid	$ 21	*(51)*	$ 165	*168*	$ 333
Income taxes paid	85	*(28)*	57	*69*	126
Other cash payments	18	*(17)*	1	*6*	7
Cash used in operating activities	$ 319	*(96)*	$ 223	*243*	$ 466
Net cash provided by operating activities	$ 1,207	*(197)*	$ 1,010	*(193)*	$ 817

e. The firm delays paying some suppliers until after the due date, and until after the start of the next period.

f. The firm sells goods for cash but promises the customers that they can return the goods for full refund after the start of the next period.

chapter 5

Introduction to Financial Statement Analysis

Learning Objectives

1. Understand the relation between the expected return and risk of investment alternatives and the role financial statement analysis can play in providing information about returns and risk.

2. Understand the usefulness of the rate of return on assets (ROA) as a measure of a firm's operating profitability independent of financing and the insights gained by disaggregating ROA into profit-margin and assets-turnover components.

3. Understand the usefulness of the rate of return on common shareholders' equity (ROCE) as a measure of profitability that incorporates a firm's particular mix of financing and the insights gained by disaggregating ROCE into profit-margin, assets-turnover, and capital-structure-leverage-ratio components.

4. Understand the strengths and weaknesses of earnings per common share as a measure of profitability.

5. Understand the distinction between short-term liquidity risk and long-term liquidity risk and the financial statement ratios used to assess these two dimensions of risk.

6. Develop skills to interpret effectively the results of an analysis of profitability and risk.

7. (Appendix) Develop skills to prepare pro forma financial statements.

8. (Appendix) Understand the usefulness of pro forma financial statements in the valuation of a firm.

5

al-Mart Stores (Wal-Mart) is the largest retailer in the world. As the financial data for a recent year in **Exhibit 5.1** make clear, Wal-Mart's sales are almost as large as the combined sales of its principal competitors, its assets are roughly two-thirds as large, but its net income significantly exceeds the combined earnings of these competitors. What is the source of Wal-Mart's competitive advantage? How has Wal-Mart's profitability changed relative to its competitors in recent years?

EXHIBIT 5.1	Financial Data for Selected Discount and Grocery Retailers (in millions of U.S. Dollars)				
Company	Headquarters	Industry	Sales	Assets	Net Income
Wal-Mart	United States	Hypermarkets	$256,329	$110,030	$9,075
Kohl's	United States	Discount	$ 10,282	$ 6,689	$ 591
Target	United States	Discount	48,163	31,392	1,841
Kroger	United States	Grocery	53,791	20,184	316
Itochu	Japan	Grocery	85,883	37,834	165
Carrefour	France	Hypermarkets	64,793	40,847	1,295
Metro AG	Germany	Hypermarkets	48,575	24,055	418
Totals			$311,487	$161,001	$4,626

Answering these questions requires that we analyze the financial statements of Wal-Mart and its competitors. This chapter introduces the tools and techniques for analyzing financial statements. Most financial statement analysis attempts to assess the profitability and the risk of a firm. The analyst examines relations between various financial statement items, expressed in the form of financial statement ratios. This chapter describes several commonly used financial statement ratios and illustrates their usefulness in assessing Wal-Mart's profitability and risk. **Problems 27, 28,** and **29** compare the profitability and risk ratios for Wal-Mart with several of its competitors listed above.

Such analyses permit the analyst (1) to evaluate the past performance and current financial position of a firm (primarily a backward-looking exercise) and (2) to project its likely future performance and condition (primarily a forward-looking exercise).

Assessments by management of the performance of competitors, assessments by shareholders of the performance of management, and assessments by government antitrust regulators of the performance of a firm use *historical* data. This chapter emphasizes such historical analyses. In contrast, an examination of the financial statement effects of changes in strategies or policies, such as adding new products or substituting debt financing for equity financing, emphasizes the analysis of *projected* data. Management prepares a set of pro forma financial statements based on these new strategies or policies to study their impact. Analysts also use pro forma financial statements in valuing a firm, such as in evaluating a potential acquisition candidate. The appendix to this chapter discusses the preparation and use of pro forma financial statements.

TERMINOLOGY NOTE

The term *pro forma statements* has different meanings depending on the context. We use the term in its classical sense to mean projected financial statements based on a particular set of assumptions. In recent years, some firms have taken to reporting net income omitting some items that ordinarily appear (such as a nonrecurring restructuring charge or gain on sale of land) or combining companies that have not theretofore been combined. These latter uses of pro forma statements generally restate historical financial data prepared under GAAP instead of showing projected data for the future. See Chapter 12 and the Glossary for discussion of the distinction.

Objectives of Financial Statement Analysis

The first question the analyst asks in analyzing a set of financial statements is, "What do I look for?" The response to this question requires an understanding of investment decisions.

To illustrate, assume that you recently inherited $25,000 and must decide what to do with the bequest. You narrow the investment decision to purchasing either a certificate of deposit at a local bank or shares of common stock of Wal-Mart, currently selling for $59 per share. You will base your decision on the **return** you anticipate from each investment and the **risk** associated with that return.

The bank currently pays interest at the rate of 3 percent annually on certificates of deposit. Because the bank will likely remain in business, you feel confident that you will earn 3 percent each year. The return from investing in the shares of Wal-Mart's common stock has two components. First, the firm paid a cash dividend in its most recent year of $0.52 per share, and you anticipate that it will continue to pay a dividend at least this large in the future. Also, the market price of Wal-Mart's stock will likely change between the date you purchase the shares and the date in the future when you sell them. The difference between the eventual selling price and the purchase price, often called a *capital gain* (or *loss*, if negative), provides the second component of the return from buying the stock.

The common stock investment involves more risk than does the certificate of deposit investment. The future profitability of Wal-Mart will likely affect future dividends and market price changes. If competitors open new stores or introduce new products or services that erode Wal-Mart's share of its sales market, future income might be less than you currently anticipate. Wal-Mart has innovated over several decades. One never knows when a new competitor will get a better idea of how to run a similar business. If Wal-Mart opens new stores, or makes acquisitions, or introduces successful new products or services, or is the first to discover new channels of retailing, future income might be greater than you currently anticipate.

Economy-wide factors, such as inflation and unemployment, and changes in international tensions will also affect the market price of Wal-Mart's shares. Also, specific industry factors, such as changes in exchange rates that affect the cost of merchandise or government regulatory actions, may influence the market price of the shares. Because most individuals prefer less risk to more risk, you will want a higher expected return if you purchase Wal-Mart's shares than if you invest in a certificate of deposit.

Theoretical and empirical research has shown that the expected return from investing in a firm relates, in part, to the expected profitability of the firm.[1] The analyst studies a firm's past earnings to understand its operating performance and to help forecast its future profitability.

---

[1]Ray Ball and Phillip Brown, "An Empirical Evaluation of Accounting Income Numbers," *Journal of Accounting Research* (Autumn 1968), 159–78; Jane A. Ou and Stephen H. Penman, "Financial Statement Analysis and the Prediction of Stock Returns." *Journal of Accounting and Economics* (November 1989), 295–329.

Investment decisions also require that the analyst assess the risk associated with the expected return.[2] A firm may find itself short of cash and unable to repay a short-term loan coming due. Or, it may have so much long-term debt in its financing structure that it has difficulty meeting the required interest and principal payments. The financial statements provide information for assessing how these and other elements of risk affect expected return.

Most financial statement analysis, therefore, explores some aspect of a firm's profitability or its risk or both. **Figure 5.1** summarizes the relation between financial statement analysis and investment decisions.

FIGURE 5.1	Relation between Financial Statement Analysis and Investment Decisions

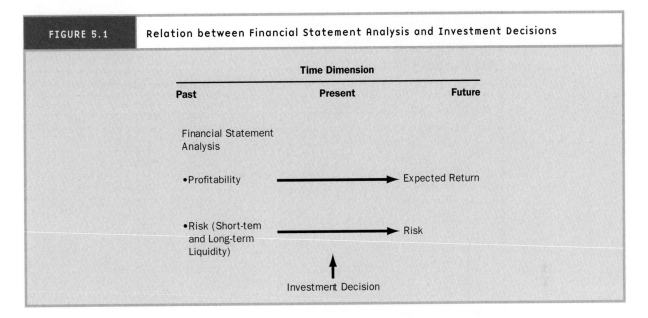

Usefulness of Ratios

Readers cannot easily answer questions about a firm's profitability and risk from the raw information in financial statements. For example, one cannot assess the profitability of a firm by noting the amount of net income—large net income could result from a large firm's earning small profits on its transactions or from a small firm's earning large profits. Comparing earnings with the assets required to generate those earnings will provide more useful information. The analyst expresses these (and other useful) relations between items in the financial statements in the form of ratios. Some ratios compare items within the income statement; some use only balance sheet data; others relate items from more than one of the three principal financial statements. Ratios aid financial statement analysis because they conveniently summarize data in a form easy to understand, interpret, and compare.

Ratios, by themselves out of context, provide little information. For example, does a rate of return on common shareholders' equity of 8.6 percent indicate satisfactory performance? After calculating the ratios, the analyst must compare them with some standard. The following list provides several possible standards:

1. The planned ratio for the period
2. The corresponding ratio during the preceding period for the same firm
3. The corresponding ratio for a similar firm in the same industry
4. The average, or other representative, ratio for other firms in the same industry

Later sections of this chapter discuss difficulties encountered in using each of these bases for comparison.

The following sections describe several ratios useful for assessing profitability and various dimensions of risk. To demonstrate the calculation of various ratios, we use data for Wal-Mart for its fiscal years ending January 31, Year 12 to Year 14, appearing in **Exhibit 5.2** (comparative

---

[2]Modern finance distinguishes between systematic (market) risk and nonsystematic (firm-specific) risk. The discussion in this chapter does not distinguish between these two dimensions of risk.

income statement), **Exhibit 5.3** (comparative balance sheet), and **Exhibit 5.4** (comparative statement of cash flows). We recommend that you trace the amounts in the various financial ratios discussed in this chapter to the amounts in Wal-Mart's financial statements.

Our analysis for Wal-Mart examines changes in its various ratios over the three-year period—a so-called **time-series analysis**. Time-series analysis contrasts with a **cross-section analysis**, which involves comparing a given firm's ratios with those of other firms for a specific period. Several problems at the end of the chapter involve cross-section analysis (see **Exercises 11**, **12**, **13**, **17**, and **18** and **Problems 28**, **29**, and **30**).

EXHIBIT 5.2	**WAL-MART STORES** **Comparative Income Statement** **(all dollar amounts in millions)**		
	For the Year Ended January 31		
	Year 12	**Year 13**	**Year 14**
Sales Revenue	$217,799	$244,524	$256,329
Other Revenues	2,013	2,139	2,516
Total Revenues	$219,812	$246,663	$258,845
Less Expenses:			
Cost of Goods Sold	$171,562	$191,838	$198,747
Selling and Administrative	36,356	41,236	44,909
Interest	1,326	1,063	996
Total	$209,244	$234,137	$244,652
Net Income before Taxes	$ 10,568	$ 12,526	$ 14,193
Income Tax Expense	3,897	4,487	5,118
Net Income	$ 6,671	$ 8,039	$ 9,075

EXHIBIT 5.3	**WAL-MART STORES** **Comparative Balance Sheet** **(all dollar amounts in millions)**			
	January 31			
	Year 11	**Year 12**	**Year 13**	**Year 14**
ASSETS				
Cash	$ 2,054	$ 2,161	$ 2,758	$ 5,199
Accounts Receivable (net)	1,768	2,000	2,108	1,254
Inventories	21,442	22,614	24,891	26,612
Prepayments	1,291	1,471	726	1,176
Total Current Assets	$26,555	$28,246	$30,483	$ 34,241
Property, Plant, and Equipment (net)	45,417	50,529	56,492	63,648
Other Noncurrent Assets	10,641	9,455	12,298	12,141
Total Assets	$82,613	$88,230	$99,273	$110,030
LIABILITIES AND SHAREHOLDERS' EQUITY				
Accounts Payable	$15,092	$15,617	$17,140	$ 19,332
Notes Payable	2,286	743	1,079	3,267
Current Portion of Long-term Debt	4,375	2,405	4,714	3,100
Other Current Liabilities	7,196	8,517	9,684	11,719
Total Current Liabilities	$28,949	$27,282	$32,617	$ 37,418
Long-term Debt	20,138	23,511	24,196	25,573
Other Noncurrent Liabilities	2,183	2,335	3,123	3,416
Total Liabilities	$51,270	$53,128	$59,936	$ 66,407
Common Stock ($.10-par value)	$ 447	$ 445	$ 440	$ 431
Additional Paid-in Capital	1,411	1,484	1,482	2,135
Retained Earnings	29,485	33,173	37,415	41,057
Total Shareholders' Equity	$31,343	$35,102	$39,337	$ 43,623
Total Liabilities and Shareholders' Equity	$88,613	$88,230	$99,273	$110,030

EXHIBIT 5.4	WAL-MART STORES Comparative Statement of Cash Flows (all dollar amounts in millions)		

	For the Year Ended January 31		
	Year 12	**Year 13**	**Year 14**
Operations			
Net Income	$ 6,671	$ 8,039	$ 9,075
Additions:			
Depreciation Expense	3,290	3,432	3,852
(Increase) Decrease in Accounts Receivable	(210)	(101)	373
(Increase) in Inventories	(1,235)	(2,236)	(1,973)
(Increase) Decrease in Prepayments	(180)	745	(450)
Increase (Decrease) in Accounts Payable	368	1,447	2,803
Increase (Decrease) in Other Current Liabilities	1,556	1,206	2,411
Cash Flow from Operations	$10,260	$12,532	$ 16,091
Investing			
Acquisition of Property, Plant, and Equipment	$(8,383)	$(9,355)	$(10,308)
Other Investing Transactions	1,237	(354)	2,046
Cash Flow from Investing	$(7,146)	$(9,709)	$ (8,262)
Financing			
Increase (Decrease) in Short-term Borrowing	$(1,533)	$ 1,836	$ 688
Increase in Long-term Borrowing	4,591	2,044	4,099
Decrease in Long-term Borrowing	(3,686)	(1,479)	(3,541)
Acquisition of Common Stock	(1,214)	(3,232)	(5,182)
Dividends	(1,249)	(1,328)	(1,569)
Other Financing Transactions	84	(67)	117
Cash Flow from Financing	$(3,007)	$(2,226)	$ (5,388)
Net Change in Cash	$ 107	$ 597	$ 2,441
Cash, Beginning of Year	2,054	2,161	2,758
Cash, End of Year	$ 2,161	$ 2,758	$ 5,199

Analysis of Profitability

A firm engages in operations, such as Wal-Mart selling merchandise in its stores, to generate net income. This section discusses three measures of **profitability**:

1. Rate of return on assets
2. Rate of return on common shareholders' equity
3. Earnings per share of common stock

Rate of Return on Assets

The **rate of return on assets (ROA)** measures a firm's performance in using assets to generate earnings independent of how the firm financed acquisition of those assets. Previous chapters described three principal business activities: investing, financing, and operating. The rate of return on assets relates the results of operating performance to the investments (assets) of a firm without regard to how the firm financed the acquisition of those investments.

The calculation of ROA is as follows:

$$ROA = \frac{\text{Net Income} + \text{Interest Expense Net of Income Tax Savings}}{\text{Average Total Assets}}$$

ROA answers the question: how well has the firm done in conducting its operations *independent of financing costs?* The numerator of ROA uses an earnings figure that excludes any expenses or distributions to the suppliers of funds. If the measure of performance in the numerator must exclude the costs of financing, then the analysis must add back the amount of interest expense because, in computing net income, the firm subtracts interest expense. Because firms can deduct interest expense in calculating taxable income, interest expense does not reduce *after-tax* net income by one dollar for each dollar of interest expense. Thus, to calculate the numerator of ROA (which measures performance independent of financing costs), the analyst adds back interest expense reduced by the income taxes that interest deductions save.

To illustrate, Wal-Mart reported interest expense for Year 14 (see **Exhibit 5.2**) of $996 million. The income tax rate is 35 percent of pretax income. Because Wal-Mart can deduct interest in computing taxable income, it saved income taxes of $348.6 million (= 0.35 × $996 million). The net after-tax cost of interest expense was $647.4 million (= $996.0 million − $348.6 million). To compute income before interest expense to lenders, the analyst adds back $647.4 million to net income. The analyst does not add back dividends paid to shareholders because the firm does not deduct them as an expense in calculating net income; net income already represents an amount before payments to suppliers of shareholders' equity capital.

Because we are computing the earnings rate for a year, the measure of investment for the denominator should reflect the average amount of assets in use during the year. A crude but usually satisfactory figure for average total assets is one-half the sum of total assets at the beginning and at the end of the year.

CONCEPTUAL NOTE

Most financial economists would subtract average noninterest-bearing liabilities (for example, accounts payable, salaries payable) from average total assets in the denominator of ROA. Economists realize that when liabilities do not provide for explicit interest charges, the creditor adjusts the terms of the contract, such as setting a higher selling price or lower discount, for those who do not pay cash immediately. ROA requires in the numerator the income amount before a firm accrues any charges to suppliers of funds. We cannot measure the interest charges implicit in the noninterest-bearing liabilities; items such as cost of goods sold and salary expense are somewhat larger because of these charges. Thus, implicit charges reduce the measure of operating income in the numerator. Subtracting average noninterest-bearing liabilities from average total assets likewise reduces the denominator for assets financed with such liabilities. The examples and problems in this book use average total assets in the denominator of the rate of return on assets, making no adjustment for noninterest-bearing liabilities.

The calculation of rate of return on assets for Wal-Mart Corporation for Year 14 is as follows:[3]

$$\frac{\text{Net Income} + \text{Interest Expense} \text{ Net of Income Tax Saving}}{\text{Average Total Assets}} = \frac{\$9{,}075 + (1.00 - 0.35)(\$996)}{(0.5)(\$99{,}273 + \$110{,}030)} = \frac{\$9{,}722.4}{\$104{,}651.5} = 9.3\%$$

Thus, for each dollar of assets used, Wal-Mart earned $0.093 during Year 14 before payments to the suppliers of financing. The rate of return on assets was 8.8 percent in Year 12 and 9.3 percent in Year 13. Thus, the rate of return increased between Year 12 and Year 13 and remained steady between Year 13 and Year 14.

One might question the rationale for a measure of return that excludes the costs of financing. After all, the firm must finance the assets and must cover the cost of the financing if it is to be profitable.

The rate of return on assets has particular relevance to the lenders, or creditors, of a firm. These creditors have a senior claim on earnings and assets relative to common shareholders. Creditors receive their return via contractual interest payments. The firm typically pays these

---

[3] Throughout the remainder of this chapter, we omit reference to the fact that the amounts for Wal-Mart are in millions; for example, "$9,075" means "$9,075 million," and "4,363 shares" means "4,363 million shares."

amounts before it makes payments, typically as dividends, to any other suppliers of financing. When extending credit or providing debt financing to a firm, creditors want to be sure that the firm can generate a rate of return from using the financing that exceeds its cost.

Common shareholders find the rate of return on assets useful in assessing financial leverage, which a later section of this chapter discusses.

Disaggregating the Rate of Return on Assets

To study changes in the rate of return on assets, the analyst can disaggregate ROA into the product of two other ratios. Improving either of these ratios will improve the overall rate of return. The disaggregation follows:

$$
\begin{array}{ccccc}
\textbf{Rate of} & & \textbf{Profit Margin for ROA} & & \textbf{Total Assets} \\
\textbf{Return} & = & \textbf{(before interest expense} & \times & \textbf{Turnover} \\
\textbf{on Assets} & & \textbf{and related income} & & \textbf{Ratio} \\
& & \textbf{tax savings) Ratio} & &
\end{array}
$$

$$
\frac{\text{Net Income} + \text{Interest Expense Net of Income Tax Savings}}{\text{Average Total Assets}} = \frac{\text{Net Income} + \text{Interest Expense Net of Income Tax Savings}}{\text{Sales}} \times \frac{\text{Sales}}{\text{Average Total Assets}}
$$

The **profit margin for ROA ratio** measures a firm's ability to control the level of expenses relative to sales, to increase selling prices relative to the level of expenses incurred, or a combination of the two. By holding down expenses or increasing selling prices, a firm can increase the profits from a given amount of sales activity and thereby improve its profit margin for ROA. The **total assets turnover ratio** measures a firm's ability to generate sales from a particular level of investment in assets, or alternatively, to control the amount of assets it uses to generate a particular level of sales. The smaller the amount of assets the firm needs to generate a given level of sales, the better (larger) its assets turnover and the more profitable is the firm.

The disaggregation of ROA for Wal-Mart for Year 14 is as follows:

$$
\frac{\text{Net Income plus Interest Expense Net of Income Tax Savings}}{\text{Average Total Assets}} = \frac{\text{Net Income plus Interest Expense Net of Income Tax Savings}}{\text{Sales}} \times \frac{\text{Sales}}{\text{Average Total Assets}}
$$

$$
\frac{\$9{,}075 + (1 - 0.35)(\$996)}{(0.5)(\$99{,}273 + \$110{,}030)} = \frac{\$9{,}075 + (1 - 0.35)(\$996)}{\$256{,}329} \times \frac{\$256{,}329}{(0.5)(\$99{,}273 + \$110{,}030)}
$$

$$
9.3\% = 3.8\% \times 2.4
$$

Exhibit 5.5 presents the disaggregation of the rate of return on assets for Wal-Mart into profit margin for ROA and total assets turnover ratios for Year 12, Year 13, and Year 14. The improvement in the rate of return on assets between Year 12 and Year 13 results from an increase in both the profit margin for ROA and the total assets turnover. On the other hand, one can attribute the stable ROA between Year 13 and Year 14 to the offsetting effects of an increased profit margin for ROA and a decreased total assets turnover. To pinpoint the causes of the changes in

EXHIBIT 5.5	WAL-MART STORES Disaggregation of Rate of Return on Assets for Year 12, Year 13, and Year 14				
	ROA	**=**	**Profit Margin for ROA Ratio**	**×**	**Total Assets Turnover Ratio**
Year 12:	8.8%	=	3.5%	×	2.5
Year 13:	9.3%	=	3.6%	×	2.6
Year 14:	9.3%	=	3.8%	×	2.4

Wal-Mart's profitability over this three-year period, we must analyze the changes in the profit margin for ROA and total assets turnover ratios further, which we will do shortly.

Firms improve their rate of return on assets by increasing the profit margin for ROA ratio, or the rate of assets turnover, or both. Some firms, however, have limited flexibility to alter one or the other of these components. For example, a firm that sells commodity products in a highly competitive market likely has little opportunity to increase its profit margin for ROA. Such a firm would need to improve its total assets turnover (for example, shortening the holding period for inventories with tighter controls) to increase its rate of return on assets. The activities of a firm that requires substantial investments in property, plant, and equipment constrain such a firm's ability to increase its rate of return on assets by increasing its assets turnover. Such a firm might have more flexibility to take actions that increase the profit margin for ROA (for example, creating brand loyalty for its products).

Analyzing Changes in the Profit Margin for ROA

Changes in a firm's expenses relative to sales cause the profit margin for ROA ratio to change. To see the relation, one can express individual expenses and net income as a percentage of sales. **Exhibit 5.6** presents such an analysis, which **Chapter 3** called a *common-size income statement*, for Wal-Mart. This analysis alters the conventional income statement format by subtracting interest expense (net of its related income tax effects) as the last expense item. The percentages on the line Income before Interest and Related Income Tax Effect correspond to the profit margin for ROA ratios in **Exhibit 5.5**. (A later section discusses the profit margin for ROCE.)

The analysis in **Exhibit 5.6** indicates that Wal-Mart's profit margin for ROA improved over the three years, primarily because cost of goods sold as a percentage of sales declined more than the selling and administrative expenses as a percentage of sales increased. The analyst should explore further with management the reasons for these changing percentages. Possible explanations for these changing expenses percentages are:

Decreasing Cost of Goods Sold to Sales Percentage

- Wal-Mart's increasing size permitted it to purchase merchandise at lower cost, either because of quantity discounts or the ability to exert bargaining power over suppliers.
- Wal-Mart shifted its sales mix toward products with lower cost of goods sold to sales percentages.
- Wal-Mart instituted improved controls over the purchase, storage, and delivery of its merchandise, reducing the cost of storage and obsolescence.

| EXHIBIT 5.6 | WAL-MART STORES Common-Size Income Statement for Year 12, Year 13, and Year 14 |

	For the Year Ended January 31		
	Year 12	Year 13	Year 14
Sales Revenue	100.0%	100.0%	100.0%
Other Revenues	0.9	0.9	1.0
Total	100.9%	100.9%	101.0%
Less Operating Expenses:			
Cost of Goods Sold	78.8%	78.4%	77.6%
Selling and Administrative	16.6	16.9	17.5
Total	95.4%	95.3%	95.1%
Income before Income Taxes and Interest	5.5%	5.6%	5.9%
Income Taxes	2.0	2.0	2.1
Income before Interest and Related Income Tax Effect (= Profit Margin for ROA)	3.5%	3.6%	3.8%
Interest Expense Net of Income Tax Effect	0.4	0.3	0.3
Net Income (= Profit Margin for ROCE)	3.1%	3.3%	3.5%

Increasing Selling and Administrative Expense to Sales Percentage

- Increased competition required Wal-Mart to increase advertising and other marketing costs to maintain its market share.
- Weak economic conditions required Wal-Mart to increase advertising and other marketing costs to stimulate demand.
- A decrease in the growth of sales required Wal-Mart to spread depreciation and other relatively fixed expenses over a smaller than anticipated sales base. Wal-Mart's sales grew 13.8 percent in Year 12, 12.3 percent in Year 13, but only 4.8 percent in Year 14. Perhaps Wal-Mart anticipated revenues would grow in Year 14 at a rate similar to those in Year 12 and Year 13 and increased the number of employees, depreciable assets, and other capacity costs accordingly.[4]

Neither the amount nor the trend in a particular ratio should, by itself, cause the analyst to invest in a firm. Ratios simply indicate areas requiring additional analysis.

Analyzing Changes in the Total Assets Turnover Ratio

You have seen how changes in the total assets turnover ratio help you understand changes in ROA. The total asset turnover results from the turnovers of the individual asset components. The analyst generally calculates separate turnover ratios for three classes of assets: accounts receivable, inventory, and fixed assets.

Accounts Receivable Turnover The rate at which accounts receivable turn over indicates how quickly a firm collects cash. The **accounts receivable turnover ratio** equals sales revenue divided by average accounts receivable during the period. In theory the numerator should include only sales made on account. Most firms, except some retailers (such as fast food outlets) that deal directly with final consumers, sell their goods and services on account. Other firms, such as Wal-Mart, sell both for cash and on account. Such firms seldom disclose the proportions of cash and credit sales in their financial statements or notes. Thus, the analyst uses sales revenue in the numerator of the accounts receivable turnover ratio, recognizing that the inclusion of sales made for cash will increase the numerator and thereby overstate the turnover ratio. The accounts receivable turnover ratio for Wal-Mart for Year 14 is as follows:

$$\frac{\text{Sales}}{\text{Average Accounts Receivable}} = \frac{\$256,329}{(0.5)(\$2,108 + \$1,254)} = 152.5 \text{ times per year}$$

The analyst often expresses the accounts receivable turnover in terms of the average number of days that elapse between the time the firm makes the sale and the time it later collects the cash, sometimes called "days accounts receivable are outstanding" or "days outstanding for receivables." To calculate this ratio, divide 365 days by the accounts receivable turnover ratio. The days outstanding for accounts receivable for Wal-Mart during Year 14 was 2.4 days (= 365 days/152.5 times per year). Its accounts receivable turnover was 115.6 during Year 12 (3.2 days) and 119 during Year 13 (3.1 days). The rapid accounts receivable turnover and small number of days on average to collect accounts receivable result from two principal causes:

- Wal-Mart makes a significant proportion of its sales for cash, which our calculations include in the numerator but not the denominator of the accounts receivable turnover ratio.
- Wal-Mart's customers use Visa, Master Card, and other third party credit cards for which Wal-Mart receives payment via electronic funds transfer from the credit card company within two to three days.

Most firms that sell to other businesses, as opposed to consumers, on account collect within 30 to 90 days. Interpreting any particular firm's accounts receivable turnover and days receivable outstanding requires knowing the terms of sale. If a firm's terms of sale are "net 30 days" and the

---

[4] Economists refer to the process of spreading relatively fixed expenses over a larger sales level as *operating leverage*, or *economies of scale*. When firms do not achieve the sales levels anticipated from a particular level of fixed expenses, economists refer to this phenomenon as *diseconomies of scale*, as may have occurred for Wal-Mart in Year 14. Managerial accounting and managerial economics textbooks discuss operating leverage more fully.

firm collects its accounts receivable in 45 days, then collections do not accord with the stated terms. Such a result warrants a review of the credit and collection activity to ascertain the cause and to guide corrective action. If the firm offers terms of "net 60 days," a days receivable outstanding of 45 days indicates that the firm handles accounts receivable well.

Many firms sell to customers on account as a strategy to stimulate sales. Customers may purchase more willingly and purchase more if they know they need only sign their name. Such firms may also encourage customers to delay paying for their purchases as a means for the selling firm to generate interest revenue through finance charges on the unpaid amounts. Thus, comparing accounts receivable turnovers over time or between firms requires an analysis of the growth rate in sales, the amount of interest revenue generated, the cost of administrating the credit-granting activity, and the losses from uncollectible accounts.

Inventory Turnover The **inventory turnover ratio** indicates how fast firms sell their inventory items, measured in terms of rate of movement of goods into and out of the firm. Inventory turnover equals cost of goods sold divided by the average inventory during the period. The inventory turnover for Wal-Mart Corporation for Year 14 is as follows:

$$\frac{\text{Cost of Goods Sold}}{\text{Average Inventory}} = \frac{\$198,747}{(0.5)(\$24,891 + \$26,612)} = 7.7 \text{ times per year}$$

Items remain in inventory an average of 47.4 days (= 365 days / 7.7 times per year) before sale. The inventory turnover for Wal-Mart was 7.8 times per year in Year 12 (46.8 days) and 8.1 times per year in Year 13 (45.1 days). The increased inventory turnover between Year 12 and 13 may result from:

- Improved inventory control systems, which reduced the levels of inventory and the cost of storage and obsolescence. This explanation is consistent with the decreased cost of goods sold to sales percentage discussed earlier.
- A shift in sales mix toward grocery or other products that turn over more quickly.

The decreased inventory turnover between Year 13 and Year 14 may result from:

- Slower growth in sales than anticipated, which resulted in more unsold inventory than anticipated. Earlier we noted that Wal-Mart's sales increased only 4.8 percent during Year 14, after increasing 13.8 percent in Year 12 and 12.3 percent in Year 13. Wal-Mart may have stocked its stores anticipating a growth in sales larger than it achieved.
- A shift in sales mix away from grocery or other products that turn over more slowly.

Managing inventory turnover involves two opposing considerations. Firms prefer to sell as many goods as possible with a minimum of assets tied up in inventories. An increase in the rate of inventory turnover between periods indicates reduced costs of financing the investment in inventory. On the other hand, management does not want to have so little inventory on hand that shortages result in lost sales. Increases in the rate of inventory turnover caused by inventory shortages could signal a loss of customers, thereby offsetting any advantage gained by decreased investment in inventory. Firms must balance these opposing considerations in setting the optimum level of inventory and, thus, the accompanying rate of inventory turnover.

Some analysts calculate the inventory turnover ratio by dividing sales, rather than cost of goods sold, by the average inventory. As long as the ratio of selling price to cost of goods sold remains relatively constant, either measure will identify changes in the trend of the inventory holding period. Using sales in the numerator will lead, however, to incorrect measures of the inventory turnover ratio for calculating the average number of days that inventory is on hand until sale.

Fixed Asset Turnover The **fixed asset turnover ratio** measures the relation between sales and the investment in fixed assets—property, plant, equipment. The notion that fixed assets "turn over" is more difficult to picture than is the case for inventory. A more appropriate title for the fixed asset turnover ratio might be the *fixed asset productivity ratio*, because it measures the amount of sales generated from a particular level of investments in fixed assets.

The fixed asset turnover ratio for Wal-Mart for Year 14 is as follows:

$$\frac{\text{Sales}}{\text{Average Fixed Inventory}} = \frac{\$256{,}329}{(0.5)(\$56{,}492 + \$63{,}648)} = 4.3 \text{ times per year}$$

Thus, $1.00 invested in fixed assets during Year 14 generated $4.30 in sales. The fixed asset turnover for Wal-Mart was 4.5 for Year 12 and 4.6 for Year 13. The decline in the fixed asset turnover in Year 14 likely relates to the decreased growth in sales. The statement of cash flows for Wal-Mart in **Exhibit 5.4** indicates that its expenditures on property, plant, and equipment increased between Year 12 and Year 14. When sales did not grow during Year 14 as rapidly as in previous years, Wal-Mart found that it had excess store capacity, causing a decline in the fixed asset turnover.

Some analysts find the reciprocal of this ratio helpful in comparing the operating characteristics of different firms. The reciprocal ratio measures dollars of fixed assets required to generate one dollar of sales. For Wal-Mart, this reciprocal is $0.23 (= $1.00/4.3). Wal-Mart required $0.23 of fixed assets to generate $1.00 of sales. Compare fixed assets per dollar of sales of AT&T, for example, with that of Safeway Stores in a recent year. AT&T has $2.70 of fixed assets per dollar of sales while Safeway Stores, a retailer with relatively modest fixed assets, requires only $0.16 (that is, only 16¢) of fixed assets per dollar of sales. AT&T has large asset requirements to generate sales; Safeway does not.

The analyst should interpret changes in the fixed asset turnover ratio cautiously. Firms often invest in fixed assets (for example, new production facilities) several periods before these assets generate sales from products manufactured in their plants or sold in their stores. Thus, a low or decreasing rate of fixed asset turnover may indicate an expanding firm preparing for future growth. On the other hand, a firm anticipating a decline in product sales could cut back its capital expenditures. Such an action could increase the fixed asset turnover ratio.

Summary of Asset Turnovers   We noted earlier that the total assets turnover ratio for Wal-Mart increased between Year 12 and Year 13 but decreased in Year 14. **Exhibit 5.7** presents the four turnover ratios discussed for Wal-Mart over this three-year period. The accounts receivable turnover ratio increased steadily over the three years, indicating either more sales for cash or faster collection from third-party credit cards. The increasing accounts receivable turnover ratio will likely not significantly impact the total assets turnover because accounts receivable comprise only 1 percent to 2 percent of total assets. Inventory and fixed assets on the other hand comprise together 80 percent to 85 percent of total assets. The turnovers for these two assets increased between Year 12 and Year 13 and decreased in Year 14. The slower growth in sales in Year 14 likely explains the decrease in the inventory and fixed asset turnovers.

Summary of the Analysis of the Rate of Return on Assets

The rate of return on assets helps one assess a firm's performance in using assets to generate earnings, independent of the financing of those assets. The rate of return on assets results from the interaction of its separate components: profit margin for ROA and total assets turnover.

- The profit margin for ROA results from the relation of the various expenses to sales.
- Total assets turnover reflects the effects of turnover ratios for accounts receivable, inventory, and fixed assets.

EXHIBIT 5.7	**WAL-MART STORES** Asset Turnover Ratios for Year 12, Year 13, and Year 14		
	Year 12	Year 13	Year 14
Total Assets Turnover	2.5	2.6	2.4
Accounts Receivable Turnover	115.6	119.0	152.5
Inventory Turnover	7.8	8.1	7.7
Fixed Asset Turnover	4.5	4.6	4.3

The analysis for Wal-Mart revealed the following:

1. The rate of return on assets increased between Year 12 and Year 13 and remained steady between Year 13 to Year 14.
2. An increased profit margin for ROA and increased total assets turnover explain the increased ROA between Year 12 and Year 13. Offsetting effects of an increased profit margin for ROA and a decreased total assets turnover explain the steady ROA between Year 13 and Year 14.
3. Decreases in the cost of goods sold to sales percentage more than offset increases in the selling and administrative expense to sales percentage to explain the improved profit margin for ROA. Possible explanations for the decreased cost of goods sold to sales percentage include (1) lower purchase, storage, and obsolescence costs related to Wal-Mart's size or improved inventory control systems, and (2) sales mix changes to higher margin products. Possible explanations for the increased selling and administrative expense to sales percentage include (1) increased marketing costs due to more intense competition or weak economic conditions, and (2) the need to spread relatively fixed administrative expenses over a smaller level of sales in Year 14 than anticipated.
4. The changes in the total assets turnover primarily reflect the effects of increasing inventory and fixed asset turnover between Year 12 and Year 13 and decreases in these turnover ratios

Problem 5.1 for Self-Study

Analyzing the rate of return on assets. Exhibit 5.8 presents profitability ratios for Abbott Corporation for three recent years. The rates of return on assets do not precisely equal profit margin for ROA times total assets turnover due to rounding.

a. Identify the likely reason for the decreasing rate of return on assets. Use common-size income statement percentages and individual asset turnover ratios in your interpretations.

b. What is the likely explanation for the decreasing cost of goods sold to sales percentage coupled with the increasing inventory turnover ratio?

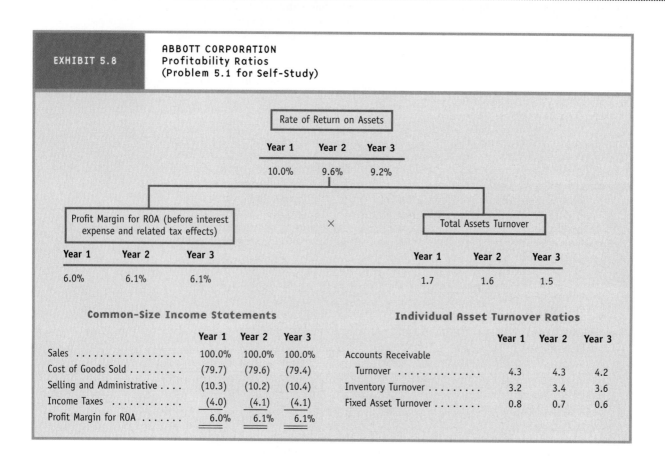

EXHIBIT 5.8

ABBOTT CORPORATION
Profitability Ratios
(Problem 5.1 for Self-Study)

Rate of Return on Assets

	Year 1	Year 2	Year 3
	10.0%	9.6%	9.2%

Profit Margin for ROA (before interest expense and related tax effects)

Year 1	Year 2	Year 3
6.0%	6.1%	6.1%

×

Total Assets Turnover

Year 1	Year 2	Year 3
1.7	1.6	1.5

Common-Size Income Statements

	Year 1	Year 2	Year 3
Sales	100.0%	100.0%	100.0%
Cost of Goods Sold	(79.7)	(79.6)	(79.4)
Selling and Administrative	(10.3)	(10.2)	(10.4)
Income Taxes	(4.0)	(4.1)	(4.1)
Profit Margin for ROA	6.0%	6.1%	6.1%

Individual Asset Turnover Ratios

	Year 1	Year 2	Year 3
Accounts Receivable Turnover	4.3	4.3	4.2
Inventory Turnover	3.2	3.4	3.6
Fixed Asset Turnover	0.8	0.7	0.6

between Year 13 and Year 14. Changes in the growth rates in sales during these years seem to explain the changes in the asset turnovers.

Rate of Return on Common Shareholders' Equity

The **rate of return on common shareholders' equity (ROCE)** measures a firm's performance in using and financing assets to generate earnings. Unlike the rate of return on assets, the rate of return on shareholders' equity explicitly considers financing costs. Thus this measure of profitability incorporates the results of operating, investing, and financing decisions. The calculation of the rate of return on common shareholders' equity is as follows:

$$\text{Rate of Return on Common Shareholders' Equity} = \frac{\text{Net Income} - \text{Dividends on Preferred Stock}}{\text{Average Common Shareholders' Equity}}$$

The Numerator To calculate the amount of earnings assignable to common shareholders' equity, the analyst subtracts all amounts required to compensate other providers of financing for the use of their funds. Expenses subtracted in computing net income already include amounts for interest expense, so the calculation of the numerator requires no further adjustment for interest. Because expenses exclude all dividends, the analyst must subtract from net income any earnings allocable to preferred stock equity, usually the dividends on preferred stock declared during the period, to measure the returns solely to the common shareholders. The analyst should not subtract dividends on common stock, because such dividends represent distributions to common shareholders of a portion of the returns generated for them during the period.

The Denominator The capital provided by common shareholders during the period equals the average par value of common stock, capital contributed in excess of par value on common stock, retained earnings, and any other common shareholders' equity accounts for the period. (Alternatively, subtract average preferred shareholders' equity from average total shareholders' equity.)

The rate of return on common shareholders' equity of Wal-Mart for Year 14 is as follows:

$$\frac{\text{Net Income} - \text{Dividends on Preferred Stock}}{\text{Average Common Shareholders' Equity}} = \frac{\$9,075 - 0}{(0.5)(\$39,337 + \$43,623)} = 21.9\%$$

The rate of return on common shareholders' equity was 20.1 percent in Year 12 and 21.6 percent in Year 13. Thus the rate of return on common shareholders' equity increased during the three years.

Relation between Return on Assets and Return on Common Shareholders' Equity

Figure 5.2 graphs the two measures of rate of return discussed thus far for Wal-Mart for Year 12, Year 13, and Year 14. **Figure 5.2** also shows the after-tax cost of borrowing each year. In each year, the rate of return on common shareholders' equity exceeds the rate of return on assets. What accounts for this relation, a normal one for profitable firms?

The rate of return on assets measures the profitability of a firm before any payments to the suppliers of financing. Each of the various providers of financing has a claim on some portion of the earnings in the numerator of the rate of return on assets. Creditors receive the contractual interest to which they have a claim; the tax savings the firm realizes from deducting interest for tax purposes reduces the interest cost to the firm. Preferred shareholders, if any, receive the stated dividend amounts on the preferred stock. Any remaining earnings belong to the common shareholders; that is, common shareholders have a residual claim on all earnings after creditors and preferred shareholders receive amounts contractually owed them. Thus,

Rate of Return on Assets → After-Tax Cost of Borrowing (interest) → Return to Preferred Shareholders (dividends) → Rate of Return on Common Shareholders' Equity (residual)

We can now see that the rate of return on common shareholders' equity will exceed the rate of return on assets whenever the rate of return on assets exceeds the after-tax cost of borrowing and any dividends required for preferred shareholders. For Year 14, the rate of return on assets for

EXHIBIT 5.9

Effects of Financial Leverage on Rate of Return on Common Shareholders' Equity (income tax rate is 30 percent of pretax income)

	Long-term Financing Equals $100,000		Income after Taxes but before Interest Expense[a]	After-tax Interest Expense[b]	Net Income	Rate of Return on Total Assets[c]	Rate of Return on Common Shareholders' Equity
	Borrowing at 10 Percent Per Year	Shareholders' Equity					
Good Earnings Year							
Leveraged Company	$40,000	$ 60,000	$10,000	$2,800	$ 7,200	10.0%	12.0%
No-Debt Company	—	100,000	10,000	—	10,000	10.0%	10.0%
Neutral Earnings Year							
Leveraged Company	40,000	60,000	7,000	2,800	4,200	7.0%	7.0%
No-Debt Company	—	100,000	7,000	—	7,000	7.0%	7.0%
Bad Earnings Year							
Leveraged Company	40,000	60,000	4,000	2,800	1,200	4.0%	2.0%
No-Debt Company	—	100,000	4,000	—	4,000	4.0%	4.0%

[a]Not including any income tax savings caused by interest charges. Income before taxes and interest for *good year* is $14,286, for *neutral year* is $10,000, for bad year is $5,714.

[b]$40,000 (borrowed) × 0.10 (interest rate) × [1 − 0.30 (income tax rate)]. The numbers shown in the preceding column for after-tax income do not include the effects of interest expense on taxes.

[c]In each year, the rate of return on total assets is the same, for both companies, as the rate of return on common shareholders' equity for No-Debt Company: 10 percent, 7 percent, and 4 percent, respectively.

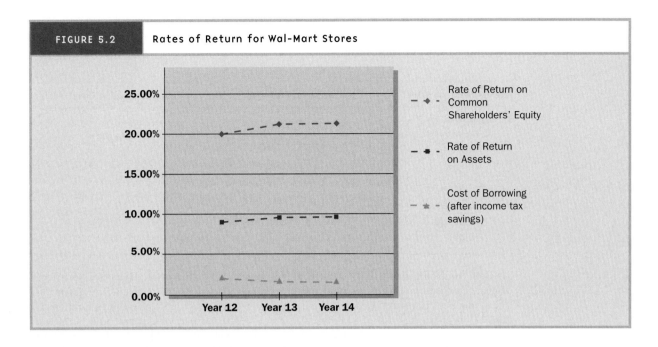

| FIGURE 5.2 | Rates of Return for Wal-Mart Stores |

Wal-Mart was 9.3 percent and the after-tax cost of liabilities was 1.0 percent {= (1.00 −0.35)($996)/[(0.5)($59,936 + $66,407)]; see **Exhibits 5.2** and **5.3**}. The return that Wal-Mart generated on assets financed with creditor's funds (9.3 percent) in excess of the cost of those funds (1.0 percent) belongs to the common shareholders. This excess return corresponds conceptually to the space in **Figure 5.2** between the line for rate of return on assets and the line for after-tax cost of borrowing. It also corresponds conceptually to the space between the line for the rate of return on assets and the rate of return on common shareholders' equity. Using lower cost borrowed funds and earning a higher rate of return on those funds that their cost increases the return to the common shareholders is a phenomenon called *financial leverage*. The common shareholders earned a higher return, but they undertook more risk in their investment. The risk results from the firm's incurring debt obligations with fixed payment amounts and dates. The next section discusses financial leverage more fully.

Financial Leverage

The term **financial leverage** describes financing with debt and preferred stock to increase the potential return to the residual common shareholders' equity. Financial leverage works as follows:

1. A firm obtains funds from creditors, preferred shareholders, and common shareholders.
2. The firm invests the funds in various assets. Each period the firm generates a return on the assets. The rate of return on assets measures this return before allocating any amounts to the suppliers of financing.
3. Creditors receive an allocated share of the return on assets equal to the interest rate on the amount borrowed. The tax deduction for the cost of the interest expense reduces the cost of this debt to the firm.
4. Preferred shareholders receive an allocated share of the return on assets equal to the preferred dividend rate on the preferred stock outstanding.
5. The common shareholders have a residual claim on all earnings in excess of the cost of debt and preferred shareholder financing. As long as a firm earns a rate of return on assets that exceeds the cost of debt and preferred shareholder financing, the common shareholders benefit. They benefit because the amount earned on assets financed with debt and the preferred shareholders' capital exceeds the amounts the firm must pay for those funds; the excess belongs to the common shareholders.

Illustration of Financial Leverage **Exhibit 5.9** explores this phenomenon. Leveraged Company and No-Debt Company both have $100,000 in assets. Leveraged Company borrows $40,000 at a 10-percent annual rate. No-Debt Company raises all its financing from common

shareholders. Both companies pay income taxes at the rate of 30 percent. Consider, first, a good earnings year. Both companies generate a rate of return on assets of 10 percent. The following table summarizes this information.

Rate of Return on Assets	→	Return to Creditors	→	Return to Common Shareholders
Leveraged Company				
$10,000	→	$2,800	→	$7,200
$100,000		$40,000		$60,000
10%		7%		12%
No-Debt Company				
$10,000	→	$ 0	→	$10,000
$100,000		$ 0		$100,000
10%		0%		10%

Both companies earn $10,000 before interest expense (but after taxes, except for tax effects of interest expense).[5] This represents a rate of return on assets for both companies of 10 percent. The creditors of Leveraged Company have a claim on this $10,000 pool of earnings from operations before financing costs of $4,000 (= 0.10 × $40,000) for interest expense. After a tax savings at 30 percent, the creditor's funds cost Leveraged Company $2,800 [= (1 − 0.30)($4,000)]. The remaining earnings from the pool, $7,200 (= $10,000 − $2,800), belong to the common shareholders. Thus, the common shareholders provided $60,000 of funds and obtained a rate of return on common shareholders' equity of 12 percent (= $7,200/$60,000). The common shareholders of No-Debt Company have a claim on the full $10,000 of earnings from operations because there is no debt in the financing structure. Thus, the common shareholders provided $100,000 of funds and obtained a rate of return on common shareholders' equity of 10 percent. Leverage increased the rate of return to shareholders of Leveraged Company because the funds contributed by the long-term debtors earned 10 percent but required an after-tax interest payment of only 7 percent. This additional 3-percent return on each dollar of assets financed by creditors increased the return to the common shareholders, as the following analysis shows.

RATE OF RETURN TO COMMON SHAREHOLDERS: GOOD EARNINGS YEAR WITH 40% DEBT

Excess Return on Assets Financed with Debt:

(0.10 − 0.07) × ($40,000) . . . . $ 1,200

Return on Assets Financed by Common Shareholders:

(0.10) × ($60,000)   6,000

Total Return to Common Shareholders . . . . $ 7,200

Common Shareholders' Equity $60,000

Rate of Return on Common Shareholders' Equity:

$7,200/$60,000 . . . .   12%

Leverage increased the return to common stock equity during the good earnings year, and a larger increase would occur if the firm financed a greater proportion of its assets with long-term borrowing, simultaneously increasing the firm's risk. For example, assume that Leveraged Company financed its assets of $100,000 with $50,000 of long-term borrowing and $50,000 of shareholders' equity. The following summarizes this example.

Rate of Return on Assets	→	Return to Creditors	→	Return to Common Shareholders
Leveraged Company				
$10,000	→	$3,500	→	$6,500
$100,000		$50,000		$50,000
10%		7%		13%

---

[5] Income before taxes and before interest expense is $14,286; $10,000 = (1.0 − 0.3) × $14,286.

Leveraged Company again generates $10,000 of earnings from operations before financing costs. The cost of the creditors funds is $3,500 [= $(1 - 0.30)(0.10 \times \$50,000)$]. Net income of Leveraged Company in this case would be $6,500 (= $10,000 - $3,500). The rate of return on common stock equity would be 13 percent (= $6,500/$50,000). This compares with a rate of return on common stock equity of 12 percent when long-term debt was only 40 percent of the total financing provided. Increasing leverage from 40 percent to 50 percent, assuming the interest rate on the borrowings stayed constant, increased the rate of return from 12 percent to 13 percent.

This 13 percent rate of return on common stock equity has the following components:

RATE OF RETURN TO COMMON SHAREHOLDERS: GOOD EARNINGS YEAR WITH 50% DEBT

Excess Return on Assets Financed with Debt:	
$(0.10 - 0.07) \times (\$50,000)$	$ 1,500
Return on Assets Financed by Common Shareholders:	
$(0.10) \times (\$50,000)$	5,000
Total Return to Common Shareholders	$ 6,500
Common Shareholders' Equity	$50,000
Rate of Return on Common Shareholders' Equity:	
$6,500/$50,000	13%

Financial leverage increases the rate of return on common stock equity when the rate of return on assets exceeds the after-tax cost of debt. The greater the proportion of debt in the financing structure, however, the greater is the risk the common shareholders bear. As it adds more debt to the financing structure, the risk of insolvency or bankruptcy becomes greater. *Insolvency* refers to a condition in which the firm has insufficient cash to pay its current debts, whereas *bankruptcy* refers to a legal condition in which liabilities usually exceed assets. Lenders, including investors in a firm's bonds, require a higher and higher return (interest rate) to compensate for this additional risk. At some point, the after-tax cost of debt will exceed the rate of return earned on assets. At this point, leverage no longer increases the potential rate of return to common stock equity. For most large manufacturing firms, liabilities represent between 30 percent and 60 percent of total financing.

Exhibit 5.9 also demonstrates the effect of financial leverage in a neutral earnings year and in a bad earnings year. In the neutral earnings year, financial leverage neither increases nor decreases the rate of return to common shareholders because the return on assets is 7 percent and the after-tax cost of long-term debt is also 7 percent. In the bad earnings year, the return on assets falls to 4 percent, below the 7 percent after-tax cost of debt. The difference between the cost of debt and the return generated on assets financed with that debt reduces the return to the common shareholders. The return on common shareholders' equity then drops below the rate of return on assets, to only 2 percent. The 2 percent rate of return on common stock equity has the following components:

RATE OF RETURN TO COMMON SHAREHOLDERS: BAD EARNINGS YEAR WITH 40% DEBT

Deficient Return on Assets Financed with Debt:	
$(0.4 - 0.07) \times (\$40,000)$	$ (1,200)
Return on Assets Financed by Common Shareholders:	
$(0.04) \times (\$60,000)$	2,400
Total Return to Common Shareholders	$ 1,200
Common Shareholders' Equity	$ 60,000
Rate of Return on Common Shareholders' Equity:	
$1,200/$60,000	2%

Clearly, financial leverage—borrowing—can work in two ways. It can enhance the owners' rate of return in good earnings years, but owners run the risk that bad earnings years will be even worse than these years would have been without the borrowing.

Disaggregating the Rate of Return on Common Shareholders' Equity

The rate of return on common shareholders' equity disaggregates into several components (in a manner similar to the disaggregation of the rate of return on assets):

$$\begin{array}{c} \text{Rate of Return} \\ \text{on Common} \\ \text{Shareholders'} \\ \text{Equity} \end{array} = \begin{array}{c} \text{Profit} \\ \text{Margin} \\ \text{for ROCE} \end{array} \times \begin{array}{c} \text{Total Assets} \\ \text{Turnover} \\ \text{Ratio} \end{array} \times \begin{array}{c} \text{Capital} \\ \text{Structure} \\ \text{Leverage} \end{array}$$

or, in terms of items from the financial statements:

$$\frac{\begin{array}{c}\text{Net Income} - \\ \text{Dividends on} \\ \text{Preferred Stock}\end{array}}{\begin{array}{c}\text{Average Common} \\ \text{Shareholders' Equity}\end{array}} = \frac{\begin{array}{c}\text{Net Income} - \\ \text{Dividends on} \\ \text{Preferred Stock}\end{array}}{\text{Sales}} \times \frac{\text{Sales}}{\begin{array}{c}\text{Average Total} \\ \text{Assets}\end{array}} \times \frac{\begin{array}{c}\text{Average Total} \\ \text{Assets}\end{array}}{\begin{array}{c}\text{Average Common} \\ \text{Shareholders' Equity}\end{array}}$$

The **profit margin ratio for ROCE** indicates the portion of the sales dollar left over for the common shareholders after covering all operating costs and subtracting all claims of creditors and preferred shareholders. It differs from the profit margin for ROA because of the subtraction for the cost of funds provided by creditors and preferred shareholders (see the last line in the profit margin panel in **Exhibit 5.6**). The total assets turnover indicates the sales generated from each dollar of assets and is identical to the total assets turnover in the disaggregation of ROA. The **capital structure leverage ratio** indicates the proportion of total assets, or total financing, provided by common shareholders contrasted with the financing provided by creditors and preferred shareholders. The larger the capital structure leverage ratio, the smaller is the proportion of financing that common shareholders provide and the larger is the proportion that creditors and preferred shareholders provide. Thus, the larger the capital structure leverage ratio, the larger is financial leverage.

The disaggregation of the rate of return on common shareholders' equity ratio for Wal-Mart for Year 14 is as follows:

$$\frac{\$9,075}{(0.5)(\$39,337 + \$43,623)} = \frac{\$9,075}{\$256,329} \times \frac{\$256,329}{(0.5)(\$99,273 + \$110,030)} \times \frac{(0.5)(\$99,273 + \$110,030)}{(0.5)(\$39,337 + \$43,623)}$$

$$21.9\% = 3.5\% \times 2.4 \times 2.5$$

Exhibit 5.10 shows the disaggregated components of the rate of return on common shareholders' equity for Wal-Mart for Year 12, Year 13, and Year 14. The increase in the rate of return on common shareholders' equity results from an increasing profit margin for ROCE over the three-year period and an increase in total assets turnover in Year 13. The increasing profit margin for ROCE results from both an increasing profit margin for ROA and a decreasing after-tax cost of debt financing (see **Figure 5.2**). The capital structure leverage ratio declined slightly during the three-year period.

EXHIBIT 5.10	**WAL-MART STORES** **Disaggregated Components of the Rate of Return on Common Shareholders' Equity**							
	Rate of Return on Common Shareholders' Equity	**=**	**Profit Margin for ROCE**	**×**	**Total Assets Turnover**	**×**	**Capital Structure Leverage Ratio**	
Year 12	20.1%	=	3.1%	×	2.5	×	2.6	
Year 13	21.6%	=	3.3%	×	2.6	×	2.5	
Year 14	21.9%	=	3.5%	×	2.4	×	2.5	

Problem 5.2 for Self-Study

Analyzing the rate of return on common shareholders' equity. Refer to the profitability analysis for Abbott Corporation in **Problem 5.1** for Self-Study. Consider the following additional data.

	Year 1	Year 2	Year 3
Profit Margin for ROCE Ratio	5.1%	4.9%	4.6%
Total Assets Turnover Ratio	1.7	1.6	1.5
Capital Structure Leverage Ratio	1.6	1.8	2.1
Rate of Return on Common Shareholders' Equity[a]	14.0%	14.2%	14.2%

[a]Amounts do not exactly equal the product of the three preceding ratios due to rounding.

a. What is the likely explanation for the increasing rate of return on common shareholders' equity?
b. Is financial leverage working to the advantage of the common shareholders in each year?

Earnings per Share of Common Stock

Earnings per share of common stock provides a third measure of profitability. Earnings per share equals net income attributable to common stock divided by the average number of common shares outstanding during the period. The numerator of ROCE and earnings per share are the same. Earnings per share for Wal-Mart for Year 14, based on 4,363 million weighted-average shares outstanding, is $2.08 (= $9,075/4,363).

A firm with securities outstanding that holders can convert into or exchange for shares of common stock may report two earnings-per-share amounts: **basic earnings per share** (the amount that results from the calculations above) and **diluted earnings per share**. Convertible bonds and convertible preferred stock permit their holders to exchange these securities directly for shares of common stock. Many firms have employee stock-option plans, which allow employees to acquire shares of the company's common stock. When holders convert their securities or when employees exercise their options, the firm will issue additional shares of common stock. Then, the amount shown as basic earnings per share will probably decrease, a phenomenon called *dilution*. When a firm has securities outstanding that, if exchanged for shares of common stock, would decrease basic earnings per share by 3 percent or more, generally accepted accounting principles require a dual presentation: basic earnings per share and diluted earnings per share.[6]

Firms that do not have convertible or other potentially dilutive securities outstanding compute earnings per share in the conventional manner. Firms with outstanding securities that have the potential for materially diluting earnings per share as conventionally computed must present dual earnings-per-share amounts.

Interpreting Earnings per Share   Accountants and financial analysts criticize earnings per share as a measure of profitability because it does not consider the amount of assets required to generate that level of earnings. Two firms with the same earnings and earnings per share will not be equally profitable if one of the firms requires more assets to generate those earnings than does the other firm.

In comparing firms, earnings-per-share amounts have limited use. For example, assume that two firms have identical earnings, common shareholders' equity, and rates of return on common shareholders' equity. One firm may have a lower earnings per share simply because it has a larger number of shares outstanding (perhaps due to the use of a lower par value for its shares or to different earnings retention policies; see **Exercise 20** at the end of this chapter).

Price-Earnings Ratio   Financial analysts often compare earnings-per-share amounts with the market price of the stock. They usually express this comparison as a price-earnings ratio

---

[6] Financial Accounting Standards Board, *Statement of Financial Accounting Standards No. 128,* "Earnings per Share," 1997.

(= market price per share/earnings per share). For example, the common stock of Wal-Mart sells for $59.00 per share at the end of Year 14. The price-earnings ratio, often called the P/E ratio, is 28.4 (= $59.00/$2.08) to 1. The analyst often expresses the relation by saying, "The stock sells at 28.4 times earnings."

Tables of stock prices and financial periodicals often present price-earnings ratios. The analyst must interpret these published P/E ratios cautiously, however. In cases in which a firm's earnings include unusual, nonrecurring gains and losses, the reader must ascertain whether the published ratio uses only income from recurring operations or final net income that includes the unusual items in the denominator. To serve their intended purpose, P/E ratios should use normal, ongoing earnings data in the denominator. The appendix to this chapter discusses more fully the use of earnings per share in the valuation of firms.

Summary of Profitability Analysis

This chapter has introduced three broad measures for assessing a firm's profitability. Because the rate of return on assets and the rate of return on common shareholders' equity relate earnings to either the assets or the assets net of liabilities required to generate those earnings, we have focused most of our attention on these two profitability measures.

Figure 5.3 summarizes the analysis discussed. Most generally (**Level 1**), the analysis concerns overall measures of profitability and the effectiveness of financial leverage. On the next level (**Level 2**), we disaggregate the overall measures of profitability into profit margin, asset turnover, and leverage components. On the third level, we further disaggregate the profit margin and asset turnover ratios to gain additional insights into reasons for changes in profitability. The depth of analysis required for an analyst to understand a particular case depends on the relative size of the observed differences or changes in profitability.

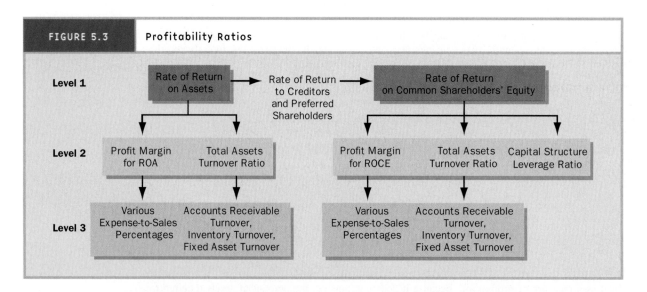

FIGURE 5.3   Profitability Ratios

Analysis of Risk

Analysts deciding between investments must consider the comparative risks. Various factors affect the risk of business firms:

1. Economy-wide factors, such as increased inflation or interest rates, unemployment, and recessions
2. Industry-wide factors, such as increased competition, lack of availability of raw materials, changes in technology, and increased government regulatory actions, such as antitrust or clean environment policies
3. Firm-specific factors, such as labor strikes, loss of facilities due to fire or other casualty, and poor health of key managerial personnel

Ultimately, analysts assess whether a firm will likely become bankrupt; creditors and investors may lose the funds they provided to a bankrupt firm.

Analysts assessing risk generally focus on the relative liquidity of a firm. Cash and near-cash assets provide a firm with the resources needed to adapt to the various types of risk; that is, liquid resources provide a firm with financial flexibility. Cash links the operating, investing, and financing activities of a firm, permitting it to run smoothly and effectively.

Assessing liquidity requires a time horizon. Consider the three questions that follow:

1. Does a firm have sufficient cash to repay a loan if it is due tomorrow?
2. Will the firm have sufficient cash to repay the same loan if it is due in six months?
3. Will the firm have sufficient cash to repay the same loan if it is due in five years?

In answering the first question, the analyst probably focuses on the amount of cash on hand and in the bank relative to the obligation coming due tomorrow. In answering the second question, the analyst compares the amount of cash expected from operations during the next six months, as well as from any new borrowings, with the obligations maturing during that period. In answering the third question, the analyst shifts the focus to the longer-run cash-generating ability of a firm relative to the amount of long-term debt that is maturing.

Measures of Short-Term Liquidity Risk

This section discusses four measures for assessing **short-term liquidity risk**: (1) the current ratio, (2) the quick ratio, (3) the cash flow from operations to current liabilities ratio, and (4) working capital turnover ratios.

Current Ratio
The **current ratio** equals current assets divided by current liabilities. Current assets comprise cash and assets that a firm expects to turn into cash or sell or consume within approximately one year of the balance sheet date. Current liabilities include obligations that will require cash (or the rendering of services) within approximately one year. Thus, the current ratio indicates a firm's ability to meet its short-term obligations. Analysts prefer a current ratio that at least exceeds 1.0.

The current ratios of Wal-Mart on January 31, Year 11, Year 12, Year 13, and Year 14, appear below:

Current Ratio		=	Current Assets / Current Liabilities
January 31, Year 11: $26,555/$28,949			0.92 to 1.0
January 31, Year 12: $28,246/$27,282			1.04 to 1.0
January 31, Year 13: $30,483/$32,617			0.93 to 1.0
January 31, Year 14: $34,241/$37,418			0.92 to 1.0

Although Wal-Mart's current ratio is less than 1.0 for three of the four years, analyst would not likely view Wal-Mart as highly risky. Wal-Mart sells either for cash or collects sales made on credit within three days. Also, Wal-Mart sells its inventory on average 47 days after purchase. Thus, Wal-Mart turns its current assets into cash quickly.

Changes in the trend of the current ratio can mislead. For example, when the current ratio exceeds 1 to 1, an increase of equal amount in both current assets and current liabilities (by acquiring inventory on account) results in a decline in the ratio, whereas equal decreases (by paying an accounts payable) result in an increased current ratio.[7]

In a recessionary period, a business may contract and use cash, a current asset, to pay its current liabilities. When the current ratio exceeds 1, such action will increase it. In a boom period,

---

[7] The general rule is that adding equal amounts to both the numerator and the denominator of a fraction moves that fraction closer to the number 1, whereas subtracting equal amounts from both the numerator and the denominator of a fraction makes that fraction diverge from the number 1. To be even more general, adding a to (subtracting a from) the numerator while adding b to (subtracting b from) the denominator of the fraction makes the fraction converge to (diverge from) the fraction a/b.

firms sometimes conserve cash by delaying payment of current liabilities, causing the reverse effect. Thus, a high current ratio may accompany deteriorating business conditions, whereas a falling ratio may accompany profitable operations.

Furthermore, management can manipulate the current ratio. It can take deliberate steps to produce a financial statement that presents a better current ratio at the balance sheet date than the average, or normal, current ratio during the rest of the year. For example, near the end of its accounting period a firm might delay normal purchases on account. Or, it might collect receivables for loans to officers, classified as noncurrent assets, and use the proceeds to reduce current liabilities. When the current ratio exceeds 1, the usual situation, such actions will increase the current ratio. Analysts refer to these manipulations as *window dressing*.

Although analysts commonly use the current ratio in financial statement analysis, its trends do not necessarily indicate liquidity problems, and management can easily manipulate it.

Quick Ratio   A variation of the current ratio is the **quick ratio** (sometimes called the **acid test ratio**). The quick ratio includes in the numerator of the fraction only those current assets that a firm could convert quickly into cash. The numerator customarily includes cash, marketable securities, and receivables. Some businesses can convert their inventory of merchandise into cash more quickly than other businesses can convert their receivables. The facts in each case will indicate whether the analyst should include receivables or exclude inventories. The denominator includes all current liabilities. A quick ratio approximately one-half of the current ratio is typical, although this varies by industry.

Assuming that the quick ratio of Wal-Mart include accounts receivable but exclude inventory, the quick ratios on January 31, Year 11, Year 12, Year 13, and Year 14, are as follows:

Quick Ratio	=	Cash, Marketable Securities, Accounts Receivable
		Current Liabilities
January 31, Year 11: ($2,054 + $1,768)/$28,949		0.13 to 1.0
January 31, Year 12: ($2,161 + $2,000)/$27,282		0.15 to 1.0
January 31, Year 13: ($2,758 + $2,108)/$32,617		0.15 to 1.0
January 31, Year 14: ($5,199 + $1,254)/$37,418		0.17 to 1.0

Wal-Mart's quick ratio, like its current ratio, remained relatively steady during the three-year period. Its quick ratio appears low, however, relative to its current ratio. Recall though that Wal-Mart, unlike most manufacturing firms, has only small amounts of accounts receivable. Wal-Mart collects cash quickly from sales on account and reinvests the cash in inventory or property, plant and equipment, pays dividends, or makes other uses of the cash. Thus, the low quick ratios are not a cause for concern.

Cash Flow from Operations to Current Liabilities Ratio   Some analysts criticize the current ratio and the quick ratio because they use balance sheet amounts at a specific time. If financial statement amounts at that time are unusually large or small, the resulting ratios will not reflect normal conditions. If management knows that analysts will evaluate the firm using one of these ratios at a particular time, it can take steps to window dress that ratio by, for example, using cash to pay off a current liability (reducing both numerator and denominator) or acquiring inventory on account (increasing both numerator and denominator).

The **cash flow from operations to current liabilities ratio** overcomes these deficiencies. The numerator of this ratio is cash flow from operations for the year. The denominator is average current liabilities for the year. A healthy firm commonly has a ratio of 40 percent or more.[8]

The cash flow from operations to current liabilities ratios for Wal-Mart for Year 12, Year 13, and Year 14 are as follows:

---

[8] Cornelius Casey and Norman Bartczak, "Using Operating Cash Flow Data to Predict Financial Distress: Some Extensions," *Journal of Accounting Research* (Spring 1985), 384–401.

Cash Flow from Operations to Current Liabilities Ratio	$=$	Cash Flow from Operations
		Average Current Liabilities

Year 12: $10,260/0.5($28,949 + $27,282)	36.5%
Year 13: $12,532/0.5($27,282 + $32,617)	41.8%
Year 14: $16,091/0.5($32,617 + $37,418)	46.0%

Thus the short-term liquidity of Wal-Mart improved between Year 12 and Year 14 and appears healthy.

Working Capital Turnover Ratios During the operating cycle, a retailing firm such as Wal-Mart

1. purchases inventory on account from suppliers,
2. sells inventory for cash or on account to customers,
3. collects amounts due from customers, and
4. pays amounts due to suppliers.

This cycle recurs for most businesses. The number of days that a firm holds inventories (that is, 365 days/inventory turnover ratio) indicates the length of the period between the purchase and the sale of inventory during each operating cycle. The number of days that a firm's receivables remain outstanding (that is, 365 days/accounts receivable turnover ratio) indicates the length of the period between the sale of inventory and the collection of cash from customers during each operating cycle.

Firms must finance their investments in inventories and accounts receivable. Suppliers typically provide a portion of the needed financing. The number of days that a firm's accounts payable remain outstanding (that is, 365 days/accounts payable turnover ratio) indicates the length of the period between the purchase of inventory on account and the payment of cash to suppliers during each operating cycle. The **accounts payable turnover ratio** equals purchases on account divided by average accounts payable. Although firms do not disclose their purchases, the analyst can approximate the amount as follows:

$$\text{Beginning Inventory} + \text{Purchases} = \text{Cost of Goods Sold} + \text{Ending Inventory}$$

Rearranging terms yields the following:

$$\text{Purchases} = \text{Cost of Goods Sold} + \text{Ending Inventory} - \text{Beginning Inventory}$$

The purchases of Wal-Mart appear below:

	Purchases	$=$	Cost of Goods Sold	$+$	Ending Inventory	$-$	Beginning Inventory
Year 12	$172,734	$=$	$171,562	$+$	$22,614	$-$	$21,442
Year 13	$194,115	$=$	$191,838	$+$	$24,891	$-$	$22,614
Year 14	$200,468	$=$	$198,747	$+$	$26,612	$-$	$24,891

The accounts payable turnover ratios for Wal-Mart for Year 12, Year 13, and Year 14 are as follows:

Accounts Payable Turnover Ratio	$=$	Purchases
		Average Accounts Payable

Year 12: $172,734/0.5($15,092 + $15,617)	11.2
Year 13: $194,115/0.5($15,617 + $17,140)	11.9
Year 14: $200,468/0.5($17,140 + $19,332)	11.0

The average number of days that payables were outstanding was 32.6 days (= 365/11.2) for Year 12, 30.7 days (= 365/11.9) for Year 13, and 33.2 days (= 365/11.0) for Year 14. Thus, the days payable were relatively steady during the three years.

Interpreting the accounts payable turnover ratio involves opposing considerations. An increase in the accounts payable turnover ratio indicates that a firm pays its obligations to suppliers more quickly, requiring cash and even wasting the benefits of cash if the firm makes payments earlier than it needs to. On the other hand, a faster accounts payable turnover means a smaller relative amount of accounts payable that the firm must pay in the near future. Most firms want to extend their payables as long as they can, but they also want to maintain their relations with suppliers. Businesses, therefore, negotiate hard for favorable payment terms and then delay paying until the last agreed moment, but they pay before that last moment.

A comparison of the days outstanding for inventories, accounts receivable, and accounts payable reveals the following:

Year	Days Inventory Held	Days Accounts Receivable Outstanding	Days Accounts Payable Outstanding
Year 12	46.8	3.2	32.6
Year 13	45.1	3.1	30.7
Year 14	47.4	2.4	33.2

Wal-Mart appears to vary the days payable in a consistent pattern with changes in the days it holds inventory. Its days receivable declined during the three-year period, increasing cash.

Summary of Short-Term Liquidity Risk Analysis   The current and quick ratios measure liquidity at a particular date. These ratios for Wal-Mart seem low. The cash flow from operations to current liabilities ratio has increased and exceeds the 40 percent benchmark for a financially healthy firm. Wal-Mart sells either for cash or collects its accounts receivable within three days of the sale. It maintains a relatively constant relation between its days inventory and days payable. Thus, Wal-Mart's short-term liquidity risk appears low.

Problem 5.3 for Self-Study

Analyzing short-term liquidity risk.   Refer to the profitability ratios for Abbott Corporation in **Problems 5.1** and **5.2** for Self-Study. Consider the following additional data:

	Year 1	Year 2	Year 3
Current Ratio	1.4	1.3	1.2
Quick Ratio	1.0	0.9	1.0
Cash Flow from Operations to Current			
Liabilities Ratio	38.2%	37.3%	36.4%
Days Accounts Receivable Outstanding	84.9	84.9	86.9
Days Inventories Held	114.1	107.4	101.4
Days Accounts Payable Outstanding	58.6	59.1	58.8

a. What is the likely explanation for the decreasing current ratio coupled with the stable quick ratio?
b. What is the likely explanation for the decline in the cash flow from operations to current liabilities ratio?
c. What is your assessment of the short-term liquidity risk of Abbott Corporation at the end of Year 3?

Measures of Long-Term Liquidity Risk

Analysts use measures of **long-term liquidity risk** to evaluate a firm's ability to meet interest and principal payments on long-term debt and similar obligations as they come due. If a firm cannot make the payments on time, it becomes insolvent and may have to reorganize or liquidate.

A firm's ability to generate profits over several years provides the best protection against long-term liquidity risk. If a firm is profitable, it will either generate sufficient cash from operations or obtain needed financing from creditors and owners. The measures of profitability discussed previously therefore apply for this purpose as well. Analysts measure long-term liquidity risk with debt ratios, the cash flow from operations to total liabilities ratio, and the interest coverage ratio.

Debt Ratios The debt ratio has several variations, but the **long-term debt ratio** commonly appears in financial analysis. It reports the portion of the firm's long-term financing that debtholders furnish. To calculate this ratio, divide total long-term debt by the sum of total long-term debt and total shareholders' equity.

Another form of the debt ratio is the **debt-equity ratio**. To calculate the debt-equity ratio, divide total liabilities (current and noncurrent) by total equities (= liabilities plus shareholders' equity = total assets). Some analysts compute the long-term debt ratio, as defined above, but call it the debt-equity ratio. *Be sure you know the definition that the writer (or speaker) has in mind when you read (or hear) this term. No other financial statement ratio has so many variations in practice.*

Exhibit 5.11 shows the long-term debt ratio and the debt-equity ratio for Wal-Mart on January 31, Year 11, Year 12, Year 13, and Year 14. In general, the higher are these ratios, the higher is the likelihood that the firm will be unable to meet fixed interest and principal payments in the future. Most firms must decide how much financial leverage, with its attendant risk, they can afford. Funds obtained from issuing bonds or borrowing from a bank have a relatively low interest cost but require fixed, periodic payments that increase the likelihood of insolvency or even bankruptcy.

EXHIBIT 5.11	Debt Ratios for Wal-Mart Stores

Long-term Debt Ratio	= $\dfrac{\text{Long-term Debt}}{\text{Long-term Debt + Shareholders' Equity}}$
January 31, Year 11: $20,138/($20,138 + $31,343)	39.1%
January 31, Year 12: $23,511/($23,511 + $35,102)	40.1%
January 31, Year 13: $24,196/($24,196 + $39,337)	38.1%
January 31, Year 14: $25,573/($25,573 + $43,623)	37.0%

Debt-Equity Ratio	= $\dfrac{\text{Total Liabilities}}{\text{Total Liabilities + Shareholders' Equity}}$
January 31, Year 11: $51,270/($51,270 + $31,343)	62.1%
January 31, Year 12: $53,128/($53,128 + $35,102)	60.2%
January 31, Year 13: $59,936/($59,936 + $39,337)	60.4%
January 31, Year 14: $66,407/($66,407 + $43,623)	60.4%

In assessing the debt ratios, analysts customarily vary the standard in relation to the stability of the firm's earnings and cash flows from operations. The more stable the earnings and cash flows, the higher is the debt ratio they deem acceptable or safe. Public utilities have high debt-equity ratios, frequently on the order of 60 to 70 percent. Banks have even higher debt ratios, typically over 90 percent. The stability of earnings and cash flows of firms in these industries makes these ratios acceptable to many investors. These investors might find such high leverage unacceptable for firms with less stable earnings and cash flows, such as a computer software developer or a biotechnology firm. Wal-Mart has debt ratios about average for a retailing firm. It uses long-term debt to finance its retail stores, warehouses, and equipment, and short-term liabilities to finance inventories. The long-term debt ratio declined slightly, whereas the debt-equity ratio was relatively stable, between the end of Year 12 and Year 14.

Because several variations of the debt ratio appear in corporate annual reports, the analyst should take care when comparing debt ratios among firms.

Cash Flow from Operations to Total Liabilities Ratio
The debt ratios do not consider the availability of liquid assets to cover various levels of debt. The **cash flow from operations to total liabilities ratio** overcomes this deficiency. This cash flow ratio resembles the one for assessing short-term liquidity risk, but here the denominator includes all liabilities (both current and noncurrent). A financially healthy company normally has a cash flow from operations to total liabilities ratio of 20 percent or more.

The cash flow from operations to total liabilities ratios for Wal-Mart are as follows:

Cash Flow from Operations to Total Liabilities Ratio	=	Cash Flow from Operations / Average Total Liabilities
Year 12: $10,260/0.5($51,270 + $53,128)		19.7%
Year 13: $12,532/0.5($53,128 + $59,936)		22.2%
Year 14: $16,091/0.5($59,936 + $66,407)		25.5%

The cash flow from operations to total liabilities ratio increased during the three years. Its level of greater than 20 percent suggests that Wal-Mart has relatively low long-term liquidity risk by this measure.

Interest Coverage Ratio
The number of times that earnings cover interest charges also measures long-term liquidity risk. The **interest coverage ratio** equals income before interest and income tax expenses divided by interest expense. This ratio attempts to indicate the relative protection that operating profitability provides bondholders, permitting them to assess the probability that a firm will fail to meet required interest payments. Analysts typically view interest coverage ratio below 3.0 as risky, although they prefer a ratio that is stable over time to one that is somewhat higher on average but varies, sometimes being higher and sometimes lower.

For Wal-Mart, the interest coverage ratios for Year 12, Year 13, and Year 14 are as follows:

Interest Coverage Ratio	=	Net Income before Interest and Income Taxes / Interest Expense
Year 12: ($6,671 + $3,897 + $1,326)/$1,326		9.0 times
Year 13: ($8,039 + $4,487 + $1,063)/$1,063		12.8 times
Year 14: ($9,075 + $5,118 + $996)/$996		15.3 times

Wal-Mart's increased profit margins coupled with relatively stable debt ratios results in increasing interest coverage ratios. The ratio level is well above the 3.0 benchmark.

If bond indentures require periodic repayments of principal on long-term liabilities, the denominator of the ratio might include such repayments. The ratio would then be called the *fixed charges coverage ratio.*

One can criticize the interest or fixed charges coverage ratios as measures for assessing long-term liquidity risk because they use earnings rather than cash flows in the numerator. Firms pay interest and other fixed payment obligations with cash, not with earnings. When the value of the ratio is relatively low (for example, two to three times), the analyst should use some measure of cash flows, such as cash flow from operations, in the numerator.

Summary of Long-Term Liquidity Risk Analysis
Long-term liquidity analysis focuses on the amount of debt (particularly long-term debt) in the financing structure of a firm and the adequacy of earnings and cash flows to service this debt (that is, to provide for interest and principal payments when due). Relatively steady debt ratios coupled with increasing profitability and cash flows from operations suggests that Wal-Mart's long-term solvency risk is low.

Problem 5.4 for Self-Study

Analyzing long-term liquidity risk.   Refer to the profitability and short-term liquidity risk ratios for Abbott Corporation in **Problems 5.1**, **5.2**, and **5.3 for Self-Study**. Consider the following additional data:

(continued)

Problem 5.4 for Self-Study *(continued)*

	Year 1	Year 2	Year 3
Long-term Debt Ratio	27.2%	33.8%	43.3%
Debt-Equity Ratio	37.5%	44.4%	52.4%
Cash Flow from Operations to Total Liabilities Ratio	16.3%	13.4%	11.1%
Interest Coverage Ratio	6.7	5.1	4.1

a. What is the likely explanation for the decrease in the cash flow from operations to total liabilities ratio?

b. What is the likely explanation for the decrease in the interest coverage ratio?

c. What is your assessment of the long-term liquidity risk of Abbott Corporation at the end of Year 3?

Limitations of Ratio Analysis

The analyst should be aware of limitations in the computations discussed in this chapter, such as the following:

1. Because ratios use financial statement data as inputs, the same factors that cause financial statements themselves to have shortcomings will affect the ratios computed from them. Such shortcomings, at least for some purposes, include the use of acquisition cost for assets rather than current replacement cost or net realizable value and the latitude permitted firms in selecting from among various generally accepted accounting principles.

2. Changes in many ratios correlate with each other. For example, the current ratio and the quick ratio often change in the same direction and proportionally. The analyst need not compute all the ratios to assess a particular dimension of profitability or risk.

3. When comparing the size of a ratio between periods for the same firm, one must recognize conditions that have changed between the periods being compared (for example, different product lines or geographic markets served, changes in economic conditions, changes in prices, changes in accounting principles, and corporate acquisitions).

4. When comparing ratios of a particular firm with those of similar firms, one must recognize differences between the firms (for example, use of different methods of accounting, differences in the methods of operations and types of financing).

Financial statement ratios alone cannot provide direct indicators of good or poor management. Such ratios indicate areas that the analyst should investigate further. For example, a decrease in the turnover of merchandise inventory, ordinarily considered an undesirable trend, may reflect the accumulation of merchandise to keep retail stores open during anticipated shortages. Such shortages may force competitors to restrict operations or to close down. The analyst must combine ratios derived from financial statements with an investigation of other facts before drawing conclusions.

An International Perspective

Analyzing the financial statements of a non-U.S. firm requires consideration of the following:

1. The format and terminology of financial statements in other countries often differs from that used in statements in the United States.

2. Economic, political, and cultural factors in other countries can differ from those in the United States in ways that affect the interpretation of financial statement ratios.

3. Firms in other countries may use accounting principles different from those of U.S. firms.

Summary

For convenient reference, **Exhibit 5.12** summarizes the calculation of the financial statement ratios discussed in this chapter.

EXHIBIT 5.12	Summary of Financial Statement Ratios

Ratio	Numerator	Denominator
Profitability Ratios		
Rate of Return on Assets	Net Income + Interest Expense (net of tax effects)[a]	Average Total Assets during the Period
Profit Margin for ROA (before interest effects)	Net Income + Interest Expense (net of tax effects)[a]	Sales
Various Expense Ratios	Various Expenses	Sales
Total Assets Turnover Ratio	Sales	Average Total Assets during the Period
Accounts Receivable Turnover Ratio	Sales	Average Accounts Receivable during the Period
Inventory Turnover Ratio	Cost of Goods Sold	Average Inventory during the Period
Fixed Asset Turnover Ratio	Sales	Average Fixed Assets during the Period
Rate of Return on Common Shareholders' Equity	Net Income − Preferred Stock Dividends	Average Common Shareholders' Equity during the Period
Profit Margin for ROCE (after interest expense and preferred dividends)	Net Income − Preferred Stock Dividends	Sales
Capital Structure Leverage Ratio	Average Total Assets during the Period	Average Common Shareholders' Equity during the Period
Earnings per Share of Common Stock[b]	Net Income − Preferred Stock Dividends	Weighted-Average Number of Common Shares Outstanding
Short-term Liquidity Ratios		
Current Ratio	Current Assets	Current Liabilities
Quick or Acid Test Ratio	Highly Liquid Assets (cash, marketable securities, and receivables)[c]	Current Liabilities
Cash Flow from Operations to Current Liabilities Ratio	Cash Flow from Operations	Average Current Liabilities during the Period
Accounts Payable Turnover Ratio	Purchases[d]	Average Accounts Payable during the Period
Days Accounts Receivable Outstanding	365 days	Accounts Receivable Turnover Ratio
Days Inventories Held	365 days	Inventory Turnover Ratio
Days Accounts Payable Outstanding	365 days	Accounts Payable Turnover Ratio
Long-term Liquidity Ratios		
Long-term Debt Ratio	Total Long-term Debt	Total Long-term Debt Plus Shareholders' Equity
Debt-Equity Ratio	Total Liabilities	Total Equities (total liabilities plus shareholders' equity)
Cash Flow from Operations to Total Liabilities Ratio	Cash Flow from Operations	Average Total Liabilities during the Period
Interest Coverage Ratio	Income before Interest and Income Taxes	Interest Expense

[a]If the parent company does not own all of a consolidated subsidiary, the calculation also adds back to net income the minority interest share of earnings. See **Chapter 11** for discussion of minority interest.

[b]This calculation is more complicated when there are convertible securities, options, or warrants outstanding.

[c]The calculation could conceivably exclude receivables for some firms and include inventories for others.

[d]Purchases = Cost of Goods Sold + Ending Inventories − Beginning Inventories.

This chapter began with the question of whether you should invest your inheritance in a certificate of deposit or in the shares of common stock of Wal-Mart. Analysis of Wal-Mart's financial statements indicates that it has been a growing, profitable company with few indications of either short-term or long-term liquidity problems. You need at least three additional inputs before making the investment decision. First, you should consult sources of information other than the financial statements (for example, articles in the financial press, the firm's statements about its spending plans for long-term assets as well as analysts' beliefs about spending needs, and new strategies of competitors) to understand a firm's future profitability and risk. Second, you must decide your attitude toward, or willingness to assume, risk. Third, you must decide if you think the stock market price of the shares makes them an attractive current purchase.[9] Before making buy/sell recommendations to investors, analysts compare their assessments of the firm's profitability and risk to the firm's share price. Analysts might recommend the purchase of shares of a poorly run company whose shares they judge underpriced rather than recommend shares of a well-run company whose shares they judge overpriced in the market. At this stage in the investment decision, the analysis requires intuition, judgment, and experience.

Problem 5.5 for Self-Study

Computing profitability and risk ratios. **Exhibit 5.13** presents an income statement for Cox Corporation for Year 2, and **Exhibit 5.14** presents comparative balance sheets as of December 31, Year 1 and Year 2. Using information from these financial statements, compute the following ratios. The income tax rate is 30 percent. Cash flow from operations totals $3,300.

EXHIBIT 5.13	COX CORPORATION Income and Retained Earnings Statement for Year 2 (Problem 5.5 for Self-Study)		
Sales Revenue.			$30,000
Less Expenses:			
Cost of Goods Sold	$18,000		
Selling.	4,500		
Administrative	2,500		
Interest.	700		
Income Taxes	1,300		
Total Expenses.			27,000
Net Income			$ 3,000
Less Dividends:			
Preferred	$ 100		
Common	700		800
Increase in Retained Earnings for Year 2			$ 2,200
Retained Earnings, December 31, Year 1.			4,500
Retained Earnings, December 31, Year 2.			$ 6,700

(continued)

---

[9] Finance texts discuss other important factors in the investment decision. Perhaps the most important question is how a particular investment fits in with the investor's entire portfolio. Modern research suggests that the suitability of a potential investment depends more on the attributes of the other components of an investment portfolio and the risk attitude of the investor than it does on the attributes of the potential investment itself.

Problem 5.5 for Self-Study *(continued)*

EXHIBIT 5.14

COX CORPORATION
Comparative Balance Sheet
December 31, Year 1 and Year 2 (Problem 5.5 for Self-Study)

	December 31	
	Year 2	Year 2
ASSETS		
Current Assets		
Cash	$ 600	$ 750
Accounts Receivable	3,600	4,300
Merchandise Inventories	5,600	7,900
Prepayments	300	380
Total Current Assets	$10,100	$13,330
Property, Plant, and Equipment		
Land	$ 500	$ 600
Buildings and Equipment (net)	9,400	10,070
Total Property, Plant, and Equipment	$ 9,900	$10,670
Total Assets	$20,000	$24,000
LIABILITIES AND SHAREHOLDERS' EQUITY		
Current Liabilities		
Notes Payable	$ 2,000	$ 4,000
Accounts Payable	3,500	3,300
Other Current Liabilities	1,500	1,900
Total Current Liabilities	$ 7,000	$ 9,200
Noncurrent Liabilities		
Bonds Payable	4,000	2,800
Total Liabilities	$11,000	$12,000
Shareholders' Equity		
Preferred Stock	$ 1,000	$ 1,000
Common Stock	2,000	2,500
Additional Paid-in Capital	1,500	1,800
Retained Earnings	4,500	6,700
Total Shareholders' Equity	$ 9,000	$12,000
Total Liabilities and Shareholders' Equity	$20,000	$24,000

a.	Rate of return on assets	m.	Diluted earnings per share
b.	Profit margin ratio for ROA	n.	Current ratio (both dates)
c.	Cost of goods sold to sales percentage	o.	Quick ratio (both dates)
d.	Selling expense to sales percentage	p.	Cash flow from operations to current liabilities ratio
e.	Total assets turnover	q.	Accounts payable turnover
f.	Accounts receivable turnover	r.	Days receivables outstanding
g.	Inventory turnover	s.	Days inventory outstanding
h.	Fixed asset turnover	t.	Days payables outstanding
i.	Rate of return on common shareholders' equity	u.	Long-term debt ratio (both dates)
j.	Profit margin ratio for ROCE	v.	Debt-equity ratio (both dates)
k.	Capital structure leverage ratio	w.	Cash flow from operations to total liabilities ratio
l.	Basic earnings per share	x.	Interest coverage ratio

Accountants use the term **pro forma financial statements** to refer to financial statements prepared under a particular set of assumptions. One set of assumptions might be that some transactions, actually reported in the firm's income statement for the year under generally accepted accounting principles, had not occurred. Such assumed-away transactions might include unusual or nonrecurring revenues, expenses, gains, and losses. Firms report pro forma earnings, in these cases, to suggest to financial statement users what the firm views as normal, recurring earnings. **Chapters 6** and **12** discuss this use of the term *pro forma financial statements.*

The traditional use of the term *pro forma financial statements* refers to projected financial statements based on some set of assumptions about the future. One set of assumptions might be that historical patterns (for example, growth rates or rates of return) will continue. Alternatively, the pro forma financial statements might reflect new assumptions about growth rates, debt levels, profitability, and so on. For example, a firm might project future sales, net income, assets, and cash flows to ascertain whether operations will generate sufficient cash flows to finance expenditures on long-term assets or whether the firm will need to borrow more. A firm might change its product lines or pricing policies and might want to estimate the impact on rates of return. A firm might project future financial statement amounts for an acquisition target to ascertain the price it should pay. This appendix describes and illustrates procedures for preparing pro forma (projected) financial statements, then shows you how to use them to value firms. In your exposure to managerial and cost accounting concepts, you will encounter the notion of a *budget.* A budget means the same thing as pro forma (projected) financial statements except that the statements projected typically have different uses and formats. Managers and analysts use pro forma financials and budgets for differing reasons, but use similar procedures to prepare them.

Preparation of Pro Forma Financial Statements

The preparation of pro forma financial statements requires the analyst to make assumptions about the future. The usefulness of the pro forma financial statements depends on the reasonableness of those assumptions. Various computer spreadsheet programs ease the calculations required in preparing these statements, but the warning "garbage-in, garbage-out" certainly applies—the results will have quality and validity no better than the input assumptions. Careful analysts bring together, preferably in a single section of their spreadsheet, a list of all assumptions made and assumed values for parameters. Well-prepared pro forma statements allow the analyst to vary critical assumptions to see how the results vary.

The preparation of pro forma financial statements typically begins with the income statement, followed by the balance sheet and then the statement of cash flows. The level of operating activity usually dictates the required amount of assets, which in turn affects the required level of financing. Amounts for the statement of cash flows come directly from the pro forma income statement and comparative balance sheets.

We follow the steps below in preparing pro forma financial statements:

1. Project operating revenues.
2. Project operating expenses other than the cost of financing and income taxes.
3. Project the assets required to support the level of projected operating activity.
4. Project the financing (liabilities and contributed capital) required to fund the level of assets in step **3**.
5. Project the cost of financing the debt projected in step **4**, income tax expense, net income, dividends, and the change in retained earnings.
6. Project the statement of cash flows from amounts on the projected balance sheet and income statement.

Exhibit 5.15 summarizes these six steps. To illustrate the preparation of pro forma financial statements, we use the data for Wal-Mart discussed previously in this chapter. We project amounts for Year 15.

Step 1: Project Operating Revenues

The projections begin with sales. The analyst studies the historical pattern of changes in sales and assesses whether this pattern will continue in the future. Among the questions raised are the following:

EXHIBIT 5.15

Preparing Pro Forma Financial Statements

Statement of Income and Retained Earnings

STEP 1: Project Operating Revenues

Sales Revenue
Other Revenues

STEP 2: Project Operating Expenses

Cost of Goods Sold
Selling and Administrative Expenses
Net Income before Interest Expense
and Income Taxes

STEP 5: Project Cost of Financing, Income Tax Expense, and the Change in Retained Earnings

Interest Expense
Income Tax Expense
Net Income
Dividends
Change in Retained Earnings

Balance Sheet

STEP 3: Project Assets

Cash
Accounts Receivable
Inventories
Other Current Assets
Investments
Fixed Assets
Other Assets

STEP 4: Project Liabilities and Contributed Capital

Accounts Payable
Notes Payable
Other Current Liabilities
Long-term Debt
Other Liabilities
Contributed Capital

STEP 5: Project Retained Earnings

Retained Earnings

Statement of Cash Flows

STEP 6: Project the Statement of Cash Flows

Operations
Net Income
Depreciation
Other Adjustments
Change in Receivables
Change in Inventories
Change in Other Current Assets
Change in Accounts Payable
Change in Other Current Liabilities
CASH FLOW FROM OPERATIONS

Investing
Acquisition of Fixed Assets
Sale of Investments
Acquisition of Investments
Other Investing Transactions
CASH FLOW FROM INVESTING

Financing
Change in Notes Payable
Change in Long-term Debt
Change in Common Stock
Dividends
Other Financing Transactions
CASH FLOW FROM FINANCING

1. Does the firm plan to change product lines or pricing policies, make acquisitions of other companies, or take other actions that would alter the historical sales pattern?
2. Does the firm expect competitors to alter their strategies or new competitors to enter the market and thereby change the market shares?
3. Will conditions in the economy affect the firm's sales? For example, do the firm's sales fluctuate with economic cycles, do they remain steady, or do they fluctuate with other variables, such as local population growth?

The assumption about sales drives most other items in the pro forma financial statements, which likely makes this assumption the most important.

Exhibit 5.2 indicates that sales revenues for Wal-Mart Corporation increased from $217,799 million to $244,524 million between Year 12 and Year 13, a growth rate of 12.3 percent [= ($244,524/$217,799) − 1]. Sales increased from $244,524 million to $256,329 million between Year 13 and Year 14, a growth rate of only 4.8 percent [= ($256,329/$244,524) − 1]. The decline in the growth rate occurred in a year when Wal-Mart did not make any large corporate acquisitions and the economy experienced recession conditions. Between Year 10 and Year 14 (income statement amounts not shown in the text), Wal-Mart's sales grew at a compound annual rate of 11.6 percent. We project Wal-Mart's revenues to increase 10 percent between Year 14 and Year 15. Thus, projected sales for Year 15 are $281,962 million (= $256,329 million × 1.10).

Other revenues have varied between 0.9 percent and 1.0 percent of sales during the last three years. We assume that other revenues will equal 1.0 percent of sales in Year 15. Projected other revenues are $2,820 million (= 0.01 × $281,962).

Step 2: Project Operating Expenses

Projecting operating expenses requires understanding the behavior of various operating costs. Does the expense item tend to vary with the level of sales, a behavior pattern characterized as a *variable cost*? Alternatively, does the expense item tend to remain relatively constant for a particular time period regardless of the level of sales, a behavior pattern characterized as a *fixed cost*? (When you study cost behavior in your managerial and economics courses, you will learn that nearly all costs vary in the long run, but appear fixed in the short run. Deciding on whether a given cost is fixed or variable requires knowing the time period envisioned for the projection.) Does the expense item have both variable- and fixed-cost characteristics, a pattern described as a *mixed cost* or a *step cost*? Does the firm have some discretion to change the amount of a fixed cost item in the short term in response to current conditions (for example, maintenance or advertising expenditures), or is there little discretion to change the level of fixed costs (for example, depreciation on equipment)? Understanding the behavior of each expense item aids in projecting its amount.

Exhibit 5.6 presents a common-size income statement for Wal-Mart for Year 12, Year 13, and Year 14. We use these common-size percentages in projecting operating expenses.

Cost of Goods Sold

Wal-Mart purchases merchandise and then marks it up to sell to customers. Thus cost of goods sold will likely vary with sales. The cost of goods sold percentage has decreased slightly during the last three years. Assume that the decrease is a result of implementing merchandise purchase and control systems in the non-U.S. retail chains that Wal-Mart acquired in recent years. We assume that Wal-Mart will benefit even further from these inventory systems in Year 15, reducing the cost of goods sold to sales percentage to 77.0 percent. Projected cost of goods sold for Year 15 is $217,111 million (= 0.77 × $281,962 million).

Selling and Administrative Expense

The ratio of selling and administrative expense to sales increased during the last three years, with most of the increase occurring in Year 14. Increased competition requiring increased expenditures on marketing partially explains the increasing percentage. Also, the significant decrease in the growth rate of sales in Year 14 likely resulted in spreading fixed costs such as depreciation, rent, and insurance over a smaller than anticipated sales base. We project sales to return to its historical growth rate in Year 15. We assume that selling and administrative expenses will equal 17 percent of sales in Year 15. Thus, projected selling and administrative expenses for Year 15 are $47,934 million (= 0.17 × $281,962 million).

Step 3: Project Assets

The projection of total assets on the balance sheet requires the analyst to make assumptions consistent with those underlying the pro forma income statement. One approach assumes a total assets turnover (that is, sales/average total assets) similar to that of previous years. For example, the total assets turnover of Wal-Mart was 2.4 during Year 14. If the firm maintains this total assets turnover during Year 15, then the calculation of its total assets at the end of Year 15 results from solving the following equation:

$$\text{Total Assets Turnover} = \frac{\text{Sales}}{\text{Average Total Assets}} = \frac{\$281,962}{(0.5)(\$110,030 + x)} = 2.4$$

Solving for the unknown in the equation yields projected total assets at the end of Year 15 of $124,938. The analyst can then use common-size balance sheet percentages to allocate this total to individual balance sheet accounts.

An alternative approach uses the historical annual growth rate in total assets of 10.2 percent during the last three years. This approach yields total assets of $121,253 million (= $110,030 million × 1.102). The analyst can then apply common-size balance sheet amounts to allocate this $121,253 million to individual balance sheet items.

A third approach uses a mixture of assets turnovers and growth rates for the various assets and then aggregates projected amounts for individual assets to compute total assets. We illustrate this approach next. We will compute last the amount of cash at the end of Year 15 as the residual (or plug) necessary to equate total assets and total liabilities plus shareholders' equity.

Accounts Receivable

For most firms, accounts receivable vary with changes in sales. Wal-Mart collects its accounts receivable so quickly (2 to 3 days after sale) that accounts receivable comprise a small proportion of total assets. We assume that accounts receivable will grow during Year 15 at the growth rate in sales. Projected accounts receivable on January 31, Year 15, are $1,379 million (= $1,254 × 1.10).

Inventory

We could use the inventory turnover to project the ending inventory for Year 15. The inventory turnover ratio was 7.8 in Year 12, 8.1 in Year 13, and 7.7 in Year 14. An earlier section suggested that the decreased inventory turnover in Year 14 may have resulted from an unexpected decrease in the growth rate in sales. We assume that sales growth will return to a more normal level in Year 15, so we use an inventory turnover of 8.1 to project ending inventory for Year 15. This inventory rate assumes that Wal-Mart can achieve still greater efficiencies in inventory management in its non-U.S. operations, consistent with our assumption for the cost of goods sold to sales percentage for Year 15. We solve for x in the following equation to project inventory at the end of Year 15.

$$\frac{\text{Cost of Goods Sold}}{\text{Average Inventory}} = \frac{\$271,111}{(0.5)(\$26,612 + x)} = 8.1$$

Using the inventory turnover of 8.1 times per year projects inventories at the end of Year 15 (x in the equation) at $26,996 million. This projected level of inventories represents only a small increase over the $26,612 of inventories at the end of Year 14, which does not seem reasonable as judged by the historical growth in inventories. This projection of a small increase in inventory when using the inventory turnover ratio is the result of the offsetting effects of a sharp drop in inventory turnover between Year 13 and Year 14. Whenever a turnover ratio changes significantly in the year preceding a projection, the projected amount for the next year compensates and usually results in unreasonable projections. Thus, we will not use the projected amounts for inventories for Wal-Mart using the inventory turnovers as discussed above.

An analysis of increase in inventories during the last three years shows an historical annual growth rate of 7.5 percent, more in line with the historical growth rate in sales. We assume that inventory at the end of Year 15 will grow at the growth rate in sales of 10 percent. Projected inventories at the end of Year 15 are $29,273 million (= $26,612 × 1.10).

Prepayments

Prepayments include rent, insurance, and similar operating expenses and usually grow at the same rate as sales. We assume that prepayments will grow during Year 15 at the projected growth rate in sales of 10 percent. Thus, prepayments at the end of Year 15 are $1,294 million (= $1,176 × 1.10).

Property, Plant, and Equipment

We could use the fixed asset turnover to project property, plant, and equipment as we attempted above for inventories. Using the fixed asset turnover in this case, however, yields unreasonable projections for property, plant, and equipment relative to the historical growth rate. We instead use the historical growth rate of property, plant and equipment for Year 11 to Year 14 of 11.9 percent. Projected property, plant, and equipment at the end of Year 15 is $71,222 million (= $63,648 million × 1.119). Growing property, plant, and equipment at a faster growth rate than sales implies that Wal-Mart will grow its store capacity or number of stores, or both, before it generates increased sales from those stores.

Other Noncurrent Assets

Other noncurrent assets primarily represent goodwill from corporate acquisitions made in previous years. GAAP does not require firms to amortize goodwill. We assume that other noncurrent assets will not change between the end of Year 14 and the end of Year 15.

Step 4: Project Liabilities and Contributed Capital

We project next the financing side of the balance sheet. The projection of liabilities and contributed capital flows directly from the projection of the level of operating activity estimated in the first two steps and the projection of total assets estimated in the preceding step.

Accounts Payable

The accounts payable turnover varied between 11.0 and 11.9 during the last three years. We project accounts payable at the end of Year 15 assuming an accounts payable turnover of 11.0. We solve the following equation to project accounts payable at the end of Year 15:

$$\frac{\text{Purchases}}{\text{Average Accounts Payable}} = \frac{\$271,111 + \$29,273 - \$26,612}{(0.5)(\$19,332 + x)} = 11.0$$

Using the turnover of 11.0 times per year projects accounts payable at the end of Year 15 at $20,627 million.

Notes Payable

Wal-Mart likely uses Notes Payable to finance inventories and other working capital needs. We assume that Notes Payable will increase at the growth rate in sales. Thus, projected Notes Payable is $3,594 million (= $3,267 × 1.10).

Current Portion of Long-term Debt

Wal-Mart discloses in notes to its financial statements that long-term debt due during Year 16, and therefore classified as a current liability on the January 31, Year 15 balance sheet, is $2,875 million.

Other Current Liabilities

Other current liabilities relate to unpaid salaries, taxes, and other operating costs. These costs tend to vary with the level of operating activity. We project that other current liabilities will grow at the growth rate in sales. We therefore project other current liabilities at the end of Year 15 to equal $12,891 million (= $11,719 × 1.10).

Bonds Payable

Wal-Mart uses long-term debt to finance the growth in its stores. We assume that bonds payable will decrease by the amount that Wal-Mart reclassifies from noncurrent liabilities to current liabilities ($2,875 million during Year 15). The remaining long-term debt will then grow at the growth rate in property, plant, and equipment of 11.9 percent. Thus, the projected amount of long-term debt at the end of Year 15 is $25,399 million [= ($25,573 − $2,875) × 1.119]. We can alter this assumption at a later stage if the firm does not need to borrow.

Other Noncurrent Liabilities

Other noncurrent liabilities include obligations for retirement plans and taxes due longer than one year into the future. These obligations vary with the level of operating activity. We therefore assume that other noncurrent liabilities will grow at the growth rate in sales. Projected other noncurrent liabilities at the end of Year 15 are $3,758 million (= $3,416 × 1.10).

Contributed Capital

We assume no change in common stock or additional paid-in capital during Year 15.

Step 5: Project Interest Expense, Income Tax Expense, Net Income, Dividends, and the Change in Retained Earnings

Interest Expense

Interest expense usually bears a relatively fixed relation to the level of borrowing. Interest expense for Wal-Mart averaged approximately 4 percent of notes and bonds payable during Year 14. Using the average amount of notes payable, current portion of long-term debt, and long-term debt for Year 15 yields projected interest expense of $1,276 million.

Income Tax Expense

The projections of sales, operating expenses, and interest expense yields income before income taxes of $18,461 million (= $281,962 + $2,820 − $217,111 − $47,934 − $1,276). Income tax expense remained a steady 36 percent of income before income taxes during the last three years. We maintain this income tax rate in projecting income tax expense for Year 15. Projected income tax expense is $6,646 million (= 0.36 × $18,461).

Retained Earnings

Retained earnings increase by the $11,815 million of net income (= $18,461 − $6,646) and decrease by dividends declared and paid. Wal-Mart's dividends have grown during the last three years at a annual growth rate of 11.9 percent. We assume that dividends in Year 15 will grow 12 percent, resulting in a dividend of $1,757 million (= $1,569 × 1.12). Thus, retained earnings at the end of Year 15 are $51,115 million (= $41,057 + $11,815 − $1,757).

   The preparation of pro forma financial statements through the first five steps results in a projected income statement (see **Exhibit 5.16**) and a projected balance sheet (see **Exhibit 5.17**). The only item on the balance sheet not yet projected is cash. We set cash as the plug that equates projected total assets with projected liabilities and shareholders' equity. Projected liabilities and shareholders' equity total $122,825 million. Projected assets other than cash equal $115,309 million (= $1,379 + $29,273 + $1,294 + $71,222 + $12,141). Projected cash is $7,516 million (=$122,825 − $115,309).

   The preparation of pro forma financial statements usually requires the analyst to plug some account to equate assets with liabilities plus shareholders' equity and have income statement amounts articulate with projected balance sheet amounts. Cash is often the plug, but not necessarily. The analyst might assume that a firm needs a certain minimum amount of cash. The

EXHIBIT 5.16	**WAL-MART STORES** **Pro Forma Income Statement for Year 15** **(all dollar amounts in millions)**		
	Year 14 **Actual**	**Assumption**	**Year 15** **Pro** **Forma**
Sales	$256,329	Growth Rate = 10%	$281,962
Other Revenues	2,516	1.0% of Sales	2,820
Total Revenues	$258,845		$284,782
Less Expenses:			
Cost of Goods Sold	$198,747	77.0% of Sales	$217,111
Selling and Administrative	44,909	17.0% of Sales	47,934
Interest	996	4.0% of Interest-Bearing Debt	1,276
Total Expenses	$244,652		$266,321
Net Income before Taxes	$ 14,193		$ 18,461
Income Tax Expense	5,118	36.0% of Net Income before	
		Taxes	$6,646
Net Income	$ 9,075	Pro Forma Net Income	$ 11,815

EXHIBIT 5.17	WAL-MART STORES Pro Forma Balance Sheet January 31, Year 15 (all dollar amounts in millions)		

	January 31, Year 14 Actual	Assumption	January 31, Year 15 Pro Forma
ASSETS			
Cash	$ 5,199	Residual	$ 7,516
Accounts Receivable	1,254	Sales Growth Rate	1,379
Inventories	26,612	Sales Growth Rate	29,273
Prepayments	1,176	Sales Growth Rate	1,294
Total Current Assets	$ 34,241		$39,462
Property, Plant, and Equipment (net)	63,648	Growth Rate = 11.9%	71,222
Other Noncurrent Assets	12,141	No Change	12,141
Total Assets	$110,030	Pro Forma Total Assets	$122,825
LIABILITIES AND SHAREHOLDERS' EQUITY			
Accounts Payable	$ 19,332	Turnover = 11.0	$ 20,627
Notes Payable	3,267	Sales Growth Rate	3,594
Current Portion of Long-term Debt	3,100	Given	2,875
Other Current Liabilities	11,719	Sales Growth Rate	12,891
Total Current Liabilities	$ 37,418		$ 39,987
Long-term Debt	25,573	Property Plant & Equipment Growth Rate .	25,399
Other Noncurrent Liabilities	3,416	Sales Growth Rate	3,758
Total Liabilities	$ 66,407		$ 69,144
Common Stock	$ 431	No Change	$ 431
Additional Paid-in Capital	2,135	No Change	2,135
Retained Earnings	41,057	12% Dividend Growth Rate	51,115
Total Shareholders' Equity	$ 43,623	Pro Forma Total Shareholders' Equity	$ 53,681
Total Liabilities and Shareholders' Equity	$110,030	Pro Forma Total Liabilities and Shareholders' Equity	$122,825

analyst might assume that the firm will invest cash in excess of this balance in marketable securities or borrow if projected cash flows suggest a balance in cash less than the minimum.

Step 6: Project the Statement of Cash Flows

The analyst can prepare a pro forma statement of cash flows directly from the pro forma income statement and pro forma balance sheet. **Exhibit 5.18** presents the pro forma statement of cash flows for Wal-Mart for Year 15. We assume that changes in other noncurrent liabilities, which include obligations for retirement plans and taxes due in later years, relate to operations. Note that the increase in cash during Year 15 of $2,317 reconciles to the change in cash on the pro forma balance sheet.

The only items not explicitly discussed previously are the addback for depreciation in the operating section and the cash outflow for acquisitions of property, plant, and equipment. Wal-Mart does not report depreciation expense on its income statement but instead includes it in selling and administrative expenses. We need to know the amount of depreciation when preparing the statement of cash flows using the indirect method. We assume that depreciation expense grows at the growth rate in property, plant, and equipment. Thus, projected depreciation for Year 15 is $4,310 million (= $3,852 × 1.119). The calculation of cash outflows to acquire property, plant, and equipment is as follows:

Property, Plant, and Equipment (net) December 31, Year 14 (**Exhibit 5.17**)	$63,648
Plus Acquisition during Year 15 (plug)	11,884
Less Depreciation Expense for Year 15 (see discussion above)	(4,310)
Property, Plant, and Equipment (net) December 31, Year 15 (**Exhibit 5.17**)	$71,222

EXHIBIT 5.18	WAL-MART STORES Pro Forma Statement of Cash Flows for Year 15 (amounts in millions)

Operations

Net Income	$ 11,815
Depreciation	4,310
Other Addbacks	342
(Increase) Decrease in Accounts Receivable	(125)
(Increase) Decrease in Inventories	(2,661)
(Increase) Decrease in Prepayments	(118)
Increase (Decrease) in Accounts Payable	1,295
Increase (Decrease) in Other Current Liabilities	1,172
Cash Flow from Operations	$ 16,030

Investing

Acquisition of Property, Plant, and Equipment	$(11,884)
Other Investing Activities	0
Cash Flow for Investing	$(11,884)

Financing

Increase (Decrease) in Short-term Borrowing	$ 327
Increase (Decrease) in Long-term Borrowing	(399)
Dividends	(1,757)
Other Financing Activities	0
Cash Flow for Financing	$ (1,829)
Change in Cash	$ 2,317
Cash, January 31, Year 14	5,199
Cash, January 31, Year 15	$ 7,516

A common source of error in preparing pro forma financial statements is to fail to reconcile the change in property, plant, and equipment (net) on the balance sheet with the amount for depreciation expense on the income statement (if disclosed) and the statement of cash flows and the amount for acquisitions on the statement of cash flows.

Analysis of Pro Forma Financial Statements

The analyst can calculate various financial statements ratios from the pro forma financial statements. **Exhibit 5.19** presents financial statements ratios for Wal-Mart based on its actual amounts for Year 12, Year 13, and Year 14 and on its pro forma amounts for Year 15. The pro forma amounts indicate a continuing increase in profitability, which ultimately results from our input assumptions. You can see how the assumptions affected profitability by noticing the following. The rate of return on assets increases because of an increased profit margin for ROA. The increased profit margin for ROA results from a decline in both the cost of goods sold to sales and the selling and administrative expense to sales percentages. The total assets turnover remains steady. The rate of return on common shareholders' equity increases because of improved operating profitability. The capital structure leverage ratio declines, the result of both reductions in long-term debt and the retention of earnings. The risk ratios do not signal any significant changes in either the short-term or long-term liquidity risk of Wal-Mart.

Valuation

Managers, security analysts, and others analyze financial statements (both historical and pro forma) to form judgments about the market value of a firm. This section briefly describes the relation between financial statement items and market values. The analyst typically values a firm by using several approaches to ascertain if a small range of values emerges. Entire textbooks and courses consider the valuation approaches introduced below.

Present Value of Future Cash Flows

Chapter 2 defined an asset as a resource with the potential to generate future cash inflows (or to reduce future cash outflows). Likewise, the common stock of a firm has value to an investor

| | EXHIBIT 5.19 | WAL-MART STORES
Financial Statement Ratio Analysis |

	Actual			Pro Forma
	Year 12	Year 13	Year 14	Year 15
Rate of Return on Assets	8.8%	9.3%	9.3%	10.8%
Profit Margin for ROA (before interest expense and related tax effects)	3.5%	3.6%	3.8%	4.5%
Total Assets Turnover	2.5	2.6	2.4	2.4
Cost of Goods Sold/Sales	78.8%	78.4%	77.6%	77.0%
Selling and Administrative Expenses/Sales	16.6%	16.9%	17.5%	17.0%
Interest Expense/Sales	0.6%	0.4%	0.4%	0.5%
Income Tax Expense/Sales	1.8%	1.8%	2.0%	2.4%
Accounts Receivable Turnover	115.6	119.0	152.5	214.1
Inventory Turnover	7.8	8.1	7.7	7.8
Fixed Asset Turnover	4.5	4.6	4.3	4.2
Rate of Return on Common Shareholders' Equity	20.1%	21.6%	21.9%	24.3%
Profit Margin Ratio for ROCE (after interest expense)	3.1%	3.3%	3.5%	4.2%
Capital Structure Leverage Ratio	2.6	2.5	2.5	2.4
Current Ratio	1.04	0.93	0.92	0.99
Quick Ratio	0.15	0.15	0.17	0.22
Cash Flow from Operations to Current Liabilities	36.5%	41.8%	46.0%	41.4%
Accounts Payable Turnover	11.2	11.9	11.0	11.0
Long-term Debt Ratio	40.1%	38.1%	37.0%	32.1%
Debt-Equity Ratio	60.2%	60.4%	60.4%	56.3%
Cash Flow from Operations to Total Liabilities	19.7%	22.2%	25.5%	23.7%
Interest Coverage Ratio	9.0	12.8	15.3	15.5

because it can generate cash inflows to the investor in the form of dividends and cash proceeds when the investor sells the shares. Dividends and cash proceeds from sales result from the future profitability and cash flows of a firm.

One valuation approach projects the net amount of cash flows a firm will generate for the common shareholders over some number of future years. Cash flow for the common shareholders equals cash flow from operating, investing, and financing activities (other than cash transactions with common shareholders). The analyst then discounts the net amount for each year at an appropriate discount rate to find the present value of these future cash flows. (The **Appendix** to this book discusses the procedure for discounting future cash flows to their equivalent present value.) Corporate finance texts discuss whether the appropriate discount rate should be the desired rate of return by the common shareholders, as we assume here, or a weighted average cost of both debt and equity financing.

Refer to the pro forma statement of cash flows for Wal-Mart for Year 15 in **Exhibit 5.18**. Cash inflow from operations totals $16,030 million, cash outflow for investing totals $11,884 million, and cash outflow from net nonowner financing is $72 million (= $327 − $399). Thus, this firm projects a positive net cash inflow for the common shareholders of $4,074 million (= $16,030 − $11,884 − $72).

Assume for purposes of illustration that pro forma financial statements for Wal-Mart reveal the amounts in columns (2) through (5) of **Exhibit 5.20**. Column (6) shows the present value of the excess cash flow when discounted at 12 percent, the assumed rate of return desired by the common shareholders. The analyst expects excess cash flow after Year 19 to increase 10 percent each year. The $186,066 million represents the present value at the end of Year 14 of this excess cash flow after Year 19. Based on the 4,310 million shares of common stock outstanding (see

EXHIBIT 5.20	Valuation of Wal-Mart Using Present Value of Cash Flows				
Year (1)	Cash Flow from Operations (2)	Cash Flow from Investing (3)	Cash Flow from Nonowner Financing (4)	Excess Cash Flow to Common Shareholders (5)	Present Value of Cash Flows to Common Shareholders (6)
15	$16,030	$(11,884)	$ (72)	$ 4,074	$ 3,637.5
16	17,632	(13,074)	(79)	4,479	3,570.6
17	19,395	(14,381)	(87)	4,927	3,506.9
18	21,335	(15,819)	(96)	5,420	3,444.5
19	23,468	(17,401)	(105)	5,962	3,383.0
After Year 19					186,066.0[a]
Total Present Value					$203,608.5
Note: Column (5) = Column (2) + Column (3) + Column (4).					

[a]Assumes a growth rate in excess cash flow of 10 percent per year and a discount rate of 12 percent. See **Problem 44** in the Appendix.

Exhibit 5.3), the analyst estimates a market value of $47.24 per share (= $203,608.5 million/4,310 million shares).[10]

Market Multiples

A second valuation approach relies on market multiples of certain financial statement items for similar firms in the market. Identifying similar firms requires the analyst to consider such factors as the type of business, growth characteristics, and size.

Price Earnings Ratios

One common valuation approach relates market prices to multiples of earnings. The chain of logic runs as follows:

The analyst uses current earnings as a surrogate for future earnings and cash flows (recall from **Chapter 3** that over sufficiently long periods, net income equals cash inflows minus cash outflows from operating, investing, and nonowner financing activities). Future cash flows of the firm provide the source of cash flows to the investor. The market multiple serves the function of a discount factor in present value calculation.[11]

---

[10] Note that the number of common shares outstanding on January 31, Year 14, of 4,310 differs from the average number of shares outstanding during Year 14 of 4,363 used in the computation of earnings per share.

[11] Actually, the discount rate and the market multiple for a no-growth firm have a reciprocal relation. Refer to the discussion of perpetuities in this book's compound interest Appendix. There you will see that the current value of an indefinite stream of constant payments, say $1 per period, is $1/r$ when the interest (or discount) rate is r per period. Thus if the discount rate is 10 percent per period, the stream has a current value of $10 (= $1/0.10), a multiple of 10, but if the discount rate is 20 percent per period, then the stream has a current value of only $5 (= $1/0.20), a multiple of 5. Market multipliers for growing firms are larger than $1/r$ because of the need to value the growth in cash flows and earnings. See **Exhibit 12.2** and the discussion of valuation in **Chapter 12**.

Assume that firms similar to Wal-Mart sell at 20 times Year 14 earnings from continuing operations. Based on the earnings of Wal-Mart for Year 14 of $9,075 million, a market multiple of 20 yields a total market value of $181,500 million, or $42.11 (= $181,500 /4,310 shares) per share.

Market-to-Book-Value Ratios

Another valuation approach relates market values to the book values of common shareholders' equity of similar firms. Book values tend to exhibit less variability over time than earnings and provide perhaps less ambiguous indications of market values.

Assume that firms similar to Wal-Mart have average market-to-book-value ratios of 4.0 at the end of Year 14. The common shareholders' equity of Wal-Mart is $43,623 million at the end of Year 14, suggesting a total market value of $174,492 million, or $40.49 (= $174,492 million/4,310 million) per share.

Summary of Valuation Approaches

These valuation approaches yielded market values for Wal-Mart of approximately $40 to $48 per share. We constructed the examples so that the values fell within a narrow range. Analysis of real data will likely show a wider range of market values, so the analyst uses judgment built over several years of practice in choosing an approach to provide a reasonable estimate. The observed market value of Wal-Mart indicated at the beginning of this chapter was $59 per share. If we trust our analysis, we would decide that the shares are too expensive for current purchase. But, we would wonder if the market has considered factors we have overlooked.

Solutions to Self-Study Problems

SUGGESTED SOLUTION TO PROBLEM 5.1 FOR SELF-STUDY

(Abbott Corporation; analyzing the rate of return on assets.)

a. The declining rate of return on assets results from a decreasing total assets turnover. The profit margin ratio for ROA was stable. The declining total assets turnover results primarily from a decreasing fixed assets turnover. Abbott Corporation has probably added productive capacity in recent years, anticipating higher sales in the future, which caused the fixed asset turnover to decline.

b. Abbott Corporation has probably implemented more effective inventory control systems, resulting in an increasing inventory turnover ratio. The more rapid inventory turnover results in fewer writedowns of inventory items for product obsolescence and physical deterioration, thereby decreasing the cost of goods sold to sales percentage.

SUGGESTED SOLUTION TO PROBLEM 5.2 FOR SELF-STUDY

(Abbott Corporation; analyzing the rate of return on common shareholders' equity.)

a. The increasing rate of return on common shareholders' equity results from an increasing proportion of debt in the financing structure. Although the rate of return on assets declined, the increase in the capital structure leverage ratio more than offset the declining operating profitability.

b. The rate of return on common shareholders' equity exceeds the rate of return on assets, suggesting that the firm's earnings on assets financed by creditors were greater than the cost of creditors' financing. The excess return benefited the common shareholders.

SUGGESTED SOLUTION TO PROBLEM 5.3 FOR SELF-STUDY

(Abbott Corporation; analyzing short-term liquidity risk.)

a. Inventories are the principal asset appearing in the current ratio but not in the quick ratio. The declining current ratio indicates that inventories are not growing as rapidly as the overall level of operations. Note the decrease in the number of days inventory items are held, suggesting that the firm exerts more effective control over the level of inventories.

b. Abbott Corporation experienced a slight increase in the number of days receivables are outstanding, which tends to decrease cash flow from operations. The decrease in the number of days a firm holds inventories increases cash flow from operations and more than offsets the effect of accounts receivable on cash flow from operations. The stable days accounts payables are outstanding also indicates that an acceleration or delay in paying accounts payable does not explain the decline in the cash flow from operations to current liabilities ratio. Most likely, declining profitability, which results in operations throwing off less cash with each revolution of the operating cycle, caused the decline. Note that the profit margin for ROA remained stable over the three years (see **Problem 5.1 for Self-Study**), whereas the profit margin ratio for ROCE decreases (see **Problem 5.2 for Self-Study**). Thus, the declining profitability results from increased financing costs, probably related to the level of debt in the financing structure.

c. Abbott Corporation's cash flow from operations to current liabilities ratio is marginally less than the 40 percent level considered desirable for a healthy firm. Its declining current ratio results from more effective inventory control systems, reducing short-term liquidity risk. A quick ratio around 1.0 indicates that the most liquid current assets are sufficient to pay current liabilities. These signals suggest a satisfactory level of short-term liquidity risk.

SUGGESTED SOLUTION TO PROBLEM 5.4 FOR SELF-STUDY

(Abbott Corporation; analyzing long-term liquidity risk.)

a. The response to question **b** in **Problem 5.3 for Self-Study** indicates that declining profitability helps explain the decrease in the cash flow from operations to total liabilities ratio. So does the increase in borrowing. This increased borrowing is both short-term and long-term, as the two debt ratios indicate.

b. The declining interest coverage ratio results primarily from increased interest expense on the increased debt loads. (Note from **Problem 5.1 for Self-Study** that the profit margin ratio for ROA was stable during the last three years.)

c. The cash flow from operations to total liabilities ratio falls below the 20 percent level considered desirable for a healthy firm. Its interest coverage ratio remains four times earnings before interest and taxes, slightly above the minimum 3.0 level expected for a healthy firm. The growth in debt appears related to increases in fixed assets (see the response to question **a** in **Problem 5.1 for Self-Study**). If Abbott Corporation experienced difficulty servicing its debt, it could perhaps sell some of these fixed assets to obtain funds. Thus, the overall long-term liquidity risk level appears reasonable.

SUGGESTED SOLUTION TO PROBLEM 5.5 FOR SELF-STUDY

(Cox Corporation; computing profitability and risk ratios.)

a. Rate of return on assets $= \dfrac{\$3,000 - (1 - 0.30)(\$700)}{(0.5)(\$20,000 + \$24,000)} = 15.9$ percent

b. Profit margin for ROA $= \dfrac{\$3,000 + (1 - 0.30)(\$700)}{\$30,000} = 11.6$ percent

c. Cost of goods sold to sales percentage $= \dfrac{\$18,000}{\$30,000} = 60.0$ percent

d. Selling expense to sales percentage $= \dfrac{\$4,500}{\$30,000} = 15.0$ percent

e. Total assets turnover $= \dfrac{\$30,000}{(0.5)(\$20,000 + \$24,000)} = 1.4$ times per year

f. Accounts receivable turnover $= \dfrac{\$30,000}{(0.5)(\$3,600 + \$4,300)} = 7.6$ times per year

g. Inventory turnover $= \dfrac{\$18,000}{(0.5)(\$5,600 + \$7,900)} = 2.7$ times per year

h. Fixed assets turnover $= \dfrac{\$30,000}{(0.5)(\$9,900 + \$10,670)} = 2.9$ times per year

i. Rate of return on common shareholders' equity $= \dfrac{\$3,000 - \$100}{(0.5)(\$8,000 + \$11,000)} = 30.5$ percent

j. Profit margin for ROCE $= \dfrac{\$3,000 - \$100}{\$30,000} = 9.7$ percent

k. Capital structure leverage ratio $= \dfrac{(0.5)(\$20,000 + \$24,00)}{(0.5)(\$8,000 + \$11,000)} = 2.3$

l. Current ratio

December 31, Year 1: $= \dfrac{\$10,100}{\$7,000} = 1.4\!:\!1$

December 31, Year 2: $= \dfrac{\$13,300}{\$9,200} = 1.4\!:\!1$

m. Quick ratio

December 31, Year 1: $= \dfrac{\$4,200}{\$7,000} = 0.6\!:\!1$

December 31, Year 2: $= \dfrac{\$5,050}{\$9,200} = 0.5\!:\!1$

n. Cash flow from operations to current liabilities ratio $= \dfrac{\$3,300}{(0.5)(\$7,000 + \$9,200)} = 40.7$ percent

o. Accounts payable turnover $= \dfrac{\$18,000 + \$7,900 - \$5,600}{(0.5)(\$3,500 + \$3,300)} = 6.0$ times per year

p. Long-term debt ratio

December 31, Year 1: $= \dfrac{\$4,000}{\$13,000} = 30.8$ percent

December 31, Year 2: $= \dfrac{\$2,800}{\$14,800} = 18.9$ percent

q. Debt-equity ratio

December 31, Year 1: $= \dfrac{\$11,000}{\$20,000} = 55.0$ percent

December 31, Year 2: $= \dfrac{\$12,000}{\$24,000} = 50.0$ percent

r. Cash flow from operations to total liabilities ratio $= \dfrac{\$3,300}{(0.5)(\$11,000 + \$12,000)} = 28.7$ percent

s. Interest coverage ratio $= \dfrac{\$3,000 + \$1,300 + \$700}{\$700} = 7.1$ times

Return and risk
Time-series analysis
Cross-section analysis
Profitability
Rate of return on assets (ROA)
Profit margin for ROA ratio
Total assets turnover ratio
Accounts receivable turnover ratio
Inventory turnover ratio
Fixed asset turnover ratio
Rate of return on common shareholders'
  equity (ROCE)
Financial leverage
Profit margin for ROCE ratio
Capital structure leverage ratio

Earnings per share
Basic and diluted earnings per share
Short-term liquidity risk
Current ratio
Quick ratio or acid test ratio
Cash flow from operations to current
  liabilities ratio
Accounts payable turnover ratio
Long-term liquidity risk
Long-term debt ratio
Debt-equity ratio
Cash flow from operations to total
  liabilities ratio
Interest coverage ratio
Pro forma financial statements

Questions, Short Exercises, Exercises, Problems, and Cases

For additional student
resources, content, and
interactive quizzes for
this chapter visit the
FACMU website:
http://facmu.swlearning.com

QUESTIONS

1. Review the meaning of the terms and concepts listed above in Key Terms and Concepts.
2. Describe several factors that might limit the comparability of a firm's financial statement ratios over several periods.
3. Describe several factors that might limit the comparability of one firm's financial statement ratios with those of another firm in the same industry.
4. "I can understand why the analyst adds back interest expense to net income in the numerator of the rate of return on assets, but I don't see why an adjustment is made for income taxes." Provide an explanation.
5. One company president stated, "The operations of our company are such that we must turn inventory over once every four weeks." A company president in another industry stated, "The operations of our company are such that we can live comfortably with a turnover of four times each year." Explain what these two company presidents probably had in mind.
6. Some have argued that for any given firm at a particular time, there is an optimal inventory turnover ratio. Explain.
7. Under what circumstances will the rate of return on common shareholders' equity exceed the rate of return on assets? Under what circumstances will it be less?
8. A company president recently stated, "The operations of our company are such that we can effectively use only a small amount of financial leverage." Explain.
9. Define financial leverage. As long as a firm's rate of return on assets exceeds its after-tax cost of borrowing, why doesn't the firm increase borrowing to as close to 100 percent of financing as possible?
10. Illustrate with amounts how a decrease in the amount of working capital (that is, current assets minus current liabilities) can accompany an increase in the current ratio.

SHORT EXERCISES

11. **Calculating and disaggregating the rate of return on assets.** Recent annual reports of Cracker Barrel Old Country Store (Cracker Barrel) and Outback Steakhouse (Outback) reveal the following for Year 13 (amounts in thousands):

	Cracker Barrel	Outback
Revenues	$2,198,182	$2,724,600
Interest Expense	8,892	1,810
Net Income	106,529	170,206
Average Total Assets	1,295,077	1,413,810

Cracker Barrel operates a chain of restaurants featuring value-priced country meals. Its restaurants are open for all meals every day. Each restaurant also sells craft items with a country theme. Outback operates a chain of restaurants featuring steaks. Each restaurant carries an Australian theme and serves primarily the dinner meal. Outback tends to locate its restaurants in buildings that were formerly restaurants that went out of business. The income tax rate for Year 13 is 35 percent.

a. Calculate the rate of return on assets for each company.

b. Disaggregate the rate of return on assets in part **a** into profit margin for ROA and total assets turnover components.

c. Comment on the relative profitability of the two companies for Year 13.

12. **Profitability analysis for two types of retailers.** Information taken from recent annual reports of two retailers appears as follows (amounts in thousands). One of these companies is Family Dollar Stores, a discount store chain, and the other is Ann Taylor Stores, a specialty retailer of apparel. The income tax rate is 35 percent. Indicate which of these companies is Family Dollar Stores and which is Ann Taylor Stores. Explain your reasoning using appropriate financial ratios.

	Company A	Company B
Sales	$1,587,708	$4,750,171
Interest Expense	6,665	—
Net Income	100,942	247,475
Average Total Assets	1,080,200	1,870,157

13. **Analyzing accounts receivable for two companies.** The annual reports of Dell Computer and Sun Microsystems, two manufacturers of computers, reveal the information below for the current year (amounts in millions). Dell Computer sells custom-order personal computers, primarily to individuals. Sun Microsystems sells higher-end computers and Internet software, primarily to businesses.

	Dell	Sun Microsystems
Sales	$41,444	$11,434
Accounts Receivable, January 1	2,586	2,745
Accounts Receivable, December 31	3,635	2,381

a. Compute the accounts receivable turnover for each company.

b. Compute the average number of days that accounts receivable are outstanding for each company.

c. Why do the accounts receivable turnovers of these two companies differ?

14. **Analyzing inventories over three years.** The following information relates to the activities of Mattel, a manufacturer of toys (amounts in millions):

	Year 11	Year 12	Year 13
Sales	$4,688	$4,885	$4,960
Cost of Goods Sold	2,539	2,524	2,531
Average Inventory	488	413	388

a. Compute the inventory turnover for each year.

b. Compute the average number of days that inventories are held each year.

c. Compute the cost of goods sold to sales percentage for each year.

d. How well has Mattel managed its inventories over the three years?

15. **Analyzing fixed asset turnover over three years.** The following information relates to The Walt Disney Company (Disney), an entertainment company (amounts in millions):

	Year 11	Year 12	Year 13
Sales	$25,172	$25,329	$27,061
Average Fixed Assets	12,609	12,843	12,729
Expenditures on Fixed Assets	1,795	1,086	1,049

a. Compute the fixed asset turnover for each year.

b. How well has Disney managed its investment in fixed assets over the three years?

16. **Calculating and disaggregating rate of return on common shareholders' equity.** Information taken from the annual reports of Exxon Mobil, a petroleum company, for three recent years appears below (amounts in millions):

	Year 11	Year 12	Year 13
Revenues	$212,785	$204,506	$246,738
Net Income	15,003	11,011	20,960
Average Total Assets	146,087	147,909	163,461
Average Common Shareholders' Equity	71,959	73,879	82,256

a. Compute the rate of return on common shareholders' equity for each year.

b. Disaggregate the rate of return on common shareholders' equity into profit margin for ROCE, total assets turnover, and capital structure leverage ratio components.

c. How has the profitability of Exxon Mobil changed over the three years?

EXERCISES

17. **Profitability analysis for two companies.** The following data show five items from the financial statements of two companies for a recent year (amounts in millions):

	Company A	Company B
For Year		
Revenues	$4,076	$4,624
Income before Interest and Related Taxes[a]	268	772
Net Income to Common Shareholders[b]	268	761
Average during Year		
Total Assets	2,472	4,392
Common Shareholders' Equity	1,903	2,595

[a]Net Income + [Interest Expense $\times$ (1 − Tax Rate)]
[b]Net Income + Preferred Stock Dividends

a. Compute the rate of return on assets for each company. Disaggregate the rate of return on assets into profit margin for ROA and total assets turnover components.

b. Compute the rate of return on common shareholders' equity for each company. Disaggregate the rate of return on common shareholders' equity into profit margin for ROCE, total assets turnover, and capital structure leverage ratio components.

c. The two companies are Harley Davidson (manufacturer of brand-name motorcycles) and Starbucks (operator of specialty retail coffee shops, primarily in rented facilities). Which of the companies corresponds to A and B? What clues did you use in reaching your conclusions?

18. **Profitability analysis for two companies.** The following data show five items from the financial statements of two companies for a recent year (amounts in millions):

	Company A	Company B
For Year		
Revenues	$30,141	$67,752
Income before Interest and Related Taxes[a]	5,679	4,989
Net Income to Common Shareholders[b]	5,641	3,077
Average during Year		
Total Assets	45,684	166,718
Common Shareholders' Equity	36,657	33,041

[a]Net Income +[Interest Expense $\times$ (1 − Tax Rate)]
[b]Net Income − Preferred Stock Dividends

The two companies are Intel (developer and manufacturer of semiconductors) and Verizon Communications (telecommunication services). Which of the companies corresponds to A and B? What clues did you use in reaching your conclusions?

19. Relating profitability to financial leverage.

a. Compute the rate of return on common shareholders' equity in each of the following independent cases.

Case	Average Total Assets	Average Interest-Bearing Debt	Average Common Share-holders' Equity	Rate of Return on Assets	After-tax Cost of Interest-Bearing Debt
A	$200	$100	$100	6%	6%
B	200	100	100	8%	6%
C	200	120	80	8%	6%
D	200	100	100	4%	6%
E	200	50	100	6%	6%
F	200	50	100	5%	6%

b. In which cases is financial leverage working to the advantage of the common shareholders?

20. Interpreting changes in earnings per share. Company A and Company B both start Year 1 with $1 million of shareholders' equity and 100,000 shares of common stock outstanding. During Year 1, both companies earn net income of $100,000, a rate of return of 10 percent on common shareholders' equity at the beginning of Year 1. Company A declares and pays $100,000 of dividends to common shareholders at the end of Year 1, whereas Company B retains all its earnings and declares no dividends. During Year 2, both companies earn net income equal to 10 percent of shareholders' equity at the beginning of Year 2.

a. Compute earnings per share for Company A and for Company B for Year 1 and for Year 2.

b. Compute the rate of growth in earnings per share for Company A and Company B, comparing earnings per share in Year 2 with earnings per share in Year 1.

c. Using the rate of growth in earnings per share as the criterion, which company's management appears to be doing a better job for its shareholders? Comment on this result.

21. Calculating and interpreting short-term liquidity ratios. Data taken from the financial statements of Nike, a designer and manufacturer of athletic footwear and apparel, appear as follows (amounts in millions):

For the Year	Year 11	Year 12	Year 13
Revenues	$9,489	$9,893	$10,697
Cost of Goods Sold	5,785	6,005	6,314
Net Income	590	668	740
Cash Flow from Operations	657	1,082	917

On December 31	Year 10	Year 11	Year 12	Year 13
Cash and Marketable Securities	$ 254	$ 304	$ 576	$ 634
Accounts Receivable	1,569	1,621	1,804	2,101
Inventories	1,446	1,424	1,374	1,515
Prepayments	327	276	401	430
Total Current Assets	$3,596	$3,625	$4,155	$4,680
Accounts Payable	$ 544	$ 432	$ 504	$ 573
Bank Loans	974	860	481	281
Other Current Liabilities	622	495	848	1,161
Total Current Liabilities	$2,140	$1,787	$1,833	$2,015

a. Compute the current and quick ratios on May 31 of each year.

b. Compute the cash flow from operations to current liabilities ratio and the accounts receivable, inventory, and accounts payable turnover ratios for Year 11, Year 12, and Year 13.

c. How has the short-term liquidity risk of Nike changed during the three-year period?

22. Calculating and interpreting short-term liquidity ratios. Data taken from the financial statements of Nokia, a cellular phone manufacturer, appear as follows (amounts in millions of euros):

For the Year	Year 3	Year 4	Year 5
Revenues	€13,326	€19,772	€30,376
Cost of Goods Sold	8,299	12,227	19,072
Net Income	1,689	2,542	3,847
Cash Flow from Operations	1,694	3,009	3,560

On December 31	Year 2	Year 3	Year 4	Year 5
Cash and Marketable Securities	€2,060	€2,891	€ 4,159	€ 4,241
Accounts Receivable	1,640	2,806	3,827	5,594
Inventories	1,230	1,292	1,772	2,263
Prepayments	501	825	1,034	1,462
Total Current Assets	€5,431	€7,814	€10,792	€13,560
Accounts Payable	€ 818	€1,357	€ 2,202	€ 2,814
Bank Loans	554	760	793	1,116
Other Current Liabilities	1,719	2,336	3,377	4,664
Total Current Liabilities	€3,091	€4,453	€ 6,372	€ 8,594

a. Compute the current and quick ratios on December 31 of each year.
b. Compute the cash flow from operations to current liabilities ratio and the accounts receivable, inventory, and accounts payable turnover ratios for Year 3, Year 4, and Year 5.
c. How has the short-term liquidity risk of Nokia changed during the three-year period?

23. Calculating and interpreting long-term liquidity ratios. Data taken from the financial statement of Ericsson, a Swedish manufacturer of cellular phone and related infrastructure equipment, appear below (amounts in millions of Swedish kroner).

For the Year	Year 2	Year 3	Year 4
Net Income before Interest and Income Taxes	Kr25,020	Kr24,293	Kr17,191
Cash Flow from Operations	7,394	12,925	(10,848)
Interest Expense	2,532	3,041	5,166

On December 31	Year 1	Year 2	Year 3	Year 4
Long-term Debt	Kr14,407	Kr19,667	Kr32,298	Kr35,247
Total Liabilities	103,483	115,152	148,895	180,208
Total Shareholders' Equity	57,364	70,320	85,616	109,217

a. Compute the long-term debt ratio and the debt-equity ratio at the end of Year 1, Year 2, Year 3, and Year 4.
b. Compute the cash flow from operations to total liabilities ratio and the interest coverage ratio for Year 2 through Year 4.
c. How has the long-term liquidity risk of Ericsson changed over this three-year period?

24. Calculating and interpreting long-term liquidity ratios. Data taken from the financial statements of Nucor, a steel manufacturer, appear below (amounts in millions):

For the Year	Year 11	Year 12	Year 13
Net Income before Interest Expense and Income Taxes	$201,371	$252,971	$ 94,029
Cash Flow from Operations	495,115	497,220	494,620
Interest Expense	22,002	22,918	27,152

On December 31	Year 10	Year 11	Year 12	Year 13
Long-term Debt	$ 460,450	$ 460,450	$ 878,550	$ 903,550
Total Liabilities	1,278,572	1,274,001	1,841,357	1,972,996
Total Shareholders' Equity	2,432,296	2,485,347	2,539,644	2,519,357

    a. Compute the long-term debt ratio and the debt-equity ratio at the end of each year.

    b. Compute the cash flow from operations to total liabilities ratio and the interest coverage ratio for Year 11 through Year 13.

    c. How has the long-term liquidity risk of Nucor changed over this three-year period?

25. Effect of various transactions on financial statement ratios. Indicate the immediate effects (increase, decrease, no effect) of each of the following independent transactions on (1) the rate of return on common shareholders' equity, (2) the current ratio, and (3) the debt-equity ratio. State any necessary assumptions.

    a. A firm purchases, on account, merchandise inventory costing $205,000.

    b. A firm sells for $150,000, on account, merchandise inventory costing $120,000.

    c. A firm collects $100,000 from customers on accounts receivable.

    d. A firm pays $160,000 to suppliers on accounts payable.

    e. A firm sells for $10,000 a machine costing $40,000 and with accumulated depreciation of $30,000.

    f. A firm declares dividends of $80,000. It will pay the dividends during the next accounting period.

    g. A firm issues common stock for $75,000.

    h. A firm acquires a machine costing $60,000. It gives $10,000 cash and signs a note for $50,000 payable five years from now for the balance of the purchase price.

26. Effect of various transactions on financial statement ratios. Indicate the effects (increase, decrease, no effect) of the following independent transactions on (1) earnings per share, (2) working capital, and (3) the quick ratio, where accounts receivable are included but merchandise inventory is excluded from quick assets. State any necessary assumptions.

    a. A firm sells for $300,000, on account, merchandise inventory costing $240,000.

    b. A firm declares dividends of $160,000. It will pay the dividends during the next accounting period.

    c. A firm purchases, on account, merchandise inventory costing $410,000.

    d. A firm sells for $20,000 a machine costing $80,000 and with accumulated depreciation of $60,000.

    e. Because of defects, a firm returns to the supplier merchandise inventory purchased for $7,000 cash. The firm receives a cash reimbursement.

    f. A firm issues 10,000 shares of $10 par value common stock on the last day of the accounting period for $15 per share. It uses the proceeds to acquire the assets of another firm composed of the following: accounts receivable, $30,000; merchandise inventory, $60,000; plant and equipment, $100,000. The acquiring firm also agrees to pay current liabilities of $40,000 of the acquired company.

PROBLEMS AND CASES

27. Calculating and interpreting profitability and risk ratios in a time series setting. Target Corporation operates retails chains under two store concepts:

    (1) Target and Target Superstores: Target stores offer a wide variety of clothing, household, electronics, sports, toys, and entertainment products at discount prices. Target stores attempt to differentiate themselves from Wal-Mart's discount stores by pushing trend merchandising with more brand name products. Target emphasizes customer service, referring to its customers as "guests" and focusing on the theme of "Expect More, Pay Less." Target Corporation attempts to differentiate itself from competitors by providing wide aisles and a less cluttered store appearance. The recent addition of Target Superstores represents Target Corporation's effort to compete directly with Wal-Mart's superstores.

    (2) Mervyn's and Marshall Field's: Mervyn's and Marshall Field's are department stores offering higher quality, brand name products at higher price points than discount stores.

Each of Target Corporation's retail chains offers its own credit card. Target Corporation grew its number of stores from 1,381 at the end of Year 12 to 1,553 at the end of Year 14. The growth rate in sales of stores open at least two full years was 2.9 percent in Year 12, 1.1 percent in Year

13, and 2.7 percent in Year 14. The U.S. economy was in a recession of a large portion of this three-year period. **Exhibit 5.21** presents segment profitability information for Target Corporation's three retail chains. The financial statements for Target Corporation for Year 12, Year 13, and Year 14 appear in **Exhibit 5.22** (balance sheet), **Exhibit 5.23** (income statement), and **Exhibit 5.24** (statement of cash flows). **Exhibit 5.25** presents financial statement ratios for Target Corporation for Year 12 and Year 13.

   a. Compute the amounts of the ratios listed in **Exhibit 5.25** for Year 14. The income tax rate applicable to interest expense deductions is 35 percent.
   b. What are the likely reasons for the changes in Target Corporation's rate of return on assets during the three-year period? Analyze the financial ratios to the maximum depth possible.
   c. What are the likely reasons for the changes in Target Corporation's rate of return on common shareholders' equity during the three-year period?
   d. How has the short-term liquidity risk of Target Corporation changed during the three-year period?
   e. How has the long-term liquidity risk of Target Corporation changed during the three-year period?

EXHIBIT 5.21	TARGET CORPORATION Segment Profitability Analysis (Problem 27)		
	Year 12	**Year 13**	**Year 14**
SALES MIX			
Target	81.8%	84.1%	85.8%
Mervyn's	10.1	8.7	7.4
Marshall Field's	7.0	6.1	5.4
Other	1.1	1.1	1.4
	100.0%	100.0%	100.0%
TARGET			
Profit Margin	7.8%	8.4%	8.4%
Total Assets Turnover	1.8	1.6	1.6
Rate of Return on Assets	13.8%	13.6%	13.6%
MERVYN'S			
Profit Margin	7.1%	6.2%	4.5%
Total Assets Turnover	1.7	1.7	1.6
Rate of Return on Assets	12.0%	10.5%	7.1%
MARSHALL FIELD'S			
Profit Margin	4.8%	5.0%	4.1%
Total Assets Turnover	1.2	1.2	1.2
Rate of Return on Assets	5.8%	6.1%	5.0%

28. **Profitability and risk analysis in a cross-sectional setting.** The chapter presents profitability and risk ratios for Wal-Mart for Year 12, Year 13, and Year 14. **Problem 27** presents or requires calculation of profitability and risk ratio for Target Corporation for these same years. This problem asks you to compare and interpret differences in the financial statement ratios for these two firms.

   a. Indicate whether Wal-Mart or Target has the higher rate of return on assets over the three-year period. Identify the likely reasons for the higher rate of return on assets, analyzing the financial ratios to the maximum depth possible.
   b. Indicate whether Wal-Mart or Target has the higher rate of return on common shareholders' equity. Identify the likely reasons for the higher rate of return on common shareholders' equity, analyzing the financial ratios to the maximum depth possible.
   c. Indicate whether Wal-Mart or Target has higher short-term liquidity risk, analyzing the financial ratios to the maximum depth possible.
   d. Indicate whether Wal-Mart or Target has higher long-term liquidity risk, analyzing the financial ratios to the maximum depth possible.

EXHIBIT 5.22	TARGET CORPORATION Comparative Balance Sheet (all dollar amounts in millions) (Problem 27)			

	January 31			
	Year 11	Year 12	Year 13	Year 14
ASSETS				
Cash	$ 356	$ 499	$ 758	$ 716
Accounts Receivable	1,941	3,831	5,565	5,776
Inventories	4,248	4,449	4,760	5,343
Prepayments	759	869	852	1,093
Total Current Assets	$ 7,304	$ 9,648	$11,935	$12,928
Property, Plant, and Equipment (net)	12,218	14,321	16,231	17,967
Other Assets	768	973	1,361	1,495
Total Assets	$20,290	$24,942	$29,527	$32,390
LIABILITIES AND SHAREHOLDERS' EQUITY				
Accounts Payable	$ 3,576	$ 4,160	$ 4,684	$ 5,448
Current Portion of Long-term Debt	857	905	975	866
Other Current Liabilities	1,868	1,989	1,864	2,000
Total Current Liabilities	$ 6,301	$ 7,054	$ 7,523	$ 8,314
Long-term Debt	6,434	8,876	11,110	11,215
Other Noncurrent Liabilities	1,036	1,152	1,451	1,796
Total Liabilities	$13,771	$17,082	$20,084	$21,325
Common Stock	$ 75	$ 75	$ 76	$ 76
Additional Paid-in Capital	902	1,098	1,256	1,341
Retained Earnings	5,542	6,687	8,111	9,648
Total Shareholders' Equity	$ 6,519	$ 7,860	$ 9,443	$11,065
Total Liabilities and Shareholders' Equity	$20,290	$24,942	$29,527	$32,390

EXHIBIT 5.23	TARGET CORPORATION Comparative Income Statement (all dollar amounts in millions) (Problem 27)		

	Year Ended January 31		
	Year 12	Year 13	Year 14
Sales Revenue	$39,114	$42,722	$46,781
Other Revenues	712	1,195	1,382
Total Revenues	$39,826	$43,917	$48,163
Expenses:			
Cost of Goods Sold	$27,143	$29,260	$31,790
Selling and Administrative	10,003	11,393	12,854
Interest	473	588	559
Income Taxes	839	1,022	1,119
Total Expenses	$38,458	$42,263	$46,322
Net Income	$ 1,368	$ 1,654	$ 1,841

29. **Profitability and risk analysis in a cross section setting.** This problem compares the profitability and risk ratios of three leading discount chains: Carrefour, Metro AG, and Wal-Mart.

Carrefour, headquartered in France, is Europe's largest retailer and the second largest retailer in the world. Sales in Year 14 totaled € 70,487 million. It segments its activities into four groups (Year 14 sales mix percentages in parentheses):

EXHIBIT 5.24	TARGET CORPORATION Comparative Statement of Cash Flows (all dollar amounts in millions) (Problem 27)		

	Year Ended January 31		
	Year 12	**Year 13**	**Year 14**
Operations			
Net Income	$ 1,368	$ 1,654	$ 1,841
Depreciation	1,079	1,212	1,320
Other Addbacks (Subtractions)	313	790	669
(Increase) in Accounts Receivable	(1,193)	(2,194)	(744)
(Increase) in Inventories	(201)	(311)	(583)
(Increase) in Prepayments	(91)	15	(255)
Increase in Accounts Payable	584	524	764
Increase in Other Current Liabilities	153	(100)	148
Cash Flow from Operations	$ 2,012	$ 1,590	$ 3,160
Investing			
Sales of Property, Plant, and Equipment	$ 32	$ 32	$ 85
Acquisition of Property, Plant, and			
Equipment	(3,163)	(3,221)	(3,004)
Other	(179)	—	—
Cash Flow from Investing	$(3,310)	$(3,189)	$(2,919)
Financing			
Increase in Long-term Borrowing	$ 3,250	$ 3,153	$ 1,200
Decrease in Long-term Borrowing	(1,601)	(1,071)	(1,272)
Acquisition of Common Stock	(20)	(14)	—
Dividends	(203)	(218)	(237)
Other	15	8	26
Cash Flow from Financing	$ 1,441	$ 1,858	$ (283)
Change in Cash	$ 143	$ 259	$ (42)
Cash, Beginning of Year	356	499	758
Cash, End of Year	$ 499	$ 758	$ 716

(1) Hypermarkets (58%): offer a wide variety of household and food products at competitively low prices under the Carrefour store brand.

(2) Supermarkets (18%): sell traditional grocery products under the Champion, Norte, GS and GB supermarkets, and other store brands.

(3) Hard Discount (8%): offer a limited variety of food products in smaller stores than those of hypermarkets and supermarkets at aggressively low prices under the Dia, Ed, and Minipreco store brands.

(4) Other (16%): includes convenience stores and wholesale stores, the latter targeted at business customers, under the SHOPI, Marche Plus, 8 A Huit, express, Contact, and Proxi store brands.

Carrefour derived approximately 51 percent of its Year 14 sales within France, 34 percent within Europe excluding France, 8 percent in Latin America, and 7 percent in Asia.

Metro AG (Metro), headquartered in Germany, generated sales of €53,595 million in Year 14. It segments its activities into four groups (Year 14 sales mix percentages in parentheses):

(1) Cash and Carry (47%): offer food and non-food products at wholesale prices, primarily to business customers, under the Metro and Makro store brands.

(2) Hypermarkets and Supermarkets (21%): offer food products under the Extra store brand and, in hypermarkets, also offer non-food products under the Real store brand.

(3) Specialty Stores (25%): two chains in this group, Media Markt and Saturn, offer electronic products and the other (Praktiker) specializes in the home improvement market.

(4) Department Stores (7%): offer a variety of household and clothing products in more upscale shopping environments under the Kauflof store brand.

EXHIBIT 5.25	TARGET CORPORATION Financial Ratio Analysis (Problem 27)			
		Year 12	Year 13	Year 14
Rate of Return on Assets		7.4%	7.5%	
Profit Margin for Rate of Return on Assets		4.3%	4.8%	
Total Assets Turnover		1.7	1.6	
Other Revenues/Sales		1.8%	2.8%	
Cost of Goods Sold/Sales		69.4%	68.5%	
Selling and Administrative Expense/Sales		25.6%	26.7%	
Interest Expense/Sales		1.2%	1.4%	
Income Tax Expense/Sales		2.1%	2.4%	
Accounts Receivable Turnover Ratio		13.6	9.1	
Inventory Turnover Ratio		6.2	6.4	
Fixed Assets Turnover Ratio		2.9	2.8	
Rate of Return on Common Shareholders' Equity		19.0%	19.1%	
Profit Margin for Rate of Return on Common Shareholders' Equity		3.5%	3.9%	
Capital Structure Leverage Ratio		3.1	3.1	
Current Ratio		1.37	1.59	
Quick Ratio		0.61	0.84	
Accounts Payable Turnover		7.1	6.7	
Cash Flow from Operations to Current Liabilities Ratio		30.1%	21.8%	
Long-term Debt Ratio		53.0%	54.1%	
Debt-Equity Ratio		68.5%	68.0%	
Cash Flow from Operations to Total Liabilities Ratio		13.0%	8.6%	
Interest Coverage Ratio		5.7	5.6	

Metro derived 53 percent of its Year 14 sales from within Germany, 45 percent from Europe excluding Germany, and 2 percent from other countries.

Wal-Mart is the largest retailer in the world with Year 14 sales of $256,329 million (€225,659 million). It segments its operations worldwide into three groups (Year 14 sales mix percentages in parentheses):

(1) Discount Stores and Superstores (68%): offer clothing, housewares, electronic equipment, pharmaceuticals, health and beauty products, sporting goods, and similar products at aggressively low prices in the discount stores and add grocery products to these non-food products in their superstores.

(2) Sam's Clubs (13%): members only warehouse stores that offer food and household products in large quantities, as well as automotive, electronic, sporting goods, and similar products at wholesale prices.

(3) International (19%): Wal-Mart has expanded internationally in recent years by acquiring established retail chains in Canada, Mexico, Germany, the United Kingdom, and other countries.

Exhibits 5.26 and **5.27** present profitability ratios for Carrefour, Metro, and Wal-Mart for Year 12 to Year 14. **Exhibit 5.28** presents risk ratios for the three firms. **Exhibit 5.29** presents selected other data for these firms. Carrefour prepares its financial statements in accordance with French accounting principles, Metro with respect to pronouncements of the International Accounting Standards Board, and Wal-Mart in accordance with U.S. accounting principles. The financial statements include the present value of commitments under all leases in property, plant, and equipment and in long-term debt. Study these financial ratios and respond to the following questions:

a. Wal-Mart consistently has the highest rate of return on assets (ROA), followed by Carrefour, and then Metro. Using information in **Exhibits 5.26** and **5.29**, suggest reasons for these differences in operating profitability.

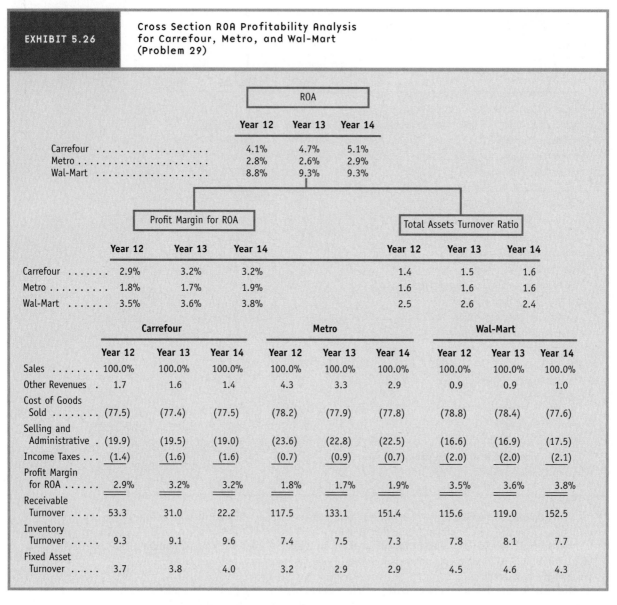

EXHIBIT 5.26 Cross Section ROA Profitability Analysis for Carrefour, Metro, and Wal-Mart (Problem 29)

ROA

	Year 12	Year 13	Year 14
Carrefour	4.1%	4.7%	5.1%
Metro	2.8%	2.6%	2.9%
Wal-Mart	8.8%	9.3%	9.3%

Profit Margin for ROA

	Year 12	Year 13	Year 14
Carrefour	2.9%	3.2%	3.2%
Metro	1.8%	1.7%	1.9%
Wal-Mart	3.5%	3.6%	3.8%

Total Assets Turnover Ratio

	Year 12	Year 13	Year 14
	1.4	1.5	1.6
	1.6	1.6	1.6
	2.5	2.6	2.4

	Carrefour			Metro			Wal-Mart		
	Year 12	Year 13	Year 14	Year 12	Year 13	Year 14	Year 12	Year 13	Year 14
Sales	100.0%	100.0%	100.0%	100.0%	100.0%	100.0%	100.0%	100.0%	100.0%
Other Revenues .	1.7	1.6	1.4	4.3	3.3	2.9	0.9	0.9	1.0
Cost of Goods Sold	(77.5)	(77.4)	(77.5)	(78.2)	(77.9)	(77.8)	(78.8)	(78.4)	(77.6)
Selling and Administrative .	(19.9)	(19.5)	(19.0)	(23.6)	(22.8)	(22.5)	(16.6)	(16.9)	(17.5)
Income Taxes ...	(1.4)	(1.6)	(1.6)	(0.7)	(0.9)	(0.7)	(2.0)	(2.0)	(2.1)
Profit Margin for ROA	2.9%	3.2%	3.2%	1.8%	1.7%	1.9%	3.5%	3.6%	3.8%
Receivable Turnover	53.3	31.0	22.2	117.5	133.1	151.4	115.6	119.0	152.5
Inventory Turnover	9.3	9.1	9.6	7.4	7.5	7.3	7.8	8.1	7.7
Fixed Asset Turnover	3.7	3.8	4.0	3.2	2.9	2.9	4.5	4.6	4.3

b. Refer to **Exhibit 5.27**. Which firm appears to have used financial leverage most effectively in enhancing the rate of return on common shareholders' equity (ROCE)? Explain your reasoning.

c. Refer to **Exhibit 5.28**. Rank order these firms in terms of their risk. Do any of these firms appear unduly risky as of the end of Year 14?

30. **Calculating and interpreting profitability and risk ratios.** The GAP and Limited Brands maintain leading market positions in the specialty apparel retailing market. The products of The GAP (jeans, blouses, shirts) are more standardized than those of Limited Brands. The products of Limited Brands are more fashion-oriented and glitzy. **Exhibit 5.30** presents comparative balance sheets for The GAP and Limited Brands at the end of Year 13 and Year 14. **Exhibit 5.31** presents an income statement for each firm for Year 14. Cash flows from operations for Year 14 were $2,171 million for The GAP and $1,062 million for Limited Brands. The income tax rate is 35 percent. On the basis of this information and appropriate financial statement ratios, which company is:

a. more profitable in Year 14?

b. less risky in terms of short-term liquidity in Year 14?

c. less risky in terms of long-term liquidity in Year 14?

31. **Interpreting profitability and risk ratios.** International Paper Company is the largest integrated paper company in the world. It grows timber in its forests, processes the harvested timber into various commodity and specialty papers in its capital-intensive plants, and distributes various paper products through wholesale and retail outlets. Its average sales mix in recent years is:

EXHIBIT 5.27	Cross Section ROCE Profitability Analysis for Carrefour, Metro, and Wal-Mart (Problem 29)

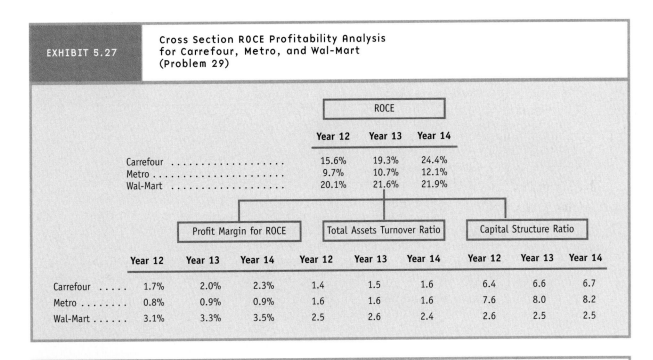

ROCE			
	Year 12	Year 13	Year 14
Carrefour	15.6%	19.3%	24.4%
Metro	9.7%	10.7%	12.1%
Wal-Mart	20.1%	21.6%	21.9%

	Profit Margin for ROCE			Total Assets Turnover Ratio			Capital Structure Ratio		
	Year 12	Year 13	Year 14	Year 12	Year 13	Year 14	Year 12	Year 13	Year 14
Carrefour	1.7%	2.0%	2.3%	1.4	1.5	1.6	6.4	6.6	6.7
Metro	0.8%	0.9%	0.9%	1.6	1.6	1.6	7.6	8.0	8.2
Wal-Mart	3.1%	3.3%	3.5%	2.5	2.6	2.4	2.6	2.5	2.5

EXHIBIT 5.28	Cross Section Risk Ratios for Carrefour, Metro, and Wal-Mart (Problem 29)

	Carrefour			Metro			Wal-Mart		
	Year 12	Year 13	Year 14	Year 12	Year 13	Year 14	Year 12	Year 13	Year 14
SHORT-TERM LIQUIDITY									
Current Ratio ...	0.67	0.64	0.65	0.87	0.84	0.73	1.04	0.93	0.92
Quick Ratio	0.24	0.28	0.27	0.19	0.14	0.14	0.15	0.15	0.17
Cash Flow from Operations/ Average Current Liabilities	13.8%	12.2%	16.9%	20.5%	19.4%	20.9%	36.5%	41.8%	46.0%
Days Receivable .	7	12	16	3	3	2	3	3	2
Days Inventory ..	39	40	38	50	49	50	47	45	47
Days Payable ...	86	90	90	79	80	82	32	31	33
LONG-TERM LIQUIDITY									
Long-term Debt Ratio	59.7%	63.2%	64.1%	78.2%	78.3%	77.1%	40.1%	38.1%	37.0%
Debt-Equity Ratio	82.2%	82.9%	83.5%	87.1%	87.3%	87.6%	60.2%	60.4%	60.4%
Cash Flow from Operations/ Average Total Liabilities	8.9%	7.5%	10.2%	8.1%	7.8%	8.9%	19.7%	22.2%	25.5%
Interest Coverage Ratio	2.8	3.4	4.0	2.2	2.7	2.4	9.0	12.8	15.3

(Problem 31 continued)

Forest Products	12%
Commodity Papers	50
Specialty Papers	16
Distribution	22
	100%

EXHIBIT 5.29	Selected Other Financial Data for Carrefour, Metro, and Wal-Mart (Problem 29)		
Growth Rate in Sales	**Year 12**	**Year 13**	**Year 14**
Carrefour	7.2%	(1.1%)	2.6%
Metro	5.5%	4.0%	4.0%
Wal-Mart	13.8%	12.3%	4.8%
Sales per Square Meter			
Carrefour	€7,593	€7,037	€7,018
Metro	€3,812	€3,884	€3,852
Wal-Mart	€5,160	€4,986	€4,005
Sales per Store			
Carrefour	€13,275,908	€12,426,107	€11,617,983
Metro	€20,019,564	€22,305,628	€22,613,924
Wal-Mart	€56,258,033	€55,771,397	€46,875,620
Square Meters per Store			
Carrefour	1,747	1,766	1,655
Metro	5,776	5,743	5,871
Wal-Mart	10,903	11,180	11,704
Fixed Assets per Square Meter			
Carrefour	€1,765	€1,574	€1,773
Metro	€1,325	€1,340	€1,359
Wal-Mart	€1,147	€1,084	€995
Sales per Employee			
Carrefour	€242,280	€223,574	€210,261
Metro	€265,087	€269,048	€270,019
Wal-Mart	€222,866	€231,003	€188,049
Personnel Cost per Employee			
Carrefour	€23,134	€21,022	€19,449
Metro	€29,778	€29,340	€28,979
Wal-Mart	€21,806	€21,836	€17,652
Exchange Rate:			
Euros per U.S. Dollar	€1.13214	€1.105807	€0.88035

Exhibit 5.32 presents financial statement ratios for International Paper for Year 8, Year 9, and Year 10. Respond to each of the following questions.

a. What are the likely reasons for the decrease in the cost of goods sold to sales percentage from 80.0 percent in Year 8 to 75.4 percent in Year 9?

b. What are the likely reasons for the decrease in the fixed asset turnover from 1.67 in Year 9 to 1.33 in Year 10?

c. Did financial leverage work to the advantage of the common shareholders in Year 10? Explain in such a way that indicates your understanding of the concept of financial leverage.

d. What are the likely reasons for the decrease in the current ratio from 1.21 in Year 9 to 1.02 in Year 10?

e. What are the likely reasons for the decrease in the cash flow from operations to total liabilities ratio from 16.3 percent in Year 9 to 9.9 percent in Year 10?

32. **Interpreting profitability and risk ratios.** Marks & Spencer operates a chain of department stories located primarily in the United Kingdom. **Exhibit 5.33** presents financial statement ratios for Marks & Spencer for Year 6, Year 7, and Year 8.

a. What are the likely reasons for the increase in the cost of goods sold to sales percentages during the three years?

b. What are the likely reasons for the increase in the selling and administrative expense to sales percentages during the three years?

c. What are the likely reasons for the decrease in the income tax expense (excluding tax effects of interest expense) to sales percentages during the three years?

| EXHIBIT 5.30 | THE GAP and LIMITED BRANDS Comparative Balance Sheet (all dollar amounts in millions) (Problem 30) |

	The GAP		Limited Brands	
	Year 13	Year 14	Year 13	Year 14
ASSETS				
Cash	$ 3,027	$ 2,261	$2,262	$ 3,129
Marketable Securities	362	2,424	—	—
Accounts Receivable	—	—	151	110
Inventories	2,048	1,704	966	943
Prepayments	303	300	227	251
Total Current Assets	$ 5,740	$ 6,689	$3,606	$ 4,433
Property, Plant, and Equipment (net)	7,976	7,504	3,752	3,655
Other Assets	385	286	2,148	1,991
Total Assets	$14,101	$14,479	$9,506	$10,079
LIABILITIES AND SHAREHOLDERS' EQUITY				
Accounts Payable	$ 1,159	$ 1,178	$ 456	$ 453
Current Maturities of Long-term Debt	500	283	—	—
Other Current Liabilities	1,067	1,031	803	939
Total Current Liabilities	$ 2,726	$ 2,482	$1,259	$ 1,392
Long-term Debt	7,095	6,633	2,807	2,854
Other Noncurrent Liabilities	621	581	580	567
Total Liabilities	$10,442	$ 9,696	$4,646	$ 4,813
Common Stock	$ 48	$ 49	$ 261	$ 262
Additional Paid-in Capital	638	732	1,693	1,674
Retained Earnings	5,261	6,263	2,906	3,417
Treasury Stock	(2,288)	(2,261)	—	(87)
Total Shareholders' Equity	$ 3,659	$ 4,783	$4,860	$ 5,266
Total Liabilities and Shareholders' Equity	$14,101	$14,479	$9,506	$10,079

| EXHIBIT 5.31 | THE GAP and LIMITED BRANDS Comparative Income Statement (all dollar amounts in millions) (Problem 30) |

	For Year 14	
	The GAP	Limited Brands
Sales Revenue	$15,854	$8,934
Other Revenues	38	63
Expenses:		
Cost of Goods Sold	(9,592)	(5,525)
Selling and Administrative	(4,089)	(2,288)
Interest	(528)	(220)
Income Taxes	(653)	(382)
Net Income	$ 1,030	$ 582

d. What are the likely reasons for the decrease in the fixed asset turnover during the three years?

e. What are the likely reasons for the increase in interest expense (net of tax effects) to sales percentages during the three years?

f. Did financial leverage work to the advantage of the common shareholders in each year? Explain.

EXHIBIT 5.32	INTERNATIONAL PAPER Financial Ratios (Problem 31)		
	Year 8	**Year 9**	**Year 10**
Profit Margin Ratio for ROA (before interest effects)	4.7%	8.2%	4.7%
Total Assets Turnover Ratio	0.87	0.95	0.77
Rate of Return on Assets	4.1%	7.8%	3.6%
Profit Margin for ROCE (after interest effects)	2.9%	5.8%	2.2%
Capital Structure Leverage Ratio	2.71	2.92	3.05
Rate of Return on Common Shareholders' Equity	6.8%	16.1%	5.1%
Cost of Goods Sold/Sales	80.0%	75.4%	79.9%
Selling & Administrative Expense/Sales	12.9%	11.9%	13.0%
Interest Expense/Sales	2.3%	2.5%	2.6%
Income Tax Expense/Sales	3.2%	5.4%	3.2%
Accounts Receivable Turnover	7.31	8.23	7.86
Inventory Turnover	5.84	6.14	5.72
Fixed Asset Turnover	1.53	1.67	1.33
Current Ratio	1.20	1.21	1.02
Quick Ratio	0.62	0.59	0.49
Cash Flow from Operations to Current Liabilities	30.9%	50.5%	32.3%
Days Accounts Receivable Outstanding	50	44	46
Days Inventories Held	62	59	64
Days Accounts Payable Outstanding	50	44	46
Long-term Debt Ratio	40.7%	45.1%	43.3%
Debt-Equity Ratio	63.5%	67.5%	66.9%
Cash Flow from Operations to Total Liabilities	11.4%	16.3%	9.9%
Interest Coverage Ratio	3.05	5.11	2.68
Growth Rate in Sales	9.4%	32.3%	1.7%
Growth Rate in Cash	11.6%	15.6%	12.8%
Growth Rate in Capital Expenditures	34.6%	69.3%	16.7%

33. **Detective analysis—identify company.** Effective financial statement analysis requires an understanding of a firm's economic characteristics. The relations between various financial statement items provide evidence of many of these economic characteristics. **Exhibit 5.34** presents common-size condensed balance sheets and income statements for 12 firms in different industries. These common-size balance sheets and income statements express various items as a percentage of operating revenues (that is, the statement divides all amounts by operating revenues for the year). A dash for a particular financial statement item does not necessarily mean that the amount is zero. It merely indicates that the amount is not sufficiently large for the firm to disclose it. The 12 companies, the country of their headquarters, and a brief description of their activities appear below.

   (1) Accor (France): World's largest hotel group, operating hotels under the names of Sofitel, Novotel, Motel 6, and others. Accor has grown in recent years by acquiring established hotel chains.

   (2) Arbed-Acier (Luxembourg): Offers flat-rolled steel products, primarily to the European automobile industry.

   (3) Carrefour (France): Operates grocery supermarkets and hypermarkets in Europe, Latin America, and Asia.

   (4) Deutsche Telekon (Germany): Europe's largest provider of wired and wireless telecommunication services. The telecommunications industry has experienced increased deregulation in recent years.

   (5) Fortis (Netherlands): Offers both insurance and banking services. Operating revenues include insurance premiums received, investment income, and interest revenue on loans.

EXHIBIT 5.33	MARKS & SPENCER Financial Ratios (Problem 32)		
	Year 6	**Year 7**	**Year 8**
Profit Margin for Rate of Return on Assets	10.8%	5.3%	4.2%
Total Assets Turnover	1.1	1.0	1.0
Rate of Return on Assets	12.0%	5.5%	4.2%
Other Revenues/Sales	3.4%	3.9%	3.9%
Cost of Goods Sold/Sales	65.6%	67.6%	68.0%
Selling and Administrative Expenses/Sales	22.5%	28.3%	29.3%
Income Tax Expense (excluding tax effects of Interest expense)/Sales	4.5%	2.5%	2.5%
Interest Expense (net of tax savings)/Sales	0.5%	0.7%	1.0%
Accounts Receivable Turnover	13.1	12.2	12.0
Inventory Turnover	11.1	10.6	10.7
Fixed Asset Turnover	2.1	1.9	1.8
Profit Margin for Rate of Return on Common Shareholders' Equity	10.3%	4.7%	3.3%
Capital Structure Leverage Ratio	1.5	1.6	1.6
Rate of Return on Common Shareholders' Equity	17.3%	7.5%	5.3%
Current Ratio	1.0	1.0	1.0
Quick Ratio	0.6	0.6	0.6
Days Accounts Payable	16	15	15
Cash Flow from Operations/Average Current Liabilities	32.6%	7.1%	24.4%
Long-term Debt Ratio	2.1%	13.7%	14.1%
Debt-Equity Ratio	33.8%	37.4%	38.8%
Cash Flow from Operations/Average Total Liabilities	27.4%	5.6%	16.9%
Interest Coverage Ratio	20.9	8.1	4.9
Sales (Year 5 = 100)	104.7	103.7	103.1
Net Income (Year 5 = 100)	109.8	49.3	34.3
Assets (Year 5 = 100)	111.6	113.9	117.0
Capital Expenditures (Year 5 = 100)	165.6	145.7	98.4

Operating expenses include amounts actually paid or amounts it expects to pay in the future on insurance coverage outstanding during the year.

(6) Interpublic Group (U.S.): Creates advertising copy for clients. Purchases advertising time and space from various media and sells it to clients. Operating revenues represent the commission or fee earned by Interpublic for advertising copy created and media time and space sold. Operating expenses include compensation paid to employees. Interpublic acquired other marketing services firms in recent years.

(7) Marks & Spencer (U.K.): Operates department stores in England and other retail stores in Europe and the United States. Offers its own credit card for customers' purchases.

(8) Nestlé (Switzerland): World's largest food processor, offering prepared foods, coffees, milk-based products, and mineral waters.

(9) Roche Holding (Switzerland): Creates, manufactures, and distributes a wide variety of prescription drugs.

(10) Sun Microsystems (U.S.): Designs, manufactures, and sells engineering workstations and servers used to maintain integrated computer networks. Sun outsources the manufacture of many of its computer components.

(11) Tokyo Electric Power (Japan): Provides electric power services, primarily to the Tokyo community. It maintains almost a monopoly position in its service area.

(12) Toyota Motor (Japan): Manufactures automobiles and offers financing services to its customers.

EXHIBIT 5.34   Data for Ratio Detective Exercise (Problem 33)

	1	2	3	4	5	6	7	8	9	10	11	12
Balance Sheet at End of Year												
Cash and Marketable Securities	4.7%	16.4%	8.9%	8.4%	16.7%	7.4%	16.1%	21.3%	72.0%	8.3%	1.4%	338.8%
Receivables	8.5	15.9	16.5	27.6	35.9	17.7	81.1	29.6	24.0	10.5	5.9	533.4
Inventories	9.9	2.8	9.9	5.8	6.4	25.7	—	1.3	20.0	2.9	—	—
Property, Plant, and Equipment Cost	40.8	20.9	59.0	69.6	88.3	130.9	23.0	110.3	83.3	278.9	535.4	15.3
Accumulated Depreciation	(15.0)	(9.1)	(33.2)	(17.8)	(50.5)	(67.7)	(11.8)	(35.5)	(35.2)	(112.5)	(284.9)	(12.9)
Net	25.8	11.8	25.8	51.8	37.8	63.2	11.2	74.8	48.1	166.4	250.5	2.4
Intercorporate Investments	4.0	14.3	3.0	0.6	18.8	10.3	1.3	10.7	7.7	22.4	16.9	41.9
Other Assets	15.0	10.9	11.7	3.6	7.1	1.9	63.5	42.1	69.1	56.3	5.4	61.9
Total Assets	67.9%	72.1%	75.8%	97.8%	122.7%	126.2%	173.2%	179.8%	240.9%	266.8%	280.1%	978.4%
Current Liabilities	37.3%	25.5%	29.7%	26.4%	42.7%	34.5%	106.0%	65.1%	48.3%	42.6%	51.3%	820.8%
Long-term Debt	12.0	6.1	6.6	9.1	22.2	23.3	22.7	49.6	56.4	95.8	167.7	76.9
Other Noncurrent Liabilities	2.1	1.8	5.9	2.3	4.2	17.2	10.6	10.9	24.5	27.8	24.7	42.2
Shareholders' Equity	16.5	38.7	33.6	60.0	53.6	51.2	33.9	54.2	111.7	100.6	36.4	38.5
Total Equities	67.9%	72.1%	75.8%	97.8%	122.7%	126.2%	173.2%	179.8%	240.9%	266.8%	280.1%	978.4%
Income Statement for Year												
Operating Revenues	100.0%	100.0%	100.0%	100.0%	100.0%	100.0%	100.0%	100.0%	100.0%	100.0%	100.0%	100.0%
Other Revenues	1.1%	2.7%	1.0%	0.2%	0.7%	2.3%	1.9%	0.3%	13.8%	0.7%	—	—
Cost of Goods Sold (excluding depreciation) or Operating Expenses	87.8	45.2	44.5	64.6	68.0	81.0	55.3	75.5	27.2	45.0	57.3	32.6
Depreciation and Amortization	3.0	4.9	4.1	3.2	5.9	5.3	2.0	7.1	9.9	23.9	19.9	—
Selling and Administrative	6.3	24.8	38.9	24.3	16.4	13.6	27.8	8.1	40.0	15.2	7.3	22.5
Interest	1.4	0.4	2.0	1.3	0.4	3.5	1.9	3.0	5.2	8.6	8.6	35.4
Research and Development	—	9.8	1.3	—	3.7	—	—	—	13.8	—	—	—
Income Taxes	1.3	5.8	3.1	2.4	2.5	0.3	5.9	3.7	4.4	3.9	2.8	2.2
All Other Items (net)	(0.8)	—	0.8	0.3	0.6	(2.1)	0.8	(1.6)	—	0.6	—	1.7
Total Expenses	99.0%	90.9%	94.7%	96.1%	97.5%	101.6%	93.7%	95.8%	100.5%	97.2%	95.9%	94.4%
Net Income	2.1%	11.8%	6.3%	4.1%	3.2%	0.7%	8.2%	4.5%	13.3%	3.5%	4.1%	5.6%

Use whatever clues you can to match the companies in **Exhibit 5.34** with the companies and industries listed above.

34. **Preparing pro forma financial statements (requires Appendix 5.1). Problem 27** presents financial statements for Target Corporation for Year 12, Year 13, and Year 14, as well as financial statement ratios.

   a. Prepare a set of pro forma financial statements for Target Corporation for Year 15 through Year 19 using the following assumptions:

   Income Statement

   1. Sales grew 9.2 percent in Year 13 and 9.5 percent in Year 14, primarily as a result of increases in the number of new stores and increases in sales of stores open more than one year. Although Target Corporation will continue to increase the number of stores, competition will likely constrain increases in same store sales. Thus, assume that sales will grow 9 percent each year between Year 15 and 19.

   2. Other revenues, representing interest of outstanding accounts receivable, have been approximately three percent of sales during the last three years. Assume that other revenues will continue at this historical pattern.

   3. The cost of goods sold to sales percentage steadily declined from 69.4 percent in Year 12 to 68.0 percent in Year 14. Target's emphasis on trend merchandising and brand name products will likely decrease this percentage somewhat in future years. Assume that the cost of goods sold to sales percentage will be 67.5 percent for Year 15 to Year 19.

   4. The selling and administrative expense percentage has steadily increased from 25.6 percent of sales in Year 12 to 27.5 percent of sales in Year 14. Increased competition will likely increase this percentage somewhat in future years. Assume that the selling and administrative expense to sales percentage will be 28.0 percent for Year 15 to Year 19.

   5. Target Corporation has engaged in long-term borrowing to construct new stores. The average interest rate on interest-bearing debt was approximately 5 percent during Year 14. Assume this interest rate for all borrowing outstanding (long-term debt, and current portion of long-term debt) for Target Corporation for Year 15 to Year 19. Compute interest expense on the average amount of interest-bearing debt outstanding each year.

   6. Target Corporation's average income tax rate as a percentage of income before income taxes has varied around 38 percent during the last three years. Assume an income tax rate of 38 percent of income before income taxes for Year 15 to Year 19.

   7. Target Corporation's dividends increased at an average annual rate of 8 percent between Year 12 and Year 14. Assume that dividends will grow 8 percent each year between Year 15 and Year 19.

   Balance Sheet

   8. Cash will be the amount necessary to equate total assets with total liabilities plus shareholders' equity.

   9. Accounts receivable will increase at the growth rate in sales.

   10. Inventory will increase at the growth rate in sales.

   11. Prepayments relate to ongoing operating costs, such as rent and insurance. Assume that prepayments will grow at the growth rate in sales.

   12. Property, plant, and equipment grew 13.7 percent annually during the most recent three years. The construction of new stores will require additional investments in property, plant, and equipment, but not at the growth rate experienced in recent years. Assume that property, plant, and equipment will grow 10 percent each year between Year 15 and Year 19.

   13. Other assets primarily include deposits made on rented facilities. Assume that other assets will grow at the growth rate in property, plant, and equipment.

   14. The accounts payable ratio declined from 7.1 in Year 12 to 6.4 during Year 14. Assume that Target Corporation will decrease its accounts payable turnover to 6.0 times per year for Year 15 to Year 19.

   15. The notes to Target Corporation's financial statements indicate that current maturities of long-term debt on January 31 of each year are as follows: Year 14, $866 (amount already appears on the January 31, Year 14, balance sheet); Year 15, $857; Year 16, $502; Year 17, $752; Year 18, $1,323; Year 19, $1,451.

   16. Other current liabilities relate to ongoing operating activities and are expected to grow at the growth rate in sales.

17. Target Corporation uses long-term debt to finance acquisitions of property, plant, and equipment. Assume that long-term debt will decrease by the amount of long-term debt reclassified as a current liability each year and then the remaining amount will increase at the growth rate in property, plant, and equipment and other assets. For example, the January 31, Year 14, balance sheet of Target Corporation shows the current portion of long-term debt to be $866. Target Corporation will repay this amount during Year 15. During Year 15, Target will reclassify $857 from long-term debt to current portion of long-term debt (see item 15 above). This will leave a preliminary balance in long-term debt of $10,358 (= $11,215 − $857). Target Corporation will increase this amount of long-term debt by the 10 percent growth rate in property, plant, and equipment and other assets. The projected amount for long-term debt on the January 31, Year 15, balance sheet is $11,394 (= $10,358 × 1.1).

18. Other noncurrent liabilities include an amount related to retirement benefits and taxes due after more than one year. Assume that other noncurrent liabilities will increase at the growth rate in sales.

19. Assume that common stock and additional paid-in capital will not change.

Statement of Cash Flows

20. Assume that depreciation expense will increase at the growth rate in property, plant, and equipment.

21. Assume that changes in other noncurrent assets on the balance sheet are an investing activity.

22. Assume that changes in other noncurrent liabilities on the balance sheet are an operating activity.

23. Assume that the amount for Other Financing Transactions is zero for Year 15 to Year 19.

b. Describe actions that Target might take to deal with the shortage of cash projected in part **a.**

c. What are the likely reasons for the projected changes in the rate of return on common shareholders' equity?

35. **Ethical issues involving financial statement ratios.** Discuss any ethical issues raised by each of the following actions.

a. Firm A is subject to a constraint in its short-term lending agreement with a bank that its current ratio at the end of each year must exceed 1.6. On December 30 of the current year, it projects that its current ratio will be only 1.4 as of the close of business on December 31. The firm has a long-term loan outstanding to its chief executive officer (CEO) that is not due for ten more years. The CEO writes a check on December 30 payable to the firm in an amount such that the current ratio on December 31 will be 1.65. Firm A renews the loan to the CEO on January 5 of the next year.

b. Firm B's rate of return on assets (ROA) has fallen below analysts' expectations in recent years because the firm, a retailer, has added a significant number of new stores (increasing assets in the denominator of ROA) prior to these stores generating earnings (ultimately increasing the numerator of ROA). Firm B decides to curtail the opening of new stores for two years in an effort to allow the earnings of new stores to catch up with the investments it made previously in store assets, thereby increasing its ROA. Management plans to restart the growth in stores after the two years.

c. Firm C has a debt-equity ratio of 30 percent, considerably lower than most of its competitors. Firm C has become the target of a takeover by a group of outside investors. This takeover group feels that Firm C could service debt up to 60 percent of its financing. They plan to borrow the necessary cash to finance the takeover and then have Firm C assume the debt. This action will result in a debt-equity ratio for Firm C of 60 percent after the takeover. The current management desires to defend the firm against this takeover attempt. It sells off a profitable division of the business and uses the cash proceeds to buy back outstanding common stock. This action has the effect of increasing the debt-equity ratio to 60 percent, making the firm less attractive because of the sale of the profitable division, and increasing the stock price that the takeover group must pay.

Part Three

Measuring *and* Reporting Assets *and* Equities Using Generally Accepted Accounting Principles

3

FACMU11

Receivables and Revenue Recognition

6

et's pause to review what you've learned thus far. **Chapter 1** provided an overview of the principal activities of business firms and showed their relation to the three principal financial statements: balance sheet, income statement, and statement of cash flows. **Chapters 2** to **4** then discussed the concepts underlying each financial statement, illustrated the accounting procedures to prepare them, and introduced tools you can use to analyze and interpret them. **Chapter 5** developed these analytical tools more fully, focusing on the analysis of profitability and risk. At this stage in your study, you probably have the sense that financial accounting is fairly precise. The illustrations in the chapter and the exercises and problems at the end of the chapter generally asked for specific numeric answers. We have purposefully presented the material thus far with this seemingly high degree of precision to ensure a solid grounding in the basic concepts and principles of financial accounting.

We are about to shift gears. Part Three **(Chapters 6** to **12)** examine **generally accepted accounting principles (GAAP)**. **Chapter 1** described GAAP as the methods that firms use to measure income for a period and financial position at the end of a period. Standard-setting bodies frequently permit more than one method of accounting for a particular transaction. Furthermore, GAAP are not cookbook rules that accountants can easily and unambiguously apply. Rather, application of GAAP requires professional judgment. Different accountants can reach different conclusions on the appropriate application of GAAP. Thus, you will encounter a higher degree of subjectivity in the remaining chapters of this book relative to the seeming precision of the first five chapters. One objective of this part of the book is to help you identify reporting areas requiring judgment and develop skills as a user to assess the appropriateness of the judgments made.

The discussion in Part Three proceeds in approximate balance sheet order:

Chapter 6: receivables and revenue recognition
Chapter 7: inventories and cost of goods sold
Chapter 8: noncurrent assets and amortization
Chapters 9 and 10: liabilities and interest expense
Chapter 11: marketable securities and long-term investments in securities of other companies
Chapter 12: shareholders' equity

Financial Reporting Environment

Chapter 1 briefly described various aspects of the financial reporting environment. Let's revisit some of the issues raised there as an introduction to our study of GAAP.

1. **What are GAAP?** GAAP are the methods of accounting that firms use to measure the results of their business transactions, with a principal aim of measuring net income for a period and financial position at the end of a period. GAAP prefer the accrual basis over the cash basis, a principle that provides a foundation for accounting. The related concept of matching expenses with associated revenues guides application of the accrual basis. Often, however, GAAP

provide specific guidance for specific issues. For example, **Chapter 7** discusses various inventory cost-flow assumptions for matching expenses with revenues. The cost-flow assumptions discussed there (first-in, first-out, or FIFO; last-in, first-out, or LIFO; weighted average) are also part of GAAP. In sum, GAAP refer to both broad principles and more specific methods for applying those broad principles to particular business transactions.

2. **Who sets GAAP?** Standard-setting bodies within each country currently set GAAP. The International Accounting Standards Board (IASB) has assumed an increasing role in recent years in promoting the establishment of more uniform GAAP worldwide. The Financial Accounting Standards Board (FASB) sets acceptable accounting principles in the United States. Standard-setting bodies refer to their pronouncements as *standards*, which are a part of GAAP.

3. **Are there alternative GAAP for a particular business transaction?** Standard-setting bodies sometimes concur that a particular method of accounting is theoretically superior to alternative methods and require that method as GAAP. For example, the allowance method of accounting for uncollectible accounts, discussed later in this chapter, provides superior matching of losses from uncollectible accounts with revenues relative to the direct charge-off method. Thus, GAAP require the allowance method for uncollectible accounts in most countries. In other cases, standard-setting bodies recognize that the economic effects of certain transactions may differ between firms and that a single method may not provide the best measures of earnings and financial position. In these cases, they allow more than one method of accounting for the transaction. For example, firms may choose from among FIFO, LIFO, and weighted average cost-flow assumptions in measuring cost of goods sold, depending on which flow assumption managers feel provides the best matching of expenses with revenues.

4. **How detailed are the rules for applying GAAP?** Standard-setting bodies generally provide broad guidelines rather than detailed rules for applying their pronouncements. They recognize that economic differences may exist between firms and that firms should have latitude to apply pronouncements to reflect these economic differences. For example, standard-setting bodies stipulate that firms should write off, or depreciate, the acquisition cost of buildings and equipment over the expected useful lives of these assets. Firms have latitude to select the depreciable life to reflect the expected intensity of use, maintenance policies, and similar factors. Firms also have latitude to select the depreciation method that sets the pattern of write-offs of the acquisition cost over an asset's depreciable life.

5. **Does the flexibility of alternative GAAP and the latitude provided firms in applying GAAP have economic consequences?** Some view the flexibility and latitude to choose and apply GAAP as allowing firms to report in a manner that best portrays their earnings and financial position. Then, according to this view, investors and lenders who use the financial statements to make decisions will allocate their capital in an economically desirable way. Critics of this view note that the flexibility and latitude provide managers with an opportunity to report as favorable results as possible within the constraints of GAAP. Managers motivated with the dual economic incentives of job security and compensation would rather report higher than lower earnings. If users of the financial statements can decipher and adjust for any games managers might have played with reported amounts, then investors will allocate capital in an economically desirable way. In this scenario, however, users of the financial statements bear the economic cost of adjusting the financial statements. If users of the financial statements cannot see through the financial statements to the games that managers might have played, then investors may misallocate capital. Thus, the flexibility and latitude of GAAP do have **economic consequences** to managers, investors, lenders, and others.

6. **What controls exist to constrain the opportunistic actions by management?** The audit by a firm's independent accountant serves as one control on management. The independent accountant makes judgments about the suitability of the accounting principles a firm selects and the reasonableness of the way the firm applies the accounting principles. For example, does an airline use longer depreciable lives for its airplanes than do its competitors? Does the firm appear to increase (or decrease) its depreciable lives over time in an effort to increase (or decrease) reported earnings? Another control is the oversight provided by government regulators, such as the Securities and Exchange Commission (SEC) in the United States. The SEC reviews the financial statements of firms with publicly traded securities and takes actions against firms that appear to violate GAAP. Security analysts who analyze financial statements and make buy, sell, or hold recommendations on a firm's common stock can also impede opportunistic actions by management.

Quality of Earnings

Investors typically use earnings to value a firm. Among the questions that investors and other users of the financial statements should ask are:

1. How well do the current period's earnings reflect the economic value added by the firm during the period and the likely amount of future economic value added from the firm's operating activities?
2. Do managers of the firm have much latitude in measuring earnings within GAAP in their particular industry and therefore have the potential for distorting measurements of economic value added?
3. Is there evidence that managers have taken advantage of this latitude and reported unusually favorable or unfavorable earnings?
4. Do earnings contain unusual or nonrecurring items of income that the investors should downplay or ignore when using earnings to value the firm?

Financial periodicals make frequent references to the **quality of earnings**. The writers of these articles appear to use the term to refer to one or some combination of the four concerns suggested by these questions. We use the term in this book in its broadest sense to include

- the representative faithfulness of earnings as a measure of value added,
- the ability managers have to use discretion in measuring and reporting earnings in their particular industry,
- the extent to which the managers have exercised this discretion, and
- the extent to which earnings include unusual or nonrecurring items.

Affirmative answers to the four questions above raise questions for a particular firm about the quality of its earnings and suggest the need for users of the financial statements to take care in using reported earnings in their decisions.

The discretion in measuring earnings can involve any of the following:

- Selecting accounting principles, or standards, when GAAP allow a choice
- Making estimates in the application of accounting principles
- Timing transactions to allow recognizing nonrecurring items in earnings.

Example 1   Retailing and manufacturing firms that carry inventories can use a FIFO, LIFO, and weighted averaged cost flow assumption in measuring cost of goods sold. Depending on the extent that acquisition or manufacturing costs change over time and the rate at which inventories turn over, this choice can significantly impact earnings. As **Chapter 7** discusses, FIFO (first-in, first-out) matches older acquisition or manufacturing costs against revenues, whereas LIFO (last-in, first-out) matches more recent such costs against revenues. Analysts generally view earnings measured using LIFO as providing a better measure of economic value added than FIFO because of this more current matching. **Chapter 7** points out, however, that firms that sell more inventory than they purchase during a particular period calculate cost of goods sold under LIFO in part using older purchase prices of earlier years, distorting the measure of economic value added. Thus, assessments of the quality of earnings sometimes require tradeoffs between these four dimensions of earnings quality.

Example 2   Fixed asset-intensive firms, such as airlines, railroads, electric utilities, and steel manufacturers, find that depreciation expense represents a large expense on their income statements. Such firms must estimate the expected useful lives and residual values of their buildings and equipment, and allocate a portion of the cost minus salvage value of these assets to each period of their use. Because many years will pass until the firm knows for certain what that life will be, some managers choose long depreciable lives that portray current management in a favorable light. The SEC, for example, accused the management of Waste Management of manipulating the lives of its garbage trucks during the 1990s to increase reported earnings. The more earnings measurement requires estimates, the greater the opportunity for management to distort earnings and the lower the quality of earnings.

Example 3   An unexpected recession in East Asia resulted in decreased earnings for a manufacturer of semiconductors. To increase earnings to the level initially anticipated for the year, the firm sold a parcel of land that it did not currently need in operations. The land had a market value larger than its book value, so selling it generated a realized gain to be reported in net income for the year. This component of net income is of low quality because the firm will not likely report similar gains on sales of land on a recurring basis.

Throughout the chapters composing Part Three you will encounter managers' choices—of accounting principles, of estimates, and of the timing of asset sales—that will affect the year-to-year reported income. To the extent managers make choices enhancing currently reported income, analysts will say the firm has a lower earnings quality. The analyst can then either adjust the reported earnings to remove any perceived bias or compensate for the bias in some other way (for example, by applying a lower multiple to earnings in arriving at an acceptable stock price). We shall say time and again, however, that over long enough time spans, reported income will equal the sum of cash inflows less the sum of cash outflows, other than cash flows resulting from transactions with owners. All the management choices that affect the quality of earnings affect *when* the firm reports its income, not its *total amount*, summed over time.

Quality of Earnings and Ethical Issues

Chapter 1 suggested some ways to think about ethical issues that confront management when they make financial reporting decisions. Among the questions that one might raise are:

1. Does the action violate a known law or regulation?
2. Has the firm provided sufficient disclosure about the action for the users of financial statements to make their own judgments about the ethics of such actions?

Each chapter in this book contains one or more questions or problems that require consideration of ethical issues. The remaining chapters of this book discuss GAAP for various business transactions. Some accounting choices that managers make require judgments as to whether the accounting falls within GAAP. Even when GAAP allow the accounting choice, the question arises as to the adequacy of disclosures.

One question of particular importance to **Chapters 6** to **12** is: Do ethical issues arise when a firm makes accounting choices within GAAP and adequately discloses information about the choice but which, however, decreases the quality of earnings? The measurement and reporting of the gain on the sale of the land by the semiconductor firm in **Example 3** conform with GAAP and, we presume, the firm adequately disclosed it. Still, the nonrecurring nature of the gain lowers the quality of earnings.

Some people would argue that an ethical issue does not arise. The reporting conforms with GAAP. The firm provided sufficient disclosures for a user to decide whether to include the gain in net income when evaluating the current period's performance and projecting future earnings. Other people would argue that an ethical issue arises because management took an action for the primary purpose of increasing earnings. Presumably, if the firm had met its earnings target without needing to include the gain, it would not have sold the land. Management purposefully managed, some would say distorted, earnings to make it and the firm look better. As with other ethical issues raised throughout this book, we do not attempt to impose our own value systems. We encourage you to identify and think carefully about possible ethical issues relating to the accounting topics discussed in this book.

Review of Income Recognition Principles

Let's review the principles of income recognition under the accrual basis of accounting from **Chapter 3**. We use the term *income* here to mean net income or earnings. The top panel of **Figure 6.1** shows the flow of operating activities for a typical manufacturing firm. A manufacturing firm

(1) acquires production facilities to permit it to engage in manufacturing and acquires raw materials for use in producing products;
(2) uses labor and other services to transform the raw materials into a salable product;
(3) identifies a customer, agrees to a selling price, and delivers the product to customers;

FIGURE 6.1   Operating Process for a Manufacturing Firm

(1) Acquire Raw Materials, Plant, and Equipment

Acquire Labor and Other Manufacturing Services and Convert Raw Materials Into Product

(3) Sell Product

(5) Collect Cash

Returns and Warranty Periods Expire

(4) Period of Holding Receivable

(2) Period of Production

(6) Periods of Returns and Warranty Services

(4) awaits collection of cash from customers, in the meantime holding an account receivable;
(5) collects cash from customers; and
(6) refunds cash for products returned by customers, or spends cash and other assets to fulfill promises under warranty.

Amount of Income The *amount* of income from these operating activities is the difference between the cash received at point **(5)** and the cash paid to suppliers of goods and services at times **(1)**, **(2)**, **(3)**, and **(4)**, as well as the cash or other assets spent during **(6)**. Income measures the economic value added from operating activities. The excess of cash inflows over cash outflows measure this economic value added.

Measurement of Income for Discrete Accounting Periods Firms measure and report their income using quarterly and annual time periods. Because the cash inflow from customers—point **(5)**—can occur in an accounting period different from the ones during which the firm pays cash out to various suppliers—times **(1)** through **(4)** and **(6)**—accrual accounting must allocate the income to one or more accounting periods.

Matching Expenses with Revenues The guideline for allocating expenses to accounting periods is to match expenses as closely as possible with revenues. In this way, income matches inputs with outputs, efforts with accomplishments. Most firms recognize revenue at the time of sale—time **(3)**. To properly measure income for the period of the sale, the firm must match against revenues the costs of producing the good or service incurred during times **(1)** and **(2)**, the cost of selling the product from time **(3)**, the cost of uncollectible accounts from time **(4)**, and the cost of returns and warranties from time **(6)**. A later section of this chapter discusses income recognition for a long-term construction contractor. We see there that construction contractors often recognize revenue during the period of construction—time **(2)**. These firms must then match appropriate portions of the total costs of construction as expenses against the revenue they recognize each period. We also see later that firms must sometimes wait until they collect cash from customers before recognizing revenue—at time **(5)**. These firms must likewise recognize all of the costs of creating and selling their good or service as expenses at time **(5)** to achieve matching.

Timing of Revenue Recognition The remaining question then is when to recognize revenue. Firms could conceivably recognize revenue at any one or more than one of the six times in **Figure 6.1**. To answer the revenue recognition timing question, GAAP set two hurdles. As soon as a firm clears the following two hurdles for a particular operating activity, GAAP permit it to recognize revenue for that activity:

1. A firm has performed all, or a substantial portion of, the services it expects to provide or, in the case of product warranties, can forecast with reasonable precision the cost of providing the future services.
2. The firm has received cash, a receivable, or some other asset capable of reasonably precise measurement or, if the firm has offered to let the customer return the product for a refund, the firm can estimate the returns with reasonable precision.

Satisfying the first criterion for revenue recognition means that a firm can estimate the total expected cash outflows related to an operating activity. If a firm cannot estimate the total expected cash outflows, it will not know the amount of expenses to match against revenue, and therefore it will not know the amount of income. Satisfying the second criterion for revenue recognition means that a firm can estimate the amount of expected cash inflows from customers. If a firm cannot estimate expected cash inflows, it will not know the amount of revenues and therefore the amount of income. Stating these criteria more succinctly, revenue recognitions requires that a firm have moved far enough down the time line in **Figure 6.1** so that it can measure all remaining uncertainty regarding cash inflows and cash outflows with reasonable precision.

The SEC in *Staff Accounting Bulletin No. 101* amplifies the criteria for revenue recognition as follows:

1. Persuasive evidence of an arrangement exists
2. Delivery has occurred or services have been performed
3. The seller's price to the buyer is fixed or determinable
4. Collectibility is reasonably assured

The second, third, and fourth criteria are similar to GAAP's two criteria stated above. The new dimension is the existence of an arrangement. The arrangement may take the form of a contract, prior business dealings with a particular customer, or customary business practices by a firm and its industry. The arrangement sets forth the responsibilities of the firm and its customers with respect to the nature and delivery of goods or services, the risks assumed by buyer and seller, the timing of cash payments, and similar factors. Having an arrangement in place permits a more informed judgment as to the second, third, and fourth criteria.

Application of Income Recognition Principles

The examples below illustrate the application of the revenue recognition criteria to several businesses.

Example 4 A magazine publisher sells subscriptions to its customers for periods of one to three years, receiving cash from customers at the beginning of the subscription period. Although the magazine publisher can measure the amount of revenue with little uncertainty, it must provide substantial future services to create, print, and deliver the magazine. Thus, it should delay the recognition of revenue and recognize proportionate parts of the subscription fee as it publishes each issue during the subscription period.

Example 5 A winery harvests grapes each year and processes them into various wines. It then bottles the wine and places it in warehouses to age for several years. Although substantial performance has occurred by the time the aging process begins, uncertainties exist as to the amount of cash the firm will collect from customers when it sells the wine. The amount of cash received will depend on the quality of the aged wine, the quantity and quality of wines offered by competitors, and similar factors. The wine producer should therefore delay recognition of revenue not only until aging finishes, but also until it identifies a customer, agrees with the customer on a selling price, and delivers the wine.

Example 6 Refer to **Example 5**. Suppose that the wine producer contracts to sell the wine to a customer at the beginning of the aging process. The wine producer agrees to age the wine in its warehouses and oversee the aging process. The selling price for the wine includes both the cost of initially producing the wine and the services involved in the aging process and subsequent bottling. The customer pays 30 percent of the selling price at the beginning of the aging process and the remainder when it takes delivery after aging. The wine producer should delay recognition of revenue until it completes the aging process and delivers the wine. The aging process is an important part of the services to be performed and the full cost of aging the wine remains uncertain. The customer might not take delivery and pay the remaining 70 percent of the selling price if the quality of the wine is poor.

Example 7 A computer software company develops banking software and sells it to commercial banks. The company promises to do the necessary programming to adapt the software to a particular bank's needs and to train the bank's employees in its use. If the bank is not satisfied with the software, it can return it within one year and receive a full refund. The software company intends to continue developing the software and promises to provide customers with updates on an if-and-when-developed basis for a period of three years. Recognizing revenue at the time of initial delivery of the software appears premature. Installation and training comprise an important part of the services provided and the firm cannot estimate their costs with reasonable precision. Substantial uncertainty also likely exists regarding returns from customers. Assuming unpredictable returns, the earliest that the computer software company should recognize revenues is the end of the one-year return period. Another issue is whether customers normally expect and receive software updates. If so, then the software company should separate the revenue from software sales from those of after-market services.

A later section of this chapter discusses the application of the revenue recognition criteria to other types of businesses.

Problem 6.1 for Self-Study

Revenue recognition. Indicate when each of the following firms should recognize revenue and briefly explain your reasoning.

a. Kodak enters into an agreement with Wal-Mart Stores to place its cameras in Wal-Mart Stores on a consignment basis. Wal-Mart, as consignee, promises to make its best efforts to sell the cameras. Kodak maintains title to the cameras until Wal-Mart sells them. When Wal-Mart sells a camera, it remits the selling price minus a fee to Kodak. Kodak takes back any damaged or defective cameras. When should Kodak recognize revenue?

b. Burlington Mills manufactures custom order athletic clothing for Nike. Near the end of the current year, Burlington Mills completed an order for athletic clothing. The order specified the goods Burlington Mills would deliver and the price Nike would pay. Nike could not take delivery at that time because it had sufficient inventory already in its distribution channel and did not have space to store the new items. Nike asked Burlington Mills to store the items in an independent warehouse for three months. Nike agreed to pay the storage costs. When should Burlington Mills recognize revenue from this transaction?

c. Nordstrom, a department store retailer, offers layaway plans to its customers. Under the plan, when the customer decides to buy the goods, Nordstrom sets them aside in its storeroom and collects a cash deposit from the customer. When the customer pays the remainder of the selling price, which they may do in several installments, Nordstrom releases the item. Nordstrom bears the risk of loss or damage to the stored items. When should Nordstrom recognize revenue?

d. Costco operates discount warehouses for sales of food and household products to customers. Purchasing from Costco requires payment of an annual membership fee, payable at the beginning of the year. Customers who cancel their memberships before year-end may receive a payment equal to a prorated portion of the membership fee. Costco can predict based on experience the likely amounts of refunds. When should Costco recognize revenue from membership fees?

e. Mall Development Corporation builds and operates shopping malls throughout the United States. It leases retail space in its shopping malls for an annual fixed rental, payable in equal monthly installments at the beginning of each month, plus an additional contingent rental, payable at the end of the year, equal to one percent of sales exceeding a stated amount. The stated amount varies by store depending on square footage leased. When should Mall Development Corporation recognize revenue from rentals?

Revenue Recognition at Time of Sale

Chapter 3 points out that most firms satisfy the criteria for revenue recognition at the time of sale or delivery of goods and services: point **(3)** in **Exhibit 6.1**. Firms have manufactured a product or created a service, identified a customer, delivered the product or service to the customer, and either received cash immediately or assessed the credit standing of customers and concluded that customers will likely pay the amount owed. The firm can estimate the amount of product returns, the cost of warranty repairs, and other after-sale costs.

When a firm satisfies the criteria for revenue recognition at the time of sale, it must estimate the effect of events that occur after the time of sale—that is, during times **(4)**, **(5)**, and **(6)** in **Figure 6.1**. Suppose, for example, that some customers do not pay the amounts owed to the firm. Or, suppose that some customers return unsatisfactory products. Recognizing revenue at the time of sale and properly matching expenses with revenues requires firms to estimate the cost of uncollectible accounts, returns, and similar items and recognize them as income reductions at the time of sale. This section discusses the accounting for such items.

Uncollectible Accounts

Whenever a firm extends credit to customers, it will almost certainly never collect from some of its customers. Most businesses should prefer to have some customers who do not pay their bills; for most firms, the optimal amount of uncollectibles is not zero. If a firm is to have no uncollectible accounts, it must screen credit customers carefully, which is costly. Furthermore, the firm would deny credit to many customers who would pay their bills even though they could not pass a credit check designed to weed out all potential uncollectibles. When the firm denies credit to potential customers, some will take their business elsewhere, and the firm will lose sales. As long as the amount collected from credit sales to a given group of customers exceeds the cost of goods sold and the other costs of serving that group of customers, the firm will be better off selling to that group than losing the sales. The rational firm should prefer granting credit to a group of customers who have a high probability of paying their bills rather than losing their business, even though some of them will not pay and the firm will, as a result, have some uncollectible accounts.

For example, assume that gross margin—selling price less cost of goods sold—on credit sales to a new group of customers, such as college sophomores, is 40 percent of credit sales. A firm could then afford uncollectible accounts of up to 40 percent of the credit sales to the new customers and still show increased net income, as long as all other costs of serving customers remain constant.

This does not suggest, of course, that a firm should grant credit indiscriminately or ignore collection efforts aimed at those who have not paid their bills. A cost-benefit analysis of credit policy should dictate a strategy that results in uncollectible accounts of an amount that is reasonably predictable before the firm makes any sales.

The principal accounting issue related to uncollected accounts concerns when firms should recognize the loss from uncollectibles. The following example illustrates the nature of the issue.

Example 8   Howarth's Home Center provides customer financing for sales of its appliances, furniture, and electronic equipment. Customers typically make monthly cash payments of a portion of the purchase price over 24 to 36 months. Despite efforts to collect amounts due and to repossess merchandise when customers fail to pay, Howarth's Home Center generally experiences losses from uncollectible accounts of 2 percent of total sales in the year of sale, 6 percent in the next year, and 4 percent in the third year. Thus the firm expects that it will ultimately not collect $12 (= 0.02 + 0.06 + 0.04)$ percent of sales made in any particular year. A summary of its recent experience appears below:

Year	Sales During Year	Accounts Deemed Uncollectible in Year					Total Uncollectibles
		2	3	4	5	6	
2	$ 800,000	$16,000	$48,000	$ 32,000	—	—	$ 96,000
3	1,200,000	—	24,000	72,000	$ 48,000	—	144,000
4	1,500,000	—	—	30,000	90,000	$60,000	180,000
		$16,000	$72,000	$134,000	$138,000	$60,000	

The accounting issue is,

- should the firm use the direct write-off method and recognize the *actual losses* from uncollectibles in the year it deems particular accounts to be uncollectible ($16,000 in Year 2, $72,000 in Year 3, $134,000 in Year 4, $138,000 in Year 5, and $60,000 in Year 6), or

- should the firm use the allowance method and recognize the total *expected losses* related to a particular year's sales in the year of the sale ($96,000 in Year 2, $144,000 in Year 3, and $180,000 in Year 4)?

Direct Write-Off Method   The **direct write-off method** recognizes losses from uncollectible accounts in the period when a firm decides that specific customers' accounts are uncollectible. For example, Howarth's Home Center decides in Year 4 that specific customers' accounts totaling $134,000 have become uncollectible. It makes the following entry using the direct write-off method:

Retained Earnings (Bad Debt Expense) (Shareholders' Equity Decrease) . . . 134,000	
Accounts Receivable (Asset Decrease)	134,000
To record losses from known uncollectible accounts.	

The direct write-off method has three important shortcomings. First, it does not usually recognize the loss from uncollectible accounts in the period in which the sale occurs and the firm recognizes revenue. For example, Howarth recognizes bad debt expense of only $16,000 in Year 2 under the direct write-off method, even though it ultimately expects not to collect $96,000 of receivables from Year 2 sales. The remaining $80,000 (= $48,000 + $32,000) appears in bad debt expense in Year 3 and Year 4, clumsily matched against those periods' sales. Based on its own expectations of collectibility of accounts, the firm recognizes too little expense in the year of sale and too much in the period of write-off.

Second, the direct write-off method provides firms with an opportunity to manage earnings each period by deciding when particular customers' accounts become uncollectible. Establishing the uncollectible status of customers' accounts requires judgment of the customers' willingness and ability to pay and the intensity of the firm's collection efforts. Firms desiring to increase (decrease) earnings for a particular period can delay (accelerate) the write-off of specific customers' accounts.

Third, the amount of accounts receivable on the balance sheet under the direct write-off method does not reflect the amount a firm expects to collect in cash. Returning to **Example 8**, assume that Howarth's Home Center collects $200,000 of the $800,000 from sales on account during Year 2. Accounts receivable at the end of Year 2 under the direct write-off method are as follows:

Total Sales on Account during Year 2	$800,000
Collections from Customers during Year 2	(200,000)
Specific Customers' Accounts Written Off as Uncollectible	(16,000)
Accounts Receivable at End of Year 2	$584,000

Howarth's Home Center expects to collect only $504,000 (= $584,000 − $48,000 − $32,000) of its accounts receivable outstanding at the end of Year 2. The $584,000 amount for accounts receivable on the balance sheet overstates the amount the firm expects to collect in cash.

Thus, the direct write-off method provides a poor matching of costs from uncollectible accounts with revenues and reports accounts receivable on the balance sheet at an amount exceeding the cash the firm expects to collect. (Double-entry recordkeeping causes these simultaneous income statement and balance sheet effects.) Consequently, GAAP do not allow firms to use the direct write-off method for financial reporting when they have significant amounts of expected uncollectible accounts and when the selling firm, such as a retail store, can reasonably predict them. Such firms must use the allowance method, explained below.

Firms must, however, use the direct write-off method for income tax reporting. Income tax laws permit firms to claim a deduction for bad debts only when a firm can demonstrate that particular customers will not pay. This is the first instance we have seen in this book of a firm's use of different accounting principles for financial reporting and for income tax reporting. This particular instance is mandatory—GAAP require one treatment and the tax law another. **Chapter 10** discusses the accounting issues raised by such differences, called *temporary differences*.

Allowance Method   When a firm can estimate with reasonable precision the amounts of uncollectibles, a necessary condition for recognizing revenue at the time of sale, GAAP require an alternative procedure, the **allowance method**, for uncollectibles. The allowance method involves estimating the amount of uncollectible accounts that will occur over time in connection with the sales of each period. The firm recognizes this amount as an expense in the period of the sale, thereby matching expenses with associated revenues. The offsetting credit reduces accounts receivable to the amount of cash the firm expects to collect from customers.

The following discussion illustrates the allowance method. Refer to **Example 8** for Howarth's Home Center, which estimates, based on past experience, that it will not collect $96,000 of the $800,000 sales on accounts during Year 2. At the end of Year 2, the firm makes the following adjusting entry.

End of Year 2		
Retained Earnings (Bad Debt Expense) (Shareholders' Equity Decrease) . . .	96,000	
Allowance for Uncollectible Accounts (Asset Decrease)		96,000
To provide for estimated uncollectible accounts relating to Year 2 sales.		

Recognizing bad debt expense of $96,000 results in matching against Year 2 sales the amount the firm does not expect to collect in cash from Year 2 sales. The credit in this entry is not to Accounts Receivable because the firm is not writing off specific customers' accounts at this time. Instead, the credit account is Allowance for Uncollectible Accounts, a contra account to Accounts Receivable. Accounts Receivable is a control account—summing the amounts in individual customer's accounts. At the time the firm reduces the gross amount of receivables to its expected net amount, the firm still does not know which specific customers will not pay, so it cannot write off any particular customer's account. Thus, it cannot credit any of the individual accounts whose sums appear in Accounts Receivable. It must credit a separate contra account, which shows the subtraction from gross receivables to derive expected net receivables. A more descriptive title for this account might be Allowance for Uncollectible Accounts—We Know Not Whom.

CONCEPTUAL NOTE

Views differ as to the type of account debited in the entry above. Some debit an expense account and others debit a revenue contra account when providing for estimated uncollectibles. Accounting for uncollectibles will reduce net income no matter which of the accounts the firm chooses to debit. Most firms debit Bad Debt Expense and include its amount among total expenses on the income statement. They reason that generating revenues implies a certain amount of bad debts. On the other hand, using a revenue contra account permits net sales to appear at the amount of cash the firm expects to collect. When a firm debits an expense account and includes it among total expenses on the income statement, net sales will overstate the amount of cash the firm expects to receive. Advocates of using a revenue contra account point out that uncollectible accounts cannot theoretically be an expense. An expense is a gone asset. Accounts that the firm did not expect to collect at the time of recording were never assets to begin with. Although we find the arguments for using a revenue contra account persuasive, we debit Bad Debt Expense in this book because most firms debit an expense, not a revenue contra, account.

Whenever a firm identifies particular customers' accounts that it judges to be uncollectible, it writes off the accounts by debiting Allowance for Uncollectible Accounts and crediting Accounts Receivable. For example, Howarth's makes the following entry at the end of Year 2 to write off the accounts of specific customers, the newly identified non-payers, totaling $16,000.

End of Year 2		
Allowance for Uncollectible Accounts (Asset Increase)	16,000	
Accounts Receivable (Asset Decrease)		16,000
To write off specific customers' accounts.		

If during Year 3 it identifies that specific customers' accounts of $72,000 are uncollectible, it makes the following entry:

End of Year 3		
Allowance for Uncollectible Accounts (Asset Increase)	72,000	
Accounts Receivable (Asset Decrease)		72,000

Note that the write-off of specific customers' accounts using the allowance method does not affect income. The income effect occurs in the year of sale, when the firm provides for estimated uncollectible accounts. Note also that the write-off of specific customers' accounts has no effect on accounts receivable (net) of the allowance for uncollectible accounts. Accounts Receivable (gross) decreases but so does the amount in the contra account for estimated uncollectibles, which the accountant subtracts in reaching the net amount for receivables on the balance sheet.

The allowance method for uncollectible accounts overcomes the three shortcomings, discussed earlier, of the direct write-off method. First, during each period, the allowance method matches against sales revenue the amount the firm does not ultimately expect to collect in cash arising from that period's sales. The allowance method provides a better matching of revenues and expenses not only in the period of sale but also in subsequent periods. Losses from uncollectible amounts of sales from Year 2 of $48,000 in Year 3 and $32,000 in Year 4 are expenses of Year 2, not Year 3 or Year 4 as with the direct write-off method.

Second, the allowance method reduces a firm's opportunity to manage earnings through the timing of write-offs. The write-off of specific customers' accounts does not affect earnings or total assets.

Third, the allowance method results in reporting accounts receivable (net) of the allowance for uncollectible accounts on the balance sheet at the amount the firm expects to collect in cash in future periods. For example, Howarth's Home Center reports accounts receivable on the balance sheet at the end of Year 2 as follows:

Accounts Receivable—Gross ($800,000 − $200,000 − $16,000)	$584,000
Less Allowance for Uncollectible Accounts ($96,000 − $16,000)	(80,000)
Accounts Receivable—Net.	$504,000

With respect to measuring economic value added each period, the allowance method, because of its better matching of bad debt expense and revenues, provides higher quality measures of earnings than the direct write-off method. The allowance method, however, requires firms to estimate the amount of uncollectibles before the time when it identifies the actual uncollectible accounts, which provides management with opportunities to manage earnings. Firms desiring to increase (decrease) earnings can underestimate (overestimate) bad debt expense. Such misestimates may not become evident for several accounting periods. Even then, management might attribute the misestimate to unexpected changes in economic conditions rather than earnings management. Thus, quality-of-earnings issues arise under both the direct write-off method and the allowance method.

Procedural Note on the Allowance Method Firms sometimes write off specific customers' accounts during an accounting period as the firm identifies the specific customers whose accounts have become uncollectible. Such firms generally wait until the end of the accounting period to recognize bad debt expense for the period. Thus, before making the provision for bad debts for the period, the firm may have a debit balance in the Allowance for Uncollectible Accounts account. This account always has a credit balance after recognizing the provision for estimated uncollectbles for the period. Because the firm will not prepare a balance sheet until after it makes its provision for the period, the debit balance in the Allowance account will never appear on the balance sheet. Still, the student may encounter a debit balance in the Allowance account before recognizing estimated uncollectibles for the period and should not let this debit balance cause confusion.

Estimating the Amount of Uncollectible Accounts Accountants use two procedures to calculate the amount of the adjustment for uncollectible accounts under the allowance method: the **percentage-of-sales procedure** and the **aging-of-accounts-receivable procedure**. The first requires fewer computations than the second, but the second provides a useful check on the first. Over time the two methods, correctly used, will give the same cumulative income and asset totals.

Percentage-of-Sales Procedure   The percentage-of-sales procedure involves the following steps:

1. Estimate the amount of uncollectible accounts that will likely occur over time in connection with sales of each period.
2. Make an entry debiting Bad Debt Expense and crediting Allowance for Uncollectible Accounts for the amount in **step 1**.

Uncollectible account amounts will likely vary directly with the volume of credit business. The firm estimates the appropriate percentage by studying its own experience or by inquiring into the experience of similar firms. These rates generally fall within the range of ¼ percent to 2 percent of credit sales.

For example, sales on account at Howarth's Home Center during Year 2 totaled $800,000. Experience indicates that 12 percent of sales become uncollectible. The relatively high percentage reflects the age and financial condition of most of the firm's customers. The entry is as follows:

Retained Earnings (Bad Debt Expense) (Shareholders' Equity Decrease) . . .	96,000	
Allowance for Uncollectible Accounts (Asset Decrease)		96,000
To provide for estimate of uncollectibles computed as a percentage of sales.		

If cash sales occur in a relatively constant proportion to credit sales, the accountant can apply the estimated uncollectibles percentage, proportionately reduced, to the total sales for the period.

Aging-of-Accounts-Receivable Procedure   The aging-of-accounts-receivable procedure involves the following steps:

1. Estimate the amount of outstanding accounts receivable that the firm does not expect to collect.
2. Adjust the balance in the Allowance for Uncollectible Accounts account so that, after the entry to recognize estimated uncollectibles, the balance in the account will equal the amount estimated in **step 1**.

Estimating the amount of outstanding accounts receivable that the firm does not expect to collect relies on information in an aging of accounts receivable. Aging accounts receivable involves classifying each customer's account as to the length of time the account has been uncollected. One set of intervals for classifying individual accounts receivable is as follows:

1. Not yet due
2. Past due 30 days or fewer
3. Past due 31 to 60 days
4. Past due 61 to 180 days
5. Past due more than 180 days

The accountant presumes that the balance in Allowance for Uncollectible Accounts should be large enough to cover substantially all accounts receivable past due for more than, say, six months and smaller portions of the more recent accounts. A firm estimates the actual portions from experience.

As an example of the adjustments to be made, assume that the balance in accounts receivable of Howarth's Home Center at the end of Year 2, before providing for estimated uncollectible accounts, is $600,000 (= $800,000 from sales on account during Year 2 minus $200,000 of cash collections). **Exhibit 6.1** presents an aging of these accounts receivable. Estimated uncollectible accounts total $98,000. The entry at the end of Year 2, assuming that Howarth's Home Center uses aging of receivables instead of percentage of sales to estimate uncollectible accounts, is as follows:

End of Year 2		
Retained Earnings (Bad Debt Expense) (Shareholders' Equity Decrease) . . .	98,000	
Allowance for Uncollectible Accounts (Asset Decrease)		98,000
To adjust the balance in the Allowance for Uncollectible Accounts to $98,000.		

	Amount	Estimated Uncollectible Percentage	Estimated Uncollectible Amounts
CLASSIFICATION OF ACCOUNTS			
Not yet due	$444,000	8.1	$36,000
1–30 days past due	75,000	20.0	15,000
31–60 days past due	40,000	40.0	16,000
61–180 days past due	25,000	60.0	15,000
More than 180 days past due	16,000	100.0	16,000
	$600,000		$98,000

EXHIBIT 6.1   Illustration of Aging Accounts Receivable

Before this entry, the Allowance account had a zero balance, so the amount debited to expense and credited to the allowance is the full amount of uncollectibles estimated by the aging analysis. In reality, the Allowance account will have some balance just before this entry—perhaps a debit balance. Then, the amounts in the debit and credit of this entry will be the plug amounts necessary to bring the balance to the estimated amount—$98,000. If, for example, the Allowance account had a $10,000 debit balance just before the adjusting entry, the amounts would be $108,000 (= $10,000 + $98,000). If the Allowance account had a $23,000 credit balance just before the adjusting entry, the amounts would be $75,000 (= $98,000 − $23,000).

Comparing Percentage-of-Sales and Aging Procedures   When the firm uses the percentage-of-sales procedure, the periodic provision for uncollectible accounts (for example, $96,000) increases (credits) the amounts provided in previous periods (zero in this case) in the account Allowance for Uncollectible Accounts. When the firm uses the aging procedure, it adjusts the balance in the account Allowance for Uncollectible Accounts (in this example, $98,000) to reflect the desired ending balance. If the percentage used under the percentage-of-sales method reasonably reflects collection experience, the balance in the allowance account should be approximately the same at the end of each period under both of these procedures of estimating uncollectible accounts.

Exhibit 6.2 illustrates the operation of the allowance method for uncollectibles over two periods. In the first period the firm uses the percentage-of-sales procedure. In the second period it uses the aging procedure. Normally, a firm would use the same method in all periods.

Dealing with Misestimates of Uncollectible Accounts   The allowance method requires estimates of uncollectible accounts. Changed economic conditions, more careful screening of credits, more aggressive collection efforts, and similar factors may cause the amount of actual uncollectible accounts to differ from the estimated amount. How should firms deal with such misestimates? Two possibilities are:

1. Make retroactive adjustments to net income of previous periods to correct for the misestimates.
2. Correct for the previous misestimates by adjusting the provision for bad debts during the current period.

GAAP require firms to follow the second approach.[1] GAAP's reasoning is that the making of estimates is an integral part of measuring earnings under the accrual basis. Presuming that firms make conscientious estimates each year, adjustments for misestimates, although recurring, should be small. Following the first approach will likely confuse users of the financial statements because of the continual restatements that would likely take place. Firms could manage earnings upward in the current year and correct later with no negative effect on any year's income.

---

[1] Accounting Principles Board, *Opinion No. 20*, "Accounting Changes," 1971.

EXHIBIT 6.2	Review of the Allowance Method of Accounting for Uncollectible Accounts

Transactions in the First Period

(1) Sales are $1,000,000.

(2) The firm collects cash of $937,000 from customers in payment of their accounts.

(3) At the end of the first period, the firm estimates that uncollectibles will be 2 percent of sales; $0.02 \times \$1,000,000 = \$20,000$.

(4) The firm writes off specific accounts totaling $7,000 as uncollectible.

Transactions in the Second Period

(5) Sales are $1,200,000.

(6) The firm writes off specific accounts totaling $22,000 during the period as information on their uncollectibility becomes known. The debit balance of $9,000 will remain in the Allowance account until the firm makes an entry at the end of the period; see **(8)**.

(7) The firm collects cash of $1,100,000 from customers in payment of their accounts.

(8) An aging of the accounts receivable shows that the amount in the Allowance account should be $16,000. The amount of the adjustment is $25,000. It is the difference between the desired $16,000 credit balance and the current $9,000 debit balance in the Allowance account.

---

(1) During First Period

| Accounts Receivable (Asset Increase) .... | 1,000,000 | |
| Retained Earnings (Sales Revenue) (Shareholders' Equity Increase) ... | | 1,000,000 |

To recognize sales on account.

(2) During First Period

| Cash (Asset Increase) .... | 937,000 | |
| Accounts Receivable (Asset Decrease) .... | | 937,000 |

To record cash collections from customers.

(3) End of First Period

| Retained Earnings (Bad Debt Expense) (Shareholders' Equity Decrease) .... | 20,000 | |
| Allowance for Uncollectible Accounts (Asset Decrease) .... | | 20,000 |

To recognize estimated uncollectible accounts for first period using the percentage-of-sales procedure.

(4) End of First Period

| Allowance for Uncollectible Accounts (Asset Increase) .... | 7,000 | |
| Accounts Receivable (Asset Decrease) .... | | 7,000 |

To write off specific customers' accounts as uncollectible. The balance in Allowance for Uncollectible Accounts is $13,000 (= $20,000 − $7,000).

(5) During Second Period

| Accounts Receivable (Asset Increase) .... | 1,200,000 | |
| Retained Earnings (Sales Revenue) (Shareholders' Equity Increase) ... | | 1,200,000 |

To recognize sales on account.

(6) During Second Period

| Allowance for Uncollectible Accounts (Asset Increase) .... | 22,000 | |
| Accounts Receivable (Asset Decrease) .... | | 22,000 |

To write off specific customers' accounts as uncollectible. The balance in Allowance for Uncollectible Accounts is now a debit of $9,000 (= $13,000 − $22,000).

(7) During Second Period

| Cash (Asset Increase) .... | 1,100,000 | |
| Accounts Receivable (Asset Decrease) .... | | 1,100,000 |

To record cash collections from customers.

(8) End of Second Period

| Retained Earnings (Bad Debt Expense) (Shareholders' Equity Decrease) .... | 25,000 | |
| Allowance for Uncollectible Accounts (Asset Decrease) .... | | 25,000 |

To recognize estimated uncollectibles for second period using aging procedure. The entry converts a debit balance of $9,000 (see entry **(6)**) to the desired credit balance of $16,000.

Summary of Accounting for Uncollectible Accounts

The accounting for uncollectible accounts using the allowance method involves four transactions or events.

(1) Sale of Goods on Account

Accounts Receivable (Asset Increase)	Selling Price	
Retained Earnings (Sales Revenue) (Shareholders' Equity Increase)		Selling Price

(2) Collection of Cash from Customers

Cash (Asset Increase)	Amount Collected	
Accounts Receivable (Asset Decrease)		Amount Collected

(3) Estimate of Expected Uncollectible Accounts

Retained Earnings (Bad Debt Expense) (Shareholders' Equity Decrease)	Estimated Uncollectible Amount	
Allowance for Uncollectible Accounts (Asset Decrease)		Estimated Uncollectible Amount

The percentage-of-sales procedure computes directly the amount of the debit, with this same amount then increasing the amount in the Allowance for Uncollectible Accounts account as a credit. The aging-of-accounts-receivable procedure computes the credit balance needed in the Allowance for Uncollectible Accounts account at the end of the period. The amount credited to the Allowance for Uncollectible Accounts account is the amount needed to bring about this needed credit balance, with this same amount then debited to Retained Earnings (Bad Debt Expense).

(4) Write-off of Actual Uncollectible Accounts using the Allowance Method

Allowance for Uncollectible Accounts (Asset Increase)	Actual Uncollectible Amount	
Accounts Receivable (Asset Decrease)		Actual Uncollectible Amount

Entries such as this can occur during the period, as the firm identifies specific uncollectible accounts, or at the end of the period, when the firm writes off a group of specific uncollectibles all at once, or both.

When a firm uses the direct write-off method, it makes the same entries for (1) and (2). It does not make entry (3). Entry (4) is as follows:

(4) Write-off of Actual Uncollectible Accounts using Direct Write-off Method

Retained Earnings (Bad Debt Expense) (Shareholders' Equity Decrease)	Actual Uncollectible Amount	
Accounts Receivable (Asset Decrease)		Actual Uncollectible Amount

Problem 6.2 for Self-Study

Accounting for uncollectible accounts. Dee's Department Store opened for business on January 2, Year 4. Sales on account during Year 4 are $5,000,000. The firm estimates that uncollectible accounts will total 2 percent of sales. Dee's writes off $40,000 of accounts as uncollectible at the end of Year 4. Collections on account during Year 4 totaled $3,500,000.

a. Present the entry on December 31, Year 4, to apply the direct write-off method for uncollectible accounts.

(continued)

Problem 6.2 for Self-Study *(continued)*

b. Present the entries on December 31, Year 4, to apply the allowance method for uncollectible accounts.

c. Sales on account during Year 5 totaled $6,000,000. Dee's writes off $110,000 of accounts as uncollectible on December 31, Year 5. Prepare the entry on December 31, Year 5, to apply the direct write-off method for Year 5.

d. Refer to part **c**. Prepare the entries on December 31, Year 5, to apply the allowance method for Year 5.

e. Dee's ages its accounts receivable on December 31, Year 5, and discovers that it needs a balance in its Allowance for Uncollectible Accounts of $75,000 at the end of Year 5. Give the additional entries on December 31, Year 5, beyond that in part **d** above, to apply the allowance method for Year 5.

The Allowance Method Applies to Many Transactions in Accounting

We have just introduced the allowance method for uncollectibles. Accountants use the allowance method when the firm knows that at the time of sale, it will experience some reduction in future cash flows (in this case for uncollected accounts) but can estimate with reasonable precision the amount at the time of sale. The allowance method permits firms to reduce reported earnings in the period of sale to the amount of the expected net cash collections.

A similar phenomenon often occurs in business transactions:

- The customer has the right to return the product for a refund and the firm can estimate with reasonable precision the amount of returns at the time of sale, or
- the customer has the right to repairs or replacement under warranty if the purchased product is defective, and the firm can estimate with reasonable precision the amount of warranty costs at the time of sale.

In these cases, the firm will use a method analogous to the allowance method for uncollectibles. **Chapter 9** illustrates the allowance method for product warranties. You should master the concepts underlying the allowance method, which means mastering its procedures and journal entries to cement your understanding of the concepts, so that you can apply these concepts in other, similar transactions. The allowance method and its analogs underpin all revenue recognition where the firm recognizes revenue before it has resolved all uncertainty about future cash flows related to the sales transaction.

Sales Discounts

Often the seller of merchandise offers a reduction from the invoice price for prompt payment. Such reductions, called **sales discounts** or cash discounts, indicate that goods may have two prices: a lower cash price and a higher price if the seller grants credit.[2] The seller offers a cash discount not only to provide an interest allowance on funds paid before the payment is due—the implied interest rate typically exceeds normal lending rates—but also to induce prompt payment so it can avoid additional bookkeeping and collection costs. The amount of sales discounts the seller expects the customers to take appears as an adjustment in measuring net sales revenue.

Sales Returns and Allowances

When a customer returns merchandise, the return cancels the sale. The firm could make an entry to reverse the sale. In analyzing sales activities, however, management may be interested in the amount of goods returned. If so, it uses a sales revenue contra account, Sales Returns, to

---

[2] See the **Glossary** at the back of the book for the definition of a discount and a summary of the various contexts in which accountants use this word.

accumulate the amount of **sales returns** for a particular period. When the firm has significant amounts of returns and can reasonably estimate their amounts, it should use an allowance method for returns. The selling firm debits a revenue contra account during the period of sale for expected returns so as to report correctly the amount of cash it expects to collect from each period's sales. GAAP do not allow a firm to recognize revenue from sales when the customers have the right to return goods unless the firm can reasonably estimate the amount of returns and it uses an allowance method to do so.[3]

Sales allowances reduce the price charged to a customer, usually after the firm has delivered the goods and the customer has found them to be unsatisfactory or damaged. The sales allowance reduces sales revenue, but the firm may desire to accumulate the amount of such adjustments in a separate sales revenue contra account. It can use an account, Sales Allowances, for this purpose.

Turning Receivables into Cash

A firm may find itself temporarily short of cash and unable to borrow from its usual sources. In such instances, it can convert accounts receivable into cash in various ways. A firm may **assign** its accounts receivable to a bank or a finance company to obtain a loan. The assigning (borrowing) company physically maintains control of the accounts receivable, collects amounts remitted by customers, and then forwards the proceeds to the lending institution. Alternatively, the firm may **pledge** its accounts receivable to the lending agency as collateral for a loan. If the borrowing firm cannot make loan repayments when due, the lending agency has the right to sell the accounts receivable to obtain payment. Finally, firms may **factor** (sell) the accounts receivable to a bank or a finance company to obtain cash. In this case, the firm sells accounts receivable to the lending institution, which physically controls the receivables and collects payments from customers. If the firm has pledged accounts receivable, a footnote to the financial statements should indicate this fact: the collection of such accounts receivable will not increase the liquid resources available to the firm to pay general trade creditors. Accounts receivable that the firm has factored or assigned do not appear on the balance sheet because the firm has sold them. **Chapter 10** discusses the difficulties in ascertaining whether a transfer of receivables is a sale (no liability appears on the balance sheet) or a collateralized loan (liability appears on the balance sheet). See *variable interest entity* in **Chapter 11** and the **Glossary**.

Illustration of Balance Sheet Presentation

The balance sheet accounts presented so far in this chapter are Accounts Receivable and the Allowance for Uncollectible Accounts. **Exhibit 6.3** shows how transactions affecting these

EXHIBIT 6.3	ALEXIS COMPANY Income Statement Illustration of Sales and Sales Adjustments Partial Income Statement for the Year Ended June 30, Year 2		
REVENUES			
Sales—Gross			$515,200
Less Sales Adjustments:			
Discounts Taken		$23,600	
Allowances		11,000	
Estimated Uncollectibles[a]		10,300	
Returns		8,600	
Total Sales Adjustments			53,500
Net Sales			$461,700

[a] Most companies call this account Bad Debt Expense and list it among the expenses.

---

[3] Financial Accounting Standards Board, *Statement of Financial Accounting Standards No. 48,* "Revenue Recognition When Right of Return Exists," 1981.

EXHIBIT 6.4	ALEXIS COMPANY Illustration of Current Assets Balance Sheet (Excerpts) June 30, Year 1 and Year 2			

	June 30, Year 1		June 30, Year 2	
CURRENT ASSETS				
Cash and Certificates of Deposit		$ 56,200		$ 63,000
Accounts Receivable, Gross	$57,200		$58,100	
Less Allowance for Uncollectible Accounts	(3,500)		(3,600)	
Accounts Receivable, Net		53,700		54,500
Merchandise Inventory[a]		67,000		72,000
Prepayments		4,300		4,800
Total Current Assets		$181,200		$194,300

[a]Additional required disclosures for this item do not appear here. See **Chapter 7**.

accounts appear in the income statement of Alexis Company. **Exhibit 6.4** illustrates the presentation of these items in the balance sheet, which includes all of the current assets for Alexis Company as of June 30, Year 1 and Year 2.

Accounts receivable appear on the balance sheet at the net amount the firm expects to collect. Firms use the allowance method to reduce the gross receivables to their expected collectible amount. The accounting involves a debit to Retained Earnings (Bad Debt Expense) and a credit to the Allowance for Uncollectible Accounts (asset contra) account in the period of sale. When the firm identifies a specific account receivable as uncollectible, it credits the specific account receivable to write it off and debits the Allowance for Uncollectible Accounts account. Periodically, the firm uses an aging-of-accounts-receivable balance to test the adequacy of the amounts debited to Bad Debt Expense.

Analyzing Information on Accounts Receivable

The financial statements contain useful information for analyzing the collectibility of accounts receivable and the adequacy of a firm's provision for uncollectible accounts. **Exhibit 6.5** presents information taken from a recent annual report of Whirlpool Corporation, a manufacturer of household appliances. The analyst might address the following questions.

1. **How quickly does the firm collect its accounts receivable?** The accounts receivable turnover ratio and the days accounts receivable outstanding, discussed in **Chapter 5**, provide the needed information.

EXHIBIT 6.5	Selected Data for Whirlpool Corporation (amounts in millions)				

	Year 4	Year 5	Year 6	Year 7
Balance Sheet				
Accounts Receivable, net of allowance for uncollectible accounts of $2.4 at the end of Year 4, $2.6 at the end of Year 5, $3.3 at the end of Year 6, and $4.4 at the end of Year 7	$ 247.0	$ 260.9	$ 323.4	$ 419.5
Income Statement				
Sales on Account	$3,987.6	$4,008.7	$4,179.0	$4,314.5
Bad Debt Expense	5.4	6.0	17.7	11.5

Year	Accounts Receivable Turnover Ratio	Days Accounts Receivable Outstanding
5	$4,008.7/0.5($247.0 + $260.9) = 15.8	365/15.8 = 23.1 days
6	$4,179.0/0.5($260.9 + $323.4) = 14.3	365/14.3 = 25.5 days
7	$4,314.5/0.5($323.4 + $419.5) = 11.6	365/11.6 = 31.5 days

Thus, the collection period increased during the three-year period.

2. **What is the uncollectible accounts experience of the firm?** The analysts can compute the amount of accounts written off using information in the Allowance for Uncollectible Accounts account.

Year	Balance at Beginning of Year	Increase for Bad Debt Expense	Accounts Written Off as Uncollectible	Balance at End of Year
5	$2.4	$ 6.0	$ 5.8 (plug)	$2.6
6	$2.6	$17.7	$17.0 (plug)	$3.3
7	$3.3	$11.5	$10.4 (plug)	$4.4

We can compare the amount of accounts written off to the average amount of gross accounts receivable each year.

Year	Accounts Written Off as Uncollectible	Accounts Receivable Net	Allowance for Uncollectible Accounts	Accounts Receivable Gross	Write-offs/ Average Gross Accounts Receivable
4		$247.0	$2.4	$249.4	
5	$ 5.8	$260.9	$2.6	$263.5	2.3%
6	$17.0	$323.4	$3.3	$326.7	5.8%
7	$10.4	$419.5	$4.4	$423.9	2.8%

Thus, consistent with the slowing accounts receivable turnover ratio, the firm experienced increased write-offs of uncollectible accounts, particularly in Year 6.

3. **Has the firm adequately provided for estimated uncollectible accounts?** We can compare the amount of bad debt expense to sales and the balance in the Allowance for Uncollectible Accounts account to gross accounts receivable to help in responding to this question.

Year	Bad Debt Expense (1)	Sales (2)	(1)/(2) = (3)	Balance in Allowance Accounts (4)	Gross Accounts Receivable (5)	(4)/(5) = (6)
5	$ 6.0	$4,008.7	0.15%	$2.6	$263.5	0.99%
6	$17.7	$4,179.0	0.42%	$3.3	$326.7	1.01%
7	$11.5	$4,314.5	0.27%	$4.4	$423.9	1.04%

The ratio of bad debt expense to sales varies considerably from year to year but in a pattern similar to write-offs of uncollectible accounts computed in **question 2** above. The balance in the allowance accounts increased as a percentage of gross accounts receivable, which one would expect with a slowing of the accounts receivable turnover.

Income Recognition at Times Different from Sale

Although most firms recognize revenue at the time of sale, many firms clear the hurdles mentioned earlier for revenue recognition at times other than the time of sale. Next, we provide examples of such firms and discuss some of the accounting issues they present.

Income Recognition Before the Sale

Firms sometimes recognize revenues and expenses before the sale or delivery of a product—time (2) in **Figure 6.1**. In these cases, the firm has typically contracted with a particular customer, agreed on a selling price, and performed substantial work to create the product.

Long-Term Contractors   The operating process for a long-term contractor (for example, building construction, shipbuilding) differs from that for a manufacturing firm (depicted in **Figure 6.1**) in three important respects:

1. The period of construction (production) may span several accounting periods.
2. The firm identifies a customer and agrees on a contract price in advance (or at least in the early stages of construction). The seller has little doubt about the ability of the customer to make the agreed-on payments.
3. The buyer often makes periodic payments of the contract price as work progresses.

The activities of contractors often meet the criteria for recognizing revenue from long-term contracts during the period of construction. The contract indicates that an arrangement exists (as required by the SEC), which shows that the contractor has identified a buyer and agreed on a price. Occasionally, the contractor collects cash in advance. More often, the contractor assesses the customer's credit and reasonably expects that the customer will pay the contract price in cash as construction progresses or afterward. Although at any given time these long-term construction contracts can require substantial future services, the contractor can estimate, with reasonable precision, the costs it will incur in providing these services. In agreeing to a contract price, the firm must have some confidence in its estimates of the total costs it will incur on the contract.

Percentage-of-Completion Method   When a firm's construction activities meet the criteria for revenue recognition as construction progresses, the firm usually recognizes revenue during the construction period using the **percentage-of-completion method**. The percentage-of-completion method recognizes a portion of the contract price as revenue during each accounting period of construction. It bases the amount of revenue, expense, and income on the proportion of total work performed during the accounting period. It measures the proportion of total work carried out during the accounting period either from engineers' estimates of the degree of completion or from the ratio of costs incurred to date to the total costs expected for the entire contract.

The actual schedule of cash collections does not affect the revenue recognition process. Even if the contract specifies that the contractor will receive the entire contract price only on completing construction, the contractor may use the percentage-of-completion method so long as it can reasonably estimate the amount of cash it will receive and the remaining costs it expects to incur in completing the job.

As the contractor recognizes revenue for portions of the contract price, it recognizes equal portions of the total estimated contract costs as expenses. Thus, the percentage-of-completion method follows the accrual basis of accounting because the method matches expenses with related revenues.

To illustrate the percentage-of-completion method, we will assume that a firm agrees to construct a bridge for $5,000,000. The firm estimates the total cost at $4,000,000, to occur as follows: Year 1, $1,500,000; Year 2, $2,000,000; and Year 3, $500,000. Thus the firm expects a total profit of $1,000,000 (= $5,000,000 − $1,500,000 − $2,000,000 − $500,000).

Assume that the firm measures the percentage of completion by using the percentage of total costs incurred and that it incurs costs as anticipated. It recognizes revenue and expense from the contract as follows:

Year	Degree of Completion	Revenue	Expense	Profit
1	$1,500,000/$4,000,000 = 37.5%	$1,875,000	$1,500,000	$ 375,000
2	$2,000,000/$4,000,000 = 50.0%	2,500,000	2,000,000	500,000
3	$ 500,000/$4,000,000 = 12.5%	625,000	500,000	125,000
		$5,000,000	$4,000,000	$1,000,000

Completed Contract Method Some firms involved with construction contracts postpone revenue recognition until they complete the construction project and its sale. Construction contractors call this method of recognizing revenue the **completed contract method**. This is the same as the **completed sale method**, a term accountants use for the usual method of recognizing revenue when a retailing or manufacturing firm makes its sales. A firm using the completed contract method in the previous example recognizes no revenue or expense from the contract during Year 1 or Year 2. In Year 3, it recognizes contract revenue of $5,000,000 and contract expenses of $4,000,000 in measuring net income. Note that total income, or profit, is $1,000,000 under both the percentage-of-completion and the completed contract methods, equal to cash inflows of $5,000,000 less cash outflows of $4,000,000.

In some cases, firms use the completed contract method because the contracts take such a short time to complete (such as a few months) that earnings reported with the percentage-of-completion method and the completed contract method do not differ significantly. In these cases, firms use the completed contract method because they find it generally easier to implement. Firms must use the completed contract method in situations when they have not found a specific buyer while construction progresses, as sometimes happens in the construction of residential housing. These situations require future marketing effort. Moreover, substantial uncertainty may exist regarding the price that the contractor will ultimately ask and the amount of cash it will collect.

If uncertainty obscures the total costs the contractor will incur in carrying out the project, it will not use the percentage-of-completion method—even when it has a contract with a specified price. If a contractor cannot reasonably estimate total costs, it cannot estimate the total income for the contract, a GAAP requirement for recognizing revenue earlier than completion of the contract. Furthermore, a firm that uses the proportion of total costs incurred each period to measure the degree of completion will not have the necessary information to allocate this total income (revenues and expenses) to each period of construction activity.

Quality-of-Earnings Issues for Long-Term Contractors

The percentage-of-completion method provides information on the profitability of a contractor as construction progresses. The completed contract method, in contrast, lumps all of the income from contracts into the period of completion. Because of the more timely reporting of operating performance in the percentage-of-completion method, GAAP require the use of this method whenever firms can make reasonable estimates of revenues and expenses.[4]

The need to make estimates under the percentage-of-completion method provides management with opportunities to manage reported earnings. Managers can either underestimate total expenses or overestimate the degree of completion to accelerate the recognition of income. Recognizing too much income during the early years of a contract means recognizing too little in later years. Thus, although the percentage-of-completion method provides better measures of a firm's value added each period than does the completed contract method, enhancing earnings quality, the need to make estimates to apply the percentage-of-completion method lowers earnings quality.

Income Recognition After the Sale

The operating process for some firms requires substantial performance after the time of sale. For other firms, it involves considerable uncertainty regarding the future amounts of cash inflows, cash outflows, or both. In these cases, recognizing income after the time of sale—at times **(4)**, **(5)**, or **(6)** in **Figure 6.1**—is appropriate.

Insurance Companies

The operating process for an insurance company involves the following steps:

1. The insurance company sells insurance policies to customers, promising to provide insurance coverage (life, health, property, liability) in the future.
2. The insurance company collects cash (premiums) from policyholders during the periods of insurance coverage.

---

[4] Financial Accounting Standards Board, *Statement of Financial Accounting Standards No. 111*, "Rescission of FASB Statement Number 32 and Technical Corrections," 1997.

3. The insurance company invests the cash received from policyholders in stocks, bonds, real estate, and other investments, periodically receiving interest, dividends, and other revenues.
4. Policyholders make claims on their insurance policies, requiring the insurance company to disburse cash.

The insurance contract requires the insurance company to provide substantial future services after the sale of the contract. Also, the insurance company cannot estimate the amount of cash it will receive from investments. The uncertainty in these steps causes the accountant to delay the recognizing of income from the time of sale to some time after the company sells the insurance.

One alternative recognizes income at the end of the period of insurance coverage (for example, at the death of the insured in the case of life insurance). At that time, the insurance company can measure with certainty the cash it received from premiums and from investments and the amount of cash it disbursed for claims. Also, the insurance company has provided the services required by the insurance contract. Such an approach, however, may inappropriately delay the recognition of income. Most policyholders pay their insurance premiums as required by the insurance contract. Insurance companies generally receive cash each period for interest and dividends from their investments. Life insurance actuaries can usually estimate the amount and timing of insurance claims. Awaiting completion of the insurance coverage period provides insufficient signals regarding the operating performance of the insurance company while it is providing the insurance coverage.

Most insurance companies therefore recognize revenues and expenses during each period of insurance coverage: time **(6)** in **Figure 6.1**. The receipt of cash from policyholders and from investments creates a relatively high degree of certainty regarding the amount of revenue. Insurance companies must, however, match against this revenue each period a portion of the ultimate cash outflow to satisfy claims. Because this cash outflow may occur several or even many years later, measuring expenses requires estimates. Actuaries study demographic and other data to estimate the likely amount and timing of policyholder claims. Accountants use this information to measure expenses each period. The need to make such estimates, however, lowers the quality of earnings for insurance companies relative to companies whose cash inflows occur closer in time to its cash outflows.

Franchisors   Companies (franchisors) such as McDonald's, Pizza Hut, and Taco Bell typically sell franchise rights to individuals (franchisees) in particular locales. These franchise rights permit the franchisee to use the franchisor's name, as well as advertising, consulting, and other services provided by the franchisor. The franchisee agrees to pay an initial franchise fee of $50,000 or even more. Most franchisees do not have the funds to pay this initial fee at the time they acquire the franchise rights. Instead, they sign a note agreeing to pay the fee over five or more years.

Franchisors usually provide most of the services required by the franchise arrangement by the time the franchisee opens for business (for example, selecting a location, constructing buildings, and acquiring equipment). Substantial uncertainty often exists, however, regarding the portion of the initial franchise fee that the franchisor will ultimately collect from its customer, the franchisee. New small businesses often fail. Franchisees can usually stop making payments and walk away from the franchise arrangement. A similar situation exists for other businesses, such as land-development companies, that sell products or services with delayed payment arrangements.

When substantial uncertainty exists at the time of sale regarding the amount (or timing or both) of cash that a firm will ultimately receive from customers, the firm delays the recognition of revenues and expenses until it receives cash: point **(5)** in **Figure 6.1**. Such sellers recognize revenue at the time of cash collection using either the installment method or the cost-recovery-first method. Unlike the cash method of accounting, however, these methods attempt to match expenses with revenues.

Installment Method   The **installment method** recognizes revenue as the seller collects parts of the selling price in cash. In parallel, this method recognizes as expenses each period the same portion of the cost of the good or service sold as the portion of total revenue recognized.

Example 9   Assume that a firm sells for $100 merchandise costing $60. Income from the transaction is $40 (= $100 − $60), cash inflow less cash outflow. The buyer agrees to pay (ignoring interest) $20, one-fifth of the total selling price, per month for five months. The installment method recognizes revenue of $20 each month as the seller receives cash. The cost of goods sold is $12 [= ($20/$100) × $60] each month, with monthly expense measured as the same proportion of total expenses as the cash collection represents of its total, one-fifth in the example. By the end of five months, the income recognized totals $40 [= 5 × ($20 − $12)].

Cost-Recovery-First Method   When the seller has substantial uncertainty about the amount of cash it will collect, it can also use the **cost-recovery-first method** of income recognition. This method matches the costs of generating revenues dollar for dollar with cash receipts until the seller recovers all such costs. Expenses equal (match) revenues in each period until the seller recovers all costs. Only when cumulative cash receipts exceed total costs will income (that is, revenue without any matching expenses) appear in the income statement.

To illustrate the cost-recovery-first method, we use information from the previous example.

Example 10   Assume the sale for $100 of merchandise costing $60, with the buyer promising to pay $20 each month for five months. Whether the buyer will pay remains uncertain (or else we would not be considering this method). If the buyer makes all payments on schedule, during each of the first three months, the seller recognizes revenue of $20 and expenses of $20. By the end of the third month, cumulative cash receipts of $60 exactly equal the cost of the merchandise sold. During the fourth and fifth months, the seller recognizes revenue of $20 per month without an offsetting expense. For the five months as a whole, the seller recognizes total income of $40, $20 in each of the last two periods, so the pattern differs from that of the installment method.

Example 11   Assume instead that the seller eventually collects only four, not five, of the expected monthly payments of $20 each. Under the cost-recovery-first method, the seller will recognize no income in the first three months, $20 in the fourth month, and $20 in total. Under the installment method, the seller would recognize $8 (= $20 − $12) each month for four months, $32 in total. Then, when the seller learns in month five that it will collect no more cash, it will have to recognize a loss of $12 (= $32 − $20) to report correctly the total income of only $20.

Use of Installment and Cost-Recovery-First Methods   GAAP permit the seller to use the installment and the cost-recovery-first methods only when the seller cannot make reasonably certain estimates of cash collection. For most sales of goods and services, past experience and an assessment of customers' credit standings provide a sufficient basis for estimating the amount of cash the seller will receive. If the seller can reasonably estimate the amount of cash it will receive, the seller may not use the installment method or the cost-recovery-first method for financial reporting and must recognize revenue no later than the time of sale.[5] When cash collection is sufficiently uncertain that GAAP allow either of these methods, then the cost-recovery-first method seems to reflect more accurately the substance of the uncertainty. The logic of the installment method assumes that the seller will eventually receive all of the promised cash or, if not, that when payments cease, the seller can repossess the goods, and, at that time, the goods still retain sufficient market value to cover the seller's as-yet-uncollected costs. If those assumptions do not hold, GAAP forbid the installment method.

Unifying Principle for Revenue Recognition   Although GAAP do not put the matter this way, we suggest you can understand revenue recognition with the following unifying principle. A firm can recognize revenue when it has delivered products or services to customers so long as the firm can estimate with reasonable statistical certainty the events remaining to complete the transaction (such as collecting cash, accepting returns, making warranty repairs and replacements). When significant uncertainty exists at the time of delivery about the events remaining to complete the transactions, firms must delay revenue recognition until the uncertainties resolve to the level of reasonable statistical certainty.

Summary Illustration of Income Recognition Methods

Exhibit 6.6 illustrates the various methods of income recognition discussed here and in **Chapter 3**. The illustration involves a contract for the construction of a bridge for $12 million. The expected and actual patterns of cash receipts and disbursements under the contract appear on page 274.

---

[5] Accounting Principles Board, *Opinion No. 10*, "Omnibus Opinion—1966," par. 12, footnote 8.

Period	Expected and Actual Cash Receipts	Expected and Actual Cash Expenditures
1	$ 1,000,000	$1,600,000
2	1,000,000	4,000,000
3	2,000,000	4,000,000
4	4,000,000	—
5	4,000,000	
Total	$12,000,000	$9,600,000

The contractor completed the bridge in Period 3. **Exhibit 6.6** indicates the contractor's periodic revenues, expenses, and income recognized during each period under the contract using the following methods:

The cash basis of accounting
The percentage-of-completion method
The completed contract (completed sale) method
The installment method
The cost-recovery-first method

No single firm could simultaneously justify all of the five methods of income recognition for financial reporting; we present them for illustrative purposes. Note that the total revenues, expenses, and income recognized for the five years are the same for all methods. Over sufficiently long time periods, total income equals cash inflows less cash outflows other than transactions with owners. The amount of income recognized each period differs, however, depending on the accounting method used.

Problem 6.3 for Self-Study

Income recognition for contractor.   Blount Construction Company contracted on May 15, Year 2, to build a bridge for a city for $4,500,000. Blount estimated that the cost of constructing the bridge would be $3,600,000. Blount incurred $1,200,000 in construction costs during Year 2, $2,000,000 during Year 3, and $400,000 during Year 4 in completing the bridge. The city paid $1,000,000 during Year 2, $1,500,000 during Year 3, and the remaining $2,000,000 of the contract price at the time the bridge was completed and approved in Year 4.

a. Calculate Blount's net income (revenue less expenses) on the contract during Year 2, Year 3, and Year 4, assuming that it uses the percentage-of-completion method.
b. Repeat part **a**, assuming that it uses the completed contract method.
c. Repeat part **a**, assuming that it uses the installment method.
d. Repeat part **a**, assuming that it uses the cost-recovery-first method.

Format and Classification within the Income Statement

Financial statement users study a firm's income statement to evaluate its past profitability and to project its likely future profitability. When assessing profitability, the analyst makes two types of distinctions regarding the nature of various income items:

1. Does the income item result from a firm's primary operating activity (creating and selling a good or service for customers) or from an activity incidental or peripheral to the primary operating activity (for example, periodic sales of equipment previously used by the firm in manufacturing)?
2. Does the income item result from an activity in which a firm will likely continue its involvement, or from an unusual transaction or event that is unlikely to recur regularly?

EXHIBIT 6.6	Comprehensive Illustration of Revenue and Expense Recognition (all dollar amounts in thousands)

Cash Basis of Accounting[a]

Period	Revenue	Expense	Income
1	$ 1,000	$1,600	$ (600)
2	1,000	4,000	(3,000)
3	2,000	4,000	(2,000)
4	4,000	—	4,000
5	4,000	—	4,000
Total	$12,000	$9,600	$2,400

Period	Percentage-of-Completion Method			Completed Contract Method		
	Revenue	Expense	Income	Revenue	Expense	Income
1	$ 2,000[d]	$1,600	$ 400	$ —	$ —	$ —
2	5,000[e]	4,000	1,000	—	—	—
3	5,000[e]	4,000	1,000	12,000	9,600	2,400
4	—	—	—	—	—	—
5	—	—	—	—	—	—
Total	$12,000	$9,600	$2,400	$12,000	$9,600	$2,400

Period	Installment Method[b]			Cost-Recovery-First Method[c]		
	Revenue	Expense	Income	Revenue	Expense	Income
1	$ 1,000	$ 800[f]	$ 200	$ 1,000	$1,000	$ 0
2	1,000	800[f]	200	1,000	1,000	0
3	2,000	1,600[g]	400	2,000	2,000	0
4	4,000	3,200[h]	800	4,000	4,000	0
5	4,000	3,200[h]	800	4,000	1,600	2,400
Total	$12,000	$9,600	$2,400	$12,000	$9,600	$2,400

[a]The cash basis is not allowed for tax or financial reporting if inventories are a material factor in generating income.

[b]The installment method is allowed for financial reporting only if extreme uncertainty exists as to the amount of cash to be collected from customers. Its use for tax purposes is independent of the collectibility of cash.

[c]The cost-recovery-first method is allowed for financial reporting only if extreme uncertainty exists as to the amount of cash to be collected from customers. It is sometimes used for tax purposes.

[d]$1,600/$9,600 \times $12,000.

[e]$4,000/$9,600 \times $12,000.

[f]$1,000/$12,000 \times $9,600.

[g]$2,000/$12,000 \times $9,600.

[h]$4,000/$12,000 $9,600.

Figure 6.2 depicts these distinctions, with examples of each.

A financial statement user who wants to evaluate a firm's ongoing operating profitability will likely focus on income items in the upper left cell. A financial statement user who wants to

FIGURE 6.2   Nature of Income Items with Examples

project net income of prior periods into the future would likely focus on the two "recurring income" cells. Income items in the nonrecurring cells should not affect ongoing assessments of profitability. This section considers the reporting of each type of income item.

Distinguishing Revenue from Gains and Expenses from Losses

Accountants distinguish between revenues and expenses on the one hand and gains and losses on the other. Revenues and expenses result from the recurring, primary operating activities of a business (upper left cell in **Figure 6.2**). Income items discussed thus far in this book fall into this first category. Gains and losses result from either peripheral activities (lower left cell) or nonrecurring activities (upper and lower right cells). A second distinction is that accounting reports revenues and expenses in gross amounts, whereas it reports gains and losses as net amounts. The following examples illustrate this distinction.

Example 12   IBM sells a computer to a customer for $400,000. The computer cost IBM $300,000 to manufacture. IBM records this sale as follows:

Cash (Asset Increase)	400,000	
Retained Earnings (Sales Revenue) (Shareholders' Equity Increase) . .		400,000
To record sale.		
Retained Earnings (Cost of Goods Sold) (Shareholders' Equity Decrease) . .	300,000	
Finished Goods Inventory (Asset Decrease)		300,000
To record the cost of goods sold.		

This transaction fits into the upper left cell of **Figure 6.2** (primary/recurring). The income statement reports both gross sales revenue and gross cost of goods sold, providing information to the financial statement user regarding both the manufacturing cost of the computer and IBM's ability to mark up this cost in setting selling prices. The $100,000 net amount never appears as a separate line item in the body of the income statement. Pretax income includes the $100,000 as part of the difference between revenues and expenses.

Example 13   The GAP, a retail clothing chain, sells computers previously used for processing data in its stores. This sale relates only peripherally to The GAP's primary operating activity, which is to sell casual clothes. Assume that the computers originally cost $500,000 and have $200,000 of accumulated depreciation at the time of sale. Thus, the computers have a net book value of $300,000. The sale of these computers for $400,000 results in the following journal entry on The GAP's books:

Cash (Asset Increase)	400,000	
Accumulated Depreciation (Asset Increase)	200,000	
Equipment (Asset Decrease)		500,000
Retained Earnings (Gain on Sale of Equipment) (Shareholders' Equity Increase)		100,000

Disposal of computers for $100,000 more than book value.

This transaction fits into the lower left cell of **Figure 6.2** (peripheral/recurring). Illustrating **net versus gross reporting of income items**, the income statement reports only the $100,000 gain on the sale, not the selling price of $400,000 nor the book value of $300,000. The income statement reports gains and losses at net instead of gross amounts because, presumably, financial statement users do not need information on the components of either peripheral or nonrecurring income items.

Note that both revenues and gains appear as credits in journal entries and increase Retained Earnings. Both expenses and losses appear as debits in journal entries and reduce Retained Earnings. To repeat, report revenues and expenses at gross amounts but gains and losses at net amounts.

An International Perspective

The IASB says that a firm should recognize revenue when

1. the seller has transferred significant risks and rewards of ownership to the buyer;
2. managerial involvement and control has passed from the seller to the buyer;
3. the seller can reliably measure the amount of revenue;
4. it is probable that the seller will receive economic benefits; and
5. the seller can reliably measure the costs (including future costs) of the transaction.[6]

You can see that these criteria do not use the same words that we have used, but the concepts do not differ from those we discuss in this chapter. The IASB explicitly states that it prefers

- the allowance method for uncollectibles when the firm recognizes the revenue,
- the percentage-of-completion method when the seller provides services, and
- the matching principles for timing of expense recognition.[7]

For construction contracts, the IASB prefers the percentage-of-completion method when the firm can "measure or reliably estimate . . . total revenue, past and future costs, and the stage of completion." If the firm cannot measure the outcome reliably, then the firm should use the cost-recovery-first method.[8]

Summary

Chapter 5 points out that financial analysts care about the operating profitability of a firm. **Chapters 3** and **6** discuss the underlying concepts, accounting procedures, and uses of the income statement. The most important underlying concepts involve the measurement of revenues and expenses following the principles of the accrual basis of accounting. The accrual basis provides operating performance measures superior to those provided by the cash basis because the accrual basis matches revenues (the results of the firm's outputs) with expenses (its inputs). Imprecision in this matching occurs when the timing of cash receipts and disbursements deviates from the timing of revenue and expense recognition. Additional interpretative issues arise when a firm's income statement includes unusual or nonrecurring income items. The financial statement user must give adequate consideration to the recurring or nonrecurring nature of various income items in both assessing a firm's past operating performance and predicting its likely future performance.

---

[6] International Accounting Standards Committee, *Statement No. 18*, "Revenue," 1984, revised and reissued 1995.

[7] *Ibid.*

[8] International Accounting Standards Committee, *Statement No. 11*, "Construction Contracts," 1980.

Appendix 6.1: Effects on the Statement of Cash Flows of Transactions Involving Accounts Receivable

From this point forward, most chapters contain an appendix describing the effects that the accounting treatments of the chapter have on the statement of cash flows. In describing effects in the derivation of cash flow from operations, we discuss both the direct and the indirect method. Recall that the direct method lists cash inflows from revenues and cash outflows for expenses. The indirect method begins the derivation of cash flow from operations with net income and then adjusts net income for noncash portions of revenues and expenses.

Accounts Receivable

The question that an analyst would raise regarding cash flows and accounts receivable is: How much cash did a firm collect from customers during a period? To illustrate the adjustments to compute cash flow from operations, consider the data in **Exhibit 6.7**.

EXHIBIT 6.7	Data Related to Accounts Receivable and Allowance for Uncollectible Accounts		
	Accounts Receivable Gross	**Allowance for Uncollectible Accounts**	**Accounts Receivable Net**
Balance, January 1, Year 10	$ 100	$(20)	$ 80
Sales on Accounts during Year 10	1,000	—	1,000
Cash Collections during Year 10	(700)	—	(700)
Bad Debt Expense for Year 10	—	(15)	(15)
Write off of Uncollectible Accounts during Year 10	(12)	12	—
Balance, December 31, Year 10	$ 388	$(23)	$ 365

Cash flow from operations is $700. To compute this amount under the direct method, subtract from sales revenue the increase in accounts receivable (net) and the amount of bad debt expense, as the following analysis shows:

Sales Revenue for Year 10	$1,000
Less Bad Debt Expense for Year 10	(15)
Less Increase in Accounts Receivable (Net) (= $365 − $80) during Year 10	(285)
Cash Inflows from Sales during Year 10	$ 700

Why subtract bad debt expense from gross sales in computing cash collected from customers? We subtract Bad Debt Expense in the income statement to reduce the gross amount of sales to the amount that the firm expects to collect in cash. In this case, the firm expects to collect only $985 in cash. Net income excludes the portion of gross sales that the firm never expects to collect in cash. Based on this rationale, some accountants treat the provision for uncollectible accounts as a revenue contra instead of as an expense. Thus, we might express the adjustment above as follows:

Sales Revenue for Year 10	$1,000
Less Estimated Uncollectibles for Year 10 (revenue contra)	(15)
Net Sales	$ 985
Less Increase in Accounts Receivable (Net) (= $365 − $80) during Year 10	(285)
Cash Inflows from Sales during Year 10	$ 700

Once we compute net sales for the period, we can measure collections of that amount. If accounts receivable (net) do not change, we collect exactly that net revenue amount. If accounts receivable (net) increase, we collect the amount of net sales less the increase in accounts receivable (net). If accounts receivable (net) decrease, we collect the amount of net sales and, in addition, the amount by which net receivables decreased.

To compute cash flow from operations under the indirect method, subtract the increase in accounts receivable (net) from revenues to reach cash flow from operations, as the following analysis shows:

Net Income for Year 10 includes Net Revenue of $1,000 − $15	$ 985
Less Increase in Accounts Receivable, Net (= $365 − $80) during Year 10	(285)
Cash Flow from Operations during Year 10	$ 700

Note that there is no need to subtract bad debt expense under the indirect method because net income already includes a subtraction for it. If the amount of accounts receivable (net) decreases during the period, add the amount of the decrease to net income in deriving cash flow from operations.

Solutions to Self-Study Problems

SUGGESTED SOLUTION TO PROBLEM 6.1 FOR SELF-STUDY

a. Should Kodak recognize revenue (1) when it initially ships the cameras to Wal-Mart, or (2) wait until the consigned cameras are sold and Wal-Mart remits the selling price minus Wal-Mart's fee back to Kodak? At the time of initial shipment to Wal-Mart, Kodak has incurred most of its costs. Experience should provide Kodak with sufficient evidence to estimate the cost of lost and damaged cameras. Thus, the first criterion for revenue recognition of substantial performance appears to be met. The second criterion, however, has not been met. The amount that Kodak receives depends on the price at which Wal-Mart sells the cameras. This price depends on the demand for cameras in general, on new products offered by competitors, and similar factors. If Wal-Mart has to mark down the selling price in order to sell certain cameras, the amount that Kodak receives will decrease. The timing of this payment is also uncertain. Wal-Mart may fail to sell some cameras and then return them to Kodak. Thus, Kodak should recognize revenue when it receives the payment from Wal-Mart or, perhaps, earlier when Wal-Mart notifies Kodak of the amounts it will remit later for sales this period.

b. Should Burlington Mills recognize revenue (1) at the completion of manufacturing and delivery to the warehouse, or (2) upon final delivery to Nike? The criteria for revenue recognition appear to be met at the completion of manufacturing and delivery to the warehouse. Burlington Mills has performed most of the work it undertook to do. Nike bears the additional cost of storage. The custom nature of the products and storage in an independent warehouse preclude Burlington Mills from selling the products to others. Nike has promised to pay for these goods and Burlington Mills can estimate the amount and timing of cash it will receive from Nike. Thus, the rewards and risks of ownership appear to shift to Nike upon delivery to the warehouse. This sort of transaction, with important differences, served as the foundation for important frauds in the 1990s. The selling firm would bill the goods to the buyer to whom it promised an unconditional right of refusal or return. The amount of goods purchased exceeded the buyer's usual quantities. In this case, with substantial returns nearly certain and unpredictable, the firm should not recognize revenue.

c. Should Nordstrom recognize revenue (1) when it receives customers' initial deposits and places the products in a storeroom, or (2) when customers make the final payment and take the products? Because Nordstrom retains the rewards and risks of ownership until the customers make the final payments and accept the merchandise, Nordstrom should not recognize revenue at the time of initial deposit. An important part of substantial performance is providing storage services. The fact of initial deposit does not satisfy the second criterion for revenue recognition, the requirement that the seller receive cash or a receivable for a specific amount. Uncertainty exists as to if and when customers will make payments after the initial deposit. Nordstrom does not have an enforceable right to the subsequent payments.

d. Costco might recognize the membership fee as revenue (1) when it receives the fee at the beginning of the year, (2) ratably over the year, or (3) at the end of the year at completion of the refund period. Costco does not meet the first criterion for revenue recognition of substantial performance at the beginning of the year because it has not yet provided services. Costco provides services during the year and has a claim on proportionate parts of the membership fee as time passes. Thus, it should recognize revenue ratably over the year. Awaiting completion of the year before recognizing any revenue probably delays recognition of revenue past the time of satisfying the revenue recognition criteria. Even so, conservative accountants might delay revenue recognition until the end of the year.

e. Mall Development Corporation satisfies the criteria for revenue recognition with respect to the fixed monthly rental each month and should recognize that portion of the revenue monthly. The ultimate amount of the revenue it will recognize on the contingent portion of the rent depends on the sales of each lessee for the year. Although Mall Development Corporation likely estimates the probable amount of contingent rent when it sets the fixed monthly rent, too much uncertainty exists as to the amount of the contingent rent to justify recognizing that portion of revenue until it knows the amount. If lessees report sales monthly, then Mall Development Corporation can begin recognizing revenue from the contingent rents as soon as the lessee reaches the stated sales threshold. Periodic recognition of the contingent rent as revenue requires, however, that Mall Development Corporation estimate the amounts of sales returns and uncollectible accounts. If it cannot reasonably estimate these amounts before the end of the year, then it must delay recognition of the contingent rent until then.

SUGGESTED SOLUTION TO PROBLEM 6.2 FOR SELF-STUDY

(Dee's Department Store; accounting for uncollectible accounts.)

a. Retained Earnings (Bad Debt Expense) (Shareholders' Equity Decrease) . .	40,000	
Accounts Receivable (Asset Decrease)		40,000
To write off uncollectible accounts using the direct write-off method for Year 4.		
b. Retained Earnings (Bad Debt Expense) (Shareholders' Equity Decrease) . .	100,000	
Allowance for Uncollectible Accounts (Asset Decrease)		100,000
To provide for estimated uncollectible accounts using the allowance method for Year 4; 0.02 × $5,000,000 = $100,000.		
Allowance for Uncollectible Accounts (Asset Increase)	40,000	
Accounts Receivable (Asset Decrease)		40,000
To write off uncollectible accounts using the allowance method for Year 4.		
c. Retained Earnings (Bad Debt Expense) (Shareholders' Equity Decrease) . .	110,000	
Accounts Receivable (Asset Decrease)		110,000
To write off uncollectible accounts using the direct write-off method for Year 5.		
d. Retained Earnings (Bad Debt Expense) (Shareholders' Equity Decrease) . .	120,000	
Allowance for Uncollectible Accounts (Asset Decrease)		120,000
To provide for estimated uncollectible accounts using the allowance method for Year 5; 0.02 × $6,000,000 = $120,000.		
Allowance for Uncollectible Accounts (Asset Increase)	110,000	
Accounts Receivable (Asset Decrease)		110,000
To write off uncollectible accounts using the allowance method for Year 5.		
e. Retained Earnings (Bad Debt Expense) (Shareholders' Equity Decrease) . .	5,000	
Allowance for Uncollectible Accounts (Asset Decrease)		5,000
To adjust the Allowance for Uncollectible Accounts to the desired ending balance of $75,000. The balance in the Allowance for Uncollectible Accounts after the entries in parts **b** and **d** is $70,000 (= $100,000 − $40,000 + $120,000 − $110,000).		

Note: Most firms would likely combine the provision for bad debts in part **d** ($120,000) and part **e** ($5,000) into a single entry.

SUGGESTED SOLUTION TO PROBLEM 6.3 FOR SELF-STUDY

(Blount Construction Company; income recognition for contractor.)

a. Percentage-of-completion method:

Year	Incremental Percentage Complete	Revenue Recognized	Expenses Recognized	Net Income
2	12/36 (0.333)	$1,500,000	$1,200,000	$300,000
3	20/36 (0.556)	2,500,000	2,000,000	500,000
4	4/36 (0.111)	500,000	400,000	100,000
Total	36/36 (1.000)	$4,500,000	$3,600,000	$900,000

b. Completed contract method:

Year	Revenue Recognized	Expenses Recognized	Net Income
2	$ 0	$ 0	$ 0
3	0	0	0
4	4,500,000	3,600,000	900,000
Total	$4,500,000	$3,600,000	$900,000

c. Installment method:

Year	Cash Collected (= revenue)	Fraction of Cash Collected	Expenses (= fraction × total cost)	Net Income
2	$1,000,000	1.0/4.5	$ 800,000	$200,000
3	1,500,000	1.5/4.5	1,200,000	300,000
4	2,000,000	2.0/4.5	1,600,000	400,000
Total	$4,500,000	1.0	$3,600,000	$900,000

d. Cost-recovery-first method:

Year	Cash Collected (= revenue)	Expenses Recognized	Net Income
2	$1,000,000	$1,000,000	$ 0
3	1,500,000	1,500,000	0
4	2,000,000	1,100,000	900,000
Total	$4,500,000	$3,600,000	$900,000

Key Terms and Concepts

Generally accepted accounting principles (GAAP)
Economic consequences
Quality of earnings
Direct write-off method
Allowance method
Percentage-of-sales procedure for estimating uncollectibles
Aging-of-accounts-receivable procedure for estimating uncollectibles
Sales discounts
Sales returns
Sales allowances
Assigning accounts receivable
Pledging accounts receivable
Factoring accounts receivable
Percentage-of-completion method
Completed contract, or completed sale, method
Installment method
Cost-recovery-first method
Net versus gross reporting of income items

For additional student resources, content, and interactive quizzes for this chapter visit the FACMU website:
http://facmu.swlearning.com

QUESTIONS

1. Review the meaning of the terms and concepts listed above in Key Terms and Concepts.

2. Which of the two methods for treating uncollectible accounts (direct write-off or allowance) results in recognizing income reductions earlier rather than later? Explain.

3. The direct write-off and the allowance method for uncollectible accounts both involve matching. How does this matching differ between the two methods?

4. **a.** Under what conditions will the direct write-off method and the allowance method result in approximately the same bad debt expense each period?

   b. Under what conditions will the direct write-off method and the allowance method result in approximately the same amount for accounts receivable (net) on the balance sheet?

5. **a.** An old wisdom in tennis holds that if your first serves are always good, you are not hitting them hard enough. An analogous statement in business might be that if you have no uncollectible accounts, you probably are not selling enough on credit. Comment on the validity and parallelism of these statements.

   b. When are more uncollectible accounts better than less uncollectible accounts?

   c. When is a higher percentage of uncollectible accounts better than a lower percentage?

6. Under what circumstances will the Allowance for Uncollectible Accounts have a debit balance during the accounting period? The balance sheet figure for the Allowance for Uncollectible Accounts at the end of the period should never show a debit balance. Why?

7. Construction companies often use the percentage-of-completion method. Why doesn't a typical manufacturing firm use this method of income recognition?

8. Both the installment method and the cost-recovery-first method recognize revenue when a firm collects cash. Why, then, does the pattern of income (that is, revenues minus expenses) over time differ under these two methods?

9. **Chapter 3** said, "From this point on in the book, all discussions assume use of the accrual basis of accounting." This chapter introduces two methods of revenue recognition based on cash—the installment and cost recovery first methods. Explain why the statement quoted from **Chapter 3** remains true.

10. "When the total amount of cash that a firm expects to collect from a customer is highly uncertain, the cost-recovery-first method seems more appropriate than the installment method." Explain.

11. Economists typically define income as an increase in value, or wealth, while a firm holds assets. Accountants typically recognize income when the criteria for revenue recognition are satisfied. Why does the accountants' approach to income recognition differ from that of economists?

12. "The usefulness of the income statement declines as the quality of earnings declines." Do you agree? Why or why not?

SHORT EXERCISES

13. **Allowance method for uncollectible accounts.** Diversified Technologies opened for business on January 2, Year 1. Sales on accounts during Year 1 totaled $126,900. Collections from customers from sales on account during Year 1 totaled $94,300. Diversified Technologies estimates that it will ultimately not collect 4 percent of sales on account. During Year 1, the firm wrote off $2,200 of accounts receivable as uncollectible. The firm uses the allowance method for uncollectible accounts.

    a. Compute the amount of bad debt expense for Year 1.

    b. Compute the net amount at which accounts receivable will appear on the balance sheet on December 31, Year 1.

14. **Aging accounts receivable.** York Company's accounts receivable show the following balances:

Age of Accounts	Balance Receivable
0–30 Days	$1,200,000
31–60 Days	255,000
61–120 Days	75,000
More than 120 Days	30,000

York Company uses the aging-of-accounts-receivable procedure for uncollectible accounts. The credit balance in the Allowance for Uncollectible Accounts is now $16,000. Analysis of recent collection experience suggests that the following percentages be used to compute the estimates of amounts that will eventually prove uncollectible: 0–30 days, half of 1.0 percent; 31–60 days, 1.0 percent; 61–120 days, 10 percent; and more than 120 days, 30 percent. Prepare the indicated entry to provide for estimated uncollectible accounts.

15. **Reconstructing events when using the allowance method.** Selected data from the accounts of Seward Corporation appear below.

	January 1	December 31
Accounts Receivable—Gross	$82,900 Dr.	$ 87,300 Dr.
Allowance for Uncollectible Accounts	8,700 Cr.	9,100 Cr.
Retained Earnings (Bad Debt Expense)	—	4,800 Dr.
Retained Earnings (Sales)	—	240,000 Cr.

The firm makes all sales on account. There were no recoveries during the year of accounts written off in previous years.

Give the journal entries for the following transactions and events during the year:

a. Sales on account
b. Provision for estimated uncollectible accounts
c. Write-off of actual uncollectible accounts
d. Collection of cash from customers from sales on account

16. **Allowance method; reconstructing journal entry from events.** (From a problem by S. A. Zeff.) During Year 6, Pandora Company wrote off $2,200 of accounts receivable as uncollectible. Pandora Company collected no cash during Year 6 of amounts it had written off in previous years. The balance in the Allowance for Uncollectibles Accounts account on the balance sheet was $3,500 at the beginning of Year 6 and $5,000 at the end of Year 6. Present the journal entry that the company made to provide for estimated uncollectibles during Year 6.

17. **Allowance method; reconstructing journal entries from events.** (From a problem by S.A. Zeff.) The balance sheets of Milton Corporation on December 31, Year 1 and Year 2, showed gross accounts receivable of $15,200,000 and $17,600,000, respectively. The balances in the Allowance for Uncollectible Accounts account at the beginning and end of Year 2 were credits of $1,400,000 and $1,550,000, respectively. The income statement for Year 2 shows that the expense for estimated uncollectible accounts was $750,000, which was 1 percent of sales. The firm makes all sales on account. There were no recoveries during Year 2 of accounts written off in previous years. Give all the journal entries made during Year 2 that have an effect on Accounts Receivable and Allowance for Uncollectible Accounts.

18. **Reconstructing events from journal entries.** Give the likely transaction or event that would result in making each of the independent journal entries that follow.

a. Retained Earnings (Bad Debt Expense) (Shareholders' Equity Decrease)	2,300	
Allowance for Uncollectible Accounts (Asset Decrease)		2,300
b. Allowance for Uncollectible Accounts (Asset Increase)	450	
Accounts Receivable (Asset Decrease)		450
c. Retained Earnings (Bad Debt Expense) (Shareholders' Equity Decrease) .	495	
Accounts Receivable (Asset Decrease)		495

19. **Percentage-of-completion and completed contract methods of income recognition.** The Shannon Construction Company agreed to build a warehouse for $6,000,000. Expected and actual costs to construct the warehouse were as follows: Year 1, $1,200,000; Year 2, $3,000,000; and Year 3, $600,000. The firm completed the warehouse in Year 3.

Compute revenue, expense, and income before income taxes for Year 1, Year 2, and Year 3 using the percentage-of-completion method and the completed contract method.

20. **Installment and cost-recovery-first methods of income recognition.** Cunningham Realty Partners sold a tract of land costing $80,000 to a manufacturing firm for $120,000. The manufacturing firm agreed to pay $30,000 per year for four years (plus interest).

Compute revenue, expense, and income before income taxes for each of the four years using the installment method and the cost-recovery-first method. Ignore interest.

EXERCISES

21. **Journal entries for the allowance method.** Data related to sales on account of Heath Company for its first three years of operations appear below:

| Year | Sales on Account | Accounts Written Off as Uncollectible in Year | | | | | |
		6	7	8	9	10	Total
6	$ 340,000	$1,800	$5,800	$ 3,000	—	—	$10,600
7	450,000	—	2,500	8,200	$ 3,400	—	14,100
8	580,000	—	—	2,900	12,700	$3,300	17,900
	$1,370,000	$1,800	$8,300	$14,100	$16,100	$3,300	$42,600

Heath Company estimates that 3 percent of sales on account will ultimately become uncollectible. Uncollectible accounts generally occur within three years of the year of sale.
a. Prepare journal entries to recognize bad debt expense and to write off uncollectible accounts for Year 6, Year 7, and Year 8 using the allowance method.
b. Does 3 percent of sales on account appear to be a reasonable rate for estimating uncollectibles?

22. **Journal entries for the allowance method.** Data related to sales on account of Schneider Corporation appear below:

| Year | Sales on Account | Accounts Written Off as Uncollectible in Year | | | | | |
		1	2	3	4	5	Total
1	$ 750,000	$1,300	$ 8,700	$ 3,900	—	—	$ 13,900
2	1,200,000	—	2,500	16,600	$ 3,800	—	22,900
3	2,400,000	—	—	3,100	37,800	$4,800	45,700
	$4,350,000	$1,300	$11,200	$23,600	$41,600	$4,800	$82,500

Schneider Corporation estimates that 2 percent of sales on account will ultimately become uncollectible. Uncollectible accounts generally occur within three years of the year of sale.
a. Prepare journal entries to recognize bad debt expense and to write off uncollectible accounts for Year 1, Year 2, and Year 3 using the allowance method.
b. Does 2 percent of sales on account appear to be a reasonable rate for estimating uncollectibles?

23. **Reconstructing events when using the allowance method.** Selected data from the accounts of Logue Corporation before recognizing bad debt expense for the year appear below:

	January 1	December 31
Accounts Receivable—Gross	$115,900 Dr.	$122,700 Dr.
Allowance for Uncollectible Accounts	18,200 Cr.	2,900 Dr.
Retained Earnings (Bad Debt Expense)	—	—
Retained Earnings (Sales)	—	450,000 Cr.

Logue Corporation estimates that 6 percent of sales, which are all on account, will become uncollectible. There were no recoveries during the year of accounts written off in previous years.
    Give journal entries for the following transactions or events of Logue Corporation that account for the changes in the accounts shown above:
a. Sales on account during the year
b. Write-off of actual uncollectible accounts during the year
c. Collection of cash from customers from sales on account during the year
d. Provision for the year for estimated uncollectible accounts

24. **Aging accounts receivable.** Dove Company's accounts receivable show the following balances by age:

Age of Accounts	Balance Receivable
0–30 Days	$1,200,000
0–30 Days	$400,000
31–60 Days	90,000
61–120 Days	40,000
More than 120 Days	20,000

The credit balance in the Allowance for Uncollectible Accounts is now $17,200.

Dove Company's independent auditors suggest that the following percentages be used to compute the estimates of amounts that will eventually prove uncollectible: 0–30 days, half of 1.0 percent; 31–60 days, 1.0 percent; 61–120 days, 10 percent; and more than 120 days, 70 percent. Prepare a journal entry that will carry out the auditors' suggestion.

25. **Effects of transactions involving suppliers and customers on cash flows.** Refer to the excerpts from the accounting records of Home and Office Depot in **Exhibit 6.8**. These are the balances in various accounts at the beginning and the end of the year. The amounts shown for sales revenue, bad debt expense, and cost of merchandise sold are their income statement amounts for the year. Home and Office Depot deals with
   * many retail customers, some of whom have not paid for goods they have purchased, and
   * many suppliers of goods, some of whom the firm has paid for orders not yet received and some of whom have delivered goods for which the firm has not yet paid.

EXHIBIT 6.8	HOME AND OFFICE DEPOT Selected Details from Financial Statements For the Current Year (Exercise 25)		
		Beginning of Year	**End of Year**
PARTIAL BALANCE SHEETS			
Accounts Receivable from Retail Customers		$ 8,000	$ 8,600
Less Allowance for Uncollectible Retail Receivables		(700)	(750)
Advances to Suppliers of Retail Merchandise		10,000	10,400
Inventory of Retail Merchandise		11,000	11,200
Total Assets		$28,300	$ 29,450
Accounts Payable to Suppliers of Retail Merchandise		7,000	7,500
All Other Accounts (Net)		21,300	21,950
Totals		$28,300	$ 29,450
PARTIAL INCOME STATEMENT FOR THE CURRENT YEAR			
Sales Revenue from Retail Customers			130,000
Bad Debt Expense		2,000	
Cost of Retail Merchandise Sold		85,000	
Less: Total Expenses			(87,000)
Income			$ 63,000

Home and Office Depot settles all its accounts with customers and suppliers with cash, never with noncash assets.
   a. Calculate the amount of cash the firm received from its customers during the year.
   b. Calculate the amount of cash the firm paid to its suppliers of retail merchandise during the year.

26. **Revenue recognition for various types of businesses.** Discuss when each of the following types of businesses is likely to recognize revenue:
   a. A shoe store
   b. A shipbuilding firm constructing an aircraft carrier under a government contract
   c. A real estate developer selling lots on long-term contracts with small down payments required

    d. A barbershop

    e. A citrus-growing firm

    f. A producer of television movies working under the condition that the rights to the movies are sold to a television network for the first three years and all rights thereafter revert to the producer

    g. A residential real estate developer who constructs only "speculative" houses and later sells the houses to buyers

    h. A producer of fine whiskey that is aged from 6 to 12 years before sale

    i. A savings and loan association lending money for home mortgages

    j. A travel agency that sells tickets in one period and has customers take trips or return tickets in the next period

    k. A printer who prints only custom-order stationery

    l. A seller to food stores of trading stamps redeemable by food store customers for various household products

    m. A wholesale food distributor

    n. A livestock rancher

    o. A shipping company that loads cargo in one accounting period, carries cargo across the ocean in a second accounting period, and unloads the cargo in a third period; the shipping is all done under contract, and cash collection of shipping charges is relatively certain.

27. Income recognition for various businesses. Discuss when each of the following businesses should recognize revenue and any income measurement issues that arise.

    a. Company A develops software and sells it to customers for an up-front fee. Company A provides these customers with password-protected access to its web site for two years after delivery of the software. With this access, customers can download certain data and other software. Company A has an obligation to provide updates on its web site.

    b. Company B develops software and sells it to newly formed storage application service providers (SAPs), who promise to pay for the software over the next two years. These SAPs in turn place the software on their web sites and sell rights to access the software to its customers.

    c. Company C develops software that it places on its web site. It sells rights to access this software on-line to its customers for a period of two years. Customers pay an up-front fee for the right to access the software.

    d. Company D maintains an auction site on the web. It charges customers an up-front fee to list products for sale and a transaction fee when a sale takes place. The transaction fee is refundable if the auction winner fails to honor its commitment to purchase the product.

    e. Company E sells products of various companies on its web site. Company E transmits customers' purchase requests to the various supplier companies, who fill the orders. Customers charge for their purchases on third-party credit cards. Company E receives a fee from the supplier companies for each item sold.

    f. Company F sells products of various companies on its web site. It promises to sell a minimum number of items each month and pays storage and insurance costs for that minimum number of units. Actual storage of these units takes place at the suppliers' warehouse. The suppliers also handle shipments to customers. Customers charge for their purchases on third-party credit cards.

    g. Company G manufactures and sells personal computers (PCs). Customers receive a $400 rebate on the purchase of the computer if they will purchase Internet access services for three years after the purchase of the computer. Customers mail their rebate coupon to the Internet service provider (called an *ISP;* for example, AOL, AT&T). The ISP bears 90 percent on the initial cost of the rebate and the PC manufacturer bears the other 10 percent. If customers do not subscribe for the full three-year period, the parties reallocate the cost of the rebate, initially borne $360 (= 0.90 × $400) by the ISP and $40 (= 0.10 × $400) by the manufacturer, resulting in the PC manufacturer's paying the ISP to reduce the ISP's share of the rebate's cost from $360 to a smaller amount.

    h. Company H sells advertising space on its web site to other companies. For an up-front fee, Company H guarantees a certain minimum number of hits, viewings, or click-throughs each month of the one-year contract period. It must return a pro rata portion of the fee if the hits and click-throughs fall short of the guarantee.

    i. Company I sells advertising space on its web site to other companies. It recently received 10,000 shares of common stock of Upstart Company in payment for certain advertising space. Upstart Company intends to make an initial public offering of its common stock in six months. At the most recent financing round, venture capitalists paid $10 per share for the common stock.

j. Company J and Company K both maintain web sites. Each company "sells" advertising space to the other company for an agreed-upon period, with no money changing hands.

PROBLEMS AND CASES

28. Analyzing changes in accounts receivable. Selected data from the financial statements of American Express appear below (amounts in millions).

	Year 4	Year 5	Year 6	Year 7
Balance Sheet				
Accounts and Notes Receivable, net of allowance for uncollectible accounts of $1,419 at the end of Year 4, $1,411 at the end of Year 5, $1,559 at the end of Year 6, and $1,728 at the end of Year 7	$41,883	$43,278	$50,049	$56,631
Income Statement				
Revenues on Account		$19,132	$21,278	$23,675
Bad Debt Expense		$ 2,187	$ 2,212	$ 2,439

a. Prepare journal entries for Year 5, Year 6, and Year 7 for the following events:
   (1) Revenues on account
   (2) Provision for estimated uncollectibles
   (3) Write-off of actual uncollectible accounts
   (4) Collection of cash from customers
b. Compute the amount of the following ratios:
   (1) Accounts receivable turnover ratio for Year 5, Year 6, and Year 7
   (2) Bad debt expense divided by revenues on account for Year 5, Year 6, and Year 7
   (3) Allowance for uncollectible accounts divided by accounts receivable (gross) at the end of Year 5, Year 6, and Year 7
   (4) Write-offs of actual uncollectible accounts divided by average accounts receivable (gross) for Year 5, Year 6, and Year 7
c. What do the ratios computed in part **b** suggest about the collection experience of American Express during the three-year period?

29. Analyzing changes in accounts receivable. The financial statements and notes for May Department Stores reveal the following for four recent years (amounts in millions):

	Year 9	Year 10	Year 11	Year 12
Total Sales	$8,330	$9,456	$10,035	$10,615
Credit Sales/Total Sales	62.2%	64.9%	66.9%	68.7%
Bad Debt Expense	$57	$64	$82	$96

	End of Year				
	Year 8	Year 9	Year 10	Year 11	Year 12
Accounts Receivable, Gross	$1,592	$2,099	$2,223	$2,456	$2,607
Less Allowance for Uncollectible Accounts	(47)	(61)	(66)	(84)	(99)
Accounts Receivable, Net	$1,545	$2,038	$2,157	$2,372	$2,508

a. Compute the amount of accounts written off as uncollectible during Year 9, Year 10, Year 11, and Year 12.
b. Compute the amount of cash collections from credit customers during Year 9, Year 10, Year 11, and Year 12.
c. Calculate the accounts receivable turnover ratio for Year 9, Year 10, Year 11, and Year 12 using total sales in the numerator and average accounts receivable (net) in the denominator.
d. Repeat part **c** but use credit sales in the numerator.
e. What are the likely reasons for the different trends in the two measures of the accounts receivable turnover ratio in parts **c** and **d**?

30. Analyzing changes in accounts receivable. Selected data from the financial statements of Sears, a retail department store chain, appear below (amounts in millions).

	Year 4	Year 5	Year 6	Year 7
Balance Sheet				
Accounts and Notes Receivable, net of allowance for uncollectible accounts of $1,113 at the end of Year 6, $974 at the end of Year 7, $760 at the end of Year 8, and $686 at the end of Year 9	$19,843	$17,972	$18,033	$17,317
Income Statement				
Sales on Account		$39,953	$39,484	$40,937
Bad Debt Expense		$ 1,287	$ 871	$ 884

a. Prepare journal entries for Year 7, Year 8, and Year 9 for the following events:
  (1) Sales on account
  (2) Bad debt Expense
  (3) Write-off of actual uncollectible accounts
  (4) Collection of cash from customers
b. Compute the amount of the following ratios:
  (1) Accounts receivable turnover ratio for Year 7, Year 8, and Year 9
  (2) Bad debt expense divided by sales on account for Year 7, Year 8, and Year 9
  (3) Allowance for uncollectible accounts divided by accounts receivable (gross) at the end of Year 7, Year 8, and Year 9
  (4) Write-offs of actual uncollectible accounts divided by average accounts receivable (gross) for Year 7, Year 8, and Year 9
c. What do the ratios computed in part **b** suggest about the collection experience of Sears during the three-year period?

31. Reconstructing transactions affecting accounts receivable and uncollectible accounts. The sales, all on account, of Pins Company in Year 10, its first year of operations, were $700,000. Collections totaled $500,000. On December 31, Year 10, Pins Company estimated that 2 percent of all sales would probably be uncollectible. On that date, Pins Company wrote off specific accounts in the amount of $8,000.

The balances in selected accounts on December 31, *Year 11*, are as follows:

Accounts Receivable (Dr.)	300,000	
Allowance for Uncollectible Accounts (Dr.)	10,000	
Retained Earnings (Bad Debt Expense)	—	—
Retained Earnings (Sales) (Cr.)		800,000

The amounts shown for bad debt expense and sales revenue are the amount, if any, recorded in the accounts during Year 11. On December 31, Year 11, Pins Company carried out an aging of its accounts receivable balances and estimated that the Year 11 ending balance of accounts receivable contained $11,000 of probable uncollectibles. That is, the allowance account should have an $11,000 ending credit balance. It made adjusting entries appropriate for this estimate. Some of the $800,000 sales during Year 11 were for cash and some were on account; the problem purposefully does not give the amounts.

a. What was the balance in the Accounts Receivable (gross) account at the end of *Year 10*? Give the amount and whether it was a debit or a credit.
b. What was the balance in the Allowance for Uncollectible Accounts account at the end of *Year 10*? Give the amount and whether it was a debit or a credit.
c. What was bad debt expense for *Year 11*?
d. What was the amount of specific accounts receivable written off as being uncollectible during *Year 11*?
e. What were total cash collections in *Year 11* from customers (for cash sales and collections from customers who had purchased on account in either Year 10 or Year 11)?
f. What was the net balance of accounts receivable included in the balance sheet asset total for December 31, *Year 11*?

32. Effect of errors involving accounts receivable on financial statement ratios. Indicate—using O/S (overstated), U/S (understated), or NO (no effect)—the pre-tax effect of each of the following errors on (1) the rate of return on assets, (2) the accounts receivable turnover, and (3) the debt equity ratio. Each of these ratios is less than 100 percent before discovering the error.

a. A firm using the allowance method neglected to provide for estimated uncollectible accounts at the end of the year.

b. A firm using the allowance method neglected to write off specific accounts as uncollectible at the end of the year.

c. A firm credited a check received from a customer to Advances from Customers even though the customer was paying for purchases previously made on account.

d. A firm recorded as a sale a customer's order received on the last day of the accounting period, even though the firm will not ship the product until the next accounting period.

e. A firm sold goods on account to a particular customer and properly recorded the transactions in the accounts. The customer returned the goods within a few days of the sale, before paying for them, but the firm neglected to record the return on the goods in its accounts. The firm normally treats sales returns as a reduction in Sales Revenue.

33. Income recognition for a nuclear generator manufacturer. General Electric Company agreed on June 15, Year 2, to construct a nuclear generator for Consolidated Edison Company. The contract price of $200 million is to be paid as follows: at the time of signing, $20 million; on December 31, Year 3, $100 million; and at completion on June 30, Year 4, $80 million. General Electric Company incurred the following costs in constructing the generator: Year 2, $42 million; Year 3, $54 million; and Year 4, $24 million. These amounts conformed to original expectations.

a. Calculate the amount of revenue, expense, and income before income taxes for Year 2, Year 3, and Year 4 under each of the following revenue recognition methods:
(1) Percentage-of-completion method
(2) Completed contract method
(3) Installment method
(4) Cost-recovery-first method

b. Which method do you believe provides the best measure of General Electric Company's performance under the contract? Why?

34. Income recognition for a contractor. On October 15, Year 1, Flanikin Construction Company contracted to build a shopping center at a contract price of $180 million. The schedule of expected and actual cash collections and contract costs is as follows:

Year	Cash Collections from Customers	Estimated and Actual Cost Incurred
1	$ 36,000,000	$ 12,000,000
2	45,000,000	36,000,000
3	45,000,000	48,000,000
4	54,000,000	24,000,000
	$180,000,000	$120,000,000

a. Calculate the amount of revenue, expense, and net income for each of the four years under the following revenue recognition methods:
(1) Percentage-of-completion method
(2) Completed contract method
(3) Installment method
(4) Cost-recovery-first method

b. Which method do you believe provides the best measure of Flanikin Construction Company's performance under the contract? Why?

35. Point-of-sale versus installment method of income recognition. The J. C. Spangle catalog division began business on January 1, Year 8. Activities of the company for the first two years are as follows:

EXHIBIT 6.9

Common-Size Income Statements for Selected Companies (Problem 37)

	Amgen	Brown-Forman	Deere	Fluor	Golden West	Merrill Lynch	Rockwell
Revenues							
Sales of Goods	98.7%	99.9%	83.6%	—	—	—	99.3%
Sales of Services	—	—	—	99.7%	2.0%	47.5%	—
Interest on Investments	1.3	0.1	16.4	0.3	98.0	52.5	0.7
Total Revenues	100.0%	100.0%	100.0%	100.0%	100.0%	100.0%	100.0%
Expenses							
Cost of Goods or Services Sold	(14.3)	(35.5)	(69.4)	(95.6)	—	(43.3)	(77.4)
Selling and Administrative	(23.4)	(33.1)	(11.4)	(.6)	(15.9)	—	(12.6)
Other Operating[a]	(26.4)	(15.4)	(3.5)	—	(3.3)	—	—
Interest	(0.7)	(1.3)	(11.0)	(0.2)	(60.4)	(47.2)	(0.9)
Income before Income Taxes	35.2%	14.7%	4.7%	3.6%	20.4%	9.5%	9.1%
Income Tax Expense	(16.1)	(5.9)	(1.6)	(1.3)	(8.4)	(3.9)	(3.5)
Net Income	19.1%	8.8%	3.1%	2.3%	12.0%	5.6%	5.6%
Revenues/Average Total Assets	0.9	1.3	0.7	3.1	0.1	0.1	1.2

[a]Represents research and development costs for Amgen and Deere, excise taxes for Brown-Forman, and a provision for loan losses by Golden West.

Year 8		Year 9
Sales, All on Account	$200,000	$300,000
Collections from Customers:		
On Year 8 Sales	90,000	110,000
On Year 9 Sales	—	120,000
Purchase of Merchandise	180,000	240,000
Inventory of Merchandise at 12/31	60,000	114,000
All Expenses Other Than Merchandise, Paid in Cash	32,000	44,000

a. Prepare income statements for Year 8 and Year 9, assuming that the company uses the accrual basis of accounting and recognizes revenue at the time of sale.

b. Prepare income statements for Year 8 and Year 9, assuming that the company uses the accrual basis of accounting and recognizes revenue at the time of cash collection following the installment method of accounting. "All Expenses Other Than Merchandise, Paid in Cash" are period expenses.

36. **Revenue recognition for a franchise.** Pickin Chicken, Inc., and Country Delight, Inc., both sell franchises for their chicken restaurants. The franchisee receives the right to use the franchisor's products and to benefit from national training and advertising programs. The franchisee agrees to pay $50,000 for exclusive franchise rights in a particular city. Of this amount, the franchisee pays $20,000 on signing the franchise agreement and promises to pay the remainder in five equal annual installments of $6,000 each starting one year after the initial signing payment.

    Pickin Chicken, Inc., recognizes franchise revenue as it signs agreements, whereas Country Delight, Inc., recognizes franchise revenue on an installment basis. In Year 2, each company sold eight franchises. In Year 3, each sold five franchises. In Year 4, neither company sold a franchise.

    a. Calculate the amount of revenue recognized by each company during Year 2, Year 3, Year 4, Year 5, Year 6, Year 7, and Year 8.

    b. When do you think a franchisor should recognize franchise revenue? Why?

37. **Income recognition for various types of business.** Most business firms recognize revenues at the time of sale or delivery of goods and services and, following the principles of the accrual basis of accounting, match expenses either with associated revenues or with the period when they consume resources in operations. Users of financial statements should maintain a questioning attitude as to the appropriateness of recognizing revenues at the time of sale and as to the timing of expense recognition. **Exhibit 6.9** presents common-size income statements for seven firms for a recent year, with all amounts expressed as a percentage of total revenues. **Exhibit 6.9** also indicates the revenues generated by each firm for each dollar of assets in use on average during the year. A brief description of the activities of each firm follows.

    Amgen engages in the development, manufacturing, and marketing of biotechnology products. Developing and obtaining approval of biotechnology products takes 10 or more years. Amgen has two principal products that it manufactures and markets and several more products in the development pipeline.

    Brown-Forman is a distiller of hard liquors. After combining the ingredients, the company ages the liquors for five or more years before sale.

    Deere manufactures farm equipment. It sells this equipment to a network of independent distributors, who in turn sell the equipment to final consumers. Deere provides financing and insurance services both to its distributors and to final consumers.

    Fluor engages in construction services on multiyear construction projects. It subcontracts most of the actual construction work and receives a fee for its services.

    Golden West is a savings and loan company. It takes deposits from customers and lends funds, primarily to individuals for home mortgages. Customers typically pay a fee (called "points") at the time of loan origination based on the amount borrowed. Their monthly mortgage payments include interest on the outstanding loan balance and a partial repayment of the principal of the loan.

    Merrill Lynch engages in the securities business. It obtains funds primarily from short-term capital market sources and invests the funds primarily in short-term, readily marketable financial instruments. It attempts to generate an excess of investment returns over the cost of the funds invested. Merrill Lynch also offers fee-based services, such as financial consulting, buying and selling securities for customers, securities underwriting, and investment management.

Rockwell is a technology-based electronics and aerospace company. It engages in research and development on behalf of its customers, which include the U.S. government (space shuttle program, defense electronics) and private-sector entities. Its contracts tend to run for many years on a constantly renewed basis.

   a. When should each of these companies recognize revenue? What unique issues does each company face in the recognition of expenses?

   b. Suggest possible reasons for differences in the net income divided by revenues percentages for these companies.

38. Meaning of Allowance for Uncollectible Accounts account. Indicate whether each of the following accurately describes the meaning of the Allowance for Uncollectible Accounts account when properly used. If the description does not apply to this account, discuss why it does not.

   a. Assets available in case customers don't later pay what they owe.

   b. Cash available in case customers don't later pay what they owe.

   c. Estimates of the amount that customers who purchased goods this period, but who have not yet paid, and won't later pay.

   d. Estimates of the amount of goods purchased by customers, whether paid or not, which we won't collect later.

   e. Estimates of the amount that customers who purchased goods at any time, but who have not yet paid, and won't later pay.

   f. Estimates of amount the firm will owe to others if its customers who purchased goods this period don't later pay what they owe.

   g. Estimates of amount the firm will owe to others if its customers who ever purchased goods don't later pay what they owe.

   h. Estimates of the amount of sales for the current period that will become bad debt expense for the current period.

   i. An amount of deferred revenue.

   j. A part of retained earnings.

39. Understanding the purpose of the Allowance for Uncollectible Accounts account. A member of the Audit Committee of a firm asks the Chief Financial Officer the following question: "How do you know the Allowance for Uncollectible Accounts is adequate?" Discuss the adequacy or inadequacy of each of the following independent responses.

   a. "I think it much more likely than not that the amount of cash and marketable securities is adequate to cover any cash shortage caused by customers' not paying what they owe."

   b. "I have checked the Bad Debt Expense for sales made this past period and found the amount reasonable."

   c. "I have performed an aging of all accounts receivable for all sales this period and found the amount reasonable."

   d. "I have performed an aging of all accounts receivable and found the amount reasonable."

   e. "We performed a detailed confirmation of receivables from customers whose accounts the firm wrote off as uncollectible this period and found the decision to write them off suitable under the circumstances."

   f. "We performed a detailed confirmation of receivables from customers whose accounts the firm has neither collected nor written off by the end of this period and found the decisions suitable under the circumstances."

   g. "I know the Allowance account was correct at the end of last period and I checked the Bad Debt Expense for this period using a percentage of sales recommended for this class of customers by the top two credit reporting agencies."

40. Ethical issues in accounting for uncollectible accounts. Sage Department Stores operates a chain of department stores throughout the United States. It provides its customers with credit cards, both to stimulate sales and to save fees the firm would otherwise incur if customers used third-party credit cards. Sage Department Stores uses the percentage-of-sales procedure to estimate the amount of bad debt expense each period. That percentage has ranged from 2.5 to 3.2 percent in recent years. It also periodically ages its account receivable to assess the reasonableness of the balance in the Allowance for Uncollectibles Accounts account. Recession conditions in the economy during the current period caused Sage Department Stores and most of its competitors to operate at a net loss. Sage Department Stores increased its provision for estimated uncollectibles during the current year to 5 percent of sales. Although the increased provision resulted in a still larger net loss than it would have reported if it had used its usual percentage, security analysts did not seem to notice. The chief financial officer was prepared, however, to defend the higher percentage on the grounds that one might expect recession conditions to lead to more uncollectible accounts. Further, the chief financial officer reasoned that the firm could take a much smaller provision during the next few years if the higher level of uncollectibles did not materialize, which would increase future earnings and show even more earnings growth. The chief financial officer also reasoned that competitors were likely to play this earnings game. To remain competitive, Sage Department Stores must play it as well. Discuss any ethical issues that you see confronting the chief financial officer of Sage Department Stores.

41. **Ethical issues in accounting for long-contracts.** Halliburton Company provides engineering and construction services under multi-year contracts to energy, industrial, and governmental customers. It has used the percentage-of-completion method of accounting for its multi-year contracts for many years. In addition to the initial contract price, its contracts call for additional payments if the customer makes changes in the plans—so-called *change orders*. The firm has not, heretofore, recognized revenue from change orders until it completes the work and collects the cash. It now decides that it can predict with reasonable precision the amount it will collect under change orders and the costs of making the changes. So, it adds the expected collections from the change orders to cash collections expected from customers and the costs of the changes to the costs expected to complete various jobs. Thus, it now recognizes income from change orders as part of its income recognition for all multi-year contracts using the percentage-of-completion method. It calls reader's attention to this change in a hard-to-understand note to the financial statements. Discuss any ethical issues that you see confronting Halliburton Company in its decision to change its income recognition method for change orders.

42. **Ethical issues in income recognition.** Qwest Communications International (Qwest), a telecommunications company, signed a $100 million contract with the Arizona Schools Facilities Board to supply high-speed Internet access to public schools in Arizona. The contract required that Qwest supply and install the computer equipment and do the necessary steps to link the computers to the Internet, a process scheduled to take over 18 months. Qwest initially intended to recognize revenue from the contract on a percentage-of-completion basis as it completed installation at each school and received payment from the State. Soon after delivery but before installation of the equipment, Qwest decided to separate the recognition of revenue for sale of the equipment from the recognition of revenue for installation services. It recognized $33 million in revenue at the time of shipment and planned to recognize $67 million as installation occurred. This change accelerated the recognition relative to the pattern initially anticipated. To allow this change in revenue recognition, Qwest's auditor required that the customer, Arizona Schools Facilities Board, formally request a separation of the hardware sales contract from the installation contract. Personnel from Qwest drafted such a request, printed it on stationery of the Arizona Schools Facilities Board, and presented to the head of the Board to sign. The head of the Board hastily signed the letter at an airport after receiving assurance that the State wouldn't actually have to pay Qwest until Qwest installed the equipment. The head of the board stated, "There was a veiled threat that if we did not sign the letter, the equipment would not be available." Discuss any ethical issues that you see confronting managers at Qwest and its auditor.

$\mathcal{I}$nventories: The Source of Operating Profits

Learning Objectives

1. Apply the principles of cost inclusions for assets to both purchased and manu- factured inventories.

2. Understand the effect of changes in the valuation of inventories subsequent to acquisition on both balance sheet and income statement amounts.

3. Understand why most firms either must make, or prefer to make, a cost flow assumption for inventories and cost of goods sold.

4. Compute cost of goods sold and ending inventory using a first-in, first-out

We continue our trek down the balance sheet and the income statement by considering the accounting for inventories, an asset, and cost of goods sold, the related expense. Inventories are a major asset for merchandising and manufacturing firms and cost of goods sold is typically their largest single expense. Such firms must make various choices in accounting for inventories. The choices made affect assessments of a firm's profitability and risk over time and can make two firms that are otherwise alike appear to differ.

Example 1 **Exhibit 1.2** in **Chapter 1** indicates that Wal-Mart Stores reported cost of goods sold of $198,747 million and net income of $9,075 million in Year 14. The ratio of cost of goods sold to net income for Wal-Mart is 21.9 to 1 (= $198,747/$9,075). Assume that Wal-Mart must make inventory choices (discussed later in this chapter) that would reduce its cost of goods sold by, say, 2 percent. A 2 percent reduction in cost of goods sold results in a $3,975 (= 0.02 × $198,747) million decrease in cost of goods sold and a corresponding increase in income before taxes. Assuming an income tax rate of 35 percent, net income would increase by $2,584 [= (1.00 − 0.35) × $3,975] million to $11,659 (= $9,075 + $2,584) million. A 2 percent decrease in cost of goods sold increases net income by 28.5 percent (= $2,584/$9,075). Thus, a seemingly small change in cost of goods sold can significantly affect net income.

Inventory Terminology

The term **inventory** means a stock of goods or other items that a firm owns and holds for sale or for further processing as part of its business operations. For example, lawnmowers are inventory of Toro, a lawnmower manufacturer, or of Lowe's, a home products store, but not of a firm that provides lawn-mowing services. Marketable securities are inventory of Merrill Lynch, a securities dealer, but not of Hewlett-Packard, a computer electronics company, which temporarily invests excess cash in such securities. *Merchandise inventory* denotes goods held for sale by a merchandising firm (retail or wholesale businesses). *Finished goods inventory* denotes goods held for sale by a manufacturing firm. The inventories of manufacturing firms also include *raw materials inventory* (materials being stored that will become part of goods to be produced) and *work-in-process inventory* (partially completed products in the factory). A later section discusses the accounting for inventories by manufacturing firms.

Asset Valuation and Income Measurement

Assets are resources that provide future benefits. Inventories are assets because firms expect to sell the inventories for cash, or cash equivalents. At the time of sale, firms consume the benefits of inventories, receiving in exchange either cash or accounts receivable. Firms recognize revenue in an amount equal to the cash-equivalent value of the asset received and recognize an expense, cost of goods sold, for the current book value, usually acquisition cost, of the inventory sold. Firms usually recognize all of the difference between the selling price and the acquisition cost of the inventory as income in the period of sale.

Example 2   Zale, Inc. operates a chain of retail jewelry stores. During the fall of Year 13, it purchased gold jewelry at an acquisition cost of $300,000. It initially marked this jewelry to sell for $750,000. A worldwide shortage of gold developed late in Year 13, leading to an increase in the amount that Zale, Inc. would have to pay to replace this jewelry to $500,000. Zale, Inc. consequently increased the selling price of the jewelry to $1,250,000. Zale, Inc. sold this jewelry in the spring and summer of Year 14 for $1,250,000. Zale, Inc. recognizes in earnings the difference between the selling price of $1,250,000 and the acquisition cost of $300,000 in Year 14 when it sells the jewelry, even though a portion of the increase in value of the jewelry occurred during Year 13. GAAP normally do not permit firms to recognize increases in the value of inventory until firms sell the inventory and a market transaction confirms the amount of the increase in value.

The market value of inventories sometimes declines below acquisition cost while firms hold the inventories awaiting sale to customers. GAAP require firms in these situations to write down the inventories and recognize an expense in the amount of the writedown. The subsequent sale of the inventory results in income equal to the difference between the selling price and the new, lower book value.

Example 3   Circuit City Stores sells computers and other electronic products. During the fall of Year 13, it purchased computer products at an acquisition cost of $300,000. It initially marked the computers to sell for $750,000. An unexpected introduction of a new computer chip late in Year 13 reduced the market value of these computers to $175,000. GAAP require that Circuit City Stores write down these computers to $175,000 and recognize a loss of $125,000 (= $300,000 acquisition cost − $175,000 market value) in Year 13. The subsequent sale of these computers in Year 14 for $175,000 results in zero net income in that year from the computers sold.

Thus, the valuation of inventory on the balance sheet closely relates to the measurement of net income. A later section discusses the valuation of inventory subsequent to acquisition more fully.

Inventory Equation

The **inventory equation** helps one understand accounting for inventory. The following equation measures all quantities in physical units:

$$\underbrace{\text{Beginning Inventory} + \text{Additions}}_{\text{Goods Available for Sale (or Use)}} - \text{Withdrawals} = \text{Ending Inventory}$$

If we begin a period with 2,000 pounds of sugar (beginning inventory) and purchase (add) 4,500 pounds during the period, then there are 6,500 (= 2,000 + 4,500) pounds available for sale or use. The term *goods available for sale* (or use) denotes the sum of Beginning Inventory plus Additions. If we use (withdraw) 5,300 pounds during the period, 1,200 pounds of sugar should remain at the end of the period (ending inventory).

The inventory equation can also appear as follows:

$$\underbrace{\text{Beginning Inventory} + \text{Additions}}_{\text{Goods Available for Sale (or Use)}} - \text{Ending Inventory} = \text{Withdrawals}$$

If we begin the period with 2,000 pounds of sugar, purchase 4,500 pounds during the period, and observe 1,200 pounds on hand at the end of the period, then we know the firm used 5,300 (= 2,000 + 4,500 − 1,200) pounds of sugar during the period.[1]

Financial statements report dollar amounts, not physical units such as pounds or cubic feet. The accountant must transform physical quantities for beginning inventory, additions, withdrawals, and ending inventory into dollar amounts in order to measure income for the period and financial

---

[1] When a firm computes the cost of goods sold each time it sells an inventory item, it uses a *perpetual inventory system*. Bar codes and serial numbers on items sold permit such continual tracking of costs. When a firm computes the cost of goods sold at the end of each period by taking a physical inventory and presuming that any items not in ending inventory were sold, it uses a *periodic inventory system*. See the Glossary for a further description of these two inventory systems. We assume use of the periodic system throughout this book.

position at the beginning and end of the period. When acquisition costs of inventory items remain constant, inventory accounting problems are minor because all items carry the same per-unit cost; physical quantities and dollar valuations change together. Any variation in the amounts recorded for inventories result only from changes in quantities. The major problems in inventory accounting arise because the per-unit acquisition costs of inventory items change over time.

Example 4 Suppose that an appliance store has a beginning inventory of one television set, TV set 1, which costs $250. Suppose further that it purchases two TV sets during the period, TV set 2 for $290 and TV set 3 later in the period for $300, and that it sells one TV set for $550. The three TV sets are physically identical; the firm acquired them at different times as their acquisition costs changed, so only their costs differ.

We can write the inventory equation as follows, measuring all quantities in dollars of cost:

Beginning Inventory + Purchases − Cost of Goods Sold = Ending Inventory

$250   + $590   −   ?   =   ?

If the firm using serial numbers or product bar codes identifies TV set 2 as the one sold, then cost of goods sold is $290 and ending inventory is $550 (= $250 + $300).

The physical similarity of some products, however, creates difficulties in identifying the products sold and the products in ending inventory. Even when technology, such as product bar codes, allows firms to keep track of the cost of each item in inventory, it may prefer not to incur the costs to do so. Firms may prefer instead to make a cost flow assumption. GAAP allow firms to assume that it sold the first TV set purchased (referred to as a *first-in, first-out,* or FIFO cost flow assumption), or the last TV set purchased (referred to as a *last-in, first-out,* or LIFO cost flow assumption), or the average TV set purchased, that is, a TV carrying the average cost of all three TV sets (referred to as a *weighted-average* cost flow assumption). A later section discusses each of these cost flow assumptions more fully.

Issues in Inventory Accounting

The remainder of this chapter discusses three issues in inventory accounting:

1. The costs included in the acquisition cost of inventory
2. The treatment of changes in the market value of inventories subsequent to acquisition
3. The cost flow assumption used to trace the movement of costs into and out of inventory

Issue 1: Costs Included in Inventory

The guiding principle for cost inclusions is that the balance sheet amount for inventory should include all costs incurred to acquire goods and prepare them for sale.

Merchandising Firms Merchandising firms, such as Wal-Mart Stores, acquire inventory items in a physical condition ready for sale. Acquisition cost includes the invoice price less any cash discounts taken for prompt payment. Acquisition cost also includes the cost of transporting, receiving, unpacking, inspecting, and shelving, as well as any costs to record the **purchases** in the accounts. The example on **page 44** in **Chapter 2**, applying the cost-inclusion principle to equipment, applies to inventory as well.

Manufacturing Firms Manufacturing firms, such as Ford Motor Company, do not acquire inventory items in a physical form ready for sale. Instead, such firms transform raw materials into finished products in their factories. The acquisition cost of manufactured inventories includes three categories of costs:

- **Direct Materials**: The cost of materials that the manufacturing firm can trace directly to units of product it manufactures. Direct materials for Ford Motor Company include the engine, car body, tires, seat cushions, and other parts that physically become part of a manufactured automobile.

- **Direct Labor**: The cost of labor to transform raw materials into a finished product. This cost for Ford Motor Company includes the compensation of factory workers on the production line.
- **Manufacturing Overhead**: A variety of indirect costs (depreciation, insurance and taxes on manufacturing facilities, supervisory factory labor, and supplies for factory equipment) that firms cannot trace directly to products manufactured but which provide a firm with productive capacity. Manufacturing overhead for Ford Motor Company includes depreciation, insurance, and property taxes on the factory building and equipment; compensation of supervisory factory labor; electricity to light, heat, and cool the factory; and costs associated with setting up a manufacturing process to do a variety of jobs. In today's economy, these indirect costs constitute an ever-larger portion of total manufacturing costs and the treatment of these costs for product costing, performance evaluation, and other management purposes has become an art in itself. *Activity-based costing* is a modern name for the process of allocating indirect costs to processes and products.

Until the manufacturing firm sells the units and recognizes revenue, it treats all manufacturing costs as **product costs**, which are assets, and accumulates the costs in various inventory accounts.

A manufacturing firm, like a merchandising firm, also incurs various marketing costs (commissions for the sales staff, depreciation, insurance and taxes on the sales staff's automobiles) and administrative costs (salary of the chief executive officer, depreciation on computer facilities used in administration). Both merchandising and manufacturing firms treat selling and administrative costs as **period expenses**. **Figure 7.1** summarizes the nature and **flow of costs** for a manufacturing firm.

Overview of the Accounting Process for a Manufacturing Firm   A manufacturing firm maintains separate inventory accounts to accumulate the product costs that it incurs at various stages of completion. The **Raw Materials Inventory** account includes (with debits) the cost of raw materials purchased but not yet transferred to the factory floor. The balance in the Raw Materials Inventory account indicates the cost of raw materials on hand in the raw materials storeroom or warehouse. When the manufacturer transfers raw materials from the raw material storeroom to the factory floor, it transfers the cost of the raw materials from the Raw Materials Inventory account (with credits) to the Work-in-Process Inventory account (with debits).

The **Work-in-Process Inventory** account accumulates (with debits) the cost of raw materials transferred from the raw materials storeroom, the cost of direct labor services used in production, and the manufacturing overhead costs incurred. When the firm completes manufacturing, it transfers the completed units from the factory floor to the finished goods storeroom. It reduces (with credits) the balance in the Work-in-Process Inventory account for the manufacturing costs assigned to the finished units and increases (with debits) the balance in the Finished Goods

FIGURE 7.1   **Diagram of Cost Flows**

| **Stage 1** | **Stage 2** | **Stage 3** |
| Acquiring Materials and Services | Production | Furnishing Goods and Services |

Inventory account. The balance in the Work-in-Process Inventory account indicates the product costs incurred thus far for units not yet finished as of the date of the balance sheet.

The **Finished Goods Inventory** account includes the total manufacturing cost of units completed but not yet sold. The sale of manufactured goods to customers results in a transfer, with credits, of their cost from the Finished Goods Inventory account to the Cost of Goods Sold, an expense reducing Retained Earnings, with debits.

Figure 7.2 shows the flow of manufacturing costs through the various inventory and other accounts. Compare the movement of amounts through the accounts in **Figure 7.2** with the parallel physical movement of inventory in **Figure 7.1**.

Illustration of the Accounting Process for a Manufacturing Firm

This section illustrates the accounting process for a manufacturing firm using information about the operations of Moon Manufacturing Company. The company began operations on January 1 by issuing 10,000 shares of $10 par value common stock for $30 per share. Transactions during January and the appropriate journal entries follow:

(1) The firm acquires a building costing $200,000 and equipment costing $50,000 for cash.

(1) Building (Asset Increase)	200,000	
Equipment (Asset Increase)	50,000	
Cash (Asset Decrease)		250,000

(2) The firm purchases raw materials costing $25,000 on account.

(2) Raw Materials Inventory (Asset Increase)	25,000	
Accounts Payable (Liability Increase)		25,000

(3) It issues, to producing departments, raw materials costing $20,000.

(3) Work-in-Process Inventory (Asset Increase)	20,000	
Raw Materials Inventory (Asset Decrease)		20,000

(4) The total payroll for January is $60,000: $40,000 paid to factory workers and $20,000 paid to marketing and administrative personnel.

(4) Work-in-Process Inventory (Asset Increase)	40,000	
Retained Earnings (Salaries Expense) (Shareholders' Equity Decrease)	20,000	
Cash (Asset Decrease)		60,000

Recall that a manufacturing firm records nonmanufacturing costs as expenses of the period when the firm consumes the services because these costs rarely create assets with future benefits. Journal entry **(4)**, as well as entries **(5)** and **(6)**, which follow, illustrates the difference between the recording of a product cost and the recording of a period expense. The debits may, on first glance, look similar, but note that the first increases an asset account and the second decreases Retained Earnings, thereby reducing shareholders' equity.

(5) The expenditures for utilities during January are $1,200. Of this amount, $1,000 is for manufacturing and the remaining $200 is for marketing and administrative activities.

(5) Work-in-Process Inventory (Asset Increase)	1,000	
Retained Earnings (Utilities Expense) (Shareholders' Equity Decrease)	200	
Cash (Asset Decrease)		1,200

These debits also split the expenditure between asset (product cost) and expense for the period.

(6) Depreciation on building and equipment during January is as follows: factory, $8,000; marketing and administrative, $2,000.

FIGURE 7.2   Flow of Manufacturing Costs through the Accounts

(6) Work-in-Process Inventory (Asset Increase)	8,000	
Retained Earnings (Depreciation Expense) (Shareholders' Equity Decrease)	2,000	
Accumulated Depreciation (Asset Decrease)		10,000

Note the split of the depreciation charge between product cost, Work-in-Process (asset), and period expense. The credit, to an asset contra account, enables the acquisition cost of the equipment to remain, unreduced, in the accounts.

(7) Units completed during January and transferred to the finished goods storeroom have a manufacturing cost of $48,500. The derivation of this amount requires the techniques of cost accounting.

| (7) Finished Goods Inventory (Asset Increase) . . . . | 48,500 | |
| Work-in-Process Inventory (Asset Decrease) . . . . | | 48,500 |

(8) Sales during January total $75,000, of which $25,000 is on account.

(8) Cash (Asset Increase)	50,000	
Accounts Receivable (Asset Increase)	25,000	
Retained Earnings (Sales Revenue) (Shareholders' Equity Increase)		75,000

(9) The cost of the goods sold during January is $42,600.

| (9) Retained Earnings (Cost of Goods Sold) (Shareholders' Equity Decrease) . . . . | 42,600 | |
| Finished Goods Inventory (Asset Decrease) . . . . | | 42,600 |

Exhibit 7.1 presents a statement of income before taxes for the firm for January.

EXHIBIT 7.1	MOON MANUFACTURING COMPANY Income Statement for the Month of January		
Sales Revenue			$75,000
Less Expenses:			
Cost of Goods Sold		$42,600	
Salaries Expense		20,000	
Utilities Expense		200	
Depreciation Expense		2,000	
Total Expenses			64,800
Income Before Taxes			$10,200

Problem 7.1 for Self-Study

Flow of manufacturing costs through the accounts.   The following data relate to the manufacturing activities of Haskell Corporation during March:

	March 1	March 31
Raw Materials Inventory	$42,400	$ 46,900
Work-in-Process Inventory	75,800	63,200
Finished Goods Inventory	44,200	46,300

(continued)

Problem 7.1 for Self-Study *(continued)*

	March 1	March 31
Factory Costs Incurred during the Month		
Raw Materials Purchased		$ 60,700
Labor Services Received		137,900
Heat, Light, and Power		1,260
Rent		4,100
Expirations of Previous Factory Acquisitions and Prepayments		
Depreciation of Factory Equipment		$ 1,800
Prepaid Insurance Expired		1,440
Other Data Relating to the Month		
Sales Revenue		$400,000
Selling and Administrative Expenses		125,000

a. Calculate the cost of raw materials used during March.
b. Calculate the cost of units completed during March and transferred to the finished goods storeroom.
c. Calculate the cost of units sold during March.
d. Calculate income before taxes for March.

Summary of the Accounting Process for Manufacturing Operations   The accounting procedures for the marketing and administrative costs of manufacturing firms resemble those for merchandising firms. The firm expenses these costs in the same period that it consumes the services. The accounting procedures for a manufacturing firm differ from those for a merchandising firm primarily in the treatment of inventories. A manufacturing firm incurs costs in transforming raw materials into finished products. Although a manufacturing firm consumes raw materials, labor services, and factory overhead services in the manufacturing process, the consumption results in the creation of an asset, partial or completed units of inventory. Until the manufacturing firm sells the units produced, it accumulates manufacturing costs in asset accounts—the Raw Materials Inventory account, the Work-in-Process Inventory account, or the Finished Goods Inventory account—depending on the stage of completion of each inventory item. The firm therefore debits product costs to inventory (asset) accounts until it sells the units produced.

Issue 2: Valuation Subsequent to Acquisition

GAAP require firms to record inventories initially at acquisition cost (**Issue 1** discussed above). The market value of inventories may change while the firm holds the inventory awaiting its sale to customers. This section discusses the treatment of increases and decreases in the market value of inventories subsequent to acquisition. Market value generally means **replacement cost**, the amount the firm would pay to acquire the inventory.

Increases in Market Value   Inventories may increase in value subsequent to acquisition for a variety of reasons. A shortage of a key raw material may increase its costs and thereby increase the replacement cost of the inventory item of which the raw material is a component. A new labor agreement may increase labor cost and thereby increase the replacement cost of manufactured inventories. If a firm were to revalue its inventories to the higher replacement cost, or market value, it would make an entry such as the following:

Inventories (Asset Increase)	X	
Retained Earnings (Unrealized Holding Gain on Inventories)		
(Shareholders' Equity Increase)		X

GAAP, however, do not permit firms to revalue inventories above acquisition cost. GAAP's reasoning is that acquisition cost valuations provide more conservative measures of assets and net income during the periods prior to sale. The increase in the market value of the inventory likely permits the firm to raise its selling price. The benefit of the increase in market value affects net income in the period of sale when the firm realizes the benefit of a higher selling price instead of recognizing the benefit during the periods while market values increased.

Decreases in Market Value Inventories can decrease in value for a variety of reasons. A competitor introduces a technologically superior product that makes a particular firm's product offering obsolete. A firm's product includes materials found to contain a health hazard. The introduction of a lower-cost raw material lowers the manufacturing cost of a product using that raw material as a component.

In contrast to the treatment of increases in market value, GAAP require firms to write down inventories when their replacement cost, or market value, declines below acquisition cost. GAAP refer to this valuation as the **lower of cost or market valuation basis**.[2] Once the firm writes down inventory, the new amount becomes the historical cost basis and the firm does not write up that amount for subsequent value increases, even if the new value remains less than the original cost.

A firm can recognize a decline of $5,000 in the market value of inventory with the following entry:

Retained Earnings (Unrealized Holding Loss on Inventory)		
(Shareholders' Equity Decrease)	5,000	
Inventory (Asset Decrease)		5,000

The account debited can appear on the income statement on a separate line. Some firms do not explicitly record the previous entry; instead, they include the unrealized holding loss as part of a higher cost of goods sold. Consider, for example, the calculations in **Exhibit 7.2** of cost of goods sold when beginning inventory is $19,000, purchases are $100,000, and ending inventory has a cost of $25,000 but has a market value of $20,000. Note that cost of goods sold is $5,000 larger when the firm values ending inventory at lower of cost or market than when it uses the acquisition cost basis for ending inventory. The loss of $5,000 does not appear separately, but income will be $5,000 smaller than when the firm uses the acquisition cost basis. To avoid misleading readers of the financial statements, the accountant should disclose in the notes the existence of large writedowns included in cost of goods sold.

The lower-of-cost-or-market basis for inventory valuation is a conservative accounting policy because (1) it recognizes losses from decreases in market value before the firm sells goods but it does not record gains from increases in market value before a sale takes place, and (2) it reports inventories on the balance sheet at amounts that are never greater, but may be less, than acquisition

EXHIBIT 7.2	Calculating Cost of Goods Sold Using Different Bases of Inventory Valuation		
		Cost Basis	Lower-of-Cost-or Market Basis
Beginning Inventory		$ 19,000	$ 19,000
Purchases		100,000	100,000
Goods Available for Sale		$119,000	$119,000
Less Ending Inventory		(25,000)	(20,000)
Cost of Goods Sold		$ 94,000	$ 99,000

---

[2] AICPA, Committee on Accounting Procedures, *Accounting Research Bulletin No. 43*, "Inventory Pricing," 1953; Chapter 4, Statements 5 and 6.

cost.[3] In other words, the lower-of-cost-or-market basis results in reporting unrealized holding losses on inventory items currently through lower net income amounts but delays reporting unrealized holding gains until the firm sells the goods.

Summary of Effect of Inventory Revaluations   Over sufficiently long time spans, income equals cash inflows minus cash outflows (other than transactions with owners). For any one unit, there is only one total gain or loss figure: the difference between its selling price and its acquisition cost. The valuation rule determines when this gain or loss appears in the financial statements over the accounting periods between acquisition and final disposition. If a firm revalued inventory upward to current replacement cost (not allowed by GAAP in the United States), the net income of the period of the inventory write-up will be higher than if the firm had used the acquisition cost basis, but if so, the net income of the later period, when the firms sells the unit, will be lower. When a firm uses the lower-of-cost-or-market basis (generally required by GAAP in the United States), the net income for the period of an inventory writedown will be lower than if the firm had used the acquisition cost basis, but if so, the net income of a later period, when the firm sells the unit, will be higher. Thus, the amount of net income for only one period depends directly on the valuation of inventory on the balance sheet.

Issue 3: Cost Flow Assumptions

Specific Identification and the Need for a Cost Flow Assumption

The accounting records typically contain information on the cost of the beginning inventory for a period, which was the ending inventory of last period. The accounting records also contain information on purchases or production costs incurred during the current period. Thus, firms can easily measure the cost of goods available for sale or use. Firms can match units sold and units in ending inventory with specific purchases or production runs by using product bar codes. Using the code, the firm can trace the unit back to its purchase invoice or cost record. An automobile dealer or a dealer in diamonds or fur coats might compute the cost of ending inventory and cost of goods sold using **specific identification**. If so, then measuring the cost of goods sold and ending inventory presents no difficulties. Refer to **Example 4**. Bar codes on the TV sets permitted the firm to identify TV set 2 as the one sold and TV sets 1 and 3 as remaining in ending inventory.

The inventory items of some firms are sufficiently similar that the firms cannot feasibly use specific identification. Lumber in a building supply store, gasoline in a storage tank, and plants in a nursery are examples. An inventory costing problem arises because of two unknowns in the inventory equation:

$$\underbrace{\text{Beginning Inventory} \quad + \quad \text{Purchases}}_{\text{Goods Available for Sale (or Use)}} \quad - \quad \text{Cost of Goods Sold} \quad = \quad \text{Ending Inventory}$$
$$\text{(known)} \qquad\qquad \text{(known)} \qquad\qquad \text{(unknown)} \qquad\qquad \text{(unknown)}$$

We know the costs of the beginning inventory and the purchases, but we do not know either the amount for cost of goods sold or the amount for ending inventory. Do we compute amounts for the units in ending inventory using the most recent costs, the oldest costs, the average cost, or some other choice? Or we could ask how to compute amounts for the cost of goods sold. Once we place an amount on one unknown quantity, the inventory equation automatically determines the amount for the other. The sum of the two unknowns, Cost of Goods Sold and Ending Inventory, must equal the cost of goods available for sale (= Beginning Inventory + Purchases). The higher the cost we assign to one unknown, the lower must be the cost we assign to the other.

If a firm finds specific identification not feasible, it must make some assumption about the flow of costs. Even when specific identification is feasible, GAAP do not require firms to use it but, instead, allow them to make a cost flow assumption. The accountant computes the acquisition

---

[3] Consult the **Glossary** for the definition of conservatism in accounting. Conservative accounting policies result in both lower asset totals and lower retained earnings totals, thus implying lower cumulative net income totals. Conservatism does not mean reporting lower income in every period. Over long-enough time spans, income will be cash-in less cash-out, other than transactions with owners. If a given accounting policy results in reporting lower income in earlier periods, it must report higher income in some subsequent periods. The conservative accounting policy results in lower income in the early periods. See **Exercise 27** at the end of this chapter.

cost applicable to the units sold and to the units remaining in inventory using one of the following **cost flow assumptions**:

    1. First-in, first-out (FIFO)   **2.** Last-in, first-out (LIFO)   **3.** Weighted average

The following demonstrations of each of these methods use the TV set example introduced earlier and repeated at the top of **Exhibit 7.3**. The example of the three TV sets illustrates most of the important points about the cost flow assumption required in accounting for inventories and cost of goods sold.

First-In, First-Out

The **first-in, first-out (FIFO)** cost flow assumption assigns the costs of the earliest units acquired to the withdrawals and assigns the costs of the most recent acquisitions to the ending inventory. This cost flow assumes that the firm uses the oldest materials and goods first. This cost flow assumption conforms to good business practice in managing physical flows, especially in the case of items that deteriorate or become obsolete. Column (1) of **Exhibit 7.3** illustrates FIFO. FIFO assumes that the firm sells TV set 1 while TV sets 2 and 3 remain in inventory. The designation *FIFO* refers to the cost flow of the units sold. A parallel description for ending inventory is last-in, still-here, or LISH.

    Think of FIFO as a conveyor belt. The first items put on the conveyor belt come off first for use or sale. The last items put on the conveyor belt remain there at the end of the period. Refer to the top panel of **Figure 7.3**. Cost of goods sold for Year 1 under FIFO uses purchases from the beginning of the year until the number of units purchased equal the number of units sold. The firm uses the cost of these purchases to measure cost of goods sold. The ending inventory for Year 1 uses the last purchases during Year 1. Cost of goods sold for Year 2 under FIFO uses the last purchases of Year 1 that comprised the ending inventory for Year 1 and the beginning inventory for Year 2, as well as sufficient purchases from Year 2 to cost all units sold. The ending inventory for Year 2 uses the last purchases during Year 2.

Last-In, First-Out

The **last-in, first out (LIFO)** cost flow assumption assigns the costs of the latest units acquired to the withdrawals and assigns the costs of the oldest units to the ending inventory. Some theorists argue that LIFO matches current costs to current revenues and, therefore, that LIFO better measures

EXHIBIT 7.3	Comparison of Cost Flow Assumptions, Historical Cost Basis

Assumed Data

Beginning Inventory:	TV Set 1 Cost	$250
Purchases:	TV Set 2 Cost	290
	TV Set 3 Cost	300
Cost of Goods Available for Sale		$840
Sales: One TV set		$550

	Cost Flow Assumption		
	FIFO	**Weighted Average**	**LIFO**
Financial Statements	**(1)**	**(2)**	**(3)**
Sales	$550	$550	$550
Cost of Goods Sold	250[a]	280[b]	300[c]
Gross Margin on Sales	$300	$270	$250
Ending Inventory	$590[d]	$560[e]	$540[f]

[a]TV set 1 costs $250.
[b]Average TV sets costs $280 (= $840/3).
[c]TV set 3 costs $300.

[d]TV sets 2 and 3 cost $290 + $300 = $590.
[e]Two average TV sets cost 2 × $280 = $560.
[f]TV sets 1 and 2 cost $250 + $290 = $540.

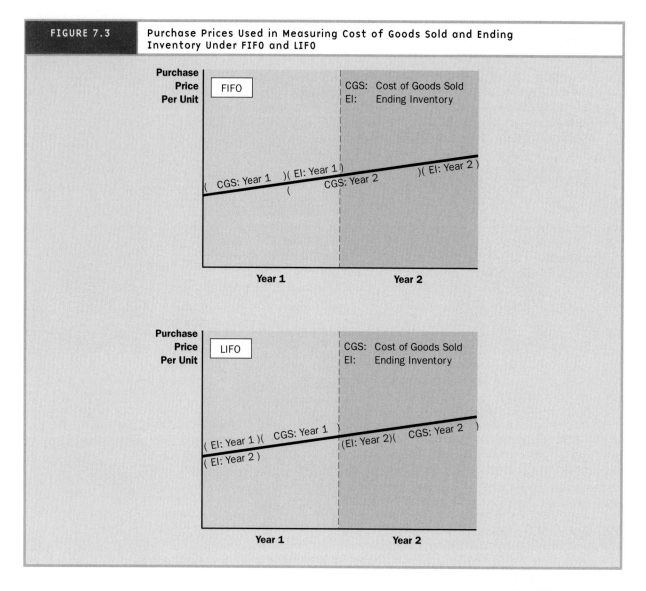

FIGURE 7.3   Purchase Prices Used in Measuring Cost of Goods Sold and Ending Inventory Under FIFO and LIFO

income. Column (3) of **Exhibit 7.3** illustrates LIFO. LIFO assumes that the firm sells TV set 3 costing $300 while the costs of TV sets 1 and 2 remain in inventory. The designation *LIFO* refers to the cost flow for the units sold. A parallel description for ending inventory is first-in, still-here, or FISH.

One might view LIFO as a coal pile. Newly purchased coal gets added to the top of the coal pile. Withdrawals likewise come off the top of the coal pile. Alternatively, think of LIFO as a stack of trays in a cafeteria. The last tray deposited on the stack is the first one next taken off. The lowest tray in the stack remains there as long as there are any trays left unused. It could, in principle, have been there for 30 years.

Refer to the lower panel of **Figure 7.3**. Cost of goods sold for Year 1 under LIFO uses purchases from the end of the year working backward through time until the number of units purchased equal the number of units sold. The firm uses the cost of these purchases to measure cost of goods sold. The ending inventory for Year 1 uses the first purchases during Year 1. Refer to the coal analogy: the coal on the bottom of the pile remains on hand at the end of Year 1. Cost of goods sold for Year 2 under LIFO likewise uses the last purchases from the end of the year backward until the number of units purchased equal the number of units sold. The ending inventory for Year 2 uses purchase prices from two time periods: (1) units equal to the number in ending inventory at the end of Year 1 use purchase prices at the beginning of Year 1, and (2) the increase in the number of units in ending inventory from Year 1 to Year 2 uses purchase prices at the beginning of Year 2. Refer to the coal analogy: a Year 2 layer of coal gets added to the layer left at the end of Year 1. The Year 1 layer carries purchase prices at the beginning of Year 1, and the Year 2 layer carries prices at the beginning of Year 2. Their sum is the total ending inventory for Year 2 under LIFO. So long as any lumps of coal remain in the pile, some will be from Year 1.

Firms have increasingly used LIFO since it first became acceptable for income tax reporting in 1939. In a period of consistently rising purchase prices and increasing inventory quantities, LIFO results in a higher cost of goods sold, a lower reported periodic income, and lower current income taxes than either the FIFO or the weighted-average cost flow assumption. You might be tempted to conclude, therefore, that LIFO always provides a lower amount of net income. Such a conclusion is incorrect, however, as we discuss later, in the context of "dips into LIFO layers."

LIFO usually does not reflect physical flows. Recall, however, that FIFO and LIFO are *cost* flow assumption, not *physical* flow assumption. Firms use LIFO not because it matches physical flows but because it produces a cost-of-goods-sold figure based on more up-to-date purchase prices and reduces income tax payments.

Weighted Average

Under the **weighted-average** cost flow assumption, a firm calculates the average of the costs of all goods available for sale (or use) during the accounting period, including the cost applicable to the beginning inventory. The weighted-average cost applies to the units sold during the period and to units on hand at the end of the period. Column (2) in **Exhibit 7.3** illustrates the weighted-average cost flow assumption. The weighted-average cost of each TV set available for sale during the period is $280 [$= \frac{1}{3} \times ($250 + $290 + $300)$]. Cost of Goods Sold is thus $280, and ending inventory is $560 (= 2 \times $280).

Comparison of Cost Flow Assumptions

Note from **Exhibit 7.3** that cost of goods sold plus ending inventory equals $840, the total cost of goods available for sale, in all three cases. When purchase prices change, no acquisition cost-based accounting method for costing ending inventory and cost of goods sold allows the accountant to show up-to-date costs on both the income statement and the balance sheet. For example, consider a period of rising prices. If measurements of cost of goods sold for the income statement use recent, higher acquisition prices, as occurs under LIFO, then older, lower acquisition prices must appear in costs of the ending inventory for the balance sheet. As long as accounting bases cost of goods sold and ending inventory on acquisition costs, financial statements can present current cost amounts in the income statement or the balance sheet but not in both.

Of the three cost flow assumptions, FIFO results in balance sheet figures that are the closest to current cost because the latest purchases dominate the ending inventory amounts. Remember LISH: last-in, still-here. The Cost of Goods Sold expense tends to be out-of-date, however, because FIFO assumes that the earlier purchase prices of the beginning inventory and the earliest purchases during the period become expenses. When purchase prices rise, FIFO usually leads to the highest reported net income of the three methods, and when purchase prices fall, it leads to the smallest.

LIFO ending inventory can contain costs of items acquired many years previously—think of those trays at the bottom of the stack. When purchase prices have been rising and inventory amounts increasing, LIFO produces balance sheet figures usually much lower than current costs. LIFO's cost-of-goods-sold figure closely approximates current costs. **Exhibit 7.4** summarizes the

EXHIBIT 7.4	Age of Information about Inventory Items		
Cost Flow Assumption	**Income Statement**	**Balance Sheet**	**Inventory-on-Hand Assumption**
FIFO	Old Purchase Prices	Current Purchase Prices	LISH
LIFO	Current Purchase Prices	Very[a] Old Purchase Prices	FISH

[a] The oldest purchase prices on the FIFO income statement are just over one year old in nearly all cases, and the average purchase price on the FIFO income statement (for a year) is slightly more than one-half year old. The larger the rate of inventory turnover, the closer the average age on the income statement is to one-half year. LIFO balance sheet items are generally much older than FIFO income statement items, with some costs from the 1940s in many cases.

differences between FIFO and LIFO. Of the cost flow assumptions (LIFO, FIFO, weighted average), LIFO usually results in the smallest net income when purchase prices are rising (highest cost of goods sold) and the largest when purchase prices are falling (lowest cost of goods sold). Also, LIFO results in the least fluctuation in gross margins in businesses in which selling prices tend to change as purchase prices of inventory items change.

The weighted-average cost flow assumption falls between the other two in its effects, but it resembles FIFO more than LIFO in its effects on the financial statements. When inventory turns over rapidly, the weighted-average inventory cost flow provides amounts virtually identical to FIFO's amounts. You can see this for yourself if you work any of **Problems 29**, **39**, and **41** at the end of the chapter. The remaining discussion treats FIFO and weighted average similarly.

Differences in cost of goods sold and inventories under the cost flow assumptions relate in part to the rate of change in the acquisition costs of inventory items. Using older purchase prices for inventories under LIFO or using older purchase prices for cost of goods sold under FIFO has little impact if prices have been stable for several years. As the rate of price change increases, the effect of using older versus more recent prices increases, resulting in larger differences in cost of goods sold and inventories between FIFO and LIFO.

Differences in cost of goods sold also relate in part to the rate of inventory turnover. As the rate of inventory turnover increases, purchases during the period make up an increasing proportion of the cost of goods available for sale. Because purchases are the same regardless of the cost flow assumption, cost of goods sold amounts will not vary as much with the choice of cost flow assumption. Consider the impact of a choice of cost flow assumption for a florist or grocery store (small effect because of fast turnover with small ending inventory relative to annual sales) versus that for a distiller of liquor that requires aging (large effect because of slow turnover with large ending inventory relative to annual sales). Even with a rapid inventory turnover, inventory amounts on the balance sheet can still differ significantly depending on the cost flow assumption. The longer a firm uses LIFO, likely the larger will be the difference between inventories based on LIFO and FIFO cost flow assumptions.

Problem 7.2 for Self-Study

Computing cost of goods sold and ending inventory under various cost flow assumptions. **Exhibit 7.5** presents data on beginning inventory, purchases, withdrawals, and ending inventory for June and July.

EXHIBIT 7.5	Data for Inventory Calculations (Problem 7.2 for Self-Study)		
	Units	**Unit Cost**	**Total Cost**
ITEM X			
Beginning Inventory, June 1	—	—	—
Purchases, June 1	100	$10.00	$1,000
Purchases, June 7	400	11.00	4,400
Purchases, June 18	100	12.50	1,250
Total Goods Available for Sale	600		$6,650
Withdrawals during June	(495)		?
Ending Inventory (June 30) and			
Beginning Inventory (July 1)	105		$?
Purchases, July 5	300	13.00	3,900
Purchases, July 15	200	13.50	2,700
Purchases, July 23	250	14.00	3,500
Total Goods Available for Sale	855		$?
Withdrawals during July	(620)		?
Ending Inventory (July 31)	235		$?

(continued)

Problem 7.2 for Self-Study *(continued)*

a. Compute the cost of goods sold and the ending inventory for June using (1) FIFO, (2) LIFO, and (3) weighted-average cost flow assumptions.

b. Compute the cost of goods sold and the ending inventory for July using (1) FIFO, (2) LIFO, and (3) weighted-average cost flow assumptions.

A Closer Look at LIFO's Effects on Financial Statements

LIFO usually presents a cost-of-goods-sold figure that reflects current costs. It also generally has the practical advantage of deferring income taxes. If a firm uses a LIFO assumption in its income tax return in the United States, it must also use LIFO in its financial reports to shareholders. This "LIFO conformity rule" results from Internal Revenue Service regulations for firms using LIFO for income tax reporting.

In the last 30 years, many firms, including DuPont, General Motors, Eastman Kodak, and Sears, have switched from FIFO to LIFO. Given the rapid rate of purchase price increases in the past, the switch from FIFO to LIFO has resulted in substantially lower cash payments for income taxes. For example, when DuPont and General Motors switched from FIFO to LIFO, they each lowered current income taxes by about $150 million. At the same time, these firms reported lower net income to shareholders than they would have reported if they had still used FIFO. The cash flow from the deferral of income taxes actually increased present value of the cash flows for these firms, despite reporting lower earnings to shareholders.

LIFO Layers   In any year when purchases exceed sales, the quantity of units in inventory increases. The amount added to inventory for that year is called a **LIFO inventory layer**. For example, assume that a firm acquires 100 TV sets each year and sells 98 TV sets each year for four years. Its inventory at the end of the fourth year contains 8 units. The cost of the 8 units under LIFO is the cost of sets numbered 1 and 2 (from the first year), 101 and 102 (from the second year), 201 and 202 (from the third year), and 301 and 302 (from the fourth year). Common terminology would say that this firm has four LIFO layers, each labeled with its year of acquisition. The physical units on hand would almost certainly be the units most recently acquired in Year 4, units numbered 393 through 400, but they would appear on the balance sheet at costs incurred for purchases during each of the four years.

To take another example, the data in **Exhibit 7.6** illustrate four LIFO inventory layers, one for each of the years shown.

Dipping into LIFO Layers   A firm using LIFO must consider the implications of dipping into old LIFO layers. LIFO reduces current taxes in periods of rising purchase prices and rising inventory quantities. If inventory quantities decline, however, the opposite effect occurs in the year of the decline: older, lower costs per unit of prior years' LIFO layers leave the balance sheet and become expenses.

If a firm must for some reason reduce end-of-period physical inventory quantities below the beginning-of-period quantities, cost of goods sold will reflect the current period's purchases plus

EXHIBIT 7.6	Data for Illustration of LIFO Layers (Inventory at January 1, Year 5)			
LIFO Layers			**Cost**	
Year Purchased		**Number of Units**	**Per Unit**	**Total Cost**
1		100	$ 50	$ 5,000
2		110	60	6,600
3		120	80	9,600
4		130	100	13,000
		460		$34,200

a portion of the older and lower costs in the beginning inventory. Such a firm will have lower cost of goods sold as well as larger reported income and larger income taxes in that period than if the firm had been able to maintain its ending inventory at beginning-of-period levels.

Example 5   Assume that LIFO inventory at the beginning of Year 5 comprises 460 units with a total cost of $34,200, as in **Exhibit 7.6**. Assume that the cost at the end of Year 5 is $120 per unit and that the income tax rate is 40 percent. If, for some reason, Year 5 ending inventory drops to 100 units, all 360 units purchased in Year 2 through Year 4 will enter cost of goods sold. These 360 units cost $29,200 (= $6,600 + $9,600 + $13,000), but the current cost of comparable units is $43,200 (= 360 units × $120 per unit). Cost of goods sold will be $14,000 smaller (= $43,200 − $29,200) than if quantities had not declined because the firm dipped into old LIFO layers. Income subject to income taxes will be $14,000 larger and income after taxes will be $8,400 larger than if the firm had purchased inventory so that quantities had not declined from 460 to 100 units. LIFO results in firms deferring taxes as long as they do not dip into LIFO layers.

Quality of Earnings and Ethical Issues from Dipping into LIFO Layers.   Because firms often control whether inventory quantities increase or decrease through their purchase or production decisions, LIFO affords firms an opportunity to manage their earnings in a particular year. Managements face the decision as to when to replenish inventories at year-end. Buy in December and these higher acquisition costs go into cost of goods sold. Wait until January of next year to purchase and the current year's cost of goods sold contains costs older, usually lower, than December's. Financially literate board members, who represent investors, and securities analysts should probe to understand how much of the current year's earnings results from managed timing of purchases or production. Analysts view firms that dip into LIFO layers to manage their earnings as having a lower quality of earnings than firms that use FIFO.

A related question is whether management faces an ethical issue when it decides to dip into LIFO layers. Some observers point out that some LIFO liquidations are either unavoidable, because of raw materials shortages for example, or good business practice, because of improved inventory control systems for example, and do not raise ethical issues. These same observers would also argue that firms that purposely dip into LIFO layers primarily to meet earnings targets do face ethical issues. Other observers point out that the timing of inventory purchases or production is so complex and subjective that disentangling these possible reasons for LIFO liquidations is not possible.

Annual Report Disclosure   Many firms using LIFO have inventory cost layers built up since the 1940s, and the costs of the early units are often as little as 10 percent of the current cost. For these firms, a dip into old layers will substantially increase income. A note from recent financial statements of The Timken Company illustrates typical disclosures when a firm dips into LIFO layers:

> During [the current year], inventory quantities were reduced as a result of ceasing manufacturing operations in Duston, England. This reduction resulted in a liquidation of LIFO inventory quantities carried at lower costs prevailing in prior years, compared to the cost of current purchases, the effect of which increased income . . . by approximately $5,700,000 or $0.09 per diluted share [approximately 10 percent].

LIFO's Effects on Purchasing Behavior   Consider the quandary faced by a purchasing manager of a LIFO firm nearing the end of a year when the quantity sold has exceeded the quantity purchased so far during the year. If the year ends with units sold exceeding units purchased, the firm will dip into old LIFO layers and will have to pay increased taxes. Assume that the purchasing manager thinks current purchase prices for the goods are abnormally high and prefers to delay making purchases until prices drop, presumably in the next year. Waiting implies dipping into old LIFO layers during this period and paying higher taxes. Buying now may entail higher inventory and carrying costs.

Example 6   Refer again to the data in **Exhibit 7.6**. Assume that the cost per unit at the end of Year 5 has risen to $120 per unit and that the inventory on hand at the end of Year 5 is 460 units, with costs as in **Exhibit 7.6**. The purchasing manager thinks the price will drop back to $105 per unit early in Year 6. An order of 50 new units arrives, which the firm will fill. The firm has two strategies:

1. The purchasing manager can refuse to acquire 50 more units for $120. Then, the 50 units sold will carry costs of $100 each (from the Year 4 layer). Taxable income will be $1,000 larger [= 50 units $\times$ ($120 − $100)] than if the firm acquires units at the end of Year 5 for $120 each.
2. The firm can acquire 50 more units for $120. Then, the firm will have paid $750 more [= 50 units $\times$ ($120 − $105)] for inventory than if it had waited until the beginning of Year 6 to acquire inventory. In this example, so long as income tax rates are less than 75 percent, the firm will probably prefer the first strategy. If the income tax rate is 35 percent, for example, the cost of the first strategy is $350 (= 0.35 $\times$ $1,000) in extra taxes, whereas the second strategy incurs extra costs of $750 to buy sooner rather than later. In reality, of course, the purchasing manager can seldom be sure about future prices and will have to make estimates for computations such as those above.

LIFO can induce firms to manage LIFO layers and cost of goods sold in a way that would be unwise in the absence of tax effects. LIFO also gives management the opportunity to manage income: under LIFO, end-of-year purchases, which the firm can manage, affect net income for the year.

LIFO Balance Sheet   LIFO usually leads to a balance sheet amount for inventory so much less than current costs that it may mislead readers of financial statements. For example, in recent years various manufacturers of steel products have reported that the cost of their ending inventory based on LIFO is about 80 percent of what it would have been had FIFO been used. Inventory on the balance sheet, reported assuming LIFO cost flow, makes up about 10 percent of total assets.

The Securities and Exchange Commission (SEC) has worried that this out-of-date information might mislead the readers of financial statements. As a result, the SEC requires firms using LIFO to disclose, in notes to the financial statements, the amounts by which inventories based on FIFO or current cost exceed their amounts as reported on a LIFO basis.[4] A note to the financial statements of Nucor Corporation, a steel manufacturer, reports that if the FIFO method of inventory accounting had been used to value all inventories, they would have been $158 million higher than reported at the end of the year and $43 million higher at the beginning of the year. Nucor's beginning inventories under LIFO amounted to $589 million and its ending inventory amounted to $560 million. Its beginning inventory under FIFO would have been $632 (= $589 + $43) million, a 7.3 percent increase. Its ending inventory would have been $718 (= $560 + $158) million, a 28.2 percent increase.

Problem 7.3 for Self-Study

Assessing the impact of a LIFO layer liquidation.   Refer to the data in **Problem 7.2 for Self-Study**. During August, the firm purchased 600 units for $15 each and sold 725 units.

a. Compute the cost of goods sold and the ending inventory for August using (1) FIFO, (2) LIFO, and (3) weighted-average cost flow assumptions.
b. Calculate the effect of the LIFO liquidation on net income before income taxes for the year.

Choosing the Cost Flow Assumption

Firms in the United States can choose a FIFO or LIFO or weighted-average cost flow assumption. The decision involves the following considerations:

1. The extent of changes in manufacturing or purchase costs: When such costs do not change significantly, then the three cost flow assumptions provide similar amounts for inventories and cost of goods sold.
2. The rate of inventory turnover: The faster the rate of inventory turnover, the smaller are the differences in inventories and cost of goods sold among the three cost flow assumptions.
3. The direction of expected changes in costs: FIFO results in higher net income and income taxes when costs increase and lower net income and income taxes when costs decrease.

---

[4] Some managers refer to the excess of FIFO or current cost over LIFO cost of inventories as the *LIFO reserve*. For reasons discussed in the Glossary at the back of the book, the term *reserve* is objectionable because it misleads some readers. Some firms nevertheless continue to use it. A term such as *inventory valuation allowance* is as descriptive as *LIFO reserve* and is less likely to mislead financial statement readers.

4. The relative emphasis on reporting higher earnings to shareholders versus saving income taxes.

5. The opportunity that LIFO provides to manage earnings by delaying purchases toward the end of the accounting period.

6. The increased recordkeeping costs of LIFO (for example, keeping track of LIFO layers for all of a firm's products) and its inconsistency with the usual physical flow of inventories.

7. Firms must use LIFO for financial reporting if they use LIFO for income tax reporting.

An annual survey of the choices that firms make in their selection of accounting principles reported for a recent year that 46 percent of the sampled firms use FIFO, 31 percent use LIFO, 20 percent use average cost, and 3 percent use other methods, including specific identification.[5] The industries with the largest percentages of firms using LIFO included firms that rely on oil as a raw material, such as chemicals, petroleum, rubber and plastic products. Retailing firms also use LIFO extensively. The industries with the smallest proportion of firms using LIFO included technology-based firms, which experience decreasing production costs, such as computers and other electronic equipment.

Analyzing Inventory Disclosures

The financial statements and notes provide helpful information for analyzing the effects of inventories and cost of goods sold on assessments of profitability and risk. This section illustrates several such analyses.

Conversion from LIFO to FIFO

As indicated above, approximately one-third of firms in the United States use a LIFO cost flow assumption, with most of the remaining firms using FIFO or weighted average. Most countries other than the United States do not allow firms to use LIFO. With the disclosures of the excess of FIFO or current cost over LIFO inventories, the analyst can compute inventories and cost of goods sold on a FIFO basis and thereby make more valid comparisons between a LIFO firm and its FIFO competitor.

To illustrate the conversion, consider the information provided on **page 311** for the inventories of Nucor Corporation. **Exhibit 7.7** summarizes this information and shows the conversion of inventories and cost of goods sold from a LIFO to a FIFO basis. The inventory amounts in the first column under LIFO come from Nucor's balance sheet and cost of goods sold and sales come from its income statement. We compute purchases using the inventory equation. The amounts disclosed for the excess of FIFO over LIFO permit the computation of beginning and ending inventories under FIFO in the third column. Purchases remain the same under LIFO and FIFO. Using the inventory equation, cost of goods sold under FIFO is $5,882 million, compared to $5,997 million under LIFO. The gross margin percentage under FIFO is 6.1 percent (= $384/$6,266), as compared to 4.3 percent (= $269/$6,266) under LIFO. The larger gross margin under FIFO suggests that acquisition costs increased during the year.

We can also compute inventory turnover ratios under LIFO and FIFO. The computations are as follows:

LIFO: $5,997/0.5($589 + $560) = 10.4 times per year
FIFO: $5,882/0.5($632 + $718) = 8.7 times per year

The inventory turnover ratio under LIFO is misleading because it uses relatively current cost in the numerator and the older cost of LIFO layers in the denominator. The inventory turnover under FIFO more accurately measures the actual turnover of inventory because it uses relatively current cost data in both the numerator and the denominator.

Consider also the current ratio (= current assets/current liabilities). Financial statement analysts use the current ratio to assess the short-term liquidity risk of a company. If a firm uses LIFO in periods of rising prices while inventory quantities increase, the amount of inventory included in the numerator of the current ratio will be smaller than it would be if the firm valued

[5] American Institute of Certified Public Accountants, *Accounting Trends and Techniques*, 2003, page 195.

	EXHIBIT 7.7	Derivation of FIFO Income Data for LIFO Company, Inventory Data from Financial Statements and Footnotes of Nucor Corporation (all dollar amounts in millions)

(Amounts shown in **boldface** appear in Nucor's financial statements. We derive other amounts as indicated.)

	LIFO Cost Flow Assumption (actually used)	+	Excess of FIFO over LIFO Amount	=	FIFO Cost Flow Assumption (hypothetical)
Beginning Inventory	$ 589		$ 43		$ 632
Purchases	5,968[a]		0		5,968
Cost of Goods Available for Sale	$ 6,557		$ 43		$ 6,600
Less Ending Inventory	560		158		718
Cost of Goods Sold	**$5,997**		$(115)		$ 5,882
Sales	**$6,266**		0		**$6,266**
Less Cost of Goods Sold	5,997		$(115)		5,882
Gross Margin on Sales	$ 269		$ 115		$ 384

[a] Computation of Purchases not presented in financial statements:

Purchases = Cost of Goods Sold + Ending Inventory − Beginning Inventory

$5,968 = $5,997 + $560 − $589

inventory at more current costs using FIFO. Hence, the unwary reader may underestimate the liquidity of a company that uses a LIFO cost flow assumption.

Identifying Operating Margin and Holding Gains

In general, the reported net income under FIFO exceeds that under LIFO during periods of rising purchase prices. This higher reported net income results from including a larger realized holding gain in reported net income under FIFO than under LIFO. This section illustrates the significance of holding gains in the calculation of net income under FIFO and LIFO.

The conventionally reported gross margin (sales minus cost of goods sold) comprises (1) an operating margin and (2) a realized holding gain (or loss). The term **operating margin** denotes the difference between the selling price of an item and its replacement cost at the time of sale. This operating margin gives some indication of a particular firm's relative advantage, such as a reputation for quality or service, in the market for its goods. The term **realized holding gain** denotes the difference between the current replacement cost of an item at the time of sale and its acquisition cost. It reflects the change in cost of an item during the period the firm holds the inventory item. Holding gains indicate increasing purchase prices and the skill (or luck) of the purchasing department in timing acquisitions.

Holding inventory generates costs. The costs are both explicit, such as for storage, and implicit, such as for the earnings forgone because the firm invests cash to acquire the inventory. Even when a firm experiences holding gains, the amount of the gain need not be sufficient to compensate the firm for its costs to hold inventory. Management should want to know about both the costs of holding inventory and the benefits.

To understand the calculation of the operating margin and the holding gain, consider the TV set example discussed in this chapter. The acquisition cost of the three items available for sale during the period is $840. Assume that the firm sells one TV set for $550. The replacement cost of the TV set at the time of sale is $320. The current replacement cost at the end of the period for each item in ending inventory is $350, or $700 total for the two items remaining. The top portion of **Exhibit 7.8** separates the conventionally reported gross margin into the operating margin and the realized holding gain.

The operating margin is the difference between the $550 selling price and the $320 replacement cost at the time of sale. The operating margin of $230 is, by definition, the same under both the FIFO and the LIFO cost flow assumptions. The realized holding gain is the difference between cost of goods sold based on replacement cost and cost of goods sold based on acquisition cost. The realized holding gain under FIFO exceeds that under LIFO because FIFO assumes that the earlier purchases at lower costs enter cost of goods sold. The larger realized holding gain explains why net income under FIFO typically exceeds that under LIFO during periods of rising prices. The smaller realized holding gains and losses under LIFO explain why earnings under LIFO tend to fluctuate less over time than under FIFO (except when a firm dips into LIFO layers). In conventional financial statements, the realized holding gain does not appear separately, as in **Exhibit 7.8**. The term **inventory profit** sometimes denotes the realized holding gain on inventory. The amount of inventory profit varies from period to period as the rate of change in the purchase prices of inventories varies. The larger the inventory profit, the less sustainable are earnings and therefore the lower is the quality of earnings.

The calculation of an **unrealized holding gain** on units in ending inventory also appears in **Exhibit 7.8**. The unrealized holding gain shows the difference between the current replacement cost of the ending inventory and its acquisition cost.[6] This unrealized holding gain on ending inventory does not appear in the firm's income statement as presently prepared under GAAP. The unrealized holding gain under LIFO exceeds that under FIFO because earlier purchases with lower costs remain in ending inventory under LIFO. The sum of the operating margin plus all holding gains (both realized and unrealized), labeled "Economic Profit" in **Exhibit 7.8**, is the same under FIFO and LIFO. FIFO recognizes most of the holding gain (that is, the realized portion) in computing net income each period. LIFO does not recognize most of the holding gain (that is, the unrealized portion) in the income statement. Instead, under LIFO, the unrealized holding gain remains unreported as long as the older acquisition costs appear on the balance sheet as ending inventory.

The total increase in wealth for a period includes both realized and unrealized holding gains. That total increase, $410 in the example, does not depend on the cost flow assumption and does not appear in financial statements under currently accepted accounting principles.

EXHIBIT 7.8	Reporting of Operating Margins and Holding Gains for TV Sets			
		Cost Flow Assumption		
		FIFO		**LIFO**
Sales Revenue		$550		$550
Less Replacement Cost of Goods Sold		320		320
Operating Margin on Sales			$230	$230
Realized Holding Gain on TV Sets				
Replacement Cost (at time of sale) of Goods Sold		$320		$320
Less Acquisition Cost of Goods Sold (FIFO—TV set 1; LIFO—TV set 3)		250		300
Realized Holding Gain on TV Sets (inventory profit)			70	20
Conventionally Reported Gross Margin[a]			$300	$250
Unrealized Holding Gain				
Replacement Cost of Ending Inventory (2 × $350)			$700	$700
Less Acquisition Cost of Ending Inventory (FIFO—TV sets 2 and 3; LIFO—TV sets 1 and 2)			590	540
Unrealized Holding Gain on TV Sets			110	160
Economic Profit on Sales and Holding Inventory of TV Sets (not reported in financial statements)			$410	$410

[a] Note that Exhibit 7.3 stops here.

---

[6] The unrealized holding gain for a given year on items on hand both at the beginning and at the end of the year is the difference between year-end current cost and beginning-of-year current cost. The examples in this chapter do not illustrate this complication; all items on hand at the end of the year are purchased during the year. See the **Glossary** definition of *inventory profit* for an illustration of the computation of holding gain for a year in which the beginning inventory includes unrealized holding gains from preceding periods.

Problem 7.4 for Self-Study

Identifying operating margins and holding gains.   Refer to the data in **Problem 7.2 for Self-Study**. Sales revenue during June was $7,500. The average replacement cost at the time of sale was $12 per unit. The replacement cost on June 30 is $12.60 per unit.

a. Calculate the operating margin, the realized holding gain, and the unrealized holding gain during June using (1) FIFO, (2) LIFO, and (3) weighted-average cost flow assumptions. Refer to **Exhibit 7.8** for the desired format for this analysis.

b. "A firm's cost flow assumption does not affect the operating margin." Explain.

c. "The FIFO cost flow assumption typically includes most of the holding gain in net income, whereas the LIFO cost flow assumption implicitly includes more of the holding gain in the balance sheet." Explain.

Effect of Dipping into LIFO Layers

GAAP require firms that dip into LIFO layers during the period to indicate the effect of the dip on cost of goods sold. Assume, for example, that Nucor Corporation disclosed the following in its notes for the year:

> Because of recession conditions in the economy, Nucor dipped into LIFO layers created in earlier years. The effect of these inventory reductions decreased cost of goods sold and increased pretax income by $15 million.

As an earlier section discussed, firms may delay purchases at the end of the year and dip into LIFO layers as a means of increasing reported earnings. Firms may also dip into LIFO layers because of improved inventory control systems that reduce the amount of inventory needed. The analyst can assess the effect of dipping into LIFO layers by recomputing cost of goods sold and earnings assuming no dipping had occurred.

Cost of goods sold for Nucor under LIFO was $5,997 million (see **Exhibit 7.7**). Without dipping into LIFO layers, cost of goods sold would have been $6,012 (= $5,997 + $15). The ratio of cost of goods sold to sales with dipping is 95.7 percent (= $5,997/$6,266). The ratio without dipping is 95.9 percent (= $6,012/$6,266).

Relating Cost of Goods Sold Percentages and Inventory Turnover Ratios

Firms often experience changes in their cost of goods sold to sales percentages and their inventory turnover ratios simultaneously. Both ratios use cost of goods sold, so the analyst might expect a relation between them. Recall from **Chapter 5** that the rate of return on assets (ROA) is the product of the profit margin for ROA and the total assets turnover. Changes in the cost of goods sold to sales percentage affect the profit margin. Changes in inventory turnovers affect the total asset turnover. The sections below describe possible explanations for various combinations of changes in the cost of goods sold to sales percentage and the inventory turnover ratio.

Increasing Cost of Goods Sold to Sales Percentage and Increasing Inventory Turnover Ratio   This combination results in a lower profit margin and an increased total assets turnover. The net effect on ROA depends on which of the two effects dominates. The firm may have shifted its sales mix toward faster moving, but more commodity-like, products that generate smaller gross margins. The firm may also have increased the proportion of manufacturing outsourced to other manufacturers. Outsourcing lowers inventories by reducing the need for raw materials and work-in-process inventories. However, the firm must share some of the profit margin with the supplier, the outsourcing firm.

Decreasing Cost of Goods Sold to Sales Percentage and Increasing Inventory Turnover Ratio   This combination increases both the profit margin and the total assets turnover and thereby increases ROA. How might this combination occur? A firm institutes improved inventory control systems that increase its inventory turnover. The savings in storage

costs and costs of obsolescence reduce the cost of goods sold to sales percentage. Another possibility is that a firm experiences an increase in demand for its products because of reductions in supply by its competitors. Inventory moves more quickly. Shortages in supply permit the firm to raise prices and thereby lower the cost of goods sold to sales percentage. Consider, also, a capital-intensive manufacturer (with variable costs lower than average costs because of significant fixed costs). The increase in demand permits the firm to lower its per-unit manufacturing costs, moving inventory more quickly and lowering its cost of goods sold to sales percentage.

Increasing Cost of Goods Sold to Sales Percentage and Decreasing Inventory Turnover Ratio   This combination decreases both the profit margin and the total assets turnover and lowers ROA. How might this combination occur? The firm experiences a buildup of obsolete inventory because competitors introduce technologically superior products. The firm has to write down the cost of the inventory to lower-of-cost-or-market or reduce selling prices to sell the inventory. Consider, also, the capital-intensive manufacturing firm. Demand weakens, resulting in a curtailment of production. The weakening of demand slows the turnover of inventory.

Decreasing Cost of Goods Sold to Sales Percentage and Decreasing Inventory
This combination increases the profit margin but decreases the total assets turnover. The net effect on ROA depends on which effect dominates. This pair could occur because the firm reduced the amount of outsourcing, permitting the firm to capture more of the gross margin. The need for more raw materials and work-in-process inventories slows the inventory turnover. Or, the firm shifts its sales mix toward higher margin differentiated products that turn over more slowly.

Other explanations could cause the various combinations discussed above. Additional combinations of changes in one of the two ratios and not in the other are also possible. Given the links between the two ratios, the analyst should remain alert to possible common explanations.

Problem 7.5 for Self-Study

Effect of cost flow assumptions on financial ratios.   Refer to the data in **Problems 7.2** and **7.3 for Self-Study**. Assume the following:

	June 30	July 31	August 31
Current Assets Excluding Inventories	$1,650	$3,480	$3,230
Current Liabilities	2,290	4,820	3,750

a. Compute the current ratio for June 30, July 31, and August 31 using (1) FIFO, (2) LIFO, and (3) weighted-average cost flow assumptions for inventories. Assume for this part that there are no differences in income taxes payable related to the three cost flow assumptions.
b. Compute the inventory turnover ratio (= cost of goods sold/average inventory) for July and August using (1) FIFO, (2) LIFO, and (3) weighted-average cost flow assumptions.

An International Perspective

Statement No. 2 of the International Accounting Standards Board supports the use of the lower-of-cost-or-market basis for the valuation of inventories, with market value based on net realizable values.[7] All major industrialized countries require the lower-of-cost-or-market method in the valuation of inventories, although the definition of market value varies across countries. *Statement No. 2* states a preference for the FIFO and weighted-average cost flow assumptions.

LIFO is an acceptable alternative, but firms should disclose how LIFO inventories differ from those valued under the lower-of-cost-or-market method. Few countries, except the United States and Japan, allow LIFO. Even in Japan, few firms use LIFO. Firms in most countries use FIFO and weighted-average cost flow assumptions. The extensive use of LIFO in the United States results from income tax considerations.

---

[7] International Accounting Standards Board, *Statement No. 2*: "Inventories," 1993.

Inventory measurements affect both the cost of goods sold on the income statement for the period and the amount shown for inventory on the balance sheet at the end of the period. The sum of the two must equal the beginning inventory plus the cost of purchases, at least in accounting based on acquisition costs and market transactions. The allocation between expense and asset depends primarily on the cost flow assumption (FIFO, LIFO, or weighted average) used.

FIFO provides inventory amounts that closely approximate current replacement costs. Costs of goods sold amounts are somewhat out of date, reflecting the cost of purchases toward the end of the previous period and the beginning of the current period. The gross margin under FIFO includes a realized holding gain for the increase in replacement cost between the time of purchase and the time of sale. The realized holding gain does not represent sustainable economic value added if the firm must replace the inventory at its currently higher costs. The amount of the holding gain depends on the change in costs between the time of purchase and sale. When inventory turns over four times a year, the elapsed time between acquisition and sale is three months. When inventory turns over six times a year, the elapsed time is only two months.

LIFO generally provides amounts for cost of goods sold that approximate current replacement cost at the time of sale. An exception occurs, however, when a firm dips into LIFO layers acquired in earlier years. The cost of goods sold amount for that period will reflect a combination of current and older acquisition costs. Inventories under LIFO may reflect very old costs, depending on how long the firm has used LIFO. A substantial unrealized holding gain on LIFO inventories exists that GAAP do not report on the balance sheet.

The weighted-average cost flow assumption provides inventory amounts similar to FIFO and cost of goods sold amounts that generally fall between those of FIFO and LIFO. When deciding on a cost flow assumption, firms must consider the effect on earnings, on taxes paid, and on recordkeeping costs.

Appendix 7.1: Effects on the Statement of Cash Flows of Transactions Involving Inventory

The question that an analyst would raise regarding cash flows and inventory is: How much cash did a firm use to purchase (merchandising firm) or produce (manufacturing firm) inventory during the year? **Exhibit 7.9** presents information to illustrate the adjustments to compute the cash paid for inventory purchases of a merchandising firm.

EXHIBIT 7.9	Data to Illustrate Cash Used to Purchase Inventory		
		Inventory	Accounts Payable
Balance, Beginning of Year		$ 100	$ 75
Purchases of Inventory on Account		1,000	1,000
Cost of Goods Sold		(800)	—
Cash Payments for Purchases on Account		—	(900)
Writedown of Inventories to Lower of Cost or Market		(50)	—
Balance, End of Year		$ 250	$ 175

The computation of cash payments for purchases of inventory under the direct method of computing cash flow from operations is as follows:

Cost of Goods Sold	$(800)
Less Increase in Inventory ($250 − $100)	(150)
Plus Increase in Accounts Payable ($175 − $75)	100
Less Writedown to Lower of Cost or Market	(50)
Cash Payments for Purchases on Account	$(900)

If firms include the loss from the writedown of inventories in cost of goods sold, as usually occurs, then the first line above becomes a negative $850. The analyst need not make a separate adjustment for the writedown of inventories in this case to compute cash payments for purchases.

The computation of cash flow from operations under the indirect method is as follows:

Net Income (for Cost of Goods Sold and Loss from Writedown of Inventories)	$(850)
Less Increase in Inventory ($250 − $100)	(150)
Plus Increase in Accounts Payable ($175 − $75)	100
Cash Flow from Operations	$(900)

The computation of cash paid for production of inventory follows these same procedures, but is more complex. The analyst must include changes in raw materials inventory, work-in-process inventory, and finished goods inventory in the change in inventory. In addition to changes in accounts payable from raw materials purchases, the analyst must include changes in other current liabilities, such as wages payable and taxes payable, to the extent that they relate to manufacturing operations. Firms seldom provide the necessary data to separate payables into the portions arising from manufacturing activities versus selling and administrative activities. Thus, computing cash paid for manufacturing costs is usually difficult.

Solutions to Self-Study Problems

SUGGESTED SOLUTION TO PROBLEM 7.1 FOR SELF-STUDY

(Haskell Corporation; flow of manufacturing costs through the accounts.)

a.	Beginning Raw Materials Inventory	$ 42,400
	Raw Materials Purchased	60,700
	Raw Materials Available for Use	$103,100
	Subtract Ending Raw Materials Inventory	46,900
	Cost of Raw Materials Used	$ 56,200
b.	Beginning Work-in-Process Inventory	$ 75,800
	Cost of Raw Materials Used (from part **a**)	56,200
	Direct Labor Costs Incurred	137,900
	Heat, Light, and Power Costs	1,260
	Rent Costs	4,100
	Depreciation of Factory Equipment	1,800
	Prepaid Insurance Costs Consumed	1,440
	Total Beginning Work-in-Process and Manufacturing Costs Incurred	$278,500
	Subtract Ending Work-in-Process Inventory	(63,200)
	Cost of Units Completed and Transferred to Finished Goods Storeroom	$215,300
c.	Beginning Finished Goods Inventory	$ 44,200
	Cost of Units Completed and Transferred to Finished Goods Storeroom (from part **b**)	215,300
	Subtract Ending Finished Goods Inventory	(46,300)
	Cost of Goods Sold	$213,200
d.	Income before taxes is $61,800 (= $400,000 − $213,200 − $125,000).	

SUGGESTED SOLUTION TO PROBLEM 7.2 FOR SELF-STUDY

(Computing cost of goods sold and ending inventory under various cost flow assumptions.)

a. See **Exhibit 7.10**.

EXHIBIT 7.10	(Suggested Solution to Problem 7.2 for Self-Study, part **a**)

	Units	Unit Cost	Total Cost FIFO	Total Cost LIFO	Total Cost Weighted Average
Beginning Inventory	—	—	—	—	
Purchases, June 1	100	$10.00	$1,000	$1,000	$1,000
Purchases, June 7	400	11.00	4,400	4,400	4,400
Purchases, June 18	100	12.50	1,250	1,250	1,250
Total Goods Available for Sale	600		$6,650	$6,650	$6,650
Withdrawals during June	(495)		(5,345)[a]	(5,595)[c]	(5,486)[e]
Ending Inventory	105		$1,305[b]	$1,055[d]	$1,164[f]

[a] $(100 \times \$10.00) + (395 \times \$11.00) = \$5,345$.

[b] $(100 \times \$12.50) + (5 \times \$11.00) = \$1,305$.

[c] $(100 \times \$12.50) + (395 \times \$11.00) = \$5,595$.

[d] $(100 \times \$10.00) + (5 \times \$11.00) = \$1,055$.

[e] $495 \times (\$6,650/600) = \$5,486$.

[f] $105 \times (\$6,650/600) = \$1,164$.

b. See **Exhibit 7.11**.

EXHIBIT 7.11	(Suggested Solution to Problem 7.2 for Self-Study, part **b**)

	Units	Unit Cost	Total Cost FIFO	Total Cost LIFO	Total Cost Weighted Average
Beginning Inventory, July 1	105	See Exhibit 7.10	$ 1,305	$ 1,055	$ 1,164
Purchases, July 5	300	$13.00	3,900	3,900	3,900
Purchases, July 15	200	13.50	2,700	2,700	2,700
Purchases, July 23	250	14.00	3,500	3,500	3,500
Total Goods Available for Sale	855		$11,405	$11,155	$11,264
Withdrawals during July	(620)		(8,115)[a]	(8,410)[c]	(8,168)[e]
Ending Inventory	235		$ 3,290[b]	$ 2,745[d]	$ 3,096[f]

[a] $\$1,305 + (300 \times \$13.00) 1 (200 \times \$13.50) + (15 \times \$14.00) = \$8,115$.

[b] $(235 \times \$14.00) = \$3,290$.

[c] $(250 \times \$14.00) + (200 \times \$13.50) + (170 \times \$13.00) = \$8,410$.

[d] $\$1,055 + (130 \times \$13.00) = \$2,745$.

[e] $620 \times (\$11,264/855) = \$8,168$.

[f] $235 \times (\$11,264/855) = \$3,096$.

SUGGESTED SOLUTION TO PROBLEM 7.3 FOR SELF-STUDY

(Assessing the impact of a LIFO layer liquidation.)
a. See **Exhibit 7.12**.
b. 125 × ($15 − $13) = $250.

EXHIBIT 7.12	(Suggested Solution to Problem 7.3 for Self-Study, part **a**)

	Units	Unit Cost	Total Cost		
			FIFO	**LIFO**	**Weighted Average**
Beginning Inventory	235	See Exhibit 7.11	$ 3,290	$ 2,745	$ 3,096
Purchases during August	600	$15	9,000	9,000	9,000
Total Goods Available for Sale	835		$ 12,290	$ 11,745	$ 12,096
Withdrawals during August	(725)		(10,640)[a]	(10,625)[c]	(10,503)[e]
Ending Inventory	110		$ 1,650[b]	$ 1,120[d]	$ 1,593[f]

[a] $3,290 + (490 × $15) = $10,640.
[b] (110 × $15) = $1,650.
[c] (600 × $15) + (125 × $13) = $10,625.
[d] $1,055 + (5 × $13) = $1,120.
[e] ($12,096/835) × 725 = $10,503.
[f] ($12,096/835) × 110 = $1,593.

SUGGESTED SOLUTION TO PROBLEM 7.4 FOR SELF-STUDY

(Identifying operating margins and holding gains.)
a. See **Exhibit 7.13**.

EXHIBIT 7.13	(Suggested Solution to Problem 7.4 for Self-Study, part **a**)

	Cost Flow Assumption		
	FIFO	**LIFO**	**Weighted Average**
OPERATING MARGIN			
Sales Revenue	$ 7,500	$ 7,500	$ 7,500
Less Replacement Cost of Goods Sold (495 × $12)	(5,940)	(5,940)	(5,940)
Operating Margin	$ 1,560	$ 1,560	$ 1,560
REALIZED HOLDING GAIN			
Replacement Cost of Goods Sold	$ 5,940	$ 5,940	$ 5,940
Acquisition Cost of Goods Sold	(5,345)	(5,595)	(5,486)
Realized Holding Gain	$ 595	$ 345	$ 454
Conventionally Reported Gross Margin	$ 2,155	$ 1,905	$ 2,014
UNREALIZED HOLDING GAIN			
Replacement Cost of Ending Inventory (105 × $12.60)	$ 1,323	$ 1,323	$ 1,323
Acquisition Cost of Ending Inventory	(1,305)	(1,055)	(1,164)
Unrealized Holding Gain	$ 18	$ 268	$ 159
Economic Profit	$ 2,173	$ 2,173	$ 2,173

b. The operating margin relates sales to the replacement cost of goods sold. The replacement cost at the time of sale depends on prices for the items at that time (even though the firm purchased no items then) and not on the prices that the firm, earlier, actually paid. In contrast, in historical cost accounting, when the firm makes a cost flow assumption, it matches one of the earlier prices with the sales revenue at the time of sale.

c. The holding gain arises because the replacement costs of inventory items increase while firms hold them. The length of the assumed holding period for goods sold under a FIFO cost flow assumption exceeds the assumed holding period under LIFO (unless a firm dips into LIFO layers of earlier years). Thus, FIFO typically reports a larger realized holding gain as part of net income. The length of the assumed holding period for goods in ending inventory under a LIFO cost flow assumption exceeds the assumed holding period under FIFO. Thus, LIFO's inventory valuation on the balance sheet reflects a larger unrealized holding gain.

SUGGESTED SOLUTION TO PROBLEM 7.5 FOR SELF-STUDY

(Effect of cost flow assumptions on financial ratios.)

a. Current Ratio

June 30	FIFO	LIFO	Weighted Average
($1,650 + $1,305)/$2,290	1.29		
($1,650 + $1,055)/$2,290		1.18	
($1,650 + $1,164)/$2,290			1.23
Current Ratio			
JULY 31			
($3,480 + $3,290)/$4,820	1.40		
($3,480 + $2,745)/$4,820		1.29	
($3,480 + $3,096)/$4,820			1.36
AUGUST 31			
($3,230 + $1,650)/$3,750	1.30		
($3,230 + $1,120)/$3,750		1.16	
($3,230 + $1,593)/$3,750			1.29

b. Inventory Turnover Ratio

	FIFO	LIFO	Weighted Average
JULY			
$8,115/0.5($1,305 + $3,290)	3.53		
$8,410/0.5($1,055 + $2,745)		4.43	
$8,168/0.5($1,164 + $3,096)			3.83
AUGUST			
$10,640/0.5($3,290 + $1,650)	4.31		
$10,625/0.5($2,745 + $1,120)		5.50	
$10,503/0.5($3,096 + $1,593)			4.48

Key Terms and Concepts

Inventory
Inventory equation
Purchases
Direct material
Direct labor
Manufacturing overhead
Product costs
Period expenses
Flow of costs
Raw Materials Inventory
Work-in-Process Inventory
Finished Goods Inventory
Replacement cost

Lower-of-cost-or-market basis
Specific identification
Cost flow assumption
First-in, first-out (FIFO)
Last-in, first-out (LIFO)
Weighted average
LIFO inventory layer
Inventory valuation allowance
Operating margin
Realized holding gain
Inventory profit
Unrealized holding gain

Questions, Short Exercises, Exercises, Problems, and Cases

QUESTIONS

1. Review the meaning of the terms and concepts listed above in Key Terms and Concepts.
2. Identify the underlying accounting principle that guides the measurement of the acquisition cost of inventories, equipment, buildings, and other assets. What is the rationale for this accounting principle?
3. "Firms may treat depreciation on equipment either as a product cost or as a period expense, depending on the type of equipment." Explain.
4. Compare and contrast the Merchandise Inventory account of a merchandising firm and the Finished Goods Inventory account of a manufacturing firm.
5. "The total income from an inventory item is the difference between the cash received from selling the item and the cash paid to acquire it. The inventory valuation method (acquisition cost, current replacement cost, lower of cost or market) is therefore largely irrelevant." Do you agree? Why or why not?
6. Assume that a firm changes its cost basis for inventory from acquisition cost to current cost, that current costs exceed acquisition costs at the end of the year of change, and that the firm sells all year-end inventory during the following year. Ignore income tax effects. What will be the impact of the change on net income for the year of change? on income for the following year? on total income over the two years?
7. "Inventory computations require cost flow assumptions only because specific identification of items sold is costly. Specific identification is theoretically superior to any cost flow assumption and eliminates the possibility of income manipulation available with some cost flow assumptions." Comment.
8. Assume no changes in physical quantities during the period. During a period of rising purchase prices, will a FIFO or a LIFO cost flow assumption result in the higher ending inventory amount? the lower amount? Which cost flow assumption will result in the higher ending inventory amount during a period of declining purchase prices? the lower inventory amount?
9. **a.** During a period of rising purchase prices, will a FIFO or a LIFO cost flow assumption result in the higher cost of goods sold? the lower cost of goods sold? Assume no changes in physical quantities during the period.
   b. Which cost flow assumption, LIFO or FIFO, will result in the higher cost of goods sold during a period of declining purchase prices? the lower cost of goods sold?
10. "LIFO provides a more meaningful income statement than FIFO, even though it provides a less meaningful balance sheet." Does it ever? Does it always?
11. Explain each of the following statements:
    a. Differences between the effects of FIFO and LIFO on the financial statements increase as the rate of change in the cost of inventory items increases.
    b. Differences between the effects of FIFO and LIFO on cost of goods sold decrease as the rate of inventory turnover increases.
    c. Differences between FIFO and LIFO amounts for inventories on the balance sheet do not decrease as the rate of inventory turnover increases.
12. Identify the reasons a firm might dip into an old LIFO layer.
13. "A firm that changes its selling prices when the acquisition costs of its inventory items change will report smoother gross margins over time under LIFO than under FIFO." Explain this statement using the concepts of operating margins and realized holding gains.
14. Suggest reasons a firm would choose a FIFO instead of a LIFO cost flow assumption for financial reporting.
15. "A firm that dips into its LIFO layers and pays additional taxes in a particular year is still better off than if had used FIFO all along." Explain. Under what circumstances will the firm be worse off?

SHORT EXERCISES

16. **Identifying inventory cost inclusions.** Intervest Corporation, a real estate developer, purchased a tract of land for $450,000. Intervest intends to develop and subdivide the land for construction of residential homes. Legal costs related to the acquisition totaled $12,000. Property taxes and insurance during the development of the land totaled $22,900. Development costs totaled $689,000. Advertising costs incurred to sell the land totaled $38,200. Identify the costs that Intervest should include in its Land Inventory account.

17. **Effect of inventory valuation on net income.** Selby Corporation, a commercial real estate developer, acquired a tract of land on September, Year 6 for $240,000. Forest fires on December, Year 6, reduced the value of this land to $160,000. In December, Year 7, a local hospital announced plans to build a new hospital near the land, increasing its market value to $420,000. Selby Corporation sold this land in February, Year 8 for $460,000. Compute the amount of income or loss related to this land for Year 6, Year 7, and Year 8 and for the three years as a whole, assuming that the firm reports the land inventory on its balance sheet using (1) acquisition cost, (2) lower of cost or market, and (3) market value.

18. **Income computation for a manufacturing firm.** Fun-in-the-Sun Tanning Lotion Company manufactures suntan lotion made from organic materials. During its first year of operations it purchased raw materials costing $78,200, of which it used $56,300 in manufacturing suntan lotions. It incurred manufacturing labor costs of $36,100 and manufacturing overhead costs of $26,800 during the year. Inventories taken at the end of the year revealed unfinished suntan lotions costing $12,700 and finished suntan lotions costing $28,500. Compute the amount of cost of goods sold for the year.

19. **Computations involving different cost flow assumptions.** Sun Health Food's purchases of vitamins during Year 10, its first year of operations, were as follows:

	Quantity	Cost per Unit	Total Cost
January 5 Purchase	460	$4.30	$ 1,978
April 16 Purchase	670	4.20	2,814
August 26 Purchase	500	4.16	2,080
November 13 Purchase	870	4.10	3,567
Totals	2,500		$10,439

The inventory on December 31 was 420 units. Compute the cost of the inventory on December 31 and the cost of goods sold for the year under each of the following cost flow assumptions:
a. FIFO
b. Weighted average
c. LIFO

20. **Effect of LIFO on financial statements over several periods.** Harmon Corporation commenced operations on January 2, Year 8. It uses a LIFO cost flow assumption. Its purchases and sales for the first three years of operations appear below:

	Purchases		Sales	
	Units	Unit Cost	Units	Unit Price
Year 8	83,000	$20.00	64,000	$32.00
Year 9	92,000	$25.00	101,000	$40.00
Year 10	120,000	$30.00	110,000	$48.00

a. Compute the amount of ending inventory for each of the three years.
b. Compute the amount of income for each of the three years.

21. **Effect of dipping into LIFO inventories.** Robertson Corporation uses a LIFO cost flow assumption for inventories and cost of goods sold. Its beginning inventory for the current year totaled $48,900 and its ending inventory totaled $42,600. Cost of goods sold for the year totaled $286,700. A note to its financial statements discloses that income before taxes would have been $2,700 lower if it had not dipped into LIFO layers during the year. Compute the purchase price of merchandise that Robertson Corporation would have had to acquire to avoid dipping into its LIFO layers.

23. **Conversion from LIFO to FIFO.** United States Steel Corporation reported inventories using LIFO of $1,030 million at the beginning of Year 13, and $1,283 million at the end of Year 13. Its cost of goods sold for Year 13 totaled $8,469 million. Inventories on a FIFO basis would exceed its inventories on a LIFO basis by $310 million at the beginning of the year and $270 million at the end of the year. Compute the amount for cost of goods sold if the firm had used a FIFO instead of a LIFO cost flow assumption.

23. **Separating operating margins and holding gains.** During Year 8, its first year of operations, Miller Corporation purchased 10,000 units at $80 each and sold 9,000 units for $100 each. On December 31, Year 8, the units had a replacement cost of $84. The average replacement cost

during Year 8 was $82. Compute the amount of operating margin, realized holding gain or loss, unrealized holding gain or loss, and economic profit for Year 8.

EXERCISES

24. **Identifying inventory cost inclusions.** Trembly Department Store commenced operations on January 2. It engaged in the following transactions during January. Identify the amount that the firm should include in the valuation of merchandise inventory.

   a. Purchases of merchandise on account during January totaled $300,000.
   b. The freight cost to transport merchandise to Trembly's warehouse was $13,800.
   c. The salary of the purchasing manager was $3,000.
   d. Depreciation, taxes, insurance, and utilities for the warehouse totaled $27,300.
   e. The salary of the warehouse manager was $2,200.
   f. The cost of merchandise that Trembly purchased in part **a** and returned to the supplier was $18,500.
   g. Cash discounts taken by Trembly from purchases on account in part **a** totaled $4,900.

25. **Income computation for a manufacturing firm.** The following data relate to General Mills, a food processor, for a recent fiscal year ending May 31 (amounts in millions):

	June 1, Year 10	May 31, Year 11
Raw Materials Inventory	$ 73.7	$101.5
Work-in-Process Inventory	100.8	119.1
Finished Goods Inventory	286.2	322.3

The company incurred manufacturing costs (direct material, direct labor, manufacturing overhead) during the fiscal year totaling $2,752.0. Sales revenue was $6,700.2, selling and administrative expenses were $2,903.7, and interest expense was $151.9. The income tax rate is 35 percent. Compute net income for the fiscal year.

26. **Income computation for a manufacturing firm.** The following data relate to Dow Chemical Corporation for a single year (amounts in millions):

	January 1	December 31
Raw Materials Inventory	$ 452	$ 373
Work-in-Process Inventory	843	837
Finished Goods Inventory	2,523	2,396

The company incurred manufacturing costs (direct material used, direct labor, and manufacturing overhead) during the year totaling $28,044. Sales revenue was $32,632, marketing and administrative expenses were $2,436, and interest expenses were $828. The income tax rate is 35 percent. Compute net income for the year.

27. **Over sufficiently long time spans, income is cash-in less cash-out; cost basis for inventory.** Duggan Company began business on January 1, Year 1. Information concerning merchandise inventories, purchases, and sales for the first three years of operations follows:

	Year 1	Year 2	Year 3
Sales	$200,000	$300,000	$400,000
Purchases	210,000	271,000	352,000
Inventories, December 31:			
At cost	60,000	80,000	115,000
At market	50,000	65,000	120,000

   a. Compute the gross margin on sales (sales minus cost of goods sold) for each year, using the lower-of-cost-or-market basis in valuing inventories.
   b. Compute the gross margin on sales (sales minus cost of goods sold) for each year, using the acquisition cost basis in valuing inventories.
   c. Indicate your conclusion about whether the lower-of-cost-or-market basis of valuing inventories is conservative.

28. **When goods available for sale exceed sales, firms can manipulate income even when they use specific identification.** Cypres, a discounter of consumer electronics, has 300 identical computers available for sale during December. It acquired these computers as follows: 100 in June for $300 each, 100 in August for $400 each, and 100 in November for $350 each. Assume that sales for December are 200 units at $600 each.

   a. Compute gross margin for December assuming FIFO.

   b. Compute gross margin for December assuming specific identification of computers sold to minimize reported income for tax purposes.

   c. Compute gross margin for December assuming specific identification of computers sold to maximize reported income for the purpose of increasing the store manager's profit-sharing bonus for the year.

29. **Computations involving different cost flow assumptions.** Arnold Company's raw material purchases during January, its first month of operations, were as follows:

	Quantity	Cost per Pound	Total Costs
1/2 Purchased	1,200 pounds	$2.20	$ 2,640
1/8 Purchased	2,200 pounds	2.25	4,950
1/15 Purchased	2,800 pounds	2.28	6,384
1/23 Purchased	1,500 pounds	2.30	3,450
1/28 Purchased	3,000 pounds	2.32	6,960
Total Goods Available for Use	10,700 pounds		$24,384

   The inventory at January 31 was 3,500 pounds. Compute the cost of the inventory on January 31 and the cost of raw materials issued to production for January under each of the following cost flow assumptions:

   a. FIFO

   b. Weighted average

   c. LIFO

30. **Effect of LIFO on financial statements over several periods.** Howell Corporation commenced operations on January 2, Year 7. Its purchases and sales for the first four years of operations appear below:

	Purchases		Sales	
	Units	Unit Cost	Units	Unit Price
Year 7	36,000	$10.00	28,000	$12.00
Year 8	40,000	10.50	38,000	12.60
Year 9	45,000	11.30	48,000	13.23
Year 10	53,000	12.40	52,000	13.89

   Howell Corporation uses a LIFO cost flow assumption. Ignore income taxes.

   a. Compute the ending inventory for each of the four years.

   b. Compute income for each of the four years.

   c. Compute the ratio of income divided by sales for each of the four years.

   d. Interpret the pattern of income-to-sales percentages computed in part **c**.

31. **Reconstructing financial statement data from information on effects of liquidations of LIFO layers.** The inventory footnote to the annual report of Chan Company reads in part as follows:

   Because of continuing high demand throughout the year, inventories were unavoidably reduced and could not be replaced. Under the LIFO system of accounting, used for many years by Chan Company, the net effect of all the inventory changes was to increase pretax income by $900,000 over what it would have been had inventories been maintained at their physical levels at the start of the year.

   The acquisition cost of Chan Company's merchandise purchases was $26 per unit during the year, after having risen erratically over past years. Its inventory positions at the beginning and the end of the year follow.

Date	Physical Count of Inventory	LIFO Cost of Inventory
January 1	200,000 units	$?
December 31	150,000 units	$600,000

    a. What was the average cost per unit of the 50,000 units removed from the January 1 LIFO inventory?

    b. What was the January 1 LIFO cost of inventory?

32. LIFO provides opportunity for income manipulation. EKG Company, a manufacturer of medical supplies, began the year with 10,000 units of product that cost $8 each. During the year, it produced another 60,000 units at a cost of $15 each. Sales for the year were expected to total 70,000 units. During November, the company needs to plan production for the remainder of the year. The company might produce no additional units beyond the 60,000 units already produced. On the other hand, the company could produce up to 100,000 additional units; the cost would be $22 per unit regardless of the quantity produced. Assume that sales are 70,000 units for the year at an average price of $30 per unit.

    a. What production level for the remainder of the year gives the largest cost of goods sold for the year? What is that cost of goods sold?

    b. What production level for the remainder of the year gives the smallest cost of goods sold for the year? What is that cost of goods sold?

    c. Compare the gross margins implied by the two production plans devised in the preceding parts.

33. Analysis of annual report; usage of LIFO. The notes to the financial statements in an annual report of Sears, Roebuck, and Company contained the following statement: "If the physical quantity of goods in inventory at [year-end and the beginning of the year] . . . were to be replaced, the estimated expenditures of funds required would exceed the amounts reported by approximately $670 million and $440 million, respectively." Sears uses LIFO.

    a. How much higher or lower would Sears's pretax reported income have been if it had valued inventories at current costs rather than with a LIFO cost flow assumption?

    b. Sears reported $606 million net income for the year. Assume tax expense equal to 35 percent of pretax income. By what percentage would Sears' net income have increased if a FIFO cost flow assumption had been used?

34. Separating operating margin from holding gains. On January 1, the merchandise inventory of Giles Computer Store comprised 200 units acquired for $300 each. During the year, the firm acquired 2,500 additional units at an average cost of $400 each and sold 2,300 units for $800 each. The replacement cost of these units at the time they were sold averaged $400 during the year. The replacement cost of units on December 31 was $500 per unit.

    a. Calculate cost of goods sold under both FIFO and LIFO cost flow assumptions.

    b. Prepare partial income statements showing gross margin on sales as revenues less cost of goods sold under both FIFO and LIFO cost flow assumptions.

    c. Prepare partial income statements, separating the gross margin on sales into operating margins and realized holding gains, under both FIFO and LIFO.

    d. Append to the bottom of the statements prepared in part **c** a statement showing the amount of unrealized holding gains and the total of realized income plus unrealized holding gains.

    e. If you did the previous steps correctly, the totals in part **d** are the same for both FIFO and LIFO. Is this equality a coincidence? Why or why not?

35. Effect of inventory errors. On December 30, Year 1, Warren Company received merchandise costing $1,000 and counted it in the December 31 listing of all items on hand. The firm included the cost of the inventory in its ending inventory on the balance sheet on December 31, Year 1. The firm received an invoice on January 4, Year 2, when it recorded the acquisition as a Year 2 acquisition. It should have recorded the acquisition for Year 1. Assume that the firm never discovered the error. Indicate the effect (overstatement, understatement, none) on each of the following amounts (ignore income taxes):

    a. Inventory, 12/31/Year 1

    b. Inventory, 12/31/Year 2

    c. Cost of goods sold, Year 1

    d. Cost of goods sold, Year 2

    e. Net income, Year 1

    f. Net income, Year 2

g. Accounts payable, 12/31/Year 1
h. Accounts payable, 12/31/Year 2
i. Retained earnings, 12/31/Year 2

PROBLEMS AND CASES

36. **Preparation of journal entries and income statement for a manufacturing firm.** Best Furniture, Inc., a furniture manufacturer, showed the following amounts in its inventory accounts on January 1:

Raw Materials Inventory	$226,800
Work-in-Process Inventory	427,900
Finished Goods Inventory.	182,700

Best Furniture engaged in the following transactions during January:
(1) Acquired raw materials costing $667,200 on account.
(2) Issued, to producing departments, raw materials costing $689,100.
(3) Paid salaries and wages during January for services received during the month as follows:

Factory Workers	$432,800
Sales Personnel	89,700
Administrative Officers	22,300

(4) Calculated depreciation on buildings and equipment during January as follows:

Manufacturing Facilities	$182,900
Selling Facilities	87,400
Administrative Facilities	12,200

(5) Incurred and paid other operating costs in cash as follows:

Manufacturing	$218,500
Selling	55,100
Administrative	34,700

(6) The cost of goods manufactured and transferred to the finished goods storeroom totaled $1,564,500.
(7) Sales on account during January totaled $2,400,000.
(8) A physical inventory taken on January 31 revealed a finished goods inventory of $210,600.
   a. Present journal entries to record the transactions and events that occurred during January.
   b. Prepare an income statement for Best Furniture, Inc. for January. Ignore income taxes.

37. **Flow of manufacturing costs through the accounts.** The following data related to the manufacturing activities of the Cornell Company during June:

	June 1	June 30
Raw Materials Inventory	$ 46,900	$ 43,600
Factory Supplies Inventory	7,600	7,700
Work-in-Process Inventory	110,900	115,200
Finished Goods Inventory	76,700	71,400

It incurred factory costs during the month as follows:

Raw Materials Purchased	$429,000
Supplies Purchased	22,300
Labor Services Received	362,100
Heat, Light, and Power	10,300
Insurance	4,200

It experienced expirations of previous factory acquisitions and prepayments as follows:

Depreciation on Factory Equipment	$36,900
Prepaid Rent Expired	3,600

Other information included the following:

Sales	$1,350,000
Selling and Administrative Expenses	246,900
Interest Expense	47,100
Income Tax Rate	40%

a. Calculate the cost of raw materials and factory supplies used during June.

b. Calculate the cost of units completed during June and transferred to the finished goods storeroom.

c. Calculate the cost of goods sold during June.

d. Calculate the amount of net income for the month of June. The income tax rate is 40 percent.

38. **Flow of manufacturing costs through the accounts.** The following data relate to the activities of Hickory Industries during April:

	April 1	April 30
Raw Materials Inventory	$ 50,600	$ 54,400
Work-in-Process Inventory	156,200	153,800
Finished Goods Inventory	76,800	79,400

It incurred factory costs during the month as follows:

Raw Materials Purchased	$182,600
Labor Services Received	144,800
Heat, Light, and Power	6,200
Depreciation	35,600

Other data relating to the month included the following:

Sales	$525,000
Selling and Administrative Expenses	82,600

a. Calculate the cost of raw materials used during April.

b. Calculate the cost of units completed during April and transferred to the finished goods storeroom.

c. Calculate net income for April. The income tax rate is 40 percent.

39. **Detailed comparison of various choices for inventory accounting.** Hartison Corporation commenced retailing operations on January 1, Year 1. It made purchases of merchandise inventory during Year 1 and Year 2 as follows:

	Quantity Purchased	Unit Price	Acquisition Cost
1/10/Year 1	1,200	$10	$12,000
6/30/Year 1	700	12	8,400
10/20/Year 1	400	13	5,200
Total Year 1	2,300		$25,600

	Quantity Purchased	Unit Price	Acquisition Cost
2/18/Year 2	600	$15	$ 9,000
7/15/Year 2	1,200	16	19,200
12/15/Year 2	800	18	14,400
Total Year 2	2,600		$42,600

Hartison Corporation sold 1,800 units during Year 1 and 2,800 units during Year 2.

a. Calculate the cost of goods sold for Year 1 using a FIFO cost flow assumption.

b. Calculate the cost of goods sold for Year 1 using a LIFO cost flow assumption.

c. Calculate the cost of goods sold for Year 1 using a weighted-average cost flow assumption.

d. Calculate the cost of goods sold for Year 2 using a FIFO cost flow assumption.

e. Calculate the cost of goods sold for Year 2 using a LIFO cost flow assumption.

f. Calculate the cost of goods sold for Year 2 using a weighted-average cost flow assumption.

g. For the two years taken as a whole, will FIFO or LIFO result in reporting the larger net income? What is the difference in net income for the two-year period under FIFO as compared with LIFO? Assume an income tax rate of 40 percent for both years.

h. Which method, LIFO or FIFO, should Hartison Corporation probably prefer and why?

40. **Continuation of preceding problem introducing current cost concepts.** (Do not attempt this problem until you have worked **Problem 39**.) Assume the same data for Hartison Corporation as given in the previous problem. In addition, assume the following:

Selling Price per Unit	
Year 1	$18
Year 2	24
Average Current Replacement Cost	
Year 1	$12
Year 2	16
Current Replacement Cost	
December 31, Year 1	$14
December 31, Year 2	18

a. Prepare an analysis for Year 1 that identifies operating margins, realized holding gains and losses, and unrealized holding gains and losses for the FIFO, LIFO, and weighted-average cost flow assumptions.

b. Repeat part **a** for Year 2.

c. Demonstrate that over the two-year period, income plus holding gains before taxes of Hartison Corporation are independent of the cost flow assumption.

41. **Detailed comparison of various choices for inventory accounting.** Burton Corporation commenced retailing operations on January 1, Year 1. Purchases of merchandise inventory during Year 1 and Year 2 appear below:

	Quantity Purchased	Unit Price	Acquisition Cost
1/10/Year 1	600	$10	$ 6,000
6/30/Year 1	200	12	2,400
10/20/Year 1	400	15	6,000
Total Year 1	1,200		$14,400

	Quantity Purchased	Unit Price	Acquisition Cost
2/18/Year 2	500	$14	$ 7,000
7/15/Year 2	500	12	6,000
12/15/Year 2	800	10	8,000
Total Year 2	1,800		$21,000

Burton Corporation sold 1,000 units during Year 1 and 1,500 units during Year 2.
   a. Calculate the cost of goods sold for Year 1 using a FIFO cost flow assumption.
   b. Calculate the cost of goods sold for Year 1 using a LIFO cost flow assumption.
   c. Calculate the cost of goods sold for Year 1 using a weighted-average cost flow assumption.
   d. Calculate the cost of goods sold for Year 2 using a FIFO cost flow assumption.
   e. Calculate the cost of goods sold for Year 2 using a LIFO cost flow assumption.
   f. Calculate the cost of goods sold for Year 2 using a weighted-average cost flow assumption.
   g. Will FIFO or LIFO result in reporting the larger net income for Year 1? Explain.
   h. Will FIFO or LIFO result in reporting the larger net income for Year 2? Explain.

42. **Continuation of preceding problem introducing current cost concepts.** (Do not attempt this problem until you have worked **Problem 41**.) Assume the same data for Burton Corporation as given in the previous problem. In addition, assume the following:

Selling Price per Unit	
Year 1	$25
Year 2	22
Average Current Replacement Cost	
Year 1	$14
Year 2	12
Current Replacement Cost	
December 31, Year 1	$16
December 31, Year 2	10

   a. Prepare an analysis for Year 1 that identifies operating margins, realized holding gains and losses, and unrealized holding gains and losses for the FIFO, LIFO, and weighted-average cost flow assumptions.
   b. Repeat part **a** for Year 2.
   c. Demonstrate that over the two-year period, income plus holding gains before taxes of Burton Corporation are independent of the cost flow assumption.

43. **Effect of FIFO and LIFO on income statement and balance sheet.** Hanover Oil Products (HOP) operates a gasoline outlet. It commenced operations on January 1. It prices its gasoline at 10 percent above its average purchase price for gasoline. Purchases of gasoline during January, February, and March appear below:

	Gallons Purchased	Unit Price	Acquisition Cost
January 1	4,000	$1.40	$ 5,600
January 13	6,000	1.46	8,760
January 28	5,000	1.50	7,500
Total	15,000		$21,860

	Gallons Purchased	Unit Price	Acquisition Cost
February 5	7,000	$1.53	$10,710
February 14	6,000	1.47	8,820
February 21	10,000	1.42	14,200
Total	23,000		$33,730

	Gallons Purchased	Unit Price	Acquisition Cost
March 2	6,000	$1.48	$ 8,880
March 15	5,000	1.54	7,700
March 26	4,000	1.60	6,400
Total	15,000		$22,980

Sales for each month were as follows:
  January: $20,840 (13,000 gallons)
  February: $35,490 (22,000 gallons)
  March: $28,648 (17,000 gallons)

a. Compute the cost of goods sold for January using both a FIFO and a LIFO cost flow assumption.

b. Repeat part **a** for February.

c. Repeat part **a** for March.

d. Why does the cost flow assumption that provides the largest cost of goods sold amount change each month?

e. Compute the cost of goods sold to sales percentage for each month using both a FIFO and a LIFO cost flow assumption.

f. Which cost flow assumption provides the most stable cost of goods sold to sales percentage over the three months? Explain why this is the case.

g. HOP deliberately allowed its inventory to decline to 1,000 gallons at the end of March because of the high purchase cost. Assume for this part that HOP had purchased 6,000 gallons on March 26 instead of 4,000, thereby maintaining an ending inventory equal to the beginning inventory for the month of 3,000 gallons. Compute the amount of cost of goods sold for March using both a FIFO and a LIFO cost flow assumption. Why are your answers the same as, or different from, those in part **c** above? Explain.

44. **Dealing with LIFO inventory layers.** (Adapted from a problem by S. A. Zeff.) The Back Store has been using a LIFO cost flow assumption for several decades. On December 31, Year 30, the company's inventory comprised the following layers:

Year 10 Layer	60,000 units at $3.00 = $180,000
Year 22 Layer	20,000 units at 6.00 = 120,000
Year 30 Layer	10,000 units at 9.00 = 90,000
	90,000 units $390,000

During Year 30, the company had bought 200,000 units at $9 each. At the end of the year, the replacement cost of units was $8. During Year 31, the company bought 250,000 units at $10 per unit, which was the average replacement cost of units for the entire year. The company sold 300,000 units at $15 each during Year 31. At the end of the year, the replacement cost of units was $11.

a. How many units did the company sell during Year 30?

b. What was the operating margin on sales, that is, the replacement cost gross margin, for Year 31?

c. What was the gross margin conventionally reported for Year 31 assuming LIFO?

d. What was the economic profit, that is, realized margin plus all holding gains, for Year 31?

e. If the company had used FIFO for both Year 30 and Year 31, what would have been the conventionally reported gross margin for Year 31?

45. **Reconstructing underlying events from ending inventory amounts.** (Adapted from CPA examination.) Burch Corporation began a merchandising business on January 1, Year 1. It acquired merchandise costing $100,000 in Year 1, $125,000 in Year 2, and $135,000 in Year 3. Information about Burch Corporation's inventory as it would appear on the balance sheet under different inventory methods follows:

December 31	LIFO Cost	FIFO Cost	Lower of FIFO Cost or Market
Year 1	$40,200	$40,000	$37,000
Year 2	36,400	36,000	34,000
Year 3	41,800	44,000	44,000

In answering each of the following questions, indicate how you deduced the answer. You may assume that in any one year, prices moved only up or down but not both.

a. Did prices go up or down in Year 1?

b. Did prices go up or down in Year 3?

c. Which inventory method would show the highest income for Year 1?

d. Which inventory method would show the highest income for Year 2?

e. Which inventory method would show the highest income for Year 3?

f. Which inventory method would show the lowest income for all three years considered as a single period?

g. For Year 3, how much higher or lower would income be on the FIFO cost basis than on the lower-of-cost-or-market basis?

46. **LIFO layers influence purchasing behavior and provide opportunity for income manipulation.** Wilson Company sells chemical compounds made from expensium. The company has used a LIFO inventory flow assumption for many years. The inventory of expensium on December 31, Year 10, comprised 4,000 pounds from Year 1 through Year 10 at prices ranging from $30 to $52 per pound. **Exhibit 7.14** shows the layers of Year 10 ending inventory.

EXHIBIT 7.14	WILSON COMPANY Layers of Year 10 Year-End Inventory (Problem 46)		
		Year 10 Year-End Inventory	
Year Acquired	**Purchase Price per Pound**	**Pounds**	**Cost**
Year 1	$30	2,000	$ 60,000
Year 6	46	200	9,200
Year 7	48	400	19,200
Year 10	52	1,400	72,800
		4,000	$161,200

Expensium costs $62 per pound during Year 11, but the purchasing agent expects its price to fall back to $52 per pound in Year 12. Sales for Year 11 require 7,000 pounds of expensium. Wilson Company wants to carry a stock of 4,000 pounds of inventory. The purchasing agent suggests that the firm decrease the inventory of expensium from 4,000 to 600 pounds by the end of Year 11 and replenish it to the desired level of 4,000 pounds early in Year 12.

The controller argues that such a policy would be foolish. If the firm allows inventories to decrease to 600 pounds, the cost of goods sold will be extraordinarily low (because Wilson will consume older LIFO layers) and income taxes will be extraordinarily high. The controller suggests that the firm plan Year 11 purchases to maintain an end-of-year inventory of 4,000 pounds. Assume that sales for Year 11 do require 7,000 pounds of expensium, that the prices for Year 11 and Year 12 are as forecast, and that the income tax rate for Wilson Company is 40 percent.

a. Calculate the cost of goods sold and the end-of-year LIFO inventory for Year 11, assuming that the firm follows the controller's advice and that inventory at the end of Year 11 is 4,000 pounds.

b. Calculate the cost of goods sold and the end-of-year LIFO inventory for Year 11, assuming that the firm follows the purchasing agent's advice and that inventory at the end of Year 11 is 600 pounds.

c. Assume the firm follows the advice of the controller, not the purchasing agent. Calculate the tax savings for Year 11 and the extra cash costs for inventory.

d. What should Wilson Company do? Consider quality of earnings and ethical issues in your response.

e. Management of Wilson Company wants to know what discretion it has to vary income for Year 11 by planning its purchases of expensium. If the firm follows the controller's policy, aftertax income for Year 11 will be $50,000. What is the range, after taxes, of income that the firm can achieve by the purposeful management of expensium purchases?

47. **Assessing the effect of LIFO versus FIFO on the financial statements. Exhibit 7.15** summarizes data taken from the financial statements and notes for Bethlehem Steel Company for three years (in millions):

a. Compute the amount of cost of goods sold for Year 9, Year 10, and Year 11, assuming that Bethlehem Steel Company had used a FIFO instead of a LIFO cost flow assumption.

b. Compute the cost of goods sold divided by sales percentages for Year 9, Year 10, and Year 11, using both LIFO and FIFO cost flow assumptions.

c. Refer to part **b**. Explain the rank-ordering of the cost of goods sold percentages for each year—that is, why does the LIFO percentage exceed the FIFO percentage or vice versa? (*Hint:* attempt to ascertain the direction of the change in inventory quantities and manufacturing costs each year.)

d. Compute the inventory turnover ratios (cost of goods sold divided by average inventories) for Year 9, Year 10, and Year 11, using both a LIFO and a FIFO cost flow assumption.

e. Which inventory turnover ratio in part **d** more accurately measures the actual inventory turnover rate? Explain your reasoning.

f. Compute the current ratio (current assets divided by current liabilities) at the end of each year using both LIFO and FIFO cost flow assumptions. Assume that the extra income taxes paid if the firm had used FIFO result in a reduction in cash. (*Hint:* the adjustment for income taxes must reflect the cumulative income tax effect between the date that Bethlehem Steel Company adopted LIFO and each year-end, not just the additional taxes payable each year.)

g. Assess the short-term liquidity risk of Bethlehem Steel Company to the extent permitted by the information presented in this problem.

EXHIBIT 7.15	BETHLEHEM STEEL COMPANY Financial Data (Problem 47)		

	For the Year Ended December 31		
	Year 9	**Year 10**	**Year 11**
Sales	$5,250.9	$4,899.2	$4,317.9
Cost of Goods Sold (LIFO)	$4,399.1	$4,327.2	$4,059.7
Net Income (Loss)	$ 245.7	$ (463.5)	$ (767.0)
Income Tax Rate	34%	34%	34%

	December 31			
	Year 8	**Year 9**	**Year 10**	**Year 11**
Inventories at FIFO Cost	$ 899.1	$ 972.8	$ 967.4	$958.3
Excess of FIFO Cost over LIFO Values	(530.1)	(562.5)	(499.1)	(504.9)
Inventories at LIFO Cost	$ 369.0	$ 410.3	$ 468.3	$453.4
Current Assets (LIFO)	$1,439.8	$1,435.2	$1,203.2	$957.8
Current Liabilities	$ 870.1	$ 838.0	$ 831.4	$931.0

48. **Interpreting inventory disclosures.** DuPont is a diversified chemicals company. Its annual report discloses inventories under LIFO of $4,409 million at the beginning of the year and $4,107 million at the end of the year and cost of goods sold of $19,476 million for the year. If the firm had used a FIFO cost flow assumption, its beginning inventory would have been $4,853

million and its ending inventory would have been $4,407 million. Sales for the year totaled $26,996 million.

a. Compute the amount for cost of goods sold for the year assuming DuPont had used a FIFO instead of a LIFO cost flow assumption.

b. Did the quantities of items in inventory increase or decrease during the year? Explain.

c. Did the manufacturing cost of items in inventory increase or decrease during the year? Explain.

d. Compute the inventory turnover ratio for DuPont under both LIFO and FIFO for the year.

e. Why does the inventory turnover ratio under LIFO exceed that under FIFO?

f. "The choice of inventory cost flow assumption affects the inventory turnover ratio but should not normally affect the accounts payable turnover ratio." Explain.

49. **Analyzing inventory disclosures.** Eli Lilly, a pharmaceutical company, uses a LIFO cost flow assumption. Amounts taken from a recent annual report appear in **Exhibit 7.16** (in millions):

EXHIBIT 7.16	ELI LILLY Financial Data (Problem 49)			
		For the Year Ended December 31		
		Year 8	**Year 9**	**Year 10**
Sales		$9,236.8	$10,002.6	$10,862.2
Cost of Goods Sold		2,015.1	2,098.0	2,055.7
		December 31		
	Year 7	**Year 8**	**Year 9**	**Year 10**
Raw Materials Inventory	$262.0	$325.1	$295.1	$230.1
Work-in-Process Inventory	459.4	435.8	372.7	380.6
Finished Goods Inventory	191.0	236.3	224.7	284.3
Total Inventories at FIFO Cost ...	$912.4	$997.2	$892.5	$895.0
Adjustment to LIFO Cost	(11.7)	2.7	7.1	(11.9)
Total Inventories at LIFO Cost ...	$900.7	$999.9	$899.6	$883.1

a. Compute the cost of goods sold for Year 8, Year 9, and Year 10 based on a FIFO cost flow assumption.

b. Did Eli Lilly appear to dip into LIFO layers in any of the three years? Explain.

c. Why is the adjustment from FIFO to LIFO a positive amount in some years and a negative amount in other years?

d. Compute the ratio of cost of goods sold to sales under both LIFO and FIFO for Year 8, Year 9, and Year 10.

e. Compute the inventory turnover ratio defined as cost of goods sold divided by average total inventories under both LIFO and FIFO for Year 8, Year 9, and Year 10.

f. Compute the costs of goods manufactured and sent to the finished goods storeroom during Year 8, Year 9, and Year 10. Use the amounts based on FIFO.

g. Compute an inventory turnover ratio for finished goods inventory defined as cost of goods sold divided by average finished goods inventory. Use the amounts based on FIFO.

h. Compute an inventory turnover ratio for work-in-process inventory defined as costs of goods manufactured (from part **f**) divided by average work-in-process inventory. Use the amounts based on FIFO.

i. Suggest reasons for the change in the cost of goods sold percentage computed in part **d** and the change in the inventory turnover ratio computed in part **e**.

50. **Ethical issuing in accounting for inventory.** Managers of firms experience pressure from securities markets to achieve earnings targets each year. Discuss ethical issues in each of the following independent actions that increase earnings for the year. Assume that the effect is material.

a. On December 10 of the current year, Firm A receives an advance of $50,000 from a hockey team for 20,000 custom-made shirts with the team's logo, which the team intends to distribute to fans entering a hockey game during the first week in January. Firm A completes the manufacturing of the shirts on December 30, intending to ship them on

December 31 before its accounting period ends. Unfortunately, a snowstorm on December 31 prevented their shipment. Firm A recorded this transaction as a sale for December, and reduced its inventory accordingly. It set the items aside in its shipping room on December 31 with a clear sign to its own personnel conducting a physical inventory on that date and to its auditors who were observing the count that the items were not to be counted as inventory.

b. Firm B uses large warehouses to store its finished goods ready for sale. After its personnel and auditors conducted a physical inventory of goods on one side of its warehouses, Firm B transported a portion of the inventory to another part of the warehouse, removing the inventory tags that indicated that the items had already been counted in inventory, and thereby included the items a second time in inventory. In this way, the firm overstated its ending inventory for the current year, understated its cost of goods sold, and overstated its earnings. This action resulted in an overstatement of the beginning inventory for the next year. Assuming a correct count of the ending inventory for the second year, the action has the result of overstating cost of goods sold for the second year and understating earnings. Net income for the two years combined, however, is correctly stated, the net result of an overstatement in the first year offset by an equal understatement in the second year.

c. Firm C manufactures high quality sunglasses that carry the endorsements of several sports personalities. In an effort to achieve sales targets for the fourth quarter of the year, Firm C pressured its independent distributors to make unusually large orders of the sunglasses. Low-priced imitations of these sunglasses hit the market soon thereafter, causing the distributors to accumulate large inventories. The distributors shipped these sunglasses back to Firm C. Firm C stored the returned sunglasses in a remote warehouse out of the view of its auditors and did not record them as returned goods.

chapter 8

Long-Lived Tangible and Intangible Assets: The Source of Operating Capacity

Learning Objectives

1. Understand the concepts distinguishing expenditures that accountants capitalize as assets, and subsequently depreciate or amortize, from expenditures that accountants expense in the period incurred.

2. Understand the concepts underlying the measurement of acquisition cost for an asset.

3. Understand depreciation and amortization as processes of cost allocation, not of valuation.

4. Develop skills to compute depreciation and amortization under various commonly used methods.

5. Develop the skills to re-compute depreciation or amortization for changes in estimates of service lives and salvage values.

6. Develop the skills to compute an impairment loss on long-lived assets.

7. Develop the skills to record the retirement of assets at various selling prices.

*C*onsider the following recent transactions of technology-based companies, which significantly affected their reported earnings and measures of their financial position.

Example 1 WorldCom (now MCI) provides telecommunication services using, in part, the telecommunication lines of other carriers. It pays these other carriers fixed amounts plus amounts based on usage each year for access to the telecommunication lines. During 2000 and the first quarter of 2001, WorldCom capitalized these costs as part of its fixed assets. Capitalizing these costs and subsequently depreciating them had the effect of increasing earnings during 2000 by $53.1 billion and in 2001 by $17.1 billion, relative to a policy of expensing these costs in the period incurred. WorldCom subsequently concluded that, according to generally accepted accounting principles (GAAP), it should have treated these access costs as an expense each period. The restatement of earnings resulted in a restated net loss of $48.9 billion for 2000, compared to reported earnings of $4.2 billion. For 2001, the restated net loss was $15.6 billion, compared to reported earnings of $1.5 billion.

Example 2 Hewlett-Packard Company (HP) acquired Compaq Computer (Compaq) in 2002 for $24.2 billion. HP allocated $793 million of the purchase price to in-process technologies, technologies not yet developed to the point of demonstrating technological feasibility. Because future benefits of expenditures on in-process technologies are uncertain, GAAP require firms to expense these amounts in the year of the acquisition. Excluding this charge, HP generated a net loss of $135 million for the year. After the charge, which provided no income tax benefit, HP reported a net loss of $928 million. Most analysts probably viewed a charge of this magnitude as nonrecurring and eliminated it in their analysis, thereby resulting in a measure of earnings with higher quality because the components are more likely to recur.

Example 3 Nortel Networks (Nortel) made 20 corporate acquisitions costing a total of $33.5 billion between 1997 and 2000 to build its Internet network. It allocated $14.5 billion of this aggregate purchase price to identifiable assets, such as accounts receivable, inventories, plant and equipment, and identifiable liabilities, such as accounts payable and long-term debt. Nortel allocated the remaining $19 billion to goodwill, an account used to represent the portion of the purchase price that Nortel could not allocate to identifiable assets and liabilities. Items in goodwill might include the skills of software engineers, customer contacts from previously installed telecommunications systems, loyal employees, and so on. Early in 2001, Nortel announced that it took a $12.3 billion charge against earnings to write down this goodwill because the acquired firms were not then worth the amount that Nortel paid for them. Combining the charge with the loss from operations resulted in a net loss of $19.2 billion for the quarter. Thus, ongoing operations produced a net loss of $6.9 billion. Analysts likely wondered whether Nortel timed the write-off of goodwill to occur in a period of otherwise poor performance, questioning the quality of earnings not only for the quarter but also for previous and succeeding periods. Analysts suspect managers of making loss periods worse by piling on losses whenever they must report any losses at all. Such piling on increases the likelihood of reporting profits in future periods.

These examples illustrate that the accounting for long-lived assets can significantly impact reported earnings and their quality. Long-lived assets include **tangible assets**, such as land, buildings, and equipment. Long-lived assets also include **intangible assets**, such as patents, brand names, customer lists, airport landing rights, franchise rights, and similar items. Long-lived assets also include investments in securities, a topic we discuss in **Chapter 11**. Questions such as the following arise in accounting for long-lived assets:

1. Should firms treat expenditures with potential long-term benefits as assets on the balance sheet or as expenses in the income statement in the year of the expenditure?
2. For expenditures treated as assets, should firms depreciate or amortize a portion of the assets' cost as expenses each period or wait until firms dispose of the assets to write off the cost?
3. For assets that firms depreciate or amortize, over what period and using what pattern of charges should firms write off the cost of the assets?
4. How should firms treat changes in expected useful lives and salvage values that become evident partway through assets' lives?
5. How should firms treat substantial declines in the market values of long-lived assets that occur because of technological change, introduction of new products by competitors, changing consumer tastes, changing government regulations, and similar factors?
6. What impact does the disposal of long-lived assets have on earnings?

The long lives and uncertain future benefits of long-lived assets create a challenge for accountants to answer these questions in a definitive, unambiguous way. Answering these questions for intangibles requires even more effort because of their lack of physical substance. The increased importance in recent years of technology and service businesses which rely more on intangibles than manufacturing businesses underscores the need to understand the accounting for long-lived assets, particularly intangibles. Users of the financial statements need to understand both the GAAP that guide firms' responses to the questions and the flexibility that firms have in applying these GAAP in assessing the quality of earnings.

Capitalization Versus Immediate Expensing

The first question addressed is: should firms treat expenditures with potential long-term benefits as (1) expenses in the period incurred, or (2) assets on the balance sheet (that is, "capitalize" their cost), which firms will subsequently write off as expenses over the estimated service life? Refer to **Figure 8.1**. Pattern **E** represents immediate write-off as an expense. Patterns **A**, **S**, **D**, and **N** represent various patterns for writing off the capitalized acquisition cost during its service life. **Figure 8.2** depicts these patterns in terms of the amount recognized as an expense each year. We discuss these patterns more fully later in the chapter.

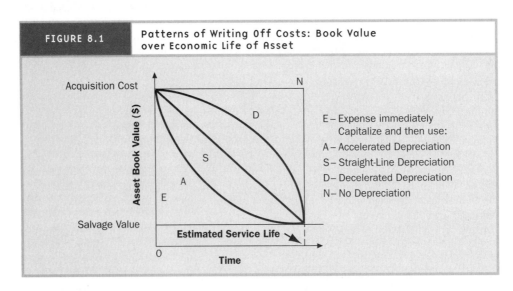

FIGURE 8.1 Patterns of Writing Off Costs: Book Value over Economic Life of Asset

E – Expense immediately
  Capitalize and then use:
A – Accelerated Depreciation
S – Straight-Line Depreciation
D – Decelerated Depreciation
N – No Depreciation

Recall the criteria from **Chapter 2** for treating an expenditure as an asset. A firm

- has acquired rights to the future use of a resource as a result of a past transaction or exchange, and

FIGURE 8.2	Patterns of Annual Depreciation Charge over Economic Life of Asset

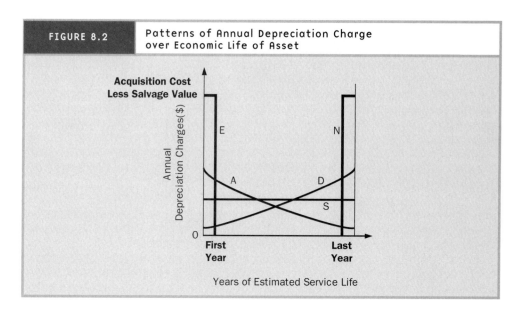

- can measure or quantify the future benefits with a reasonable degree of precision.[1]

The exchange of cash for a resource with future service potential satisfies the first criterion. Satisfying the second criterion is more difficult because of the extended period of time that must pass before expected future benefits materialize. Also, satisfying the second criterion is even more difficult for intangible assets than for tangible assets because of the difficulty of observing the realization of benefits. The following examples illustrate the application of these two criteria for capitalization versus immediate expensing.

Example 4 General Motors acquires land and a building for a factory. The land and buildings provide General Motors with future benefits. The external market exchange between an independent buyer and seller sets the minimum value of the expected future benefits. The land and buildings therefore appear as assets on General Motors' balance sheet.

Example 5 Wal-Mart self-constructs new stores using individuals on its payroll as well as outside contractors. The new stores, once completed, provide Wal-Mart with future benefits. This example differs from **Example 4** in that Wal-Mart (1) incurs part of the cost internally, and (2) makes expenditures over time to construct the stores instead of acquiring a completed asset. Wal-Mart presumably decided to construct the stores itself instead of having an outside contractor do the work because of lower cost, or higher quality, or both. The accountant presumes that all expenditures incurred during construction are assets. If, at completion, the total cost of the stores exceeds their market value, Wal-Mart will write down the cost to the market value and recognize a loss. If the market value of the completed stores exceeds Wal-Mart's cost to construct them, Wal-Mart will not recognize a gain or construction profit. Rather, it will enjoy the future benefit of using the stores over time with depreciation charges less than they would have been had Wal-Mart paid an independent contractor to build it.

Example 6 Merck, a pharmaceutical firm, acquires a patent on a new drug from its creator for $30 million. The patent gives Merck an exclusive legal right to manufacture and market the drug for 20 years, although the time-consuming drug approval process has reduced the economic life to a shorter time period. The external market transaction between an independent buyer and seller for the patent fixes both Merck's right to the patent and the minimum value to Merck. The patent therefore appears on Merck's balance sheet as an asset.

Example 7 Merck spends $40 million each year on research to identify, develop, and test new drugs to combat infectious diseases. This example differs from **Example 6** in that Merck (1)

---

[1] This second criterion is not part of the FASB's formal definition of an asset (see the **Glossary**) but is a criterion for recognizing an asset in practice.

incurs the costs internally, and (2) does not acquire a completed asset. Merck would not engage in research if it did not expect future benefits. The difficulty is identifying the portion of each year's expenditures that leads to future benefits and the portion that does not. GAAP require the firm to treat all research and development (R&D) expenditures as expenses in the period incurred, instead of recognizing a portion of such expenditures as assets.[2] GAAP's rationale is that future benefits of R&D expenditures are too uncertain to justify recognizing as an asset. **Example 5** and **Example 7** are similar in that each firm incurs costs internally for an uncompleted resource. Accountants act as though they favor the physical over the intangible and are more willing to capitalize the cost of the building, a tangible asset, than the research, an intangible resource. Accountants do not have a choice here, because GAAP require the expensing of the R&D costs.

Example 8   Microsoft Corporation incurs various costs internally to develop new computer software for sale to customers. Such costs result from planning, designing, coding, and testing the software to establish its technological feasibility. GAAP treat costs incurred prior to the point of establishing technological feasibility like all other internally incurred R&D costs: Microsoft must expense the costs in the period incurred.[3] GAAP allow firms to capitalize as assets software costs incurred after the point of technological feasibility. Thus, a firm that takes existing software and adapts it to meet the needs of particular customers could capitalize the costs incurred between the technological feasibility stage of the software and the time it releases the adaptation to customers.

Example 9   Merck acquires a biotechnology firm engaged in the early development of drugs using DNA technologies. Of the $25 million purchase price, it allocates $20 million to the value of potential drugs in the pipeline, call *in-process technologies*. The biotechnology firm has expensed its R&D costs each year as required by GAAP (see **Example 7**). Merck acquires the in-process technologies in an external market transaction with an independent seller, which establishes the existence and value of the technologies. The technologies, however, are not a completed resource. GAAP currently require firms to expense the cost of in-process technologies in the year acquired, thereby not reporting any portion of the amount as an asset.[4] GAAP's reasoning is the same as for internally incurred R&D: future benefits are too uncertain to justify recognizing an asset. The FASB is considering requiring that firms capitalize, not expense, the cost of acquired in-process technologies, which have reached the stage of technological feasibility, similar to the treatment of software, above.

Example 10   Refer to **Example 3**. Nortel negotiated with the selling firms to establish the purchase price of each acquired firm. Nortel used appraisals and other means to establish the market value of the identifiable assets and liabilities of each firm. GAAP require the acquiring firm to allocate a portion of the purchase price to intangibles, even though they do not appear as assets on the books of the acquired company at the time of the acquisition. For the purchasing firm to recognize an intangible, the asset must (1) arise from contractual or other rights, or (2) be separable (that is, capable of being separated from the acquired enterprise and sold, transferred, licensed, rented, or exchanged).[5] Thus, Nortel might allocate a portion of the purchase price to contractual rights as a licensee to sell another firm's products in Japan. Nortel might also allocate a portion of the purchase price to specific proved technologies as long as the technologies meet the test of separability.

Example 11   Refer to **Examples 3** and **10**. Nortel allocates to goodwill any excess of its purchase price for each entity over the amount assigned to identifiable net assets (= assets less liabilities). GAAP presume that on the date of acquisition the negotiations between an independent buyer and seller establish the total value of the enterprise acquired. To the extent that Nortel can establish the existence and value of specific assets and liabilities, it allocates the purchase price to these items. Any remaining portion of the purchase price not so allocated must result from other valuable resources that Nortel cannot separately identify. Thus, goodwill appears on the balance sheet as an asset on the date of the acquisition to represent the totality of those assets it cannot identify.

---

[2] Financial Accounting Standards Board, *Statement of Financial Accounting Standards No. 2,* "Accounting for Research and Development Costs," 1974.

[3] Financial Accounting Standards Board, *Statement of Financial Accounting Standards No. 86,* "Accounting for the Costs of Computer Software to Be Sold, Leased or Otherwise Marketed," 1985.

[4] Financial Accounting Standards Board, *Interpretation No. 4,* "Applicability of FASB Statement No. 2 to Business Combinations Accounted for by the Purchase Method," 1975.

[5] Financial Accounting Standards Board, *Statement of Financial Accounting Standards No. 142,* "Goodwill and Other Intangible Assets," 2001.

Figure 8.3 summarizes GAAP's treatment of expenditures on resources with potential long-term benefits. We can make the following generalizations:

1. Firms capitalize as assets expenditures made to acquire or self-construct tangible assets. The physical existence of tangible assets provides evidence of the existence of an asset. Unless information indicates otherwise, the presumption is that the amount the firm paid to acquire the tangible assets is the best evidence of its value on the date of acquisition.
2. Firms expense as incurred expenditures made internally to develop intangibles. The absence of an external market validation of the existence and value of a completed intangible leads GAAP to require the immediate expensing of these expenditures.
3. Firms can generally treat expenditures made to acquire completed intangibles externally as assets. A firm must expense in the period acquired the cost of in-process technologies. Although the firm acquired the in-process technologies voluntarily and in an arm's-length, external transaction, GAAP view these as unproved technologies. Goodwill is neither a contractual right nor a separable resource but appears as an asset on the date of a corporate acquisition.

FIGURE 8.3	Treatment of Expenditures with Potential Long-Term Benefits	
	Nature of Resource	
	Tangible	**Intangible**
Acquired Internally	Self-constructed Buildings and Equipment (asset)	Research and Development (expense) Advertising (expense) Employee Training (expense) Software Development Costs: 　Pre-technological feasibility (expense) 　Post-technological feasibility (asset)
Acquired Externally	Land, Buildings, and Equipment (asset)	Patent (asset) Proved Technologies (asset) In-Process Technologies (expense) Goodwill (asset)

The accounting for expenditures with potential long-term benefits has been, and continues to be, one of the most controversial topics faced by standard setters. Inconsistencies between the treatment of tangibles and intangibles and between costs incurred internally and externally permeate GAAP. The user of the financial statements should keep such inconsistencies in mind when comparing a manufacturing firm with significant tangible assets and a technology or service firm with significant intangibles, or when comparing a firm that develops brand names and other intangibles internally and one that acquires such intangibles by acquiring them from other firms.

Measurement of Acquisition Cost

The acquisition cost of a long-lived asset, whether tangible or intangible, includes all costs incurred to prepare it for rendering services. The acquisition cost of a piece of equipment, for example, will be the sum of the invoice price (less any discounts), transportation costs, installation charges, and any other costs incurred before the equipment is ready for use. Also consider the following, more complex, example.

Example 12　Refer to **Example 4.** General Motors incurs the following costs in searching for and acquiring the land and building:

1. Purchase price of land with an existing building, $1,000,000
2. Fees paid to lawyer in handling purchase contracts, $10,000
3. Transfer taxes paid to local real estate taxing authorities, $2,000

4. Salaries earned by management personnel during the search for the site and the negotiation of its purchase, $8,000
5. Operating expenditures for company automobiles used during the search, $75
6. Depreciation charges for company automobiles used during the search, $65
7. Fees paid to consulting engineer for a report on the structural soundness of the building, its current value, and the estimated cost of making needed repairs, $15,000
8. Uninsured costs to repair automobiles damaged in a multi-vehicle accident during the search, $3,000
9. Profits lost on sales the company failed to make because, during the search, management paid insufficient attention to a potential new customer, $20,000

The first six cost items relate to the search for, and acquisition of, the land and building. General Motors should accumulate these items in a temporary Land and Building account. Some firms would treat items **5** and **6** as expenses of the period because of their immaterial amount, but strictly applying accounting theory will capitalize these costs as an asset. After completing the acquisition of the land and building, General Motors should allocate the accumulated costs of $1,020,140 (= $1,000,000 + $10,000 + $2,000 + $8,000 + $75 + $65) between these two assets. Accounting requires such division of costs, or allocation, because the firm will depreciate the building but not the land. The allocation uses the relative market values of the land and building. For example, if the engineer in item **7** estimates the current value of the existing building to be $250,000, then the firm might allocate 25 percent (= $250,000/$1,000,000) of the combined costs of $1,020,140 to the building and 75 percent to the land.

Item **7** relates to the building only, so the accountant includes the cost of the engineer's report in the cost of the building.

Accountants would not agree on the treatment of item **8**, repair costs for the accident. Some would think it is part of the cost of the site, to be allocated to the land and the building. Others would report it as an expense of the period. Probably all practicing accountants would classify it as an expense for financial reporting so that the firm could bolster its argument for calling it a current tax deduction in computing taxable income.

Item **9**, forgone profits, does not result from an expenditure. The firm did not incur this cost in an arm's-length transaction with outsiders. Historical cost accounting would not record this cost, called an *opportunity cost*, in any account.

Example 13   Refer to **Example 6**. Merck's acquisition cost for the patent includes the $30 million paid to its creator. Merck also pays an attorney $800,000 in legal fees to evaluate its legal rights under the patent and $1,800 to register the patent. Merck's acquisition cost is therefore $30,801,800 (= $30,000,000 + $800,000 + $1,800).

Self-Constructed Asset   When a firm, such as Wal-Mart Stores in **Example 5**, constructs its own buildings or equipment, it will record many entries in these asset accounts for the labor, material, and overhead costs incurred. GAAP require the firm to include (capitalize) **interest paid during construction** as part of the cost of the asset it constructs.[6] Accounting's capitalizing interest results from reasoning that the firm must incur financing costs in self-constructing an asset just as it must incur labor and material costs. The accountant computes the amount of financing costs from the entity's actual borrowings and interest payments. The amount represents the interest cost that the firm incurred during periods of asset acquisition and that, in principle, the firm could have avoided if it had not acquired the assets. The inclusion of interest stops after the firm has finished constructing the asset.

If the firm borrows new funds in connection with the asset being constructed, it will use the interest rate on that borrowing. If the expenditures on construction exceed such new borrowings, then the interest rate applied to the excess is the weighted-average rate the firm pays for its other borrowings. The total amount of interest capitalized cannot exceed total interest costs for the period. The capitalization of interest in the acquisition cost of assets during construction reduces otherwise reportable interest expense and thereby increases income during periods of construction. In later periods, the asset will have higher depreciation charges, reducing income. Total expense over the life of the asset will equal the cash expenditure; capitalizing interest into the asset's cost delays expense recognition from the times of borrowing to the times of using the asset.

---

[6] Financial Accounting Standards Board, *Statement of Financial Accounting Standards No. 34*, "Capitalization of Interest Costs," 1979.

Example 14 Refer to **Example 5**. Assume the following long-term debt structure for Wal-Mart Stores:

Construction Loan at 5 Percent on Building under Construction	$1,000,000
Other Borrowings at 6 Percent Average Rate	3,600,000
Total Long-term Debt	$4,600,000

The account Building under Construction has an average balance during the year of $3,000,000. Wal-Mart Stores bases the amount of interest to be capitalized on all of the new construction-related borrowings ($1,000,000) and enough of the older borrowings ($2,000,000) to bring the total to $3,000,000. The firm computes interest capitalized as follows:

$1,000,000 × 0.05	$ 50,000
$2,000,000 × 0.06	120,000
$3,000,000	$170,000

The entries to record interest and to capitalize the required amounts might be as follows:

Retained Earnings (Interest Expense) (Shareholders' Equity Decrease)	266,000	
Interest Payable (Liability Increase)		266,000
To record all interest as expense: $266,000 [= (0.05 × $1,000,000) + (0.06 × $3,600,000) = $50,000 + $216,000].		
Building under Construction (Asset Increase)	170,000	
Retained Earnings (Interest Expense) (Shareholders' Equity Increase)		170,000
The amount capitalized reduces interest expense and increases the recorded cost of the building.		

The firm might combine the preceding two entries into one as follows:

Retained Earnings (Interest Expense) (Shareholders' Equity Decrease)	96,000	
Building under Construction (Asset Increase)	170,000	
Interest Payable (Liability Increase)		266,000
The amount for Interest Expense is a plug.		

The firm must disclose, in notes to the financial statements, both total interest for the year, $266,000, and the amount capitalized, $170,000. The income statement will report interest expense, $96,000 in this example. Interest capitalization in earlier years will cause the depreciation of the building in future years to exceed its amount without capitalization. Over the life of the asset, from construction through retirement, capitalizing interest does not change total income because larger depreciation charges later exactly offset the increased income that lower interest charges cause during the construction period. Over sufficiently long time spans, total expenses incurred for using assets must equal total cash expenditures made to acquire them.

Problem 8.1 for Self-Study

Calculating the acquisition cost of fixed assets. Jensen Company purchased land with a building as the site for a new plant it planned to construct. The company received bids from several independent contractors for demolition of the old building and construction of the new one. It rejected all bids and undertook demolition and construction using company labor, facilities, and equipment.

(continued)

Problem 8.1 for Self-Study *(continued)*

It debited or credited amounts for all transactions relating to these properties to a single account, Construction in Process. Descriptions of various items in the Construction in Process account appear below. Jensen Company will close the Construction in Process account at the completion of construction. It will remove all amounts in it and reclassify them into the following accounts:

1. Land account
2. Building account
3. Retained Earnings (revenue, gain, expense, or loss) account
4. Some balance sheet account other than Land, Building, or Retained Earnings

Reclassify the amounts of the following transactions into one or more of these accounts. If you use **4** (some other balance sheet account), indicate the nature of the account.

a. Cost of land, including old building
b. Legal fees paid to bring about purchase of land and to transfer its title
c. Invoice cost of materials and supplies used in construction
d. Direct labor and materials costs incurred in demolishing old building
e. Direct costs of excavating raw land to prepare it for the foundation of the new building
f. Discounts earned for prompt payment of item **c**
g. Interest for the year on notes issued to finance construction
h. Amounts equivalent to interest on Jensen Company's own funds that it used in construction but that it would have invested in marketable securities if it had used an independent contractor; it debited the amount to Construction in Process and credited Interest Revenue so that the cost of the real estate would be comparable to the cost if it had purchased the building from an independent contractor
i. Depreciation during the construction period on trucks used both in construction and in regular company operations
j. Proceeds of sale of materials salvaged from the old buildings; the firm had debited these to Cash and credited Construction in Process
k. Cost of building permits
l. Salaries of certain corporate engineering executives; these represent costs for both Salary Expense and Construction in Process, with the portion debited to Construction in Process representing an estimate of the portion of the time spent during the year on planning and construction activities for the new building
m. Payments for property taxes on the plant site (its former owner owed these taxes but Jensen Company assumed responsibility to pay them)
n. Payments for property taxes on plant site during construction period
o. Insurance premiums to cover workers engaged in demolition and construction activities; the insurance policy contains various deductible clauses, requiring the company to pay the first $5,000 of damages from any accident
p. Cost of injury claims for $2,000 paid by the company because the amount was less than the deductible amount in the policy
q. Costs of new machinery to be installed in the building
r. Installation costs for the machinery in item **q**
s. Profit on construction of the new building (computed as the difference between the lowest independent contractor's bid and the actual construction cost); the firm debited this to Construction in Process and credited Retained Earnings (Construction Revenue)

Treatment of Acquisition Cost over Life of Asset

The second question we address in accounting for long-term assets is: should firms write off a portion of the acquisition costs of assets as expenses each period or wait until the firms dispose of the assets to write off the cost? Refer again to **Figures 8.1** and **8.2**. Writing off a portion of the acquisition cost each period corresponds to patterns A, S, and D, whereas writing off the acquisition cost at disposal corresponds to pattern N. The guiding principle to respond to this question is matching:

- If a firm consumes the services of long-lived assets over time in generating revenues, then the firm should write off a portion of the asset's cost each period to match against the revenues.
- If the firm does not consume the services of long-lived assets as time passes, then it should not write off a portion of its cost each period. Instead, the asset should remain on the balance sheet at acquisition cost. If the firm later sells or abandons the asset, it removes the acquisition cost from the asset account, offsetting that cost against the proceeds, if any, from selling the asset to measure the gain or loss on disposal.

Accountants refer to the periodic write-off of the acquisition cost of a tangible asset, such as buildings and equipment, as **depreciation**. Accountants use the term **amortization** to refer to the periodic write-off of intangible assets.

Example 15 Refer to **Examples 5** and **14**. Wal-Mart Stores consumes the services of the store building over time in generating revenues. It should therefore write off, or depreciate, the acquisition cost minus estimated salvage value over the building's expected useful life. During the building's useful life, it would not write off the portion of the asset's acquisition cost equal to the estimated salvage value but instead match that cost against any proceeds from selling the building at the end of the asset's useful life.

Example 16 Refer to **Examples 6** and **13** where Merck acquires a patent from its creator. Patents have a legal life of 20 years. However, new technologies may shorten the economic life of the patent before the 20-year legal life expires. Merck should write off, or amortize, the acquisition cost of the patent over its expected useful life, the shorter of the economic life and the legal life.

Example 17 Refer to **Examples 3** and **11** for Nortel. The portion of the purchase price of an acquired company that Nortel allocates to goodwill represents the excess cost of the acquired entity as a whole over the amounts that Nortel can attribute to identifiable assets and liabilities. As **Example 3** discusses, goodwill might include trained scientists, other knowledgeable employees, reputation for quality products, and loyal customers. GAAP view goodwill as having an *indefinite* life, which you should not confuse with an *infinite* life. Thus, GAAP do not permit firms to amortize goodwill.[7] Firms must, however, test goodwill annually for a loss in value, a topic discussed later in the section on impairment losses.

Depreciation and Amortization: Fundamental Concepts

The third question accounting addresses in dealing with long-term assets is: how should firms spread the acquisition cost of long-lived assets over their expected service lives? We address this question by discussing the fundamental concepts underlying depreciation and amortization and then describe and illustrate depreciation and amortization methods that firms use.

Depreciation and Amortization: A Process of Cost Allocation The acquisition cost of a long-lived asset is the cost of a series of future services. The asset is a prepayment, similar to prepaid rent or insurance, a payment in advance for services the firm will receive. As the firm uses the asset in each accounting period, it treats a portion of the cost of the asset as the cost of the service received.

Accountants cannot compute a uniquely correct amount for the periodic charge for depreciation or amortization. Long-lived assets benefit several accounting periods. Accountants and economists call such an asset a **joint cost** of several accounting periods because each of the periods of the asset's use benefits from its services. There is usually no single correct way to allocate a joint cost.

Firms select a depreciation or amortization method for a long-lived asset. That method allocates the cost minus salvage value to each period of expected useful life of the asset in a systematic, predetermined manner.

---

[7] Financial Accounting Standards Board, *Statement of Financial Accounting Standards No. 142,* "Goodwill and Other Intangible Assets," 2001.

Depreciation and Amortization: Return of Investment   A firm attempts to generate a return on investments the firm makes. Before a firm can earn a return, as measured by net income, it must generate larger revenues than all costs. One might view costs incurred as the investment required to generate revenues. Revenues cover the costs in that the net assets generated convert the costs of assets' services back into cash or other assets. Depreciation and amortization are the costs of the services of long-lived assets that revenue must cover before a firm earns a return on investment.

In historical cost accounting, the process of depreciation and amortization allows for a return of the acquisition cost of the asset, no more and no less. Because the costs of services provided by long-lived assets generally increase over time, accountants increasingly recognize that basing depreciation and amortization on acquisition costs will not, in most cases, expense amounts sufficiently large to maintain the productive capacity of the business. That is, if a firm sets aside an amount of cash each period equal to depreciation and amortization expense, it would not likely have enough cash at the end of the life of the long-lived asset to replace it. By now, you should be comfortable with the notion that recognizing depreciation expense has nothing to do with setting aside a fund of cash for acquiring new and replacement assets.

Depreciation and Amortization: Not a Measure of the Decline in Economic Value   Depreciation and amortization involve cost allocation, not valuation. In ordinary conversation and in economics, *depreciation* and *amortization* frequently mean a decline in **value**. Over the entire service life of a long-lived asset, the asset's value declines from acquisition until the firm retires it from service. The charge made to each accounting period does not measure the decline in economic value during the period but rather represents a process of cost allocation—a systematic process, but one in which the firm has some freedom to choose. If, in a given period, an asset increases in value, the firm still records depreciation and amortization during that period. There have been two partially offsetting processes: (1) a holding gain on the asset for the increase in market value, which historical cost-based accounting does not usually recognize, and (2) an allocation of the asset's acquisition cost to the period of benefit, which accounting does recognize.

Depreciation and Amortization: Measurement

Measuring the amount of depreciation or amortization of long-lived assets requires firms to:

1. Measure the depreciable or amortizable basis of the asset
2. Estimate its service life
3. Decide the pattern of expiration of asset cost over its service life

This section discusses each of the three items.

Depreciable or Amortizable Basis of Long-Lived Assets: Cost Less Salvage Value

Historical cost accounting bases depreciation and amortization charges on the acquisition cost less the estimated salvage value of long-lived assets. The terms **salvage value** and **net residual value** refer to the estimated proceeds on the disposition of an asset less all removal and selling costs. At any time before a firm retires an asset, it can only estimate the salvage value. Hence, before retirement, the term *salvage value* and *estimated salvage value* are synonyms. Because firms recover salvage value through the proceeds of sales, it need not depreciate or amortize that amount.

For buildings, common practice assumes a zero salvage value. This treatment rests on the assumption that the cost to be incurred in tearing down the buildings will approximate the sales value of the scrap materials recovered. Other tangible assets, however, may have substantial salvage value. For example, a car rental firm will replace its automobiles at a time when other owners can use the cars for several years more. The rental firm will be able to recover a substantial part of acquisition cost from selling used cars. Intangible assets related to a contractual right, such as landing rights at an airport or franchise rights to sell a franchiser's products, generally expire at a specific time. The residual value of such intangibles is zero. Identifiable intangibles acquired in a corporate acquisition that embody the attribute of separability, such as customer lists or brand names, may have salvage values, depending on the length of time the firm expects to use the intangibles.

Salvage value can be negative. Consider, for example, the cost of dismantling a nuclear electricity-generating plant. At the time the firm acquires the plant, it estimates the fair value at that date of the dismantling cost. The fair value of dismantling costs can be either a current market price for the future cost or the present value of the expected cash outflows. A provider of nuclear plant dismantling services might be willing to assume all risks of dismantling the plant 25 or 30 years hence for an agreed-upon price at the time of acquisition of the plant, which provides evidence of a current market price for this future service. Alternatively, the owner of the power plant might estimate the expected cost of obtaining the dismantling services or engaging in the dismantling itself in 25 to 30 years and then discounting the expected cash outflows to a present value. It adds this fair value to the asset and recognizes a liability of equal amount. The firm computes depreciation based on both the cost of the plant assets and fair value of the obligation to dismantle the nuclear power plant because the firm must recover this cost through depreciation during the asset's useful life.[8]

Estimates of salvage value are necessarily subjective. Disputes over salvage values have led in the past to many disagreements between the Internal Revenue Service and taxpayers. Partly to reduce such controversy, the Internal Revenue Code provides that firms may ignore salvage value entirely in calculating depreciation and amortization for tax reporting. When calculating depreciation and amortization in problems in this text, take the salvage value into account unless the problem gives explicit contrary instructions, such as for declining balance depreciation methods.

Estimating Service Life

The second factor in measuring depreciation and amortization is the expected **service life** of long-lived assets. In making the estimate, the accountant must consider both **physical and functional factors** that limit the life of the assets. Physical factors for tangible assets include such things as ordinary wear and tear from use, chemical action such as rust, and the effects of wind and rain. The most important functional factor for both tangible and intangible assets is obsolescence. Inventions, for example, may result in new processes that reduce the unit cost of production to the point where a firm finds continued operation of old equipment uneconomical, even though the equipment may be relatively unimpaired physically. Computers may work as well as ever, but firms replace them because new, smaller computers occupy less space and compute faster. Although display cases and storefronts may not have worn out, retail stores replace them to make the store look better. Technology-based intangibles can become obsolete overnight. Although the legal life of a patent on a drug is 20 years, the expected economic life of the drug may be as short as 8 or 10 years.

Despite abundant data from experience, estimating service lives for financial reporting presents the most difficult task in the depreciation and amortization calculation. Because obsolescence typically results from forces outside the firm, accountants have particular difficulty estimating its effect on the service life. This difficulty leads accountants to evaluate their estimates of service lives every few years and change the depreciation and amortization amounts going forward, a later topic in this chapter.

Estimates of service lives, like estimates of salvage value, have caused considerable controversy in the past between the Internal Revenue Service and taxpayers. The Congress created the **Modified Accelerated Cost Recovery System (MACRS)** to alleviate disagreements about service lives for depreciable, tangible assets. MACRS groups almost all depreciable assets into one of seven classes and specifies the depreciable lives and annual depreciation amounts for each class. The seven classes are as follows:

Class	Examples
3-year	Some racehorses; almost no others
5-year	Cars, trucks, some manufacturing equipment, research and development property
7-year	Office equipment, railroad cars, locomotives
10-year	Vessels, barges, and land improvements

(continued)

---

[8] Financial Accounting Standards Board, *Statement of Financial Accounting Standards No. 143*, "Accounting for Asset Retirement Obligations," 2001.

Class	Examples
20-year	Municipal sewers
27.5-year	Residential rental property
39-year	Nonresidential buildings acquired after 1993; otherwise 31.5 years

The MACRS generally results in depreciating buildings, equipment, and other tangible assets faster than their economic service lives. Although most firms use MACRS for income tax reporting, they must use the estimated service life for financial reporting. The Internal Revenue Code specifies that firms must amortize intangibles acquired in a corporate asset acquisition over 15 years. Firm must amortize other intangibles acquired, such as a patent from its creator, over the expected useful life of the intangible.

Earnings Quality Issue

Management estimates the depreciable lives and salvage values of depreciable assets. Management can shade those estimates to manage income. Management at Waste Management Inc. increased salvage value so much that over several years the company increased pre-tax income by about $600 million, when total pre-tax income for the period was on the order of $3.3 billion. Thus, the fudged depreciation charges represent about 20 percent of pretax income for the period of the fraud. Whenever the amount of depreciation expenses will materially change income, as it does for a fixed-asset intensive business like Waste Management, the analyst will worry about earnings quality. In the case of Waste Management's fraud, the savvy analyst, at least with hindsight, can spot a large and increasing deviation between net income and cash flow from operations.

Pattern of Depreciation and Amortization

After measuring the asset's acquisition cost and estimating both its salvage value and its service life, the firm has fixed the total of depreciation and amortization charges and the time span over which to recognize those costs. If the firm estimates salvage value of zero, it will depreciate or amortize the entire cost. The firm must select the pattern for allocating those charges to the specific years of the service life.

Depreciation of tangible assets based on the passage of time follows one of three basic patterns. These appear as A (accelerated), S (straight-line), and D (decelerated) in **Figures 8.1** and **8.2**. Amortization of intangible assets follows pattern S, not always by GAAP rule but in usual practice. You can more easily understand the terms *accelerated* and *decelerated* if you compare in **Figure 8.2** the depreciation charges in the early years with the straight-line method. Accelerated depreciation methods write off the depreciable basis of tangible assets more quickly during the early years of the asset's life as compared with straight-line depreciation amounts. Accelerated depreciation methods recognize less depreciation during the later years relative to straight-line depreciation. Over the service life of depreciable assets, total depreciation charges using accelerated and straight-line methods are the same. Only their timing differs. GAAP do not allow decelerated depreciation for financial reporting. Managerial accounting texts discuss this method because of its useful managerial accounting applications.

The next section illustrates the calculation of depreciation using the following acceptable methods under GAAP.

1. Straight-line (time) method (pattern S)
2. Production or use (straight-line use) method
3. Accelerated depreciation (pattern A):
    a. Declining-balance methods
    b. Sum-of-the-years'-digits method
    c. Modified Accelerated Cost Recovery System for income tax reporting

When acquiring or retiring a long-lived asset during an accounting period, the firm should calculate depreciation and amortization only for that portion of the period during which it uses the asset.

Straight-Line (Time) Method Firms most commonly use the **straight-line (time) method** for financial reporting to depreciate tangible assets and amortize intangible assets. The straight-line method divides the acquisition cost of the assets, less any estimated salvage value, by the number of years of its expected service life, to calculate the annual depreciation or amortization.

$$\text{Annual Depreciation or Amortization} = \frac{\text{Cost Less Estimated Salvage Value}}{\text{Estimated Life in Years}}$$

For example, if a machine costs $5,000, has an estimated salvage value of $200, and has an expected service life of five years, the annual depreciation will be $960 [= ($5,000 − $200)/5]. If a patent acquired from its creator for $30,000 has an expected service life of 5 years and zero salvage value, the annual amortization will be $6,000 (= $30,000/5). Occasionally, instead of a positive salvage value, the cost of removal exceeds the gross proceeds on disposition. Add this excess of removal costs over the gross proceeds to the cost of the asset in making the calculation. Thus, if a firm constructs a building for $3,500,000 and estimates a cost of $500,000 to remove it at the end of 25 years, the annual depreciation will be $160,000 [= ($3,500,000 + $500,000)/25]. By the end of the 22nd year, the accumulated depreciation will exceed the original cost of the building. Rather than show an Accumulated Depreciation account with a balance larger than the asset's cost, accounting shows the excess as a liability, such as Liability for Removal Costs.

Production or Use (Straight-Line Use) Method Firms do not use all assets uniformly over time. Manufacturing plants often have seasonal variations in operations, so that they use certain machines 24 hours a day at one time of the year and 8 hours or less a day at another time of the year. Trucks do not receive the same amount of use in each year of their lives. The straight-line (time) method of depreciation may result in depreciation patterns unrelated to usage patterns.

When the rate of usage of a depreciable asset varies over time and the firm can estimate the total usage over its life, the firm can use a **straight-line (use) method** based on actual usage each period. For example, a firm could base depreciation of a truck for a period on the ratio of miles driven during the period to total miles the firm expects to drive over the truck's life. The depreciation cost per unit (mile) of use is as follows:

$$\text{Depreciation or Amortization Cost per Unit} = \frac{\text{Cost Less Estimated Salvage Value}}{\text{Estimated Number of Units}}$$

Assume that a truck cost $54,000, has an estimated salvage value of $4,000, and will provide 200,000 miles of use before retirement. The depreciation per mile is $0.25 [= ($54,000 − $4,000)/200,000]. If the truck operates 24,000 miles in a given year, the depreciation charge is $6,000 (= 24,000 × $0.25).

Accelerated Depreciation The earning power of some depreciable assets declines as they grow older. Cutting tools lose some of their precision; printing presses require more frequent shutdowns for repairs; rent receipts from an old office building fall below those from a new one. Some assets provide more and better services in the early years of their lives and require increasing amounts of maintenance as they grow older. These cases justify accelerated depreciation methods, which recognize larger depreciation charges in early years and smaller depreciation charges in later years. GAAP do not *require* firms to use an accelerated method when the firm expects asset usage to be accelerated. As a later section discusses, GAAP provide firms considerable flexibility in choosing their depreciation method.

Even when a firm computes depreciation charges for a year on an accelerated method, it allocates amounts within a year on a straight-line basis. Thus, depreciation charges for a month are 1/12 the annual amount.

Declining-Balance Methods Under **declining-balance methods**, the depreciation charge results from multiplying a fixed rate times the net book value of the asset (cost less accumulated depreciation without subtracting salvage value) at the start of each period. Because the net book value declines from period to period, the result is a declining periodic charge for depreciation throughout the life of the asset. Even though the method does not subtract salvage value from cost, the depreciation stops when net book value reaches salvage value. Because the declining-balance method applies a fixed rate to a declining, but always positive, book value, declining-balance methods never fully depreciate an asset's cost. A firm using a declining balance method must therefore switch to straight-line at some point in the asset's life.

EXHIBIT 8.1

200 Percent Declining-Balance Depreciation with Switch to Straight-Line as Appropriate, Asset Costing $5,000 with Five-Year Life and $200 Salvage Value (Asset is retired at start of Year 6, when book value = $200.)

Start of Year	Acquisition Cost (1)	Accumulated Depreciation as of Jan. 1 (2)	Net Book Value as of Jan. 1 (3)	Double Declining-Balance Depreciation Rate (4)	Double Declining-Balance Depreciation Charge for the Year (5)	Net Book Value as of Jan. 1 Less Salvage Value of $200 (6)	Straight-Line Depreciation for Year (7)	Depreciation Charge for Year (8)
1	$5,000	$ 0	$5,000	40%	$2,000	$4,800	$960	$2,000
2	5,000	2,000	3,000	40	1,200	2,800	700	1,200
3	5,000	3,200	1,800	40	720	1,600	533	720
4	5,000	3,920	1,080	40	432	880	440	440[a]
5	5,000	4,360	640	40	256	440	440	440
6	5,000	4,800	200					440
								$4,800

Column (1), given.

Column (2) = column (2), previous period + column (8), previous period.

Column (3) = column (1) − column (2).

Column (4) = 2/life of asset in years = 2/5.

Column (5) = column (3) × column (4).

Column (6) = column (3) − salvage value, $200.

Column (7) = column (6)/remaining life in years: 5 for first row; 4 for second row; 3 for third row; 2 for fourth row; 1 for fifth row. This is the charge resulting from using straight-line for the first time in this year.

Column (8) = larger of column (5) and column (7).

[a] Firm switches to straight-line method in fourth year, when straight-line depreciation charges first exceed double declining-balance depreciation charges.

The fixed rate that firms use to apply declining-balance depreciation is usually some multiple of $1/n$, where n is the expected service life of the asset. The double declining-balance method uses a multiple of 2. Thus, an asset with a 5-year life will have a fixed rate of 40 percent ($= 2 \times 1/5$). The depreciation charge is 40 percent times the book value of the asset at the start of each year. Refer to our earlier example illustrating the straight-line (time) method. The firm acquires a machine costing $5,000 with a $200 salvage value and a five-year life. **Exhibit 8.1** illustrates the double declining-balance method. To depreciate the machine to its $200 salvage value at the end of five years, the firm switches to the straight-line method at the beginning of Year 4. Firms generally switch when depreciation under the straight-line method exceeds depreciation for that year under the double declining-balance method. If the firm continued to use the double declining-balance method for Year 4, depreciation would be $432 ($= 0.4 \times \$1,080$). Depreciation on the straight-line method is $440 [$= (\$1,080 - \$200)/2$].

Firms sometimes use fixed rates of 1.25 or 1.5 times $1/n$ when applying the declining-balance method.

Sum-of-the-Years'-Digits Method   Under the **sum-of-the-years'-digits method**, the depreciation charge results from applying a fraction, which decreases from year to year, to the cost less salvage value of the asset. The fraction's numerator and denominator are as follows:

- Numerator—the number of years of remaining life at the beginning of the year of the depreciation calculation
- Denominator—the sum of all digits of the estimated service life.

If the service life is n years, the denominator for the sum-of-the-years'-digits method is $1 + 2 + \ldots + n$. Consider the example above of a machine with a five-year life. The sum-of-the-years'-digits is 15 ($= 1 + 2 + 3 + 4 + 5$). **Exhibit 8.2** shows the depreciation charges under the sum-of-the-years'-digits method for the machine costing $5,000 and having a salvage value of $200.

EXHIBIT 8.2	Sum-of-the-Years'-Digits Depreciation, Asset with Five-Year Life, $5,000 Cost, and $200 Estimated Salvage Value			
Year	Acquisition Cost Less Salvage Value (1)	Remaining Life in Years (2)	Fraction $=(2)/15$ (3)	Depreciation Charge for the Year $=(3)\times(1)$ (4)
1	$4,800	5	5/15	$1,600
2	4,800	4	4/15	1,280
3	4,800	3	3/15	960
4	4,800	2	2/15	640
5	4,800	1	1/15	320
				$4,800

Modified Accelerated Cost Recovery System for Income Tax Reporting (MACRS)   Firms generally use MACRS to compute depreciation for income tax reporting. MACRS specifies the percentage of an asset's cost that firms may write off as depreciation each year for various defined classes of assets. MACRS derives these percentages using 1.5 and 2.0 declining-balance methods. MACRS assumes that firms acquire depreciable assets at the midpoint of the first year, regardless of the acquisition date. The MACRS percentages for 5-year property, for example, are 0.20, 0.32, 0.192, 0.115, 0.115, and 0.058. Thus, the five years of depreciation run from the midpoint of the first year to the midpoint of the sixth year. Firms rarely judge MACRS appropriate for financial reporting.

Problem 8.2 for Self-Study

Calculating periodic depreciation. Markam Corporation acquires a new machine costing $20,000 on January 2, Year 3. The firm expects

- To use the machine for five years,
- To operate it for 24,000 hours during that time,
- To recoup an estimated salvage value of $2,000 at the end of five years.

Calculate the depreciation charge for each of the five years using the following:

a. The straight-line (time) method
b. The sum-of-the-years'-digits method
c. The double declining-balance method, switching to the straight-line method in the fourth year
d. The straight-line (use) method; expected operating times are 5,000 hours each year for four years and 4,000 hours in the fifth year

Factors in Choosing the Depreciation and Amortization Method

Depreciation and amortization affect both income reported in the financial statements and taxable income on tax returns. Firms generally use straight-line amortization for intangibles for both financial and tax reporting. GAAP allow firms more flexibility in choosing their depreciation method for financial reporting. Firms will likely choose different depreciation methods for financial and tax reporting purposes. If so, the difference between depreciation in the financial statements and on the tax return leads to an issue in accounting for income taxes, which **Chapter 10** discusses.

Tax Reporting In selecting depreciation methods for tax reporting, the firm should try to maximize the present value of the reductions in tax payments from claiming depreciation. When tax rates stay constant over time, earlier deductions have greater value than later ones because a dollar saved today has greater value than a dollar saved tomorrow. Congress has presented business firms with several permissible alternatives under MACRS for computing the amount of depreciation to deduct each year. A firm will usually choose the alternative that meets the general goal of allowing it to pay the least amount of tax, as late as possible, within the law. Accountants call this goal the *least and latest rule*.

Financial Reporting Financial reporting for long-lived assets seeks an income statement that realistically measures the expiration of the assets' benefits and provides a reasonable pattern of cost allocation. No one knows, however, just how much service potential of a long-lived asset expires in any one period. The cost of the long-lived asset jointly benefits all the periods of use, and accountants have found no single correct way to allocate such joint costs. Financial statements should report depreciation charges based on reasonable estimates of asset expirations. Most U.S. firms use the straight-line method for financial reporting. Analysts understand that accelerated methods provide higher-quality earnings measures than do straight-line methods, but the differences are minor. Analysts will not likely downgrade a company because it uses the straight-line depreciation method.

Accounting for Periodic Depreciation and Amortization

In recording periodic depreciation and amortization, the accountant debits either an expense (a component of Retained Earnings) or a product cost account. Depreciation of factory buildings and equipment used in manufacturing operations, a product cost, becomes part of the cost of work-in-process and finished goods inventories. The amortization of a patent on a semiconductor that a firm embeds in its product is likewise a product cost. The cost for amortization of a customer list becomes either amortization expense or selling expense, depending on whether the firm classifies expenses by their nature or by their function. The cost of depreciation of office equipment becomes either depreciation expense or administrative expense.

In recording amortization of intangibles, the accountant usually records the matching credit directly to the asset account, such as Patent or Customer List. In recording depreciation of tangible assets, the accountant could, in principle, likewise record the matching credit directly in the asset account, such as Buildings or Equipment. In practice, most firms credit a contra-asset account, Accumulated Depreciation. This leaves the acquisition cost of the asset undisturbed and permits the analyst to compute both the amount written off through depreciation and the undepreciated acquisition cost. When the firm credits the asset account directly, an analysis of the accounts would disclose only the undepreciated acquisition cost. A later section of this chapter shows how the analyst can use this information to make useful inferences. Whether the firm uses a contra-asset account does not affect net assets.

The entry to record periodic depreciation of office facilities, a period expense first illustrated in **Chapter 3**, is as follows:

Retained Earnings (Depreciation or Administrative Expense) (Shareholders' Equity Decrease)	1,500	
Accumulated Depreciation (Asset Decrease)		1,500

The entry to record periodic depreciation of manufacturing facilities, a product cost first illustrated in **Chapter 7**, is as follows:

Work-in-Process Inventory (Asset Increase)	1,500	
Accumulated Depreciation (Asset Decrease)		1,500

The entry to record a patent's amortization embedded in a product is as follows:

Work-in-Process Inventory (Asset Increase)	1,500	
Patent (Asset Decrease)		1,500

The entry to record amortization of a customer list is as follows:

Retained Earnings (Amortization or Selling Expense) (Shareholders' Equity Decrease)	1,500	
Customer List (Asset Decrease)		1,500

The Work-in-Process Inventory account is an asset. Product costs, such as depreciation on manufacturing facilities, accumulate in the Work-in-Process Inventory account until the firm completes goods produced and transfers them to Finished Goods Inventory. The Accumulated Depreciation account remains open at the end of the period and appears on the balance sheet as a deduction from the asset account to which it is contra. The balance in the Accumulated Depreciation account usually represents the total charges in all accounting periods up through the balance sheet date for the depreciation on assets currently in use. The terms *book value* and *net book value* of an asset refer to the difference between the balance of an asset account and the balance of its accumulated depreciation account.

Impact of New Information about Long-Lived Assets

This chapter has considered thus far the acquisition and depreciation or amortization of long-lived assets based on transactions and knowledge at the time of initial acquisition. New information often comes to light over the life of tangible or intangible assets that firms must incorporate into their accounting for these assets. This section discusses the following items:

1. Changes in expected service lives or salvage values
2. Additional expenditures to maintain or improve the assets
3. Changes in the market value of assets

Changes in Service Lives or Salvage Values

The original depreciation or amortization schedule for a particular asset sometimes requires changing. A firm periodically re-estimates the service life and salvage value. The accuracy of the estimates improves as retirement approaches. If changing from the old to the new estimates would have a material impact, the firm must change the depreciation or amortization schedule. The generally accepted procedure makes no adjustment for the past misestimate but spreads the remaining book value less the new estimate of salvage value over the new estimate of the remaining service life of the asset.

The rationale for adjusting current and future depreciation or amortization charges instead of correcting past charges rests on the nature and role of estimates in accounting. The accountant makes estimates for depreciable lives and salvage values, uncollectible accounts, warranty costs, and similar items based on the available information at the time of the estimate. Changes in estimates occur regularly and users should learn to expect such changes, most of which do not materially impact the financial statements. Requiring firms to restate previously issued financial statements each year for changes in estimates might confuse users and undermine the credibility of the statements. Retroactive restatement might also provide management with an opportunity to inflate earnings of earlier periods, knowing that any adjustment will not affect future earnings. **Chapter 12** discusses these issues more fully.

To understand the **treatment of changes in periodic depreciation or amortization**, assume the following facts, illustrated in **Figure 8.4**. A firm

- purchases an office machine on January 1, Year 1, for $9,200,
- estimates that it will use the machine for 15 years, and
- estimates a salvage value of $200.

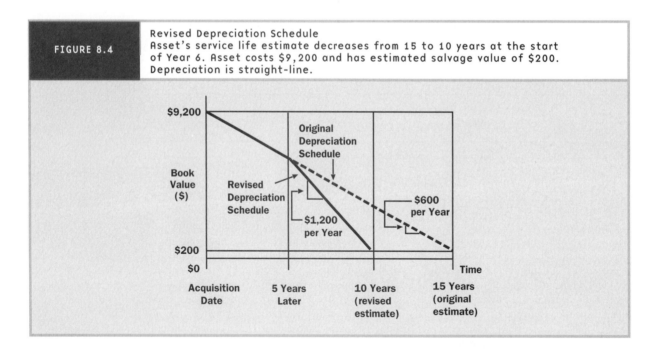

FIGURE 8.4

Revised Depreciation Schedule
Asset's service life estimate decreases from 15 to 10 years at the start of Year 6. Asset costs $9,200 and has estimated salvage value of $200. Depreciation is straight-line.

The depreciation charge recorded for each of the years from Year 1 through Year 5 under the straight-line method has been $600 [= ($9,200 − $200)/15]. On December 31, Year 6, before closing the books for the year, the firm decides that

- the machine will have a total useful life of only 10 years, and
- the salvage estimate of $200 remains reasonable.

The accepted procedure for recognizing this substantial decrease in service life revises the future depreciation so that the correct total will accumulate in the Accumulated Depreciation account at the end of the revised service life. The firm makes no adjustments of amounts previously recorded. In our example, the total amount of acquisition cost yet to be depreciated before the Year 6 change is $6,000 [= ($9,200 − $200) − (5 × $600)]. The new estimate of the remaining life is five years (the year just ended plus the next four), so the new annual depreciation charge is $1,200 (= $6,000/5). The accounting changes the amount recorded for annual depreciation in the current and future years, from $600 to $1,200. The depreciation entry on December 31, Year 6, and each year thereafter would be as follows:

Retained Earnings (Depreciation Expense) (Shareholders' Equity Decrease)	1,200	
Accumulated Depreciation (Asset Decrease)		1,200
To record depreciation for Year 6 based on revised estimates.		

Figure 8.4 illustrates the revised depreciation path.

Problem 8.3 for Self-Study

Adjustments for changes in estimates. Central States Electric Company constructs a nuclear power-generating plant at a cost of $200 million. It expects the plant to last 50 years before retiring the plant from service. The company estimates that at the time it retires the plant from service, it will incur $20 million in "decommissioning" costs (costs to dismantle the plant and dispose of the radioactive materials). The firm computes and charges straight-line depreciation once per year, at year-end.

During the company's 11th year of operating the plant, Congress enacts new regulations governing nuclear waste disposal. The estimated decommissioning costs increase from $20 million to $24 million. During the 31st year of operation, the firm revises the life of the plant. It will last 60 years in total, not 50 years.

a. What is the depreciation charge for the first year?
b. What is the depreciation charge for the 11th year?
c. What is the depreciation charge for the 31st year?

Additional Expenditures to Maintain or Improve Long-Lived Assets

Firms often spend cash for maintenance, repairs, and improvements during a tangible asset's life. Distinguishing between these purposes affects reported periodic income because firms immediately expense expenditures for maintenance and repairs but will debit to an asset account expenditures for improvements, and then depreciate or amortize those amounts in future periods.

Maintenance and Repairs A firm services and repairs an asset to maintain its expected operating condition. **Maintenance** includes routine costs such as for cleaning and adjusting. **Repairs** include the costs of restoring an asset's service potential after breakdowns or other damage. Expenditures for these items do not extend the estimated service life or otherwise increase productive capacity beyond the firm's original expectations for the asset. Because these expenditures restore future benefits to originally estimated levels, accounting treats such expenditures as expenses of the period when the firm makes the expenditure. In practice, to distinguish repairs from maintenance is difficult. Because expenditures for both become immediate expenses, accountants need not devote energy to distinguishing between them.

The repair policy a firm adopts will affect the depreciation rate for its assets. If, for example, a firm checks and services its assets often, the assets are likely to last longer than otherwise, and the depreciation rate will be lower.

Improvements Expenditures for **improvements**, sometimes called *betterments*, make an asset perform better than before. Such expenditures may increase the asset's life or reduce its operating cost or increase its rate of output. Because the expenditure improves the asset's service potential, accounting treats such an expenditure as an asset acquisition. The firm has acquired new future benefits. When the firm makes the expenditure, it can debit a new asset account or the existing asset account. Subsequent depreciation charges will increase.

Example 18   Assume a firm suffers a loss to its building in a fire. The firm spends $200,000 to replace the loss. It judges that $160,000 of the expenditure replaces long-lived assets lost in the fire, and $40,000 represents improvements to the building. It could make the following single journal entry.

Building (Asset Increase)	40,000	
Retained Earnings (Loss from Fire) (Shareholders' Equity Decrease)	160,000	
Cash (Asset Decrease)		200,000
To record loss and subsequent expenditure.		

The following two entries are equivalent and may be easier to understand:

Retained Earnings (Loss from Fire) (Shareholders' Equity Decrease)	160,000	
Building (Asset Decrease)		160,000
To record loss from fire.		
Building (Asset Increase)	200,000	
Cash (Asset Decrease)		200,000
To record expenditures on building.		

Distinguishing Maintenance and Repairs from Improvements   Accountants must distinguish maintenance and repairs from improvements because of the effect on periodic income. Some expenditures may both repair and improve. Consider expenditures to replace a roof damaged in a hurricane. The firm installs a new roof purposefully designed to be stronger than the old one so that it will support the air conditioning equipment the firm plans to install. Clearly, part of the expenditure represents repair and part, improvement.

The accountant must make judgments and allocate costs between maintenance and repairs and improvements. When in doubt, the accountant tends to call the expenditure a repair because of conservatism. The firm may also believe that expensing the item for financial reporting will support its immediate deduction for income tax reporting.

Problem 8.4 for Self-Study

Distinguishing repairs from improvements.   Purdy Company acquired two used trucks from Foster Company. Although the trucks were not identical, they both cost $15,000. Purdy knew when it negotiated the purchase price that the first truck required extensive engine repair, estimated to cost $4,000. The repair was made the week after acquisition and actually cost $4,200. Purdy Company thought the second truck was in normal operating condition when it negotiated the purchase price but discovered, after taking possession of the truck, that it required new bearings. The firm made this repair, costing $4,200, during the week after acquisition.

a. What costs should Purdy Company record in the accounts for the two trucks?
b. If the amounts recorded in part **a** are different, distinguish between the two repairs.

Changes in the Market Value of Assets

A firm acquires assets for their future benefits. The world changes, and expected future benefits change, sometimes increasing and sometimes decreasing in value. GAAP do not permit firms to write up the book value of their tangible and intangible long-lived assets when market values increase. This prohibition rests on conservatism. Accountants do not recognize increases in market value until the firm sells the assets, thereby realizing and validating the value increase.

Accounting treats value decreases differently. GAAP do not allow assets whose values have declined substantially to remain on the balance sheet at amortized acquisition cost. When a firm has information indicating that its assets have declined in market value or will provide a smaller future benefit than originally anticipated, GAAP may require the firm to recognize an impairment loss. GAAP distinguish three categories of long-lived assets for purposes of measuring and recognizing impairment losses:

1. All long-lived assets except intangibles not subject to amortization. This category includes property, plant, equipment, patents, franchise rights, and similar assets. These assets provide a firm with benefits over a predictable, finite period of time.
2. Intangibles, other than goodwill, not subject to amortization. This category includes brand names and trademarks. Firms do not amortize these intangibles because they provide benefits to a firm over an *indefinite* period of time.
3. Goodwill.

Asset Impairment for Long-Lived Assets Other Than Goodwill
GAAP require a three-step procedure for measuring impairments for long-lived assets other than goodwill:

1. The test for an impairment loss on all long-lived assets except intangibles not subject to amortization (**category 1** above) compares the undiscounted cash flows from the assets with their book values. An asset **impairment loss** arises when the book values of the assets exceed the undiscounted cash flows. The amount of the impairment loss is the excess of the book values of the assets over their fair values (either market value or present value of expected cash flows). (If you are unfamiliar with the notion of discounting, see the **Appendix**.)
2. The test for an impairment loss on intangibles not subject to amortization, other than goodwill (**category 2** above), compares the book values of the assets to their market values. The amount of the impairment loss is the excess of the book values over their market values.
3. At the time the firm judges that an impairment loss has occurred, the firm writes down the book value of the asset to its current fair value. That fair value is (a) the market value of the asset or, (b) if the firm cannot ascertain the market value, the net present value of the expected future cash flows.[9]

In requiring that the firm use undiscounted cash flows to test for an asset impairment in **step 1**, the FASB reasoned that a loss has not occurred if the firm can recover in future cash flows an amount at least equal to or larger than the current book value. The use of undiscounted, instead of discounted, cash flows seems theoretically unsound. The economic value of an asset may decline below its book value but the firm would recognize no impairment because the undiscounted future cash flows from the asset exceed its book value. We illustrate the application of the impairment test and the subsequent revaluations with examples.

Basic Impairment Example
Miller Company owns an apartment building that originally cost $20 million and by the end of the current period has accumulated depreciation of $5 million, with net book value of $15 (= $20 − $5) million. Miller Company had originally expected to collect rentals of $1.67 million each year for 30 years before selling the building for $8 million. Unanticipated placement of a new shopping center has caused Miller Company to reassess the future rentals. Miller Company expects the building to provide rentals for only 15 more years before Miller will sell it. Miller Company uses a discount rate of 12 percent per year in discounting expected rentals from the building.

Example 19
Miller now expects to receive annual rentals of $1.35 million per year for 15 years and to sell the building for $5 million after 15 years; these payments, in total, have a present value of $10.1 million when discounted at 12 percent per year. The building has a market value of $10 million today.

GAAP deem that no impairment loss has occurred because the expected undiscounted future cash flows of $25.25 [= ($1.35 × 15) + $5] million exceed the book value of $15 million. The firm has suffered an economic loss but will not recognize any loss in its accounts.

Example 20
Assume next that Miller expects to receive annual rentals of $600,000 per year for 15 years and to sell the building for $3 million after 15 years; these payments, in total, have a present value of $4.6 million when discounted at 12 percent per year. The building has a market value of $4 million today.

Miller has an asset impairment loss because the book value of $15 million exceeds the expected undiscounted future cash flows of $12.0 [= ($0.6 × 15) + $3] million. Miller

---

[9] Financial Accounting Standards Board, *Statement of Financial Accounting Standards No. 121*, "Accounting for the Impairment of Long-Lived Assets and for Long-Lived Assets to Be Disposed Of," 1995.

measures the impairment loss as the excess of the book value of the building of $15 million over its market value of $4 million. Miller accounts for the impairment by removing the building's acquisition cost and the accumulated depreciation from the accounts and establishing a new asset cost equal to current fair value, which is market value because the firm can estimate that amount. The journal entries (with amounts in millions) would be as follows:

Accumulated Depreciation (Asset Increase)	5.0	
Apartment Building (New Valuation) (Asset Increase)	4.0	
Retained Earnings (Loss on Impairment) (Shareholders' Equity Decrease) . .	11.0	
Apartment Building (Acquisition Cost) (Asset Decrease)		20.0

The loss appears on the income statement. Note that the firm uses undiscounted amounts to decide there is an impairment loss but uses market values to measure the loss in this example.

Example 21   As in **Example 20**, Miller expects to receive annual rentals of $600,000 per year for 15 years and to sell the building for $3 million after 15 years, which, discounted at 12 percent per year, has a present value of $4.6 million. Because of new housing code regulations, Miller Company cannot readily find a buyer or anyone who will quote a market value. FASB *Statement of Financial Accounting Standards No. 121* says that in such a case, fair value is the present value of future cash flows, or $4.6 million.

An asset impairment has occurred because the book value of $15 million exceeds the expected undiscounted future cash flows of $12.0 [= ($0.6 × 15) + $3] million. Miller Company measures the impairment loss as the excess of the book value of the building of $15 million over the present value of the future cash flows of $4.6 million. The firm accounts for the impairment loss by removing the building's acquisition cost and the accumulated depreciation from the accounts. It establishes a new asset cost equal to the current fair value, which is the present value of expected cash flows because the firm cannot estimate market value. The journal entries (with amounts in millions) could be as follows:

Accumulated Depreciation (Asset Increase)	5.0	
Apartment Building (New Valuation) (Asset Increase)	4.6	
Retained Earnings (Loss on Impairment) (Shareholders' Equity Decrease) . .	10.4	
Apartment Building (Acquisition Cost) (Asset Decrease)		20.0

The loss appears on the income statement.

Asset Impairment for Goodwill   As an earlier section discussed, FASB *Statement of Financial Accounting Standards No. 142* does not allow firms to amortize goodwill in measuring net income each period. Firms must, however, test annually for impairment in the value of goodwill. If impairment occurs, firms must write down goodwill and recognize an impairment loss. Firms must first apply the procedures above for measuring and recognizing impairment losses on assets other than goodwill. Firms then follow these two steps:[10]

1. **Test for Impairment of Goodwill.** Ascertain the current fair market value of a reporting unit that includes goodwill. The reporting unit is generally a previously acquired company in which the acquiring firm allocated a portion of the purchase price to goodwill. If the current fair value of a reporting unit that includes goodwill on its balance sheet falls below the net book value of its assets (including goodwill) less liabilities, then an impairment loss on goodwill may have occurred. In usual business terminology, this loss occurs when the book value of a firm exceeds its market value. GAAP do not require that the reporting unit have shares that separately trade in the market place to apply the impairment test. In the absence of such shares, however, measuring the current fair value of the reporting unit presents a challenge.

---

[10] Financial Accounting Standards Board, *Statement of Financial Accounting Standards No. 142,* "Goodwill and Other Intangible Assets," 2001.

2. **Measure the Amount of the Goodwill Impairment Loss.** Measuring the amount of the impairment loss of goodwill involves:
   a. allocating the current market value from **step 1** to identifiable assets and liabilities of the reporting unit based on their current fair values (either market values or current values of expected cash flows),
   b. allocating any excess current market value to goodwill,
   c. comparing the amount allocated to goodwill in **step 2b** with the book value of goodwill,
   d. recognizing an impairment loss on goodwill to write the book value of goodwill down to its current market value, computed in **step 2b**.

This computation parallels the initial computation of goodwill when the reporting unit first recognized it at the time of a corporate acquisition. The accountant uses the allocations described in **steps 2a** and **2b** solely for purposes of measuring the amount of the impairment loss to goodwill. The accountant does not record these allocated amounts in the accounts, except to the extent that they impact the amount of any impairment loss recognized before measuring an impairment loss on goodwill. The following example illustrates the application of this procedure.

Example 22 Burns, Philp and Company Limited (B-P), a food ingredients company, spent $100 million to acquire the long-lived tangible assets and brand names of Tone's Spices. B-P intended to sell Tone's Spices in warehouse stores like Sam's Clubs and Costco warehouses. B-P allocated $15 million to long-lived tangible assets, $35 million to brand names, and the remaining $50 million to goodwill. Within days of the acquisition, market pressure from its competitor, McCormick Spices, forced B-P to offer higher-than-anticipated cash discounts and slotting fees (for the rights to put spices into the club stores and warehouses) to its large customers. B-P judged that the expected undiscounted future cash flows from the Tone's operations had declined to only $90 million and the market value of the Tone's operations had dropped to $60 million.

B-P first applies the provisions for identifying and measuring an impairment loss on the long-lived tangible assets and brand names. Assume that $25 million of the $90 million undiscounted cash flows relates to long-lived tangible assets, $50 million relates to brand names, and $15 million relates to goodwill. Assume also that the fair value of the long-lived tangible assets is $15 million and the fair value of the brand names is $25 million. No impairment loss arises on the long-lived tangible assets because the undiscounted cash flows of $25 million exceed the book value of $15 million. An impairment loss arises on the brand names because the book value of $35 million exceeds their fair value of $25 million. The firm recognizes an impairment loss on the brand names of $10 million (= $35 million − $25 million). The book value of the entity after recognizing the impairment loss is $90 million (= $15 million for long-lived tangible assets + $25 million for brand names + $50 million for goodwill).

B-P may have incurred an impairment loss on its goodwill because the market value of the entity of $60 million is less than the book value of $90 million (**step 1** above).

B-P next allocates the $60 million current market value of Tone's to the long-lived tangible assets ($15 million—already measured), to the brand names ($25 million—already measured), and to goodwill ($20 million—plug) solely for the purpose of measuring the amount of the goodwill impairment loss. The book value of goodwill of $50 million exceeds its implied market value of $20 million by $30 million. B-P therefore recognizes an impairment loss on the goodwill. The journal entries would be as follows (with amounts in millions), with the first one made at the time of acquisition and the second on discovery of the impairment:

Land, Buildings, and Equipment (Asset Increase)	15.0	
Brand Names (Asset Increase)	35.0	
Goodwill on Acquisition of Tone's Spices (Asset Increase)	50.0	
Cash (Asset Decrease)		100.0
To record the acquisition of Tone's Spices for $100 million cash.		
Retained Earnings (Loss on Impairments) (Shareholders' Equity Decrease) . .	40.0	
Brand Names (Asset Decrease)		10.0
Goodwill on Acquisition of Tone's Spices (Asset Decrease)		30.0
To record asset impairment losses.		

The loss appears on the income statement. Recording this loss reduces the book value to $60 (= $15 + $25 + 20) million, its current fair value.

Problem 8.5 for Self-Study

Measuring impairment losses. Real Estate Financing Corporation (REFC) acquired the assets of Key West Financing Corporation (KWFC) on June 1, Year 6, for $250 million. On the date of the acquisition, KWFC's assets consisted of loans receivable with a market value of $120 million and real estate leased to businesses and individuals with a market value of $60 million. Thus, REFC allocated $70 (= $250 − $120 − $60) million of the purchase price to goodwill. On October 15, Year 8, a hurricane hit Key West and severely damaged many homes and businesses. Information related to the assets of KWFC on October 15, Year 8, is as follows (amounts in millions):

	Book Value	Undiscounted Cash Flows	Market Value
Loans Receivable	$140	$160	$125
Real Estate	80	65	50
Goodwill	70		
Total	$290		

a. Assume that the market value of KWFC on October 15, Year 8, after the hurricane is $310 million. Compute the amount of any asset impairment losses.

b. Assume that the market value of KWFC on October 15, Year 8, after the hurricane is $220 million. Compute the amount of any asset impairment losses.

Retirement of Assets

The final question asked regarding long-lived assets is: how does disposal of an asset affect earnings? Its owner can dispose of an asset through sale, abandonment, or trade-in on another asset.

Sale of Asset The firm records the consideration received from the sale (usually cash), eliminates any amounts, both debits and credits, in the accounts related to the asset sold, and recognizes a gain or loss for the difference. Because sales of long-lived assets are usually peripheral to a firm's principal business activities, accountants record the gain or loss net instead of gross. That is, the firm does not record the amount received as revenue and the book value of the asset sold as an expense. Rather, the firm nets the two amounts and reports only the gain or loss.

Before making the entry to record the sale, the firm records an entry to bring depreciation and amortization up to date. That is, the firm records the depreciation and amortization that has occurred between the start of the current accounting period and the date of disposition. When a firm retires an asset from service, it removes the cost of the asset and, in the case of tangible, depreciable assets, the related amount of accumulated depreciation from the books. As part of this entry, the firm records the amount received from the sale, a debit, and the amount of net book value removed from the books, a net credit (that is, a credit to the asset account and a smaller debit to the accumulated depreciation account). Typically, these two—debit for retirement proceeds and net credit to remove the asset from the accounts—differ from each other. The excess of the proceeds received on retirement over the book value is a gain (if positive) or a loss (if negative, that is, if net book value exceeds proceeds).

To understand the retirement of an asset, assume sales equipment costs $5,000, has an expected life of four years and a salvage value of $200. The firm has depreciated this asset on a straight-line basis at $1,200 [= ($5,000 − $200)/4] per year. The firm has recorded depreciation for two years and sells the equipment at midyear in the third year. The firm records the depreciation from the start of the accounting period to the date of sale: $600 [= 1/2 × ($5,000 − $200)/4].

Retained Earnings (Depreciation Expense) (Shareholders' Equity Decrease)	600	
Accumulated Depreciation (Asset Decrease)		600
To record depreciation charges up to the date of sale.		

The book value of the asset is now its cost less 2 1/2 years of straight-line depreciation of $1,200 per year or $2,000 [= ($5,000 − (2 1/2 × $1,200)) = ($5,000 − $3,000)]. The entry to record the retirement of the asset depends on the amount of the selling price.

1. Suppose the firm sells the equipment for cash at its book value of $2,000. The entry to record the sale would be as follows:

Cash (Asset Increase)	2,000	
Accumulated Depreciation (Asset Increase)	3,000	
Equipment (Asset Decrease)		5,000

When firms sell a long-lived asset during its life at its book value or at the end of its service life for an amount equal to the expected salvage used in computing depreciation or amortization, then no gain or loss arises.

2. Suppose the firm sells the equipment for $2,300 cash, more than its book value. The entry to record the sale would be as follows:

Cash (Asset Increase)	2,300	
Accumulated Depreciation (Asset Increase)	3,000	
Equipment (Asset Decrease)		5,000
Retained Earnings (Gain on Retirement of Equipment) (Shareholders' Equity Increase)		300

The gain on retirement recognizes that, given the information now available, the firm charged too much depreciation. The gain appears on the income statement. The gain restores to Retained Earnings the excess past depreciation charges.

3. Suppose the firm sells the equipment for $1,500 cash, less than its book value. The entry to record the sale would be as follows:

Cash (Asset Increase)	1,500	
Accumulated Depreciation (Asset Increase)	3,000	
Retained Earnings (Loss on Retirement of Equipment) (Shareholders' Equity Decrease)	500	
Equipment (Asset Decrease)		5,000

The loss on retirement recognizes that, given the information now available, the firm charged too little depreciation in the past. The loss appears on the income statement. The loss reduces Retained Earnings for the shortfall in past depreciation charged, in effect increasing depreciation charges all at once.

Abandonment of Asset   Firms will sometimes abandon assets if there is no market for the asset. Examples include an automobile severely damaged in an accident or a machine requiring an overhaul that is not cost-effective. The firm eliminates the book value of the asset and recognizes a loss in an amount equal to the book value.

Trading in an Asset   Instead of selling an asset to retire it from service, the firm may trade it in on a new asset. This is common practice for automobiles. Think of a trade-in transaction as a sale of the old asset followed by a purchase of the new asset. The accounting for trade-in transactions determines simultaneously the gain or loss on disposal of the old asset and the acquisition cost recorded for the new asset. The procedures depend on the similarity of the old and new assets, data available about the market value of the asset traded in, and the cash equivalent cost of the new asset. Intermediate accounting texts explain the various procedures. See also the **Glossary** entry for *trade-in transaction*.

Financial Statement Presentation

This section discusses the presentation of long-lived assets in the balance sheet and income statement. **Appendix 8.1** discusses their presentation in the statement of cash flows.

Balance Sheet

The balance sheet separates noncurrent from current assets. Tangible long-lived assets typically appear under the title Property, Plant, and Equipment, among the noncurrent assets. Firms generally disclose the assets' acquisition cost and accumulated depreciation in one of the three ways illustrated with the following data from a recent annual report of the General Electric Company (with dollar amounts in millions):

1. All information is listed in the balance sheet.

Property, Plant, and Equipment	
Acquisition Cost	$25,168
Less Accumulated Depreciation	(11,557)
Property, Plant, and Equipment—Net	$13,611

2. Acquisition cost is omitted from the balance sheet.

Property, Plant, and Equipment, less	
Accumulated Depreciation of $11,557	$13,611

3. Acquisition cost and accumulated depreciation are omitted from the balance sheet but are detailed in the notes.

Property, Plant, and Equipment—Net (Note 10)	$13,611

Note 10 to the Financial Statement
Property, plant, and equipment have an acquisition cost of $25,168 and accumulated depreciation of $11,557.

Firms typically disclose the amounts for land, buildings, and equipment separately in notes to the financial statements.

Because firms generally do not use an accumulated amortization account for intangibles, the balance sheet presents intangibles in a format similar to the last one above.

Income Statement

Depreciation and amortization expenses appear in the income statement, sometimes disclosed separately and sometimes, particularly for manufacturing firms, as part of cost of goods sold expense. United States Steel Corporation lists depreciation expense separately from other costs of goods sold, explicitly noting that cost of goods sold excludes depreciation. General Electric includes depreciation expense in cost of goods sold and separately discloses the amount of depreciation in the notes. Gain or loss on retirement of plant assets appears on the income statement, but often the amounts are so small that some "Other" caption includes them.

Analyzing Financial Statement Disclosures of Long-Lived Assets

Property, Plant and Equipment

The financial statements and notes provide useful information for analyzing changes in property, plant, and equipment. **Exhibit 8.3** presents information for Wal-Mart Stores for three recent years. This section illustrates insights provided by these disclosures.

Fixed Asset Turnover   **Chapter 5** discussed the fixed asset turnover, a measure of the amount of sales generated from property, plant, and equipment. The computation of the fixed asset turnover for Wal-Mart Stores is as follows:

Year 12: $217,799/0.5($45,417 + $50,529)	4.5
Year 13: $244,524/0.5($50,529 + $56,492)	4.6
Year 14: $256,329/0.5($56,492 + $63,648)	4.3

EXHIBIT 8.3	Selected Data for Wal-Mart Stores (all dollar amounts in millions)			

| | Year Ended January 31 | | | |
	Year 11	Year 12	Year 13	Year 14
Balance Sheet				
Land	$10,466	$ 11,311	$ 12,318	$ 13,809
Buildings and Improvements	32,607	36,862	42,161	48,066
Fixtures and Transportation				
Equipment	13,843	15,224	16,739	19,130
Total	$56,916	$ 63,397	$ 71,218	$ 81,005
Less Accumulated				
Depreciation	(11,499)	(12,868)	(14,726)	(17,357)
Total	$45,417	$ 50,529	$ 56,492	$ 63,648

| | For the Year | | |
	Year 12	Year 13	Year 14
Income Statement			
Sales	$217,799	$244,524	$256,329
Depreciation Expense	3,290	3,432	3,852

Sales increased 12.2 percent between Year 12 and Year 13, but only 4.8 percent between Year 13 and Year 14. **Chapter 5** suggested that Wal-Mart likely continued adding new stores in Year 14, but the decreased growth in sales caused its fixed asset turnover to decline.

Proportion of Depreciable Assets Written Off Because Wal-Mart Stores uses the straight-line depreciation method, we can compare the amount in accumulated depreciation with the acquisition cost of depreciable assets to approximate the fraction of the depreciable life of its assets Wal-Mart Stores has used.

Year 11: $11,499/($32,607 + $13,843)	24.8%
Year 12: $12,868/($36,862 + $15,224)	24.7%
Year 13: $14,726/($42,161 + $16,739)	25.0%
Year 14: $17,357/($48,066 + $19,130)	25.8%

One possible explanation for the increasing percentage is that Wal-Mart decreased the rate of growth in new buildings and equipment, allowing accumulated depreciation to catch up with new investments in depreciable assets. In fact, the growth in depreciable assets actually increased during the three-year period. Another possible explanation is that Wal-Mart increased the proportion of the shorter-lived fixtures and transportation relative to the longer-lived buildings. In fact, the proportion of short-lived assets decreased relative to buildings during the three-year period. One explanation consistent with the increasing percentage is that Wal-Mart had an increasing percentage of fully depreciated assets on its books. To make these calculations, you need to know both acquisition cost and accumulated depreciation.

Average Life of Depreciable Assets We can calculate the average total life of depreciable assets by dividing the average acquisition cost of depreciable assets by depreciation expense each year. The computations are as follows:

Year 12: 0.5($32,607 + $13,843 + $36,862 + $15,224)/$3,290	15.0 years
Year 13: 0.5($36,862 + $15,224 + $42,161 + $16,739)/$3,432	16.2 years
Year 14: 0.5($42,161 + $16,739 + $48,066 + $19,130)/$3,852	16.4 years

Because depreciation expense is an amount for the year, we use the average amount of depreciable assets at acquisition cost in use during the year. We exclude land because it is not depreciated. The average life increased, reflecting a higher proportion of store buildings and warehouses with 20- to 25-year lives and a smaller proportion of fixtures and transportation equipment with 5- to 10-year lives.

Average Age of Depreciable Assets   We can calculate the average age of depreciable assets by dividing the average amount of accumulated depreciation by depreciation expense each year. The computations are as follows:

Year 12: 0.5($11,499 + $12,868)/$3,290	3.7
Year 13: 0.5($12,868 + $14,726)/$3,432	4.0
Year 14: 0.5($14,726 + $17,357)/$3,852	4.2

The increase in the average age reflects the increasing proportion of buildings and the decreasing proportion of fixtures and transportation equipment among depreciable assets.

Intangibles

Analysis of the disclosures regarding intangibles provides less insight for the following reasons:

1. Internally developed intangibles generally do not appear on the balance sheet.
2. Firms that grow through corporate acquisitions usually will report intangibles on the balance sheet, whereas companies that grow internally usually will not report intangibles.
3. Intangibles that do appear on the balance sheet usually appear net of amortization, so the analysts cannot perform the analyses illustrated above for property, plant, and equipment.

The absence of intangibles on the balance sheet, particularly those related to technologies and brand names, has caused many financial statement users to criticize GAAP in recent years. An investor in a firm's common stock may want to estimate the value of such intangibles when deciding to purchase or sell the firm's shares. The investor can use information in the financial statements to help in these valuations. One approach to valuation computes the present value of the cash flows derived from a brand name, technology, or other intangible.

Exhibit 8.4 illustrates how one might value the Tootsie Roll family of brands (Tootsie Roll, Charms, and Junior Mints, among others) at more than $200 million based on the present value of the cash flows it generates. The method involves four steps, each labeled in the exhibit; all but one typically involves subjective judgment. The interaction of these judgments produces a range of final estimates, which shows the imprecision of the process. This imprecision makes U.S. accountants reluctant to audit and attest to such valuations.

EXHIBIT 8.4	Illustration of Steps to Estimate the Value of a Brand Name Using Present Value of Discounted Cash Flows Caused by the Tootsie Roll Family of Brands (all dollar amounts in millions)		
	Worldwide Sales		$ 312.7
	Cost of Goods Sold and Operating Expenses		(248.6)
	[1] Operating Margin (20 percent)		$ 64.1
	Employed Physical Capital	$188.1	
	Subtract Pretax Profit on Physical Capital Required at 12 Percent		(22.6)
	[2] Profit Generated by Brand		$ 41.5
	Subtract Income Taxes at 37 Percent		(15.3)
	[3] Net Brand Profits		$ 26.2
	Multiply by After-tax Capitalization Factor		× 8.0
	[4] Estimated Brand Value		$ 209.6

1. The first step attempts to measure the cash flow that the brand, in this example Tootsie Roll, generates. The computation shows brand revenues less brand operating expenses, all of which ultimately result in cash flows. A more precise computation adjusts revenues and expenses for changes in receivables and payables, but **Exhibit 8.4** does not illustrate this sub-step. Brand revenues in excess of operating expenses for the year are $64.1 million.

2. The next step computes the cost of the physical capital—such as land, factories, inventories, and other components of working capital, assets for distributing the branded product—used to produce the cash flow. Tootsie Roll devotes about $188 million of assets to the production and distribution of Tootsie Roll products. (Computing this amount may require estimates and approximations.) **Exhibit 8.4** assumes that Tootsie Roll expects to earn 12 percent per year, before taxes, on its assets. Thus, Tootsie Roll must earn $22.6 (= 0.12 × $188) million from the Tootsie Roll family of products just to pay the cost of the physical capital devoted to the production of products carrying the Tootsie Roll brand. That leaves $41.5 (= $64.1 − $22.6) million of pretax profits attributable to the nonphysical assets, in this case the brands themselves. We base this calculation on the historical cost of the physical assets, but one might prefer to use some measure of their current cost.

3. **Exhibit 8.4** assumes that Tootsie Roll must pay income taxes at the rate of 37 percent of taxable income, so that after taxes, the brands generate $26.2 [= (1.00 − 0.37) × $41.5] million of after-tax cash flows for the year.

4. Now comes the toughest part of the estimation: how long does the analyst expect the cash flows from the brand to last, and how risky are they? If the analyst expected the brand-generated cash flow, $26.2 million per year, to persist for just one year, the analyst would value the brand at the amount of those cash flows—$26.2 million. If the analyst expected the brand values to last indefinitely and used an after-tax discount rate of 10 percent per year, then the analysis would result in a brand valuation of $262 million (= $26.2 million × 1/0.10). (See the discussion of the valuation of perpetuities in the **Appendix** at the back of the book, at **Examples 15** and following.) **Exhibit 8.4** shows a multiplier (like a price/earnings ratio) of 8, which suggests that the brand is worth about $209 million (= 8 × $26.2 million).[11]

Problem 8.6 for Self-Study

Sensitivity of brand valuation to estimates. Refer to the computations of brand value for Tootsie Roll in **Exhibit 8.4** and observe the sensitivity of the final valuation to these estimates.

a. Recompute the brand value assuming a pretax charge for physical capital of 10 percent per year and a multiplier for brand cash flows of 10.

b. Recompute the brand value assuming a pretax charge for physical capital of 20 percent per year and a multiplier for brand cash flows of 6.

An International Perspective

The accounting for long-lived assets in most developed countries closely parallels that in the United States. Firms commonly value long-lived assets at acquisition, or historical, cost. France permits periodic revaluations of buildings and equipment to current market values. Few firms perform these revaluations, however, because the French immediately tax the unrealized gains. As a result of the book-tax conformity requirement in France, few firms choose to revalue their buildings and equipment for financial reporting. Firms in Great Britain also periodically revalue their buildings and equipment to current market value. Unlike in France, in Great Britain the revaluations do not result in immediate taxation. Refer to

---

[11] Examine **Table 4** at the back of the book. Notice that a multiplier of 8 implies a discount rate of 8 percent for cash flows lasting 13 years or 10 percent for cash flows lasting 17 years or 12.5 percent for cash flows lasting forever (in perpetuity). The **Appendix** at the back of the book explains **Table 4** and how to use it. A comprehensive discussion of brand valuation from an accounting perspective appears in Patrick Barwise, Christopher Higson, Andrew Likierman, and Paul Marsh, *Accounting for Brands* (London: London Business School and The Institute of Chartered Accountants of England and Wales, 1989). See Carol J. Simon and Mary W. Sullivan, "The Measurement and Determinants of Brand Equity: A Financial Approach," *Marketing Science* 12, no. 1 (Winter 1993): 28–52, for the classic study of the economies of brand valuation. Simon and Sullivan find that of all the food-product brand names they examined, Tootsie Roll had the highest ratio of brand value to other asset value.

Exhibit 2.7, a balance sheet for Rolls Royce. This firm revalued its tangible assets (it also purchased additional tangible assets). The off-setting credit for the revaluation is to the account Revaluation Reserve, shown among Capital and Reserves on the balance sheet.

Depreciation accounting in developed countries also closely parallels that in the United States. Firms use both straight-line and accelerated depreciation methods. In countries where financial and tax reporting closely conform (such as Japan and Germany), firms tend to use accelerated depreciation methods for both financial and tax reporting. When firms in Great Britain recognize depreciation on revalued plant assets, they charge the depreciation on the revalued amount above historical cost to the Revaluation Reserve account. Thus, neither the initial unrealized holding gain nor depreciation of this unrealized gain flows through the income statement. The income statement includes depreciation based on historical cost amounts only.

The International Accounting Standards Board (IASB) has specified accounting procedures for impairments somewhat different from the procedures used in the United States.[12] Firms compare the recoverable amount of an asset (its net selling price or present value of expected cash flows) to the book value of the asset to determine if an asset impairment has occurred. In the United States, recall, the test compares undiscounted cash flows to the book value of the asset.

The IASB has also specified accounting

principles for intangibles somewhat different from those used in the United States.[13] For expenditures on development—the "D" of R&D, the stage following research where the firm has found something with commercial value—the IASB requires that the firm capitalize those costs into an asset account if the future economic benefits will flow from the expenditures and the firm can reliably measure the costs. This reporting standard precludes the recognition of intangibles, whether developed internally or acquired in external market transactions, if the intangible does not meet the definition of an asset. It specifically excludes from recognition as assets the results of expenditures on research, advertising, and employee training. *IRS No. 38* provides for the amortization of intangibles over their useful lives. It sets forth 20 years as the maximum amortization period unless firms can justify a longer life.

Both the FASB and the IASB have said they want to bring U.S. and international accounting standards closer to each other. The issues in the preceding paragraphs are likely areas for convergence. We shall not be surprised to see the FASB requiring a different treatment for development from that for research. The FASB has so much on its agenda that it is not likely to change its impairment tests in the direction of the IASB's, but we suspect that if the FASB were addressing this issue anew today, it would use the IASB's discounted tests, rather than the current undiscounted ones.

Summary

This chapter started by setting forth a series of questions regarding the accounting for long-lived assets. We repeat those questions here and summarize GAAP's response to each.

1. Should firms treat expenditures with potential long-term benefits as assets on the balance sheet or as expenses in the income statement in the year of the expenditure? The criteria applied in practice to treat an expenditure as an asset requires that the firm:

   - have acquired rights to the future use of a resource as a result of a past transaction or exchange, and
   - be able to measure or quantify the future benefits with a reasonable degree of precision.

   Firms easily apply these criteria to tangible assets, such as buildings and equipment, because of their physical attributes. Considerable controversy surrounds the recognition of many intangibles, particularly for research and development, brand names, and software development costs.

2. For expenditures treated as assets, should firms depreciate or amortize a portion of the assets as expenses each period or wait until firms dispose of the assets to write off the cost? The response to this question depends on when the firm expects to consume the service benefits of the assets. Firms depreciate or amortize the cost of long-lived assets whose service benefits

---

[12] International Accounting Standards Board, *International Reporting Standards 36*, "Impairment of Assets," 1998.

[13] International Accounting Standards Board, *International Reporting Standards 38*, "Recognizing Intangibles," 1998.

diminish over time. Examples are buildings, equipment, and patents. Firms do not depreciate or amortize the cost of long-lived assets when service benefits do not diminish with time, such as for land and goodwill. Firms must test these, and all other, assets for impairment in value.

3. For assets that firms depreciate or amortize, over what period and using what pattern of charges should firms write off the cost of the assets? Firms write off the cost of assets over their expected service life. Most firms choose to write off an equal amount each year using the straight-line method. Some firms use accelerated methods for tangible assets.

4. How should firms treat new information about expected useful lives or salvage value? GAAP require firms to depreciate or amortize the book value at the time of the change in estimate over the revised remaining useful life, thereby spreading the effect of the misestimate of the past over the current and future years.

5. How should firms treat substantial declines in the market values of long-lived assets that occur because of technological change, introduction of new products by competitors, changing consumer tastes, and similar factors? Firms must test assets for impairment in value. GAAP specify different tests for goodwill and assets other than goodwill.

6. What impact does the disposal of long-lived assets have on earnings? Firms record any proceeds of disposal, eliminate the book value of the asset, and record a gain or loss for the difference (except for some trade-ins).

GAAP's responses to each of these questions provide guidance to firms in accounting for their long-lived assets. Firms have considerable latitude within GAAP, however, to apply the general principles. Firms must make estimates of service lives and salvage values for depreciation and amortization, choose their depreciation method, make estimates of market values in allocating the aggregate purchase price in corporate acquisitions and measuring asset impairments, and time asset sales for gain or loss. The opportunities open to firms to manage earnings with respect to long-lived assets cause analysts to consider the impact on the quality of earnings.

Appendix 8.1: Effects on the Statement of Cash Flows of Transactions Involving Long-Lived Tangible and Intangible Assets

The statement of cash flows reports as investing activities both the cash used for acquisition of tangible or intangible assets and the cash provided by their retirement. It usually shows adjustments for depreciation, amortization, asset impairments, and gains and losses on disposal in deriving cash from operations when the firm uses the indirect method.

Retirement Entries in the Statement of Cash Flows

When the firm sells a tangible or intangible asset for cash, it reports that cash in the Investing section as a nonoperating source, Proceeds from Disposition of Noncurrent Assets. Usually, the firm sells a tangible or intangible asset for an amount different from its book value at the time of sale. Thus, the retirement generates a loss (proceeds less than book value) or a gain (proceeds greater than book value).

Loss on Retirement

The Investing section of the statement shows all the proceeds from selling the tangible or intangible asset. None of that cash results from operations. When firms report cash flow from operations using the direct method, they need not make adjustments for the loss on retirement. In the indirect format for operating cash flow, the statement of cash flows begins with net income, which includes the loss on sale. Because the sale is a (dis)investing—not an operating—activity, the presentation must add back the amount of the loss in deriving operating cash flows. The addback presentation resembles the addback for depreciation expense.

Gain on Retirement

The gain on retirement increases net income, but the cash from retirement produces (dis)investing, not operating, cash flow. When the statement of cash flows presents cash from operations using the indirect format, it must subtract the amount of the gain from net income so that operating cash flow will exclude the cash from retirement, properly classified among investing activities.

Depreciation and Amortization Charges

Whether or not depreciation and amortization charges appear in the statement of cash flows depends on whether the firm chooses to use the direct method or the indirect method for reporting cash generated by operations. A firm using the direct method reports only receipts minus expenditures for operating activities. A firm using the indirect method reports net income—revenues minus expenses—along with various addbacks and subtractions to convert the amount into receipts minus expenditures. Because depreciation and amortization expenses reduce income but use no cash currently, an addback for depreciation and amortization expenses appears in the derivation of cash from operations. Most firms use the indirect method and show such an addback.

Depreciation Charges for a Manufacturing Firm   Chapter 7 introduced the notion, repeated in this chapter, that manufacturing firms typically do not debit all depreciation charges to depreciation expense. Rather, such firms debit depreciation on manufacturing facilities to the Work-in-Process Inventory account. The firm transfers the depreciation costs from Work-in-Process to Finished Goods Inventory at the same time that it transfers the goods from the production line to the finished goods warehouse. Then, the depreciation cost remains in Finished Goods Inventory until the firm sells the goods embodying the depreciation. Only then do the depreciation costs become expenses—part of Cost of Goods Sold. Conventionally, however, a manufacturing firm adds back all depreciation charges for a given period in its derivation of cash from operations for the same period in which the firm incurred those charges.

- If the firm has sold the goods embodying the depreciation, the addback cancels the depreciation included in Cost of Goods Sold.
- If the firm has not yet sold the inventory embodying the depreciation, then the current asset inventories will increase by the amount of any depreciation embodied in the Work-in-Process accounts. Recall that in the indirect method, the firm subtracts the increase in inventory accounts in deriving cash flows from operations. (Refer to **Exhibit 4.12**. Note that the addback on line 4 and the subtraction on line 5 increase by the same amount.)

Thus, whether the firm sells or keeps in inventory the manufactured goods embodying the depreciation charges, it will add back all depreciation charges, manufacturing and other, to net income in deriving operating cash flows. If the firm has not sold the goods, the subtraction for the increase in inventory will cancel just the right part—the depreciation charges in ending inventory—of the addback.

Asset Impairment Losses

The recognition of an impairment loss involves a debit for the impairment loss and a credit to the asset account. The impairment loss reduces net income but does not use cash. Thus, like depreciation and amortization charges, the accountant adds back the impairment loss to net income in deriving cash flow from operations using the direct method.

Noncash Acquisitions of Plant and Intangible Assets

Firms often borrow funds from a lender to acquire plant and intangible assets from a third party. A firm, for example, might borrow $5 million from an insurance company and use the cash to acquire a building from a developer. The loan appears on the statement of cash flows as a financing activity, and the acquisition of the building appears as an investing activity.

Firms sometimes give consideration other than cash to the seller (the developer in the above example) in acquiring plant and intangible assets. The consideration might be a mortgage note or the firm's shares. Because these investing and financing transactions involve a bartering that does not use cash, they do not appear on the statement of cash flows. The firm must report such transactions in a supplementary schedule or note.

SUGGESTED SOLUTION TO PROBLEM 8.1 FOR SELF-STUDY

(Jensen Company; calculating the acquisition cost of fixed assets.)
(1) a, b, d, j, l, m, o, p
(2) c, e, f, g, i, k, l, n, o, p
(3) h, i, p, s
(4) i, q, r

COMMENTS AND EXPLANATIONS

d. Removing the old building makes the land ready to accept the new one. These costs apply to the land, not to the new building. For tax purposes, the firm might prefer to allocate this cost to the building because it can depreciate the building, but not the land.

f. The reduction in cost of materials and supplies will reduce the cost of the building. The actual accounting entries depend on the method used to record the potential discount. This book does not discuss these issues.

h. Although one capitalizes explicit interest, one may not capitalize opportunity-cost interest or interest imputed on one's own funds used. The adjusting entry credits Construction in Process and debits Retained Earnings (Interest Revenue). The debit reduces income, removing the revenue that had been recognized by the company.

i. Computation of the amounts to be allocated requires an estimate. Once the firm estimates amounts, it debits them to Building or to Retained Earnings (Depreciation Expense) and Work-in-Process Inventory, as appropriate, for the regular company operations.

j. Credit to Land account, reducing its cost.

l. Allocate to Land and Building, based on an estimate of how time was spent. Given the description, most of these costs are probably for the building.

m. Include as part of the cost of the land.

n. Capitalize as part of the Building account for the same reasons that a firm capitalizes interest during construction. Some accountants would treat this item as an expense. In any case, the firm can treat this item as an expense for tax reporting.

o. Allocate the costs for insuring workers to the same accounts as the wages for those workers.

p. Most accountants would treat this as an expense or a loss for the period. Others would capitalize it as part of the cost of the building for the same reason that they capitalized the explicit insurance cost. If, however, the company was irrational in acquiring insurance policies with deductible clauses, this item would be an expense or loss. Accounting usually assumes that most managements make rational decisions most of the time. In any case, one can treat this item as an expense or a loss for tax reporting.

q. Debit to Machinery and Equipment account, an asset account separate from Building.

r. Treat the same as the preceding item; installation costs are part of the cost of the asset; see **Chapter 2**.

s. Recognizing revenue is incorrect. Credit the Construction in Process account and debit the Construction Revenue account.

SUGGESTED SOLUTION TO PROBLEM 8.2 FOR SELF-STUDY

(Markam Corporation; calculating periodic depreciation.)
a. Straight-Line Method:

Years 3–7: ($20,000 − $2,000)/5 = $3,600 each year
Total: $3,600 × 5 = $18,000

b. Sum-of-the-Years'-Digits Method:

Year 3: 5/15 × ($20,000 − $2,000) = $ 6,000
Year 4: 4/15 × ($20,000 − $2,000) =   4,800
Year 5: 3/15 × ($20,000 − $2,000) =   3,600
Year 6: 2/15 × ($20,000 − $2,000) =   2,400
Year 7: 1/15 × ($20,000 − $2,000) =   1,200
        Total $18,000

c. Double Declining-Balance Method:

Year 3: $2/5 \times \$20,000 =$	$ 8,000
Year 4: $2/5 \times (\$20,000 - \$8,000) =$	4,800
Year 5: $2/5 \times (\$20,000 - \$8,000 - \$4,800) =$	2,880
Year 6: $1/2 \times (\$4,320^{a} - \$2,000) =$	1,160
Year 7: $1/2 \times (\$4,320 - \$2,000) =$	1,160
Total	$18,000

[a] $\$20,000 - \$8,000 - \$4,800 - \$2,880 = \$4,320$

d. Units-of-Production Method:

Years 3–6: $5,000 \times \$0.75^{a} = \$3,750$ per year
Year 7: $4,000 \times \$0.75^{a} = \$3,000$
Total $[(\$3,750 \times 4) + \$3,000] = \$18,000$

[a] $(\$20,000 - \$2,000)/24,000 = \$0.75$ per hour

SUGGESTED SOLUTION TO PROBLEM 8.3 FOR SELF-STUDY

(Central States Electric Company; adjustments for changes in estimates.)
(All dollar amounts in millions.)
a. $4.4 per year $= (\$200 + \$20)/50$ years
b. $4.5 per year $= [\$200 + \$20 + \$4 - (\$4.4$ per year $\times 10$ years$)]/40$ years remaining life
 $= (\$224 - \$44)/40$
 $= \$180/40$
c. $3.0 per year $= [\$180 - (\$4.5 \times 20$ years$)]/30$ years remaining life
 $= (\$180 - \$90)/30$
 $= \$90/30$

SUGGESTED SOLUTION TO PROBLEM 8.4 FOR SELF-STUDY

(Purdy Company; distinguishing repairs from improvements.)
a. Record the first truck at $19,200. Record the second truck at $15,000; debit $4,200 to expense or loss.
b. When Purdy Company acquired the first truck, it knew it would have to make the "repair," which is an improvement. The purchase price was lower because of the known cost to be incurred. At the time of acquisition, the firm anticipated the cost as required to produce the expected service potential of the asset. The fact that the cost was $4,200, rather than "about $4,000," does not seem to violate Purdy Company's expectations at the time it acquired the truck. If the repair had cost significantly more than $4,000—say, $7,000—then the excess could be a loss or an expense.

Purdy Company believed that the second truck was operable when it agreed on the purchase price. Purdy Company incurred the cost of the repair to achieve the level of service potential it thought it had acquired. There are no more future benefits after the repair than it had anticipated at the time of acquisition. Therefore, the $4,200 is an expense or a loss.

SUGGESTED SOLUTION TO PROBLEM 8.5 FOR SELF-STUDY

(Real Estate Financing Corporation; measuring impairment losses.)
a. The undiscounted cash flows related to the loans receivable of $160 million exceed their book value of $140 million, so no impairment loss arises for the receivables. For real estate, the book value of $80 million exceeds their undiscounted cash flows of $65 million, so Real Estate Financing Corporation recognizes an impairment loss of $30 (= $50 − $80) million. The book value of the firm after recognizing the impairment loss is $260 million (= $140 for loans receivable + $50 million for real estate + $70 million for goodwill). The market value of the firm of $310 million exceeds the book value of $260 million, so no impairment loss on goodwill arises.
b. The answers for the loans receivable and the real estate in part **a** apply here as well. In this case, however, the book value of the firm of $260 million exceeds the market value of $220

million, so an impairment loss of goodwill arises. To measure the impairment loss, the accountant attributes $125 million of the market value of $220 million to loans receivable, $50 million to real estate, and $45 million to goodwill. Comparing the market value of goodwill of $45 million to the book value of goodwill of $70 million yields an impairment loss of $25 million.

SUGGESTED SOLUTION TO PROBLEM 8.6 FOR SELF-STUDY

(Tootsie Roll; sensitivity of brand valuations to estimates)

TOOTSIE ROLL
Illustration of Steps to Estimate the Value of a Brand Name Using Present Value of Discounted Cash Flows Caused by the Tootsie Roll Family of Brands with Variations in Assumptions
(all dollar amounts in millions)

			Part a	Part b
Worldwide Sales			$312.7	$ 312.7
Operating Expenses			(248.6)	(248.6)
[1] Operating Margin (20 percent)			$ 64.1	$ 64.1
Employed Physical Capital		$188.1		
Subtract Pretax Profit on Physical Capital				
Required at 10 (part **a**) or 20 (part **b**) Percent			(18.8)	(37.6)
[2] Profit Generated by Brand			$ 45.3	$ 26.5
Subtract Income Taxes at 37 Percent			(16.8)	(9.8)
[3] Net Brand Profits			$ 28.5	$ 16.7
Multiply by Aftertax Capitalization Factor			10.0	6.0
[4] Estimated Brand Value			$ 285.0	$ 100.2

Key Terms and Concepts

Tangible assets
Intangible assets
Interest paid during construction
Depreciation
Amortization
Joint cost
Value
Salvage value
Net residual value
Service life
Physical and functional factors
Modified Accelerated Cost Recovery System
  (MACRS)

Straight-line (time and use) methods
Declining-balance methods
Sum-of-the-years'-digits method
Treatment of changes in periodic depreciation
  or amortization (estimates of useful lives
  and residual values of long-lived assets)
Maintenance
Repairs
Improvements
Impairment loss

Questions, Short Exercises, Exercises, Problems, and Cases

QUESTIONS

1. Review the meaning of the terms and concepts listed above in **Key Terms and Concepts**.

2. A particular firm's property department maintains buildings and equipment used in manufacturing, selling, and administrative activities. The salaries of personnel in the property department during the current period may appear as an expense during the current period, as an expense next period, or as an expense during several future periods. Explain.

3. A manufacturing firm receives a bid from a local construction company to build a warehouse for $300,000. The firm decides to build the warehouse itself and does so at a cost of $250,000. Why is it that GAAP do not permit the firm to record the warehouse at $300,000 and recognize revenue of $50,000? How will net income differ if the firm follows the generally accepted procedure versus recording the warehouse at $300,000?

For additional student resources, content, and interactive quizzes for this chapter visit the FACMU website:
http://facmu.swlearning.com

4. **a.** What is the effect of capitalizing interest on reported net income summed over all the periods of the life of a given self-constructed asset, from building through use until eventual retirement? Contrast with a policy of expensing interest as incurred.

   b. Consider a company engaging in increasing dollar amounts of self-construction activity each period during periods when interest rates do not decline. What is the effect on reported income each year of capitalizing interest in contrast to expensing interest as incurred?

5. **a.** "Accounting for depreciating assets would be greatly simplified if accounting periods were only long enough or assets' lives short enough." What is the point of the quotation?

   b. "The major purpose of depreciation accounting is to provide funds for the replacement of assets as they wear out." Do you agree? Explain.

6. "Showing both acquisition cost and accumulated depreciation amounts separately provides a rough indication of the relative age of the firm's long-lived assets."

   a. Assume that the Dickens Company acquired an asset several years ago with a depreciable cost of $100,000 and no salvage value. Accumulated depreciation as of December 31, recorded on a straight-line basis, is $60,000. The depreciation charge for the year is $10,000. What is the asset's total depreciable life? How old is the asset?

   b. Assume straight-line depreciation. Devise a formula that, given the depreciation charge for the year and the asset's accumulated depreciation, you can use to estimate the age of the asset.

7. Some critics of the required accounting for changes in estimates of service lives of depreciable assets characterize it as the "always wrong" method. Why do you think these critics use this characterization?

8. "Applying the accounting for repairs versus betterments often comes down to a matter of materiality." Explain.

9. A firm expects to use a delivery truck for five years. At the end of three years, the transmission wears out and requires replacement at a cost of $4,000. The firm argues that it should capitalize this expenditure because without it the useful life is zero and with it the useful life will be another three years. Comment on the firm's reasoning relative to GAAP.

10. A firm sold for $10,000 a machine that originally cost $30,000 and had accumulated depreciation of $24,000 (book value = $6,000). Why does accounting include a gain on the sale of the machine of $4,000 in the income statement instead of showing sales revenue of $10,000 and cost of machine sold of $6,000?

11. Relate the concept of return of capital to the criterion under generally accepted accounting principles for deciding whether an impairment loss on assets other than intangibles not requiring amortization and goodwill has occurred.

12. Suggest reasons why generally accepted accounting procedures permit firms engaged in mineral exploration, such as for oil or gold, to capitalize and subsequently amortize exploration costs but require firms engaged in research and development, such as pharmaceutical companies, to expense the costs in the year incurred.

13. A firm that incurs research and development costs to develop a patented product must expense these costs as incurred. A firm that purchases that same patent from its creator, however, capitalizes the expenditure as an asset and amortizes it. What is the rationale for this different treatment of the patent?

SHORT EXERCISES

14. **Calculating acquisition costs of long-lived assets.** Outback Steakhouse opened a new restaurant on the site of an existing building. It paid the owner $260,000 for the land and building, of which it attributes $52,000 to the land and $208,000 to the building. Outback incurred legal costs of $12,600 to conduct a title search and prepare the necessary legal documents for the purchase. It then paid $35,900 to renovate the building to make it suitable for Outback's use. Property and liability insurance on the land and building for the first year was $12,000, of which $4,000 applied to the period during renovation and $8,000 applied to the period after opening. Property taxes on the land and building for the first year totaled $15,000, of which $5,000 applied to the period during renovation and $10,000 applied to the period after opening. Calculate the amounts that Outback Steakhouse should include in the Land account and in the Building account.

15. **Calculating interest capitalized during construction.** Target Stores constructed new stores during Year 14. The average balance in the Construction-in-Process account excluding Year 14's capitalized interest costs was $3,400,000 during the year. Target Stores engaged in borrowing

directly related to these stores in the amount of $2,000,000, which carries an interest rate of 6 percent. Target Stores has other borrowing outstanding totaling $8,000,000 at an average interest rate of 7 percent. Compute the amount of interest capitalized in the Construction-in-Process account during Year 14.

16. **Computing depreciation expense.** Office Depot acquired a forklift truck on January 1 of the current year for $40,000. The vehicle has an estimated useful life of six years and $4,000 estimated salvage value. Compute the amount of depreciation expense for the current year under the straight-line, double declining-balance, and sum-of-the-years'-digits depreciation methods. Round calculations to the nearest dollar.

17. **Change in depreciable life and salvage value.** Thomson Financial acquired a computer on January 1, Year 12, for $10,000,000. The computer had an estimated useful life of six years and $1,000,000 estimated salvage value. The firm uses the straight-line depreciation method. On January 1, Year 14, Thomson Financial discovers that new technologies make it likely that the computer will last only four years in total and that the estimated salvage value will be only $600,000. Compute the amount of depreciation expense for Year 14 for this change in depreciable life and salvage value. Assume that the change does not represent an impairment loss.

18. **Distinguishing repairs versus betterments.** Disney World experienced damage from a tornado at Space Mountain, one of its most popular attractions. It paid $30,200 to replace steel reinforcements to the structure damaged by the tornado, $86,100 for a new roof torn off by the tornado, $26,900 for a new air conditioning system that was housed on the roof, and $12,600 to replace carpeting damaged by water. Disney World estimates that higher quality steel used as replacements added 20 percent more structural support in terms of weight-bearing capacity. The new air conditioning system provides 25 percent more cooling power than the unit previously installed in the attraction. Compute the amount of these expenses that Disney World should treat as a repair and the amount it should treat as a betterment.

19. **Computing the amount of an impairment loss on tangible long-lived assets.** Wildwood Properties owns an apartment building that has a book value of $15,000,000 on January 1, Year 14. The highway department has decided to construct a new highway near the building, which substantially decreases its attractiveness to tenants. Wildwood Properties estimates that it will now collect rentals from the building of $1,400,000 a year for the next six years and that it will sell the building at the end of that time for $4,000,000. An appropriate interest rate to discount cash flows for this building is 10 percent. Assume that all cash flows occur at the end of the year. Compute the amount of any impairment loss that Wildwood Properties should recognize.

20. **Computing the gain or loss on sale of equipment.** Federal Express acquired a delivery truck on January 1, Year 10, for $48,000. It estimated that the truck would have a six-year useful life and $6,000 salvage value. Federal Express uses the straight-line depreciation method. On July 1, Year 14, Federal Express sells the truck for $14,000. Give the journal entries that Federal Express makes on July 1, Year 14, to recognize depreciation for Year 14 and the sale of the truck.

EXERCISES

21. **Classifying expenditure as asset or expense.** For each of the following expenditures or acquisitions, indicate the type of account debited. Classify the account as (1) asset other than product cost, (2) product cost (Work-in-Process Inventory), or (3) expense. If the account debited is an asset account, specify whether it is current or noncurrent.
    a. $150 for repairs of office machines
    b. $1,500 for emergency repairs to an office machine
    c. $250 for maintenance of delivery trucks
    d. $5,000 for a machine acquired in return for a three-year note
    e. $4,200 for research and development staff salaries
    f. $3,100 for newspaper ads
    g. $6,400 for wages of factory workers engaged in production
    h. $3,500 for wages of factory workers engaged in installing equipment the firm has purchased
    i. $2,500 for salaries of the office workforce
    j. $1,000 for legal fees incurred in acquiring an ore deposit
    k. $1,200 for a one-year insurance policy beginning next month
    l. $1,800 for U.S. Treasury notes, to be sold to pay the next installment due on income taxes
    m. $4,000 for royalty payment for the right to use a patent used in manufacturing
    n. $10,000 for purchase of a trademark
    o. $100 filing fee for copyright registration application

p. $1,850 to purchase computer software used in recordkeeping

q. $8,600 to purchase from its creator initial research on a possible drug to treat hypertension

22. **Cost of self-constructed assets.** Assume that Bolton Company purchased a plot of land for $90,000 as a factory site. A small office building sits on the plot, conservatively appraised at $20,000. The company plans to use the office building after making some modifications and renovations (item **(4)** below). The company had plans drawn for a factory and received bids for its construction. It rejected all bids and decided to construct the factory itself. Management believes that plant asset accounts should include the following additional items:

(1)	Materials and Supplies for Factory Building	$200,000
(2)	Excavation of Land	12,000
(3)	Labor on Construction of Factory Building	140,000
(4)	Cost of Remodeling Old Building into Office Building	13,000
(5)	Interest Paid on Cash Borrowed by Bolton to Construct Factory[a]	6,000
(6)	Interest Forgone on Bolton's Own Cash Used	9,000
(7)	Cash Discounts on Materials Purchased for Factory Building	7,000
(8)	Supervision by Management on Factory Building	10,000
(9)	Workers' Compensation Insurance Premiums on Labor in **(3)**	8,000
(10)	Payment of Claims for Injuries During Construction of Factory Building Not Covered by Insurance	3,000
(11)	Clerical and Other Expenses on Construction of Factory Building	8,000
(12)	Paving of Streets and Sidewalks	5,000
(13)	Architect's Plans and Specifications of Factory Building	4,000
(14)	Legal Costs of Conveying Land	2,000
(15)	Legal Costs of Injury Claim during Construction of Factory Building	1,000
(16)	Income Credited to Retained Earnings Account (the difference between the forgone cost and the lowest contractor's bid)	11,000

[a] This interest is the entire amount of interest paid during the construction period.

Show in detail the items Bolton should include in the following accounts: Land, Factory Building, Office Building, and Site Improvements. Explain the reason for excluding any of these items from the four accounts.

23. **Cost of self-developed product.** Duck Vehicle Manufacturing Company incurs various costs in developing a new, amphibious vehicle for use in providing tours on land and water. Indicate the accounting treatment for each of the following expenditures.

(1)	Salaries of company engineers to design the new vehicle	$325,000
(2)	Cost of prototype of new vehicle built by external contractor	278,200
(3)	Cost of supplies and salaries of personnel to test prototype	68,900
(4)	Fees paid to Environmental Protection Agency to test emissions of new vehicle	15,200
(5)	Legal fees incurred to register and establish a patent on the new vehicle	12,500
(6)	Cost of castings, or molds, for metal parts of new vehicle	46,000
(7)	Cost of local permits to commence manufacturing the new vehicle	5,000
(8)	Cost of manufacturing the first vehicle for a customer	167,600

24. **Amount of interest capitalized during construction.** Nucor, a steel manufacturer, self-constructs a new manufacturing facility in Vermont. At the start of Year 14, the Construction-in-Process account had a balance of $30 million. Construction activity occurred uniformly throughout the year. At the end of Year 14, the balance was $60 million before capitalization of interest for the year. The outstanding borrowings of the company during the year were as follows:

New Construction Loans at 8 Percent per Year	$ 25,000,000
Old Bond Issues Averaging 6 Percent Rate	100,000,000
Total Interest-Bearing Debt	$125,000,000

    a. Compute the amount of interest capitalized in the Construction-in-Process account for Year 14.

    b. Present journal entries for interest for Year 14.

    c. On December 31, Year 15, Nucor completed the manufacturing facility and put it to work. Average Construction-in-Process for Year 15 was $110 million. The debt listed above remained outstanding throughout the construction project and the firm did not issue any additional interest-bearing debt during this time. Present journal entries for Year 15 related to interest expense and interest capitalization.

25. **Capitalizing interest during construction.** Nebok Company recently constructed a new headquarters building. Its Construction-in-Process account showed a balance of $23,186,000 on May 31, Year 9, and $68,797,000 on May 31, Year 10, before capitalization of interest for the year. Construction activity occurred evenly throughout the year. Nebok Company completed construction during Year 11. Nebok Company's note on long-term debt revealed the following (amounts in thousands):

	May 31	
	Year 9	**Year 10**
8.5% unsecured term loan	$25,000	$25,000
12.5% loan secured by real estate	15,600	15,100
14.0% loan secured by real estate	10,900	9,600
Total	$51,500	$49,700

None of this debt relates specifically to construction of the headquarters building. Interest expense before capitalization of interest for the year ending May 31, Year 10, is $5,480,000.

    a. Compute the amount of interest capitalized in the Construction-in-Process account for the year.

    b. Present journal entries for interest for the year.

    c. Nebok Company's net income before interest expense and income taxes for the year is $16,300,000. Nebok Company is subject to a 35 percent income tax rate. Compute net income for the year ending May 31, Year 10.

    d. Compute the interest coverage ratio (equals net income before interest expense and income taxes divided by interest expense) using the amounts computed in part **c**.

    e. Repeat part **d** using the interest expense before capitalization of interest of $5,480,000 in the denominator.

    f. Which measure of the interest coverage ratio provides a more appropriate measure for assessing risk?

26. **Calculations for various depreciation methods.**   Alcoa acquires a machine for $88,800. It expects the machine to last six years and to operate for 30,000 hours during that time. Estimated salvage value is $4,800 at the end of the machine's useful life. Calculate the depreciation charge for each of the first three years using each of the following methods:

    a. The straight-line (time) method

    b. The sum-of-the-years'-digits method

    c. The declining-balance method using a 33 percent rate

    d. The straight-line (use) method, with the following operating times: first year, 4,500 hours; second year, 5,000 hours; third year, 5,500 hours

27. **Calculations for various depreciation methods.** On January 1, Year 8, assume that Luck Delivery Company acquired a new truck for $30,000. It estimated the truck to have a useful life of five years and no salvage value. The company closes its books annually on December 31. Indicate the amount of the depreciation charge for each year of the asset's life under the following methods:

    a. The straight-line method

    b. The declining-balance method at twice the straight-line rate, with a switch to straight-line in Year 11

    c. The sum-of-the-years'-digits method

    d. MACRS depreciation, assuming that the truck belongs to the five-year property class. The proportions of the asset's cost written off each year are 0.20, 0.32, 0.192, 0.115, 0.115, 0.058. (*Hint:* charge depreciation for each of six calendar years.)

    e. Assume now that the firm acquired the truck on April 1, Year 8. Indicate the amount of the depreciation charge for each of the years from Year 8 to Year 13, using the sum-of-the-years'-digits method. (*Hint:* the firm allocates depreciation charges for a year, regardless of the depreciation method, on a straight-line basis to periods within a year.)

28. **Revision of estimated service life changes depreciation schedule.** Slow Poke Delivery Company buys a new machine for $80,000 on January 1, Year 12. It estimates that the machine will last 10 years and have a salvage value of $8,000. Early in Year 14, it discovers that the machine will last only an additional six years, or eight years total (with no change in estimated salvage value). Present a table showing the depreciation charges for each year from Year 12 to Year 15, using each of the following methods (round calculations to the nearest dollar):

    a. The straight-line method

    b. The sum-of-the-years'-digits method

29. **Journal entries for revising estimate of life.** Give the journal entries for the following selected transactions of Florida Manufacturing Corporation. The company uses the straight-line method of calculating depreciation and reports on a December 31 year-end.

    a. The firm purchases a cutting machine on November 1, Year 14, for $180,000. It estimates that the machine will have a useful life of 12 years and a salvage value of $7,200 at the end of that time. Give the journal entry for the depreciation at December 31, Year 14.

    b. Record the depreciation for the year ending December 31, Year 15.

    c. In August, Year 20, the firm estimates that the machine will probably have a total useful life of 14 years and a $3,840 salvage value. Record the depreciation for the year ending December 31, Year 20.

    d. The firm sells the machine for $40,000 on March 31, Year 25. Record the entries of that date, assuming that the firm records depreciation as indicated in part **c.**

30. **Working backward to derive proceeds from disposition of plant assets.** The balance sheets of Wilcox Corporation at the beginning and end of the year contained the following data:

	Beginning of Year	End of Year
Property, Plant, and Equipment (at cost)	$400,000	$550,000
Accumulated Depreciation	180,000	160,000
Net Book Value	$220,000	$390,000

During the year, Wilcox Corporation sold machinery and equipment at a gain of $4,000. It purchased new machinery and equipment at a cost of $230,000. Depreciation charges on machinery and equipment for the year amounted to $50,000. Calculate the proceeds Wilcox Corporation received from the sale of the machinery and equipment.

31. **Computing the amount of impairment loss.** Tillis Corporation acquired the assets of Kieran Corporation (Kieran) on January 1, Year 6, for $2,400,000. On this date, the market values of the assets of Kieran were as follows: land, $400,000; building, $600,000; equipment, $900,000. On June 15, Year 8, a competitor introduced a new product that will likely significantly affect future sales of Kieran's products. It will also affect the value of Kieran's property, plant, and equipment because of their specialized nature in producing Kieran's existing products. The following information relates to the property, plant, and equipment of Kieran on June 15, Year 8:

	Book Value	Undiscounted Cash Flows	Market Value
Land	$ 550,000	$575,000	$550,000
Building	580,000	600,000	580,000
Equipment	1,200,000	950,000	800,000

The market value of Kieran as an entity on June 15, Year 8, is $2,200,000.

Compute the amount of impairment loss recognized on each of Kieran's property, plant, and equipment on June 15, Year 8.

32. **Journal entries to correct accounting errors.** Give correcting entries for the following situations. In each case, the firm uses the straight-line method of depreciation and closes its books annually on December 31. Recognize all gains and losses currently.

   a. A firm purchased a computer for $3,000 on January 1, Year 3. It depreciated the computer at a rate of 25 percent of acquisition cost per year. On June 30, Year 5, it sold the computer for $800 and acquired a new computer for $4,000. The bookkeeper made the following entry to record the transaction:

Equipment (Asset Increase)	3,200	
Cash (Asset Decrease)		3,200

   b. A firm purchased a used truck for $7,000. Its cost, when new, was $12,000. The bookkeeper made the following entry to record the purchase:

Truck (Asset Increase)	12,000	
Accumulated Depreciation (Asset Decrease)		5,000
Cash (Asset Decrease)		7,000

   c. A firm purchased a testing mechanism on April 1, Year 6, for $1,200. It depreciated the testing mechanism at a 10 percent annual rate. A burglar stole the testing mechanism on June 30, Year 8. The firm had not insured against this theft. The bookkeeper made the following entry:

Retained Earnings (Theft Loss) (Shareholders' Equity Decrease)	1,200	
Testing Mechanism (Asset Decrease)		1,200

33. **Effect of transaction on statement of cash flows.** (Requires coverage of **Appendix 8.1**.) Refer to the simplified statement of cash flows in **Exhibit 4.12**. Numbers appear on 11 of the lines in the statement. Ignore the unnumbered lines in responding to the questions that follow.

   Assume that the accounting cycle is complete for the period and that the firm has prepared all of the financial statements. It then discovers that it has overlooked a transaction. It records that transaction in the accounts and corrects all of the financial statements. For each of the following transactions, indicate which of the numbered lines of the statement of cash flows change and the amount and direction of the change. Ignore income tax effects.

   a. A firm sells for $3,000 cash a machine that cost $10,000 and that has $6,000 of accumulated depreciation.

   b. A firm sells for $5,000 cash a machine that cost $10,000 and that has $6,000 of accumulated depreciation.

   c. A firm trades in an old machine on a new machine. The old machine cost $10,000 and has $6,000 of accumulated depreciation. The new machine has a cash price of $9,000. The firm receives a trade-in allowance for the old machine of $5,000 and pays $4,000. Following GAAP, the firm records no gain or loss on trade-in but records the new machine at $8,000.

   d. A fire destroys a warehouse. The loss is uninsured. The warehouse cost $90,000 and at the time of the fire had accumulated depreciation of $40,000.

   e. Refer to the facts of part **d.** The fire also destroyed inventory costing $60,000. The loss is uninsured. Record the effects of only these new facts.

PROBLEMS AND CASES

34. **Improvements versus repairs or maintenance.** The balance sheet of May Department Stores includes a building with an acquisition cost of $800,000 and accumulated depreciation of $660,000. The firm depreciates the building on a straight-line basis over 40 years. The remaining service life of the building and its depreciable life are both seven years. On January 2 of the current year, the firm makes an expenditure of $28,000 on the entrance ramps and stairs of the store. Indicate the accounting for the current year if May Department Stores made the

expenditure of $28,000 under each of the following circumstances. Consider each of these cases independently, except where noted. Ignore income tax effects.

a. Management decided that improved entrances would make the store more attractive and that new customers would come. The ramps and stairs are a worthwhile investment.

b. A flood on New Year's Day ruined the entrance ramps and stairs previously installed. The firm carried no insurance coverage for this sort of destruction. The new ramps and stairs are physically identical to the old ones. The old ones had a book value of $28,000 at the time of the flood.

c. Vandals destroyed the ramps and stairs on New Year's Day. May carried no insurance for this sort of destruction. The ramps and stairs installed are physically identical to the old ones, which had a book value of $28,000 at the time of the destruction.

d. The old entrances were not handicapped-accessible. Management had previously considered replacing its old entrances with new, handicapped-accessible ones but had decided that there was zero benefit to the firm in doing so. It installed new entrance ramps and stairs because a new law required that all stores have such ramps and stairs on the street level. The alternative to installing the new ramps was to shut down the store. In responding to this part, assume zero benefits result from the new ramps. Part **e** considers the more realistic case of some benefits.

e. Management had previously considered replacing its old entrances with new ones but had decided that the handicapped-accessible ramps and stairs were worth only $7,000 (that is, would produce future benefits of only $7,000) and so were not a worthwhile investment. The new law (see part **d**), however, now requires the store to do so (or else shut down), and management installs the new entrance facilities.

35. **Capitalizing versus expensing; if capitalized, what amortization period?** In each of the following situations, compute the amounts of revenue, gain, expense, and loss appearing on the income statement for the year and the amount of asset appearing on the balance sheet as of the end of the year. Show the journal entry or entries required, and provide reasons for your decisions. The firm uses straight-line amortization. The reporting period is the calendar year. Consider each of the situations independently, except where noted.

a. Because of a new fire code, MCB Upholstery Shop must install an additional fire escape on its building. Management previously considered installing the additional fire escape. It rejected the idea because it had already installed a modern sprinkler system, which was even more cost-effective. The new code gives management no alternative except to close the store. MCB acquires the fire escape for $28,000 cash on January 1. It expects to demolish the building seven years from the date it installs the fire escape.

b. Many years ago, a firm acquired shares of stock in General Electric Company for $100,000. On December 31, the firm acquired a building with an appraised value of $1 million. The company paid for the building by giving up its shares in General Electric Company at a time when equivalent shares traded on the New York Stock Exchange for $1,050,000.

c. Same data as in part **b**, except that the shares of stock represent ownership in Small Timers, Inc., whose shares trade on a regional stock exchange. The last transaction in shares of Small Timers, Inc., occurred on December 27. Using the prices of the most recent trades, the shares of stock of Small Timers, Inc., given in exchange for the building have a market value of $1,050,000.

d. Oberweis Dairy decides that it can save $3,500 a year for 10 years by switching from small panel trucks to larger delivery vans. To do so requires remodeling costs of $18,000 for various garages. The first fleet of delivery vans will last for five years, and the garages will last for 20 years. Oberweis remodeled the garages on January 1.

e. A company manufactures aircraft. During the current year, it made all sales to the government under defense contracts. The company spent $400,000 on institutional advertising to keep its name before the business community. It expects to resume sales of small jet planes to corporate buyers in two years.

f. AT&T runs a large laboratory that has, over the years, found marketable ideas and products worth tens of millions of dollars. On average, the successful products have a life of 10 years. Assume that expenditures for the laboratory this year were $1,500,000.

g. A textile manufacturer gives $250,000 to the Textile Engineering Department at Georgia Tech for basic research in fibers. The results of the research, if any, will belong to the general public.

h. On January 1, assume that Mazda incurs costs of $6 million for specialized machine tools necessary to produce a new-model automobile. Such tools last for six years, on average, but Mazda expects to produce the new model automobile for only three years.

i. On January 1, assume that United Airlines purchased a fleet of airplanes for $100 million cash. United Airlines expects the airplanes to have a useful life of 10 years and zero salvage value. At the same time, the airline purchased for cash $20 million of spare parts for use with those airplanes. The spare parts have no use, now or in the future, other than replacing broken or worn-out airplane parts. During the first year of operation, United Airlines used no spare parts.

j. Refer to the data in **i.** In the second year of operation, United Airlines used $1 million of spare parts.

36. Accounting for intangibles. In Year 1, Epstein Company acquired the assets of Falk Company, which included various intangibles. Discuss the accounting for the acquisition in Year 1, and in later years, for each of the following items.

a. Registration of the trademark Thyrom® for thyristors expires in three years. Epstein Company believes that the trademark has a fair market value of $100,000. It expects to continue making and selling Thyrom thyristors indefinitely.

b. The design patent covering the ornamentation of the containers for displaying Thyrom thyristors expires in five years. Epstein Company thinks that the design patent has a fair market value of $30,000 and expects to continue making the containers indefinitely.

c. Epstein Company views an unpatented trade secret on a special material used in manufacturing thyristors as having a fair market value of $200,000.

d. Refer to the trade secret in part **c.** Suppose that in Year 2 a competitor discovers the trade secret but does not disclose the secret to other competitors. How should Epstein Company change its accounting policies?

e. During Year 1, Epstein Company produced a sales promotion film, Using Thyristors for Fun and Profit, at a cost of $45,000. It licensed the film to purchasers of thyristors for use in training their employees and customers. Epstein has copyrighted the film.

37. Interpreting disclosures regarding property, plant, and equipment. Mead Corporation reports the following information in its financial statements and notes for a recent year (amounts in millions):

	December 31	
	Year 7	**Year 8**
Property, Plant, and Equipment (at cost)	$ 3,824.0	$ 3,938.5
Accumulated Depreciation	(1,803.7)	(1,849.3)
Property, Plant, and Equipment (net)	$ 2,020.3	$ 2,089.2

	For Year 8
Depreciation Expense	$ 188.1
Expenditures on Property, Plant, and Equipment	315.6
Proceeds from Sales of Property, Plant, and Equipment	38.7
Sales	4,557.5

a. Give the journal entries for the transactions and events that account for the changes in the Property, Plant, and Equipment account and the Accumulated Depreciation account for Year 8.

b. Mead Corporation uses the straight-line depreciation method for financial reporting. Estimate the average *total* life of property, plant, and equipment in use during Year 8.

c. Refer to part **b.** Estimate the average age to date of property, plant, and equipment in use during Year 8.

d. Compute the fixed asset turnover for Year 8.

e. Mead Corporation uses accelerated depreciation for income tax purposes. From information in the financial statement note on income taxes (discussed in **Chapter 10**), the balance in the accumulated depreciation account using accelerated depreciation would have been $2,810.2 million on December 31, Year 7, and $2,830.5 million on December 31, Year 8. Compute the fixed asset turnover ratio using accelerated depreciation.

38. Interpreting disclosures regarding property, plant, and equipment. PepsiCo reports the following information in its financial statements and notes in a recent year (amounts in millions):

	December 31	
	Year 6	Year 7
Property, Plant, and Equipment (at cost)	$14,250.0	$16,130.1
Accumulated Depreciation	(5,394.4)	(6,247.3)
Property, Plant, and Equipment (net)	$ 8,855.6	$ 9,882.8

	For Year 7
Sales	$28,472.4
Depreciation Expense	1,200.0
Expenditures on Property, Plant, and Equipment	2,253.2
Proceeds from Sales of Property, Plant, and Equipment	55.3

a. Give the journal entries for the transactions and events that account for the changes in the Property, Plant, and Equipment account and the Accumulated Depreciation account during Year 7.

b. PepsiCo uses the straight-line depreciation method for financial reporting. Estimate the average *total* life of property, plant, and equipment in use during Year 7.

c. Refer to part **b**. Estimate the average age to date of property, plant, and equipment in use during Year 7.

d. Compute the fixed asset turnover for Year 7.

e. PepsiCo uses accelerated depreciation for income tax purposes. From information in the financial statement note on income taxes (discussed in **Chapter 10**), the balance in the accumulated depreciation account using accelerated depreciation would have been $7,018.8 on December 31, Year 6, and $7,736.7 on December 31, Year 7. Compute the fixed asset turnover ratio using accelerated depreciation.

39. **Effect on net income of changes in estimates for depreciable assets.** American Airlines has $3 billion of assets, including airplanes costing $2.5 billion with net book value of $1.6 billion. It earns net income equal to approximately 6 percent of total assets. American Airlines depreciates its airplanes for financial reporting purposes on a straight-line basis over 10-year lives to a salvage value equal to 10 percent of acquisition cost. American announces a change in depreciation policy; it will use 14-year lives and salvage values equal to 12 percent of original cost. The airplanes are all four years old. Assume an income tax rate of 35 percent.

Calculate the approximate impact on net income of the change in depreciation policy. Compute both dollar and percentage effects. What conjectures about the earnings quality of an airline can you derive from these computations?

40. **Recording transactions involving tangible and intangible assets.** Present journal entries for each of the following transactions of Moon Macrosystems:

a. Acquired computers costing $400,000 and computer software costing $40,000 on January 1, Year 6. Moon expects the computers to have a service life of 10 years and $40,000 salvage value. It expects the computer software to have a service life of four years and zero salvage value.

b. Paid $20,000 to install the computers in the office. Paid $10,000 to install and test the computer software.

c. Recorded depreciation and amortization using the straight-line method for Year 6 and Year 7. Moon records a full year of depreciation in the year of acquisition. Treat depreciation and amortization as a period expense.

d. On January 1, Year 8, new software offered on the market made the software acquired above completely obsolete. Give any required journal entry.

e. On January 2, Year 8, Moon revised the depreciable life of the computers to a total of 14 years and the salvage value to $56,000. Give the entry to record depreciation for Year 8.

f. On December 31, Year 9, Moon sold the computers for $260,000. Give the required journal entries for Year 9.

41. **Recognizing and measuring impairment losses.** Give the journal entry to recognize an impairment loss, if appropriate, in each of the following cases. If a loss does not qualify as an impairment loss, explain the reason, and indicate the appropriate accounting.

a. Commercial Realty Corporation leases office space to tenants in Boston. One of its office buildings originally cost $80 million and has accumulated depreciation of $20 million. The city of Boston has announced its intention to construct an exit ramp from a nearby expressway on one side of the office building. Rental rates in the building will likely decrease as a result. The expected future undiscounted cash flows from rentals and from disposal of the building decreased from $120 million before the announcement to $50 million afterward. The market value of the building decreased from $85 million before the announcement to $32 million afterward.

b. Refer to part **a**. Assume that the undiscounted cash flows totaled $70 million and that the market value totaled $44 million after the announcement.

c. Medical Services Corporation plans, and then builds, its own office building and clinic. It originally anticipated that the building would cost $15 million. The physicians in charge of overseeing construction had medical practices so busy that they did not closely track costs, which ultimately reached $25 million. The expected future cash flows from using the building total $22 million, and the market value of the building totals $16 million.

d. Medco Pharmaceuticals acquired New Start Biotechnology two years ago for $40 million. Medco allocated $25 million to a patent held by New Start and $15 million to goodwill. By the end of the current period, Medco has written down the book value of the patent to $20 million. A competitor recently received approval for a biotechnology drug that will reduce the value of the patent that Medco acquired from New Start. The expected future undiscounted cash flows from sales of the patented drug total $18 million, and the market value of the patent is $12 million. The market value of the former New Start Biotechnology operation owned by Medco is now $25 million.

e. Chicken Franchisees, Inc., acquires franchise rights in the Atlanta area for Chicken Delight Restaurants, a national restaurant chain. The franchise rights originally cost $15 million; since acquisition, Chicken Franchisees has written down the book value to $10 million. Chicken Delight Restaurants recently received negative publicity because the chickens it delivered to its franchisees contained potentially harmful pesticides. As a result, business has declined. Chicken Franchisees estimates that the future undiscounted cash flows associated with the Chicken Delight name total $6 million and that the franchise rights have market value of $3 million.

42. **Expensing versus capitalizing research and development costs.** Pfizer, a pharmaceutical company, plans to spend $90 million on research and development (R&D) at the beginning of each of the next several years to develop new drugs. As a result of the R&D expenditure for a given year, it expects pre-tax income (not counting R&D expense) to increase by $36 million a year for three years, including the year of the expenditure itself. Pfizer has other pre-tax income of $30 million per year. The controller of Pfizer is curious about the effect on the financial statements of following one of two accounting policies with respect to R&D expenditures:

(1) Expensing the R&D costs in the year of expenditure (the policy required in the United States)

(2) Capitalizing the R&D costs and amortizing them over three years, including the year of the expenditure itself (the policy allowed in certain other countries)

Assume that the company does spend $90 million at the beginning of each of four years and that the planned increase in income occurs. Ignore income tax effects.

a. Prepare a four-year condensed summary of income before income taxes, assuming that Pfizer follows policy **(1)** and expenses R&D costs as incurred.

b. Prepare a four-year condensed summary of income before income taxes, assuming that Pfizer follows policy **(2)** and capitalizes R&D costs, then amortizes them over three years. Also compute the amount of Deferred R&D Costs (asset) appearing on the balance sheet at the end of each of the four years.

c. In what sense is policy **(1)** a conservative policy?

d. Ascertain the effect on income before income taxes and on the balance sheet if Pfizer continues to spend $90 million each year and the pre-tax income effects continue as in the first four years.

43. **Valuation of the brand name.** Ross Laboratories sells various formulations of infant baby food around the world under the brand name Similac. In a recent year, worldwide sales less operating expenses were $600 million. Ross Laboratories employed $500 million of physical capital to produce and sell this food. Estimate the value of the Similac brand assuming the following:

a. Ross Laboratories charges 10 percent, before taxes, for physical capital, pays income taxes at the rate of 40 percent of pre-tax income, and uses a price/earnings ratio (capitalization factor) of 17.

b. Ross Laboratories charges 20 percent, before taxes, for physical capital, pays income taxes at the rate of 40 percent of pre-tax income, and uses a price/earnings ratio (capitalization factor) of 8.

44. Ethical issues in capitalization versus expensing policy. Refer to **Example 1** involving the treatment of access costs by WorldCom.

    a. Assume that you were the chief financial officer of WorldCom. What case might you make to your external auditors to justify the capitalization of the access costs in fixed assets?

    b. What is GAAP's rationale for the expensing of such costs in the period incurred?

    c. Do WorldCom's actions to capitalize these costs pose ethical issues? Explain.

chapter 9

Liabilities: Introduction

Learning Objectives

1. Understand and apply the concept of an accounting liability to obligations with uncertain payment dates and amounts.

2. Develop the skills to compute the issue price, book value, and current market value of various debt obligations in an amount equal to the present value of the future cash flows.

3. Understand the effective interest method and apply it to debt amortization for various long-term debt obligations.

4. Understand the accounting procedures for debt retirements, whether at or before maturity.

Chapters **9**, **10**, and **12** examine the accounting concepts and procedures for the right-hand side of the balance sheet, which shows the sources of a firm's financing. The funds used to acquire assets come from two sources: owners and nonowners. **Chapter 12** discusses shareholders' equity. This chapter and **Chapter 10** discuss obligations incurred by a business as a result of raising funds from nonowners. Banks and creditors providing debt on a long-term basis understand their role as providers of funds. Suppliers and employees who do not require immediate cash payment for goods provided or services rendered usually do not think of themselves as contributing to a firm's funds, but they do contribute. Likewise, customers who advance cash to a firm before delivery of a good or service provide funds to the firm. The obligations of a business to these nonowners who contribute funds are liabilities.

A thorough understanding of liabilities requires knowledge of compound interest and present value computations. These computations allow valid comparisons between payments made at different times because they take into account the interest that cash can earn over time. The **Appendix** at the back of the book describes and illustrates compound interest and present value. Understanding all the material in this chapter requires that you master the material in the **Appendix**. Without such mastery, you will have to accept on faith some of the computations in this chapter.

Lenders often, as part of the loan agreement, require the borrower to manage its operations and its financing so as to keep defined financial ratios above or below specified levels. If the ratios violate the constraints, the lender will have additional rights, such as to require early repayment of the loan. These lending constraints provide protection for the lender. For example, the lending agreement might require a debt-equity ratio no larger than 60 percent or an interest coverage ratio no less than 3.0. To set the limits for the ratios, the lender must understand GAAP's definition of a liability, so that it can write the lending agreement to achieve the goal the lender has in mind with respect to the borrower's acceptable and unacceptable levels of total debt. To illustrate, consider the data in **Exhibit 9.1** for Wal-Mart. The first column of amounts shows the reported

EXHIBIT 9.1	Selected Balance Sheet Data for Wal-Mart Stores January 31, Year 14 (amounts in millions)		
		Reported	**Restated**
Current Liabilities		$ 37,418	$ 37,418
Long-term Debt		25,573	27,290
Other Noncurrent Liabilities		3,416	3,416
Obligations under Operating Leases		—	5,487
Guarantees of Debt of Others		—	2,110
Total		$ 66,407	$ 75,721
Shareholders' Equity		43,623	39,796
Total		$110,030	$115,517
Debt-Equity Ratio (Total Liabilities/Total Sources of Financing)		60.4%	65.5%

liabilities on January 31, Year 14. Wal-Mart's debt-equity ratio, defined as total liabilities divided by total sources of financing, is 60.4 percent. The second column of amounts shows additional information about Wal-Mart's obligations, some of which GAAP do not require Wal-Mart to report as a liability.

The restated amounts differ from the reported amounts for the following reasons:

1. Long-term Debt: Interest rates have declined since Wal-Mart issued its long-term debt and the market value of this debt has consequently increased. (A later section of this chapter explains why this occurs.)
2. Obligations under Operating Leases: Wal-Mart has signed lease agreements for land, buildings, and equipment that do not appear on its balance sheet as liabilities. **Chapter 10** explains why such leases, called *operating leases,* do not appear on the balance sheet under GAAP. Yet, Wal-Mart has obligated itself to make these payments, which it will likely pay according to the schedule already known by the balance sheet date.
3. Guarantees of Debt of Others: Wal-Mart has guaranteed the debt of some of its suppliers. In the event the suppliers do not pay, Wal-Mart must pay the debt. A later section of this chapter explains why GAAP do not normally require firms to recognize obligations for guarantees of others' debt as a liability.

In computing the restated debt-equity ratio, we assume that the excess of market value over the book value of the long-term debt and the potential losses from the debt guarantees reduce shareholders' equity.

This example illustrates why you should understand the obligations that GAAP require firms to recognize as liabilities and the potential obligations that GAAP allow firms to leave off of the balance sheet.

Basic Concepts of Liabilities

Liability Recognition

Nearly all liabilities are obligations, but not all obligations are liabilities. According to the Financial Accounting Standards Board (FASB), accounting generally recognizes an entity's obligation as a **liability** if the obligation meets three criteria.[1]

1. The obligation involves a probable future sacrifice of resources—a future transfer of cash, goods, or services or the forgoing of a future cash receipt—at a specified or ascertainable date. The firm can measure, with reasonable precision, the cash equivalent value of resources needed to satisfy the obligation.
2. The firm has little or no discretion to avoid the transfer.
3. The transaction or event giving rise to the entity's obligation has already occurred. (We suggest to our students that they understand this third FASB criterion by saying that for an obligation to be a liability, it must arise from something other than an executory contract, that is, the obligation arises from something other than a mere exchange of promises.)

Example 1   General Electric has borrowed $75 million by issuing bonds that require it to pay interest of 4 percent every six months for 20 years and to repay the $75 million at the end of 20 years. This borrowing arrangement obligates General Electric to make definite cash payments in the future at specified times and is a liability, titled Bonds Payable.

Example 2   Avon Products' employees have earned wages and salaries that Avon will not pay until the next payday, two weeks after the end of the current accounting period. Avon owes suppliers substantial amounts for materials they sold to Avon, but Avon need not pay these debts for 10 to 30 days after the end of the period. Avon owes the federal and state governments for taxes, but need not make payments until next month. Although the payment dates are not necessarily fixed, Avon can estimate those dates with reasonable precision. Each of these items therefore

---

[1] Financial Accounting Standards Board, *Statement of Financial Accounting Concepts No. 6,* "Elements of Financial Statements," 1985, par. 36.

meets the three criteria for a liability. The items appear as liabilities under titles such as Wages Payable, Salaries Payable, Accounts Payable, and Taxes Payable.

Example 3   When Sony USA sells television sets, it gives a warranty to repair or replace any faulty parts or faulty sets within one year after sale. This obligation meets the three criteria of a liability. Because some television sets will surely need repair, the future sacrifice of resources is probable. Sony has the obligation to make repairs. The transaction giving rise to the obligation, the sale of the television set, has already occurred. Sony does not know the amount with certainty, but Sony's experience with its television sets permits a reasonably precise estimate of the expected costs of repairs or replacements. The repairs or replacements will occur within a time span that Sony estimates with reasonable precision. Sony USA will thus show Estimated Warranty Liability on its balance sheet.

Example 4   The Boston Red Sox receives $2,400,000 from the sale of tickets for the upcoming baseball season. *Sports Illustrated* receives $1,750,000 for the sale of magazine subscriptions for the next three years. The American Automobile Association receives $840,000 from the sale of memberships for the next two years. These advances from customers obligate the firms to provide services in the future. The amount of the cash advance serves as a measure of the liability until the firms provide the services.

Example 5   Columbia Pictures has signed a binding contract to supply films to Cineplex Odeon, a chain of movie theaters, within the next six months. In this case, there is an obligation, definite time, and definite amount (of goods, if not cash), but no past or current transaction has occurred. **Chapter 2** pointed out that accounting does not recognize assets or liabilities for **executory contracts**—the mere exchange of promises with no mutual performance. Without some mutual performance, there is no current or past benefit. Thus no accounting liability arises in this case.

Example 6   Online Corporation has signed a contract promising to employ its president for the next five years and to pay the president a salary of $750,000 per year. The salary will increase in future years at the same rate of increase as the Consumer Price Index, published by the U.S. government. Online Corporation has an obligation to make payments (although the president may quit at any time without penalty). The payments are for reasonably certain amounts and will occur at definite times. At the time Online signs the contract, no mutual performance has occurred; the contract is purely executory. Because no exchange has occurred, no liability appears on the balance sheet. A liability will, of course, arise as the president performs services over time and earns the salary.

Example 7   ChevronTexaco Corporation has signed a contract with Tenneco Oil Pipeline Company to ship at least 10,000 barrels of crude oil per month for the next three years. ChevronTexaco must pay for the shipping services, even if it does not ship the oil. An arrangement such as this, called a *throughput contract,* does not qualify as an accounting liability because accounting views actual shipment, which has not yet occurred, as the event causing a liability. ChevronTexaco will disclose the obligation in notes. Similarly, obligations for take-or-pay contracts, in which the purchaser must pay for certain quantities of goods even if the purchaser does not take delivery of the goods, are not formal liabilities. Firms obligating themselves with take-or-pay contracts must disclose them.[2] Accounting views both throughput and take-or-pay contracts as executory.

Example 8   Smokers have sued Philip Morris, a subsidiary of Altria, in a lawsuit alleging damages of $6 billion. The smokers claim that the company knowingly withheld information about the harmful effects of smoking and that misleading advertising about Marlboro cigarettes injured them. Shook, Hardy & Bacon, lawyers from Kansas City retained by the corporation, think that Philip Morris can mount an adequate defense to the charges. Because Philip Morris has no obligation to make a payment at a reasonably definite time, it has no liability. The notes to the financial

---

[2] Financial Accounting Standards Board, *Statement of Financial Accounting Standards No. 47,* "Disclosure of Long-Term Obligations," 1981.

statements will disclose the existence of the lawsuit, but normally no liability will appear on the balance sheet.

Example 9 Citibank extends $800 million in lines of credit to its customers, agreeing to make loans up to this amount as customers need funds. Because the line of credit is an executory contract (a mere exchange of promises), accounting does not recognize it as a liability. Citibank discloses the amount of such lending commitments in the notes to its financial statements.

Summary of Liability Recognition **Figure 9.1** classifies obligations into six groups based on the degree to which they satisfy the criteria for liability recognition. Accounting recognizes obligations in the first four groups as liabilities. As the examples above illustrate, accounting typically does not recognize as liabilities obligations under mutually unexecuted contracts. The exclusion of executory contracts from liabilities has created controversy in accounting. **Chapter 10** discusses commitments arising from a long-term lease, an executory contract that accounting recognizes as a liability if the lease agreement satisfies certain conditions.

Contingencies: Potential Obligations

The question of whether to recognize contingent, or potential, obligations as liabilities causes controversy. One criterion for deciding whether an obligation qualifies as a liability is that the firm will make a probable future sacrifice of resources. The world of business and law contains many uncertainties. At any given time a firm may find itself potentially liable for events that have occurred in the past. Accounting does not recognize contingencies of this nature as liabilities. They are potential future obligations rather than current obligations. The potential obligations arise from events that occurred in the past but whose outcome remains uncertain. Whether an item becomes a liability—and, if it does, the size of the liability—depends on a future event, such as the outcome of a lawsuit.

Suppose that an employee sues Mattel, the toy manufacturer, in a formal court proceeding for damages from an accident. The court has scheduled a trial sometime after the end of this accounting period. If Mattel's lawyers and auditors agree that the court will likely rule in favor of Mattel (or that any adverse settlement will be small), then Mattel will not recognize a liability on its balance sheet. The notes to the financial statements, however, must disclose significant contingencies.

FIGURE 9.1	Classifications of Accounting Liabilities by Degree of Certainty				

Obligations with Fixed Payment Dates and Amounts	Obligations with Fixed Payment Amounts but Estimated Payment Dates	Obligations for Which the Firm Must Estimate Both Timing and Amount of Payment	Obligations Arising from Advances from Customers on Unexecuted Contracts and Agreements	Obligations under Mutually Unexecuted Contracts	Contingent Obligations
Notes Payable	Accounts Payable	Warranties Payable [a]	Rental Fees Received in Advance	Purchase Commitments [b]	Unsettled Lawsuits [c]
Interest Payable	Taxes Payable			Employment Commitments	Financial Instruments with Off-Balance-Sheet Risk [c]
Bonds Payable			Subscription Fees Received in Advance		

Most Certain ⟵————————————————————————⟶ Least Certain

⟵———— Recognized as Accounting Liabilities ————⟶ ⟵—— Not Generally Recognized as ——⟶ Accounting Liabilities

[a] If the firm cannot estimate the future warranty cost with reasonable precision, it will not recognize revenue at the time of sale, so there is no liability.

[b] If the market price of a purchase commitment for inventory is less than the contract price, the firm recognizes a loss and a liability in the amount of the loss.

[c] If an obligation meets certain criteria for a loss contingency, the firm recognizes this obligation as a liability. See the discussion later in this chapter.

Both the FASB and the International Accounting Standards Board (IASB) have said that a firm should recognize an estimated loss from a contingency in the accounts only if the contingency meets both of the following conditions: (a) information available before issuance of the financial statements indicates that it is probable that an event has impaired an asset or has caused the firm to incur a liability, and (b) the firm can reasonably estimate the amount of the loss.[3]

When information indicates that events have probably impaired an asset or led to a liability and when the firm has estimated the amount but the amount is a range, then the firm should use the lower end of the range. For example, if Mattel estimates the loss in a range from $1 million to $5 million, it must record the liability at $1 million.

TERMINOLOGY NOTE

In stating the conditions, quoted above, for the firm to record a liability, the FASB has said that the loss must be *probable,* but the FASB has not defined what it means by *probable.* In recent years, the FASB has discussed whether probable means "more likely than not"—any probability above 50 percent—or something larger, such as 80 to 85 percent. Currently, most accountants and auditors appear to use *probable* to mean 80 to 85 percent or larger. The FASB has used the phrase *more likely than not* when it means a probability greater than 50 percent. In contrast, the IASB has defined *probable* to mean "more likely than not."[4] The difference in meanings of the word *probable* can matter in applying accounting principles, and we expect the two standard-setting bodies to reconcile this difference within the next few years.

Example 10   A toy manufacturer, such as Mattel, has sold products for which the Consumer Protection Agency has discovered a safety hazard. The toy manufacturer thinks it probable that it has incurred a liability. This potential obligation meets condition **b** if the firm's experience or other information enables it to make a reasonable estimate of the loss. The journal entry would be as follows:

Retained Earnings (Loss from Damage Claim) (Shareholders' Equity Decrease)	1,000,000	
Estimated Liability for Damages (Liability Increase)		1,000,000
To recognize estimated liability for expected damage arising from safety hazard on toys sold.		

This entry debits a loss account (presented among Other Expenses on the income statement) and credits an **estimated liability**, which should appear on the balance sheet as a current liability, similar to the Estimated Warranty Liability account. In practice, an account with the title Estimated Liability for Damages would seldom, if ever, appear in published financial statements because firms fear that a court or jury might perceive it as an admission of guilt. Such an admission would likely affect the outcome of the lawsuit. Most firms would combine the liability account with others for financial statement presentation and GAAP approve this aggregated disclosure unless the amount is materially large.

Contingency Disclosure   Accounting uses the term **contingency**, or sometimes *contingent liability*, only when it recognizes the item not in the accounts but rather in the notes. A recent annual report of Kodak illustrates the disclosure of contingencies. Its note on contingencies starts with 12 paragraphs over 3 pages giving moderate detail about environmental remediation issues, which end as follows:

---

[3] Financial Accounting Standards Board, *Statement of Financial Accounting Standards No. 5,* "Accounting for Contingencies," 1975; International Accounting Standards Board, *Statement No. 37,* "Provisions, Contingent Liabilities, and Contingent Assets," 1998.

[4] International Accounting Standards Board, *Statement No. 37.*

Estimates of the amount and timing of future costs of environmental remediation requirements are necessarily imprecise because of the continuing evolution of environmental laws and regulatory requirements, the availability and application of technology, the identification of presently unknown remediation sites and the allocation of costs among the potentially responsible parties. Based upon information presently available, such future costs are not expected to have a material effect on the Company's competitive or financial position. However, such costs could be material to results of operations in a particular future quarter or year.

Then, Kodak's note on contingencies presents 20 paragraphs covering another 3 pages on other commitments and contingencies, ending with:

The Company and its subsidiary companies are involved in lawsuits, claims, investigations and proceedings, including product liability, commercial, environmental, and health and safety matters, which are being handled and defended in the ordinary course of business. There are no such matters pending that the Company and its General Counsel expect to be material in relation to the Company's business, financial position or results of operations.

Constructive Liabilities

As this book goes to press, the FASB is struggling with the concept of *constructive liability*, and whether firms should record them. You can understand the definition of constructive liability here, but you need to master some of the material in **Chapter 12** on recurring and nonrecurring income before you can understand why constructive liabilities have become an issue. Firms have discovered that by recording constructive liabilities, they give themselves more wiggle room, more flexibility, in reporting income and, more important, in reporting patterns of income over time.

A **constructive liability** arises, not from an obligation, but from management intent. Assume management has decided it will close a plant and knows that it will reduce the labor force, laying off current employees and making severance payments in amounts yet to be determined. It can recognize an expense, often euphemistically called *Restructuring Charges*, with a journal entry such as:

Retained Earnings (Restructuring Charges) (Shareholders' Equity Decrease)	1,000	
Liability for Severance Pay to Employees (Liability Increase)		1,000

Now the firm has established a liability. Later, when it discharges workers and makes a $200 cash payment for severance benefits, it can record the following entry:

Liability for Severance Pay to Employees (Liability Decrease)	200	
Cash (Asset Decrease)		200

No controversy arises from the above, conservative accounting. Issues arise from different circumstances. Assume management finds that the initial $1,000 charge for estimated severance payments was $300 too large, that the charge should have been only $700. At the later time when it finds the initial charge was too large, it will make the following entry to reverse part of the initial charge:

Liability for Severance Pay to Employees (Liability Decrease)	300	
Retained Earnings (Reversal of Restructuring Charges) (Shareholders' Equity Increase)		300
Reversal of prior charge; reversal appears in income for the current year.		

Management reduced income in the year of initial charge by $1,000 and then increased income in the reversal year by $300. The FASB suspects that firms are using this ability to record initial intent with later reversals as a way to manage income and requires firms to present the increase in income in the current year in the same place in the income statement as the decrease in income had appeared in the earlier year.[5] Analysts say that the mere ability of firms to reduce income and then later increase income based on its own intent, without obligation, reduces the quality of earnings.

Liability Valuation

In historical cost accounting, liabilities appear on the balance sheet at the present value of payments that a firm expects to make in the future. The interest rate a firm uses in computing the present value amount throughout the life of a liability is the interest rate appropriate for the specific borrower at the time it initially incurred the liability. That is, the firm uses the historical interest rate.

As **Chapter 2** mentions, most current liabilities appear at the undiscounted amount payable because of the immaterially small difference between the amount ultimately payable and its present value.

Liability Classification

The balance sheet generally classifies liabilities as current or noncurrent. Firms separate current from noncurrent liabilities based on the length of time that will elapse before the borrower must make payment. Current liabilities fall due within the operating cycle, usually one year, and noncurrent liabilities fall due later.

Current Liabilities

Current liabilities, those due within the current operating cycle, normally one year, include accounts payable to creditors, short-term notes payable, payroll accruals, taxes payable, and current portion of long-term debt. A firm continually discharges current liabilities and replaces them with new ones in the course of business operations.

The firm will not pay these obligations for several weeks or months after the current balance sheet date. They have present value less than the amount to be paid. Even so, accountants show these items at the full amount owed because, considering the small difference between the amount owed and its present value, a separate accounting for this difference as interest expense would not be cost-effective.

Accounts Payable to Creditors

A firm seldom pays for goods and services as received. It defers payment until it receives a bill from the supplier. Then it may not pay the bill immediately but instead accumulate it with other bills until a specified time of the month when it pays all bills. Because these accounts do not accrue explicit interest, management tries to obtain as much funding as possible from its creditors by delaying payment as long as possible. Failure to keep scheduled promises to creditors can lead to poor credit ratings and to restrictions on future credit. The Marmon Group, a Chicago-based conglomerate, has instructed its purchasing agents to negotiate for as long a grace period as they can before payments become due, but instructs the controllers always to pay bills by the due date.

Short-Term Notes and Interest Payable

Firms obtain financing for less than a year from banks or other creditors in return for a short-term note called a *note payable*. The borrower records a liability. As time passes, the borrower makes entries, usually adjusting entries, debiting Interest Expense and crediting Interest Payable. When the borrower makes payments, the entry credits Cash and debits Interest Payable and, perhaps, Notes Payable. Payment amounts go first to reduce the liability for Interest Payable and then, if the amount exceeds the balance in the Interest Payable account, to reduce the principal for Notes Payable.

---

[5] See Paragraph 19 of *Statement of Financial Accounting Standards No. 146,* "Accounting for Costs Associated with Exit or Disposal Activities," 2002.

Wages, Salaries, and Other Payroll Items

When employees earn wages, they owe part of their earnings to governments for income and other taxes. They may also owe other amounts for union dues and insurance plans. Although these amounts form part of the employer's wage expense, the employer does not pay them directly to employees but pays them, on employees' behalf, to the governments, unions, and insurance companies.

In addition, the employer must pay various payroll taxes and may have agreed to pay for other fringe benefits because employees earned wages.

Employers often provide paid vacations to employees who have worked for a specified period, such as six months or one year. The employer must accrue the costs of the earned but unused vacations (including the payroll taxes and fringe benefits on them) at the time the employees earn them, not at the later time when employees take vacations and receive their wages. This treatment results in charging each quarter of the year with a portion of the cost of vacations rather than allocating all costs to the summer, when most employees take the majority of their vacation days.

Example 11 Assume that the Sacramento Radio Shack's employees earn $100,000 and that the employees owe taxes averaging 40 percent of these amounts for federal income taxes, state income taxes, Social Security taxes, and Medicare taxes. In addition, employees in aggregate owe $500 for union dues to be withheld by the employer and $3,000 for health insurance plans.

Radio Shack must pay various payroll taxes averaging 18 percent of gross wages. In addition, the employer owes $4,500 to Fireman's Fund for payments to provide life and health insurance coverage. Employees have earned vacation pay estimated to be $4,000; Radio Shack estimates employer payroll taxes and fringe benefits to be 18 percent of the gross amount.

The journal entries that follow record these wages. If production workers had earned some of the wages, the firm would debit some of the amounts to Work-in-Process Inventory rather than to Wages and Salaries Expense.

Retained Earnings (Wages and Salaries Expense) (Shareholders' Equity Decrease)	100,000	
Taxes Payable to Various Governments (Liability Increase)		40,000
Withheld Dues Payable to Union (Liability Increase)		500
Insurance Premiums Payable (Liability Increase)		3,000
Wages and Salaries Payable (Liability Increase)		56,500
To record wage expense; plug for $56,500 actually payable to employees.		
Retained Earnings (Wages and Salaries Expense) (Shareholders' Equity Decrease)	22,500	
Payroll Taxes Payable (Liability Increase)		18,000
Insurance Premiums Payable (Liability Increase)		4,500
To record employer's expense for amounts not payable directly to employees. The debit is a plug.		
Retained Earnings (Wages and Salaries Expense) (Shareholders' Equity Decrease)	4,720	
Estimated Vacation Wage and Fringes Payable (Liability Increase) . . .		4,720
To record estimate of vacation pay and fringes thereon earned during the current period: 0.18 × $4,000 = $720.		

Income Taxes Payable

Businesses organized as corporations must pay federal income taxes based on their taxable income from business activities. In contrast, businesses organized as partnerships or sole proprietorships do not pay income taxes. Instead the Internal Revenue Service taxes the income of the business entity as income of the individual partners or the sole proprietor. Each partner or sole proprietor adds his or her share of business income to income from all other (non-business) sources in preparing an individual income tax return. **Chapter 10** discusses more fully the accounting for income taxes.

Deferred Performance Liabilities: Advances from Customers

Another current liability arises when a firm receives cash from customers for goods or services it will deliver in the future. It discharges this liability, unlike the preceding ones, by delivering goods or services rather than by paying cash. When the firm discharges the liability it will recognize revenue.

An example of this type of liability is the Houston Rockets' advance sale of basketball game tickets for ten games for, say, $2,000,000. At the time of the sale, the Rockets record the following entry:

Cash (Asset Increase)	2,000,000	
Advances from Customers (Liability Increase)		2,000,000

The Rockets sell tickets for cash but earn no revenue until the organization renders the service when the team plays. These deferred performance obligations qualify as liabilities. The firm credits an account such as Advances from Customers or Liability for Advance Sales. After a game, the firm has discharged its obligation so it recognizes (credits) revenue and reduces (debits) the liability.

Advances from Customers (Liability Decrease)	200,000	
Retained Earnings (Game Ticket Sales Revenue) (Shareholders'		
Equity Increase)		200,000

After the first game and the entry above, the Advances from Customers (Liability) account has a balance of $1,800,000.

Deferred performance liabilities arise also in connection with the sale of magazine subscriptions, airline tickets, and service contracts.

Deferred Performance Liabilities: Product Warranties

A similar deferred performance liability arises when a firm provides a warranty for service or repairs for some period after a sale. At the time of the sale, the firm can only estimate the likely amount of warranty liability.

Example 12 J&R Music World makes sales of $280,000 during the accounting period and estimates that it will eventually use an amount equal to 4 percent of the sales revenue to satisfy warranty claims. The expense for warranties is $11,200 (= 0.04 × $280,000). It will make the following entry:

Accounts Receivable (Asset Increase)	280,000	
Retained Earnings (Warranty Expense) (Shareholders' Equity Decrease) . . .	11,200	
Retained Earnings (Sales) (Shareholders' Equity Increase)		280,000
Estimated Warranty Liability (Liability Increase)		11,200
To record sales and estimated liability for warranties on items sold.		

Note that this entry recognizes the warranty expense in the period when the firm recognizes revenue, even though it will make the repairs in a later period. The accounting matches warranty expense with associated revenue. Because it recognizes the expense, it creates the liability. In this case, the firm knows neither the amount nor the due date of the liability for sure, but it can estimate both with reasonable precision. FASB *Statement of Financial Accounting Standards No. 5*, "Accounting for Contingencies," requires the accrual of the expense and the related warranty liability when the firm can "reasonably estimate" the amount.

As J&R makes expenditures of $1,750 in the next period for repairs under the warranty, the entry is as follows:

Estimated Warranty Liability (Liability Decrease)	1,750	
Cash [or other assets consumed for repairs] (Asset Decrease)		1,750
To record repairs made. Recognize no expense now; the firm recognized all expense in the period of sale.		

Note that *actual* expenditures to satisfy warranty claims do not affect net income. The net income effect occurs in the year of sale when the firm estimates the *expected* amount of expenditures that it will make in all future periods to satisfy warranty claims arising from products sold in a particular year. With experience, the firm will adjust the percentage of sales that it charges to Warranty Expense. It attempts to maintain the Estimated Warranty Liability account at each balance sheet date with a credit balance that reasonably estimates the actual cost of repairs to be made under warranties outstanding at that time. The accounting for warranties resembles the allowance method for uncollectibles discussed in **Chapter 6**.

A firm may not use the allowance method of accounting for warranties (or for bad debts) in tax reporting. In tax reporting, taxpayers recognize expense in the period when they use cash or other assets to discharge the obligation. This creates a temporary difference between financial statement pretax income and taxable income, discussed in the next chapter.

Problem 9.1 for Self-Study

Journal entries for transactions involving current liabilities.   Prepare journal entries for each of the following transactions of Ashton Corporation during January, the first month of operations. The firm closes its books monthly.

a. January 2: The firm borrows $10,000 on a 9-percent, 90-day note from First National Bank.

b. January 3: The firm acquires merchandise costing $8,000 from suppliers on account.

c. January 10: The firm receives $1,500 from a customer as a deposit on merchandise that Ashton Corporation expects to deliver in February.

d. Month of January: The firm sells merchandise costing $6,000 to customers on account for $12,000.

e. Month of January: The firm pays suppliers $8,000 of the amount owed for purchases of merchandise on account and collects $7,000 of amounts owed by customers.

f. January 31: Products sold during January include a two-year warranty. Ashton Corporation estimates that warranty claims will equal 8 percent of sales. No customer made warranty claims during January.

g. January 31: Employees earned wages of $4,000 for the month of January. The firm must withhold from the amounts it pays to employees, as follows: 20 percent for income taxes, 10 percent for Social Security taxes, and $200 for union dues. In addition, the employer must pay Social Security taxes of 10 percent and unemployment taxes of 3.5 percent. These wages and taxes remain unpaid at the end of January.

h. January 31: The firm accrues interest expense on the bank loan (see transaction **a**).

i. January 31: The firm accrues income tax expense, but makes no payment, at a rate of 40 percent on net income during January.

j. February 1: Ashton Corporation pays employees their January wages net of withholdings.

k. February 10: The firm delivers merchandise costing $800 to the customer in transaction **c** in full satisfaction of its order.

l. February 15: The firm remits payroll taxes and union dues to government and union authorities.

m. February 20: A customer who purchased merchandise during January returns goods for warranty repairs. The repairs cost the firm $220, which it paid in cash.

Long-Term Liabilities

The principal long-term liabilities are mortgages, notes, bonds, and leases. Borrowers usually pay interest on long-term liabilities at regular intervals during the life of a long-term obligation, whereas they pay interest on short-term debt in a lump sum at maturity. Borrowers often repay the principal of long-term obligations in installments or accumulate special funds for retiring long-term liabilities.

Accounting for all long-term liabilities generally rests on a single, unified set of concepts. We outline these concepts, and the related procedures, next and illustrate them throughout the rest of this chapter and **Chapter 10**.

Concepts and Methods for Recording Long-Term Liabilities

In return for promising to make future payments, the borrower receives cash (or other assets with a measurable cash-equivalent value). The borrower initially records a long-term liability for that amount. By definition, the book value of the borrowing at any time equals the present value of all the then-remaining promised payments using the historical market interest rate applicable at the time the firm originally incurred the liability.

Sometimes a borrower knows the amount of cash received from a loan, the market interest rate at that time, and the various future times when it must pay. In this case, it uses the interest rate at the time of the loan and the elapsed time between payments to compute the amounts it must pay at the various future dates.

More often, however, a borrower knows the amount of cash received as well as the amounts and due dates of cash repayments, but the loan does not explicitly state the market interest rate or, perhaps, states it incorrectly. Finding the market interest rate implied by the receipt of a given amount of cash now in return for a series of promised future repayments requires a process called "finding the internal rate of return." The *internal rate of return* is the interest rate that discounts a series of future cash flows to its present value. Some refer to this rate as the *implicit rate of return*. The **Appendix** at the end of the book illustrates the process of finding the internal rate of return.

The borrower uses the original, or historical, market interest rate, either specified or computed at the time the borrower receives the loan, throughout the life of the loan to compute interest expense. When the borrower makes a cash payment, a portion (perhaps all) of the payment represents interest. Any excess of cash payment over interest expense reduces the borrower's liability for the principal amount. If a given payment is less than the interest expense accrued since the last payment date, then the liability principal increases by the excess of interest expense over cash payment.

Borrowers can retire long-term liabilities in several ways, but the accounting process is the same for all. The borrower debits the liability account for its current book value, credits cash, and recognizes any difference as a gain (when book value exceeds cash disbursement, a credit) or a loss (when cash disbursement exceeds book value, a debit) on retirement of debt.

Mortgages and Notes

In a **mortgage** contract, the lender (such as a bank) takes legal title to certain property of the borrower, with the provision that the title reverts to the borrower when the borrower repays the loan in full. (In a few states, the lender merely acquires a lien on the borrower's property rather than legal title to it.) The mortgaged property is **collateral** for the loan. The customary terminology designates the lender as the **mortgagee** and the borrower as the **mortgagor**.

TERMINOLOGY NOTE

Accountants generally use the word *collateral,* rather than *security,* in this context. Whether the loan is secured requires legal judgment; moreover, accountants do not want to imply that the value of the collateral will be sufficient to satisfy the debt, as the word *secured* might imply. When you borrow money to finance a home purchase, you give the bank a mortgage, a form of IOU, and the bank accepts the mortgage and lends you cash. Common usage often says "the borrower gets a mortgage from the bank" whereas the correct statement is "the borrower gets a mortgage loan from the bank" because the borrower gives the mortgage to the bank, which provides the funds in return for the promise to pay built into the mortgage.

As long as the mortgagor (borrower) makes the payments required by the mortgage agreement, the mortgagee (lender) does not have the ordinary rights of an owner to possess and use the property. If the mortgagor defaults by failing to make the periodic payments, the mortgagee can usually arrange to sell the property for its benefit through a process called *foreclosure*. The mortgagee has first rights to the proceeds from the foreclosure sale for satisfying any unpaid claim. If funds remain, the mortgagee pays them to the mortgagor. If the proceeds are too small to pay the remaining loan, the lender becomes an unsecured creditor of the borrower for the unpaid balance.

A note payable resembles a mortgage payable except that the borrower does not pledge property as collateral.

Illustration of Accounting for a Mortgage

Some of the more common problems in accounting for mortgages appear in the following illustration. On October 1, Year 1, Western Company borrows $125,000 for five years from the Home Savings and Finance Company to obtain funds for additional working capital. As collateral, Western Company pledges to Home Savings and Finance Company several parcels of land that it owns and that are on its books at a cost of $50,000. The mortgage specifies that interest will accrue on the unpaid balance of the amounts owed at a rate of 12 percent per year compounded semiannually (that is, 6 percent interest will accrue every six months). The borrower must make payments on April 1 and October 1 of each year. Western agrees to make 10 payments over the five years of the mortgage so that when it makes the last payment on October 1, Year 6, it will have paid the loan and all interest. The contract calls for the first nine payments to be $17,000 each. The tenth payment will discharge the balance of the loan. Western Company's accounting periods end on December 31 each year. (The derivation of the semiannual payment of $17,000 appears in **Example 11** in the **Appendix** at the end of the book.)

The entries from the time Western issues the mortgage through December 31, Year 2, follow:

10/1/Year 1	Cash (Asset Increase)	125,000	
	Mortgage Payable (Liability Increase)		125,000
	To record loan obtained from Home Savings and Finance Company for five years at 12 percent compounded semiannually.		

As **Example 11** in the **Appendix** shows, $125,000 approximately equals the present value of 10 semiannual cash payments of $17,000, each discounted at 12 percent compounded semiannually.

12/31/Year 1	Retained Earnings (Interest Expense) (Shareholders' Equity Decrease)	3,750	
	Interest Payable (Liability Increase)		3,750
	To record adjusting entry: interest expense on mortgage from 10/1/Year 1 to 12/31/Year 1.		

Interest expense on the loan for the first six months is $7,500 (= 0.12 × $125,000 × 6/12). To simplify the calculations, accounting typically assumes that the interest accrues evenly over the six-month period. Thus interest expense for the three-month period (October, November, and December) equals one-half of the $7,500, or $3,750.

4/1/Year 2	Retained Earnings (Interest Expense) (Shareholders' Equity Decrease)	3,750	
	Interest Payable (Liability Decrease)	3,750	
	Mortgage Payable (Liability Decrease)	9,500	
	Cash (Asset Decrease)		17,000
	To record cash payment made: interest expense on mortgage from 1/1/Year 2 to 4/1/Year 2, payment of six months' interest, and reduction of loan by the difference: $9,500 = $17,000 − $7,500.		

After the cash payment on April 1, Year 2, the unpaid amount of the loan is $115,500 (= $125,000 − $9,500). Interest expense during the second six-month period accrues on this unpaid amount.

10/1/Year 2	Retained Earnings (Interest Expense) (Shareholders' Equity Decrease)	6,930	
	Mortgage Payable (Liability Decrease)	10,070	
	Cash (Asset Decrease)		17,000
	To record cash payment made: interest expense for the period 4/1/Year 2 to 10/1/Year 2 is $6,930 [= 0.12 × ($125,000 − $9,500) × 6/12]; the loan balance declines by the difference: $10,070 = $17,000 − $6,930.		
12/31/Year 2	Retained Earnings (Interest Expense) (Shareholders' Equity Decrease)	3,163	
	Interest Payable (Liability Increase)		3,163
	To record adjusting entry: interest expense from 10/1/Year 2 to 12/31/Year 2 = [0.12 × ($125,000 − $9,500 − $10,070) × 3/12].		

Amortization Schedule   **Exhibit 9.2** presents an amortization schedule for this mortgage. For each period it shows the balance at the beginning of the period, the interest expense for the period, the cash payment for the period, the reduction in principal for the period, and the balance at the end of the period. (The last payment, $16,781 in this case, often differs slightly from the others because of the cumulative effect of rounding payments to the nearest dollar or hundred dollars.) All long-term liabilities have analogous amortization schedules, which aid in

EXHIBIT 9.2	**Amortization Schedule for $125,000 Mortgage (or Note), Repaid in 10 Semiannual Installments of $17,000, Interest Rate of 12 Percent, Compounded Semiannually (6 percent compounded each six months)**

Semiannual Journal Entry

Retained Earnings (Interest Expense) (Shareholders' Equity Decrease) ...	Amount in Column **(3)**
Mortgage (or Note) Payable (Liability Decrease)	Amount in Column **(5)**
Cash (Asset Decrease)	Amount in Column **(4)**

6-Month Period (1)	Loan Balance Start of Period (2)	Interest Expense for Period (3)	Payment (4)	Portion of Payment Reducing Principal (5)	Loan Balance End of Period (6)
0					$125,000
1	$125,000	$7,500	$17,000	$ 9,500	115,500
2	115,500	6,930	17,000	10,070	105,430
3	105,430	6,326	17,000	10,674	94,756
4	94,756	5,685	17,000	11,315	83,441
5	83,441	5,006	17,000	11,994	71,447
6	71,447	4,287	17,000	12,713	58,734
7	58,734	3,524	17,000	13,476	45,258
8	45,258	2,715	17,000	14,285	30,973
9	30,973	1,858	17,000	15,142	15,831
10	15,831	950	16,781	15,831	0

Note: In preparing this table, we rounded calculations to the nearest dollar.

Column (2) = column (6) from previous period.

Column (3) = 0.06 × column (2).

Column (4) is given, except row 10, where it is the amount such that column (4) = column (2) + column (3).

Column (5) = column (4) − column (3).

Column (6) = column (2) − column (5).

understanding the timing of payments to discharge the liability. Amortization schedules for various long-term liabilities appear throughout this chapter and the next.

Problem 9.2 for Self-Study

Accounting for an interest-bearing note.   Sapra Company receives cash of $112,434 in return for a three-year, $100,000 note, promising to pay $15,000 at the end of one year, $15,000 at the end of two years, and $115,000 at the end of three years. The market interest rate on the original issue date of the note is 10 percent.

a. Prepare an amortization schedule similar to **Exhibit 9.2** for the life of the note.
b. Prepare journal entries that Sapra Company would make on three dates: the date of issue, six months after the date of issue (assuming Sapra closes the books then), and one year after the date of issue (assuming Sapra makes a cash payment then).

Contracts and Long-Term Notes: Interest Imputation

Firms often finance the acquisition of buildings, equipment, and other fixed assets using interest-bearing notes, which the previous section discussed. Some borrowing arrangements do not state an explicit interest rate. Instead, the purchase price includes carrying charges, and the buyer pays the total over a specified number of months. The contract does not mention the charge for interest. The principal on the note in this case includes **implicit interest**.

Generally accepted accounting principles (GAAP) require that all long-term monetary liabilities, including those carrying no explicit interest, appear on the balance sheet at the present value of the future cash payments. To compute a present value requires an interest rate, sometimes in this context called a *discount rate*. In historical cost accounting, the discounting process uses the historical (or original) interest rate appropriate for the particular borrower at the time it incurred the obligation. That rate will have depended on the amount and terms of the borrowing arrangement as well as on the risk that the borrower will default on its obligations. The rate is known as the **implicit (imputed) interest rate**. The excess of the par, or face, value of the liability over its present value represents interest to be recognized over the period of the loan. The next two sections discuss two acceptable ways to compute the present value of the liability and the amount of imputed interest.

The first approach uses the market value of the asset acquired as a basis for computing the present value of the liability.

Example 13   Hixon Saab can purchase a piece of equipment for $105,000 cash. The firm purchases the equipment in return for a single-payment note with a face amount of $160,000 payable in three years. The implied interest rate is about 15 percent per year; that is, $105,000 grows at 15 percent in one year to $120,750 (= $105,000 × 1.15), in two years to about $139,000 (= $120,750 × 1.15), and in three years to about $160,000 (= $139,000 × 1.15). The journal entry using this approach would be as follows:

Equipment (Asset Increase)	105,000	
Note Payable (Liability Increase)		105,000

To record purchase of equipment using the known cash price. The firm infers the interest rate for the note from the known cash price of the equipment and the face amount of the note.

At the end of each accounting period that intervenes between the acquisition of the equipment and repayment of the note, Hixon Saab makes journal entries for depreciation of the equipment. We do not show these here. The firm must also make journal entries to recognize interest expense. Assume that Hixon Saab issued the note at the beginning of a year. The entries for the three years would be as follows:

(1) Retained Earnings (Interest Expense) (Shareholders' Equity		
Decrease)	15,750	
Note Payable (Liability Increase)		15,750

Entry made one year after issuance of note.

Interest is $0.15 \times \$105,000$. The firm does not pay $15,750 in cash but adds it to the principal amount of the liability.

(2) Retained Earnings (Interest Expense) (Shareholders' Equity Decrease)	18,113	
Note Payable (Liability Increase)		18,113
Entry made one year after entry (1), two years after issuance of note.		

Interest is $0.15 \times (\$105,000 + \$15,750)$.

(3) Retained Earnings (Interest Expense) (Shareholders' Equity Decrease)	21,137	
Note Payable (Liability Increase)		21,137
Entry made one year after entry (2), at maturity of note to increase liability to its maturity amount, $160,000.		

Interest $= \$160,000 - (\$105,000 + \$15,750 + \$18,113)$, which is approximately equal to $0.15 \times (\$105,000 + \$15,750 + \$18,113)$; the difference represents the accumulated rounding error caused by using 15 percent as the implicit interest rate rather than the exact rate, which is 15.074 percent.

(4) Note Payable (Liability Decrease)	160,000	
Cash (Asset Decrease)		160,000
To repay note at maturity.		

Of the $160,000 paid at maturity, $55,000 represents interest accumulated on the note since its issue.

Use of Market Interest Rate to Establish Market Value of Asset and Present Value of Note   If the firm purchased used equipment with the same three-year note, it might be unable to establish a reliable estimate of the current market value of the asset acquired. To find the present value of the note, the firm would discount the payments using the interest rate it would have to pay for a similar loan in the open market at the time that it acquired the equipment. The firm would continue to use this rate throughout the life of the note. GAAP allow this second method for quantifying the amount of the liability and computing the imputed interest.

Example 14   Refer to the data in **Example 13**. When Hixon Saab borrows using single-payment notes with maturity of three years, it pays interest of 12 percent compounded annually, rather than 15 percent. The present value at 12 percent per year of the $160,000 note due in three years is $113,885 (= $160,000 × 0.71178; see **Appendix Table 2** at the back of the book, 3-period row, 12-percent column). The entry to record the purchase of used equipment paid for with the note would be as follows:

Equipment (Asset Increase)	113,885	
Note Payable (Liability Increase)		113,885
To record purchase of equipment. The firm infers the cost of equipment from known interest rate.		

The firm would make entries at the end of each period to recognize interest expense (using the 12 percent borrowing rate) and to increase the principal amount of the liability. After the third period, the principal amount of the liability would be $160,000.

Total Expense Is Independent of Interest Rate   In **Example 13**, the buyer records the equipment of $105,000 and recognizes $55,000 of imputed interest. In **Example 14**, the buyer records the equipment at $113,885 and recognizes $46,115 of imputed interest. The expense over the combined lives of the note and the equipment—interest plus depreciation—will total the same amount, $160,000, no matter which interest rate the buyer uses. Over sufficiently long time periods, total expense equals total cash expenditure; accrual accounting affects only the timing of the expense recognition.

Long-Term Notes Held as Receivables   A borrower's long-term note payable is the lender's long-term asset, a note receivable. GAAP require the lender to show the asset in the Long-Term Note Receivable account at its present value. The rate at which the lender discounts the note should, in theory, equal the rate the borrower uses. In practice, the two rates sometimes differ because the lender and the borrower reach different conclusions regarding the borrower's default risk, sometimes called *credit risk*. The lender's accounting mirrors the borrower's: the lender has interest revenue, whereas the borrower has interest expense.

Problem 9.3 for Self-Study

Accounting for note with imputed interest rate.   Bens Company purchased a fork-lift truck from Roulstone's Auto Agency. The truck had a list price of $25,000, but sellers often offer discounts of 8 to 20 percent from list prices for purchases of this sort. Bens Company paid for the truck by giving a noninterest-bearing note due two years from the date of purchase. The note had a maturity value of $28,730. The rate of interest that Bens Company paid to borrow on secured two-year loans ranged from 10 percent to 15 percent during the period when the purchase occurred.

a. Record the acquisition of the truck on Bens Company's books, computing the fair market value of the truck using a 10 percent discount from list price.

b. What imputed interest rate will Bens use for computing interest expense throughout the loan if it records the acquisition as in part **a**?

c. Record the acquisition of the truck on Bens Company's books, assuming that the estimated interest rate Bens Company must pay to borrow is reliable and is 12 percent per year.

d. Record the acquisition of the truck on Bens Company's books, assuming that the interest rate Bens Company must pay to borrow is 1 percent per month.

e. Prepare journal entries to record the loan and to record interest over two years, assuming that Bens records the truck at $23,744 and that the interest rate implicit in the loan is 10 percent per year.

f. This book has stressed that over sufficiently long time periods, total expense is equal to total cash outflow. In what sense is the total expense for this transaction the same, independent of the interest rate (and, therefore, the interest expense)?

Bonds

When a firm can borrow funds from one lender, the firm usually issues mortgages or notes. When it needs larger amounts, the firm may have to borrow from the general investing public with a bond issue. Corporations and governmental units are the usual issuers. Bond issues have the following features:

1. A firm or its investment banker writes a **bond indenture**, or agreement, which gives the terms of the loan and the rights and duties of the borrower and other parties to the contract. To provide some protection to bondholders, bond indentures typically limit the borrower's right to declare dividends, to make other distributions to owners, and to acquire other businesses.
2. The borrower can prepare engraved bond certificates, although this practice is disappearing. Each one represents a portion of the total loan. The usual minimum denomination is $1,000. The federal government has issued some bonds in denominations as small as $50.
3. If the borrower pledges property as collateral for the loan (such as in a mortgage bond), the indenture names a trustee to hold title to the property serving as collateral. The trustee, usually a bank, acts as the representative of the bondholders.
4. The borrower or trustee appoints an agent, usually a bank, to act as *registrar* and *disbursing agent*. The borrower deposits interest and principal payments with the disbursing agent, who distributes the funds to the bondholders.

5. Some bonds are **coupon bonds**. Coupons attached to the bond certificate represent promises to make periodic payments throughout the life of the bond. When a coupon comes due, the bondholder cuts it off and deposits it with a bank. Then the bank sends the coupon, as it would with a check it received, through the bank clearing system to the disbursing agent, who deposits the payment in the bondholder's account at the bank. In recent years, most bonds are registered, which means that the borrower records the name and address of the bondholder and sends the periodic payments to the registered owner, who need not clip coupons and redeem them.

6. The borrower usually issues the entire loan to an investment banking firm or to a group of investment bankers known as a *syndicate*, which takes over the responsibility for selling the bonds to the investing public. Members of the syndicate usually bear the risks and rewards of interest rate fluctuations during the period while they are selling the bonds to the public.

Types of Bonds   Mortgage bonds carry a mortgage on real estate as collateral for the repayment of the loan. Issuers of *collateral trust bonds* usually hand over stocks and bonds of other corporations to the trustee. The most common type of corporate bond, except in the railroad and public utility industries, is the **debenture bond**. This type carries no special collateral; instead, the borrower issues it on the general credit of the business. For added protection to the bondholders, the bond indenture usually includes provisions that limit the dividends that the borrower can declare or the amount of subsequent long-term debt that it can incur. Common terminology refers to such provisions as *covenants* or *debt covenants*. **Convertible bonds** are debentures that the holder (lender) can exchange, possibly after some specific period of time has elapsed, for a specific number of common or, perhaps, preferred shares, of the borrower.

From the viewpoint of the issuer (borrower), all bonds require future cash outflows in return for a current or previous cash inflow. The pattern of future cash outflows varies across bonds depending on the provisions in the bond indenture.

Example 15   Ford Motor Company issues $250 million of 10 percent, semiannual, 20-year bonds. The bond indenture requires Ford to pay interest of $12.5 million each six months for 20 years and to repay the $250 million principal at the end of 20 years.

Example 16   DaimlerChrysler Corporation issues $180 million of 15-year bonds. The bond indenture requires DaimlerChrysler to pay $13.1 million each six months for 15 years. Each periodic payment includes interest plus repayment of a portion of the principal. (Common terminology refers to such bonds as **serial bonds**.)

Example 17   General Motors Corporation (GM) issues bonds that do not require a periodic cash payment (common terminology refers to such bonds as **zero coupon bonds**), but it promises a single payment of $300 million at the end of 10 years. The $300 million paid after 10 years includes both interest and principal.

COMPUTATIONAL NOTE

By the time you have completed the Appendix to this book, you should be able to work out the implicit interest rate in this GM bond issue, given the amount of initial issue proceeds. To take an example, assume GM receives $140 million for this issue. Then the implicit interest rate is just under 8 percent per year. See Table 2 at the back of the book, 10-period column and 8-percent row; the factor is 0.46319. Multiply that factor by $300 million, and notice that you get slightly less than $140 million, which indicates that 8 percent slightly overstates the implicit rate, which is 7.92 percent. Later in this section, we show the derivation of proceeds for this note assuming a 10-percent rate. Over the life of the bond issue, GM will record $160 million of interest expense, all of which it will pay at maturity along with the $140 million originally borrowed.

The bond indenture indicates the par value or face value of a bond. The par value is usually an even amount (for example, $250 million in **Example 15**, $180 million in **Example 16**, and

$300 million in **Example 17**). Bonds requiring periodic payments (called *coupon* payments if the bonds have coupons) use the par value as the base for computing the amount of the cash payment. For example, the Ford Motor Company bonds in **Example 15** require the payment of 10 percent of the par amount each year, payable in two installments. The semiannual payment is $12.5 million (= 0.10 × $250 million × 0.5).

TERMINOLOGY NOTE

Almost everyone in business refers to the periodic payments as *interest payments*. This term causes confusion because, as you will soon see, the amount of interest expense for a period almost never equals the amount of these payments for that same period. The periodic payment will always include some amount to pay interest to the lender, but not necessarily all interest accrued since the last payment. If the payment exceeds all accrued interest, then the payment will discharge some of the principal amount. Both payment of interest and payment of principal serve to reduce the debt, so one all-purpose term used for the payments is *debt service payments*. We urge you not to call them, or to think of them as, interest payments until you have understood why they do not equal interest expense. You will never be wrong to call them *debt service payments*.

Proceeds of a Bond Issue

The price at which a firm issues bonds on the market depends on two factors: the future cash payments that the bond indenture requires the firm to make; and the discount rate that the market deems appropriate given the risk of the borrower, the general level of interest rates in the economy, and other factors. The issuing price equals the present value of the required cash flows discounted at the appropriate market interest rate.

Example 18   Refer to **Example 15**. The time line for this semiannual bond covers 40 six-month periods and is as follows:

Assume that the market charges Ford an interest rate of 10 percent, compounded semiannually. Ford will receive $250 million for its bond issue, computed as follows:

Required Cash Flows	Present Value Factor for 10 Percent Interest Rate Compounded Semiannually for 20 Years	Present Value of Required Cash Flows
$250.0 million at end of 20 years	0.14205[a]	$ 35.5
$12.5 million every six months for 20 Years	17.15909[b]	214.5
Issue Price		$250.0

[a]Table 2, 5-percent column and 40-period row.
[b]Table 4, 5-percent column and 40-period row.

Example 19   Refer to **Example 16**. The time line for this serial bond covers 30 six-month periods and is as follows:

Assume that the market deems that an appropriate interest rate for DaimlerChrysler's bonds on the date of issue is also 10 percent, compounded semiannually. The issue price of Daimler-Chrysler's bonds is $201.4 million, computed as follows:

Required Cash Flows	Present Value Factor for 10 Percent Interest Rate Compounded Semiannually for 15 Years	Present Value of Required Cash Flows
$13.1 million every six months for 15 years	15.37245[a]	$201.4
Issue Price		$201.4

[a]Table 4, 5-percent column and 30-period row.

Example 20 Refer to **Example 17**. The time line for this zero coupon bond covers 10 one-year periods and is as follows:

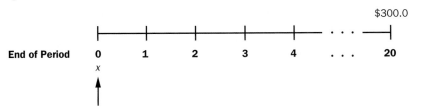

Assume that the market deems that 10 percent, compounded annually, is an appropriate interest rate on the date of issue for GM bonds. The issue price is $113.1 million, computed as follows:

Required Cash Flows	Present Value Factor for 10 Percent Interest Rate Compounded Semiannually for 10 Years	Present Value of Required Cash Flows
$300 million at end of 10 years	0.38554[a]	$115.7
Issue Price		$115.7

[a]Table 2, 10-percent column and 10-period row.

The issue price will usually differ from the par value of the bonds. (The Ford example above, where the price and the value equal each other, is rare, but we include it for teaching purposes.) The difference arises because the coupon interest rate stated in the bond indenture differs from the interest rate that the market charges the issuer to borrow.

If the market required rate exceeds the coupon rate, the bonds will sell for less than par value. The difference between the par value and the selling price is known as the *discount* on the bonds. The zero coupon bonds of GM in **Example 20** have a par value of $300 million, an issue price of $115.7 million and a discount of $184.3 (= $300.0 − $115.7) million. The 10-percent rate required by the lenders before they will purchase these bonds exceeds the bonds' promised periodic payment rate, zero in this case. Purchasing the GM bonds for $115.7 million and receiving $300 million 10 years later yields the purchasers a return of 10 percent compounded annually. That is, $300 million is the future value of $115.7 million invested to yield 10 percent compounded annually for 10 years. The $184.3 million will be the amount of interest GM will accrue over the 10-year life of the bonds.

If the coupon rate exceeds the market-required rate, the bonds will sell for more than par value. The difference between the selling price and the par value is known as the *premium* on the bond. The DaimlerChrysler bonds in **Example 19** have an issue price of $201.4 million, a par value of $180 million, and a premium of $21.4 (= $201.4 − $180.0) million. Purchasing the DaimlerChrysler bonds for $201.4 million and receiving $13.1 million every six months for 15 years yields the lenders a return of 10 percent compounded semiannually.

If the coupon rate equals the market-required rate, a rare occurrence, the bonds will sell for par value. The Ford Motor Company bonds in **Example 18** have a coupon rate and a market required rate of 10 percent compounded semiannually. The issue price of $250 million equals the par value of the bonds. Purchasing these bonds for $250 million and receiving $12.5 million every six months for 20 years and $250 million at the end of 20 years yields the purchaser 10 percent compounded semiannually.

The presence of a discount or premium by itself indicates nothing about the credit risk of the borrower. A solid firm, such as General Electric, with a small credit risk that would enable it to borrow funds at 8 percent, might issue 7-percent bonds that would sell at a discount. In contrast, an untested firm with a lower credit standing that requires it to pay 15 percent on loans might issue 18-percent bonds that would sell at a premium.

Issued at Par   The Macaulay Corporation issues $100,000 face value of 12-percent semiannual coupon debenture bonds on July 1, Year 1. Macaulay must repay the principal amount five years later, on July 1, Year 6. Macaulay owes periodic payments (coupons) on January 1 and July 1 of each year. The coupon payments promised at each payment date total $6,000. **Figure 9.2** presents a time line for the two sets of cash flows associated with this bond. Assume that the market rate of interest for Macaulay on July 1, Year 1, exactly equals 12 percent compounded semiannually. Then, the calculation of the loan proceeds would be as follows (the **Appendix** at the back of the book explains the present value calculations):

(a) Present Value of $100,000 to Be Paid at the End of Five Years .... $ 55,839

(Table 2 at the back of the book shows the present value of $1 to be paid in 10 periods at 6 percent per period to be $0.55839; $100,000 × 0.55839 = $55,839.)

(b) Present Value of $6,000 to Be Paid Each Six Months for Five Years 44,161

(Table 4 shows the present value of an ordinary annuity of $1 per period for 10 periods discounted at 6 percent to be $7.36009; $6,000 × 7.36009 = $44,161.)

Total Proceeds $100,000

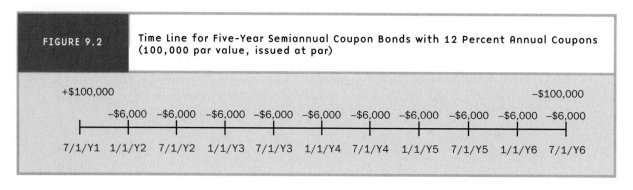

| FIGURE 9.2 | **Time Line for Five-Year Semiannual Coupon Bonds with 12 Percent Annual Coupons (100,000 par value, issued at par)** |

Common terminology quotes bond prices as a percentage of par value. The issue price of these bonds is 100.0 (that is, 100 percent of par), which implies that the market interest rate is 12 percent, compounded semiannually, the same as the coupon rate.

Issued at Less Than Par   Assume that Macaulay Corporation issued these same bonds at a price to yield 14 percent compounded semiannually. The cash flows promised after July 1, Year 1, associated with these bonds (periodic payments plus repayment of principal) equal those in the time line in **Figure 9.2**. The market discounts these future cash flows to their present value using a 14 percent discount rate compounded semiannually. The calculation of the issue proceeds (that is, initial market price) follows:

(a) Present Value of $100,000 to Be Paid at the End of Five Years	$50,835
(Present value of $1 to be paid in 10 periods at 7 percent per period is $0.50835; $100,000 × 0.50835 = $50,835.)	
(b) Present Value of $6,000 to Be Paid Each Six Months for Five Years	42,141
(Present value of an ordinary annuity of $1 per period for 10 periods discounted at 7 percent per period = $7.02358; $6,000 × 7.02358 = $42,141.)	
Total Proceeds	$92,976

Assume Macaulay issues these bonds at 92.98 for $92,980. This implies a market yield of slightly less than 14 percent compounded semiannually.

Issued at More than Par   Assume that Macaulay Corporation issued the bonds at a price to yield 10 percent compounded semiannually. The cash flows promised after July 1, Year 1, again equal those in **Figure 9.2**. The market discounts these future cash flows at 10 percent compounded semiannually. The calculation of the proceeds follows:

(a) Present Value of $100,000 to Be Paid at the End of Five Years	$ 61,391
(Present value of $1 to be paid in 10 periods at 5 percent per period is $0.61391; $100,000 × 0.61391 = $61,391.)	
(b) Present Value of $6,000 to Be Paid Each Six Months for Five Years	46,330
(Present value of an ordinary annuity of $1 per period for 10 periods, discounted at 5 percent per period = $7.72173; $6,000 × 7.72173 = $46,330.)	
Total Proceeds	$107,721

Assume Macaulay issues these bonds at 107.72 (that is, 107.72 percent of par) for $107,720. The price would imply a market yield of slightly more than 10 percent compounded semiannually.

Bond Tables   One need not make these tedious calculations every time one analyzes a bond issue. **Bond tables** show the results of calculations like those just described. **Tables 5** and **6** at the back of the book illustrate such tables. **Table 5** shows the price for 10-percent semiannual coupon bonds as a percent of par for various market interest rates (yields) and years to maturity. **Table 6** shows market rates and implied prices for 12-percent semiannual coupon bonds. (Most calculators make the calculations represented by these tables in a few seconds. Spreadsheet program financial functions make the calculations even faster. We urge you to learn how to use and interpret the tables because you will need the resulting understanding to know which financial functions to use in your spreadsheet and which data to input to the functions.)

The percentages of par shown in these tables represent the present value of the bond indicated. Because the tables give factors as a percent of par, the user must multiply them by 10 to find the price of a $1,000 bond. If you have never used bond tables before now, turn to **Table 6** after the Appendix at the back of the book, and find in the 5-year row the three different prices for the three different market yields used in the preceding examples. Notice further that a bond will sell at par if and only if it has a market yield equal to its coupon rate.

These tables apply both when a corporation issues a bond and when an investor later resells it. Computing the market price will be the same in either case. The following generalizations describe bond prices:

1. When the market interest rate equals the coupon rate, the market price will equal par.
2. When the market interest rate exceeds the coupon rate, the market price will be less than par.
3. When the market interest rate is less than the coupon rate, the market price will exceed par.

Problem 9.4 for Self-Study

Calculating the issue price of bonds.   Engel Corporation issues $1,000,000 face-value bonds on January 1, Year 1. The bonds carry a 10-percent coupon rate, payable in two installments on June 30 and December 31 each year. The bonds mature on December 31, Year 10.

(continued)

Problem 9.4 for Self-Study *(continued)*

Compute the issue price of these bonds assuming that the market requires the following yields:

a. 8 percent compounded semiannually
b. 10 percent compounded semiannually
c. 12 percent compounded semiannually

Accounting for Bonds Issued at Par   The following illustrates bonds issued at par. We use the data presented in the previous sections for the Macaulay Corporation bonds issued at par, and we assume that the firm closes its books semiannually on June 30 and December 31. The entry at the time of issue follows:

7/1/Year 1	Cash (Asset Increase)	100,000	
	Debenture Bonds Payable (Liability Increase)		100,000
	$100,000 of 12-percent, five-year, semi-annual coupon bonds issued at par.		

The borrower would make entries for interest at the end of the accounting period and on the payment dates. Entries through January 1, Year 2, would be as follows:

12/31/Year 1	Retained Earnings (Interest Expense) (Shareholders' Equity Decrease)	6,000	
	Interest Payable (Liability increase)		6,000
	To record interest expense for six months.		
1/1/Year 2	Interest Payable (Liability Decrease)	6,000	
	Cash (Asset Decrease)		6,000
	To record payment of six months' interest.		

Bond Issued between Payment Dates   The actual date when a firm issues a bond seldom coincides with one of the periodic payment dates. Assuming that Macaulay brought these same bonds to market on September 1, rather than July 1, at par, the borrower would expect the purchasers of the bonds to pay for two months of periodic payments in advance. On the first coupon, Macaulay Corporation promises a full $6,000 for six months' debt service, but it would have had the use of the borrowed funds for only four months. The purchasers of the bonds would pay $100,000 plus two months' interest of $2,000 (= 0.12 × $100,000 × 2/12) and would get the $2,000 back when Macaulay redeemed the first coupons. The journal entry made by Macaulay Corporation, the issuer, would be as follows:

9/1/Year 1	Cash (Asset Increase)	102,000	
	Bonds Payable (Liability Increase)		100,000
	Interest Payable (Liability Increase)		2,000
	To record issue of bonds at par between payment dates.		

The purchasers pay an amount equal to interest for the first two months but will get it back when the borrower pays for the first coupon.

Accounting for Bonds Issued at Less than Par   The following illustrates bonds issued at less than par. Assume the data presented above where the Macaulay Corporation issued 12-percent, $100,000-par value, five-year bonds to yield 14 percent compounded semiannually. Earlier, we derived the issue price to be $92,976. The journal entry at issue would be as follows:

7/1/Year 1	Cash (Asset Increase)	92,976	
	Debenture Bonds Payable (Liability Increase)		92,976

The issuance of these bonds for $92,976, instead of for the $100,000 par value, indicates that lenders demand more than 12 percent from Macaulay Corporation, the borrower. If purchasers of these bonds paid the $100,000 par value, they would earn only 12 percent compounded semi-annually, the coupon rate. Purchasers desiring a rate of return of 14 percent will not buy until the market price drops to $92,976. At this price, purchasers of the bonds will earn the 14 percent return they require. The return will comprise 10 coupon payments of $6,000 each over the next five years plus $7,024 (= $100,000 − $92,976) as part of the payment at maturity.

For Macaulay Corporation, the total interest expense over the life of the bonds will equal $67,024 (= periodic payments totaling $60,000 plus $7,024 paid at maturity). The accounting for these payments allocates the total interest expense of $67,024 to the periods of the loan using the effective interest method, explained next. Following the next discussion will be easier if you refer to **Exhibit 9.3**.

EXHIBIT 9.3	Effective Interest Amortization Schedule for $100,000 of 12-Percent, Semiannual Coupon, Five-Year Bonds Issued for 92.976 Percent of Par to Yield 14 Percent, Interest Compounded Semiannually

Semiannual Journal Entry

Retained Earnings (Interest Expense)(Shareholders' Equity Decrease) . . . . . . 　　Amount in Column (3)

　　Cash (Asset Decrease) . . . . 　　　　　　Amount in Column (4)

　　Debenture Bonds Payable (Liability Increase) . . . . 　　　　　　Amount in Column (5)

Period (6-Month Intervals) (1)	Liability at Start of Period (2)	Effective Interest: 7 Percent per Period (3)	Coupon Rate: 6 Percent of Par (4)	Increase in Recorded Book Value of Liability (5)	Liability at End of Period (6)
0					$ 92,976
1	$92,976	$ 6,508	$ 6,000	$ 508	93,484
2	93,484	6,544	6,000	544	94,028
3	94,028	6,582	6,000	582	94,610
4	94,610	6,623	6,000	623	95,233
5	95,233	6,666	6,000	666	95,899
6	95,899	6,713	6,000	713	96,612
7	96,612	6,763	6,000	763	97,375
8	97,375	6,816	6,000	816	98,191
9	98,191	6,873	6,000	873	99,064
10	99,064	6,936	6,000	936	100,000
Total		$67,024	$60,000	$7,024	

Note: In preparing this table, we rounded calculations to the nearest dollar.

Column (2) = column (6) from previous period.

Column (3) = 0.07 × column (2), except for period 10, where it is a plug.

Column (4) is given.

Column (5) = column (3) − column (4), except for period 10, where it is a plug.

Column (6) = column (2) + column (5).

Interest Expense under the Effective Interest Method

Interest Expense under the Effective Interest Method Under the **effective interest method**, interest expense each period equals the market interest rate at the time the firm initially issued the bonds (14 percent compounded semiannually, which is 7 percent per six months, in this example) multiplied by the book value of the liability at the beginning of the interest period. For example, interest expense for the period from July 1, Year 1, to December 31, Year 1, the first six-month period, is $6,508 (= 0.07 × $92,976). The bond indenture provides that the borrower repay only $6,000 (= 0.06 × $100,000) on January 1, Year 2. This amount equals the coupon rate times the par value of the bonds. The difference between the interest expense of $6,508 and the interest then payable of $6,000 increases the book value of the bond. The borrower will pay this amount as part of the principal payment at maturity. The journal entry made on December 31, Year 1, to recognize interest for the last six months of Year 1 follows:

12/31/Year 1	Retained Earnings (Interest Expense) (Shareholders' Equity Decrease)	6,508	
	Interest Payable (Liability Increase)		6,000
	Debenture Bonds Payable (Liability Increase)		508
	To recognize interest expense for six months.		

The Interest Payable account will appear as a current liability on the balance sheet at the end of Year 1. Debenture Bonds Payable of $93,484 (= $92,976 + $508) will appear on the balance sheet as a noncurrent liability.

On January 1, Year 2, the borrower makes the first periodic cash payment.

1/1/Year 2	Interest Payable (Liability Decrease)	6,000	
	Cash (Asset Decrease)		6,000
	To record payment of interest for six months.		

Interest expense for the second six months (from January 1, Year 2, through June 30, Year 2) is $6,544 (= 0.07 × $93,484). It exceeds the $6,508 for the first six months because the recorded book value of the liability at the beginning of the second six months has grown. The journal entry on June 30, Year 2, to record interest expense follows:

6/30/Year 2	Retained Earnings (Interest Expense) (Shareholders' Equity Decrease)	6,544	
	Interest Payable (Liability Increase)		6,000
	Debenture Bonds Payable (Liability Increase)		544
	To recognize interest expense for six months.		

An amortization schedule for these bonds over their five-year life appears in **Exhibit 9.3**. Column **(3)** shows the periodic interest expense, and column **(6)** shows the book value that appears on the balance sheet at the end of each period.

The effective interest method of recognizing interest expense on a bond has the following financial statement effects:

1. Interest expense on the income statement will equal a constant percentage of the recorded liability at the beginning of each interest period. This percentage will equal the market interest rate for these bonds when the borrower issued them. When the borrower issues bonds for less than par value, the dollar amount of interest expense will increase each period as the recorded book value amount increases.
2. On the balance sheet at the end of each period, the bonds will appear at the present value of the remaining cash outflows discounted at the market interest rate measured when the borrower initially issued the bonds. For example, on July 1, Year 2, just after the borrower has made a coupon payment, the remaining cash payments have present value computed as follows:

(a) Present Value of $100,000 to Be Paid at the End of Four Years	$58,201
(Table 2 shows the present value of $1 to be paid at the end of eight periods discounted at 7 percent to be $0.58201; $100,000 × 0.58201 = $58,201.)	
(b) Present Value of Eight Remaining Semiannual Interest Payments Discounted at 14 Percent Compounded Semiannually	35,827
(Table 4 shows the present value of an ordinary annuity of $1 per period for eight periods discounted at 7 percent to be $5.97130; $6,000 × 5.97130 = $35,827.)	
Total Present Value	$94,028

The amount $94,028 appears in column **(6)** of **Exhibit 9.3** for the liability at the end of the second six-month period.

Accounting for Bonds Issued at More than Par

The following discussion illustrates bonds issued at more than par. Assume the data presented where the Macaulay Corporation issued 12-percent, $100,000-par value, five-year bonds to yield approximately 10-percent compounded semiannually. The issue price, derived previously, was $107,721. The journal entry at the time of issue follows:

7/1/Year 1	Cash (Asset Increase)	107,721	
	Debenture Bonds Payable (Liability Increase)		107,721

The firm borrows $107,721. The issuance of these bonds for $107,721, instead of the $100,000 par value, indicates that 12 percent exceeds the interest rate the purchasers (lenders) demand. If purchasers of these bonds paid the $100,000 par value, they would earn 12 percent compounded semiannually, the coupon rate. Purchasers requiring a rate of return of only 10 percent will bid up the market price to $107,721. At this price, purchasers of the bonds will earn only the 10 percent return they demand. Their return comprises 10 coupon payments of $6,000 each over the next five years reduced by the $7,721 (= $107,721 − $100,000) paid as part of initial amount transferred to the borrower but not repaid at maturity.

For Macaulay Corporation, the total interest expense over the life of the bonds equals $52,279 (= periodic payments totaling $60,000 less $7,721 received at the time of original issue but not repaid at maturity). Following the next discussion will be easier if you refer to **Exhibit 9.4**.

EXHIBIT 9.4	**Effective Interest Amortization Schedule for $100,000 of 12-Percent, Semiannual Coupon, Five-Year Bonds Issued for 107.721 Percent of Par to Yield 10 Percent, Compounded Semiannually**

Semiannual Journal Entry

Retained Earnings (Interest Expense)(Shareholders' Equity Decrease) ...... Amount in Column **(3)**
Debenture Bonds Payable (Liability Decrease) .... Amount in Column **(5)**
    Cash (Asset Decrease) .... Amount in Column **(4)**

Period (6-Month Intervals) (1)	Liability at Start of Period (2)	Effective Interest: 5 Percent per Period (3)	Coupon Rate: 6 Percent of Par (4)	Decrease in Recorded Book Value of Liability (5)	Liability at End of Period (6)
0					$107,721
1	$107,721	$ 5,386	$ 6,000	$ 614	107,107
2	107,107	5,355	6,000	645	106,462
3	106,462	5,323	6,000	677	105,785
4	105,785	5,289	6,000	711	105,074
5	105,074	5,245	6,000	746	104,328
6	104,328	5,216	6,000	784	103,544
7	103,544	5,177	6,000	823	102,721
8	102,721	5,136	6,000	864	101,857
9	101,857	5,093	6,000	907	100,950
10	100,950	5,050	6,000	950	100,000
Total		$52,279	$60,000	$7,721	

Note: In preparing this table, we rounded calculations to the nearest dollar.
Column (2) = column (6) from previous period.
Column (3) = 0.05 × column (2), except for period 10, where it is a plug.
Column (4) is given.
Column (5) = column (4) − column (3), except for period 10, where it is a plug.
Column (6) = column (2) − column (5).

Interest Expense under the Effective Interest Method   Under the effective interest method, interest expense each period equals the market interest rate at the time the firm initially issued the bonds (10 percent compounded semiannually, equals 5 percent per six months, in this example), multiplied by the recorded book value of the liability at the beginning of the interest period. For example, interest expense for the period from July 1, Year 1, to December 31, Year 1, the first six-month period, is $5,386 (= 0.05 × $107,721). The bond indenture requires the borrower to pay $6,000 (= 0.06 × $100,000) on January 1, Year 2. This amount equals the coupon rate times the face value of the bonds. The difference between the payment of $6,000 and the interest expense of $5,386 reduces the amount of the liability. The journal entry made on December 31, Year 1, to recognize interest for the last six months of Year 1 follows:

12/31/Year 1	Retained Earnings (Interest Expense) (Shareholders' Equity Decrease)	5,386	
	Debenture Bonds Payable (Liability Decrease)	614	
	Interest Payable (Liability Increase)		6,000
	To recognize interest expense for six months.		

The Interest Payable account appears as a current liability on the balance sheet at the end of Year 1. Debenture Bonds Payable has a new balance of $107,107 (= $107,721 − $614), which appears as a noncurrent liability.

On January 1, Year 2, the borrower makes the first periodic cash payment and the following entry:

1/1/Year 2	Interest Payable (Liability Decrease)	6,000	
	Cash (Asset Decrease)		6,000
	To record payment of interest for six months.		

Interest expense for the second six months (from January 1, Year 2, through June 30, Year 2) equals $5,355 (= 0.05 × $107,107). Because the amount of the liability has declined from the beginning of the preceding period to the beginning of the current period, the amount of interest expense for the period declines from $5,386 for the first six months, and the borrower records it as follows:

6/30/Year 2	Retained Earnings (Interest Expense) (Shareholders' Equity Decrease)	5,355	
	Debenture Bonds Payable (Liability Decrease)	645	
	Interest Payable (Liability Increase)		6,000
	To recognize interest expense for six months.		

An amortization schedule for these bonds over their five-year life appears in **Exhibit 9.4**. Column **(3)** shows the periodic interest expense, and column **(6)** shows the book value that appears on the balance sheet at the end of the period.

The effective interest method of recognizing interest expense on a bond has the following financial statement effects:

1. Interest expense on the income statement equals a constant percentage of the recorded liability at the beginning of each interest period. This percentage equals the market interest rate when the borrower first issued the bonds. When the borrower issues bonds for more than par value, the dollar amount of interest expense will decrease each period as the unpaid liability decreases to the amount to be paid at maturity.

2. On the balance sheet at the end of each period, the bonds will appear at the present value of the remaining cash flows discounted at the market interest rate when the borrower initially issued the bonds. For example, on July 1, Year 2, just after the borrower has made the coupon payment, the remaining cash payments have present value computed as follows:

(a) Present Value of $100,000 to Be Paid at the End of Four Years	$ 67,684

(Table 2 shows the present value of $1 to be paid at the end of eight periods discounted at 5 percent to be $0.67684; $100,000 × 0.67684 = $67,684.)

(b) Present Value of Eight Remaining Semiannual Interest Payments Discounted at 10 Percent, Compounded Semiannually	38,779

(Table 4 shows the present value of an ordinary annuity of $1 per period for eight periods discounted at 5 percent to be $6.46321; $6,000 × 6.46321 = $38,779.)

Total Present Value	$106,463

The amount $106,462, different because of rounding effects, appears in column **(6)** of **Exhibit 9.4** for the liability at the end of the second six-month period.

Problem 9.5 for Self-Study

Preparing journal entries to account for bonds. Refer to **Problem 9.4 for Self-Study**. Prepare the journal entries on January 1, June 30, and December 31, Year 1, to account for the bonds, assuming each of the following market-required interest rates at the time the firm issued the bonds:

a. 8 percent compounded semiannually
b. 10 percent compounded semiannually
c. 12 percent compounded semiannually

Bond Retirement Many bonds remain outstanding until the stated maturity date. Refer to **Exhibit 9.3**, where Macaulay Corporation issued the 12-percent coupon bonds to yield 14 percent. The company pays the final coupon, $6,000, and the face amount, $100,000, on the stated maturity date. The entries are as follows:

7/1/Year 6	Retained Earnings (Interest Expense) (Shareholders' Equity Decrease)	6,936	
	Cash (Asset Decrease)		6,000
	Debenture Bonds Payable (Liability Increase)		936
	See row for Period 10 of **Exhibit 9.3**.		
	Debenture Bonds Payable (Liability Decrease)	100,000	
	Cash (Asset Decrease)		100,000
	To record retirement at maturity of bonds.		

Retirement before Maturity A firm sometimes purchases its own bonds on the open market before maturity. Because market interest rates constantly change, the purchase price will seldom equal the recorded book value of the bonds. Assume that Macaulay Corporation originally issued its 12-percent coupon bonds to yield 14 percent compounded semiannually. Assume that three years later, on June 30, Year 4, interest rates in the marketplace have increased so that the market currently requires Macaulay Corporation to pay a 15-percent interest rate. Refer to **Table 6** in the appendix at the back of the book, 2-year row, 15-percent column; there you see that 12-percent bonds with two years until maturity sell in the marketplace for 94.9760 percent of par when the current interest rate is 15 percent compounded semiannually.

The principles of historical cost accounting do not constrain the pricing of bonds in the marketplace. Even though Macaulay Corporation shows Debenture Bonds Payable on the balance sheet at $96,612 (see row for Period 6 of **Exhibit 9.3**), the marketplace puts a price of only $94,976 on the entire bond issue. From the point of view of the marketplace, these bonds are the same as two-year bonds issued on June 30, Year 4, at an effective yield of 15 percent, so they carry a discount of $5,024 (= $100,000 − $94,976).

If on June 30, Year 4, Macaulay Corporation purchased $10,000 of par value of its own bonds, it would have to pay only $9,498 (= 0.94976 × $10,000) for those bonds, which have a book value of $9,661. Macaulay would make the following journal entries at the time of purchase:

6/30/Year 4	Retained Earnings (Interest Expense) (Shareholders' Equity Decrease)	6,713	
	Interest Payable (Liability Increase)		6,000
	Debenture Bonds Payable (Liability Increase)		713
	See row for Period 6 of **Exhibit 9.3**.		
	Interest Payable (Liability Decrease)	6,000	
	Cash (Asset Decrease)		6,000
	To record payment of coupons, as usual.		
	Debenture Bonds Payable (Liability Decrease)	9,661	
	Cash (Asset Decrease)		9,498
	Retained Earnings (Gain on Retirement of Bonds) (Shareholders' Equity Increase)		163
	To record purchase of bonds for less than the current amount shown in the accounting records.		

Historical cost accounting calls the entry to make debits equal credits in recording the retirement a *gain*. This gain arises because the firm can retire a liability recorded at one amount, $9,661, for a smaller cash payment, $9,498. The borrower earned this gain as interest rates increased between Year 1 and Year 4. Historical cost accounting reports the gain in the period when the borrower realizes it—that is, in the period when the borrower retires the bonds. This phenomenon parallels the economic events that occur when a firm invests in land, holds the land as its value increases, sells the land in a subsequent year, and reports all the gain in the year of sale. The phenomenon results from the historical cost accounting convention of recording amounts at historical cost and not recording increases in wealth until the firm realizes those increases in arm's-length transactions with outsiders.

A Quality-of-Earnings Issue   During recent years, interest rates have increased from their levels a few years earlier. Many companies had issued bonds at prices near par, with coupon rates of only 3 or 4 percent per year. When interest rates increased, these bonds traded in the market for substantial discounts from face value. Companies can repurchase their own bonds, recording substantial gains in the process. (In one year, an airline reported profits after seven consecutive years of losses. The airline, now bankrupt, had gains on bond retirement that year in excess of the entire amount of reported net income.) Such gains do not form part of high-quality earnings because of their nonrecurring nature.

Serial Bonds   The bond indenture may require the issuing firm to make a provision for partial early retirement of the bond issue. Such requirements generally take one of two forms. One, for serial bonds, provides that stated portions of the principal amount will come due on a series of maturity dates. The DaimlerChrysler Corporation bonds in **Example 16** are serial bonds.

Sinking Fund Bonds   The other major type of partial early retirement provision in bond indentures requires the firm to accumulate a fund of cash or other assets to use to pay the bonds when the maturity date arrives or to reacquire and retire portions of the bond issue. Financial terminology refers to these funds as **sinking funds**, although *bond retirement funds* would be more descriptive. The trustee of the bond issue usually holds the assets of the sinking fund. The fund appears on the balance sheet of the borrower as a noncurrent asset in the Investments section.

Right of Offset.   Why do we show the sinking fund of the preceding paragraph as an asset separate from the liability that the firm will pay off with the fund of cash? To take a concrete example, assume a firm with outstanding bonds of $100 million, appearing as a liability, and a $60 million fund of cash, appearing as an asset in a separate fund. The firm plans to use the cash to pay off part of the bond debt. One might think that a superior financial disclosure on the balance sheet would be to show only the net liability of $40 (= $100 − $60) million. Managers prefer to offset liabilities with cash funds, such as this. To understand why, think about the effect on the debt-equity ratio of reducing liabilities and assets by the same amount: the debt-equity ratio will decline and the firm will appear less risky.[6] Standard setters are aware of managers' wish to

---

[6] Firms with assets greater than liabilities, that is, all solvent firms, have debt-equity ratios less than 1.0. When we subtract equal amounts from the numerator and denominator of a fraction less than 1.0, the fraction gets smaller; refer to footnote **7** in **Chapter 5**, on page 207.

offset liabilities with assets. GAAP allow it only in the rare case when the asset has a contractual right of offset, that is the borrower owes the lender and the lender owes the borrower and each agrees the other can offset the two items to discharge the debts. That is, the asset must be a receivable from the lender to whom the firm owes an offsetting liability and the asset specifically gives its holder the right to use the asset to discharge the liability. A firm can use some bonds issued by the U.S. Treasury, which it holds as assets, to pay U.S. income tax obligations, and if the firm holds such bonds, it can use the bonds to offset liabilities for income taxes payable.

Refunded Bonds   Most bond indentures make no provision for **bond refunding**, that is, for making serial repayments or for accumulating sinking funds for bond retirement. The market judges these bonds to be protected with property held by trustees as collateral or with the high credit standing of the issuer. In such cases, the borrower may pay the entire bond liability at maturity out of cash in the bank at that time. Quite commonly, however, the firm refunds the bond issue. That is, it issues a new set of bonds to obtain the funds to retire the old ones when they come due. Accounting records the issue of the new bonds and the retirement of the old bonds as separate transactions.

Callable Bonds   A common provision gives the issuing company the option to retire portions of the bond issue before maturity if it so desires, but the provision does not require the company to do so. To facilitate such reacquisition and retirement of the bonds, the bond indenture provides that the bonds be *callable*. That is, the issuing company has the right, but not the obligation, to reacquire its bonds before stated maturity at prices specified in the bond indenture. When the borrower calls the bonds, the trustee will not immediately pay a subsequent coupon presented for redemption. Rather, the trustee will notify the holder to present all remaining coupons and the bond principal for payments equal to the call price plus accrued interest.

The indenture usually sets the **call price** initially higher than the par value and provides a declining schedule for the call price as the maturity date approaches. Because the borrower may exercise the call provision at a time when the coupon rate exceeds the market interest rate, the market usually prices callable bonds at something less than the price of otherwise similar but noncallable bonds.

Assume, for example, that a firm issued 12-percent semiannual coupon bonds at a discount, implying a borrowing rate higher than 12 percent. Later, market interest rates and the firm's credit standing allow it to borrow at 10 percent. Assume the borrower has recorded all accrued interest expense and the bonds have a current book value of $98,000, including accrued interest. If the borrower calls $100,000 of par value of these bonds at 105 percent of par, the entry would be as follows:

Debenture Bonds Payable (Liability Decrease)	98,000	
Retained Earnings (Loss on Retirement of Bonds) (Shareholders' Equity Decrease)	7,000	
Cash		105,000
To record bonds called and retired.		

The market rate of interest that a firm must pay to borrow depends on two factors: the general level of interest rates and its own creditworthiness. If the market rate of interest has risen since the borrower issued the bonds (or if the firm's credit rating has declined), the bonds will sell in the market at less than issue price. A firm that wanted to retire such bonds would not call them because the call price would typically exceed the face value. Instead the firm would probably purchase its bonds on the open market and realize a gain on the bonds' retirement.

Unifying Principles of Accounting for Long-Term Liabilities

Long-term liabilities obligate the borrowing firm to pay specified amounts at definite times more than one year in the future. We now state a single set of principles to describe the balance sheet presentation of all long-term liabilities and a single procedure for computing that amount and the amount of interest expense. First, we describe the amounts on the balance sheet, a "state description" (like a blueprint). Then, we describe the process for computing the amounts, a "process description" (like a recipe).

State Description   All long-term liabilities appear on the balance sheet at the present value of the remaining future payments. The present value computations use the historical rate of interest—the market interest rate on the date the borrower incurred the obligation.

Process Description   The methods of computing balance sheet amounts for all long-term liabilities and their related expenses embody identical concepts and follow the same procedures:

1. Record the liability at the cash (or cash equivalent) value received. This amount equals the present value of the future contractual payments discounted using the market interest rate for the borrower on the date the loan begins. (Sometimes the borrower must compute the original issue market interest rate by finding the internal rate of return. See the **Appendix** at the back of the book.)
2. At any subsequent time when the firm makes a cash payment or an adjusting entry for interest, it computes interest expense as the book value of the liability at the beginning of the interest period (which includes any interest added in prior periods) multiplied by the historical interest rate. The accountant debits this amount to Interest Expense and credits it to the liability account. If the firm makes a cash payment, the accountant debits the liability accounts and credits Cash.

The effect will change the book value of the liabilities to a number closer to par value (or leave the amount at par if book value already equals par value) for the start of the next period. If the accountant follows these procedures, the liabilities on the balance sheet will always satisfy the state description above. The liabilities will have book value equal to the present value of the remaining future payments discounted at the historical market interest rate.

Amortization schedules, such as in **Exhibits 9.2**, **9.3**, **9.4**, **9.5**, and **10.1** (in **Chapter 10**), illustrate this unchanging procedure for a variety of long-term liabilities. The next problem for self-study focuses on the procedure.

Problem 9.6 for Self-Study

Unifying principles of accounting for long-term liabilities.   This problem illustrates the unifying principles of accounting for long-term liabilities described just above. Assume that a firm closes its books once per year, making adjusting entries once per year. On the date the firm borrows, the market requires it to pay interest at the rate of 10 percent per year, compounded annually for all loans spanning a two-year period. Note the following steps:

1. Compute the initial issue proceeds received by the firm issuing the obligation (that is, borrowing the cash) on the date of issue.
2. Give the journal entry for issue of the liability and receipt of cash.
3. Show the journal entry or entries for interest accrual and cash payment, if any, at the end of the first year, and re-compute the book value of all liabilities related to the borrowing at the end of the first year. Combine the liability accounts for the main borrowing and accrued interest into a single account called Monetary Liability.
4. Show the journal entry or entries for interest accrual and cash payment at the end of the second year, and re-compute the book value of all liabilities related to the borrowing at the end of the second year.

Perform the above steps for each of the following borrowings:

a. The firm issues a single-payment note on the first day of the first year, promising to pay $1,000 on the last day of the second year.
b. The firm issues a 10-percent annual coupon bond, promising to pay $100 on the last day of the first year and $1,100 (= $1,000 + $100) on the last day of the second year.
c. The firm issues an 8-percent annual coupon bond, promising to pay $80 on the last day of the first year and $1,080 (= $1,000 + $80) on the last day of the second year.
d. The firm issues a 12-percent annual coupon bond, promising to pay $120 on the last day of the first year and $1,120 (= $1,000 + $120) on the last day of the second year.
e. The firm issues a level-payment note (like a mortgage or installment note), promising to pay $576.19 on the last day of the first year and another $576.19 on the last day of the second year.

A liability obligates a firm to make a (probable) future sacrifice of resources. The firm can estimate the amount of that obligation and its timing with reasonable certainty. The transaction causing the obligation has already occurred; in other words, the obligation arises from other than an executory contract.

Accounting initially records long-term liabilities at the cash-equivalent value the borrower receives (which equals the present value of the future cash flows the borrower promises, discounted at the market interest rate for that borrower at the time of issue). As the maturity date of the liability draws near, the book value of the liability approaches the amount of the final cash payment. To compute interest expense throughout the accounting life of the liability, historical cost accounting uses the borrower's market interest rate on the date the borrower incurred the liability. Interest expense for any period is the book value of the liability at the start of the period multiplied by the historical interest rate.

Borrowers retire liabilities in different ways. In each case, the borrower debits the liability retired for its book value, credits the asset given up, and recognizes gain or loss on retirement.

Appendix 9.1: Effects on the Statement of Cash Flows of Transactions Involving Long-Term Liabilities

Because expenditures for interest do not usually equal interest expense, and debt service payments sometimes discharge principal as well as interest, you need to think about how the transactions for long-term liabilities affect the statement of cash flows.

Interest Expense Exceeds Debt Service Payments—Example is Bonds Issued for Less than Par

Here, interest expense exceeds debt service payments, that is, coupon payments for a bond issue. Refer to **Exhibit 9.3** for the first period. Interest expense reported for the first six months is $6,508 (= $6,000 in coupon payments and $508 in increased principal amount). Notice that the borrower used only $6,000 of cash for the expense. Liabilities increased by $6,508. A cash payment of $6,000 followed. The remainder of the interest expense, $508, increased the noncurrent liability Debenture Bonds Payable.

Direct Method of Computing Cash Flows from Operations. The entire coupon payment of $6,000, paid in cash, discharged part of interest expense of $6,508, which exceeds the amount of the coupon payments. Hence, the expenditure for interest expense equals the coupon payments of $6,000.

Indirect Method of Computing Cash Flows from Operations. When the firm uses the indirect method, interest expense has already reduced the beginning number, net income, in the example, by $6,508. So, in deriving cash flows from operations, we add back the part of the expense, $508, which did not use cash.

The principles here apply to all long-term debt where interest expense exceeds debt service payments.

Debt Service Payments Exceed Interest Expense—Example is Bonds Issued for More than Par

Here, expenditures for debt service, the coupons of a bond issue, exceed interest expense. Refer to **Exhibit 9.4** for the first period of a bond issued at a premium. Interest expense reported for the first six months is $5,386 (= $6,000 in coupon payments reduced by $614 which pays back part of the borrowed principal). The borrower used only $5,386 for interest expense, although it paid $6,000 in cash. Cash flow from operations goes down by $5,386 and Financing uses of cash to discharge debt increases by $614. (In practice, some accountants ignore this distinction and show all the cash expenditure as operating. We do not illustrate this practice in this text as it is conceptually wrong, and therefore harder to understand.[7])

Direct Method of Computing Cash Flows from Operations.
The operating expenditure is the amount of interest expense, $5,386. The remainder of the expenditure of cash, $614, appears as a Financing use of cash, to reduce the principal amount of the debt.

Indirect Method of Computing Cash Flows from Operations.
Income has already been reduced by interest expense of $5,386. The rest of the expenditure, $614, appears, just as above, in the Financing use of cash, to reduce the principal amount of the debt.

The principles here apply to all long-term debt where debt service payments exceed interest expense.

Gain or Loss on Debt Retirement

When a firm retires debt for cash, it reports the cash expenditure in the Financing section as a nonoperating use, Cash Used to Reduce Debt. In most cases, the amount of cash the firm uses to retire a liability differs from the book value of the liability at the time of retirement. Thus, the retirement generates a gain (when book value exceeds cash used) or a loss (when cash used exceeds book value).

The Financing section of the statement shows all the cash used to retire the liability; that use of cash had nothing to do with operations. When the statement of cash flows presents cash from operations with the indirect format, the computation starts with net income. That figure includes the gain or loss on the repurchase of the liability. Because the repurchase is a financing, not an operating, use of cash, the accountant subtracts the amount of the gain or adds back the amount of the loss in deriving operating cash flows. See line **(4)**, for addition of the loss, and line **(5)**, for the subtraction of the gain, of **Exhibit 4.12**.

Solutions to Self-Study Problems

SUGGESTED SOLUTION TO PROBLEM 9.1 FOR SELF-STUDY
(Ashton Corporation; journal entries for transactions involving current liabilities.)

a. January 2

Cash (Asset Increase)	10,000	
Note Payable (Liability Increase)		10,000

To record 90-day, 9-percent bank loan.

b. January 3

Merchandise Inventory (Asset Increase)	8,000	
Accounts Payable (Liability Increase)		8,000

To record purchases of merchandise on account.

c. January 10

Cash (Asset Increase)	1,500	
Advances from Customer (Liability Increase)		1,500

To record advance from customer on merchandise scheduled for delivery in February.

d. Month of January

Accounts Receivable (Asset Increase)	12,000	
Retained Earnings (Sales Revenue) (Shareholders' Equity Increase) . .		12,000

To record sales on account during January.

Retained Earnings (Cost of Goods Sold) (Shareholders' Equity Decrease)	6,000	
Merchandise Inventory (Asset Decrease)		6,000

To record the cost of merchandise sold.

---

[7] We think this practice stems from accountants' not being clear in their distinctions between interest payments, debt service payments, and interest expense.

e. Month of January

Accounts Payable (Liability Decrease)	8,000	
Cash (Asset Decrease)		8,000

To record payments to suppliers for purchases on account.

Cash (Asset Increase)	7,000	
Accounts Receivable (Asset Decrease)		7,000

To record collections from customers for sales on account.

f. January 31

Retained Earnings (Warranty Expense) (Shareholders' Equity Decrease)	960	
Estimated Warranty Liability (Liability Increase)		960

To record estimated warranty cost for goods sold during January; $0.08 \times \$12,000 = \$960$.

g. January 31

Retained Earnings (Wages Expense) (Shareholders' Equity Decrease)	4,000	
U.S. Withholding Taxes Payable (Liability Increase)		800
Social Security Taxes Payable (Liability Increase)		400
Withheld Union Dues Payable (Liability Increase)		200
Wages Payable (Liability Increase)		2,600

To record January wages net of taxes and union dues withheld.

Retained Earnings (Wages Expense) (Shareholders' Equity Decrease)	540	
Social Security Taxes Payable (Liability Increase)		400
Unemployment Taxes Payable (Liability Increase)		140

To record employer's share of payroll taxes.

h. January 31

Retained Earnings (Interest Expense) (Shareholders' Equity Decrease)	75	
Interest Payable (Liability Increase)		75

To record interest expense on notes payable for January; $\$10,000 \times 0.09 \times 30/360 = \$75$.

i. January 31

Retained Earnings (Income Tax Expense) (Shareholders' Equity Decrease) .	170	
Income Tax Payable (Liability Increase)		170

To accrue income taxes payable for January: $0.40 \times (\$12,000 - \$6,000 - \$960 - \$4,000 - \$540 - \$75) = \$170$.

j. February 1

Wages Payable (Liability Decrease)	2,600	
Cash (Asset Decrease)		2,600

To pay employees their January wages net of withholdings.

k. February 10

Advances from Customers (Liability Decrease)	1,500	
Retained Earnings (Sales Revenue) (Shareholders' Equity Increase) ..		1,500

To record the sale of merchandise to customer.

Retained Earnings (Cost of Goods Sold) (Shareholders' Equity Decrease)	800	
Merchandise Inventory (Asset Decrease)		800

To record the cost of merchandise sold.

l. February 15

U.S. Withholding Taxes Payable (Liability Decrease)	800	
Social Security Taxes Payable (Liability Decrease)	800	
Unemployment Taxes Payable (Liability Decrease)	140	
Withheld Union Dues Payable (Liability Decrease)	200	
Cash (Asset Decrease)		1,940

To record payment of payroll taxes and union dues.

m. February 20

Estimated Warranty Liability (Liability Decrease)	220	
Cash (Asset Decrease)		220

To record the cost of warranty repairs on products sold during January.

SUGGESTED SOLUTION TO PROBLEM 9.2 FOR SELF-STUDY

(Sapra Company; accounting for an interest-bearing note.)
a. See **Exhibit 9.5**.

EXHIBIT 9.5	Amortization Schedule for Note with Face Value of $100,000 Issued for $112,434, Bearing Interest at the Rate of 15 Percent of Face Value per Year, Issued to Yield 10 Percent (Problem 9.2 for Self-Study)

Yearly Periods (1)	Loan Balance Start of Period (2)	Interest Expense for Period (3)	Payment (4)	Portion of Payment Reducing Book Value of Liability (5)	Loan Balance End of Period (6)
0					$112,434
1	$112,434	$11,243	$ 15,000	$ 3,757	108,677
2	108,677	10,868	15,000	4,132	104,545
3	104,545	10,455	115,000	104,545	0

Column (2) = column (6) from previous period.
Column (3) = 0.10 × column (2).
Column (4) is given.
Column (5) = column (4) − column (3).
Column (6) = column (2) − column (5).

b. **Date of Issue**

Cash (Asset Increase)	112,434	
Note Payable (Liability Increase)		112,434

Proceeds of issue of note.

Six Months after Issue

Retained Earnings (Interest Expense) (Shareholders' Equity Decrease)	5,622	
Interest Payable (Liability Increase)		5,622

See **Exhibit 9.5**; accrual of six months' interest = $11,243/2.

One Year after Issue

Retained Earnings (Interest Expense) (Shareholders' Equity Decrease)	5,621	
Interest Payable (Liability Decrease)	5,622	
Note Payable (Liability Decrease)	3,757	
Cash (Asset Decrease)		15,000

Interest expense for the remainder of the first year and cash payment made. Excess of cash payment over interest expense reduces note principal.

SUGGESTED SOLUTION TO PROBLEM 9.3 FOR SELF-STUDY

(Bens Company; accounting for note with imputed interest rate.)

a.

Truck (Asset Increase)	22,500	
Note Payable (Liability Increase)		22,500

0.90 × $25,000 = $22,500.

b. $28,730/$22,500 = 1.27689$. The truck has fair market value of $22,500 (= 0.90 \times $25,000)$; $(1 + r)^2 = 1.27689$, which implies that $r = \sqrt{1.27689} - 1.00 = 0.13$, or 13 percent per year. In other words, $22,500 grows to $28,730 in two years when the interest rate is 13 percent per period.

c. Truck (Asset Increase)	22,903	
Note Payable (Liability Increase)		22,903
$(1.12)^{-2} = 0.79719; 0.79719 \times 28,730 = $22,903.$		

d. $(1.01)^{-24} = 0.78757$. (See **Table 2** at the end of the book, 24-period row, 1-percent column.) $0.78757 \times $28,730 = $22,627$.

Truck (Asset Increase)	22,627	
Note Payable (Liability Increase)		22,627

e. Truck (Asset Increase)	23,744	
Note Payable (Liability Increase)		23,744
Year 1:		
Retained Earnings [Interest Expense (= $0.10 \times $23,744$)] (Shareholders' Equity Decrease)	2,374	
Note Payable (Liability Increase)		2,374
Year 2:		
Retained Earnings {Interest Expense [= $0.10 \times ($23,744 + $2,374$)]} (Shareholders' Equity Decrease)	2,612	
Note Payable (Liability Increase)		2,612
Balance in Note Payable Account at End of Year 2		$28,730

f. Total expense equals interest expense on the note plus depreciation on the truck. Interest expense is $28,730 less the amount at which the firm records the truck. Depreciation expense is equal to the amount at which Bens records the truck less estimated salvage value. Thus, over the life of the truck or two years, whichever is longer, the total expense equals $28,730 less the salvage value of the truck.

SUGGESTED SOLUTION TO PROBLEM 9.4 FOR SELF-STUDY

(Engel Corporation; calculating the issue price of bonds.)

a.

Required Cash Flows	Present Value Factor for 8 Percent Interest Rate Compounded Semiannually for 10 Years	Present Value of Required Cash Flows
$1,000,000 at end of 10 years	0.45639[a]	456,390
$50,000 every six months for 10 years	13.59033[b]	679,516
Issue Price		$1,135,906

[a]Table 2, 4-percent column and 20-period row.
[b]Table 4, 4-percent column and 20-period row.

b.

Required Cash Flows	Present Value Factor for 10 Percent Interest Rate Compounded Semiannually for 10 Years	Present Value of Required Cash Flows
$1,000,000 at end of 10 years	0.37689[a]	$376,890
$50,000 every six months for 10 years	12.46221[b]	623,110
Issue Price		$1,000,000

[a]Table 2, 5-percent column and 20-period row.
[b]Table 4, 5-percent column and 20-period row.

c.

Required Cash Flows	Present Value Factor for 12 Percent Interest Rate Compounded Semiannually for 10 Years	Present Value of Required Cash Flows
$1,000,000 at end of 10 years	0.31180[a]	$311,800
$50,000 every six months for 10 years	11.46992[b]	573,496
Issue Price		$885,296

[a]Table 2, 6-percent column and 20-period row.
[b]Table 4, 6-percent column and 20-period row.

SUGGESTED SOLUTION TO PROBLEM 9.5 FOR SELF-STUDY

(Engel Corporation; preparing journal entries to account for bonds.)

a. January 1

Cash (Asset Increase)	1,135,906	
Bonds Payable (Liability Increase)		1,135,906

To record issue of $1,000,000-par value, 10-percent semiannual coupon bonds priced to yield 8 percent compounded semiannually.

June 30

Retained Earnings (Interest Expense) (Shareholders' Equity Decrease) = 0.04 × 1,135,906	45,436	
Bonds Payable (Liability Decrease)	4,564	
Cash (Asset Decrease) = 0.05 × $1,000,000		50,000

To record interest expense and amount paid for first six months.

December 31

Retained Earnings (Interest Expense) (Shareholders' Equity Decrease) = 0.04 × ($1,135,906 − $4,564)	45,254	
Bonds Payable (Liability Decrease)	4,746	
Cash (Asset Decrease) = 0.05 × $1,000,000		50,000

To record interest expense and amount payable for second six months.

b. January 1

Cash (Asset Increase)	1,000,000	
Bonds Payable (Liability Increase)		1,000,000

To record issue of $1,000,000-par value, 10-percent semiannual coupon bonds priced to yield 10 percent compounded semiannually.

June 30

Retained Earnings (Interest Expense) (Shareholders' Equity Decrease) = 0.05 × $1,000,000	50,000	
Cash (Asset Decrease) = 0.05 × $1,000,000		50,000

To record interest expense and amount paid for first six months.

December 31

Retained Earnings (Interest Expense) (Shareholders' Equity
   Decrease) = 0.05 × $1,000,000   50,000

    Cash (Asset Decrease) = 0.05 = $1,000,000   50,000

To record interest expense and amount paid for second six months.

c. January 1

Cash (Asset Increase)   885,296

    Bonds Payable (Liability Increase)   885,296

To record issue of $1,000,000-par value, 10-percent semiannual coupon
bonds priced to yield 12 percent compounded semiannually.

June 30

Retained Earnings (Interest Expense) (Shareholders' Equity
   Decrease) = 0.06 × $885,296   53,118

    Cash (Asset Decrease) = 0.05 × $1,000,000   50,000

    Bonds Payable (Liability Increase)   3,118

To record interest expense and amount paid for first six months.

December 30

Retained Earnings (Interest Expense) (Shareholders' Equity
   Decrease) = 0.06 × ($885,296 + $3,118)   53,305

    Cash (Asset Decrease) = 0.05 × $1,000,000   50,000

    Bonds Payable (Liability Increase)   3,305

To record interest expense and amount payable for second six months.

SUGGESTED SOLUTION TO PROBLEM 9.6 FOR SELF-STUDY

(Unifying principles of accounting for long-term liabilities.)

    Exhibit 9.6 shows the accounting for five types of long-term monetary liabilities stated at the present value of future cash flows in columns labeled **a.** through **e.** The accounting for each of these monetary liabilities follows a common procedure.

	EXHIBIT 9.6	Accounting for Long-term Monetary Liabilities Based on the Present Value of Future Cash Flows (Problem 9.6 for Self-Study)

	a. Single-Payment Note of $1,000 Maturing in Two Years			b. Two-Year Annual Coupon Bond—10 Percent ($100) Coupons		
	Amount	Dr.	Cr.	Amount	Dr.	Cr.
(1) Compute Present Value of Future Contractual Payments Using Historical Interest Rate on Day Monetary Liability is First Recorded. Rate is 10.0 Percent.						
(a) 1 Year Hence	$ 0			$ 100.00		
(b) 2 Years Hence	$1,000.00			$1,100.00		
Multiply Payment by Present Value Factors (Table 2).						
0.90909 × (a)	$ 0			$ 90.91		
0.82645 × (b)	826.45			909.09		
(c) Total Present Value	$ 826.45			$1,000.00		
(2) Record Initial Liability and Cash or Other Assets Received from Step 1.						
Cash or Other Assets (Assets Increase)		826.45			1,000.00	
Monetary Liability (Liability Increase) ..			826.45			1,000.00
(3) First Recording (payment date or end of period): End of First Year						
(a) Compute Interest Expense as Monetary Liability × Historical Interest Rate.						
Amount on Line 1(c) × 0.10	$ 82.64			$ 100.00		
(b) Record Interest Expense.						
Retained Earnings (Interest Expense) (Shareholders' Equity Decrease)		82.64			100.00	
Monetary Liability (Liability Increase)			82.64			100.00
(c) Record Cash Payment (if any).						
Monetary Liability (Liability Decrease) .		—			100.00	
Cash (Asset Decrease)			—			100.00
(d) Compute Book Value of Monetary Liability.						
Beginning Balance	$ 826.45			$1,000.00		
Add Interest Expense	82.64			100.00		
Subtotal	$ 909.09			$1,100.00		
Subtract Cash Payment (if any)	—			(100.00)		
= Ending Balance	$ 909.09			$1,000.00		
(4) Second Recording: End of Second Year						
(a) Compute Interest Expense as Monetary Liability × Historical Interest Rate.						
Amount on Line 3(d) × 0.10	$ 90.91			$ 100.00		
(b) Record Interest Expense						
Retained Earnings (Interest Expense) (Shareholders' Equity Decrease)		90.91			100.00	
Monetary Liability (Liability Increase) .			90.91			100.00
(c) Record Cash Payment (if any).						
Monetary Liability (Liability Decrease) .		1,000.00			1,100.00	
Cash (Asset Decrease)			1,000.00			1,100.00
(d) Compute Book Value of Monetary Liability.						
Beginning Balance	$ 909.09			$1,000.00		
Add Interest Expense	90.91			100.00		
Subtotal	$1,000.00			$1,100.00		
Subtract Cash Payment (if any)	(1,000.00)			(1,100.00)		
= Ending Balance	$ 0			$ 0		

c. Two-Year Annual Coupon Bond—8 Percent ($80) Coupons			d. Two-Year Annual Coupon Bond—12 Percent ($120) Coupons			e. Two-Year Level-Payment Note— Annual Payments of $576.19		
Amount	Dr.	Cr.	Amount	Dr.	Cr.	Amount	Dr.	Cr.
$ 80.00			$ 120.00			$ 576.19		
$1,080.00			$1,120.00			$ 576.19		
$72.73			$ 109.09			$ 523.81		
892.57			925.62			476.19		
$ 965.30			$1,034.71			$1,000.00		
	965.30			1,034.71			1,000.00	
		965.30			1,034.71			1,000.00
$ 96.53			$ 103.47			$ 100.00		
	96.53			103.47			100.00	
		96.53			103.47			100.00
	80.00			120.00			576.19	
		80.00			120.00			576.19
$ 965.30			$1,034.71			$1,000.00		
96.53			103.47			100.00		
$1,061.83			$1,138.18			$1,100.00		
(80.00)			(120.00)			(576.19)		
$ 981.83			$1,018.18			$ 523.81		
$ 98.18			$ 101.82			$ 52.38		
	98.18			101.82			52.38	
		98.18			101.82			52.38
	1,080.00			1,120.00			576.19	
		1,080.00			1,120.00			576.19
$ 981.83			$1,018.18			$ 523.81		
98.18			101.82			52.38		
$1,080.01			1,120.00			$ 576.19		
(1,080.00)			(1,120.00)			(576.19)		
$0[a]			$ 0			$ 0		

[a]Rounding error of $0.01.

1. Compute the initial amount of cash received by the borrower as well as the historical interest rate. Sometimes you will know both of these. Sometimes you will know the cash received and you must calculate the interest rate. Sometimes, as **Exhibit 9.6** illustrates in all five cases, you will know the interest rate and must compute the initial cash received.

   a. To compute the initial amount of cash received, given the contractual payments and the market interest rate, multiply each of the contractual payments by the present value factor (as from **Table 2** at the back of the book) for a single payment of $1 to be received in the future. **Exhibit 9.6** shows the present value factors at 10-percent interest for payments to be received in 1 year (0.90909) and in 2 years (0.82645).

   b. Computing the market interest rate, given the initial cash proceeds and the series of contractual payments, requires finding the *internal rate of return* of the series of cash flows. The Appendix at the back of the book illustrates this process. **Exhibit 9.6** shows that only the 10-percent coupon bond and the level-payment note have initial cash proceeds equal to $1,000. The difference in amounts arises because each of the items has a different present value, in spite of the fact that some people might, loosely speaking, call each a "$1,000 liability."

2. Record a journal entry debiting cash and crediting the monetary liability with the amount of cash received. This presentation showing the common theme uses the generic account title Monetary Liability, although in practice a firm would use more descriptive titles.

3. At every contractual payment date and at the end of an accounting period, compute interest expense as the book value of the liability at the beginning of the period (which includes the principal liability account and the Interest Payable account if the firm keeps these amounts in separate accounts) multiplied by the historical interest rate. Debit the computed amount to interest expense and credit the liability account.

   If the borrower makes a cash payment, credit cash and debit the liability. The book value of the liability is now equal to the beginning balance plus interest expense recorded less cash payments made, if any.

   Exhibit 9.6 does not illustrate this fact directly, but if you were to return to **step 1** at this point and compute the present value of the remaining contractual payments using the historical interest rate (10 percent in the examples), that present value would equal the book value computed after **step 3**.

4. At each payment date, or at each period-end closing date, repeat **step 3**. Eventually, when the borrower makes the final payment (as illustrated at the bottom of **Exhibit 9.6**), it will have discharged the entire amount of the liability plus interest. The remaining liability is zero. The accounting has amortized the liability to zero at the same time that the firm has extinguished its obligation.

Key Terms and Concepts

Liability	Coupon bonds
Executory contract	Debenture bonds
Estimated liability	Convertible bonds
Contingency	Serial bonds
Constructive liability	Zero coupon bonds
Mortgage	Bond tables
Collateral	Effective interest method
Mortgagee, mortgagor	Sinking fund
Implicit interest	Bond refunding
Implicit (imputed) interest rate	Right of offset
Bond indenture	Call price

Questions, Short Exercises, Exercises, Problems, and Cases

QUESTIONS

1. Review the meaning of the terms and concepts listed above in **Key Terms and Concepts**.
2. For each of the following items, indicate whether the item meets all of the criteria of a liability. If so, how does the firm value it?

a. Interest accrued but not paid on a note

b. Advances from customers for goods and services to be delivered later

c. Confirmed orders from customers for goods and services to be delivered later

d. Bonds payable

e. Product warranties

f. Damages the company must pay if it loses a pending lawsuit

g. Future costs of restoring strip-mining sites after completing mining operations

h. Contractual promises to purchase natural gas for each of the next 10 years

i. Promises by an airline to provide free flights in the future if customers accumulate a certain number of miles at regular fares

For additional student resources, content, and interactive quizzes for this chapter visit the FACMU website: **http://facmu.swlearning.com**

3. What is the amount of the liability recognized in each of the independent cases below?

   a. A plaintiff files a lawsuit against a company. The probability is 90 percent that the company will lose. If it loses, the amount of the loss will most likely be $100,000.

   b. A cereal company issues redeemable coupons for "free" boxes of cereal. Now, it issues one million coupons that promise the retailer who redeems the coupons $1 per coupon. The probability of redemption of any one coupon is 9 percent.

4. "Firms should obtain as much financing as possible from suppliers through accounts payable because it is a free source of capital." Do you agree? Why or why not?

5. The Francis W. Parker School, a private lower school, has a reporting year ending June 30. It hires teachers for a 10-month period: September of one year through June of the following year. It contracts to pay teachers in 12 monthly installments over the period September of one year through August of the next year. For the current academic year, suppose that the total contractual salaries to be paid to teachers is $3,600,000. How should the school account for this amount in the financial statements issued June 30, at the end of the academic year?

6. A magazine publisher offers a reduced annual subscription fee if customers pay for three years in advance. Under this subscription program, the magazine publisher receives from customers $45,000, which it credits to the account Advances from Customers. The estimated cost of publishing and distributing magazines for these customers is $32,000. Why does accounting report a liability of $45,000 instead of $32,000?

7. A noted accountant once remarked that the optimal number of faulty TV sets for Sony to sell is "not zero," even if Sony promises to repair all faulty Sony sets that break down, for whatever reason, within two years of purchase. Why could the optimal number be "not zero"?

8. Describe the similarities and differences between the allowance method for uncollectibles (see **Chapter 6**) and the allowance method for estimated warranty costs.

9. What factors determine the amount a firm actually receives when it offers a bond issue to the market?

10. Distinguish between the following sets of terms for bonds. Under what circumstances will they be the same? Under what circumstances will they differ?

    a. Par value and face value

    b. Par value and book value

    c. Book value and current market value

11. "Using the market interest rate at the time of issue to account for bonds in subsequent periods provides a book value for bonds that is consistent with using historical, or acquisition, cost valuations for assets." Explain.

12. If the Deer Valley Ski Association borrows $1,000,000 by issuing, at par, 20-year, 10-percent bonds with semiannual coupons, the total interest expense over the life of the issue is $2,000,000 ($= 20 \times 0.10 \times \$1,000,000$). If Deer Valley undertakes a 20-year mortgage or note with an implicit borrowing rate of 10 percent, the annual payments are $1,000,000/8.51356 = $117,460. (See **Table 4** at the end of the book, 20-period row, 10-percent column.) The total mortgage payments are $2,349,200 ($= 20 \times \$117,460$), and the total interest expense over the life of the note or mortgage is $1,349,200 ($= \$2,349,200 - \$1,000,000$).

    Why are the amounts of interest expense different for these two types of borrowing for the same length of time at identical interest rates?

13. Define *zero coupon bonds*. What are the advantages of a zero coupon bond to the issuer and to the investor?

14. A call premium is the difference between the call price of a bond and its par (face) value. What is the purpose of such a premium?

15. Critics of historical cost accounting for long-term debt argue that the procedures give management unreasonable opportunity to "manage" income with the timing of bond retirements. What phenomenon do these critics have in mind?

SHORT EXERCISES

16. **Recognition of a loss contingency.** While shopping in a store on July 5, Year 6, a customer slips on the floor and sustains back injuries. On January 15, Year 7, the customer sues the store for $1 million. The case comes to trial on April 30, Year 7. The jury renders its verdict on June 15, Year 7, and finds the store liable for negligence. The jury grants a damage award of $400,000 to the customer. The store, on June 25, Year 7, appeals the decision to a higher court on the grounds that the lower court failed to admit certain evidence. The higher court rules on November 1, Year 7, that the trial court should have admitted the evidence. The trial court rehears the case beginning on March 21, Year 8. Another jury, on April 20, Year 8, again finds the store liable for negligence and awards $500,000. On May 15, Year 8, the store pays the $500,000 judgment. When should the store recognize a loss from these events? Explain your reasoning.

17. **Journal entries for payroll.** During the current period, suppose that McGee Associates' office employees earned wages of $700,000. McGee withheld 30 percent of this amount for payments for various income and payroll taxes. In addition, McGee must pay 10 percent of gross wages for the employer's share of various taxes. McGee has promised to contribute 4 percent of gross wages to a profit-sharing fund, which workers will share as they retire. Employees earned vacation pay estimated to be $14,000; estimated fringe benefits are 20 percent of that amount.
    a. Prepare journal entries for these wage-related items.
    b. What is total wage and salary expense?

18. **Allowance method for uncollectibles and warranties.** A firm estimates both uncollectible accounts and warranty repair costs using a percentage of sales. Assume that the combined Bad Debt Expense and Warranty Expense computed with the percentage-of-sales method totals $20,000. At the end of the period, the firm also performs aging analyses of both receivables and outstanding warranty obligations and finds that the implied total expense should be $19,000. What will be the firm's combined bad debt and warranty expense for the year? Explain.

19. **Amortization schedule for note where explicit interest differs from market rate of interest.** Blaydon Company acquires a computer from Orange Computer Company. The cash price (fair market value) of the computer is $36,157. Blaydon Company gives a three-year, interest-bearing note with maturity value of $40,000. The note requires annual interest payments of 8 percent of face value, or $3,200 per year. The interest rate implicit in the note is 12 percent per year.
    a. Prepare an amortization schedule for the note.
    b. Prepare journal entries for Blaydon Company over the life of the note.

20. **Computing the issue price of bonds.** Compute the issue price of each of the following bonds.
    a. $10,000,000-face value, zero coupon bonds due in 20 years, priced on the market to yield 12 percent compounded semiannually.
    b. $10,000,000-face value, serial bonds repayable in equal semiannual installments of $500,000, which includes coupon payments and repayment of principal, for 20 years, priced on the market to yield 6 percent.

21. **Using bond tables; computing interest expense.** Refer to **Table 5** at the back of the book for 10-percent semiannual coupon bonds. On January 1, Year 1, assume that Florida Edison Company issued $1 million face value, 10 percent semiannual coupon bonds maturing in 10 years (on December 31, Year 10) at a price to yield 12 percent per year, compounded semiannually. Use the effective interest method of computing interest expense.
    a. What were the proceeds of the original issue?
    b. What was the interest expense for the first half of Year 1?
    c. What was the interest expense for the second half of Year 1?
    d. What was the book value of the bonds on January 1, Year 6 (when the bonds have five years until maturity)?
    e. What was the interest expense for the first half of Year 6?

22. **Amortization schedule for bonds.** Womack Company issues 10-percent semiannual coupon bonds maturing five years from the date of issue. The coupons, each dated for January 1 and July 1 of each year, promise 5 percent of the face value, 10 percent total for a year. The firm issues the bonds to yield 8 percent, compounded semiannually.
    a. What are the initial issue proceeds received by Womack Company?
    b. Construct an amortization schedule, similar to that in **Exhibit 9.4**, for this bond issue.
    c. Assume that at the end of the third year of the bond's life, Womack Company reacquires $10,000 face value of bonds for 103 percent of par and retires them. Give the journal entry to record the retirement.

EXERCISES

23. **Accounting for uncollectible accounts and warranties.** Hurley Corporation sells household appliances (for example, refrigerators, dishwashers) to customers on account. The firm also provides warranty services on products sold. Hurley *estimates* that 2 percent of sales will ultimately become uncollectible and that warranty costs will equal 6 percent of sales. *Actual* uncollectible accounts and warranty expenditures generally occur within three years of the time of sale. Amounts in selected accounts appear below.

December 31:	Year 8	Year 9	Year 10
Accounts Receivable, net of Allowance for Uncollectible Accounts of $355 on December 31, Year 8, $405 on December 31, Year 9, and $245 on December 31, Year 10	$7,000	$7,750	$6,470
Estimated Warranty Liability	1,325	1,535	1,720

For the Year:	Year 9	Year 10
Sales Revenue	$18,000	$16,000

a. Prepare an analysis that explains the change in the Allowance for Uncollectible Accounts account during Year 9 and Year 10.
b. Prepare an analysis that explains the change in the Estimated Warranty Liability account during Year 9 and Year 10.

24. **Journal entries for coupons.** Morrison's Cafeteria sells coupons that customers may use later to purchase meals. Each coupon book sells for $25 and has a face value of $30; that is, the customer can use the book to purchase meals with menu prices of $30. On January 1, redeemable unused coupons that Morrison's had sold for $4,000 were outstanding. Cash inflows during the next three months appear below:

	January	February	March
Cash-paying Customers	$48,000	$48,500	$50,000
Sale of Coupon Books	2,100	2,200	2,400
Total Cash Receipts	$50,100	$50,700	$52,400

Customers returned coupons with a discounted face value for meals as follows: January, $1,600; February, $2,300; March $2,100.

a. Prepare journal entries for January, February, and March to reflect the above information.
b. What effect, if any, do the coupon sales and redemptions have on the liabilities on the March 31 balance sheet?

25. **Journal entries for service contracts.** Abson Corporation began business on January 1. Abson sells copiers to business firms. It also sells service contracts to maintain and repair copiers for $600 per year. When a customer signs a contract, Abson collects the $600 fee and credits Service Contract Fees Received in Advance. Abson recognizes revenues on a quarterly basis during the year in which the coverage is in effect. For purposes of computing revenue, Abson assumes that all sales of service contracts occur midway through each quarter. Sales of contracts and service expenses for its first year of operations appear below:

	Sales of Contracts	Service Expenses
First Quarter	$180,000 (300 contracts)	$ 32,000
Second Quarter	300,000 (500 contracts)	71,000
Third Quarter	240,000 (400 contracts)	105,000
Fourth Quarter	120,000 (200 contracts)	130,000

a. Prepare journal entries for the first three quarters of the year for Abson Corporation. Assume that the firm prepares quarterly reports on March 31, June 30, and September 30.
b. What is the balance in the Service Contract Fees Received in Advance account on December 31?

26. **Journal entries for estimated warranty liabilities and subsequent expenditures.** A new appliance introduced by Maypool Corporation carries a two-year warranty against defects. The firm *estimates* that the total cost of warranty claims over the two-year period on appliances sold in a particular year (for example, Year 1) will equal 4 percent of sales revenue in the year of sale (that is, Year 1). The firm will incur *actual* warranty costs over the two-year period following the time of sale. Sales (all on account) and actual warranty expenditures (all paid in cash) for the first two years of the appliance's life were as follows:

	Sales	Actual Warranty Expenditures
Year 1	$1,200,000	$12,000
Year 2	1,500,000	50,000

    a. Prepare journal entries for the events of Year 1 and Year 2. Closing entries are not required.
    b. What is the balance in the Estimated Warranty Liability account at the end of Year 2?

27. **Journal entries for estimated warranty liabilities and subsequent expenditures.** Global Motors Corporation offers three-year warranties against defects on the sales of its automobiles. The firm *estimates* that the total cost of warranty claims over the three-year warranty period on automobiles sold in a particular year (for example, Year 1) will equal 6 percent of sales revenue in the year of sale (that is, Year 1). The firm will incur *actual* warranty costs over the three-year period following the time of sale. Sales (all for cash) and actual warranty costs incurred on automobiles under warranty (60 percent in cash and 40 percent in parts) appear below:

	Sales	Actual Warranty Costs Incurred during Year on Automobiles under Warranty
Year 1	$ 800,000	$22,000
Year 2	1,200,000	55,000
Year 3	900,000	52,000

    a. Prepare journal entries for the events of Year 1, Year 2, and Year 3. Closing entries are not required.
    b. What is the balance in the Estimated Warranty Liability account at the end of Year 3?

28. **Journal entry for short-term note payable.** On December 1, Sung Company obtained a 60-day loan for $50,000 from the City State Bank at an annual interest rate of 6 percent. On the maturity date, the bank renewed the note for another 30 days, and Sung Company issued a check to the bank for the accrued interest. Sung Company closes its books annually at December 31.

    a. Present entries on the books of Sung Company to record the issue of the note, the year-end adjustment, the renewal of the note, and the payment of cash at maturity of the renewed note.
    b. Present entries at the maturity date of Sung Company's original note for the following variations in the settlement of the note.
      (1) Sung pays the original note at maturity.
      (2) Sung Company renews the note for 30 days; the new note bears interest at 9 percent per annum. Sung did not pay interest on the old note at maturity.

29. **Computing the issue price of bonds.** Compute the issue price of each of the following bonds.
    a. $1,000,000-face value, zero coupon bonds due in 20 years, priced on the market to yield 12 percent compounded semiannually.
    b. $1,000,000-face value, serial bonds repayable in equal semiannual installments of $50,000 for 20 years, priced on the market to yield 6 percent.
    c. $1,000,000-face value, 10-percent semiannual coupon bonds, with interest payable each six months and the principal due in 20 years, priced on the market to yield 8 percent.
    d. $1,000,000-face value semiannual coupon bonds, with an annual coupon rate of 6 percent for the first ten years and 14 percent for the second ten years and the principal due in 20 years, priced on the market to yield 10 percent.

30. **Accounting for bonds.** Several years ago, Huergo Dooley Corporation (HDC) issued $2,000,000-face value, 8-percent semiannual coupon bonds on the market priced to yield 10 percent, compounded semiannually. The bonds require HDC to make semiannual payments of 4 percent of face value, on June 30 and December 31 of each year. The bonds mature on December 31, Year 5.

   a. Compute the book value of these bonds on January 1, Year 1.

   b. Give HDC's journal entry to recognize interest expense and cash payments on June 30, Year 1.

   c. Give HDC's journal entry to recognize interest expense and cash payments on December 31, Year 1.

   d. On January 1, Year 2, these bonds traded in the market at a price to yield 6 percent, compounded semiannually. On this date, HDC repurchased 20 percent of these bonds on the open market and retired them. Give its journal entry to record the repurchase.

31. Computing the issue price of bonds and interest expense. O'Brien Corporation issues $8,000,000-par value, 8-percent semiannual coupon bonds maturing in 20 years. The market initially prices these bonds to yield 6 percent compounded semiannually.

   a. Compute the issue price of these bonds.

   b. Compute interest expense for the first six-month period.

   c. Compute interest expense for the second six-month period.

   d. Compute the book value of the bonds after the second six-month period.

   e. Use present value computations to verify the book value of the bonds after the second six-month period as computed in part **d** above.

32. Computing the issue price of bonds and interest expense. Robinson Company issues $5,000,000-par value, 8-percent semiannual coupon bonds maturing in 10 years. The market initially prices these bonds to yield 10 percent compounded semiannually.

   a. Compute the issue price of these bonds.

   b. Compute interest expense for the first six-month period.

   c. Compute interest expense for the second six-month period.

   d. Compute the book value of the bonds after the second six-month period.

   e. Use present value computations to verify the book value of the bonds after the second six-month period as computed in part **d** above.

33. Using bond tables. Refer to **Table 6** for 12-percent semiannual coupon bonds issued to yield 11 percent per year compounded semiannually. All of the questions that follow refer to the $1 million face value of such bonds issued by Centrix Company.

   a. What are the initial issue proceeds for bonds issued to mature in 25 years?

   b. What is the book value of those bonds after five years?

   c. What is the book value of the bonds when they have 15 years until maturity?

   d. What are the initial issue proceeds for bonds issued to mature in 15 years? (Compare your answer to part **c**.)

   e. Write an expression for interest expense for the last six months before maturity.

   f. If the market rate of interest on the bonds is 13 percent compounded semiannually, what is the market value of the bonds when they have 15 years to maturity?

   g. When the bonds have 10 years until maturity, they trade in the market for 112.46 percent of par. What is the effective market rate at that time?

34. Journal entries for bond coupon payments and retirement. (Adapted from a problem by S. Zeff.) On December 31, Year 7, at the close of Mendoza Corporation's fiscal year, the company has outstanding $1 million face value of 12-percent semiannual coupon bonds, with payments due on July 1 and December 31 each year through the bonds' maturity date of December 31, Year 16. The company issued the bonds at a market yield (interest rate) of 10 percent, compounded semiannually. On December 31, Year 7, the market interest rate for similar bonds is 14 percent, compounded semiannually. The company uses the effective interest method of accounting for these bonds, rounds computations to the nearest dollar, and closes its books once per year, on December 31.

   a. Give the journal entries to record the company's interest expense for both the first and the second payments during Year 7.

   b. Suppose the firm repurchases one-half of the bonds for cash in the open market on December 31, Year 7, at the price implied by the market interest rate of 14 percent compounded semiannually on that date. Give the journal entry, ignoring income taxes.

   c. How would the gain or loss in **b** appear on the income statement?

35. Amortization schedule for bonds. Seward Corporation issues on January 2, Year 1, 8-percent semiannual coupon bonds maturing three years from the date of issue. The coupons, dated for January 1 and July 1 of each year, each promise 4 percent of the face value, 8 percent total for a year. The firm issues the bonds to yield 10 percent, compounded semiannually.

   a. What are the issue proceeds received by Seward Corporation?

   b. Construct an amortization schedule, similar to that in **Exhibit 9.3**, for this bond issue.

   c. Give the journal entries relating to these bonds for the first year. Seward Corporation uses a calendar year for its accounting period.

d. Assume that on January 2, Year 3, Seward Corporation reacquires $20,000 face value of these bonds for 102 percent of par and retires them. Give the journal entry to record the retirement.

36. **Journal entries to account for bonds.** Brooks Corporation issues $100,000 face value, 10-year bonds on January 2, Year 2. The bonds' coupons, dated June 30 and December 31 of each year, each promise 4 percent of face value, 8 percent total for a year. The market initially prices the bonds to yield 6 percent compounded semiannually.
    a. Compute the issue price of the bonds.
    b. Give the journal entries to account for these bonds during Year 2.
    c. Brooks Corporation reacquires these bonds on the open market on January 2, Year 3, at a time when the market prices the bonds to yield 10 percent compounded semiannually. Give the journal entry to record the reacquisition.

PROBLEMS AND CASES

37. **Allowance method for warranties; reconstructing transactions.** Assume that Central Appliance sells appliances, all for cash. It debits all acquisitions of appliances during a year to the Merchandise Inventory account. The company provides warranties on all its products, guaranteeing to make required repairs, within one year of the date of sale, for any of its appliances that break down. The company has many years of experience with its products and warranties.

    Exhibit 9.7 contains summary data and financial statement excerpts for Central Appliance for the end of Year 1 and for some of the events during Year 2. The firm made entries to the Estimated Liability for Warranty Repairs account during Year 2 as it made repairs, which converted the credit balance at the end of Year 1 into a debit balance of $15,000 at the end of Year 2. That is, before the firm makes its entry to recognize warranty expense for the entire year, the Estimated Liability for Warranty Repairs account has a *debit* balance of $15,000. Also, the Merchandise Inventory account, to which the firm has debited all purchases of inventory, has a balance of $820,000 before the adjusting entry for Cost of Goods Sold, so that Goods Available for Sale totaled $820,000. Central Appliance makes its adjusting entries and closes its books only once each year, at the end of the year.

EXHIBIT 9.7	CENTRAL APPLIANCE (Problem 37)		
Balance Sheet Excerpts		**End of Year 1**	
Merchandise Inventory		$100,000	
All Other Accounts		110,000	
Total Assets		$210,000	
Estimated Liability for Warranty Repairs		$ 6,000	
All Other Accounts		204,000	
Total Liabilities and Owners' Equity		$210,000	
Income Statements Excerpts		**Year 1**	**Year 2**
Sales Revenue		$800,000 Cr.	$1,000,000 Cr.
Warranty Expense		(18,000) Dr.	?

At the end of Year 2, the management of Central Appliance analyzes the appliances sold within the preceding 12 months. It classifies all appliances still covered by warranty as follows: those sold on or before June 30 (more than six months old), those sold after June 30 but on or before November 30 (more than one month but less than six months old), and those sold on or after December 1. Assume that it estimates that one-half of 1 percent of the appliances sold more than six months ago will require repair, 5 percent of the appliances sold one to six months before the end of the year will require repair, and 8 percent of the appliances sold within the last month will require repair. From this analysis, management estimates that $5,000 of repairs will still have to be made in Year 3 on the appliances sold in Year 2. Items remaining in ending inventory on December 31, Year 2, had cost $120,000.

a. What were the total acquisitions of merchandise inventory during Year 2?

b. What was the cost of goods sold for Year 2?

c. What was the dollar amount of repairs made during Year 2?

d. What was the warranty expense for Year 2?

e. Give journal entries for repairs made during Year 2, for the warranty expense for Year 2, and for cost of goods sold for Year 2.

38. **Accounting for zero-coupon debt.** When Time Warner, Inc., announced its intention to borrow about $500 million by issuing 20-year zero coupon (single-payment) notes, *The Wall Street Journal* reported the following:

> NEW YORK—Time Warner Inc. announced an offering of debt that could yield the company as much as $500 million . . . . The media and entertainment giant said that it would offer $1.55 billion principal amount of zero-coupon . . . notes due [in 20 years] . . . through Merrill Lynch. . . . Zero-coupon debt is priced at a steep discount to principal, [which] is fully paid at maturity . . . . A preliminary prospectus . . . didn't include the issue price and yield of the notes.[8]

Assume Time Warner borrows funds at the beginning of Year 1 and pays $1.55 billion in a single payment at the end of Year 20.

a. Assume the yield of the notes is 6 percent per year, compounded annually. What initial issue proceeds will Time Warner, Inc., realize from issuing these notes? That is, how much cash will Time Warner receive on issuing the notes?

b. Assume the initial issue proceeds from these notes is $500 million. What is the annual yield on these notes?

c. Assume the initial issue proceeds from these notes is $400 million and their annual yield is 7 percent compounded annually. What interest expense will Time Warner record for Year 1, the first year the notes are outstanding?

d. Assume the initial issue proceeds from these notes is $400 million and their annual yield is 7 percent compounded annually. What interest expense will Time Warner record for Year 20, the last year the notes are outstanding?

39. **Accounting for long-term bonds.** The notes to the financial statements of Aggarwal Corporation for Year 4 reveal the following information with respect to long-term debt. *All interest rates in this problem assume semiannual compounding and the effective interest method of amortization.*

	December 31, Year 3	December 31, Year 4
$800,000 zero coupon notes due December 31, Year 13, initially priced to yield 10 percent	$ 301,512	?
$1,000,000, 7 percent bonds due December 31, Year 8. Interest is payable on June 30 and December 31. The bonds were initially priced to yield 8 percent	?	$966,336
$1,000,000, 9 percent bonds due December 31, Year 19. Interest is payable on June 30 and December 31. The bonds were initially priced to yield 6 percent	$1,305,832	?

a. Compute the book value of the zero coupon notes on December 31, Year 4. A zero coupon note requires no periodic cash payments; only the face value is payable at maturity. Do not overlook the italicized sentence above.

b. Compute the amount of interest expense for Year 4 on the 7 percent bonds.

c. On July 1, Year 4, Aggarwal Corporation acquires half of the 9-percent bonds ($500,000 face value) in the market for $526,720 and retires them. Give the journal entry to record this retirement.

d. Compute the amount of interest expense on the 9-percent bonds for the second half of Year 4.

[8] *The Wall Street Journal,* December 8, 1992, p. A6.

40. **Accounting for long-term bonds.** The notes to the financial statements of Wal-Mart Stores reveal the following information with respect to long-term debt. *All interest rates in this problem assume semiannual compounding and the effective interest method of amortization.*

	January 31	
	Year 11	**Year 12**
$100,000,000-par value of 9-percent debenture bonds due January 31, Year 20, initially priced on the market to yield 12 percent	$ 83,758,595	?
? par value zero coupon bonds due July 31, Year 16, initially priced on the market to yield 8 percent	$162,395,233	$175,646,684
$400,000,000 face value 9.25-percent notes due January 31, Year 20, initially priced on the market to yield ? percent	$400,000,000	$400,000,000

a. Compute the amount of interest expense on the 9 percent coupon bonds for fiscal year Year 12. Do not overlook the italicized sentence above.

b. Compute the book value of the 9 percent bonds on January 31, Year 12.

c. Compute the par value of the zero coupon bonds.

d. Compute the initial market yield on the $400,000,000 notes.

41. **Comparison of straight-line and effective interest methods of amortizing debt discount.** IBM established IBM Credit Corporation (IBMCC) on May 1, Year 1. On July 1, Year 1, IBMCC issued $150 million of zero coupon notes due July 1, Year 8. These notes promise to pay a single amount of $150 million at maturity, seven years after issue date. IBMCC marketed these notes to yield 14 percent compounded semiannually. IBMCC may at any time redeem these notes, in part or in whole, for 100 percent of the principal amount.

IBMCC computes interest expense for financial reporting using the effective interest method but amortizes "original-issue discount" on the notes in equal semiannual amounts for tax reporting. That is, if IBMCC issued the $150 million face value of notes for $66 million, the *original-issue discount* is $84 (= $150 − $66) million and the semiannual interest expense each period is $6 [= $84/(7 years × 2 periods per year)] million per year. Assume an income tax rate of 40 percent. The financial statements of IBMCC present the following data about long-term debt on December 31, Year 1:

(all dollar amounts in thousands)	
14 3/8 Percent Notes Due July, Year 6	$100,000
Zero Coupon Notes Due July, Year 8 (Face Value of $150,000)	62,238
	$162,238

a. Calculate the proceeds to IBMCC from issuing the zero coupon notes.

b. Compute the amount of interest expense reported on the income statement for these notes for the six-month period ending December 31, Year 1.

c. Compute the amount of the interest deduction on the tax return for Year 1 resulting from these notes. Assuming IBMCC can fully deduct this amount on its income tax return, how much does this reduce the income taxes payable that IBMCC would otherwise compute?

d. What was the amount of "Unamortized Discount" that relates only to the zero coupon notes on the balance sheet at the end of Year 1?

e. A news story in Year 2 reported the following:

[T]he Treasury wants to plug a tax loophole that has enabled companies to borrow billions of dollars cheaply. . . . At issue is a tax break granted to companies issuing . . . "zero-coupon" bonds . . . and other deeply discounted debt instruments, which pay very low interest rates.

Describe the advantages to issuers and purchasers of zero coupon bonds. Give your interpretation of the tax loophole alleged by the U.S. Treasury. Be specific in your response by indicating the dollar amount of the "loophole" that IBMCC used in Year 1. What tax policy with respect to interest on zero coupon notes would you recommend?

42. **Ethical issues of managing income and the debt-equity ratio through bond retirement.** Suppose that Quaker Oats Company issued $40 million of 5-percent semiannual coupon bonds many years ago at par. The bonds now have 20 years until scheduled maturity. Because market interest rates have risen to 9 percent, the market value of the bonds has dropped to 63 percent of par. Quaker Oats has $5 million of current liabilities and $35 million of shareholders' equity in addition to the $40 million of long-term debt in its financial structure. The debt-equity ratio (= total liabilities/total liabilities plus shareholders' equity) is 56 percent [= ($40 + $5)/($5 + $40 + $35)]. (Shareholders' equity includes an estimate of the current year's income.) The president of Quaker Oats is concerned about boosting reported income for the year, which is about $8 million in the absence of any other actions. Also, the debt-equity ratio appears to be larger than that of other firms in the industry. The president wonders what the impact on net income and the debt-equity ratio would be if the company issues at par new 9-percent semiannual coupon bonds to mature in 20 years and uses the proceeds to retire the outstanding bond issue. Assume that such action is taken and that any gain on bond retirement is taxable immediately, at the rate of 40 percent.

    a. Prepare the journal entries for the issue of new bonds in the amount required to raise funds to retire the old bonds, for the retirement of the old bonds, and for the income tax effects.

    b. What is the effect on income for the year? Give both dollar and percentage amounts.

    c. What is the debt-equity ratio after the transaction?

    d. Discuss any ethical concerns raised by these considerations.

43. **Accounting for bonds in a troubled debt restructuring.** On January 1, 1985, First National Bank (FNB) acquired $10 million of face value bonds issued on that date by Occidental Oceanic Power Systems (OOPS). The bonds carried 12 percent semiannual coupons and were to mature 20 years from the issue date. OOPS issued the bonds at par.

    By 2005, OOPS was in severe financial difficulty and threatened to default on the bonds. After much negotiation with FNB (and other creditors), it agreed to repay the bond issue but only on less burdensome terms. OOPS agreed to pay 5 percent per year, semiannually, for 25 years and to repay the principal on January 1, 2030, or 25 years after the negotiation. FNB will receive $250,000 every six months starting July 1, 2005, and $10 million on January 1, 2030. By January 1, 2005, OOPS was being charged 20 percent per year, compounded semiannually, for its new long-term borrowings.

    a. What is the value of the bonds that FNB holds? In other words, what is the present value of the newly promised cash payments when discounted at OOPS's current borrowing rate of 20 percent per year, compounded semiannually?

    b. Repeat part **a**, but use the market interest rate at the time of initial issue, 12 percent, compounded semiannually, to calculate the present value of the newly promised cash payments.

    c. Consider three accounting treatments for this negotiation (called a "troubled debt restructuring" by the FASB in its *Statement of Financial Accounting Standards No. 114*).

       (1) Write down the bonds to the value computed in part **a**, and base future interest revenue computations on that new book value and the new historical interest rate of 20 percent per year, compounded semiannually.

       (2) Write down the bonds to the value computed in part **b**, and base future interest revenue computations on that new book value and the old historical interest rate of 12 percent per year, compounded semiannually.

       (3) Make no entry to record the negotiation, and record interest revenue as the amount of cash, $250,000, that FNB receives semiannually.

       Over the new life of the bond issue, how will total income vary as a function of the method chosen?

    d. Which of the three methods listed in **c** would you recommend? Why?

44. **Discounting warranty obligations.** GAAP require long-term monetary liabilities to appear at the present value of the future cash flows discounted at the market rate of interest appropriate to the monetary items at the time the firm initially recorded them. The Accounting Principles Board *Opinion No. 21* specifically excludes from present-value valuation those obligations that arise from warranties. The *Opinion* requires that warranties, being nonmonetary liabilities, be stated at the estimated cost of providing warranty goods and services in the future.

    Assume that the estimated future costs of a three-year warranty plan on products sold during Year 1 are as follows:

Year of Expected Expenditure		Expected Cost
2	....	$ 500,000
3	....	600,000
4	....	900,000
Total	....	$2,000,000

Actual costs coincided with expectations as to both timing and amount.

  a. Prepare the journal entries for each of the years 1 through 4 for this warranty plan following current GAAP.

  b. Now assume that GAAP allow these liabilities to appear at their present value. Prepare the journal entries for each of the years 1 through 4 for this warranty plan, assuming that the firm states warranty liability at the present value of the future costs discounted at 10 percent. To simplify the calculations, assume that the firm incurs all warranty costs on December 31 of each year.

  c. What theoretical arguments can you offer for the valuation basis in part **b**?

45. **Effects on statement of cash flows. Exhibit 4.12** in **Chapter 4** provides a simplified statement of cash flows with numbered lines. For each of the transactions that follow, indicate the number(s) of the line(s) affected by the transaction and state the amount and direction (increase or decrease) of the effect. If the transaction affects net income on line **(1)** or cash on line **(11)**, be sure to indicate if it increases or decreases the line. Ignore income tax effects.

  a. The firm issues bonds for $100,000 cash.

  b. The firm issues a note with a fair market value of $100,000 for a building.

  c. The firm retires, for $90,000 cash, bonds with a book value of $100,000.

  d. The firm calls for $105,000 and retires bonds with a book value of $100,000.

  e. The firm records interest expense and expenditures for the first half of a year on bonds. The bonds have a face value of $100,000 and a book value at the beginning of the year of $90,000. The coupon rate is 10 percent, paid semiannually in arrears, and the bonds were originally issued to yield 12 percent, compounded semiannually.

  f. The firm records interest expense and expenditures for the first half of a year on bonds. The bonds have a face value of $100,000 and a book value at the beginning of the year of $105,000. The coupon rate is 12 percent, paid semiannually in arrears, and the bonds were originally issued to yield 10 percent, compounded semiannually.

46. **Ethical issues.** Several years ago, the firm issued bonds with an annual coupon rate of 5 percent. In today's market, those bonds yield 11 percent. The market value of the bonds had declined below book value by $50 million. Management considers issuing at par new bonds with coupon rate of 11 percent and using the proceeds to retire the outstanding issue, recognizing a gain of $50 million.

  Comment on any ethical issues pertinent for management's consideration.

chapter 10

*L*iabilities: Off-Balance-Sheet Financing, Leases, Deferred Income Taxes, and Retirement Benefits

Learning Objectives

1. Understand (a) why firms attempt to structure debt financing to keep debt off the balance sheet and (b) how standard-setters have refined the concept of an accounting liability to reduce off-balance-sheet financing abuses.

2. Distinguish between operating leases and capital leases on the bases of their economic characteristics, accounting criteria, and financial statement effects.

3. Understand why firms may recognize revenues and expenses for financial reporting in a period different from that used for tax reporting and the

*C*hapter 9 discussed the concept of an accounting liability and illustrated its application to current liabilities and long-term debt. This chapter explores liabilities further by considering four controversial accounting topics of the past decade: off-balance-sheet financing, leases, deferred taxes, and retirement benefits.

Off-Balance-Sheet Financing

In 1980, *Forbes* magazine noted, "The basic needs of humans are simple: to get enough food, to find shelter, and to keep debt off the balance sheet." Accounting standard setters and financial engineers continually battle: the standard setters to devise rules to get debt onto the balance sheet and the financial engineers to devise transactions that both comply with the rules and keep debt off the balance sheet. Breaking the rules but making it appear otherwise is fraud; complying with the rules but keeping debt off the balance sheet is acceptable and, in some circles, highly regarded, even rewarded. This section discusses the rationale for off-balance-sheet financing and illustrates several financing arrangements to keep debt off the balance sheet.

Rationale for Off-Balance-Sheet Financing

Firms often attempt to structure their financing to keep debt off the balance sheet (that is, to obtain funds without increasing liabilities on the balance sheet). They hope to show lower liabilities on the balance sheet and thereby to improve the debt ratios that analysts use to assess the financial risk of a firm. Reasons frequently cited for **off-balance-sheet financing** include the following:

1. It lowers the cost of borrowing. Unwary lenders may ignore off-balance-sheet financing and set lower interest rates for loans than the underlying risk levels warrant.
2. It avoids violating debt covenants. Covenants in existing debt contracts may restrict a firm's increasing debt ratios above defined levels. Structuring an off-balance-sheet financing arrangement permits the firm to obtain needed funds without affecting the debt ratios. It also provides a cushion in the event that the firm must engage in on-balance-sheet financing in the future.

The first rationale for off-balance-sheet financing assumes that some lenders, credit-rating agencies, and others who assess financial risks do not possess the knowledge, skills, and information needed to identify and deal appropriately with such financing arrangements. Even though firms have little evidence that financial statement users systematically ignore these obligations, firms often structure their financings as though they believe that assumption. Standard-setting bodies have required increased disclosures of off-balance-sheet financings in recent years to alert financial statement users.

Structuring Off-Balance-Sheet Financing

Off-balance-sheet financings generally fall into one of the two categories of obligations that accounting does not recognize as liabilities: executory contracts and contingent obligations (see **Figure 9.1**).

Executory Contracts   Firms frequently sign contracts promising to pay defined amounts in the future in return for future benefits. For a firm's obligation to qualify as an accounting liability, the firm must have received a past or current benefit in return for the obligation—the event or transaction must already have happened. If the firm will receive the benefit in the future, accounting treats the obligation as an executory contract and typically does not recognize a liability.

Example 1   Delta Airlines needs additional aircraft to expand internationally. Delta could borrow the needed funds and purchase the aircraft. This arrangement places additional debt on the balance sheet. Instead, Delta signs a lease agreeing to pay the owner of the aircraft certain amounts each year for 12 years. Delta paints its name on the aircraft, uses them in operations, and makes the required lease payments. The usual accounting assumes that Delta receives benefits when it uses the aircraft, not when it initially signs the lease. Thus, Delta obtains financing for its flight equipment without showing a liability on the balance sheet.

Example 2   Boise Cascade and Georgia-Pacific Corporation (forest products companies) need additional pulp-processing capacity. Each firm could borrow the needed funds and build its own manufacturing plant. Instead, they form a joint venture to build a pulp-processing plant suitable for their joint needs. Each firm agrees to use one-half of the new plant's capacity each year for 20 years and to pay half of all operating and debt service costs. The joint venture uses the purchase commitments of Boise Cascade and Georgia-Pacific to obtain a loan to build the facility. Accounting views the purchase commitments as executory contracts—all benefits occur in the future—and therefore neither firm will recognize a liability. The loan appears as a liability of the balance sheet of the joint venture. Thus, each firm obtains financing for the plant without showing a liability on its balance sheet.

Contingent Obligations   As an alternative to borrowing funds and using a particular asset as collateral, a firm might obtain funds by "selling" the asset with the understanding that the firm will give cash back to the "purchaser" under stated conditions. Such sales usually provide that the selling firm must repay cash to the purchaser in the future if, for example, the asset sold generates less cash for the purchaser than anticipated at the time of "sale." If such payments do not meet the criteria for a loss contingency, as discussed in **Chapter 9**, then the firm treats the transaction as a sale, keeping debt off the balance sheet, instead of as a loan collateralized by the asset.

Example 3   Sears extends credit to its customers to purchase appliances, furniture, and other goods. Sears could borrow from banks using its accounts receivable as collateral, thereby placing debt on the balance sheet. Sears would use collections from customers to repay the bank loans with interest. Instead, Sears "sells" the accounts receivable to the banks. The amount Sears expects to collect from receivables sold exceeds the amount of cash Sears receives from the banks. This excess provides the banks with their expected return, or interest income on their "loan" to Sears. Sears agrees to collect the receivables from customers and remit the cash to the banks. Sears will probably treat this transaction as a sale and thus avoid placing debt on the balance sheet.

Example 4   Seagram Company, a distiller of liquors, ages its whiskeys for approximately ten years. The firm must pay the costs to produce the whiskey and to store it during aging. Using the whiskey as collateral, Seagram could borrow the necessary funds; however, this would lead to increased liabilities. Instead, it "sells" the whiskey to the banks. Seagram oversees the aging process on behalf of the banks. At the completion of the aging, Seagram assists banks in finding a buyer. The banks bear the risk of changes in selling prices for the whiskey. Seagram will probably treat this transaction as a sale and thereby avoid placing debt on the balance sheet.

Example 5   **Chapter 4** described the Enron/Merrill Lynch Nigerian barge transactions. In these, Enron allegedly sold barges anchored in Nigeria for a fair value greater than book value to Merrill Lynch. Later, Enron repurchased the barges for a price roughly equal to the initial transaction price plus an amount equivalent to interest at a market rate. **Chapter 4** emphasized the effect of the transaction on income and cash flow from operations. Here, consider the transaction as a device of Enron's for keeping a borrowing from Merrill Lynch, the lender, off the balance sheet. Some would say that Enron borrowed funds from Merrill Lynch, using barges as collateral, and later repaid the financing.

The Financial Accounting Standards Board (FASB) has dealt with various off-balance-sheet financing arrangements on a case-by-case basis. A unifying theme appears in the FASB rules:

- First, the accountant identifies the party that enjoys the economic benefits of the item in each transaction and that bears the economic risks of holding it.
- Then, the accountant identifies the party that *needs* financing.

When the party *needing* financing controls the benefits and risks, the transaction usually leads to recognizing a liability on the balance sheet of the controlling party. When the party *providing* the financing controls the benefits and risks, the debt does not appear as a liability on the balance sheet of the firm needing financing.

Example 6   Refer to **Example 1**, but assume that Delta signs a lease for 20 years. Also assume that each aircraft Delta leases has a useful life of approximately 20 years and that the required lease payments compensate the owner of the aircraft (that is, the lessor) for the cost of the aircraft plus a reasonable return for the level of risk incurred. Then Delta has rights to use nearly all the economic benefits of the aircraft and bears the risks of technological obsolescence, overcapacity during economic downturns, and similar factors. Because Delta controls the enjoyment of economic benefits and bears the economic risks, it will, following FASB rules discussed later, likely report its lease commitment as a liability. If, as in **Example 1**, the lease spans a period substantially shorter than the expected useful life of the aircraft and if the economics of the transaction virtually require that the lessor either sell the aircraft at the end of the lease period or re-lease them to another airline, then the lessor enjoys the benefits and bears the risks of ownership. In this case, the lease commitment will not appear as a liability on Delta's balance sheet. The next section of this chapter more fully discusses the accounting for leases.

Example 7   Refer to **Example 2**. Suppose that the lender requires Boise Cascade to guarantee payment of the loan in case the joint venture defaults. Suppose also that Georgia-Pacific Corporation experiences severe financial difficulties and fails to pay its share of operating and debt service costs. Boise Cascade bears most of the economic risk of this joint venture and should probably recognize a liability. If the lender relies solely on the joint venture to repay the loan and does not require either Boise Cascade or Georgia-Pacific Corporation to guarantee the loan, then the debt will probably not appear on the balance sheet of either company. The loan would appear as a liability on the books of the joint venture only.

Example 8   Refer to **Example 3**. Assume that Sears must transfer additional uncollected receivables to the lender/purchaser banks for any receivables judged uncollectible. Assume further that Sears must transfer additional uncollected receivables to the banks if interest rates rise above a specified level. In this case, Sears bears credit and interest rate risks and treats the transfer of receivables as a loan and not as a sale, with debt appearing on its balance sheet. If, instead, the banks bear credit and interest rate risks, Sears records the transfer of receivables as a sale; no debt related to the transaction appears on its balance sheet.

Example 9   Refer to **Example 4**. Assume that Seagram guarantees an ultimate selling price that provides the lender with both a return of the original "purchase price" and coverage of storage and interest costs. Seagram bears the economic risks and must show a liability on its balance sheet. Assume, in contrast, that the lender does not require Seagram to guarantee a minimum selling price for the whiskey (for example, the lender might conclude that the quality of Seagram whiskey and a favorable market outlook for whiskey make such a guarantee unnecessary). Then Seagram will likely record the transaction as a sale and not a loan.

Example 10   Refer to **Example 5**. Enron appears not to have given Merrill Lynch a written commitment to repay the loan, but a gentleman's agreement, a handshake. Even an unwritten agreement that Enron would repay would make the transaction a loan under GAAP. Without a written agreement, however, an accountant or auditor cannot easily discover the economic substance of the transaction.

Firms continue to create innovative financing schemes to keep debt off the balance sheet. The FASB continues to consider the appropriate accounting for each transaction as it arises. Some accountants think that there will never be a satisfactory solution until accounting requires the recording of a liability whenever a firm has an obligation to pay a reasonably definite amount at a reasonably definite time, independent of the executory nature of the contract.

Balance Sheet Quality Issues

A parallel concept to quality of earnings is quality of the balance sheet. To what extent does the balance sheet portray the economic resources of a firm and the economic claims on those resources? Previous chapters discussed quality issues on the asset side of the balance sheet with respect to receivables arising from revenue recognition, LIFO inventories, valuation of long-lived assets at acquisition cost, and exclusion from the balance sheet of intangibles developed internally. Firms' attempts to keep debt off the balance sheet affect balance sheet quality as well. Understating the liabilities of a firm can mislead statement users when they assess the risk of the firm. GAAP attempt to define when an obligation is and is not a liability. However, obligations sometimes have some, but not all, attributes of a liability. GAAP require firms to disclose information about such obligations in notes to the financial statements. Statement users should study these notes when assessing the risk of a firm and make their own judgments about whether to exclude such obligations.

Ethical Issues in Off-Balance-Sheet Financing

Do firms confront ethical issues when engaging in off-balance-sheet financing? One view argues that ethical issues do not arise so long as firms structure their off-balance-sheet financing arrangements to comply with GAAP. GAAP set the rules and firms do their best to comply. Another view argues that ethical issues do arise. The continuing efforts of standard-setting bodies to change and refine their standards to react to firms' efforts to work around the spirit, if not the letter, of the standards evidences that firms do not strive to reflect economic reality, but merely to keep debt off the balance sheet.

Problem 10.1 for Self-Study

Attempting off-balance-sheet financing.   Assume that International Paper Company (IP) needs $75 million of additional financing but, because of restrictions in existing debt covenants, cannot, except at prohibitive cost, put more debt on its balance sheet. Instead of borrowing funds, it creates a trust to which, on January 1, it transfers cutting rights to a mature timber tract. The trust will pay for these rights by borrowing $75 million for five years from a bank, with interest at 14 percent. The trust promises to make five equal installment payments, one on December 31 of each year.

The trust will harvest and sell timber each year to obtain funds to make the loan payments and to pay operating costs. At current prices, the value of the standing wood exceeds by ten percent the amounts the trust will need to service the loan and to pay the ongoing operating costs (including wind, fire, and erosion insurance). The future selling price of timber will determine the trust's actions, as follows:

- If the selling price of timber declines in the future, the trust will harvest more timber and sell it to service the debt and to pay other operating costs.
- If the selling price of timber increases in the future, the trust will harvest timber at the level originally planned but will invest any cash left over after paying for debt service and operating costs, to provide a cushion for possible future price decreases. At the end of five years, the trust will distribute the value of any cash or uncut timber to IP.

IP will not guarantee the debt. The bank, however, has the right to inspect the tract at any time and to replace IP's forest-management personnel with managers of its own choosing if it feels that IP is mismanaging the tract.

a. Identify IP's economic returns and risks in this arrangement.
b. Identify the economic returns and risks in this arrangement for the bank lending the funds.
c. Should IP treat this transaction as a loan (a liability will appear on IP's balance sheet) or as a sale (no liability will appear on IP's balance sheet)? Explain your reasoning.

Leases

Many firms acquire rights to use assets through long-term leases. **Examples 1** and **6** above, in which Delta Airlines signed leases to acquire the use of airplanes, illustrate such financing arrangements. A company seeking office space might agree to lease a floor of a building for 5 years or an entire building for 40 years, promising to pay a fixed periodic fee for the duration of the lease. Promising to make a series of lease payments commits the firm just as surely as a bond indenture or a mortgage and, often, results in similar accounting. This section examines two methods of accounting for long-term leases: the operating lease method, which keeps debt off the balance sheet, and the capital lease method, which puts it on.

To understand these two methods, suppose that Food Barn wants to acquire a computer that has a three-year life and costs $45,000. Assume that Food Barn must pay 15 percent per year to borrow funds for three years. The computer manufacturer will sell the equipment for $45,000 or lease it for three years. Food Barn must pay for property taxes, maintenance, and repairs of the computer whether it purchases or leases. Food Barn signs the lease on January 1, Year 1, and promises to make payments on the lease on December 31, Year 1, Year 2, and Year 3. In practice, a lessee (the "buyer" or "tenant") usually makes payments in advance, but assuming the payments occur at year-end makes the computations simpler in these illustrations. Compound interest computations show that each lease payment must be $19,709.[1]

Operating Lease Method

In an **operating lease**, the owner, or lessor (the "landlord"), enjoys the rewards and bears most of the risks of ownership. For example, the lease may require the lessee (the user or "tenant") to make fixed periodic payments. The lessor in this case benefits from decreases in interest rates (the lessor receives the fixed periodic amount) but bears the risk of interest rate increases (the lessor cannot increase the fixed periodic payment). The lease may specify that the lessee return the leased asset to the lessor at the end of the lease term. The lessor must then re-lease the asset to some other firm to obtain a portion of its return. The lessor bears the risk of technological change and other factors that would affect its ability to lease the asset to others. If the computer manufacturer, and not Food Barn, bears most of the risks of ownership, accounting considers the lease to be an executory contract and treats it as an operating lease. Food Barn would make no entry on January 1, Year 1, when it signs the lease. It makes the following entry on December 31, Year 1, Year 2, and Year 3:

December 31 of each year		
Retained Earnings (Rent Expense) (Shareholders' Equity Decrease)	19,709	
Cash (Asset Decrease)		19,709
To recognize annual expense of leasing computer.		

Capital Lease Method

In a **capital lease**, the lessee enjoys the rewards and bears most of the risks of ownership. If the periodic rental payments vary with changes in interest rates, then Food Barn, not the computer manufacturer, bears interest rate risk. If the lease period approximately equals the useful life of the leased asset, then Food Barn bears the risk of technological changes and other factors that affect the market value of the asset. If Food Barn, not the computer manufacturer, bears most of the risks of ownership, accounting views the arrangement as an executed contract—a form of borrowing to purchase the computer. Food Barn must account for it as a capital lease.[2] This

---

[1] The present value of $1 paid at the end of this year and each of the next two years equals $2.28323 when discounted at an annual rate of 15 percent. See **Table 4** at the end of the book, 15-percent column, 3-period row. Because the lease payments must have a present value of $45,000, each payment must equal $45,000/2.28323 = $19,709.

[2] Financial Accounting Standards Board, *Statement of Financial Accounting Standards No. 13*, "Accounting for Leases," 1976, reissued and reinterpreted 1980.

treatment recognizes the signing of the lease as the simultaneous acquisition of a long-term asset and the incurring of a long-term liability for lease payments. At the time Food Barn signs the lease, it records both the leased asset and the lease liability at the present value of the required cash payments, $45,000 in the example. The entry at the time Food Barn signed its three-year lease would be as follows:

January 1, Year 1		
Leased Asset—Computer (Asset Increase)	45,000	
Lease Liability (Liability Increase)		45,000
To recognize acquisition of the asset and the related liability.		

At the end of the year, Food Barn must make two separate entries—one related to the asset and one to the liability. First, it must depreciate the leased asset over its useful life. The first entry made at the end of each year records this depreciation. Assuming that Food Barn uses the straight-line depreciation method, it makes the following entries at the end of Year 1, Year 2, and Year 3:

December 31 of each year		
Retained Earnings (Depreciation Expense [on Computer]) (Shareholders' Equity Decrease)	15,000	
Accumulated Depreciation—Computer (Asset Decrease)		15,000

The second entry made at the end of each year recognizes that the debt service payment—the lease payment—pays interest and, in part, reduces the liability itself. The entries made at the end of each of the three years, based on the amortization schedule in **Exhibit 10.1**, would be as follows:

December 31, Year 1		
Retained Earnings (Interest Expense)(Shareholders' Equity Decrease)	6,750	
Lease Liability (Liability Decrease)	12,959	
Cash (Asset Decrease)		19,709
To recognize lease payment, interest on liability for the year (0.15 × $45,000 = $6,750), and the plug for reduction in the liability. The present value of the liability after this entry is $32,041 = $45,000 − $12,959.		
December 31, Year 2		
Retained Earnings (Interest Expense)(Shareholders' Equity Decrease)	4,806	
Lease Liability (Liability Decrease)	14,903	
Cash (Asset Decrease)		19,709
To recognize lease payment, interest on liability for the year (0.15 × $32,041 = $4,806), and the plug for reduction in the liability. The present value of the liability after this entry is $17,138 = $32,041 − $14,903.		
December 31, Year 3		
Retained Earnings (Interest Expense)(Shareholders' Equity Decrease)	2,571	
Lease Liability (Liability Decrease)	17,138	
Cash (Asset Decrease)		19,709
To recognize lease payment, interest on liability for the year (0.15 × $17,138 = $2,571), and the plug for reduction in the liability. The present value of the liability after this entry is zero (= $17,138 − $17,138).		

Exhibit 10.1 shows the amortization schedule for this lease. Note that it has the same form as the mortgage amortization schedule in **Exhibit 9.2**.

EXHIBIT 10.1	Amortization Schedule for $45,000 Lease Liability, Accounted for as a Capital Lease, Repaid in Three Annual Installments of $19,709 Each, Interest Rate 15 percent, Compounded Annually

Annual Journal Entry

Retained Earnings (Interest Expense) (Shareholders' Equity Decrease) . . .   Amount in Column **(3)**

Liability—Present Value of Lease Obligation (Liability Decrease) . . . . . .   Amount in Column **(5)**

   Cash (Asset Decrease) . . . .   Amount in Column **(4)**

Year (1)	Lease Liability Start of Year (2)	Interest Expense for Year (3)	Payment (4)	Portion of Payment Reducing Lease Liability (5)	Lease Liability End of Year (6)
0					$45,000
1	$45,000	$6,750	$19,709	$12,959	32,041
2	32,041	4,806	19,709	14,903	17,138
3	17,138	2,571	19,709	17,138	0

Column (2) = column (6), previous period.

Column (3) = 0.15 × column (2).

Column (4) is given.

Column (5) = column (4) − column (3).

Column (6) = column (2) − column (5).

Accounting Method Determines Timing, but Not Amount, of Total Expense

In the capital lease method, the expense over the three years totals $59,127, comprising $45,000 (= $15,000 + $15,000 + $15,000) for depreciation expense and $14,127 (= $6,750 + $4,806 +$2,571) for interest expense. This exactly equals the total rent expense of $59,127 recognized under the operating lease method described previously ($19,709 × 3 = $59,127). The capital lease method recognizes expense sooner than does the operating lease method, as **Exhibit 10.2** summarizes. But over sufficiently long time periods, expense equals cash expenditure. The operating lease method and the capital lease method differ in the timing, but not in the total amount, of expense. The capital lease method recognizes both the leased asset and the lease liability on the balance sheet, whereas the operating lease recognizes neither.

EXHIBIT 10.2	Comparison of Expense Recognized under Operating and Capital Lease Methods

Year	Expense Recognized Each Year Under		
	Operating Lease Method	Capital Lease Method	
1	$19,709	$21,750 (=	$15,000 + $ 6,750)
2	19,709	19,806 (=	15,000 + 4,806)
3	19,709	17,571 (=	15,000 + 2,571)
Total	$59,127[a]	$59,127 (=	$45,000[b] + $14,127[c])

[a]Rent expense

[b]Depreciation expense

[c]Interest expense

Choosing the Accounting Method

When a transaction increases both an asset and a liability of a solvent firm, the debt-equity ratio (= total liabilities divided by total equities) increases, making the company appear more risky. Thus, given a choice, some managers prefer not to show an asset and a related liability on the balance sheet. Either borrowing funds to purchase an asset or obtaining an asset's service through a capital lease records new assets and liabilities on the balance sheet, increasing debt ratios. So, some managers prefer operating leases for acquiring asset services. Many managers would also prefer to recognize expenses later rather than sooner for financial reporting. Their preferences have led managers to structure asset acquisitions so that the financing takes the form of an operating lease. Meanwhile, the FASB has tried to specify rules for curtailing the use of the operating lease accounting treatment for leases that transfer risks and rewards of ownership from the lessor to the lessee. Analysts' reports suggest that the capital lease method provides higher quality measures of financial position.

Conditions Requiring Capital Lease Accounting
The FASB has provided rules for classifying long-term leases.[3] A firm must account for a lease as a capital lease if the lease meets any one of four conditions. If the lease meets none of the four conditions, the firm treats the lease as an operating lease.

1. It transfers ownership to the lessee at the end of the lease term.
2. Transfer of ownership at the end of the lease term seems likely because the lessee (user) has a "bargain purchase" option. (A "bargain purchase" option gives the lessee the right to purchase the asset at a specified future time for a price less than the currently predicted fair market value of the asset at the future time.)
3. The lease extends for at least 75 percent of the asset's life.
4. The present value of the minimum contractual lease payments equals or exceeds 90 percent of the fair market value of the asset at the time the lessee signs the lease. The present value computation uses a discount rate appropriate for the creditworthiness of the lessee.

These criteria attempt to identify who enjoys the economic benefits and bears the economic risks of the leased asset. The FASB's rules reflect the concepts that when the lessor bears the risks of a lease, it is an operating lease, but that when the lessee bears the risks, it is a capital lease. If the leased asset, either automatically or for a bargain price, becomes the property of the lessee at the end of the lease period, then the lessee enjoys all of the economic benefits of the asset and incurs all risks of ownership. If the life of the lease extends for most of the expected useful life of the asset (the FASB specifies 75 percent or more), then the lessee enjoys most of the economic benefits of the asset, particularly when we measure them in present values, and incurs most of the risk of technological obsolescence.

Lessees who want to treat a lease as an operating lease, rather than a capital lease, can usually structure the leasing contract to avoid the first three conditions. Avoiding the fourth condition is more difficult because it requires lessors to bear more risk than they might desire. The fourth condition compares the present value of the lessee's contractual minimum lease payments with the fair market value of the asset at the time the lessee signs the lease. The lessor presumably could either sell the asset for its fair market value or lease it to the lessee for a set of lease payments set forth in the lease contract. The present value of the minimum lease payments has the economic character of a purchase price in that the lessee has committed to make payments just as it would commit to make payments in an installment purchase. The FASB says, in effect, that if this present value (lessee's purchase price) equals or exceeds 90 percent of the asset's fair market value (lessor's alternative selling price) at the inception of the lease, then the lessee has effectively purchased the asset and must account for the asset as though it had.

Note on the Risks of the Leasing Business
What is the major long-term asset of Hertz or of Avis? Used cars: Hertz and Avis must deal on a daily basis with an inventory of used cars and will bear the loss should government regulations make obsolete the current stock of used cars because, for example, they consume too much gasoline or do not have passenger airbags. Thus, Hertz and Avis bear the risk of obsolescence and treat their leases of automobiles as operating leases. Hertz and Avis, of course, price their car rentals to compensate for the obso-

---

[3] *Ibid.*, par. 7.

lescence risks they bear. A manufacturer of airplanes such as Boeing may find the new airplane business sufficiently risky that it does not want to bear the additional risks of being in the used airplane business, so Boeing might require its lease customers to sign long-term leases in which the lessee guarantees a certain minimum residual value for the leased asset. In this case, the lessee bears the risk of obsolescence; Boeing likely treats the leases as capital leases.

Consequence of Lessors' Desire to Avoid Used Asset Risk   Lessors of assets, such as airplanes and computers, do not want to lease an asset under conditions in which they have more than 10 percent of the asset's original market value at risk. When the lessee returns the asset to the lessor, the lessor must renew the lease or sell it in order to capture the benefits originally expected from the asset and to realize all the profit inherent in its original manufacture. Many lessors will not accept such risks without additional payment from the lessee. A lease that meets the fourth condition above has transferred the risks and rewards of ownership from the lessor to the lessee. In economic substance, the lessee has acquired an asset and has agreed to pay for it under a long-term installment payment contract. Accounting recognizes that contract as the lessee's long-term liability.

Effects on Lessor   Lessors, such as Boeing for aircraft and IBM for computers, manufacture and then lease assets to lessees. Other lessors, such as financial institutions, purchase assets from the manufacturer and then lease the asset to lessees.

The lessor (landlord) generally uses the same criteria as does the lessee (tenant) for classifying a lease as a capital lease or an operating lease. When the lessor signs an operating lease, the lessor recognizes rent revenue each period in amounts that mirror rent expense for the lessee. The lessor also depreciates the leased asset over time. When the lessor is the manufacturer and signs a capital lease, the lessor recognizes revenue in an amount equal to the present value of all future lease payments and recognizes expense (analogous to cost of goods sold) in an amount equal to the book value of the leased asset at the time of signing the capital lease. The difference between the revenue and the expense is the lessor's income on the "sale" of the asset. Only manufacturers of leased assets recognize this type of income. When the lessor is either the manufacturer or a financial institution, the capital lease is a means of financing for the lessee. The lessor records the lease receivable like any other long-term receivable—at the present value of the future cash flows. It recognizes interest revenue over the collection period of the payments with entries that are mirror images of the lessee's entries for interest expense. The entries made by the lessor of the computer to Food Barn appear below. These entries assume that the lessor manufactured the computer at a cost of $39,000.

Operating Lease Method by Lessor
January 1, Year 1

Equipment (Computer Leased to Customers) (Asset Increase)	39,000	
Inventory (Asset Decrease)		39,000

To record the transfer of product from inventory to equipment (in hands of lessee).

December 31 of each year

Cash (Asset Increase)	19,709	
Retained Earnings (Rent Revenue) (Shareholders' Equity Increase)		19,709

To recognize annual revenue from renting computer.

December 31 of each year

Retained Earnings (Depreciation Expense) (Shareholders' Equity Decrease) . .	13,000	
Accumulated Depreciation—Computer (Asset Decrease)		13,000

To recognize depreciation on rented computer ($13,000 = $39,000/3).

Capital Lease Method by Lessor
January 1, Year 1

Lease Receivable (Asset Increase)	45,000	
Retained Earnings (Sales Revenue) (Shareholders' Equity Increase)		45,000

To recognize the "sale" of a computer for a series of future cash flows with a present value of $45,000.

Retained Earnings (Cost of Goods Sold) (Shareholders' Equity Decrease) . . .	39,000	
Inventory (Asset Decrease)		39,000

To record the cost of the computer "sold" as an expense.

(continued)

December 31, Year 1

Cash (Asset Increase)	19,709	
Retained Earnings (Interest Revenue) (Shareholders' Equity Increase) ..		6,750
Lease Receivable (Asset Decrease)		12,959

To recognize lease receipt, interest on receivable, and reduction in receivable for Year 1. See supporting calculations in the lessee's journal entries and in **Exhibit 10.1.**

December 31, Year 2

Cash (Asset Increase)	19,709	
Retained Earnings (Interest Revenue) (Shareholders' Equity Increase) ..		4,806
Lease Receivable (Asset Decrease)		14,903

To recognize lease amounts for Year 2.

December 31, Year 3

Cash (Asset Increase)	19,709	
Retained Earnings (Interest Revenue) (Shareholders' Equity Increase) ..		2,571
Lease Receivable (Asset Decrease)		17,138

To recognize lease amounts for Year 3.

Lessors tend to prefer capital lease accounting for financial reporting because it enables them to recognize all income from the sale of the asset on the date the parties sign the lease while spreading the interest revenue over the life of the lease. The operating lease method recognizes all lease revenue—which implicitly includes manufacturing profit and interest—gradually over time as the lessor receives lease payments. Lessors, however, recognize the preference of lessees to structure leases as operating leases. Because the lessor and lessee apply the same criteria to classify a lease as either an operating lease or a capital lease, lessors tend to accommodate the preferences of lessees, their customers, but set rental payments to compensate for any additional risk the lessor bears.

Income Tax Consideration in Lease Arrangements

Leasing has become an industry separate from manufacturing. That is, companies such as General Electric Capital Services buy computers from, say, IBM and lease them to end-users. The leasing industry developed in part because the users of computers, airplanes, and other depreciable assets did not have sufficient taxable income to take advantage of accelerated depreciation deductions. A tax deduction has value only to the extent the taxpayer has taxable income against which to offset the deduction, reducing taxes otherwise payable. Any organization without taxable income, whether a not-for-profit, or a municipality, or a taxpayer with no earnings, cannot take advantage of a deduction, such as for depreciation. Other entities, such as financial institutions or manufacturers of leased equipment, have sufficient taxable income to benefit from these deductions. These parties structure leases as operating leases for income tax purposes so that the lessors claim depreciation deductions and save taxes. Lessees attempt to negotiate with the lessors to obtain lower lease payments, which in effect transfer some of the benefits of reduced taxes to the lessee.

The rules for classifying a lease as operating or capital for income tax purposes differ from the FASB rules discussed here for financial reporting. Thus, leases sometimes appear as operating leases for tax purposes and capital leases for financial reporting, or vice versa.

Bundling in Lease Arrangements

In the last 50 years, leases have become a common method for users to finance acquisition of long-term assets. Think about the copying machine down the hall from where you work; likely your school or business chooses to lease it from the manufacturer, such as Canon or Xerox, rather than buy it. Increasingly, customers, such as your school, want to acquire a full package of services from the supplier. In the case of a copier, this would mean buying toner and other supplies, as well as a contract for ordinary maintenance and emergency service. As a result, companies such as Xerox quote a single price to the user to cover a complete package of goods and services: for example, the copier, toner, and combined maintenance/service contract. The customer makes a single monthly payment and Xerox confronts the accounting problem of separating the single payment into components—part for copier rental, part for toner, and part for the service/maintenance contract. GAAP provide little guidance other than require that the revenues from each of the components bear a reasonable relation to the fair market price of the item sold separately. In the case of Xerox, it has much data on separate sales of toner and maintenance/service contracts, but few separate transactions where it has sold a stand-alone copier, with no extras. Hence, the lessor must use some methods to disaggregate the total rental payment into the parts for toner and service, which is easy, and the rest into the part that is for interest and the part for equipment, which is hard. Xerox found itself in trouble with the SEC in how it split the total lease payment into a part for the sales price of the copier and part for the interest revenue implicit in the financing. One of the cases at the end of this chapter explores the issue. The FASB, with the EITF and the SEC, is attempting to provide more guidance to lessors who deal in bundled contracts.[4]

Problem 10.2 for Self-Study

Operating and capital lease methods for lessee and lessor. On January 2, Year 1, Holt Book Store will acquire a delivery van that a local automobile dealer sells for $25,000. The dealer offers Holt Book Store the option of leasing the van for four years, with rentals of $8,231 due on December 31 of each year. Holt Book Store must return the van at the end of four years, although the automobile dealer anticipates that the resale value of the van after four years will be negligible. The automobile dealer acquired the van from the manufacturer for $23,500. The automobile dealer considers 12 percent an appropriate interest rate to charge Holt Book Store to finance the acquisition.

a. Does this lease qualify as an operating lease or as a capital lease for financial reporting according to the four criteria specified by the FASB? Explain.
b. Assume for this part that the lease qualifies as an operating lease. Give the journal entries made by Holt Book Store over the first two years of the life of the lease.
c. Repeat part **b** for the automobile dealership. Use straight-line depreciation and zero estimated salvage value.
d. Assume for this part that the lease qualifies as a capital lease. Give the journal entries made by Holt Book Store over the first two years of the life of the lease.
e. Repeat part **d** for the automobile dealership.
f. Compute the amount of expenses that Holt Book Store recognizes during each of the four years under the operating lease method and the capital lease method.
g. Compute the amount of revenues and expenses that the automobile dealership recognizes during each of the four years under the operating lease method and the capital lease method.
h. Why are the lessee's total expenses the same under the operating and the capital lease methods? Why is the lessor's total revenue, or income, the same under the operating and the capital lease methods?
i. Why do the total expenses of the lessee differ from the total income of the lessor?

Income Tax Accounting and Deferred Income Taxes

The amount that a firm reports as income before income taxes for financial reporting usually differs from the amount of taxable income that appears on its income tax return.

The difference between book and taxable income arises from two factors:

1. **Permanent differences**—book income includes revenues (such as interest revenue on municipal bonds) or expenses that taxable income never includes.
2. **Temporary differences**—book income includes revenues or expenses (such as depreciation on long-lived assets and bad debt expense) in one accounting period whereas taxable income includes them in a different period.

---

[4] See *EITF 00–21: Revenue Arrangements with Multiple Deliverables*, FASB, January 2003.

TERMINOLOGY NOTE

We find the correct term *income before income taxes for financial reporting* too cumbersome to use throughout this section. Instead, we use *book income* to refer to income before income taxes reported in the financial statements, and we use *taxable income* to refer to the amount reported in the income tax return. Similarly, the terms book purposes and *tax purposes* distinguish the financial statements from the tax return. We use the term *pre-tax income* to refer to an item on the financial statements and the term *taxable income* to refer to an item on the tax return. You will be less likely to confuse yourself and others if you also use these terms this way. The term *book basis* means the amortized cost—that is, acquisition cost less accumulated depreciation from the financial statements—and *tax basis* means the cost for tax purposes less the sum of prior depreciation deductions on the tax return.

Firms compute **income tax payable** for a particular period using taxable income as the base, deriving the amount from computations on the tax return. Taxable income excludes permanent differences and uses the accounting methods that a firm selects for income tax purposes.

A more controversial issue concerns the appropriate base for computing **income tax expense**, which appears on the income statement. Should income tax expense equal the income taxes actually payable each period based on taxable income, or should income tax expense equal income taxes actually payable each period plus (minus) the income taxes a firm expects to pay (save) in the future when temporary differences reverse?

Advocates of setting income tax expense equal to income taxes currently payable view income taxes similar to other taxes (such as property taxes, sales taxes, or payroll taxes). Government entities define the tax base (for example, assessed value of property, sales, or payroll costs) and apply a tax rate to this tax base to measure the taxes due each period. Some accountants want to follow the same procedure for income taxes by reporting income tax expense equal to income taxes payable currently.

Advocates of setting income tax expense equal to income taxes currently payable plus (minus) income taxes payable (saved) in the future when temporary differences reverse use the *matching convention* to support their position. (Permanent differences never reverse, never affect cash outflows for income taxes, and therefore should not affect income tax expense.) The current period's book income includes revenues and expenses that ultimately affect cash outflows for income taxes. Proponents argue that proper matching of income tax expense with pretax book income requires firms to include the future income tax effects of temporary differences in measuring income tax expense in the periods when temporary differences originate, not when they reverse. Moreover, they say, assets provide future benefits; long-lived assets provide a future benefit in the form of reduced taxes payable caused by taking depreciation deductions on the tax return. If the firm uses some extra benefits in early years, it ought to show the liability for greater taxes in later years.

Example 11   **Exhibit 10.3** shows data for Burns Corporation for a six-year period. This exhibit shows why accounting for income taxes presents a problem for firms with temporary differences. Burns Corporation acquires equipment that costs $120,000 and that has a six-year life with no expected salvage value. Columns **[1]** and **[5]** show Burns Corporation's income *before depreciation expense and income tax expense* of $100,000 for each of the six years of the asset's life.

Columns **[1]** through **[4]** show data from Burns Corporation's income tax return for each of the six years: Column **[2]** shows the (accelerated) depreciation deductions, column **[3]** (= **[1]** − **[2]**) shows taxable income, and column **[4]** shows income taxes payable computed as 40 percent of taxable income from column **[3]**.

The data in columns **[5]** through **[7]** come from the financial statements. Column **[6]** shows the (straight-line) depreciation expense, and column **[7]** shows pre-tax income equal to column **[5]** minus column **[6]**.

Assume, contrary to generally accepted accounting principles (GAAP), that firms report income tax expense equal to income tax payable. In the Burns example, this means that income tax expense equals the amounts in column **[4]**, resulting in the hypothetical net income numbers in column **[8]**. The caption on column **[8]** does not say *Net Income* because GAAP do not report net income this way. Column **[8]** represents pre-tax financial statement income less income taxes payable.

Note the time series of income numbers in column **[8]**: up about 11.6 percent from Year 1 to Year 2, down 11.3 percent from Year 2 to Year 3, and down in each of the next three years by varying amounts. Recall, from **Chapter 3**, that the income statement intends to help the reader understand *why* income behaves over time as it does. When operations remain the same year after year and tax rates do not change, the reader will expect net income not to change. Looking at the amounts in column **[8]** (if they were net income figures), the reader of Burns Corporation's income statements will wonder, "What's going on with this company?" The answer is: nothing unusual. Burns does the same thing for six years, and its performance remains constant over the six-year period. Yet if the accountant sets income tax expense equal to income taxes payable, reported earnings vary from year to year. Reported income behaves strangely over time because of temporary differences: in each year the depreciation deduction on the tax return differs from depreciation expense in the financial statements.

GAAP require firms to base income tax expense on pre-tax income in the financial statements. Thus, when pre-tax income remains the same, $80,000 (= $100,000 − $20,000) in this example, income tax expense also remains the same, $32,000 (= 0.40 × $80,000). Net income is $48,000 (= $80,000 − $32,000) each year, as column **[10]** shows. This illustration assumes there are no permanent differences.

Recording Income Tax Expense

Exhibit 10.3 illustrates that income tax expense differs from income tax payable each year. The accountant debits or credits this difference to a **deferred income tax liability** account. The journal entry to record income taxes for Year 1 is as follows:

Year 1

Retained Earnings (Income Tax Expense) (Shareholders' Equity Decrease)	32,000	
Income Tax Payable (Liability Increase)		30,400
Deferred Tax Liability (Liability Increase)		1,600

The credit to the Deferred Tax Liability account equals the 40 percent tax rate times the difference between the depreciation deduction of $24,000 on the tax return and the depreciation expense of $20,000 on the financial statements. The deferred tax liability, $1,600 in this example for Burns, represents the income taxes that the taxpayer will pay in future years when the temporary difference reverses.

Burns will make similar entries during Year 2 and Year 3, adding $7,360 [= 0.40 × ($38,400 − $20,000)] to the Deferred Tax Liability account in Year 2 and $1,120 [= 0.40 × ($22,800 − $20,000)] in Year 3. See **Exhibit 10.4**, which tracks the Deferred Tax Liability account over the six years of this example. The balance in the Deferred Tax Liability account at the end of Year 3 is $10,080 (= $1,600 + $7,360 + $1,120). This amount equals the 40 percent income tax rate times the cumulative difference between tax depreciation of $85,200 (= $24,000 + $38,400 + $22,800) and book depreciation of $60,000 (= $20,000 × 3); note that the deferred tax liability equals $10,080 [= 0.40 × ($85,200 − $60,000)].

The temporary differences for depreciation begin to reverse in Year 4. The journal entry to recognize income tax expense for Year 4 is as follows:

Year 4

Retained Earnings (Income Tax Expense) (Shareholders' Equity Decrease)	32,000	
Deferred Tax Liability (Liability Decrease)	2,240	
Income Tax Payable (Liability Increase)		34,240

Depreciation expense recognized for financial reporting, $20,000, exceeds the depreciation deduction for tax purposes, $14,400. The income taxes currently payable because the temporary difference reversed are $2,240 [= 0.40 × ($20,000 − 14,400)].

EXHIBIT 10.3

BURNS CORPORATION
Computation of Income Taxes over Six-Year Life of Equipment
(Equipment Costs $120,000 and Has Six-Year Life)

Information from (or Based on) Tax Returns

Year	Income before Depreciation and Taxes [1]	Depreciation Deduction on Tax Return [2]	Taxable Income [3]	Income Taxes Payable [4]
1	$100,000	$ 24,000	$ 76,000	$ 30,400
2	100,000	38,400	61,600	24,640
3	100,000	22,800	77,200	30,880
4	100,000	14,400	85,600	34,240
5	100,000	13,200	86,800	34,720
6	100,000	7,200	92,800	37,120
Totals		$120,000	$480,000	$192,000

Information from (or Based on) Financial Statements

				Not Allowed by GAAP		Accounting Required by GAAP	
Year	Income before Depreciation and Taxes [5]	Depreciation Expense [6]	Pre-Tax Income = $100,000 − $20,000 [7]	Pre-Tax Income Less Income Taxes Payable [8]	Percentage Change in Column [8] [9]	Pre-Tax Income Less Income Taxes at 40% of Pre-Tax Income [10]	Percentage Change in Column [10] [11]
1	$100,000	$ 20,000	$ 80,000	$ 49,600		$ 48,000	—
2	100,000	20,000	80,000	55,360	11.6%	48,000	—
3	100,000	20,000	80,000	49,120	−11.3%	48,000	—
4	100,000	20,000	80,000	45,760	−6.8%	48,000	—
5	100,000	20,000	80,000	45,280	−1.0%	48,000	—
6	100,000	20,000	80,000	42,880	−5.3%	48,000	—
Totals		$120,000	$480,000	$288,000		$288,000	

[1] = Given   [3] = [1] − [2]   [5] = Given   [7] = [5] − [6]   [9] = ([8] this year/[8] last year) − 1
[2] = Given   [4] = 0.40 × [3]   [6] = $120,000/6   [8] = [7] − [4]   [10] = (1.00 − 0.40) × [7]

EXHIBIT 10.4	Deferred Income Tax Liability Account over 6-Year Period (Amounts with Check Mark [✓] Appear on Balance Sheet)

Opening Credit Balance, Year 1	$ —	✓
Credit, Addition for Year 1	1,600	[1]
Balance, End of Year 1	$ 1,600	✓
Credit, Addition for Year 2	7,360	[2]
Balance, End of Year 2	$ 8,960	✓
Credit, Addition for Year 3	1,120	[3]
Balance, End of Year 3	$10,080	✓
Debit, Subtraction for Year 4	(2,240)	[4]
Balance, End of Year 4	$ 7,840	✓
Debit, Subtraction for Year 5	(2,720)	[5]
Balance, End of Year 5	$ 5,120	✓
Debit, Subtraction for Year 6	(5,120)	[6]
Balance, End of Year 6	$ —	✓

Burns will make entries similar to the above in Year 5, reducing the Deferred Tax Liability by $2,720 [= 0.40 × ($20,000 − $13,200)], and in Year 6, reducing the Deferred Tax Liability account by $5,120 [= 0.40 × ($20,000 − $7,200)]. The reductions in the Deferred Tax Liability account during these three years total $10,080 (= $2,240 + $2,720 + $5,120). The balance in this account at the end of Year 6 is zero. The zero balance indicates that total lifetime depreciation amounts on the equipment both for financial reporting and for income tax reporting are the same: $120,000.

Problem 10.3 for Self-Study

Computing income tax expense.   Wade Corporation acquires a machine on January 1, Year 1, costing $80,000 and having a four-year useful life and zero salvage value. Wade uses accelerated depreciation on its income tax return. For taxes, it deducts the following:

- 33 percent of the cost of the machine in Year 1
- 44 percent in Year 2
- 15 percent in Year 3
- 8 percent in Year 4

The firm uses the straight-line depreciation method for financial reporting. Income before depreciation and income taxes is $100,000, and the income tax rate is 40 percent.

a. Compute the amount of income taxes currently payable for each year.
b. Compute the amount of income tax expense for each year.
c. Give the journal entries for income taxes for each year.

A Further Look at GAAP for Income Taxes

The illustration for Burns Corporation in the previous section showed that income tax expense each period equaled pre-tax income for financial reporting multiplied by the income tax rate; in each year, income tax expense was $32,000 (= 0.40 × $80,000). Income tax expense also equaled income taxes currently payable plus the change in the Deferred Tax Liability account. For example, income tax expense for Year 1 equals income taxes currently payable of $30,400 plus the increase in the Deferred Tax Liability account of $1,600, and income tax expense for Year 4 equals income taxes currently payable of $34,240 reduced by the $2,240 amount by which the Deferred Tax Liability account decreased. The Deferred Tax Liability account changed each year in the amount of the tax effect of the temporary differences between depreciation in the financial statements and on the tax return.

The FASB requires a more complex accounting for income taxes than given in this simple illustration for Burns Corporation, for the following reasons:

1. The income tax rate that firms will have to pay in the future might change, and if so, the amount in the Deferred Tax Liability account will not represent the amount of taxes that the firm must pay later.
2. Temporary differences might create **deferred tax assets** instead of deferred tax liabilities. A deferred tax asset arises when a firm recognizes an expense earlier for financial reporting than for tax reporting. For example, for financial reporting, a firm provides for estimated warranty costs in the year it sells the warranted product but claims a tax deduction later, when it makes actual expenditures for warranty repairs. Similarly, for financial reporting, a firm reports Bad Debt Expense in the year it makes a credit sale but claims a tax deduction only later, when it writes off specific uncollectible accounts. These temporary differences create deferred tax assets.
3. GAAP require firms to recognize a **deferred tax asset valuation allowance** (similar in concept to an allowance for uncollectible accounts) to reduce the balance in the Deferred Tax Asset account to the amount the firm expects to realize in tax savings in the future.

Thus, the Deferred Tax Asset or Deferred Tax Liability accounts on the balance sheet can change each period because of (1) temporary differences originating or reversing during the current period, (2) changes in income tax rates expected to apply in future periods when temporary differences reverse, and (3) changes in the valuation allowance for Deferred Tax Assets.

The illustration for Burns Corporation in **Exhibit 10.3** assumed that only the first of the three factors affected deferred income taxes each year. In such cases, we can measure income tax expense using pre-tax income amounts from the financial statements and plug the difference between income tax expense and income tax payable to deferred asset or liability accounts on the balance sheet.

Because the second and third factors often occur, GAAP require firms to measure income tax expense with a procedure more complex than the one we illustrate here.[5] The International Accounting Standards Board has issued rules virtually the same as the FASB rules illustrated here.[6]

Problem 10.4 for Self-Study

Working backward to components of book and tax income.   Dominiak Company reports the following information about its financial statements and tax return for a year:

Depreciation Expense from Financial Statements	$270,000
Financial Statement Pretax Income	160,000
Income Tax Expense from Financial Statements	36,000
Income Taxes Payable from Tax Returns	24,000

The federal and state governments combine to tax taxable income at a rate of 40 percent. Permanent differences result from municipal bond interest that appears as revenue in the financial statements but is exempt from income taxes. Temporary differences result from the use of accelerated depreciation for tax returns and straight-line depreciation for financial reporting.

Reconstruct the income statement for financial reporting and for tax reporting for the year, identifying temporary differences and permanent differences.

Disclosure of Income Taxes in Financial Statements

Notes to the financial statements provide additional information regarding a firm's income tax expense. **Exhibit 10.5** illustrates these disclosures for General Products Company. Firms report four items of information:

---

[5] We discuss and illustrate this more general but more complex procedure on the web site that the publisher has made available for this book. To view this material, go to the publisher's web site (refer to the book's preface for a description of the site).

[6] International Accounting Standards Board, *International Accounting Standards No. 12*, "Income Taxes," revised 1996.

EXHIBIT 10.5	GENERAL PRODUCTS COMPANY Illustrative Disclosure in Notes about Income Taxes Excerpts from Financial Statements[a] (all dollar amounts in millions)		

	Year 2	Year 3	Year 4
Income Before Income Taxes			
Domestic	$2,158	$2,208	$2,262
Foreign	612	747	750
Total	$2,770	$2,955	$3,012
Components of Income Tax Expense			
Income Taxes Currently Payable:			
Domestic	$ 716	$ 762	$ 711
Foreign	166	221	177
Income Taxes Deferred	(13)	(21)	14
Income Tax Expense	$ 869	$ 962	$ 902
Reconciliation from Statutory to Effective Income Tax Rates			
U.S. Federal Statutory Rate	35.0%	35.0%	35.0%
Reduction in Taxes Resulting from:			
Income from Tax-Exempt Investments	(1.6)	(1.2)	(1.7)
Exclusion of 80% of Intercorporate Dividends Received	(0.5)	(0.1)	(0.8)
Foreign Income Taxed at Rate Lower than 35%	(1.5)	(1.1)	(2.6)
Effective Income Tax Rate[b]	31.4%	32.6%	29.9%

	End of Year			
COMPONENTS OF DEFERRED TAX ASSETS AND LIABILITIES	Year 1	Year 2	Year 3	Year 4
Deferred Tax Assets				
Uncollectible Accounts Receivable[c]	$ 45	$ 55	$ 72	$ 90
Warranty Liability[d]	67	93	126	161
Valuation Allowance[e]	(5)	(7)	(12)	(15)
Total Deferred Tax Assets	$107	$141	$186	$236
Deferred Tax Liabilities				
Depreciable Assets[f]	$126	$142	$155	$213
Installment Accounts Receivable[g]	25	30	41	47
Total Deferred Tax Liabilities	$151	$172	$196	$260

Authors' Notes (Notes such as these do not usually appear in published financial statements):

[a] Adapted from disclosures of General Electric and Sears, Roebuck.

[b] Income Tax Expense/Income before Income Tax Expense.

[c] General Products Company uses the allowance method for book purposes and, as required, the direct write-off method for tax purposes.

[d] For book purposes, General Products Company recognizes estimated warranty expense (and the related liability) at the time of sale, but, as required, it takes a tax deduction for warranty costs only when repairs and replacements under warranty are actually made.

[e] Adjustment to reflect the amount of deferred tax assets General Products expects to realize.

[f] General Products uses accelerated depreciation for tax purposes and straight-line depreciation for book purposes.

[g] General Products sells certain products on an installment-payment plan, for which it recognizes revenue for book purposes when it makes the sale and for tax purposes when it collects cash from customers using the installment method.

1. *Components of Income before Income Taxes.* This section indicates the amount of book income before income taxes that a firm derives from both its domestic and its foreign operations.
2. *Components of Income Tax Expense.* This section indicates the amount of income taxes currently payable and the amount deferred because of temporary differences. It also separates the total taxes currently payable into the portions payable to U.S. and foreign government entities.

3. *Reconciliation from Statutory to Effective Income Tax Rates.* The **effective tax rate** equals (book) income tax expense divided by book income before income taxes. The effective tax rate of 29.9 percent for Year 4 equals $902 million income tax expense divided by $3,012 million income before income taxes. This section of the income tax note explains why the effective tax rate differs from the **statutory tax rate** of 35 percent. The differences result primarily from differences in tax rate (for example, General Products operates in countries whose average tax rate is less than the U.S. rate of 35 percent) and from permanent differences. Examples of permanent differences are the exclusion from taxable income of interest from state and municipal bonds and a portion of the dividend received from intercorporate investments. The U.S. system taxes income at the corporate level and again, after the corporation pays dividends to shareholders, at the personal level. To keep from taxing corporate income every time one corporation pays dividends to another, the system provides an exemption from taxes for part of the dividends that one corporation pays to another. See *double taxation* in the **Glossary**.

4. *Components of Deferred Tax Assets and Liabilities.* This section discloses the types of temporary differences that result in the deferred tax asset and the deferred tax liability on the balance sheet each period. The change in these deferred tax accounts on the balance sheet equals the deferred portion of income tax expense each period.

The journal entries to record income tax expense for General Products Company each year are as follows:

Year 2		
Retained Earnings (Income Tax Expense) (Shareholders' Equity Decrease) ..	869	
Deferred Tax Asset [= $141 − $107] (Asset Increase)	34	
Deferred Tax Liability (= $172 − $151) (Liability Increase)		21
Cash or Income Tax Payable (= $716 + $166) (Asset Decrease or (Liability Increase)		882
Year 3		
Retained Earnings (Income Tax Expense) (Shareholders' Equity Decrease) ..	962	
Deferred Tax Asset [= $186 − $141] (Asset Increase)	45	
Deferred Tax Liability [= $196 + $172] (Liability Increase)		24
Cash or Income Tax Payable [= $762 + $221] (Asset Decrease or (Liability Increase)		983
Year 4		
Retained Earnings (Income Tax Expense) (Shareholders' Equity Decrease) ..	902	
Deferred Tax Asset [= $236 − $186] (Asset Increase)	50	
Deferred Tax Liability [= $260 − $196] (Liability Increase)		64
Cash or Income Tax Payable [= $711 + $177] (Asset Decrease or (Liability Increase)		888

Criticisms of Deferred Tax Accounting

Some accountants have criticized the accounting for deferred income taxes, for several reasons.

Benefits and Costs Ignored Requiring firms to record income tax expense currently on temporary differences for which the income tax law permits firms to delay payment fails to allow net income to show the economic benefit realized. Likewise, permitting firms to exclude from income tax expense currently the tax effects of temporary differences that require an immediate cash outflow, such as those created by bad debt expense, fails to allow net income to show the economic cost incurred. Cash flow from operations in the statement of cash flows, however, reflects this cash savings or cash outflow.

Not an Asset nor an Obligation An asset is a resource that provides future benefits. A liability is an obligation that requires a future sacrifice of resources, usually cash. A growing firm finds that its deferred tax asset and its deferred tax liability grow continually. For example, the book amount for warranty expense based on the current period's sales exceeds the tax amount for warranty expense based on warranty expenditures. The firm has this pattern of warranty expense and expenditure year after year, so expense exceeds expenditure year after year. The resulting continual growth in the deferred tax asset suggests that the firm never receives the benefits of future tax deductions. Another example: The depreciation deduction on the income tax return using an accelerated depreciation method exceeds depreciation expense on the financial statements using the straight-line method. The firm acquires new assets each year and so has this pattern of book expense and tax deduction, year after year. The continual growth in the deferred tax liability suggests that the firm never pays these income taxes.

Proponents of deferred tax accounting argue that firms do not continually grow. Firms experience decreased sales and earnings, often thereby experiencing reversals of previous temporary differences. Proponents of deferred tax accounting also argue that individual temporary differences do reverse but that new temporary differences of larger amounts replace them. Thus, firms do realize the benefits of deferred tax assets and must pay deferred tax liabilities. These proponents argue that the deferred tax accounts on the balance sheet do not differ from accounts receivable and accounts payable. New accounts continually replace old accounts, but these accounts still represent assets and liabilities. Critics of deferred tax accounting counter that governmental entities impose income taxes on aggregate taxable income, not on individual temporary differences.

Undiscounted Amount Deferred tax liabilities appear at undiscounted amounts on the balance sheet. Other long-term liabilities, such as bonds and capitalized leases, appear at the present value of future cash flows discounted at an interest rate appropriate to the obligation on the date the firm first records the obligation. When the FASB issued *Statement No. 109*, "Accounting for Income Taxes," in 1992, it indicated its desire to defer consideration of the discounting of deferred taxes for several reasons, including the complexity of the process and the FASB's wish to consider discounting in a broad context as it applies to several accounting issues.

Deferred Compensation: Pension Benefits and Other Deferred Compensation

Most employers provide retirement benefits to their employees. Typical benefits include pensions, health insurance, and life insurance. Some employers set aside cash during the employees' working years to ensure the availability of funds to pay these retirement benefits later. Other firms use a pay-as-you-go system, paying for retirement benefits as retired employees receive them.

The employer must count as expense the cost of these retirement benefits in measuring net income. The accounting question arises whether firms should recognize the expense during the years while employees render services or later, when the firm pays the benefits during the employees' retirement. The matching convention of accrual accounting requires that firms recognize the expense during employees' working years because the labor services of those years generate revenues. The cost of **deferred compensation** does not differ from the cost of current compensation (that is, salaries and wages). Employees agree to render services currently for a package of compensation, some of which the employees receive immediately and some of which the employees receive later. Delaying the recognition of deferred compensation costs until employees retire results in an expense without a matching revenue from those employees' services and overstates income of the period when the firm earned the revenue.

This section discusses the accounting issues for pension benefit plans. The accounting for other retirement benefits follows similar principles. Under a pension plan, an employer promises to make payments to employees after they retire. Private pension plan systems have grown in number and size over the last several decades. For many individuals, the present value of their pension benefits is their major financial asset, and for many firms, the present value of their pension promises forms a significant obligation. The variety of details about pension plans can hide their basic structure, which we discuss next.

Pension Plan Structure and Definitions

Employer This section discusses the structure of a pension plan from the viewpoint of the employer.

1. The employer sets up a pension plan specifying the eligibility of employees, the types of promises made to employees, the method of funding, and the pension plan administrator. Some employers promise to contribute a certain amount to the pension plan each period for each employee (usually based on an employee's salary), without specifying the benefits the employee will receive during retirement. The amounts employees eventually receive depend on the investment performance of the pension plan. Common terminology refers to such plans as **defined contribution pension plans**. Other employers specify the benefit that employees will receive during retirement. The employer must contribute sufficient amounts to the pension plan so that those contributions plus earnings from investments made with those contributions will be sufficient to pay the specified benefit. Common terminology refers to such plans as **defined benefit pension plans**.

2. The employer computes pension expense each period. Pension expense under a defined contribution plan equals the amount contributed for the period. The FASB prescribes the measurement of pension expense for a defined benefit plan, but we do not discuss these details in this book.[7] The employer debits Pension Expense and credits Pension Liability, following a process called *expensing pension obligations*.

3. The employer transfers cash to a separate pension fund each period according to some formula. The employer debits Pension Liability and credits Cash, following a process called *funding pension obligations*.

4. If cumulative pension expenses exceed cumulative pension funding, a pension liability appears on the employer's balance sheet. If cumulative pension funding exceeds cumulative pension expenses, a pension asset appears on the employer's balance sheet. In addition, the FASB requires firms to report a pension liability on the balance sheet if the present value of pension commitments to employees exceeds the assets in the pension fund.

Pension Plan   The pension plan carries out the following steps.

1. The plan receives cash each period from the employer. The plan invests this cash in bonds, capital stock, real estate, and other investments to generate income. The plan pays cash to retired employees each period. The assets in the pension plan change each period as follows:

$$
\begin{array}{rl}
 & \text{Assets at Beginning of the Period} \\
\pm & \text{Actual Earnings on Pension Plan Investments} \\
+ & \text{Contributions Received from the Employer} \\
- & \text{Payments to Retirees} \\
\hline
= & \text{Assets at End of the Period}
\end{array}
$$

The assets in the pension fund do not appear on the balance sheet of the employer, although the net of the plans assets and liabilities will likely appear in some form on the employer's balance sheet.

2. The pension plan computes the amount of the pension liability each period. The liability of a defined contribution plan equals the assets in the pension fund. The computation of the pension liability for a defined benefit plan uses the pension benefit formula underlying the pension plan and depends on assumptions about employee turnover, mortality, interest rates, and other factors. The liability of a defined benefit pension plan equals the present value of the expected amounts payable to employees.

The typical benefit formula takes into account the employee's length of service and some measure of average earnings. For example, the employer might promise to pay each employee during retirement an annual pension equal to a stated percentage of the average annual salary during the five highest-paid working years for that employee. The percentage might increase by 2 percentage points for each year of service, so that an employee with 40 years of service receives an annual pension equal to 80 percent of that employee's average salary during the five highest-paid working years.[8]

---

[7] Financial Accounting Standards Board, *Statement of Financial Accounting Standards No. 87*, "Employer's Accounting for Pensions," 1985.

[8] We discuss and illustrate more of the accounting concepts and methods for pensions and pension plans on the web site that the publisher has made available for this book. To view this material, which includes problems for self-study as well as exercises and other problems, go to the publisher's web site (refer to the book's preface for a description of the site).

Deferred Compensation: Health Care and Other Benefits

Health care, insurance, and other benefits resemble, in concept, pension benefits. Employers promise to provide benefits to employees during retirement. The present value of these commitments, called **health care benefits obligation**, represents an economic obligation of the employer. Until the FASB issued its rules in the early 1990s, few firms had either recognized an expense for these obligations or set aside cash to fund them. The FASB requires firms to recognize expenses for employees' health care and similar benefits and to recognize liabilities for the firms' underfunded obligations to pay for these benefits.[9] Firms may recognize the full liability in one year or recognize it piecemeal over several years.

An International Perspective

Leases

Most industrialized countries maintain a distinction between operating leases and capital leases (often called *financing leases*). The criteria for a capital lease in Japan, Germany, and France follow income tax laws, whereas standard-setting bodies set the criteria in the United States, Canada, and the United Kingdom. The criteria in each case attempt to identify the entity enjoying the rewards and bearing the risk of the asset.

Income Tax Accounting

Countries that permit firms to select different methods of accounting for financial and tax reporting (such as the United States, Canada, and Great Britain) require deferred tax accounting. Firms provide deferred taxes for all temporary differences in the United States and Canada, whereas firms in Great Britain provide deferred taxes only when a firm expects that a liability for deferred taxes will materialize. The book/tax conformity requirement in France, Japan, and Germany largely eliminates the need for deferred tax accounting in these countries.

Retirement Benefits

The types of retirement benefits that employers provide for employees vary across industrialized countries. The law in Germany, France, and most socialized countries guarantees employees their rights to retirement benefits. Japan has historically provided a severance benefit, although pension benefits have increased in use. Disclosures about retirement benefits in most countries contain less detail than in the United States.

Summary

Analyzing a firm's risk involves an assessment of the adequacy of a firm's assets and cash flows to pay obligations as they come due. This chapter discusses commitments and obligations that accounting may not recognize as liabilities (certain asset sales with recourse provisions or operating leases), may partially recognize (some pension, health care, and other retirement benefits), or may recognize in an amount larger than the expected cash outflow (deferred tax liability). Effective analysis of risk requires an understanding of the accounting for each of these obligations and commitments.

Appendix 10.1: Effects on the Statement of Cash Flows of of Transactions Involving Liabilities

Leases

When firms account for leases as operating leases, the amount reported as rent revenue (by the lessor) or rent expense (by the lessee) usually equals the lessee's cash payment to the lessor. In

---

[9] Financial Accounting Standards Board, *Statement of Financial Accounting Standards No. 106*, "Employers' Accounting for Postretirement Benefits Other Than Pensions," 1990.

the direct method of computing cash flow from operations, the cash inflow or outflow equals the amount of revenue or expense. In the indirect method, the accountant makes no adjustment to net income to compute cash flow from operations. The lessee may either prepay or delay payment of the rental fee. In the direct method, the amount of the cash inflow or outflow will therefore differ from the amount of revenue or expense. In the indirect method, the accountant includes the change in the lessee's account Prepaid Rent (Rental Fees Received in Advance, for the lessor) or the lessee's account Rent Payable (Rent Receivable, for the lessor) as an addition to, or subtraction from, net income to compute cash flow from operations.

At the time that a lessee signs a lease accounted for as a capital lease, it debits an asset account for the leased asset and credits a lease liability account. The signing of a capital lease is an investing and a financing activity that does not affect cash. Lessees must report such transactions in a supplementary schedule or notes to the statement of cash flows.

During the lease period, the lessee depreciates the leased asset. The accountant adds back depreciation expense to net income when computing cash flow from operations with the indirect method. The lessee treats lease payments partially as interest expense and partially as a repayment of the lease liability. Refer to the example for Food Barn in the chapter. The firm made the following entry on December 31, Year 1:

December 31, Year 1

Retained Earnings (Interest Expense) (Shareholders' Equity Decrease)	6,750	
Lease Liability (Liability Decrease)	12,959	
Cash (Asset Decrease)		19,709

To recognize lease payment, interest on liability for the year (0.15 × $45,000 = $6,750), and the plug for reduction in the liability. The present value of the liability after this entry is $32,041 = $45,000 − $12,959.

In the direct method, $6,750 appears as an operating use of cash and $12,959 appears as a financing use of cash. In the indirect method, the portion of the cash payment representing interest expense, $6,750 above, requires no adjustment when converting net income to cash flow from operations. The portion of the cash payment representing repayment of the lease liability, $12,959 above, will appear as a financing use of cash to reduce debt.

Deferred Income Taxes

Refer to **Example 11, Exhibit 10.3**, for Burns Corporation. Firms using the direct method for presenting cash flow from operations show the amounts paid for income taxes in the computation of operating expenditures. In the indirect method, firms must add back or subtract amounts from net income to compute cash flow from operations. In the first year, income tax expense of $32,000 exceeds income taxes payable of $30,400 by $1,600. That $1,600 of tax expense did not use cash. The statement of cash flows requires an addback to net income in deriving cash flow from operations. The $1,600 of expense increases the noncurrent liability for deferred income taxes. Income tax expense exceeds income taxes payable in the second and third years, requiring addbacks in those years as well. In the fourth, fifth, and sixth years, the firm uses more cash than the amount of the expense. For the sixth year, for example, the firm uses $37,120 cash to pay taxes but reports income tax expense of only $32,000 in the income statement. Consequently, it must subtract $5,120 (= $37,120 − $32,000) in the statement of cash flows to derive cash flow from operations when the firm uses the indirect method.

Solutions to Self-Study Problems

SUGGESTED SOLUTION TO PROBLEM 10.1 FOR SELF-STUDY

(International Paper Company; attempting off-balance-sheet financing.)

a. IP receives an immediate benefit of $75 million cash on January 1. IP retains a residual interest in the cash and uncut timber at the end of five years. IP's principal risk is that the bank will replace IP's forest-management personnel with managers of its own choosing who might mismanage the property. For example, to control operating costs, the new managers might not remove stumpage from harvested trees or might not replant new seedlings.

b. The bank has rights to an uncertain future revenue stream of 14 percent of the unpaid balance of the loan. Factors affecting this uncertainty include

- the absence of a loan guarantee by IP,
- the adequacy of 10 percent excess timber to cover interest, operating costs, and decreases in selling prices, and
- a fixed yield on the loan regardless of changes in interest rates.

c. Timber and pulp prices vary significantly each year depending on economic conditions, availability and usage of fixed-asset-intensive pulp-processing plants, and foreign competition. The key factor affecting the accounting treatment of this transaction is the adequacy of the 10 percent excess timber intended to cushion the bank against timber price decreases. If the amount of timber transferred to the trust will likely assure the bank of repayment of its loan with interest, then the bank bears little risk and IP would recognize a liability. If the amount of timber transferred creates significant uncertainty that the bank will receive the loan repayment with interest, then IP will treat the transaction as a sale and not recognize a liability. Accountants will likely use probability analysis to judge the significance of the uncertainty. The higher the probability that the cushion is adequate, the more IP retains the risks and rewards of future price movements and will need to recognize a liability. Accountants will examine the historical distribution of timber prices to judge the probability that prices will fall enough to wipe out the cushion. The auditor will likely judge the cushion inadequate, keeping debt off IP's balance sheet, only if the probability of its being too small drops below 50 percent. Because the conservative accounting treatment (the one that leads to IP's recognizing a liability) results when the bank's cushion is adequate, the outside auditor might drop the cutoff even lower.

SUGGESTED SOLUTION TO PROBLEM 10.2 FOR SELF-STUDY

(Holt Book Store and automobile dealer; operating and capital lease methods for lessee and lessor.)
a. Application of the four criteria is as follows:
  (1) Ownership transferred to lessee at end of lease term: not satisfied.
  (2) Lease contains a bargain purchase option for lessee: not satisfied.
  (3) Lease period extends for at least 75 percent of asset's life: satisfied.
  (4) Present value of contractual lease payments equals or exceeds 90 percent of fair market value of the asset at the time lessee signs the lease: satisfied. The present value of the lease payments when discounted at 12 percent is $25,000 (= $8,231 \times 3.03735$), which equals the $25,000 market value of the asset on January 2, Year 1. The lease is therefore a capital lease.
b. December 31 of each year:

Retained Earnings (Rent Expense) (Shareholders' Equity Decrease)	8,231	
Cash (Asset Decrease)		8,231
To recognize annual expense of renting delivery van.		

c. January 2, Year 1:

Equipment [delivery van leased to customer] (Asset Increase)	23,500	
Inventory (Asset Decrease)		23,500
To record transfer of delivery van from inventory to equipment.		

December 31 of each year:

Cash (Asset Increase)	8,231	
Retained Earnings (Rent Revenue) (Shareholders' Equity Increase) . .		8,231
To recognize annual revenue from renting delivery van.		

Retained Earnings (Depreciation Expense) (Shareholders' Equity Decrease)	5,875	
Accumulated Depreciation (Asset Decrease)		5,875
To recognize depreciation on leased van; $5,875 = $23,500/4.		

d. January 2, Year 1:

Leased Asset—Delivery Van (Asset Increase)	25,000	
Lease Liability (Liability Increase)		25,000
To recognize acquisition of delivery van and the related liability.		

December 31, Year 1:

Retained Earnings (Interest Expense [0.12 × $25,000]) (Shareholders' Equity Decrease)	3,000	
Lease Liability (Liability Decrease)	5,231	
Cash (Asset Decrease)		8,231
To record first lease payment. The book value of the lease liability after this entry is $19,769 (= $25,000 − $5,231).		

December 31, Year 1:

Retained Earnings (Depreciation Expense [$25,000/4]) (Shareholders' Equity Decrease)	6,250	
Accumulated Depreciation (Asset Decrease)		6,250
To record depreciation expense for Year 1.		

December 31, Year 2:

Retained Earnings (Interest Expense [0.12 × $19,769]) (Shareholders' Equity Decrease)	2,372	
Lease Liability (Liability Decrease)	5,859	
Cash (Asset Decrease)		8,231
To record second lease payment. The book value of the lease liability after this entry is $13,910 (= $19,769 − $5,859).		

December 31, Year 2:

Retained Earnings (Depreciation Expense [$25,000/4]) (Shareholders' Equity Decrease)	6,250	
Accumulated Depreciation (Asset Decrease)		6,250
To record depreciation expense for Year 2.		

e. January 2, Year 1:

Lease Receivable (Asset Increase)	25,000	
Retained Earnings (Sales Revenue) (Shareholders' Equity Increase) ..		25,000
To record sale of delivery van.		

January 2, Year 1:

Retained Earnings (Cost of Goods Sold) (Shareholders' Equity Decrease) ..	23,500	
Inventory (Asset Decrease)		23,500
To record cost of delivery van sold.		

December 31, Year 1:

Cash (Asset Increase)	8,231	
Retained Earnings (Interest Revenue) (Shareholders' Equity Increase)		3,000
Lease Receivable (Asset Decrease)		5,231
To record lease receipt for Year 1; amounts mirror those for lessee.		

December 31, Year 2:

Cash (Asset Increase)	8,231	
Retained Earnings (Interest Revenue) (Shareholders' Equity Increase)		2,372
Lease Receivable (Asset Decrease)		5,859
To record lease receipt for Year 2; amounts mirror those for lessee.		

f.

	Operating Lease Method	Capital Lease Method		
Year	Rent Expense	Interest Expense	+ Depreciation Expense	= Total
1	$ 8,231	$3,000	$ 6,250	$ 9,250
2	8,231	2,372	6,250	8,622
3	8,231	1,669[a]	6,250	7,919
4	8,231	883[b]	6,250	7,133
	$32,924	$7,924 +	$25,000 =	$32,924

[a] 12 × $13,910 = $1,669. Book value of lease liability after this entry is $7,348 [= $13,910 − ($8,231 − $1,669)].
[b] 12 × $7,348 = $882, which differs from $883 due to rounding.

g.

	Operating Lease Method			Capital Lease Method		
Year	Rent Revenue	− Depreciation Expense	= Total	Gain from Sale	+ Interest Revenue	= Total
1	$ 8,231	$ 5,875	$2,356	$1,500	$3,000	$4,500
2	8,231	5,875	2,356	—	2,372	2,372
3	8,231	5,875	2,356	—	1,669	1,669
4	8,231	5,875	2,356	—	883	883
	$32,924 −	$23,500 =	$9,424	$1,500 +	$7,924 =	$9,424

h. The lessee's total expenses equal cash outflows, and the lessor's total revenue, or income, equals cash inflows minus cash outflows. The operating and the capital lease methods recognize the revenues and expenses associated with these cash flows in different periods.

i. The lessee's total expenses equal its total cash outflows of $32,924 (= $8,231 × 4). The lessor's total income equals cash inflows of $32,924 (= $8,231 × 4) minus cash outflows of $23,500. Although the lessor's receipts equal the lessee's payments, the lessor must pay for the goods, which reduces its income with a subtraction for cost of goods sold (or depreciation, depending on method). This cost of goods sold accounts for the difference between the lessee's expense and the lessor's income.

SUGGESTED SOLUTION TO PROBLEM 10.3 FOR SELF-STUDY

(Wade Corporation; computing income tax expense.)

a.

Year	Income before Depreciation and Income Taxes [1]	Deduction on Tax Return [2]	Taxable Income [3]	Income Tax Payable [4]
1	$100,000	$26,400	$ 73,600	$ 29,440
2	$100,000	35,200	64,800	25,920
3	$100,000	12,000	88,000	35,200
4	$100,000	6,400	93,600	37,440
Totals	$400,000	$80,000	$320,000	$128,000

Column [1] is given.
Column [2] = $80,000 × 0.33 for Year 1, 0.44 for Year 2, 0.15 for Year 3, and 0.08 for Year 4.
Column [3] = [1] − [2].
Column [4] = 0.40 × [3].

b.

Year	Income before Depreciation and Income Taxes [1]	Depreciation Expense [2]	Income before Income Taxes [3]	Income Tax Expense [4]
1	$100,000	$20,000	$ 80,000	$ 32,000
2	100,000	20,000	80,000	32,000
3	100,000	20,000	80,000	32,000
4	100,000	20,000	80,000	32,000
Totals	$400,000	$80,000	$320,000	$128,000

Column [1] is given.
Column [2] = $80,000/4 = $20,000.
Column [3] = [1] − [2].
Column [4] = 0.40 × [3].

c. **Year 1**

Retained Earnings (Income Tax Expense) (Shareholders' Equity Decrease)	32,000	
Income Tax Payable (Liability Increase)		29,440
Deferred Tax Liability (Liability Increase)		2,560

Year 2

Retained Earnings (Income Tax Expense) (Shareholders' Equity Decrease)	32,000	
Income Tax Payable (Liability Increase)		25,920
Deferred Tax Liability (Liability Increase)		6,080

Year 3

Retained Earnings (Income Tax Expense) (Shareholders' Equity Decrease)	32,000	
Deferred Tax Liability (Liability Decrease)	3,200	
Income Tax Payable (Liability Increase)		35,200

Year 4

Retained Earnings (Income Tax Expense) (Shareholders' Equity Decrease)	32,000	
Deferred Tax Liability (Liability Decrease)	5,440	
Income Tax Payable (Liability Increase)		37,440

SUGGESTED SOLUTION TO PROBLEM 10.4 FOR SELF-STUDY

(Dominiak Company; working backward to components of book and tax income.) See **Exhibit 10.6**.

	Financial Statements	Type of Difference	Income Tax Return
EXHIBIT 10.6 — DOMINIAK COMPANY — Illustration of Temporary Differences and Permanent Differences (Suggested Solution to Problem 10.4 for Self-Study)			
Operating Income except Depreciation	$ 360,000 (6)	—	$ 360,000 (4)
Depreciation	(270,000) (g)	Temporary	(300,000) (3)
Municipal Bond Interest	70,000 (5)	Permanent	—
Taxable Income			$ 60,000 (2)
Pretax Income	$ 160,000 (g)		
Income Taxes Payable at 40 Percent			$ 24,000 (g)
Income Tax Expense at 40 Percent of $90,000 = $160,000 − $70,000, Which Is Book Income Excluding Permanent Differences	(36,000) (g)		
Net Income	$ 124,000 (1)		

Order and derivation of computations:

(g) Given.

(1) $124,000 = $160,000 − $36,000.

(2) $60,000 = $24,000/0.40.

(3) Temporary difference for depreciation is ($36,000 − $24,000)/0.40 = $30,000. Because income taxes payable are less than income tax expense, we know that depreciation deducted on tax return exceeds depreciation expense on financial statements. Thus the depreciation deduction on the tax return is $300,000 = $270,000 + $30,000.

(4) $360,000 = $300,000 + $60,000.

(5) Financial statement income before taxes, excluding permanent differences, is $90,000 = $36,000/0.40. Financial statement income before taxes, including permanent differences, is $160,000. Hence permanent differences are $160,000 − $90,000 = $70,000.

(6) $160,000 + $270,000 − $70,000 = $360,000. See also **(4)**, for check.

Key Terms and Concepts

Off-balance-sheet financing
Operating lease
Capital lease
Book basis
Tax basis
Permanent differences
Temporary differences
Income tax payable
Income tax expense

Deferred income tax liability
Deferred tax assets
Deferred tax asset valuation allowance
Effective tax rate
Statutory tax rate
Deferred compensation
Defined contribution pension plan
Defined benefit pension plan
Health care benefits obligation

Questions, Short Exercises, Exercises, Problems, and Cases

QUESTIONS

1. Review the meaning of the terms and concepts listed in **Key Terms and Concepts**.
2. "The concern with off-balance-sheet financing is overstated. As long as the notes to the financial statements provide information about the transaction, the analyst can incorporate the financing into debt ratios as appropriate." Do you agree or disagree? Explain.

For additional student resources, content, and interactive quizzes for this chapter visit the FACMU website:
http://facmu.swlearning.com

3. Compare and contrast the financial statement effects of achieving off-balance-sheet financing through an executory contract versus an asset sale with recourse, where the seller of the assets will reimburse the buyer for any shortfall in collections from the purchased asset.

4. Explain why the following question is important for lease accounting: "Who enjoys the potential rewards and bears the risks of an asset?"

5. In what ways is the economic substance of a lessee's capital lease similar to, and different from, that of purchasing the equipment using the proceeds of a loan repayable in installments?

6. Distinguish between the lessee's accounting for a capital lease and for the purchase of equipment using the proceeds of a loan repayable in installments.

7. In what sense is the total expense from a lease independent of the lessee's method of accounting for it?

8. "The lessor recognizes the same amount of income (revenue minus expenses) over the term of a lease as the lessee recognizes expenses." Do you agree or disagree? Explain.

9. "The rationale for deferred tax accounting rests on the matching convention." Explain.

10. "One might view deferred income taxes as an interest-free loan from the government." Do you agree? Why or why not?

11. You have been called to testify before a congressional committee on income taxation. One committee member states: "My staff has added up the amounts shown for Deferred Tax Liability on the balance sheets of the 500 largest U.S. corporations. If we collected these amounts immediately, we could reduce the national deficit by billions of dollars. After all, I have to pay my taxes as they become due each year. Why shouldn't corporations have to do the same?" How would you respond?

12. How should an analyst wanting to study the debt-equity ratio (= total liabilities/total equities, or total sources of financing) of a business treat the deferred income tax liability?

13. Under what circumstances will a firm report a deferred tax asset on the balance sheet? Under what circumstances will a firm report a deferred tax liability on the balance sheet?

14. Most firms report income tax expense at a percentage of pretax book income that differs from the statutory federal income tax rate. What might cause this difference?

15. "The principal accounting issues involving deferred compensation plans relate to the matching convention in accounting." Explain.

16. Suggest reasons why the total assets and total liabilities of a pension plan do not appear, but their net amount does appear, on the employer's balance sheet.

17. What are the economic and accounting differences between a defined-benefit pension plan and a defined-contribution plan?

18. Under what circumstances will a firm report a pension fund asset on its balance sheet? a pension fund liability?

SHORT EXERCISES

19. **Using accounts receivable to achieve off-balance-sheet financing.** Cypres Appliance Store has $100,000 of accounts receivable on its books on January 2, Year 2. These receivables are due on December 31, Year 2. The firm desires to use these accounts receivables to obtain financing.

    a. Prepare journal entries during Year 2 for the transactions in parts (i) and (ii) below:
       (i) The firm borrows $89,286 from its bank, using the accounts receivable as collateral. The loan is repayable on December 31, Year 2, with interest at 12 percent.
       (ii) The firm sells the accounts receivable to the bank for $89,286. It collects amounts due from customers on these accounts and remits the cash to the bank.

    b. Compare and contrast the income statement and balance sheet effects of these two transactions.

    c. How should Cypres Appliance Store attempt to structure this transaction to ensure that it qualifies as a sale instead of a collateralized loan?

20. **Using inventory to achieve off-balance-sheet financing.** P. J. Lorimar Company grows and ages tobacco. On January 2, Year 5, the firm has aging tobacco with a cost of $200,000 and a current market value of $300,000. P. J. Lorimar Company wants to use this tobacco to obtain financing. The firm uses a December 31 year-end.

    a. Prepare journal entries during Year 5 and Year 6 for the transactions in parts (i) and (ii) below:
       (i) The firm borrows $300,000 from its bank, using the tobacco inventory as collateral. The loan is repayable on December 31, Year 6, with interest at 10 percent per year compounded annually. Assume zero storage costs. The firm expects to sell the tobacco on December 31, Year 6, for $363,000.

(ii) The firm sells the tobacco inventory to the bank for $300,000. It promises to sell the inventory on behalf of the bank at the end of two years and remit the proceeds to the bank.

b. Compare and contrast the income statement and balance sheet effects of these two transactions.

c. How should P. J. Lorimar Company attempt to structure this transaction to ensure that it qualifies as a sale instead of a collateralized loan?

21. **Preparing lessee's journal entries for an operating lease and a capital lease.** General Motors Corporation (GM) sells a luxury minivan for $24,000. FedUp Delivery Services agrees to lease a minivan for a monthly rental of $750 for three years. FedUp Delivery Services will return the minivan to GM at the end of the lease period. GM then expects to lease the minivan to Rent-a-Wreck for the remaining two years of its useful life. The appropriate interest rate for a three-year collateralized loan for FedUp Delivery Services is 12 percent compounded monthly. Assume that FedUp Delivery Services makes all rental payments at the end of each month.

a. Is the lease with FedUp Delivery Services an operating lease or a capital lease?

b. Assume that this lease is an operating lease. Give the journal entries for FedUp Delivery Services at the time it signs the lease and at the end of each of the first two months of the lease period.

c. Repeat part **b** assuming that the lease is a capital lease. FedUp Delivery Services uses the straight-line depreciation method and records depreciation monthly.

22. **Preparing lessor's journal entries for an operating lease and a capital lease.** Sun Microsystems manufactures an engineering workstation for $7,200 and sells it for $12,000. Although the workstation has a physical life of approximately ten years, rapid technological change limits its expected useful life to three years. Sun leases a workstation to Design Consultants for the three-year period beginning January 2, Year 2. The annual rental payments of $4,386.70 are due at the beginning of each year. The interest rate appropriate for discounting cash flows is 10 percent. Sun uses a calendar year as its reporting period.

a. Does this lease qualify as an operating lease or a capital lease?

b. Assume that this lease qualifies as an operating lease. Give the journal entries for Sun over the three-year lease period.

c. Repeat part **b** assuming that the lease qualifies as a capital lease.

23. **Preparing journal entries for income tax expense.** The income tax note to the financial statements of Ingersoll-Rand for three recent years shows the following (amounts in millions):

	Year 9	Year 10	Year 11
Components of Income Tax Expense			
Currently Payable	$110,975	$105,537	$104,615
Deferred	(43,575)	(15,537)	14,185
Total Income Tax Expense	$ 67,400	$ 90,000	$118,800

Assume that all deferred taxes relate to the use of accelerated depreciation for income tax purposes and the straight-line method for financial reporting.

a. Give the journal entry to record income tax expense for Year 9, Year 10, and Year 11.

b. Describe the likely reasons for the pattern of currently payable and deferred income taxes for each of the three years.

24. **Computations and journal entries for income taxes with both temporary and permanent differences.** Sung Company reported the following amounts for book and tax purposes for its first three years of operations:

	Year 1	Year 2	Year 3
Pretax Book Income	$560,000	$500,000	$620,000
Taxable Income	600,000	450,000	560,000

The differences between book income and taxable income result from different depreciation methods. The income tax rate was 40 percent during all years.

a. Give the journal entry to record income tax expense for each year.

b. Assume for this part that the firm included $10,000 of interest on state and municipal bonds in the pretax book income amounts shown above for each year but properly excluded these amounts from the taxable income amounts shown above. Give the journal entry to record income tax expense for each year.

25. **Deriving permanent and temporary differences from financial statement disclosures.** Pownall Company reports the following information for a year:

Book Income before Income Taxes	$318,000
Income Tax Expense	156,000
Income Taxes Payable for This Year	48,000
Income Tax Rate on Taxable Income	40 percent

The company has both permanent and temporary differences between book income and taxable income.

a. What is the amount of temporary differences for the year? Give the amount, and indicate whether the effect is to make book income larger or smaller than taxable income.

b. What is the amount of permanent differences for the year? Give the amount, and indicate whether the effect is to make book income larger or smaller than taxable income.

EXERCISES

26. **Applying the capital lease criteria.** Boeing manufactures a jet aircraft at a cost of $50 million. The usual selling price for this aircraft is $60 million, and its typical useful life is 25 years. American Airlines desires to lease this aircraft from Boeing. The parties contemplate the following alternatives for structuring the lease. Indicate whether each arrangement qualifies as an operating lease or a capital lease. Assume that all cash flows occur at the end of each year.

a. American will lease the aircraft for 20 years at an annual rental of $6 million. At the end of 20 years, American will return the aircraft to Boeing. The interest rate appropriate to a 20-year collateralized loan for American is 10 percent.

b. American will lease the aircraft for 15 years at an annual rental of $7.2 million. At the end of 15 years, American will return the aircraft to Boeing. The interest rate appropriate for a 15-year collateralized loan for American is 10 percent.

c. American will lease the aircraft for 10 years at an annual rental of $5.5 million. At the end of 10 years, American has the option of returning the aircraft to Boeing or purchasing it for $55 million. The interest rate appropriate for a 10-year collateralized loan for American is 8 percent.

d. American will lease the aircraft for 18 years at an annual rental of $6.2 million, and will return the aircraft at the end of the lease term. In addition, American will pay a fee of $1,500 per hour for each hour over 5,000 hours per year that American flies the aircraft. American's average usage of its aircraft is currently 6,200 hours per year. The interest rate appropriate for an 18-year collateralized loan for American is 10 percent.

27. **Preparing lessee's journal entries for an operating lease and a capital lease.** On January 2, Year 6, Baldwin Products, as lessee, leases a machine used in its operations. The annual lease payment of $10,000 is due on December 31 of Year 6, Year 7, and Year 8. The machine reverts to the lessor at the end of three years. The lessor can either sell the machine or lease it to another firm for the remainder of its expected total useful life of five years. Baldwin Products could borrow on a three-year collateralized loan at 12 percent. The market value of the machine at the inception of the lease is $30,000.

a. Is this lease an operating lease or a capital lease?

b. Assume that this lease qualifies as an operating lease. Give the journal entries for Baldwin Products over the three-year lease period.

c. Assume that this lease qualifies as a capital lease. Repeat part **b**.

d. Compute the total expenses for the three-year period under the operating and capital lease methods.

28. **Preparing journal entries for income tax expense.** The income tax note to the financial statements of L.A. Gear for three recent years reports the amounts on the next page (amounts in thousands). The deferred taxes relate to uncollectible accounts. Assume that L.A. Gear has only deferred tax assets, no deferred tax liabilities.

a. Give the journal entry to record income tax expense for Year 4, Year 5, and Year 6.

b. Describe the likely reasons for the pattern of currently payable and deferred income taxes for each of the three years.

	Year 4	Year 5	Year 6
Components of Income Tax Expense			
Currently Payable	$37,919	$12,884	$(17,184)
Deferred	(3,555)	(3,492)	(5,543)
Total Income Tax Expense	$34,364	$ 9,392	$(22,727)

29. **Effect of temporary differences on income taxes.** Woodward Corporation purchases a new machine for $50,000 on January 1, Year 1. The machine has a four-year estimated service life and an estimated salvage value of zero. After paying the cost of running and maintaining the machine, the firm enjoys a $25,000-per-year excess of revenues over expenses (except depreciation and taxes). In addition to the $25,000 from the machine, other pretax income each year is $35,000. Woodward uses straight-line depreciation for financial reporting and MACRS for tax reporting. The MACRS depreciation percentages for this machine are 33 percent in the first year, 44 percent in the second, 15 percent in the third, and 8 percent in the fourth. Depreciation is Woodward's only temporary difference. Woodward pays combined federal and local income taxes at a rate of 40 percent of taxable income.
   a. Compute the amount of income taxes currently payable for each of the four years.
   b. Compute the book value of the machine for financial reporting and the tax basis of the machine for tax reporting at the end of each of the four years. The tax basis is the amortized cost for income tax purposes.
   c. Compute the amount of income tax expense for each of the four years.
   d. Give the components of the journal entries to record income tax expense and income tax payable for Year 1 through Year 4.

30. **Reconstructing information about income taxes.** Lilly Company reports the following information about its financial statements and tax return for a year:

Depreciation Expense from Financial Statements	$322,800
Financial Statement Pretax Income	190,800
Income Tax Expense from Financial Statements	42,000
Income Taxes Payable from Tax Returns	27,600

The federal and state governments combine to tax taxable income at a rate of 40 percent. Permanent differences result from municipal bond interest that appears as revenue in the financial statements but is exempt from income taxes. Temporary differences result from the use of accelerated depreciation for tax returns and straight-line depreciation for financial reporting.

   Reconstruct the income statement for financial reporting and for tax reporting for the year, identifying temporary differences and permanent differences.

31. **Effects of leases on statement of cash flows.** Refer to the simplified statement of cash flows in **Exhibit 4.12**. Eleven of the lines in the statement are numbered. Ignore the unnumbered lines in considering the transactions below.

   Assume that the accounting cycle is complete for the period and that a firm has prepared all of its financial statements. It then discovers that it has overlooked a transaction. It records that transaction in the accounts and corrects all of the financial statements. For each of the following transactions, indicate which of the numbered lines of the statement of cash flows change and the amount and direction (increase or decrease) of any change. Ignore income tax effects except when the problem explicitly mentions taxes.

   For the following transactions, assume that the leased asset has an economic life of ten years, costs $100,000, and requires lease payments of $19,925 per year, payable at the end of each year.
   a. The lessor, using the operating lease method, records depreciation for the year.
   b. The lessor, using the operating lease method, records receipt of a cash payment for the year. The lessor has not previously recognized revenue.
   c. The lessee, using the operating lease method, records payment of cash for the year. The lessee has not previously recognized expense.
   d. The lessee records the signing of a capital lease. The present value of the future cash payments when discounted at 15 percent is $100,000.
   e. The lessee, using the capital lease method, records payment of cash for the first year and uses an interest rate of 15 percent per year. Interest is $15,000, and $4,925 is a payment of principal.

32. Effects of income taxes on statement of cash flows. Refer to the instructions in the preceding exercise. For each of the following transactions, indicate which of the numbered lines of the statement of cash flows change and by how much. Assume an income tax rate of 40 percent of taxable income.

a. Pretax financial statement income is $200,000. Depreciation claimed on the tax return exceeds depreciation expense on the financial statements by $50,000. The firm makes an entry to record income tax expense and accrual of amounts payable because it has made no previous entry.

b. Pretax financial statement income is $300,000. Warranty deductions allowed on the tax return are less than warranty expense on the financial statements by $40,000. The firm makes an entry to record income tax expense and payment of amounts payable because it has made no previous entry for taxes.

c. Pretax financial statement income is $300,000. Bad debt expense on the financial statements exceeds deductions for bad debts allowed on the tax return by $40,000. The firm makes an entry to record income tax expense and payment of amounts payable because it has made no previous entry for taxes.

d. A firm records nontaxable municipal bond interest revenue of $10,000. It has made no previous entry for this interest. The firm records all effects of this transaction, including income tax effects (if any).

PROBLEMS AND CASES

33. Financial statement effects of operating and capital leases. Excerpts from the notes to the financial statements of Wal-Mart Stores for the year ending January 31, Year 9, appear below (amounts in millions).

Long-Term Lease Obligations. The company and certain of its subsidiaries maintain long-term leases for stores and equipment. Aggregate minimum annual rentals at January 31, Year 9, under leases appear below. Assume that Wal-Mart makes lease payments at the end of each fiscal year.

Fiscal Year Ending January 31:	Capital Leases	Operating Leases
Year 10	$ 204.7	$ 249.3
Year 11	205.2	238.2
Year 12	204.6	229.6
Year 13	204.8	220.7
Year 14	204.7	224.1
After Year 14	2,859.7	2,409.6
Total	$ 3,883.7	$3,571.5
Less Interest at 11 Percent	(2,189.5)	
Capital Lease Liability	$ 1,694.2	

a. Prepare the journal entry to record cash payments under capital leases during fiscal Year 10.

b. Prepare the journal entry to record cash payments under operating leases during fiscal Year 10.

c. Assume that the present value of Wal-Mart's operating lease commitments when discounted at 12 percent is $1,586.5 million on January 31, Year 9, and that these leases have a remaining life of 15 years. Give the journal entries to convert these operating leases into capital leases as of January 31, Year 9, and to account for them as capital leases for the year ending January 31, Year 10.

34. Financial statement effects of operating and capital leases. Excerpts from the notes to the financial statements of American Airlines for a recent year reveal the following (amounts in millions):

	December 31	
	Year 10	Year 11
Leased Asset (net of accumulated depreciation)	$1,716	$1,878
Lease Liability	$2,233	$2,403

Future minimum commitments under leases with lease periods extending beyond one year appear below.

Year	Capital Leases December 31, Year 10	Capital Leases December 31, Year 11	Operating Leases December 31, Year 10	Operating Leases December 31, Year 11
11	$ 268	—	$ 946	—
12	281	$ 273	924	$ 982
13	268	300	920	967
14	250	280	931	939
15	245	276	912	954
16	240	270	915	961
Later Years	2,164	2,440	14,463	16,420
	$3,716	$3,839	$20,011	$21,223
Interest Portion (8%)	(1,483)	(1,436)		
Capitalized Lease Obligation	$2,233	$2,403		

a. Assume that American Airlines makes all lease payments at the end of each year. Prepare an analysis that explains how the liability for capital leases increased from $2,233 million on December 31, Year 10, to $2,403 million on December 31, Year 11.

b. Prepare an analysis that explains how the leasehold asset increased from $1,716 million on December 31, Year 10, to $1,878 million on December 31, Year 11.

c. Give the journal entries to account for capital leases during Year 11.

d. Give the journal entries to account for operating leases during Year 11.

e. The present value at 10 percent of American's *operating* lease commitments is $7,793 million on December 31, Year 10, and $8,164 million on December 31, Year 11. The leases have an average remaining useful life of 22 years on each date. Prepare the journal entries to convert these operating leases into capital leases as of December 31, Year 10, and to account for the leases as capital leases during Year 11.

35. **Comparison of borrow/buy with operating and capital leases.** Carom Sports Collectibles Shop plans to acquire, as of January 1, Year 1, a computerized cash register system that costs $100,000 and has a five-year life and no salvage value. The company is considering two plans for acquiring the system:

(1) *Outright purchase.* To finance the purchase, the firm will issue $100,000 of par-value, 10-percent semiannual coupon bonds issued January 1, Year 1, at par. The bonds mature in five years.

(2) *Lease.* The lease requires five annual payments on December 31, Year 1, Year 2, Year 3, Year 4, and Year 5. The lease payments are such that they have a present value of $100,000 on January 1, Year 1, when discounted at 10 percent per year.

The firm will use straight-line amortization methods for all depreciation and amortization computations for assets.

a. Verify that the amount of the required lease payment is $26,380 by constructing an amortization schedule for the five payments. Note that there will be a $2 rounding error in the fifth year. Nevertheless, you may treat each payment as being $26,380 in the rest of the problem.

b. What balance sheet accounts are affected if the firm selects plan (1)? What if the firm uses plan (2) and the operating lease method? What if the firm selects plan (2) and it uses the capital lease method?

c. What is the total depreciation and interest expense for the five years under plan (1)?

d. What is the total expense for the five years under plan (2) if the firm was able to account for the lease as an operating lease? as a capital lease?

e. Why are the answers in part d the same? Why do the answers in part c differ from those in part d?

f. What is the total expense for Year 1 under plan (1)? under plan (2) accounted for as an operating lease? under plan (2) accounted for as a capital lease?

g. Repeat part f for Year 5.

36. **Accounting for lease by lessor and lessee.** IBM manufactures a particular computer for $6,000 and sells it for $10,000. Adair Corporation needs this computer in its operations and contemplates three ways of acquiring it on January 1, Year 11. The computer has a three-year estimated useful life and zero salvage value. Both firms use the straight-line depreciation method.

   (1) *Outright purchase.* Adair Corporation will borrow $10,000 from its bank and purchase the computer from IBM. The bank loan bears interest at 8 percent annually and requires payments of $3,880, which includes principal and interest, on December 31 of Year 11, Year 12, and Year 13.

   (2) *Operating lease.* Adair Corporation will lease the computer from IBM and account for it as an operating lease. IBM sets the annual payment due on December 31, Year 11, Year 12, and Year 13 at $3,810.

   (3) *Capital lease.* Adair Corporation will lease the computer from IBM and account for it as a capital lease, using an annual interest rate of 7 percent. The annual payment due on December 31 of Year 11, Year 12, and Year 13 is $3,810.

   a. Give the journal entries on the books of Adair Corporation on January 1, Year 11, December 31, Year 11, and December 31, Year 12 related to the loan and acquisition of the equipment assuming the outright purchase alternative.

   b. Repeat part **a** assuming the operating lease alternative.

   c. Repeat part **a** assuming the capital lease alternative.

   d. Give the journal entries on the books of IBM on January 1, Year 11, December 31, Year 11, and December 31, Year 12 related to the sale of the equipment assuming the outright sale alternative.

   e. Repeat part **d** assuming the operating lease alternative.

   f. Repeat part **d** assuming the capital lease alternative.

   g. Prepare a schedule of the total expenses incurred by Adair Corporation for Year 11, Year 12, and Year 13 under each of the three alternatives.

   h. Prepare a schedule of the total revenues and total expenses recognized by IBM for Year 11, Year 12, and Year 13 under each of the three alternatives.

37. **Financial statement effects of capitalizing operating leases.** Selected data (in millions) for three U.S. airlines appear below.

	American	Delta	United
Long-term Debt on Balance Sheet, End of Year	$7,878	$3,121	$ 3,617
Shareholders' Equity (Deficit), End of Year	3,380	1,827	(267)
Net Income (Loss), for Year	228	408	77
Present Value of Operating Lease Commitments, End of Year	8,164	7,307	10,645

   a. Compute the ratio of (long-term debt)/(long-term debt plus shareholders' equity) for the three airlines using amounts reported on the balance sheet.

   b. Repeat part **a** but include the present value of operating lease commitments in long-term debt.

   c. Suggest reasons why these airlines prefer to treat these leases as operating leases.

   d. Suggest how these airlines might have structured their leases to qualify as operating leases.

   e. Suggest reasons why airlines tend to lease rather than purchase their aircraft.

38. **Interpreting income tax disclosures.** Deere & Company manufactures agricultural and industrial equipment, which it sells through independent distributors. Deere recognizes revenue for financial reporting at the time it ships equipment to its independent distributors. It recognizes revenue for tax purposes using the installment method. Distributors have no rights to return unsold equipment, unless it is faulty. Deere rebates a portion of the selling price to distributors if they sell a certain volume of products each year. Deere also provides financing services to retail customers for Deere products sold by its independent distributors.

   The income tax note for Deere for Year 10 and Year 11 appears in **Exhibit 10.7** (amounts in millions).

   a. Give the journal entry to record income tax expense for Year 10.

   b. Was book income before income taxes larger or smaller than taxable income for Year 10? Explain.

   c. Give the journal entry to record income tax expense for Year 11.

   d. Was book income before income taxes larger or smaller than taxable income for Year 11? Explain.

	EXHIBIT 10.7	DEERE & COMPANY Income Tax Disclosures (all dollar amounts in millions) (Problem 38)		

	Year 10	Year 11
Income before Income Taxes	$588	$ (26)
Income Tax Expense		
Current	$124	$ 95
Deferred	58	$(100)
Total	$182	$ (5)
Income Taxes on Income before Income Taxes at the Statutory Tax Rate of 35%	$206	$ (9)
Tax-Exempt Interest	(30)	(3)
Foreign Tax Rates	6	7
Income Tax Expense (credit)	$182	$ (5)

	September 30		
	Year 9	Year 10	Year 11
COMPONENTS OF DEFERRED TAXES			
Deferred Tax Assets			
Uncollectible Accounts	$ 36	$ 44	$70
Sales Rebates and Allowances	22	37	58
Pensions	41	35	44
Valuation Allowance	(22)	(34)	(23)
Net Deferred Tax Assets	$ 77	$ 82	$ 149
Deferred Tax Liabilities			
Installment Sales Receivable	$126	$167	$ 127
Depreciable Assets	186	208	215
Deferred Tax Liability	$312	$375	$ 342

    e. What is the likely reason for the direction of change in the deferred liability relating to installment sales between Year 10 and Year 11?

    f. Assume that the income tax rate applicable to Year 11 and future years did not change during Year 11. Depreciation expense for book purposes was $209 million during Year 11. Compute the amount of depreciation expense Deere recognized for tax purposes for Year 11.

39. Interpreting income tax disclosures. Exhibit 10.8 presents data from the income tax note for Sun Microsystems for Year 5, Year 6, and Year 7 (amounts in millions). No changes occurred in the income tax rates applicable to Years 5 through 7 or to future years.

    a. Give the journal entry to record income tax expense for Year 5. You may combine federal, foreign, state, and local taxes.

    b. Was book income before income taxes larger or smaller than taxable income for Year 5? Explain.

    c. Repeat part **a** for Year 6.

    d. Repeat part **b** for Year 6.

    e. Repeat part **a** for Year 7.

    f. Repeat part **b** for Year 7.

    g. What was the likely direction of change in expenditures on depreciable assets between Year 6 and Year 7? Explain.

40. Interpreting income tax disclosures. Refer to the income tax note for General Products Company in **Exhibit 10.5** in this chapter. The income tax rate applicable to Year 1 through Year 4 and future years did not change.

    a. Was book income before income taxes larger or smaller than taxable income during Year 3? Explain.

    b. Was book income before income taxes larger or smaller than taxable income during Year 4? Explain.

EXHIBIT 10.8	**SUN MICROSYSTEMS** **Income Tax Disclosures (all dollar amounts in millions)** **(Problem 39)**			

	Year 5	Year 6	Year 7
INCOME (LOSS) BEFORE TAXES			
Domestic	$130	$ 49	$250
International	94	235	274
	$224	$284	$524

	Year 5	Year 6	Year 7
TAXES ON INCOME			
Current—Federal	$ 38	$ 28	$123
Foreign	38	60	57
State and Local	6	4	10
Deferred—Federal	(14)	(5)	(17)
Foreign	3	(5)	(11)
State and Local	(4)	6	5
	$ 67	$ 88	$167
EFFECTIVE TAX RATE			
Federal Tax Rate	35%	35%	35%
State and Local Taxes	2	2	1
Nontaxable Interest Revenue	(3)	(2)	(1)
Foreign Tax Rates	(4)	(5)	(6)
Other	—	1	3
	30%	31%	32%

	December 31			
	Year 4	Year 5	Year 6	Year 7
COMPONENTS OF DEFERRED TAXES				
Deferred Tax Assets				
Pension	$ 68	$ 73	$ 85	$ 101
Inventories	74	77	89	94
Deferred Tax Assets	$ 142	$ 150	$ 174	$ 195
Deferred Tax Liabilities				
Depreciation	$ 14	$ 7	$ 27	$ 25
Deferred Tax Liabilities	$ 14	$ 7	$ 27	$ 25

c. What is the likely interpretation of the increasing deferred tax asset for both uncollectible accounts receivable and warranty liability?

d. By how much did depreciation claimed on the tax return for Year 4 exceed book depreciation?

41. Behavior of deferred income tax account when a firm acquires new assets every year. Equilibrium Company has adopted a program of purchasing a new machine each year. It uses MACRS on its income tax return and straight-line depreciation on its financial statements. Each machine costs $12,000 installed, has an economic life of six years for financial reporting, and is in the five-year property class for MACRS. MACRS deductions are 20, 32, 19, 12, 11, and 6 percent of cost in each of the first six years, respectively.

a. Calculate the total depreciation deduction on the tax return for each of the first seven years in accordance with MACRS.

b. Calculate depreciation for each year using the straight-line method of depreciation.

c. Calculate the annual difference in depreciation charges using the results from parts **a** and **b**.

d. Calculate the annual increase in the Deferred Tax Liability account for the balance sheet by multiplying the tax rate, 40 percent, by the amount found in the preceding part.

e. Calculate year-end balances for the Deferred Tax Liability account on the balance sheet.

f. If Equilibrium Company continues to follow its policy of buying a new machine every year for $12,000, what will happen to the balance in the Deferred Tax Liability account on the balance sheet?

42. Attempts to achieve off-balance-sheet financing. (Adapted from materials by R. Dieter, D. Landsittel, J. Stewart, and A. Wyatt.) Shiraz Company wants to raise $50 million cash but, for various reasons, does not want to do so in a way that results in a newly recorded liability. It is sufficiently solvent and profitable that its bank is willing to lend up to $50 million at the prime interest rate. Shiraz Company's financial executives have devised six different plans, described in the following sections.

Plan 1: Transfer of Receivables with Recourse. Shiraz Company will transfer to Credit Company its long-term accounts receivable, which call for payments over the next two years. Credit Company will pay an amount equal to the present value of the receivables less an allowance for uncollectibles as well as a discount because it is paying now but will collect cash later. Shiraz Company must repurchase from Credit Company at face value any receivables that become uncollectible in excess of the allowance. In addition, Shiraz Company may repurchase any of the receivables not yet due at face value less a discount specified by formula and based on the prime rate at the time of the initial transfer. (This option permits Shiraz Company to benefit if an unexpected drop in interest rates occurs after the transfer.) The accounting issue is whether the transfer is a sale (Shiraz Company debits Cash, credits Accounts Receivable, and debits an expense or loss on transfer) or whether the transfer is merely a loan collateralized by the receivables (Shiraz Company debits Cash and credits Notes Payable at the time of transfer).

Plan 2: Product Financing Arrangement. Shiraz Company will transfer inventory to Credit Company, who will store the inventory in a public warehouse. Credit Company may use the inventory as collateral for its own borrowings, whose proceeds will be used to pay Shiraz Company. Shiraz Company will pay storage costs and will repurchase all the inventory within the next four years at contractually fixed prices plus interest accrued for the time elapsed between the transfer and later repurchase. The accounting issue is whether Shiraz has sold the inventory to Credit Company, with later repurchases treated as new acquisitions for Shiraz's inventory, or whether Shiraz has merely borrowed from Credit Company, with the inventory remaining on Shiraz's balance sheet.

Plan 3: Throughput Contract. Shiraz Company wants a branch line of a railroad built from the main rail line to carry raw material directly to its own plant. It could, of course, borrow the funds and build the branch line itself. Instead, it will sign an agreement with the railroad to ship specified amounts of material each month for ten years. Even if it does not ship the specified amounts of material, it will pay the agreed shipping costs. The railroad will take the contract to its bank and, using it as collateral, borrow the funds to build the branch line. The accounting issue is whether Shiraz Company should debit an asset for future rail services and credit a liability for payments to the railroad. The alternative is to make no accounting entry except when Shiraz makes payments to the railroad.

Plan 4: Construction Joint Venture. Shiraz Company and Mission Company will jointly build a plant to manufacture chemicals that both companies need in their production processes. Each will contribute $5 million to the project, called Chemical. Chemical will borrow another $40 million from a bank, with Shiraz, only, guaranteeing the debt. Shiraz and Mission are each to contribute equally to future operating expenses and debt service payments of Chemical, but in return for guaranteeing the debt, Shiraz will have an option to purchase Mission's interest for $20 million four years later. The accounting issue is whether Shiraz Company, which will ultimately be responsible for all debt service payments, should recognize a liability for the funds that Chemical borrowed. Alternatively, the debt guarantee is merely a commitment that Shiraz Company must disclose in notes to its financial statements.

Plan 5: Research and Development Partnership. Shiraz Company will contribute a laboratory and preliminary findings about a potentially profitable gene-splicing discovery to a partnership, called Venture. Venture will raise funds by selling the remaining interest in the partnership to outside investors for $2 million and by borrowing $48 million from a bank, with Shiraz Company guaranteeing the debt. Although Venture will operate under the management of Shiraz Company, it will be free to sell the results of its further discoveries and development efforts to anyone, including Shiraz Company. Shiraz Company has no obligation to purchase any of Venture's output. The accounting issue is whether Shiraz Company should recognize the liability. (Would it make any difference if Shiraz Company did not guarantee the loan but had either the option to purchase or an obligation to purchase the results of Venture's work?)

Plan 6: Hotel Financing. Shiraz Company owns and operates a profitable hotel. It could use the hotel as collateral for a conventional mortgage loan. Instead, it considers selling the hotel to a partnership for $50 million cash. The partnership will sell ownership interests to outside investors for $5 million and borrow $45 million from a bank on a conventional mortgage loan, using the hotel as collateral. Shiraz Company guarantees the debt. The accounting issue is whether Shiraz Company should record the liability for the guaranteed debt of the partnership. Discuss whether Shiraz Company should recognize any of these obligations or commitments as a liability on its balance sheet.

43. **Bundled leases and related earnings quality and ethical issues for Xerox Corporation.** Assume that Xerox enters into a seven-year lease with Ford Motor Company for a constellation of copying equipment. The lease requires Ford to pay to Xerox $14,816.12 at the end of each of the seven years following the date of Xerox's delivering and installing the equipment on Ford premises. The copying equipment cost Xerox $23,000 to manufacture.

The lease requires that Xerox will provide Ford with on-site emergency service and regular maintenance at no cost additional to the annual payment. Such service contracts ordinarily cost $2,000 per year. The lease requires that Xerox will provide Ford with all toner and other supplies at no cost additional to the annual payment. Such supply contracts ordinarily cost the user $1,200 per year, if the user purchases these separately. Assume, unrealistically, that firms would make these payments at the end of the year.

Because Xerox cannot readily establish the stand-alone sales price of the equipment in comparable transactions, it cannot make a direct estimate of the revenue for the equipment element of its bundled leases. Instead, Xerox directly estimates the financing revenues. To this end, Xerox developed procedures to measure the fair value of the financing revenue included in its total revenue from bundled leases. Xerox has estimated from publicly available data that Ford Motor Company ordinarily must pay 15 percent per year, compounded annually, to finance over seven years any purchases for equipment being leased.

a. Compute the amount of each payment attributable to the equipment and financing, combined.

b. Compute the present value of Xerox's collections attributable for the equipment and financing, combined.

c. Construct an amortization schedule to allocate the total receipts for equipment and financing into those two components. Use the 15 percent rate suitable for Ford. What is total interest revenue for the 7 years?

d. Compute Xerox's gross profit from the equipment on signing the lease.

e. If Xerox were to estimate a lower interest rate for Ford, but all the other data remain unchanged, would Xerox's gross profit recognized at the time the lease begins increase or decrease?

f. Re-do parts **c** and **d** using a 12 percent rate as suitable for Ford. If you do the computations correctly, you will see that gross profit increases by 18.5 percent, which meant several hundred million dollars of income in the case of Xerox.

g. What ethical issues might accompany Xerox's estimation of Ford's borrowing rate? How do these estimates affect Xerox's quality of earnings?

chapter 11

Marketable Securities, Derivatives, and Investments

Learning Objectives

1. Understand why firms acquire securities of other firms and how the purpose of the investment governs the method of accounting for that investment.

2. Develop skills to apply the market value method to minority, passive investments, including financial derivatives.

3. Develop skills to apply the equity method to minority, active investments, contrasting its financial statement effects with those of the market value method.

4. Understand the concepts underlying consolidated financial statements for majority, active investments, contrasting the financial statement effects of consolidation with those of the equity method.

5. Understand when a firm must consolidate a variable interest entity, for which it does not have conventional control, but does have parent-like characteristics.

For a variety of reasons, corporations often acquire the securities (bonds, preferred stock, common stock) of other entities.

Example 1   Southwest Airlines sells airline tickets and receives cash prior to providing transportation services. Rather than let the cash remain idle in its bank account, Southwest Airlines acquires U.S. Treasury Notes. The firm earns interest while it holds the notes and will sell the notes when it needs the cash for operations.

Example 2   Merck, a pharmaceutical company, acquires shares of common stock of several firms engaged in biotechnology research. Merck will benefit from increases in the market prices of these shares if the research efforts are successful.

Example 3   The Coca-Cola Company owns 40 percent of the common stock of Coca-Cola Enterprises, a bottler of its soft drinks. This ownership percentage permits The Coca-Cola Company to exert significant influence over the operations of Coca-Cola Enterprises and keep the affiliate's debt off the parent's balance sheet.

Example 4   Walt Disney owns all of the common stock of ABC/Capital Cities. Walt Disney can control both the broad policy and the day-to-day business decisions of ABC/Capital Cities.

Overview of the Accounting and Reporting of Investments in Securities

The accounting for investments in securities depends on (1) the expected holding period, and (2) the purpose of the investment.

Expected Holding Period

The expected holding period determines where investments in securities appear in the balance sheet. Securities that firms expect to sell within the next year appear as **Marketable Securities** in the Current Assets section of the balance sheet. In **Example 1**, Southwest Airlines would likely include the U.S. Treasury Notes in Marketable Securities. Securities that firms expect to hold for more than one year from the date of the balance sheet appear in **Investments in Securities**, which firms include in a separate section of the balance sheet between Current Assets and Property, Plant and Equipment. The investments in biotechnology companies by Merck in **Example 2** and the investment in Coca-Cola Enterprises by The Coca-Cola Company in **Example 3** appear in Investments in Securities. A later section explains that Walt Disney would prepare consolidated financial statements with ABC/Capital Cities. The consolidation procedure requires Walt Disney to eliminate its Investment in ABC/Capital Cities account and replace it with that firm's individual assets and liabilities. Thus, the Investment in ABC/Capital Cities account will not appear on the balance sheet. Although we and others use the phrase *investment in securities* to refer broadly to all investments in the bonds, capital stock, and other financial instruments of other entities, the preferred usage reserves the word *investment* for holdings with a long-term purpose.

Purpose of the Investments

The purpose of the investment in securities and the percentage of voting stock that one corporation owns of another determine the accounting for the investment. Refer to **Figure 11.1**, which identifies three types of investments.

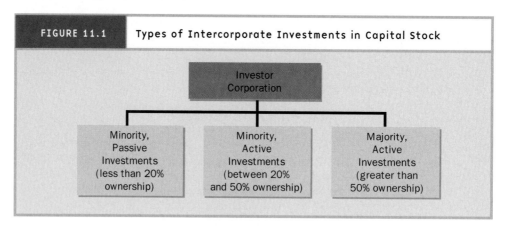

FIGURE 11.1 Types of Intercorporate Investments in Capital Stock

1. In **minority, passive investments**, an investor views acquiring bonds or shares of capital stock of another corporation as a worthwhile expenditure and acquires them for the interest, dividends and capital gains (increases in the market prices) anticipated from owning them. The acquiring company owns such a small percentage of the other corporation's shares that it cannot control or exert **significant influence** over the other company. Southwest Airlines' investment in U.S. Treasury notes in **Example 1** and Merck's investments in the common stock of biotechnology companies in **Example 2** are minority, passive investments. Occasionally, an owner of a small percentage of the shares has the contractual right to elect one or more members of the board of directors. If so, the acquiring company, even though a small percentage holder, could exercise significant influence. Generally accepted accounting principles (GAAP) view investments of less than 20 percent of the voting stock of another company as minority, passive investments in most cases.[1] The owner may intend to hold these shares for relatively short time spans and classify them as current assets or for a longer time and classify them as investments.

2. In **minority, active investments**, an investor acquires shares of another corporation so that it can exert significant influence over the other company's activities. The investor might seek broad policy-making influence through representation on the other corporation's board of directors. Many different entities own the shares of most publicly held corporations, and most of these have not collaborated in voting their shares, although this is changing. Therefore, an owner can exert significant influence over another corporation with ownership of less than a majority of the voting stock. The investment by The Coca-Cola Company in the shares of Coca-Cola Enterprises in **Example 3** is a minority, active investment. GAAP view investments of between 20 and 50 percent of the voting stock of another company as minority, active investments "unless evidence indicates that significant influence cannot be exercised."[2] Minority, active investments appear under investments on the balance sheet.

3. In **majority, active investments**, an investor acquires shares of another corporation so that it can control the other company both at the broad policy-making level and at the day-to-day

[1] Accounting Principles Board, *Opinion No. 18,* "The Equity Method of Accounting for Investments in Common Stock," 1971.

[2] Ibid.; *Financial Accounting Standards Board, Interpretation No. 35,* "Criteria for Applying the Equity Method of Accounting for Investments in Common Stock," 1981.

operational level. Refer to **Example 4**. Walt Disney acquired ABC/Capital Cities to add television broadcasting to its entertainment capabilities. GAAP view ownership of more than 50 percent of the voting stock of another company as implying an ability to control, unless there is evidence to the contrary. An investor cannot exercise control over a corporation, despite owning a majority of the voting stock, if a court effectively controls the corporation in bankruptcy proceedings or if the investor owns shares in a foreign company whose government restricts the withdrawal of assets from the country.

This chapter describes and illustrates the accounting for each of these three types of investments. Throughout our discussion, we will designate the acquiring corporation as P, for purchaser or for parent, depending on the context, and the acquired corporation as S, for seller or for subsidiary.

Minority, Passive Investments

Valuation of Securities at Acquisition

A firm initially records the acquisition of securities at acquisition cost, which includes the purchase price plus any commissions, taxes, and other costs incurred. For example, if a firm acquires securities classified as Marketable Securities for $10,000 plus $300 for commissions and taxes, the entry is as follows:

Marketable Securities (Asset Increase)	10,300	
Cash (Asset Decrease)		10,300

Dividends on equity securities become revenue when declared. Interest on debt securities becomes revenue when earned. Assume that a firm holds equity securities earning $250 through dividend declarations and debt securities earning $300 from interest earned and that it has not yet received these amounts in cash. The entry is as follows:

Dividends and Interest Receivable (Asset Increase)	550	
Retained Earnings (Dividend Revenue) (Shareholders' Equity Increase) ...		250
Retained Earnings (Interest Revenue) (Shareholders' Equity Increase)		300

The valuation of minority, passive investments at the date of acquisition or the recording of dividends and interest presents no new issues. Valuing securities after acquisition, however, departs from acquisition cost accounting.

Valuation of Securities after Acquisition

The Financial Accounting Standards Board (FASB) *Statement of Financial Accounting Standards No. 115*[3] requires firms to classify minority, passive investments in securities into three categories:

1. Debt securities for which a firm has both the positive intent and the ability to hold to maturity—shown on the balance sheet at an amount based on acquisition cost
2. Debt and equity securities, as well as derivatives, held as trading securities—shown on the balance sheet at market value, with changes in market value of securities held at the end of the accounting period reported each period in income
3. Debt and equity securities, as well as derivatives, held as securities available for sale—shown on the balance sheet at market value, with changes in market value of securities held at the end of the accounting period not affecting reported income until the firm sells, or otherwise disposes of, the securities

---

[3] Financial Accounting Standards Board, Statement of *Financial Accounting Standards No. 115*, "Accounting for Certain Investments in Debt and Equity Securities," 1993.

This three-way classification resulted from one of the most contentious battles ever to involve the attention of accounting standard-setters, including the FASB and several of its predecessor organizations. We discuss the controversy at the end of this section.

Debt Securities Held to Maturity   Firms sometimes acquire debt securities with the intention of holding these securities until maturity, as in the next example.

Example 5   Consolidated Edison, an electric utility, has $100 million of bonds payable outstanding that mature in five years. The utility acquires U.S. government securities whose periodic interest payments and maturity value exactly equal those on the utility's outstanding bonds. The firm intends to use the cash received from the government bonds to make required interest and principal payments on its own bonds.

A Practice of Corporate Finance   Some students ask why a business would purchase bonds and then use the cash throwoff from those bonds to make debt service payments, rather than use cash to retire the bonds immediately. After firms issue bonds, the broad investing public holds these securities. The subsequent transaction costs the firm would incur if it were to attempt to contact all of the holders and then persuade them to turn in their bonds for cash make the effort too expensive to be cost-effective. Instead the firm uses the cash to acquire other bonds whose cash throwoffs approximately match the cash needs for debt service. Corporate finance courses treat transactions such as these. Here, the presentation emphasizes the accounting for the transaction, not why the firm enters into it.

Accounting for Debt Held to Maturity   Debt securities for which a firm has a positive intent and ability to hold to maturity appear in the Investments section of the balance sheet at amortized acquisition cost. A firm initially records these debt securities at acquisition cost. This acquisition cost will differ from the maturity value of the debt if the coupon rate on the bonds differs from the required market yield on the bonds at the time the firm acquired them. The firm must amortize any difference between acquisition cost and maturity value over the life of the debt as an adjustment to interest revenue. The amortization procedure involves the same compound interest computation that **Chapter 9** introduced for the issuer of the bonds.

The holder of the debt records interest revenue each period at an amount equal to the book value of the investment in debt at the start of the period, multiplied by the market rate of interest applicable to that debt on the day the firm acquired it. It debits the Investment account and credits Interest Revenue, which increases Retained Earnings. Then, if it receives cash, it debits Cash and credits the Investment account. The result of this process is a new book value (called the *amortized cost*) for use in the computations during the next period. See **Exhibit 9.6**. The holder of the debt securities in those illustrations makes the same entries, with reversed debits and credits.

Problem 11.1 for Self-Study

Accounting for an interest-bearing note receivable.   (Compare with **Problem 9.2** for Self-Study.) General Electric Capital Services (GECS) lends $112,434 to Sapra Company. GECS lends the cash of $112,434 in return for a three-year, $100,000 note, in which Sapra Company promises to pay $15,000 after one year, $15,000 after two years, and $115,000 after three years. The market interest rate on the original issue date of the note is 10 percent.

a. Prepare an amortization schedule, similar to that in **Exhibit 9.2**, for the life of the note. Change the column headings as follows: Column (2) is Note Receivable Balance Start of Period; Column (3) is Interest Revenue for Period; Column (6) is Note Receivable Balance End of Period.

b. Prepare journal entries that GECS would make on three dates: the date of issue, six months after the date of issue (assuming GECS closes the books then), and one year after the date of issue (assuming GECS receives a cash payment from Sapra then).

Trading Securities   Firms sometimes purchase and sell debt and equity securities for the short-term profit potential—some would say for *speculation*. The term *trading* implies active and frequent buying and selling with the objective of generating profits from short-term differences in market prices. Acquisition and disposition of trading securities are operating activities. Commercial banks, for example, often trade securities in different capital markets worldwide to take advantage of temporary differences in market prices. Other financial firms, such as thrift institutions, insurance companies, and brokerage firms, also trade securities. Manufacturers, retailers, and other nonfinancial firms occasionally invest funds for trading purposes, but such situations are unusual. Firms include trading securities in Marketable Securities in the Current Assets section of the balance sheet.

Firms initially record trading securities at acquisition cost. FASB *Statement No. 115* requires firms to report trading securities at *market value* on the balance sheet. The FASB justifies this departure from acquisition cost accounting on two factors: (1) active securities markets provide objective measures of market values, and (2) market values provide financial statement users with the most relevant information for assessing the success of a firm's trading activities over time.

The income statement reports the debit (loss) for decreases in the market value and the credit (gain) for increases in the market value of trading securities in an account with a title such as *Unrealized Holding Loss* (or *Gain* or *Gains and Losses, net*) *on Valuation of Trading Securities*.

Example 6   First Insurance acquired shares of Sun Microsystems' common stock on December 28, Year 3, for $400,000. The market value of these securities on December 31, Year 3, was $435,000. First Insurance sold these shares on January 3, Year 4, for $480,000. The journal entries to record these transactions appear below.

December 28, Year 3		
Marketable Securities (Asset Increase)	400,000	
Cash (Asset Decrease)		400,000
To record acquisition of trading securities.		
December 31, Year 3		
Marketable Securities (Asset Increase)	35,000	
Retained Earnings (Unrealized Holding Gain on Trading Securities)		
(Shareholders' Equity Increase)		35,000
To revalue trading securities to market value and recognize an unrealized holding gain in income.		
January 3, Year 4		
Cash (Asset Increase)	480,000	
Marketable Securities (Asset Decrease)		435,000
Retained Earnings (Realized Gain on Sale of Trading Securities)		
(Shareholders' Equity Increase)		45,000
To record the sale of trading securities at a gain.		

The total income from the purchase and sale of these securities is $80,000 (equals cash inflows of $480,000 minus cash outflows of $400,000). The required accounting allocates $35,000 to Year 3, the change in market value during that year, and $45,000 to Year 4, the change in market value during that year.

Securities Available for Sale   FASB *Statement No. 115* classifies securities that are neither debt securities held to maturity nor trading securities as *securities available for sale*. Securities available for sale that a firm intends to sell within one year appear in Marketable Securities in the Current Assets section of the balance sheet. All others appear in Investments in Securities. Acquisition and disposition of securities available for sale, whether current or noncurrent, are investing activities. The FASB requires firms to report these securities at market value on the balance sheet. Securities in this category often trade in active securities markets and therefore have easily measurable market values. Firms typically acquire these securities for an operating purpose (for example, investment of temporarily excess cash or investment in a supplier) rather than for their short-term profit potential, the typical reason for investments in trading securities.

Accounting for Securities Available for Sale   Firms initially record investments in securities available for sale at acquisition cost. FASB *Statement No. 115* requires firms to report securities available for sale at market value on the balance sheet. *The unrealized holding gain or holding loss each period does not affect income immediately, as is the case with trading securities, but instead increases or decreases Accumulated Other Comprehensive Income, a separate shareholders' equity account.* Accumulated Other Comprehensive Income is a shareholders' equity account, which shows the sum of all increases and decreases in shareholders' equity that have not yet appeared in net income. **Chapter 12** discusses this account and the related accounts for its periodic components, called Other Comprehensive Income. Holding gains and losses on securities available for sale affect net income only when the firm sells these securities. The FASB's reasoning for delaying the recognition of holding gains and losses in earnings is that firms do not acquire securities classified as available for sale for the short-term returns, as with trading securities, but for support of an operating activity. Also, including unrealized gains and losses in earnings might result in significant earnings changes that could easily reverse during future periods.

Example 7   Nike has temporarily excess cash and acquires common stock of Merck for $400,000 on November 1, Year 3. The market value of these shares is $435,000 on December 31, Year 3. Nike sells these shares on August 15, Year 4, for $480,000. The journal entries to record these transactions are as follows:

November 1, Year 3		
Marketable Securities (Asset Increase)	400,000	
Cash (Asset Decrease)		400,000
To record acquisition of securities available for sale.		
December 31, Year 3		
Marketable Securities (Asset Increase)	35,000	
Accumulated Other Comprehensive Income (Unrealized Holding Gain on Securities Available for Sale) (Shareholders' Equity Increase)		35,000
To revalue securities available for sale to market value and record an unrealized gain. Don't overlook the fact that the increase in shareholders' equity appears directly in the Shareholders' Equity section and in other comprehensive income, but not in net income.		
August 15, Year 4		
Cash (Asset Increase)	480,000	
Marketable Securities (Asset Decrease)		400,000
Retained Earnings (Realized Gain on Sale of Securities Available for Sale) (Shareholders' Equity Increase)		80,000
To record the sale of securities available for sale at a gain based on acquisition cost.		

If Nike intended to hold the shares of Merck for more than one year, then it would debit or credit Investment in Securities instead of Marketable Securities in the three entries above.

The total income from the purchase and sale of these securities is $80,000 (equals cash inflow of $480,000 minus cash outflow of $400,000). The required accounting allocates the full gain to the year of sale, even though the balance sheet reports changes in market value of the assets as they occur. At the time of sale, or later in the period when the firm makes adjusting entries, it must make the following entry:

August 15, Year 4 (or later, at time of adjusting entries)		
Accumulated Other Comprehensive Income (Unrealized Holding Gain on Securities Available for Sale) (Shareholders' Equity Decrease)	35,000	
Marketable Securities (Asset Decrease)		35,000
To eliminate the previously recorded effects of changes in market values of securities available for sale.		

The credit in this entry reduces the asset valuation: the firm no longer holds the security, so the accounting must remove from the balance sheet not only the asset's acquisition cost—as in the first August 15 entry above—but also the increases in market value included in the asset's valuation. The debit removes the unrealized gain from Accumulated Other Comprehensive Income in shareholders' equity. Total shareholders' equity has increased by $80,000 while this firm held the securities, and the Gain on Sale account shows all that gain, which increases Retained Earnings.

We can summarize the effects as follows:

- In the year of purchase, asset valuation and shareholders' equity both increased by $35,000 from the increase in market value, but the increase has no effect on net income or Retained Earnings. The shareholders' equity account showing the increase is part of Accumulated Other Comprehensive Income.
- In the next year, asset valuation and shareholders' equity increased another $45,000. Retained Earnings increases by $80,000—the full gain on holding the securities. The shareholders' equity account for Unrealized Gain must decrease by $35,000 (= $80,000 − $45,000), just equal to the amounts of the market gain increase that the firm recorded in periods before the firm sold the security and realized the gain.

Summary of Accounting for Securities Available for Sale
The accounting for securities available for sale involves three transactions or events.

1. Acquisition of Securities Available for Sale

Marketable Securities (Asset Increase)	Acquisition Cost
Cash (Asset Decrease)	Acquisition Cost

2. Revaluation to Market Value at End of Each Accounting Period

Marketable Securities (Asset Increase)	Increase in Market Value above Book Value
Accumulated Other Comprehensive Income (Unrealized Holding Gain on Securities Available for Sale) (Shareholders' Equity Increase)	Increase in Market Value above Book Value
Accumulated Other Comprehensive Income (Unrealized Holding Loss on Securities Available for Sale) (Shareholders' Equity Decrease)	Decrease in Market Value below Book Value
Marketable Securities (Asset Decrease)	Decrease in Market Value below Book Value

The unrealized holding gain and loss accounts are Accumulated Other Comprehensive Income accounts, that is, shareholders' equity accounts, not income statement accounts. The accountant can make separate entries for each security held or a single, combined entry for the portfolio of securities.

3. Sale of Securities Available for Sale

Cash (Asset Increase)	Proceeds of Sale
Marketable Securities (Asset Decrease)	Acquisition Cost
Retained Earnings (Realized Gain on Sale of Securities Available for Sale) (Shareholders' Equity Increase)	Plug Amount
Securities sold for amount larger than acquisition cost.	
Cash (Asset Increase)	Proceeds of Sale
Retained Earnings (Realized Loss on Sale of Securities Available for Sale) (Shareholders' Equity Decrease)	Plug Amount
Marketable Securities (Asset Decrease)	Acquisition Cost
Securities sold for amount smaller than acquisition cost.	

The realized gain or loss accounts appear in the income statement as increases or decreases to Retained Earnings. Once the firm has sold the securities, it no longer has an unrealized gain or loss from holding these securities. The final step in the accounting eliminates from the balance sheet the recording of the unrealized holding gain or loss. The next entry eliminates any excess of the book value of the securities sold over their original acquisition cost.

Accumulated Other Comprehensive Income (Unrealized Holding Gain on Securities Available for Sale) (Shareholders' Equity Decrease)	Excess of Book Value over Acquisition Cost	
Marketable Securities (Asset Decrease)		Excess of Book Value over Acquisition Cost

These securities had risen in value between the time of acquisition and the time of sale. The firm had recorded an unrealized holding gain and an increase in the value of the securities. Now it eliminates both the unrealized holding gain and the securities themselves.

When the firm sells securities, it records the realized gain (or loss) as the difference between sales price and acquisition cost. It reduces the carrying amount of securities by the amount of acquisition cost in the entry recognizing the gain (or loss). The above entry reduces the carrying amount of the securities for the increases recorded since acquisition. After this entry, the balance in the securities account for the securities sold is zero because the firm no longer holds these specific securities. The firm can make this entry at the time of sale of an individual security or at the end of the period as part of the revaluation of the portfolio of securities.

If the firm had recorded unrealized holding losses on the securities before it sold them, the final entry, made at time of sale or the end of the period, would be:

Marketable Securities (Asset Increase)	Excess of Acquisition Cost over Book Value	
Accumulated Other Comprehensive Income (Unrealized Holding Loss on Securities Available For Sale) (Shareholders' Equity Increase)		Excess of Acquisition Cost over Book Value

When the firm sells securities, it records the loss as the difference between sales price and acquisition cost. It reduces the carrying amount of securities by the amount of acquisition cost in the entry recognizing the loss, which creates a credit balance in the securities account for the security sold. This entry restores the balance in that account to zero. The firm can make this entry at the time of sale of an individual security or at the end of the period as part of the revaluation of the portfolio of securities.

An Earnings Quality Issue   The unrealized holding gain on securities available for sale appears in other comprehensive income period by period, and its cumulative amount resides in the Accumulated Other Comprehensive Income account on the balance sheet. Whenever management wishes, it can sell securities with unrealized holding gains (or losses) and transfer through net income to retained earnings the entire unrealized holding gain (or loss). To the extent a firm has unrealized holding gains and losses in Accumulated Other Comprehensive Income, the firm can decide the amounts to report in any period as realized gains and losses, affecting the quality of earnings. Analysts do not have difficulty in understanding the potential for management to use the unrealized gains and losses to manage earnings and report possibly misleading financial statements.

Reclassification of Securities

The firm's purpose for holding certain securities may change, requiring it to transfer securities from one of the three categories to another one. The firm transfers the security at its market value at the time of the transfer. FASB *Statement No. 115* prescribes the accounting for any unrealized gain or loss at the time of the transfer, a topic discussed in intermediate accounting principles textbooks.

Problem 11.2 for Self-Study

Accounting for securities available for sale. Transactions involving Conlin Corporation's marketable securities available for sale appear in **Exhibit 11.1**.

EXHIBIT 11.1	CONLIN CORPORATION (Problem 11.2 for Self-Study)

					Market Value	
Security	Date Acquired	Acquisition Cost	Date Sold	Selling Price	Dec. 31, Year 2	Dec. 31, Year 3
A	2/3/Year 2	$ 40,000	—	—	$ 38,000	$ 33,000
B	7/15/Year 2	75,000	9/6/Year 3	$78,000	79,000	—
C	11/27/Year 2	90,000	—	—	93,000	94,000
		$205,000			$210,000	$127,000

a. Give the journal entries to account for these securities during Year 2 and Year 3.
b. How would the journal entries in part **a** differ if Conlin Corporation acquired these securities available for sale as long-term investments?
c. How would the journal entries in part **a** differ if Conlin Corporation classified these securities as trading securities?

Disclosures about Securities

FASB *Statement No. 115* requires the following disclosures each period:

1. The aggregate market value, gross unrealized holding gains, gross unrealized holding losses, and amortized cost for debt securities held to maturity and debt and equity securities available for sale
2. The proceeds from sales of securities available for sale, and the gross realized gains and gross realized losses on those sales
3. The change during the period in the net unrealized holding gain or loss on securities available for sale included in a separate shareholders' equity account
4. The change during the period in the net unrealized holding gain or loss on trading securities included in earnings

In addition, firms often show the gross gains and gross losses included in earnings from transfers of securities from the available-for-sale category. **Exhibit 11.2**, expanded from **Exhibit 6.4**, illustrates these disclosures.

Controversy Surrounding the Accounting for Marketable Securities

The accounting for minority, passive investments in securities has been controversial. We try to give the flavor of the controversy without the details. The accounting issues are as follows:

- Whether to report these securities at acquisition cost (or some method based on acquisition cost) or at market value on the balance sheet date
- If reported at market value, whether to report the changes in market value from period to period as part of that period's income, or await the period when the firm sells or otherwise disposes of the security to record the gain or loss in income

EXHIBIT 11.2	ALEXIS COMPANY Detailed Illustration of Current Assets Balance Sheet (Excerpts) June 30, Year 1 and Year 2

	June 30, Year 1		June 30, Year 2	
Current Assets				
Cash in Change and Petty Cash Funds		$ 800		$ 1,000
Cash in Bank		11,000		13,000
Cash Held as Compensating Balances		1,500		1,500
Certificates of Deposit		7,500		8,000
Marketable Securities at Market Value (see Note A)		25,000		27,000
Notes Receivable (see Note B)		10,000		12,000
Interest and Dividends Receivable		400		500
Accounts Receivable, Gross	$57,200		$58,100	
Less Allowance for Uncollectible Accounts	(3,500)		(3,600)	
Accounts Receivable, Net		53,700		54,500
Merchandise Inventory[a]		67,000		72,000
Prepayments		4,300		4,800
Total Current Assets		$181,200		$194,300

Note A. Gross unrealized holding gains and gross unrealized holding losses on Marketable Securities are as follows:

	June 30, Year 1	June 30, Year 2
Gross Unrealized Holding Gains	$ 7,000	$ 7,000
Gross Unrealized Holding Losses	(1,000)	(10,000)
Net Unrealized Holding Gain (Loss)	$ 6,000	$ (3,000)

The net unrealized holding gain (loss) changed during the year as follows:

Net Unrealized Holding Gain, June 30, Year 1	$ 6,000
Unrealized Holding Gain on Securities Sold	1,000
Unrealized Holding Loss for Year Ending June 30, Year 2	(10,000)
Net Unrealized Holding Loss, June 30, Year 2	$ (3,000)

Note B. The amount shown for Notes Receivable does not include notes with a face amount of $2,000 that have been discounted with recourse at The First National Bank. The company is contingently liable for these notes, should the makers not honor them at maturity. The estimated amount of the company's liability is zero.

[a]Additional required disclosures for this item do not appear here. See **Chapter 7**.

Nonfinancial Firms   For nonfinancial firms, the primary controversy surrounds the treatment of financial derivatives that these firms use in reducing, that is, hedging, their risks of exposure to fluctuations in interest rates or in prices of raw materials that the firm will need to acquire later. The next section of this chapter discusses the accounting for such hedges. Before the FASB *Statement of Financial Accounting Standards No. 133,* "Accounting for Derivative Instruments and Hedging Activities," in 1998, nonfinancial firms engaging in hedges of forecasted transactions feared that the FASB would require them to show the gains and losses in income each period. The FASB had proposed such treatment; however, under pressure from nonfinancial firms, it ruled that such gains and losses need not appear in net income but only in comprehensive income, until subsequent events unfolded.

Financial Firms   Financial firms, such as commercial and investment banks, generally hold substantial positions in marketable securities among their assets. The accounting for marketable securities impacts not only the amounts these firms reports as assets, but also the amounts they report as earnings and shareholders' equity. Financial firms typically carry higher debt-equity ratios than nonfinancial firms. The recording of marketable securities at market value results in an increase in the debt-equity ratio when market values decrease (shareholders' equity declines with no change in liabilities). Increased debt-equity ratios usually get the attention of bank regulators. To understand how the accounting interacts with the regulations to make financial firms, particularly banks, sensitive to market value accounting, refer to **Problem 52** at the end of this chapter.

Firms incur various risks in carrying out their business operations. A fire may destroy a warehouse of a retail chain and disrupt the flow of merchandise to stores. An automobile accident involving a member of the sales staff may injure the employee or others and damage the firm's automobile. A firm's products may injure customers and subject the firm to lawsuits. Most firms purchase property, medical, and liability insurance against such risks. The insurance shifts the risk of the loss, at least up to the limits in the insurance policy, to the insurance company. The firm pays insurance premiums for the right to shift the risk of these losses.

Firms engage in other transactions that subject them to risks. Consider the following scenarios.

Example 8 Firm A, a U.S. firm, orders a machine on June 30, Year 1, for delivery on June 30, Year 2, from a British supplier for £10,000 (currency in Great Britain pounds sterling). The exchange rate between the U.S. dollar and the British pound is currently $1.60 per £1, indicating a purchase price of $16,000. Firm A worries that the value of the U.S. dollar will decline between June 30, Year 1, and June 30, Year 2, when it must convert U.S. dollars into British pounds, requiring it to pay more than $16,000 to purchase the machine.

Example 9 Firm B holds a note receivable from a customer dated January 1, Year 1, for the customer's purchase of manufacturing equipment. The note has a face value of $100,000 and bears interest at the rate of 8 percent each year. Interest is receivable annually on December 31 and the note matures on December 31, Year 3. The customer has the option of repaying the note for its face value of $100,000, plus accrued interest, prior to maturity. Firm B knows that the customer will pay off early only if interest rates drop. In that event, the market value of the note would exceed $100,000, but Firm B would receive only $100,000 from the customer, not its higher market value. Firm B worries that the value of the note will increase if interest rates decrease but that if the customer pays off early, it will not capture the benefits of the higher interest rate it negotiated with the customer.

Example 10 Firm C gives a note payable to a supplier on January 1, Year 1, to acquire manufacturing equipment. The note has a face value of $100,000 and bears interest at the prime lending rate. The prime lending rate is 8 percent on January 1, Year 1. The supplier resets the interest rate each December 31 to establish the interest charge for the next calendar year. Interest is payable on December 31 of each year and the note matures on December 31, Year 3. Firm C worries that interest rates will increase above 8 percent during the term of the note and negatively affect its cash flows.

Example 11 Firm D holds 10,000 gallons of whiskey in inventory on October 31, Year 1. Firm D expects to complete aging this whiskey by March 31, Year 2, at which time it intends to sell the whiskey. Uncertainties about the quality of the aged whiskey and economic conditions at the time, however, make predicting the selling price on March 31, Year 2, difficult.

Most firms face risks of economic losses from changes in interest rate, foreign exchange rates, and commodity prices. Firms can purchase financial instruments to lessen these business risks. Typically, these are marketable securities and their accounting follows the principles for marketable securities, with some exceptions. The general term used for the financial instrument is a **derivative**. This section discusses the nature, use, accounting, and reporting of derivative instruments. Financial Accounting Standards Board *Statement of Financial Accounting Standards No. 133*[4] and Statement of *Financial Accounting Standards No. 138*[5] set forth the required accounting for derivative instruments, a form of marketable security.

Nature and Use of Derivative Instruments

A derivative is a financial instrument that obtains its value from some other financial item. An option to purchase a share of stock derives its value from the market price of the stock. A

---

[4] Financial Accounting Standards Board, *Statement of Financial Accounting Standards No. 133,* "Accounting for Derivative Instruments and Hedging Activities," 1998.

[5] Financial Accounting Standards Board, *Statement of Financial Accounting Standards No. 138,* "Accounting for Certain Derivative Instruments and Certain Hedging Activities, an Amendment to FASB Statement No. 133," 2000.

commitment to purchase a certain amount of foreign currency in the future derives its value from changes in the exchange rate for that currency. Firms use the derivative instrument to hedge the risk of losses from changes in interest rates, foreign exchange rates, and commodity prices. The general idea is that changes in the value of the derivative instrument offset changes in the value of an asset or liability or changes in future cash flows, thereby neutralizing, or at least reducing, the economic loss. Let's reconsider the four examples above.

Example 12   Refer to **Example 8**. Firm A desires to incur a cost now to eliminate the effect of changes in the exchange rate between the U.S. dollar and British pound while it awaits delivery of the equipment. It purchases a **forward foreign exchange contract** from a bank on June 30, Year 1, in which it promises to pay a fixed U.S. dollar amount on June 30, Year 2, in exchange for £10,000 received then. The forward foreign exchange rate between U.S. dollars and British pounds on June 30, Year 1, for settlement on June 30, Year 2, establishes the number of U.S. dollars it must deliver. Assume that the forward rate on June 30, Year 1, for settlement of the forward contract on June 30, Year 2, is $1.64 per £1. By purchasing the forward contract, Firm A locks in the cost of the equipment at $16,400 (= £10,000 pounds × $1.64 per £1).

Example 13   Refer to **Example 9**. Firm B wants to neutralize the effect of changes in the market value of the note receivable caused by changes in market interest rates. It engages in a **swap contract** with its bank. The swap has the effect of allowing Firm B to exchange its fixed interest rate obligation for a variable interest rate obligation. The market value of the note remains at $100,000 as long as the variable interest rate in the swap is the same as the variable rate used by the Firm B to revalue the note while it is outstanding.

Example 14   Refer to **Example 10**. Firm C wants to protect itself against increases in the variable interest rate above the initial 8 percent rate. It, too, engages in a swap contract with its bank. The swap has the effect of allowing Firm C to exchange its variable interest rate obligation for a fixed interest rate obligation. The swap fixes its annual interest expense and cash expenditure to 8 percent of the $100,000 note. By engaging in the swap, Firm C cannot take advantage of decreases in interest rates below 8 percent, which it could have done with its variable rate note, but it no longer bears risk, with attendant costs, that the rate will rise above 8 percent.

Example 15   Refer to **Example 11**. Firm D would like to fix the price at which it can sell the whiskey in its inventory on March 31, Year 2. It acquires a **forward commodity contract** in which it promises to sell 10,000 gallons of whiskey on March 31, Year 2, at a fixed price. The forward price of whiskey on October 31, Year 1, for delivery on March 31, Year 2, is $320 per gallon. Thus, it locks in a total cash inflow from selling the whiskey of $3,200,000.

Forward contracts and swap contracts illustrate two types of derivative instruments. Banks and other financial intermediaries structure derivatives to suit the particular needs of their customers. Thus, the nature and complexity of derivatives vary widely. We confine our discussion to swap contracts to illustrate the accounting and reporting of derivatives.

With these examples of derivatives in mind, consider the following elements of a derivative:

1. A derivative has one or more **underlyings**. An underlying is a variable such as a specified interest rate, or commodity price, or foreign exchange rate. The underlying in **Example 12** is the foreign exchange rate, in **Examples 13** and **14** is an interest rate, and in **Example 15** is the price of whiskey.
2. A derivative has one or more **notional amounts**. A notional amount is a number of currency units, bushels, shares, or other units specified in the contract. The notional amount in **Example 12** is £10,000, in **Examples 13** and **14** is the $100,000 face value of the note, and in **Example 15** is 10,000 gallons of whiskey.
3. A derivative often requires no initial investment, although it might. The firm usually acquires a derivative by exchanging promises with a **counterparty**, such as a commercial or investment bank. The exchange of promises is a mutually unexecuted contract.
4. Derivatives typically require, or permit, **net settlement**. Firm A in **Example 12** will not deliver $16,400 and receive in exchange £10,000. Firm A will actually purchase £10,000 in the market on June 20, Year 2, at the exchange rate on that date, when it needs the British pounds to purchase the equipment. Then, Firm A will receive cash from the counterparty to the extent that the exchange rate on June 30, Year 2 exceeds $1.64 per £1 and must pay the counterparty on this date to the extent that the exchange rate is less than $1.64 per £1. Firm B

in **Example 13** will receive from its customer the 8 percent interest established in the fixed rate note. If the variable interest rate used in the swap contract increases to 10 percent, the counterparty will pay Firm B an amount equal to 2 percent (= 0.10 − 0.08) of the notional amount of the note, $100,000. Receiving interest of 8 percent from the customer and receiving cash of 2 percent from the counterparty results in net interest receipts of 10 percent. If the variable interest rate decreases to 5 percent, Firm B still receives the customer's interest of 8 percent as specified in the original note. It would then pay the counterparty 3 percent (= 0.08 − 0.05), resulting in total interest collection equal to the variable rate of 5 percent.

Because many derivatives require no initial investment, that is, no initial cash payment to the counterparty, historical cost accounting makes little sense for these instruments, which have zero initial cost, but potentially large positive or negative values later. This has led both the FASB and the IASB to require that firms record derivatives at their fair value on the balance sheet date.

Accounting for Derivatives

A firm must recognize derivatives in its balance sheet as assets or liabilities, depending on the rights and obligations under the contract. The forward contract in **Example 12** is an asset and the commitment to purchase the equipment is a liability. The swap contracts in **Examples 13** and **14** may be assets or liabilities, depending on the level of interest rates—that is, whether at the balance sheet date the holder of the derivative would be entitled to receive assets or have to pay the counterparty. The forward contract in **Example 15** may be an asset or liability, depending on the price of whiskey.

Firms must revalue the derivatives to market value each period. (Common terminology refers to this as *marking to market*.) The revaluation amount, in addition to increasing or decreasing the derivative asset or liability, also affects either (1) net income immediately (like a trading security), or (2) other comprehensive income immediately and net income later (like securities available for sale).

The income effect of a change in the market value of a derivative depends on the nature of the hedge for which a firm acquires the derivative and whether the firm has chosen to use **hedge accounting**.

Generally accepted accounting principles (GAAP) classify derivatives as (1) speculative investments, or (2) fair value hedges, or (3) cash flow hedges. Firms usually acquire derivatives to hedge particular risks. Thus, firms typically classify derivatives as either fair value hedges or cash flow hedges. Firms must choose to designate each derivative as one or the other, depending on their general hedging strategy and purpose in acquiring the particular derivative instrument. If a firm chooses not to designate a particular derivative as either a fair value hedge or a cash flow hedge, GAAP require that the firm account for the derivative as a speculative investment.

Speculative Investment   Firms must revalue derivatives held as speculative investments to market value each period and, like trading securities, recognize the resulting gain or loss in earnings.

Fair Value Hedges   Derivative instruments acquired to hedge exposure to changes in the fair value of an asset or liability are **fair value hedges**. Fair value hedges are of two general types: (1) hedges of a *recognized* asset or liability, and (2) hedges of an *unrecognized* firm commitment. Firm B in **Examples 9** and **13** entered into the interest swap agreement to neutralize the effect of changes in interest rates on the market value of its notes receivable, a recorded asset. Firm A in **Examples 8** and **12** acquired the forward foreign exchange contract to neutralize the effect of changes in exchange rates on its commitment to purchase the equipment. The FASB defines these derivative instruments as fair value hedges.

Cash Flow Hedges   Derivative instruments acquired to hedge exposure to variability in expected future cash flows are **cash flow hedges**. Cash flow hedges are of two general types: (1) hedges of cash flows of an *existing* asset or liability, and (2) hedges of cash flows of *forecasted* transactions. Firm C in **Examples 10** and **14** entered into the interest swap agreement to neutralize changes in cash flows for interest payments on its variable rate notes payable. Firm D in **Examples 11** and **15** acquired the forward contract on whiskey to protect itself from changes in the selling price of whiskey on March 31, Year 2. These derivative instruments are therefore cash flow hedges.

A particular derivative could be either a fair value hedge or a cash flow hedge, depending on the firm's reason for engaging in the hedge. Both the forward foreign exchange contract in **Example 12** and the forward whiskey price contract in **Example 15** protect the firms' cash flows. The firms could conceivably classify both derivative instruments as cash flow hedges. Firm A in **Example 12** acquires the derivative to protect the value of equipment acquired and therefore classifies it as a fair value hedge. Firm D in **Example 15** acquires the derivative to protect its cash flows from changes in the price of whiskey and therefore classifies it as a cash flow hedge. One suspects that the FASB views the firm commitment to purchase the equipment by Firm A as having the economic substance of an asset and a liability, even though accounting treats it as a mutually unexecuted contract, whereas it views the forecasted transaction by Firm D to sell whiskey in the future as too uncertain to have the economic attributes of an asset at this point.

Treatment of Hedging Gains and Losses   GAAP allow firms to choose whether to designate a particular derivative as hedging the risk of a change in market value (fair value hedges) or a change in cash flows (cash flow hedges). If firms choose not to designate the derivative as either a fair value hedge or a cash flow hedge, then firms must account for the derivative as a speculative investment. The derivative appears at market value, with fluctuations recognized in net income. The hedged item remains on the balance sheet at historical cost because, although the firm has acquired an instrument that economically hedges the item, the firm has chosen not to account for the pair as a hedge.

If firms designate a derivative as a fair value hedge, GAAP require firms to revalue both the hedged item and the related derivative instrument to market value each period and to recognize gains and losses from changes in the market value in *net income* each period while the firm holds them. If the hedge is fully effective, the gain (loss) on the derivative will precisely offset the loss (gain) on the asset or liability hedged. The net effect on earnings is zero. If the hedge is not fully effective, the net gain or loss increases or decreases earnings to the degree the offset is incomplete.

If firms designate a derivative as a cash flow hedge, GAAP require firms to revalue the derivative instrument to market value each period but to include gains and losses from changes in the market values of such derivatives in *accumulated other comprehensive income* each period to the extent the financial instrument is "highly effective" in neutralizing the risk. Firms must include the ineffective portion in net income currently. FASB *Statement No. 133* gives general guidelines but leaves to professional judgment the meaning of "highly effective." The firm removes the accumulated amount in other comprehensive income related to a particular derivative instrument and transfers it to net income either periodically during the life of the derivative instrument or at the time of settlement, depending on the type of derivative instrument used.

The logic for the FASB's different treatment of gains and losses from changes in fair value of financial instruments results from applying the matching principle. In a fair value hedge of a recognized asset or liability, both the hedged asset (or liability) and its related derivative generally appear on the balance sheet. The firm revalues both the hedged asset (or liability) and its derivative to fair value each period and reports the gain or loss on the hedged asset (or liability) and the loss or gain on the derivative in net income. The net gain or loss indicates the effectiveness of the hedge in neutralizing the risk. In a cash flow hedge of an anticipated transaction, the hedged cash flow commitment does not appear on the balance sheet but the derivative instrument does appear. Recognizing a gain or loss on the derivative instrument in net income each period but recognizing the loss or gain on the anticipated transaction at the time an actual transaction occurs results in poor matching. Thus, the firm classifies the gain or loss on the derivative instrument in other comprehensive income and then, later, reclassifies it to net income when it records the actual transaction.

The logic for the FASB's different treatment would seem to break down for fair value hedges related to a firm commitment. GAAP usually do not recognize the firm commitment as an asset or a liability.

Summary of Accounting for Derivatives as Marketable Securities

Derivatives appear on the balance sheet at fair market value.

- **Trading Security Treatment—Gains and losses on speculative securities, fair value hedges reported in current earnings, and the ineffective portion of cash flow hedges.** The holder will include in current earnings the gains and losses on all speculative derivatives, fair value hedges, and the ineffective portion of cash flow hedges.

- **Securities Available for Sale Treatment—Gains and losses on effective cash flow hedges reported initially in other comprehensive income.** The holder will exclude from current earnings, but include in Accumulated Other Comprehensive Income, the gains and losses on derivatives used effectively to hedge cash flows.
- **Disclosures Related to Derivative Instruments** Several FASB pronouncements affect disclosures about derivative instruments. FASB *Statement No. 107*[6] requires firms to disclose the book, or carrying, value and the fair value of financial instruments. Financial instruments impose on one entity a right to receive cash and an obligation on another entity to pay cash. Financial instruments include accounts receivable, notes receivable, notes payable, bonds payable, forward contracts, swap contracts, and most derivatives. Fair value is the current amount of cash for which two willing parties would agree to exchange the instrument for cash.

FASB *Statement No. 133* requires the following disclosures (among others) with respect to derivatives.

1. A description of the firm's risk management strategy and how particular derivatives help accomplish the firm's hedging objectives. The description should distinguish between derivative instruments designated as fair value hedges, cash flow hedges, and all other derivatives.
2. For fair value and cash flow hedges, firms must disclose the net gain or loss recognized in earnings resulting from the hedge's ineffectiveness (that is, not offsetting the risk hedged) and the line on the income statement that includes this net gain or loss.
3. For cash flow hedges, firms must describe the transactions or events that will result in reclassifying gains and losses from other comprehensive income to net income and the estimated amount of such reclassifications during the next 12 months.
4. The net amount of gains and losses recognized in earnings because a hedged firm's commitment no longer qualifies as a fair value hedge or a hedged forecasted transaction no longer qualifies as a cash flow hedge.

FASB Statement of *Financial Accounting Standards No. 105*[7] requires a firm to disclose the nature and extent of risk of loss if the counterparty to a derivative instrument failed to perform according to the contractual terms. For example, a firm involved in an interest swap with a bank experiencing financial difficulty would need to disclose this credit risk and the amount of the loss that would result if the bank failed to perform. A firm contracting with a single bank for a large portion of its derivatives would need to disclose this concentration of credit risk.

Dealing with Uncertainty by Using Measurement, Not Recognition

The business world is uncertain. For example, will the firm lose a lawsuit? Until recently, GAAP dealt with uncertainty through its rules for recognizing a liability, not measuring its amount. For example *SFAS No. 5*[8] says the firm will record a liability for the lawsuit only if losing is probable, which has come to mean a likelihood of 80 percent or greater. If the firm recognizes liability for such a probable loss, the amount will be the most likely amount for the loss, or the minimum amount if the most likely amount falls in a range with no number more likely than any other. Assume the mostly likely loss is $10 million. Then, the liability for the loss in a lawsuit will appear on the books either at zero or at $10 million. Assume, further, that the firm has a 60 percent chance of losing and if it loses the amount will be $10 million. Its expected loss is $6 (= $0.60 \times 10) million, but, even so, the balance sheet number will be either zero or $10 million.

Example. Assume the firm faces 100 such lawsuits, each presenting a 60 percent chance of losing $10 million an a 40 percent chance of winning. Then, with near statistical certainty, the

---

[6] Financial Accounting Standards Board, *Statement of Financial Accounting Standards No. 107,* "Disclosures about Fair Value of Financial Instruments," 1991.

[7] Financial Accounting Standards Board, *Statement of Financial Accounting Standards No. 105,* "Disclosures of Information about Financial Instruments with Off-Balance-Sheet Risk and Financial Instruments with Concentrations of Credit Risk," 1990.

[8] Financial Accounting Standards Board, *Statement of Financial Accounting Standards No. 5,* "Accounting for Contingencies," 1975.

firm will have an obligation to pay about $600 million (= $100 \times 0.60 \times \$10$ million), but current GAAP will show no liability as the events individually do not rise to the level of certainty to warrant recognition.

If we were to record the liability for any one lawsuit at its expected value, $6 million, then we could say that the GAAP deals with uncertainty not by recognition—a binary choice of yes or no—but with measurement. The FASB *is* beginning to deal with uncertainty with measurement, not recognition. An example is the accounting for derivatives, which are neither assets nor liabilities until prices of the underlyings change. GAAP deal with the uncertainty of future price change, not with recognition criteria, but measurement rules: if the item results in an expected payment (or receipt), measure the liability (asset) with the market value of the amount.

Minority, Active Investments

When an investor owns less than a majority of the voting stock of another corporation, the accountant must judge when the investor can exert significant influence. For the sake of uniformity, GAAP presume that one company can significantly influence another company when the investor company owns 20 percent or more of the voting stock of the other company. An investor can exert significant influence even when owning less than 20 percent, but then its management must convince the independent accountants that the company can do so. Analysts become suspicious when they see an investor changing its ownership from just below 20 percent to just above, or vice versa. They suspect that the investor is trying to manage earnings, in ways discussed below, by changing its accounting techniques to suit the circumstances.

Recent trends in corporate governance are changing the way minority shareholders should view the voting power inherent in their shares. Consider a large, public company like IBM or General Electric whose shares are so widely owned that the largest single voting block of the shares might be 4 percent of the total outstanding. Many pension funds, mutual funds, and state retirement trusts (such as CALPERS, the California Public Employees Retirement System) own substantial investments in virtually all public companies. These fiduciaries collectively own enough shares that if they were to act in concert, they could control the boards and, hence, the actions of the companies whose shares they hold. These fiduciaries have increasingly acted in concert when deciding how to vote on pivotal corporate governance issues. When they act in concert, they can overwhelm the voting power of minority share holdings otherwise large enough to exert significant influence.

Minority, active investments, generally those where the investor owns between 20 and 50 percent, require the **equity method** of accounting. Under the equity method, the investor firm recognizes as revenue (expense) each period its share of the net income (loss) of the other firm. The investor recognizes dividends received from S as a return of investment, not as income. In the discussion that follows, we designate the investor firm as P and the firm whose shares it owns as S.

Equity Method: Rationale

To understand why GAAP require the equity method for minority, active investments, review the financial statement effects of using the **market value method** for such investments. Under the market value method for securities available for sale, P recognizes net income effects only when it receives a dividend (revenue) or sells some of the investment (gain or loss). (P does recognize amounts in comprehensive income for unrealized holding gains and losses, but the amount of comprehensive income for a period does not typically appear on the income statement.) Suppose, as often happens, that S follows a policy of financing its own growing operations through retaining earnings, consistently declaring dividends less than its net income. The market price of S's shares will probably increase to reflect this retention of assets. Under the market value method, P reports net income only from the dividends it receives. Because P, by assumption, exerts significant influence over S, it can affect S's dividend policy, which in turn affects P's net income. When P can so easily manage its own net income (via dividends from S), the market value method will not reasonably reflect P's earnings from investing in S. The equity method better measures a firm's earnings from its investment when, because of its ownership interest, it can exert significant influence over the operations and dividend policy of the investee firm. Most analysts agree that the equity method provides higher quality earnings than does the market value method when the owner can exert significant influence over the operations and financial policies of the affiliated company.

Equity Method: Procedures

The equity method records the initial purchase of an investment at acquisition cost, just as for minority, passive investments. Each period, Company P treats as revenue its proportionate share of the periodic earnings, not the dividends, of Company S. Company P treats dividends declared by S as a reduction in P's investment in S account.

Suppose that P acquires 30 percent of the outstanding shares of S for $600,000. The entry to record the acquisition is as follows:

(1) Investment in Stock of S (Asset Increase)	600,000	
Cash (Asset Decrease)		600,000
Investment made in 30 percent of Company S.		

Between the time of the acquisition and the end of P's next accounting period, S reports income of $80,000. P, using the equity method, records the following:

(2) Investment in Stock of S (Asset Increase)	24,000	
Retained Earnings (Equity in Earnings of Affiliate) (Shareholders' Equity Increase)		24,000
To record 30 percent of income earned by investee, accounted for using the equity method.		

The account Equity in Earnings of Affiliate is a revenue account. If S declares and pays a dividend of $30,000 to holders of common stock, P receives $9,000 (= 0.30 × $30,000) and records the following:

(3) Cash (Asset Increase)	9,000	
Investment in Stock of S (Asset Decrease)		9,000
To record dividends received from investee, accounted for using the equity method, and the resulting reduction in the Investment account.		

Notice the credit to the Investment in S account. P records income earned by S as an increase in investment. The dividend returns part of the investment and decreases the Investment account.

Hint: Students often have difficulty understanding journal entry **(3)**, particularly the credit by the investor when the investee company pays a dividend. The transactions and entries resemble those for an individual's ordinary savings account at a local bank. Assume that you put $600,000 in a savings account, that later the bank adds interest of 4 percent (or $24,000) to the account, and that still later you withdraw $9,000 from the savings account. You can record journal entries **(1)** through **(3)** for these three events, with slight changes in the account titles: Investment in S changes to Savings Account, and Equity in Earnings of Affiliate changes to Interest Revenue. The cash withdrawal reduces the amount invested in the savings account. Similarly, the payment of a cash dividend by an investee company accounted for with the equity method reduces the investor's investment in the company. The investor, Company P, owns a sufficiently large percentage of the voting shares that it can effectively require Company S to pay a dividend, just as you can require the savings bank to remit cash to you almost whenever you choose.

Suppose that S subsequently reports earnings of $100,000 and also pays dividends of $40,000. P's entries are as follows:

(4) Investment in Stock of S (Asset Increase)	30,000	
Retained Earnings (Equity in Earnings of Affiliate) (Shareholders' Equity Increase)		30,000
(5) Cash (Asset Increase)	12,000	
Investment in Stock of S (Asset Decrease)		12,000
To record revenue and dividends from investee, accounted for using the equity method.		

P's Investment in S account now has a balance of $633,000 as follows:

Investment in Shares of Company S

Initial Investment	$600,000	[1]
First Share of Income	24,000	[2]
First Dividend Received	(9,000)	[3]
Second Share of Income	30,000	[4]
Second Dividend Received	(12,000)	[5]
Ending Balance	$633,000	

Assume now that P sells one-fourth of its investment in S for $165,000. The entry is:

(6) Cash (Asset Increase)	165,000	
Investment in Stock of S (Asset Decrease)		158,250
Retained Earnings (Gain on Sale of Investment in S) (Shareholders' Equity Increase)		6,750

Cost of investments sold is $158,250 = 1/4 \times $633,000.

After the sale, the balance in the investment account is $474,750, as follows.

Investment in Shares of Company S

Initial Investment	$600,000	[1]
First Share of Income	24,000	[2]
First Dividend Received	(9,000)	[3]
Second Share of Income	30,000	[4]
Second Dividend Received	(12,000)	[5]
Balance Before Disposal	$633,000	
Less Cost of Shares Sold,		
25 Percent of Total	(158,250)	[6]
Book Value of Remaining Shares	$474,750	

Excess Purchase Price on Acquisition of Equity Method Investment

P may pay more for its investment than its proportion of the book value of the net assets (= assets − liabilities), or shareholders' equity, of S at the date of acquisition. For example, assume that P acquires 25 percent of the stock of S for $400,000 when S has total shareholders' equity of $1 million. P's cost exceeds book value acquired by $150,000 [= $400,000 − (0.25 × $1,000,000)]. P may pay an amount that differs from the book value of S's recorded net assets because the market values of the net assets differ from their book values or because of unrecorded assets (for example, trade secrets) or unrecorded liabilities (for example, an unsettled lawsuit). GAAP previously required firms to write off this excess acquisition cost over a period not to exceed 40 years.[9] Beginning with investments made after June 30, 2001, firms do not have the option to amortize this excess to the extent it relates to goodwill. Firms may also discontinue amortizing goodwill from investments made prior to July 1, 2001, as soon as they adopt *Statement No. 142*.[10] Firms must still amortize the excess to the extent it relates to other assets or liabilities. GAAP's rationale for the different treatment of goodwill is that it has an indefinite life, whereas other assets and liabilities typically have a definite life. **Chapter 8** discusses the accounting for goodwill and other long-lived assets, including their impairment.

Summary of Equity Method

On the balance sheet, an investment accounted for with the equity method appears in the Investments section. The amount shown generally equals the acquisition cost of the shares plus P's share of S's undistributed earnings since the date P acquired the shares. On the income statement, P generally shows its share of S's income as revenue each

---

[9] Accounting Principles Board, *Opinion No. 17*, "Intangible Assets," 1970.

[10] Financial Accounting Standards Board, *Statement of Financial Accounting Standards No. 142*, "Goodwill and Other Intangible Assets," 2001.

period. The exceptions in the preceding sentence occur when the original purchase price exceeds the proportionate share of the book value acquired. The accounting method used by the investor, P, does not affect the financial statements of the investee, S.

Problem 11.3 for Self-Study

Journal entries to apply the equity method for long-term investments in securities. Exhibit 11.3 summarizes data about the minority, active investments of Equity Investing Group. Assume that any excess of acquisition cost over the book value of the net assets acquired relates to equipment with a 10-year remaining life on January 1, Year 1. Prepare the journal entries to do the following:

a. Record the acquisition of these securities on January 1, Year 1.
b. Apply the equity method for Year 1.
c. Apply the equity method for Year 2.
d. Record the sale of Security E on January 2, Year 3, for $190,000.

EXHIBIT 11.3	EQUITY INVESTING GROUP (Problem 11.3 for Self-Study)

Security	Date Acquired	Acquisition Cost	Ownership Percentage	Book Value of Net Assets on January 1, Year 1	Earnings (Loss) Year 1	Earnings (Loss) Year 2	Dividends Year 1	Dividends Year 2
D	1/1/Year 1	$ 80,000	40%	$200,000	$ 40,000	$ 50,000	$10,000	$12,000
E	1/1/Year 1	190,000	30	500,000	120,000	(40,000)	30,000	—
F	1/1/Year 1	200,000	20	800,000	200,000	50,000	60,000	60,000

Majority, Active Investments

When one firm, P, owns more than 50 percent of the voting stock of another company such as S, P can control the activities of S. P can control both broad policy-making and day-to-day operations. Common usage refers to the majority investor as the **parent** and to the majority-owned company as the **subsidiary**. GAAP require the parent to combine the financial statements of majority-owned companies with those of the parent, in **consolidated financial statements**.[11]

Reasons for Legally Separate Corporations

Business firms have several reasons for preferring to operate as a group of legally separate corporations rather than as a single entity. From the standpoint of the parent company, the more important reasons for maintaining legally separate subsidiary companies include the following:

1. To reduce the parent's risk. Separate corporations may mine raw materials, transport them to a manufacturing plant, produce the product, and sell the finished product to the public. If any one part of the total process proves to be unprofitable or inefficient, losses from insolvency will fall only on the owners and creditors of the one subsidiary corporation. (Some drug firms acquire subsidiaries to make and market medical products in the hope that if something goes wrong in future years, the parent firm will not be liable for losses of the customers of the subsidiary. Individuals who believe the subsidiary's products have harmed them often sue the parent and sometimes succeed in "piercing the corporate veil.")

---

[11] Financial Accounting Standards Board, *Statement of Financial Accounting Standards No. 94*, "Consolidation of All Majority-Owned Subsidiaries," 1987.

2. To meet more effectively the requirements of state corporation laws and tax legislation. If an organization does business in a number of states, it often faces overlapping and inconsistent taxation, regulations, and requirements. Organizing separate corporations to conduct operations in the various states can sometimes reduce administrative costs.

3. To expand or diversify with a minimum of capital investment. A firm may absorb another company by acquiring a controlling interest in its voting stock. The firm may accomplish this result with a substantially smaller capital investment, as well as with less difficulty, inconvenience, and risk, than if it constructs a new plant or starts a new line of business.

4. To sell an unwanted operation with a minimum of administrative, legal, and other costs. Firms generally save costs if they sell the common stock of a subsidiary rather than trying to sell each of its assets and transfer all known and, perhaps, unknown liabilities to a buyer.

Purpose of Consolidated Statements

For a variety of reasons, then, a single economic entity may exist in the form of a parent and several legally separate subsidiaries. (General Electric Company, for example, comprises more than 50 large legally separate companies.) A consolidation of the financial statements of the parent and each of its subsidiaries presents the results of operations, financial position, and cash flows of an affiliated group of companies under the control of a parent as if the group of companies composed a single entity. The parent and each subsidiary are legally separate entities, but they operate as one centrally controlled **economic entity**. Consolidated financial statements generally provide more useful information to the shareholders of the parent corporation than do separate financial statements for the parent and each subsidiary.

Consolidated financial statements also generally provide more helpful information than does the equity method. The parent, because of its voting interest, can effectively control the use of all of the subsidiary's assets. Consolidation of the individual assets, liabilities, revenues, and expenses of both the parent and the subsidiary provides a more realistic picture of the operations and financial position of the single economic entity.

In a legal sense, consolidated statements merely supplement, and do not replace, the separate statements of the individual corporations, although common practice presents only the consolidated statements in published annual reports.

Example 16   General Motors, General Electric, and IBM, among others, have wholly owned finance subsidiaries. These subsidiaries make a portion of their loans to customers who want to purchase the products of the parent company. The parent company consolidates the financial statements of these subsidiaries. These subsidiaries have billions of dollars of assets, mostly receivables. Statement readers may misunderstand the relative liquidity of firms preparing consolidated statements, which combine the parent's assets—largely noncurrent manufacturing plant and equipment—with the more liquid assets of the finance subsidiary. This suggests preparing separate statements for the manufacturing parent and for the financial subsidiary. The counterargument suggests that these entities operate as a single integrated unit, so that consolidated financial statements more accurately depict the nature of their operating relations. For many years, General Electric has shown the separate financial statements of its finance subsidiaries in addition to the consolidated statements.

Example 17   A major mining corporation owns a mining subsidiary in South America. The government of the country enforces stringent control over cash payments outside the country. The company cannot control the use of all the assets, despite owning a majority of the voting shares. Therefore, it does not prepare consolidated statements with the subsidiary. The parent company will probably carry the investment on its books at cost.

The Purchase Transaction

In a corporate acquisition, one corporation acquires all, or substantially all, of another corporation's common shares. The **purchase method** views a corporate acquisition as conceptually identical to the purchase of any single asset (for example, inventory or a machine). The purchaser records the intercorporate investment in the common stock of the acquired company at the *market value of the consideration given*. The purchaser allocates the purchase price to the identifiable assets and liabilities to record them at market values on the date of acquisition. The purchaser will record any assets acquired independent of whether the purchased company showed those assets on its books. For example, the purchased company owns patents and trademarks not recorded on its balance sheet. The purchasing company will show those assets on its balance sheet at their market value. The purchaser allocates any remaining excess to goodwill. That is, **goodwill** is the excess of purchase price of another company, or division, over the fair value of the net assets acquired, independent of whether those assets appeared on the books of the acquired company.

Problem 11.4 for Self-Study

Financial statement effects of the purchase method.   Exhibit 11.4 presents balance sheet data for Powell Corporation and Steele Corporation as of January 1, Year 8. On this date, Powell Corporation exchanges 2,700 shares of its common stock, selling for $20 per share, for all of the common stock of Steele Corporation.

Prepare a consolidated balance sheet for Powell Corporation and Steele Corporation on January 1, Year 8, using the purchase method. Powell Corporation allocates any excess cost to property, plant, and equipment and to goodwill.

EXHIBIT 11.4	POWELL CORPORATION AND STEELE CORPORATION Financial Statement Data for January 1, Year 8 (Problem 11.4 for Self-Study)		
	Historical Cost		**Current Market Value**
	Powell Corp.	**Steele Corp.**	**Steele Corporation**
ASSETS			
Current Assets	$10,000	$ 7,000	$ 7,000
Property, Plant, and Equipment (net)	30,000	18,000	23,000
Goodwill	—	—	40,000
Total Assets	$40,000	$25,000	$70,000
EQUITIES			
Liabilities	$25,000	$16,000	$16,000
Common Stock ($1 par value)	1,000	1,000	1,000
Additional Paid-in Capital	9,000	5,000	5,000
Retained Earnings	5,000	3,000	3,000
Unrecorded Excess of Market Value over Historical Costs	—	—	45,000
Total Equities	$40,000	$25,000	$70,000

The Boundaries of the Consolidated Entity

The usual criterion for preparing consolidated financial statements is that one entity has voting control, more than 50 percent, of another company's common stock. For more complicated business arrangements, voting control may not adequately measure control. Consider the following business arrangement of Company P, which wants to borrow to finance the acquisition of an airplane, but does not want the debt to appear on its balance sheet.

1. Company P gives $100,000 to an unrelated party; think of the local Red Cross. This is a one-time payment to induce the Red Cross to own 100 percent of the shares of Company S. The Red Cross buys these shares for $60,000 cash, contributing the cash to Company S in return for the shares.
2. Company S borrows $50 million from a group of Lenders; think of a group of banks, which it uses to buy the airplane that Company P wants to use. It agrees to repay the loan with monthly installments for 10 years, at the rate of $717,500 per month, which implies a loan at about 1 percent per month fully paid off with 120 (= 10 years × 12) payments.

3. Company P provides a written guarantee to the Lenders that it will make any debt service payment that Company S fails to make on time. Without the guarantee, the Lenders would not lend to Company S, as the airplane itself does not provide sufficient collateral to satisfy cautious lenders worried about possible loss in market value of an asset in such a volatile industry.

4. Company P makes a business arrangement with Company S; in this example, Company P agrees to use the airplane and pay $717,500 per month to rent the airplane. Company P might agree to pay Company S a bit more to cover Company S's transactions costs.

Figure 11.2 depicts this structure.

In this arrangement, the Red Cross owns all Company S and controls it in the sense that voting shares convey control. Company P, however, enjoys the risks and rewards of using the airplane. If the airplane becomes obsolete, Company P bears the cost. If the rental arrangement turns out to be a bargain, Company P will enjoy the gains. Firms have organized entities such as Company S to turn accounts receivable into cash without explicit borrowing, and to finance research and development efforts. Ford, Kimberly-Clark, and Boeing have used them.

Arrangements such as those described for leases in the illustration became popular in the late 1980s. Then, in 1990, the FASB and the SEC, through the Emerging Issues Task Force (EITF), formerly recognized this sort of arrangement. It coined the phrases, which it never defined, *special purpose entity* and *special purpose vehicle* to describe the entity, such as Company S in this example. It specifically allowed Company P to engage in this sort of leasing arrangement, and keep the transaction off its books, other than the cash payments to Company S. Although that 1990 ruling, *EITF Consensus 90-15*,[12] applied only to leases, financial engineers soon turned its principles to other arrangements, such as securitizing accounts receivable. Eventually, after the collapse of Enron, which had built itself, in part, on shaky special purpose entities, the FASB tightened the rules for keeping such entities off the balance sheet.[13]

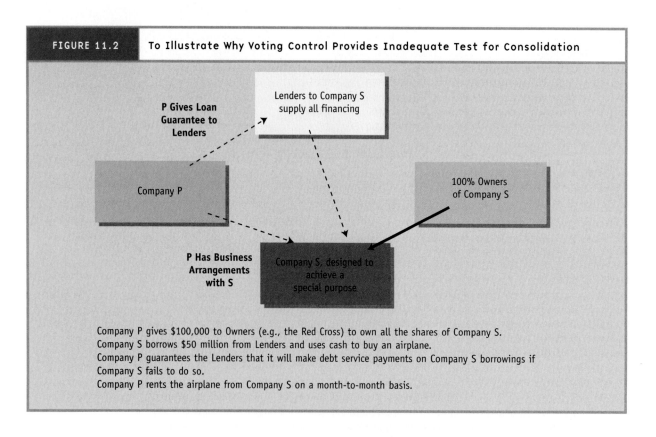

| FIGURE 11.2 | To Illustrate Why Voting Control Provides Inadequate Test for Consolidation |

P Gives Loan Guarantee to Lenders

Lenders to Company S supply all financing

Company P

100% Owners of Company S

P Has Business Arrangements with S

Company S, designed to achieve a special purpose

Company P gives $100,000 to Owners (e.g., the Red Cross) to own all the shares of Company S.
Company S borrows $50 million from Lenders and uses cash to buy an airplane.
Company P guarantees the Lenders that it will make debt service payments on Company S borrowings if Company S fails to do so.
Company P rents the airplane from Company S on a month-to-month basis.

---

[12] Emerging Issue Task Force, *EITF Issue 90-15*, "Impact of Nonsubstantive Lessors, Residual Value Guarantees, and Other Provisions in Leasing Transactions," July 1991.

[13] *FASB Interpretation no. 46*, "Consolidation of Variable Interest Entities," 2003.

The FASB defined the new term *variable interest entity (VIE)* to refer to entities such as Company S in our illustration. A variable interest entity will exist whenever the owner holds equity so small that the entity requires other financial support to sustain its activities. The FASB means that the owner must have contributed assets larger than the expected losses of the entity. The FASB's rule suggests that unless the owners have contributed 10 percent or more of the total financing, then the entity is a VIE. (In the illustration, assuming a total financing of $50 million, the owner must have invested at least $5 million for Company S not to be a VIE.) The FASB requires that the *primary beneficiary* of the VIE consolidate the VIE. A company, such as Company P in the illustration, will be a primary beneficiary if it absorbs (or receives) the majority of the variability of the outcomes of the VIE. In the case where a company, like Company P, guarantees the debt of the VIE, then the guarantor will be the primary beneficiary.

Disclosure of Consolidation Policy

The summary of significant accounting principles, a required part of the financial statement notes, must include a statement about the **consolidation policy** of the parent. If an investor does not consolidate a significant majority-owned subsidiary, the notes will disclose that fact. A recent annual report of American Home Products Corporation contained the following (bracketed remarks do not appear in the original):

> Notes to Consolidated Financial Statements
> 1. *Summary of Significant Accounting Policies*: . . . Principles of Consolidation: The accompanying consolidated financial statements include the accounts of the Company and its subsidiaries with the exception of those subsidiaries described in **Note 3** which are accounted for on a cash basis . . . .
> 3. *Provision for Impairment of Investment in Certain Foreign Locations*: [During the preceding year], the Corporation recorded a charge of $50,000,000 recognizing the impairment of its investment in its subsidiaries in South America, except for its investment in Brazil. The provision was made after determining that the continued imposition of constraints such as dividend restrictions, exchange controls, price controls, and import restrictions in these countries so severely impede management's control of the economic performance of the businesses that continued inclusion of these subsidiaries in the consolidated financial statements is inappropriate. The Company is continuing to operate these businesses, which for the most part are self-sufficient; however, the investments have been deconsolidated and earnings are recorded on a cash [similar to the market value method] basis. Net sales from these operations aggregated $97,790,000, $95,084,000, and $100,045,000 [in the last three years] . . . . Net income included in the consolidated statements of income was approximately $2,200,000 . . . and $2,000,000 [for the last two years].

Understanding Consolidated Statements

This section discusses three concepts essential for understanding consolidated financial statements:

1. The need for intercompany eliminations
2. The meaning of consolidated net income
3. The nature of the external minority interest

We illustrate the concepts for understanding consolidated statements with the data in **Exhibit 11.5** for Company P and Company S.

- **Column (1)** shows the balance sheet and income statement for Company P.
- **Column (2)** shows the balance sheet and income statement for Company S.
- **Column (3)** sums the amounts from **columns (1)** and **(2),** but these amounts do not represent the correct amounts for the consolidated statements.
- **Column (4)** presents the correct consolidated financial statements.

The following discussion explains why the correct amounts in **column (4)** differ from the sums in **column (3)**.

EXHIBIT 11.5	Illustrative Data for Preparation of Consolidated Financial Statements

| | Single-Company Statements | | Combined | Consolidated |
	Company P (1)	Company S (2)	(3) = (1) + (2)	(4)
CONDENSED BALANCE SHEETS ON DECEMBER 31, YEAR 4				
Assets				
Accounts Receivable	$ 200,000	$ 25,000	$ 225,000	$ 213,000
Investment in Stock of Company S (using equity method)	705,000	—	705,000	—
Other Assets	2,150,000	975,000	3,125,000	3,125,000
Total Assets	$3,055,000	$1,000,000	$4,055,000	$3,338,000
Equities				
Accounts Payable	$ 75,000	$ 15,000	$ 90,000	$ 78,000
Other Liabilities	70,000	280,000	350,000	350,000
Common Stock	2,500,000	500,000	3,000,000	2,500,000
Retained Earnings	410,000	205,000	615,000	410,000
Total Equities	$3,055,000	$1,000,000	$4,055,000	$3,338,000
CONDENSED INCOME STATEMENTS FOR YEAR 4				
Revenues				
Sales	$ 900,000	$ 250,000	$1,150,000	$1,110,000
Equity in Earnings of Company S	48,000	—	48,000	—
Total Revenues	$ 948,000	$ 250,000	$1,198,000	$1,110,000
Expenses				
Cost of Goods Sold (excluding depreciation)	$ 440,000	$ 80,000	$ 520,000	$ 480,000
Depreciation Expense	120,000	50,000	170,000	170,000
Administrative Expense	80,000	40,000	120,000	120,000
Income Tax Expense	104,000	32,000	136,000	136,000
Total Expenses	$ 744,000	$ 202,000	$ 946,000	$ 906,000
Net Income	$ 204,000	$ 48,000	$ 252,000	$ 204,000
Dividends Declared	(50,000)	(13,000)	(63,000)	(50,000)
Increase in Retained Earnings for the Year	$ 154,000	$ 35,000	$ 189,000	$ 154,000

Need for Intercompany Eliminations   State corporation laws typically require each legally separate corporation to maintain its own accounting records. Thus, during the accounting period, each corporation will record transactions of that entity with all other entities (both affiliated and nonaffiliated). At the end of the period, each corporation will prepare its own financial statements. The consolidation, or combining, of these financial statements basically involves summing the amounts for various financial statement items across the separate company statements. The accountant must adjust the amounts resulting from the summation, however, to eliminate double-counting resulting from **intercompany transactions**.

The guiding principle is that consolidated financial statements will reflect the results that the affiliated group would report if it were a single company. Consolidated financial statements reflect the transactions between the consolidated group of entities and others outside the entity. Thus, to take a simple example, if one affiliate company sells goods to another, the consolidation must remove from the financial statements the effects of this intercompany transaction.

Eliminating Double-Counting of Intercompany Payables   Separate company records indicate that $12,000 of Company S's accounts receivable represent amounts receivable from Company P. **Column (3)** counts the current assets underlying this transaction twice: once as part of

Accounts Receivable on Company S's books and a second time as Cash (Other Assets) on Company P's books. Also, the liability shown on Company P's books appears in the combined amount for Accounts Payable in **column (3)**. The consolidated group does not owe this $12,000 to an outsider. To eliminate double-counting on the asset side and to report Accounts Payable at the amount payable to outsiders, the consolidation process must eliminate $12,000 from the amounts for Accounts Receivable and Accounts Payable in **column (3)**. In **column (4)**, the consolidated Accounts Receivable and Accounts Payable both total $12,000 less than their sum in **column (3)**.

If either company holds bonds or long-term notes of the other, the consolidation process will eliminate the investment and related liability in the consolidated balance sheet. It will also eliminate the "borrower's" interest expense and the "lender's" interest revenue from the consolidated income statement.

Eliminating Double-Counting of Investment

Company P's balance sheet shows an asset, Investment in Stock of Company S, which represents P's investment in S's net assets. The subsidiary's balance sheet shows its individual assets. When **column (3)** adds the two balance sheets, the sum shows both Company P's investment in Company S's assets and S's actual assets. The consolidation process must eliminate Company P's account, Investment in Stock of Company S, $705,000, from the sum of the balance sheets. Because the consolidated balance sheet must maintain the accounting equation, the process must make corresponding eliminations of $705,000 from the equities.

To understand the eliminations from the equities in the balance sheet, recall that the right-hand side shows the *sources* of the firm's financing. Financing for Company S comes from creditors (liabilities of $295,000) and from owners (shareholders' equity of $705,000). Company P owns 100 percent of Company S's voting shares. Thus the financing for the assets of the consolidated entity comes from the creditors of both companies and from Company P's shareholders. In other words, the equities of the consolidated entity are the liabilities of both companies plus the shareholders' equity of Company P alone. **Column (3)** adds the shareholders' equity accounts of Company S to those of Company P. It counts the financing from Company P's shareholders twice (once on the parent's books and once on the subsidiary's books). Hence, when the consolidation process eliminates Company P's investment account ($705,000) from the sum of the two companies' assets, it eliminates the shareholders' equity accounts of Company S ($500,000 of common stock and $205,000 of retained earnings). See **column (4)**.

Learning Aid

When we prepare a consolidated balance sheet for two entities, we must deal with two sets of assets, two sets of liabilities, and two sets of shareholders' equity accounts. Which assets, liabilities, and shareholders' equity accounts provide a better understanding of the entity operating as one economic whole? The parent's balance sheet shows on one line, Investment in Subsidiary, the net assets of the subsidiary, whose individual amounts appear on the subsidiary's balance sheet. The individual components of net assets of the subsidiary provide more helpful information than does the single asset, Investment in Subsidiary. Thus, we eliminate the Investment in Subsidiary account and replace it with the individual assets and liabilities of the subsidiary. The shareholders' equity of the parent financed the subsidiary's shareholders' equity. Because the sources of the assets already appear as the parent's shareholders' equity, we eliminate the subsidiary's shareholders' equity when we eliminate the parent's investment account. As a result, a consolidated balance sheet reports the individual assets of the parent and the subsidiary, except the Investment in Subsidiary account, the individual liabilities of both entities, and the shareholders' equity of the parent.

Back to Basics

By now, you should understand that Retained Earnings represents a source of financing for assets, not a pool of assets. Owners of P provide the financing to the consolidated group, so the consolidation process eliminates the retained earnings of S. Some students cannot understand what happens to S's retained earnings, which apparently disappear in consolidation. The difficulty stems from confusing Retained Earnings with assets, rather than understanding it as one of the sources of financing provided by shareholders, a component of shareholders' equity.

Eliminating Intercompany Sales

The consolidation process must eliminate intercompany transactions from the sum of the income statements so that the consolidated income statement will present only the consolidated entity's transactions with outsiders. Consider intercompany sales. Separate company records indicate that Company S sold merchandise at its cost of $40,000 to Company P for $40,000 during the year. None of this inventory remains in Company P's inventory on December 31. Therefore, the merchandise inventory items sold appear in Sales Revenue both on Company

S's books (sale to Company P) and on Company P's books (sale to outsiders). Thus, **column (3)** overstates sales of the consolidated entity to outsiders. Likewise, Cost of Goods Sold of both companies in **column (3)** counts twice the cost of the goods sold, first by Company S to Company P and then by Company P to outsiders. The consolidation process eliminates the effects of the intercompany sale from Company S to Company P. See **column (4)** for Sales and Cost of Goods Sold.

A Realistic Complication

We simplified the above example by having Company S sell the goods to Company P at cost, $40,000, so that you can easily see that the consolidation process reduces both sales and cost of goods sold by $40,000. Often S sells the goods to P for a price larger than S's cost. Assume, now, that S sold goods costing $30,000 to P for $40,000, goods that P later sold to outsiders for $45,000. The consolidation process still eliminates $40,000 from both combined sales and combined cost of goods sold. The transactions remaining in the consolidated income statement will be P's sales to outsiders for $45,000 and S's cost of $30,000, just as if they were a single company selling, for $45,000, goods that cost $30,000. This realistic complication becomes more complex when Company P has not yet, by the end of the accounting period, sold all the goods it bought from Company S. In that case, Company S has recorded a profit on the goods remaining in inventory, which the consolidation must eliminate. We do not illustrate this complication.

Eliminating Double-Counting of Income

Company P's accounts show Equity in Earnings of Company S of $48,000. Company S's records show individual revenues and expenses that net to $48,000. When **column (3)** sums the revenues and expenses of the two companies, it counts that income twice. The consolidation process must eliminate the account Equity in Earnings of Company S. See **column (4)** for Equity in Earnings.

Consolidated Income

The amount of consolidated net income for a period exactly equals the amount that the parent would show on its separate company books if it used the equity method for all its subsidiaries. That is, consolidated net income is as follows:

Parent Company's Net Income from Its Own Activities	+	Parent Company's Share of Subsidiaries' Net Income	−	Profit (or + Loss) on Intercompany Transactions

A consolidated income statement differs from a parent's income statement using the equity method only in the components presented. The equity method for an unconsolidated subsidiary shows the parent's share of the subsidiary's net income minus gain (or plus loss) on intercompany transactions on a single line, Equity in Earnings of Unconsolidated Subsidiary. A consolidated income statement combines the individual revenues and expenses of the subsidiary (less intercompany adjustments) with those of the parent. The consolidation process eliminates the account Equity in Earnings of Unconsolidated Subsidiary.

TERMINOLOGY NOTE

Accountants sometimes refer to the equity method as a *one-line consolidation* because the revenues less the expenses of the subsidiary appear in the one account Equity in Earnings of Unconsolidated Subsidiary. Applying the equity method in realistic situations sometimes presents ambiguities. The guiding principle: treat the items in such a way that the parent's net income equals the same amount that it would show if it consolidated the investment rather than used the equity method for it.

External Minority Interest in Consolidated Subsidiary

Often, the parent does not own 100 percent of the voting stock of a consolidated subsidiary. The parent refers to the owners of the remaining shares of voting stock as the external minority shareholders or the **minority interest**. These shareholders have provided a portion or fraction of the subsidiary's financing and have a claim to this same fraction of its net assets (= total assets − total liabilities) shown on the subsidiary's separate corporate records. They also have a claim to the same fraction of the earnings of the subsidiary. Do not confuse this minority interest in a consolidated subsidiary with a firm's own minority investments, discussed earlier. The minority interest represents ownership by others outside the parent and its economic entity. The parent's minority investments represent its ownership of shares of other companies in which the parent owns less than 50 percent of the shares.

The Minority Interest in Net Assets in the Consolidated Balance Sheet Assume now that the parent owns less than 100 percent of the subsidiary's shares—80 percent to be concrete. The minority shareholders own 20 percent of the subsidiary. Should the parent's consolidated statements show (1) only its 80 percent fraction of each of the assets and liabilities of the subsidiary or (2) all of the subsidiary's assets and liabilities?

The parent, with its controlling voting interest, can direct the use of *all* the subsidiary's assets and liabilities, not merely the 80 percent it owns claim to. The generally accepted accounting principle, therefore, shows all of the assets and liabilities of the subsidiary. The consolidated balance sheet and income statement will disclose the interest of the minority shareholders in the consolidated, but less-than-wholly-owned subsidiary.

The amount of the **minority interest** appearing in the balance sheet generally results from multiplying the common shareholders' equity of the subsidiary by the minority's percentage of ownership. For example, if the common shareholders' equity (= assets − liabilities) of a consolidated subsidiary totals $500,000, and the minority owns 20 percent of the common stock, the minority interest will appear on the consolidated balance sheet as $100,000 (= 0.20 × $500,000). The minority interest appears in the shareholders' section of the consolidated balance sheet, clearly labeled to distinguish it from the sources of financing provided by the parent's shareholders.

The parent's consolidated income statement shows all the subsidiary's revenues less all the subsidiary's expenses and so includes all of the subsidiary's income even though that amount does not appear with a separate caption. The minority shareholders claim part of this income, typically an amount equal to the subsidiary's net income multiplied by the minority's percentage of ownership. The consolidated income statement subtracts the minority's share of the subsidiary's income in calculating consolidated net income, which shows the parent's shareholders' claim on the income of the entire group of companies.[14]

Limitations of Consolidated Statements

The consolidated statements, provided for the parent's shareholders, do not replace the statements of individual corporations.

- Creditors must rely on the resources of the one corporation to which they loaned funds. They may misunderstand the protection for their loans if they use only a consolidated statement combining the data of a company that is sound with the data of one that is verging on insolvency.
- A corporation can declare dividends against only its own retained earnings.
- When the parent company does not own all of the shares of the subsidiary, the minority shareholders can judge the dividend constraints, both legal and financial, only by inspecting the subsidiary's statements.

Problem 11.5 for Self-Study

Understanding consolidation concepts. **Exhibit 11.6** presents income statement data and **Exhibit 11.7** presents balance sheet data for Parent and its 80-percent-owned Sub. The first two columns in each exhibit show amounts taken from the separate-company accounting records of each firm. The third column sums the amounts in the first two columns. The fourth column shows consolidated amounts for Parent and Sub after making intercompany eliminations.

a. Does the account Investment in Sub (equity method) on the Parent's books include any excess acquisition cost relative to the book value of the shareholders' equity of Sub?
b. Suggest four ways in which the data in **Exhibits 11.6** and **11.7** confirm that Parent owns 80 percent of Sub.
c. Why does the amount for accounts receivable in **column (3)** of **Exhibit 11.7** differ from the amount in **column (4)**?

(continued)

[14] We discuss and illustrate more of the accounting for minority interest, as well as special purpose entities and proportional consolidation, topics too advanced to discuss in the text, on the web site that the publisher has made available for this book (see the **Preface**).

Problem 11.5 for Self-Study *(continued)*

d. Explain why the account Investment in Sub does not appear on the consolidated balance sheet.

e. Why does the total shareholders' equity of $692 on the consolidated balance sheet equal the shareholders' equity on Parent's separate-company books?

f. Compute the amount of intercompany sales during Year 1.

g. Explain why the $80 for Equity in Earnings of Sub does not appear on the consolidated income statement.

h. Why does the account Minority Interest in Earnings of Sub appear on the consolidated income statement but not on the income statements of either Parent or Sub?

| EXHIBIT 11.6 | PARENT AND SUB
Income Statement Data for Year 1
(Problem 11.5 for Self-Study) |

	Separate Company Books		Combined (3) = (1) + (2)	Consolidated (4)
	Parent (1)	Sub (2)		
Sales	$ 4,000	$ 2,000	$ 6,000	$ 5,500
Equity in Earnings of Sub	80	—	80	—
Cost of Goods Sold	(2,690)	(1,350)	(4,040)	(3,540)
Selling and Administrative Expenses	(1,080)	(480)	(1,560)	(1,560)
Interest Expense	(30)	(20)	(50)	(50)
Income Tax Expense	(70)	(50)	(120)	(120)
Minority Interest in Earnings of Sub	—	—	—	(20)
Net Income	$ 210	$ 100	$ 310	$ 210

| EXHIBIT 11.7 | PARENT AND SUB
Balance Sheet Data, December 31, Year 1
(Problem 11.5 for Self-Study) |

	Separate Company Books		Combined (3) = (1) + (2)	Consolidated (4)
	Parent (1)	Sub (2)		
ASSETS				
Cash	$ 125	$ 60	$ 185	$ 185
Accounts Receivable	550	270	820	795
Inventories	460	210	670	670
Investment in Sub (equity method) . . .	192	—	192	—
Property, Plant, and Equipment (net) . .	680	380	1,060	1,060
Total Assets	$2,007	$920	$2,927	$2,710
LIABILITIES AND SHAREHOLDERS' EQUITY				
Accounts Payable	$ 370	$170	$ 540	$ 515
Notes Payable	400	250	650	650
Other Current Liabilities	245	60	305	305
Long-term Debt	300	200	500	500
Total Liabilities	$1,315	$680	$1,995	$1,970
Minority Interest Net Assets of Sub	—	—	—	$ 48
Common Stock	$ 200	$ 50	$ 250	$ 200
Retained Earnings	492	190	682	492
Total Shareholders' Equity	$ 692	$240	$ 932	$ 692
Total Liabilities and Shareholders' Equity	$2,007	$920	$2,927	$2,710

An International Perspective

Most countries outside of the United States require that the accounting for minority, passive investments use the lower-of-cost-or-market method, not the market value method. The accounting for minority and majority, active investments closely parallels practices in the United States: the equity method for minority, active investments and consolidation for majority investments. Practices for these active investments have become similar, however, only in recent years. Countries such as Germany and Japan have historically followed a strict legal definition of the corporate entity, with all intercorporate investments reported at acquisition cost and dividends received reported as the only revenues from these investments. The movement toward the use of the equity method and consolidation reflects increasing recognition that the economic entity likely differs from the legal entity and that financial statements based on the economic entity provide more useful information to users.

The International Accounting Standards Board (IASB) requires the equity method for investments where the holder exerts significant influence and has no plans to sell its investment in the near future.[15] The IASB expresses a preference for the consolidation of controlled entities, even if the investor owns less than 50 percent of the shares, and allows the cost method, the lower-of-cost-or-market method, the market value method, and the equity method for noncontrolling investments.[16]

As this book goes to press, the IASB is struggling with a treatment for derivative financial instruments—under what conditions to require these appear at market value. The IASB does not have an equivalent of a Statement of Other Comprehensive Income or a balance sheet account Accumulated Other Comprehensive Income. Instead, for items such as unrealized holding gains or losses on effective cash flow hedges, the IASB uses a separate account in shareholders' equity.

Summary

Businesses acquire the bonds or capital stock in other entities for a variety of reasons and in a variety of ways. The investor records the acquisition of the bonds or capital stock of another entity at the cash given or the market value of other consideration exchanged. The account debited for equity securities, either Marketable Securities or Investment in Securities, depends on the expected holding period.

Investment in S (Asset Increase)	X	
Cash or Other Consideration Given (Asset Decrease)		X

The accounting for investments in equity securities subsequent to acquisition depends on the ownership percentage:

- The market value method generally applies when the parent owns less than 20 percent.
- The equity method generally applies when the parent owns at least 20 percent but not more than 50 percent of the stock of another company.
- The equity method applies also when the investor company can exercise significant influence even though it owns less than 20 percent.
- The investor generally prepares consolidated statements when it owns more than 50 percent of the voting shares of another company.

The accounting for investments in debt securities subsequent to acquisition depends on the ability and intent of the investor to hold the security until it matures:

- The market value method generally applies when the investor does not have both the ability and intent to hold to maturity, with treatment as security available for sale or as trading security determined by the holder's intent.

---

[15] International Accounting Standards Board, *International Accounting Standard No. 28,* "Investments in Associates," 1989, revised in 1998.

[16] International Accounting Standards Board, *International Accounting Standard No. 27,* "Consolidated Financial Statements," 1989.

FIGURE 11.3   Roadmap to Investments

- The amortized cost method generally applies when the investor has both the ability and intent to hold the debt security to its maturity.

Figure 11.3 summarizes the structure of accounting for holdings of securities, and **Exhibit 11.8** summarizes the accounting for investments subsequent to acquisition.

EXHIBIT 11.8	Effects of Various Methods of Accounting for Long-term Investments in Corporate Securities		
Method of Accounting	**Balance Sheet**	**Income Statement**	**Statement of Cash Flows— Cash Flows from Operations**
Market value method for securities available for sale (generally used when ownership percentage is less than 20 percent)	Investment account appears at current market value as a noncurrent asset. Unrealized holding gains and losses appear in a separate shareholders' equity account.	Dividends declared by investee appear as revenue of investor. Gains and losses (from acquisition cost) appear in income only when realized in arm's-length transactions with outsiders.	Dividends received from investee are included in cash provided by operations of investors.
Market value method for trading securities (generally used when ownership percentage is less than 20 percent)	Investment account appears at current market value as a noncurrent asset. Unrealized holding gains and losses appear in income statement and effects increase or decrease the Retained Earnings account.	Dividends declared by investee appear as revenue of investor. Gains and losses (from then-current book value) appear in income when realized in arm's-length transactions with outsiders.	Dividends received from investee are included in cash provided by operations of investors. Under indirect method, add back unrealized holding losses and subtract unrealized holding gains included in income of the period.
Equity method (generally used when ownership percentage is at least 20 percent but not more than 50 percent)	Investment account appears at acquisition cost plus share of investee's net income less share of investee's dividends since acquisition. More advanced: also, less amortization of excess of purchase price over book value acquired.	Equity in investee's net income is part of revenue in the period that investee earns income. Reduce income by the amount, if any, of amortization of excess purchase price over book value acquired.	Cash from operations increases only by the amount of dividend received. In indirect method, deduct equity in investee's undistributed earnings from net income to derive cash provided by operations of investor. More advanced: if amortization of excess purchase price, then add back the amount amortized during current period.
Consolidation (generally used when ownership percentage exceeds 50 percent)	Eliminate investment account and replace it with individual assets and liabilities of subsidiary. Show minority interest in subsidiary's net assets among equities. Eliminate intercompany assets and liabilities.	Combine individual revenues and expenses of subsidiary with those of parent. Subtract minority interest in subsidiary's net income.	Combine individual sources and uses of cash of subsidiary with those of parent. In indirect method, add minority interest in net income to obtain cash provided by operations.
Amortized Cost Method (used only for debt where holder has both intent and ability to hold to maturity)	Original cost plus accrued interest not yet received in cash.	Book value at start of period multiplied by historical interest rate—market interest rate on date of acquisition of debt.	If holder acquired debt at a price below par, then cash flow from operations includes only the interest payment received. If the holder acquired the debt at a price above par, then cash flow from operations will include the amount of interest for the period, with the remainder of the cash received appearing as a financing receipt for redemption of debt.

The market value method for securities available for sale recognizes net income only when the investor becomes entitled to receive interest or dividends, or when it sells the securities.

Changes in the market value of securities available for sale appear in other comprehensive income, not net income. The market value method for trading securities recognizes in net income unrealized holding gains and losses from changes in the market value each period and any additional gain or loss realized at the time of sale.

Consolidated statements and the equity method have the same effect on net income. The parent shows as income its proportional share of the acquired firm's periodic income after acquisition, after eliminating the effects of intercompany transactions. In the equity method, this share appears on a single line of the income statement. Income statement amounts of revenues and expenses are larger in consolidation because the consolidated income statement combines the revenues and expenses of the acquired company with those of the parent. Balance sheet components under the consolidation method will exceed those under the equity method; the consolidated balance sheet substitutes the individual assets and liabilities of the acquired company for the parent company's Investment in the Subsidiary account.

Appendix 11.1: Effects on the Statement of Cash Flows of Investments in Securities

Investments in Debt with Both Ability and Intent to Hold to Maturity

Amortized Cost Method Acquisitions of debt securities are investing transactions. If the firm uses the direct method for cash flow from operations, it will show in cash inflow the debt service payments it receives so long as that amount does not exceed interest income for the period. Any excess reduces the amount of the asset for the investment in debt and appears as a negative investment activity, as though the holder sold some of the asset. If the firm uses the indirect method, it will subtract from net income any amounts by which interest revenue exceeds debt service collections. It will add back to net income any amounts by which debt service collections exceed interest revenue.

Investments in Equity Securities and Debt Without Ability and Intent to Hold to Maturity

Market Value Method Acquisitions of trading securities are operating activities; acquisitions of securities available for sale are investing transactions.[17] When Company P uses the market value method to account for its investment in Company S, all dividend revenues recognized in computing net income also generally produce cash. Therefore, calculating cash flow from operations normally requires no adjustment to revenues (direct method) or net income (indirect method). When firms do not receive cash equal to the amount of dividend revenue, there will be a subtraction from dividend revenue (direct method) or net income (indirect method) for increases in the Dividends Receivable account or additions for decreases in that account.

Changes in the Marketable Securities account and the Investment in Securities account and in the account for Unrealized Holding Gains or Losses, which arise in the market value method, do not appear in the statement of cash flows for Securities Available for Sale. These changes in market value do not affect cash, so require no adjustment when computing cash flow from operations under either the direct or the indirect method. In contrast, holding gains and losses on trading securities do appear in income but do not affect cash flow, so they do require an adjustment to net income in deriving cash flow from operations if the firm uses the indirect method. For holding gains (losses) on trading securities, income has increased (decreased), but not cash from operations, so the indirect method shows a subtraction (addition) for those holding gains (losses).

---

[17] Financial Accounting Standards Board, *Statement of Financial Accounting Standards No. 102*, "Statement of Cash Flows—Exemption of Certain Enterprises and Classification of Cash Flows from Certain Securities Acquired for Resale," paragraph 26, 1989.

Equity Method   Under the direct method, the firm shows the dividends received as an operating cash flow. Accounting for investments using the equity method requires an adjustment to net income to compute cash flow from operations if the firm uses the indirect method in its statement of cash flows. Suppose that Company P prepares its financial statements at the end of a year during which occurred transactions (1) through (5) described in the section "Equity Method: Procedures" on page 493. Company P reported revenue from its investment in S of $54,000. This amount results from summing the revenue recognized in transactions (2) and (4). P's income (ignoring income tax effects) increased $54,000 because of its investment. However, P's cash increased by only $21,000—transactions (3) and (5)—as a result of S's dividends. Consequently, in computing cash flow from operations, P must subtract from net income an amount equal to the excess of revenue over cash flow, or $33,000 (= $54,000 − $21,000), to show that cash did not increase by as much as the amount of revenue recognized under the equity method.

If a firm acquires an investment for an amount that exceeds the book value of the underlying net assets, the firm must write off the excess purchase price over the expected useful life of the item (other than goodwill). The expense does not use cash and requires an addback to net income when the firm computes cash flow from operations using the indirect method.

Consolidation   The accountant prepares a consolidated statement of cash flows from the consolidated balance sheet and income statement. Advanced accounting texts discuss the adjustments unique to a consolidated statement of cash flows, such as for a minority interest in a consolidated subsidiary. You should be able to recognize, however, that the minority interest in income subtracted (or, in losses added) on the consolidated income statement does not affect cash flow from operations, so the firm using the indirect method will show an addback (subtraction) for the minority interest in income (loss).

Solutions to Self-Study Problems

SUGGESTED SOLUTION TO PROBLEM 11.1 FOR SELF-STUDY

(General Electric Capital Services and Sapra Company; accounting for an interest-bearing note receivable.)

a. See **Exhibit 9.5**; the numbers remain the same; only the column captions change.

b. *Date of Issue*

Notes Receivable (Asset Increase)	112,434	
Cash (Asset Decrease)		112,434

GECS lends cash to Sapra and receives note.

Six Months after Issue

Interest Receivable (Asset Increase)	5,622	
Retained Earnings (Interest Revenue) (Shareholders' Equity Increase)		5,622

See **Exhibit 9.5**; accrual of six months' interest = $11,243/2.

One Year after Issue

Cash (Asset Increase)	15,000	
Interest Receivable (Asset Decrease)		5,622
Retained Earnings (Interest Revenue) (Shareholders' Equity Increase)		5,621
Notes Receivable (Asset Decrease)		3,757

Interest revenue for the remainder of the first year and cash received. Excess of cash payment over interest expense reduces note principal.

SUGGESTED SOLUTION TO PROBLEM 11.2 FOR SELF-STUDY

(Conlin Corporation; accounting for securities available for sale.)

a. **(1)** *February 3, Year 2*

Marketable Securities [A] (Asset Increase)	40,000	
Cash (Asset Decrease)		40,000

To record acquisition of Security A.

(2) *July 15, Year 2*

Marketable Securities [B] (Asset Increase)	75,000	
Cash (Asset Decrease)		75,000

To record acquisition of Security B.

(3) *November 27, Year 2*

Marketable Securities [C] (Asset Increase)	90,000	
Cash (Asset Decrease)		90,000

To record acquisition of Security C.

(4) *December 31, Year 2*

Accumulated Other Comprehensive Income (Unrealized Holding Loss on Security A Available for Sale) (Shareholders' Equity Decrease)	2,000	
Marketable Securities [A] (Asset Decrease)		2,000

To revalue Security A to market value.

(5) *December 31, Year 2*

Marketable Securities [B] (Asset Increase)	4,000	
Accumulated Other Comprehensive Income (Unrealized Holding Gain on Security B Available For Sale) (Shareholders' Equity Increase)		4,000

To revalue Security B to market value.

(6) *December 31, Year 2*

Marketable Securities [C] (Asset Increase)	3,000	
Accumulated Other Comprehensive Income (Unrealized Holding Gain on Security C Available for Sale) (Shareholders' Equity Increase)		3,000

To revalue Security C to market value.

Note: The accountant could combine entries **(4)**, **(5)**, and **(6)** above as follows:

December 31, Year 2

Marketable Securities (Asset Increase)	5,000	
Accumulated Other Comprehensive Income (Unrealized Holding Gain (net) on Securities Available for Sale) (Shareholders' Equity Increase)		5,000

To revalue the portfolio of marketable securities available for sale to market value.

(7) *September 6, Year 3*

Cash (Asset Increase)	78,000	
Marketable Securities [B] (Asset Decrease)		75,000
Retained Earnings (Realized Gain on Sale of Security B Available for Sale) (Shareholders' Equity Increase)		3,000

To record sale of Security B at a gain equal to the difference between selling price and acquisition cost and include the realized gain in net income.

(8) *September 6, Year 3, or December 31, Year 3*

Accumulated Other Comprehensive Income (Unrealized Holding Gain on Security B Available for Sale) (Shareholders' Equity Decrease)	4,000	
Marketable Securities (B) (Asset Decrease)		4,000

To eliminate the effects of changes previously recorded in the market values of securities available for sale.

(9) *December 31, Year 3*

Accumulated Other Comprehensive Income (Unrealized Holding Loss on Security A Available for Sale) (Shareholders' Equity Decrease)	5,000	
Marketable Securities [A] (Asset Decrease)		5,000

To revalue Security A to market value.

(10) *December 31, Year 3*

Marketable Securities [C] (Asset Increase)	1,000	
Accumulated Other Comprehensive Income (Unrealized Holding Gain on Security C Available for Sale) (Shareholders' Equity Increase)		1,000

To revalue Security C to market value.

Note: The accountant could combine entries **(8)**, **(9)**, and **(10)** above as follows:

December 31, Year 3

Accumulated Other Comprehensive Income (Unrealized Holding Gain [net] on Securities Available for Sale) (Shareholders' Equity Decrease)	8,000	
Marketable Securities (Asset Decrease)		8,000

To revalue the portfolio of marketable securities available for sale to market value.

b. The journal entries are identical except that the account titled Marketable Securities becomes Investment in Securities.

c. The first three journal entries are identical. The unrealized holding gain or loss accounts in entries **(4)**, **(5)**, **(6)**, **(9)**, and **(10)** are income statement accounts when the firm classifies the securities as trading securities. Entry **(7)** is as follows:

September 6, Year 3

Cash (Asset Increase)	78,000	
Retained Earnings (Realized Loss from Sale of Trading Security B) (Shareholders' Equity Decrease)	1,000	
Marketable Securities [B] (Asset Decrease)		79,000

To record sale of trading security for less than its book value at the time of sale.

If the security were a trading security, the firm would not make Entry **(8)**.

SUGGESTED SOLUTION TO PROBLEM 11.3 FOR SELF-STUDY

(Equity Investing Group; journal entries to apply the equity method for long-term investments in securities.)

a.

Investment in Securities [D] (Asset Increase)	80,000	
Investment in Securities [E] (Asset Increase)	190,000	
Investment in Securities [F] (Asset Increase)	200,000	
Cash (Asset Decrease)		470,000

b.

Investment in Securities [D] (0.40 × $40,000) (Asset Increase)	16,000	
Investment in Securities [E] (0.30 × $120,000) (Asset Increase)	36,000	
Investment in Securities [F] (0.20 × $200,000) (Asset Increase)	40,000	
Retained Earnings (Equity in Earnings of Affiliates) (Shareholders' Equity Increase)		92,000
Cash (Asset Increase)	25,000	
Investment in Securities [D] (0.40 × $10,000) (Asset Decrease) ..		4,000
Investment in Securities [E] (0.30 × $30,000) (Asset Decrease) ..		9,000
Investment in Securities [F] (0.20 × $60,000) (Asset Decrease) ..		12,000
Retained Earnings (Depreciation Expense) (Shareholders' Equity Decrease)	8,000	
Investment in Securities [E] (Asset Decrease)		4,000
Investment in Securities [F] (Asset Decrease)		4,000

Security	Book Value of Investee on January 1, Year 1	Ownership Percentage	Share of Book Value Acquired	Acquisition Cost of Investment	Excess Acquisition Cost	Annual Amortization for 10 Years
D	$200,000	40%	$ 80,000	$ 80,000	—	—
E	500,000	30	150,000	190,000	$40,000	$4,000
F	800,000	20	160,000	200,000	40,000	4,000

c.

Investment in Securities [D] (0.40 × $50,000) (Asset Increase)	20,000	
Investment in Securities [F] (0.20 × $50,000) (Asset Increase)	10,000	
Investment in Securities [E] (0.30 × $40,000) (Asset Decrease) ...		12,000
Retained Earnings (Equity in Net Earnings of Affiliates) (Shareholders' Equity Increase)		18,000[b]
Cash (Asset Increase)	16,800	
Investment in Securities [D] (0.40 × $12,000) (Asset Decrease) ...		4,800
Investment in Securities [F] (0.20 × $60,000) (Asset Decrease) ...		12,000
Retained Earnings (Depreciation Expense) (Shareholders' Equity Decrease)	8,000	
Investment in Securities [E] (Asset Decrease)		4,000
Investment in Securities [F] (Asset Decrease)		4,000

d.

Cash (Asset Increase)	190,000	
Retained Earnings (Loss on Sale of Investment in Securities) (Shareholders' Equity Decrease)	7,000	
Investment in Securities [E] (Asset Decrease)		197,000
$197,000 = $190,000 + $36,000 − $9,000 − $4,000 − $12,000 − $4,000.		

SUGGESTED SOLUTION TO PROBLEM 11.4 FOR SELF-STUDY

(Powell Corporation and Steele Corporation; financial statement effects of the purchase method.)

Exhibit 11.9 presents the consolidated balance sheet of January 1, Year 8, using the purchase method.

EXHIBIT 11.9	POWELL CORPORATION AND STEELE CORPORATION Consolidated Balance Sheet, January 1, Year 8 (Problem 11.4 for Self-Study)

	Purchase Method
ASSETS	
Current Assets	$ 17,000
Property, Plant, and Equipment (net)	53,000
Goodwill	40,000
Total Assets	$110,000
EQUITIES	
Liabilities	$ 41,000
Common Stock	3,700[a]
Additional Paid-in Capital	60,300[b]
Retained Earnings	5,000
Total Equities	$110,000

[a]$3,700 = $1,000 + (2,700 × $1).
[b]$60,300 = $9,000 + (2,700 × 19).

SUGGESTED SOLUTION TO PROBLEM 11.5 FOR SELF-STUDY

(Parent and Sub; understanding consolidation concepts.)

a. No. The investment account shows a balance of $192, which equals 80 percent of Sub's shareholders' equity ($192 = 0.80 × $240).

b. (1) The account Investment in Sub has a balance of $192, which equals 80 percent of the shareholders' equity of Sub. This clue supports the 80 percent ownership only because no unamortized excess acquisition cost exists (see the response to question **a**).

   (2) The minority interest in the net assets of Sub is $48, which equals 20 percent of the shareholders' equity of Sub ($48 = 0.20 × $240).

   (3) The account Equity in Earnings of Sub on Parent's books has a balance of $80 for Year 1, which equals 80 percent of the net income of Sub for Year 1 ($80 = 0.80 × $100).

   (4) The account Minority Interest in Earnings of Sub has a balance of $20 for Year 1 ($20 = 0.20 × $100).

c. Parent and Sub have intercompany accounts receivable and accounts payable. Combined accounts receivable exceed consolidated accounts receivable by $25 (= $820 − $795), the same as the excess of combined accounts payable over consolidated accounts payable ($25 = $540 − $515).

d. Double-counting results if both the investment account and the individual assets and liabilities of Sub appear on the consolidated balance sheet.

e. The $240 of Sub's shareholders' equity disappears in consolidation. As a result the only remaining shareholders' equity amount is the $692 of Parent. The elimination of the $240 of Sub's shareholders' equity proceeds as follows:

Elimination of Investment in Sub	$192
Recognition of Minority Interest in Net Assets of Sub	48
Total	$240

f. $500 (= $6,000 − $5,500 or $4,040 − $3,540).

g. Consolidated amounts include individual revenues, expenses, and minority interest in earnings, which net to $80. Double-counting this earnings results if the accountant does not eliminate the equity in earnings account.

h. The separate-company income statements report the total revenues and expenses of each entity without regard to who owns the common stock of each company. The consolidated income statement shows the earnings allocable to the shareholders of the parent company. These shareholders have a claim on all of the earnings of Parent but on only 80 percent of the earnings of Sub. Consolidated revenues and expenses included the combined amounts for both companies, adjusted for intercompany transactions. The minority interest in net income of Sub shows the portion of Sub's net income not subject to a claim by Parent's shareholders.

Key Terms and Concepts

Marketable securities	Cash flow hedge
Investments in securities	Equity method
Minority, passive investments	Market value method
Significant influence	Parent
Minority, active investments	Subsidiary
Majority, active investments	Consolidated financial statements
Derivative	Economic entity
Forward foreign exchange contract	Purchase method
Swap contract	Goodwill
Forward commodity contract	Variable interest entity (VIE)
Underlyings	Primary beneficiary
Notional amounts	Consolidation policy
Counterparty	Intercompany transactions
Net settlement	Minority interest (income statement)
Hedge accounting	Minority interest (balance sheet)
Fair value hedge	

QUESTIONS

1. Review the meaning of the terms and concepts listed above in Key Terms and Concepts.

2. "The classification of securities on the balance sheet as a current asset (Marketable Securities) or as a noncurrent asset (Investment in Securities) depends on a firm's intent." Explain.

3. Distinguish between the following pairs of terms:
   a. Debt securities classified as "held to maturity" versus "available for sale"
   b. Equity securities classified as "trading securities" versus "available for sale"
   c. Amortized acquisition cost versus market value of debt securities
   d. Unrealized holding gain or loss on trading securities versus on securities available for sale
   e. Realized gain or loss on trading securities versus on securities available for sale

4. What is the GAAP justification for including unrealized holding gains and losses on trading securities in income but reporting unrealized holding gains and losses on securities available for sale in Accumulated Other Comprehensive Income, a separate shareholders' equity account?

5. "The realized gain or loss from the sale of a particular security classified as available for sale will likely differ in amount from the realized gain or loss if the firm had classified that same security as a trading security." Explain.

6. "Reporting marketable securities available for sale at market values on the balance sheet but not including the unrealized holding gains and losses in income is inconsistent and provides opportunity for earnings management." Do you agree? Why or why not?

7. Compare and contrast each of the following pairs of accounts:
   a. For securities available for sale: Unrealized Holding Gain (or Loss) on Marketable Equity Securities and Unrealized Holding Gain (or Loss) on Investments in Securities
   b. Dividend Revenue, and Equity in Earnings of Unconsolidated Affiliates
   c. Equity in Earnings of Unconsolidated Affiliate, and Minority Interest in Earnings of Consolidated Subsidiary
   d. Minority Interest in Earnings of Consolidated Subsidiary, and Minority Interest in Net Assets of Consolidated Subsidiary

8. "Dividends received or receivable from another company are either a revenue in calculating net income or a return of investment, depending on the method of accounting the investor uses." Explain.

9. Why is the equity method sometimes described as a *one-line consolidation*? Consider both the balance sheet and the income statement in your response.

10. When is a derivative also a hedge? When is it not also a hedge? Can management manipulate earnings by its choice of whether to use hedge accounting?

11. Distinguish between a fair value hedge and a cash flow hedge.

12. When will a firm not show in income the periodic gain or loss caused by the change in fair value of a derivative?

13. Distinguish between minority investments in other companies and the minority interest in a consolidated subsidiary.

14. "Accounting for an investment in a subsidiary using the equity method and not consolidating it yields the same net income as consolidating the subsidiary. Total assets will differ, however, depending on whether or not the investor consolidates the subsidiary." Explain.

15. Why does GAAP require firms to write off over time any portion of an excess purchase price allocated to buildings and equipment but not goodwill?

SHORT EXERCISES

16. **Accounting principles for marketable securities.** For each of the following items, describe its accounting using one of the following four systems:
    (1) Measured at fair value with changes appearing in net income
    (2) Measured at amortized cost
    (3) Measured at fair value with changes appearing in other comprehensive income equity (FASB) or directly in shareholders' equity (IASB)
    (4) Measurement depends on whether firm uses hedge accounting
    a. A derivative judged to be effective used to hedge forecast sales
    b. Derivatives appearing as liabilities; these derivatives do not hedge assets or liabilities or anticipated transactions.

c. Traded debt issued by others that the firm has purchased with ability to hold to maturity, but intent after the current year is uncertain. The firm frequently buys and sells debt of this sort.

d. Marketable equity securities held for an indefinite period as securities available for sale.

17. **Working backward from data on marketable securities transaction.** (Adapted from a problem by S. A. Zeff.) During Year 3, Fischer/Black Co. purchased equity securities classified as securities available for sale. On May 22, Year 4, the company recorded the following correct journal entry to record the sale of the equity securities:

Cash (Asset Increase)	16,000	
Retained Earnings (Realized Loss) (Shareholders' Equity Decrease)	5,000	
Accumulated Other Comprehensive Income (Unrealized Holding Loss) (Shareholders' Equity Decrease)		3,000
Marketable Securities (Asset Decrease)		18,000

a. What was the acquisition cost of these securities in Year 3?

b. What was the market value of these securities at the end of Year 3?

c. What is the total amount of securities gain or loss that Fischer/Black reports on the income statement for Year 4?

18. **Working backward from data on marketable securities transaction.** (Adapted from a problem by S. A. Zeff.) On December 12, Year 2, Canning had purchased 2,000 shares of Werther. By December 31, the market price of these shares had dropped by $1,000. On March 2, Year 3, Canning sold the 2,000 shares for $18,000 and reported a realized gain on the transaction of $4,000.

a. What was the acquisition cost of these securities if Canning had accounted for them as trading securities?

b. What was the acquisition cost of these securities if Canning had accounted for them as securities available for sale?

19. **Reconstructing events from journal entries.** Give the likely transaction or event that would result in making each of the independent journal entries that follow:

a.

Accumulated Other Comprehensive Income (Unrealized Loss on Securities Available for Sale) (Shareholders' Equity Decrease)	4,000	
Marketable Securities (Asset Decrease)		4,000

b.

Cash (Asset Increase)	1,100	
Retained Earnings (Realized Loss on Sale of Securities Available for Sale) (Shareholders' Equity Decrease)	200	
Marketable Securities (Asset Decrease)		1,300

c.

Marketable Securities (Asset Increase)	750	
Accumulated Other Comprehensive Income (Unrealized Holding Gain on Securities Available for Sale) (Shareholders' Equity Increase)		750

d.

Cash (Asset Increase)	1,800	
Marketable Securities (Asset Decrease)		1,700
Retained Earnings (Realized Gain on Sale of Securities Available for Sale) (Shareholders' Equity Increase)		100

20. **Equity method entries.** Hanna Company purchased 100 percent of the common stock of Denver Company on January 2 for $550,000. The common stock of Denver Company at this date was $200,000, and the retained earnings balance was $350,000. During the year, net income of Denver Company was $120,000; dividends declared were $30,000. Hanna Company uses the equity method to account for the investment. Give the journal entries that Hanna Company made during the year to account for its investment in Denver Company.

21. **Working backward to consolidation relations.** Laesch Company, as parent, owns shares in Lily Company. Laesch Company has owned them since it formed Lily Company. Lily Company has never declared a dividend. Laesch Company has retained earnings from its own operations independent of intercorporate investments of $100,000. The consolidated balance sheet shows no goodwill and shows retained earnings of $156,000. Consider each of the following questions independently of the others:

   a. If the parent owns 80 percent of its consolidated subsidiary, what are the retained earnings of the subsidiary?

   b. If the subsidiary has retained earnings of $77,000, what fraction of the subsidiary does the parent own?

   c. If the parent had not consolidated the subsidiary but instead had accounted for it using the equity method, how much revenue would the parent company have recognized from the investment?

22. **Working backward from consolidated income statements.** Dealco Corporation published a consolidated income statement for the year, shown in **Exhibit 11.10**. The unconsolidated affiliate retained 25 percent of its earnings of $140 million during the year, having paid out the rest as dividends. The consolidated subsidiary earned $280 million during the year and declared no dividends.

EXHIBIT 11.10	DEALCO CORPORATION Consolidated Income Statement (Exercise 22)		
REVENUES			
Sales			$1,400,000
Equity in Earnings of Unconsolidated Affiliate			56,000
Total Revenues			$1,456,000
EXPENSES			
Cost of Goods Sold (excluding depreciation)			$ 910,000
Administrative Expense			140,000
Depreciation Expense			161,000
Amortization of Goodwill			7,000
Income Tax Expenses:			
Currently Payable		$ 58,800	
Deferred		14,000	72,800
Total Expenses			$1,290,800
Income of the Consolidated Group			$ 165,200
Less Minority Interest in Earnings of Consolidated Subsidiary			(42,000)
Net Income to Shareholders			$ 123,200

   a. What percentage of the unconsolidated affiliate does Dealco Corporation own?

   b. What dividends did Dealco Corporation receive from the unconsolidated affiliate during the year?

   c. What percentage of the consolidated subsidiary does Dealco Corporation own?

EXERCISES

23. **Classifying securities.** Firms must classify minority, passive investments in securities along two dimensions:

- Purpose of investment: debt securities held to maturity, trading securities, or securities available for sale
- Length of expected holding period: current asset (Marketable Securities) or noncurrent asset (Investment in Securities)

Classify each of the securities below along each of these two dimensions.

   a. A forest products company plans to construct a pulp-processing plant beginning in April of next year. It issues common stock for $200 million on December 10 of this year to help finance construction. The company invests this $200 million in U.S. government debt securities to generate income until it needs the cash for construction.

   b. An electric utility has bonds payable outstanding for $100 million that mature in five years. The electric utility acquires U.S. government bonds that have a maturity value of $100 million in five years. The firm plans to use the proceeds from the government bonds to repay its own outstanding bonds.

   c. A commercial bank acquires bonds of the state of New York to generate tax-exempt interest revenue. The bank plans to sell the bonds when it needs cash for loans and other ongoing operating needs.

   d. A pharmaceutical company acquires common stock of a biogenetic engineering company that conducts research in human growth hormones. The pharmaceutical company hopes the investment will lead to strategic alliances or joint ventures in the future.

   e. A commercial bank maintains a department that regularly purchases and sells securities on stock exchanges around the world. This department acquires common stock of Toyota on the New York Stock Exchange because it thinks the market price does not fully reflect favorable news about Toyota.

   f. A U.S. computer company has bonds outstanding that are payable in French francs. The bonds mature in installments during the next five years. The computer company purchases a French winery's bonds, denominated in French francs, that mature in seven years. The computer company will sell a portion of the bonds of the French winery each year to obtain the French francs needed to repay its franc-denominated bonds.

24. **Journal entries to apply the market value method to short-term investments in securities.** Events related to Vermont Company's investment in the common stock of Texas Instruments appear below. Vermont Company closes its books on December 31 of each year.

   8/21   Vermont Company purchases 1,000 shares of Texas Instruments' common stock for $45 per share as an investment of temporarily excess cash (classified as Securities Available for Sale).

   9/13   The stockbroker for Vermont Company calls to report that the shares of Texas Instruments closed on the preceding day at $49 per share.

   9/30   Texas Instruments declares a dividend of $0.50 per share.

   10/25 Vermont Company receives a dividend check from Texas Instruments for $550.

   12/31 The stockbroker calls Vermont Company to report that Texas Instruments' shares closed the year at $51 per share. Vermont Company closes its books for the year.

   1/20   Vermont Company sells 600 shares for $55 per share, the closing price for the day.

   Prepare dated journal entries as required by these events. Ignore income taxes.

25. **Journal entries to apply the market value method to short-term investments in securities.** Events related to Elston Corporation's investments of temporarily excess cash appear below. The firm classifies these investments as Securities Available for Sale.

Security	Date Acquired	Acquisition Cost	Market Value on December 31		Date Sold	Selling Price
			Year 4	Year 5		
A	10/15/Year 4	$28,000	$25,000	–	2/10/Year 5	$24,000
B	11/2/Year 4	49,000	55,000	$53,000	7/15/Year 6	57,000

Elston received no dividends on Security A. It received dividends from Security B of $1,000 on December 31, Year 4, and $1,200 on December 31, Year 5. Prepare dated journal entries for the events related to these investments, assuming that the accounting period is the calendar year.

   a. Acquisition of securities

   b. Receipt of dividends

c. Revaluation on December 31
d. Sale of securities

26. **Journal entries to apply the market value method for short-term investments in securities.** Events related to Simmons Corporation's investments of temporarily excess cash appear below. The firm classifies these investments as Securities Available for Sale.

Security	Date Acquired	Acquisition Cost	Market Value on December 31 Year 6	Market Value on December 31 Year 7	Date Sold	Selling Price
S	6/13/Year 6	$12,000	$13,500	$15,200	2/15/Year 8	$14,900
T	6/13/Year 6	29,000	26,200	31,700	8/22/Year 8	28,500
U	6/13/Year 6	43,000	—	—	10/11/Year 6	39,000

None of these three securities paid dividends. Prepare dated journal entries for the events related to these investments, assuming that the accounting period is the calendar year.
a. Acquisition of securities
b. Revaluation on December 31
c. Sale of securities

27. **Amount of income recognized under various methods of accounting for investments.** On January 1, Apollo Corporation acquired common stock of Venus Corporation. At the time of acquisition, the book value and the fair market value of Venus Corporation's net assets were $500 million. During the year, Venus Corporation earned $80 million and declared dividends of $20 million. The market value of shares increased by 15 percent during the year. How much income would Apollo Corporation report for the year related to its investment under the assumption that it took the following actions?
a. Paid $75 million for 15 percent of the common stock and uses the market value method to account for its investment in Venus Corporation as securities available for sale.
b. Paid $120 million for 15 percent of the common stock and uses the market value method to account for its investment in Venus Corporation as securities available for sale.
c. Paid $150 million for 30 percent of the common stock and uses the equity method to account for its investment in Venus Corporation.

28. **Balance sheet and income effects of alternative methods of accounting for investments.** On January 1, Trusco acquired common stock of USP Company. At the time of acquisition, the book value and the market value of USP's net assets were $400 million. During the current year, USP earned $50 million and declared dividends of $30 million. Indicate the amount shown for Investment in USP on the balance sheet on December 31 and the amount of income Trusco would report for the year related to its investment under the assumption that Trusco did the following:
a. Paid $40 million for a 10 percent interest in USP and uses the market value method for securities available for sale. The market value of USP on December 31 was $400 million.
b. Same as part a except that the market value of USP on December 31 was $390 million.
c. Paid $45 million for a 10 percent interest in USP and uses the market value method for securities available for sale. The market value of USP on December 31 was $450 million.
d. Paid $120 million for a 30 percent interest in USP and uses the equity method.
e. Paid $160 million for a 30 percent interest in USP and uses the equity method. The firm neither amortizes any goodwill nor finds it impaired.

29. **Journal entries to apply the market value method for long-term investments in securities.** The following information summarizes data about the long-term minority, passive investments in securities of Randle Company for its first two years of operations. Randle Company classifies these investments as Securities Available for Sale.

Security	Date Acquired	Acquisition Cost	Date Sold	Selling Price	Market Value Dec. 31, Year 1	Market Value Dec. 31, Year 2
M	4/10/Year 1	$ 37,000	10/15/Year 2	$43,000	$ 35,000	—
N	7/11/Year 1	31,000			38,000	45,000
O	9/29/Year 1	94,000			87,000	89,000
		$162,000			$160,000	$134,000

Randle Company received dividends on December 31 of each year as follows:

Security	Year 1	Year 2
M	$1,500	—
N	1,400	$1,600
O	5,000	4,000

Prepare journal entries to account for these investments in securities during Year 1 and Year 2 using the market value method.

30. **Journal entries to apply the market value method for long-term investments in securities.** The following information summarizes data about the long-term minority, passive investments in securities of Blake Company. Blake Company classifies these investments as Securities Available for Sale.

					Market Value	
Security	Date Acquired	Acquisition Cost	Date Sold	Selling Price	Dec. 31, Year 4	Dec. 31, Year 5
F	7/9/Year 3	$93,700	10/29/Year 4	$89,700	—	—
G	7/2/Year 4	42,800			$38,300	$36,900
H	10/19/Year 4	29,600	9/17/Year 5	32,300	31,600	—
I	2/9/Year 5	18,100			—	20,700

The market value of the investment in Security F totaled $91,200 on December 31, Year 3. Assume that none of the investees paid dividends during Year 4 or Year 5. Prepare journal entries to account for these investments in securities during Year 4 and Year 5 using the market value method.

31. **Journal entries to apply the equity method of accounting for investments in securities.** Wood Corporation made three long-term intercorporate investments on January 2. Data relating to these investments for the year appear below.

Company	Percentage Acquired	Book Value and Market Value of Net Assets on January 2	Acquisition Cost	Net Income (Loss) for the Year	Dividends Declared during the Year
Knox Corporation	50%	$700,000	$350,000	$70,000	$30,000
Vachi Corporation	30	520,000	196,000	40,000	15,000
Snow Corporation	20	400,000	100,000	(24,000)	—

Give the journal entries to record the acquisition of these investments and to apply the equity method during the year. The firm neither amortizes any goodwill nor finds it impaired.

32. **Journal entries to apply the equity method of accounting for investments in securities.** The following information summarizes data about the minority, active investments of Stebbins Corporation.

Security	Date Acquired	Acquisition Cost	Ownership Percentage	Book Value of Net Assets on January 1, Year 1	Earnings (Loss) Year 1	Earnings (Loss) Year 2	Dividends Year 1	Dividends Year 2
R	1/1/Year 1	$250,000	25%	$800,000	$200,000	$225,000	$125,000	$130,000
S	1/1/Year 1	325,000	40	750,000	120,000	75,000	80,000	80,000
T	1/1/Year 1	475,000	50	950,000	(150,000)	50,000	—	—

Company R owns a building with 10 years of remaining life and with a market value exceeding its book value by $160,000. $40,000 of this amount applies to the shares Stebbins Corporation owns. Stebbins Corporation attributes the rest of any excess of purchase price over book value acquired to goodwill. The building has a 10-year remaining life. The market values of the recorded net assets of Company S and Company T equal their book values.

The firm neither amortizes any goodwill nor finds it impaired.

a. Give the journal entries to record the acquisition of these investments and to apply the equity method during Year 1 and Year 2.

b. Stebbins Corporation sells Security R on January 1, Year 3, for $275,000. Give the journal entry to record the sale.

33. **Journal entries under various methods of accounting for investments.** Mulherin Corporation made three long-term investments on January 2. Data relating to these investments appear below.

Company	Percentage Acquired	Book Value and Market Value of Net Assets on January 2	Acquisition Cost	Net Income (Loss) for the Year	Dividends Declared during the Year	Market Value on Shares Held on December 31
Hanson	15%	$2,000,000	$ 320,000	$200,000	$ 40,000	$ 305,000
Maloney	30	2,000,000	680,000	500,000	180,000	700,000
Quinn	100	2,000,000	2,800,000	600,000	310,000	1,950,000

Assume that these were the only intercorporate investments of Mulherin Corporation. Maloney Company has a patent developed from its internal research efforts that has a market value exceeding book value of zero on January 2. Mulherin's 30 percent share of that excess is $80,000. The patent has a 10-year remaining life on this date. Any excess purchase price from the acquisition of Quinn Company relates to goodwill. The firm neither amortizes any goodwill nor finds it impaired.

Give the journal entries on Mulherin Corporation's books to record these acquisitions of common stock and to account for the intercorporate investments under GAAP. Mulherin Corporation accounts for its investment in Quinn Corporation using the equity method on its separate-company books.

34. **Consolidation policy and principal consolidation concepts.** CAR Corporation manufactures computers in the United States. It owns 75 percent of the voting stock of Charles Electronics, 80 percent of the voting stock of Alexandre du France Software Systems (in France), and 90 percent of the voting stock of R Credit Corporation (a finance company). CAR Corporation prepares consolidated financial statements consolidating Charles Electronics, uses the equity method for R Credit Corporation, and treats its investment in Alexandre du France Software Systems as securities available for sale. Data from the annual reports of these companies appear below. There are no intercompany transactions.

	Percentage Owned	Net Income	Dividends	Accounting Method
CAR Corporation Consolidated	—	$1,200,000	$ 84,000	—
Charles Electronics	75%	120,000	48,000	Consolidated
Alexandre du France Software Systems[a]	80	96,000	60,000	Market Value (Securities Available for Sale)
R Credit Corporation	90	144,000	120,000	Equity

[a]Market value of shares exceeds cost.

a. Which, if any, of the companies does CAR incorrectly account for according to GAAP?

Assuming the accounting methods and accounting itself for the three subsidiaries shown above are correct, answer the following questions:

b. How much of the net income reported by CAR Corporation Consolidated results from the operations of the three subsidiaries?

c. What is the amount of the minority interest now shown on the income statement, and how does it affect net income of CAR Corporation Consolidated?

d. If CAR had consolidated all three subsidiaries, what would have been the net income of CAR Corporation Consolidated?

e. If CAR had consolidated all three subsidiaries, what minority interest would appear on the income statement?

35. **Equity method entries, earnings quality, and ethics.** Bush Corporation acquired significant influence over Cheney Computer Company on January 2 by purchasing 20 percent of its outstanding stock for $100 million. Bush attributes the entire excess of cost over book value acquired to a patent, which it amortizes over 10 years. The shareholders' equity accounts of Cheney Computer Company appeared as follows on January 2 and December 31 of the current year (amounts in millions):

	Jan. 2	Dec. 31
Common Stock	$300	$300
Retained Earnings	120	190

Cheney Computer had earnings of $100 million and declared dividends of $30 million during the year. The accounts receivable of Bush Corporation at December 31 included $600,000 due from Cheney Computer. Bush Corporation accounts for its investment in Cheney Computer using the equity method.

a. Give the journal entries to record the acquisition of the shares of Cheney Computer and to apply the equity method during the year on the books of Bush Corporation.

b. Bush Corporation considers reducing its ownership from 20 percent to 19.5 percent so that it no longer has to use the equity method. Comment on this possibility and its implications for earnings quality and ethics.

36. **Equity method entries.** Vogel Company is a subsidiary of Joyce Company. Joyce Company accounts for its investment in Vogel Company using the equity method on its single-company books. Present journal entries for the following selected transactions. Record the set of entries on the books of Vogel Company separately from the set of entries on the books of Joyce Company.

(1) On January 2, Joyce Company acquired on the market, for cash, 100 percent of the common stock of Vogel Company. The outlay was $420,000. The total contributed capital of Vogel Company's stock outstanding was $300,000; the retained earnings balance was $80,000. Joyce attributes the excess of cost over book value acquired to an internally developed patent that has a ten-year remaining useful life on January 2.

(2) Vogel Company purchased materials for $29,000 from Joyce Company on account at the latter's cost.

(3) Vogel Company obtained an advance of $6,000 from Joyce Company. Vogel Company deposited the funds in the bank.

(4) Vogel Company paid $16,000 on the purchases in (2).

(5) Vogel Company repaid $4,000 of the loan received from Joyce Company in (3).

(6) Vogel Company declared and paid a dividend of $20,000 during the year.

37. **Working backwards from data which has eliminated intercompany transactions.** (Adapted from a problem by S. A. Zeff.) Alpha owns 100 percent of Omega and consolidates Omega in an entity called Alpha/Omega. Beginning in Year 2, Alpha sold merchandise to Omega at a price 50 percent larger than Alpha's costs. Omega sold some, but not all, of these goods to customers at a further markup. Excerpts from the single-company statements of Alpha and Omega and from the consolidated financial statements of Alpha/Omega appear below.

	Single-Company Statements		Consolidated Financial Statements
	Alpha	**Omega**	
Sales Revenue	$450,000	$250,000	$620,000
Cost of Goods Sold	300,000	210,000	430,000
Merchandise Inventory	60,000	50,000	100,000

a. What was the total sales price at which Alpha sold goods to Omega during Year 2?

b. What was Omega's cost of the goods it had purchased from Alpha but has not yet sold by the end of Year 2? What was Alpha's cost of those goods? Which of those two numbers appears in the total Merchandise Inventory on the consolidated balance sheet?

38. **Working backward from purchase data.** (Adapted from a problem by S. A. Zeff.) On May 1, Year 1, Homer acquired the assets and agreed to take on and pay off the liabilities of Tonga in exchange for 10,000 of Homer's common shares. Homer accounted for the acquisition of the net assets of Tonga using the purchase method. On the date of acquisition, Tonga's book value

of depreciable assets exceeded Homer's estimate of their market value, but Homer judged all other items on Tonga's books to reflect market value on that date, so that the purchase price exceeded the fair value of the identifiable assets, generating goodwill. On the date of the acquisition, Tonga's shareholders' equity was $980,000 and its liabilities totaled $80,000. Tonga reported no goodwill on its balance sheet.

Homer made the following journal entry to record the acquisition:

Current Assets (Asset Increase)	210,000	
Depreciable Assets (net) (Asset Increase)	700,000	
Goodwill (Asset Increase)	120,000	
Liabilities (Liability Increase)		80,000
Common Stock—Par (Shareholders' Equity Increase)		150,000
Additional Paid-in Capital (Shareholders' Equity Increase)		800,000

    a. What was the book value on Tonga's books of its total assets just before the acquisition?
    b. What was the book value of depreciable assets of Tonga just before the acquisition?

39. **Financial statement effects of revaluations required by the purchase method.** Bristol-Myers Corporation and Squibb, both pharmaceutical companies, agreed to merge as of January 2, Year 10. Bristol-Myers exchanged 234 million shares of its common stock for the outstanding shares of Squibb. The shares of Bristol-Myers sold for $55 per share on the merger date, resulting in a transaction with a market value of $12.87 billion. Assume that the market value of buildings and equipment of Squibb exceeds their book value by $2,500 million, the market value of patents exceeds their book value by $6,400 million, and that the market values of all other recorded assets and liabilities equal their book values. The buildings and equipment have a ten-year remaining useful life and the patents have a five-year remaining useful life as of January 2, Year 10. Condensed balance sheet data on January 2, Year 10, appear below (amounts in millions).

	Bristol-Myers	Squibb
Assets	$5,190	$3,083
Liabilities	1,643	1,682
Shareholders' Equity	3,547	1,401
	$5,190	$3,083

    a. Prepare a condensed consolidated balance sheet on the date of the merger assuming that the firms accounted for the merger using the purchase method. Show any amount for goodwill separately.
    b. Projected net income for Year 10 before considering the effects of the merger are $1,225 for Bristol-Myers and $523 for Squibb. Compute the amount of consolidated net income projected for Year 10 for Bristol-Myers and Squibb using the purchase method.

40. **Effect of transactions involving the market value methods on the statement of cash flows.** Refer to the simplified statement of cash flows in **Exhibit 4.12**. Numbers appear on 11 of the lines in the statement. Ignore the unnumbered lines in considering the transactions below. Assume that the accounting cycle is complete for the period and that the firm has prepared all of its financial statements. It then discovers that it has overlooked a transaction. It records the transaction in the accounts and corrects all of the financial statements. For each of the following transactions or events, indicate which of the numbered lines of the statement of cash flows change and the amounts and directions of the changes (increase or decrease). Ignore income tax effects.
    a. A firm purchased equity securities costing $59,800 during the period. The firm classifies these as short-term Securities Available for Sale.
    b. A firm sold for $47,900 equity securities classified as short-term Securities Available for Sale. The securities originally cost $42,200 and had a book value of $44,000 at the time of sale.
    c. A firm sold for $18,700 equity securities classified as short-term Securities Available for Sale. The securities originally cost $25,100 and had a book value of $19,600 at the time of sale.
    d. A particular equity security purchased during the period for $220,500 had a market value of $201,500 at the end of the accounting period. The firm classifies the security as a short-term Security Available for Sale. The firm has already recorded the purchase.

    e. Assume the same information as in part **d** except that the market value of the security at the end of the accounting period is $227,900.

    f. A firm receives a dividend of $8,000 on shares held as a long-term Security Available for Sale and accounted for using the market value method.

    g. A firm writes down, from $10,000 to $8,000, Securities Available for Sale accounted for with the market value method.

41. Effect of transactions involving the equity method on the statement of cash flows. Refer to the preceding exercise and use those instructions for the following items.

    a. A 40-percent-owned affiliate accounted for using the equity method earns $25,000 and pays dividends of $10,000.

    b. A 40-percent-owned affiliate accounted for using the equity method reports a loss for the year of $12,500.

    c. A firm amortizes $3,000 of the excess of the purchase price over the book value of the underlying net assets in a 40-percent-owned affiliate. The excess related to a patent.

42. Effect of errors involving securities available for sale on financial statement ratios. Indicate using O/S (overstated), U/S (understated), or NO (no effect) the pre-tax effect of each of the following errors on (1) the rate of return on assets, and (2) the debt-equity ratio. Each of these ratios is between zero and 100 percent before management discovered the error.

    a. A firm holding equity securities classified as short-term Securities Available for Sale neglected to write down the securities to market value at the end of the year.

    b. A firm holding equity securities classified as long-term Securities Available for Sale neglected to write up the securities to market value at the end of the year.

    c. A firm holding equity securities classified as long-term Securities Available for Sale recorded dividends received by debiting Cash and crediting the Investment account.

    d. A firm holding equity securities accounted for using the equity method credited a check received for dividends from the investment to Dividend Revenue.

    e. A firm holding equity securities accounted for using the equity method neglected to amortize excess purchase price related to undervalued depreciable assets.

43. Effect of errors on financial statements. Using the notation O/S (overstated), U/S (understated), or NO (no effect), indicate the effects on assets, liabilities, shareholders' equity, and net income of each of the independent errors that follow. Ignore income tax effects.

    a. In applying the market value method to minority, passive investments in securities, a firm incorrectly credits dividends received to the investment account.

    b. The market value of minority, passive investments in securities at the end of a firm's first year of operations was $5,000 less than cost. The firm neglected to make the required journal entry in applying the market value method.

    c. In applying the equity method, P correctly accrues its share of S's net income for the year. However, when receiving a dividend, P credits Dividend Revenue.

    d. P acquired 30 percent of S on January 1 of the current year for an amount in excess of the book value of S's net assets. The excess relates to patents. P correctly accounted for its share of S's net income and dividends for the year but neglected to amortize any of the excess purchase price.

    e. During the current year, P sold inventory items to S, its wholly owned subsidiary, at a profit. S sold these inventory items, and S paid P for them before the end of the year. The firms made no elimination entry for this intercompany sale on the consolidation work sheet.

    f. Refer to part **e**. Assume that S owes P $10,000 for intercompany purchases at year-end. The firm made no elimination entry for this intercompany debt.

    g. P owns 90 percent of S. P treats the minority interest in consolidated subsidiaries as a liability. In preparing a consolidated work sheet, the firms made no entry to accrue the minority interest's share of S's net income or of S's net assets.

PROBLEMS AND CASES

44. Journal entries and financial statement presentation of short-term securities available for sale. The following information summarizes data about Dostal Corporation's marketable securities held as current assets and as Securities Available for Sale.

Security	Date Acquired	Acquisition Cost	Date Sold	Selling Price	Market Value Dec. 31, Year 1	Market Value Dec. 31, Year 2
A.........	2/5/Year 1	$60,000	6/5/Year 2	$72,000	$66,000	—
B.........	8/12/Year 1	25,000	—	—	20,000	$23,000
C.........	1/22/Year 2	82,000	—	—	—	79,000
D.........	2/25/Year 2	42,000	6/5/Year 2	39,000	—	—
E.........	3/25/Year 2	75,000	—	—	—	80,000

a. Give all journal entries relating to these marketable equity securities during Year 1 and Year 2, assuming that the accounting period is the calendar year.

b. Provide a suitable presentation of marketable securities in the balance sheet and related notes on December 31, Year 1.

c. Provide a suitable presentation of marketable securities in the balance sheet and related notes on December 31, Year 2.

45. **Journal entries and financial statement presentation of long-term securities available for sale.** The following information summarizes data about Rice Corporation's investments in equity securities held as noncurrent assets and as Securities Available for Sale.

Security	Date Acquired	Acquisition Cost	Date Sold	Selling Price	Market Value Dec. 31, Year 1	Market Value Dec. 31, Year 2
A.........	3/5/Year 1	$40,000	10/5/Year 2	$52,000	$45,000	—
B.........	5/12/Year 1	80,000	—	—	70,000	$83,000
C.........	3/22/Year 2	32,000	—	—	—	27,000
D.........	5/25/Year 2	17,000	10/5/Year 2	16,000	—	—
E.........	5/25/Year 2	63,000	—	—	—	67,000

a. Give all journal entries relating to these equity securities during Year 1 and Year 2, assuming that the accounting period is the calendar year.

b. Provide a suitable presentation of investments in securities in the balance sheet and related notes on December 31, Year 1.

c. Provide a suitable presentation of investments in securities in the balance sheet and related notes on December 31, Year 2.

46. **Reconstructing transactions involving short-term securities available for sale.** The financial statements of Zeff Corporation reveal the following information with respect to Securities Available for Sale:

	December 31 Year 1	December 31 Year 2
Balance Sheet		
Marketable Securities at Market Value	$187,000	$195,000
Net Unrealized Holding Gain on Securities Available for Sale	12,000	10,000
Income Statement		Year 2
Realized Gain on Sale of Securities Available for Sale		$4,000

a. What was the cost of the marketable securities sold?

b. What was the unrealized holding gain on the securities sold at the time of sale?

c. What was the unrealized holding gain during Year 2 on securities still held by the end of Year 2?

d. What was the cost of marketable securities purchased during Year 2?

47. **Analysis of financial statement disclosures for securities available for sale.** Exhibit 11.11 reproduces data about the marketable equity securities held as securities available for sale for

Sunshine Mining Company for a recent year, with dates changed for convenience. Assume that Sunshine held no current marketable securities at the end of Year 1, sold no current marketable securities during Year 2, purchased no noncurrent marketable securities during Year 2, and transferred no noncurrent marketable securities to the current portfolio during Year 2. The income statement for Year 2 shows a realized loss on sale of noncurrent marketable securities of $3,068,000.

a. What amount of net unrealized holding gain or loss on noncurrent marketable securities appears on the balance sheet for the end of Year 1?

b. What amount of net unrealized gain or loss on noncurrent securities appears on the balance sheet for the end of Year 2?

c. What were the proceeds of the sale of noncurrent marketable securities sold during Year 2?

d. What amount of unrealized holding gain or loss on marketable securities appears on the income statement for Year 2?

EXHIBIT 11.11	SUNSHINE MINING COMPANY Data on Marketable Equity Securities (all dollar amounts in thousands) (Problem 47)		
Marketable Equity Securities		**Acquisition Cost**	**Market Value**
At December 31, Year 2:			
Current Marketable Securities		$ 7,067	$ 4,601
Noncurrent Marketable Securities		$ 6,158	$ 8,807
At December 31, Year 1:			
Noncurrent Marketable Securities		$21,685	$11,418

48. **Effect of various methods of accounting for marketable equity securities.** Information related to marketable equity securities of Callahan Corporation appears below.

Security	Acquisition Cost in Year 1	Dividends Received during Year 1	Market Value on Dec. 31, Year 1	Selling Price in Year 2	Dividends Received during Year 2	Market Value on Dec. 31, Year 2
G	$18,000	$ 800	$16,000	$14,500	$ 200	—
H	25,000	1,500	24,000	26,000	500	—
I	12,000	1,000	14,000	—	1,500	$17,000
	$55,000	$3,300	$54,000	$40,500	$2,200	$17,000

a. Assume that these securities represent trading securities. Indicate the nature and amount of income recognized during Year 1 and Year 2 and the presentation of information about these securities on the balance sheet on December 31, Year 1 and Year 2.

b. Repeat part **a** assuming that these securities are securities available for sale held as temporary investments of excess cash by Callahan Corporation.

c. Repeat part **a** assuming that these securities represent long-term investments by Callahan Corporation held as securities available for sale.

d. Compute the combined income for Year 1 and Year 2 under each of the three treatments of these securities in parts **a**, **b**, and **c**. Why do the combined income amounts differ? Will total shareholders' equity differ? Why or why not?

49. **Analysis of financial statement disclosures related to marketable securities and quality of earnings.** Citibank reports the following information relating to its marketable securities classified as Securities Available for Sale for a recent year (amounts in millions):

	December 31	
	Year 10	**Year 11**
Marketable Securities at Acquisition Cost	$14,075	$13,968
Gross Unrealized Holding Gains	957	1,445
Gross Unrealized Holding Losses	(510)	(218)
Marketable Securities at Market Value	$14,522	$15,195

Cash proceeds from sales and maturities of marketable securities totaled $37,600 million in Year 11. Gross realized gains totaled $443 million and gross realized losses totaled $113 million during Year 11. The book value of marketable securities sold or matured totaled $37,008 million. Interest and dividend revenue during Year 11 totaled $1,081 million. Purchases of marketable securities totaled $37,163 million during Year 11.

a. Give the journal entries to record the sale of marketable securities during Year 11.

b. Analyze the change in the net unrealized holding gain from $447 million on December 31, Year 10, to $1,227 million on December 31, Year 11.

c. Compute the total income (both realized and unrealized) *occurring during Year 11* on Citibank's investments in securities.

d. How might the judicious selection of marketable securities sold during Year 11 permit Citibank to report an even larger net realized gain? Comment on the quality of earnings and ethics issues this option raises.

50. **Journal entries for various methods of accounting for intercorporate investments.** Rockwell Corporation acquired, as long-term investments, shares of common stock of Company R, Company S, and Company T on January 2. These are the only long-term investments in securities that Rockwell Corporation holds. Data relating to the acquisitions follow.

Company	Percentage Acquired	Book Value and Market Value of Total Net Assets on January 2	Acquisition Cost	Net Income for Year	Dividends Declared for Year	Market Value of Shares Owned on December 31
R	10%	$6,000,000	$ 648,000	$1,200,000	$480,000	$ 624,000
S	30	6,000,000	2,040,000	1,200,000	480,000	2,052,000
T	100	6,000,000	6,000,000	1,200,000	480,000	6,300,000

a. Give the journal entries made to acquire the shares of Company R and to account for the investment during the year, using the market value method.

b. Give the journal entries made to acquire the shares of Company S and to account for the investment during the year, using the equity method. Any excess cost relates to goodwill. The firm neither amortizes any goodwill nor finds it impaired.

c. Give the journal entries made to acquire the shares of Company T and to account for the investment during the year, using the equity method.

51. **Effect of intercorporate investment policies on financial statements.** Coca-Cola Company (Coke) and PepsiCo (Pepsi) dominate the soft drink industry in the United States and maintain leading market positions in many other countries. Coke has followed a policy of holding a 49 percent ownership interest in its bottlers, whereas Pepsi wholly owns its bottling operations. **Exhibit 11.12** presents selected balance sheet data for Coke and Pepsi for Year 11.

The first column shows amounts for Coke as reported, with Coke using the equity method to account for investments in its bottlers. The second column shows amounts for Coke's bottlers as reflected in a note to Coke's financial statements. The third column shows consolidated amounts for Coke and its bottlers. The 51 percent external interest in these bottlers appears on a line between liabilities and shareholders' equity. The fourth column shows amounts for Pepsi as reported, with its bottlers consolidated.

a. Compute the rate of return on assets for Year 11 under each of the four treatments in **Exhibit 11.12**. Assume an income tax rate of 34 percent. Also assume that the amounts shown for total assets in **Exhibit 11.12** approximate the average assets for Year 11.

b. Compute the ratio of total liabilities to total assets at the end of Year 11 under each of the four treatments in **Exhibit 11.12**.

c. Evaluate the operating profitability and risk of Coke versus Pepsi using the ratios computed in questions a and b.

d. Suggest reasons why Coke might choose to own 49 percent of its bottlers whereas Pepsi holds 100 percent of its bottlers.

EXHIBIT 11.12	COKE and PEPSI Financial Statement Data for Year 11 (all dollar amounts in millions) (Problem 51)			
	Coke as Reported (1)	**Coke's Bottlers (2)**	**Coke as Consolidated with Bottlers (3)**	**Pepsi as Reported (4)**
ASSETS				
Current Assets	$4,143	$ 2,153	$ 6,296	$ 4,081
Investment in Bottlers	2,025	—	—	—
Property, Plant, and Equipment	3,112	8,957	12,069	5,711
Goodwill	—	—	310	5,845
Total Assets	$9,280	$11,110	$18,675	$15,637
LIABILITIES AND SHAREHOLDERS' EQUITY				
Current Liability	$4,296	$ 2,752	$ 7,048	$ 3,264
Long-term Liabilities	1,133	4,858	5,991	7,469
External Interest in Bottlers	—	—	1,785	—
Shareholders' Equity	3,851	3,500	3,851	4,904
Total Liabilities and Shareholders' Equity	$9,280	$11,110	$18,675	$15,637
Net Income for Year 11	$1,364	$ 290	$ 1,364	$ 1,091
Interest Expense for Year 11	$ 231	$ 452	$ 683	$ 689

52. Interaction of regulation and accounting rules for financial institutions, particularly banks. Exhibit 11.13 illustrates the key features of a banking or thrift institution. Because regulators and investors view the banking business—borrowing funds and lending them to others at higher rates—as less risky than most other businesses, they allow banks and thrifts to carry smaller shareholders' equity as a percentage of total equities than do most nonfinancial firms. That is, banks have, with the blessing of regulators, higher financial leverage than non-financial firms.

   Exhibit 11.13 illustrates a thrift institution that regulators allow to have shareholders' equity equal to only 8 percent of assets. (The effects illustrated here would be even more dramatic with a capital ratio of 5 percent or less, which many banks use.) Other realistic assumptions, used for illustration, are as follows:

* Liabilities can be 11.5 times as large as owners' equity; this follows from the assumption that owners' equity is 8 percent of total equities, so that liabilities can be 92 percent of total equities.
* Liabilities cost 5.5 percent (interest expense) each year.
* Assets earn 7.0 percent (interest revenues) each year.
* Variable operating expenses are 0.4 percent of total assets.
* Fixed operating expenses are 0.1 percent of the bank's starting asset position of $1,000.
* There are no income taxes.

Key features of a bank are that (1) they tend to borrow funds for short terms, such as through accepting cash into checking and savings accounts or by issuing short-term certificates of deposits, while (2) they lend funds for longer terms, such as for home mortgages or customers' auto purchases.

   The top panel of **Exhibit 11.13** shows the balance sheet for the bank as it starts in business. The firm starts with contributed capital of $80; it borrows $920, giving it $1,000 of equities and funds available for lending. It lends $1,000, earning 7 percent on those assets. It pays interest on its $920 of borrowings, pays its operating expenses, and reports income of $14.4.

   Now, let the market value of the bank's financial assets—loans—increase by 5 percent, or $50, as shown in the second panel. Show this increase on the balance sheet. The transactions are as follows:

(1) Assets increase in value by $50, so Retained Earnings increase by $50.

(2) The bank uses the extra owners' equity of $50 to borrow an additional $575 (= 11.5 × $50), which it lends to new customers, increasing total assets by $575.

The income statement shows more revenues and more expenses, but rates of return change little from those of the original bank. Note, however, the effect on the bank's size: a 5 percent increase in market value allows the bank to increase its assets and size by 62.5 percent, from $1,000 in assets to $1,625 in assets. This creates no problem for the bank. Bank managers are happy because their compensation often depends on bank size, not just bank profitability.

Now, go back to the original bank and let the market value of the bank's financial assets decrease by 5 percent, or $50, as shown in the third panel. Observe this decrease on the balance sheet. The transactions are as follows:

(3) Assets decrease in value by $50, so Retained Earnings decrease by $50.

(4) The bank's decrease in owners' equity requires it to reduce borrowings by $575 (= 11.5 × $50). In order to pay back its creditors and to reduce assets, it must reduce its lendings by $575.

The income statement shows smaller revenues and smaller expenses, but rates of return change little from those of the original bank. Note, however, the effect on the bank's size: a 5 percent decrease in market value has forced the bank to reduce its size by 62.5 percent, from $1,000 in assets to $375 in assets. This creates a major problem for the bank. The problem arises because the bank must shrink in size, by a lot and quickly. The bank's assets comprise loans it has made to customers, typically long-term loans. The bank cannot easily recall those loans without incurring significant cost. (The typical loan gives the bank's customer the right to prepay the loan whenever the customer wants but does not allow the bank to call in the loan at the bank's whim.) Perhaps the bank will have to sell its assets to others, at a loss, to raise cash to reduce its own borrowings and its size.

Whatever it does, the bank has a problem. This problem arises because the bank shows the losses on its balance sheet and must reduce owners' equity because of this loss. Bankers understand this feature of market value accounting for assets, and they have, historically, been the most vocal opponents of such accounting for financial assets. For many years, bankers have prevailed in keeping the changes in market values of their assets off the balance sheet.

Many banks' assets are not marketable securities but are loans, which do not trade in the marketplace. The FASB does not require the marking to market value of nonmarketable financial assets. For such assets, banks use the amortized cost method, illustrated in **Problem 11.1** for Self-Study. For marketable debt securities, the bank will use market value accounting for trading securities or the amortized cost method (debt held to maturity), depending on its holding intention and ability. So long as the bank can show that it has both the ability and the intent to hold a loan until it matures, the bank need not show changes in that loan's market value on the balance sheet.

Repeat the analysis in **Exhibit 11.13**, using a capital ratio of 5 percent instead of 8 percent, and set the changes in market value of assets first to an increase of 4 percent and then to a decrease of 4 percent.

EXHIBIT 11.13	Effects of Changing Market Value of Assets on a Bank's Activities (Problem 52) Bank has Capital Ratio of 5 percent

Step [1]: Market Value of Assets Increases, Also Increasing Owners' Equity.
Step [2]: Bank Increases Lending to Maintain Capital (Leverage) Ratio at 5 Percent.
Step [3]: Market Value of Original Bank Decreases, Decreasing Owners' Equity.
Step [4]: Bank Decreases Lending to Maintain Capital (Leverage) Ratio at 5 Percent.
Operating Income Excludes Gains and Losses in Market Value of Assets Held.

Balance Sheet

Partial Income Statement

Rate of Return On:

Original Bank, before Market Value Changes

Assets		Equities		Revenues as % of Assets			
		Liabilities:					
$1,000 Original		Borrowings $950		7.0%	$70.0		
				Interest Expense			
				5.5%	(52.3)		
		Owners' Equity:		Operating Expense			
		Contributed Capital . . . 50		% of Assets			
		Retained Earnings. . . . 0		0.4%	(4.0)	Assets 1.3%	
		Total Owners' Equity . . $50		Fixed costs . . . . . (1.0)		Owners'	
$1,000		Totals $1,000		Operating Income . . .$12.8		Equity 25.5%	

Market Value of Assets Increases   4.0%

Assets		Equities		Revenues as % of Assets			
		Liabilities:					
$1,000 Original		Original Borrowings . . .$950		7.0%	$126.0		
				Interest Expense			
				5.5%	(94.1)		
[1] 40 Market Value Increase				Operating Expense			
[2] 760 New Lending		[2] New Borrowing 760		% of Assets			
				0.4%	(7.2)		
		Owners' Equity:		Fixed costs . . . . . (1.0)			
		Contributed Capital . . . 50					
		[1] Retained Earnings. . . . 40					
		Total Owners' Equity . . $90				Assets 1.3%	
						Owners'	
$1,800		Totals $1,800		Operating Income . . .$23.8		Equity 26.4%	

Market Value of Assets Decreases   −4.0%

Assets		Equities		Revenues as % of Assets			
		Liabilities:					
$1,000 Original		Original Borrowings . . .$950		7.0%	$14.0		
				Interest Expense			
				5.5%	(10.5)		
[3] (40) Market Value Decline				Operating Expense			
[4] (760) Reduce Lending		[4] Reduce Borrowings . . .(760)		% of Assets			
				0.4%	(0.8)		
		Owners' Equity:		Fixed costs . . . . . (1.0)			
		Contributed Capital . . . 50					
		[3] Retained Earnings. . . . (40)					
		Total Owners' Equity . . $10				Assets 0.9%	
						Owners'	
$200		Totals $200		Operating Income $1.8		Equity 17.5%	

chapter 12

Shareholders' Equity: Capital Contributions, Distributions, and Earnings

Learning Objectives

1. Understand the different priority claims of common and preferred shareholders on the assets of a firm and the disclosure of those claims in the shareholders' equity section of the balance sheet.

2. Understand the concepts underlying, and apply the accounting procedures for, the issuance of capital stock, particularly with respect to capital stock issued under various option arrangements.

3. Understand the concepts underlying, and apply the accounting procedures for, cash, property, and stock dividends.

4. Understand the concepts underlying, and apply the accounting procedures for, the acquisition and reissue of treasury stock.

5. Understand why the format for reporting income matters and master the concept that different kinds of income require different formats.

6. Understand the distinction between *earnings* and *comprehensive income*.

7. Develop the skills to interpret disclosures about changes in shareholders' equity accounts.

*C*hapters **6** to **11** discussed generally accepted accounting principles for various assets and liabilities. Changes in assets and liabilities often cause shareholders' equity to change. Changes in shareholders' equity result from three types of transactions:

1. **Capital Contributions:** Firms issue common or preferred stock to obtain funds to finance various operating and investing activities.
2. **Distributions:** Firms distribute assets to shareholders either in the form of a dividend or the repurchase of common or preferred stock.
3. **Earnings Transactions:** Firms use assets financed by creditors and owners to generate earnings.

Exhibit 12.1 presents the shareholders' equity section of the balance sheet of The Coca-Cola Company (Coke). Previous chapters discussed the items marked in boldface. Let's review the important concepts:

1. Shareholders' equity is a residual interest. It represents the shareholders' claim on the assets of a firm insofar as the assets exceed the amounts claimed by the higher-priority, often called *senior*, creditors. Coke reports total assets of $24,501 million, liabilities of $12,701 million, and shareholders' equity of $11,800 million at the end of Year 12. Thus, lenders finance approximately half of Coke's assets and shareholders finance the other half.
2. All firms issue common stock. Firms may also issue preferred stock, which has a claim on the assets of a firm senior to that of the common shareholders. Coke does not have preferred stock outstanding in Year 11 and Year 12.
3. Common and preferred stock usually have a par or stated value. Coke's common stock has a $0.25 par value per share. Firms report amounts received from issuing common and preferred stock in excess of the par or stated value as Additional Paid-in Capital. Note that the amounts in Additional Paid-in Capital for Coke exceed the amounts in Common Stock, indicating that Coke issued shares for substantially more than $0.25 par value, a common practice among publicly traded firms.
4. Firms accumulate information about revenues and expenses during a reporting period to enable the preparation of the income statement. The amount of net income for a period increases net assets and retained earnings. Coke reported net income for Year 12 of $3,050 million.
5. Firms may periodically distribute net assets generated by earnings to shareholders as a dividend. Firms reduce net assets and retained earnings for the distribution. Coke declared dividends of $1,987 million during Year 12, representing a distribution equal to approximately two-thirds of net income for the year. Retained earnings increased $1,063 million during Year 12 (= $3,050 − $1,987 = $24,506 − $23,443).
6. Retained earnings on the balance sheet provides a measure of the cumulative net assets generated by earnings in excess of dividends declared. Note that retained earnings for Coke substantially exceeds the capital provided by issuing common stock. The retention of net assets from operations represents a substantial source of funds for most businesses.

EXHIBIT 12.1	Disclosure of Shareholders' Equity for The Coca-Cola Company (amounts in millions)

	December 31	
	Year 11	Year 12
Preferred Stock	none	none
Common Stock: $0.25-par Value, 5,600 Shares Authorized, 3,491.8 Shares Issued	$ 873	$ 873
Additional Paid-in Capital	3,520	3,857
Retained Earnings	23,443	24,506
Accumulated Other Comprehensive Income (Loss)	(2,788)	(3,047)
Total	$ 25,048	$ 26,189
Less Cost of Treasury Stock	(13,682)	(14,389)
Total Shareholders' Equity	$ 11,366	$ 11,800

This chapter explores these concepts in greater depth and expands the discussion of shareholders' equity by considering:

1. The reasons for issuing preferred stock and the different rights which firms might grant to various preferred stockholders.
2. The use of various options arrangements as a means of enhancing the issuance of additional common stock.
3. The reasons for repurchasing shares of common or preferred stock and the accounting for such share repurchases. **Exhibit 12.1** indicates that Coke had repurchased $13,682 million of its own stock as of December 31, Year 11 and $14,389 million as of December 31, Year 12. These repurchases substantially reduced total shareholders' equity.
4. The reporting of earnings transactions, particularly the distinction between net income and other comprehensive income. **Exhibit 12.1** indicates that Coke reports a reduction in shareholders' equity for negative amounts of Accumulated Other Comprehensive Income (that is, losses) at the end of each year. What is the purpose of classifying certain earnings transactions in Other Comprehensive Income instead of net income? What types of transactions or events give rise to Other Comprehensive Income?

We begin with capital contributions. We then move to distributions and finish the chapter with the reporting of earnings transactions.

TERMINOLOGY NOTE

Of all the words used in business, accounting, and finance, the word *capital* is one of the most ambiguous. It can mean *cash* ("The firm raised capital with a stock issue"), or *long-term assets* ("The firm's capital assets have depreciable lives between 7 and 10 years"), or all sources of funding, that is, all items on the right side of the balance sheet ("The firm's weighted average cost of capital is 11 percent"), or shareholders' equity or, as in this chapter, that part of shareholders' equity arising from owner's contributions of cash and other assets. We recommend that you use this word to mean only contributed capital, but the rest of the world will continue to use the word to mean whatever is convenient for the speaker at the time. You should be attuned to the various meanings and understand what a particular user means at a particular time by the word *capital*. See the discussion in the Glossary for *capital*.

Most large, publicly traded firms operate as **corporations**. The corporate form has at least three advantages:

1. The corporate form provides the owner (shareholder) with limited liability; that is, should the corporation become insolvent, creditors can claim the assets of the corporate entity only. The corporation's creditors cannot claim the assets of the individual owners. On the other hand, to settle debts of partnerships and sole proprietorships, creditors have a claim on the owners' business and personal assets.
2. The corporate form allows the firm to raise funds by issuing shares. The general public can acquire the shares in varying amounts. Individual investments can range from a few dollars to billions of dollars.
3. The corporate form makes transfer of ownership interests relatively easy because owners can sell their shares to others without interfering with the ongoing operations of the firm. The transfer is a transaction between shareholders and does not directly involve the firm whose shares are exchanged.

The corporation has legal status separate from its owners. Individuals or other entities make capital contributions under a contract between themselves and the corporation. Because those who contribute funds receive certificates for shares of stock, business usage calls them *stockholders* or *shareholders*.

Various laws and contracts govern the rights and obligations of a shareholder:

1. The corporation laws of the state in which incorporation takes place
2. The articles of incorporation or the **corporate charter** (This contract sets out the agreement between the firm and the state in which the business incorporates. The state grants to the firm the privileges of operating as a corporation for certain stated purposes and of obtaining its capital through the issue of shares of stock.)
3. The **corporate bylaws** (The board of directors adopts bylaws, which are the rules and regulations governing the internal affairs of the corporation.)
4. The **capital stock contract** (Each type of **capital stock** has its own provisions on matters such as voting, sharing in earnings, distributing assets generated by earnings, and sharing in assets in case of dissolution.)

Preferred Shareholders' Equity

Owners of **preferred stock** generally have a claim on the assets of a firm in the event of bankruptcy that is senior to the claim of common shareholders. Preferred shares also carry special rights. The senior status and special rights may induce certain investors to purchase preferred stock of a firm, even though they would be unwilling to purchase common stock of the same firm. The senior status and special rights reduce the risks of preferred shareholders relative to common shareholders. Preferred shareholders should therefore expect a lower return than common shareholders.

Although the rights of preferred shares vary from issue to issue, a preferred share usually entitles its holder to dividends at a certain rate, which the firm must pay before it can pay dividends to common shareholders. Firms may sometimes postpone or omit preferred dividends. Most preferred shares, however, have **cumulative dividend rights**, which means that a firm must pay all current and previously postponed preferred dividends before it can pay any dividends on common shares.

In recent years, corporations have made many of their preferred stock callable. The corporation can reacquire **callable preferred shares** at a specified price, which may vary according to a preset time schedule. If financing becomes available at a cost lower than the rate fixed for the preferred shares, the issuing firm may want to reduce its financing costs by issuing some new securities and then exercising its option to reacquire the callable shares at a fixed price. Some naïve critics think callability benefits only the firm issuing callable shares. The callability option provides a valuable alternative to the issuing firm but makes the shares less attractive to potential owners of the shares. Other things being equal, a firm will issue callable shares at a lower price than that for noncallable shares. The purchaser of the callable shares benefits from acquiring the callable shares at the lower price.

Firms sometimes issue preferred shares with a conversion feature. **Convertible preferred shares** give their holder the option to convert them into a specified number of common shares at a specified time. The conversion option may appear advantageous to both the individual shareholder and the corporation. The preferred shareholders enjoy the security of a relatively assured dividend as long as they hold the shares and senior status to common shareholders in the event of bankruptcy. The shareholders also have the option to realize capital appreciation by converting the shares into common stock if the market price of the common shares rises sufficiently. Because of this option, changes in the market price of the convertible preferred shares will often parallel changes in the market price of the common shares. The firm may also benefit from the conversion option. By including it in the issue, the firm is usually able to specify a lower dividend rate on the preferred stock than otherwise would have been required to issue the shares for a given price.

Example 1   Global Crossing Ltd. is a telecommunications firm in bankruptcy. It reports several issues of convertible preferred stock outstanding at the end of Year 12. One issue carries a 6¾ percent cumulative dividend rate and is convertible into 6.31 shares of Global Crossing common stock. The preferred shares have senior rights as to dividends and in liquidation to all classes of common stock but are junior to all indebtedness of the firm.

Some preferred share issues carry mandatory redemption features; that is, the issuing firm must repurchase the shares from their holders, paying a specified dollar amount at a specified future time. Because such **redeemable preferred shares** have some of the characteristics of debt, firms must disclose them as liabilities on the balance sheet.[1]

Example 2   Global Crossing Ltd. also reports mandatory redeemable preferred stock outstanding. This preferred stock carries a 10⅛ percent cumulative dividend based on a $100 liquidation value. The preferred stock outstanding at the end of Year 12 is subject to mandatory redemption on December 1, Year 18 at the $100 liquidation value plus any dividends in arrears. This preferred stock is senior to all other classes of preferred and common stock but junior to all indebtedness of the firm in the case of dividends and in liquidation.

Common Shareholders' Equity

Firms need not issue preferred stock. All firms, however, must issue **common stock**. Common shareholders have a claim on the assets of a firm after creditors and preferred shareholders have received amounts promised to them. Frequently, corporations grant voting rights only to common shares, giving their holders the right to elect members of the board of directors and decide certain broad corporate policies (spelled out in the stock contract).

Issuing Capital Stock

Firms may issue capital stock (preferred or common) for cash or for noncash assets or under various option arrangements.

Issue for Cash

Firms usually issue shares for cash at the time of their initial incorporation and at periodic intervals as they need additional shareholder funds. Firms often issue shares to employees instead of paying them directly in cash for a portion of their compensation. The issue price for preferred stock usually approximates its par value. Firms generally issue common shares for amounts greater than **par (or stated) value**. Typically, individuals who purchase newly issued shares from a seasoned corporation pay a price larger than that paid by the original owners. The larger price compensates current shareholders for the additional assets accumulated through the retention of earnings, as well as for increases in the market values of assets over their book values. The firm credits the excess of issue proceeds over par (or stated) value to the **Additional Paid-in Capital account**.

If a firm issues par-value shares, the credit to the Additional Paid-in Capital account always equals the difference between the amount received and the par value of the shares issued. Thus

---

[1] Financial Accounting Standards Board, *Statement of Financial Accounting Standards No. 150*, "Accounting for Certain Financial Instruments with Characteristics of both Liabilities and Equity," 2003.

the entry to record the issue of 1,000 common shares with a par value of $10 per share for $100,000 is as follows:

Cash (Asset Increase)	100,000	
Common Stock—$10 Par Value (Shareholders' Equity Increase)		10,000
Additional Paid-in Capital (Shareholders' Equity Increase)		90,000
To record the issue of common shares for cash in an amount greater than par value.		

Issue for Noncash Assets

Firms occasionally issue common stock for assets other than cash. For example, a firm might want to acquire the assets of another firm in an effort to expand or diversify its operations. The firm records the shares issued at an amount equal to the market value of the assets received or, if the firm cannot make a reasonable estimate, at the market value of the shares issued.[2]

Assume that a firm issues 1,000 shares of its common stock with a par value of $10 per share in the acquisition of another firm's assets having the following market values: accounts receivable, $6,000; inventories, $12,000; land, $10,000; building, $62,000; and equipment, $10,000. The journal entry to record the exchange is as follows:

Accounts Receivable (Asset Increase)	6,000	
Inventories (Asset Increase)	12,000	
Land (Asset Increase)	10,000	
Building (Asset Increase)	62,000	
Equipment (Asset Increase)	10,000	
Common Stock—$10 Par Value (Shareholders' Equity Increase)		10,000
Additional Paid-in Capital (Shareholders' Equity Increase)		90,000
To record the issue of common shares for noncash assets in amount greater than par value. The amount for Additional Paid-in Capital is a plug.		

If the firm issues 100 shares with $10 par value to employees for $10,000 of compensation, instead of paying cash, the entry would be as follows:

Retained Earnings (Compensation Expense) (Shareholders' Equity Decrease)	10,000	
Common Stock—$10 Par Value (Shareholders' Equity Increase)		1,000
Additional Paid-in Capital (Shareholders' Equity Increase)		9,000
To record the issue of common shares instead of cash for wages of $10,000 paid to employees.		

Issue under Option Arrangements

Corporations often give various individuals or entities the right, or option, to acquire shares of common stock at a price that is less than the market price of the shares at the time they exercise the option.

Example 3 Ford, IBM, and other corporations with publicly traded common shares give **stock options** to their top managers each period as an element of their compensation. The stock options permit the employees to purchase shares of common stock at a price usually set equal to the market price of the stock at the time the firm grants the stock option. Employees exercise these stock options at a later time, after the stock price has increased. Firms adopt stock option plans to motivate employees to take actions that will increase the market value of a firm's common shares. Some firms issue employee stock options as a way to conserve cash. Likewise, firms issue

---

[2] Accounting Principles Board, *Opinion No. 29*, "Accounting for Nonmonetary Transactions," 1973.

stock rights to current shareholders, which give the shareholders the right to purchase shares of common or preferred stock at a specified price.

Example 4   Firms sometimes issue bonds with **stock warrants** attached. The bond contract gives the holder the right to receive periodic interest payments and the principal amount at maturity. The stock warrant permits the holder to exchange the warrant and a specified amount of cash for shares of the firm's common stock. Attaching a stock warrant permits the firm to issue bonds at a lower interest cost than would be required for bonds without such a warrant attached.

Example 5   Firms sometimes issue bonds or shares of preferred stock (see **Example 1** for Global Crossing, Ltd.) that are convertible into shares of common stock. The holders receive periodic interest or preferred dividend payments before conversion and usually maintain a senior claim on the firm's assets relative to the common shareholders. The conversion into common stock usually does not require any additional cash investment at the time of conversion. Including the conversion option in a debt or preferred stock issue permits the firm to pay a lower interest or preferred dividend rate than it would have to pay without the conversion option.

Each of these options has economic value. Accounting historically has not recognized the value of the options at the time firms grant them. Some accountants have argued that measuring the value of the option requires too much subjectivity to justify recognition in the accounts. Research in finance demonstrates valuation approaches that seem to meet accountants' standards for reliable measurement. Consequently, the FASB has proposed to require the recognition of the value of these options in the accounting records.

Employee Stock Option Plans   An understanding of the accounting for stock options requires several definitions. Refer to **Figure 12.1**. The *grant date* is the date a firm gives a stock option to employees. The *vesting date* is the first date employees can exercise their stock options. The *exercise date* is the date employees exchange the option and cash for shares of common stock. The *exercise price* is the price specified in the stock option contract for purchasing the common stock. The *market price* is the price of the stock as it trades in the market. Firms usually structure stock option plans so that a period of time elapses between the grant date and the vesting date. Firms may either preclude employees from exercising the option for one or more years (a service condition), require that the firm achieve specified levels of profitability (a performance condition), or achieve particular market prices for its common stock (a market condition) before employees can exercise their options. Delaying the vesting date increases the likelihood that the employee continues to work for the firm.

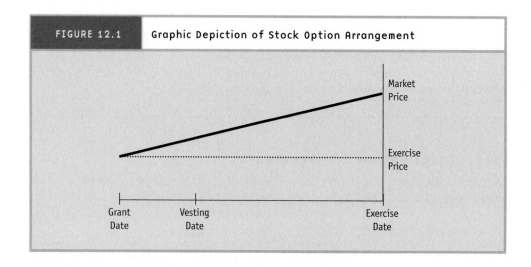

FIGURE 12.1   **Graphic Depiction of Stock Option Arrangement**

The value of a stock option results from two elements:

1. the benefit realized on the exercise date because the market price of the stock exceeds the exercise price (the **benefit element**), and
2. the length of the period during which the holder can exercise the option (the **time value element**).

One cannot know the amount of the benefit element before the exercise date. In general, stock options with exercise prices less than the current market price of the stock (described as *in the money*) have a higher value than stock options with exercise prices exceeding the current market price of the stock (described as *out of the money*). The time value element of an option's value results from the potential benefit it provides its holder for increases in the market price of the stock during the exercise period. An option provides the holder the right to enjoy the benefits of market price increases for the stock. This second element of an option will have more value the longer the exercise period and the more volatile the market price of the stock. Note that a stock option may have an exercise price that exceeds the current market price (zero value for the first element) but still have a value because of the possibility that the market price will exceed the exercise price on the exercise date (positive value for the second element). As the expiration date of the option approaches, the value of the second element approaches zero.[3]

Example 6   In a recent year, Microsoft Corporation granted their employees 1,604 million options to purchase shares of its common stock. The weighted average option price for options granted during the year was $26.88. This weighted average option price compares to a low and high market price for the stock for the year of $21.42 and $29.12 respectively, suggesting that Microsoft likely set the option price approximately equal to the market price of the stock at the time of the grant. Microsoft applied an option-pricing model and derived a value of $12.08 per option, or $19,376 million (= 1,604 × $12.08) for all options granted during the year. Microsoft reported net income of $9,993 million for the year.

Political Pressures on Standard Setters   Employees accept stock options instead of cash compensation because of the potential economic benefit they can realize if the market price of the shares increases above the option price (the stock options ultimately become worthless if the market price of the stock never exceeds the option price). Thus, stock options have a potential economic opportunity cost to firms issuing them and a potential economic benefit to employees. The concepts of accounting studied throughout this book suggest that firms should recognize this economic cost as an expense during the period(s) that firms realize the benefits of employees' services related to the stock options.

Despite the conceptual rationale for expense recognition, firms have historically not recognized any expense relating to stock options. The justification generally offered for not recognizing an expense is that employees receive no benefit when the option price equals or exceeds the market price. This view, however, ignores the fair value of the options, which results from the potential future benefit because the market price might exceed the option price. Proponents acknowledge that some benefit might result, but firms cannot reliably measure that benefit at the time of the grant.

In the mid-1990s, the FASB proposed that firms recognize the cost of stock options as an expense in measuring earnings. The FASB proposal met with extensive resistance at that time. Firms found the proposed accounting would substantially reduce earnings. Although most large, publicly traded firms grant stock options to their employees, firms in technology industries in particular rely heavily on stock options as an element of employee compensation and lobbied against the proposed accounting. Although their arguments centered on the difficulty of reliably measuring the value of stock options, one suspects that the negative earnings impact of this attractive form of compensation was the real driver. The FASB at the time bowed to pressure from companies and from some members of Congress and altered its proposed accounting. The FASB gave firms the option of either (1) recognizing the value of stock options as an expense, or (2) continuing the practice at the time of recognizing no expense whenever the option price equaled or exceeded the market price of the stock at the time of granting the option. Most firms chose the second approach. Firms that followed this second approach, however, would still value the stock options granted each year and disclose in notes to the financial statement what net income would have been if they had reported under the first method. Microsoft in **Example 6** disclosed that its net income—if it had amortized the cost of options granted over the period of benefit—would have been $7,531 million, instead of the $9,993 million it reported on the income statement.

Reported earnings abuses stemming from Enron, Global Crossing, and other firms beginning around 2000 raised the public's interest in corporate reporting and particularly on the compensation of top management. Frequent articles appeared in the financial press indicating that

---

[3] For an elaboration on the theory of option pricing, see Fischer Black and Myron Scholes, "The Pricing of Options and Corporate Liabilities," *Journal of Political Economy* (May–June 1973), pp. 637–54.

most firms did not recognize the cost of stock options when measuring net income. Armed with disclosures similar to those of Microsoft above, the public became aware of the extensive use and cost of stock options and put pressure on the Congress to do something about it. Some firms, particularly those in non-technology industries for which the cost of stock options was relatively small, voluntarily switched their accounting to begin recognizing the cost of stock options as an expense. Technology firms continued to resist.

Public pressure and support from the Congress led the FASB and the IASB to reconsider the accounting for stock options. As this book goes to press, the IASB has issued a reporting standard and the FASB has issued an Exposure Draft of a reporting standard that will require the recognition of an expense for stock options when measuring net income beginning in 2006.[4] The section below illustrates the accounting expected from these new reporting standards.

The accounting for stock options will likely involve the following:

1. Measuring the fair value of stock options on the date of the grant using an option-pricing model. Option valuation models incorporate information about the current market price, the exercise price, the expected time between grant and exercise, the expected market price volatility of the stock, the expected dividends, and the risk-free interest rate.
2. Amortizing the fair value of the stock options over the expected period of benefit, which is usually the period from the date of the grant to the date of vesting. The firm debits Retained Earnings (Compensation Expense) and credits Additional Paid-in Capital (Stock Options) for the amount amortized.
3. When employees exercise their options, the firm debits Cash for the proceeds, debits Additional Paid-in Capital (Stock Options) for any amounts credited to that account in step **2** above, credits Common Stock for the par value of the shares issued, and credits Additional Paid-in Capital for any excess of the value of the options plus the cash proceeds over the par value of the shares issued.

Example 7   Fiala Corporation awards options to employees on January 1, Year 1, to acquire 1,000 shares of $5 par value common stock at an exercise price of $35 per share. The firm uses an option-pricing model to value the options at $8,000. It expects to receive benefits of enhanced employee services for the two-year period between the grant date and the vesting date. Employees exercise the options on December 31, Year 4, when the market price of the stock is $50 per share. Fiala Corporation makes the following entries:

January 1, Year 1
No entry.

December 31, Year 1

Retained Earnings (Compensation Expense) (Shareholders' Equity Decrease)	4,000	
Additional Paid-in Capital (Stock Options) (Shareholders' Equity Increase)		4,000

December 31, Year 2

Retained Earnings (Compensation Expense) (Shareholders' Equity Decrease)	4,000	
Additional Paid-in Capital (Stock Options) (Shareholders' Equity Increase)		4,000

December 31, Year 4

Cash (1,000 × $35) (Asset Increase)	35,000	
Additional Paid-in Capital (Stock Options) (Shareholders' Equity Decrease)	8,000	
Common Stock—Par Value (1,000 × $5) (Shareholders' Equity Increase)		5,000
Additional Paid-in Capital {$8,000 + [1,000 × ($35 − $5)]} (Shareholders' Equity Increase)		38,000

---

[4] International Accounting Standards Board, *International Financial Reporting Standard 2*, "Share-based Payment," 2004; Financial Accounting Standards Board, *Proposed Statement of Financial Accounting Standard*, "Share-based Payment," 2004.

This accounting recognizes an expense as the firm receives the benefits ($4,000 each in both Year 1 and Year 2), and increases contributed capital for both the cash equivalent value of employees' services rendered to obtain the common stock ($8,000) and the cash received when employees exercise their options ($35,000).

Stock Rights   Like stock options, stock rights give their holder the right to acquire shares of stock at a specified price. The major differences between stock options and stock rights are as follows:

- Firms grant stock options to employees. Employees receive them as a form of compensation and may not transfer or sell them to others.
- Firms grant stock rights to current shareholders. The rights usually trade in public markets.

Firms issue stock rights to raise new capital from current shareholders. The granting of stock rights to current shareholders requires no accounting entries. GAAP ignore any value inherent in the stock right on the date of the grant. When holders exercise the rights, the firm records the issue of shares at the price paid just as it records the issue of new shares for cash.

Stock Warrants   Firms issue stock warrants to the general investing public for cash. Assume that a corporation issues warrants for $15,000 cash. The warrants allow holders to purchase 10,000 shares for $20 each. The entry is as follows:

Cash (Asset Increase)	15,000	
Common Stock Warrants (Shareholders' Equity Increase)		15,000
To record the issue of warrants to the public. The accountant normally includes the Common Stock Warrants account with Additional Paid-in Capital for balance sheet presentation.		

When warrant holders exercise their rights, the firm issues 10,000 shares of $5 par value common stock in exchange for the warrants plus $200,000 and records the following entry:

Cash (Asset Increase)	200,000	
Common Stock Warrants (Shareholders' Equity Decrease)	15,000	
Common Stock—$5 Par Value (Shareholders' Equity Increase)		50,000
Additional Paid-in Capital (Shareholders' Equity Increase)		165,000
To record the issue of 10,000 shares for $200,000 cash and the redemption of warrants. (The amount originally received for the warrants transfers to Additional Paid-in Capital.)		

If the warrants expire before the holders exercise them, the firm records the following entry:

Common Stock Warrants (Shareholders' Equity Decrease)	15,000	
Additional Paid-in Capital (Shareholders' Equity Increase)		15,000
To record the expiration of common stock warrants and the transfer to permanent contributed capital.		

Firms sometimes attach common stock warrants to a bond or preferred stock, which the holder can detach and redeem separately from the bond or preferred stock. The holder receives periodic interest or preferred dividends and holds an option to purchase common shares. When the accountant can objectively measure the value of the stock warrants separately from the value of the associated bond or preferred stock, the accounting allocates the issue price between the two securities.

To illustrate, assume that a firm issues 20-year, $1,000,000 bonds with 7-percent semiannual coupons. The bonds contain stock warrants, which their holders can either sell on the open market or exercise to acquire 10,000 shares of common stock for $200,000. The issue price for the bonds and warrants is $1,050,000. Immediately after issue, the bonds sell on the market for $1,035,000 and the warrants sell for $15,000. The accountant records the issue of the bonds as follows:

Cash (Asset Increase)	1,050,000	
Bonds Payable (Liability Increase)		1,035,000
Common Stock Warrants (Shareholders' Equity Increase)		15,000

The subsequent accounting for the bonds follows the procedures discussed in **Chapter 9** for bonds issued above or below par value. The accounting for the warrants follows the procedures illustrated above for warrants issued for cash.

If the accountant cannot objectively measure the value of the stock warrants separately from the value of the bond or preferred stock, the accounting credits the full issue price to the bond or preferred stock and none of the price to the common stock warrants.

Convertible Bonds or Preferred Stock

Convertible bonds and convertible preferred stock permit their owner either to hold the security as a bond or preferred stock or to convert the security into shares of common stock. The market value of the conversion option does not trade independently of the bond or preferred stock, as was the case above for bonds or preferred stock issued with a separable stock warrant. Thus, the accountant has greater difficulty allocating the issue price of a convertible bond or convertible preferred stock between its debt or preferred stock attributes and its conversion feature.

The required accounting allocates the full issue price to the bonds or preferred stock and none of the price to the conversion feature. Suppose, for example, that Johnson Company's credit rating would allow it to issue $100,000 of ordinary 10-year, 14-percent semiannual coupon bonds at par. The firm prefers to issue convertible bonds with a lower coupon rate. Assume that Johnson Company issues at par $100,000 of 10-year, 10-percent semiannual coupon bonds, but the holder of each $1,000 bond can convert it into 50 shares of Johnson Company $5 par value common stock. (Holders in aggregate can convert the entire issue into 5,000 shares.) Accounting requires the following entry:

Cash (Asset Increase)	100,000	
Convertible Bonds Payable (Liability Increase)		100,000
To record the issue of convertible bonds at par.		

This entry effectively treats convertible bonds just like ordinary, nonconvertible bonds, and it records the value of the conversion feature at zero.

An alternative treatment, but one not currently permitted, allocates a portion of the issue price to the conversion feature. **Appendix Table 5** (for 10-percent coupon bonds) indicates that 10-percent, 10-year semiannual (nonconvertible) coupon bonds sell for about 79 percent of par for an issuer with a market borrowing rate of 14 percent. Thus, if the firm can issue 10-percent convertible bonds at par, the conversion feature must be worth about 21 ($= 100 - 79$) percent of par. This indicates that the bond buyers have paid 21 percent of the proceeds from the bond issue as a capital contribution for the right to acquire common stock later. If GAAP allowed the accountant to record the substance of the issue of these 10-percent convertible bonds at par, the entry would be as follows:

Cash (Asset Increase)	100,000	
Convertible Bonds Payable (Liability Increase)		79,000
Additional Paid-in Capital (Shareholders' Equity Increase)		21,000
To record the issue of 10-percent semiannual coupon convertible bonds at a time when ordinary 10-percent bonds could be issued for 79 percent of par. GAAP do not allow this entry.		

Notice that the calculation of the amounts for this entry requires knowing the proceeds of an issue of nonconvertible bonds with other features similar to the convertible bonds. Because auditors often believe that they are unable to reliably estimate this information, GAAP do not currently allow the previous journal entry.[5] The entry under GAAP simply debits Cash and credits Convertible Bonds Payable for $100,000.

---

[5] As this book goes to press, the FASB is studying the accounting for convertible bonds. Given the FASB's recent moves to recognize the value of various options, the required accounting for convertible bonds in the future may follow this alternative treatment.

The usual entry to record the conversion of bonds into shares ignores current market prices in the interest of simplicity and merely shows the swap of shares for bonds at their book value. For example, assume that the common stock of Johnson Company increases in the market to $30 a share, so that the holder of one $1,000 bond, convertible into 50 shares, can convert it into shares with a market value of $1,500. If holders convert all the convertible issue into common shares at this time, the firm would issue 5,000 shares of $5 par value stock on conversion and make the following journal entry:

Convertible Bonds Payable (Liability Decrease)	100,000	
Common Shares—$5 Par (Shareholders' Equity Increase)		25,000
Additional Paid-in Capital (Shareholders' Equity Increase)		75,000
To record the conversion of 100 convertible bonds with book value of $100,000 into 5,000 shares of $5 par value stock.		

An allowable alternative treatment recognizes that market prices provide information useful in quantifying the market value of the shares issued. Under the alternative treatment, with $30 market price per share and $150,000 fair market value of the 5,000 shares issued on conversion, the journal entry would be as follows:

Convertible Bonds Payable (Liability Decrease)	100,000	
Retained Earnings (Loss on Conversion of Bonds) (Shareholders' Equity Decrease)	50,000	
Common Shares—$5 Par (Shareholders' Equity Increase)		25,000
Additional Paid-in Capital (Shareholders' Equity Increase)		125,000
To record the conversion of 100 convertible bonds into 5,000 shares of $5 par value stock at a time when the market price is $30 per share.		

The alternative entry results in the same total shareholders' equity, with smaller retained earnings but larger contributed capital. It results from treating the conversion as the following two separate transactions:

Cash (Asset Increase)	150,000	
Common Shares—$5 Par (Shareholders' Equity Increase)		25,000
Additional Paid-in Capital (Shareholders' Equity Increase)		125,000
To record issue of 5,000 shares of $5 par value stock at $30 per share.		
Convertible Bonds Payable (Liability Decrease)	100,000	
Retained Earnings (Loss on Retirement of Bonds) (Shareholders' Equity Decrease)	50,000	
Cash (Asset Decrease)		150,000
To record the retirement by purchase for $150,000 of 100 convertible bonds carried on the books at $100,000.		

Problem 12.1 for Self-Study

Journal entries for capital contributions. Prepare the journal entries to record the following transactions for Healy Corporation during Year 1.

a. Issued 100,000 of $10 par value common stock for $14 per share on January 2.
b. Issued 10,000 shares of common stock on January 2 in the acquisition of a patent. The firm has no separate information about the fair value of the patent.
c. Issued 2,000 shares of $100 convertible preferred stock on March 1 for $100 per share. Holders may convert each share of preferred stock into four shares of common stock.
d. Sold 10,000 common warrants on the open market on June 1 for $5 per warrant. Holders can exchange each warrant and $24 in cash for a share of common stock.

(continued)

Problem 12.1 for Self-Study (continued)

e. Holders of 600 shares of convertible preferred stock (see **c**) exchanged their shares for common stock on September 15. The market price of the common stock on this date was $26 per share. Record the conversion using the book values.

f. Holders of 4,000 common stock warrants exchanged their warrants (see **d**) and $96,000 in cash for common stock on November 20. The market price of the common stock on this date was $32 per share.

g. Granted options to employees to purchase 5,000 shares of common stock for $35 per share on December 31. The value of these options is $25,000 and the firm expects to realize all benefits of these options in future years.

Corporate Distributions

Firms use net assets (= assets – liabilities) to generate more net assets through the earnings process. Some firms retain some or all of the net assets generated by earnings, causing net assets to increase, along with retained earnings, the component of shareholders' equity showing the cause of that increase in net assets. The retention of assets generated by earnings generally results in an increase in the market price of the firm's common shares. Most firms do not retain all of the net assets generated by earnings but, instead, pay a dividend to the common shareholders. Each common shareholder receives the same dividend per share as all other common shareholders. This section discusses corporate dividend policies and the accounting for dividends.

Firms may also choose to use the net assets generated by earnings to repurchase shares of its common stock. Cash flows out of the firm to shareholders, as it does with a cash dividend. In the case of share repurchases, only shareholders selling their shares to the firm receive cash. This section discusses business reasons for stock repurchases and the accounting for such repurchases.

Dividends

The board of directors has the legal authority to declare dividends. The directors, in considering whether to declare dividends, must conclude that declaring a dividend is both legal (under law and contract) and financially expedient.

Legal Limits on Dividends—Statutory (by Law)   State corporation laws limit directors' freedom to declare dividends. These limitations attempt to protect a firm's creditors. Without these limits, directors might dissipate the firm's assets for the benefit of shareholders, harming the creditors. Neither directors nor shareholders are liable for the corporation's debts.

Generally, the laws provide that the board may not declare dividends "out of capital," that is, debited against the contributed capital accounts, which result from fund-raising transactions with owners, but must declare them "out of earnings" by debiting them against the retained earnings account, which results from operating transactions. The wording and the interpretation of this rule vary among states. "Capital" usually means the total amount paid in by shareholders. Some states allow corporations to declare dividends out of the earnings of the current period even though the Retained Earnings account has a debit (negative) balance because of accumulated losses from previous periods.

For most companies, statutory limits do not influence the accounting for shareholders' equity and dividends. A balance sheet does not provide all the legal details of amounts available for dividends, but it should disclose information necessary for the user to apply the legal rules of the corporation's state of incorporation. For example, state statutes can provide that the corporation "may acquire its own shares only in amounts less than retained earnings." In other words, dividends cannot exceed the amount of retained earnings reduced by the cost of currently held repurchased shares. If a firm acquires its own shares under these constraints, the amount of future dividends it might otherwise declare declines. The firm must disclose this fact in a note to the financial statements.[6]

---

[6] Accounting Principles Board, *Opinion No. 6*, "Status of Accounting Research Bulletins," 1965.

The firm can meet the statutory requirements for declaring dividends by building up a balance in retained earnings. Such a balance does not mean that the firm has a fund of cash available for the dividends. Some readers of financial statements mistakenly believe that retained earnings represent cash available for dividends. This error often results from the confusion of assets (such as cash) and sources of assets (such as retained earnings). Retained earnings represent the source of the increased net assets, which do not necessarily, or even usually, take the form of cash.

Managing cash requires the techniques of corporate finance; a firm must anticipate cash needs for dividends just as it anticipates cash needs for the purchase of equipment, the retirement of debts, and so on. A prudent firm might borrow from the bank to pay the regular dividend if its financial condition justifies the resulting increase in liabilities.

Legal Limits on Dividends—Contractual   Contracts with bondholders, other lenders, and preferred shareholders often limit dividend payments and thereby compel the retention of earnings. A bond contract may require that total liabilities not exceed the total amount of shareholders' equity or that the retirement of the debt be made "out of earnings." Such a provision involves curtailing dividends so that the necessary debt service payments, plus any dividends, do not exceed the amount of earnings for the period. This provision forces the shareholders to increase their investment in the business by limiting the amount of dividends that the board might otherwise declare for them. Financial statement notes must disclose significant limitations on dividend declarations.

The notes to a financial statement of Sears, Roebuck and Co. contain the following disclosure:

> Dividend payments are restricted by several statutory and contractual factors, including: Certain indentures relating to the long-term debt of Sears, Roebuck and Co., which represent the most restrictive contractual limitation on the payment of dividends, provide that the company cannot take specified actions, including the declaration of cash dividends, which would cause its consolidated unencumbered assets, as defined [in the indentures, not in the annual report], to fall below 150 percent of its consolidated liabilities, as defined. At . . . [year-end], $11.2 billion in retained income [of a total of $12.7 billion of retained earnings] could be paid in dividends to shareholders under the most restrictive indentures. [Sears declared dividends for the year of approximately $700 million.]

Dividends and Corporate Financial Policy   Directors usually declare dividends less than the legal maximum. The directors may allow retained earnings to increase as a matter of corporate financial policy for several reasons:

1. Available cash did not increase by as much as the amount of earnings, so maximum dividends would require raising more cash.
2. Restricting dividends in prosperous years may permit continued level or steadily growing dividend payments in poor years.
3. The firm may need funds for expansion of working capital or plant and equipment.
4. Reducing the amount of borrowings, rather than paying dividends, may seem prudent.
5. The firm can distribute the funds to shareholders with lower tax burdens for them by using the cash to repurchase shares.

Accounting for Dividends

A firm may pay dividends in cash, other assets, or shares of its common stock.

Cash Dividends   When the board of directors declares a **cash dividend**, the entry is as follows:

Retained Earnings (Dividends Declared) (Shareholders' Equity Decrease) . .	150,000	
Dividends Payable (Liability Increase)		150,000
To record declaration of dividends.		

Once the board of directors declares a dividend, the dividend becomes a legal liability of the corporation. Dividends Payable appears as a current liability on the balance sheet if the firm has not yet paid the dividends at the end of the accounting period. When the firm pays the dividends, the entry is as follows:

Dividends Payable (Liability Decrease)	150,000	
Cash (Asset Decrease)		150,000

Property Dividends   Corporations sometimes distribute assets other than cash when paying a dividend; such a dividend is known as a **dividend in kind** or a **property dividend**. The accounting for such dividends resembles that for cash dividends, except that when the firm pays the dividend, it credits the asset given up, rather than cash. The amount debited to Retained Earnings equals the fair market value of the assets distributed. When this market value differs from the book value of the asset distributed, a gain or loss arises. The firm reports any gain or loss as part of earnings for the period.

Stock Dividends   The retention of earnings may lead to a substantial increase in shareholders' equity, as the firm accumulates assets which it keeps invested in the business. Many of these investments commit assets for the long term; they represent relatively permanent commitments by shareholders to the business. The permanency results from the firm's having invested the net assets generated by the earnings process in operating assets such as inventories and fixed assets. To indicate such a permanent commitment of assets generated by reinvested earnings, the board of directors may declare a **stock dividend**. The accounting involves a debit to the Retained Earnings account and a credit to the contributed capital accounts. The stock dividend does not affect total shareholders' equity. It reallocates amounts from Retained Earnings to the contributed capital accounts. When the firm declares a stock dividend, shareholders receive additional shares of stock in proportion to their existing holdings. If, for example, the firm issues a 5-percent stock dividend, each shareholder receives one additional share for every 20 shares held before the dividend.

GAAP require firms to record the value of the newly issued shares based on the market value of the shares issued. For example, the directors of a corporation may decide to declare a stock dividend of 10,000 additional shares of common stock with a par value of $10 per share at a time when the market price of a share is $40. The entry would be as follows:

Retained Earnings (Dividend Declared) (Shareholders' Equity Decrease) ...	400,000	
Common Stock—$10 Par (Shareholders' Equity Increase)		100,000
Additional Paid-in Capital (Shareholders' Equity Increase)		300,000
To declare a stock dividend, recorded using market price of shares to quantify the amounts: $40 × 10,000 shares = $400,000.		

The stock dividend relabels a portion of the retained earnings that had been legally available for dividend declarations as a more permanent form of shareholders' equity. A stock dividend formalizes the fact that the firm has used some funds represented by past earnings to expand plant facilities, or to replace assets at increased prices, or to retire bonds. The firm does not have this cash available for cash dividends. The stock dividend does not affect the availability of cash that the firm has already invested; the stock dividend signals the commitment to investment, perhaps more clearly than before, to readers of the balance sheet.

Stock dividends have little economic substance for shareholders. More shares of common stock represent the same ownership percentage. If the shareholders each receive the same type of shares as they already own, each shareholder's proportionate interest in the capital of the corporation and proportionate voting power do not change. Although the book value per common share (total common shareholders' equity divided by number of common shares outstanding) decreases, the shareholder has a proportionately larger number of shares, so the total book value of each shareholder's interest remains unchanged. The market value per share should decline, but all else being equal, the total market value of an individual's shares will not change. To describe such a distribution of shares as a "dividend"—meaning a distribution of assets generated by earnings— may mislead some readers, but the terminology is generally accepted.

Stock Splits

Stock splits (or, more technically, split-ups) resemble stock dividends. The corporation issues additional shares of stock to shareholders in proportion to their existing holdings. The firm receives no additional assets. A stock split usually results in a reduction in the par value of all the stock in the issued class. A corporation may, for example, have 1,000 shares of $10 par value stock outstanding and, by a stock split, exchange those shares for 2,000 shares of $5 par value stock (a two-for-one split) or for 4,000 shares of $2.50 par value stock (a four-for-one split) or for any number of shares of no-par stock. If the shares outstanding have no par value, the shareholders keep the existing certificates and receive the new ones. Firms sometimes engage in **reverse stock splits**, in which they increase the par value of stock and reduce the number of shares outstanding.

A stock split or reverse stock split does not require a journal entry if, as in the examples above, the par value changes in proportion to the new number of shares. If the change in par value is not in proportion to the new number of shares, the firm increases or decreases Additional Paid-in Capital. The amount of retained earnings usually does not change. The amount shown in the Common Stock account represents a different number of shares. Of course the firm must record the new number of shares held by each shareholder in the subsidiary capital stock records.

Distinguishing a stock dividend from a stock split can sometimes cause difficulties. For example, is a 50-percent increase in the number of shares accounted for as a stock dividend, using the market value of the stock, or as a 1.5-for-one stock split, using the par value of the stock? Usually firms treat small-percentage distributions, say less than a 25-percent increase in the number of shares, as stock dividends and larger ones as stock splits.

A stock split (or a stock dividend) usually reduces the market value per share, all else equal, in inverse proportion to the split (or dividend). Thus a two-for-one split could be expected to result in a 50-percent reduction in the market price per share. Likewise, a reverse stock split usually increases the market value per share in inverse proportion to the reverse split. Therefore, management has used stock splits and reverse stock splits to keep the market price per share in what management believes is an acceptable trading range. For example, the board of directors might think that a market price of $60 to $80 is an effective trading range for its stock. If the share price has risen to $150 in the market, the board of directors may declare a two-for-one split. (This subjective judgment almost never has supporting evidence. Warren Buffett, chairman of Berkshire-Hathaway, refused to split the common shares until they sold in the marketplace for over $33,000 per share. When he did make lower cost shares available, the new shares had restrictions that required them to trade in blocks costing over $10,000 per trade. Buffett appears not to believe that his company's share price suffers as a result.) For certain, stock splits and dividends result in increased record-keeping costs.

Problem 12.2 for Self-Study

Journal entries for dividends and stock splits.   The shareholders' equity section of the balance sheet of Baker Corporation on January 1, Year 5, appears below:

Shareholders' Equity

Common Stock, $10 par value, 25,000 shares issued and outstanding	$250,000
Additional Paid-in Capital	50,000
Retained Earnings	150,000
Total	$450,000

Prepare journal entries for each of the following transactions of Baker Corporation for Year 5. Ignore income taxes.

a. March 31: The board of directors declares a cash dividend of $0.50 per share. The firm will pay the dividend on April 15.

b. April 15: The firm pays the dividend declared on March 31.

c. June 30: The board of directors declares and distributes a 10-percent stock dividend. The market price per share on this date is $15.

d. December 31: The board of directors declares a 2-for-1 stock split and changes the par value of the common shares from $10 to $5.

Stock Repurchases

When a corporation reacquires its own previously issued common shares, accounting calls these **treasury stock** or **treasury shares**. Refer to the disclosure of shareholders' equity for Coke in **Exhibit 12.1**. Coke has repurchased shares of its common stock in an amount equal to just over one-half of its total shareholders' equity before treasury stock transactions. Reasons for reacquiring outstanding common stock include the following:

1. To use in various option arrangements. When holders of stock options, stock rights, stock warrants, and convertible securities exercise their options, firms usually receive less cash (or market value of other consideration) than the market value of the common stock at the time. Reacquiring treasury shares and then issuing an equal number of new shares under various option arrangements may keep the total number of shares outstanding the same, thereby avoiding dilution of the voting interest of ongoing shareholders and perhaps maintaining earnings per share.
2. To serve as a worthwhile investment of excess cash. Some firms believe that their own shares provide a good investment. Evidence supports the notion that share prices increase after news becomes public that a firm intends to or has reacquired its own shares. Such shares do not receive dividends, nor do they have voting rights, because corporation laws do not consider them to be outstanding shares for these purposes. Firms can reissue the treasury shares when they need cash.
3. To defend against an unfriendly takeover bid. Many firms received unfriendly takeover bids in recent years. To defend against the takeover attempt, firms used available cash to repurchase shares of common stock on the market. Two different motives appear to be at work here:

   - This action reduces the amount of common shareholders' equity and increased the proportion of debt in the capital structure, making the firm more risky and therefore less attractive to an unfriendly bidder. Some firms even borrow cash to repurchase shares, which affects the debt ratio even more than using already available cash to reacquire shares.
   - The acquisition of shares uses available cash and thereby reduces the attractiveness of the company to outsiders who have believed that the available cash makes the company an attractive target.

4. To distribute cash to shareholders in a tax-advantaged way. Rather than pay dividends to all shareholders, many of whom will owe personal income taxes on the entire dividend amount, the firm can buy back shares from those who wish to raise cash. Many shareholders will have lower tax rates on receipts from sales of shares than on dividend receipts.

Accounting for Treasury Shares

Accounting for treasury shares—share repurchases—follows from the fundamental principle that a corporation does not report a gain or loss on transactions involving its own shares. Even though the firm may sell (technically, reissue) the shares for more than their acquisition cost, the accounting does not report the economic gain as accounting income. Similarly, the firm may subsequently reissue shares for less than their acquisition cost, but even so, the economic loss will not reduce net income. The required accounting views treasury stock purchases and sales as capital, not operating, transactions and therefore debits (for economic losses) or credits (for economic gains) the contributed capital accounts for the adjustments for reissue of treasury shares. The amounts bypass the income statement, comprehensive income, and, generally, the Retained Earnings account.

When a firm reacquires common shares, it debits a Treasury Shares—Common account (a shareholders' equity contra account) with the total amount paid to reacquire the shares.

Treasury Shares—Common (Shareholders' Equity Decrease)	11,000	
Cash (Asset Decrease)		11,000
To record $11,000 paid to reacquire 1,000 common shares. Treasury Shares—Common is a contra account to shareholders' equity.		

If the firm later reissues treasury shares for cash, it debits Cash with the amount received and credits the Treasury Shares—Common account with the cost of the shares. If it reissues treasury shares at the conversion of bonds or preferred stock into common stock, it debits the convertible bonds or preferred stock instead of debiting cash. The reissue price will usually differ from the amount paid to acquire the treasury shares. If the reissue price exceeds the acquisition price, the credit to make the entry balance is to the Additional Paid-in Capital account. Assuming that the above firm reissued for $14,000 the 1,000 shares reacquired previously, the entry would be as follows:

Cash (Asset Increase)	14,000	
Treasury Shares—Common (Shareholders' Equity Increase)		11,000
Additional Paid-in Capital (Shareholders' Equity Increase)		3,000

To reissue 1,000 shares of treasury stock at a price greater than acquisition cost. The $3,000 economic "gain" does not appear on the income statement as an accounting gain.

If the amount paid for the treasury shares exceeds the reissue price, the firm debits the balance to Additional Paid-in Capital, so long as that account has a sufficiently large credit balance. To the extent the required debit exceeds the credit balance in the Additional Paid-in Capital account, the firm reduces that account to zero and debits the excess to retained earnings. This debit to the Retained Earnings account resembles a dividend; it does not appear as an expense or a loss reported on the income statement.

The Treasury Shares account appears as a subtraction from total shareholders' equity on the balance sheet; see **Exhibit 12.1** for Coke.

Problem 12.3 for Self-Study

Journal entries for treasury stock transactions. Prepare journal entries for the following transactions of Crissie Corporation.

a. Reacquired 2,000 shares of $10 par value common stock on January 15 for $45 per share.
b. Issued 1,200 shares of treasury stock to employees upon the exercise of stock options at a price of $48 per share on April 26.
c. Reacquired 3,000 shares of $10 par value common stock for $52 per share on August 15.
d. Issued 1,600 shares of treasury stock to holders of 800 shares of convertible preferred stock, which had a book value of $80,000 on November 24. Crissie Corporation uses a first-in, first-out assumption on reissues of treasury stock and uses book values to record conversions of preferred stock.
e. Sold 1,500 shares of treasury stock on the open market for $47 per share on December 20.

Reporting Earnings Transactions

What purpose does the income statement serve? We argue that it is *not* "to show earnings for the period." The reader of the financial statements can generally ascertain earnings by subtracting the beginning balance of the Retained Earnings account from its ending balance and adding dividends. Accountants provide an income statement so managers and investors can see the *causes* of earnings. Then a reader can compare a company's performance with other companies (cross-section analysis) or with the company itself over time (time-series analysis), to make more informed projections about the future.

Previous chapters concentrated on *measuring* the results of earnings transactions. Next, we focus on *reporting*, or *disclosing*, earnings transactions in the financial statements. To motivate an understanding of the issues involved in reporting earnings transactions, consider the earnings data for Bernard Corporation in **Exhibit 12.2**. To simplify the illustration, we assume that revenues result in immediate cash receipts and expenses require immediate cash expenditures. Thus, income flows equal cash flows.

Suppose that an analyst wished to value Bernard Corporation using the present value of the cash flows of its individual activities, some recurring, some not. Assume that the cash flows in **Exhibit 12.2** are after tax. Also assume the discount rate appropriate for finding the present value of Bernard Company's cash flows is 10 percent per year. Corporate finance classes discuss the

EXHIBIT 12.2	BERNARD COMPANY Measurement of Firm's Market Value from Cash Flow Data

	Cash Flows Occur at the End of Each Period								Present Value of Activity Using Discount Rate of 10%
Activities of the Firm	Period Number								
	1	2	3	4	5	6	7	8	
1. Recurring	$100	$100	$100	$100	$100	$100	$100	$100	$1,000.00
2. Recurring, but Growing at 6% per Year	30	32	34	36	38	40	43	45	750.00
3. Cyclic	115	0	115	0	115	0	115	0	602.38
4. Nonrecurring	120	0	0	0	0	0	0	0	109.09
5. Recurring	(40)	(40)	(40)	(40)	(40)	(40)	(40)	(40)	(400.00)
6. Nonrecurring	(70)	0	0	0	0	0	0	0	(63.64)
Income for Year 1	$255								

Present Value [= Fair Market Value] of Entire Firm **$1,997.83**

issues related to choosing the discount rate and the **Appendix** to this book introduces the techniques of present value analysis. You need not have studied the **Appendix** if you will take on faith the derivation of the numbers in the right-hand column of **Exhibit 12.2**.

Bernard Company engages in six activities, numbered 1 through 6, shown in **Exhibit 12.2**.

Activity 1. The first activity generates $100 per year, with the cash flow at the end of each year, indefinitely. The present value of this activity is $1,000 (= $100/0.10). See **Example 18** in the **Appendix**. Investors sometimes call this process of deriving market value from a series of future cash flows *capitalizing earnings*. The analyst might say that the earnings of $100 have a *price/earnings ratio* of 10 or that the earnings "deserve [or carry] a multiple of 10."

Activity 2. The second activity generates $30 at the end of the first year, and a cash flow that grows by 6 percent per year thereafter. The present value of this activity is $750 [= $30/(0.10 − 0.06)]. See **Example 19** in the **Appendix**. The price/earnings ratio (or multiple) for these cash flows is 25, because of their growth. Management that is interested in higher market prices for its firm's shares wants investors to think of the company as a growth stock, because investors put higher values on growing-earnings companies than on stable-earnings companies.

Activity 3. The third activity is cyclic, generating $115 per year at the end of each odd-numbered year. The present value of this activity is $602.38. See **Example 20** in the **Appendix**.

Activity 4. The fourth activity is nonrecurring, generating a single cash flow of $120 at the end of the first year, with present value of $109.09 (= $120/1.10) at the start of the first year.

Activity 5. The fifth activity, an expenditure (outflow), uses $40 of cash each year, at the end of each year. The present value of this activity is −$400 (= −$40/0.10).

Activity 6. The sixth activity, a single expenditure (outflow), uses $70 cash at the end of the first year and has present value of −$63.64 (= −$70/1.10).

The value of the firm is the sum of the present values of its individual activities, $1,998 in **Exhibit 12.2**. In this example, most of the value of this firm comes from the recurring activities. In deriving firm values, investors generally care about recurring activities more than nonrecurring ones, because recurring activities add value each year, while nonrecurring activities, by definition, happen once or infrequently.

Exhibit 12.2 shows the net earnings for Year 1 of $255. How can analysts and investors deduce the value of the company from this one year's earnings statement? They can't. This firm is too complex for even a sophisticated user to derive the value from a single column of data, without further information. Investors and analysts need to know about the components of a firm's earnings and their recurring versus nonrecurring nature so that they can make estimates of the market value of the firm. Analysts feel more confident estimating the value of firms with recurring activities than with nonrecurring activities. Analysts may also want to include changes in the market value of a firm's assets and liabilities in their valuation of a company even though GAAP may not include these market value changes in earnings.

Overview of GAAP Reporting of Earnings Transactions

The sections that follow discuss the reporting of various earnings items. We begin by providing an overview of this reporting.

1. GAAP require that firms initially report the results of most earnings transactions in the income statement instead of bypassing the income statement and reporting the amounts in some other shareholders' equity account. This reporting reflects the emphasis most analysts and investors place on the income statement when evaluating a firm's earnings performance and the concern that statement users may overlook earnings transactions reported elsewhere.
2. GAAP recognize that some earnings transactions are central to a firm's principal business activities and recur, while others are peripheral or nonrecurring. GAAP require firms to report items in their income statements in various categories to inform statement users about the nature of income items.
3. Changes in the market value of assets and liabilities affect the value of a firm as they occur. GAAP recognize some of these value changes in net income as they occur even though the firm has not yet sold the asset for cash or settled the liability, events that confirm the amount of the value change. GAAP delay reporting value changes of other assets and liabilities in net income until confirming events occur. In the meantime, GAAP include such value changes in Other Comprehensive Income, a component of shareholders' equity.
4. Firms sometimes discover errors in amounts previously reported, change their accounting principles, or change estimates made in applying their accounting principles. GAAP require firms to retroactively restate previously reported amounts for corrections of errors and changes in accounting principles but adjust current and future amounts for changes in accounting estimates.

We examine the reporting of four types of earnings transactions:

1. Recurring versus nonrecurring
2. Central versus peripheral
3. Unrealized versus realized gains and losses from changes in the market values of assets and liabilities
4. Adjustments for errors and changes in accounting principles and accounting estimates

The issues discussed affect the quality of earnings. Firms have incentives to report good earnings news in ways that make it appear recurring and central, but to report bad earnings news as nonrecurring and peripheral. Analysts must sort through the various components of earnings, recognizing possible biases injected by management, and apply appropriate multiples to the earnings components in valuing firms. GAAP attempt to aid this process by requiring firms to classify earnings transactions in particular ways in the financial statements. In recent years firms often reported so-called *pro forma earnings*, which each firm defines in its own way. Typically pro forma earnings remove the effects of nonrecurring events which have reduced net income, so that pro forma earnings exceed GAAP earnings. We rarely see pro forma earnings lower than GAAP earnings. As this book goes to press, regulators express concern about the lack of reporting discipline in pro forma earnings and firms remain free to say what they please. Analysts learn to suspect the earnings of firms that report nonrecurring items year after year.

Reporting Recurring/Nonrecurring and Central/Peripheral Activities

An analyst likely asks two questions when using a firm's past profitability to project its likely future profitability:

1. Does the earnings item result from an activity in which a firm will likely continue its involvement, or does the earnings item result from an unusual transaction or event that is unlikely to recur regularly?

2. Does the earnings item result from a firm's primary operating activity (creating and selling a good or service for customers) or from an activity incidental or peripheral to the primary operating activity (for example, periodic sales of equipment previously used by the firm in manufacturing)?

Figure 12.2 depicts these distinctions, with examples of each.

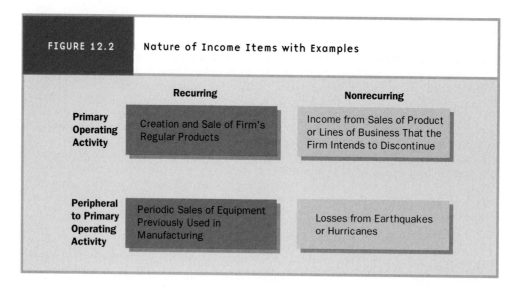

FIGURE 12.2   **Nature of Income Items with Examples**

	Recurring	**Nonrecurring**
Primary Operating Activity	Creation and Sale of Firm's Regular Products	Income from Sales of Product or Lines of Business That the Firm Intends to Discontinue
Peripheral to Primary Operating Activity	Periodic Sales of Equipment Previously Used in Manufacturing	Losses from Earthquakes or Hurricanes

A financial statement user who wants to evaluate a firm's ongoing operating profitability will likely focus on earnings items in the upper left cell. A financial statement user who wants to project earnings of prior periods into the future would likely focus on the two *recurring earnings* cells. Earnings items in the nonrecurring cells should not affect ongoing assessments of profitability. This section considers the reporting of each type of earnings item.

Measurement of Earnings Effect

Accountants distinguish between revenues and expenses on the one hand and gains and losses on the other. Revenues and expenses result from the recurring, primary operating activities of a business (upper left cell in **Figure 12.2**). Earnings items in this first category are the ordinary, recurring operating activities of the firm. Gains and losses result from either peripheral activities (lower left cell) or nonrecurring activities (upper and lower right cells). A second distinction is the reporting of revenues and expenses at gross amounts, whereas accounting reports gains and losses at net amounts. The following examples illustrate this distinction.

Example 8   IBM sells a computer to a customer for $400,000. The computer cost IBM $300,000 to manufacture. IBM records this sale as follows:

Cash (Asset Increase)	400,000	
Retained Earnings (Sales Revenue) (Shareholders' Equity Increase) . .		400,000
To record sale.		
Retained Earnings (Cost of Goods Sold) (Shareholders' Equity Decrease) . .	300,000	
Finished Goods Inventory (Asset Decrease)		300,000
To record the cost of goods sold.		

This transaction fits into the upper left cell of **Figure 12.2** (primary/recurring). The income statement reports both sales revenue and cost of goods sold, providing information to the financial statement user regarding both the manufacturing cost of the computer and IBM's ability to mark up this cost in setting selling prices. Retained earnings increase by $100,000 as a result of this transaction. Notice that the $100,000 amount does not itself appear in the income statement. Rather, income increases by $100,000 as a result of sales of $400,000 offset with cost of goods sold of $300,000.

Example 9   The GAP, a retail clothing chain, sells computers previously used for processing data in its stores. This sale relates only peripherally to The GAP's primary operating activity, which is to sell casual clothes. Assume that the computers originally cost $500,000 and have $200,000 of accumulated depreciation at the time of sale. Thus, the computers have a net book value of $300,000. The sale of these computers for $400,000 results in the following journal entry on The GAP's books:

Cash (Asset Increase)	400,000	
Accumulated Depreciation (Asset Increase)	200,000	
Equipment (Asset Decrease)		500,000
Retained Earnings (Gain on Sale of Equipment) (Shareholders' Equity Increase)		100,000
Disposal of computers for $100,000 more than book value.		

This transaction fits into the lower left cell of **Figure 12.2** (peripheral/recurring). The income statement reports only the $100,000 gain on the sale, not the selling price of $400,000 and the book value of $300,000. The income statement reports gains and losses at net, instead of gross, amounts because, presumably, financial statement users do not care about information on the individual components comprising peripheral or nonrecurring earnings items. The gain on the sale increases retained earnings by $100,000.

Note that both revenues and gains appear as credits in journal entries and increase Retained Earnings. Both expenses and losses appear as debits in journal entries and reduce Retained Earnings. To repeat, revenues and expenses report operating or central items as gross amounts; gains and losses report nonrecurring or peripheral items as net amounts.

Classifications in the Income Statement

Income statements contain some or all of the following sections or categories, depending on the nature of a firm's earnings for the period:

1. Earnings from continuing operations
2. Earnings, gains, and losses from discontinued operations
3. Extraordinary gains and losses

The majority of income statements include only the first section. **Exhibit 12.3** presents an income statement for Hypothetical Company that includes all three sections.

Earnings from Continuing Operations   Revenues, gains, expenses, and losses from the continuing areas of business activity of a firm appear in the first section of the income statement, **Earnings from Continuing Operations**. This section includes earnings derived from a firm's primary business activities as well as from activities peripherally related to operations. The key distinction is that the firm expects these sources of earnings to continue. Firms without the nonrecurring categories of earnings for a particular year (discussed next) need not use the title *Earnings from Continuing Operations* in their income statements. In this case, absence of nonrecurring types of earnings implies that all reported revenues, gains, expenses, and losses relate to continuing operations. Firms often report a subtotal within the continuing operations section of the income statement, labeled *operating income*, to report the revenues and expenses from the firm's primary business activity of creating and selling goods or services. Revenues from marketable securities and investments in securities, interest expense on borrowings, and gains and losses from peripheral activities appear separately as *nonoperating income* in the continuing operations section of the income statement.

			EXHIBIT 12.3	HYPOTHETICAL COMPANY Income Statement (all dollar amounts in millions)

	Year 6	Year 7	Year 8
EARNINGS FROM CONTINUING OPERATIONS			
Sales	$ 240	$ 265	$ 295
Cost of Goods Sold	(144)	(154)	(165)
Selling and Administrative Expenses	(50)	(58)	(67)
Operating Income	$ 46	$ 53	$ 63
Interest Revenue	4	5	7
Interest Expense	(15)	(19)	(22)
Gain on Sale of Equipment	4	9	3
Income from Continuing Operations before			
Taxes	$ 39	$ 48	$ 51
Income Taxes	(13)	(16)	(17)
Income from Continuing Operations	$ 26	$ 32	$ 34
EARNINGS, GAINS, AND LOSSES FROM DISCONTINUED OPERATIONS			
Income (Loss) from Operations of Business Sold			
in Year 6 (net of income taxes)	$ 16	$ (4)	$ 2
Gain on Sale of Division (net of income taxes)	—	—	40
Income from Discontinued Operations	$ 16	$ (4)	$ 42
EXTRAORDINARY GAINS AND LOSSES			
Loss from Hurricane (net of income taxes)	—	$ (12)	—
Net Income	$ 42	$ 16	$ 76
EARNINGS PER COMMON SHARE			
Continuing Operations	$2.60	$3.04	$3.09
Discontinued Operations	1.60	(0.38)	3.82
Extraordinary Items	—	(1.14)	—
Net Income	$4.20	$1.52	$6.91

Earnings, Gains, and Losses from Discontinued Operations   Sometimes a firm sells a major division or segment of its business during the year or contemplates its sale within a foreseeable time after the end of the accounting period. If so, it must disclose separately any earnings, gains, and losses related to that segment. The separate disclosure appears in the next section of the income statement, **Earnings, Gains, and Losses from Discontinued Operations**, alerting the financial statement reader that the firm does not expect this source of earnings to continue.[7] Firms report the earnings, gain, or loss net of income tax effects. This section follows the section presenting Earnings from Continuing Operations.

Extraordinary Gains and Losses   A separate section of the income statement presents **Extraordinary Gains and Losses**. For an item to be extraordinary, it must generally meet both of the following:

1. Unusual in nature, and
2. Infrequent in occurrence.[8]

An example of an item likely to be extraordinary for most firms is a loss from an earthquake or confiscation of assets by a foreign government. Firms report extraordinary items net of their tax effects.

---

[7] Accounting Principles Board, *Opinion No. 30*, "Reporting the Results of Operations," 1973.
[8] *Ibid.*

Unrealized Gains and Losses from Changes in Market Values of Assets and Liabilities

The FASB has increasingly required firms to report certain assets and liabilities at their current market values at the end of each period instead of their historical, or acquisition, costs. Examples discussed in previous chapters include:

1. Valuation of inventories at lower of cost or market (**Chapter 7**).
2. Valuation of fixed assets and intangibles at current market value when evidence indicates that an asset impairment has occurred (**Chapter 8**).
3. Valuation of financial instruments, including derivatives used to hedge risk, at market value (**Chapter 10**).
4. Valuation of marketable equity securities at market value (**Chapter 11**).

When a firm writes assets and liabilities up or down to market value, the question arises as to how it should treat the offsetting credit (gain) or debit (loss). At the time of the revaluation, the firm has not yet **realized** the gains or losses. That is, the firm has not yet sold the asset or settled the liability with a transaction involving cash. In some cases, GAAP require firms to **recognize** the gains and losses, that is, to include them, even though not yet realized, in earnings in the period of the revaluation. Firms include losses from the writedown of inventories, fixed assets, and intangibles in computing earnings in the period of the revaluation. Firms include gains and losses from the revaluation of financial instruments classified as fair value hedges in earnings each period as market values of the hedged financial instrument and its derivative change.

The FASB has been reluctant, however, to require firms to include in earnings all unrealized gains and losses from the revaluation of assets and liabilities. We suspect the reason has to do with the volatility that some unrealized gains and losses inject into the reported income of companies with a large fraction of their assets in the form of marketable securities and other financial instruments. The reluctance stems from the preferences of the firms preparing the statements, not from the preferences of the rule makers themselves. Including all unrealized gains and losses on marketable equity securities in earnings each period, for example, will cause reported earnings to fluctuate (in response to fluctuations in market prices) more than it would otherwise.

Many, probably most, managers prefer to report stable earnings in contrast to fluctuating earnings. All else equal, the less risky the earnings stream—that is, the less volatile are reported earnings—the higher will be the market price of the firm's shares. Financial institutions in particular do not like fluctuations in net income; see **Problem 52** at the end of **Chapter 11** for a discussion of why. Managers have succeeded over the years in lobbying the FASB to keep many fluctuating components of income out of reported earnings. Unrealized gains and losses have typically appeared on a separate line in the shareholders' equity section of the balance sheet.

The FASB has become increasingly concerned that users of financial statements might overlook these value changes if they appear on the comparative balance sheet only and not in the income statement. As a consequence, the FASB requires firms to disclose unrealized gains and losses that historically have bypassed the income statement in a category called **other comprehensive income**.[9]

Other comprehensive income *for a reporting period* includes changes in the market value of marketable equity securities available for sale and changes in the market value of derivatives used as cash flow hedges. Other comprehensive income also includes unrealized gains and losses from translating the financial statements of foreign units into U.S. dollars and certain changes in pension liabilities, topics covered in advanced financial accounting courses. **Accumulated other comprehensive income**, a shareholders' equity account on the balance sheet, reports the *cumulative* amounts of other comprehensive income as of the date of the balance sheet. **Comprehensive income** equals net income on the traditional income statement plus other comprehensive income for the period.

Firms have considerable flexibility as to how they report other comprehensive income each period. They can:

1. Include it in a combined statement of net income and other comprehensive income, in effect appending it to the bottom of the traditional income statement.
2. Include it in a separate statement of other comprehensive income.
3. Include it in a statement of changes in shareholders' equity.

---

[9] Financial Accounting Standards Board, *Statement of Financial Accounting Standards No. 130*, "Reporting Comprehensive Income," 1997.

Exhibit 12.4 shows the required disclosure of comprehensive income in the first two of the allowed formats—as part of a combined earnings and comprehensive income statement, and as part of a separate statement of comprehensive income. We illustrate the third format, as part of a statement explaining the reasons for changes in shareholders' equity accounts, later in this chapter in **Exhibit 12.6**.

EXHIBIT 12.4	Reporting Comprehensive Income, Two Allowed Formats

ONE-STATEMENT APPROACH
Statement of Net Income and Comprehensive Income

Revenues		$100,000
Expenses		(25,000)
Gain on Sale of Securities		2,000
Other Gains and Losses		8,000
Earnings from Continuing Operations before Income Tax		$ 85,000
Income Tax Expense		(21,250)
Earnings before Discontinued Operations and Extraordinary Items		$ 63,750
Discontinued Operations, Net of Tax		30,000
Extraordinary Items, Net of Tax		(30,500)
Net Income (or, as preferred by the FASB, Earnings)		**$ 63,250**
Other Comprehensive Income, Net of Tax:		
Foreign Currency Translation Adjustments		7,000
Unrealized Gains and Losses on Securities:		
Unrealized Holding Gains Arising during Period	$13,000	
Less: Reclassification Adjustment for Gain Included in Net Income (Earnings)	(1,500)	11,500
Minimum Pension Liability Adjustment		(2,500)
Other Comprehensive Income (Loss)		**$ 16,000**
Comprehensive Income (Loss)		**$ 79,250**

TWO-STATEMENT APPROACH
Statement of Net Income

Revenues		$100,000
Expenses		(25,000)
Gain on Sale of Securities		2,000
Other Gains and Losses		8,000
Earnings from Continuing Operations before Income Tax		$ 85,000
Income Tax Expense		(21,250)
Earnings before Discontinued Operations and Extraordinary Items		$ 63,750
Discontinued Operations, Net of Tax		30,000
Extraordinary Items, Net of Tax		(30,500)
Net Income (or, as preferred by the FASB, Earnings)		**$ 63,250**

Statement of Comprehensive Income

Net Income (or, as preferred by the FASB, Earnings)		**$ 63,250**
Other Comprehensive Income, Net of Tax:		
Foreign Currency Translation Adjustments		7,000
Unrealized Gains and Losses on Securities:		
Unrealized Holding Gains Arising during Period	$13,000	
Less: Reclassification Adjustment for Gain Included in Net Income (Earnings)	(1,500)	11,500
Minimum Pension Liability Adjustment		(2,500)
Other Comprehensive Income (Loss)		**$ 16,000**
Comprehensive Income (Loss)		**$ 79,250**

TERMINOLOGY NOTE

The FASB faced an issue in naming the amount that we call *net income* in the traditional income statement. Use of the term *net* implies that it is a bottom-line number. Yet firms that append other comprehensive income to the bottom of their income statements need a label to differentiate traditional net income from the combined amounts of traditional net income plus other comprehensive income. The FASB expressed a preference to eliminate the term *net income* altogether, to label traditional net income as *earnings*, and to label the combined amounts of earnings and other comprehensive income as *comprehensive income*. The FASB gave firms wide latitude, not only in their choice of reporting formats, but in their choice of terminology. Most firms choose to follow the third reporting format above, leaving the traditional income statement unchanged. Thus, we will continue to use *net income* to designate the bottom line of the traditional income statement.

Adjustments for Errors and Accounting Changes

Firms occasionally obtain new information about amounts included in net income of prior periods or change either their accounting principles or estimates used in applying their accounting principles. Consider the following examples:

1. Dell Computer Corporation discovers that it neglected to count $250,000 of inventory items stored in a warehouse in Texas at the end of last year. In consequence, Dell understated its earnings last period.
2. JC Penney has used a LIFO cost flow assumption for inventories and cost of goods sold for many years. It decides during the current year to change to a FIFO cost flow assumption. Earnings of prior years would differ if JC Penney had used a FIFO, instead of a LIFO, cost flow assumption.
3. American Airlines depreciates its aircraft over a 20-year life. More fuel-efficient aircraft now available on the market leads American Airlines to begin slowly replacing its existing aircraft with the new aircraft. American Airlines reduces the depreciable life of its existing aircraft, which increases current and future depreciation charges relative to the recent past.

Each of these three examples requires the accountant to decide whether to (1) retroactively restate prior years' earnings, (2) include an adjustment for the correction or accounting change in the current year's earnings, or (3) correct or adjust earnings of the current and future periods (so-called prospective adjustment).

Advocates of retroactive restatement view past earnings as useful to the extent they permit predictions of future earnings. Retroactive restatement results in computing earnings for prior years on the same basis as earnings of the current and future years, thereby enhancing earnings predictions.

Advocates of including adjustments for these items in the income statement of the current year argue that all earnings items should initially appear in the income statement of some period. In this way, the cumulative series of income statements includes all earnings items. The financial statement reader will less likely overlook the items if they appear in the income statement than if firms record the amounts as an adjustment of prior years' earnings. Adequate disclosure of the nature of each item in the income statement will permit the financial statement user to assess its importance when evaluating the firm's profitability. Probably with good reason, some on this side of the argument suggest that if managers have the discretion to leave such items out of the current year's income statement, many of them will find ways to justify restating prior years' earnings for income-reducing adjustments and including in earnings of the current period only income-enhancing adjustments. Virtually all theorists agree that giving managers the discretion to report good news and bad news as they see fit will lead to less useful financial statements unless auditors become more critical of their clients' accounting than they have been.

Advocates of adjusting earnings prospectively argue that restating previously reported amounts reduces the credibility of the financing reporting process. Advocates also argue that such adjustments are a normal, recurring part of the accounting process. Prospective adjustment avoids the connotation that prior years' earnings were computed incorrectly.

GAAP distinguish the accounting for (1) corrections of errors, (2) adjustments for changes in accounting principles, and (3) adjustments for changes in accounting estimates.

Reporting Correction of Errors   Errors result from such actions as miscounting inventories, miscalculations, and misapplying accounting principles. The example above for Dell Computer illustrates an accounting error. The accountant makes a **correction of errors**, if material, by retroactively restating earnings of prior periods and adjusting the beginning balance in Retained Earnings for the current period.[10] Dell Computer's understatement of inventory at the end of last period resulted in an overstatement of cost of goods sold last period, as the following analysis shows:

Cost of Goods Sold		Beginning Inventory	+	Purchases	−	Ending Inventory
Overstated $250,000	=	0	+	0	−	Understated $250,000

The firm retroactively restates net income of last period and makes the following entry (ignoring income tax effects) this period:

Merchandise Inventory (Asset Increase)	250,000	
Retained Earnings (Shareholders' Equity Increase)		250,000
To correct inventory error. Firm overstated last period's cost of goods sold and understated earnings.		

Reporting Changes in Accounting Principles   JC Penney's change from a LIFO to a FIFO cost flow assumption is a **change in accounting principle**. Assuming that firms can compute the amount of earnings for prior periods under the new accounting principle, GAAP is expected to require firms to retroactively restate prior years' earnings to reflect the new accounting principle.[11] Assume that inventory at the end the last year for JC Penney was $450 million under LIFO and $525 million under FIFO. The entry to record the change in accounting principle is as follows (in millions):

Merchandise Inventory (Asset Increase)	75	
Retained Earnings (Shareholders' Equity Increase)		75
To restate inventory and retained earnings retroactively for a change from LIFO to FIFO.		

JC Penney would also restate net income for each prior year reported in its financial statements using a FIFO cost flow assumption.

Reporting Changes in Accounting Estimates   As time passes, new information becomes available that sharpens estimates required to apply accounting principles. Examples include the amount of uncollectible accounts and the useful lives of depreciable assets. The example above for American Airlines is a change in accounting estimate. Earlier chapters have pointed out that accountants do not correct revenues and expenses of previous periods to incorporate new information. Instead, the accountant allows the effect of the change in estimate to affect current and future periods' earnings.[12] Refer, for example, to **Figure 8.4**, which illustrates the effect of a change in depreciable life on depreciation expense. Rather than correct Retained Earnings directly, the firm adjusts current and future depreciation charges, but not past ones, to take into account the book value at the time the new information arrives and the new information itself.

---

[10] Accounting Principles Board, *Opinion No. 20,* "Accounting Changes," 1971. As this book goes to press, the FASB plans to issue a new reporting standard on accounting changes. The proposed standard does not change the accounting for corrections of errors.

[11] The accounting for changes in accounting principles under *Opinion No. 20* requires recognition in the current period's income statement of the cumulative effect of the the change, instead of the retroactive restatement expected under the current proposed standard.

[12] The proposed standard does not change the accounting for changes in estimates.

Accrual accounting requires frequent, ongoing changes in estimates. Restating the financial statements of previous years, which would require changing the opening balance of retained earnings for the current period, each time a firm changes an estimate will add complexity to the task of understanding financial statements and might reduce their credibility. This approach would also provide management with methods for boosting earnings of the current period by lowering the already-reported earnings of previous periods in order to raise current and future periods' earnings.

Changes in estimates do not always relate to recurring accrual accounting measurements, such as depreciable lives. Some changes in estimates concern unusual or nonrecurring events. Consider, for example, the following:

- A court this period finds a firm responsible for an act that occurred several years previously and caused injury. The damage award differs from the amount that the firm previously recognized with a debit to a loss and a credit to a liability.
- The Internal Revenue Service assesses additional income taxes on a firm's taxable income of previous years. The amount previously recognized as income tax expense for those years understates the final amount payable.

These events provide new information regarding measurements made in previous periods. Even though the events do not recur, GAAP treat them similarly to changes in estimates for recurring items. The earnings effect of these items appears in the income statement of the current period, appropriately disclosed, not in retained earnings as a direct adjustment.

Problem 12.4 for Self-Study

Journal entries for earnings and retained earnings transactions.   Prepare journal entries for each of the following transactions of Able Corporation for Year 5. Ignore income taxes.

a. January 15: As a result of a computer software error the preceding December, the firm failed to record depreciation on office facilities totaling $35,000.

b. March 20: An earthquake in California causes an uninsured loss of $70,000 to a warehouse.

c. December 31: The firm acquired its office building six years before December 31, Year 5. The building cost $400,000, had zero estimated salvage value, and had a 40-year life. The firm uses the straight-line depreciation method. Able Corporation now estimates that the building will have a total useful life of 30 years instead of 40 years. Record depreciation expense on the building for Year 5 and any required adjustment to depreciation of previous years.

Earnings and Book Value per Share

Publicly held firms must show **earnings per common share** data in the body of the income statement.[13] Earnings per common share result from dividing net earnings minus preferred stock dividends by the average number of outstanding common shares during the accounting period. Firms reporting more than one of the three categories of earnings items must disclose earnings per common share for each reported category. See **Exhibit 12.3** for categories and the disclosure. Issues in calculating earnings per common share go beyond the scope of this book. **Problem 40** at the end of this chapter illustrates some of the calculations.

Most firms also report **book value per common share** in their annual reports. Book value per common share equals total common shareholders' equity divided by the number of shares outstanding on the date of the balance sheet.

Appendix 5.1 indicates that investors often apply multiples to earnings per common share and book value per common share in deciding on a reasonable market price for a firm's shares.

---

[13] Financial Accounting Standards Board, *Statement of Financial Accounting Standards No. 128,* "Earnings per Share," 1997.

An International Perspective

Firms in all industrialized countries and in most developing countries around the world prepare financial statements based on the accrual, rather than the cash, basis of accounting. The particular measurement rules used in applying the accrual basis differ among countries.

The format and classification of earnings items within the income statement vary across countries. The general measurement and disclosure principles discussed in this book should permit the reader of the financial statements to understand and interpret various income statement formats. Refer to the income statement for Wellcome PLC, a British pharmaceutical company, in **Exhibit 12.5**. Although this financial statement uses terminology different from that used in this book, the reader should be able to infer the nature of various items.

EXHIBIT 12.5	WELLCOME PLC Group Profit and Loss Account (all currency amounts in millions)		
		Year 7	**Year 8**
Turnover		£1,147.4	£1,272.2
Operating Costs:			
Raw Materials and Consumables		(246.9)	(245.4)
Other External Charges		(401.5)	(424.4)
Staff Costs		(309.1)	(337.4)
Depreciation		(38.8)	(44.1)
Change in Stocks of Finished Goods and Work in Progress		36.5	18.7
Other Operating Charges		(10.3)	(6.7)
Trading Profit		£ 177.3	£ 232.9
Net Interest Payable		(8.2)	(11.7)
Profit on Ordinary Activities before Taxation		£ 169.1	£ 221.2
Tax on Profit from Ordinary Activities		(71.4)	(89.4)
Profit on Ordinary Activities Attributable to Shareholders		£ 97.7	£ 131.8

Title Used in Exhibit 12.5	**Title Used in this Book**
Group Profit and Loss Account	Income (or, sometimes, Earnings) Statement
Turnover	Sales Revenue
Stocks	Inventories
Trading Profit	Operating Earnings
Profit on Ordinary Activities	Earnings from Continuing Operations

Wellcome's statement in **Exhibit 12.5** classifies operating costs according to their nature (for example, raw materials, labor, depreciation) instead of by the functional activity (for example, cost of goods sold, marketing expenses, administrative expenses). European companies often classify expenses by nature. One item seldom seen in annual reports of U.S. companies is "Change in Stocks of Finished Goods and Work in Process." Wellcome reports among its operating costs on the income statement actual raw materials, labor, and overhead costs incurred during the year. Recall the inventory equation:

$$\text{Cost of Goods Sold} = \text{Beginning Inventory} + \text{Purchases} - \text{Ending Inventory}$$
$$= \text{Purchases} - (\text{Ending Inventory} - \text{Beginning Inventory})$$
$$= \text{Purchases} - (\text{Change in Inventory})$$

Wellcome shows all purchases in its income statement, so it must subtract the increase in inventory to compute Cost of Goods Sold. For example, at the end of Year 8, £18.7 million of costs included in various operating cost items in the income statement actually apply to units in process or in finished goods at the end of Year 8 and not to units sold. Netting this £18.7 million against the actual total cost results in the proper matching of costs against revenues.

The annual reports to shareholders must explain the changes in all shareholders' equity accounts.[14] The reconciliation of retained earnings may appear in the balance sheet, in a statement of earnings and retained earnings, or in a separate statement. The reconciliation of Other Comprehensive Income may also appear in a separate statement.

Exhibit 12.6 shows the consolidated statement of shareholders' equity for Michigan Company (information adapted from the annual report of Ford Motor Company). The two-year comparative statement shows separate columns for common stock at par, additional paid-in capital, retained earnings, accumulated other comprehensive income, treasury shares, and total shareholders' equity. The statement shows opening balances, net income, cash dividends, unrealized gains and losses on securities available for sale, stock issued under employee option plans, common stock retired, and common stock issued on conversion of convertible bonds.

The FASB suggested that firms use a reporting format reconciling the beginning balance of Other Comprehensive Income, its components for a year, and the ending balance in a format such as the one below, which uses data for the General Electric Company (GE) for a recent year (dollar amounts in millions):

Accumulated Other Comprehensive Income, Beginning of Year	$1,340
Components of Other Comprehensive Income for Year (= $264 + $60; see below)	324
Accumulated Other Comprehensive Income, End of Year	$1,664

Some firms find this reporting distasteful because, we suspect, they do not want to point to any total other than net income as deserving the title *income*. Hence, they find various ways to re-label both the balance sheet beginning and ending balances as well as the components of other comprehensive income for the year. GE, for example, shows just under the income statement a separate Statement of Changes in Share Owners' Equity, which has the following components (dollar amounts in millions). Note: The information in brackets *does not appear* in the GE report; we add this information here for clarity.

Changes in Share Owners' Equity		
Balance [of Share Owners' Equity], January 1		$34,438
Dividends and other transactions [treasury share acquisitions and dispositions] with share owners		(5,178)
Changes other than transactions with share owners		
Increases attributable to net earnings [net income for year]	$9,296	
Unrealized gains (losses) on investment securities	264	
Currency translation adjustments [another component of other comprehensive income]	60	
Total changes other than transactions with share owners		9,620
Balance at December 31		$38,880

What is other comprehensive income for the year? It is $324 (= $264 + $60), but unsophisticated readers of financial statements will likely not know this because of the method of disclosures. GE shows the beginning and ending balances of Other Comprehensive Income, which it calls *Nonowner changes other than earnings*, in the note reconciling all of the changes in the components of shareholders' equity.

Journal Entries for Changes in Shareholders' Equity

Exhibit 12.7 reconstructs the journal entries of Michigan Company for Year 1 and Year 2. The amounts in the entries in **Exhibit 12.7** represent millions of dollars, and the numbers of the journal entries correspond to the lines in **Exhibit 12.6** to which they correspond.

---

[14] Accounting Principles Board, *Opinion No. 12*, "Omnibus Opinion—1967," 1967.

EXHIBIT 12.6

MICHIGAN COMPANY (adapted from Ford Motor Company)
Consolidated Statement of Shareholders' Equity
(all dollar amounts in millions)

Line Number[a]		Shares	Amount	Additional Paid-in Capital	Retained Earnings	Accumulated Other Comprehensive Income	Treasury Shares	Total Shareholders' Equity
	Balance, January 1, Year 1	101.5	$253.7	$379.5	$5,328.1	$137.7	$(56.5)	$6,042.5
(1)	Net Income				906.5			906.5
(2)	Unrealized Gain (Loss) on Securities Available for Sale					46.2		46.2
	Comprehensive Income							952.2
(3)	Cash Dividends				(317.1)			(317.1)
(4)	Common Stock Issued under Certain Employee Stock Plans	0.2	0.5	9.9				10.4
(5)	Conversion of Debentures			0.6			10.2	10.8
(6)	Common Stock Retired	(2.5)	(6.2)	(9.5)	(140.9)			(156.6)
	Balance, December 31, Year 1	99.2	$248.0	$380.5	$5,776.6	$183.9	$(46.3)	$6,542.7
(1)	Net Income				360.9			360.9
(2)	Unrealized Gain (Loss) on Securities Available for Sale					(53.7)		(53.7)
	Comprehensive Income							307.2
(3)	Cash Dividends				(298.1)			(298.1)
(4)	Common Stock Issued under Certain Employee Stock Plans	0.1	0.2	1.8				2.0
(5)	Conversion of Debentures			1.4			30.6	32.0
(6)	Common Stock Retired	(5.7)	(14.2)	(21.8)	(194.0)			(230.0)
	Balance, December 31, Year 2	93.6	$234.0	$361.9	$5,645.4	$130.2	$(15.7)	$6,355.8

[a]This caption and the line numbers do not appear on the original statement. The line numbers correspond to the journal entries in **Exhibit 12.7.**

EXHIBIT 12.7	MICHIGAN COMPANY (adapted from Ford Motor Company) Journal Entries Illustrating Transactions Involving Shareholders' Equity, Years 1 and 2 (all dollar amounts in millions)		

Entry and Explanation	Year 1	Year 2
(1) No journal entry required because revenues and expenses for the year that net to net income are already recorded in retained earnings.		
(2) Marketable Security Investments Available for Sale (Asset Increase)	46.2	
Other Comprehensive Income (Unrealized Holding Gain (Loss) on Securities Available for Sale) (Shareholders' Equity Increase)		46.2
Other Comprehensive Income (Unrealized Holding Gain (Loss) on Securities Available for Sale) (Shareholders' Equity Decrease)		53.7
Marketable Security Investments Available for Sale (Asset Decrease)		53.7
To record increase in market value in Year 1 (decrease in market value in Year 2) with increase in asset account in Year 1 (decrease in asset account in Year 2). Matching credit in Year 1 (debit in Year 2) is to Accumulated Other Comprehensive Income, a shareholders' equity account, bypassing the income statement.		
(3) Retained Earnings (Dividend Declared) (Shareholders' Equity Decrease)	317.1	298.1
Cash (or Dividends Payable) (Asset Decrease or Liability Increase)	317.1	298.1
Cash dividends declared.		
(4) Cash (Asset Increase)	10.4	2.0
Common Stock (Shareholders' Equity Increase)	0.5	0.2
Additional Paid-in Capital (Shareholders' Equity Increase)	9.9	1.8
Common stock issued under certain employee stock plans.		
(5) Convertible Debentures (Bonds) (Liability Decrease)	10.8	32.0
Treasury Stock (Shareholders' Equity Increase)	10.2	30.6
Additional Paid-in Capital (Shareholders' Equity Increase)	0.6	1.4
Common stock issued on conversion of convertible debentures (bonds). The shares "issued" on conversion were shares reissued from a block of treasury shares that had cost $10.2 (for Year 1) and $30.6 (for Year 2).		
(6) Common Stock (Shareholders' Equity Decrease)	6.2	14.2
Additional Paid-in Capital (Shareholders' Equity Decrease)	9.5	21.8
Retained Earnings (Shareholders' Equity Decrease)	140.9	194.0
Cash (Asset Decrease)	156.6	230.0
Retirement of common stock acquired for cash. When a firm acquires shares for the treasury, it usually debits a Treasury Stock account, shown as a contra to all of shareholders' equity. In this case, the firm "retires" the shares, so the journal entry identifies the specific amounts for Common Stock, Additional Paid-in Capital, and Retained Earnings corresponding to these shares. The debits are to these accounts instead of to a single contra account.		

An International Perspective on Shareholders' Equity

The accounting for shareholders' equity in most developed countries closely parallels that in the United States.

- Contributed capital accounts increase when firms issue shares of common or preferred stock.
- Revenues, gains, expenses, and losses affect the measurement of periodic earnings and retained earnings.
- Dividends reduce retained earnings and either reduce corporate assets (cash dividends or dividends in kind) or increase other shareholders' equity accounts (stock dividends).

Accounting in many other countries, unlike in the United States, uses **shareholders' equity reserve accounts**. Reserve accounts have credit balances and generally appear in the shareholders' equity section of the balance sheet.

Foreign firms often use a reserve account to disclose to financial statement readers that the firm will not declare dividends against a portion of retained earnings. Firms in the United States can achieve the same result by declaring a stock dividend.

TERMINOLOGY NOTE

GAAP in the United States discourage the use of the word *reserve*. Here's why. Think about the word *reserve* as used in ordinary English. Do you think it refers to something in accounting with a debit balance or a credit balance? When we ask this question, almost all students respond, "Debit," thinking of things like oil reserves and cash set aside for a rainy day. In accounting, the word *reserve* always means an account with a credit balance: Reserve for Depreciation means Accumulated Depreciation, not cash set aside to acquire new equipment; Reserve for Bad Debts means the Allowance for Uncollectible Accounts, not cash set aside in case customers do not pay their bills; Reserve for Warranties means the Estimated Liability for Warranties, not cash set aside to pay for warranty repairs. Since the word *reserve* causes so much confusion, most accountants in the United States do not use it. (We still encounter accountants, even young ones, who use the term, but we do not understand why anyone interested in clarity would use this word in accounting.)

Example 10   Japanese accounting standards require that firms declaring dividends transfer from retained earnings to a permanent legal capital account a specified percentage of the dividend each period. Japanese firms make this entry in addition to the usual entry for dividends. To illustrate, Oji Paper Company declared and paid a ¥10 million dividend during a recent year and made the following entry (amounts in millions):

Retained Earnings (Dividends Declared and Paid) (Shareholders' Equity Decrease)	10	
Cash (Asset Decrease)		10
To record declaration and payment of cash dividend.		

The firm also made the following entry:

Retained Earnings (Shareholders' Equity Decrease)	3	
Permanent Legal Capital (Shareholders' Equity Increase)		3
To reclassify 30 percent of dividends out of retained earnings and into a permanent capital account.		

The second entry effectively marks a portion of retained earnings as unavailable to support dividend declarations. Including the ¥3 million in a capital account indicates to the reader of the financial statements that the firm cannot declare dividends up to the full amount of retained earnings.

Example 11   French accounting standards permit firms to reclassify a portion of retained earnings to a capital account to indicate that the firm cannot declare dividends up to the full amount of retained earnings, at least temporarily. An annual report of Société National Elf Acquitaine revealed the following:

Reserves:	
Legal	€ 100
Long-term Capital Gains.	3,885
Operating Costs	7,300
Unappropriated	5,227

This disclosure indicates that the firm may declare dividends against €5,227 of retained earnings but not against retained earnings €11,285 (= €100 + €3,885 + €7,300), which represent net assets permanently or temporarily not available for payment as dividends. For example, suppose a customer is suing the firm for €20,000. Although the firm feels that it has an adequate defense, it might lose. The firm could make the following entry when the customer files the suit.

Retained Earnings (unappropriated) (Shareholders' Equity Decrease)	20,000	
Operating Risk Reserve (Shareholders' Equity Increase)		20,000
To reclassify a portion of retained earnings into an operating risk reserve.		

Assume now that the firm loses the suit and incurs an uninsured liability of €12,000. The entry, assuming immediate cash payment, is as follows:

Retained Earnings (Loss from Damage Suit) (Shareholders' Equity Decrease)	12,000	
Cash (Asset Decrease)		12,000

Because the firm has now settled the lawsuit, it reclassifies the operating risk reserve back to retained earnings with the following entry:

Operating Risk Reserve (Shareholders' Equity Decrease)	20,000	
Retained Earnings (Shareholders' Equity Increase)		20,000

A second use of reserve accounts relates to revaluations of assets. Accounting regulations in Great Britain and France permit firms to revalue periodically their fixed and other assets.

Example 12   Refer to **Exhibit 2.7**, which shows the balance sheet of Rolls-Royce, a British company. During the current year, this firm revalued its fixed assets, with debits. It credited a revaluation reserve account. The firm will charge (debit) future depreciation and amortization of these revalued amounts to the revaluation reserve account, not to the earnings statement. Neither the initial revaluation nor the subsequent depreciation or amortization enters the earnings statement.

The reader of financial statements issued by firms outside of the United States will frequently encounter various accounts containing the word *reserve* appearing in the shareholders' equity section of the balance sheet. Reserve accounts, even outside the United States, *always* have a credit balance. The reader must be wary of these accounts for the following reasons:

1. Firms rarely set aside assets in the amount of the reserve for the purpose indicated by the title of the reserve (for example, "reserve for plant replacement," "reserve for business risks"). Because of the balance sheet equality of assets and equities, one can conclude only that there are assets in some form (for example, equipment or goodwill) equal to the amount of the reserve. But the assets would be there even if the amounts remained in the Retained Earnings account, without the firm's re-labeling them as reserves.
2. Firms increase and decrease reserves for a variety of purposes (such as reclassifying retained earnings and revaluing assets). The reader should understand the nature of each reserve and the events that cause its amounts to change.

Comprehensive Presentation of Cash Flows, Income, and Changes in Shareholder Wealth

The book has discussed the purpose, underlying concepts, preparation, and interpretation of the three principal financial statements that firms prepare each period:

- Balance Sheet: a report on the financial position of a firm at a point in time.
- Income Statement: a report on the results of a firm's operating activities for a period of time.
- Statement of Cash Flows: a report on the net cash flows from a firm's operating, investing, and financing activities for a period of time.

Exhibit 12.8 presents a summary statement for Wal-Mart Stores that relates various key measures from these three principal financial statements. **Exhibit 12.8** is not a required financial statement according to GAAP. We use it here primarily as a summary device. We discuss each of the elements in **Exhibit 12.8** next.

EXHIBIT 12.8	WAL-MART STORES Consolidated Statement of Net Income, Comprehensive Income, Shareholders' Wealth (also showing Cash Flow from Operations) (amounts in millions)		

Fiscal Year Ended January 31:	Year 11	Year 12	Year 13
CASH PROVIDED BY OPERATING ACTIVITIES			
Sources of Cash			
Cash Received from Customer	$ 190,907	$ 217,589	$ 244,423
Cash Received from Other Revenues.	1,966	2,013	2,139
Uses of Cash			
Payments to Merchandise Suppliers.	$(147,121)	$(169,139)	$(189,195)
Payments to Other Suppliers of Goods and Services	(31,082)	(34,980)	(39,285)
Payment of Interest	(1,374)	(1,326)	(1,063)
Payment of Income Taxes	(3,692)	(3,897)	(4,487)
Net Cash Provided by Operations	$ 9,604	$ 10,260	$ 12,532
EXPENSES, GAINS, AND LOSSES TO CONVERT			
Cash Flow from Operations to Net Income			
Depreciation	(2,868)	(3,290)	(3,432)
CHANGES IN OPERATING ACCOUNTS TO CONVERT			
Cash Flow from Operations to Net Income			
Increase (Decrease) in:			
Accounts Receivable	422	210	101
Inventories	1,795	1,235	2,236
Prepayments	(75)	180	(745)
(Increase) Decrease in:			
Accounts Payable	(2,061)	(368)	(1,447)
Other Current Liabilities	(522)	(1,556)	(1,206)
Net Income	$ 6,295	$ 6,671	$ 8,039
CHANGES IN OTHER COMPREHENSIVE INCOME			
Foreign Currency Translation	(1,126)	(472)	1,113
Cash Flow Hedges	897	(112)	(148)
Minimum Pension Liability	—	—	(206)
Comprehensive Income	$ 6,066	$ 6,087	$ 8,798
CHANGES IN FAIR VALUES OF ASSETS AND LIABILITIES			
Land	?	?	?
Buildings and Equipment	?	?	?
Brand Names and Other Intangibles.	?	?	?
Long-term Liabilities	?	?	?
Total Change in Shareholder Wealth	?	?	?

Cash Flows from Operations

The top panel (shaded in green) shows the computation of cash flow from operations using the direct method (see the discussion in **Chapter 4**). The amounts in this panel result from cash transactions between Wal-Mart and its customers and suppliers. The existence of actual cash flows permits the auditor to trace and verify the amounts in this top panel with a high degree of reliability. Although firms have some flexibility to manage the timing of their operating cash flows (for example, by delaying the payments of suppliers), the amounts in this panel are not as subject to management as amounts in other sections of this statement.

Adjustment to Convert Cash Flow from Operations to Net Income   The middle section (shaded in yellow) down to the line for Net Income shows the conversion of cash flow from operations to net income. Recall from **Chapter 4** that firms calculating cash flow from operations using the indirect method begin with net income and then convert it to cash flow from operations. This panel moves in the opposite direction. Revenue and expense that do not involve an operating cash flow in the period when firms recognize the revenue or expense appear in this section as additions to or subtractions from cash flow from operations. Depreciation, for example, is an expense in measuring net income but does not affect cash flow from operations. We therefore subtract depreciation from cash flow from operations to compute net income. Note that the indirect method of computing cash flow from operations adds depreciation to net income to zero out its effect when computing cash flow from operations. Because we are moving in the opposite direction in this case, we must now subtract depreciation. Other items that might appear in this section are deferred income taxes, gains and losses from sales of property, plant, and equipment, and equity in undistributed earnings of affiliates.

The middle section also includes changes in operating working capital accounts other than cash. These are the same items that appear in the conversion of net income to cash flow from operations using the indirect method but, because **Exhibit 12.8** moves in the opposite direction, the adjustments carry the opposite sign. For example, accounts receivable increase each year for Wal-Mart. The top panel of **Exhibit 12.8** shows the amount of cash received each year by Wal-Mart from sales to customers. An increase in accounts receivable for a year means that Wal-Mart sold more goods on account than it collected from customers. The conversion of cash flow from operations to net income requires that we convert cash collections from customers to sales revenue, resulting in an addition for the increase in accounts receivable.

The amounts shaded in yellow in this section represent allocations of amounts from actual transactions. For example, depreciation allocates the cost of depreciable assets over their expected periods of benefit. Auditors can verify the acquisition cost of the depreciable assets by examining purchase invoices, cancelled checks, and other documents. However, firms must estimate the expected period of benefit of the depreciable assets and the depreciation method that will allocate this cost over those future periods. Take another example. The change in accounts receivable results from the net effects of sales on account, cash collections from customers, and estimates of uncollectible accounts. The sales transaction and the collection of cash are easily verifiable. Firms must estimate the amount of uncollectible accounts. To the extent that actual uncollectible accounts differ from estimates amounts, income gets shifted between accounting periods. The amounts in this section result from applying GAAP to compute net income on an accrual basis. Recall that accrual accounting attempts to match expenses with revenues to obtain a measure of operation performance that relates inputs to outputs. The estimates required to apply GAAP to achieve this matching, however, inject a degree of subjectivity into the measurement process and provide management with a greater opportunity to manage net income than to manage cash flow from operations.

Adjustments to Convert Net Income to Comprehensive Income   The next section, also shaded in yellow, shows changes in the values of assets and liabilities for which GAAP require firms to revalue the asset or liability but do not permit inclusion of the resulting unrealized gain or loss in net income. Instead, firms include these unrealized gains and losses in other comprehensive income until such time as the firm realizes the gains or losses in market transactions. Wal-Mart includes amounts for foreign currency translation, cash flow hedges, and minimum pension liability. This book discussed these items only briefly. A fuller study of these items would show that their computation requires information about exchange rates, interest rates, discount rates, and rates of return on investments, all of which can differ in the future from the current levels used to measure their amounts. The amounts included in other comprehensive income therefore represent only an estimate of the ultimate amount. Because they represent only estimates of amounts firms will realize later, the amounts are less reliable measures of wealth changes than cash flow from operations. Nonetheless, they do provide information to permit the user to track estimated wealth changes over time and, in that sense, provide more useful information than if firms made no such disclosures.

Changes in Fair Values of Assets and Liabilities   The final section (shaded in red) shows changes in the fair value of assets and liabilities for which GAAP generally require valuation at acquisition cost or its equivalent (for example, land, buildings, equipment, long-term liabilities) or do not recognize the items as an asset or liability (for example, internally-developed intangibles or unsettled lawsuits). Changes in the value of these items affect the wealth of shareholders, even though GAAP do not permit either revaluation of the asset or liability or inclusion of the unrealized gain or loss in net income or other comprehensive income. **Exhibit 12.8** shows no amounts for these items because GAAP generally do not require firms to report such fair values in notes to the financial statements. Users must obtain information about such value changes from other sources. For items with active markets, such as land and buildings, users can obtain more reliable measures of fair value changes than for items with less active markets, such as specially designed equipment or internally developed intangibles. We include this last section to emphasize the need to consider such value changes in measuring the change in wealth of shareholders.

Summary of Comprehensive Presentation of Cash Flows, Income, and Changes in Shareholders' Wealth
Exhibit 12.8 illustrates four categories of items that affect the value of a firm. GAAP treat each of these categories differently:

Category 1: Cash receipts and disbursements related to operations, which appear in the statement of cash flows.
Category 2: Accrual accounting adjustments to operating cash flows to derive net income. Firms report the net income amount in the income statement, showing the revenues and expenses for the period that net to this net income amount.
Category 3: Unrealized changes in the value of certain assets and liabilities that accountants can measure with sufficient reliability to justify revaluation of the asset or liability but whose ultimate amount when realized may differ. GAAP require firms to include unrealized changes in value in Other Comprehensive Income.
Category 4: Unrealized changes in the value of certain assets and liabilities that accountants cannot measure with sufficient reliability to justify recognition of the value change either in the valuation of assets and liabilities or in shareholders' equity.

As one moves from category **1** to category **4**, the opportunity for management to manage earnings to its advantage increases. GAAP draw a line after category **2** as to amounts firms can include in reported net income, recognizing that even at this level firms must make choices in applying GAAP that provide opportunities for managing earnings. GAAP recognize the potential information value of items in category **3** for tracking changes in the value of a firm but view the amounts as sufficiently tentative to justify excluding them from net income. GAAP view the value changes in category **4** as sufficiently unreliable to justify including them in the financial statements, even though these value changes may play an important role in the value of a firm.

Summary

The shareholders' equity section of the balance sheet reports the equity, or interests, of preferred and common shareholders in the net assets of a firm. The equity of the preferred shareholders usually approximates the par value of the preferred shares. The remaining shareholders' equity accounts relate to the equity of the common shareholders. The equity of the common shareholders equals the sum of the amounts appearing in the Common Stock, Additional Paid-in Capital, Retained Earnings, Accumulated Other Comprehensive Income, Treasury Stock, and other common-share equity accounts. The user of the financial statements gains insight into capital contributions, earnings, other comprehensive income, dividends, and treasury stock transactions only by studying changes in the individual accounts.

Appendix 12.1: Effects on the Statement of Cash Flows of Transactions Involving Shareholders' Equity

With the exception of earnings, most transactions affecting shareholders' equity accounts appear in the statement of cash flows as financing transactions.

Capital Contributions

Firms that issue preferred or common stock for cash report the transaction as a financing activity. If the firm receives an asset other than cash (for example, building, equipment, or patent), it does not report the transaction as investing and financing activities that involve cash. The firm discloses the transaction in a supplementary schedule or note to the financial statements.

Stock Options, Rights, and Warrants

The firm reports the cash received from the issuance of stock under options, rights, or warrants arrangements as a financing activity. When a firm recognizes a compensation expense related to stock options, it must add back the expense to earnings when computing cash flow from operations under the indirect method.

Conversions of Bonds or Preferred Stock

The firm does not report the conversion of convertible bonds or convertible preferred stock into common stock as a financing activity that involves cash. The firm discloses this transaction in a supplementary schedule or note to the financial statements.

Treasury Stock Transactions

Reacquisitions and reissuances of a firm's capital stock (that is, treasury stock) appear as financing activities in the statement of cash flows.

Dividends

Dividends that a firm declares and pays in cash during a period appear as financing activities. If a portion of the dividend paid during the current period relates to dividends declared during the previous period or if the firm does not pay all dividends declared during the current period by the end of the period, then the amount in the Dividends Payable account will change. The change in the Dividends Payable account, a current liability, appears in the Financing section of the statement of cash flows as an adjustment to the amount of dividends declared. The adjustment converts dividends declared during the period to the amount of dividends paid in cash. Until this point of the book, all changes in current assets and liabilities, other than cash, marketable securities, and short-term borrowings, appeared as adjustments to net earnings in deriving cash provided by operations when the firm uses the indirect method in the statement of cash flows. Because all dividend activities are financing, the change in the Dividends Payable account must appear in the Financing section.

Firms sometimes issue property dividends (that is, dividends payable in inventory, equipment, or some other asset). Such dividends do not use cash and therefore appear in a supplementary schedule or note to the financial statements. If the firm recognized a gain or loss at the time that it distributed the property dividend, it subtracts the gain or adds back the loss to earnings when computing cash flow from operations under the indirect method.

Stock dividends, likewise, do not involve cash and therefore do not appear in the statement of cash flows. Nor do such dividends appear in a supplementary schedule or note because they do not usually change the equity ownership of the firm.

Solutions to Self-Study Problems

SUGGESTED SOLUTION TO PROBLEM 12.1 FOR SELF-STUDY

(Healy Corporation; journal entries for capital contributions.)

a. *January 2, Year 1*

Cash (Asset Increase)	1,400,000	
Common Stock—$10 Par (Shareholders' Equity Increase).		1,000,000
Additional Paid-in Capital (Shareholders' Equity Increase).		400,000

Issue of 100,000 shares of $10-par value common stock for $14 per share.

b. *January 2, Year 1*

Patent (Asset Increase)	140,000	
Common Stock—$10 Par (Shareholders' Equity Increase)		100,000
Additional Paid-in Capital (Shareholders' Equity Increase)		40,000

Issue of 10,000 shares of $10-par value common stock in exchange for a patent. The value of the patent is not easily determinable, so use the issue price of $14 per share from part **a.**

c. *March 1, Year 1*

Cash (Asset Increase)	200,000	
Preferred Stock (Shareholders' Equity Increase)		200,000

Issue of 2,000 shares of convertible preferred stock at par value.

d. *June 1, Year 1*

Cash (Asset Increase)	50,000	
Common Stock Warrants (Shareholders' Equity Increase).		50,000

Issue of 10,000 common stock warrants for $5 per warrant.

e. *September 15, Year 1*

Preferred Stock (Shareholders' Equity Decrease)	60,000	
Common Stock—$10 Par (Shareholders' Equity Increase)		24,000
Additional Paid-in Capital (Shareholders' Equity Increase)		36,000

To record the conversion of 600 preferred shares into 2,400 common shares at book value.

f. *November 20, Year 1*

Cash (Asset Increase)	96,000	
Common Stock Warrants (Shareholders' Equity Decrease)	20,000	
Common Stock—$10 Par (Shareholders' Equity Increase)		40,000
Additional Paid-in Capital (Shareholders' Equity Increase)		76,000

Issue of 4,000 shares of common stock in exchange for 4,000 stock warrants and $96,000 cash.

g. No entry in Year 1. The firm must amortize the $25,000 over the expected period of benefit in future years.

SUGGESTED SOLUTION TO PROBLEM 12.2 FOR SELF-STUDY

(Baker Corporation; journal entries for dividends and stock splits.)

a. *March 31*

Retained Earnings (Shareholders' Equity Decrease)	12,500	
Dividends Payable (Liability Increase)		12,500

To record declaration of cash dividend of $0.50 per share on 25,000 shares.

b. *April 15*

Dividends Payable (Liability Decrease)	12,500	
Cash (Asset Decrease)		12,500

To pay cash dividend declared on March 31.

c. *June 30*

Retained Earnings (Shareholders' Equity Decrease)	37,500	
Common Stock (Shareholders' Equity Increase)		25,000
Additional Paid-in Capital (Shareholders' Equity Increase)		12,500

To record issuance of 10 percent stock dividend: $0.10 \times 25,000 = 2,500$ shares; $2,500 \times \$15 = \$37,500$.

d.

Common Stock, $10 par value (Shareholders' Equity Decrease)	275,000	
Common Stock, $5 par value (Shareholders' Equity Increase)		275,000

To record 2-for-1 stock split. Alternatively, the firm might make no formal entry in the accounting records.

SUGGESTED SOLUTION TO PROBLEM 12.3 FOR SELF-STUDY

(Crissie Corporation; journal entries for treasury stock transactions.)

a. *January 15*

Treasury Shares—Common (Shareholders' Equity Decrease)	90,000	
Cash (Asset Decrease)		90,000

Paid $90,000 to reacquire 2,000 common shares at $45 per share.

b. *April 26*

Cash (Asset Increase)	57,600	
Treasury Shares—Common (Shareholders' Equity Increase)		54,000
Additional Paid-in Capital (Shareholders' Equity Increase)		3,600

Reissue of 1,200 shares of treasury stock costing $45 per share; treasury shares reissued to employees under stock option plan with an exercise price of $48 per share.

c. *August 15*

Treasury Shares—Common (Shareholders' Equity Decrease)	156,000	
Cash (Asset Decrease)		156,000

Paid $156,000 to reacquire 3,000 common shares at $52 per share.

d. *November 24*

Preferred Stock (Shareholders' Equity Decrease)	80,000	
Treasury Stock (Shareholders' Equity Increase)		77,600
Additional Paid-in Capital (Shareholders' Equity Increase)		2,400

Reissue of 1,600 shares of treasury stock with a cost of $77,600 [= (800 × $45) + (800 × $52)] in exchange for convertible preferred stock with a book value of $80,000.

e. *December 20*

Cash (Asset Increase)	70,500	
Additional Paid-in Capital (Shareholders' Equity Decrease)	7,500	
Treasury Stock (Shareholders' Equity Increase)		78,000

Reissue of 1,500 shares of treasury stock costing $52 per share; treasury shares sold on the open market for $47 per share.

SUGGESTED SOLUTION TO PROBLEM 12.4 FOR SELF-STUDY

(Able Corporation; journal entries for earnings and retained earnings transactions.)

a. *January 15*

Retained Earnings (Shareholders' Equity Decrease)	35,000	
Accumulated Depreciation (Asset Decrease)		35,000

To correct error in prior year's depreciation with direct charge to retained earnings.

b. *March 20*

Retained Earnings (Loss from Earthquake) (Shareholders' Equity Decrease)	70,000	
Building (Asset Decrease)		70,000

To record loss from earthquake in an income statement account.

c. *December 31*

Retained Earnings (Depreciation Expense) (Shareholders' Equity Decrease)	14,000	
Accumulated Depreciation (Asset Decrease)		14,000

Original depreciation: $400,000/40 = $10,000 per year. Book value on January 1, Year 5 is $350,000 [= $400,000 − ($10,000 × 5)]. Depreciation for Year 5 is $14,000 (= $350,000/25).

Key Terms and Concepts

Corporation	Dividend in kind or property dividend
Corporate charter	Stock dividend
Corporate bylaws	Stock split
Capital stock contract	Reverse stock split
Capital stock	Treasury shares, treasury stock
Preferred stock	Earnings from continuing operations
Cumulative dividend rights	Earnings, gains, and losses from discontinued
Callable preferred shares	operations
Convertible preferred shares	Extraordinary gains and losses
Redeemable preferred shares	Realize v. recognize
Common stock	Other comprehensive income
Par or stated value	Accumulated other comprehensive income
Additional Paid-in Capital account	Comprehensive income
Stock options	Correction of error
Stock rights	Change in accounting principle
Stock warrants	Changes in estimates
Benefit element in stock option	Earnings per common share
Time value element in stock option	Book value per common share
Convertible bonds	Shareholders' equity reserve accounts
Cash dividend	

Questions, Short Exercises, Exercises, Problems, and Cases

QUESTIONS

For additional student resources, content, and interactive quizzes for this chapter visit the FACMU website:
http://facmu.swlearning.com

1. Review the meaning of the terms and concepts listed in Key Terms and Concepts.
2. The chapter states that the amount in various common shareholders' equity accounts represents the equity of the common shareholders in the net assets of a firm. If a bankrupt firm sold its assets and used the proceeds to pay creditors, preferred shareholders, and common shareholders, would these common shareholders likely receive an amount equal to the amount in the common shareholders' equity accounts on the balance sheet? Explain.
3. "The accounting for stock options, stock dividends, and treasury stock cloud the distinction between capital transactions and operating transactions." Explain.
4. A firm contemplates issuing 10,000 shares of $100 par value preferred stock. The preferred stock promises a $4 per share annual dividend. The firm considers making this preferred stock either callable, convertible, or subject to mandatory redemption. Will the issue price be the same in each of these three cases? Explain.
5. Compare and contrast a stock option, a stock right, and a stock warrant. How does the accounting for these three differ?
6. Stock option valuation models indicate that the value of a stock option increases with the volatility of the stock, increases with the time between the grant date and the expected exercise date, and decreases with increases in the discount rate. Explain.
7. GAAP require firms to amortize the value of stock options as an expense over the periods the firm expects to receive employee services as a result of granting the option. What is the theoretical rationale for this amortization?
8. Compare the position of a shareholder who receives a cash dividend with that of one who receives a stock dividend.
9. A firm that sells inventory for more than its acquisition cost realizes an economic gain that accountants include in earnings, but a firm that sells treasury stock for more than its acquisition cost realizes an economic gain that accountants exclude from earnings. What is the rationale for the difference in treatment of these economic gains?
10. A security analyst states: "Accountants could increase the usefulness of income statements if they included only recurring income items in the income statement and reported nonrecurring items directly in retained earnings, bypassing the income statement." Do you agree?
11. Why should GAAP exclude from earnings items of other comprehensive income such as holding gains and losses on securities held available for sale?
12. Distinguish between the nature of, and accounting for (1) a correction of an error in previously issued financial statements, (2) the adjustment for a change in accounting principle, and (3) the

adjustment for a change in an accounting estimate made in preparing previously issued financial statements.

SHORT EXERCISES

13. **Journal entry to issue common stock.** Office Depot issues 10 million shares of $2 par value common stock for $12.50 per share. Give the journal entry to record this transaction.

14. **Accounting for stock options.** Intel grants 100,000 stock options to employees on December 31, Year 13, permitting them to purchase 100,000 shares of Intel $1 par value common stock for $30 per share. An option-pricing model indicates that the value of each option on this date is $12. Intel expects to receive the benefit of enhanced employee services for the next three years. On December 31, Year 18, employees exercise these options when the market price of the stock is $40 per share. Compute the pre-tax effect of this option plan on the earnings of Intel for Year 13 through Year 18.

15. **Accounting for conversion of bonds.** Symantec has convertible bonds outstanding with a face value of $10,000,000 and a book value of $10,255,000. Holders of the bonds convert them into 100,000 shares of $10 par value common stock. The common stock sells for $105 per share on the market. Give the journal entries to record the conversion of the bonds using the (1) book value method, and (2) the market value method.

16. **Accounting for declaration and payment of a dividend.** Wyeth Corporation has 100,000 shares of $100 par value, 4-percent preferred stock outstanding. On December 10, Year 13, Wyeth Corporation declares the annual dividend on these preferred shares for Year 13. The dividend is paid on January 10, Year 14. Give the journal entries for these transactions.

17. **Accounting for treasury stock transactions.** On July 15, Year 13, PepsiCo purchased 75,000 shares of its common stock for $55 per share. On February 10, Year 14, PepsiCo reissued 50,000 shares of this common stock on the market for $62 per share. Give the journal entries to record these transactions.

18. **Computation of net income and comprehensive income.** Champion Enterprises reports the following items for Year 13 (amounts in millions): income from continuing operations, $126.7; extraordinary loss from hurricane, $10.3; other comprehensive income, $17.9; loss from discontinued operations, $26.9. Compute the amount of net income and the amount of comprehensive income for Year 13.

19. **Treatment of accounting errors, changes in accounting principles, and changes in accounting estimates.** A firm computes net income for Year 12 of $1,500 and for Year 13 of $1,800, its first two years of operations. Before issuing its financial statements for Year 13, the firm discovers that an item requires an income-reducing adjustment of $400 after taxes. Indicate the amount of net income for Year 12 and Year 13 assuming (1) the item is an error in the computation of depreciation expense for Year 12 (Year 13 depreciation expense is correct as computed), (2) the item is the change in net income for Year 12 as a result of adopting a new method of accounting for stock options in Year 13 (Year 13 stock option expense reflects the new accounting principle), and (3) the item is the change in estimated uncollectible accounts for Year 12 as a result of worsened credit losses experienced in Year 13; the firm included the adjustment amount in bad debt expense for Year 13.

EXERCISES

20. **Journal entries to record the issuance of capital stock.** Prepare journal entries to record the issuance of capital stock in each of the independent cases below. You may omit explanations for the journal entries. A firm does the following:
    a. Issues 50,000 shares of $5 par value common stock for $30 per share.
    b. Issues 20,000 shares of $100 par value convertible preferred stock at par.
    c. Issues 16,000 shares of $10 par value common stock in the acquisition of a patent. The shares of the firm traded on a stock exchange for $15 per share on the day of the transaction. The seller listed the patent for sale at $250,000.
    d. Issues 25,000 shares of $1 par value common stock in exchange for convertible preferred stock with a par and book value of $400,000. The common shares traded on the market for $18 per share on the date of the transaction. Use the book value method to record the conversion.
    e. Issues 5,000 shares of $10 par value common stock to employees as a bonus for reaching sales goals for the year. The shares traded for $12 per share on the day of the transaction.

21. **Journal entries for the issuance of capital stock.** Prepare journal entries to record the issuance of capital stock in each of the independent cases below. You may omit explanations for the journal entries. A firm does the following:

    a. Issues 20,000 shares of $10 par value common stock in the acquisition of inventory with a market value of $175,000, land valued at $220,000, a building valued at $1,400,000, and equipment valued at $405,000.

    b. Issues 10,000 shares of $100 par value preferred stock at par. The preferred stock is subject to mandatory redemption in five years.

    c. Issues 5,000 shares of $1 par value common stock upon the exercise of stock warrants. The firm had issued the stock warrants several years previously for $8 per warrant and properly recorded the sale of the warrants in the accounts. The exercise price is $24 plus one warrant for each share of common stock.

    d. Issues 20,000 shares of $10 par value common stock upon the conversion of 10,000 shares of $50 par value convertible preferred stock originally issued for par. Record the conversion using book values.

22. **Journal entries for employee stock options.** Morrissey Corporation grants 50,000 stock options to its managerial employees on December 31, Year 13, to purchase 50,000 shares of its $1 par value common stock for $60 per share. The market price of a share of common stock on this date is $50 per share. Employees must wait two years before the options vest and they can exercise the options and this two-year period is the expected period of benefit from the stock options. A financial consulting firm estimates that the market value of these options on the grant date is $400,000. On June 30, Year 15, holders of 30,000 options exercise their options at a time when the market price of the stock is $65 per share. On November 15, Year 16, holders of the remaining options exercise them at a time when the market price of the stock is $72 per share.

    Present journal entries to record the effects of the transactions related to stock options during Year 13, Year 14, Year 15, and Year 16 following the market value method. The firm reports on a calendar-year basis. Ignore income tax effects.

23. **Journal entries for employee stock options.** Watson Corporation grants 20,000 stock options to its managerial employees on December 31, Year 6, to purchase 20,000 shares of its $10 par value common stock for $25 per share. The market price of a share of common stock on this date is $18 per share. Employees must work for another two years before they can exercise the options. A financial consulting firm estimates that the market value of these options on the grant date is $75,000. On April 30, Year 9, holders of 15,000 options exercise their options at a time when the market price of the stock is $30 per share. On September 15, Year 10, holders of the remaining options exercise them at a time when the market price of the stock is $38 per share.

    Present journal entries to record these transactions on December 31, Year 6, Year 7, and Year 8; on April 30, Year 9; and on September 15, Year 10 following the market value method. Assume that the firm receives any benefits of the stock option plan during Year 6, Year 7, and Year 8 and that the firm reports on a calendar-year basis. Ignore income tax effects.

24. **Journal entries for stock warrants.** Kiersten Corporation sells 60,000 common stock warrants for $4 each on February 26, Year 12. Each warrant permits its holder to purchase a share of the firm's $10 par value common stock for $30 per share at any time during the next two years. The market price of the common shares was $20 per share on February 26, Year 12. Holders of 40,000 warrants exercised their warrants on June 6, Year 14, at a time when the market price of the stock was $38 per share. Kiersten Corporation experienced a major uninsured loss from a fire late in Year 14 and its market price fell immediately to $22 per share. The market price remained around $22 until the stock warrants expired on February 26, Year 16. Present journal entries on February 26, Year 12; June 6, Year 14; and February 26, Year 16, relating to these stock warrants.

25. **Journal entries for convertible bonds.** Higgins Corporation issues $1 million of 20-year, $1,000 face value, 10-percent semiannual coupon bonds at par on January 2, Year 1. Each $1,000 bond is convertible into 40 shares of $1 par value common stock. Assume that Higgins Corporation's credit rating is such that it could issue 15-percent semiannual, nonconvertible bonds at par. On January 2, Year 5, holders convert their bonds into common stock. The common stock has a market price of $45 per share on January 2, Year 5.

    a. Present the journal entries made under GAAP on January 2, Year 1, and January 2, Year 5, to record the issue and conversion of these bonds. Use the book value method to record the conversion.

    b. Assume for this part that the firm allocates a portion of the issue price on January 2, Year 1, to the conversion option (GAAP do not allow this treatment). Give the journal entry on January 2, Year 1.

26. Journal entries to correct errors and adjust for changes in estimates. Prepare journal entries to record each of the following items for Uncertainty Corporation for Year 13. Ignore income tax effects.

   a. Discovers on January 15, Year 13, that it neglected to amortize a patent during Year 12 in the amount of $12,000.

   b. Discovers on January 20, Year 13, that it recorded the sale of a machine on December 30, Year 12, for $6,000 with the following journal entry:

Cash (Asset Increase)	6,000	
Retained Earnings (Loss on Sale of Machine) (Shareholders' Equity Decrease)	4,000	
Machine (acquisition cost) (Asset Decrease)		10,000

The machine had accumulated depreciation of $7,000 on the date of the sale.

   c. Changes the depreciable life of a building as of December 31, Year 13, from a total useful life of 30 years to a total of 42 years. The building has an acquisition cost of $2,400,000 and is 11 years old as of December 31, Year 13. The firm has not recorded depreciation for Year 13. It uses the straight-line method and zero estimated salvage value.

   d. The firm has used 2 percent of sales as its estimate of uncollectible accounts for several years. Its actual losses have averaged only 1.50 percent of sales. As a consequence, the Allowance for Estimated Uncollectibles account has a credit balance of $25,000 at the end of Year 13 before making the provision for Year 13. An aging of customers' accounts suggests that the firm needs $35,000 in the allowance account at the end of Year 13 to cover estimated uncollectibles. Sales for Year 13 are $1,000,000.

27. Journal entries for dividends. Give journal entries, if required, for the following transactions, which are unrelated unless otherwise specified:

   a. A firm declares the regular quarterly dividend on its 6 percent, $100 par value preferred stock. There are 30,000 shares authorized and 15,000 shares issued, of which the firm has previously reacquired 2,000 shares and holds them in the treasury.

   b. The firm pays the dividend on the preferred stock (see part **a**).

   c. A company declares and issues a stock dividend of $300,000 of no-par common stock to its common shareholders.

   d. The shares of no-par stock of the corporation sell on the market for $200 a share. To bring the market value down to a more popular price and thereby broaden the distribution of its stockholdings, the board of directors votes to issue four extra shares to shareholders for each share they already hold. The corporation issues the shares.

28. Journal entries for dividends. Prepare journal entries for the following transactions of Watt Corporation. The firm has 20,000 shares of $15 par value common stock outstanding on January 1, Year 6. The balance in the Additional Paid-in Capital account on this date is $200,000.

   a. Declares a dividend of $0.50 per share on March 31, Year 6.

   b. Pays the dividend in part **a** on April 15, Year 6.

   c. Declares and distributes a 10 percent stock dividend on June 30, Year 6. The market price of the stock is $20 on this date.

   d. Declares a $0.50 per share dividend on September 30, Year 6.

   e. Pays the dividend in part **d** on October 15, Year 6.

   f. Declares a 3-for-2 stock split on December 31, Year 6, but does not alter the par value.

29. Journal entries for treasury stock transactions. Prepare journal entries to record the following treasury stock transactions of Danos Corporation.

   a. Purchases 10,000 shares of $10 par value common stock for $30 per share.

   b. Issues 6,000 treasury shares to employees under stock option plans. The exercise price is $32 per share. Assume that the market price of the common stock on the exercise date is $35 per share. The stock options had a value of $6 a share when issued, which the firm has already amortized to expense.

   c. Purchases 7,000 shares of common stock for $38 per share.

   d. Issues 8,000 treasury shares in the acquisition of land valued at $300,000. Danos Corporation uses a FIFO assumption for reissues of treasury stock.

   e. Sells the 3,000 remaining shares of treasury stock for $36 per share.

30. Journal entries for treasury stock transactions. Prepare journal entries to record the following treasury stock transactions of Melissa Corporation.

   a. Purchases 10,000 shares of $5 par value common stock for $12 per share.

b. Issues 6,000 treasury shares upon the conversion of bonds with a book value of $72,000. Melissa Corporation records bond conversions using the book value method.

c. Purchases 20,000 shares of common stock for $15 per share.

d. Issues 24,000 treasury shares and 6,000 newly issued shares of common stock in the acquisition of land with a market value of $540,000.

31. Effects on statement of cash flows. Refer to the simplified statement of cash flows in **Exhibit 4.12**. Numbers appear on 11 of the lines in the statement. Ignore the unnumbered lines in considering the following transactions.

Assume that a firm has completed the accounting cycle for the period and prepared all of the financial statements. It then discovers that it has overlooked a transaction. It records the transaction in the accounts and corrects all of the financial statements. For each of the following transactions, indicate which of the numbered lines of the statement of cash flows changes and by how much. Ignore income tax effects.

a. The firm issues common shares for $200,000.

b. The firm repurchases for $75,000 common shares originally issued at par for $50,000 and retires them.

c. Holders of convertible bonds with a book value of $100,000 and a market value of $240,000 convert them into common shares with a par value of $10,000 and a market value of $240,000. Respond assuming that the firm uses (1) the book value method to record bond conversions, and (2) the market value method to record bond conversions.

d. The firm issues for $15,000 treasury shares that have been previously acquired for $20,000.

e. The directors declare a stock dividend. The par value of the shares issued is $1,000, and their market value is $300,000.

f. The directors declare a cash dividend of $70,000, but the firm has not yet paid it.

g. The firm pays a previously declared cash dividend of $70,000.

h. Holders of stock rights exercise them. The shares issued have a par value of $1,000 and a market value of $35,000 on the date of exercise. The firm receives the exercise price of $20,000 in cash.

PROBLEMS AND CASES

32. Transactions to incorporate and run a business. The following events relate to shareholders' equity transactions of Wilson Supply Company during the first year of its existence. Present journal entries for each of the transactions.

a. January 2. The firm files articles of incorporation with the State Corporation Commission. The authorized capital stock consists of 5,000 shares of $100 par value preferred stock that offers an 8-percent annual dividend, and 50,000 shares of no-par common stock. The original incorporators acquire 300 shares of common stock at $30 per share; the firm collects cash for the shares. It assigns a stated value of $30 per share to the common stock.

b. January 6. The firm issues 2,000 shares of common stock for cash at $30 per share.

c. January 8. It issues 4,000 shares of preferred stock at par.

d. January 9. The firm issues certificates for the shares of preferred stock.

e. January 12. The firm acquires the tangible assets and goodwill of Richardson Supply, a partnership, in exchange for 1,000 shares of preferred stock and 12,000 shares of common stock. It values the tangible assets acquired as follows: inventories, $50,000; land, $80,000; buildings, $210,000; and equipment, $120,000.

f. July 3. The directors declare the semiannual dividend on preferred stock outstanding, payable July 25, to shareholders of record on July 12.

g. July 5. The firm operated profitably for the first six months, and it decides to expand. The company issues 25,000 shares of common stock for cash at $33 per share.

h. July 25. It pays the dividend on preferred stock declared on July 3.

i. October 2. The directors declare a dividend of $1 per share on the common stock, payable October 25, to shareholders of record on October 12.

j. October 25. The firm pays the dividend on common stock declared on October 2.

33. Reconstructing transactions involving shareholders' equity. Fisher Company began business on January 1. Its balance sheet on December 31 contained the shareholders' equity section in **Exhibit 12.9**.

EXHIBIT 12.9	FISHER COMPANY Shareholders' Equity as of December 31 (Problem 33)	
Common Stock ($10 par value)		$60,000
Additional Paid-in Capital		31,440
Retained Earnings		12,000
Less Unrealized Holding Loss on Securities Available for Sale		(2,000)
Less 360 Shares Held in Treasury		(7,200)
Total Shareholders' Equity		$94,240

During the year, Fisher Company engaged in the following transactions:

(1) Issued shares for $15 each.

(2) Acquired a block of 600 shares for the treasury in a single transaction.

(3) Reissued some of the treasury shares.

(4) Sold for $10,000 securities available for sale with original cost of $6,000. At the end of the year, securities available for sale had original cost of $12,000 and market value of $14,000.

Assuming that these were all of the common stock transactions during the year, answer the following questions:

a. How many shares did Fisher Company issue for $30?

b. What was the price at which it acquired the treasury shares?

c. How many shares did it reissue from the block of treasury shares?

d. What was the price at which it reissued the treasury shares?

e. What journal entries did it make during the year?

f. In which statement or statements will Fisher Company report the various gains and losses on its holdings of securities available for sale?

34. **Reconstructing transactions involving shareholders' equity.** Shea Company began business on January 1. Its balance sheet on December 31 contained the shareholders' equity section shown in **Exhibit 12.10**.

EXHIBIT 12.10	SHEA COMPANY Shareholders' Equity as of December 31 (Problem 34)	
Common Stock ($5 par value)		$100,000
Additional Paid-in Capital		509,600
Retained Earnings		50,000
Less Unrealized Holding Loss on Securities Available for Sale		(7,000)
Less 1,200 Shares Held in Treasury		(33,600)
Total Shareholders' Equity		$619,000

During the year, Shea Company engaged in the following transactions:

(1) Issued shares for $30 each.

(2) Acquired a block of 2,000 shares for the treasury in a single transaction.

(3) Reissued some of the treasury shares.

(4) Sold for $12,000 securities available for sale that had originally cost $14,000. At the end of the year, securities available for sale, still on hand, that had originally cost $25,000 had market value of $18,000.

Assuming that these were the only common stock transactions during the year, answer the following questions:

a. How many shares did Shea Company issue for $30 each?

b. What was the price at which it acquired the treasury shares?

c. How many shares did it reissue from the block of treasury shares?

d. What was the price at which it reissued the treasury shares?

e. What journal entries did it make during the year?

f. In which statement or statements will Shea Company report the various gains and losses on its holdings of securities available for sale?

35. Accounting for stock options. Lowe Corporation grants stock options to its managerial employees on December 31 of each year. Employees may acquire one share of common stock with each stock option. Lowe Corporation sets the exercise price equal to the market price of its common stock on the date of the grant. Employees must continue working for two years after the date of the grant before the options vest and employees can exercise them. This two-year period is the period of benefit. **Exhibit 12.11** presents information for the stock options granted by Lowe Corporation on December 31 of each year.

EXHIBIT 12.11	Stock Option Data for Lowe Corporation (Problem 35)		
Year	**Options Granted during Year**	**Option Price per Share**	**Option Value per Share**
1	5,000	$18	$2.40
2	6,000	$22	$3.00
3	7,000	$25	$3.14
4	8,000	$30	$3.25
5	9,000	$38	$5.33

Assume that Lowe Corporation accounts for its stock options using the market value method. Calculate the effect of the stock options on net income before income taxes for Years 1 to 5.

36. Comprehensive review of accounting for shareholders' equity. The shareholders' equity section of the balance sheet of Alex Corporation at December 31 is as follows:

Shareholders' Equity

Common Stock—$10 Par Value, 250,000 Shares Authorized and 50,000 Shares Outstanding	$ 500,000
Additional Paid-in Capital	250,000
Retained Earnings	1,500,000
Total Shareholders' Equity	$2,250,000

a. Calculate the total book value and the book value per common share as of December 31.
b. For each of the following transactions or events, give the appropriate journal entry and compute the total book value and the book value per common share of Alex Corporation after the transaction. The transactions and events are independent of one another, except where noted.
  (1) Declares a 10-percent stock dividend when the market price of Alex Corporation's common stock is $30 per share.
  (2) Declares a 2-for-1 stock split and reduces the par value of the common stock from $10 to $5 per share. The firm issues the new shares immediately.
  (3) Purchases 5,000 shares of Alex Corporation's common stock on the open market for $25 per share and holds the shares as treasury stock.
  (4) Purchases 5,000 shares of Alex Corporation's common stock on the open market for $15 per share and holds the shares as treasury stock.
  (5) Sells the shares acquired in **(3)** for $35 per share.
  (6) Sells the shares acquired in **(3)** for $20 per share.
  (7) Sells the shares acquired in **(3)** for $15 per share.
  (8) Officers exercise options to acquire 5,000 shares of Alex Corporation stock for $15 per share.
  (9) Same as **(8)**, except that the exercise price is $50 per share.
  (10) Holders of convertible bonds with a book value of $150,000 and a market value of $170,000 exchanged them for 10,000 shares of common stock having a market value of $17 per share. The firm recognizes no gain or loss on the conversion of bonds.

(11) Same as **(10)**, except that the firm recognizes gain or loss on the conversion of bonds into stock. Ignore income tax effects.

   c. Using the results from part **b**, summarize the transactions and events that result in a reduction in
   (1) total book value, and
   (2) book value per share.

37. **Reconstructing events affecting shareholders' equity. Exhibit 12.12** reproduces the statement of changes in shareholders' equity accounts for Neslin Company for Year 2.
   a. Identify the most likely events or transactions for each of the events numbered **(1)** to **(7)** in the exhibit. The events are not independent of one another.
   b. Prepare journal entries for each of these events or transactions.

38. **Journal entries for changes in shareholders' equity. Exhibit 12.13** presents a statement of changes in shareholders' equity for Wal-Mart Stores for Year 11. Prepare journal entries for each of these transactions or events. The corporate acquisition involved an investment in the common stock of another entity.

39. **Treasury shares and their effects on performance ratios. Exhibit 12.14** presents the changes in common shareholders' equity of Merck for Year 3 through Year 5. Merck regularly purchases shares of its common stock and reissues them in connection with stock option plans. It will usually issue a small number of new common shares when it requires fractional shares to complete a stock option transaction. Earnings per common share were $2.70 in Year 3, $3.20 in Year 4, and $3.83 in Year 5.
   a. Give the journal entries for Year 5 to record (1) the issue of common shares in connection with stock option plans, and (2) the purchase of treasury stock.
   b. Compute the percentage change in net income and in earnings per share between Year 3 and Year 4, and between Year 4 and Year 5. Why do the percentage changes in earnings per share exceed the percentage changes in net income in both Year 4 and Year 5?
   c. Compute the book value per outstanding common share at the end of Year 3, Year 4, and Year 5, and the percentage change in book value per share between Year 3 and Year 4, and between Year 4 and Year 5. Why are the percentage changes in book value per common share less than the percentage changes in both net income and earnings per share?
   d. Compute the rate of return on common shareholders' equity for Year 3, Year 4, and Year 5.
   e. Do the treasury stock purchases appear to be motivated primarily by the need to satisfy commitments under stock option plans? Explain.

40. **Case introducing earnings-per-share calculations for a complex capital structure.** The Layton Ball Corporation has a relatively complicated capital structure—that is, it raises funds using a variety of financing devices. In addition to common shares, it has issued stock options, warrants, and convertible bonds. **Exhibit 12.15** summarizes some pertinent information about these items. Net income for the year is $9,500, and the income tax rate used in computing income tax expense is 40 percent of pretax income.
   a. First, ignore all items of capital except for the common shares. Calculate earnings per common share.
   b. In past years, employees have been issued options to purchase shares of stock. **Exhibit 12.15** indicates that the price of the common stock throughout the current year has remained steady at $25 but that holders of the stock options could exercise them at any time for $15 for each share. That is, the option allows the holder to surrender it along with $15 cash and receive one share in return. Thus the number of shares would increase, which would decrease the earnings-per-share figure. The company would, however, have more cash. Assume that the holders of options tender them, along with $15 each, to purchase shares. Assume that the company uses the cash to purchase shares for its own treasury at a price of $25 each. Compute a new earnings-per-share figure. The firm does not count shares in its own treasury in the denominator of the earnings-per-share calculation.
   c. **Exhibit 12.15** indicates that there were also warrants outstanding in the hands of the public. The warrant allows the holder to turn in that warrant, along with $30 cash, to purchase one share of stock. If holders exercised the warrants, the number of outstanding shares would increase, which would reduce earnings per share. However, the company would have more cash, which it could use to purchase shares for the treasury, reducing the number of shares outstanding. Assume that all holders of warrants exercise them. Assume that the company uses the cash to purchase outstanding shares for the treasury. Compute a new earnings-per-share figure. Ignore the information about options and the calculations in part **b** at this point. Note that a rational warrants holder would not exercise the warrants for $30 when they can purchase a share for $25.

EXHIBIT 12.12

NESLIN COMPANY
Statement of Changes in Shareholders' Equity Accounts for Year 2
(Problem 37)

	Market Value per Share^a	Number of Shares	Par Value	Additional Paid-in Capital	Retained Earnings	Accumulated Other Comprehensive Income	Treasury Stock	Total Shareholders' Equity
Balances, Dec. 31, Year 1	$50	100,000	$1,000,000	$5,400,000	$ 9,600,000	$1,200,000	—	$17,200,000
Events Causing Changes								
(1)	52	20,000	200,000	840,000	—	—	—	1,040,000
(2)	55	(4,000)	—	—	—	—	$(220,000)	(220,000)
(3)	48	3,000	—	(21,000)	—	—	165,000	144,000
(4)	60	1,000	—	5,000	—	—	55,000	60,000
(5)	62	—	—	—	2,400,000	—	—	2,400,000
(6)	63	—	—	—	—	(150,000)	—	(150,000)
(7)	63	—	—	—	(1,200,000)	—	—	(1,200,000)
Balances, Dec. 31, Year 2		120,000	$1,200,000	$6,224,000	$10,800,000	$1,050,000	—	$19,274,000

^aBefore event.

EXHIBIT 12.13

WAL-MART STORES
Statement of Changes in Shareholders' Equity Accounts for Year 11
(all dollar amounts in thousands) (Problem 38)

	Number of Shares	Common Stock	Additional Paid-in Capital	Retained Earnings	Accumulated Other Comprehensive Income	Treasury Shares	Total Shareholders' Equity
Balance, January 31, Year 10	566,135	$ 56,613	$180,465	$3,728,482	$763,488	—	$4,729,048
(1) Net Income	—	—	—	1,291,024	—	—	1,291,024
(2) Cash Dividends	—	—	—	(158,889)	—	—	(158,889)
(3) Exercise of Stock Options	662	66	3,754	—	—	—	3,820
(4) Two-for-One Stock Split	568,797	56,680	(56,680)	—	—	—	—
(5) Shares Issued in Corporate Acquisition	10,366	1,037	273,659	—	—	—	274,696
(6) Purchase of Shares	—	—	—	—	—	$(25,826)	(25,826)
(7) Mark Securities to Market	—	—	—	—	(57,086)	—	(57,086)
Balance, January 31, Year 11	1,145,960	$114,396	$401,198	$4,860,617	$706,402	$(25,826)	$6,056,787

EXHIBIT 12.14	MERCK & CO. Analysis of Changes in Common Shareholders' Equity (all dollar amounts in millions) (Problem 39)

| | Common Stock[a] | | | Treasury Stock | | |
	Shares	Amount	Retained Earnings	Shares	Amount	Total
December 31, Year 2	1,483.168	$4,667.8	$10,942.0	(235.342)	$(4,470.8)	$11,139.0
Net Income	—	—	3,376.6	—	—	3,376.6
Dividends	—	—	(1,578.0)	—	—	(1,578.0)
Stock Options Exercised	0.295	74.7	—	14.104	294.3	369.0
Treasury Stock Purchased	—	—	—	(33.377)	(1,570.9)	(1,570.9)
December 31, Year 3	1,483.463	$4,742.5	$12,740.6	(254.615)	$(5,747.4)	$11,735.7
Net Income	—	—	3,870.5	—	—	3,870.5
Dividends	—	—	(1,793.4)	—	—	(1,793.4)
Stock Options Exercised	0.156	225.0	—	15.982	426.0	651.0
Treasury Stock Purchased	—	—	—	(38.384)	(2,493.3)	(2,493.3)
December 31, Year 4	1,483.619	$4,967.5	$14,817.7	(277.017)	$(7,814.7)	$11,970.5
Net Income	—	—	4,596.5	—	—	4,596.5
Dividends	—	—	(2,094.8)	—	—	(2,094.8)
Stock Options Exercised	0.307	286.5	—	14.183	427.6	714.1
Treasury Stock Purchased	—	—	—	(27.444)	(2,572.8)	(2,572.8)
December 31, Year 5	1,483.926	$5,254.0	$17,319.4	(290.278)	$(9,959.9)	$12,613.5

[a]Includes Additional Paid-in Capital.

d. The firm also has convertible bonds outstanding. Each convertible bond entitles the holder to trade in that bond for 10 shares. If holders convert the bonds, the number of shares would increase, which would tend to reduce earnings per share. On the other hand, the company would not have to pay interest and thus would have no interest expense on the bond because it would no longer be outstanding. This would tend to increase income and earnings per share. Assume that all holders of convertible bonds convert their bonds into shares. Compute a new net income figure (do not forget income tax effects on income of the interest saved) and a new earnings-per-share figure. Ignore the information about options and warrants and the calculations in parts **b** and **c** at this point.

e. Now consider all the previous calculations. Which sets of assumptions from parts **b**, **c**, and **d** lead to the lowest possible earnings per share when they are all made simultaneously? Compute a new earnings per share under the most restrictive set of assumptions about reductions in earnings per share.

f. Accountants publish several earnings-per-share figures for companies with complicated capital structures and complicated events during the year. *The Wall Street Journal*, however, publishes only one figure in its daily columns (where it reports the price-earnings ratio—the price of a share of stock divided by its earnings per share). Which of the figures computed previously for earnings per share do you think *The Wall Street Journal* should report as the earnings-per-share figure? Why?

41. Case for discussion: Value of stock options. (The text does not give an explicit answer to this question but provides a sufficient basis to enable students to discuss the question.) Below is an excerpt from an article from the *San Francisco Examiner*, a leading Silicon Valley newspaper, which appeared at the height of the controversy over the accounting for employee stock options.

EXHIBIT 12.15	LAYTON BALL CORPORATION Information on Capital Structure for Earnings-per-Share Calculations (Problem 40)

Assume the following data about the capital structure and earnings for the Layton Ball Corporation for the year:	
Number of Common Shares Outstanding throughout the Year	2,500 shares
Market Price per Common Share throughout the Year	$25
Options Outstanding during the Year:	
Number of Shares Issuable on Exercise of Options	1,000 shares
Exercise Price per Share	$15
Warrants Outstanding during the Year:	
Number of Shares Issuable on Exercise of Warrants	2,000 shares
Exercise Price per Share	$30
Convertible Bonds Outstanding:	
Number (issued 15 years ago)	100 bonds
Proceeds per Bond at Time of Issue (= par value)	$1,000
Shares of Common Issuable on Conversion (per bond)	10 shares
Coupon Rate (per year)	4 percent

For example, if StartUp Inc. recruits the brilliant software designer Joe Bithead . . . by offering him the option to buy 10,000 shares of StartUp's stock at its current price of a penny a share, what's the value of Joe's grant? If StartUp goes belly up, as 80 percent of new high-tech firms do, the grant is worthless. . . . If, on the other hand, after five years of struggle, StartUp manages to create a successful product and outperforms its competitors, the company's stock might sell for $10 a share on the public market. For a penny each, Joe can buy the 10,000 shares. . . . He unloads them in the market for a $100,000 profit.

The accounting question is, What cost, if any, does StartUp incur on Day 1 of the grant to Bithead of an option to acquire 10,000 shares five years hence for $0.01 per share? StartUp shares trade in public stock markets on the date of grant at $0.01 per share. Because the word *cost* has so many meanings (see *cost terminology* in the **Glossary**), make the question operational and specific by considering the following.

Imagine that you are the financial executive of StartUp and that Goldman Sachs offers to relieve you of the obligation to deliver the shares to Bithead. That is, Goldman will take a payment from you today and will deliver the shares to Bithead if he exercises the options but will do nothing otherwise, except keep your cash. How much are you willing to pay Goldman *today* to relieve you of your obligation to Bithead? That is, you pay Goldman now and they later deliver shares to Bithead if he exercises his options. No one can be sure of the exact answer, given the sketchy data, but which of the following ranges do you think most likely?

a. $0 to $10
b. $10 to $100
c. $100 to $1,000
d. $1,000 to $10,000
e. $10,000 to $100,000
f. Some other answer (indicate answer)

42. **Ethical issues in accounting for stock options.** Throughout the deliberations on the accounting for stock options during the last decade, managers of business firms, particularly in technology industries, have argued against the recognition of an expense for stock options. These managers emphasize the difficulty in measuring reliably the cost of stock options until employees actually exercise them. Yet the managers of these firms receive a substantial proportion of their compensation in the form of stock options. Discuss any ethical issues raised by the position of these managers.

appendix

Compound Interest: Concepts and Applications

Learning Objectives

1. Begin to master compound interest concepts of future value, present value, present discounted value of single sums and annuities, discount rates, interest rates, and internal rates of return on cash flows.

2. Apply those concepts to problems of finding the single payment or, in the context of annuities, the amount for a series of payments required to meet a specified objective.

3. Begin using perpetuity growth models in valuation analysis.

4. Learn how to find the interest rate to satisfy a stated set of conditions, such as to make the present value of a stream of cash flows equal a specified amount.

5. Begin to learn how to construct a problem of the types described above from a description of a business or an accounting situation.

O wners of cash, like owners of other scarce resources, can permit borrowers to rent the use of their cash for a period of time. Payment for the rental of cash differs little from other rental payments, such as those made to a landlord for the use of property or to a car rental agency for the use of a car. *Interest* is payment for the use of cash. Accounting must record transactions for both the lender and the borrower caused by lenders' providing cash to borrowers.

Accountants and managers deal with interest calculations for other reasons. Expenditures for an asset most often precede the receipts for services produced by that asset. Cash received later has smaller value than cash received sooner. The difference in timing affects the amount of profit from a firm's acquiring an asset. Amounts of cash received at different times have different values. Managers use interest calculations to make valid comparisons among amounts of cash paid or received at different times. Accountants and analysts use interest-related calculations involving present values to help them estimate the values of entire divisions and firms.

Contracts involving a series of cash payments over time, such as bonds, mortgages, notes, and leases, have **present values**. The present value of a series of payments represents the single amount of cash one would pay now to receive the entire series of future cash payments.

Compound Interest Concepts

Contracts typically state interest cost as a percentage of the amount borrowed per unit of time. Examples are 12 percent per year and 1 percent per month, which differ from one another. When the statement of interest cost does not explicitly state a period, then the rate applies to a year, so that "interest at the rate of 12 percent" means 12 percent per year. Some inflation-ravaged countries, such as Brazil, quote interest rates for a month.

The amount borrowed or lent is the **principal**. **Compound interest** means that the amount of interest earned during a period increases the principal, which is thus larger for the next interest period. For example, if you deposit $1,000 in a savings account that pays compound interest at the rate of 6 percent per year, you will earn $60 by the end of one year. If you do not withdraw the $60, then $1,060 will earn interest during the second year. During the second year, your principal of $1,060 will earn $63.60 in interest: $60 on the initial deposit of $1,000 and $3.60 on the $60 earned the first year. By the end of the second year, your principal will total $1,123.60.

When only the original principal earns interest during the entire life of the loan, the interest due at the time the borrower repays the loan is called **simple interest**. Simple interest calculations ignore interest on previously earned interest. If the lender may withdraw interest earned, or the borrower must make periodic payments with further interest charges for late payments, then compound interest techniques will still apply.

Simple Interest Rarely Applies to Economic Calculations but Accounting Often Uses it for Convenience

The use of simple interest calculations in accounting arises in the following way: if you borrow $10,000 at a rate of 12 percent per year but compute interest for any month as $100 (= $10,000 × 0.12 × 1/12), you are using a simple interest calculation.

Nearly all economic calculations, however, involve compound interest. When firms use simple interest to compute amounts for periods less than a year, some distortion of periodic numbers results, but no harm. Early periods get charged "too much" interest and later periods get charged "too little," but the distortions are minor.

Power of Compound Interest   The force, or effect, of compound interest exceeds the intuition of many people. For example, compounded annually at 8 percent, cash doubles itself in nine years. Put another way, if you invest $100 at 8 percent compounded annually, you will have $200 in nine years. If you were to invest $1 in the stock market at age 25 and leave it there for 45 years and the market increased for the next 45 years the way it has for the last 20 years, you would have over $150 by the time you reached age 70.

Problems involving compound interest generally fall into two groups with respect to time.

- First, we may want to know the future value of cash invested or loaned today, as in the two examples in the preceding paragraph.
- Second, we may want to know the present value, or today's value, of cash to be received or paid at later dates. (If I want to have $1,000,000 available at retirement, how much must I invest today?)

In addition, the accountant must sometimes find the interest rate implicit in specified payment streams. For example, assume a bank will lend you $1,000 in return for your promise to repay $91.70 per month for one year or $73.24 per month for 15 months. You might want to know that the implied rate of interest is 1.5 percent per month for the first offer and 1.2 percent per month for the second.

Future Value

If you invest $1 today at 12 percent compounded annually, it will grow to $1.12000 at the end of one year, $1.25440 at the end of two years, $1.40493 at the end of three years, and so on, according to the following formula:

$$F_n = P(1 + r)^n,$$

where

$$
\begin{aligned}
F_n &= \text{accumulation or future value} \\
P &= \text{one-time investment today} \\
r &= \text{interest rate per period} \\
n &= \text{number of periods from today}
\end{aligned}
$$

The amount F_n is the **future value** of the present payment, P, compounded at r percent per period for n periods. **Table 1** at the back of the book on page **604** shows the future values of $P = \$1$ for various numbers of periods and for various interest rates. Extracts from that table appear here in **Table A.1**.

Example Problems in Computing Future Value

Example 1   How much will $1,000 deposited today at 8 percent compounded annually grow to in 10 years?

Refer to **Table A.1**, 10-period row, 8-percent column. One dollar deposited today at 8 percent will grow to $2.15892; therefore, $1,000 will grow to $1,000 × $(1.08)^{10} = \$1,000 \times 2.15892 = \$2,158.92$.

Example 2   Macaulay Corporation deposits $10,000 in an expansion fund today. The fund will earn 12 percent per year. How much will the $10,000 grow to in 20 years if Macaulay leaves the entire fund and all interest earned on it deposited in the fund?

One dollar deposited today at 12 percent will grow to $9.64629 in 20 years. Therefore, $10,000 will grow to $96,463 (= $10,000 × 9.64629) in 20 years.

TABLE A.1	(Excerpt from Table 1) Future Value of $1 at 8 Percent and 12 Percent per Period $F_n = (1 + r)^n$

Number of Periods = n	Rate = r	
	8 Percent	12 Percent
1	1.08000	1.12000
2	1.16640	1.25440
3	1.25971	1.40493
10	2.15892	3.10585
20	4.66096	9.64629

Present Value

The preceding section developed the computation of the future value, F_n, of a sum of cash, P, deposited or invested today. You know P, and you calculate F_n. This section deals with the problems of calculating how much principal, P, you must invest today in order to have a specified amount, F_n, at the end of n periods. You know the future amount, F_n, the interest rate, r, and the number of periods, n; you want to find P. In order to have $1 one year from today when deposits earn 8 percent, you must invest P of $0.92593 today. That is, $F_1 = P(1.08)^1$ or $1 = \$0.92593 \times 1.08$. Because $F_n = P(1 + r)^n$, dividing both sides of the equation by $(1 + r)^n$ yields

$$\frac{F_n}{(1 + r)^n} = P,$$

or

$$P = \frac{F_n}{(1 + r)^n} = F_n (1 + r)^{-n}.$$

Present Value Terminology

The number $(1 + r)^{-n}$ equals the present value of $1 to be received after n periods when interest accrues at r percent per period. Accountants often use the words *discount* and **discounted value** in this context as follows. The discounted present value of $1 to be received n periods in the future is $(1 + r)^{-n}$ when the discount rate is r percent per period for n periods. The number r is the **discount rate**, and the number $(1 + r)^{-n}$ is the **discount factor** for n periods. A discount factor $(1 + r)^{-n}$ is the reciprocal, or inverse, of a number, $(1 + r)^{-n}$, in **Table A.1**. Portions of **Table 2** at the back of the book on page **605**, which shows discount factors or, equivalently, present values of $1 for various interest (or discount) rates for various numbers of periods, appear in **Table A.2**.

Example Problems in Computing Present Values

Example 3 What is the present value of $1 due 10 years from now if the interest rate (equivalently, the discount rate) r is 8 percent per year?

From **Table A.2**, 8-percent column, 10-period row, the present value of $1 to be received 10 periods hence at 8 percent is $0.46319.

Example 4 (This is **Example 14** in **Chapter 9**.) You issue a single-payment note that promises to pay $160,000 three years from today in exchange for used equipment. How much is that promise worth today if the discount rate appropriate for such notes is 12 percent per period? (An accountant needs to know the answer to the question to record the acquisition cost of the used equipment just acquired.)

One dollar paid three years hence discounted at 12 percent has a present value of $0.71178. Thus, the promise is worth $160,000 \times 0.71178 = \$113,885$. (Record the equipment at a cost of $113,885.)

TABLE A.2	(Excerpt from Table 2) Present Value of $1 at 8 Percent and 12 Percent per Period $P = F_n(1 + r)^{-n}$	

| Number of Periods = n | Rate = r | |
	8 Percent	12 Percent
1	0.92593	0.89286
2	0.85734	0.79719
3	0.79383	0.71178
10	0.46319	0.32197
20	0.21455	0.10367

Changing the Compounding Period: Nominal and Effective Rates

"Twelve percent, compounded annually" states the price for a loan; this means that interest increases, or converts to, principal once a year at the rate of 12 percent. Often, however, the price for a loan states that compounding is to take place more than once a year. A savings bank may advertise that it pays 6 percent, compounded quarterly. This means that at the end of each quarter the bank credits savings accounts with interest calculated at the rate of 1.5 percent (= 6 percent/4). The investor can withdraw the interest payment or leave it on deposit to earn more interest.

The sum of $10,000 invested today at 12 percent, compounded annually, grows to a future value one year later of $11,200. If the rate of interest is 12 percent compounded semiannually, the bank adds 6 percent interest to the principal every six months. At the end of the first six months, $10,000 will have grown to $10,600; that amount will grow to $10,600 × 1.06 = $11,236 by the end of the year. Twelve percent compounded semiannually is equivalent to 12.36 percent compounded annually. Suppose that the bank quotes interest as 12 percent, compounded quarterly. It will add an additional 3 percent of the principal every three months. By the end of the year, $10,000 will grow to $10,000 × $(1.03)^4$ = $10,000 × 1.12551 = $11,255. At 12 percent compounded monthly, $1 will grow to $1 × $(1.01)^{12}$ = $1.12683 and $10,000 will grow to $11,268. Thus, 12 percent compounded monthly provides the same ending amount as 12.68 percent compounded annually. Common terminology would say that *12 percent compounded monthly* has an "effective rate of 12.68 percent compounded annually" or is "equivalent to 12.68 percent compounded annually."

For a given nominal rate, such as the 12 percent in the examples above, the more often interest compounds, the higher the effective rate of interest paid. If a nominal rate, r, compounds m times per year, the effective rate equals $(1 + r/m)^m - 1$.

In practice, to solve problems that require computation of interest quoted at a nominal rate r percent per period compounded m times per period for n periods, use the tables for rate r/m and m × n periods. For example, 12 percent compounded quarterly for five years is equivalent to the rate found in the interest tables for r = 12/4 = 3 percent for m × n = 4 × 5 = 20 periods.

Some savings banks advertise that they compound interest daily or even continuously. The mathematics of calculus provides a mechanism for finding the effective rate when interest is compounded continuously. If interest compounds continuously at nominal rate r per year, the effective annual rate is $e^r - 1$, where e is the base of the natural logarithms. Six percent per year compounded continuously is equivalent to 6.1837 percent compounded annually. Twelve percent per year compounded continuously is equivalent to 12.75 percent compounded annually. Do not confuse the compounding period with the payment period. Some banks, for example, compound interest daily but pay interest quarterly. You can be sure that these banks do not employ clerks or even computers to calculate interest every day. They derive an equivalent effective rate to apply at the end of each quarter.

Example Problems in Changing the Compounding Period

Example 5 What is the future value five years hence of $600 invested at 16 percent compounded semiannually?

Sixteen percent compounded two times per year for five years is equivalent to 8 percent per period compounded for 10 periods. **Table A.1** shows the value of $F_{10} = (1.08)^{10}$ to be 2.15892. Six hundred dollars, then, would grow to $600 \times 2.15892 = \$1,295.35$.

Example 6   How much cash must you invest today at 16 percent compounded semiannually in order to yield \$10,000 in 10 years from today?

Sixteen percent compounded two times a year for 10 years is equivalent to 8 percent per period compounded for 20 periods. The present value, **Table A.2**, of \$1 received 20 periods hence at 8 percent per period is \$0.21455. That is, \$0.21455 invested today for 20 periods at an interest rate of 8 percent per period will grow to \$1. To have \$10,000 in 20 periods (10 years), you must invest \$2,146 (= \$10,000 \times \$0.21455) today.

Example 7   A local department store offers its customers credit and advertises its interest rate at 18 percent per year, compounded monthly at the rate of 1.5 percent per month. What is the effective annual interest rate?

One and one-half percent per month for 12 months is equivalent to $(1.015)^{12} - 1 = 19.562$ percent per year. See **Table 1**, 12-period row, 1.5-percent column, where the factor is 1.19562.

Under truth in lending legislation, lenders must disclose the effective annual interest rate, called the **APR** or *annual percentage rate*, to borrowers.

Example 8   If prices increased at the rate of 6 percent during each of two consecutive six-month periods, how much did prices increase during the entire year?

If a price index is 100.00 at the start of the year, it will be $100.00 \times (1.06)^2 = 112.36$ at the end of the year. The price change for the entire year is $(112.36/100.00) - 1 = 12.36$ percent.

Annuities

An annuity is a series of equal payments, one per period for periods equally spaced through time. Examples of annuities include monthly rental payments, semiannual corporate bond coupon payments, and annual payments to a lessor under a lease contract. Armed with an understanding of the tables for future and present values, you can solve any annuity problem. Annuities arise so often, however, and their solution is so tedious without special tables or calculator functions that annuity problems merit special study and the use of special tables or functions.

The common computer spreadsheet programs such as Microsoft Excel® include functions for annuity and other compound interest functions. Knowing which function to use to solve a given problem and which values for the variables to insert into the formula requires the same clear understanding required to use the tables. Hence, if you want to use spreadsheet functions, you must master the use of the tables in this book or gain equivalent knowledge.

Terminology for Annuities

An annuity involves equally spaced payments of equal amounts. If either the time between payments or the amounts of the payments vary, then the stream is not an annuity. An annuity with payments occurring at the end of each period is an **ordinary annuity (annuity in arrears)**. Semiannual corporate bonds usually promise that debt service (coupon) payments will be paid in arrears or, equivalently, that the first payment will not occur until after the bond has been outstanding for six months. An annuity with payments occurring at the beginning of each period is an *annuity due* or an *annuity in advance*. Rent paid at the beginning of each month is an annuity due. In a **deferred annuity**, the first payment occurs sometime later than the end of the first period.

Annuity payments can go on forever. Such annuities are *perpetuities*. Bonds that promise payments forever are *consols*. The British and the Canadian governments have issued consols from time to time. A perpetuity can be in arrears or in advance. The only difference between the two is the timing of the first payment.

Annuities can be confusing. Studying them is easier with a time line such as the one shown below.

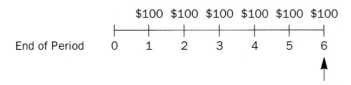

A time line marks the end of each period, numbers the period, shows the payments to be received or paid, and shows the time in which the accountant wants to value the annuity. The time line above represents an ordinary annuity (in arrears) for six periods of $100 to be valued at the end of period 6. The end of period 0 is *now*. The first payment occurs one period from now.

Ordinary Annuities (Annuities in Arrears)

The future values of ordinary annuities appear in **Table 3** at the back of the book on page **606**, portions of which **Table A.3** reproduces.

Consider an ordinary annuity for three periods at 12 percent. The time line for the future value of such an annuity is as follows:

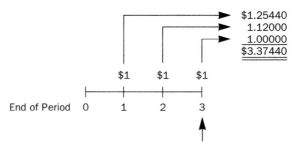

The $1 received at the end of the first period earns interest for two periods, so it grows to $1.25440 at the end of period 3 (see **Table A.1**). The $1 received at the end of the second period grows to $1.12000 by the end of period 3, and the $1 received at the end of period 3 is, of course, worth $1.00000 at the end of period 3. The entire annuity is worth $3.37440 at the end of period 3. This amount appears in **Table A.3** for the future value of an ordinary annuity for three periods at 12 percent. Factors for the future value of an annuity for a particular number of periods sum the factors for the future value of $1 for each of the periods. The future value of an ordinary annuity is as follows:

$$\begin{array}{ccc} \text{Future Value of} \\ \text{Ordinary Annuity} \end{array} = \begin{array}{c} \text{Periodic} \\ \text{Payment} \end{array} \times \begin{array}{c} \text{Factor for} \\ \text{the Future} \\ \text{Value of an} \\ \text{Ordinary Annuity} \end{array}$$

Thus,

$$\$3.37440 \quad = \quad \$1 \quad \times \quad 3.37440$$

TABLE A.3	(Excerpt from Table 3) Future Value of an Ordinary Annuity of $1 per Period at 8 Percent and 12 Percent

Number of Periods = n	Rate = r	
	8 Percent	**12 Percent**
1	1.00000	1.00000
2	2.08000	2.12000
3	3.24640	3.37440
5	5.86660	6.35285
10	14.48656	17.54874
20	45.76196	72.05244

Table 4 at the back of the book on page **607** shows the present value of ordinary annuities. **Table A.4** reproduces excerpts from **Table 4.**

The time line for the present value of an ordinary annuity of $1 per period for three periods, discounted at 12 percent, is as follows:

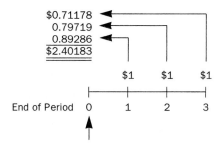

The $1 due at the end of period 1 has a present value of $0.89286, the $1 due at the end of period 2 has a present value of $0.79719, and the $1 due at the end of period 3 has a present value of $0.71178. Each of these numbers comes from **Table A.2**. The present value of the annuity sums these individual present values, $2.40183, shown in **Table A.4**.

The present value of an ordinary annuity for *n* periods is the sum of the present value of $1 received one period from now plus the present value of $1 received two periods from now, and so on until we add on the present value of $1 received *n* periods from now. The present value of an ordinary annuity is as follows:

$$\begin{matrix}\text{Present Value} \\ \text{of an} \\ \text{Ordinary Annuity}\end{matrix} = \begin{matrix}\text{Periodic} \\ \text{Payment}\end{matrix} \times \begin{matrix}\text{Factor for} \\ \text{the Present} \\ \text{Value of an} \\ \text{Ordinary Annuity}\end{matrix}$$

Thus,

$$\$2.40183 \quad = \quad \$1 \quad \times \quad 2.40183$$

Example Problems Involving Ordinary Annuities

Example 9   You plan to invest $1,000 at the end of each of the next 10 years in a savings account. The savings account accumulates interest of 8 percent compounded annually. What will be the balance in the savings account at the end of 10 years?

The time line for this problem is as follows:

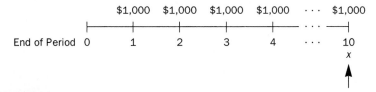

TABLE A.4	(Excerpt from Table 4) Present Value of an Ordinary Annuity of $1 per Period at 8 Percent and 12 Percent

| Number of | Rate = *r* | |
Periods = *n*	8 Percent	12 Percent
1	0.92593	0.89286
2	1.78326	1.69005
3	2.57710	2.40183
5	3.99271	3.60478
10	6.71008	5.65022
20	9.81815	7.46944

The symbol x denotes the amount you must calculate. **Table A.3** indicates that the factor for the future value of an annuity at 8 percent for 10 periods is 14.48656. Thus,

Future Value of an Ordinary Annuity	=	Periodic Payment	×	Factor for the Future Value of an Ordinary Annuity
x	=	$1,000	×	14.48656
x	=	$14,487		

Example 10   You want to receive $600 every six months, starting six months hence, for the next five years. How much must you invest today if the funds accumulate at the rate of 8 percent compounded semiannually?

The time line is as follows:

The factor from **Table 4** for the present value of an annuity at 4 percent (= 8 percent per year/2 semiannual periods per year) for 10 (= 2 periods per year × 5 years) periods is 8.11090. Thus,

Present Value of an Ordinary Annuity	=	Periodic Payment	×	Factor for the Present Value of an Ordinary Annuity
x	=	$600	×	8.11090
x	=	$4,866.54		

If you invest $4,866.54 today, the principal plus interest compounded on the principal will provide sufficient funds that you can withdraw $600 every six months for the next five years.

Example 11   (This example also appears on page **396** in **Chapter 9** as the Western Company mortgage problem.) A company borrows $125,000 from a savings and loan association. The interest rate on the loan is 12 percent compounded semiannually. The company agrees to repay the loan in equal semiannual installments over the next five years, with the first payment six months from now. What is the required semiannual payment?

The time line is as follows:

This problem resembles **Example 10** because both involve periodic future payments discounted to today. **Example 10** gives the periodic payments and asks for the present value. **Example 11** gives the present value and asks for the periodic payment. **Table 4** indicates that the present value of an annuity at 6 percent (= 12 percent per year/2 semiannual periods per year) for 10 periods (=2 periods per year × 5 years) is 7.36009. Thus,

Present Value of an Ordinary Annuity	=	Periodic Payment	×	Factor for the Present Value of an Ordinary Annuity
$125,000	=	x	×	7.36009
x	=	$\dfrac{\$125,000}{7.36009}$		
x	=	$16,983		

To find the periodic payment, divide the present value amount of $125,000 by the present value factor. (**Exhibit 9.2** presents the amortization table for this loan. That exhibit shows the amount of each semiannual payment as $17,000, rather than $16,983, and the last payment as $16,781, less than $17,000, to compensate for the extra $17 paid in each of the preceding periods and the interest on those amounts.)

Example 12 (This example also appears on page **441** in **Chapter 10** as the Food Barn lease problem.) A company signs a lease acquiring the right to use property for three years. The company will make lease payments of $19,709 annually at the end of this and the next two years. The discount rate is 15 percent per year. What is the present value of the lease payments?

The time line is as follows:

The factor from **Table 4** for the present value of an annuity at 15 percent for three periods is 2.28323. Thus,

$$
\begin{array}{ccccc}
\text{Present Value} & & & & \text{Factor for} \\
\text{of an} & = & \text{Periodic} & \times & \text{the Present} \\
\text{Ordinary Annuity} & & \text{Payment} & & \text{Value of an} \\
& & & & \text{Ordinary Annuity} \\
x & = & \$19{,}709 & \times & 2.28323 \\
x & = & \$45{,}000 & &
\end{array}
$$

The Food Barn example in **Chapter 10** gives the cost of the equipment, $45,000, and we compute the periodic rental payment with an annuity factor. Thus,

$$
\begin{array}{ccccc}
\text{Present Value} & & & & \text{Factor for} \\
\text{of an} & = & \text{Periodic} & \times & \text{the Present} \\
\text{Ordinary Annuity} & & \text{Payment} & & \text{Value of an} \\
& & & & \text{Ordinary Annuity} \\
\$45{,}000 & = & x & \times & 2.28323 \\
x & = & \dfrac{\$45{,}000}{2.28323} & & \\
x & = & \$19{,}709 & &
\end{array}
$$

Example 13 A company promises to make annual payments to a pension fund at the end of each of the next 30 years. The payments must have a present value today of $100,000. What must the annual payment be if the fund expects to earn interest at the rate of 8 percent per year?

The time line is as follows:

$$
\begin{array}{ccccccc}
& x & x & x & x & \cdots & x \\
\vdash\!\!-\!\!-\!\!+\!\!-\!\!+\!\!-\!\!+\!\!-\!\!+\!\!-\!\!\cdots\!\!-\!\dashv \\
\text{End of Period} \quad 0 & 1 & 2 & 3 & 4 & \cdots & 30 \\
\$100{,}000 & & & & & &
\end{array}
$$

Table 4 indicates that the factor for the present value of $1 paid at the end of the next 30 periods at 8 percent per period is 11.25778. Thus,

$$
\begin{array}{ccccc}
\text{Present Value} & & & & \text{Factor for} \\
\text{of an} & = & \text{Periodic} & \times & \text{the Present} \\
\text{Ordinary Annuity} & & \text{Payment} & & \text{Value of an} \\
& & & & \text{Ordinary Annuity} \\
\$100{,}000 & = & x & \times & 11.25778 \\
x & = & \dfrac{\$100{,}000}{11.25778} & & \\
x & = & \$8{,}883 & &
\end{array}
$$

Example 14   Mr. Mason is 62 years old. He wants to invest equal amounts on his 63rd, 64th, and 65th birthdays so that starting on his 66th birthday he can withdraw $50,000 on each birthday for 10 years. His investments will earn 8 percent per year. How much should he invest on the 63rd through 65th birthdays?

The time line for this problem is as follows:

At 65, Mr. Mason needs to have accumulated a fund equal to the present value of an annuity of $50,000 per period for 10 periods, discounted at 8 percent per period. The factor from **Table A.4** for 8 percent and 10 periods is 6.71008. Thus,

$$
\begin{array}{ccc}
\text{Present Value} & & \text{Factor for} \\
\text{of an} & = \text{Periodic} \times & \text{the Present} \\
\text{Ordinary Annuity} & \text{Payment} & \text{Value of an} \\
& & \text{Ordinary Annuity} \\
x & = \$50,000 \times & 6.71008 \\
x & = \$335,500 &
\end{array}
$$

The time line now appears as follows:

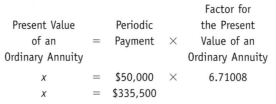

The question now becomes, how much must Mr. Mason invest on his 63rd, 64th, and 65th birthdays to accumulate to a fund of $335,500 on his 65th birthday? The factor for the future value of an annuity for three periods at 8 percent is 3.24640. Thus,

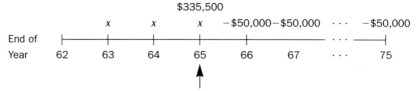

$$
\begin{array}{ccc}
\text{Future Value} & & \text{Factor for} \\
\text{of an} & = \text{Periodic} \times & \text{the Future} \\
\text{Ordinary Annuity} & \text{Payment} & \text{Value of an} \\
& & \text{Ordinary Annuity} \\
\$335,500 & = x \times & 3.24640 \\
x & = \dfrac{\$335,500}{3.24640} & \\
x & = \$103,350 &
\end{array}
$$

The solution above expresses all calculations in terms of equivalent amounts on Mr. Mason's 65th birthday. That is, the present value of an annuity of $50,000 per period for 10 periods at 8 percent equals the future value of an annuity of $103,350 per period for three periods at 8 percent, and both of these amounts equal $335,500. You could work this problem by selecting any common time period between Mr. Mason's 62nd and 75th birthdays.

One alternative expresses all calculations in terms of equivalent amounts on Mr. Mason's 62nd birthday. To solve the problem in this way, first find the present value on Mr. Mason's 65th birthday of an annuity of $50,000 per period for 10 periods ($335,500 = $50,000 × 6.71008). Discount $335,500 back three periods using **Table 2** for present value of single payments: $266,330 = $335,500 × 0.79383. The result is the present value of the payments to be made to Mr. Mason measured as of his 62nd birthday. Then, find the amounts that Mr. Mason must invest on his 63rd, 64th, and 65th birthdays to have a present value on his 62nd birthday equal to $266,330. The calculation is as follows:

$$
\begin{array}{ccc}
\text{Present Value} & & \text{Factor for} \\
\text{of an} & = \text{Periodic} \times & \text{the Present} \\
\text{Ordinary Annuity} & \text{Payment} & \text{Value of an} \\
& & \text{Ordinary Annuity} \\
\$266,330 & = x \times & 2.57710 \\
x & = \$103,350 &
\end{array}
$$

We computed the same amount, $103,350, above.

A periodic payment to be received forever is a **perpetuity**. Future values of perpetuities are undefined. One dollar to be received at the end of every period discounted at rate r percent has a present value of $\$1/r$. Observe what happens in the expression for the present value of an ordinary annuity of $\$A$ per payment as n, the number of payments, approaches infinity:

$$P_A = \frac{A[1 - (1 + r)^{-n}]}{r}$$

As n approaches infinity, $(1 + r)^{-n}$ approaches 0, so that P_A approaches $A(1/r)$. If the first payment of the perpetuity occurs now, the present value is $A[1 + 1/r]$.

Examples of Perpetuities

Example 15   The Canadian government offers to pay $30 every six months forever in the form of a perpetual bond. What is that bond worth if the discount rate is 10 percent compounded semiannually?

Ten percent compounded semiannually is equivalent to 5 percent per six-month period. If the first payment occurs six months from now, the present value is $30/0.05 = $600. If the first payment occurs today, the present value is $30 + $600 = $630.

Example 16   Every two years, the Bank of Tokyo gives ¥5 million (Japanese yen) to the university to provide a scholarship for an entering student in a two-year business administration course. If the university credits 6 percent per year to its investment accounts, how much must the bank give to the university to provide such a scholarship every two years forever, starting two years hence?

A perpetuity in arrears assumes one payment at the end of each period. Here, the period is two years. Six percent compounded once a year over two years is equivalent to a rate of $(1.06)^2 - 1 = 0.12360$ or 12.36 percent compounded once per two-year period. Consequently, the present value of the perpetuity paid in arrears every two years is ¥40.45 (= ¥5/0.1236). A gift of ¥40.45 million will provide a ¥5 million scholarship forever. If the university will award the first scholarship now, the gift must be ¥45.45 (= ¥40.45 + ¥5.00) million.

Example 17   (This example illustrates the **relief from royalty method** for valuing trademarks.) Burns, Philp & Company (B-P) wants to value its trademark for Fleischmann's Yeast using the relief from royalty method. B-P estimates that sales of the product will continue at the rate of $100 million per year in perpetuity and that if it had to pay a royalty to another firm that owned the trademark, it would have to pay 4 percent of sales at the end of each year. It uses a discount rate of 10 percent per year in computing present values. What is the value of the trademark under these assumptions?

If B-P paid royalties of 4 percent of sales, these would total $4 (= 0.04 × $100) million per year, in perpetuity. The present value of a perpetual stream of payments of $4 million per year, discounted at 10 percent per year, is $40 (= $4/0.10) million. Under these assumptions, the trademark has a value of $40 million.

B-P, more realistically, might estimate that sales will grow each year by, say, 2 percent more than the rate of inflation. When one assumes that a perpetuity's payments, which start at p per period, $4 million in this example, will grow at a constant rate g, 2 percent in this example, then the value of the perpetuity is $p/(r - g) = \$4/(0.10 - 0.02) = \$50$ million in this example.

The next three examples all refer to the data in **Exhibit 12.2**, where we evaluate the six individual activities of Bernard Company to find the value of the entire firm.

Example 18   Bernard Company's Activity 1 generates $100 per year, with the cash flow at the end of the year, indefinitely. The present value of this activity is $1,000 (= $100/ 0.10). Investors sometimes call this process of deriving market value from a series of future cash flows *capitalizing earnings*. The analyst might say that the earnings of $100 have a *price/earnings ratio* of 10 or that the earnings "deserve [or carry] a multiple of 10." The price/earnings ratio for a perpetuity is the reciprocal of the discount rate. In the example, where the discount rate is 10 percent per period, the price/earnings ratio is 10.

Example 19   Bernard Company's second activity generates $30 at the end of the first year, and a cash flow that grows by 6 percent per year thereafter. The present value of this activity is $750 [= $30/(0.10 − 0.06)]: If the cash flow starts at $1 per year and grows at rate *g* per year, then the present value of the growing cash flows is $1/(*r* − *g*). This is the **perpetuity with growth** formula. This example and the formula for it assume the cash flows and growth last *forever*. *Forever* is a long time. Sometimes students derive silly results from assuming *forever*, particularly when the growth rate is large. We have seen analysts project growth rates so much larger than the growth of the U.S. economy that after 50 or so years, the analyzed company projects sales larger than the entire U.S. gross domestic product. Use these perpetuity-based, arithmetic tools to learn and to make approximations, but do not expect firms to grow *forever* at high growth rates.

Example 20   Bernard Company's third activity is cyclic, generating $115 per year at the end of each odd-numbered year. The present value of this activity is $602.38, derived as follows. Think of this series of cash flows as a perpetuity with $115 per period, but each period is two years long. Then, when the discount rate is 10 percent per year, the discount rate for a two-year period must be 21 percent [= (1.10 × 1.10) − 1]. The cash flows from Year 2 onwards have present value of $547.62 (= $115/0.21) at the start of Year 2 and present value of $497.84 (= $547.62/1.10) at the start of Year 1. The $115 cash flow received at the end of Year 1 has present value of $104.54 (= $115/1.10) at the start of Year 1. The entire series has present value of $602.38 (= $497.84 + $104.54) at the start of Year 1.

The preceding examples computed a future value or a present value given the interest rate and stated cash payment. Or, they computed the required payments given their known future value or

Implicit Interest Rates: Finding Internal Rates of Return

their known present value. In other calculations, however, you know the present or the future value and the periodic payments; you must find the implicit interest rate. For example, **Chapter 9** illustrates a case in which you know that the cash price of some equipment is $10,500 and that the firm acquired the asset in exchange for a single-payment note. The note has a face value of $16,000 and matures in three years. To compute interest expense over the three-year period, you must know the **implicit interest rate (internal rate of return)**. The time line for this problem is as follows:

The implicit interest rate is *r*, such that

(A.1) $$0 = \$10{,}500 - \frac{\$16{,}000}{(1 + r)^3}$$

(A.2) $$\$10{,}500 = \frac{\$16{,}000}{(1 + r)^3}$$

That is, the present value of $16,000 discounted three periods at *r* percent per period is $10,500. The present value of all current and future cash flows discounted at *r* per period must be zero. In general, to find such an *r* requires trial and error. In cases where *r* appears only in one term, as here, you can find *r* analytically. Here *r* = ($16,000/$10,500)^{1/3} − 1 = 0.1507 = 15.1 percent.

The general procedure is *finding the internal rate of return of a series of cash flows*. The internal rate of return of a series of cash flows is the discount rate that makes the net present values of that series of cash flows equal to zero. The steps in finding the internal rate of return are as follows:

1. Make an educated guess, called the "trial rate," at the internal rate of return. If you have no idea what to guess, try zero.
2. Calculate the present value of all the cash flows (including the one at the end of Year 0).

3. If the present value of the cash flows is zero, stop. The current trial rate is the internal rate of return.
4. If the amount found in step **2** is less than zero, try a larger interest rate as the trial rate and go back to step **2**.
5. If the amount found in step **2** is greater than zero, try a smaller interest rate as the new trial rate and go back to step **2**.

The iterations below illustrate the process for the example in **Equation A.1**.

| | | Net Present Value: | |
Iteration Number	Trial Rate = r	Right-Hand Side of Equation A.1
1	0.0%	−$5,500
2	10.0	−1,521
3	15.0	−20
4	15.5	116
5	15.2	34
6	15.1	7

With a trial rate of 15.1 percent, the right-hand side is close enough to zero that you can use 15.1 percent as the implicit interest rate in making the adjusting entries for interest expense. Continued iterations would find trial rates even closer to the true rate, which is about 15.0739 percent.

Finding the internal rate of return for a series of cash flows can be tedious; you should not attempt it unless you have at least a calculator. An exponential feature, which allows the computation of $(1 + r)$ raised to various powers, helps. Computer spreadsheets, such as Microsoft Excel®, have a built-in function to find the internal rate of return.

Example Problem Involving Implicit Interest Rates

Example 21 Alexis Company acquires a machine with a cash price of $10,500. It pays for the machine by giving a note for $12,000, promising to make payments equal to 7 percent of the face value, $840 ($= 0.07 \times \$12,000$), at the end of each of the next three years and a single payment of $12,000 in three years. What is the interest rate implicit in the loan?

The time line for this problem is as follows:

$10,500   −$840   −$840   −$12,840

End of Year   0   1   2   3

The implicit interest rate is r, such that

(A.3) $$\$10,500 = \frac{\$840}{(1 + r)} + \frac{\$840}{(1 + r)^2} + \frac{\$12,840}{(1 + r)^3}$$

Compare this formulation to that in **Equation A.1**. Note that the left-hand side equals 0 in **Equation A.1** but not in **Equation A.3**. You may use any left-hand side that you find convenient for the particular context.

The iteration process finds an internal rate of return of 12.2 percent to the nearest tenth of 1 percent:

Iteration Number	Trial Rate	Right-Hand Side of Equation A.3
1	7.0%	$12,000
2	15.0	9,808
3	11.0	10,827
4	13.0	10,300
5	12.0	10,559
6	12.5	10,428
7	12.3	10,480

8	12.2	10,506
9	12.1	10,532

Accountants typically use one of four kinds of compound interest calculations: (1) the present value or (2) the future value of (3) a single payment or of (4) a series of payments. In working annuity problems, you may find a time line helpful in deciding the particular kind of annuity involved. Computer spreadsheet programs have a built-in function to perform the computations described in this appendix.

Present value	APR
Principal	Ordinary annuity (annuity in arrears)
Compound interest	Deferred annuity
Simple interest	Perpetuity
Future value	Perpetuity with growth
Discounted value	Relief from royalty method
Discount rate	Implicit interest rate (internal rate of return)
Discount factor	

QUESTIONS

1. Review the terms and concepts listed above in Key Terms and Concepts.
2. What is interest?
3. Distinguish between simple and compound interest.
4. Distinguish between the discounted present value of a stream of future payments and their net present value. If there is no distinction, then so state.
5. Distinguish between an annuity due and an ordinary annuity.
6. Describe the implicit interest rate for a series of cash flows and a procedure for finding it.
7. Does the present value of a given amount to be paid in 10 years increase or decrease if the interest rate increases? Suppose that the amount is due in 5 years? 20 years? Does the present value of an annuity to be paid for 10 years increase or decrease if the discount rate decreases? Suppose that the annuity is for 5 years? 20 years?
8. Rather than pay you $1,000 a month for the next 20 years, the person who injured you in an automobile accident is willing to pay a single amount now to settle your claim for injuries. Would you rather use an interest rate of 6 percent or 12 percent in computing the present value of the lump-sum settlement? Comment or explain.
9. The perpetuity with growth formula involves several assumptions. Which one seems least plausible?

SHORT EXERCISES

Short exercises 10 through 15 involve calculations of present and future value for single payments and for annuities. To make the exercises more realistic, we do not give specific guidance with each individual exercise.

10. Mr. Altgeldt has $5,000 to invest. He wants to know how much it will amount to if he invests it at the following rates:
   a. 6 percent per year for 21 years
   b. 8 percent per year for 33 years
11. Mme. Barefield wishes to have $150,000 at the end of 8 years. How much must she invest today to accomplish this purpose if the interest rate is

    a. 6 percent per year?
    b. 8 percent per year?
12. Mr. Case plans to set aside $4,000 each year, the first payment to be made on January 1, 2005, and the last on January 1, 2010. How much will he have accumulated by January 1, 2010, if the interest rate is
    a. 6 percent per year?
    b. 8 percent per year?
13. Ms. Namura wants to have ¥45 million on her 65th birthday. She asks you to tell her how much she must deposit on each birthday from her 58th to 65th, inclusive, in order to receive this amount. Assume the following interest rates:
    a. 8 percent per year
    b. 12 percent per year
14. If Mr. Enmetti invests 90,000 on June 1 of each year from 2001 to 2011 inclusive, how much will he have accumulated on June 1, 2012 (note that one year elapses after last payment) if the interest rate is
    a. 5 percent per year?
    b. 10 percent per year?
15. Ms. Fleming has £145,000 with which she purchases an annuity on February 1, 2006. The annuity consists of six annual receipts, the first to be received on February 1, 2007. How much will she receive in each payment? Assume the following interest rates:
    a. 8 percent per year
    b. 12 percent per year

EXERCISES

16. In the preceding **Short Exercises 10** through **15**, you computed a number. To do so, first you must decide on the appropriate factor from the tables, and then you use that factor in the appropriate calculation. Notice that you could omit the last step. You could write an arithmetic expression showing the factor you want to use without actually copying down the number and doing the arithmetic. For example, the notation $T(i, p, r)$ means Table i (1, 2, 3, or 4), row p (periods 1 to 20, 22, 24 . . . , 40, 45, 50, 100), and column r (interest rates from 1/2 percent up to 20 percent). Thus, $T(3, 16, 12)$ would be the factor in **Table 3** for 16 periods and an interest rate of 12 percent per period, which is 42.75328. Using this notation, you can write an expression for any compound interest problem. A clerk or a computer can evaluate the expression.
    You can check that you understand this notation by observing that the following are true statements:

$$T(1, 20, 8) = 4.66096$$
$$T(2, 12, 5) = 0.55684$$
$$T(3, 16, 12) = 42.75328$$
$$T(4, 10, 20) = 4.19247$$

    In the following questions, write an expression for the answer using the notation introduced here, but do not attempt to evaluate the expression.
    a. Work the **a** parts of **Exercises 10** through **15**.
    b. How might your instructor use this notation to write examination questions on compound interest without having to supply you with tables?
17. **Effective interest rate.** State the rate per period and the number of periods in the following:
    a. 12 percent per year, for 5 years, compounded annually
    b. 12 percent per year, for 5 years, compounded semiannually
    c. 12 percent per year, for 5 years, compounded quarterly
    d. 12 percent per year, for 5 years, compounded monthly

    Exercises 18 through 26 involve calculations of present and future value for single payments and for annuities. To make the exercises more realistic, we do not give specific guidance with each individual exercise.
18. Compute the future value of the following:
    a. $100 invested for 5 years at 4 percent compounded annually
    b. $500 invested for 15 periods at 2 percent compounded once per period
    c. $200 invested for 8 years at 3 percent compounded semiannually

d. $2,500 invested for 14 years at 8 percent compounded quarterly

e. $600 invested for 3 years at 12 percent compounded monthly

19. Compute the present value of the following:

   a. $100 due in 30 years at 4 percent compounded annually

   b. $250 due in 8 years at 8 percent compounded quarterly

   c. $1,000 due in 2 years at 12 percent compounded monthly

20. Compute the amount (future value) of an ordinary annuity (an annuity in arrears) of the following:

   a. 13 rental payments of $100 at 1 percent per period

   b. 8 rental payments of $850 at 6 percent per period

   c. 28 rental payments of $400 at 4 percent per period

21. Mr. Grady agrees to lease a certain property for 10 years, at the following annual rental, payable in advance:

Years 1 and 2—$1,000 per year

Years 3 to 6—$2,000 per year

Years 7 to 10—$2,500 per year

What single immediate sum will pay all of these rents, discounted at

   a. 6 percent per year?

   b. 8 percent per year?

   c. 10 percent per year?

22. To establish a fund that will provide a scholarship of $3,000 per year indefinitely, with the first award to occur now, how much must a donor deposit if the fund earns

   a. 6 percent per period?

   b. 8 percent per period?

23. Consider the scholarship fund in the preceding question. Suppose that the first scholarship award occurs one year from now and the donor wants the scholarship to grow by 2 percent per year. How much should the donor deposit if the fund earns

   a. 6 percent per period?

   b. 8 percent per period?

   Suppose that the first scholarship award occurs five years from now but is to grow at 2 percent per year after Year 5, the time of the first $3,000 award. How much should the donor deposit if the fund earns

   c. 6 percent per year?

   d. 8 percent per year?

24. An old agreement obliges the state to help a rural county maintain a bridge by paying $60,000 now and every two years thereafter forever toward the expenses. The state wants to discharge its obligation by paying a single sum to the county now for the payment due and all future payments. How much should the state pay the county if the discount rate is

   a. 8 percent per year?

   b. 12 percent per year?

25. Find the interest rate implicit in a loan of $100,000 that the borrower discharges with two annual installments of $55,307 each, paid at the end of Years 1 and 2.

26. A single-payment note promises to pay $140,493 in three years. The issuer exchanges the note for equipment having a fair market value of $100,000. The exchange occurs three years before the maturity date on the note. What interest rate will the accounting impute for the single-payment note?

27. A single-payment note promises $67,280 at maturity. The issuer of the note exchanges it for land with a fair market value of $50,000. The exchange occurs two years before the maturity date on the note.

   a. What interest rate will the accounting impute for this single-payment note?

   b. Using the imputed interest rate (sometimes called the *implicit interest* rate), construct an amortization schedule for the note. Show book value of the note at the start of each year, interest for each year, the amount reducing or increasing book value each year, and book value at the end of the year.

28. **Finding implicit interest rates; constructing amortization schedules.** Berman Company purchased a plot of land for possible future development. The land had fair market value of $86,000. Berman Company gave a three-year interest-bearing note. The note had face value of $100,000 and provided for interest at a stated rate of 8 percent. The note requires payments of

$8,000 at the end of each of three years, the last payment coinciding with the maturity of the note's face value of $100,000.

a. What is the interest rate implicit in the note, accurate to the nearest tenth of 1 percent?

b. Construct an amortization schedule for the note for each year. Show the book value of the note at the start of the year, interest for the year, payment for the year, amount reducing or increasing the book value of the note for each payment, and the book value of the note at the end of each year. Use the interest rate found in part **a**. See **Exhibit 10.3** for an example of an amortization schedule.

29. **Find equivalent annual rate offered for purchase discounts.** The terms of sale "2/10, net/30" mean that the buyer can take a discount of 2 percent from gross invoice price by paying the invoice within 10 days; otherwise, the buyer must pay the full amount within 30 days.

a. Write an expression for the implied annual rate of interest being offered by viewing the entire discount as interest for funds received sooner rather than later. (Note that by not taking the discount, the buyer borrows 98 percent of the gross invoice price for 20 days.)

b. The tables at the back of the book do not permit the exact evaluation of the expression derived in part **a**. The rate of interest implied is 44.59 percent per year. Use the tables to convince yourself that this astounding (to some) answer must be close to correct.

PROBLEMS AND CASES

Problems 30 through 44 involve using future value and present value techniques, including perpetuities, to solve a variety of realistic problems. We give no hints as to the specific calculation with the problems.

30. An oil-drilling company figures that it must spend $30,000 for an initial supply of drill bits and that it must spend $10,000 every month to replace the worn-out bits. What is the present value of the cost of the bits if the company plans to be in business indefinitely and discounts payments at 1 percent per month?

31. If you promise to leave $35,000 on deposit at the Dime Savings Bank for four years, the bank will give you a new large, flat-screen Sony TV today and your $35,000 back at the end of four years. How much are you paying today for the TV, in effect, if the bank pays other customers 8 percent interest compounded quarterly (2 percent paid four times per year)?

32. When Mr. Shafer died, his estate after taxes amounted to $300,000. His will provided that Mrs. Shafer would receive $24,000 per year starting immediately from the principal of the estate and that the balance of the principal would pass to the Shafers' children upon Mrs. Shafer's death. The state law governing this estate provided for a dower option. If Mrs. Shafer elects the dower option, she renounces the will and can have one-third of the estate in cash now. The remainder will then pass immediately to their children. Mrs. Shafer wants to maximize the present value of her bequest. Should she take the annuity or elect the dower option if she will receive five payments and discounts payments at

a. 8 percent per year?

b. 12 percent per year?

(Note this problem explicitly states that Mrs. Shafer will receive five payments. In reality, life expectancy is uncertain. The correct calculation combines a mortality table with the present value tables. Actuaries deal with such calculations.)

33. Mrs. Heileman occasionally drinks beer. (Guess which brand.) She consumes one case in 20 weeks. She can buy beer in disposable cans for $25.20 per case or for $24.00 per case of returnable bottles if she pays a $3.00 refundable deposit at the time of purchase. If her discount rate is 1/2 percent per week, how much in present value dollars does she save by buying the returnables and thereby losing the use of the $3.00 deposit for 20 weeks?

34. When General Electric Company first introduced the Lucalox ceramic, screw-in light bulb, the bulb cost three and one-half times as much as an ordinary bulb but lasted five times as long. An ordinary bulb cost $1.00 and lasted about eight months. If a firm has a discount rate of 12 percent compounded three times a year, how much would it save in present-value dollars by using one Lucalox bulb?

35. Oberweis Dairy switched from delivery trucks with regular gasoline engines to ones with diesel engines. The diesel trucks cost $2,000 more than the ordinary gasoline trucks but $600 per year less to operate. Assume that Oberweis saves the operating costs at the end of each month. If Oberweis uses a discount rate of 1 percent per month, approximately how many months, at a minimum, must the diesel trucks remain in service for the switch to be sensible?

36. On January 1, Year 1, assume that Levi Strauss opened a new textile plant to produce synthetic fabrics. The plant is on leased land; 20 years remain on the nonrenewable lease.

The cost of the plant was $20 million. Net cash flow to be derived from the project is estimated to be $3,000,000 per year. The company does not normally invest in such projects unless the anticipated yield is at least 12 percent.

On December 31, Year 1, the company finds cash flows from the plant to be $2,800,000 for the year. On the same day, farm experts predict cotton production will be unusually low for the next two years. Levi Strauss estimates the resulting increase in demand for synthetic fabrics will boost cash flows to $3,500,000 for each of the next two years. Subsequent years' estimates remain unchanged. Ignore tax considerations.

a. Calculate the present value of the future expected cash flows from the plant when it opened.

b. What is the present value of the plant on January 1, Year 2, immediately after the re-estimation of future cash flows?

c. On January 2, Year 2, the day following the cotton production news release, a competitor announces plans to build a synthetic fabrics plant to open in three years. Levi Strauss keeps its Year 2 to Year 4 estimates but reduces the estimated annual cash flows for subsequent years to $2,000,000. What is the value of Levi Strauss's present plant on January 1, Year 2, after the new projections?

d. On January 2, Year 2, an investor contacts Levi Strauss about purchasing a 20 percent share of the plant. If the investor expects to earn at least a 12 percent annual return on the investment, what is the maximum amount that the investor can pay? Assume that the investor and Levi Strauss both know all relevant information and use the same estimates of annual cash flows.

37. **Finding implicit interest rates (truth-in-lending laws reduce the type of deception suggested by this problem).** Friendly Loan Company advertises that it is willing to lend money for five years at the low rate of 8 percent per year. A potential borrower discovers that a five-year, $10,000 loan requires that the borrower pay the 8 percent interest in advance, with interest deducted from the loan proceeds. The borrower will collect $6,000 [= $10,000 − (= 5 × 0.08 × $10,000)] in cash and must repay the "$10,000" loan in five annual installments of $2,000, one each at the end of the next five years.

Compute the effective interest rate implied by these loan terms.

38. **Deriving net present value of cash flows for decision to dispose of asset.** Suppose that yesterday Black & Decker Company purchased and installed a made-to-order machine tool for fabricating parts for small appliances. The machine cost $100,000. Today, Square D Company offers a machine tool that will do exactly the same work but costs only $50,000. Assume that the discount rate is 12 percent, that both machines will last for five years, that Black & Decker will depreciate both machines on a straight-line basis with no salvage value for tax purposes, that the income tax rate is and will continue to be 40 percent, and that Black & Decker earns sufficient income that it can use any loss from disposing of or depreciating the "old" machine to offset other taxable income.

How much, at a minimum, must the "old" machine fetch on resale at this time to make purchasing the new machine worthwhile?

39. **Computation of present value of cash flows; untaxed acquisition, no change in tax basis of assets.** The balance sheet of Lynch Company shows net assets of $100,000 and owners' equity of $100,000. The assets are all depreciable assets with remaining lives of 20 years. The income statement for the year shows revenues of $700,000, depreciation of $50,000 (= $1,000,000 ÷ 20 years), no other expenses, income taxes of $260,000 (40 percent of pretax income of $650,000), and net income of $390,000.

Bages Company is considering purchasing all of the stock of Lynch Company. It is willing to pay an amount equal to the present value of the cash flows from operations for the next 20 years discounted at a rate of 10 percent per year.

The transaction will be a tax-free exchange; that is, after the purchase, the tax basis of the assets of Lynch Company will remain unchanged, so that depreciation charges will remain at $50,000 per year and income taxes will remain at $260,000 per year. Revenues will be $700,000 per year for the next 20 years.

a. Compute the annual cash flows produced by Lynch Company.

b. Compute the maximum amount Bages Company should be willing to pay.

40. **Computation of the present value of cash flows; taxable acquisition, changing tax basis of assets.** Refer to the data in the preceding problem. Assume now that the acquisition is taxable, so that the tax basis of the assets acquired changes after the purchase. If the purchase price is $V, then depreciation charges will be $V/20 per year for 20 years. Income taxes will be 40 percent of pretax income. What is the maximum Bages Company should be willing to pay for Lynch Company?

41. **Valuation of intangibles with perpetuity formulas.** When the American Basketball Association (ABA) merged with the National Basketball Association (NBA), the owners of the ABA St. Louis Spirits agreed to dissolve their team and not enter the NBA. In return, the owners received a promise in perpetuity from the NBA that the NBA would pay to the Spirits' owners an amount each year equal to 40 percent of the TV revenues that the NBA paid to any one of its regular teams. Currently, the owners receive $4 million per year. The NBA wants to pay a single amount to the owners now and not have to pay more in the future. Of course, the owners prefer to collect more, rather than less, but here they want to know the reasonable minimum that will make them indifferent to the single payment in lieu of receiving the annual payments in perpetuity. Ignore income tax effects.

   a. Assume the owners expect the TV revenues to remain constant, so that they can expect $4 million per year in perpetuity and use an interest rate of 8 percent in their discounting calculations. What minimum price should these owners be willing to accept?

   b. Refer to the specifications for the preceding question. If the owners use a smaller interest rate for discounting, will the minimum price they are willing to accept increase, decrease, or remain unchanged?

   c. The owners use an 8-percent discount rate, and they expect TV revenues to increase by 2 percent per year in perpetuity. What minimum price should the owners be willing to accept?

   d. Refer to the specifications in c. If the owners use a smaller interest rate for discounting, will the minimum price they are willing to accept increase, decrease, or remain unchanged?

   e. Refer to the specifications in c. If the owners assume a smaller rate for growth in future receipts from the NBA, will the minimum price they are willing to accept increase, decrease, or remain unchanged?

42. **(Adapted from a problem by S. Zeff.)** Lexie T. Colleton is the chief financial officer of Ragazze, and one of her duties is to give advice on investment projects. Today's date is December 31, Year 0. Colleton requires that, to be acceptable, new investments must provide a positive net present value after discounting cash flows at 12 percent per year.

    A proposed investment is the purchase of an automatic gonculator, which involves an initial cash disbursement on December 31, Year 0. The useful life of the machine is nine years, through Year 9. Colleton expects to be able to sell the machine for cash of $30,000 on December 31, Year 9. She expects commercial production to begin on December 31, Year 1.

    Ragazze will depreciate the machine on a straight-line basis. Ignore income taxes.

    During Year 1, the break-in year, Ragazze will perform test runs in order to put the machine in proper working order. Colleton expects that the total cash outlay for this purpose will be $20,000, incurred at the end of Year 1.

    Colleton expects that the cash disbursements for regular maintenance will be $60,000 at the end of each of Years 2 through 5, inclusive, and $100,000 at the end of each of Years 6 through 8, inclusive.

    Colleton expects the cash receipts (net of all other operating expenses) from the sale of the product that the machine produces to be $130,000 at the end of each year from Year 2 through Year 9, inclusive.

    a. What is the maximum price that Ragazze can pay for the automatic gonculator on December 31, Year 0, and still earn a positive net present value of cash flows?

    b. Independent of your answer to part a, assume the purchase price is $250,000, which Ragazze will pay with an installment note requiring four equal annual installments starting December 31, Year 1, and an implicit interest rate of 10 percent per year. What is the amount of each payment?

43. **(Adapted from a problem by S. Zeff.)** William Marsh, CEO of Gulf Coast Manufacturing, wishes to know which of two strategies he has chosen for acquiring an automobile has lower present value of cost.

    Strategy L. Acquire a new Lexus, keep it for six years, then trade it in on a new car.

    Strategy M. Acquire a new Mercedes-Benz, trade it in after three years on a second Mercedes-Benz, keep that for another three years, then trade it in on a new car.

    Data pertinent to these choices appear below. Assume that Marsh will receive the trade-in value in cash or as a credit toward the purchase price of a new car. Ignore income taxes and use a discount rate of 10 percent per year. Gulf Coast Manufacturing depreciates automobiles on a straight-line basis over 8 years for financial reporting, assuming zero salvage value at the end of 8 years.

    a. Which strategy has lower present value of costs?

b. What role, if any, do depreciation charges play in the analysis and why?

	Lexus	Mercedes-Benz
Initial Cost at the Start of Year 1	$60,000	$ 45,000
Initial Cost at the Start of Year 4		48,000
Trade-in Value		
End of Year 3		23,000
End of Year 6[2]	16,000	24,500
Estimated Annual Cash Operating Costs,		
Except Major Servicing	4,000	4,500
Estimated Cash Cost of Major Servicing		
End of Year 4	6,500	
End of Year 2 and End of Year 5		2,500

[2] At this time Lexus is 6 years old; second Mercedes-Benz is 3 years old.

44. (Wal Mart Stores; perpetuity growth model derivation of results in Chapter 5.) Refer to the discussion on page **226** in **Chapter 5**. There, in estimating the value of a share of common stock of Wal-Mart Stores, we computed the present value of excess cash flows at the end of Year 14 (= beginning of Year 15) to be $203.6 billion. This exercise requires you to confirm that computation.

To compute the amount for the years after Year 19, note we assume that the excess cash flows are $5.962 billion at the end of Year 9 and grow at the rate of 10 percent per year thereafter. That means the cash flows for the end of Year 20 are $6.558 (= $1.10 \times$ $5.962) billion. You can use the perpetuity growth model to verify that the present value at the end of Year 19 of that growing stream of payments is $327.9 billion. That is, if a payment (in this case $6.558 billion), grows at rate g (in this case, 10 percent) per period forever, the discount rate is r (in this case, 12 percent) per period, and the first payment flows at the end of the first period, then the present value of that stream is $327.9 [= $6.558/($r - g$) = $6.558/(0.12 - 0.10)]$ million. Then, we discount that amount to the end of Year 14 to derive $186.1 billion. Analysts describe the $186.1 million valuation in such computations as the *terminal value*.

(We do not expect that Wal-Mart's excess cash flows could increase forever at 10 percent per year. After a century or so, such a firm would be larger than the rest of the entire U.S. economy, combined. We use such computations to estimate values. When the discount rate (here 12 percent per year) exceeds the growth rate (here 10 percent per year) by a substantial amount (here only 2 percentage points), the present value of payments far in the future, say more than 40 years out, is negligible.)

a. Reproduce the numbers in Column **(6)** on page **226** using the data from Column **(5)** and the appropriate present value computations.

b. Re-do the valuation changing the growth rate from Year 19 from 10 percent to 9 percent.

c. Re-do the valuation changing the growth rate from Year 19 from 10 percent to 5 percent.

d. Comment on the sensitivity of this valuation modeling tool to the effect of assumed growth rates on terminal values.

45. (Fast Growth Start-Up Company; valuation involving perpetuity growth model assumptions.) Fast Growth Start-Up Company (FGSUC) has a new successful internet business model. It earned $100 million of after-tax free cash flows this year. The company proposes to go public and the company's internal financial staff suggests to the board of directors that a valuation of $2.5 billion seems reasonable for the company. The investment banking firm's analyst and the financial staff at the company agree that the growth rate in free cash flows will be 25 percent per year for several years before the growth rate drops back to one more closely resembling the growth rate in the economy as a whole, which all assume to be 4 percent per year. Assume that the after-tax discount rate suitable for such a new venture is 15 percent per year.

How many years of growth in after-tax free cash flow of 25 percent per year will the FGSUC need to earn to justify a market valuation of $2.5 billion? Do not attempt to work this problem without using a spreadsheet program.

Compound Interest, Annuity, and Bond Tables

TABLE 1

Future Value of $1

$$F_n = P(1 + r)^n$$

r = interest rate; n = number of periods until valuation; P = $1

Periods = n	½%	1%	1½%	2%	3%	4%	5%	6%	7%	8%	10%	12%	15%	20%	25%
1	1.00500	1.01000	1.01500	1.02000	1.03000	1.04000	1.05000	1.06000	1.07000	1.08000	1.10000	1.12000	1.15000	1.20000	1.25000
2	1.01003	1.02010	1.03023	1.04040	1.06090	1.08160	1.10250	1.12360	1.14490	1.16640	1.21000	1.25440	1.32250	1.44000	1.56250
3	1.01508	1.03030	1.04568	1.06121	1.09273	1.12486	1.15763	1.19102	1.22504	1.25971	1.33100	1.40493	1.52088	1.72800	1.95313
4	1.02015	1.04060	1.06136	1.08243	1.12551	1.16986	1.21551	1.26248	1.31080	1.36049	1.46410	1.57352	1.74901	2.07360	2.44141
5	1.02525	1.05101	1.07728	1.10408	1.15927	1.21665	1.27628	1.33823	1.40255	1.46933	1.61051	1.76234	2.01136	2.48832	3.05176
6	1.03038	1.06152	1.09344	1.12616	1.19405	1.26532	1.34010	1.41852	1.50073	1.58687	1.77156	1.97382	2.31306	2.98598	3.81470
7	1.03553	1.07214	1.10984	1.14869	1.22987	1.31593	1.40710	1.50363	1.60578	1.71382	1.94872	2.21068	2.66002	3.58318	4.76837
8	1.04071	1.08286	1.12649	1.17166	1.26677	1.36857	1.47746	1.59385	1.71819	1.85093	2.14359	2.47596	3.05902	4.29982	5.96046
9	1.04591	1.09369	1.14339	1.19509	1.30477	1.42331	1.55133	1.68948	1.83846	1.99900	2.35795	2.77308	3.51788	5.15978	7.45058
10	1.05114	1.10462	1.16054	1.21899	1.34392	1.48024	1.62889	1.79085	1.96715	2.15892	2.59374	3.10585	4.04556	6.19174	9.31323
11	1.05640	1.11567	1.17795	1.24337	1.38423	1.53945	1.71034	1.89830	2.10485	2.33164	2.85312	3.47855	4.65239	7.43008	11.64153
12	1.06168	1.12683	1.19562	1.26824	1.42576	1.60103	1.79586	2.01220	2.25219	2.51817	3.13843	3.89598	5.35025	8.91610	14.55192
13	1.06699	1.13809	1.21355	1.29361	1.46853	1.66507	1.88565	2.13293	2.40985	2.71962	3.45227	4.36349	6.15279	10.69932	18.18989
14	1.07232	1.14947	1.23176	1.31948	1.51259	1.73168	1.97993	2.26090	2.57853	2.93719	3.79750	4.88711	7.07571	12.83918	22.73737
15	1.07768	1.16097	1.25023	1.34587	1.55797	1.80094	2.07893	2.39656	2.75903	3.17217	4.17725	5.47357	8.13706	15.40702	28.42171
16	1.08307	1.17258	1.26899	1.37279	1.60471	1.87298	2.18287	2.54035	2.95216	3.42594	4.59497	6.13039	9.35762	18.48843	35.52714
17	1.08849	1.18430	1.28802	1.40024	1.65285	1.94790	2.29202	2.69277	3.15882	3.70002	5.05447	6.86604	10.76126	22.18611	44.40892
18	1.09393	1.19615	1.30734	1.42825	1.70243	2.02582	2.40662	2.85434	3.37993	3.99602	5.55992	7.68997	12.37545	26.62333	55.51115
19	1.09940	1.20811	1.32695	1.45681	1.75351	2.10685	2.52695	3.02560	3.61653	4.31570	6.11591	8.61276	14.23177	31.94800	69.38894
20	1.10490	1.22019	1.34686	1.48595	1.80611	2.19112	2.65330	3.20714	3.86968	4.66096	6.72750	9.64629	16.36654	38.33760	86.73617
22	1.11597	1.24472	1.38756	1.54598	1.91610	2.36992	2.92526	3.60354	4.43040	5.43654	8.14027	12.10031	21.64475	55.20614	135.5253
24	1.12716	1.26973	1.42950	1.60844	2.03279	2.56330	3.22510	4.04893	5.07237	6.34118	9.84973	15.17863	28.62518	79.49685	211.7582
26	1.13846	1.29526	1.47271	1.67342	2.15659	2.77247	3.55567	4.54938	5.80735	7.39635	11.91818	19.04007	37.85680	114.4755	330.8722
28	1.14987	1.32129	1.51722	1.74102	2.28793	2.99870	3.92013	5.11169	6.64884	8.62711	14.42099	23.88387	50.06561	164.8447	516.9879
30	1.16140	1.34785	1.56308	1.81136	2.42726	3.24340	4.32194	5.74349	7.61226	10.06266	17.44940	29.95992	66.21177	237.3763	807.7936
32	1.17304	1.37494	1.61032	1.88454	2.57508	3.50806	4.76494	6.45339	8.71527	11.73708	21.11378	37.58173	87.56507	341.8219	1262.177
34	1.18480	1.40258	1.65900	1.96068	2.73191	3.79432	5.25335	7.25103	9.97811	13.69013	25.54767	47.14252	115.80480	492.2235	1972.152
36	1.19668	1.43077	1.70914	2.03989	2.89828	4.10393	5.79182	8.14725	11.42394	15.96817	30.91268	59.13557	153.15185	708.8019	3081.488
38	1.20868	1.45953	1.76080	2.12230	3.07478	4.43881	6.38548	9.15425	13.07927	18.62528	37.40434	74.17966	202.54332	1020.675	4814.825
40	1.22079	1.48886	1.81402	2.20804	3.26204	4.80102	7.03999	10.28572	14.97446	21.72452	45.25926	93.05097	267.86355	1469.772	7523.164
45	1.25162	1.56481	1.95421	2.43785	3.78160	5.84118	8.98501	13.76461	21.00245	31.92045	72.89048	163.9876	538.76927	3657.262	22958.87
50	1.28323	1.64463	2.10524	2.69159	4.38391	7.10668	11.46740	18.42015	29.45703	46.90161	117.3909	289.0022	1083.65744	9100.438	70064.92
100	1.64667	2.70481	4.43205	7.24465	19.21863	50.50495	131.5013	339.3021	867.7163	2199.761	13780.61	83522.27	117×10^4	828×10^5	491×10^7

TABLE 2

Present Value of $1
$P = F_n(1 + r)^{-n}$
r = discount rate; n = number of periods until payment; F_n = $1

Periods = n	½%	1%	1½%	2%	3%	4%	5%	6%	7%	8%	10%	12%	15%	20%	25%
1	.99502	.99010	.98522	.98039	.97087	.96154	.95238	.94340	.93458	.92593	.90909	.89286	.86957	.83333	.80000
2	.99007	.98030	.97066	.96117	.94260	.92456	.90703	.89000	.87344	.85734	.82645	.79719	.75614	.69444	.64000
3	.98515	.97059	.95632	.94232	.91514	.88900	.86384	.83962	.81630	.79383	.75131	.71178	.65752	.57870	.51200
4	.98025	.96098	.94218	.92385	.88849	.85480	.82270	.79209	.76290	.73503	.68301	.63552	.57175	.48225	.40960
5	.97537	.95147	.92826	.90573	.86261	.82193	.78353	.74726	.71299	.68058	.62092	.56743	.49718	.40188	.32768
6	.97052	.94205	.91454	.88797	.83748	.79031	.74622	.70496	.66634	.63017	.56447	.50663	.43233	.33490	.26214
7	.96569	.93272	.90103	.87056	.81309	.75992	.71068	.66506	.62275	.58349	.51316	.45235	.37594	.27908	.20972
8	.96089	.92348	.88771	.85349	.78941	.73069	.67684	.62741	.58201	.54027	.46651	.40388	.32690	.23257	.16777
9	.95610	.91434	.87459	.83676	.76642	.70259	.64461	.59190	.54393	.50025	.42410	.36061	.28426	.19381	.13422
10	.95135	.90529	.86167	.82035	.74409	.67556	.61391	.55839	.50835	.46319	.38554	.32197	.24718	.16151	.10737
11	.94661	.89632	.84893	.80426	.72242	.64958	.58468	.52679	.47509	.42888	.35049	.28748	.21494	.13459	.08590
12	.94191	.88745	.83639	.78849	.70138	.62460	.55684	.49697	.44401	.39711	.31863	.25668	.18691	.11216	.06872
13	.93722	.87866	.82403	.77303	.68095	.60057	.53032	.46884	.41496	.36770	.28966	.22917	.16253	.09346	.05498
14	.93256	.86996	.81185	.75788	.66112	.57748	.50507	.44230	.38782	.34046	.26333	.20462	.14133	.07789	.04398
15	.92792	.86135	.79985	.74301	.64186	.55526	.48102	.41727	.36245	.31524	.23939	.18270	.12289	.06491	.03518
16	.92330	.85282	.78803	.72845	.62317	.53391	.45811	.39365	.33873	.29189	.21763	.16312	.10686	.05409	.02815
17	.91871	.84438	.77639	.71416	.60502	.51337	.43630	.37136	.31657	.27027	.19784	.14564	.09293	.04507	.02252
18	.91414	.83602	.76491	.70016	.58739	.49363	.41552	.35034	.29586	.25025	.17986	.13004	.08081	.03756	.01801
19	.90959	.82774	.75361	.68643	.57029	.47464	.39573	.33051	.27651	.23171	.16351	.11611	.07027	.03130	.01441
20	.90506	.81954	.74247	.67297	.55368	.45639	.37689	.31180	.25842	.21455	.14864	.10367	.06110	.02608	.01153
22	.89608	.80340	.72069	.64684	.52189	.42196	.34185	.27751	.22571	.18394	.12285	.08264	.04620	.01811	.00738
24	.88719	.78757	.69954	.62172	.49193	.39012	.31007	.24698	.19715	.15770	.10153	.06588	.03493	.01258	.00472
26	.87838	.77205	.67902	.59758	.46369	.36069	.28124	.21981	.17220	.13520	.08391	.05252	.02642	.00874	.00302
28	.86966	.75684	.65910	.57437	.43708	.33348	.25509	.19563	.15040	.11591	.06934	.04187	.01997	.00607	.00193
30	.86103	.74192	.63976	.55207	.41199	.30832	.23138	.17411	.13137	.09938	.05731	.03338	.01510	.00421	.00124
32	.85248	.72730	.62099	.53063	.38834	.28506	.20987	.15496	.11474	.08520	.04736	.02661	.01142	.00293	.00079
34	.84402	.71297	.60277	.51003	.36604	.26355	.19035	.13791	.10022	.07305	.03914	.02121	.00864	.00203	.00051
36	.83564	.69892	.58509	.49022	.34503	.24367	.17266	.12274	.08754	.06262	.03235	.01691	.00653	.00141	.00032
38	.82735	.68515	.56792	.47119	.32523	.22529	.15661	.10924	.07646	.05369	.02673	.01348	.00494	.00098	.00021
40	.81914	.67165	.55126	.45289	.30656	.20829	.14205	.09722	.06678	.04603	.02209	.01075	.00373	.00068	.00013
45	.79896	.63905	.51171	.41020	.26444	.17120	.11130	.07265	.04761	.03133	.01372	.00610	.00186	.00027	.00004
50	.77929	.60804	.47500	.37153	.22811	.14071	.08720	.05429	.03395	.02132	.00852	.00346	.00092	.00011	.00001
100	.60729	.36971	.22563	.13803	.05203	.01980	.00760	.00295	.00115	.00045	.00007	.00001	.00000	.00000	.00000

TABLE 3

Future Value of Annuity of $1 in Arrears

$$P_F = \frac{(1 + r)^n - 1}{r}$$

r = interest rate; n = number of payments

No. of Payments = n	½%	1%	1½%	2%	3%	4%	5%	6%	7%	8%	10%	12%	15%	20%	25%
1	1.00000	1.00000	1.00000	1.00000	1.00000	1.00000	1.00000	1.00000	1.00000	1.00000	1.00000	1.00000	1.00000	1.00000	1.00000
2	2.00500	2.01000	2.01500	2.02000	2.03000	2.04000	2.05000	2.06000	2.07000	2.08000	2.10000	2.12000	2.15000	2.20000	2.25000
3	3.01503	3.03010	3.04523	3.06040	3.09090	3.12160	3.15250	3.18360	3.21490	3.24640	3.31000	3.37440	3.47250	3.64000	3.81250
4	4.03010	4.06040	4.09090	4.12161	4.18363	4.24646	4.31013	4.37462	4.43994	4.50611	4.64100	4.77933	4.99338	5.36800	5.76563
5	5.05025	5.10101	5.15227	5.20404	5.30914	5.41632	5.52563	5.63709	5.75074	5.86660	6.10510	6.35285	6.74238	7.44160	8.20703
6	6.07550	6.15202	6.22955	6.30812	6.46841	6.63298	6.80191	6.97532	7.15329	7.33593	7.71561	8.11519	8.75374	9.92992	11.25879
7	7.10588	7.21354	7.32299	7.43428	7.66246	7.89829	8.14201	8.39384	8.65402	8.92280	9.48717	10.08901	11.06680	12.91590	15.07349
8	8.14141	8.28567	8.43284	8.58297	8.89234	9.21423	9.54911	9.89747	10.25980	10.63663	11.43589	12.29969	13.72682	16.49908	19.84186
9	9.18212	9.36853	9.55933	9.75463	10.15911	10.58280	11.02656	11.49132	11.97799	12.48756	13.57948	14.77566	16.78584	20.79890	25.80232
10	10.22803	10.46221	10.70272	10.94972	11.46388	12.00611	12.57789	13.18079	13.81645	14.48656	15.93742	17.54874	20.30372	25.95868	33.25290
11	11.27917	11.56683	11.86326	12.16872	12.80780	13.48635	14.20679	14.97164	15.78360	16.64549	18.53117	20.65458	24.34928	32.15042	42.56613
12	12.33556	12.68250	13.04121	13.41209	14.19203	15.02581	15.91713	16.86994	17.88845	18.97713	21.38428	24.13313	29.00167	39.58050	54.20766
13	13.39724	13.80933	14.23683	14.68033	15.61779	16.62684	17.71298	18.88214	20.14064	21.49530	24.52271	28.02911	34.35192	48.49660	68.75958
14	14.46423	14.94742	15.45038	15.97394	17.08632	18.29191	19.59863	21.01507	22.55049	24.21492	27.97498	32.39260	40.50471	59.19592	86.94947
15	15.53655	16.09690	16.68214	17.29342	18.59891	20.02359	21.57856	23.27597	25.12902	27.15211	31.77248	37.27971	47.58041	72.03511	109.6868
16	16.61423	17.25786	17.93237	18.63929	20.15688	21.82453	23.65749	25.67253	27.88805	30.32428	35.94973	42.75328	55.71747	87.44213	138.1085
17	17.69730	18.43044	19.20136	20.01207	21.76159	23.69751	25.84037	28.21288	30.84022	33.75023	40.54470	48.88367	65.07509	105.9306	173.6357
18	18.78579	19.61475	20.48938	21.41231	23.41444	25.64541	28.13238	30.90565	33.99903	37.45024	45.59917	55.74971	75.83636	128.1167	218.0446
19	19.87972	20.81090	21.79672	22.84056	25.11687	27.67123	30.53900	33.75999	37.37896	41.44626	51.15909	63.43968	88.21181	154.7400	273.5558
20	20.97912	22.01900	23.12367	24.29737	26.87037	29.77808	33.06595	36.78559	40.99549	45.76196	57.27500	72.05244	102.44358	186.6880	342.9447
22	23.19443	24.47159	25.83758	27.29898	30.53678	34.24797	38.50521	43.39229	49.00574	55.45676	71.40275	92.50258	137.63164	271.0307	538.1011
24	25.43196	26.97346	28.63352	30.42186	34.42647	39.08260	44.50200	50.81558	58.17667	66.76476	88.49733	118.15524	184.16784	392.4842	843.0329
26	27.69191	29.52563	31.51397	33.67091	38.55304	44.31174	51.11345	59.15638	68.67647	79.95442	109.18177	150.33393	245.71197	567.3773	1319.489
28	29.97452	32.12910	34.48148	37.05121	42.93092	49.96758	58.40258	68.52811	80.69769	95.33883	134.20994	190.69889	327.10408	819.2233	2063.952
30	32.28002	34.78489	37.53868	40.56808	47.57542	56.08494	66.43885	79.05819	94.46079	113.28321	164.49402	241.33268	434.74515	1181.881	3227.174
32	34.60862	37.49407	40.68829	44.22703	52.50276	62.70147	75.29883	90.88978	110.21815	134.21354	201.13777	304.84772	577.10046	1704.109	5044.710
34	36.96058	40.25770	43.93309	48.03380	57.73018	69.85791	85.06696	104.18375	128.25876	158.62667	245.47670	384.52098	765.36535	2456.118	7884.609
36	39.33610	43.07688	47.27597	51.99437	63.27594	77.59831	95.83632	119.12087	148.91346	187.10215	299.12681	484.46312	1014.34568	3539.009	12321.95
38	41.73545	45.95272	50.71989	56.11494	69.15945	85.97034	107.70955	135.90421	172.56102	220.31595	364.04343	609.83053	1343.62216	5098.373	19255.30
40	44.15885	48.88637	54.26789	60.40198	75.40126	95.02552	120.79977	154.76197	199.63511	259.05652	442.59256	767.09142	1779.09031	7343.858	30088.66
45	50.32416	56.48107	63.61420	71.89271	92.71986	121.0294	159.7002	212.7435	285.7493	386.5056	718.9048	1358.230	3585.12846	18281.31	91831.50
50	56.64516	64.46318	73.68283	84.57940	112.7969	152.6671	209.3480	290.3359	406.5289	573.7702	1163.909	2400.018	7217.71628	45497.19	280255.7
100	129.33370	170.4814	228.8030	312.2323	607.2877	1237.624	2610.025	5638.368	12381.66	27484.52	137796.1	696010.5	783×10^4	414×10^6	196×10^8

Note: To convert from this table to values of an annuity in advance, determine the annuity in arrears above for one more period and subtract 1.00000.

TABLE 4

Present Value of Annuity of $1 in Arrears

$$P_A = \frac{1 - (1 + r)^{-n}}{r} \times \$1.00$$

r = discount rate; n = number of payments

n Periods = Payments

$$P_A \longrightarrow \sum \binom{\text{Individual Values}}{\text{from Table 2}}$$

$$\binom{\text{Value in}}{\text{Table 4}} \longrightarrow \sum \binom{\text{Individual Values}}{\text{from Table 2}}$$

No. of Payments = n	½%	1%	1½%	2%	3%	4%	5%	6%	7%	8%	10%	12%	15%	20%	25%
1	.99502	.99010	.98522	.99039	.97087	.96154	.95238	.94340	.93458	.92593	.90909	.89286	.86957	.83333	.80000
2	1.98510	1.97040	1.95588	1.94156	1.91347	1.88609	1.85941	1.83339	1.80802	1.78326	1.73554	1.69005	1.62571	1.52778	1.44000
3	2.97025	2.94099	2.91220	2.88388	2.82861	2.77509	2.72325	2.67301	2.62432	2.57710	2.48685	2.40183	2.28323	2.10648	1.95200
4	3.95050	3.90197	3.85438	3.80773	3.71710	3.62990	3.54595	3.46511	3.38721	3.31213	3.16987	3.03735	2.85498	2.58873	2.36160
5	4.92587	4.85343	4.78264	4.71346	4.57971	4.45182	4.32948	4.21236	4.10020	3.99271	3.79079	3.60478	3.35216	2.99061	2.68928
6	5.89638	5.79548	5.69719	5.60143	5.41719	5.24214	5.07569	4.91732	4.76654	4.62288	4.35526	4.11141	3.78448	3.32551	2.95142
7	6.86207	6.72819	6.59821	6.47199	6.23028	6.00205	5.78637	5.58238	5.38929	5.20637	4.86842	4.56376	4.16042	3.60459	3.16114
8	7.82296	7.65168	7.48593	7.32548	7.01969	6.73274	6.46321	6.20979	5.97130	5.74664	5.33493	4.96764	4.48732	3.83716	3.32891
9	8.77906	8.56602	8.36052	8.16224	7.78611	7.43533	7.10782	6.80169	6.51523	6.24689	5.75902	5.32825	4.77158	4.03097	3.46313
10	9.73041	9.47130	9.22218	8.98259	8.53020	8.11090	7.72173	7.36009	7.02358	6.71008	6.14457	5.65022	5.01877	4.19247	3.57050
11	10.67703	10.36763	10.07112	9.78685	9.25262	8.76048	8.30641	7.88687	7.49867	7.13896	6.49506	5.93770	5.23371	4.32706	3.65640
12	11.61893	11.25508	10.90751	10.57534	9.95400	9.38507	8.86325	8.38384	7.94269	7.53608	6.81369	6.19437	5.42062	4.43922	3.72512
13	12.55615	12.13374	11.73153	11.34837	10.63496	9.98565	9.39357	8.85268	8.35765	7.90378	7.10336	6.42355	5.58315	4.53268	3.78010
14	13.48871	13.00370	12.54338	12.10625	11.29607	10.56312	9.89864	9.29498	8.74547	8.24424	7.36669	6.62817	5.72448	4.61057	3.82408
15	14.41662	13.86505	13.34323	12.84926	11.93794	11.11839	10.37966	9.71225	9.10791	8.55948	7.60608	6.81086	5.84737	4.67547	3.85926
16	15.33993	14.71787	14.13126	13.57771	12.56110	11.65230	10.83777	10.10590	9.44665	8.85137	7.82371	6.97399	5.95423	4.72956	3.88741
17	16.25863	15.56225	14.90765	14.29187	13.16612	12.16567	11.27407	10.47726	9.76322	9.12164	8.02155	7.11963	6.04716	4.77463	3.90993
18	17.17277	16.39827	15.67256	14.99203	13.75351	12.65930	11.68959	10.82760	10.05909	9.37189	8.20141	7.24967	6.12797	4.81219	3.92794
19	18.08236	17.22601	16.42617	15.67846	14.32380	13.13394	12.08532	11.15812	10.33560	9.60360	8.36492	7.36578	6.19823	4.84350	3.94235
20	18.98742	18.04555	17.16864	16.35143	14.87747	13.59033	12.46221	11.46992	10.59401	9.81815	8.51356	7.46944	6.25933	4.86958	3.95388
22	20.78406	19.66038	18.62082	17.65805	15.93692	14.45112	13.16300	12.04158	11.06124	10.20074	8.77154	7.64465	6.35866	4.90943	3.97049
24	22.56287	21.24339	20.03041	18.91393	16.93554	15.24696	13.79864	12.55036	11.46933	10.52876	8.98474	7.78432	6.43377	4.93710	3.98111
26	24.32402	22.79520	21.39863	20.12104	17.87684	15.98277	14.37519	13.00317	11.82578	10.80998	9.16095	7.89566	6.49056	4.95632	3.98791
28	26.06769	24.31644	22.72672	21.28127	18.76411	16.66306	14.89813	13.40616	12.13711	11.05108	9.30657	7.98442	6.53351	4.96967	3.99226
30	27.79405	25.80771	24.01584	22.39646	19.60044	17.29203	15.37245	13.76483	12.40904	11.25778	9.42691	8.05518	6.56598	4.97894	3.99505
32	29.50328	27.26959	25.26714	23.46833	20.38877	17.87355	15.80268	14.08404	12.64656	11.43500	9.52638	8.11159	6.59053	4.98537	3.99663
34	31.19555	28.70267	26.48173	24.49859	21.13184	18.41120	16.19290	14.36814	12.85401	11.58693	9.60857	8.15656	6.60910	4.98984	3.99797
36	32.87102	30.10751	27.66068	25.48884	21.83225	18.90828	16.54685	14.62099	13.03521	11.71719	9.67651	8.19241	6.62314	4.99295	3.99870
38	34.52985	31.48466	28.80505	26.44064	22.49246	19.36786	16.86789	14.84602	13.19347	11.82887	9.73265	8.22099	6.63375	4.99510	3.99917
40	36.17223	32.83469	29.91585	27.35548	23.11477	19.79277	17.15909	15.04630	13.33171	11.92461	9.77905	8.24378	6.64178	4.99660	3.99947
45	40.20720	36.09451	32.55234	29.49016	24.51871	20.72004	17.77407	15.45583	13.60552	12.10840	9.86281	8.28252	6.65429	4.99863	3.99983
50	44.14279	39.19612	34.99969	31.42361	25.72976	21.48218	18.25593	15.76186	13.80075	12.23348	9.91481	8.30450	6.66051	4.99945	3.99994
100	78.54264	63.02888	51.62470	43.09835	31.59891	24.50500	19.84791	16.61755	14.26925	12.49432	9.99927	8.33323	6.66666	5.00000	4.00000

Note: To convert from this table to values of an annuity in advance, determine the annuity in arrears above for one fewer period and add 1.00000.

TABLE 5

Bond Values in Percent of Par: 10 Percent Semiannual Coupons

Bond value $= 10/r + (100 - 10/r)(1 + r/2)^{-2n}$

$r =$ yield to maturity; $n =$ years to maturity

Market Yield Percent per Year Compounded Semiannually

Years to Maturity	8.0	9.0	9.5	10	10.5	11.0	12.0	13.0	14.0	15.0	20.0
0.5	100.9615	100.4785	100.2387	100.0	99.7625	99.5261	99.0566	98.5915	98.1308	97.6744	95.4545
1.0	101.8861	100.9363	100.4665	100.0	99.5368	99.0768	98.1666	97.2691	96.3840	95.5111	91.3223
1.5	102.7751	101.3745	100.6840	100.0	99.3224	98.6510	97.3270	96.0273	94.7514	93.4987	87.5657
2.0	103.6299	101.7938	100.8917	100.0	99.1186	98.2474	96.5349	94.8613	93.2256	91.6267	84.1507
2.5	104.4518	102.1950	101.0899	100.0	98.9251	97.8649	95.7876	93.7665	91.7996	89.8853	81.0461
5.0	108.1109	103.9564	101.9541	100.0	98.0928	96.2312	92.6399	89.2168	85.9528	82.8398	69.2772
9.0	112.6593	106.0800	102.9803	100.0	97.1339	94.3770	89.1724	84.3513	79.8818	75.7350	58.9929
9.5	113.1339	106.2966	103.0838	100.0	97.0393	94.1962	88.8419	83.8979	79.3288	75.1023	58.1754
10.0	113.5903	106.5040	103.1827	100.0	96.9494	94.0248	88.5301	83.4722	78.8120	74.5138	57.4322
15.0	117.2920	108.1444	103.9551	100.0	96.2640	92.7331	86.2352	80.4120	75.1819	70.4740	52.8654
19.0	119.3679	109.0250	104.3608	100.0	95.9194	92.0976	85.1540	79.0312	73.6131	68.8015	51.3367
19.5	119.5845	109.1148	104.4017	100.0	95.8854	92.0357	85.0509	78.9025	73.4701	68.6525	51.2152
20.0	119.7928	109.2008	104.4408	100.0	95.8531	91.9769	84.9537	78.7817	73.3366	68.5140	51.1047
25.0	121.4822	109.8810	104.7461	100.0	95.6068	91.5342	84.2381	77.9132	72.3985	67.5630	50.4259
30.0	122.6235	110.3190	104.9381	100.0	95.4591	91.2751	83.8386	77.4506	71.9216	67.1015	50.1642
40.0	123.9154	110.7827	105.1347	100.0	95.3175	91.0345	83.4909	77.0728	71.5560	66.7690	50.0244
50.0	124.5050	110.9749	105.2124	100.0	95.2666	90.9521	83.3825	76.9656	71.4615	66.6908	50.0036

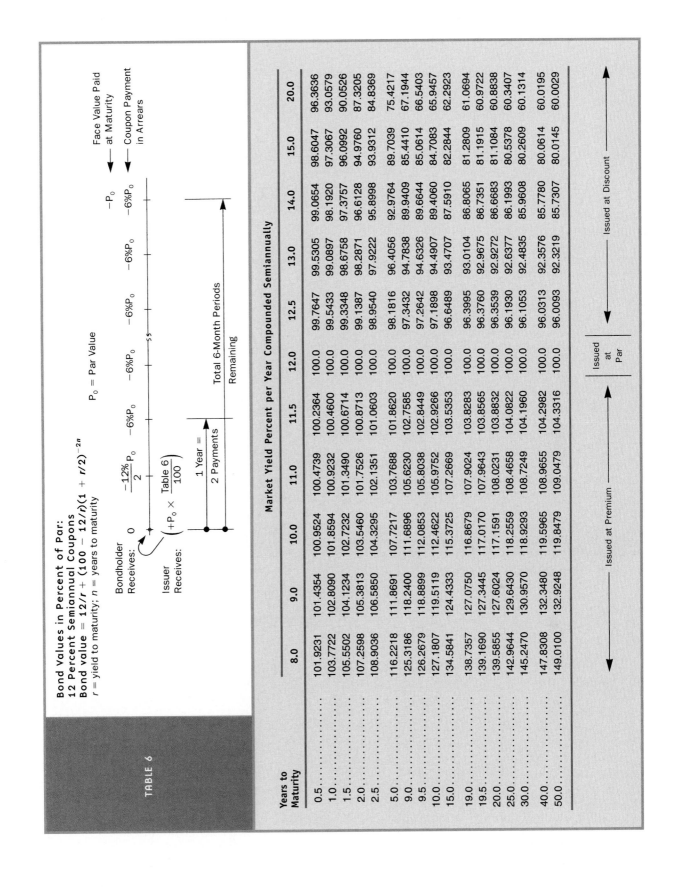

TABLE 6

Bond Values in Percent of Par:
12 Percent Semiannual Coupons
Bond value $= 12/r + (100 - 12/r)(1 + r/2)^{-2n}$
r = yield to maturity; n = years to maturity

P_0 = Par Value

Bondholder Receives: $0 \quad \dfrac{-12\% P_0}{2} \quad -6\% P_0 \quad -6\% P_0 \quad -6\% P_0 \quad -6\% P_0 \quad -6\% P_0 \quad -6\% P_0 \quad -6\% P_0$

Face Value Paid at Maturity

Coupon Payment in Arrears

Issuer Receives: $\left(+P_0 \times \dfrac{\text{Table 6}}{100} \right)$

1 Year = 2 Payments

Total 6-Month Periods Remaining

$-P_0$

Market Yield Percent per Year Compounded Semiannually

Years to Maturity	8.0	9.0	10.0	11.0	11.5	12.0	12.5	13.0	14.0	15.0	20.0
0.5	101.9231	101.4354	100.9524	100.4739	100.2364	100.0	99.7647	99.5305	99.0654	98.6047	96.3636
1.0	103.7722	102.8090	101.8594	100.9232	100.4600	100.0	99.5433	99.0897	98.1920	97.3067	93.0579
1.5	105.5502	104.1234	102.7232	101.3490	100.6714	100.0	99.3348	98.6758	97.3757	96.0992	90.0526
2.0	107.2598	105.3813	103.5460	101.7526	100.8713	100.0	99.1387	98.2871	96.6128	94.9760	87.3205
2.5	108.9036	106.5850	104.3295	102.1351	101.0603	100.0	98.9540	97.9222	95.8998	93.9312	84.8369
5.0	116.2218	111.8691	107.7217	103.7688	101.8620	100.0	98.1816	96.4056	92.9764	89.7039	75.4217
9.0	125.3186	118.2400	111.6896	105.6230	102.7585	100.0	97.3432	94.7838	89.9409	85.4410	67.1944
9.5	126.2679	118.8899	112.0853	105.8038	102.8449	100.0	97.2642	94.6326	89.6644	85.0614	66.5403
10.0	127.1807	119.5119	112.4622	105.9752	102.9266	100.0	97.1898	94.4907	89.4060	84.7083	65.9457
15.0	134.5841	124.4333	115.3725	107.2669	103.5353	100.0	96.6489	93.4707	87.5910	82.2844	62.2923
19.0	138.7357	127.0750	116.8679	107.9024	103.8283	100.0	96.3995	93.0104	86.8065	81.2809	61.0694
19.5	139.1690	127.3445	117.0170	107.9643	103.8565	100.0	96.3760	92.9675	86.7351	81.1915	60.9722
20.0	139.5855	127.6024	117.1591	108.0231	103.8832	100.0	96.3539	92.9272	86.6683	81.1084	60.8838
25.0	142.9644	129.6430	118.2559	108.4658	104.0822	100.0	96.1930	92.6377	86.1993	80.5378	60.3407
30.0	145.2470	130.9570	118.9293	108.7249	104.1960	100.0	96.1053	92.4835	85.9608	80.2609	60.1314
40.0	147.8308	132.3480	119.5965	108.9655	104.2982	100.0	96.0313	92.3576	85.7780	80.0614	60.0195
50.0	149.0100	132.9248	119.8479	109.0479	104.3316	100.0	96.0093	92.3219	85.7307	80.0145	60.0029

← Issued at Premium | Issued at Par | Issued at Discount →

Glossary

The definitions of many words and phrases in the glossary use other glossary terms. In a given definition, we *italicize* terms that themselves (or variants thereof) appear elsewhere under their own listings. The cross-references generally take one of two forms:

1. absorption costing. See *full absorption costing.*
2. ABC. *Activity-based costing.*

Form (1) refers you to another term for discussion of this boldfaced term. Form (2) tells you that this bold-faced term is synonymous with the *italicized* term, which you can consult for discussion if necessary.

A

AAA. *American Accounting Association.*

Abacus. A scholarly journal containing articles on theoretical aspects of accounting, published by Blackwell Publishers for the Accounting Foundation of the University of Sydney.

abatement. A complete or partial cancellation of a levy imposed by a government unit.

ABC. *Activity-based costing.*

abnormal spoilage. Actual spoilage exceeding that expected when operations are normally efficient. Usual practice treats this cost as an *expense* of the period rather than as a *product cost.* Contrast with *normal spoilage.*

aboriginal cost. In public utility accounting, the *acquisition cost* of an *asset* incurred by the first *entity* devoting that asset to public use; the cost basis for most public utility regulation. If regulators used a different cost basis, then public utilities could exchange assets among themselves at ever-increasing prices in order to raise the rate base and, then, prices based on them.

absorbed overhead. *Overhead costs* allocated to individual products at some *overhead rate;* also called *applied overhead.*

absorption costing. See *full absorption costing.*

Abstracts of the EITF. See *Emerging Issues Task Force.*

Accelerated Cost Recovery System (ACRS). A form of accelerated depreciation that Congress enacted in 1981 and amended in 1986, so that now most writers refer to it as *MACRS,* or *Modified Accelerated Cost Recovery System.* The system provides percentages of the asset's cost that a firm depreciates each year for tax purposes. The percentages derive, roughly, from 150-percent *declining-balance depreciation* methods. ACRS ignores salvage value. We do not generally use these amounts for *financial accounting.*

accelerated depreciation. In calculating *depreciation* charges, any method in which the charges become progressively smaller each period. Examples are *double declining-balance depreciation* and *sum-of-the-years'-digits depreciation* methods.

acceptance. A written promise to pay; equivalent to a *promissory note.*

account. A device for representing the amount (*balance*) for any line (or a part of a line) in the *balance sheet* or *income statement.* Because income statement accounts explain the changes in the balance sheet account Retained Earnings, the definition does not require the last three words of the preceding sentence. An account is any device for accumulating additions and subtractions relating to a single *asset, liability,* or *owners' equity* item, including *revenues* and *expenses.*

account analysis method. A method of separating *fixed costs* from *variable costs* based on the analyst's judgment of whether the cost is fixed or variable. Based on their names alone, the analyst might classify *direct labor* (*materials*) *costs* as variable and *depreciation* on a factory building as fixed. In our experience, this method results in too many fixed costs and not enough variable costs—that is, analysts have insufficient information to judge management's ability to reduce costs that appear to be fixed.

account form. The form of *balance sheet* in which *assets* appear on the left and *equities* appear on the right. Contrast with *report form.* See *T-account.*

accountability center. *Responsibility center.*

accountancy. The British word for *accounting.* In the United States, it means the theory and practice of accounting.

accountant's comments. Canada: a written communication issued by a public accountant at the conclusion of a review engagement. It consists of a description of the work performed and a statement that, under the terms of the engagement, the accountant has not performed an audit and consequently expresses no opinion. (Compare *auditor's report; denial of opinion.*)

accountant's opinion. *Auditor's report.*

accountant's report. *Auditor's report.*

accounting. A system conveying information about a specific *entity.* The information is in financial terms and will appear in accounting statements only if the accountant can measure it with reasonable precision. The *AICPA* defines accounting as a service activity whose "function is to provide quantitative information, primarily financial in nature, about economic entities that is intended to be useful in making economic decisions."

accounting adjustments. *Prior-period adjustments,* changes in accounting principles accounted for on a cumulative basis, and corrections of errors. See *accounting changes.* The *FASB* indicates that it will tend to call these items "accounting adjustments," not "accounting changes," when it requires the reporting of *comprehensive income.*

Accounting and Tax Index. A publication that indexes, in detail, the accounting literature of the period. Published by UMI, a subsidiary of ProQuest Company.

accounting changes. As defined by *APB Opinion No. 20,* a change in (1) an *accounting principle* (such as a switch from *FIFO* to *LIFO* or from *sum-of-the-years'-digits depreciation* to *straight-line depreciation*), (2) an accounting estimate (such as estimated useful lives or salvage value of depreciable assets and estimates of *warranty* costs or *uncollectible accounts*), or (3) the reporting *entity*. The firm should disclose changes of type (1). It should include in reported earnings for the period of change the cumulative effect of the change on *retained earnings* at the start of the period during which it made the change. The firm should treat changes of type (2) as affecting only the period of change and, if necessary, future periods. The firm should disclose reasons for changes of type (3) in statements reporting on operations of the period of the change, and it should show the effect of the change on all other periods, for comparative purposes. In some cases (such as a change from *LIFO* to other inventory *flow assumptions* or a change in the method of accounting for long-term construction contracts), *GAAP* treat changes of type (1) like changes of type (3). That is, for these changes the firm should restate all statements shown for prior periods to show the effect of adopting the change for those periods as well. See *all-inclusive (income) concept* and *accounting errors*.

accounting conventions. Methods or procedures used in accounting. Writers tend to use this term when the method or procedure has not yet received official authoritative sanction by a pronouncement of a group such as the *APB, EITF, FASB,* or *SEC*. Contrast with *accounting principles*.

accounting cycle. The sequence of accounting procedures starting with *journal entries* for various transactions and events and ending with the *financial statements* or, perhaps, the *post-closing trial balance*.

accounting deficiency. Canada: a failure to adhere to generally accepted *accounting principles* or to disclose essential information in *financial statements*.

accounting entity. See *entity*.

accounting equation. *Assets = Equities; Assets = Liabilities + Owners' Equity.*

accounting errors. Arithmetic errors and misapplications of *accounting principles* in previously published financial statements. The firm corrects these during the current period with direct *debits* or *credits* to *retained earnings*. In this regard, the firm treats them like *prior-period adjustments,* but technically *APB Opinion No. 9* does not classify them as prior-period adjustments. See *accounting changes,* and contrast with changes in accounting estimates as described there.

accounting event. Any occurrence that is recorded in the accounting records.

Accounting Horizons. Quarterly journal of the *American Accounting Association.*

accounting methods. *Accounting principles;* procedures for carrying out accounting principles.

accounting period. The time period between consecutive *balance sheets;* the time period for which the firm prepares *financial statements* that measure *flows,* such as the *income statement* and the *statement of cash flows.* See *interim statements.*

accounting policies. *Accounting principles* adopted by a specific *entity.*

accounting principles. The methods or procedures used in accounting for events reported in the *financial*

statements. We tend to use this term when the method or procedure has received official authoritative sanction from a pronouncement of a group such as the *APB, EITF, FASB,* or *SEC*. Contrast with *accounting conventions* and *conceptual framework.*

Accounting Principles Board. See *APB.*

accounting procedures. See *accounting principles.* However, this term usually refers to the methods for implementing accounting principles.

accounting rate of return. Income for a period divided by average investment during the period; based on income, rather than discounted cash flows, and hence a poor decision-making aid or tool. See *ratio.*

Accounting Research Bulletin (ARB). The name of the official pronouncements of the former *Committee on Accounting Procedure (CAP)* of the AICPA. The committee issued fifty-one bulletins between 1939 and 1959. *ARB No. 43* restated and codified the parts of the first forty-two bulletins not dealing solely with definitions.

Accounting Research Study (ARS). One of a series of studies published by the Director of Accounting Research of the *AICPA* and "designed to provide professional accountants and others interested in the development of accounting with a discussion and documentation of accounting problems." The AICPA published fifteen such studies in the period 1961–73.

Accounting Review. Scholarly publication of the *American Accounting Association.*

Accounting Series Release (ASR). See *SEC.*

accounting standards. *Accounting principles.*

Accounting Standards Executive Committee (AcSEC). The senior technical committee of the *AICPA* authorized to speak for the AICPA in the areas of *financial accounting* and reporting as well as *cost accounting.*

accounting system. The procedures for collecting and summarizing financial data in a firm.

Accounting Terminology Bulletin (ATB). One of four releases of the Committee on Terminology of the *AICPA* issued in the period 1953–57.

Accounting Trends and Techniques. An annual *AICPA* publication that surveys the reporting practices of 600 large corporations. It presents tabulations of specific practices, terminology, and disclosures along with illustrations taken from individual annual reports.

accounts payable. A *liability* representing an amount owed to a *creditor;* usually arising from the purchase of *merchandise* or materials and supplies, not necessarily due or past due; normally, a *current liability.*

accounts receivable. Claims against a *debtor;* usually arising from sales or services rendered, not necessarily due or past due; normally, a *current asset.*

accounts receivable turnover. Net sales on account divided by average accounts receivable. See *ratio.*

accretion. Occurs when a *book value* grows over time, such as a *bond* originally issued at a *discount;* the correct technical term is "accretion," not "amortization." This term also refers to an increase in economic worth through physical change caused by natural growth, usually said of a natural resource such as timber. Contrast with *appreciation.* See *amortization.*

accrual. Recognition of an *expense* (or *revenue*) and the related *liability* (or *asset*) resulting from an *accounting event,* frequently from the passage of time but not signaled by an explicit cash transaction; for example, the recognition of interest expense or revenue (or wages, salaries, or rent) at the end of a period even though the firm makes no explicit cash transaction at that time. Cash flow follows accounting recognition; contrast with *deferral.*

accrual basis of accounting. The method of recognizing *revenues* as a firm sells *goods* (or delivers them) and as it renders *services,* independent of the time when it receives cash. This system recognizes *expenses* in the period when it recognizes the related revenue, independent of the time when it pays cash. *SFAC No. 1* says, "Accrual accounting attempts to record the financial effects on an enterprise of transactions and other events and circumstances that have cash consequences for the enterprise in the periods in which those transactions, events, and circumstances occur rather than only in the periods in which cash is received or paid by the enterprise." Contrast with the *cash basis of accounting.* See *accrual* and *deferral.* We could more correctly call this "accrual/deferral" accounting.

accrue. See *accrued,* and contrast with *incur.*

accrued. Said of a *revenue* (*expense*) that the firm has earned (recognized) even though the related *receivable* (*payable*) has a future due date. We prefer not to use this adjective as part of an account title. Thus, we prefer to use Interest Receivable (Payable) as the account title rather than Accrued Interest Receivable (Payable). See *matching convention* and *accrual.* Contrast with *incur.*

accrued depreciation. An incorrect term for *accumulated depreciation.* Acquiring an asset with cash, capitalizing it, and then amortizing its cost over periods of use is a process of *deferral* and allocation, not of *accrual.*

accrued payable. A *payable* usually resulting from the passage of time. For example, *salaries* and *interest* accrue as time passes. See *accrued.*

accrued receivable. A *receivable* usually resulting from the passage of time. See *accrued.*

accumulated benefit obligation. See *projected benefit obligation* for definition and contrast.

accumulated depreciation. A preferred title for the asset *contra account* that shows the sum of *depreciation* charges on an asset since the time the firm acquired it. Other account titles are *allowance* for *depreciation* (acceptable term) and *reserve* for *depreciation* (unacceptable term).

accumulated other comprehensive income. *Balance sheet* amount in *owners' equity* showing the total of all *other comprehensive income* amounts from all prior periods.

accurate presentation. The qualitative accounting objective suggesting that information reported in financial statements should correspond as precisely as possible with the economic effects underlying transactions and events. See *fair presentation* and *full disclosure.*

acid test ratio. *Quick ratio.*

acquisition cost. Of an *asset,* the net *invoice* price plus all *expenditures* to place and ready the asset for its intended use. The other expenditures might include legal fees, transportation charges, and installation costs.

ACRS. *Accelerated Cost Recovery System.*

AcSEC. *Accounting Standards Executive Committee* of the *AICPA.*

activity accounting. *Responsibility accounting.*

activity-based costing (ABC). Method of assigning *indirect costs,* including nonmanufacturing *overhead costs,* to products and services. ABC assumes that almost all overhead costs associate with activities within the firm and vary with respect to the *drivers* of those activities. Some practitioners suggest that ABC attempts to find the drivers for all indirect costs; these people note that in the long run, all costs are *variable,* so *fixed* indirect costs do not occur. This method first assigns costs to activities and then to products based on the products' usage of the activities.

activity-based depreciation. *Production method* (*depreciation*).

activity-based management (ABM). Analysis and management of activities required to make a product or to produce a service. ABM focuses attention to enhance activities that add value to the customer and to reduce activities that do not. Its goal is to satisfy customer needs while making smaller demands on costly resources. Some refer to this as "activity management."

activity basis. *Costs* are *variable* or *fixed* (*incremental* or *unavoidable*) with respect to some activity, such as production of units (or the undertaking of some new project). Usage calls this activity the "activity basis."

activity center. Unit of the organization that performs a set of tasks.

activity variance. *Sales volume variance.*

actual cost (basis). *Acquisition* or *historical cost.* Also contrast with *standard cost.*

actual costing (system). Method of allocating costs to products using actual *direct materials,* actual *direct labor,* and actual *factory overhead.* Contrast with *normal costing* and *standard costing.*

actuarial. An adjective describing computations or analyses that involve both *compound interest* and probabilities, such as the computation of the *present value* of a life-contingent *annuity.* Some writers use the word even for computations involving only one of the two.

actuarial accrued liability. A 1981 report of the Joint Committee on Pension Terminology (of various actuarial societies) agreed to use this term rather than *prior service cost.*

ad valorem. A method of levying a tax or duty on goods by using their estimated value as the tax base.

additional paid-in capital. An alternative acceptable title for the *capital contributed in excess of par* (or *stated*) *value account.*

additional processing cost. *Costs* incurred in processing *joint products* after the *split-off point.*

adequate disclosure. An auditing standard that, to achieve *fair presentation* of *financial statements,* requires *disclosure* of *material* items. This *auditing standard* does not, however, require publicizing all information detrimental to a company. For example, the company may face a lawsuit, and disclosure might require a *debit* to a *loss* account and a *credit* to an *estimated liability.* But the court might view the making of this entry as an admission of liability, which could adversely affect the outcome of the suit. The firm should debit expense or loss for the expected loss, as required by *SFAS No. 5,* but need not use such accurate account titles that the court can spot an admission of liability.

adjunct account. An *account* that accumulates additions to another account. For example, Premium on Bonds Payable is adjunct to the liability Bonds Payable; the effective liability is the sum of the two account balances at a given date. Contrast with *contra account.*

adjusted acquisition (historical) cost. Sometimes said of the *book value* of a *plant asset,* that is, *acquisition cost* less *accumulated depreciation.* Also, cost adjusted to a *constant-dollar* amount to reflect *general price-level changes.*

adjusted bank balance of cash. The *balance* shown on the statement from the bank plus or minus amounts, such as for unrecorded deposits or outstanding checks, to reconcile the bank's balance with the correct cash balance. See *adjusted book balance of cash.*

adjusted basis. The *basis* used to compute gain or loss on the disposition of an *asset* for tax purposes. See also *book value.*

adjusted book balance of cash. The *balance* shown in the firm's account for cash in bank plus or minus amounts, such as for *notes* collected by the bank or bank service charges, to reconcile the account balance with the correct cash balance. See *adjusted bank balance of cash.*

adjusted trial balance. *Trial balance* taken after *adjusting entries* but before *closing entries.* Contrast with *pre-*and *post-closing trial balances.* See *unadjusted trial balance* and *post-closing trial balance.* See also *work sheet.*

adjusting entry. An entry made at the end of an *accounting period* to record a *transaction* or other *accounting event* that the firm has not yet recorded or has improperly recorded during the accounting period; an entry to update the accounts. See *work sheet.*

adjustment. An *account* change produced by an *adjusting entry.* Sometimes accountants use the term to refer to the process of restating *financial statement* amounts to *constant dollars.*

administrative costs (expenses). *Costs (expenses)* incurred for the firm as a whole, in contrast with specific functions such as manufacturing or selling; includes items such as salaries of top executives, general office rent, legal fees, and auditing fees.

admission of partner. Occurs when a new partner joins a *partnership.* Legally, the old partnership dissolves, and a new one comes into being. In practice, however, the firm may keep the old accounting records in use, and the accounting entries reflect the manner in which the new partner joined the firm. If the new partner merely purchases the interest of another partner, the accounting changes the name for one capital account. If the new partner contributes *assets* and *liabilities* to the partnership, then the firm must recognize them. See *bonus method.*

ADR. See *asset depreciation range.*

advances from (by) customers. A preferred title for the *liability* account representing *receipts* of *cash* in advance of delivering the *goods* or rendering the *service.* After the firm delivers the goods or services, it will recognize *revenue.* Some refer to this as "deferred revenue" or "deferred income," terms likely to confuse the unwary because the item is not yet *revenue* or *income.*

advances to affiliates. *Loans* by a parent company to a *subsidiary;* frequently combined with "investment in subsidiary" as "investments and advances to subsidiary" and shown as a *noncurrent asset* on the parent's *balance sheet.* The consolidation process eliminates these advances in *consolidated financial statements.*

advances to suppliers. A preferred term for the *asset* account representing *disbursements* of cash in advance of receiving *assets* or *services.*

adverse opinion. An *auditor's report* stating that the financial statements are not fair or are not in accord with *GAAP.*

affiliated company. A company controlling or controlled by another company.

after closing. Post-closing; a *trial balance* at the end of the period.

after cost. *Expenditures* to be made after *revenue* recognition. For example, *expenditures* for *repairs* under warranty are after cost. Proper recognition of after cost involves a debit to expense at the time of the sale and a credit to an *estimated liability.* When the firm discharges the liability, it debits the estimated liability and credits the assets consumed.

AG (Aktiengesellschaft). Germany: the form of a German company whose shares can trade on the stock exchange.

agency fund. An account for *assets* received by governmental units in the capacity of trustee or agent.

agency theory. A branch of economics relating the behavior of *principals* (such as owner nonmanagers or bosses) and that of their *agents* (such as nonowner managers or subordinates). The principal assigns responsibility and authority to the agent, but the agent's own risks and preferences differ from those of the principal. The principal cannot observe all activities of the agent. Both the principal and the agent must consider the differing risks and preferences in designing incentive contracts.

agent. One authorized to transact business, including executing contracts, for another.

aging accounts receivable. The process of classifying *accounts receivable* by the time elapsed since the claim came into existence for the purpose of estimating the amount of uncollectible accounts receivable as of a given date. See *sales contra, estimated uncollectibles,* and *allowance for uncollectibles.*

aging schedule. A listing of *accounts receivable,* classified by age, used in *aging accounts receivable.*

AICPA (American Institute of Certified Public Accountants). The national organization that represents *CPAs.* See *AcSEC.* It oversees the writing and grading of the Uniform CPA Examination. Each state sets its own requirements for becoming a CPA in that state. See *certified public accountant.* Web Site: www.aicpa.org.

all-capital earnings rate. *Rate* of return on assets.

all-current method. *Foreign currency translation* in which all *financial statement* items are translated at the *current exchange rate.*

all-inclusive (income) concept. A concept that does not distinguish between *operating* and *nonoperating revenues* and *expenses.* Thus, the only entries to retained earnings are for *net income* and *dividends.* Under this concept, the *income statement* reports all *income, gains,* and *losses;* thus, net income includes events usually reported as *prior-period adjustments* and as *corrections of errors.* GAAP do not include this concept in its pure form, but *APB Opinions No. 9* and *No. 30* move far in this direction. They do permit retained earnings entries for prior-period adjustments and correction of errors.

allocate. To divide or spread a *cost* from one *account* into several accounts, to several products or activities, or to several periods.

allocation base. The systematic method that assigns *joint costs* to *cost objectives.* For example, a firm might assign the cost of a truck to periods based on miles driven during the period; the allocation base is miles. Or the firm might assign the cost of a factory supervisor to a product based on *direct labor* hours; the allocation base is direct labor hours.

allocation of income taxes. See *deferred income tax.*

allowance. A balance sheet *contra account* generally used for *receivables* and depreciable assets. See *sales (or purchase) allowance* for another use of this term.

allowance for funds used during construction. In accounting for public utilities, a *revenue* account *credited* for *implicit interest* earnings on *shareholders' equity* balances. One principle of public utility regulation and rate setting requires that customers should pay the full costs of producing the services (e.g., electricity) that they use, nothing more and nothing less. Thus, an electric utility must capitalize into an *asset* account the full costs, but no more, of producing a new electric power-generating plant. One of the costs of building a new plant is the *interest* cost on cash tied up during construction. If *funds* are explicitly borrowed by an ordinary business, the journal entry for interest of $1,000 is typically:

Interest Expense	1,000	
Interest Payable		1,000
Interest expense for the period.		

If the firm is constructing a new plant, then another entry would be made, capitalizing interest into the plant-under-construction account:

Construction Work-in-Progress	750	
Interest Expense		750
Capitalize relevant portion of interest relating to construction work in progress into the asset account.		

The cost of the *plant asset* increases; when the firm uses the plant, it charges *depreciation.* The interest will become an expense through the depreciation process in the later periods of use, not currently as the firm pays for interest. Thus, the firm reports the full cost of the electricity generated during a given period as expense in that period. But suppose, as is common, that the electric utility does not explicitly borrow the funds but uses some of its own funds, including funds raised from equity issues as well as from debt. Even though the firm incurs no explicit interest expense or other explicit expense for capital, the funds have an *opportunity cost.* Put another way, the plant under construction will not have lower economic cost just because the firm used its own cash rather than borrowing. The public utility using its own funds, on which it would have to pay $750 of interest if it had explicitly borrowed the funds, will make the following entry:

Construction Work-in-Progress	750	
Allowance for Funds Used		
during Construction		750
Recognition of interest, an opportunity cost, on own funds used.		

The allowance account is a form of *revenue,* to appear on the income statement, and the firm will close it to Retained Earnings, increasing it. On the *statement of cash flows* it is an income or revenue item not producing funds, and so the firm must subtract it from net income in deriving *cash provided by operations. SFAS No. 34* specifically prohibits nonutility companies from capitalizing, into plant under construction, the opportunity cost (interest) on their own funds used.

allowance for uncollectibles (accounts receivable). A *contra account* that shows the estimated *accounts receivable* amount that the firm expects not to collect. When the firm uses such an allowance, the actual write-off of specific accounts receivable (*debit* allowance, *credit* specific customer's account) does not affect *revenue* or *expense* at the time of the write-off. The firm reduces revenue when it debits *bad debt expense* (or, our preference, a revenue contra account) and credits the allowance; the firm can base the amount of the credit to the allowance on a percentage of sales on account for a period of time or compute it from *aging accounts receivable.* This contra account enables the firm to show an estimated receivables amount that it expects to collect without identifying specific uncollectible accounts. See *allowance method.*

allowance method. A method of attempting to match all *expenses* of a transaction with their associated *revenues;* usually involves a debit to expense and a credit to an *estimated liability,* such as for estimated warranty expenditures, or a debit to a revenue (*contra*) account and a credit to an asset (*contra*) account, such as in some firms' accounting for uncollectible accounts. See *allowance for uncollectibles* for further explanation. When the firm uses the allowance method for *sales discounts,* the firm records sales at gross invoice prices (not reduced by the amounts of discounts made available). The firm *debits* an estimate of the amount of discounts to be taken to a revenue contra account and *credits* an allowance account, shown contra to *accounts receivable.*

American Accounting Association (AAA). An organization primarily for academic accountants but open to all interested in accounting. It publishes the *Accounting Review* and several other journals.

American Institute of Certified Public Accountants. See *AICPA*.

American Stock Exchange (AMEX) (ASE). A public market where various corporate *securities* are traded.

AMEX. *American Stock Exchange.*

amortization. Strictly speaking, the process of liquidating or extinguishing ("bringing to death") a *debt* with a series of payments to the *creditor* (or to a *sinking fund*). From that usage has evolved a related use involving the accounting for the payments themselves: "amortization schedule" for a mortgage, which is a table showing the allocation between *interest* and *principal*. The term has come to mean writing off ("liquidating") the cost of an asset. In this context it means the general process of *allocating* the *acquisition cost* of an asset either to the periods of benefit as an *expense* or to *inventory* accounts as a *product cost*. This is called *depreciation* for *plant assets, depletion* for *wasting assets* (natural resources), and "amortization" for *intangibles*. *SFAC No. 6* refers to amortization as "the accounting process of reducing an amount by periodic payments or write-downs." The expressions "unamortized debt discount or premium" and "to amortize debt discount or premium" relate to *accruals,* not to *deferrals.* The expressions "amortization of long-term assets" and "to amortize long-term assets" refer to deferrals, not accruals. Contrast with *accretion*.

amortized cost. A measure required by *SFAS No. 115* for *held-to-maturity securities*. This amount results from applying the method described at *effective interest method*. The firm records the security at its initial cost and computes the *effective interest rate* for the security. Whenever the firm receives cash from the issuer of the security or whenever the firm reaches the end of one of its own *accounting periods* (that is, reaches the time for its own *adjusting entries*), it takes the following steps. It multiplies the amount currently recorded on the books by the effective interest rate (which remains constant over the time the firm holds the security). It debits that amount to the debt security account and credits the amount to Interest Revenue. If the firm receives cash, it debits Cash and credits the debt security account. The firm recomputes the book value of the debt security as the book value before these entries plus the increase for the interest revenue less the decrease for the cash received. The resulting amount is the amortized cost for the end of that period.

analysis of variances. See *variance analysis*.

annual report. A report prepared once a year for shareholders and other interested parties. It includes a *balance sheet*, an *income statement*, a *statement of cash flows,* a reconciliation of changes in *owners' equity* accounts, a *summary of significant accounting principles*, other explanatory *notes,* the *auditor's report,* and comments from management about the year's events. See *10-K* and *financial statements*.

annuitant. One who receives an *annuity*.

annuity. A series of payments of equal amount, usually made at equally spaced time intervals.

annuity certain. An *annuity* payable for a definite number of periods. Contrast with *contingent annuity*.

annuity due. An *annuity* whose first payment occurs at the start of period 1 (or at the end of period 0). Contrast with *annuity in arrears*.

annuity in advance. An *annuity due*.

annuity in arrears. An *ordinary annuity* whose first payment occurs at the end of the first period.

annuity method of depreciation. See *compound interest depreciation*.

antidilutive. Said of a *potentially dilutive* security that will increase *earnings per share* if its holder *exercises* it or *converts* it into common stock. In computing *primary* and *fully diluted earnings per share,* the firm must assume that holders of antidilutive securities will not exercise their options or convert securities into common shares. The opposite assumption would lead to increased reported earnings per share in a given period.

APB. Accounting Principles Board of the *AICPA*. It set *accounting principles* from 1959 through 1973, issuing 31 *APB Opinions* and 4 *APB Statements*. The *FASB* superseded it.

APB Opinion. The name for the APB pronouncements that compose much of *generally accepted accounting principles;* the APB issued 31 APB Opinions from 1962 through 1973.

APB Statement. The *APB* issued four *APB Statements* between 1962 and 1970. The *Statements* were approved by at least two-thirds of the board, but they state recommendations, not requirements. For example, *Statement No. 3* (1969) suggested the publication of *constant-dollar* financial statements but did not require them.

APBs. An abbreviation used for *APB Opinions*.

applied cost. A *cost* that a firm has *allocated* to a department, product, or activity; not necessarily based on actual costs incurred.

applied overhead. *Overhead costs* charged to departments, products, or activities. Also called *absorbed overhead*.

appraisal. In valuing an *asset* or *liability,* a process that involves expert opinion rather than evaluation of explicit market transactions.

appraisal method of depreciation. The periodic *depreciation* charge that equals the difference between the beginning-of-period and the end-of-period appraised values of the *asset* if that difference is positive. If negative, there is no charge. Not based on *historical cost,* this method is thus not generally accepted.

appreciation. An increase in economic value caused by rising market prices for an *asset*. Contrast with *accretion*.

appropriated retained earnings. See *retained earnings, appropriated*.

appropriation. In governmental accounting, an *expenditure* authorized for a specified amount, purpose, and time.

appropriation account. In governmental accounting, an account set up to record specific authorizations to spend. The governmental unit credits this account with appropriation amounts. At the end of the period, the unit closes to (debits) this account all *expenditures* during the period and all *encumbrances* outstanding at the end of the period.

approximate net realizable value method. A method of assigning joint costs to *joint products* based on revenues minus *additional processing costs* of the end products.

ARB. *Accounting Research Bulletin.*

arbitrage. Strictly speaking, the simultaneous purchase in one market and sale in another of a *security* or commodity in hope of making a *profit* on price differences in the different markets. Often writers use this term loosely when a trader sells an item that is somewhat different from the item purchased; for example, the sale of shares of common stock and the simultaneous purchase of a *convertible bond* that is convertible into identical common shares. The trader hopes that the market will soon see that the similarities of the items should make them have equal market values. When the market values converge, the trader closes the positions and profits from the original difference in prices, less trading costs.

arbitrary. Having no causation basis. Accounting theorists and practitioners often, properly, say, "Some cost allocations are arbitrary." In that sense, the accountant does not mean that the allocations are capricious or haphazard but does mean that theory suggests no unique solution to the allocation problem at hand. Accountants require that arbitrary allocations be systematic, rational, and consistently followed over time.

arm's length. A transaction negotiated by unrelated parties, both acting in their own self-interests; the basis for a *fair market value* estimation or computation.

arrears. *Cumulative dividends* that the firm has not yet declared. See *annuity in arrears* for another context.

ARS. *Accounting Research Study.*

articles of incorporation. Document filed with state authorities by persons forming a corporation. When the state returns the document with a certificate of incorporation, the document becomes the corporation's *charter.*

articulate. The relation between any operating statement (for example, *income statement* or *statement of cash flows*) and comparative balance sheets, where the operating statement explains (or reconciles) the change in some major balance sheet category (for example, *retained earnings* or *working capital*).

ASE. *American Stock Exchange.*

ASR. *Accounting Series Release.*

assess. To value property for the purpose of property taxation; to levy a charge on the owner of property for improvements thereto, such as for sewers or sidewalks. The taxing authority computes the assessment.

assessed valuation. For real estate or other property, a dollar amount that a government uses as a basis for levying taxes. The amount need not have some relation to *market value.*

asset. *SFAC No. 6* defines assets as "probable future economic benefits obtained or controlled by a particular entity as a result of past transactions. . . . An asset has three essential characteristics: (a) it embodies a probable future benefit that involves a capacity, singly or in combination with other assets, to contribute directly or indirectly to future net cash inflows, (b) a particular entity can obtain the benefit and control others' access to it, and (c) the transaction or other event giving rise to the entity's right to or control of the benefit has already

occurred." A footnote points out that "probable" means that which we can reasonably expect or believe but that is not certain or proved. You may understand condition (c) better if you think of it as requiring that a future benefit cannot be an asset if it arises from an *executory contract,* a mere exchange of promises. Receiving a purchase order from a customer provides a future benefit, but it is an executory contract, so the order cannot be an asset. An asset may be *tangible* or *intangible,* short-term (current) or long-term (noncurrent).

asset depreciation range (ADR). The range of *depreciable lives* allowed by the *Internal Revenue Service* for a specific depreciable *asset.*

asset turnover. Net sales divided by average assets. See *ratio.*

assignment of accounts receivable. Transfer of the legal ownership of an account receivable through its sale. Contrast with *pledging* accounts receivable, where the receivables serve as *collateral* for a *loan.*

ATB. *Accounting Terminology Bulletin.*

at par. A *bond* or *preferred shares* issued (or selling) at *face amount.*

attachment. The laying claim to the *assets* of a borrower (or debtor) by a lender (or creditor) when the borrower has failed to pay debts on time.

attest. An auditor's rendering of an *opinion* that the *financial statements* are fair. Common usage calls this procedure the "attest function" of the CPA. See *fair presentation.*

attestor. Typically independent *CPAs,* who *audit financial statements* prepared by management for the benefit of users. The *FASB* describes accounting's constituency as comprising preparers, attestors, and users.

attribute measured. The particular *cost* reported in the balance sheet. When making physical measurements, such as of a person, one needs to decide the units with which to measure, such as inches or centimeters or pounds or grams. One chooses the attribute height or weight independently of the measuring unit, English or metric. Conventional accounting uses *historical cost* as the attribute measured and *nominal dollars* as the measuring unit. Some theorists argue that accounting would better serve readers if it used *current cost* as the attribute measured. Others argue that accounting would better serve readers if it used *constant dollars* as the measuring unit. Some, including us, think accounting should change both the measuring unit and the attribute measured. One can measure the attribute historical cost in nominal dollars or in constant dollars. One can also measure the attribute current cost in nominal dollars or constant dollars. Choosing between the two attributes and the two measuring units implies four different accounting systems. Each of these four has its uses.

attribute(s) sampling. The use of sampling technique in which the observer assesses each item selected on the basis of whether it has a particular qualitative characteristic in order to ascertain the rate of occurrence of this characteristic in the population. See also *estimation sampling.* Compare *variables sampling.* Example of attributes sampling: take a sample population of people, note the fraction that is male (say, 40 percent), and then infer that the entire population contains 40 percent males. Example of variables sampling: take a sample population of people, observe the weight of each sample point, compute the mean of those sampled people's weights (say 160 pounds), and then infer that the mean weight of the entire population equals 160 pounds.

audit. Systematic inspection of accounting records involving analyses, tests, and *confirmations*. See *internal audit*.

audit committee. A committee of the board of directors of a *corporation,* usually comprising outside directors, who nominate the independent auditors and discuss the auditors' work with them. If the auditors believe the shareholders should know about certain matters, the auditors, in principle, first bring these matters to the attention of the audit committee; in practice, the auditors may notify management before they notify the audit committee.

Audit Guides. See *Industry Audit Guides*.

audit program. The procedures followed by the *auditor* in carrying out the *audit*.

audit trail. A reference accompanying an entry, or *post,* to an underlying source record or document. Efficiently checking the accuracy of accounting entries requires an audit trail. See *cross-reference*.

Auditing Research Monograph. Publication series of the *AICPA*.

auditing standards. Standards promulgated by the *PCAOB* for auditors to follow in carrying out their attest functions. The PCAOB began operations in earnest in 2003, and initially has said that is would use the standards originally promulgated by the *AICPA*, including general standards, standards of field work, and standards of reporting. According to the AICPA, these standards "deal with the measures of the quality of the performance and the objectives to be attained" rather than with specific auditing procedures. As time passes, the PCAOB will substitute its rules for those of the AICPA.

Auditing Standards Board. *AICPA* operating committee that promulgates auditing rules. The new operations of the *PCAOB*, after 2003, render uncertain what this Board will do.

auditor. Without a modifying adjective, usually refers to an external auditor—one who checks the accuracy, fairness, and general acceptability of accounting records and statements and then *attests* to them. See *internal auditor*.

auditor's opinion. *Auditor's report*.

auditor's report. The auditor's statement of the work done and an opinion of the *financial statements*. The auditor usually gives unqualified ("clean") opinions but may qualify them, or the auditor may disclaim an opinion in the report. Often called the "accountant's report." See *adverse opinion*.

AudSEC. The former Auditing Standards Executive Committee of the *AICPA,* now functioning as the *Auditing Standards Board*.

authorized capital stock. The number of *shares* of stock that a corporation can issue; specified by the *articles of incorporation*.

available for sale, securities. *Marketable securities* a firm holds that are classified as neither *trading securities* nor *held-to-maturity (debt) securities*. This classification is important in *SFAS No. 115,* which requires the owner to carry marketable equity securities on the balance sheet at market value, not at cost. Under *SFAS No. 115,* the income statement reports *holding gains and losses* on trading securities but not on securities available for sale. The required accounting *credits* (*debits*) holding gains (losses) on securities available for sale directly to an *owners' equity* account. On sale, the firm reports realized gain or loss as the difference between the selling price and the original cost, for trading securities, and as the difference between the selling price and the book value at the beginning of the period of sale, for securities available for sale and for debt securities held to maturity. By their nature, however, the firm will only rarely sell debt securities "held to maturity."

average. The arithmetic mean of a set of numbers; obtained by summing the items and dividing by the number of items.

average collection period of receivables. See *ratio*.

average-cost flow assumption. An inventory *flow assumption* in which the cost of units equals the *weighted average* cost of the *beginning inventory* and purchases. See *inventory equation*.

average tax rate. The rate found by dividing *income tax* expense by *net income* before taxes. Contrast with *marginal tax rate* and *statutory tax rate*.

avoidable cost. A *cost* that ceases if a firm discontinues an activity; an *incremental* or *variable cost*. See *programmed cost*.

B

backflush costing. A method of *allocating indirect costs* and *overhead;* used by companies that hope to have zero or small *work-in-process inventory* at the end of the period. The method *debits* all *product costs* to *cost of goods sold* (or *finished goods inventory*) during the period. To the extent that work in process actually exists at the end of the period, the method then debits work-in-process and *credits* cost of goods sold (or finished goods inventory). This method is "backflush" in the sense that costing systems ordinarily, but not in this case, allocate first to work-in-process and then forward to cost of goods sold or to finished goods. Here, the process allocates first to cost of goods sold (or finished goods) and then, later if necessary, to work-in-process.

backlog. Orders for which a firm has insufficient *inventory* on hand for current delivery and will fill in a later period.

backlog depreciation. In *current cost accounting,* a problem arising for the *accumulated depreciation* on *plant assets.* Consider an *asset* costing $10,000 with a 10-year life depreciated with the straight-line method. Assume that a similar asset has a current cost of $10,000 at the end of the first year but $12,000 at the end of the second year. Assume that the firm bases the depreciation charge on the average current cost during the year, $10,000 for the first year and $11,000 for the second. The depreciation charge for the first year is $1,000 and for the second is $1,100 (= 0.10 x $11,000), so the *accumulated depreciation account* is $2,100 after two years. Note that at the end of the second year, the firm has used 20 percent of the asset's future benefits, so the accounting records based on current costs must show a *net book value* of $9,600 (= 0.80 x $12,000), which results only if accumulated depreciation equals $2,400, so that book value equals $9,600 (= $12,000 – $2,400). But the sum of the depreciation charges equals only $2,100 (= $1,000 + $1,100). The *journal entry* to increase the accumulated depreciation account requires a *credit* to that account of $300. The backlog depreciation question arises: what account do we debit? Some theorists would *debit* an *income* account, and others would *debit* a *balance sheet owners' equity* account without reducing current-period earnings. The answer to the question of what to debit interrelates with how the firm records the *holding gains* on the asset. When the firm debits the asset account for $2,000 to increase the recorded amount from $10,000 to $12,000, it records a holding gain of $2,000 with a credit. Many theorists believe that whatever account the firm credits for the holding gain is the same account that the firm should debit for backlog depreciation. This is sometimes called "catch-up depreciation."

bad debt. An *uncollectible account;* see *bad debt expense* and *sales contra, estimated uncollectibles.*

bad debt expense. The name for an *account debited* in both the *allowance method* for *uncollectible accounts* and the *direct write-off method.* Under the allowance method, some prefer to treat the account as a revenue contra, not as an expense, and give it an account title such as Uncollectible Accounts Adjustment.

bad debt recovery. Collection, perhaps partial, of a specific account receivable previously written off as uncollectible. If a firm uses the *allowance method,* it will usually *credit* the *allowance* account, assuming that it has correctly assessed the amount of bad debts but has merely misjudged the identity of one of the nonpaying customers. If the firm decides that its charges for bad debts have been too large, it will credit the Bad Debt Expense account. If the firm uses the *direct write-off* method, it will credit a *revenue account.*

bailout period. In a *capital budgeting* context, the total time that elapses before accumulated cash inflows from a project, including the potential *salvage value* of assets at various times, equal or exceed the accumulated cash outflows. Contrast with *payback period,* which assumes completion of the project and uses terminal salvage value. Bailout, in contrast with payback, takes into account, at least to some degree, the *present value* of the cash flows after the termination date that the analyst is considering. The potential salvage value at any time includes some estimate of the flows that can occur after that time.

balance. As a noun, the opening balance in an *account* plus the amounts of increases less the amounts of decreases. (In the absence of a modifying adjective, the term means closing balance, in contrast to opening balance. The closing balance for a period becomes the opening balance for the next period.) As a verb, "balance" means to find the value of the arithmetic expression described above.

balance sheet. Statement of financial position that shows Total *Assets* = Total *Liabilities* + *Owners' Equity.* The *balance sheet* usually classifies Total Assets as (1) *current assets,* (2) *investments,* (3) *property, plant, and equipment,* or (4) *intangible assets.* The balance sheet accounts composing Total Liabilities usually appear under the headings Current Liabilities and Long-term Liabilities.

balance sheet account. An account that can appear on a balance sheet; a *permanent account.* Contrast with *temporary account.*

balanced scorecard. A set of performance targets, not all expressed in dollar amounts, for setting an organization's goals for its individual employees or groups or divisions. A community relations employee might, for example, set targets in terms of number of employee hours devoted to local charitable purposes.

balloon. Most *mortgage* and *installment loans* require relatively equal periodic payments. Sometimes the loan requires relatively equal periodic payments with a large final payment. Usage calls the large final payment a "balloon" payment and the loan, a "balloon" loan. Although a coupon bond meets this definition, usage seldom, if ever, applies this term to bond loans.

bank balance. The amount of the balance in a checking account shown on the *bank statement.* Compare with *adjusted bank balance of cash,* and see *bank reconciliation schedule.*

bank prime rate. See *prime rate.*

bank reconciliation schedule. A schedule that explains the difference between the book balance of the cash in a bank account and the bank's statement of that amount; takes into account the amount of items such as checks that have not cleared or deposits that have not been recorded by the bank, as well as errors made by the bank or the firm.

bank statement. A statement sent by the bank to a checking account customer showing deposits, checks cleared, and service charges for a period, usually one month.

bankrupt. Occurs when a company's *liabilities* exceed its *assets* and the firm or one of its creditors has filed a legal petition that the bankruptcy court has accepted under the bankruptcy law. A bankrupt firm is usually, but need not be, *insolvent.*

base stock method. A method of inventory valuation that assumes that a firm must keep on hand at all times a minimum normal, or base stock, of goods for effective continuity of operations. The firm values this base quantity at *acquisition cost* of the inventory on hand in the earliest period when inventory was on hand. Firms may not use this method, either for financial reporting or for tax reporting, but most theorists consider it to be the forerunner of the *LIFO* cost flow assumption.

basic accounting equation. *Accounting equation.*

basic cost-flow equation. *Cost-flow equation.*

basic earnings per share (BEPS). *Net income* to *common shareholders,* divided by the weighted average number of common shares *outstanding* during the period. Required by *SFAS No. 128* and by *IASB.* See *primary earnings per share (PEPS)* for contrast. Because BEPS does not deal with *com-mon-stock equivalents,* it will almost always give a larger earnings-per-share figure than PEPS.

basis. *Acquisition cost,* or some substitute therefor, of an *asset* or *liability* used in computing gain or loss on disposition or retirement; *attribute measured.* This term appears in both *financial* and *tax reporting,* but the basis of a given item need not be the same for both purposes.

basis point. One one-hundreth (=1/100). Terminology usually quotes *interest rates* in percentage terms, such as "5.60 percent" or "5.67 percent." The difference between those two interest rates is described as "7 basis points" or seven one hundreths of one percent. Financial writers often extend this usage to other contexts involving decimals. For example, if the mean grade point average in the class is 3.25 and a given student scores 3.30, we might say that the student scored "5 basis points" above the class average.

basket purchase. Purchase of a group of *assets* (and *liabilities*) for a single price; the acquiring firm must assign *costs* to each item so that it can record the individual items with their separate amounts in the *accounts.*

bear. One who believes that security prices will fall. A "bear market" refers to a time when stock prices are generally declining. Contrast with *bull.*

bearer bond. See *registered bond* for contrast and definition.

beginning inventory. Valuation of *inventory* on hand at the beginning of the *accounting period,* equals *ending inventory* from the preceding period.

behavioral congruence. *Goal congruence.*

benchmarking. Process of measuring a firm's performance, products, and services against standards based on best levels of performance achievable or, sometimes, achieved by other firms.

benefit element (of stock options). The amount by which the *market value* of a *share* exceeds the *exercise price* of the *stock option.*

BEPS. *Basic earnings per share.*

betterment. An *improvement,* usually *capitalized,* not *expensed.*

bid. An offer to purchase, or the amount of the offer.

big bath. A *write-off* of a substantial amount of costs previously treated as *assets;* usually occurs when a corporation drops a business line that earlier required a large investment but that proved to be unprofitable. The term is sometimes used to describe a situation in which a corporation takes a large write-off in one period in order to free later periods of gradual write-offs of those amounts. In this sense it frequently occurs when the top management of the firm changes.

Big 4; Final 4. The four largest U.S. *public accounting* partnerships; in alphabetical order: Andersen; Deloitte & Touche (U.S. national practice of the international firm Deloitte Touche Tohmatsu); Ernst & Young; KPMG Peat Marwick; and Pricewaterhouse Coopers.

Big N. The largest U.S. *public accounting* partnerships. When we first prepared this glossary, there were eight such partnerships, referred to as the "Big 8." See *Big 4.* The term "Big N" came into use when various of the *Big 8* proposed to merge with each other and the ultimate number of large partnerships was in doubt, which it still is.

bill. An *invoice* of charges and *terms of sale* for *goods* and *services;* also, a piece of currency.

bill of materials. A specification of the quantities of *direct materials* that a firm expects to use to produce a given job or quantity of output.

blocked currency. Currency that the holder, by law, cannot withdraw from the issuing country or exchange for the currency of another country.

board. *Board of directors.*`

board of directors. The governing body of a corporation; elected by the shareholders.

bond. A certificate to show evidence of debt. The *par value* is the *principal* or face amount of the bond payable at maturity. The *coupon rate* is the amount of the yearly payments divided by the principal amount. Coupon bonds have attached coupons that the holder can redeem at stated dates. Increasingly, firms issue not coupon bonds but registered bonds; the firm or its agent keeps track of the owners of registered bonds. Normally, bonds call for semiannual payments.

bond conversion. The act of exchanging *convertible bonds* for *preferred* or *common shares.*

bond discount. From the standpoint of the issuer of a *bond* at the issue date, the excess of the *par value* of a bond over its initial sales price and, at later dates, the excess of par over the sum of the following two amounts: initial issue price and the portion of discount already *amortized;* from the standpoint of a bondholder, the difference between par value and selling price when the bond sells below par.

bond indenture. The contract between an issuer of *bonds* and the bondholders.

bond premium. Exactly parallel to *bond discount* except that the issue price (or current selling price) exceeds *par value.*

bond ratings. Corporate and *municipal bond* issue ratings, based on the issuer's existing *debt* level, its previous record of payment, the *coupon rate* on the bonds, and the safety of the *assets* or *revenues* that are committed to paying off *principal* and *interest.* Moody's Investors Service and Standard & Poor's Corporation publish bond ratings: Moody's top rating is Aaa; Standard & Poor's is AAA.

bond redemption. Retirement of *bonds.*

bond refunding. To incur *debt,* usually through the issue of new *bonds,* intending to use the proceeds to retire an *outstanding* bond issue.

bond sinking fund. See *sinking fund.*

bond table. A table showing the current price of a *bond* as a function of the *coupon rate,* current (remaining) term *maturity,* and effective *yield to maturity* (or *effective rate*).

bonus. Premium over normal *wage* or *salary,* paid usually for meritorious performance.

bonus method. One of two methods to recognize an excess, say $10,000, when a *partnership* admits a new partner and when the new partner's capital account is to show an amount larger than the amount of *tangible* assets that he or she contributes. First, the old partners may transfer $10,000 from themselves to the new partner. This is the bonus method. Second, the partnership may recognize goodwill in the amount of $10,000, with the credit to the new partner's capital account. This is the *goodwill method.* (Notice that the new partner's percentage of total ownership differs under the two methods.) If the new partner's capital account is to show an amount smaller than the tangible assets that he or she contributed, then the old partners will receive bonus or goodwill, depending on the method.

book. As a verb, to record a transaction; as a noun, usually plural, the *journals* and *ledgers;* as an adjective, see *book value.*

book cost. *Book value.*

book inventory. An *inventory* amount that results not from physical count but from the amount of beginning inventory plus *invoice* amounts of net purchases less invoice amounts of *requisitions* or withdrawals; implies a *perpetual inventory* method.

book of original entry. *Journal.*

book value. The amount shown in the books or in the *accounts* for an *asset, liability,* or *owners' equity* item. The term is generally used to refer to the *net* amount of an *asset* or group of assets shown in the account that records the asset and reductions, such as for *amortization,* in its cost. Of a firm, it refers to the excess of total assets over total liabilities; *net assets.*

book value per share of common stock. Common *shareholders' equity* divided by the number of shares of common stock outstanding. See *ratio.*

bookkeeping. The process of analyzing and recording transactions in the accounting records.

boot. The additional cash paid (or received) along with a used item in a trade-in or exchange transaction for another item. See *trade-in.*

borrower. See *loan.*

branch. A sales office or other unit of an enterprise physically separated from the home office of the enterprise but not organized as a legally separate *subsidiary.* Writers seldom use this term to refer to manufacturing units.

branch accounting. An accounting procedure that enables the firm to report the financial position and operations of each *branch* separately but later combine them for published statements.

breakeven analysis. See *breakeven chart.*

breakeven chart. Two kinds of breakeven charts appear here. The charts use the following information for one month. Revenue is $30 per unit.

Cost Classification	Variable Cost, Per Unit	Fixed Cost, Per Month
Manufacturing costs:		
Direct material	$ 4	—
Direct labor	9	—
Overhead	4	$3,060
Total manufacturing costs	$17	$3,060
Selling, general, and administrative costs	5	1,740
Total costs	$22	$4,800

The cost-volume-profit graph presents the relation between changes in volume to the amount of *profit,* or *income.* Such a graph shows total *revenue* and total *costs* for each volume level, and the user reads profit or loss at any volume directly from the chart. The profit-volume graph does not show revenues and costs but more readily indicates profit (or loss) at various output levels.

(a) Cost-Volume-Profit Graph

(b) Profit-Volume Graph

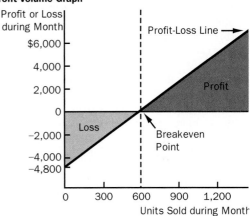

Keep in mind two caveats about these graphs:

1. Although the curve depicting *variable cost* and total cost appears as a straight line for its entire length, at low or high levels of output, variable cost will probably differ from $22 per unit. The variable cost figure usually results from studies of operations at some broad central area of production, called the *relevant range.* The chart will not usually provide accurate results for low (or high) levels of activity. For this reason, the total cost and the profit-loss curves sometimes appear as dotted lines at lower (or higher) volume levels.

2. This chart, simplistically, assumes a single-product firm. For a multiproduct firm, the horizontal axis would have to be stated in dollars rather than in physical units of output. Breakeven charts for multiproduct firms necessarily assume that the firm sells constant proportions of the several products, so that changes in this mixture, as well as in costs or selling prices, invalidate such a chart.

breakeven point. The volume of sales required so that total *revenues* equals total *costs;* may be expressed in units (*fixed costs* ÷ *contribution per unit*) or in sales dollars [selling price per unit × (fixed costs ÷ contribution per unit)].

budget. A financial plan that a firm uses to estimate the results of future operations; frequently used to help control future operations. In governmental operations, budgets often become the law. See *standard costs* for further elaboration and contrast.

budgetary accounts. In governmental accounting, the accounts that reflect estimated operations and financial condition, as affected by estimated *revenues, appropriations,* and *encumbrances.* Contrast with *proprietary accounts,* which record the transactions.

budgetary control. Management of governmental (nongovernmental) unit in accordance with an official (approved) *budget* in order to keep total expenditures within authorized (planned) limits.

budgeted cost. See *standard costs* for definition and contrast.

budgeted statements. *Pro forma statements* prepared before the event or period occurs.

bull. One who believes that security prices will rise. A "bull market" refers to a time when stock prices are generally rising. Contrast with *bear.*

burden. See *overhead costs.*

burn rate. A new business usually begins life with cash-absorbing operating losses but with a limited amount of cash. The "burn rate" measures how long the new business can survive before operating losses must stop or the firm must receive a new infusion of cash. Writers usually express the burn rate in months.

business combination. As defined in *APB Opinion No. 16,* the bringing together into a single accounting *entity* of two or more incorporated or unincorporated businesses. The new entity will account for the *merger* either with the *purchase method* or the *pooling-of-interests method.* See *conglomerate.*

business entity. *Entity; accounting entity.*

BV (*besloten vennootschap*). Netherlands: a private limited-liability company.

bylaws. The rules adopted by the shareholders of a corporation; specify the general methods for carrying out the functions of the corporation.

by-product. A *joint product* whose sales value is so small relative to the sales value of the other joint product(s) that it does not receive normal accounting treatment. The costs assigned to by-products reduce the costs of the main product(s). Accounting allocates by-products a share of joint costs such that the expected gain or loss at their sale is zero. Thus, by-products appear in the *accounts* at *net realizable value.*

C

C corporation. In tax terminology, a corporation paying its own income taxes. Contrast with *S corporation.*

CA. *Chartered accountant.*

call. An option to buy *shares* of a publicly traded corporation at a fixed price during a fixed time span. Contrast with *put.*

call premium. See *callable bond.*

call price. See *callable bond.*

callable bond. A *bond* for which the issuer reserves the right to pay a specific amount, the call price, to retire the obligation before its *maturity* date. If the issuer agrees to pay more than the *face amount* of the bond when called, the excess of the payment over the face amount is the "call premium."

called-up share capital. UK: *common stock* at *par value.*

Canadian Institute of Chartered Accountants. The national organization that represents *chartered accountants* in Canada. Web Site: www.cica.ca.

cancelable lease. See *lease.*

CAP. *Committee on Accounting Procedure.*

capacity. Stated in units of product, the amount that a firm can produce per unit of time; stated in units of input, such as *direct labor* hours, the amount of input that a firm can use in production per unit of time. A firm uses this measure of output or input in allocating *fixed costs* if the amounts producible are normal, rather than maximum, amounts.

capacity cost. A *fixed cost* incurred to provide a firm with the capacity to produce or to sell. Consists of *standby costs* and *enabling costs.* Contrast with *programmed costs.*

capacity variance. *Production volume variance.*

capital. *Owners' equity* in a business; often used, equally correctly, to mean the total assets of a business; sometimes used to mean *capital assets.* Sometimes used to mean *funds* raised. This word causes confusion in accounting and finance. Uninformed users mix up the funds (and their uses) with the sources of the funds. Consider the following transactions. A firm raises $100 cash from investors and uses the $100 to acquire *inventory* and *plant assets.* Did the investors "invest capital" of $100 or did the firm "invest capital" of $100? You will hear "invest capital" used for both sides of that transaction. Now focus on the firm who issued the shares and received the cash. Some would say the first transaction, the issue of shares, "raised capital." (If you ask of a person who answers this way, "What is the *capital,* the increase in owners' equity or the increased cash?" you will not get a clear answer, consistent across all such people.) Others would say only the second transaction, spending the cash, raised capital and only then for the plant assets, not the inventory. When a regulator focuses on a bank's capital ratios, it looks to the right-hand side of the balance sheet, not to how the firm has invested its funds. Sometimes bank regulators will take the owners' equity total and subtract from that amount the amount of intangible assets, resulting in a total with no clear conception, which they call "tangible capital." See *cost of capital* for further discussion of the confusion between the cost of raising funds and the return to, or *opportunity cost* of, investing funds. The confusion is so prevalent that we tend to avoid using the word.

capital asset. Properly used, a designation, for income tax purposes, that describes property held by a taxpayer except *cash,* inventoriable *assets,* goods held primarily for sale, most depreciable property, *real estate, receivables,* certain *intangibles,* and a few other items. Sometimes writers use this term imprecisely to describe *plant* and *equipment,* which are clearly not capital assets under the income-tax definition. Writers often use the term to refer to an *investment* in *securities.*

capital budget. Plan of proposed outlays for acquiring long-term *assets* and the means of *financing* the acquisition.

capital budgeting. The process of choosing *investment* projects for an enterprise by considering the *present value* of cash flows and deciding how to raise the funds the investment requires.

capital consumption allowance. The term used for *depreciation expense* in national income accounting and the reporting of funds in the economy.

capital contributed in excess of par (or stated) value. A preferred title for the account that shows the amount received by the issuer for *capital stock* in excess of *par (or stated) value.*

capital expenditure (outlay). An *expenditure* to acquire long-term *assets.*

capital gain. The excess of proceeds over *cost,* or other *basis,* from the sale of a *capital asset* as defined by the Internal Revenue Code. If the taxpayer has held the capital asset for a sufficiently long time before sale, then the gain is taxed at a rate lower than that used for other gains and ordinary income.

capital lease. A *lease* treated by the *lessee* as both the borrowing of funds and the acquisition of an *asset* to be *amortized.* The lessee (tenant) recognizes both the *liability* and the asset on its balance sheet. Expenses consist of *interest* on the *debt* and *amortization* of the asset. The *lessor* (landlord) treats the lease as the sale of the asset in return for a series of future cash receipts. Contrast with *operating lease.*

capital loss. A negative capital gain; see *capital gain.*

capital rationing. In a *capital budgeting* context, the imposition of constraints on the amounts of total capital expenditures in each period.

capital stock. The ownership shares of a corporation. Consists of all classes of *common* and *preferred shares.*

capital structure. The composition of a corporation's equities; the relative proportions of short-term debt, long-term debt, and *owners' equity.*

capital surplus. An inferior term for *capital contributed in excess of par (or stated) value.*

capitalization of a corporation. A term used by investment analysts to indicate *shareholders' equity* plus bonds outstanding.

capitalization of earnings. The process of estimating the *fair value* of a firm by computing the *net present value* of the predicted *net income* (not *cash flows*) of the firm for the future.

capitalization rate. An *interest rate* used to convert a series of payments or receipts or earnings into a single *present value.*

capitalize. To record an *expenditure* that may benefit a future period as an *asset* rather than to treat the expenditure as an *expense* of the period of its occurrence. Whether expenditures for advertising or for research and development should be capitalized is controversial, but *SFAS No. 2* forbids capitalizing *R&D* costs. We believe GAAP should allow firms to capitalize expenditures when they lead to future benefits and thus meet the criterion to be an asset.

carryback, carryforward, carryover. The use of losses or tax credits in one period to reduce income taxes payable in other periods. Two common kinds of carrybacks exist: for net operating losses and for *capital losses.* They apply against taxable income. In general, carrybacks are for three years, with the earliest year first. The taxpayer can carry forward operating losses for fifteen years. Corporate capital loss carryforwards are for five years. Individuals can carry forward capital losses indefinitely.

carrying cost. Costs (such as property taxes and insurance) of holding, or storing, *inventory* from the time of purchase until the time of sale or use.

carrying value (amount). *Book value.*

CASB (Cost Accounting Standards Board). A board authorized by the U.S. Congress to "promulgate cost-accounting standards designed to achieve uniformity and consistency in the cost-accounting principles followed by defense contractors and subcontractors under federal contracts." The *principles* the CASB promulgated since 1970 have considerable weight in practice wherever the *FASB* has not established a standard. Congress allowed the CASB to go out of existence in 1980 but reinstated it in 1990.

cash. Currency and coins, negotiable checks, and balances in bank accounts. For the *statement of cash flows,* "cash" also includes *marketable securities* held as *current assets.*

cash basis of accounting. In contrast to the *accrual basis of accounting,* a system of accounting in which a firm recognizes *revenues* when it receives *cash* and recognizes *expenses* as it makes *disbursements.* The firm makes no attempt to match *revenues* and *expenses* in measuring *income.* See *modified cash basis.*

cash budget. A schedule of expected cash *receipts* and *disbursements.*

cash change equation. For any *period,* the change in *cash* equals the change in *liabilities* plus the change in *owners' equity* minus the change in noncash *assets.*

cash collection basis. The *installment method* for recognizing *revenue.* Do not confuse with the *cash basis of accounting.*

cash conversion cycle. *Cash cycle.*

cash cycle. The period of time during which a firm converts *cash* into *inventories,* inventories into *accounts receivable,* and *receivables* back into cash. Sometimes called *earnings cycle.*

cash disbursements journal. A specialized *journal* used to record *expenditures* by *cash* and by *check.* If a *check register* is also used, a cash disbursements journal records only expenditures of currency and coins.

cash discount. A sales or purchase price reduction allowed for prompt payment.

cash dividend. See *dividend.*

cash equivalent. According to *SFAS No. 95,* "short-term, highly liquid investments that are both readily convertible to known amounts of cash [and] so near their maturity that they present insignificant risk of changes in value because of changes in interest rates. . . . Examples of items commonly considered to be cash equivalents are Treasury bills, commercial paper, [and] money market funds."

cash equivalent value. A term used to describe the amount for which an *asset* could be sold. Sometimes called *market value* or *fair market price (value).*

cash flow. Cash *receipts* minus *disbursements* from a given *asset,* or group of assets, for a given period. Financial analysts sometimes use this term to mean *net income + depreciation + depletion + amortization.* See also *operating cash flow* and *free cash flow.*

cash flow from operations. Receipts from customers and from investments less expenditures for inventory, labor, and services used in the usual activities of the firm, less interest expenditures. See *statement of cash flows* and *operations*. Same as *cash provided by operations*.

cash-flow hedge. A hedge of an exposure to variability in the cash flows of a recognized *asset* or *liability* or of a forecasted transaction, such as expected future foreign sales.

cash flow statement. *Statement of cash flows*.

cash provided by operations. An important subtotal in the *statement of cash flows*. This amount equals the total of revenues producing *cash* less *expenses* requiring cash. Often, the amount appears as *net income* plus expenses not requiring cash (such as depreciation charges) minus revenues not producing cash (such as revenues recognized under the *equity method* of accounting for a long-term investment). The statement of cash flows maintains the same distinctions between *continuing operations, discontinued operations,* and *income* or *loss* from *extraordinary items* as does the *income statement*.

cash receipts journal. A specialized *journal* used to record all *receipts* of *cash*.

cash (surrender) value of life insurance. An amount equal not to the face value of the policy to be paid in the event of death but to the amount that the owner could realize by immediately canceling the policy and returning it to the insurance company for cash. A firm owning a life insurance policy reports it as an asset at an amount equal to this value.

cash yield. See *yield*.

cashier's check. A bank's own *check* drawn on itself and signed by the cashier or other authorized official. It is a direct obligation of the bank. Compare with *certified check*.

catch-up depreciation. *Backlog depreciation*.

CCA. *Current cost accounting; current value accounting*.

central corporate expenses. General *overhead expenses* incurred in running the corporate headquarters and related supporting activities of a corporation. Accounting treats these expenses as *period expenses*. Contrast with *manufacturing overhead. Line of business reporting* must decide how to treat these expenses—whether to allocate them to the individual segments and, if so, how to allocate them.

central processing unit (CPU). The computer system component that carries out the arithmetic, logic, and data transfer.

certificate. The document that is the physical embodiment of a *bond* or a *share of stock;* a term sometimes used for the *auditor's report*.

certificate of deposit. A form of *deposit* in a bank or thrift institution. Federal law constrains the rate of interest that banks can pay to their depositors. Current law allows banks to pay a rate higher than the one allowed on a *time deposit* if the depositor promises to leave funds on deposit for several months or more. When the bank receives such funds, it issues a certificate of deposit. The depositor can withdraw the funds before maturity by paying a penalty.

certified check. The *check* of a depositor drawn on a bank. The bank inserts the words "accepted" or "certified" on the face of the check, with the date and a signature of a bank official. The check then becomes an obligation of the bank. Compare with *cashier's check*.

certified financial statement. A financial statement attested to by an independent *auditor* who is a *CPA*.

certified internal auditor. See *CIA*.

certified management accountant. *CMA*.

certified public accountant (CPA). An accountant who has satisfied the statutory and administrative requirements of his or her jurisdiction to be registered or licensed as a public accountant. In addition to passing the Uniform CPA Examination administered by the *AICPA,* the CPA must meet certain educational, experience, and moral requirements that differ from jurisdiction to jurisdiction. The jurisdictions are the 50 states, the District of Columbia, Guam, Puerto Rico, and the Virgin Islands.

CGA (Certified General Accountant). Canada: an accountant who has satisfied the experience, education, and examination requirements of the Certified General Accountants' Association.

chain discount. A series of *discount* percentages. For example, if a chain discount of 10 and 5 percent is quoted, then the actual, or *invoice*, price is the nominal, or list, price times 0.90 times 0.95, or 85.5, percent of invoice price.

change fund. Coins and currency issued to cashiers, delivery drivers, and so on.

changes, accounting. See *accounting changes*.

changes in financial position. See *statement of cash flows*.

charge. As a noun, a *debit* to an account; as a verb, to debit.

charge off. To treat as a *loss* or *expense* an amount originally recorded as an *asset;* use of this term implies that the charge is not in accord with original expectations.

chart of accounts. A list of names and numbers, systematically organized, of *accounts*.

charter. Document issued by a state government authorizing the creation of a corporation.

chartered accountant(s) (CA). The title used in Australia, Canada, and Scotland for an accountant who has satisfied the requirements of the institute of his or her jurisdiction to be qualified to serve as a *public accountant*. In the UK other than Scotland, members use the initials ACA or FCA: *A* means Associate and *F* means Fellow; the Associate has less experience than does the Fellow. A partnership of chartered accountants signs its firm name with the letters *CA*. In Canada, each provincial institute or order has the right to administer the examination and set the standards of performance and ethics for Chartered Accountants in its province. For a number of years, however, the provincial organizations have pooled their rights to qualify new members through the Inter-provincial Education Committee, and the result is that there are nationally set and graded examinations given in English and French. Deviation from the pass/fail grade awarded by the Board of Examiners (a subcommittee of the Inter-provincial Education Committee) is rare.

check. The Federal Reserve Board defines a check as "a *draft* or order upon a bank or banking house purporting to be drawn upon a deposit of funds for the payment at all events of a certain sum of money to a certain person therein named or to him or his order or to bearer and payable instantly on demand." It must contain the phrase "pay to the order of." The amount shown on the check must be clearly readable, and the check must have the signature of the drawer. The drawer need not date the check. In the accounts, the drawer usually reduces the *balance* in the *cash account* when it issues the check, not later when the check clears the bank. See *remittance advice.*

check register. A *journal* to record *checks* issued.

CIA (Certified Internal Auditor). One who has satisfied certain requirements of the *Institute of Internal Auditors* including experience, ethics, education, and passing examinations.

CICA. *Canadian Institute of Chartered Accountants.*

CIF (cost, insurance, and freight). In contracts, a term used along with the name of a given port, such as New Orleans, to indicate that the quoted price includes insurance, handling, and freight charges up to delivery by the seller at the given port.

circulating capital. *Working capital.*

clean opinion. See *auditor's report.*

clean surplus concept. The notion that all entries to the *retained earnings* account must record *net income* and *dividends.* See *comprehensive income.* Contrast with *current operating performance concept.* This concept, with minor exceptions, now controls *GAAP.* (See *APB Opinions No. 9* and *No. 30.*)

clearing account. An account containing amounts to be transferred to another account(s) before the end of the *accounting period.* Examples are the *income summary* account (whose balance transfers to *retained earnings*) and the purchases account (whose balance transfers to *inventory* or to *cost of goods sold*).

close. As a verb, to transfer the *balance* of a *temporary* or *contra* or *adjunct account* to the main account to which it relates; for example, to transfer *revenue* and *expense* accounts directly, or through the *income summary* account, to an *owners' equity* account or to transfer *purchase discounts* to purchases.

closed account. An *account* with equal *debits* and *credits,* usually as a result of a *closing entry.* See *ruling an account.*

closing entries. closing process. The *entries* that accomplish the transfer of balances in *temporary accounts* to the related *balance sheet accounts.* See *work sheet.*

closing inventory. *Ending inventory.*

CMA (Certified Management Accountant) certificate. Awarded by the *Institute of Certified Management Accountants* of the *Institute of Management Accountants* to those who pass a set of examinations and meet certain experience and continuing-education requirements.

CoCoA. *Continuously Contemporary Accounting.*

coding of accounts. The numbering of *accounts,* as for a *chart of accounts,* that is necessary for computerized accounting.

coinsurance. Common condition of insurance policies that protect against hazards such as fire or water damage. These often specify that the owner of the property may not collect the full amount of insurance for a loss unless the insurance policy covers at least some specified "coinsurance" percentage, usually about 80 percent, of the *replacement cost* of the property. Coinsurance clauses induce the owner to carry full, or nearly full, coverage.

COLA. Cost-of-living adjustment. See *indexation.*

collateral. *Assets* pledged by a *borrower* who will surrender those assets if he or she fails to repay a *loan.*

collectible. Capable of being converted into *cash*—now if due, later otherwise.

collusion. Cooperative effort by employees to commit fraud or another unethical act.

combination. See *business combination.*

comfort letter. A letter in which an auditor conveys negative assurances as to unaudited financial statements in a prospectus or draft financial statements included in a preliminary prospectus.

commercial paper. Short-term notes issued by corporate borrowers.

commission. Employee remuneration, usually expressed as a percentage, based on an activity rate, such as sales.

committed costs. *Capacity costs.*

Committee on Accounting Procedure (CAP). Predecessor of the *APB.* The *AICPA*'s principles-promulgating body from 1939 through 1959. Its 51 pronouncements are *Accounting Research Bulletins.*

common cost. *Cost* resulting from the use of *raw materials,* a facility (for example, plant or machines), or a service (for example, fire insurance) that benefits several products or departments. A firm must allocate this cost to those products or departments. Common costs result when two or more departments produce multiple products together even though the departments could produce them separately; *joint costs* occur when two or more departments must produce multiple products together. Many writers use "common costs" and "joint costs" synonymously. See *joint cost, indirect costs, overhead;* and *sterilized allocation.*

common-dollar accounting. *Constant-dollar accounting.*

common monetary measuring unit. For U.S. corporations, the dollar. See also *stable monetary unit assumption* and *constant-dollar accounting.*

common shares. *Shares* representing the class of owners who have residual claims on the *assets* and *earnings* of a *corporation* after the firm meets all *debt* and *preferred shareholders'* claims.

common-size statement. A *percentage statement* usually based on total *assets* or *net sales* or *revenues.*

common-stock equivalent. A *security* whose primary value arises from its holder's ability to exchange it for *common shares;* includes *stock options, warrants,* and also *convertible bonds* or *convertible preferred stock* whose *effective interest rate* at the time of issue is less than two-thirds the average Aa corporate bond yield. See *bond ratings.*

company-wide control. See *control system.*

comparative (financial) statements. *Financial statements* showing information for the same company for different times, usually two successive years for balance sheets and three for *income* and *cash flow statements.* Nearly all published financial statements are in this form. Contrast with *historical summary.*

compensating balance. The amount required to be left on deposit for a loan. When a bank lends funds to customers, it often requires that the customers keep on deposit in their checking accounts an amount equal to some percentage— say, 20 percent—of the loan. Such amounts effectively increase the *interest rate*. The borrower must disclose the amounts of such balances in *notes* to the *financial statements*.

completed contract method. Recognizing *revenues* and *expenses* for a job or order only when the firm finishes it, except that when the firm expects a loss on the contract, the firm must recognize all revenues and expenses in the period when the firm first foresees a loss. Accountants generally use this term only for long-term contracts. This method is otherwise equivalent to the *sales basis of revenue recognition*.

completed sales basis. See *sales basis of revenue recognition*.

compliance audit. Objectively obtaining and evaluating evidence regarding assertions, actions, and events to ascertain the degree of correspondence between them and established performance criteria.

compliance procedure. An *audit* procedure used to gain evidence as to whether the prescribed internal controls are operating effectively.

composite cost of capital. See *cost of capital*.

composite depreciation or **composite life method.** *Group depreciation* when the items are of unlike kind. The term also applies when the firm depreciates as a whole a single item (for example, a crane, which consists of separate units with differing service lives, such as the chassis, the motor, the lifting mechanism, and so on), rather than treating each of its components separately.

compound entry. A *journal entry* with more than one *debit* or more than one *credit* or both. See *trade-in transaction* for an example.

compound interest. *Interest* calculated on *principal* plus previously undistributed interest.

compound interest depreciation. A method designed to hold the *rate of return* on an asset constant. First find the *internal rate of return* on the cash inflows and outflows of the asset. The periodic depreciation charge equals the cash flow for the period less the internal rate of return multiplied by the asset's book value at the beginning of the period. When the cash flows from the asset are constant over time, usage sometimes refers to the method as the "annuity method" of depreciation.

compounding period. The time period, usually a year or a portion of a year, for which a firm calculates *interest*. At the end of the period, the borrower may pay interest to the lender or may add the interest (that is, convert it) to the principal for the next interest-earning period.

comprehensive budget. *Master budget.*

comprehensive income. Defined in *SFAC No. 3* as "the change in equity (net assets) of an entity during a period from transactions and other events and circumstances from nonowner sources. It includes all changes in equity during a period except those resulting from investments by owners and distributions to owners." In this definition, "equity" means *owners' equity* or *shareholders' equity*. *SFAS No. 130* requires firms to report comprehensive income as part of a statement showing *earnings* (primarily from realized transactions), comprehensive income (with additions for all other changes in owners' equity, primarily *holding gains and losses* and *foreign exchange gains and losses*), and comprehensive income

plus *accounting adjustments*. The *FASB* encourages the discontinuation of the term "net income." The terms "earnings" and "comprehensive income" denote different concepts, with totals different from that of the old "net income." *SFAS No. 130* requires that the firm report comprehensive income in a format having the same prominence as other *financial statements*. We cannot predict which "income total"—earnings or comprehensive income—users of financial statements will focus on. See *Exhibits 12.4* and *12.6* for the three formats the FASB suggests firms use.

comptroller. Same meaning and pronunciation as *controller*.

conceptual framework. A coherent system of interrelated objectives and fundamentals, promulgated by the *FASB* primarily through its *SFAC* publications, expected to lead to consistent standards for *financial accounting* and reporting.

confidence level. The measure of probability that the actual characteristics of the population lie within the stated precision of the estimate derived from a sampling process. A sample estimate may be expressed in the following terms: "Based on the sample, we are 95 percent sure [confidence level] that the true population value is within the range of X to Y [precision]." See *precision*.

confirmation. A formal memorandum delivered by the customers or suppliers of a company to its independent *auditor* verifying the amounts shown as receivable or payable. The auditor originally sends the confirmation document to the customer. If the auditor asks that the customer return the document whether the *balance* is correct or incorrect, usage calls it a "positive confirmation." If the auditor asks that the customer return the document only if it contains an error, usage calls it a "negative confirmation."

conglomerate. *Holding company*. This term implies that the owned companies operate in dissimilar lines of business.

conservatism. A *reporting objective* that calls for anticipation of all *losses* and *expenses* but defers recognition of *gains* or *profits* until they are *realized* in *arm's-length* transactions. In the absence of certainty, report events to minimize cumulative income. Conservatism does not mean reporting low income in every *accounting period*. Over long-enough time spans, income is cash-in less cash-out. If a (conservative) reporting method shows low income in early periods, it must show higher income in some later period.

consignee. See *on consignment*.

consignment. See *on consignment*.

consignor. See *on consignment*.

consistency. Treatment of like *transactions* in the same way in consecutive periods so that financial statements will be more comparable than otherwise; the reporting policy implying that a reporting *entity*, once it adopts specified procedures, should follow them from period to period. See *accounting changes* for the treatment of inconsistencies.

consol. A *bond* that never matures; a *perpetuity* in the form of a bond; originally issued by Great Britain after the Napoleonic wars to consolidate debt issues of that period. The term arose as an abbreviation for "consolidated annuities."

consolidated financial statements. Statements that are issued by legally separate companies and that show financial position and income as they would appear if the companies were one economic *entity*.

constant dollar. A hypothetical unit of *general purchasing power*, denoted "C$" by the *FASB*.

constant-dollar accounting. Accounting that measures items in *constant dollars*. See *historical cost/constant-dollar accounting* and *current cost/nominal-dollar accounting*. Sometimes called "general price level– adjusted accounting" or "general purchasing power accounting."

constant-dollar date. The time at which the *general purchasing power* of one *constant dollar* exactly equals the *general purchasing power* of one *nominal dollar;* that is, the date when C$1 = $1. When the constant-dollar date is midperiod, the nominal amounts of *revenues* and *expenses* spread evenly throughout the period equal their constant-dollar amounts but end-of-period *balance sheet* amounts measured in constant midperiod dollars differ from their nominal-dollar amounts. When the constant-dollar date is at the end of the period, the constant-dollar amounts equal the nominal-dollar amounts on a balance sheet for that date.

constrained share company. Canada: a public company whose *charter* specifies that people who are Canadian citizens or who are corporations resident in Canada must own a prescribed percentage of the shares.

constructive liability. *FASB's* term for an item recorded as an accounting *liability,* which the firm has no obligation to pay but intends to pay. An example is the liability with related *expense* that management establishes for future cash payments for severance payments for employees it intends to discharge in a restructuring.

constructive receipt. An item included in taxable income when the taxpayer can control funds whether or not it has received cash. For example, *interest* added to *principal* in a savings account is constructively received.

Consumer Price Index (CPI). A *price index* computed and issued monthly by the Bureau of Labor Statistics of the U.S. Department of Labor. The index attempts to track the price level of a group of goods and services purchased by the average consumer. The CPI is used in *constant-dollar accounting*.

contingency. A potential *liability.* If a specified event occurs, such as a firm's losing a lawsuit, it would recognize a liability. The notes disclose the contingency, but so long as it remains contingent, it does not appear in the balance sheet. *SFAS No. 5* requires treatment as a contingency until the outcome is "probable" and the amount of payment can be reasonably estimated, perhaps within a range. When the outcome becomes probable (the future event is "likely" to occur) and the firm can reasonably estimate the amount (using the lower end of a range if it can estimate only a range), then the firm recognizes a liability in the accounts, rather than just disclosing it. A *material* contingency may lead to a qualified, "*subject to*" auditor's opinion. Firms do not record *gain* contingencies in the accounts but merely disclose them in notes.

contingent annuity. An *annuity* whose number of payments depends on the outcome of an event whose timing is uncertain at the time the annuity begins; for example, an annuity payable until death of the *annuitant*. Contrast with *annuity certain*.

contingent issue (securities). Securities issuable to specific individuals at the occurrence of some event, such as the firm's attaining a specified level of earnings.

contingent liability. *Contingency.* Avoid this term because it refers to something not (yet) a *liability* on the *balance sheet.*

contingent obligation. *Contingency.*

continuing appropriation. A governmental *appropriation* automatically renewed without further legislative action until altered or revoked or expended.

continuing operations. See *income from continuing operations.*

continuity of operations. The assumption in accounting that the business *entity* will continue to operate long enough to carry out its current plans. The *going-concern assumption.*

continuous budget. A *budget* that adds a future period as the current period ends. This budget, then, always reports on the same number of periods.

continuous compounding. *Compound interest* in which the *compounding period* is every instant of time. See *e* for the computation of the equivalent annual or periodic rate.

continuous improvement. Modern *total quality management (TQM)* practitioners believe that the process of seeking quality is never complete. This attitude reflects that assumption, seeking always to improve activities.

continuous inventory method. The *perpetual inventory* method.

Continuously Contemporary Accounting (CoCoA). A name coined by the Australian theorist Raymond J. Chambers to indicate a combination of *current value accounting* in which the *measuring unit* is *constant dollars* and the *attribute measured* is *exit value.*

contra account. An *account,* such as *accumulated depreciation,* that accumulates subtractions from another account, such as machinery. Contrast with *adjunct account.*

contributed capital. Name for the *owners' equity* account that represents amounts paid in, usually in *cash,* by owners; the sum of the balances in *capital stock* accounts plus *capital contributed in excess of par (or stated) value* accounts. Contrast with *donated capital.*

contributed surplus. An inferior term for *capital contributed in excess of par value.*

contribution approach. *Income statement* preparation method that reports *contribution margin,* by separating *variable costs* from *fixed costs,* in order to emphasize the importance of cost-behavior patterns for purposes of planning and control.

contribution margin. *Revenue* from *sales* less all variable *expenses.* Contrast with *gross margin.*

contribution margin ratio. *Contribution margin* divided by *net sales;* usually measured from the price and cost of a single unit; sometimes measured in total for companies with multiple products.

contribution per unit. Selling price less *variable costs* per unit.

contributory. Said of a *pension plan* in which employees, as well as employers, make payments to a pension *fund*. Note that the provisions for *vesting* apply only to the employer's payments. Whatever the degree of vesting of the employer's payments, employees typically gets back all their payments, with interest, in case of death or other cessation of employment before retirement.

control (controlling) account. A summary *account* with totals equal to those of entries and balances that appear in individual accounts in a *subsidiary ledger*. Accounts Receivable is a control account backed up with an account for each customer. Do not change the balance in a control account unless you make a corresponding change in one of the subsidiary accounts.

control system. A device used by top management to ensure that lower-level management carries out its plans or to safeguard assets. Control designed for a single function within the firm is "operational control"; control designed for autonomous segments that generally have responsibility for both revenues and costs is "divisional control"; control designed for activities of the firm as a whole is "companywide control." Systems designed for safeguarding *assets* are "internal control" systems.

controllable cost. A *cost* influenced by the way a firm carries out operations. For example, marketing executives control advertising costs. These costs can be *fixed* or *variable*. See *programmed costs* and managed costs.

controlled company. A company in which an individual or corporation holds a majority of the voting shares. An owner can sometimes exercise effective control even though it owns less than 50 percent of the shares.

controller. A title for the chief accountant of an organization; often spelled *comptroller*.

conversion. The act of exchanging a convertible security for another security.

conversion audit. An examination of changeover procedures, and new accounting procedures and files, that takes place when a significant change in the accounting system (e.g., a change from a manual to a computerized system or a change of computers) occurs.

conversion cost. *Direct labor* costs plus factory *overhead* costs incurred in producing a product; that is, the cost to convert raw materials to finished products. *Manufacturing cost*.

conversion period. *Compounding period;* also, period during which the holder of a *convertible bond* or *convertible preferred stock* can convert it into *common shares*.

convertible bond. A *bond* whose owner may convert it into a specified number of shares of *capital stock* during the *conversion period*.

convertible preferred stock. *Preferred shares* whose owner may convert them into a specified number of *common shares*.

cookie jar accounting. When a firm records a *loss*, such as for an *asset impairment*, it *debits* loss and *credits* an *asset account*. If management thinks the market expects a loss, then it can increase the amount of the reported loss even larger than actual. It knows that future *income* can be made to be larger by the amount of the excess loss recognized currently and management can choose the time for the future *earnings* boost. Arthur Levitt, Jr.,

former Chairman of the *SEC,* criticized this practice and called it "cookie jar accounting," because firms can overstate losses or expenses on one period to store, as in a jar, reportable earnings for discretionary reporting in the future.

cooperative. An incorporated organization formed for the benefit of its members (owners), who are either producers or consumers, in order to acquire for them profits or savings that otherwise accrue to middlemen. Members exercise control on the basis of one vote per member.

coproduct. A product sharing production facilities with another product. For example, if an apparel manufacturer produces shirts and jeans on the same line, these are coproducts. Distinguish coproducts from *joint products* and *by-products* that, by their very nature, a firm must produce together, such as the various grades of wood a lumber factory produces.

copyright. Exclusive right granted by the government to an individual author, composer, playwright, or the like for the life of the individual plus 50 years. If a firm receives the copyright, then the right extends 75 years after the original publication. The *economic life* of a copyright can be less than the legal life, such as, for example, the copyright of this book.

core deposit intangible. A bank borrows funds from its customers, called "depositors," who open checking and savings accounts. Those depositors can take out their funds at any time, but usually don't. The amount that depositors leave on deposit for long periods of time are called "core deposits." The bank lends those funds to other customers, called "borrowers," at *interest rates* larger than the amount it pays the depositors for the funds. (For checking accounts, the rate the bank pays depositors is often zero.) The fact that the depositors can remove their funds at any time, but, on average, leave amounts on deposit relatively permanently means that the bank can lend those funds for relatively long periods of time, usually at higher interest rates, than it can charge for shorter-term loans. (See *yield curve*.) The bank's ability to borrow from some customers at a low rate and lend to other customers at a high rate creates wealth for the bank. Bankers and banking analysts call the cause of this wealth the "core deposit intangible." It represents an *asset* not recognized in the financial statements by the bank that created with wealth, although some *SEC* commissioners have expressed the thought that accounting should recognize such items as assets. When one bank buys another in a *purchase,* however, it will pay for this asset and will record it as an asset. Usually, the acquiring bank does not use the specific account title "Core Deposit Intangible," but instead uses the account title *Goodwill*.

corner. The control, of a quantity of shares or a commodity, sufficiently large that the holder can control the market price.

corporation. A legal entity authorized by a state to operate under the rules of the entity's *charter*.

correcting entry. An *adjusting entry* that properly records a previously, improperly recorded *transaction*. Do not confuse with entries that correct *accounting errors*.

correction of errors. See *accounting errors*.

cost. The sacrifice, measured by the *price* paid or to be paid, to acquire *goods* or *services*. See *acquisition cost* and *replacement cost.* Terminology often uses "cost" when referring to the valuation of a good or service acquired. When writers use the word in this sense, a cost is an *asset.* When the benefits of the acquisition (the goods or services acquired) expire, the cost becomes an *expense* or *loss.* Some writers, however, use "cost" and "expense" as synonyms. Contrast with *expense.* The word "cost" appears in more than 50 accounting terms, each with sometimes subtle distinctions in meaning. See *cost terminology* for elaboration. Clarity requires that the user include with the word "cost" an adjective or phrase to be clear about intended meaning.

cost accounting. Classifying, summarizing, recording, reporting, and allocating current or predicted *costs;* a subset of *managerial accounting.*

Cost Accounting Standards Board. See *CASB.*

cost accumulation. Bringing together, usually in a single *account,* all *costs* of a specified activity. Contrast with *cost allocation.*

cost allocation. Assigning *costs* to individual products or time periods. Contrast with *cost accumulation.*

cost-based transfer price. A *transfer price* based on *historical costs.*

cost behavior. The functional relation between changes in activity and changes in *cost;* for example: *fixed* versus *variable costs; linear* versus *curvilinear cost.*

cost/benefit criterion. Some measure of *costs* compared with some measure of *benefits* for a proposed undertaking. If the costs exceed the benefits, then the analyst judges the undertaking not worthwhile. This criterion will not yield good decisions unless the analyst estimates all costs and benefits flowing from the undertaking.

cost center. A unit of activity for which a firm accumulates *expenditures* and *expenses.*

cost driver. A factor that causes an activity's costs. See *driver* and *activity basis.*

cost-effective. Among alternatives, the one whose benefit, or payoff, per unit of cost is highest; sometimes said of an action whose expected benefits exceed expected costs whether or not other alternatives exist with larger benefit-cost ratios.

cost estimation. The process of measuring the functional relation between changes in activity levels and changes in cost.

cost flow assumption. See *flow assumption.*

cost-flow equation. Beginning Balance + Transfers In = Transfers Out + Ending Balance; BB + TI = TO + EB.

cost flows. Costs passing through various classifications within an entity. See *flow of costs* for a diagram.

cost method (for investments). In accounting for an investment in the *capital stock* or *bonds* of another company, method in which the firm shows the investment at *acquisition cost* and treats only *dividends* declared or *interest receivable* as *revenue;* not allowed by *GAAP.*

cost method (for treasury stock). The method of showing *treasury stock* in a *contra account* to all other items of *shareholders' equity* in an amount equal to that paid to reacquire the stock.

cost object(ive). Any activity for which management desires a separate measurement of *costs.* Examples include departments, products, and territories.

cost of capital. *Opportunity cost* of funds invested in a business; the rate of return that rational owners require an asset to earn before they will devote that asset to a particular purpose; sometimes measured as the average annual rate that a company must pay for its *equities.* In *efficient capital markets,* this cost is the *discount rate* that equates the expected *present value* of all future cash flows to common shareholders with the market value of common stock at a given time. Analysts often measure the cost of capital by taking a *weighted average* of the firm's *debt* and various *equity securities.* We sometimes call the measurement so derived the "composite cost of capital," and some analysts confuse this measurement of the cost of capital with the cost of capital itself. For example, if the equities of a firm include substantial amounts for the *deferred income tax liability,* the composite cost of capital will underestimate the true cost of capital, the required rate of return on a firm's assets, because the deferred income tax liability has no explicit cost.

cost of goods manufactured. The sum of all costs allocated to products completed during a period, including materials, labor, and *overhead.*

cost of goods purchased. Net purchase price of goods acquired plus costs of storage and delivery to the place where the owner can productively use the items.

cost of goods sold. Inventoriable *costs* that firms *expense* because they sold the units; equals *beginning inventory* plus *cost of goods purchased* or *manufactured* minus *ending inventory.*

cost of sales. Generally refers to *cost of goods sold,* occasionally to *selling expenses.*

cost or market, whichever is lower. See *lower of cost or market.*

cost percentage. One less *markup percentage; cost* of *goods available for sale* divided by selling prices of goods available for sale (when FIFO is used); *cost* of *purchases* divided by selling prices of purchases (when LIFO is used). See *markup* for further detail on inclusions in the calculation of cost percentage.

cost pool. *Indirect cost pool;* groupings or aggregations of costs, usually for subsequent analysis.

cost principle. The *principle* that requires reporting *assets* at *historical* or *acquisition cost,* less accumulated *amortization.* This principle relies on the assumption that cost equals *fair market value* at the date of acquisition and that subsequent changes are not likely to be significant.

cost-recovery-first method. A method of *revenue* recognition that *credits inventory* as the firm receives cash collections and continues until the firm has collected cash equal to the sum of all costs. Only after the firm has collected cash equal to costs does it recognize *income.* A firm may not use this method in financial reporting unless the total amount of collections is highly uncertain. It is never allowed for income tax reporting. Contrast with the *installment method,* allowed for both book and tax, in which the firm credits *constant* proportions of each cash collection both to cost and to income.

cost sheet. Statement that shows all the elements composing the total cost of an item.

cost structure. For a given set of total costs, the percentages of fixed and variable costs, typically two percentages adding to 100 percent.

cost terminology. The word "cost" appears in many accounting terms. The accompanying exhibit classifies some of these terms according to the distinctions between the terms in accounting usage. Joel Dean was, to our knowledge, the first to attempt such distinctions; we have used some of his ideas here. We discuss some of the terms in more detail under their own listings.

cost-to-cost. The *percentage-of-completion method* in which the firm estimates the fraction of completion as the ratio of costs incurred to date divided by the total costs the firm expects to incur for the entire project.

cost-volume-profit analysis. A study of the sensitivity of *profits* to changes in units sold (or produced) or costs or prices.

cost-volume-profit graph (chart). A graph that shows the relation between *fixed costs, contribution per unit, break-even point,* and *sales.* See *breakeven chart.*

costing. The process of calculating the cost of activities, products, or services; the British word for *cost accounting.*

counterparty. The term refers to the opposite party in a legal contract. In accounting and finance, a frequent usage arises when an entity purchases (or sells) a *derivative* financial contract, such as an *option, forward contract,* and *futures contract.*

coupon. That portion of a *bond* document redeemable at a specified date for payments. Its physical form resembles a series of tickets; each coupon has a date, and the holder either deposits it at a bank, just like a check, for collection or mails it to the issuer's agent for collection.

coupon rate. Of a *bond,* the amount of annual coupons divided by par value. Contrast with *effective rate.*

covenant. A promise with legal validity. A loan covenant specifies the terms under which the lender can force the borrower to repay funds otherwise not yet due. For example, a *bond* covenant might say that the *principal* of a bond issue falls due on December 31, 2010, unless the firm's *debt-equity ratio* falls below 40 percent, in which case the amount becomes due immediately.

CPA. See *certified public accountant.* The *AICPA* suggests that no periods appear in the abbreviation.

CPI. *Consumer price index.*

CPP. Current purchasing power; usually used, primarily in the UK, as an adjective modifying the word "accounting" to mean the accounting that produces *constant-dollar financial statements.*

Cr. Abbreviation for *credit,* always with initial capital letter. Quiz: what do you suppose *Cr.* stands for? For the answer, see *Dr.*

creative accounting. Selection of *accounting principles* and interpretation of transactions or events designed to manipulate, typically to increase but sometimes merely to smooth, reported *income from continuing operations;* one form of *fraudulent financial reporting.* Many attempts at creative accounting involve premature *revenue recognition.*

Cost Terminology: Distinctions among Terms Containing the Word "Cost"

Terms (Synonyms Given in Parentheses)			Distinctions and Comments
			1. The following pairs of terms distinguish the basis measured in accounting.
Historical Cost (Acquisition Cost)	v.	Current Cost	A distinction used in financial accounting. Current cost can be used more specifically to mean replacement cost, net realizable value, or present value of cash flows. "Current cost" is often used narrowly to mean replacement cost.
Historical Cost (Actual Cost)	v.	Standard Cost	The distinction between historical and standard costs arises in product costing for inventory valuation. Some systems record actual costs; others record the standard costs.
			2. The following pairs of terms denote various distinctions among historical costs. For each pair of terms, the sum of the two kinds of costs equals total historical cost used in financial reporting.
Variable Cost	v.	Fixed Cost (Constant Cost)	Distinction used in breakeven analysis and in the design of cost accounting systems, particularly for product costing. See *(4)*, below, for a further subdivision of fixed costs and *(5)*, below, for the economic distinction between marginal and average cost closely paralleling this one.
Traceable Cost	v.	Common Cost (Joint Cost)	Distinction arises in allocating manufacturing costs to product. Common costs are allocated to product, but the allocations are more or less arbitrary. The distinction also arises in preparing segment reports and in separating manufacturing from nonmanufacturing costs.
Direct Cost	v.	Indirect Cost	Distinction arises in designing cost accounting systems and in product costing. Direct costs can be traced directly to a cost object (e.g., a product, a responsibility center), whereas indirect costs cannot.

(continued on next page)

Terms (Synonyms Given in Parentheses)			Distinctions and Comments
Out-of-Pocket Cost (Outlay Cost; Cash Cost)	v.	Book Cost	Virtually all costs recorded in financial statements require a cash outlay at one time or another. The distinction here separates expenditures to occur in the future from those already made and is used in making decisions. Book costs, such as for depreciation, reduce income without requiring a future outlay of cash. The cash has already been spent. See future cost v. past cost in (5), below.
Incremental Cost (Marginal Cost; Differential Cost)	v.	Unavoidable Cost (Inescapable Cost; Sunk Cost)	Distinction used in making decisions. Incremental costs will be incurred (or saved) if a decision is made to go ahead (or to stop) some activity, but not otherwise. Unavoidable costs will be reported in financial statements whether the decision is made to go ahead or not, because cash has already been spent or committed. Not all unavoidable costs are book costs, such as, for example, a salary that is promised but not yet earned and that will be paid even if a no-go decision is made.
			The economist restricts the term marginal cost to the cost of producing one more unit. Thus the next unit has a marginal cost; the next week's output has an incremental cost. If a firm produces and sells a new product, the related new costs would properly be called incremental, not marginal. If a factory is closed, the costs saved are incremental, not marginal.
Escapable Cost	v.	Inescapable Cost (Unavoidable Cost)	Same distinction as incremental cost v. unavoidable cost, but this pair is used only when the decision maker is considering stopping something—ceasing to produce a product, closing a factory, or the like. See next pair.
Avoidable Cost	v.	Unavoidable Cost	A distinction sometimes used in discussing the merits of variable and absorption costing. Avoidable costs are treated as product costs and unavoidable costs are treated as period expenses under variable costing.
Controllable Cost	v.	Uncontrollable Cost	The distinction here is used in assigning responsibility and in setting bonus or incentive plans. All costs can be affected by someone in the entity; those who design incentive schemes attempt to hold a person responsible for a cost only if that person can influence the amount of the cost.

3. In each of the following pairs, used in historical cost accounting, the word "cost" appears in one of the terms where "expense" is meant.

Expired Cost	v.	Unexpired Cost	The distinction is between expense and asset.
Product Cost	v.	Period Cost	The terms distinguish product cost from period expense. When a given asset is used, is its cost converted into work-in-process and then finished goods on the balance sheet until the goods are sold, or is it an expense shown on this period's income statement? Product costs appear on the income statement as part of cost of goods sold in the period when the goods are sold. Period expenses appear on the income statement with an appropriate caption for the item in the period when the cost is incurred or recognized.

4. The following subdivisions of fixed (historical) costs are used in analyzing operations. The relation between the components of fixed costs is as follows:

$$\underbrace{\text{Fixed Costs}} = \underbrace{\text{Capacity Costs}} + \underbrace{\text{Programmed Costs}}$$

Semifixed Costs + "Pure" Fixed Costs	+	Fixed Portions of Semi-variable Costs	Standby Costs	+	Enabling Costs

Capacity Cost (Committed Cost)	v.	Programmed Cost (Managed Cost; Discretionary Cost)	Capacity costs give a firm the capability to produce or to sell. Programmed costs, such as for advertising or research and development, may not be essential, but once a decision to incur them is made, they become fixed costs.
Standby Cost	v.	Enabling Cost	Standby costs will be incurred whether capacity, once acquired, is used or not, such as property taxes and depreciation on a factory. Enabling costs, such as for a security force, can be avoided if the capacity is unused.

(continued on next page)

Terms (Synonyms Given in Parentheses)			Distinctions and Comments
Semifixed Cost	v.	Semivariable Cost	A cost that is fixed over a wide range but that can change at various levels is a semifixed cost or "step cost." An example is the cost of rail lines from the factory to the main rail line, where fixed cost depends on whether there are one or two parallel lines but is independent of the number of trains run per day. Semivariable costs combine a strictly fixed component cost plus a variable component. Telephone charges usually have a fixed monthly component plus a charge related to usage.
			5. The following pairs of terms distinguish among economic uses or decision-making uses or regulatory uses of cost terms.
Fully Absorbed Cost	v.	Variable Cost (Direct Cost)	Fully absorbed costs refer to costs where fixed costs have been allocated to units or departments as required by generally accepted accounting principles. Variable costs, in contrast, may be more relevant for making decisions, such as setting prices.
Fully Absorbed Cost	v.	Full Cost	In full costing, all costs, manufacturing costs as well as central corporate expenses (including financing expenses), are allocated to products or divisions. In full absorption costing, only manufacturing costs are allocated to products. Only in full costing will revenues, expenses, and income summed over all products or divisions equal corporate revenues, expenses, and income.
Opportunity Cost	v.	Outlay Cost (Out-of-Pocket Cost)	Opportunity cost refers to the economic benefit forgone by using a resource for one purpose instead of for another. The outlay cost of the resource will be recorded in financial records. The distinction arises because a resource is already in the possession of the entity with a recorded historical cost. Its economic value to the firm, opportunity cost, generally differs from the historical cost; it can be either larger or smaller.
Future Cost	v.	Past Cost	Effective decision making analyzes only present and future outlay costs, or out-of-pocket costs. Opportunity costs are relevant for profit maximizing; past costs are used in financial reporting.
Short-Run Cost	v.	Long-Run Cost	Short-run costs vary as output is varied for a given configuration of plant and equipment. Long-run costs can be incurred to change that configuration. This pair of terms is the economic analog of the accounting pair, see (2) above, variable and fixed costs. The analogy is not perfect because some short-run costs are fixed, such as property taxes on the factory, from the point of view of breakeven analysis.
Imputed Cost	v.	Book Cost	In a regulatory setting some costs, for example the cost of owners' equity capital, are calculated and used for various purposes; these are imputed costs. Imputed costs are not recorded in the historical costs accounting records for financial reporting. Book costs are recorded.
Average Cost	v.	Marginal Cost	The economic distinction equivalent to fully absorbed cost of product and variable cost of product. Average cost is total cost divided by number of units. Marginal cost is the cost to produce the next unit (or the last unit).
Differential Cost (Incremental Cost)	v.	Variable Cost	Whether a cost changes or remains fixed depends on the activity basis being considered. Typically, but not invariably, costs are said to be variable or with respect to an activity basis such as changes in production levels. Typically, but not invariably, costs are said to be incremental or not with respect to an activity basis such as the undertaking of some new venture. For example, consider the decision to undertake the production of food processors, rather than food blenders, which the manufacturer has been making. To produce processors requires the acquisition of a new machine tool. The cost of the new machine tool is incremental with respect to a decision to produce food processors instead of food blenders but, once acquired, becomes a fixed cost of producing food processors. If costs of direct labor hours are going to be incurred for the production of food processors or food blenders, whichever is produced (in a scenario when not both are to be produced), such costs are variable with respect to production measured in units but are not incremental with respect to the decision to produce processors rather than blenders. This distinction is often blurred in practice, so a careful understanding of the activity basis being considered is necessary to understand the concepts being used in a particular application.

credit. As a noun, an entry on the right-hand side of an *account;* as a verb, to make an entry on the right-hand side of an account; records increases in *liabilities, owners' equity, revenues,* and *gains;* records decreases in *assets* and *expenses.* See *debit and credit conventions.* This term also refers to the ability or right to buy or borrow in return for a promise to pay later.

credit bureau. An organization that gathers and evaluates data on the ability of a person to meet financial obligations and sells this information to its clients.

credit loss. The amount of accounts receivable that the firm finds, or expects to find, *uncollectible.*

credit memorandum. A document used by a seller to inform a buyer that the seller is crediting (reducing) the buyer's account receivable because of *errors, returns,* or *allowances;* also, the document provided by a bank to a depositor to indicate that the bank is increasing the depositor's balance because of some event other than a deposit, such as the collection by the bank of the depositor's *note receivable.*

creditor. One who lends. In the UK, *account payable.*

critical path method (CPM). A method of *network analysis* in which the analyst estimates normal duration time for each activity within a project. The critical path identifies the shortest completion period based on the most time-consuming sequence of activities from the beginning to the end of the network. Compare *PERT.*

cross-reference (index). A number placed beside each *account* in a *journal entry* indicating the *ledger* account to which the record keeper posted the entry and placing in the ledger the page number of the journal where the record keeper first recorded the journal entry; used to link the *debit* and *credit* parts of an entry in the ledger accounts back to the original entry in the journal. See *audit trail.*

cross-section analysis. Analysis of *financial statements* of various firms for a single period of time; contrast with *time-series analysis,* in which analysts examine statements of a given firm for several periods of time.

Crown corporation. Canada and UK: a corporation that is ultimately accountable, through a minister of the Crown, to Parliament or a legislature for the conduct of its affairs.

cum div. (dividend). The condition of shares whose quoted market price includes a declared but unpaid dividend. This condition pertains between the declaration date of the dividend and the record date. Compare *ex div. (dividend).*

cum rights. The condition of securities whose quoted market price includes the right to purchase new securities. Compare *ex rights.*

cumulative dividend. Preferred stock *dividends* that, if not paid, accrue as a commitment that the firm must pay before it can declare dividends to common shareholders.

cumulative preferred shares. *Preferred* shares with *cumulative dividend* rights.

current assets. *Cash* and other *assets* that a firm expects to turn into cash, sell, or exchange within the normal operating cycle of the firm or one year, whichever is longer. One year is the usual period for classifying asset balances on the balance sheet. Current assets include *cash,* *marketable securities, receivables, inventory,* and *current prepayments.*

current cost. *Cost* stated in terms of current values (of *productive capacity*) rather than in terms of *acquisition cost.* See *net realizable value* and *current selling price.*

current cost accounting. The *FASB's* term for *financial statements* in which the *attribute measured* is *current cost.*

current cost/nominal-dollar accounting. Accounting based on *current cost* valuations measured in *nominal dollars.* Components of *income* include an *operating margin* and *holding gains and losses.*

current exchange rate. The rate at which the holder of one unit of currency can convert it into another at the end of the *accounting period* being reported on or, for *revenues, expenses, gains,* and *losses,* the date of recognition of the transaction.

current exit value. *Exit value.*

current fund. In governmental accounting, a synonym for *general fund.*

current funds. *Cash* and other assets readily convertible into cash; in governmental accounting, funds spent for operating purposes during the current period; includes *general,* special revenue, *debt service,* and *enterprise funds.*

current (gross) margin. See *operating margin based on current costs.*

current liability. A debt or other obligation that a firm must discharge within a short time, usually the *earnings cycle* or one year, normally by expending *current assets.*

current operating performance concept. The notion that reported *income* for a period ought to reflect only ordinary, normal, and recurring operations of that period. A consequence is that *extraordinary* and nonrecurring items are entered directly in the Retained Earnings account. Contrast with *clean surplus concept.* This concept is no longer acceptable. (See *APB Opinion No. 9* and *No. 30.*)

current ratio. Sum of *current assets* divided by sum of *current liabilities.* See *ratio.*

current realizable value. *Realizable value.*

current replacement cost. Of an *asset,* the amount currently required to acquire an identical asset (in the same condition and with the same service potential) or an asset capable of rendering the same service at a current *fair market price.* If these two amounts differ, use the lower. Contrast with *reproduction cost.*

current selling price. The amount for which an *asset* could be sold as of a given time in an *arm's-length* transaction rather than in a forced sale.

current service costs. *Service costs* of a *pension plan.*

current value accounting. The form of accounting in which all assets appear at *current replacement cost* (*entry value*) or *current selling price* or *net realizable value* (*exit value*) and all *liabilities* appear at *present value.* Entry and exit values may differ from each other, so theorists have not agreed on the precise meaning of "current value accounting."

current yield. Of a *bond,* the annual amount of *coupons* divided by the current market price of the bond. Contrast with *yield to maturity.*

currently attainable standard cost. *Normal standard cost.*

curvilinear (variable) cost. A continuous, but not necessarily linear (straight-line), functional relation between activity levels and *costs.*

customers' ledger. The *ledger* that shows *accounts receivable* of individual customers. It is the *subsidiary ledger* for the *control account* Accounts Receivable.

cutoff rate. *Hurdle rate.*

D

data bank. An organized file of information, such as a customer name and address file, used in and kept up-to-date by a processing system.

database. A comprehensive collection of interrelated information stored together in computerized form to serve several applications.

database management system. Generalized software programs used to handle physical storage and manipulation of databases.

days of average inventory on hand. See *ratio.*

days of grace. The days allowed by law or contract for payment of a debt after its due date.

DCF. *Discounted cash flow.*

DDB. *Double declining-balance depreciation.*

debenture bond. A *bond* not secured with *collateral.*

debit. As a noun, an entry on the left-hand side of an *account;* as a verb, to make an entry on the left-hand side of an account; records increases in *assets* and *expenses;* records decreases in *liabilities, owners' equity,* and *revenues.* See *debit and credit conventions.*

debit and credit conventions. The conventional use of the *T-account* form and the rules for debit and credit in *balance sheet accounts* (see below). The equality of the two sides of the *accounting equation* results from recording equal amounts of *debits* and *credits* for each *transaction.*

Typical Asset Account

Opening Balance Increase + Dr. Ending Balance	Decrease − Cr.

Typical Liability Account

Decrease − Dr.	Opening Balance Increase + Cr. Ending Balance

Typical Owners' Equity Account

Decrease − Dr.	Opening Balance Increase + Cr. Ending Balance

Revenue and expense accounts belong to the owners' equity group. The relation and the rules for debit and credit in these accounts take the following form:

Owners' Equity

Decrease − Dr.	Increase + Cr.

Expenses		**Revenues**	
Dr.	Cr.	Dr.	Cr.
+	−	−	+
*			*

*Normal balance before closing

debit memorandum. A document used by a seller to inform a buyer that the seller is debiting (increasing) the amount of the buyer's *accounts receivable.* Also, the document provided by a bank to a depositor to indicate that the bank is decreasing the depositor's *balance* because of some event other than payment for a *check,* such as monthly service charges or the printing of checks.

debt. An amount owed. The general name for *notes, bonds, mortgages,* and the like that provide evidence of amounts owed and have definite payment dates.

debt capital. *Noncurrent liabilities.* See *debt financing,* and contrast with *equity financing.*

debt-equity ratio. Total *liabilities* divided by total equities. See *ratio.* Some analysts put only total shareholders' equity in the denominator. Some analysts restrict the numerator to *long-term debt.*

debt financing. *Leverage.* Raising *funds* by issuing *bonds, mortgages,* or *notes.* Contrast with *equity financing.*

debt guarantee. See *guarantee.*

debt ratio. *Debt-equity ratio.*

debt service fund. In governmental accounting, a *fund* established to account for payment of *interest* and *principal* on all general-obligation *debt* other than that payable from special *assessments.*

debt service payment. The payment required by a lending agreement, such as periodic coupon payment on a bond or installment payment on a loan or a lease payment. It is sometimes called "interest payment," but this term will mislead the unwary. Only rarely will the amount of a debt service payment equal the interest expense for the period preceding the payment. A debt service payment will always include some amount for interest, but the payment will usually differ from the interest expense.

debt service requirement. The amount of cash required for payments of *interest,* current maturities of *principal* on outstanding *debt,* and payments to *sinking funds* (corporations) or to the debt service fund (governmental).

debtor. One who borrows; in the UK, *account receivable.*

decentralized decision making. Management practice in which a firm gives a manager of a business unit responsibility for that unit's *revenues* and *costs,* freeing the manager to make decisions about prices, sources of supply, and the like, as though the unit were a separate business that the manager owns. See *responsibility accounting* and *transfer price.*

declaration date. Time when the *board of directors* declares a *dividend.*

declining-balance depreciation. The method of calculating the periodic *depreciation* charge by multiplying the *book value* at the start of the period by a constant percentage. In pure declining-balance depreciation, the constant percentage is $1 - ns/c$, where n is the *depreciable life*, s is *salvage value*, and c is *acquisition cost*. See *double declining-balance depreciation*.

deep discount bonds. Said of *bonds* selling much below (exactly how much is not clear) *par value*.

defalcation. Embezzlement.

default. Failure to pay *interest* or *principal* on a *debt* when due.

defeasance. Transaction with the economic effect of *debt retirement* that does not retire the debt. When *interest rates* increase, many firms find that the *market value* of their outstanding *debt* has dropped substantially below its *book value*. In *historical cost accounting* for debt retirements, retiring debt with a *cash* payment less than the book value of the debt results in a gain (generally, an *extraordinary item*). Many firms would like to retire the outstanding debt issues and report the gain. Two factors impede doing so: (1) the gain can be a taxable event generating adverse *income tax* consequences; and (2) the transaction costs in retiring all the debt can be large, in part because the firm cannot easily locate all the debt holders or persuade them to sell back their bonds to the issuer. The process of "defeasance" serves as the economic equivalent to retiring a debt issue while it saves the issuer from experiencing adverse tax consequences and from actually having to locate and retire the bonds. The process works as follows. The debt-issuing firm turns over to an independent trustee, such as a bank, amounts of cash or low-risk government bonds sufficient to make all debt service payments on the outstanding debt, including bond retirements, in return for the trustee's commitment to make all debt service payments. The debt issuer effectively retires the outstanding debt. It debits the liability account, credits Cash or Marketable Securities as appropriate, and credits Extraordinary Gain on Debt Retirement. The trustee can retire debt or make debt service payments, whichever it chooses. For income tax purposes, however, the firm's debt remains outstanding. The firm will have taxable interest *deductions* for its still-outstanding debt and taxable interest *revenue* on the investments held by the trustee for debt service. In law, the term "defeasance" means "a rendering null and void." This process renders the outstanding debt economically null and void, without causing a taxable event.

defensive interval. A financial *ratio* equal to the number of days of normal cash *expenditures* covered by *quick assets*. It is defined as follows:

$$\frac{\text{Quick Assets}}{(\text{All Expenses Except Amortization and Others Not Using Funds} \div 365)}$$

The denominator of the ratio is the cash expenditure per day. Analysts have found this ratio useful in predicting *bankruptcy*.

deferral. The accounting process concerned with past *cash receipts* and *payments;* in contrast to *accrual;* recognizing a liability resulting from a current cash receipt (as for magazines to be delivered) or recognizing an asset from a current cash payment (as for prepaid insurance or a long-term depreciable asset).

deferral method. See *flow-through method* (of accounting for the *investment credit*) for definition and contrast.

deferred annuity. An *annuity* whose first payment occurs sometime after the end of the first period.

deferred asset. *Deferred charge.*

deferred charge. *Expenditure* not recognized as an *expense* of the period when made but carried forward as an *asset* to be *written off* in future periods, such as for advance rent payments or insurance premiums. See *deferral*.

deferred cost. *Deferred charge.*

deferred credit. Sometimes used to indicate *advances from customers*.

deferred debit. *Deferred charge.*

deferred expense. *Deferred charge.*

deferred gross margin. *Unrealized gross margin.*

deferred income. *Advances from customers.*

deferred income tax (liability). An *indeterminate-term liability* that arises when the pretax income shown on the tax return is less than what it would have been had the firm used the same *accounting principles* and *cost basis* for *assets* and *liabilities* in tax returns as it used for financial reporting. *SFAS No. 109* requires that the firm debit income tax *expense* and credit deferred income tax with the amount of the taxes delayed by using accounting principles in tax returns different from those used in financial reports. See *temporary difference, timing difference, permanent difference,* and *installment sales*. If, as a result of temporary differences, cumulative taxable income exceeds cumulative reported income before taxes, the deferred income tax account will have a *debit* balance, which the firm will report as a *deferred charge*.

deferred revenue. Sometimes used to indicate *advances from customers*.

deferred tax. See *deferred income tax*.

deficit. A *debit balance* in the Retained Earnings account; presented on the balance sheet in a *contra account* to shareholders' equity; sometimes used to mean negative *net income* for a period.

defined-benefit plan. A *pension plan* in which the employer promises specific dollar amounts to each eligible employee; the amounts usually depend on a formula that takes into account such things as the employee's earnings, years of employment, and age. The employer adjusts its cash contributions and pension expense to *actuarial* experience in the eligible employee group and investment performance of the pension *fund*. This is sometimes called a "fixed-benefit" pension plan. Contrast with *money purchase plan*.

defined-contribution plan. A *money purchase (pension) plan* or other arrangement, based on formula or discretion, in which the employer makes cash contributions to eligible individual employee *accounts* under the terms of a written plan document. The trustee of the funds in the account manages the funds, and the employee-beneficiary receives at retirement (or at some other agreed time) the amount in the fund. The employer makes no promise about that amount. Profit-sharing pension plans are of this type.

deflation. A period of declining *general price-level changes*.

demand deposit. *Funds* in a *checking account* at a bank.

demand loan. See *term loan* for definition and contrast.

denial of opinion. Canada: the statement that an *auditor,* for reasons arising in the *audit,* is unable to express an opinion on whether the *financial statement*s provide *fair presentation.*

denominator volume. Capacity measured in the number of units the firm expects to produce this period; when divided into *budgeted fixed costs,* results in fixed costs applied per unit of product.

department(al) allocation. Obtained by first accumulating *costs* in *cost pools* for each department and then, using separate rates, or sets of rates, for each department, allocating from each cost pool to products produced in that department.

dependent variable. See *regression analysis.*

depletion. Exhaustion or *amortization* of a *wasting asset* or *natural resource.* Also see *percentage depletion.*

depletion allowance. See *percentage depletion.*

deposit intangible. See *core deposit intangible.*

deposit, sinking fund. Payments made to a *sinking fund.*

deposit method (of revenue recognition). A method of *revenue* recognition that is the same as the *completed sale* or *completed contract method.* In some contexts, such as when the customer has the right to return goods for a full refund or in retail land sales, the customer must make substantial payments while still having the right to back out of the deal and receive a refund. When the seller cannot predict with reasonable precision the amount of cash it will ultimately collect and when it will receive cash, the seller must *credit* Deposits, a *liability account,* rather than *revenue.* (In this regard, the accounting differs from that in the completed contract method, in which the account credited offsets the *Work-in-Process* inventory account.) When the *sale* becomes complete, the firm credits a revenue account and *debits* the Deposits account.

deposits (by customers). A *liability* that the firm *credits* when receiving *cash* (as in a bank, or in a grocery store when the customer pays for soda-pop bottles with cash to be repaid when the customer returns the bottles) and when the firm intends to discharge the liability by returning the cash. Contrast with the liability account *Advances from Customers,* which the firm credits on receipt of cash, expecting later to discharge the liability by delivering goods or services. When the firm delivers the goods or services, it credits a *revenue* account.

deposits in transit. Deposits made by a firm but not yet reflected on the *bank statement.*

depreciable cost. That part of the *cost* of an asset, usually *acquisition cost* less *salvage value,* that the firm will charge off over the life of the asset through the process of *depreciation.*

depreciable life. For an *asset,* the time period or units of activity (such as miles driven for a truck) over which the firm allocates the *depreciable cost.* For tax returns, depreciable life may be shorter than estimated *service life.*

depreciation. *Amortization of plant assets;* the process of allocating the cost of an asset to the periods of benefit—the *depreciable life;* classified as a *production cost* or a *period expense,* depending on the asset and whether the firm uses *full absorption* or *variable costing.* Depreciation methods described in this glossary include the *annuity method, appraisal method, composite method, compound interest method, declining-balance method, production method, replacement method, retirement method, straight-line method, sinking fund method,* and *sum-of-the-years'-digits method.*

depreciation reserve. An inferior term for *accumulated depreciation.* See *reserve.* Do not confuse with a replacement *fund.*

derivative (financial instrument). A financial instrument, such as an option to purchase a share of stock, created from another, such as a share of stock; an instrument, such as a *swap,* whose value depends on the value of another asset called the "underlying"—for example, the right to receive the difference between the interest payments on a fixed-rate five-year loan for $1 million and the interest payments on a floating-rate five-year loan for $1 million. To qualify as a derivative under *FASB* rules, *SFAS No. 133,* the instrument has one or more underlyings, and one or more notional amounts or payment provisions or both, it either does not require an initial net investment or it requires one smaller than would be required for other types of contracts expected to have a similar response to changes in market factors, and its terms permit settlement for cash in lieu of physical delivery or the instrument itself trades on an exchange. See also *forward contract* and *futures contract.*

detective controls. *Internal controls* designed to detect, or maximize the chance of detection of, errors and other irregularities.

determination. See *determine.*

determine. A term often used (in our opinion, overused) by accountants and those who describe the accounting process. A leading dictionary associates the following meanings with the verb "determine": settle, decide, conclude, ascertain, cause, affect, control, impel, terminate, and decide upon. In addition, accounting writers can mean any one of the following: measure, allocate, report, calculate, compute, observe, choose, and legislate. In accounting, there are two distinct sets of meanings: those encompassed by the synonym "cause or legislate" and those encompassed by the synonym "measure." The first set of uses conveys the active notion of causing something to happen, and the second set of uses conveys the more passive notion of observing something that someone else has caused to happen. An accountant who speaks of cost or income "determination" generally means measurement or observation, not causation; management and economic conditions cause costs and income to be what they are. One who speaks of accounting principles "determination" can mean choosing or applying (as in "determining depreciation charges" from an allowable set) or causing to be acceptable (as in the *FASB*'s "determining" the accounting for *leases*). In the long run, income is cash-in less cash-out, so management and economic conditions "determine" (cause) income to be what it is. In the short run, reported income is a function of accounting principles chosen and applied, so the accountant "determines" (measures) income. A question such as "Who determines income?" has, therefore, no unambiguous answer. The meaning of "an accountant determining acceptable accounting principles" is also vague. Does the clause mean merely choosing one principle from the set of generally acceptable principles, or does it mean using professional judgment to decide that some of the generally accepted principles are not correct under the current circumstances? We try never to use "determine" unless we mean "cause." Otherwise we use "measure," "report," "calculate," "compute," or whatever specific verb seems appropriate. We suggest that careful writers will always "determine" to use the most specific verb to convey meaning. "Determine" seldom best describes a process in which those who make decisions often differ from those who apply technique. The term *predetermined (factory) overhead rate* contains an appropriate use of the word.

development stage enterprise. As defined in *SFAS No. 7,* a firm whose planned principal *operations* have not commenced or, having commenced, have not generated significant *revenue*. The financial statements should identify such enterprises, but no special *accounting principles* apply to them.

diagnostic signal. See *warning signal* for definition and contrast.

differentiable cost. The cost increments associated with infinitesimal changes in volume. If a total cost curve is smooth (in mathematical terms, differentiable), then we say that the curve graphing the derivative of the total cost curve shows differentiable costs.

differential. An adjective used to describe the change (increase or decrease) in a *cost, expense, investment, cash flow, revenue, profit,* and the like as the firm produces or sells one or more additional (or fewer) units or undertakes (or ceases) an activity. This term has virtually the same meaning as *incremental,* but if the item declines, "decremental" better describes the change. Contrast with *marginal,* which means the change in cost or other item for a small (one unit or even less) change in number of units produced or sold.

differential analysis. Analysis of *differential costs, revenues, profits, investment, cash flow,* and the like.

differential cost. See *differential.*

dilution. A potential reduction in *earnings per share* or *book value* per share by the potential *conversion* of securities or by the potential exercise of *warrants* or *options.*

dilutive. Said of a *security* that will reduce *earnings per share* if it is exchanged for *common shares.*

dip(ping) into LIFO layers. See *LIFO inventory layer.*

direct access. Access to computer storage where information can be located directly, regardless of its position in the storage file. Compare *sequential access.*

direct cost. Cost of *direct material* and *direct labor* incurred in producing a product. See *prime cost.* In some accounting literature, writers use this term to mean the same thing as *variable cost.*

direct costing. Another, less-preferred, term for *variable costing.*

direct-financing (capital) lease. See *sales-type (capital) lease* for definition and contrast.

direct labor (material) cost. Cost of labor (material) applied and assigned directly to a product; contrast with *indirect labor (material).*

direct labor variance. Difference between actual and *standard direct labor* allowed.

direct method. See *statement of cash flows.*

direct posting. A method of bookkeeping in which the firm makes *entries* directly in *ledger accounts,* without using a *journal.*

direct write-off method. See *write-off method.*

disbursement. Payment by *cash* or by *check.* See *expenditure.*

DISC (domestic international sales corporation). A U.S. *corporation,* usually a *subsidiary,* whose *income* results primarily from exports. The parent firm usually defers paying *income tax* on 50 percent of a DISC's income for a long period. Generally, this results in a lower overall corporate tax for the *parent* than would otherwise be incurred.

disclaimer of opinion. An *auditor's report* stating that the auditor cannot give an opinion on the *financial statements.* Usually results from *material* restrictions on the scope of the audit or from material uncertainties, which the firm has been unable to resolve by the time of the audit, about the accounts.

disclosure. The showing of facts in *financial statements, notes* thereto, or the *auditor's report.*

discontinued operations. See *income from discontinued operations.*

discount. In the context of *compound interest, bonds,* and *notes,* the difference between *face amount* (or *future value*) and *present value* of a payment; in the context of *sales* and *purchases,* a reduction in price granted for prompt payment. See also *chain discount, quantity discount,* and *trade discount.*

discount factor. The reciprocal of one plus the *discount rate.* If the discount rate is 10 percent per period, the discount factor for three periods is $1/(1.10)^3 = (1.10)^{-3} = 0.75131.$

discount rate. *Interest rate* used to convert future payments to *present values.*

discounted bailout period. In a *capital budgeting* context, the total time that must elapse before discounted value of net accumulated cash flows from a project, including potential *salvage value* at various times of assets, equals or exceeds the *present value* of net accumulated cash outflows. Contrast with *discounted payback period.*

discounted cash flow (DCF). Using either the *net present value* or the *internal rate of return* in an analysis to measure the value of future expected cash *expenditures* and *receipts* at a common date. In discounted cash flow analysis, choosing the alternative with the largest *internal rate of return* may yield wrong answers given *mutually exclusive projects* with differing amounts of initial investment for two of the projects. Consider, to take an unrealistic example, a project involving an initial investment of $1, with an *IRR* of 60 percent, and another project involving an initial investment of $1 million, with an IRR of 40 percent. Under most conditions, most firms will prefer the second project to the first, but choosing the project with the larger IRR will lead to undertaking the first, not the second. Usage calls this shortcoming of choosing between alternatives based on the magnitude of the internal rate of return, rather than based on the magnitude of the *net present value* of the cash flows, the "scale effect."

discounted payback period. The shortest amount of time that must elapse before the discounted *present value* of cash inflows from a project, excluding potential *salvage value,* equals the discounted present value of the cash outflows.

discounting a note. See *note receivable discounted* and *factoring.*

discounts lapsed (lost). The sum of *discounts* offered for prompt payment that the purchaser did not take because the discount period expired. See *terms of sale.*

discovery sampling. Acceptance sampling in which the analyst accepts an entire population if and only if the sample contains no disparities.

discovery value accounting. See *reserve recognition accounting.*

discretionary cost center. See *engineered cost center* for definition and contrast.

discretionary costs. *Programmed costs.*

Discussion Memorandum. A neutral discussion of all the issues concerning an accounting problem of current concern to the *FASB.* The publication of such a document usually signals that the FASB will consider issuing an *SFAS* or *SFAC* on this particular problem. The discussion memorandum brings together material about the particular problem to facilitate interaction and comment by those interested in the matter. A public hearing follows before the FASB will issue an *Exposure Draft.*

dishonored note. A *promissory note* whose maker does not repay the loan at *maturity,* for a *term loan,* or on demand, for a *demand loan.*

disintermediation. Moving funds from one interest-earning account to another, typically one promising a higher rate. Federal law regulates the maximum *interest rate* that both banks and savings-and-loan associations can pay for *time deposits.* When free-market interest rates exceed the regulated interest ceiling for such time deposits, some depositors withdraw their funds and invest them elsewhere at a higher interest rate. This process is known as "disintermediation."

distributable income. The portion of conventional accounting net income that the firm can distribute to owners (usually in the form of *dividends*) without impairing the physical capacity of the firm to continue operations at current levels. Pretax distributable income is conventional pretax income less the excess of *current cost* of goods sold and *depreciation* charges based on the replacement cost of *productive capacity* over cost of goods sold and depreciation on an *acquisition cost basis.* Contrast with *sustainable income.* See *inventory profit.*

distributable surplus. Canada and UK: the statutory designation to describe the portion of the proceeds of the issue of shares without *par value* not allocated to share capital.

distributed processing. Processing in a computer information network in which an individual location processes data relevant to it while the operating system transmits information required elsewhere, either to the central computer or to another local computer for further processing.

distribution expense. *Expense* of selling, advertising, and delivery activities.

dividend. A distribution of assets generated from *earnings* to owners of a corporation. The firm may distribute cash (cash dividend), stock (stock dividend), property, or other securities (dividend in kind). Dividends, except stock dividends, become a legal liability of the corporation when the corporation's board declares them. Hence, the owner of stock ordinarily recognizes *revenue* when the board of the corporation declares the dividend, except for stock dividends. See also *liquidating dividend* and *stock dividend.*

dividend yield. *Dividends* declared for the year divided by market price of the stock as of the time for which the analyst computes the yield.

dividends in arrears. Dividends on *cumulative preferred stock* that the corporation's board has not yet declared in accordance with the preferred stock contract. The corporation must usually clear such arrearages before it can declare dividends on *common shares.*

dividends in kind. See *dividend.*

division. A more or less self-contained business unit that is part of a larger family of business units under common control.

divisional control. See *control system.*

divisional reporting. See *segment reporting.*

dollar sign rules. In accounting statements or schedules, place a dollar sign beside the first figure in each column and beside any figure below a horizontal line drawn under the preceding figure.

dollar-value LIFO method. A form of *LIFO* inventory accounting with inventory quantities (*layers*) measured in dollar, rather than physical, terms. The method adjusts for changing prices by using specific price indexes appropriate for the kinds of items in the inventory.

domestic international sales corporation. See *DISC.*

donated capital. A *shareholders' equity* account credited when the company receives gifts, such as land or buildings, without issuing shares or other owners' equity interest in return. A city might donate a plant site hoping the firm will build a factory and employ local residents. Do not confuse with *contributed capital.*

double declining-balance depreciation (DDB). *Declining-balance depreciation* in which the constant percentage used to multiply by book value in computing the depreciation charge for the year is $2/n$, where n is the *depreciable life* in periods. Omit *salvage value* from the depreciable amount. Thus if the asset cost $100 and has a depreciable life of five years, the depreciation in the first year would be $40 = 2/5 \times 100, in the second year would be $24 = 2/5 \times ($100 - $40)$, and in the third year would be $14.40 = 2/5 \times ($100 - $40 - $24)$. By the fourth year, the remaining undepreciated cost could be depreciated under the straight-line method at $10.80 = 1/2 \times ($100 - $40 - $24 - $14.40)$ per year for tax purposes. Note that salvage value does not affect these computations except that the method will not depreciate the book value below salvage value.

double entry. In recording transactions, a system that maintains the equality of the accounting equation or the balance sheet. Each entry results in recording equal amounts of *debits* and *credits*.

double T-account. *T-account* with an extra horizontal line showing a change in the account balance to be explained by the subsequent entries into the account.

Plant

42,000	

This account shows an increase in the asset account, plant, of $42,000 to be explained. Such accounts are useful in preparing the *statement of cash flows;* they are not a part of the formal record-keeping process.

double taxation. Occurs when the taxing authority (U.S. or state) taxes corporate income as earned (first tax) and then the same taxing authority taxes the aftertax income, distributed to owners as dividends, again as personal income tax (second tax).

doubtful accounts. *Accounts receivable* that the firm estimates to be *uncollectible*.

Dr. The abbreviation for *debit,* always with the initial capital letter. *Dr.* is a shortened form of the word *debitor,* and *Cr.* comes from the word *creditor.* In the early days of double-entry record keeping in the UK, the major asset was accounts receivable, called *creditors,* and the major liability was accounts payable, called *debitors.* Thus the *r* in *Cr.* does not refer to the *r* in *credit* but to the second *r* in *creditor.*

draft. A written order by the first party, called the drawer, instructing a second party, called the drawee (such as a bank) to pay a third party, called the payee. See also *check, cashier's check, certified check, NOW account, sight draft,* and *trade acceptance.*

drawee. See *draft.*

drawer. See *draft.*

drawing account. A *temporary account* used in *sole proprietorships* and *partnerships* to record payments to owners or partners during a period. At the end of the period, the firm closes the drawing account by crediting it and debiting the owner's or partner's share of income or, perhaps, his or her capital account.

drawings. Payments made to a *sole proprietor* or to a *partner* during a period. See *drawing account.*

driver, cost driver. A cause of costs incurred. Examples include processing orders, issuing an engineering change order, changing the production schedule, and stopping production to change machine settings. The notion arises primarily in product costing, particularly *activity-based costing.*

drop ship(ment). Occurs when a distributor asks a manufacturer to send an order directly to the customer (ordinarily a manufacturer sends goods to a distributor, who sends the goods to its customer). Usage calls the shipment a "drop shipment" and refers to the goods as "drop shipped."

dry-hole accounting. See *reserve recognition accounting* for definition and contrast.

dual-transactions assumption (fiction). Occurs when an analyst, in understanding cash flows, views transactions not involving *cash* as though the firm first generated cash and then used it. For example, the analyst might view the issue of *capital stock* in return for the *asset* land as though the firm issued stock for *cash* and then used cash to acquire the land. Other examples of transactions that could involve the dual-transaction assumption are the issue of a *mortgage* in return for a noncurrent asset and the issue of stock to bondholders on *conversion* of their *convertible bonds.*

dual transfer prices. Occurs when the *transfer price charged* to the buying *division* differs from that *credited* to the selling division. Such prices make sense when the selling division has excess capacity and, as usual, the *fair market value* exceeds the *incremental cost* to produce the goods or services being transferred.

duality. The *double entry* record-keeping axiom that every *transaction* must result in equal *debit* and *credit* amounts.

dumping. A foreign firm's selling a good or service in the United States at a price below market price at home or, in some contexts, below some measure of cost (which concept is not clearly defined). The practice is illegal in the United States if it harms (or threatens to harm) a U.S. industry.

E

e. The base of natural logarithms; 2.71828. . . . If *interest* compounds continuously during a period at stated rate of *r* per period, then the effective *interest rate* is equivalent to interest compounded once per period at rate *i* where $i = e^r - 1$. Tables of e^r are widely available. If 12 percent annual interest compounds continuously, the effective annual rate is $e^{.12} - 1 = 12.75$ percent. Interest compounded continuously at rate *r* for *d* days is $e^{rd/365} - 1$. For example, interest compounded continuously for 92 days at 12 percent is $e^{.12 \times 92/365} - 1 = 3.07$ percent.

earn-out. For two merging firms, an agreement in which the amount paid by the acquiring firm to the acquired firm's shareholders depends on the future earnings of the acquired firm or, perhaps, of the *consolidated entity.*

earned surplus. A term that writers once used, but no longer use, for *retained earnings.*

earnings. A term with no precise meaning but used to mean *income* or sometimes *profit.* The *FASB,* in requiring that firms report *comprehensive income,* encouraged firms to use the term "earnings" for the total formerly reported as *net income.* Firms will likely only slowly change from using the term "net income" to the term "earnings."

earnings, retained. See *retained earnings.*

earnings cycle. The period of time, or the series of transactions, during which a given firm converts *cash* into *goods* and *services,* then sells goods and services to customers, and finally collects cash from customers. *Cash cycle.*

earnings per share (of common stock). *Net income* to common shareholders (net income minus *preferred dividends*) divided by the average number of *common shares* outstanding; see also *primary earnings per share* and *fully diluted earnings per share.* See *ratio.*

earnings per share (of preferred stock). *Net income* divided by the average number of *preferred shares* outstanding during the period. This ratio indicates how well income covers (or protects) the preferred dividends; it does not indicate a legal share of *earnings.* See *ratio.*

earnings statement. *Income statement.*

easement. The acquired right or privilege of one person to use, or have access to, certain property of another. For example, a public utility's right to lay pipes or lines under the property of another and to service those facilities.

EBIT. *Earnings* before *income taxes;* acronym used by analysts.

EBITDA. *Earnings* before *income taxes, depreciation,* and *amortization;* acronym used by analysts to focus on a particular measure of *cash flow* used in valuation. This is not the same as, but is similar in concept to, *cash flow from operations.* Some analysts exclude *nonrecurring* items from this total.

economic consequences. The *FASB* says that in setting *accounting principles,* it should take into account the real effects on various participants in the business world. It calls these effects "economic consequences."

economic depreciation. Decline in *current cost* (or *fair value*) of an *asset* during a period.

economic entity. See *entity.*

economic life. The time span over which the firm expects to receive the benefits of an *asset.* The economic life of a *patent, copyright,* or *franchise* may be less than the legal life. *Service life.*

economic order quantity (EOQ). In mathematical *inventory* analysis, the optimal amount of stock to order when demand reduces inventory to a level called the "reorder point." If A represents the *incremental cost* of placing a single order, D represents the total demand for a period of time in units, and H represents the incremental holding cost during the period per unit of inventory, then the economic order quantity is $EOQ = \sqrt{2AD/H}$. Usage sometimes calls EOQ the "optimal lot size."

ED. *Exposure Draft.*

EDGAR. Electronic Data, Gathering, Analysis, and Retrieval system; rules and systems adopted by the *SEC* in 1993 to ensure that all the paperwork involved in the filings submitted by more than 15,000 public companies are electronically submitted.

EDP. *Electronic data processing.*

effective interest method. In computing *interest expense* (or *revenue*), a systematic method that makes the interest expense (revenue) for each period divided by the amount of the net *liability* (*asset*) at the beginning of the period equal to the *yield rate* on the liability (asset) at the time of issue (acquisition). Interest for a period is the yield rate (at time of issue) multiplied by the net liability (asset) at the start of the period. The *amortization* of discount or premium is the *plug* to give equal *debits* and *credits.* (Interest expense is a debit, and the amount of debt service payment is a credit.)

effective (interest) rate. Of a liability such as a bond, the *internal rate of return* or *yield to maturity* at the time of issue. Contrast with *coupon rate.* If the borrower issues the bond for a price below *par,* the effective rate is higher than the coupon rate; if it issues the bond for a price greater than par, the effective rate is lower than the coupon rate. In the context of *compound interest,* the effective rate occurs when the *compounding period* on a *loan* differs from one year, such as a nominal interest rate of 12 percent compounded monthly. The effective interest is the single rate that one could use at the end of the year to multiply the *principal* at the beginning of the year and give the same amount as results from compounding interest each period during the year. For example, if 12 percent per year compounds monthly, the effective annual interest rate is 12.683 percent. That is, if you compound \$100 each month at 1 percent per month, the \$100 will grow to \$112.68 at the end of the year. In general, if the nominal rate of r percent per year compounds m times per year, then the effective rate is $(1 + r/m)^m - 1$.

efficiency variance. A term used for the *quantity variance* for materials or labor or *variable overhead* in a *standard costing system.*

efficient capital market. A market in which security prices reflect all available information and react nearly instantaneously and in an unbiased fashion to new information.

efficient market hypothesis. The finance supposition that security prices trade in *efficient capital markets.*

EITF. *Emerging Issues Task Force.*

electronic data processing. Performing computations and other data-organizing steps in a computer, in contrast to doing these steps by hand or with mechanical calculators.

eligible. Under income tax legislation, a term that restricts or otherwise alters the meaning of another tax or accounting term, generally to signify that the related assets or operations may receive a specified tax treatment.

eliminations. In preparing *consolidated statements, work sheet* entries made to avoid duplicating the amounts of *assets, liabilities, owners' equity, revenues,* and *expenses* of the consolidated *entity* when the firm sums the accounts of the *parent* and *subsidiaries.*

Emerging Issues Task Force (EITF). A group convened by the *FASB* to deal more rapidly with accounting issues than the FASB's due-process procedures can allow. The task force comprises about 20 members from public accounting, industry, and several trade associations. It meets every six weeks. Several FASB board members usually attend and participate. The chief accountant of the *SEC* has indicated that the SEC will require that published financial statements follow guidelines set by a consensus of the EITF. The EITF requires that nearly all its members agree on a position before that position receives the label of "consensus." Such positions appear in *Abstracts of the EITF,* published by the FASB. Since 1984, the EITF has become one of the promulgators of *GAAP.*

employee stock option. See *stock option.*

Employee Stock Ownership Trust (or Plan). See *ESOT.*

employer, employee payroll taxes. See *payroll taxes.*

enabling costs. A type of *capacity cost* that a firm will stop incurring if it shuts down operations completely but will incur in full if it carries out operations at any level. Examples include costs of a security force or of a quality-control inspector for an assembly line. Contrast with *standby costs.*

encumbrance. In governmental accounting, an anticipated *expenditure* or *funds* restricted for an anticipated expenditure, such as for outstanding purchase orders. *Appropriations* less expenditures less outstanding encumbrances yields unencumbered balance.

ending inventory. The *cost* of *inventory* on hand at the end of the *accounting period;* often called "closing inventory." Ending inventory from the end of one period becomes the *beginning inventory* for the next period.

endorsee. See *endorser.*

endorsement. See *draft.* The *payee* signs the draft and transfers it to a fourth party, such as the payee's bank.

endorser. A *note* or *draft payee,* who signs the note after writing "Pay to the order of X," transfers the note to person X, and presumably receives some benefit, such as cash, in return. Usage refers to person x as the "endorsee." The endorsee then has the rights of the payee and may in turn become an endorser by endorsing the note to another endorsee.

engineered cost center. Responsibility center with sufficiently well-established relations between inputs and outputs that the analyst, given data on inputs, can predict the outputs or, conversely, given the outputs, can estimate the amounts of inputs that the process should have used. Consider the relation between pounds of flour (input) and loaves of bread (output). Contrast discretionary cost center, where such relations are so imprecise that analysts have no reliable way to relate inputs to outputs. Consider the relation between advertising the corporate logo or trademark (input) and future revenues (output).

engineering method (of cost estimation). To estimate unit cost of product from study of the materials, labor, and *overhead* components of the production process.

enterprise. Any business organization, usually defining the accounting *entity.*

enterprise fund. A *fund* that a governmental unit establishes to account for acquisition, operation, and maintenance of governmental services that the government intends to be self-supporting from user charges, such as for water or airports and some toll roads.

entity. A person, *partnership, corporation,* or other organization. The *accounting entity* that issues accounting statements may not be the same as the entity defined by law. For example, a *sole proprietorship* is an accounting entity, but the individual's combined business and personal assets are the legal entity in most jurisdictions. Several affiliated corporations may be separate legal entities but issue *consolidated financial statements* for the group of companies operating as a single economic entity.

entity theory. The corporation view that emphasizes the form of the *accounting equation* that says *assets = equities.* Contrast with *proprietorship theory.* The entity theory focuses less on the distinction between *liabilities* and *shareholders' equity* than does the proprietorship theory. The entity theory views all equities as coming to the corporation from outsiders who have claims of differing legal standings. The entity theory implies using a *multiple-step* income statement.

entry value. The *current cost* of acquiring an asset or service at a *fair market price. Replacement cost.*

EOQ. *Economic order quantity.*

EPS. *Earnings per share.*

EPVI. *Excess present value index.*

equalization reserve. An inferior title for the allowance or *estimated liability* account when the firm uses the *allowance method* for such things as maintenance expenses. Periodically, the accountant will debit maintenance *expense* and credit the allowance. As the firm makes *expenditures* for maintenance, it will debit the allowance and credit cash or the other asset used in maintenance.

equities. *Liabilities* plus *owners' equity.* See *equity.*

equity. A claim to *assets;* a source of assets. *SFAC No. 3* defines equity as "the residual interest in the assets of an entity that remains after deducting its liabilities." Thus, many knowledgeable people use "equity" to exclude liabilities and count only owners' equities. We prefer to use the term to mean all liabilities plus all owners' equity because there is no other single word that serves this useful purpose. We fight a losing battle.

equity financing. Raising *funds* by issuing *capital stock.* Contrast with *debt financing.*

equity method. In accounting for an *investment* in the stock of another company, a method that debits the proportionate share of the earnings of the other company to the investment account and credits that amount to a *revenue* account as earned. When the investor receives *dividends,* it debits *cash* and credits the investment account. An investor who owns sufficient shares of stock of an unconsolidated company to exercise significant control over the actions of that company must use the equity method. It is one of the few instances in which the firm recognizes revenue without an increase in *working capital.*

equity ratio. *Shareholders' equity* divided by total *assets.* See *ratio.*

equivalent production. *Equivalent units.* **equivalent units (of work).** The number of units of completed output that would require the same costs that a firm would actually incur for the production of completed and partially completed units during a period. For example, if at the beginning of a period the firm starts 100 units and by the end of the period has incurred costs for each of these equal to 75 percent of total costs to complete the units, then the equivalent units of work for the period would be 75. This is used primarily in *process costing* calculations to measure in uniform terms the output of a continuous process.

ERISA (Employee Retirement Income Security Act of 1974). The federal law that sets most *pension plan* requirements.

error accounting. See *accounting errors.*

escalator clause. Inserted in a purchase or rental contract, a clause that permits, under specified conditions, upward adjustments of price.

escapable cost. *Avoidable cost.*

ESOP (Employee Stock Ownership Plan). See *ESOT.*

ESOT (Employee Stock Ownership Trust). A trust *fund* that is created by a corporate employer and that can provide certain tax benefits to the corporation while providing for employee stock ownership. The corporate employer can contribute up to 25 percent of its payroll per year to the trust. The corporation may deduct the amount of the contribution from otherwise taxable income for federal *income tax* purposes. The trustee of the assets must use them for the benefit of employees—for example, to fund death or retirement benefits. The assets of the trust are usually the *common shares,* sometimes nonvoting, of the corporate employer. For an example of the potential *tax shelter,* consider the case of a corporation with $1 million of *debt* outstanding, which it wants to retire, and an annual payroll of $2 million. The corporation sells $1 million of common stock to the ESOT. The ESOT borrows $1 million with the loan guaranteed by, and therefore a *contingency* of, the corporation. The corporation uses the $1 million proceeds of the stock issue to retire its outstanding debt. (The debt of the corporation has been replaced with the debt of the ESOT.) The corporation can contribute $500,000 (= 0.25 × $2 million payroll) to the ESOT each year and treat the contribution as a deduction for tax purposes. After a little more than two years, the ESOT has received sufficient funds to retire its loan. The corporation has effectively repaid its original $1 million debt with pretax dollars. Assuming an income tax rate of 40 percent, it has saved $400,000 (= 0.40 × $1 million) of aftertax dollars *if* the $500,000 expense for the contribution to the ESOT for the pension benefits of employees would have been made, in one form or another, anyway. Observe that the corporation could use the proceeds ($1 million in the example) of the stock issued to the ESOT for any of several different purposes: financing expansion, replacing plant assets, or acquiring another company. Basically this same form of pretax-dollar financing through pensions is available with almost any corporate pension plan, with one important exception. The trustees of an ordinary pension trust must invest the assets prudently, and if they do not, they are personally liable to the employees. Current judgment about prudent investment requires diversification— trustees should invest pension trust assets in a wide variety of investment opportunities. (The trustee may not ordinarily invest more than 10 percent of a pension trust's assets in the parent's common stock.) Thus the ordinary pension trust cannot, in practice, invest all, or even most, of its assets in the parent corporation's stock. This constraint does not apply to the investments of an ESOT. The trustee may invest all ESOT assets in the parent company's stock. The ESOT also provides a means for closely held corporations to achieve wider ownership of shares without *going public*. The laws enabling ESOTs provide for the independent professional appraisal of shares not traded in public markets and for transactions between the corporation and the ESOT or between the ESOT and the employees to be based on the appraised values of the shares.

estate planning. The arrangement of an individual's affairs to facilitate the passage of assets to beneficiaries and to minimize taxes at death.

estimated expenses. See *after cost*.

estimated liability. The preferred terminology for estimated costs the firm will incur for such uncertain things as repairs under *warranty*. An estimated liability appears on the *balance sheet*. Contrast with *contingency*.

estimated revenue. A term used in governmental accounting to designate revenue expected to accrue during a period independent of whether the government will collect it during the period. The governmental unit usually establishes a *budgetary account* at the beginning of the budget period.

estimated salvage value. Synonymous with *salvage value* of an *asset* before its retirement.

estimates, changes in. See *accounting changes*.

estimation sampling. The use of sampling technique in which the sampler infers a qualitative (e.g., fraction female) or quantitative (e.g., mean weight) characteristic of the population from the occurrence of that characteristic in the sample drawn. See *attribute(s) sampling; variables sampling.*

EURL (entreprise unipersonnelle à responsabilité limitée). France: similar to *SARL* but having only one shareholder.

ex div. (dividend). Said of *shares* whose market price quoted in the market has been reduced by a *dividend* already declared but not yet paid. The *corporation* will send the dividend to the person who owned the share on the *record date*. One who buys the share ex dividend will not receive the dividend although the corporation has not yet paid it.

ex rights. The condition of securities whose quoted market price no longer includes the right to purchase new securities, such rights having expired or been retained by the seller. Compare *cum rights*.

except for. Qualification in *auditor's report,* usually caused by a change, approved by the auditor, from one acceptable accounting principle or procedure to another.

excess present value. In a *capital budgeting* context, *present value* (of anticipated net cash inflows minus cash outflows including initial cash outflow) for a project. The analyst uses the *cost of capital* as the *discount rate*.

excess present value index. *Present value* of future *cash* inflows divided by initial cash outlay.

exchange. The generic term for a transaction (or, more technically, a reciprocal transfer) between one entity and another; in another context, the name for a market, such as the New York Stock Exchange.

exchange gain or loss. The phrase used by the *FASB* for *foreign exchange gain or loss*.

exchange rate. The *price* of one country's currency in terms of another country's currency. For example, the British pound sterling might be worth U.S.$1.60 at a given time. The exchange rate would be stated as "one pound is worth one dollar and sixty cents" or "one dollar is worth £.625" (= £1/$1.60).

excise tax. Tax on the manufacture, sale, or consumption of a commodity.

executory contract. A mere exchange of promises; an agreement providing for payment by a payor to a payee on the performance of an act or service by the payee, such as a labor contract. Accounting does not recognize benefits arising from executory contracts as *assets,* nor does it recognize obligations arising from such contracts as *liabilities*. See *partially executory contract*.

exemption. A term used for various amounts subtracted from gross income in computing taxable income. Usage does not call all such subtractions "exemptions." See *tax deduction.*

exercise. Occurs when owners of an *option* or *warrant* purchase the security that the option entitles them to purchase.

exercise price. See *option.*

exit value. The proceeds that would be received if assets were disposed of in an *arm's-length transaction. Current selling price; net realizable value.*

expected value. The mean or arithmetic *average* of a statistical distribution or series of numbers.

expected value of (perfect) information. Expected *net benefits* from an undertaking with (perfect) information minus expected net benefits of the undertaking without (perfect) information.

expendable fund. In governmental accounting, a *fund* whose resources, *principal,* and earnings the governmental unit may distribute.

expenditure. Payment of *cash* for goods or services received. Payment may occur at the time the purchaser receives the goods or services or at a later time. Virtually synonymous with *disbursement* except that disbursement is a broader term and includes all payments for goods or services. Contrast with *expense.*

expense. As a noun, a decrease in *owners' equity* accompanying the decrease in *net assets* caused by selling goods or rendering services or by the passage of time; a "gone" (net) asset; an expired cost. Measure expense as the *cost* of the (net) assets used. Do not confuse with *expenditure* or *disbursement,* which may occur before, when, or after the firm recognizes the related expense. Use the word "cost" to refer to an item that still has service potential and is an asset. Use the word "expense" after the firm has used the asset's service potential. As a verb, "expense" means to designate an expenditure—past, current, or future—as a current expense.

expense account. An *account* to accumulate *expenses; closed* to *retained earnings* at the end of the accounting period; a *temporary owners' equity* account; also used to describe a listing of expenses that an employee submits to the employer for reimbursement.

experience rating. A term used in insurance, particularly unemployment insurance, to denote changes from ordinary rates to reflect extraordinarily large or small amounts of claims over time by the insured.

expired cost. An *expense* or a *loss.*

Exposure Draft (ED). A preliminary statement of the *FASB* (or the *APB* between 1962 and 1973) showing the contents of a pronouncement being considered for enactment by the board.

external reporting. Reporting to shareholders and the public, as opposed to internal reporting for management's benefit. See *financial accounting,* and contrast with *managerial accounting.*

extraordinary item. A *material expense* or *revenue* item characterized both by its unusual nature and by its infrequency of occurrence; appears along with its income tax effects separately from ordinary income and *income from discontinued operations* on the *income statement.* Accountants would probably classify a *loss* from an earthquake as an extraordinary item. Accountants treat gain (or loss) on the retirement of *bonds* as an extraordinary item under the terms of *SFAS No. 4.*

F

face amount (value). The nominal amount due at *maturity* from a *bond* or *note* not including the contractual periodic payment that may also come due on the same date. Good usage calls the corresponding amount of a stock certificate the *par* or *stated value,* whichever applies.

factoring. The process of buying *notes* or *accounts receivable* at a *discount* from the holder owed the debt; from the holder's point of view, the selling of such notes or accounts. When the transaction involves a single note, usage calls the process "discounting a note."

factory. Used synonymously with *manufacturing* as an adjective.

factory burden. *Manufacturing overhead.*

factory cost. *Manufacturing cost.*

factory expense. *Manufacturing overhead. Expense* is a poor term in this context because the item is a *product cost.*

factory overhead. Usually an item of *manufacturing cost* other than *direct labor* or *direct materials.*

fair market price (value). See *fair value.*

fair presentation (fairness). One of the qualitative standards of financial reporting. When the *auditor's report* says that the *financial statements* "present fairly . . . ," the auditor means that the accounting alternatives used by the entity all comply with *GAAP.* In recent years, however, courts have ruled that conformity with *generally accepted accounting principles* may be insufficient grounds for an opinion that the statements are fair. *SAS No. 5* requires that the auditor judge the accounting principles used in the statements to be "appropriate in the circumstances" before attesting to fair presentation.

fair value, fair market price (value). Price (value) negotiated at *arm's length* between a willing buyer and a willing seller, each acting rationally in his or her own self-interest. The accountant may estimate this amount in the absence of a monetary transaction. This is sometimes measured as the present value of expected cash flows.

fair-value hedge. A hedge of an exposure to changes in the *fair value* of a recognized *asset* or *liability* or of an unrecognized firm commitment.

FASAC. *Financial Accounting Standards Advisory Council.*

FASB (Financial Accounting Standards Board). An independent board responsible, since 1973, for establishing *generally accepted accounting principles.* Its official pronouncements are *Statements of Financial Accounting Concepts* (SFAC), *Statements of Financial Accounting Standards* (SFAS), and *FASB Interpretations.* See also *Discussion Memorandum* and *Technical Bulletin.* Web Site: www.fasb.org.

FASB Interpretation. An official *FASB* statement interpreting the meaning of *Accounting Research Bulletins, APB Opinions,* and *Statements of Financial Accounting Standards.*

FASB Technical Bulletin. See *Technical Bulletin.*

favorable variance. An excess of actual *revenues* over expected revenues; an excess of *standard cost* over actual cost.

federal income tax. *Income tax* levied by the U.S. government on individuals and corporations.

Federal Insurance Contributions Act. See *FICA.*

Federal Unemployment Tax Act. See *FUTA.*

feedback. The process of informing employees about how their actual performance compares with the expected or desired level of performance, in the hope that the information will reinforce desired behavior and reduce unproductive behavior.

FEI. *Financial Executives Institute.*

FICA (Federal Insurance Contributions Act). The law that sets *Social Security taxes* and benefits.

fiduciary. Someone responsible for the custody or administration of property belonging to another; for example, an executor (of an estate), agent, receiver (in *bankruptcy*), or trustee (of a trust).

FIFO (first-in, first-out). The *inventory flow assumption* that firms use to compute *ending inventory* cost from most recent purchases and *cost of goods sold* from oldest purchases including beginning inventory. FIFO describes cost flow from the viewpoint of the income statement. From the balance sheet perspective, *LISH* (last-in, still-here) describes this same cost flow. Contrast with *LIFO.*

finance. As a verb, to supply with *funds* through the *issue* of stocks, bonds, notes, or mortgages or through the retention of earnings.

financial accounting. The accounting for *assets, equities, revenues,* and *expenses* of a business; primarily concerned with the historical reporting, to external users, of the *financial position* and operations of an *entity* on a regular, periodic basis. Contrast with *managerial accounting.*

Financial Accounting Foundation. The independent foundation (committee), governed by a board of trustees, that raises funds to support the *FASB* and *GASB.*

Financial Accounting Standards Advisory Council (FASAC). A committee of academics, preparers, attestors, and users giving advice to the *FASB* on matters of strategy and emerging issues. The council spends much of each meeting learning about current developments in standard-setting from the FASB staff.

Financial Accounting Standards Board. *FASB.*

Financial Executives Institute (FEI). An organization of financial executives, such as chief accountants, *controllers,* and treasurers, of large businesses. In recent years, the FEI has been a critic of the FASB because it views many of the FASB requirements as burdensome while not *cost-effective.*

financial expense. An *expense* incurred in raising or managing *funds.*

financial flexibility. As defined by *SFAC No. 5,* "the ability of an entity to take effective actions to alter amounts and timing of cash flows so it can respond to unexpected needs and opportunities."

financial forecast. See *financial projection* for definition and contrast.

financial instrument. The *FASB* defines this term as follows: "Cash, evidence of an ownership interest in an entity, or a contract that both:

[a] imposes on one entity a contractual obligation (1) to deliver cash or another financial instrument to a second entity or (2) to exchange financial instruments on potentially unfavorable terms with the second entity, and

[b] conveys to that second entity a contractual right (1) to receive cash or another financial instrument from the first entity or (2) to exchange other financial instruments on potentially favorable terms with the first entity."

financial leverage. See *leverage.*

financial position (condition). Statement of the *assets* and *equities* of a firm; displayed as a *balance sheet.*

financial projection. An estimate of *financial position,* results of *operations,* and changes in cash flows for one or more future periods based on a set of assumptions. If the assumptions do not represent the most likely outcomes, then auditors call the estimate a "projection." If the assumptions represent the most probable outcomes, then auditors call the estimate a "forecast." "Most probable" means that management has evaluated the assumptions and that they are management's judgment of the most likely set of conditions and most likely outcomes.

financial ratio. See *ratio.*

financial reporting objectives. Broad objectives that are intended to guide the development of specific *accounting standards;* set out by *FASB SFAC No. 1.*

Financial Reporting Release. Series of releases, issued by the SEC since 1982; replaces the *Accounting Series Release.* See *SEC.*

financial statements. The *balance sheet, income statement, statement of retained earnings, statement of cash flows,* statement of changes in *owners' equity accounts,* statement of *comprehensive income,* and *notes* thereto.

financial structure. *Capital structure.*

financial vice-president. Person in charge of the entire accounting and finance function; typically one of the three most influential people in the company.

financial year. Australia and UK: term for *fiscal year.*

financing activities. Obtaining resources from (a) owners and providing them with a return on and a return of their *investment* and (b) *creditors* and repaying amounts borrowed (or otherwise settling the obligation). See *statement of cash flows.*

financing lease. *Capital lease.*

finished goods (inventory account). Manufactured product ready for sale; a *current asset* (inventory) account.

firm. Informally, any business entity. (Strictly speaking, a firm is a *partnership.*)

firm commitment. The *FASB,* in *SFAS No. 133,* defines this as "an agreement with an unrelated party, binding on both parties and usually legally enforceable,"which requires that the firm promise to pay a specified amount of a currency and that the firm has sufficient disincentives for nonpayment that the firm will probably make the payment. A firm commitment resembles a *liability,* but it is an *executory contract,* so is not a liability. *SFAS No. 133* allows the firm to recognize certain financial *hedges* in the balance sheet if they hedge firm commitments. The *FASB* first used the term in *SFAS No. 52* and *No. 80* but made the term more definite and more important in *SFAS No. 133.* This is an early, perhaps the first, step in changing the recognition criteria for assets and liabilities to exclude the test that the future benefit (asset) or obligation (liability) not arise from an executory contract.

first-in, first-out. See *FIFO*.

fiscal year. A period of 12 consecutive months chosen by a business as the *accounting period* for *annual reports,* not necessarily a *natural business year* or a calendar year.

FISH. An acronym, conceived by George H. Sorter, for *first-in, still-here.* FISH is the same cost flow assumption as *LIFO*. Many readers of accounting statements find it easier to think about inventory questions in terms of items still on hand. Think of LIFO in connection with *cost of goods sold* but of FISH in connection with *ending inventory.* See *LISH*.

fixed assets. *Plant assets.*

fixed assets turnover. *Sales* divided by average total *fixed assets.*

fixed benefit plan. A *defined-benefit plan.*

fixed budget. A plan that provides for specified amounts of *expenditures* and *receipts* that do not vary with activity levels; sometimes called a "static budget." Contrast with *flexible budget.*

fixed charges earned (coverage) ratio. *Income* before *interest expense* and *income tax expense* divided by interest expense.

fixed cost (expense). An *expenditure* or *expense* that does not vary with volume of activity, at least in the short run. See *capacity costs,* which include *enabling costs* and *standby costs,* and *programmed costs* for various subdivisions of fixed costs. See *cost terminology.*

fixed interval sampling. A method of choosing a sample: the analyst selects the first item from the population randomly, drawing the remaining sample items at equally spaced intervals.

fixed liability. *Long-term* liability.

fixed manufacturing overhead applied. The portion of *fixed manufacturing overhead cost* allocated to units produced during a period.

fixed overhead variance. Difference between *actual fixed manufacturing costs* and fixed manufacturing costs applied to production in a *standard costing system.*

flexible budget. *Budget* that projects receipts and expenditures as a function of activity levels. Contrast with *fixed budget.*

flexible budget allowance. With respect to manufacturing overhead, the total cost that a firm should have incurred at the level of activity actually experienced during the period.

float. *Checks* whose amounts the bank has *added* to the depositor's bank account but whose amounts the bank has not yet reduced from the *drawer's* bank account.

flow. The change in the amount of an item over time. Contrast with *stock.*

flow assumption. An assumption used when the firm makes a *withdrawal* from *inventory.* The firm must compute the cost of the withdrawal by a flow assumption if the firm does not use the *specific identification* method. The usual flow assumptions are *FIFO, LIFO,* and *weighted average.*

flow of costs. *Costs* passing through various classifications within an *entity* engaging, at least in part, in manufacturing activities. See the diagram on the next page for a summary of *product* and *period cost* flows.

flow-through method. Accounting for the *investment credit* to show all income statement benefits of the credit in the year of acquisition rather than spreading them over the life of the asset acquired (called the "deferral method"). The *APB* preferred the deferral method in *Opinion No. 2* (1962) but accepted the flow-through method in *Opinion No. 4* (1964). The term also applies to *depreciation* accounting in which the firm uses the *straight-line method* for financial reporting and an *accelerated depreciation* method for tax reporting. Followers of the flow-through method would not recognize a *deferred tax liability.* APB Opinion No. 11 prohibits the use of the flow-through approach in financial reporting, although some regulatory commissions have used it.

FOB. Free on board some location (for example, FOB shipping point, FOB destination). The *invoice* price includes delivery at seller's expense to that location. Title to goods usually passes from seller to buyer at the FOB location.

folio. A page number or other identifying reference used in posting to indicate the source of entry.

footing. Adding a column of figures.

footnotes. More detailed information than that provided in the *income statement, balance sheet, statement of retained earnings,* and *statement of cash flows.* These are an integral part of the statements, and the *auditor's report* covers them. They are sometimes called "notes."

forecast. See *financial projection* for definition and contrast.

foreclosure. Occurs when a lender takes possession of property for his or her own use or sale after the borrower fails to make a required payment on a *mortgage.* Assume that the lender sells the property but that the proceeds of the sale are too small to cover the outstanding balance on the loan at the time of foreclosure. Under the terms of most mortgages, the lender becomes an unsecured creditor of the borrower for the still-unrecovered balance of the loan.

foreign currency. For *financial statements* prepared in a given currency, any other currency.

foreign currency translation. Reporting in the currency used in financial statements the amounts denominated or measured in a different currency.

foreign exchange gain or loss. Gain or loss from holding *net* foreign *monetary items* during a period when the *exchange rate* changes.

foreign sales corporation. See *FSC*.

forfeited share. A share to which a subscriber has lost title because of nonpayment of a *call.*

Form 10-K. See *10-K.*

Form 20-F. See *20-F.*

forward contract. An agreement to purchase or sell a specific commodity or financial instrument for a specified price, the *forward price,* at a specified date. Contrast with *futures contract.* Typically, forward contracts are not traded on organized exchanges (unlike *futures contract*), so the parties to the agreement sacrifice liquidity but gain flexibility in setting contract quantities, qualities, and settlement dates.

Flow of Costs (and Sales Revenue)

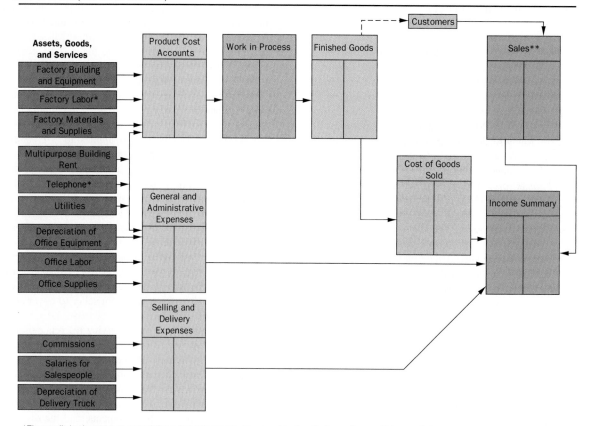

*The credit in the entry to record these items is usually to a payable; for all others, the credit is usually to an asset, or to an asset contra account.

**When the firm records sales to customers, it credits the Sales account. The debit is usually to Cash or Accounts Receivable.

forward-exchange contract. An agreement to exchange at a specified future date currencies of different countries at a specified rate called the "forward rate."

forward price. The price of a commodity for delivery at a specified future date; in contrast to the "spot price," the price of that commodity on the day of the price quotation.

franchise. A privilege granted or sold, such as to use a name or to sell products or services.

fraudulent conveyance. A transfer of goods or cash that a court finds illegal. *Creditors* of a *bankrupt* firm usually receive less than the firm owed them. For example, a creditor of a bankrupt firm might collect from the trustee of the bankrupt firm only $0.60 for every dollar the bankrupt firm owed. Creditors, anticipating bankruptcy, sometimes attempt to persuade the firm to pay the debt in full before the firm declares bankruptcy, reducing the net assets available to other creditors. Bankruptcy laws have rules forbidding such transfers from a near-bankrupt firm to some of its creditors. Such a transfer is called a "fraudulent conveyance." Courts sometimes ask accountants to judge whether a firm had liabilities exceeding assets even before the firm went into bankruptcy. When the court can find that economic bankruptcy occurred before legal bankruptcy, it will declare transfers of assets to creditors after economic bank-

ruptcy to be fraudulent conveyances and have the assets returned to the trustees (or to a legal entity called the "bankrupt's estate") for redistribution to all creditors.

fraudulent financial reporting. Intentional or reckless conduct that results in materially misleading *financial statements*. See *creative accounting*.

free cash flow. This term has no standard meaning. Some financial statement analysts use it to mean *cash flow from operations + interest expense + income tax expense*. Others mean the excess of cash flow from operations over cash flow for investing. Usage varies so much that you should ascertain the meaning intended in context by this phrase.

free on board. *FOB.*

freight-in. The *cost* of freight or shipping incurred in acquiring *inventory*, preferably treated as a part of the cost of *inventory;* often shown temporarily in an *adjunct account* that the acquirer closes at the end of the period with other purchase accounts to the inventory account.

freight-out. The *cost* of freight or shipping incurred in selling *inventory,* treated by the seller as a selling *expense* in the period of sale.

FSC (foreign sales corporation). A foreign *corporation* engaging in certain export activities, some of whose *income* the United States exempts from federal *income tax.* A U.S. corporation need pay no income taxes on *dividends* distributed by an FSC out of *earnings* attributable to certain foreign income.

full absorption costing. The *costing* method that assigns all types of manufacturing costs (*direct material, direct labor, fixed* and *variable overhead*) to units produced; required by *GAAP;* also called "absorption costing." Contrast with *variable costing.*

full costing, full costs. The total cost of producing and selling a unit; often used in *long-term* profitability and pricing decisions. Full cost per unit equals *full absorption cost* per unit plus *marketing, administrative, interest,* and other *central corporate expenses,* per unit. The sum of full costs for all units equals total costs of the firm.

full disclosure. The reporting policy requiring that all significant or *material* information appear in the financial statements. See *fair presentation.*

fully diluted earnings per share. For *common stock,* smallest *earnings per share* figure that one can obtain by computing an earnings per share for all possible combinations of assumed *exercise* or *conversion* of *potentially dilutive securities.* This figure must appear on the *income statement* if it is less than 97 percent of earnings available to common shareholders divided by the average number of common shares outstanding during the period.

fully vested. Said of a *pension plan* when an employee (or his or her estate) has rights to all the benefits purchased with the employer's contributions to the plan even if the employee does not work for this employer at the time of death or retirement.

function. In governmental accounting, said of a group of related activities for accomplishing a service or regulatory program for which the governmental unit has responsibility; in mathematics, a rule for associating a number, called the dependent variable, with another number (or numbers), called independent variable(s).

functional classification. *Income statement* reporting form that classifies *expenses* by function, that is, cost of goods sold, administrative expenses, financing expenses, selling expenses. Contrast with *natural classification.*

functional currency. Currency in which an entity carries out its principal economic activity.

fund. An *asset* or group of assets set aside for a specific purpose. See also *fund accounting.*

fund accounting. The accounting for resources, obligations, and *capital* balances, usually of a not-for-profit or governmental *entity,* which the entity has segregated into *accounts* representing logical groupings based on legal, donor, or administrative restrictions or requirements. The groupings are "funds." The accounts of each fund are *self-balancing,* and from them one can prepare a *balance sheet* and an operating statement for each fund. See *fund* and *fund balance.*

fund balance. In governmental accounting, the excess of assets of a *fund* over its liabilities and reserves; the not-for-profit equivalent of *owners' equity.*

funded. Said of a *pension plan* or other obligation when the firm has set aside *funds* for meeting the obligation when it comes due. The federal law for pension plans requires that the firm fund all *normal costs* when it recognizes them as expenses. In addition, the firm must fund *prior*

service cost of pension plans over 30 or over 40 years, depending on the circumstances.

funding. Replacing *short-term* liabilities with *long-term* debt.

funds. Generally *working capital;* current assets less current liabilities; sometimes used to refer to *cash* or to cash and *marketable securities.*

funds provided by operations. See *cash provided by operations.*

funds statement. An informal name often used for the *statement of cash flows.*

funny money. Said of securities, such as *convertible preferred stock, convertible bonds, options,* and *warrants,* that have aspects of *common shares* but that did not reduce reported *earnings per share* before the issuance of *APB Opinion No. 9* in 1966 and *No. 15* in 1969.

FUTA (Federal Unemployment Tax Act). Provides for taxes to be collected at the federal level, to help subsidize the individual states' administration of their unemployment compensation programs.

future value. Value at a specified future date of a sum increased at a specified *interest rate.*

futures contract. An agreement to purchase or sell a specific commodity or financial instrument for a specified price, at a specific future time or during a specified future period. Contrast with *forward contract.* When traded on an organized exchange, the exchange sets the minimum contract size and expiration date(s). The exchange requires that the holder of the contract settle in cash each day the fluctuations in the value of the contract. That is, each day, the exchange marks the contract to market value, called the "(daily) settlement price." A contract holder who has lost during the day must put up more cash, and a holder who has gained receives cash.

G

GAAP. *Generally accepted accounting principles;* a plural noun. In the UK and elsewhere, this means "generally accepted accounting practices."

GAAS. *Generally accepted auditing standards;* a plural noun. Do not confuse with *GAS.*

gain. In *financial accounting* contexts, the increase in *owners' equity* caused by a transaction that is not part of a firm's typical, day-to-day operations and not part of owners' *investment* or *withdrawals.* Accounting distinguishes the meaning of the term "gain" (or *loss*) from that of related terms. First, gains (and losses) generally refer to nonoperating, incidental, peripheral, or nonroutine transactions: gain on sale of land in contrast to *gross margin* on *sale* of *inventory.* Second, gains and losses are *net* concepts, not gross concepts: gain or loss results from subtracting some measure of *cost* from the measure of inflow. *Revenues* and *expenses,* on the other hand, are gross concepts; their difference is a net concept. Gain is non-routine and net, *profit* or *margin* is routine and net; revenue from *continuing operations* is routine and gross; revenue from *discontinued operations* is nonroutine and gross. Loss is net but can be either routine ("loss on sale of inventory") or not ("loss on disposal of segment of business").

In *managerial accounting* and lay contexts, the difference between some measure of *revenue* or *receipts* or *proceeds* and some measure of costs, such as direct costs or variable costs or fully absorbed costs or full costs (see *cost terminology*). Because the word can have so many different meanings, careful writers should be explicit to designate one.

gain contingency. See *contingency*.

GAS. *Goods available for sale*. Do not confuse with *GAAS*.

GASB (Governmental Accounting Standards Board). An independent body responsible, since 1984, for establishing accounting standards for state and local government units. It is part of the *Financial Accounting Foundation,* parallel to the *FASB,* and currently consists of five members.

GbR (Gesellschaft des bürgerlichen Rechtes). Germany: a *partnership* whose members agree to share in specific aspects of their own separate business pursuits, such as an office. This partnership has no legal form and is not a separate accounting *entity*.

GDP Implicit Price Deflator (index). A *price index* issued quarterly by the Office of Business Economics of the U.S. Department of Commerce. This index attempts to trace the price level of all *goods and services* composing the *gross domestic product*. Contrast with *Consumer Price Index*.

gearing. UK: *financial leverage*.

gearing adjustment. A *revenue* representing part of a *holding gain*. Consider a firm that has part of its assets financed by *noncurrent liabilities* and that has experienced *holding gains* on its *assets* during a period. All the increase in wealth caused by the holding gains belongs to the owners; none typically belongs to the lenders. Some British accounting authorities believe that published *income statements* should show part of the holding gain in *income* for the period. The part they would report in income is the fraction of the gain equal to the fraction that debt composes of total financing; for example, if debt equals 40 percent of total equities and the holding gain equals $100 for the period, the amount to appear in income for the period would be $40. Usage calls that part the "gearing adjustment."

general debt. A governmental unit's debt legally payable from general revenues and backed by the full faith and credit of the governmental unit.

general expenses. *Operating expenses* other than those specifically identified as cost of goods sold, selling, and administration.

general fixed asset (group of accounts). Accounts showing a governmental unit's long-term assets that are not accounted for in *enterprise, trust,* or intragovernmental service funds.

general fund. A nonprofit entity's assets and liabilities not specifically earmarked for other purposes; the primary operating fund of a governmental unit.

general journal. The formal record in which the firm records transactions, or summaries of similar transactions, in *journal entry* form as they occur. Use of the adjective "general" usually implies that the journal has only two columns for cash amounts or that the firm also uses various *special journals,* such as a *check register* or *sales journal.*

general ledger. The name for the formal *ledger* containing all the financial statement accounts. It has equal debits and credits, as evidenced by the *trial balance*. Some of the accounts in the general ledger may be *control accounts,* supported by details contained in *subsidiary ledgers*.

general partner. *Partnership* member who is personally liable for all debts of the partnership; contrast with *limited partner*.

general price index. A measure of the aggregate prices of a wide range of goods and services in the economy at one time relative to the prices during a base period. See *Consumer Price Index* and *GDP Implicit Price Deflator*. Contrast with *specific price index*.

general price level–adjusted statements. See *constant-dollar accounting*.

general price-level changes. Changes in the aggregate prices of a wide range of goods and services in the economy. These price measurements result from using a *general price index*. Contrast with *specific price changes*.

general purchasing power. The command of the dollar over a wide range of goods and services in the economy. The general purchasing power of the dollar is inversely related to changes in a general price index. See *general price index*.

general purchasing-power accounting. See *constant-dollar accounting*.

generally accepted accounting principles (GAAP). As previously defined by the *CAP, APB,* and now the *FASB,* the conventions, rules, and procedures necessary to define accepted accounting practice at a particular time; includes both broad guidelines and relatively detailed practices and procedures. In the United States the FASB defines GAAP to include accounting pronouncements of the *SEC* and other government agencies as well as a variety of authoritative sources, such as this book.

generally accepted auditing standards (GAAS). The *PCAOB* has explicitly stated that it began compiling its auditing promulgations with *GAAS,* as issued by the *AICPA,* but "a reference to generally accepted auditing standards in auditors' reports is no longer appropriate or necessary." The phrase has referred to the standards, as opposed to particular procedures, that the AICPA promulgated (in *Statements on Auditing Standards*) and that concern "the auditor's professional quantities" and "the judgment exercised by him in the performance of his examination and in his report." Currently, there have been ten such standards: three general ones (concerned with proficiency, independence, and degree of care to be exercised), three standards of field work, and four standards of reporting. The first standard of reporting requires that the *auditor's report* state whether the firm prepared the *financial statements* in accordance with *generally accepted accounting principles*. Thus, before the PCAOB became the auditing rulemaker, the typical auditor's report says that the auditor conducted the examination in accordance with generally accepted auditing standards and that the firm prepared the statements in accordance with generally accepted accounting principles. The report will not refer to the standards of the Public Company Accounting Oversight Board (United States). See *auditor's report.*

geographic segment. A single operation or a group of operations that are located in a particular geographic area and that generate revenue, incur costs, and have assets used in or associated with generating such revenue.

G4+1. A group concerned with unifying accounting standards across countries. It originally comprised the *FASB, CICA* (Canada), the Accounting Standards Board (UK), and the Australian Accounting Standards Board, plus the *IASB.* Hence, the name: a group of four national standard-setters plus the *IASB.* The group now includes participants from New Zealand.

GIE (groupement d'intérêt économique). France: a joint venture, normally used for exports and research-and-development pooling.

GmbH (Gesellschaft mit beschränkter Haftung). Germany: a private company with an unlimited number of shareholders. Transfer of ownership can take place only with the consent of other shareholders. Contrast with *AG.*

goal congruence. The idea that all members of an organization have incentives to perform for a common interest, such as *shareholder* wealth maximization for a *corporation.*

going-concern assumption. For accounting purposes, accountants' assumption that a business will remain in operation long enough to carry out all its current plans. This assumption partially justifies the *acquisition cost* basis, rather than a *liquidation* or *exit value* basis, of accounting.

going public. Said of a business when its *shares* become widely traded rather than being closely held by relatively few shareholders; issuing shares to the general investing public.

goods. Items of merchandise, supplies, raw materials, or finished goods. Sometimes the meaning of "goods" is extended to include all *tangible* items, as in the phrase "goods and services."

goods available for sale. The sum of *beginning inventory* plus all acquisitions of merchandise or finished goods during an *accounting period.*

goods-in-process. *Work-in-process.*

goodwill. The excess of cost of an acquired firm (or operating unit) over the current *fair market value* of the separately identifiable *net assets* of the acquired unit. Before the acquiring firm can recognize goodwill, it must assign a *fair market value* to all identifiable assets, even when not recorded on the books of the acquired unit. For example, if a firm has developed a *patent* that does not appear on its books because of *SFAS No. 2,* if another company acquires the firm, the acquirer will recognize the patent at an amount equal to its estimated fair market value. The acquirer will compute the amount of goodwill only after assigning values to all assets it can identify. Informally, the term indicates the value of good customer relations, high employee morale, a well-respected business name, and so on, all of which the firm or analyst expects to result in greater-than-normal earning power.

goodwill method. A method of accounting for the *admission* of a new partner to a *partnership* when the new partner will receive a portion of capital different from the value of the *tangible* assets contributed as a fraction of tangible assets of the partnership. See *bonus method* for a description and contrast.

Governmental Accounting Standards Advisory Council. A group that consults with the *GASB* on agenda, technical issues, and the assignment of priorities to projects. It comprises more than a dozen members representing various areas of expertise.

Governmental Accounting Standards Board. *GASB.*

GPL (general price level). Usually used as an adjective modifying the word "accounting" to mean *constant-dollar accounting.*

GPLA (general price level–adjusted accounting). *Constant-dollar accounting.*

GPP (general purchasing power). Usually used as an adjective modifying the word "accounting" to mean *constant-dollar accounting.*

graded vesting. Said of a *pension plan* in which not all employees currently have fully *vested* benefits. By law, the benefits must vest according to one of several formulas as time passes.

grandfather clause. An exemption in new accounting *pronouncements* exempting transactions that occurred before a given date from the new accounting treatment. For example, *APB Opinion No. 17,* adopted in 1970, exempted *goodwill* acquired before 1970 from required *amortization.* The term "grandfather" appears in the title to *SFAS No. 10.*

gross. Not adjusted or reduced by deductions or subtractions. Contrast with *net,* and see *gain* for a description of how the difference between net and gross affects usage of the terms *revenue, gain, expense,* and *loss.*

gross domestic product (GDP). The market value of all goods and services produced by capital or labor within a country, regardless of who owns the capital or of the nationality of the labor; most widely used measure of production within a country. Contrast with gross national product (GNP), which measures the market value of all goods and services produced with capital owned by, and labor services supplied by, the residents of that country regardless of where they work or where they own capital. In the United States in recent years, the difference between GDP and GNP equals about two-tenths of 1 percent of GDP.

gross margin. *Net sales* minus *cost of goods sold.*

gross margin percent. $100 \times (1 - \text{cost of goods sold/net sales}) = 100 \times (\text{gross margin/net sales}).$

gross national product (GNP). See *gross domestic product* for definition and contrast.

gross price method (of recording purchase or sales discounts). The firm records the *purchase* (or *sale*) at the *invoice price,* not deducting the amounts of *discounts* available. Later, it uses a *contra* account to purchases (or sales) to record the amounts of discounts taken. Since information on discounts lapsed will not emerge from this system, most firms should prefer the *net price method* of recording purchase discounts.

gross profit. *Gross margin.*

gross profit method. A method of estimating *ending inventory* amounts. First, the firm measures *cost of goods sold* as some fraction of sales; then, it uses the *inventory equation* to value *ending inventory*.

gross profit ratio. *Gross margin* divided by *net sales*.

gross sales. All *sales* at *invoice* prices, not reduced by *discounts, allowances, returns,* or other adjustments.

group depreciation. In calculating *depreciation* charges, a method that combines similar assets rather than depreciating them separately. It does not recognize gain or loss on retirement of items from the group until the firm sells or retires the last item in the group. See *composite life method*.

Group of 4 Plus 1. See *G4+1*.

guarantee. A promise to answer for payment of debt or performance of some obligation if the person liable for the debt or obligation fails to perform. A guarantee is a *contingency* of the *entity* making the promise. Often, writers use the words "guarantee" and "warranty" to mean the same thing. In precise usage, however, "guarantee" means some person's promise to perform a contractual obligation such as to pay a sum of cash, whereas "warranty" refers to promises about pieces of machinery or other products. See *warranty*.

H

half-year convention. In *tax accounting* under *ACRS,* and sometimes in *financial accounting,* an assumption that the firm acquired *depreciable assets* at midyear of the year of acquisition. When the firm uses this convention, it computes the *depreciation charge* for the year as one-half the charge that it would have used if it had acquired the assets at the beginning of the year.

hardware. The physical equipment or devices forming a computer and peripheral equipment.

hash total. Used to establish accuracy of data processing; a control that takes the sum of data items not normally added together (e.g., the sum of a list of part numbers) and subsequently compares that sum with a computer-generated total of the same values. If the two sums are identical, then the analyst takes some comfort that the two lists are identical.

Hasselback. An annual directory of accounting faculty at colleges and universities; gives information about the faculty's training and fields of specialization. James R. Hasselback, of Florida State University, has compiled the directory since the 1970s; Prentice-Hall distributes it. On-line, you can find it at the Rutgers University accounting Web Site: www.rutgers .edu/Accounting/.

health-care benefits obligation. At any time, the present value of the non-pension benefits promised by an employer to employees during their retirement years.

hedge. To reduce, perhaps cancel altogether, one risk the entity already bears, by purchasing a security or other financial instrument. For example, a farmer growing corn runs the risk that corn prices may decline before the corn matures and can be brought to market. Such a farmer can arrange to sell the corn now for future delivery, hedging the risk of corn price changes. A firm may have a *receivable* denominated in German marks due in six months. It runs the risk that the exchange rate between the dollar and

the mark will change and the firm will receive a smaller number of dollars in the future than it would receive from the same number of marks received today. Such a firm may hedge its exposure to risk of changes in the exchange rate between dollars and German marks in a variety of ways.

held-to-maturity securities. *Marketable debt securities* that a firm expects to, and has the ability to, hold to *maturity;* a classification important in *SFAS No. 115,* which generally requires the owner to carry marketable securities on the balance sheet at market value, not at cost. Under *SFAS No. 115,* the firm may show held-to-maturity debt securities at *amortized cost.* If the firm lacks either the expectation or the intent to hold the debt security to its maturity, then the firm will show that security at market value as a security *available for sale*.

hidden reserve. An amount by which a firm has understated *owners' equity,* perhaps deliberately. The understatement arises from an undervaluation of *assets* or overvaluation of *liabilities.* By undervaluing assets on this period's *balance sheet,* the firm can overstate *net income* in some future period by disposing of the asset: actual *revenues* less artificially low cost of assets sold yields artificially high net income. No *account* in the *ledger* has this title.

hire-purchase agreement (contract). UK: a *lease* containing a purchase *option*.

historical cost. *Acquisition cost; original cost; a sunk cost.*

historical cost/constant-dollar accounting. Accounting based on *historical cost* valuations measured in *constant dollars.* The method restates *nonmonetary items* to reflect changes in the *general purchasing power* of the dollar since the time the firm acquired specific *assets* or incurred specific *liabilities.* The method recognizes a *gain* or *loss* on *monetary items* as the firm holds them over time periods when the general purchasing power of the dollar changes.

historical exchange rate. The rate at which one currency converts into another at the date a transaction took place. Contrast with *current exchange rate*.

historical summary. A part of the *annual report* that shows items, such as *net income, revenues, expenses, asset* and *equity* totals, *earnings per share,* and the like, for five or ten periods including the current one. Usually not as much detail appears in the historical summary as in *comparative statements,* which typically report as much detail for the two preceding years as for the current year. Annual reports may contain both comparative statements and a historical summary.

historical valuation. Showing balance sheet amounts at acquisition cost, sometimes reduced for *accumulated amortization;* sometimes reduced to *lower of cost or market*.

holdback. Under the terms of a contract, a portion of the progress payments that the customer need not pay until the contractor has fulfilled the contract or satisfied financial obligations to subcontractors.

holding company. A company that confines its activities to owning *stock* in, and supervising management of, other companies. A holding company usually owns a controlling interest in—that is, more than 50 percent of the voting *stock* of—the companies whose stock it holds.

Contrast with *mutual fund*. See *conglomerate*. In British usage, the term refers to any company with controlling interest in another company.

holding gain or loss. Difference between end-of-period price and beginning-of-period price of an asset held during the period. The financial statements ordinarily do not separately report realized holding gains and losses. Income does not usually report unrealized gains at all, except on *trading securities*. See *lower of cost or market*. See *inventory profit* for further refinement, including *gains* on *assets* sold during the period.

holding gain or loss net of inflation. Increase or decrease in the *current cost* of an asset while it is held; measured in units of *constant dollars*.

horizontal analysis. *Time-series analysis.*

horizontal integration. An organization's extension of activity in the same general line of business or its expansion into supplementary, complementary, or compatible products. Compare *vertical integration*.

house account. An account with a customer who does not pay sales commissions.

human resource accounting. A term used to describe a variety of proposals that seek to report the importance of human resources—knowledgeable, trained, and loyal employees—in a company's earning process and total assets.

hurdle rate. Required rate of return in a *discounted cash flow* analysis.

hybrid security. *Security,* such as a *convertible bond,* containing elements of both *debt* and *owners' equity.*

hypothecation. The *pledging* of property, without transfer of title or possession, to secure a loan.

I

IAA. *Interamerican Accounting Association.*

IASB. *International Accounting Standards Board.*

ICMA (Institute of Certified Management Accountants). See *CMA* and *Institute of Management Accountants.*

ideal standard costs. *Standard costs* set equal to those that a firm would incur under the best-possible conditions.

IIA. *Institute of Internal Auditors.*

IMA. *Institute of Management Accountants.*

impairment. Reduction in *market value* of an *asset.* When the firm has information indicating that its long-lived *assets,* such as *plant,* identifiable *intangibles,* and *goodwill,* have declined in *market value* or will provide a smaller future benefit that originally anticipated, it tests to see if the decline in value is so drastic that the expected future cash flows from the asset have declined below *book value.* If then-current book value exceeds the sum of expected cash flows, an asset impairment has occurred. At the time the firm judges that an impairment has occurred, the firm writes down the book value of the asset to its then-current *fair value,* which is the market value of the asset or, if the firm cannot assess the market value, the expected *net present value* of the future cash flows.

impairment loss. See *impairment.* This term refers to the amount by which the firm writes down the asset.

implicit interest. *Interest* not paid or received. See *interest, imputed.* All transactions involving the deferred payment or receipt of cash involve interest, whether explicitly stated or not. The implicit interest on a single-payment *note* equals the difference between the amount collected at maturity and the amount lent at the start of the loan. One can compute the implicit *interest rate* per year for loans with a single cash inflow and a single cash outflow from the following equation:

$$\left[\frac{\text{Cash Received at Maturity}}{\text{Cash Lent}} \right]^{(1|t)} - 1$$

where *t* is the term of the loan in years; *t* need not be an integer.

imprest fund. *Petty cash fund.*

improvement. An *expenditure* to extend the useful life of an *asset* or to improve its performance (rate of output, cost) over that of the original asset; sometimes called "betterment." The firm capitalizes such expenditures as part of the asset's cost. Contrast with *maintenance* and *repair.*

imputed cost. A cost that does not appear in accounting records, such as the *interest* that a firm could earn on cash spent to acquire inventories rather than, say, government bonds. Or, consider a firm that owns the buildings it occupies. This firm has an imputed cost for rent in an amount equal to what it would have to pay to use similar buildings owned by another or equal to the amount it could collect from someone renting the premises from the firm. *Opportunity cost.*

imputed interest. See *interest, imputed.*

in the black (red). Operating at a profit (loss).

in-process R&D. When one firm acquires another, the acquired firm will often have *research and development* activities under way that, following *GAAP,* it has *expensed.* The acquiring firm will pay for these activities to the extent they have value and will then, following GAAP, write off the activities. For each dollar of in-process R&D the acquiring firm identities and immediately *expenses,* it will have one less dollar of *goodwill* or other assets to *amortize.* Some acquirers have overstated the valuations of acquired in-process R&D in order to increase immediate *write-offs* and subsequent, recurring *income.*

incentive compatible compensation. Said of a compensation plan that induces managers to act for the interests of owners while acting also in their own interests. For example, consider that a time of rising prices and increasing inventories when using a *LIFO* cost flow assumption implies paying lower *income taxes* than using *FIFO.* A bonus scheme for managers based on accounting *net income* is not incentive-compatible because owners likely benefit more under LIFO, whereas managers benefit more if they report using FIFO. See *LIFO conformity rule* and *goal congruence.*

income. *Excess* of *revenues* and *gains* over *expenses* and *losses* for a period; *net income.* The term is sometimes used with an appropriate modifier to refer to the various intermediate amounts shown in a *multiple-step income statement* or to refer to revenues, as in "rental income." See *comprehensive income.*

income accounts. *Revenue* and *expense accounts.*

income before taxes. On the *income statement,* the difference between all *revenues* and *expenses* except *income tax* expense. Contrast with *net income.*

income determination. See *determine.*

income distribution account. *Temporary account* sometimes debited when the firm declares *dividends;* closed to *retained earnings.*

income from continuing operations. As defined by *APB Opinion No. 30,* all *revenues* less all *expenses* except for the following: results of operations (including *income tax* effects) that a firm has discontinued or will discontinue; *gains* or *losses,* including income tax effects, on disposal of segments of the business; gains or losses, including income tax effects, from *extraordinary items;* and the cumulative effect of *accounting changes.*

income from discontinued operations. *Income,* net of tax effects, from parts of the business that the firm has discontinued during the period or will discontinue in the near future. Accountants report such items on separate lines of the *income statement,* after *income from continuing operations* but before *extraordinary items.*

income (revenue) bond. See *special revenue debt.*

income smoothing. A method of timing business *transactions* or choosing *accounting principles* so that the firm reports smaller variations in *income* from year to year than it otherwise would. Although some managements set income smoothing as an objective, no standard-setter does.

income statement. The statement of *revenues, expenses, gains,* and *losses* for the period, ending with *net income* for the period. Accountants usually show the *earnings-per-share* amount on the income statement; the *reconciliation* of beginning and ending balances of *retained earnings* may also appear in a combined statement of income and retained earnings. See *income from continuing operations, income from discontinued operations, extraordinary items, multiple-step,* and *single-step.*

income summary. In problem solving, an *account* that serves as a surrogate for the *income statement.* In using an income summary, close all *revenue* accounts to the Income Summary as *credits* and all *expense* accounts as *debits.* The *balance* in the account, after you make all these *closing entries,* represents income or loss for the period. Then, close the income summary balance to retained earnings.

income tax. An annual tax levied by the federal and other governments on the income of an entity.

income tax allocation. See *deferred income tax (liability)* and *tax allocation:intra-statement.*

incremental. An adjective used to describe the increase in *cost, expense, investment, cash flow, revenue, profit,* and the like if the firm produces or sells one or more units or if it undertakes an activity. See *differential.*

incremental cost. See *incremental.*

incur. Said of an obligation of a firm, whether or not that obligation is *accrued.* For example, a firm incurs interest expense on a loan as time passes but accrues that interest only on payment dates or when it makes an *adjusting entry.*

indenture. See *bond indenture.*

independence. The mental attitude required of the *CPA* in performing the *attest* function. It implies that the CPA is impartial and that the members of the auditing CPA firm own no stock in the corporation being audited.

independent accountant. The *CPA* who performs the *attest* function for a firm.

independent variable. See *regression analysis.*

indeterminate-term liability. A *liability* lacking the criterion of being due at a definite time. This term is our own coinage to encompass the *minority interest.*

indexation. An attempt by lawmakers or parties to a contract to cope with the effects of *inflation.* Amounts fixed in law or contracts are "indexed" when these amounts change as a given measure of price changes. For example, a so-called escalator clause (COLA—cost of living allowance or adjustment) in a labor contract might provide that hourly wages will be increased as the *Consumer Price Index* increases. Many economists have suggested the indexation of numbers fixed in the *income tax* laws. If, for example, the personal *exemption* is \$2,500 at the start of the period, if prices rise by 10 percent during the period, and if the personal exemption is indexed, then the personal exemption would automatically rise to \$2,750 (= \$2,500 + 0.10 × \$2,500) at the end of the period.

indirect cost pool. Any grouping of individual costs that a firm does not identify with a *cost objective.*

indirect costs. Production costs not easily associated with the production of specific goods and services; *overhead costs.* Accountants may *allocate* them on some *arbitrary* basis to specific products or departments.

indirect labor (material) cost. An *indirect cost* for labor (material), such as for supervisors (supplies).

indirect method. See *statement of cash flows.*

individual proprietorship. *Sole proprietorship.*

Industry Audit Guides. A series of *AICPA* publications providing specific accounting and *auditing principles* for specialized situations. Audit guides have been issued covering government contractors, state and local government units, investment companies, finance companies, brokers and dealers in securities, and many other subjects.

inescapable cost. A *cost* that the firm or manager cannot avoid (see *avoidable*) because of an action. For example, if management shuts down two operating rooms in a hospital but still must employ security guards in unreduced numbers, the security costs are "inescapable" with respect to the decision to close the operating rooms.

inflation. A time of generally rising prices.

inflation accounting. Strictly speaking, *constant-dollar accounting.* Some writers incorrectly use the term to mean *current cost accounting.*

information circular. Canada: a document, accompanying the notice of a shareholders' meeting, prepared in connection with the solicitation of proxies by or on behalf of the management of the corporation. It contains information concerning the people making the solicitation, election of directors, appointment of auditors, and other matters to be acted on at the meeting.

information system. A system, sometimes formal and sometimes informal, for collecting, processing, and communicating data that are useful for the managerial functions of decision making, planning, and control and for financial reporting under the *attest* requirement.

inherent interest rate. *Implicit interest* rate.

insolvent. Unable to pay debts when due; said of a company even though *assets* exceed *liabilities.*

installment. Partial payment of a debt or partial collection of a receivable, usually according to a contract.

installment contracts receivable. The name used for *accounts receivable* when the firm uses the *installment method* of recognizing revenue. Its *contra account, unrealized gross margin,* appears on the balance sheet as a subtraction from the amount receivable.

installment sales. Sales on account when the buyer promises to pay in several separate payments, called *installments.* The seller may, but need not, account for such sales using the *installment method.* If the seller accounts for installment sales with the sales *basis of revenue recognition* for financial reporting but with the installment method for income tax returns, then it will have *deferred income tax* (*liability*).

installment (sales) method. Recognizing *revenue* and *expense* (or *gross margin*) from a sales transaction in proportion to the fraction of the selling price collected during a period; allowed by the *IRS* for income tax reporting but acceptable in *GAAP* (*APB Opinion No. 10*) only when the firm cannot estimate cash collections with reasonable precision. See *realized* (and *unrealized*) *gross margin.*

Institute of Certified Management Accountants (ICMA). See *CMA* and *Institute of Management Accountants.*

Institute of Internal Auditors (IIA). The national association of accountants who are engaged in internal auditing and are employed by business firms; administers a comprehensive professional examination. Those who pass the exam qualify to be designated *CIA* (Certified Internal Auditor).

Institute of Management Accountants (IMA). Formerly, the National Association of Accountants, NAA; a society open to those engaged in management accounting; parent organization of the *ICMA,* which oversees the *CMA* program.

insurance. A contract for reimbursement of specific losses; purchased with insurance premiums. "Self-insurance" is not insurance but is merely the noninsured's willingness to assume the risk of incurring losses while saving the premium.

intangible asset. A nonphysical right that gives a firm an exclusive or preferred position in the marketplace. Examples are *copyright, patent, trademark, goodwill, organization costs, capitalized* advertising cost, computer programs, licenses for any of the preceding, government licenses (e.g., broadcasting or the right to sell liquor), *leases,* franchises, mailing lists, exploration permits, import and export permits, construction permits, and marketing quotas. Invariably, accountants define "intangible" using a "for example" list, as we have just done, because accounting has been unable to devise a definition of "intangible" that will include items such as those listed above but exclude stock and bond certificates. Accountants classify these items as tangibles,

even though they give their holders a preferred position in receiving dividends and interest payments.

Interamerican Accounting Association (IAA). An organization, headquartered in Miami, devoted to facilitating interaction between accounting practitioners in the Americas.

intercompany elimination. See *eliminations.*

intercompany profit. Profit within an organization. If one *affiliated company* sells to another, and the goods remain in the second company's *inventory* at the end of the period, then the first company has not yet realized a *profit* by a sale to an outsider. The profit is "intercompany profit," and the accountant eliminates it from net *income* when preparing *consolidated income statements* or when the firm uses the *equity method.*

intercompany transaction. *Transaction* between a *parent company* and a *subsidiary* or between subsidiaries in a *consolidated entity;* the accountant must eliminate the effects of such a transaction when preparing *consolidated financial statements.* See *intercompany profit.*

intercorporate investment. Occurs when a given *corporation* owns *shares* or *debt* issued by another.

interdepartment monitoring. An *internal control* device. The advantage of allocating *service department costs* to *production departments* stems from the incentives that this gives those charged with the costs to control the costs incurred in the service department. That process of having one group monitor the performance of another is interdepartment monitoring.

interest. The charge or cost for using cash, usually borrowed funds. Interest on one's own cash used is an *opportunity cost, imputed interest.* The amount of interest for a loan is the total amount paid by a borrower to a lender less the amount paid by the lender to the borrower. Accounting seeks to allocate that interest over the time of the loan so that the interest rate (= interest charge/amount borrowed) stays constant each period. See *interest rate* for discussion of the quoted amount. See *effective interest rate* and *nominal interest rate.*

interest, imputed. The difference between the face amount and the present value of a promise. If a borrower merely promises to pay a single amount, sometime later than the present, then the face amount the borrower will repay at *maturity* will exceed the present value (computed at a *fair market* interest rate, called the "imputed interest rate") of the promise. See also *imputed cost.*

interest factor. One plus the *interest* rate.

interest method. See *effective interest method.*

interest rate. A basis used for computing the cost of borrowing funds; usually expressed as a ratio between the number of currency units (e.g., dollars) charged for a period of time and the number of currency units borrowed for that same period of time. When the writers and speakers do not state a period, they almost always mean a period of one year. See *interest, simple interest, compound interest, effective* (*interest*) *rate,* and *nominal interest rate.*

interest rate swap. See *swap.*

interfund accounts. In governmental accounting, the accounts that show transactions between funds, especially interfund receivables and payables.

interim statements. Statements issued for periods less than the regular, annual *accounting period*. The *SEC* requires most corporations to issue interim statements on a quarterly basis. In preparing interim reports, a problem arises that the accountant can resolve only by understanding whether interim reports should report on the interim period (1) as a self-contained accounting period or (2) as an integral part of the year so that analysts can make forecasts of annual performance. For example, assume that at the end of the first quarter, a retailer has dipped into old LIFO layers, depleting its *inventory,* so that it computes *LIFO cost of goods sold* artificially low and *net income* artificially high, relative to the amounts the firm would have computed if it had made the "normal" purchases, equal to or greater than sales. The retailer expects to purchase inventory sufficiently large so that when it computes cost of goods sold for the year, there will be no *dips into old LIFO layers* and income will not be artificially high. The first approach will compute the quarterly income from low cost of goods sold using data for the dips that have actually occurred by the end of the quarter. The second approach will compute quarterly income from cost of goods sold assuming that purchases were equal to "normal" amounts and that the firm did not dip into old LIFO layers. *APB Opinion No. 28* and the *SEC* require that interim reports be constructed largely to satisfy the second purpose.

internal audit, internal auditor. An *audit* conducted by the firm's own employees, called "internal auditors," to ascertain whether the firm's *internal control* procedures work as planned. Contrast with an external audit conducted by a *CPA*.

internal controls. Policies and procedures designed to provide management with reasonable assurances that employees behave in a way that enables the firm to meet its organizational goals. See *control system.*

internal rate of return (IRR). The discount rate that equates the net *present value* of a stream of cash outflows and inflows to zero.

internal reporting. Reporting for management's use in planning and control. Contrast with *external reporting* for financial statement users.

Internal Revenue Service (IRS). Agency of the U.S. Treasury Department responsible for administering the Internal Revenue Code and collecting income and certain other taxes.

International Accounting Standards Board (IASB). An organization that promotes the international harmonization of accounting standards. Web Site: www.iasb.org.uk.

International Organization of Securities Commissions. *IOSCO.*

interperiod tax allocation. See *deferred income tax (liability).*

interpolation. The estimation of an unknown number intermediate between two (or more) known numbers.

Interpretations. See *FASB Interpretation.*

intrastatement tax allocation. See *tax allocation: intrastatement.*

inventoriable costs. *Costs* incurred that the firm adds to the cost of manufactured products; *product costs (assets)* as opposed to *period expenses.*

inventory. As a noun, the *balance* in an asset *account,* such as raw materials, supplies, work-in-process, and finished goods; as a verb, to calculate the *cost* of goods on hand at a given time or to count items on hand physically.

inventory equation. *Beginning inventory* + net additions − withdrawals = *ending inventory.* Ordinarily, additions are net purchases, and withdrawals are *cost of goods sold.* Notice that ending inventory, appearing on the balance sheet, and cost of goods sold, appearing on the income statement, must add to a fixed sum. The larger is one; the smaller must be the other. In valuing inventories, the firm usually knows beginning inventory and net purchases. Some inventory methods (for example, some applications of the *retail inventory method*) measure costs of goods sold and use the equation to find the cost of ending inventory. Most methods measure cost of ending inventory and use the equation to find the cost of goods sold (withdrawals). In *current cost* (in contrast to *historical cost*) *accounting,* additions (in the equation) include holding gains, whether realized or not. Thus the current cost inventory equation is as follows: Beginning Inventory (at Current Cost) + Purchases (where Current Cost is Historical Cost) + Holding Gains (whether Realized or Not) − Ending Inventory (at Current Cost) = Cost of Goods Sold (Current Cost).

inventory holding gains. See *inventory profit.*

inventory layer. See *LIFO inventory layer.*

inventory profit. A term with several possible meanings. Consider the data in the accompanying illustration. The firm uses a *FIFO cost flow assumption* and derives its *historical cost* data. The assumed *current cost* data resemble those that the FASB suggested in *SFAS No. 89.* The term *income from continuing operations* refers to revenues less expenses based on current, rather than historical, costs. To that subtotal, add realized holding gains to arrive at realized (conventional) income. To that, add unrealized holding gains to arrive at economic income. The term "inventory profit" often refers (for example, in some *SEC* releases) to the realized holding gain, $110 in the illustration. The amount of inventory profit will usually be material when the firm uses FIFO and when prices rise. Other analysts, including us, prefer to use the term "inventory profit" to refer to the total *holding gain,* $300 (= $110 + $190, both realized and unrealized), but writers use this meaning less often. In periods of rising prices and increasing inventories, the realized holding gains under a FIFO cost flow assumption will exceed those under LIFO. In the illustration, for example, assume under LIFO that the historical cost of goods sold is $4,800, that historical LIFO cost of beginning inventory is $600, and that historical LIFO cost of ending inventory is $800. Then income from continuing operations, based on current costs, remains $350 (= $5,200 − $4,850), realized holding gains are $50 (= $4,850 − $4,800), realized income is $400 (= $350 + $50), the unrealized holding gain for the year is $250 [= ($1,550 − $800) − ($1,100 − $600)], and economic income is $650 (= $350 + $50 + $250). The cost flow assumption has only one real effect on this series of calculations: the split of the total holding gain into realized and unrealized portions. Thus, economic income does not depend on the cost flow assumption. Holding gains total

$300 in the illustration. The choice of cost flow assumption determines the portion reported as realized.

inventory turnover. Number of times the firm sells the average *inventory* during a period; *cost of goods sold* for a period divided by average inventory for the period. See *ratio.*

inventory valuation allowance. A preferred term for the difference between the *FIFO* (or *current cost*) of *inventory* and its *LIFO* valuation. Many in business refer to this as the "LIFO reserve." See *reserve* for an explanation of why we dislike that term.

invested capital. *Contributed capital.*

investee. A company in which another entity, the "investor," owns stock.

investing activities. Acquiring and selling *securities* or productive *assets* expected to produce *revenue* over several *periods.*

investment. An *expenditure* to acquire property or other *assets* in order to produce *revenue;* the asset so acquired; hence a *current* expenditure made in anticipation of future income; said of other companies' *securities* held for the long term and appearing in a separate section of the *balance sheet;* in this context, contrast with *marketable securities.*

Inventory Profit Illustration

	(Historical) Acquisition Cost Assuming FIFO	Current Cost
ASSUMED DATA		
Inventory, 1/1	$ 900	$1,100
Inventory, 12/31	1,160	1,550
Cost of Goods Sold for the Year	4,740	4,850
Sales for the Year	$5,200	$5,200
INCOME STATEMENT FOR THE YEAR		
Sales	$5,200	$5,200
Cost of Goods Sold	4,740	4,850
(1) Income from Continuing Operations		$ 350
Realized Holding Gains		110[a]
(2) Realized Income = Conventional Net Income (under FIFO)	$ 460	$ 460
Unrealized Holding Gain		190[b]
(3) Economic Income		$ 650

[a]Realized holding gain during a period is current cost of goods sold less historical cost of goods sold; for the year the realized holding gain under FIFO is $110 = $4,850 − $4,740. Some refer to this as "inventory profit."

[b]The total unrealized holding gain at any time is current cost of inventory on hand at that time less historical cost of that inventory. The unrealized holding gain during a period is unrealized holding gain at the end of the period less the unrealized holding gain prior to this year is: $200 = $1,100 − $900. Unrealized holding gain during the year = ($1,550 − $1,160) − ($1,100 − 900) = $390 − $200 = $190.

investment center. A *responsibility center,* with control over *revenues, costs,* and *assets.*

investment credit. A reduction in income tax liability sometimes granted by the federal government to firms that buy new equipment. This item is a credit in that the taxpayer deducts it from the tax bill, not from pretax income. The tax credit has been a given percentage of the purchase price of the assets purchased. The government has changed the actual rules and rates over the years. As of 1999, there is no investment credit. See *flow-through method* and *carryforward.*

investment decision. The decision whether to undertake an action involving production of goods or services; contrast with *financing decision.*

investment tax credit. *Investment credit.*

investment turnover ratio. A term that means the same thing as *total assets turnover ratio.*

investments. A balance sheet heading for tangible assets held for periods longer than the operating cycle and not used in revenue production (assets not meeting the definitions of *current assets* or *property, plant, and equipment*).

invoice. A document showing the details of a sale or purchase *transaction.*

IOSCO (International Organization of Securities Commissions). The name, since 1983, of a confederation of regulators of securities and futures markets. Members come from over 80 countries. The IOSCO encourages the *IASB* to eliminate accounting alternatives and to ensure that accounting standards are detailed and complete, with adequate disclosure requirements, and that financial statements are user-friendly.

I.O.U. An informal document acknowledging a debt, setting out the amount of the debt and signed by the debtor.

IRR. *Internal rate of return.*

IRS. *Internal Revenue Service.*

isoprofit line. On a graph showing feasible production possibilities of two products that require the use of the same, limited resources, a line showing all feasible production possibility combinations with the same *profit* or, perhaps, *contribution margin.*

issue. A corporation exchange of its stock (or *bonds*) for cash or other *assets.* Terminology says the corporation "issues," not "sells," that stock (or bonds). Also used in the context of withdrawing supplies or materials from inventory for use in operations and of drawing a *check.*

issued shares. Those shares of *authorized capital stock* that a *corporation* has distributed to the shareholders. See *issue.* Shares of *treasury stock* are legally issued but are not *outstanding* for the purpose of voting, *dividend declarations,* and *earnings-per-share* calculations.

J

JIT. See *just-in-time inventory.*

job cost sheet. A schedule showing actual or budgeted inputs for a special order.

job development credit. The name used for the *investment credit* in the 1971 tax law, since repealed, on this subject.

job (-order) costing. Accumulation of *costs* for a particular identifiable batch of product, known as a job, as it moves through production.

joint cost. Cost of simultaneously producing or otherwise acquiring two or more products, called joint products, that a firm must, by the nature of the process, produce or acquire together, such as the cost of beef and hides of cattle. Generally, accounting allocates the joint costs of production to the individual products in proportion to their respective sales value (or, sometimes and usually not preferred, their respective physical quantities) at the *split-off* point. Other examples include *central corporate expenses* and *overhead* of a department when it manufactures several products. See *common cost* and *sterilized allocation.*

joint cost allocation. See *joint cost.*

joint product. One of two or more outputs with significant value that a firm must produce or acquire simultaneously. See *by-product* and *joint cost.*

journal. The place where the firm records transactions as they occur; the book of original entry.

journal entry. A dated *journal* recording, showing the accounts affected, of equal *debits* and *credits,* with an explanation of the *transaction,* if necessary.

Journal of Accountancy. A monthly publication of the *AICPA.*

Journal of Accounting and Economics. Scholarly journal published by the William E. Simon Graduate School of Business Administration of the University of Rochester.

Journal of Accounting Research. Scholarly journal containing articles on theoretical and empirical aspects of accounting; published by the Graduate School of Business of the University of Chicago.

journal voucher. A *voucher* documenting (and sometimes authorizing) a *transaction,* leading to an entry in the *journal.*

journalize. To make an entry in a *journal.*

judgment(al) sampling. A method of choosing a sample in which the analyst subjectively selects items for examination, in contrast to selecting them by statistical methods. Compare *random sampling.*

junk bond. A low-rated *bond* that lacks the merit and characteristics of an investment-grade bond. It offers high yields, typically in excess of 15 percent per year, but also possesses high risk of default. Sometimes writers, less pejoratively, call these "high-yield bonds." No clear line separates junk from nonjunk bonds.

just-in-time inventory (production) (JIT). In managing *inventory* for manufacturing, system in which a firm purchases or manufactures each component just before the firm uses it. Contrast with systems in which firms acquire or manufacture many parts in advance of needs. JIT systems have much smaller carrying costs for inventory, ideally none, but run higher risks of incurring *stockout* costs.

K

k. Two to the tenth power (2^{10} or 1,024), when referring to computer storage capacity. The one-letter abbreviation derives from the first letter of the prefix "kilo-" (which means 1,000 in decimal notation).

Kaizen costing. A management concept that seeks continuous improvements, likely occurring in small incremental amounts, by refinements of all components of a production process.

KG (Kommanditgesellschaft). Germany: similar to a general partnership (*OHG*) except that some of its members

may limit their liability. One of the partners must be a *general partner* with unlimited liability.

kiting. A term with slightly different meanings in banking and auditing contexts. In both, however, it refers to the wrongful practice of taking advantage of the *float,* the time that elapses between the deposit of a *check* in one bank and its collection at another. In the banking context, an individual deposits in Bank A a check written on Bank B. He (or she) then writes checks against the deposit created in Bank A. Several days later, he deposits in Bank B a check written on Bank A, to cover the original check written on Bank B. Still later, he deposits in Bank A a check written on Bank B. The process of covering the deposit in Bank A with a check written on Bank B and vice versa continues until the person can arrange an actual deposit of cash. In the auditing context, kiting refers to a form of *window dressing* in which the firm makes the amount of the account Cash in Bank appear larger than it actually is by depositing in Bank A a check written on Bank B without recording the check written on Bank B in the *check register* until after the close of the *accounting period.*

know-how. Technical or business information that is of the type defined under *trade secret* but that a firm does not maintain as a secret. The rules of accounting for this *asset* are the same as for other *intangibles.*

L

labor variances. The *price* (or *rate*) and *quantity* (or *usage*) *variances* for *direct labor* inputs in a *standard costing system.*

laid-down cost. Canada and UK: the sum of all direct costs incurred for procurement of goods up to the time of physical receipt, such as invoice cost plus customs and excise duties, freight, and cartage.

land. An *asset* shown at *acquisition cost* plus the *cost* of any nondepreciable *improvements;* in accounting, implies use as a plant or office site rather than as a *natural resource,* such as timberland or farmland.

lapping (accounts receivable). The theft, by an employee, of cash sent in by a customer to discharge the latter's *payable.* The employee conceals the theft from the first customer by using cash received from a second customer. The employee conceals the theft from the second customer by using cash received from a third customer, and so on. The process continues until the thief returns the funds or can make the theft permanent by creating a fictitious *expense* or receivable write-off or until someone discovers the fraud.

lapse. To expire; said of, for example, an insurance policy or discounts that are made available for prompt payment and that the purchaser does not take.

last-in, first-out. See *LIFO.*

layer. See *LIFO inventory layer.*

lead time. The time that elapses between placing an order and receiving the *goods* or *services* ordered.

learning curve. A mathematical expression of the phenomenon that incremental unit costs to produce decrease as managers and labor gain experience from practice.

lease. A contract calling for the lessee (user) to pay the lessor (owner) for the use of an asset. A cancelable lease allows the lessee to cancel at any time. A noncancelable lease requires payments from the lessee for the life of the lease and usually shares many of the economic characteristics of *debt financing*. Most long-term noncancelable leases meet the usual criteria for classifying them as *liabilities*, and GAAP require the firm to show them as liabilities. *SFAS No. 13* and the *SEC* require disclosure, in notes to the financial statements, of the commitments for long-term noncancelable leases. See *capital lease* and *operating lease*.

leasehold. The *asset* representing the right of the lessee to use leased property. See *lease* and *leasehold improvement*.

leasehold improvement. An *improvement* to leased property. The firm should *amortize* it over the *service life* or the life of the lease, whichever is shorter.

least and latest rule. Paying the least amount of taxes as late as possible within the law to minimize the *present value* of tax payments for a given set of operations. Sensible taxpayers will follow this rule. When a taxpayer knows that tax rates will increase later, the taxpayer may reduce the present value of the tax burden by paying smaller taxes sooner. Each set of circumstances requires its own computations.

ledger. A book of accounts; book of final entry. See *general ledger* and *subsidiary ledger*. Contrast with *journal*.

legal capital. The amount of *contributed capital* that, according to state law, the firm must keep permanently in the firm as protection for creditors.

legal entity. See *entity*.

lender. See *loan*.

lessee. See *lease*.

lessor. See *lease*.

letter stock. Privately placed *common shares;* so called because the *SEC* requires the purchaser to sign a letter of intent not to resell the shares.

leverage. More than proportional result from extra effort or financing. Some measure of output increases faster than the measure of input. "Operating leverage" refers to the tendency of *net income* to rise at a faster rate than sales in the presence of *fixed costs*. A doubling of sales, for example, usually implies a more than doubling of net income. "Financial leverage" (or "capital leverage") refers to an increase in rate of return larger than the increase in explicit financing costs—the increased rate of return on *owners' equity* (see *ratio*) when an *investment* earns a return larger than the after-tax *interest rate* paid for *debt* financing. Because the interest charges on debt usually do not change, any *incremental* income benefits owners and none benefits debtors. When writers use the term "leverage" without a qualifying adjective, the term usually refers to financial leverage, the use of *long-term* debt in securing *funds* for the *entity*.

leveraged lease. A special form of lease involving three parties: a *lender,* a *lessor,* and a *lessee*. The lender, such as a bank or insurance company, lends a portion, say 80 percent, of the cash required for acquiring the *asset*. The lessor puts up the remainder, 20 percent, of the cash required. The lessor acquires the asset with the cash, using the asset as security for the loan, and leases it to the lessee on a *noncancelable* basis. The lessee makes periodic lease payments to the lessor, who in turn makes payments on the loan to the lender. Typically, the lessor has no obligation for the debt to the lender other than transferring a portion of the receipts from the lessee. If the lessee should default on the required lease payments, then the lender can repossess the leased asset. The lessor usually has the right to benefit from the tax deductions for *depreciation* on the asset, for *interest expense* on the loan from the lender, and for any *investment credit*. The lease is leveraged in the sense that the lessor, who takes most of the risks and enjoys most of the rewards of ownership, usually borrows most of the funds needed to acquire the asset. See *leverage*.

liability. An obligation to pay a definite (or reasonably definite) amount at a definite (or reasonably definite) time in return for a past or current benefit (that is, the obligation arises from a transaction that is not an *executory contract*); a probable future sacrifice of economic benefits arising from present obligations of a particular *entity* to *transfer assets* or to provide services to other entities in the future as a result of past *transactions* or events. *SFAC No. 6* says that "probable" refers to that which we can reasonably expect or believe but that is neither certain nor proved. A liability has three essential characteristics: (1) the obligation to transfer assets or services has a specified or knowable date, (2) the entity has little or no discretion to avoid the transfer, and (3) the event causing the obligation has already happened, that is, it is not executory.

lien. The right of person A to satisfy a claim against person B by holding B's property as security or by seizing B's property.

life annuity. A *contingent annuity* in which payments cease at the death of a specified person(s), usually the *annuitant(s)*.

LIFO (last-in, first-out). An *inventory* flow assumption in which the *cost of goods sold* equals the cost of the most recently acquired units and a firm computes the *ending inventory cost* from the costs of the oldest units. In periods of rising prices and increasing inventories, LIFO leads to higher reported expenses and therefore lower reported income and lower balance sheet inventories than does FIFO. Contrast with *FIFO*. See *FISH* and *inventory profit*.

LIFO conformity rule. The *IRS* rule requiring that companies that use a *LIFO cost flow assumption* for *income taxes* must also use LIFO in computing *income* reported in *financial statements* and forbidding the disclosure of pro forma results from using any other cost flow assumption.

LIFO, dollar-value method. See *dollar-value LIFO method*.

LIFO inventory layer. A portion of LIFO inventory cost on the *balance sheet*. The *ending inventory* in physical quantity will usually exceed the *beginning inventory*. The *LIFO cost flow assumption* assigns to this increase in physical quantities a cost computed from the prices of the earliest purchases during the year. The LIFO inventory then consists of layers, sometimes called "slices," which typically consist of relatively small amounts of physical quantities from each of the past years when purchases in physical units exceeded sales in units. Each layer carries the prices from near the beginning of the period when the firm acquired it. The earliest layers will typically (in periods of rising prices) have prices much less than current prices. If inventory quantities should decline in a subsequent period—a "dip into old LIFO layers"—the latest layers enter cost of goods sold first.

LIFO reserve. *Unrealized holding gain* in *ending inventory:* current or *FIFO historical* cost of ending inventory less LIFO *historical cost.* A better term for this concept is "excess of current cost over LIFO historical cost." See *reserve.*

limited liability. The legal concept that shareholders of corporations are not personally liable for debts of the company.

limited partner. A *partnership* member who is not personally liable for debts of the partnership. Every partnership must have at least one *general partner,* who is fully liable.

line-of-business reporting. See *segment reporting.* **line of credit.** An agreement with a bank or set of banks for short-term borrowings on demand.

linear programming. A mathematical tool for finding profit-maximizing (or cost-minimizing) combinations of products to produce when a firm has several products that it can produce but faces linear constraints on the resources available in the production processes or on maximum and minimum production requirements.

liquid. Said of a business with a substantial amount (the amount is unspecified) of *working capital,* especially *quick assets.*

liquid assets. *Cash, current marketable securities,* and sometimes, *current receivables.*

liquidating dividend. A *dividend* that a firm declares in the winding up of a business to distribute its assets to the shareholders. Usually the recipient treats this as a return of *investment,* not as *revenue.*

liquidation. Payment of a debt; sale of assets in closing down a business or a segment thereof.

liquidation value per share. The amount each *share* of stock will receive if the *board* dissolves a corporation; for *preferred stock* with a liquidation preference, a stated amount per share.

liquidity. Refers to the availability of *cash,* or near-cash resources, for meeting a firm's obligations.

LISH. An acronym, conceived by George H. Sorter, for *last-in, still-here.* LISH is the same cost flow assumption as *FIFO.* Many readers of accounting statements find it easier to think about inventory questions in terms of items still on hand. Think of FIFO in connection with *cost of goods sold* but of LISH in connection with *ending inventory.* See *FISH.*

list price. The published or nominally quoted price for goods.

list price method. See *trade-in transaction.*

loan. An arrangement in which the owner of property, called the lender, allows someone else, called the borrower, the use of the property for a period of time, which the agreement setting up the loan usually specifies. The borrower promises to return the property to the lender and, often, to make a payment for the use of the property. This term is generally used when the property is *cash* and the payment for its use is *interest.*

LOCOM. *Lower of cost or market.*

long-lived (term) asset. An asset whose benefits the firm expects to receive over several years; a *noncurrent* asset, usually includes *investments, plant assets,* and *intangibles.*

long-term (construction) contract accounting. The *percentage-of-completion method* of *revenue* recognition; sometimes used to mean the *completed contract method.*

long-term debt ratio. *Noncurrent liabilities* divided by total *assets.*

long-term liability (debt). *Noncurrent liability.*

long-term, long-run. A term denoting a time or time periods in the future. How far in the future depends on context. For some securities traders, "long-term" can mean anything beyond the next hour or two. For most managers, it means anything beyond the next year or two. For government policymakers, it can mean anything beyond the next decade or two. For geologists, it can mean millions of years.

long-term solvency risk. The risk that a firm will not have sufficient *cash* to pay its *debts* sometime in the *long run.*

loophole. Imprecise term meaning a technicality allowing a taxpayer (or *financial statements*) to circumvent the intent, without violating the letter, of the law (or *GAAP*).

loss. Excess of *cost* over net proceeds for a single transaction; negative *income* for a period; a cost expiration that produced no *revenue.* See *gain* for a discussion of related and contrasting terms and how to distinguish loss from *expense.*

loss contingency. See *contingency.*

lower of cost or market (LOCOM). A basis for valuation of *inventory.* This basis sets inventory value at the lower of *acquisition cost* or *current replacement cost* (market), subject to the following constraints. First, the market value of an item used in the computation cannot exceed its *net realizable value*—an amount equal to selling price less reasonable costs to complete production and to sell the item. Second, the market value of an item used in the computation cannot be less than the net realizable value minus the normal *profit* ordinarily realized on disposition of completed items of this type. The basis chooses the lower-of-cost-or-market valuation as the lower of acquisition *cost* or replacement cost (*market*) subject to the upper and lower bounds on replacement cost established in the first two steps. Thus,

Market Value = Midvalue of (Replacement Cost, Net Realizable Value, Net Realizable Value Less Normal Profit Margin)

Lower of Cost or Market Valuation = Minimum (Acquisition Cost, Market Value)

The accompanying exhibit illustrates the calculation of the lower-of-cost-or-market valuation for four inventory items. Notice that each of the four possible outcomes occurs once in measuring lower of cost or market. Item 1 uses acquisition cost; item 2 uses net realizable value;

item 3 uses replacement cost; and item 4 uses net realizable value less normal profit margin.

	Item			
	1	**2**	**3**	**4**
Calculation of Market Value				
(a) Replacement Cost	$92	$96	$92	$96
(b) Net Realizable Value	95	95	95	95
(c) Net Realizable Value Less Normal Profit Margin [= (b) − $9]	86	86	86	86
(d) Market = Midvalue [(a), (b), (c)]	92	95	92	95
Calculation of Lower of Cost or Market				
(e) Acquisition Cost	90	97	96	90
(f) Market [= (d)]	92	95	92	95
(g) Lower of Cost or Market = Minimum [(e), (f)]	90	95	92	90

A taxpayer may not use the lower-of-cost-or-market basis for inventory on tax returns in combination with a *LIFO cost flow assumption.* In the context of inventory, once the firm writes down the asset, it establishes a new "original cost" basis and ignores subsequent increases in market value in the accounts.

The firm may apply lower of cost or market to individual items of inventory or to groups (usually called *pools*) of items. The smaller the group, the more *conservative* the resulting valuation.

Omit hyphens when you use the term as a noun, but use them when you use the term as an adjectival phrase.

Ltd., Limited. UK: a private limited corporation. The name of a private limited company must include the word "Limited" or its abbreviation "Ltd."

lump-sum acquisition. *Basket purchase.*

M

MACRS. *Modified Accelerated Cost Recovery System.* See *Accelerated Cost Recovery System.* Since 1986, MACRS has been the accelerated depreciation method required for U.S. income tax purposes.

maintenance. *Expenditures* undertaken to preserve an *asset's* service potential for its originally intended life. These expenditures are *period expenses* or *product costs.* Contrast with *improvement,* and see *repair.*

make-or-buy decision. A managerial decision about whether the firm should produce a product internally or purchase it from others. Proper make-or-buy decisions in the short run result only when a firm considers *incremental costs* in the analysis.

maker (of note) (of check). One who signs a *note* to borrow; one who signs a *check;* in the latter context, synonymous with "drawer." See *draft.*

management. Executive authority that operates a business.

management accounting. See *managerial accounting.*

Management Accounting. Monthly publication of the *IMA.*

management audit. An audit conducted to ascertain whether a firm or one of its operating units properly carries out its objectives, policies, and procedures; generally applies only to activities for which accountants can specify qualitative standards. See *audit* and *internal audit.*

management by exception. A principle of management in which managers focus attention on performance only if it differs significantly from that expected.

management by objective (MBO). A management approach designed to focus on the definition and attainment of overall and individual objectives with the participation of all levels of management.

management information system (MIS). A system designed to provide all levels of management with timely and reliable information required for planning, control, and evaluation of performance.

management's discussion and analysis (MD&A). A discussion of management's views of the company's performance; required by the *SEC* to be included in the *10-K* and in the *annual report* to shareholders. The information typically contains discussion of such items as liquidity, results of *operations, segments,* and the effects of *inflation.*

managerial (management) accounting. Reporting designed to enhance the ability of management to do its job of decision making, planning, and control. Contrast with *financial accounting.*

manufacturing cost. Cost of producing goods, usually in a factory.

manufacturing expense. An imprecise, and generally incorrect, alternative title for *manufacturing overhead.* The term is generally incorrect because these costs are usually *product costs,* not expenses.

manufacturing overhead. General manufacturing *costs* that are not directly associated with identifiable units of product and that the firm incurs in providing a capacity to carry on productive activities. Accounting treats *fixed* manufacturing overhead cost as a *product cost* under *full absorption costing* but as an *expense* of the period under *variable costing.*

margin. *Revenue* less specified expenses. See *contribution margin, gross margin,* and *current margin.*

margin of safety. Excess of actual, or budgeted, sales over *breakeven* sales; usually expressed in dollars but may be expressed in units of product.

marginal cost. The *incremental cost* or *differential cost* of the last unit added to production or the first unit subtracted from production. See *cost terminology* and *differential* for contrast.

marginal costing. *Variable costing.*

marginal revenue. The increment in *revenue* from the sale of one additional unit of product.

marginal tax rate. The amount, expressed as a percentage, by which income taxes increase when taxable income increases by one dollar. Contrast with *average tax rate.*

markdown. See *markup* for definition and contrast.

markdown cancellation. See *markup* for definition and contrast.

market-based transfer price. A *transfer price* based on external market data rather than internal company data.

market price. See *fair value.*

market rate. The rate of *interest* a company must pay to borrow *funds* currently. See *effective rate.*

market value. *Fair market value.*

marketable equity securities. *Marketable securities* representing *owners' equity* interest in other companies, rather than *loans* to them.

marketable securities. Other companies' stocks and *bonds* held that can be readily sold on stock exchanges or over-the-counter markets and that the company plans to sell as cash is needed; classified as *current assets* and as part of "cash" in preparing the *statement of cash flows.* If the firm holds these same securities for *long-term* purposes, it will classify them as *noncurrent assets. SFAS No. 115* requires that all marketable equity and all debt securities (except those debt securities the holder has the ability and intent to hold to maturity) appear at market value on the balance sheet. The firm reports changes in market value in income for *trading securities* but debits holding losses (or credits holding gains) directly to owners' equity accounts for *securities available for sale.*

marketing costs. Costs incurred to sell; includes locating customers, persuading them to buy, delivering the goods or services, and collecting the sales proceeds.

markon. See *markup* for definition and contrast.

markup. The difference between the original selling price of items acquired for *inventory* and the cost. Precise usage calls this "markon," although many business people use the term "markup." Because of confusion of this use of "markup" with its precise definition (see below), terminology sometimes uses "original markup." If the originally established retail price increases, the precise term for the amount of price increase is "markup," although terminology sometimes uses "additional markup." If a firm reduces selling price, terminology uses the terms "markdown" and "markup cancellation." "Markup cancellation" refers to reduction in price following "additional markups" and can, by definition, be no more than the amount of the additional markup; "cancellation of additional markup," although not used, is descriptive. "Markdown" refers to price reductions from the original retail price. A price increase after a markdown is a "markdown cancellation." If original cost is $12 and original selling price is $20, then markon (original markup) is $8; if the firm later increases the price to $24, the $4 increase is markup (additional markup); if the firm later lowers the price to $21, the $3 reduction is markup cancellation; if the firm further lowers the price to $17, the $4 reduction comprises $1 markup cancellation and $3 markdown; if the firm later increases the price to $22, the $5 increase comprises $3 of markdown cancellation and $2 of markup (additional markup). Accountants track markup cancellations and markdowns separately because they deduct the former (but not the latter) in computing the selling prices of goods available for sale for the denominator of the *cost percentage* used in the conventional *retail inventory method.*

markup cancellation. See *markup* for definition and contrast.

markup percentage. *Markup* divided by (acquisition cost plus *markup*).

master budget. A *budget* projecting all *financial statements* and their components.

matching convention. matching principle. The concept of recognizing cost expirations (*expenses*) in the same accounting period during which the firm recognizes related *revenues;* combining or simultaneously recognizing the revenues and expenses that jointly result from the same *transactions* or other events.

material. As an adjective, it means relatively important, capable of influencing a decision (see *materiality*); as a noun, *raw material.*

materiality. The concept that accounting should disclose separately only those events that are relatively important (no operable definition yet exists) for the business or for understanding its statements. *SFAC No. 2* suggests that accounting information is material if "the judgment of a reasonable person relying on the information would have been changed or influenced by the omission or misstatement."

materials variances. *Price* and *quantity variances* for *direct materials* in *standard costing systems;* difference between actual cost and standard cost.

matrix. A rectangular array of numbers or mathematical symbols.

matrix inverse. For a given square *matrix* **A**, the matrix, $\mathbf{A}^{-1}$ such that $\mathbf{A}\mathbf{A}^{-1} = \mathbf{A}^{-1}\mathbf{A} = \mathbf{I}$, the identity matrix. Not all square matrices have inverses. Those that do not are "singular"; those that do are nonsingular.

maturity. The date at which an obligation, such as the *principal* of a *bond* or a *note,* becomes due.

maturity value. The amount expected to be collected when a loan reaches *maturity.* Depending on the context, the amount may be *principal* or principal and *interest.*

MBO. *Management by objective.*

MD&A. *Management's discussion and analysis* section of the *annual report.*

measuring unit. See *attribute measured* for definition and contrast.

merchandise. *Finished goods* bought by a retailer or wholesaler for resale; contrast with finished goods of a manufacturing business.

merchandise costs. Costs incurred to sell a product, such as commissions and advertising.

merchandise turnover. *Inventory turnover* for merchandise. See *ratio.*

merchandising business. As opposed to a manufacturing or service business, one that purchases (rather than manufactures) *finished goods* for resale.

merger. The joining of two or more businesses into a single *economic entity.* See *holding company.*

minority interest. A *balance sheet account* on *consolidated statements* showing the *equity* in a less-than-100-percent-owned *subsidiary* company; equity allocable to those who are not part of the controlling (majority) interest; may be classified either as shareholders' equity or as a liability of *indeterminate term* on the consolidated balance sheet. The *income statement* must subtract the minority interest in the current period's income of the less-than-100-percent-owned subsidiary to arrive at consolidated *net income* for the period.

minority investment. A holding of less than 50 percent of the *voting stock* in another corporation; accounted for with the *equity method* when the investor owns sufficient shares that it can exercise "significant influence" and as *marketable securities* otherwise. See *mutual fund.*

minutes book. A record of all actions authorized at corporate *board of directors* or shareholders' meetings.

MIS. *Management information system.*

mix variance. One of the *manufacturing variances.* Many *standard cost* systems specify combinations of inputs—for example, labor of a certain skill and materials of a certain quality grade. Sometimes combinations of inputs used differ from those contemplated by the standard. The mix variance attempts to report the cost difference caused by those changes in the combination of inputs.

mixed cost. A *semifixed* or a *semivariable* cost.

Modified Accelerated Cost Recovery System (MACRS). Name used for the *Accelerated Cost Recovery System,* originally passed by Congress in 1981 and amended by Congress in 1986.

modified cash basis. The *cash basis of accounting* with long-term assets accounted for using the *accrual basis of accounting.* Most users of the term "cash basis of accounting" actually mean "modified cash basis."

monetary assets and liabilities. See *monetary items.*

monetary gain or loss. The firm's *gain* or *loss* in *general purchasing power* as a result of its holding *monetary assets* or liabilities during a period when the *general purchasing power of the dollar* changes; explicitly reported in *constant-dollar accounting.* During periods of *inflation,* holders of net monetary assets lose, and holders of net monetary liabilities gain, general purchasing power. During periods of *deflation,* holders of net monetary assets gain, and holders of net monetary liabilities lose, general purchasing power.

monetary items. Amounts fixed in terms of dollars by statute or contract; *cash, accounts receivable, accounts payable,* and *debt.* The distinction between monetary and nonmonetary items is important for *constant-dollar accounting* and for *foreign exchange gain or loss* computations. In the foreign exchange context, account amounts denominated in dollars are not monetary items, whereas amounts denominated in any other currency are monetary.

monetary-nonmonetary method. *Foreign currency translation* that translates all *monetary items* at the *current exchange rate* and translates all *nonmonetary items* at the *historical rate.*

money. A word seldom used with precision in accounting, at least in part because economists have not yet agreed on its definition. Economists use the term to refer to both a medium of exchange and a store of value. See *cash* and *monetary items.* Consider a different set of issues concerning the phrase, "making money." Lay terminology uses this to mean "earning income" whether, as a result, the firm increased its cash balances or other net assets. The user does not typically mean that the firm has increased cash equal to the amount of net income, although the unaware listeners often think the phrase means this. Given that usage equates "making money" with "earning income," in this sense "money" has a

credit balance not a debit balance. Since cash typically has a debit balance, the phrase "making money" is even more troublesome. Consider the following language from the U.S. statutes on forfeitures required of some who commit illegal acts: ". . . the amount of money acquired through illegal transactions . . ." Does the law mean the cash left over after the lawbreaker has completed the illegal transactions, the income earned from the transactions, or something else? Sometimes "making money" means avoiding a cost, not recognized in financial accounting. Consider the following sets of questions and see how you have to think to decide whether, in a given question, "money" refers to a debit or a credit. Assume I start with $10 in cash.

1. I took a cab and it cost $10; I spent money. Did the cabbie make money? Does the cabbie have money?
2. I decided to walk, so I didn't spend $10. Did I make money?
3. I canceled the trip. Did I make money?

"Money" sometimes refers to debits and sometimes to credits; "making money" sometimes means earning accounting income and sometimes avoiding a cost, not reported in accounting, so careful writing about accounting avoids the word.

money purchase plan. A *pension plan* in which the employer contributes a specified amount of cash each year to each employee's pension fund; sometimes called a *defined-contribution plan;* contrast with *defined-benefit plan.* The plan does not specify the benefits ultimately received by the employee, since these benefits depend on the rate of return on the cash invested. As of the mid-1990's, most corporate pension plans were defined-benefit plans because both the law and *generally accepted accounting principles* for pensions made defined-benefit plans more attractive than money purchase plans. *ERISA* makes money purchase plans relatively more attractive than they had been. We expect the relative number of money purchase plans to continue to increase.

mortality table. Data of life expectancies or probabilities of death for persons of specified age and sex.

mortgage. A claim given by the borrower (mortgagor) to the lender (mortgagee) against the borrower's property in return for a loan.

moving average. An *average* computed on observations over time. As a new observation becomes available, analysts drop the oldest one so that they always compute the average for the same number of observations and use only the most recent ones.

moving average method. *Weighted-average inventory method.*

multiple-step. Said of an *income statement* that shows various subtotals of *expenses* and *losses* subtracted from *revenues* to show intermediate items such as *operating income,* income of the enterprise (operating income plus *interest* income), income to investors (income of the enterprise less *income taxes*), net income to shareholders (income to investors less interest charges), and income retained (net income to shareholders less dividends). See *entity theory.*

municipal bond. A *bond* issued by a village, town, or city. *Interest* on such bonds is generally exempt from federal *income taxes* and from some state income taxes. Because bonds issued by state and county governments often have these characteristics, terminology often calls such bonds "municipals" as well. These are also sometimes called "taxexempts."

mutual fund. An investment company that issues its own stock to the public and uses the proceeds to invest in securities of other companies. A mutual fund usually owns less than 5 or 10 percent of the stock of any one company and accounts for its investments using current *market values*. Contrast with *holding company*.

mutually exclusive (investment) projects. Competing investment projects in which accepting one project eliminates the possibility of undertaking the remaining projects.

N

NAARS. *National Automated Accounting Research System.*

NASDAQ (National Association of Securities Dealers Automated Quotation System). A computerized system to provide brokers and dealers with price quotations for securities traded *over the counter* as well as for some *NYSE* securities.

National Association of Accountants (NAA). Former name for the *Institute of Management Accountants (IMA)*.

National Automated Accounting Research System (NAARS). A computer-based information-retrieval system containing, among other things, the complete text of most public corporate annual reports and *Forms 10-K*. Users may access the system through the *AICPA*.

natural business year. A 12-month period chosen as the reporting period so that the end of the period coincides with a low point in activity or inventories. See *ratio* for a discussion of analyses of financial statements of companies using a natural business year.

natural classification. *Income statement* reporting form that classifies *expenses* by nature of items acquired, that is, materials, wages, salaries, insurance, and taxes, as well as depreciation. Contrast with *functional classification*.

natural resources. Timberland, oil and gas wells, ore deposits, and other products of nature that have economic value. Terminology uses the term *depletion* to refer to the process of *amortizing* the cost of natural resources. Natural resources are "nonrenewable" (for example, oil, coal, gas, ore deposits) or "renewable" (timberland, sod fields); terminology often calls the former "wasting assets." See also *reserve recognition accounting* and *percentage depletion*.

negative confirmation. See *confirmation*.

negative goodwill. See *goodwill*. When a firm acquires another company, and the *fair market value* of the *net assets* acquired exceeds the purchase price, *APB Opinion No. 16* requires that the acquiring company reduce the valuation of noncurrent assets (except *investments* in *marketable securities*) until the purchase price equals the adjusted valuation of the fair market value of net assets acquired. If, after the acquiring company reduces the valuation of noncurrent assets to zero, the valuation of the remaining net assets acquired still exceeds the purchase price, then the difference appears as a credit balance on the balance sheet as negative goodwill. For negative goodwill to exist, someone must be willing to sell a company for less than the fair market value of net current assets and marketable securities. Because such bargain purchases are rare, one seldom sees negative goodwill in the financial statements. When it does appear, it generally signals unrecorded obligations, such as a contingency related to a pending lawsuit.

negotiable. Legally capable of being transferred by *endorsement*. Usually said of *checks* and *notes* and sometimes of *stocks* and *bearer bonds*.

negotiated transfer price. A *transfer price* set jointly by the buying and the selling divisions.

net. Reduced by all relevant deductions.

net assets. Total *assets* minus total *liabilities*; equals the amount of *owners' equity*. Often, we find it useful to split the balance sheet into two parts: owners' equity and all the rest. The "rest" is total assets less total liabilities. To take an example, consider one definition of *revenue*: the increase in owners' equity accompanying the net assets increase caused by selling goods or rendering services. An alternative, more cumbersome way to say the same thing is: the increase in owners' equity accompanying the assets increase or the liabilities decrease, or both, caused by selling goods or rendering services. Consider the definition of *goodwill*: the excess of purchase price over the fair market value of identifiable net assets acquired in a purchase transaction. Without the phrase "net assets," the definition might be as follows: the excess of purchase price over the fair market value of identifiable assets reduced by the fair market value of identifiable liabilities acquired in a purchase transaction.

net bank position. From a firm's point of view, *cash* in a specific bank less *loans* payable to that bank.

net book value. *Book value*.

net current asset value (per share). *Working capital* divided by the number of common shares outstanding. Some analysts think that when a common share trades in the market for an amount less than net current asset value, the shares are undervalued and investors should purchase them. We find this view naive because it ignores, generally, the efficiency of capital markets and, specifically, unrecorded obligations, such as for executory contracts and contingencies, not currently reported as *liabilities* in the *balance sheet* under *GAAP*.

net current assets. *Working capital* = *current assets* − *current liabilities*.

net income. The excess of all *revenues* and *gains* for a period over all *expenses* and *losses* of the period. The FASB is proposing to discontinue use of this term and substitute *earnings*. See *comprehensive income*.

net loss. The excess of all *expenses* and *losses* for a period over all *revenues* and *gains* of the period; negative *net income*.

net markup. In the context of *retail inventory methods*, *markups* less markup cancellations; a figure that usually ignores *markdowns* and markdown cancellations.

net of tax method. A nonsanctioned method for dealing with the problem of *income tax allocation*; described in

APB Opinion No. 11. The method subtracts deferred tax items from specific *asset* amounts rather than showing them as a deferred credit or *liability*.

net of tax reporting. Reporting, such as for *income from discontinued operations, extraordinary items,* and *prior-period adjustments,* in which the firm adjusts the amounts presented in the *financial statements* for all income tax effects. For example, if an extraordinary loss amounted to $10,000, and the marginal tax rate was 40 percent, then the extraordinary item would appear "net of taxes" as a $6,000 loss. Hence, not all a firm's income taxes necessarily appear on one line of the income statement. The reporting allocates the total taxes among *income from continuing operations, income from discontinued operations, extraordinary items,* cumulative effects of *accounting changes,* and *prior-period adjustments.*

net operating profit. *Income from continuing operations.*

net present value. Discounted or *present value* of all cash inflows and outflows of a project or of an *investment* at a given *discount rate*.

net price method (of recording purchase or sales discounts). Method that records a *purchase* (or *sale*) at its *invoice* price less all *discounts* made available, under the assumption that the firm will take nearly all discounts offered. The purchaser debits, to an *expense* account, discounts lapsed through failure to pay promptly. For purchases, management usually prefers to know about the amount of discounts lost because of inefficient operations, not the amounts taken, so that most managers prefer the net price method to the *gross price method*.

net realizable (sales) value. Current selling price less reasonable costs to complete production and to sell the item. Also, a method for *allocating joint costs* in proportion to *realizable values* of the joint products. For example, joint products A and B together cost $100; A sells for $60, whereas B sells for $90. Then a firm would allocate to A ($60/$150) × $100 = 0.40 × $100 = $40 of cost while it would allocate to B ($90/$150) × $100 = $60 of cost.

net sales. Sales (at gross invoice amount) less *returns, allowances,* freight paid for customers, and *discounts* taken.

net working capital. *Working capital;* the term "net" is redundant in accounting. Financial analysts sometimes mean *current assets* when they speak of working capital, so for them the "net" is not redundant.

net worth. A misleading term with the same meaning as *owners' equity.* Avoid using this term; accounting valuations at historical cost do not show economic worth.

network analysis. A project planning and scheduling method, usually displayed in a diagram, that enables management to identify the interrelated sequences that it must accomplish to complete the project.

New York Stock Exchange (NYSE). A public market in which those who own seats (a seat is the right to participate) trade various corporate *securities*.

next-in, first-out. See *NIFO*.

NIFO (next-in, first-out). A *cost flow assumption,* one not allowed by GAAP. In making decisions, many managers consider *replacement costs* (rather than *historical costs*) and refer to them as NIFO costs.

no par. Said of *stock* without a *par value*.

nominal accounts. *Temporary accounts,* such as *revenue* and *expense* accounts; contrast with *balance sheet accounts*. The firm *closes* all nominal accounts at the end of each *accounting period*.

nominal amount (value). An amount stated in dollars, in contrast to an amount stated in *constant dollars*. Contrast with *real amount (value)*.

nominal dollars. The measuring unit giving no consideration to differences in the *general purchasing power of the dollar* over time. The face amount of currency or coin, a *bond,* an *invoice,* or a *receivable* is a nominal-dollar amount. When the analyst adjusts that amount for changes in *general purchasing power,* it becomes a *constant-dollar* amount.

nominal interest rate. A rate specified on a *debt* instrument; usually differs from the market or *effective rate;* also, a rate of *interest* quoted for a year. If the interest compounds more often than annually, then the *effective interest rate* exceeds the nominal rate.

noncancelable. See *lease*.

nonconsolidated subsidiary. An *intercorporate investment* in which the parent owns more than 50 percent of the shares of the *subsidiary* but accounts for the investment with the *cost method*.

noncontributory. Said of a *pension plan* in which only the employer makes payments to a pension *fund*. Contrast with *contributory*.

noncontrollable cost. A cost that a particular manager cannot *control*.

noncurrent. Of a *liability,* due in more than one year (or more than one *operating cycle*); of an *asset,* the firm will enjoy the future benefit in more than one year (or more than one operating cycle).

nonexpendable fund. A governmental fund whose *principal,* and sometimes earnings, the entity may not spend.

noninterest-bearing note. A *note* that does not specify explicit interest. The *face value* of such a note will exceed its *present value* at any time before *maturity* value so long as *interest rates* are positive. *APB Opinion No. 21* requires that firms report the present value, not face value, of long-term noninterest-bearing notes as the *asset* or *liability* amount in financial statements. For this purpose, the firm uses the *historical interest rate*. See *interest, imputed*.

nonmanufacturing costs. All *costs* incurred other than those necessary to produce goods. Typically, only manufacturing firms use this designation.

non-monetary items. All items that are not monetary. See *monetary items*.

nonoperating. In the *income statement* context, said of *revenues* and *expenses* arising from *transactions* incidental to the company's main line(s) of business; in the *statement of cash flows* context, said of all financing and investing sources or uses of cash in contrast to cash provided by operations. See *operations*.

nonprofit corporation. An incorporated *entity,* such as a hospital, with owners who do not share in the earnings. It usually emphasizes providing services rather than maximizing income.

nonrecurring. Said of an event that is not expected to happen often for a given firm. *APB Opinion No. 30* requires firms to disclose separately the effects of such events as part of *ordinary* items unless the event is also unusual. See *extraordinary* item.

nonvalue-added activity. An activity that causes costs without increasing a product's or service's value to the customer.

normal cost. Former name for *service cost* in accounting for pensions and other postemployment benefits.

normal costing. Method of charging costs to products using actual *direct materials,* actual *direct labor,* and predetermined *factory overhead* rates.

normal costing system. *Costing* based on *actual material* and *labor* costs but using *predetermined overhead* rates per unit of some *activity* basis (such as *direct labor hours* or machine hours) to apply overhead to production. Management decides the rate to charge to production for overhead at the start of the period. At the end of the period the accounting multiplies this rate by the actual number of units of the base activity (such as actual direct labor hours worked or actual machine hours used during the period) to apply overhead to production.

normal spoilage. Costs incurred because of ordinary amounts of spoilage. Accounting prorates such costs to units produced as *product costs.* Contrast with *abnormal spoilage.*

normal standard cost, normal standards. The *cost* a firm expects to incur under reasonably efficient operating conditions with adequate provision for an average amount of rework, spoilage, and the like.

normal volume. The level of production that will, over a time span, usually one year, satisfy purchasers' demands and provide for reasonable *inventory* levels.

note. An unconditional written promise by the maker (borrower) to pay a certain amount on demand or at a certain future time.

note receivable discounted. A *note* assigned by the holder to another. The new holder of the note typically pays the old holder an amount less than the *face value* of the note, hence the word "discounted." If the old holder assigns the note to the new holder with recourse, the old holder has a *contingent liability* until the maker of the note pays the debt. See *factoring.*

notes. Some use this word instead of *footnotes* when referring to the detailed information included by management as an integral part of the *financial statements* and covered by the *auditor's report.*

NOW (negotiable order of withdrawal) account. Negotiable order of withdrawal. A *savings account* whose owner can draw an order to pay, much like a *check* but technically not a check, and give it to others, who can redeem the order at the savings institution.

number of days sales in inventory (or receivables). Days of average inventory on hand (or average collection period for receivables). See *ratio.*

NV (naamloze vennootschap). Netherlands: a public limited liability company.

NYSE. *New York Stock Exchange.*

O

OASD(H)I. *Old Age, Survivors, Disability, and (Hospital) Insurance.*

objective. See *reporting objectives* and *objectivity.*

objective function. In *linear programming,* the name of the profit (or cost) criterion the analyst wants to maximize (or minimize).

objectivity. The reporting policy implying that the firm will not give formal recognition to an event in financial statements until the firm can measure the magnitude of the events with reasonable accuracy and check that amount with independent verification.

obsolescence. An asset's *market value* decline caused by improved alternatives becoming available that will be more *cost-effective.* The decline in market value does not relate to physical changes in the asset itself. For example, computers become obsolete long before they wear out. See *partial obsolescence.*

Occupational Safety and Health Act. *OSHA.*

off-balance-sheet financing. A description often used for an obligation that meets all the tests to be classified a liability except that the obligation arises from an *executory contract* and, hence, is not a *liability.* Consider the following example. Miller Corporation desires to acquire land costing $25 million, on which it will build a shopping center. It could borrow the $25 million from its bank, paying interest at 12 percent, and buy the land outright from the seller. If so, both an asset and a liability will appear on the balance sheet. Instead, it borrows $5 million and purchases for $5 million from the seller an *option* to buy the land from the seller at any time within the next six years for a price of $20 million. The option costs Miller Corporation $5 million immediately and provides for continuing "option" payments of $2.4 million per year, which precisely equal Miller Corporation's borrowing rate multiplied by the remaining purchase price of the land: $2.4 million = 0.12 × $20 million. Although Miller Corporation need not continue payments and can let the option lapse at any time, it also has an obligation to begin developing on the site immediately. Because Miller Corporation has invested a substantial sum in the option, will invest more, and will begin immediately developing the land, Miller Corporation will almost certainly exercise its option before expiration. The seller of the land can take the option contract to the bank and borrow $20 million, paying interest at Miller Corporation's borrowing rate, 12 percent per year. The continuing option payments from Miller Corporation will be sufficient to enable the seller to make its payments to the bank. *Generally accepted accounting principles* view Miller Corporation as having acquired an option for $5 million rather than having acquired land costing $25 million in return for $25 million of debt. The firm will not recognize debt on the balance sheet until it borrows more funds to exercise the option.

off-balance-sheet risk. A contract that exposes an entity to the possibility of loss but that does not appear in the financial statements. For example, a *forward-exchange contract* generally does not appear on the balance sheet because it is an *executory contract.* The contract may reduce or increase the entity's exposure to foreign-exchange risk (the chance of loss due to unfavorable changes in the foreign-exchange rate). It may also expose the entity to credit risk (the chance of loss that occurs when the *counterparty* to the contract cannot fulfill the contract terms). *SFAS No. 105* requires entities to describe contracts with off-balance-sheet risk.

OHG (Offene Handelsgesellschaft). Germany: a general *partnership*. The partners have unlimited *liability*.

Old Age, Survivors, Disability, and (Hospital) Insurance, or OASD(H)I. The technical name for Social Security under the Federal Insurance Contributions Act (*FICA*).

on consignment. Said of goods delivered by the owner (the consignor) to another (the consignee) to be sold by the consignee. On delivery of the goods from the consignor to the consignee, the consignor can, but need not, make an entry transferring the goods at cost from Finished Goods Inventory to another *inventory account*, such as Goods out on Consignment. The consignor recognizes *revenue* only when the consignee has sold the goods to customers. Under such an arrangement, the owner of the goods bears the inventory holding costs until the ultimate seller (consignee) sells them. The owner also bears the risk that the items will never sell to final customers, but manufacturers or distributors who provide generous return options to their customers can achieve this aspect of consignment sales in an outright sale. The consignment protects the consignor from the consignee's bankruptcy, as the arrangement entitles the owner either to the return of the property or to payment of a specified amount. The goods are *assets* of the consignor. Such arrangements provide the consignor with better protection than an outright *sale on account* to the consignee in *bankruptcy*. In event of bankruptcy, the ordinary seller, holding an account receivable, had no special claim to the return of the goods, whereas a consignor can reclaim the goods without going through bankruptcy proceedings, from which the consignor might recover only a fraction of the amounts owed to it.

on (open) account. Said of a *purchase* (or *sale*) when the seller expects payment sometime after delivery and the purchaser does not give a *note* evidencing the *debt*. The purchaser has generally signed an agreement sometime in the past promising to pay for such purchases according to an agreed time schedule. When the firm sells (purchases) on open account, it *debits* (*credits*) Accounts Receivable (*Payable*).

one-line consolidation. Said of an *intercorporate investment* accounted for with the *equity method*. With this method, the *income* and *balance sheet* total *assets* and *equities* amounts are identical to those that would appear if the parent consolidated the investee firm, even though the income from the investment appears on a single line of the income statement and the net investment appears on a single line in the Assets section of the balance sheet.

one-write system. A system of bookkeeping that produces several records, including original documents, in one operation by the use of reproductive paper and equipment that provides for the proper alignment of the documents.

open account. Any *account* with a nonzero *debit* or *credit* balance. See *on (open) account*.

operating. An adjective used to refer to *revenue* and *expense* items relating to the company's main line(s) of business. See *operations*.

operating accounts. *Revenue, expense,* and *production cost accounts.* Contrast with *balance sheet accounts*.

operating activities. For purposes of the *statement of cash flows,* all *transactions* and *events* that are neither *financing activities* nor *investing activities*. See *operations*.

operating budget. A formal *budget* for the *operating cycle* or for a year.

operating cash flow. *Cash flow from operations.* Financial statement analysts sometimes use this term to mean *cash flow from operations* − *capital expenditures* − *dividends.* This usage leads to such ambiguity that the reader should always confirm the definition that the writer uses before drawing inferences from the reported data.

operating cycle. *Earnings cycle.*

operating expenses. *Expenses* incurred in the course of *ordinary* activities of an *entity;* frequently, a classification including only *selling, general,* and *administrative expenses,* thereby excluding *cost of goods sold, interest,* and *income tax* expenses. See *operations*.

operating lease. A *lease* accounted for by the *lessee* without showing an *asset* for the lease rights (*leasehold*) or a *liability* for the lease payment obligations. The lessee reports only rental payments during the period, as *expenses* of the period. The asset remains on the lessor's *books,* where rental collections appear as *revenues.* Contrast with *capital lease*.

operating leverage. Usually said of a firm with a large proportion of *fixed costs* in its *total costs.* Consider a book publisher or a railroad: such a firm has large costs to produce the first unit of service; then, the *incremental costs* of producing another book or transporting another freight car are much less than the *average cost,* so the *gross margin* on the sale of the subsequent units is relatively large. Contrast this situation with that, for example, of a grocery store, where the *contribution margin* equals less than 5 percent of the selling price. For firms with equal profitability, however defined, we say that the one with the larger percentage increase in income from a given percentage increase in dollar sales has the larger operating leverage. See *leverage* for contrast of this term with "financial leverage." See *cost terminology* for definitions of terms involving the word "cost."

operating margin. *Revenues* from *sales* minus *cost of goods sold* and *operating expenses*.

operating margin based on current costs. *Revenues* from *sales* minus *current cost* of goods sold; a measure of operating efficiency that does not depend on the *cost flow assumption* for *inventory;* sometimes called "current (gross) margin." See *inventory profit* for illustrative computations.

operating ratio. See *ratio*.

operational control. See *control system*.

operations. A word not precisely defined in *accounting.* Generally, analysts distinguish operating activities (producing and selling *goods* or *services*) from financing activities (raising funds) and *investing activities.* Acquiring goods on account and then paying for them one month later, though generally classified as an operating activity, has the characteristics of a financing activity. Or consider the transaction of selling plant assets for a price in excess of book value. On the *income statement,* the gain appears as part of income from operations ("continuing operations" or "discontinued" operations, depending on the circumstances), but the *statement of cash flows* reports all the funds received below the Cash from Operations section, as a nonoperating source of cash, "disposition of noncurrent assets." In income tax accounting, an "operating loss" results whenever deductions exceed taxable revenues.

opinion. The *auditor's report* containing an attestation or lack thereof; also, *APB Opinion.*

opinion paragraph. Section of *auditor's report,* generally following the *scope paragraph* and giving the auditor's conclusion that the *financial statements* are (rarely, are not) in accordance with *GAAP* and present fairly the *financial position,* changes in financial position, and the results of *operations.*

opportunity cost. The *present value* of the *income* (or *costs*) that a firm could earn (or save) from using an *asset* in its best alternative use to the one under consideration.

opportunity cost of capital. *Cost of capital.*

option. The legal right to buy or sell something during a specified period at a specified price, called the *exercise* price. If the right exists during a specified time interval, it is known as an "American option." If it exists for only one specific day, it is known as a "European option." Do not confuse employee stock options with *put* and *call* options, traded in various public markets.

ordinary annuity. An *annuity in arrears.*

ordinary income. For income tax purposes, reportable *income* not qualifying as *capital gains.*

organization costs. The *costs* incurred in planning and establishing an *entity;* example of an *intangible* asset. The firm must treat these costs as *expenses* of the period, even though the *expenditures* clearly provide future benefits and meet the test to be *assets.*

original cost. *Acquisition cost;* in public utility accounting, the acquisition cost of the *entity* first devoting the *asset* to public use. See *aboriginal cost.*

original entry. Entry in a *journal.*

OSHA (Occupational Safety and Health Act). The federal law that governs working conditions in commerce and industry.

other comprehensive income. According to the FASB, *comprehensive income* items that are not themselves part of earnings. See *comprehensive income.* To define comprehensive income does not convey its essence. To understand comprehensive income, you need to understand how it differs from *earnings* (or *net income*), the concept measured in the *earnings (income) statement.* The term *earnings* (or *net income*) refers to the sum of all components of comprehensive income *minus* the components of other comprehensive income.

outlay. The amount of an *expenditure.*

outlier. Said of an observation (or data point) that appears to differ significantly in some regard from other observations (or data points) of supposedly the same phenomenon; in a *regression analysis,* often used to describe an observation that falls far from the fitted regression equation (in two dimensions, line).

out-of-pocket. Said of an *expenditure* usually paid for with cash; an *incremental* cost.

out-of-stock cost. The estimated decrease in future *profit* as a result of losing customers because a firm has insufficient quantities of *inventory* currently on hand to meet customers' demands.

output. Physical quantity or monetary measurement of *goods* and *services* produced.

outside director. A corporate board of directors member who is not a company officer and does not participate in the corporation's day-to-day management.

outstanding. Unpaid or uncollected; when said of *stock,* refers to the shares issued less *treasury stock;* when said of *checks,* refers to a check issued that did not clear the *drawer's* bank prior to the *bank statement* date.

over-and-short. Title for an *expense account* used to account for small differences between book balances of cash and actual cash and vouchers or receipts in *petty cash* or *change funds.*

overapplied (overabsorbed) overhead. Costs applied, or *charged,* to product and exceeding actual *overhead costs* during the period; a *credit balance* in an overhead account after overhead is assigned to product.

overdraft. A *check* written on a checking account that contains funds less than the amount of the check.

overhead costs. Any *cost* not directly associated with the production or sale of identifiable goods and services; sometimes called "burden" or "indirect costs" and, in the UK, "oncosts"; frequently limited to manufacturing overhead. See *central corporate expenses* and *manufacturing overhead.*

overhead rate. Standard, or other predetermined rate, at which a firm applies *overhead costs* to products or to services.

over-the-counter. Said of a *security* traded in a negotiated transaction, as on *NASDAQ,* rather than in an auctioned one on an organized stock exchange, such as the *New York Stock Exchange.*

owners' equity. *Proprietorship; assets* minus *liabilities; paid-in capital* plus *retained earnings* of a corporation; partners' capital accounts in a *partnership;* owner's capital account in a *sole proprietorship.*

P

paid-in capital. Sum of balances in *capital stock* and *capital contributed in excess of par (or stated) value* accounts; same as *contributed capital* (minus *donated capital*). Some use the term to mean only *capital contributed in excess of par (or stated value).*

paid-in surplus. See *surplus.*

P&L. Profit-and-loss statement; *income statement.*

paper profit. A *gain* not yet realized through a *transaction;* an *unrealized holding gain.*

par. See *at par* and *face amount.*

par value. *Face amount* of a *security*.

par value method. In accounting for *treasury stock,* method that *debits* a common stock account with the *par value* of the shares required and allocates the remaining debits between the *Additional Paid-in Capital* and *Retained Earnings* accounts. Contrast with *cost method*.

parent company. Company owning more than 50 percent of the voting shares of another company, called the *subsidiary*.

Pareto chart. A graph of a skewed statistical distribution. In many business settings, a relatively small percentage of the potential population causes a relatively large percentage of the business activity. For example, some businesses find that the top 20 percent of the customers buy 80 percent of the goods sold. Or, the top 10 percent of products account for 60 percent of the revenues or 70 percent of the profits. The statistical distribution known as the Pareto distribution has this property of skewness, so a graph of a phenomenon with such skewness has come to be known as a Pareto chart, even if the underlying data do not actually well fit the Pareto distribution. Practitioners of *total quality management* find that in many businesses, a small number of processes account for a large fraction of the quality problems, so they advocate charting potential problems and actual occurrences of problems to identify the relatively small number of sources of trouble. They call such a chart a "Pareto chart."

partial obsolescence. One cause of decline in *market value* of an *asset.* As technology improves, the economic value of existing *assets* declines. In many cases, however, it will not pay a firm to replace the existing asset with a new one, even though it would acquire the new type rather than the old if it did make a new acquisition currently. In these cases, the accountant should theoretically recognize a loss from partial obsolescence from the firm's owning an old, out-of-date asset, but *GAAP* do not permit recognition of partial obsolescence until the sum of future cash flows from the asset total less than book value; see *impairment.* The firm will carry the old asset at *cost* less *accumulated depreciation* until the firm retires it from service so long as the *undiscounted* future *cash flows* from the asset exceed its book value. Thus management that uses an asset subject to partial obsolescence reports results inferior to those reported by a similar management that uses a new asset. See *obsolescence*.

partially executory contract. *Executory contract* in which one or both parties have done something other than merely promise.

partially funded. Said of a *pension plan* in which the firm has not funded all earned benefits. See *funded* for funding requirements.

partially vested. Said of a *pension plan* in which not all employee benefits have *vested.* See *graded vesting*.

participating dividend. *Dividend* paid to preferred shareholders in addition to the minimum preferred dividends when the *preferred stock* contract provides for such sharing in earnings. Usually the contract specifies that dividends on *common shares* must reach a specified level before the preferred shares receive the participating dividend.

participating preferred stock. *Preferred stock* with rights to *participating dividends*.

partner's drawing. A payment made to a partner and debited against his or her share of income or capital. The name of a *temporary account,* closed to the partner's capital account, to record the debits when the partner receives such payments.

partnership. Contractual arrangement between individuals to share resources and operations in a jointly run business. See *general* and *limited partner* and *Uniform Partnership Act*.

patent. A right granted for up to 20 years by the federal government to exclude others from manufacturing, using, or selling a claimed design, product, or plant (e.g., a new breed of rose) or from using a claimed process or method of manufacture; an *asset* if the firm acquires it by purchase. If the firm develops it internally, current *GAAP* require the firm to *expense* the development costs when incurred.

payable. Unpaid but not necessarily due or past due.

pay-as-you-go. Said of an *income tax* scheme in which the taxpayer makes periodic payments of income taxes during the period when it earns the income to be taxed; in contrast to a scheme in which the taxpayer owes no payments until the end of, or after, the period when it earned the income being taxed (called PAYE—pay-as-you-earn—in the UK). The phrase is sometimes used to describe an *unfunded pension plan,* or retirement benefit plan, in which the firm makes payments to pension plan beneficiaries from general corporate funds, not from cash previously contributed to a fund. Under this method, the firm debits expense as it makes payments, not as it incurs the obligations. This is not acceptable as a method of accounting for pension plans, under *SFAS No. 87,* or as a method of *funding,* under *ERISA*.

payback period. Amount of time that must elapse before the cash inflows from a project equal the cash outflows.

payback reciprocal. One divided by the *payback period.* This number approximates the *internal rate of return* on a project when the project life exceeds twice the payback period and the cash inflows are identical in every period after the initial period.

PAYE (pay-as-you-earn). See *pay-as-you-go* for contrast.

payee. The person or entity who receives a cash payment or who will receive the stated amount of cash on a *check.* See *draft*.

payout ratio. *Common stock dividends* declared for a year divided by net *income* to common stock for the year; a term used by financial analysts. Contrast with *dividend yield*.

payroll taxes. Taxes levied because the taxpayer pays salaries or wages; for example, *FICA* and unemployment compensation insurance taxes. Typically, the employer pays a portion and withholds part of the employee's wages.

P/E ratio. *Price-earnings ratio*.

Pension Benefit Guarantee Corporation (PBGC). A federal corporation established under *ERISA* to guarantee basic pension benefits in covered pension plans by administering terminated pension plans and placing *liens* on corporate assets for certain unfunded pension liabilities.

pension fund. *Fund,* the assets of which the trustee will pay to retired ex-employees, usually as a *life annuity;* generally held by an independent trustee and thus not an *asset* of the employer.

pension plan. Details or provisions of employer's contract with employees for paying retirement *annuities* or other benefits. See *funded, vested, service cost, prior service cost, money purchase plan,* and *defined-benefit plan.*

per books. An expression used to refer to the *book value* of an item at a specific time.

percent. Any number, expressed as a decimal, multiplied by 100.

percentage depletion (allowance). Deductible *expense* allowed in some cases by the federal *income tax* regulations; computed as a percentage of gross income from a *natural resource* independent of the unamortized cost of the *asset.* Because the amount of the total deductions for tax purposes usually exceeds the cost of the asset being *depleted,* many people think the deduction is an unfair tax advantage or *loophole.*

percentage-of-completion method. Recognizing *revenues* and *expenses* on a job, order, or contract (1) in proportion to the *costs* incurred for the period divided by total costs expected to be incurred for the job or order ("cost to cost") or (2) in proportion to engineers' or architects' estimates of the incremental degree of completion of the job, order, or contract during the period. Contrast with *completed contract method.*

percentage of sales method. Measuring *bad debt expense* as a fraction of *sales revenue.* When the firm uses this method, it must periodically check the adequacy of the *allowance for uncollectibles* by *aging accounts receivable.* See *allowance method* for contrast.

percentage statement. A statement containing, in addition to (or instead of) dollar amounts, ratios of dollar amounts to some base. In a percentage *income statement,* the base is usually either *net sales* or total *revenues,* and in a percentage *balance sheet,* the base is usually total *assets.*

period. *Accounting period.*

period cost. An inferior term for *period expense.*

period expense (charge). *Expenditure,* usually based on the passage of time, charged to operations of the accounting period rather than *capitalized* as an asset. Contrast with *product cost.*

periodic inventory. In recording *inventory,* a method that uses data on beginning inventory, additions to inventories, and ending inventory to find the cost of withdrawals from inventory. Contrast with *perpetual inventory.*

periodic procedures. The process of making *adjusting entries* and *closing entries* and preparing the *financial statements,* usually by use of *trial balances* and *work sheets.*

permanent account. An account that appears on the *balance sheet.* Contrast with *temporary account.*

permanent difference. Difference between reported income and taxable income that will never reverse and, hence, requires no entry in the *deferred income tax (liability)* account; for example, nontaxable state and municipal *bond* interest that will appear on the financial statements. Contrast with *temporary difference.* See *deferred income tax liability.*

permanent file. The file of working papers that are prepared by a public accountant and that contain the information required for reference in successive professional engagements for a particular organization, as distinguished from working papers applicable only to a particular engagement.

perpetual annuity. *Perpetuity.*

perpetual inventory. *Inventory* quantity and amount records that the firm changes and makes current with each physical addition to or withdrawal from the stock of goods; an inventory so recorded. The records will show the physical quantities and, frequently, the dollar valuations that should be on hand at any time. Because the firm explicitly computes *cost of goods sold,* it can use the *inventory equation* to compute an amount for what *ending inventory* should be. It can then compare the computed amount of ending inventory with the actual amount of ending inventory as a *control* device to measure the amount of *shrinkages.* Contrast with *periodic inventory.*

perpetuity. An *annuity* whose payments continue forever. The *present value* of a perpetuity in *arrears* is p/r where p is the periodic payment and r is the *interest rate* per period. If a perpetuity promises \$100 each year, in arrears, forever and the interest rate is 8 percent per year, then the perpetuity has a value of $\$1,250 = \$100/0.08$.

perpetuity (with) growth model. See *perpetuity.* A *perpetuity* whose cash flows grow at the rate g per period and thus has *present value* of $1/(r - g)$. Some call this the "Gordon Growth Model" because Myron Gordon wrote about applications of this formula and its variants in the 1950s. John Burr Williams wrote about them in the 1930s.

personal account. *Drawing account.*

PERT (Program Evaluation and Review Technique). A method of *network analysis* in which the analyst makes three time estimates for each activity—the optimistic time, the most likely time, and the pessimistic time—and gives an expected completion date for the project within a probability range.

petty cash fund. Currency and coins maintained for expenditures that the firm makes with cash on hand.

physical units method. A method of allocating a *joint cost* to the *joint products* based on a physical measure of the joint products; for example, allocating the cost of a cow to sirloin steak and to hamburger, based on the weight of the meat. This method usually provides nonsensical (see *sterilized allocation*) results unless the physical units of the joint products tend to have the same value.

physical verification. *Verification,* by an *auditor,* performed by actually inspecting items in *inventory, plant assets,* and the like, in contrast to merely checking the written records. The auditor may use statistical sampling procedures.

planning and control process. General name for the management techniques comprising the setting of organizational goals and *strategic plans, capital budgeting, operations* budgeting, comparison of plans with actual results, performance evaluation and corrective action, and revisions of goals, plans, and budgets.

plant. *Plant assets.*

plant asset turnover. Number of dollars of *sales* generated per dollar of *plant assets;* equal to sales divided by average *plant assets.*

plant assets. *Assets* used in the revenue-production process. Plant assets include buildings, machinery, equipment, land, and natural resources. The phrase "property, plant, and equipment" (though often appearing on balance sheets) is therefore a redundancy. In this context, "plant" used alone means buildings.

plantwide allocation method. A method for *allocating overhead costs* to product. First, use one *cost pool* for the entire plant. Then, allocate all costs from that pool to products using a single overhead *allocation* rate, or one set of rates, for all the products of the plant, independent of the number of departments in the plant.

PLC (public limited company). UK: a publicly held *corporation.* Contrast with *Ltd.*

pledging. The borrower assigns *assets* as security or *collateral* for repayment of a loan.

pledging of receivables. The process of using expected collections on *accounts receivable* as *collateral* for a loan. The borrower remains responsible for collecting the receivable but promises to use the proceeds for repaying the debt.

plow back. To retain *assets* generated by earnings for continued investment in the business.

plug. Process for finding an unknown amount. For any *account,* beginning balance + additions − deductions = ending balance; if you know any three of the four items, you can find the fourth with simple arithmetic, called "plugging." In making a *journal entry,* often you know all *debits* and all but one of the *credits* (or vice versa). Because *double-entry* bookkeeping requires equal debits and credits, you can compute the unknown quantity by subtracting the sum of the known credits from the sum of all the debits (or vice versa), also called "plugging." Accountants often call the unknown the "plug." For example, in amortizing a *discount* on *bonds payable* with the *straight-line depreciation* method, *interest expense* is a plug: interest expense = interest payable + discount amortization. See *trade-in transaction* for an example. The term sometimes has a bad connotation for accountants because plugging can occur in a slightly different context. During the process of preparing a *preclosing trial balance* (or *balance sheet*), often the sum of the debits does not equal the sum of the credits. Rather than find the error, some accountants are tempted to force equality by changing one of the amounts, with a plugged debit or credit to an account such as Other Expenses. No harm results from this procedure if the amount of the error is small compared with asset totals, since spending tens or hundreds of dollars in a bookkeeper's or accountant's time to find an error of a few dollars will not be *cost-effective.* Still, most accounting teachers rightly disallow this use of plugging because exercises and problems set for students provide enough information not to require it.

point of sale. The time, not the location, at which a *sale* occurs.

pooling-of-interests method. Accounting for a *business combination* by adding together the *book value* of the assets and *equities* of the combined firms; generally leads to a higher reported *net income* for the combined firms than results when the firm accounts for the business combination as a purchase because the *market values* of the merged assets generally exceed their book values. *GAAP* no longer allows this treatment in the U.S. Contrast with *purchase method.* Called *uniting-of-interests method* by the *IASB* and allowed by it under some conditions.

population. The entire set of numbers or items from which the analyst samples or performs some other analysis.

positive confirmation. See *confirmation.*

post. To record entries in an *account* to a *ledger,* usually as transfers from a *journal.*

post-closing trial balance. *Trial balance* taken after the accountant has *closed* all *temporary accounts.*

post-statement events. Events that have *material* impact and that occur between the end of the *accounting period* and the formal publication of the *financial statements.* Even though the events occur after the end of the period being reported on, the firm must disclose such events in notes if the auditor is to give a *clean opinion.*

potentially dilutive. A *security* that its holder may convert into, or exchange for, common stock and thereby reduce reported *earnings per share; options, warrants, convertible bonds,* and *convertible preferred stock.*

PPB. *Program budgeting.* The second "P" stands for "plan."

practical capacity. Maximum level at which a plant or department can operate efficiently.

precision. The degree of accuracy for an estimate derived from a sampling process, usually expressed as a range of values around the estimate. The analyst might express a sample estimate in the following terms: "Based on the sample, we are 95 percent sure [confidence level] that the true population value is within the range of X to Y [precision]." See *confidence level.*

preclosing trial balance. *Trial balance* taken at the end of the period before *closing entries;* in this sense, an *adjusted trial balance;* sometimes taken before *adjusting entries* and then synonymous with *unadjusted trial balance.*

predatory prices. Setting prices below some measure of cost in an effort to drive out competitors with the hope of recouping losses later by charging monopoly prices. Illegal in the United States if the prices set are below long-run variable costs. We know of no empirical evidence that firms are successful at recoupment.

predetermined (factory) overhead rate. Rate used in applying *overhead costs* to products or departments developed at the start of a period. Compute the rate as estimated overhead cost divided by the estimated number of units of the overhead allocation base (or *denominator volume*) activity. See *normal costing.*

preemptive right. The privilege of a *shareholder* to maintain a proportionate share of ownership by purchasing a proportionate share of any new stock issues. Most state corporation laws allow corporations to pay shareholders to waive their preemptive rights or state that preemptive rights exist only if the *corporation charter* explicitly grants them. In practice, then, preemptive rights are the exception rather than the rule.

preference as to assets. The rights of *preferred shareholders* to receive certain payments before common shareholders receive payments in case the board dissolves the corporation.

preferred shares. *Capital stock* with a claim to *income* or *assets* after *bondholders* but before *common shares*. *Dividends* on preferred shares are *income distributions,* not *expenses*. See *cumulative preferred stock*.

premium. The excess of issue (or market) price over *par value*. For a different context, see *insurance*.

premium on capital stock. Alternative but inferior title for *capital contributed in excess of par (or stated) value*.

prepaid expense. An *expenditure* that leads to a *deferred charge* or *prepayment*. Strictly speaking, this is a contradiction in terms because an *expense* is a gone asset, and this title refers to past *expenditures,* such as for rent or insurance premiums, that still have future benefits and thus are *assets*. We try to avoid this term and use "prepayment" instead.

prepaid income. An inferior alternative title for *advances from customers*. Do not call an item *revenue* or *income* until the firm earns it by delivering goods or rendering services.

prepayments. *Deferred charges; assets* representing *expenditures* for future benefits. Rent and insurance premiums paid in advance are usually current prepayments.

present value. Value today (or at some specific date) of an amount or amounts to be paid or received later (or at other, different dates), discounted at some *interest* or *discount rate;* an amount that, if invested today at the specified rate, will grow to the amount to be paid or received in the future.

price. The quantity of one *good* or *service,* usually *cash,* asked in return for a unit of another good or service. See *fair value*.

price-earnings (P/E) ratio. At a given time, the market value of a company's *common share,* per share, divided by the *earnings per* common *share* for the past year. The analyst usually bases the denominator on *income from continuing operations* or, if the analyst thinks the current figure for that amount does not represent a usual situation—such as when the number is negative or, if positive, close to zero—on some estimate of the number. See *ratio*.

price index. A series of numbers, one for each period, that purports to represent some *average* of prices for a series of periods, relative to a base period.

price level. The number from a *price index* series for a given period or date.

price level-adjusted statements. *Financial statements* expressed in terms of dollars of uniform purchasing power. The statements restate *nonmonetary* items to reflect changes in general *price levels* since the time the firm acquired specific *assets* and incurred *liabilities*. The statements recognize a *gain* or *loss* on *monetary items* as the firm holds them over time periods when the general *price level changes*. Conventional financial statements show *historical costs* and ignore differences in purchasing power in different periods.

price variance. In accounting for *standard costs,* an amount equal to (actual cost per unit – standard cost per unit) times actual quantity.

primary earnings per share (PEPS). Net *income* to common shareholders plus *interest* (net of tax effects) or *dividends* paid on *common-stock equivalents* divided by (weighted average of common shares outstanding plus the net increase in the number of common shares that would become *outstanding* if the holders of all common stock equivalents were to exchange them for common shares with cash proceeds, if any, used to retire common shares). As of 1997 and *SFAS No. 128,* replaced with *basic earnings per share*.

prime cost. Sum of *direct materials* plus *direct labor* costs assigned to product.

prime rate. The loan rate charged by commercial banks to their creditworthy customers. Some customers pay even less than the prime rate and others, more. The *Federal Reserve Bulletin* is the authoritative source of information about historical prime rates.

principal. An amount on which *interest* accrues, either as *expense* (for the borrower) or as *revenue* (for the lender); the *face amount* of a *loan;* also, the absent owner (principal) who hires the manager (agent) in a "principal-agent" relationship.

principle. See *generally accepted accounting principles*.

prior-period adjustment. A *debit* or *credit* that is made directly to *retained earnings* (and that does not affect *income* for the period) to adjust earnings as calculated for prior periods. Such adjustments are now rare. Theory suggests that accounting should correct for errors in accounting estimates (such as the *depreciable life* or *salvage value* of an asset) by adjusting retained earnings so that statements for future periods will show correct amounts. But *GAAP* require that corrections of such estimates flow through current, and perhaps future, *income statements*. See *accounting changes* and *accounting errors*.

prior service cost. *Present value* at a given time of a *pension plan's* retroactive *benefits*. "Unrecognized prior service cost" refers to that portion of prior service cost not yet *debited* to *expense*. See *actuarial accrued liability* and *funded*. Contrast with *normal cost*.

pro forma statements. Hypothetical statements; financial statements as they would appear if some event, such as a *merger* or increased production and sales, had occurred or were to occur; sometimes spelled as one word, "proforma."

probable. In many of its definitions, the *FASB* uses the term "probable." See, for example, *asset, firm commitment, liability*. A survey of practicing accountants revealed that the average of the probabilities that those surveyed had in mind when they used the term "probable" was 85 percent. Some accountants think that any event whose outcome is greater than 50 percent should be called "probable." The FASB uses the phrase "more likely than not" when it means greater than 50 percent.

proceeds. The *funds* received from the disposition of assets or from the issue of securities.

process costing. A method of *cost accounting* based on average costs (total cost divided by the *equivalent units* of work done in a period); typically used for assembly lines or for products that the firm produces in a series of steps that are more continuous than discrete.

product. *Goods* or *services* produced.

product cost. Any *manufacturing cost* that the firm can— or, in some contexts, should—debit to an *inventory* account. See *flow of costs,* for example. Contrast with *period expenses.*

product life cycle. Time span between initial concept (typically starting with research and development) of a good or service and the time when the firm ceases to support customers who have purchased the good or service.

production cost. *Manufacturing cost.*

production cost account. A *temporary account* for accumulating *manufacturing costs* during a period.

production department. A department producing salable *goods* or *services;* contrast with *service department.*

production method (depreciation). One form of *straight-line depreciation.* The firm assigns to the depreciable asset (e.g., a truck) a *depreciable life* measured not in elapsed time but in units of output (e.g., miles) or perhaps in units of time of expected use. Then the *depreciation* charge for a period is a portion of depreciable cost equal to a fraction computed as the actual output produced during the period divided by the expected total output to be produced over the life of the asset. This method is sometimes called the "units-of-production (or output) method."

production method (revenue recognition). *Percentage-of-completion method* for recognizing *revenue.*

production volume variance. Standard fixed *overhead* rate per unit of normal *capacity* (or base activity) times (units of base activity budgeted or planned for a period minus actual units of base activity worked or assigned to product during the period); often called a "volume variance."

productive capacity. One *attribute measured* for *assets.* The *current cost* of *long-term assets* means the cost of reproducing the productive capacity (for example, the ability to manufacture one million units a year), not the cost of reproducing the actual physical assets currently used (see *reproduction cost*). *Replacement cost* of productive capacity will be the same as reproduction cost of assets only in the unusual case when no technological improvement in production processes has occurred and the relative prices of goods and services used in production have remained approximately the same as when the firm acquired the currently used goods and services.

profit. Excess of *revenues* over *expenses* for a *transaction;* sometimes used synonymously with *net income* for the period.

profit and loss account. UK: *retained earnings.*

profit-and-loss sharing ratio. The fraction of *net income* or loss allocable to a partner in a *partnership;* need not be the same fraction as the partner's share of capital.

profit-and-loss statement. *Income statement.*

profit center. A *responsibility center* for which a firm accumulates both *revenues* and *expenses.* Contrast with *cost center.*

profit margin. *Sales* minus all *expenses.*

profit margin percentage. *Profit margin* divided by *net sales.*

profit maximization. The doctrine that the firm should account for a given set of operations so as to make reported *net income* as large as possible; contrast with

conservatism. This concept in accounting differs from the profit-maximizing concept in economics, which states that the firm should manage operations to maximize the present value of the firm's wealth, generally by equating *marginal costs* and *marginal revenues.*

profit-sharing plan. A *defined-contribution plan* in which the employer contributes amounts based on *net income.*

profit variance analysis. Analysis of the causes of the difference between budgeted profit in the *master budget* and the profits earned.

profit-volume analysis (equation). Analysis of effects, on *profits,* caused by changes in volume or *contribution margin* per unit or *fixed costs.* See *breakeven chart.*

profit-volume graph. See *breakeven chart.*

profit-volume ratio. *Net income* divided by net sales in dollars.

profitability. Some measure of the firm's ability to earn *income* relative to the size of the firm or its *revenues.*

profitability accounting. *Responsibility accounting.*

program budgeting (PPB). Specification and analysis of inputs, outputs, costs, and alternatives that link plans to *budgets.*

programmed cost. A *fixed cost* not essential for carrying out operations. For example, a firm can control costs for research and development and advertising designed to generate new business, but once it commits to incur them, they become fixed costs. These costs are sometimes called managed costs or *discretionary costs.* Contrast with *capacity costs.*

progressive tax. Tax for which the rate increases as the taxed base, such as income, increases. Contrast with *regressive tax.*

project financing arrangement. As defined by *SFAS No. 47,* the financing of an investment project in which the lender looks principally to the *cash flows* and *earnings* of the project as the source of funds for repayment and to the *assets* of the project as *collateral* for the loan. The general *credit* of the project entity usually does not affect the terms of the financing either because the borrowing entity is a *corporation* without other assets or because the financing provides that the lender has no direct *recourse* to the entity's owners.

projected benefit obligation. The *actuarial present value* at a given date of all pension benefits attributed by a *defined-benefit pension* formula to employee service rendered before that date. The analyst measures the obligation using assumptions as to future compensation levels if the formula incorporates future compensation, as happens, for example, when the plan bases the eventual pension benefit on wages of the last several years of employees' work lives. Contrast to "accumulated benefit obligation," where the analyst measures the obligation using employee compensation levels at the time of the measurement date.

projected financial statement. *Pro forma* financial statement.

projection. See *financial projection* for definition and contrast.

promissory note. An unconditional written promise to pay a specified sum of cash on demand or at a specified date.

proof of journal. The process of checking the arithmetic accuracy of *journal entries* by testing for the equality of all *debits* and all *credits* since the last previous proof.

property dividend. A *dividend in kind.*

property, plant, and equipment. See *plant assets.*

proportionate consolidation. Canada: a presentation of the *financial statements* of any investor-investment relationship, whereby the investor's pro rata share of each *asset, liability, income* item, and *expense* item appears in the *financial statements* of the investor under the various *balance sheet* and *income statement* headings.

proprietary accounts. See *budgetary accounts* for definition and contrast in the context of governmental accounting.

proprietorship. *Assets* minus *liabilities* of an *entity;* equals *contributed capital* plus *retained earnings.*

proprietorship theory. The corporation view that emphasizes the form of the *accounting equation* that says *assets − liabilities = owners' equity;* contrast with *entity theory.* The major implication of a choice between these theories deals with the treatment of *subsidiaries.* For example, the proprietorship theory views *minority interest* as an *indeterminate-term liability.* The proprietorship theory implies using a *single-step income statement.*

prorate. To *allocate* in proportion to some base; for example, to allocate *service department* costs in proportion to hours of service used by the benefited department or to allocate *manufacturing variances* to product sold and to product added to *ending inventory.*

prorating variances. See *prorate.*

prospectus. Formal written document describing *securities* a firm will issue. See *proxy.*

protest fee. Fee charged by banks or other financial agencies when the bank cannot collect items (such as *checks*) presented for collection.

provision. Part of an *account* title. Often the firm must recognize an *expense* even though it cannot be sure of the exact amount. The entry for the estimated expense, such as for *income taxes* or expected costs under *warranty,* is as follows:

Expense (Estimated)	X	
Liability (Estimated)		X

American terminology often uses "provision" in the expense account title of the above entry. Thus, Provision for Income Taxes means the estimate of income tax expense. (British terminology uses "provision" in the title for the estimated liability of the above entry, so that Provision for Income Taxes is a balance sheet account.)

proxy. Written authorization given by one person to another so that the second person can act for the first, such as to vote shares of stock; of particular significance to accountants because the *SEC* presumes that management distributes financial information along with its proxy solicitations.

public accountant. Generally, this term is synonymous with *certified public accountant.* Some jurisdictions, however, license individuals who are not CPAs as public accountants.

public accounting. That portion of accounting primarily involving the *attest* function, culminating in the *auditor's report.*

PuPU. Acronym for *purchasing power unit;* conceived by John C. Burton, former chief accountant of the *SEC.* Those who think that *constant-dollar accounting* is not particularly useful poke fun at it by calling it "PuPU accounting."

purchase allowance. A reduction in sales *invoice price* usually granted because the purchaser received *goods* not exactly as ordered. The purchaser does not return the goods but agrees to keep them for a price lower than originally agreed upon.

purchase discount. A reduction in purchase *invoice price* granted for prompt payment. See *sales discount* and *terms of sale.*

purchase investigation. An investigation of the financial affairs of a company for the purpose of disclosing matters that may influence the terms or conclusion of a potential acquisition.

purchase method. Accounting for a *business combination* by adding the acquired company's assets at the price paid for them to the acquiring company's assets. Contrast with *pooling-of-interests method.* The firm adds the acquired assets to the books at current values rather than original costs; the subsequent *amortization expenses* usually exceed those (and reported income is smaller than that) for the same business combination accounted for as a pooling of interests. *GAAP* in the U.S. require that the acquirer use the purchase method but other countries still allow the pooling-of-interests method.

purchase order. Document issued by a buyer authorizing a seller to deliver goods, with the buyer to make payment later.

purchasing power gain or loss. *Monetary gain or loss.*

push-down accounting. An accounting method used in some *purchase transactions.* Assume that Company A purchases substantially all the *common shares* of Company B but that Company B must still issue its own *financial statements.* The question arises, shall Company B change the *basis* for its *assets* and *equities* on its own books to the same updated amounts at which they appear on Company A's *consolidated financial statements?* Company B uses "push-down accounting" when it shows the new asset and equity bases reflecting Company A's purchase, because the method "pushes down" the new bases from Company A (where *GAAP* require them) to Company B (where the new bases would not appear in *historical cost accounting*). Since 1983, the *SEC* has required push-down accounting under some circumstances.

put. An option to sell *shares* of a publicly traded corporation at a fixed price during a fixed time span. Contrast with *call.*

Q

qualified report (opinion). *Auditor's report* containing a statement that the auditor was unable to complete a satisfactory examination of all things considered relevant or that the auditor has doubts about the financial impact of some *material* item reported in the financial statements. See *except for* and *subject to*.

quality. In modern usage, a product or service has quality to the extent it conforms to specifications or provides customers the characteristics promised them.

quality of earnings. A phrase with no single, agreed-upon meaning. Some who use the phrase use it with different meanings on different occasions. "Quality of earnings" has an accounting aspect and a business cycle aspect.

In its accounting aspect, managers have choices in measuring and reporting *earnings*. This discretion can involve any of the following: selecting *accounting principles* or standards when *GAAP* allow a choice; making estimates in the application of accounting principles; and timing transactions to allow recognizing *nonrecurring* items in earnings. In some instances the range of choices has a large impact on reported earnings and in others, small. (1) Some use the phrase "quality of earnings" to mean the degree to which management can affect reported income by its choices of accounting estimates even though the choices recur every period. These users judge, for example, insurance companies to have low-quality earnings. Insurance company management must reestimate its liabilities for future payments to the insured each period, thereby having an opportunity to report periodic earnings within a wide range. (2) Others use the phrase to mean the degree to which management actually takes advantage of its flexibility. For them, an insurance company that does not vary its methods and estimating techniques, even though it has the opportunity to do so, has high-quality earnings. (3) Some have in mind the proximity in time between *revenue* recognition and cash collection. For them, the smaller the time delay, the higher will be the quality. (4) Still others use the phrase to mean the degree to which managers who have a choice among the items with large influence on earnings choose the ones that result in income measures that are more likely to recur. For them, the more likely an item of earnings is to recur, the higher will be its quality. Often these last two groups trade off with each other. Consider a dealer leasing a car on a long-term *lease,* receiving monthly collections. The dealer who uses *sales-type lease* accounting scores low on proximity of revenue recognition (all at the time of signing the lease) to cash collection but highlights the nonrepetitive nature of the transaction. The leasing dealer who uses *operating lease* accounting has perfectly matching revenue recognition and cash collection, but the *recurring* nature of the revenue gives a misleading picture of a repetitive transaction. The phrase "item of earnings" in (4) is ambiguous. The writer could mean the underlying economic event (which occurs when the lease for the car is signed) or the revenue recognition (which occurs every time the dealer using operating lease accounting receives cash). Hence, you should try to understand what other speakers and writers mean by "quality of earnings" when you interpret what they say and write. Some who refer to "earnings quality" suspect that managers will usually make choices that enhance current earnings and present the firm in the best light, independent of the ability of the firm to generate similar earnings in the future. In this book, particularly in *Chapter 14*, we use the term in the first sense—opportunity to manage earnings, not necessarily exploitation of that opportunity.

In the business cycle aspect, management's action often has no impact on the stability and recurrence of earnings. Compare a company that sells consumer products and likely has sales repeating every week with a construction company that builds to order. Companies in noncyclical businesses, such as some public utilities, likely have more stable earnings than ones in cyclical businesses, such as steel. Some use "quality of earnings" to refer to the stability and recurrence of basic revenue-generating activities. Those who use the phrase this way rarely associate earnings quality with accounting issues.

quality of financial position. Because of the *articulation* of the *income statement* with the *balance sheet,* the factors that imply a high (or low) *quality of earnings* also affect the balance sheet. Users of this phrase have in mind the same accounting issues as they have in mind when they use the phrase "quality of earnings."

quantitative performance measure. A measure of output based on an objectively observable quantity, such as units produced or *direct costs* incurred, rather than on an unobservable quantity or a quantity observable only nonobjectively, like quality of service provided.

quantity discount. A reduction in purchase price as quantity purchased increases. The Robinson-Patman Act constrains the amount of the discount. Do not confuse with *purchase discount.*

quantity variance. *Efficiency variance;* in *standard cost* systems, the standard price per unit times (actual quantity used minus standard quantity that should be used).

quasi-reorganization. A *reorganization* in which no new company emerges or no court has intervened, as would happen in *bankruptcy.* The primary purpose is to rid the balance sheet of a *deficit* (negative *retained earnings*) and give the firm a "fresh start."

quick assets. *Assets* readily convertible into *cash;* includes cash, current marketable securities, and current receivables.

quick ratio. Sum of (cash, current marketable securities, and current receivables) divided by *current liabilities;* often called the "acid test ratio." The analyst may exclude some nonliquid receivables from the numerator. See *ratio.*

R

R^2. The proportion of the statistical variance of a *dependent variable* explained by the equation fit to *independent variable(s)* in a *regression analysis.*

Railroad Accounting Principles Board (RAPB). A board brought into existence by the Staggers Rail Act of 1980 to advise the Interstate Commerce Commission on accounting matters affecting railroads. The RAPB was the only cost-accounting body authorized by the government during the decade of the 1980s (because Congress ceased funding the CASB during the 1980s). The RAPB incorporated the pronouncements of the CASB and became the government's authority on cost accounting principles.

R&D. See *research and development.*

random number sampling. For choosing a sample, a method in which the analyst selects items from the *population* by using a random number table or generator.

random sampling. For choosing a sample, a method in which all items in the population have an equal chance of being selected. Compare *judgment(al) sampling.*

RAPB. *Railroad Accounting Principles Board.*

rate of return on assets. *Return on assets.*

rate of return on common stock equity. See *ratio.*

rate of return on shareholders' (owners') equity. See *ratio.*

rate of return (on total capital). See *ratio* and *return on assets.*

rate variance. *Price variance,* usually for *direct labor costs.*

ratio. The number resulting when one number divides another. Analysts generally use ratios to assess aspects of profitability, solvency, and liquidity. The commonly used financial ratios fall into three categories: (1) those that summarize some aspect of *operations* for a period, usually a year, (2) those that summarize some aspect of *financial position* at a given moment—the moment for which a balance sheet reports, and (3) those that relate some aspect of operations to some aspect of financial position. *Exhibit 5.11* lists the most common financial ratios and shows separately both the numerator and the denominator for each ratio.

For all ratios that require an average balance during the period, the analyst often derives the average as one half the sum of the beginning and the ending balances. Sophisticated analysts recognize, however, that particularly when companies use a fiscal year different from the calendar year, this averaging of beginning and ending balances may mislead. Consider, for example, the rate of *return on assets* of Sears, Roebuck & Company, whose fiscal year ends on January 31. Sears chooses a January 31 closing date at least in part because inventories are at a low level and are therefore easy to count—it has sold the Christmas merchandise, and the Easter merchandise has not yet all arrived. Furthermore, by January 31, Sears has collected for most Christmas sales, so receivable amounts are not unusually large. Thus at January 31, the amount of total assets is lower than at many other times during the year. Consequently, the denominator of the rate of return on assets, total assets, for Sears more likely represents the smallest amount of total assets on hand during the year rather than the average amount. The return on assets rate for Sears and other companies that choose a fiscal year end to coincide with low points in the inventory cycle is likely to exceed the ratio measured with a more accurate estimate of the average amounts of total assets.

raw material. Goods purchased for use in manufacturing a product.

reacquired stock. *Treasury shares.*

real accounts. *Balance sheet accounts,* as opposed to *nominal accounts.* See *permanent accounts.*

real amount (value). An amount stated in *constant dollars.* For example, if the firm sells an investment costing $100 for $130 after a period of 10 percent general *inflation,* the *nominal amount* of *gain* is $30 (= $130 − $100) but the real amount of gain is C$20 (= $130 − 1.10 ×

$100), where "C$" denotes constant dollars of purchasing power on the date of sale.

real estate. *Land* and its *improvements,* such as landscaping and roads, but not buildings.

real interest rate. Interest rate reflecting the productivity of capital, not including a premium for inflation anticipated over the life of the loan.

realizable value. *Fair value* or, sometimes, *net realizable (sales) value.*

realization convention. The accounting practice of delaying the recognition of *gains* and *losses* from changes in the market price of *assets* until the firm sells the assets. However, the firm recognizes unrealized losses on *inventory* (or *marketable securities* classified as *trading securities*) prior to sale when the firm uses the *lower-of-cost-or-market* valuation basis for inventory (or the *fair value* basis for marketable securities).

realize. To convert into *funds;* when applied to a *gain* or *loss,* implies that an *arm's-length transaction* has taken place. Contrast with *recognize;* the firm may recognize a loss (as, for example, on *marketable equity securities*) in the financial statements even though it has not yet realized the loss via a transaction.

realized gain (or loss) on marketable equity securities. An income statement account title for the difference between the proceeds of disposition and the *original cost* of *marketable equity securities.*

realized holding gain. See *inventory profit* for definition and an example.

rearrangement costs. Costs of reinstalling assets, perhaps in a different location. The firm may, but need not, *capitalize* them as part of the assets cost, just as is done with original installation cost. The firm will *expense* these costs if they merely maintain the asset's future benefits at their originally intended level before the relocation.

recapitalization. *Reorganization.*

recapture. Name for one kind of tax payment. Various provisions of the *income tax* rules require a refund by the taxpayer (recapture by the government) of various tax advantages under certain conditions. For example, the taxpayer must repay tax savings provided by *accelerated depreciation* if the taxpayer prematurely retires the item providing the tax savings.

receipt. Acquisition of *cash.*

receivable. Any *collectible,* whether or not it is currently due.

receivable turnover. See *ratio.*

reciprocal holdings. Company A owns stock of Company B, and Company B owns stock of Company A; or Company B owns stock of Company C, which owns stock of Company A.

recognize. To enter a transaction in the accounts; not synonymous with *realize.*

reconciliation. A calculation that shows how one balance or figure derives from another, such as a reconciliation of retained earnings or a *bank reconciliation schedule.* See *articulate.*

record date. The date at which the firm pays *dividends* on payment date to those who own the stock.

recourse. The rights of the lender if a borrower does not repay as promised. A recourse loan gives the lender the right to take any of the borrower's assets not exempted from such taking by the contract. See also *note receivable discounted.*

recovery of unrealized loss on trading securities. An *income statement account title* for the *gain* during the current period on *trading securities.*

recurring. Occurring again; occurring repetitively; in accounting, an adjective often used in describing *revenue* or *earnings.* In some contexts, the term "recurring revenue" is ambiguous. Consider a construction contractor who accounts for a single long-term project with the *installment method,* with revenue recognized at the time of each cash collection from the customer. The recognized revenue is recurring, but the transaction leading to the revenue is not. See *quality of earnings.*

redemption. Retirement by the issuer, usually by a purchase or *call,* of *stocks* or *bonds.*

redemption premium. *Call premium.*

redemption value. The price a corporation will pay to retire *bonds* or *preferred stock* if it calls them before *maturity.*

refinancing. An adjustment in the *capital structure* of a *corporation,* involving changes in the nature and amounts of the various classes of *debt* and, in some cases, *capital* as well as other components of *shareholders' equity. Asset* carrying values in the accounts remain unchanged.

refunding bond issue. Said of a *bond* issue whose proceeds the firm uses to retire bonds already *outstanding.*

register. A collection of consecutive entries, or other information, in chronological order, such as a check register or an insurance register that lists all insurance policies owned. If the firm records entries in the register, it can serve as a *journal.*

registered bond. A bond for which the issuer will pay the *principal* and *interest,* if registered as to interest, to the owner listed on the books of the issuer; as opposed to a bearer bond, in which the issuer must pay the possessor of the bond.

registrar. An *agent,* usually a bank or trust company, appointed by a corporation to keep track of the names of shareholders and distributions to them.

registration statement. Required by the Securities Act of 1933, statement of most companies that want to have owners of their securities trade the securities in public markets. The statement discloses financial data and other items of interest to potential investors.

regression analysis. A method of *cost estimation* based on statistical techniques for fitting a line (or its equivalent in higher mathematical dimensions) to an observed series of data points, usually by minimizing the sum of squared deviations of the observed data from the fitted line. Common usage calls the cost that the analysis explains the "dependent variable"; it calls the variable(s) we use to estimate cost behavior "independent variable(s)." If we use more than one independent variable, the term for the analysis is "multiple regression analysis." See R^2, *standard error,* and *t-value.*

regressive tax. Tax for which the rate decreases as the taxed base, such as income, increases. Contrast with *progressive tax.*

Regulation S-K. The *SEC's* standardization of nonfinancial statement disclosure requirements for documents filed with the SEC.

Regulation S-T. The *SEC's* regulations specifying formats for electronic filing and the *EDGAR* system.

Regulation S-X. The *SEC's* principal accounting regulation, which specifies the form and content of financial reports to the SEC.

rehabilitation. The improving of a used *asset* via an extensive repair. Ordinary *repairs* and *maintenance* restore or maintain expected *service potential* of an asset, and the firm treats them as *expenses.* A rehabilitation improves the asset beyond its current service potential, enhancing the service potential to a significantly higher level than before the rehabilitation. Once rehabilitated, the asset may be better, but need not be, than it was when new. The firm will *capitalize expenditures* for rehabilitation, like those for *betterments* and *improvements.*

reinvestment rate. In a *capital budgeting* context, the rate at which the firm invests cash inflows from a project occurring before the project's completion. Once the analyst assumes such a rate, no project can ever have multiple *internal rates of return.* See *Descartes' rule of signs.*

relative performance evaluation. Setting performance targets and, sometimes, compensation in relation to the performance of others, perhaps in different firms or divisions, who face a similar environment.

relative sales value method. See *net realizable (sales) value.*

relevant cost. Cost used by an analyst in making a decision. *Incremental cost; opportunity cost.*

relevant range. Activity levels over which costs are linear or for which *flexible budget* estimates and *breakeven charts* will remain valid.

remit earnings. An expression likely to confuse a reader without a firm understanding of accounting basics. A firm generates *net assets* by earning *income* and retains net assets if it does not declare *dividends* in the amount of net income. When a firm declares dividends and pays the cash (or other net assets), some writers would say the firm "remits earnings." We think the student learns better by conceiving earnings as a *credit balance.* When a firm pays dividends it sends net assets, things with debit balances, not something with a credit balance, to the recipient. When writers say firms "remit earnings," they mean the firms send assets (or net assets) that previous earnings have generated and reduce *retained earnings.*

remittance advice. Information on a *check stub,* or on a document attached to a check by the *drawer,* that tells the *payee* why a payment is being made.

rent. A charge for use of land, buildings, or other assets.

reorganization. In the *capital structure* of a corporation, a major change that leads to changes in the rights, interests, and implied ownership of the various security owners; usually results from a *merger* or an agreement by senior security holders to take action to forestall *bankruptcy.*

repair. An *expenditure* to restore an *asset's* service potential after damage or after prolonged use. In the second sense, after prolonged use, the difference between repairs and maintenance is one of degree and not of kind. A repair is treated as an *expense* of the period when incurred. Because the firm treats repairs and maintenance similarly in this regard, the distinction is not important. A repair helps to maintain capacity at the levels planned when the firm acquired the *asset.* Contrast with *improvement.*

replacement cost. For an asset, the current fair market price to purchase another, similar asset (with the same future benefit or service potential). *Current cost.* See *reproduction cost* and *productive capacity.* See also *distributable income* and *inventory profit.*

replacement cost method of depreciation. Method in which the analyst augments the original-cost *depreciation* charge with an amount based on a portion of the difference between the *current replacement cost* of the asset and its *original cost.*

replacement system of depreciation. See *retirement method of depreciation* for definition and contrast.

report. *Financial statement; auditor's report.*

report form. *Balance sheet* form that typically shows *assets* minus *liabilities* as one total. Then, below that total appears the components of *owners' equity* summing to the same total. Often, the top section shows *current* assets less current liabilities before *noncurrent assets* less noncurrent liabilities. Contrast with *account form.*

reporting objectives (policies). The general purposes for which the firm prepares *financial statements.* The *FASB* has discussed these in *SFAC No. 1.*

representative item sampling. Sampling in which the analyst believes the sample selected is typical of the entire population from which it comes. Compare *specific item sampling.*

reproduction cost. The *cost* necessary to acquire an *asset* similar in all physical respects to another asset for which the analyst requires a *current value.* See *replacement cost* and *productive capacity* for contrast.

required rate of return (RRR). *Cost of capital.*

requisition. A formal written order or request, such as for withdrawal of supplies from the storeroom.

resale value. *Exit value; net realizable value.*

research and development (R&D). A form of economic activity with special accounting rules. Firms engage in research in hopes of discovering new knowledge that will create a new product, process, or service or of improving a present product, process, or service. Development translates research findings or other knowledge into a new or improved product, process, or service. *SFAS No. 2* requires that firms expense costs of such activities as incurred on the grounds that the future benefits are too uncertain to warrant *capitalization* as an asset. This treatment seems questionable to us because we wonder why firms would continue to undertake R&D if there was no expectation of future benefit; if future benefits exist, then R&D *costs* should be assets that appear, like other assets, at *historical cost.*

reserve. The worst word in accounting because almost everyone not trained in accounting, and some who are, misunderstand it. The common confusion is that "reserves" represent a pool of *cash* or other *assets* available when the firm needs them. Wrong. Cash always has a *debit balance.* Reserves always have a *credit* balance. When properly used in accounting, "reserves" refer to an account that appropriates *retained earnings* and restricts dividend declarations. Appropriating retained earnings is itself a poor and vanishing practice, so the word should seldom appear in accounting. In addition,

"reserve" was used in the past to indicate an asset *contra account* (for example, "reserve for depreciation") or an *estimated liability* (for example, "reserve for warranty costs"). In any case, reserve accounts have *credit* balances and are not pools of *funds,* as the unwary reader might infer. If a company has set aside a pool of *cash* (or *marketable securities*) to serve some specific purpose such as paying for a new factory, then it will call that cash a *fund.* No other word in accounting causes so much misunderstanding by nonexperts as well as by "experts" who should know better. A leading unabridged dictionary defines "reserve" as "cash, or assets readily convertible into cash, held aside, as by a corporation, bank, state or national government, etc. to meet expected or unexpected demands." This definition is absolutely wrong in accounting. Reserves are not funds. For example, the firm creates a contingency fund of $10,000 by depositing cash in a fund and makes the following entry:

Dr. Contingency Fund	10,000	
Cr. Cash		10,000

The following entry may accompany the previous entry, if the firm wants to appropriate retained earnings:

Dr. Retained Earnings	10,000	
Cr. Reserve for Contingencies		10,000

The transaction leading to the first entry has economic significance. The second entry has little economic impact for most firms. The problem with the word "reserve" arises because the firm can make the second entry without the first—a company can create a reserve, that is, appropriate retained earnings, without creating a fund. The problem results, at least in part, from the fact that in common usage, "reserve" means a pool of assets, as in the phrase "oil reserves." The *Internal Revenue Service* does not help in dispelling confusion about the term "reserves." The federal *income tax* return for corporations uses the title "Reserve for Bad Debts" to mean "Allowance for Uncollectible Accounts" and speaks of the "Reserve Method" in referring to the *allowance method* for estimating *revenue* or *income* reductions from estimated *uncollectibles.*

reserve recognition accounting (RRA). One form of *accounting* for natural resources. In exploration for natural resources, the problem arises of how to treat the expenditures for exploration, both before the firm knows the outcome of the efforts and after it knows the outcome. Suppose that the firm spends $10 million to drill 10 holes ($1 million each) and that nine of them are dry whereas one is a gusher containing oil with a *net realizable value* of $40 million. Dry hole, or *successful efforts,* accounting would expense $9 million and *capitalize* $1 million, which the firm will *deplete* as it lifts the oil from the ground. *SFAS No. 19,* now suspended, required *successful efforts costing.* Full costing would expense nothing but would capitalize the $10 million of drilling costs that the firm will deplete as it lifts the oil from the single productive well. Reserve recognition accounting would capitalize $40 million, which the firm will deplete as it lifts the oil, with a $30 million *credit* to *income* or *contributed capital*. The *balance sheet* shows the *net realizable value* of proven oil and gas reserves. The *income statement* has three sorts of items: (1) current income resulting from production or "lifting profit," which is the *revenue* from sales of oil and gas less the expense based on the current valuation amount at which these items have appeared on the balance sheet, (2) profit or loss from exploration efforts in which the current value of new discoveries is revenue and all the exploration cost is expense, and (3) gain or loss on changes in current value during the year, which accountants in other contexts call a *holding gain or loss*.

reset bond. A bond, typically a *junk bond*, that specifies that periodically the issuer will reset the coupon rate so that the bond sells at *par* in the market. Investment bankers created this type of instrument to help ensure the purchasers of such bonds of getting a fair rate of return, given the riskiness of the issuer. If the issuer gets into financial trouble, its bonds will trade for less than par in the market. The issuer of a reset bond promises to raise the interest rate and preserve the value of the bond. Ironically, the reset feature has often had just the opposite effect. The default risk of many issuers of reset bonds has deteriorated so much that the bonds have dropped to less than 50 percent of par. To raise the value to par, the issuer would have to raise the interest rate to more than 25 percent per year. That rate is so large that issuers have declared bankruptcy rather than attempt to make the new large interest payments; this then reduces the market value of the bonds rather than increases them.

residual income. In an external reporting context, a term that refers to *net income* to *common shares* (= net income less *preferred stock dividends*). In *managerial accounting,* this term refers to the excess of income for a *division* or *segment* of a company over the product of the *cost of capital* for the company multiplied by the average amount of capital invested in the division during the period over which the division earned the income.

residual security. A *potentially dilutive security. Options, warrants, convertible bonds,* and *convertible preferred stock.*

residual value. At any time, the estimated or actual *net realizable value* (that is, proceeds less removal costs) of an *asset,* usually a depreciable *plant asset.* In the context of depreciation accounting, this term is equivalent to *salvage value* and is preferred to *scrap value* because the firm need not scrap the asset. It is sometimes used to mean net *book value.* In the context of a *noncancelable* lease, it is the estimated value of the leased asset at the end of the lease period. See *lease.*

resources supplied. *Expenditures* made for an activity.

resources used. *Cost driver* rate times cost driver volume.

responsibility accounting. Accounting for a business by considering various units as separate entities, or *profit centers,* giving management of each unit responsibility for the unit's *revenues* and *expenses.* See *transfer price.*

responsibility center. An organization part or *segment* that top management holds accountable for a specified set of activities. Also called "accountability center." See *cost center, investment center, profit center,* and *revenue center.*

restricted assets. Governmental resources restricted by legal or contractual requirements for specific purpose.

restricted retained earnings. That part of *retained earnings* not legally available for *dividends.* See *retained earnings, appropriated.* Bond indentures and other loan contracts can curtail the legal ability of the corporation to declare dividends without formally requiring a retained earnings appropriation, but the firm must disclose such restrictions.

retail inventory method. Ascertaining cost amounts of *ending inventory* as follows (assuming *FIFO*): cost of ending inventory = (selling price of *goods available for sale* − sales) × *cost percentage.* The analyst then computes cost of goods sold from the inventory equation; costs of beginning inventory, purchases, and ending inventory are all known. (When the firm uses *LIFO,* the method resembles the *dollar-value LIFO method.*) See *markup.*

retail terminology. See *markup.*

retained earnings. Net *income* over the life of a corporation less all *dividends* (including capitalization through *stock dividends*); *owners' equity* less *contributed capital.*

retained earnings, appropriated. An *account* set up by crediting it and debiting *retained earnings;* used to indicate that a portion of retained earnings is not available for dividends. The practice of appropriating retained earnings is misleading unless the firm marks all capital with its use, which is not practicable, nor sensible, since capital is fungible—all the *equities* jointly fund all the *assets.* The use of formal retained earnings appropriations is declining.

retained earnings statement. A *reconciliation* of the beginning and the ending balances in the *retained earnings account;* required by *generally accepted accounting principles* whenever the firm presents *comparative balance sheets* and an *income statement.* This reconciliation can appear in a separate statement, in a combined statement of income and retained earnings, or in the balance sheet.

retirement method of depreciation. A method in which the firm records no entry for *depreciation expense* until it retires an *asset* from service. Then, it makes an entry *debiting* depreciation expense and *crediting* the asset account for the cost of the asset retired. If the retired asset has a *salvage value,* the firm reduces the amount of the debit to depreciation expense by the amount of salvage value with a corresponding debit to cash, receivables, or salvaged materials. The "replacement system of depreciation" is similar, except that the debit to depreciation expense equals the cost of the new asset less the salvage value, if any, of the old asset. Some public utilities used these methods. For example, if the firm acquired ten telephone poles in Year 1 for $60 each and replaces them in Year 10 for $100 each when the salvage value of the old poles is $5 each, the accounting would be as follows:

Retirement Method

Plant Assets	600	
Cash		600
To acquire assets in Year 1.		
Depreciation Expense	550	
Salvage Receivable	50	
Plant Assets		600
To record retirement and depreciation in Year 10.		
Plant Assets	1,000	
Cash		1,000
To record acquisition of new assets in Year 10.		

Replacement Method

Plant Assets	600	
Cash		600
To acquire assets in Year 1.		
Depreciation Expense	950	
Salvage Receivable	50	
Cash		1,000
To record depreciation on old asset in amount quantified by net cost of replacement asset in Year 10.		

The retirement method is like *FIFO* in that it records the cost of the first assets as depreciation and puts the cost of the second assets on the balance sheet. The replacement method is like *LIFO* in that it records the cost of the second assets as depreciation expense and leaves the cost of the first assets on the balance sheet.

retirement plan. *Pension plan.*

retroactive benefits. In initiating or amending a *defined-benefit pension plan,* benefits that the benefit formula attributes to employee services rendered in periods prior to the initiation or amendment. See *prior service costs.*

return. A schedule of information required by governmental bodies, such as the tax return required by the *Internal Revenue Service;* also the physical return of merchandise. See also *return on investment.*

return on assets (ROA). *Net income* plus after-tax *interest charges* plus *minority interest* in income divided by average total *assets;* perhaps the single most useful ratio for assessing management's overall operating performance. Most financial economists would subtract average noninterest-bearing *liabilities* from the denominator. Economists realize that when liabilities do not provide for explicit interest charges, the creditor adjusts the terms of contract, such as setting a higher selling price or lower discount, to those who do not pay cash immediately. (To take an extreme example, consider how much higher salary a worker who receives a salary once per year, rather than once per month, would demand.) This ratio requires in the numerator the income amount before the firm accrues any charges to suppliers of funds. We cannot measure the interest charges implicit in the noninterest-bearing liabilities because they cause items such as cost of goods sold and salary expense to be somewhat larger, since the interest is implicit. Sub-

tracting their amounts from the denominator adjusts for their implicit cost. Such subtraction assumes that assets financed with noninterest-bearing liabilities have the same rate of return as all the other assets.

return on investment (ROI), return on capital. *Income* (before distributions to suppliers of capital) for a period; as a rate, this amount divided by average total assets. The analyst should add back *interest,* net of tax effects, to *net income* for the numerator. See *ratio.*

revenue. The *owners' equity* increase accompanying the *net assets* increase caused by selling goods or rendering services; in short, a service rendered; *sales* of products, merchandise, and services and earnings from *interest, dividends, rents,* and the like. Measure revenue as the expected *net present value* of the net assets the firm will receive. Do not confuse with *receipt* of *funds,* which may occur before, when, or after revenue is recognized. Contrast with *gain* and *income.* See also *holding gain.* Some writers use the term *gross income* synonymously with *revenue;* avoid such usage.

revenue center. Within a firm, a *responsibility center* that has control only over revenues generated. Contrast with *cost center.* See *profit center.*

revenue expenditure. A term sometimes used to mean an *expense,* in contrast to a capital *expenditure* to acquire an *asset* or to discharge a *liability.* Avoid using this term; use *period expense* instead.

revenue received in advance. An inferior term for *advances from customers.*

reversal (reversing) entry. An *entry* in which all *debits* and *credits* are the credits and debits, respectively, of another entry, and in the same amounts. The accountant usually records a reversal entry on the first day of an *accounting period* to reverse a previous *adjusting entry,* usually an *accrual.* The purpose of such entries is to make the book-keeper's tasks easier. Suppose that the firm pays salaries every other Friday, with paychecks compensating employees for the two weeks just ended. Total salaries accrue at the rate of $5,000 per five-day workweek. The bookkeeper is accustomed to making the following entry every other Friday:

(1) Salary Expense	10,000	
Cash		10,000
To record salary expense and salary payments.		

If the firm delivers paychecks to employees on Friday, November 25, then the *adjusting entry* made on November 30 (or perhaps later) to record accrued salaries for November 28, 29, and 30 would be as follows:

(2) Salary Expense	3,000	
Salaries Payable		3,000
To charge November operations with all salaries earned in November.		

The firm would close the Salary Expense account as part of the November 30 closing entries. On the next payday, December 9, the salary entry would be as follows:

(3) Salary Expense	. . . .	7,000	
Salaries Payable	. . . .	3,000	
Cash	. . . .		10,000

To record salary payments split between expense for December (seven days) and liability carried over from November.

To make entry *(3)*, the bookkeeper must look back into the records to see how much of the debit is to Salaries Payable accrued from the previous month in order to split the total debits between December expense and the liability carried over from November. Notice that this entry forces the bookkeeper both (a) to refer to balances in old accounts and (b) to make an entry different from the one customarily made, entry *(1)*. The reversing entry, made just after the books have been closed for the second quarter, makes the salary entry for December 9 the same as that made on all other Friday paydays. The reversing entry merely *reverses* the adjusting entry *(2)*:

| (4) Salaries Payable | . . . . | 3,000 | |
| Salary Expense | . . . . | | 3,000 |

To reverse the adjusting entry.

This entry results in a zero balance in the Salaries Payable account and a credit balance in the Salary Expense account. If the firm makes entry *(4)* just after it closes the books for November, then the entry on December 9 will be the customary entry *(1)*. Entries *(4)* and *(1)* together have exactly the same effect as entry *(3)*.

The procedure for using reversal entries is as follows: the firm makes the required adjustment to record an accrual (*payable* or *receivable*) at the end of an *accounting period;* it makes the closing entry as usual; as of the first day of the following period, it makes an entry reversing the adjusting entry; when the firm makes (or receives) a payment, it records the entry as though it had not recorded an adjusting entry at the end of the preceding period. Whether a firm uses reversal entries affects the record-keeping procedures but not the financial statements.

This term is also used to describe the entry reversing an incorrect entry before recording the correct entry.

reverse stock split. A stock split in which the firm decreases the number of shares *outstanding*. See *stock split*.

revolving fund. A fund whose amounts the firm continually spends and replenishes; for example, a *petty cash fund*.

revolving loan. A *loan* that both the borrower and the lender expect to renew at *maturity*.

right. The privilege to subscribe to new *stock* issues or to purchase stock. Usually, securities called *warrants* contain the rights, and the owner of the warrants may sell them. See also *preemptive right*.

risk. A measure of the variability of the *return on investment*. For a given expected amount of return, most people prefer less risk to more risk. Therefore, in rational markets, investments with more risk usually promise, or investors expect to receive, a higher rate of return than investments with lower risk. Most people use "risk" and "uncertainty" as synonyms. In technical language, however, these terms have different meanings. We use "risk" when we know the probabilities attached to the various outcomes, such as the probabilities of heads or tails in the flip of a fair coin. "Uncertainty" refers to an event for which we can only estimate the probabilities of the outcomes, such as winning or losing a lawsuit.

risk-adjusted discount rate. Rate used in discounting cash flows for projects more or less risky than the firm's average. In a *capital budgeting* context, a decision analyst compares projects by comparing their net *present values* for a given *interest* rate, usually the cost of capital. If the analyst considers a given project's outcome to be much more or much less risky than the normal undertakings of the company, then the analyst will use a larger interest rate (if the project is riskier) or a smaller interest rate (if less risky) in discounting, and the rate used is "risk-adjusted."

risk-free rate. An interest rate reflecting only the pure interest rate plus an amount to compensate for inflation anticipated over the life of a loan, excluding a premium for the risk of default by the borrower. Financial economists usually measure the risk-free rate in the United States from U.S. government securities, such as Treasury bills and notes.

risk premium. Extra compensation paid to employees or extra *interest* paid to lenders, over amounts usually considered normal, in return for their undertaking to engage in activities riskier than normal.

ROA. *Return on assets.*

ROI. *Return on investment;* usually used to refer to a single project and expressed as a ratio: *income* divided by average *cost* of *assets* devoted to the project.

royalty. Compensation for the use of property, usually a patent, copyrighted material, or natural resources. The amount is often expressed as a percentage of receipts from using the property or as an amount per unit produced.

RRA. *Reserve recognition accounting.*

RRR. Required rate of return. See *cost of capital*.

rule of 69. Rule stating that an amount of cash invested at r percent per period will double in $69/r + 0.35$ periods. This approximation is accurate to one-tenth of a period for interest rates between 1/4 and 100 percent per period. For example, at 10 percent per period, the rule says that a given sum will double in $69/10 + 0.35 = 7.25$ periods. At 10 percent per period, a given sum actually doubles in 7.27+ periods.

rule of 72. Rule stating that an amount of cash invested at r percent per period will double in $72/r$ periods. A reasonable approximation for interest rates between 4 and 10 percent but not nearly as accurate as the *rule of 69* for interest rates outside that range. For example, at 10 percent per period, the rule says that a given sum will double in $72/10 = 7.2$ periods.

rule of 78. The rule followed by many finance companies for allocating earnings on *loans* among the months of a year on the sum-of-the-months'-digits basis when the borrower makes equal monthly payments to the lender. The sum of the digits from 1 through 12 is 78, so the rule allocates 12/78 of the year's earnings to the first month, 11/78 to the second month, and so on. This approximation allocates more of the early payments to interest and less to principal than does the correct, compound-interest method. Hence, lenders still use this method even though present-day computers can make the compound-interest computation as easily as they can carry out the approximation. See *sum-of-the-years'-digits depreciation*.

ruling (and balancing) an account. The process of summarizing a series of entries in an *account* by computing a new *balance* and drawing double lines to indicate that the new balance summarizes the information above the double lines. An illustration appears below. The steps are as follows: (1) Compute the sum of all *debit* entries including opening debit balance, if any— $1,464.16. (2) Compute the sum of all credit entries including opening credit balance, if any— $413.57. (3) If the amount in (1) exceeds the amount in (2), then write the excess as a credit with a checkmark— $1,464.16 − $413.57 = $1,050.59. (4) Add both debit and credit columns, which should both now sum to the same amount, and show that identical total at the foot of both columns. (5) Draw double lines under those numbers and write the excess of debits over credits as the new debit balance with a checkmark. (6) If the amount in (2) exceeds the amount in (1), then write the excess as a debit with a check-mark. (7) Do steps (4) and (5) except that the excess becomes the new credit balance. (8) If the amount in (1) equals the amount in (2), then the balance is zero, and only the totals with the double lines beneath them need appear.

Rutgers Accounting Web Site. See http://www.rutgers.edu/Accounting/ for a useful compendium of accounting information.

S

S corporation. A corporation taxed like a *partnership*. Corporation (or partnership) agreements allocate the periodic *income* to the individual shareholders (or partners) who report these amounts on their individual *income tax* returns. Contrast with *C corporation*.

SA (société anonyme). France: A *corporation*.

SAB. *Staff Accounting Bulletin* of the *SEC*.

safe-harbor lease. A form of *tax-transfer lease*.

safety stock. Extra items of *inventory* kept on hand to protect against running out.

salary. Compensation earned by managers, administrators, and professionals, not based on an hourly rate. Contrast with *wage*.

sale. A *revenue* transaction in which the firm delivers *goods* or *services* to a customer in return for cash or a contractual obligation to pay.

sale and leaseback. A *financing* transaction in which the firm sells improved property but takes it back for use on a long-term *lease*. Such transactions often have advantageous income tax effects but usually have no effect on *financial statement income*.

sales activity variance. *Sales volume variance*.

sales allowance. A sales *invoice* price reduction that a seller grants to a buyer because the seller delivered *goods* different from, perhaps because of damage, those the buyer ordered. The seller often accumulates amounts of such adjustments in a temporary *revenue contra account* having this, or a similar, title. See *sales discount*.

sales basis of revenue recognition. Recognition of *revenue* not when a firm produces goods or when it receives orders but only when it has completed the sale by delivering the goods or services and has received cash or a claim to cash. Most firms recognize revenue on this basis. Compare with the *percentage-of-completion method* and the *installment method*. This is identical with the *completed contract method*, but the latter term ordinarily applies only to *long-term* construction projects.

sales contra, estimated uncollectibles. A title for the contra-revenue account to recognize estimated reductions in income caused by *accounts receivable* that will not be collected. See *bad debt expense, allowance for uncollectibles,* and *allowance method*.

sales discount. A sales *invoice* price reduction usually offered for prompt payment. See *terms of sale* and *2/10, n/30*.

sales return. The physical return of merchandise. The seller often accumulates amounts of such returns in a temporary revenue contra account.

An Open Account, Ruled and Balanced
(Steps indicated in parentheses correspond to steps described in "ruling an account.")

	Date 2007	Explanation	Ref.	Debit (1)	Date 2007	Explanation	Ref.	Credit (2)	
	Jan. 2	Balance	θ	100.00					
	Jan. 13		VR	121.37	Sept. 15		J	.42	
	Mar. 20		VR	56.42	Nov. 12		J	413.15	
	June 5		J	1,138.09	Dec. 31	Balance	θ	1,050.59	(3)
	Aug. 18		J	1.21					
	Nov. 20		VR	38.43					
	Dec. 7		VR	8.64					
(4)	2001			1,464.16	2001			1,464.16	(4)
(5)	Jan. 1	Balance	θ	1,050.59					

sales-type (capital) lease. A form of *lease.* See *capital lease.* When a manufacturer (or other firm) that ordinarily sells goods enters a capital lease as *lessor,* the lease is a "salestype lease." When a financial firm, such as a bank or insurance company or leasing company, acquires the asset from the manufacturer and then enters a capital lease as lessor, the lease is a "direct-financing-type lease." The manufacturer recognizes its ordinary profit (sales price less *cost of goods sold,* where sales price is the *present value* of the contractual lease payments plus any down payment) on executing the sales-type capital lease, but the financial firm does not recognize profit on executing a capital lease of the direct-financing type.

sales value method. *Relative sales value method.* See *net realizable value method.*

sales volume variance. Budgeted *contribution margin* per unit times (planned sales volume minus actual sales volume).

salvage value. Actual or estimated selling price, net of removal or disposal costs, of a used *plant asset* that the firm expects to sell or otherwise retire. See *residual value.*

SAR. *Summary annual report.*

SARL (société à responsabilité limitée). France: a *corporation* with limited liability and a life of no more than 99 years; must have at least two and no more than 50 *shareholders.*

SAS. *Statement on Auditing Standards* of the *AICPA.*

scale effect. See *discounted cash flow.*

scatter diagram. A graphic representation of the relation between two or more variables within a population.

schedule. A supporting set of calculations, with explanations, that show how to derive figures in a *financial statement* or tax return.

scientific method. *Effective interest method* of amortizing *bond discount* or *premium.*

scrap value. *Salvage value* assuming the owner intends to junk the item. A *net realizable value. Residual value.*

SEC (Securities and Exchange Commission). An agency authorized by the U.S. Congress to regulate, among other things, the financial reporting practices of most public corporations. The SEC has indicated that it will usually allow the *FASB* to set accounting principles, but it often requires more disclosure than the FASB requires. The SEC states its accounting requirements in its *Accounting Series Releases (ASR), Financial Reporting Releases, Accounting and Auditing Enforcement Releases, Staff Accounting Bulletins* (these are, strictly speaking, interpretations by the accounting staff, not rules of the commissioners themselves), and *Regulations S-X.* See also *registration statement, 10-K,* and *20-F.*

secret reserve. *Hidden reserve.*

Securities and Exchange Commission. *SEC.*

security. Document that indicates ownership, such as a *share* of *stock,* or indebtedness, such as a *bond,* or potential ownership, such as an *option* or *warrant.*

security available for sale. According to *SFAS No. 115* (1993), a *debt* or *equity security* that is not a *trading security,* or a debt security that is not a *security held to maturity.*

security held to maturity. According to *SFAS No. 115* (1993), a *debt security* the holder has both the ability and the intent to hold to *maturity;* valued in the *balance sheet* at amortized acquisition cost: the book value of the security at the end of each period is the book value at the beginning of the period multiplied by the historical *yield* on the security (measured as of the time of purchase) less any cash the holder receives at the end of this period from the security.

segment (of a business). As defined by *APB Opinion No. 30,* "a component of an *entity* whose activities represent a separate major line of business or class of customer. . . . [It maybe] a *subsidiary,* a division, or a department, . . . provided that its *assets,* results of *operations,* and activities can be clearly distinguished, physically and operationally for financial reporting purposes, from the other assets, results of operations, and activities of the entity." In *SFAS No. 14,* a segment is defined as a "component of an enterprise engaged in promoting a product or service or a group of related products and services primarily to unaffiliated customers . . . for a profit." *SFAS No. 131* defines operating segments using the "management approach" as components of the enterprise engaging in revenue- and expense-generating business activities "whose operating results are regularly reviewed by the enterprise's chief operating decision maker to make decisions about resources... and asset performance."

segment reporting. Reporting of *sales, income,* and *assets* by *segments of a business,* usually classified by nature of products sold but sometimes by geographical area where the firm produces or sells goods or by type of customers; sometimes called "line of business reporting." The accounting for segment income does not allocate *central corporate expenses* to the segments.

self-balancing. A set of records with equal *debits* and *credits* such as the *ledger* (but not individual accounts), the *balance sheet,* and a *fund* in nonprofit accounting.

self-check(ing) digit. A digit forming part of an account or code number, normally the last digit of the number, which is arithmetically derived from the other numbers of the code and is used to detect errors in transcribing the code number. For example, assume the last digit of the account number is the remainder after summing the preceding digits and dividing that sum by nine. Suppose the computer encounters the account numbers 7027261-7 and 9445229-7. The program can tell that something has gone wrong with the encoding of the second account number because the sum of the first seven digits is 35, whose remainder on division by 9 is 8, not 7. The first account number does not show such an error because the sum of the first seven digits is 25, whose remainder on division by 9 is, indeed, 7. The first account number may be in error, but the second surely is.

self-insurance. See *insurance.*

self-sustaining foreign operation. A foreign operation both financially and operationally independent of the reporting enterprise (owner) so that the owner's exposure to exchange-rate changes results only from the owner's net investment in the foreign entity.

selling and administrative expenses. *Expenses* not specifically identifiable with, or assigned to, production.

semifixed costs. *Costs* that increase with activity as a step function.

semivariable costs. *Costs* that increase strictly linearly with activity but that are positive at zero activity level. Royalty fees of 2 percent of sales are variable; royalty fees of $1,000 per year plus 2 percent of sales are semivariable.

senior securities. *Bonds* as opposed to *preferred stock; preferred stock* as opposed to *common stock*. The firm must meet the senior security claim against *earnings* or *assets* before meeting the claims of less-senior securities.

sensitivity analysis. A study of how the outcome of a decision-making process changes as one or more of the assumptions change.

sequential access. Computer-storage access in which the analyst can locate information only by a sequential search of the storage file. Compare *direct access.*

serial bonds. An *issue* of *bonds* that mature in part at one date, another part on another date, and so on. The various maturity dates usually occur at equally spaced intervals. Contrast with *term bonds.*

service basis of depreciation. *Production method.*

service bureau. A commercial data-processing center providing service to various customers.

service cost, (current) service cost. *Pension plan expenses incurred* during an *accounting period* for employment services performed during that period. Contrast with *prior service cost.* See *funded.*

service department. A department, such as the personnel or computer department, that provides services to other departments rather than direct work on a salable product. Contrast with *production department.* A firm must allocate costs of service departments whose services benefit manufacturing operations to *product costs* under *full absorption costing.*

service life. Period of expected usefulness of an asset; may differ from *depreciable life* for income tax purposes.

service potential. The future benefits that cause an item to be classified as an *asset.* Without service potential, an item has no future benefits, and accounting will not classify the item as an asset. *SFAC No. 6* suggests that the primary characteristic of service potential is the ability to generate future net cash inflows.

services. Useful work done by a person, a machine, or an organization. See *goods.*

setup. The time or costs required to prepare production equipment for doing a job.

SFAC. *Statement of Financial Accounting Concepts of the FASB.*

SFAS. *Statement of Financial Accounting Standards.* See *FASB.*

shadow price. An opportunity cost. A *linear programming* analysis provides as one of its outputs the potential value of having available more of the scarce resources that constrain the production process, for example, the value of having more time available on a machine tool critical to the production of two products. Common terminology refers to this value as the "shadow price" or the "dual value" of the scarce resource.

share. A unit of *stock* representing ownership in a corporation.

share premium. UK: *additional paid-in capital* or *capital contributed in excess of par value.*

shareholders' equity. *Proprietorship* or *owners' equity* of a corporation. Because *stock* means inventory in Australia, the UK, and Canada, their writers use the term "shareholders' equity" rather than the term "stockholders' equity."

short-run. The opposite of *long-run* or *long-term.*

short-term. Current; ordinarily, due within one year.

short-term liquidity risk. The risk that an *entity* will not have enough *cash* in the *short run* to pay its *debts.*

shrinkage. An excess of *inventory* shown on the *books* over actual physical quantities on hand; can result from theft or shoplifting as well as from evaporation or general wear and tear. Some accountants, in an attempt to downplay their own errors, use the term to mean record-keeping mistakes that they later must correct, with some embarrassment, and that result in material changes in reported income. One should not use the term "shrinkage" for the correction of mistakes because adequate terminology exists for describing mistakes.

shutdown cost. Those fixed costs that the firm continues to incur after it has ceased production; the costs of closing down a particular production facility.

sight draft. A demand for payment drawn by Person A to whom Person B owes cash. Person A presents the *draft* to Person B's (the debtor's) bank in expectation that Person B will authorize his or her bank to disburse the funds. Sellers often use such drafts when selling goods to a new customer in a different city. The seller is uncertain whether the buyer will pay the bill. The seller sends the *bill* of lading, or other evidence of ownership of the goods, along with a sight draft to the buyer's bank. Before the warehouse holding the goods can release them to the buyer, the buyer must instruct its bank to honor the sight draft by withdrawing funds from the buyer's account. Once the bank honors the sight draft, it hands to the buyer the bill of lading or other document evidencing ownership, and the goods become the property of the buyer.

significant influence. A firm will use the *equity method* of accounting for its *investment* in another when it has significant influence over the *investee company. GAAP* do not define this term, but give examples of it: representation on the *board of directors,* participation in policy making processes, *material* intercompany transactions, interchange of managerial personnel, and technological dependency. Ultimately, the accountant must judge whether the investor's influence is significant.

simple interest. *Interest* calculated on *principal* where interest earned during periods before maturity of the loan does not increase the principal amount earning interest for the subsequent periods and the lender cannot withdraw the funds before maturity. Interest = principal × interest rate × time, where the rate is a rate per period (typically a year) and time is expressed in units of that period. For example, if the *rate* is annual and the time is two months, then in the formula, use 2/12 for *time.* Simple interest is seldom used in economic calculations except for periods of less than one year and then only for computational convenience. Contrast with *compound interest.*

single-entry accounting. Accounting that is neither *self-balancing* nor *articulated.* That is, it does not rely on equal *debits* and *credits.* The firm makes no *journal entries* and must *plug* to derive *owners' equity* for the *balance sheet.*

single proprietorship. *Sole proprietorship.*

single-step. Said of an *income statement* in which *ordinary revenue* and *gain* items appear first, with their total. Then come all ordinary *expenses* and *losses,* with their total. The difference between these two totals, plus the effect of *income from discontinued operations* and *extra-ordinary items,* appears as *net income.* Contrast with *multiple-step* and see *proprietorship theory.*

sinking fund. *Assets* and their earnings earmarked for the retirement of bonds or other long-term obligations. Earnings of sinking fund investments become taxable income of the company.

sinking fund method of depreciation. Method in which the periodic charge is an equal amount each period so that the *future value* of the charges, considered as an *annuity,* will accumulate at the end of the depreciable life to an amount equal to the *acquisition cost* of the asset. The firm does not necessarily, or even usually, accumulate a *fund* of cash. Firms rarely use this method.

skeleton account. *T-account.*

slide. The name of the error made by a bookkeeper in recording the digits of a number correctly with the decimal point misplaced; for example, recording $123.40 as $1,234.00 or as $12.34. If the only errors in a *trial balance* result from one or more slides, then the difference between the sum of the *debits* and the sum of the *credits* will be divisible by nine. Not all such differences divisible by nine result from slides. See *transposition error.*

SMAC (Society of Management Accountants of Canada). The national association of accountants whose provincial associations engage in industrial and governmental accounting. The association undertakes research and administers an educational program and comprehensive examinations; those who pass qualify to be designated CMA (Certified Management Accountants), formerly called RIA (Registered Industrial Accountant).

SNC (société en nom collectif). France: a *partnership.*

soak-up method. The *equity method.*

Social Security taxes. Taxes levied by the federal government on both employers and employees to provide *funds* to pay retired persons (or their survivors) who are entitled to receive such payments, either because they paid Social Security taxes themselves or because Congress has declared them eligible. Unlike a *pension plan,* the Social Security system does not collect funds and invest them for many years. The tax collections in a given year pay primarily for benefits distributed that year. At any given time the system has a multitrillion-dollar unfunded obligation to current workers for their eventual retirement benefits. See *Old Age, Survivors, Disability, and (Hospital) Insurance.*

software. The programming aids, such as compilers, sort and report programs, and generators, that extend the capabilities of and simplify the use of the computer, as well as certain operating systems and other control programs. Compare *hardware.*

sole proprietorship. A firm in which all *owners' equity* belongs to one person.

solvent. Able to meet debts when due.

SOP. *Statement of Position* (of the *AcSEC* of the *AICPA*).

sound value. A phrase used mainly in appraisals of *fixed assets* to mean *fair market price* (*value*) or *replacement cost* in present condition.

source of funds. Any *transaction* that increases *cash* and *marketable securities* held as *current assets.*

sources and uses statement. *Statement of cash flows.*

SOYD. *Sum-of-the years'-digits depreciation.*

SP (société en participation). France: a silent *partnership* in which the managing partner acts for the partnership as an individual in transacting with others who need not know that the person represents a partnership.

special assessment. A compulsory levy made by a governmental unit on property to pay the costs of a specific improvement or service presumed not to benefit the general public but only the owners of the property so assessed; accounted for in a special assessment fund.

special journal. A *journal,* such as a sales journal or cash disbursements journal, to record *transactions* of a similar nature that occur frequently.

special purpose entity (vehicle). SPE (SPV). A term unknown by laymen until the Enron shambles of 2001. A legal entity—corporation or partnership or trust—with substantial owners' equity provided by investors other than the firm organizing the SPE. The independent owners must have significant risks and rewards of ownership. A parent firm, such as Enron, establishes the SPE to transfer assets and debt off its balance sheet. Some of Enron's SPE's appear not to have satisfied all the GAAP tests to be kept off the balance sheet. Many SPE's have a legitimate purpose. Consider, for example, a firm that wishes to sell its accounts receivable. It sells the receivables to a corporation in which others have provided owners' equity funding. The corporation runs the risks (or will reap the rewards) of collecting less (or more) from the receivables than the organizers of the SPE forecast.

special revenue debt. A governmental unit's debt backed only by revenues from specific sources, such as tolls from a bridge.

specific identification method. Method for valuing *ending inventory* and *cost of goods sold* by identifying actual units sold and remaining in inventory and summing the actual costs of those individual units; usually used for items with large unit values, such as precious jewelry, automobiles, and fur coats.

specific item sampling. Sampling in which the analyst selects particular items because of their nature, value, or method of recording. Compare *representative item sampling.*

specific price changes. Changes in the market prices of specific *goods* and *services.* Contrast with *general price-level changes.*

specific price index. A measure of the price of a specific good or service, or a small group of similar goods or services, at one time relative to the price during a base period. Contrast with *general price index.* See *dollar-value LIFO method.*

spending variance. In *standard cost systems,* the rate or *price variance* for *overhead costs.*

split. *Stock split.* Sometimes called "split-up."

split-off point. In accumulating and allocating costs for *joint products,* the point at which all costs are no longer *joint costs* but at which an analyst can identify costs associated with individual products or perhaps with a smaller number of *joint products.*

spoilage. See *abnormal spoilage* and *normal spoilage.*

spot price. The price of a commodity for delivery on the day of the price quotation. See *forward price* for contrast.

spreadsheet. For many years, a term that referred specifically to a *work sheet* organized like a *matrix* that provides a two-way classification of accounting data. The rows and columns both have labels, which are *account* titles. An entry in a row represents a *debit,* whereas an entry in a column represents a *credit.* Thus, the number "100" in the "cash" row and the "accounts receivable" column records an entry debiting cash and crediting accounts receivable for $100. A given row total indicates all debit entries to the account represented by that row, and a given column total indicates the sum of all credit entries to the account represented by the column. Since personal-computer software has become widespread, this term has come to refer to any file created by programs such as Lotus 1-2-3® and Microsoft Excel®. Such files have rows and columns, but they need not represent debits and credits. Moreover, they can have more than two dimensions.

squeeze. A term sometimes used for *plug.*

SSARS. *Statement on Standards for Accounting and Review Services.*

stabilized accounting. *Constant-dollar accounting.*

stable monetary unit assumption. In spite of *inflation,* which appears to be a way of life, the assumption that underlies historical cost/nominal-dollar accounting—namely that one can meaningfully add together current dollars and dollars of previous years. The assumption gives no specific recognition to changing values of the dollar in the usual *financial statements.* See *constant-dollar accounting.*

Staff Accounting Bulletin. An interpretation issued by the staff of the Chief Accountant of the *SEC* "suggesting" how the accountants should apply various *Accounting Series Releases* in practice. The suggestions are part of *GAAP.*

stakeholder. An individual or group, such as employees, suppliers, customers, and shareholders, who have an interest in the corporation's activities and outcomes.

standard cost. Anticipated *cost* of producing a unit of output; a predetermined cost to be assigned to products produced. Standard cost implies a norm—what costs should be. Budgeted cost implies a forecast—something likely, but not necessarily, a "should," as implied by a norm. Firms use standard costs as the benchmark for gauging good and bad performance. Although a firm may similarly use a budget, it need not. A budget may be a planning document, subject to changes whenever plans change, whereas standard costs usually change annually or when technology significantly changes or when costs of labor and materials significantly change.

standard costing. *Costing* based on *standard costs.*

standard costing system. *Product costing* using *standard costs* rather than actual costs. The firm may use either *full absorption* or *variable costing* principles.

standard error (of regression coefficients). A measure of the uncertainty about the magnitude of the estimated parameters of an equation fit with a *regression analysis.*

standard manufacturing overhead. *Overhead costs* expected to be incurred per unit of time and per unit produced.

standard price (rate). Unit price established for materials or labor used in *standard cost systems.*

standard quantity allowed. The direct material or direct labor (inputs) quantity that production should have used if it had produced the units of output in accordance with preset *standards.*

standby costs. A type of *capacity cost,* such as property taxes, incurred even if a firm shuts down operations completely. Contrast with *enabling costs.*

stated capital. Amount of capital contributed by shareholders; sometimes used to mean *legal capital.*

stated value. A term sometimes used for the *face amount of capital stock,* when the *board* has not designated a *par value.* Where there is stated value per share, capital *contributed in excess of stated value* may come into being.

statement of affairs. A *balance sheet* showing immediate *liquidation* amounts rather than *historical costs,* usually prepared when *insolvency* or *bankruptcy* is imminent. Such a statement specifically does not use the *going-concern assumption.*

statement of cash flows. A schedule of *cash receipts and payments,* classified by *investing, financing,* and *operating activities;* required by the *FASB* for all for-profit companies. Companies may report operating activities with either the direct method (which shows only receipts and payments of cash) or the indirect method (which starts with *net income* and shows adjustments for *revenues* not currently producing cash and for *expenses* not currently using cash). "Cash" includes cash equivalents such as Treasury bills, commercial paper, and *marketable securities* held as *current assets.* This is sometimes called the "funds statement." Before 1987, the FASB required the presentation of a similar statement called the *statement of changes in financial position,* which tended to emphasize *working capital,* not cash.

statement of changes in financial position. As defined by *APB Opinion No. 19,* a statement that explains the changes in *working capital* (or cash) balances during a period and shows the changes in the working capital (or cash) accounts themselves. The *statement of cash flows* has replaced this statement.

statement of charge and discharge. A financial statement, showing *net assets* or *income,* drawn up by an executor or administrator, to account for receipts and dispositions of cash or other assets in an estate or trust.

Statement of Financial Accounting Concepts (SFAC). One of a series of *FASB* publications in its *conceptual framework* for *financial accounting* and reporting. Such statements set forth objectives and fundamentals to be the basis for specific financial accounting and reporting standards.

Statement of Financial Accounting Standards (SFAS). See *FASB*.

statement of financial position. *Balance sheet.*

Statement of Position (SOP). A recommendation, on an emerging accounting problem, issued by the *AcSEC* of the *AICPA*. The AICPA's Code of Professional Ethics specifically states that *CPAs* need not treat *SOPs* as they do rules from the *FASB*, but a CPA would be wary of departing from the recommendations of an *SOP*.

statement of retained earnings (income). A statement that reconciles the beginning-of-period and the end-of-period balances in the *retained earnings* account. It shows the effects of *earnings, dividend declarations,* and *prior-period adjustments*.

statement of significant accounting policies (principles). A summary of the significant *accounting principles* used in compiling an *annual report;* required by *APB Opinion No. 22*. This summary may be a separate exhibit or the first *note* to the financial statements.

Statement on Auditing Standards (SAS). A series addressing specific auditing standards and procedures. *No. 1* (1973) of this series codifies all statements on auditing standards previously promulgated by the *AICPA*.

Statement on Standards for Accounting and Review Services (SSARS). Pronouncements issued by the *AICPA* on unaudited *financial statements* and unaudited financial information of nonpublic entities.

static budget. *Fixed budget.* Budget developed for a set level of the driving variable, such as production or sales, which the analyst does not change if the actual level deviates from the level set at the outset of the analysis.

status quo. Events or cost incurrences that will happen or that a firm expects to happen in the absence of taking some contemplated action.

statutory tax rate. The tax rate specified in the *income tax* law for each type of income (for example, *ordinary income, capital gain or loss*).

step allocation method. *Step-down method.*

step cost. *Semifixed cost.*

step-down method. In *allocating service department* costs, a method that starts by allocating one service department's costs to *production departments* and to all other service departments. Then the firm allocates a second service department's costs, including costs allocated from the first, to production departments and to all other service departments except the first one. In this fashion, a firm may allocate all service departments costs, including previous allocations, to production departments and to those service departments whose costs it has not yet allocated.

step(ped) cost. *Semifixed cost.*

sterilized allocation. Desirable characteristics of cost allocation methods. Optimal decisions result from considering *incremental costs* only. Optimal decisions never require *allocations* of *joint* or *common costs*. A "sterilized allocation" causes the optimal decision choice not to differ from the one that occurs when the accountant does not allocate joint or common costs "sterilized" with respect to that decision. Arthur L. Thomas first used the term in this context. Because *absorption costing* requires that product costs absorb all manufacturing costs and because some allocations can lead to bad decisions, Thomas (and we) advocate that the analyst choose a sterilized allocation scheme that will not alter the otherwise optimal decision. No single allocation scheme is always sterilized with respect to all decisions. Thus, Thomas (and we) advocate that decisions be made on the basis of incremental costs before any allocations.

stewardship. Principle by which management is accountable for an *entity's* resources, for their efficient use, and for protecting them from adverse impact. Some theorists believe that accounting has as a primary goal aiding users of *financial statements* in their assessment of management's performance in stewardship.

stock. A measure of the amount of something on hand at a specific time. In this sense, contrast with *flow.* See *inventory* and *capital stock.*

stock appreciation rights. An employer's promise to pay to the employee an amount of *cash* on a certain future date, with the amount of cash being the difference between the *market value* of a specified number of *shares* of stock in the employer's company on the given future date and some base price set on the date the rights are granted. Firms sometimes use this form of compensation because changes in tax laws in recent years have made *stock options* relatively less attractive. *GAAP* compute compensation based on the difference between the market value of the shares and the base price set at the time of the grant.

stock dividend. A so-called *dividend* in which the firm distributes additional *shares* of *capital stock* without cash payments to existing shareholders. It results in a *debit* to *retained earnings* in the amount of the market value of the shares issued and a *credit* to *capital stock* accounts. Firms ordinarily use stock dividends to indicate that they have permanently reinvested earnings in the business. Contrast with a *stock split*, which requires no entry in the capital stock accounts other than a notation that the *par* or *stated value* per share has changed.

stock option. The right to purchase or sell a specified number of shares of *stock* for a specified price at specified times. Employee stock options are purchase rights granted by a corporation to employees, a form of compensation. Traded stock options are *derivative* securities, rights created and traded by investors, independent of the corporation whose stock is optioned. Contrast with *warrant*.

stock right. See *right.*

stock split(-up). Increase in the number of common shares outstanding resulting from the issuance of additional shares to existing shareholders without additional capital contributions by them. Does not increase the total *value* (or *stated value*) of *common shares* outstanding because the *board* reduces the par (or stated) value per share in inverse proportion. A three-for-one stock split reduces par (or stated) value per share to one-third of its former amount. A stock split usually implies a distribution that increases the number of shares outstanding by 20 percent or more. Compare with *stock dividend*.

stock subscriptions. See *subscription* and *subscribed stock.*

stock warrant. See *warrant.*

stockholders' equity. See *shareholders' equity.*

stockout. Occurs when a firm needs a unit of *inventory* to use in production or to sell to a customer but has none available.

stockout costs. *Contribution margin* or other measure of *profits* not earned because a seller has run out of *inventory* and cannot fill a customer's order. A firm may incur an extra cost because of delay in filling an order.

stores. *Raw materials,* parts, and supplies.

straight-debt value. An estimate of the *market value* of a *convertible bond* if the bond did not contain a conversion privilege.

straight-line depreciation. Method in which, if the *depreciable life* is *n* periods, the periodic *depreciation* charge is 1/*n* of the *depreciable cost;* results in equal periodic charges. Accountants sometimes call it "straight-time depreciation."

strategic plan. A statement of the method for achieving an organization's goals.

stratified sampling. In choosing a *sample,* a method in which the investigator first divides the entire *population* into relatively homogeneous subgroups (strata) and then selects random samples from these subgroups.

street security. A stock certificate in immediately transferable form, most commonly because the issuing firm has registered it in the name of the broker, who has endorsed it with "payee" left blank.

Subchapter S corporation. A firm legally organized as a *corporation* but taxed as if it were a *partnership.* Tax terminology calls the corporations paying their own income taxes *C corporations.*

subject to. In an *auditor's report,* qualifications usually caused by a *material* uncertainty in the valuation of an item, such as future promised payments from a foreign government or outcome of pending litigation.

subordinated. *Debt* whose claim on income or assets has lower priority than claims of other debt.

subscribed stock. A *shareholders' equity* account showing the capital that the firm will receive as soon as the share-purchaser pays the subscription price. A subscription is a legal contract, so once the share-purchaser signs it, the firm makes an entry *debiting* an *owners' equity contra account* and *crediting* subscribed stock.

subscription. Agreement to buy a *security* or to purchase periodicals, such as magazines.

subsequent events. *Poststatement events.*

subsidiary. A company in which another company owns more than 50 percent of the voting shares.

subsidiary ledger. The *ledger* that contains the detailed accounts whose total appears in a *controlling account* of the *general ledger.*

subsidiary (ledger) accounts. The *accounts* in a *subsidiary ledger.*

successful efforts costing. In petroleum accounting, the *capitalization* of the drilling costs of only those wells that contain gas or oil. See *reserve recognition accounting* for an example.

summary annual report (SAR). Condensed financial statements distributed in lieu of the usual *annual report.*

Since 1987, the *SEC* has allowed firms to include such statements in the annual report to shareholders as long as the firm includes full, detailed statements in SEC filings and in *proxy* materials sent to shareholders.

summary of significant accounting principles. *Statement of significant accounting policies (principles).*

sum-of-the-years'-digits depreciation (SYD, SOYD). An *accelerated depreciation* method for an asset with *depreciable life* of *n* years where the charge in period *i* ($i = 1, \ldots, n$) is the fraction $(n + 1 - i)/[n(n + 1)/2]$ of the *depreciable cost.* If an asset has a depreciable cost of $15,000 and a five-year depreciable life, for example, the depreciation charges would be $5,000 (= 5/15 × $15,000) in the first year, $4,000 in the second, $3,000 in the third, $2,000 in the fourth, and $1,000 in the fifth. The name derives from the fact that the denominator in the fraction is the sum of the digits 1 through *n*.

sunk cost. Past *costs* that current and future decisions cannot affect and, hence, that are irrelevant for decision making aside from *income tax* effects. Contrast with *incremental costs* and *imputed costs.* For example, the *acquisition cost* of machinery is irrelevant to a decision of whether to scrap the machinery. The current *exit value* of the machinery is the *opportunity cost* of continuing to own it, and the cost of, say, the electricity to run the machinery is an incremental cost of its operation. Sunk costs become relevant for decision making when the analysis requires taking *income taxes* (*gain* or *loss* on disposal of asset) into account, since the cash payment for income taxes depends on the tax basis of the asset. Avoid this term in careful writing because it is ambiguous. Consider, for example, a machine costing $100,000 with current *salvage* value of $20,000. Some (including us) would say that $100,000 (the *gross* amount) is "sunk"; others would say that only $80,000 (the *net* amount) is "sunk."

supplementary statements (schedules). Statements (schedules) in addition to the four basic *financial statements* (*balance sheet, income statement, statement of cash flows,* and the *statement of retained earnings*).

surplus. A word once used but now considered poor terminology; prefaced by "earned" to mean *retained earnings* and prefaced by "capital" to mean *capital contributed in excess of par (or stated) value.*

surplus reserves. *Appropriated retained earnings.* A phrase with nothing to recommend it: of all the words in accounting, *reserve* is the most objectionable, and *surplus* is the second-most objectionable.

suspense account. A *temporary account* used to record part of a transaction before final analysis of that transaction. For example, if a business regularly classifies all sales into a dozen or more different categories but wants to deposit the proceeds of cash sales every day, it may credit a sales suspense account pending detailed classification of all sales into Durable Goods Sales, Women's Clothing Sales, Men's Clothing Sales, Housewares Sales, and so on.

sustainable income. The part of *distributable income* (computed from *current cost* data) that the firm can expect to earn in the next accounting period if it continues operations at the same levels as were maintained during the current period. *Income from discontinued operations,* for example, may be distributable but not sustainable.

swap. A currency swap is a financial instrument in which the holder promises to pay to (or receive from) the *counterparty* the difference between *debt* denominated in one currency (such as U.S. dollars) and the payments on debt denominated in another currency (such as German marks). An interest-rate swap typically obligates the party and counterparty to exchange the difference between fixed- and floating-rate interest payments on otherwise similar loans.

S-X. See *Regulation S-X.*

SYD. *Sum-of-the-years'-digits depreciation.*

T

T-account. Account form shaped like the letter T with the title above the horizontal line. *Debits* appear on the left of the vertical line, *credits* on the right.

take-home pay. The amount of a paycheck; earned wages or *salary* reduced by deductions for *income taxes, Social Security taxes,* contributions to fringe-benefit plans, union dues, and so on. Take-home pay might be as little as half of earned compensation.

take-or-pay contract. As defined by *SFAS No. 47,* a purchaser-seller agreement that provides for the purchaser to pay specified amounts periodically in return for products or services. The purchaser must make specified minimum payments even if it does not take delivery of the contracted products or services.

taking a bath. To incur a large loss. See *big bath.*

tangible. Having physical form. Accounting has never satisfactorily defined the distinction between tangible and intangible assets. Typically, accountants define intangibles by giving an exhaustive list, and everything not on the list is defined as tangible. See *intangible asset* for such a list.

target cost. *Standard cost.* Sometimes, target price less expected profit margin.

target price. Selling price based on customers' value in use of a good or service, constrained by competitors' prices of similar items.

tax. A nonpenal, but compulsory, charge levied by a government on income, consumption, wealth, or other basis, for the benefit of all those governed. The term does not include fines or specific charges for benefits accruing only to those paying the charges, such as licenses, permits, special assessments, admission fees, and tolls.

tax allocation: interperiod. See *deferred income tax liability.*

tax allocation: intrastatement. The showing of income tax effects on *extraordinary items, income from discontinued operations,* and *prior-period adjustments,* along with these items, separately from income taxes on other income. See *net-of-tax reporting.*

tax avoidance. See *tax shelter* and *loophole.*

tax basis of assets and liabilities. A concept important for applying *SFAS No. 109* on *deferred income taxes.* Two *assets* will generally have different *book values* if the firm paid different amounts for them, *amortizes* them on a different schedule, or both. Similarly a single asset will generally have a book value different from what it will have for tax purposes if the firm recorded different

acquisition amounts for the asset for book and for tax purposes, amortizes it differently for book and for tax purposes, or both. The difference between financial book value and income tax basis becomes important in computing deferred income tax amounts. The adjusted cost in the financial records is the "book basis," and the adjusted amount in the tax records is the "tax basis." Differences between book and tax basis can arise for *liabilities* as well as for assets.

tax credit. A subtraction from taxes otherwise payable. Contrast with *tax deduction.*

tax deduction. A subtraction from *revenues* and *gains* to arrive at taxable income. Tax deductions differ technically from tax *exemptions,* but both reduce gross income in computing taxable income. Both differ from *tax credits,* which reduce the computed tax itself in computing taxes payable. If the tax rate is the fraction t of pretax income, then a *tax credit* of \$1 is worth \$1/t of *tax deductions.* Deductions appear on tax returns, *expenses* appear on *income statements.*

tax evasion. The fraudulent understatement of taxable revenues or overstatement of deductions and expenses or both. Contrast with *tax shelter* and *loophole.*

tax-exempts. See *municipal bonds.*

tax shelter. The legal avoidance of, or reduction in, *income taxes* resulting from a careful reading of the complex income-tax regulations and the subsequent rearrangement of financial affairs to take advantage of the regulations. Often writers use the term pejoratively, but the courts have long held that a taxpayer has no obligation to pay taxes any larger than the legal minimum. If the public concludes that a given tax shelter is "unfair," then Congress can, and has, changed the laws and regulations. The term is sometimes used to refer to the investment that permits tax avoidance. See *loophole.*

tax shield. The amount of an *expense,* such as *depreciation,* that reduces taxable income but does not require *working capital.* Sometimes this term includes expenses that reduce taxable income and use working capital. A depreciation deduction (or *R&D expense* in the expanded sense) of \$10,000 provides a tax shield of \$3,700 when the marginal tax rate is 37 percent.

taxable income. *Income* computed according to *IRS* regulations and subject to *income taxes.* Contrast with income, net income, income before taxes (in the *income statement*), and *comprehensive income* (a *financial reporting* concept). Use the term "pretax income" to refer to income before taxes on the income statement in financial reports.

tax-transfer lease. One form of *capital lease.* Congress has in the past provided business with an incentive to invest in qualifying *plant and equipment* by granting an *investment credit,* which, though it occurs as a reduction in *income taxes* otherwise payable, effectively reduces the purchase price of the assets. Similarly, Congress continues to grant an incentive to acquire such assets by allowing the *Modified Accelerated Cost Recovery System* (*MACRS,* form of unusually *accelerated depreciation*). Accelerated depreciation for tax purposes allows a reduction of taxes paid in the early years of an asset's life, providing the firm with an increased *net present value* of *cash flows.* The *IRS* administers both of these incentives through the income tax laws, rather than paying an outright cash payment. A business with no taxable income in many cases had difficulty reaping the benefits of the investment credit or of accelerated depreciation because Congress had not provided for tax refunds to those who acquire qualifying assets but who have no taxable income. In principle, a company without taxable income could lease from another firm with taxable income an asset that it would otherwise purchase. The second firm acquires the asset, gets the tax-reduction benefits from the acquisition, and becomes a lessor, leasing the asset (presumably at a lower price reflecting its own costs lowered by the tax reductions) to the unprofitable company. Before 1981, tax laws discouraged such leases. That is, although firms could enter into such leases, they could not legally transfer the tax benefits. Under certain restrictive conditions, the tax law now allows a profitable firm to earn tax credits and take deductions while leasing to the firm without tax liability in such leases. These are sometimes called "safe-harbor leases."

Technical Bulletin. The *FASB* has authorized its staff to issue bulletins to provide guidance on financial accounting and reporting problems. Although the FASB does not formally approve the contents of the bulletins, their contents are part of *GAAP.*

technology. The sum of a firm's technical *trade secrets* and *know-how,* as distinct from its *patents.*

temporary account. *Account* that does not appear on the *balance sheet; revenue* and *expense* accounts, their *adjuncts* and *contras, production cost accounts, dividend distribution accounts,* and purchases-related accounts (which close to the various inventories); sometimes called a "nominal account."

temporary difference. According to the *SFAS No. 109* (1992) definition: "A difference between the tax basis of an asset or liability and its reported amount in the financial statements that will result in taxable or deductible amounts in future years." Temporary differences include *timing differences* and differences between *taxable income* and pretax income caused by different cost bases for assets. For example, a plant asset might have a cost of $10,000 for financial reporting but a basis of $7,000 for income tax purposes. This temporary difference might arise because the firm has used an accelerated depreciation method for tax but straight-line for book, or the firm may have purchased the asset in a transaction in which the fair value of the asset exceeded its tax basis. Both situations create a temporary difference.

temporary investments. Investments in *marketable securities* that the owner intends to sell within a short time, usually one year, and hence classifies as *current assets.*

10-K. The name of the annual report that the *SEC* requires of nearly all publicly held corporations.

term bonds. A *bond issue* whose component bonds all mature at the same time. Contrast with *serial bonds.*

term loan. A loan with a *maturity* date, as opposed to a demand loan, which is due whenever the lender requests payment. In practice, bankers and auditors use this phrase only for loans for a year or more.

term structure. A phrase with different meanings in *accounting* and *financial economics.* In accounting, it refers to the pattern of times that must elapse before *assets* turn into, or produce, *cash* and the pattern of times that must elapse before *liabilities* require cash. In financial economics, the phrase refers to the pattern of interest rates as a function of the time that elapses for loans to come due. For example, if six-month loans cost 6 percent per year and 10-year loans cost 9 percent per year, this is called a "normal" term structure because the longer-term loan carries a higher rate. If the six-month loan costs 9 percent per year and the 10-year loan costs 6 percent per year, the term structure is said to be "inverted." See *yield curve.*

terms of sale. The conditions governing payment for a sale. For example, the terms *2/10, n(et)/30* mean that if the purchaser makes payment within 10 days of the invoice date, it can take a *discount* of 2 percent from *invoice* price; the purchaser must pay the invoice amount, in any event, within 30 days, or it becomes overdue.

theory of constraints (TOC). Concept of improving operations by identifying and reducing bottlenecks in process flows.

thin capitalization. A state of having a high *debt-equity ratio.* Under income tax legislation, the term has a special meaning.

throughput contract. As defined by *SFAS No. 47,* an agreement that is signed by a shipper (processor) and by the owner of a transportation facility (such as an oil or natural gas pipeline or a ship) or a manufacturing facility and that provides for the shipper (processor) to pay specified amounts periodically in return for the transportation (processing) of a product. The shipper (processor) must make cash payments even if it does not ship (process) the contracted quantities.

throughput contribution. Sales dollars minus the sum of all short-run variable costs.

tickler file. A collection of *vouchers* or other memoranda arranged chronologically to remind the person in charge of certain duties to make payments (or to do other tasks) as scheduled.

time-adjusted rate of return. *Internal rate of return.*

time cost. *Period cost.*

time deposit. Cash in bank earning interest. Contrast with *demand deposit.*

time value element (of stock options). All else equal, the longer one has to exercise an *option,* the more valuable that option. This term refers to the part of an option's value on a date caused by the option's not expiring until sometime after that date. All else equal, the more volatile the *market price* of the *security* receivable on exercise, the more valuable is this element.

time-series analysis. See *cross-section analysis* for definition and contrast.

times-interest (charges) earned. Ratio of pretax *income* plus *interest* charges to interest charges. See *ratio.*

timing difference. The major type of *temporary difference* between taxable income and pretax income reported to shareholders; reverses in a subsequent period and requires an entry in the *deferred income tax* account; for example, the use of *accelerated depreciation* for tax returns and *straight-line depreciation* for financial reporting. Contrast with *permanent difference.*

Toronto Stock Exchange (TSE). A public market where various corporate securities trade.

total assets turnover. *Sales* divided by average total *assets*.

total quality management (TQM). Concept of organizing a company to excel in all its activities in order to increase the quality of products and services.

traceable cost. A *cost* that a firm can identify with or assign to a specific product. Contrast with a *joint cost*.

trade acceptance. A *draft* that a seller presents for signature (acceptance) to the buyer at the time it sells goods. The draft then becomes the equivalent of a *note receivable* of the seller and a *note payable* of the buyer.

trade credit. Occurs when one business allows another to buy from it in return for a promise to pay later. Contrast with "consumer credit," which occurs when a business extends a retail customer the privilege of paying later.

trade discount. A *list price discount* offered to all customers of a given type. Contrast with a *discount* offered for prompt payment and with *quantity discount*.

trade-in. Acquiring a new *asset* in exchange for a used one and perhaps additional cash. See *boot* and *trade-in transaction*.

trade-in transaction. The accounting for a trade-in; depends on whether the firm receives an asset "similar" to (and used in the same line of business as) the asset traded in and whether the accounting is for *financial statements* or for *income tax* returns. Assume that an old asset cost $5,000, has $3,000 of *accumulated depreciation* (after recording depreciation to the date of the trade-in), and hence has a *book value* of $2,000. The old asset appears to have a market value of $1,500, according to price quotations in used asset markets. The firm trades in the old asset on a new asset with a list price of $10,000. The firm gives up the old asset and $5,500 cash (*boot*) for the new asset. The generic entry for the trade-in transaction is as follows:

New Asset	A		
Accumulated Depreciation (Old Asset)	3,000		
Adjustment on Exchange of Asset	B or	B	
Old Asset		5,000	
Cash		5,500	

(1) The *list price* method of accounting for trade-ins rests on the assumption that the list price of the new asset closely approximates its market value. The firm records the new asset at its list price (A = $10,000 in the example); B is a *plug* (= $2,500 credit in the example). If B requires a *debit* plug, the Adjustment on Exchange of Asset is a *loss;* if B requires a *credit* plug (as in the example), the adjustment is a *gain*.

(2) Another theoretically sound method of accounting for trade-ins rests on the assumption that the price quotation from used-asset markets gives a market value of the old asset that is a more reliable measure than the market value of the new asset determined by list price. This method uses the *fair market price (value)* of the old asset, $1,500 in the example, to determine B (= $2,000 book value − $1,500 assumed proceeds on disposition = $500 debit or loss). The exchange results in a loss if the book value of the old asset exceeds its market value and in a gain if the market value exceeds the book value. The firm records the new asset on the books by plugging for A (= $7,000 in the example).

(3) For income tax reporting, the taxpayer must recognize neither gain nor loss on the trade-in. Thus the taxpayer records the new asset for tax purposes by assuming B is zero and plugging for A (= $7,500 in the example). In practice, firms that want to recognize the loss currently will sell the old asset directly, rather than trading it in, and acquire the new asset entirely for cash.

(4) *Generally accepted accounting principles (APB Opinion No. 29)* require a variant of these methods. The basic method is (1) or (2), depending on whether the list price of the new asset (1) or the quotation of the old asset's market value (2) provides the more reliable indication of market value. If the basic method requires a debit entry, or loss, for the Adjustment on Exchange of Asset, then the firm records the trade-in as in (1) or (2) and recognizes the full amount of the loss currently. If, however, the basic method requires a credit entry, or gain, for the Adjustment on Exchange of Asset, then the firm recognizes the gain currently if the old asset and the new asset are not "similar." If the assets are similar and the party trading in receives no cash, then it recognizes no gain and the treatment resembles that in (3); that is B = 0, plug for A. If the assets are similar and the firm trading in receives cash—a rare case—then it recognizes a portion of the gain currently. The portion of the gain recognized currently is the fraction cash received/ fair market value of total consideration received. (When the firm uses the list price method, (1), it assumes that the market value of the old asset is the list price of the new asset plus the amount of cash received by the party trading in.)

A summary of the results of applying *GAAP* to the example follows.

More Reliable Information as to Fair Market Value	Old Asset Compared with New Asset	
	Similar	Not Similar
New Asset List Price	A = $7,500 B = 0	A = $10,000 B = 2,500 gain
Old Asset Market Price	A = $7,000 B = 500 loss	A = $ 7,000 B = 500 loss

trade payables (receivables). *Payables (receivables)* arising in the ordinary course of business transactions. Most *accounts payable (receivable)* are of this kind.

trade secret. Technical or business information such as formulas, recipes, computer programs, and marketing data not generally known by competitors and maintained by the firm as a secret; theoretically capable of having an indefinite, finite life. A famous example is the secret process for Coca-Cola® (a registered *trademark* of the company). Compare with *know-how*. The firm will capitalize this intangible asset only if purchased and then will amortize it over a period not to exceed 40 years. If the firm develops the intangible internally, the firm will *expense* the costs as incurred and show no asset.

trademark. A distinctive word or symbol that is affixed to a product, its package, or its dispenser and that uniquely identifies the firm's products and services. See *trademark right*.

trademark right. The right to exclude competitors in sales or advertising from using words or symbols that are so similar to the firm's *trademarks* as possibly to confuse consumers. Trademark rights last as long as the firm continues to use the trademarks in question. In the United States, trademark rights arise from use and not from government registration. They therefore have a legal life independent of the life of a registration. Registrations last 20 years, and the holder may renew them as long as the holder uses the trademark. Although a trademark right might have an indefinite life, *GAAP* require amortization over some estimate of its life, not to exceed 40 years. Under *SFAS No. 2*, the firm must *expense* internally developed trademark rights.

trading on the equity. Said of a firm engaging in *debt financing;* frequently said of a firm doing so to a degree considered abnormal for a firm of its kind. *Leverage*.

trading securities. *Marketable securities* that a firm holds and expects to sell within a relatively short time; a classification important in *SFAS No. 115*, which requires the owner to carry marketable equity securities on the balance sheet at market value, not at cost. Contrast with *available for sale, securities* and *held-to-maturity securities*. Under *SFAS No. 115*, the balance sheet reports trading securities at market value on the balance sheet date, and the income statement reports *holding gains and losses* on trading securities. When the firm sells the securities, it reports realized gain or loss as the difference between the selling price and the market value at the last balance sheet date.

transaction. A *transfer* (of more than promises—see *executory contract*) between the accounting *entity* and another party or parties.

transfer. Under *SFAC No. 6*, consists of two types: "reciprocal" and "nonreciprocal." In a reciprocal transfer, or "exchange," the entity both receives and sacrifices. In a nonreciprocal transfer, the entity sacrifices but does not receive (examples include gifts, distributions to owners) or receives but does not sacrifice (investment by owner in entity). *SFAC No. 6* suggests that the term "internal transfer" is self-contradictory and that writers should use the term "internal event" instead.

transfer agent. Usually a bank or trust company designated by a corporation to make legal transfers of *stock* (*bonds*) and, perhaps, to pay *dividends* (*coupons*).

transfer price. A substitute for a *market,* or *arm's-length, price* used in *profit,* or *responsibility center, accounting* when one segment of the business "sells" to another segment. Incentives of profit center managers will not coincide with the best interests of the entire business unless a firm sets transfer prices properly.

transfer-pricing problem. The problem of setting *transfer prices* so that both buyer and seller have *goal congruence* with respect to the parent organization's goals.

translation adjustment. The effect of *exchange-rate* changes caused by converting the value of a net investment denominated in a *foreign currency* to the entity's reporting currency. *SFAS No. 52* requires firms to translate their net investment in relatively self-contained foreign operations at the *balance sheet* date. Year-to-year changes in value caused by exchange-rate changes accumulate in an *owners' equity* account, sometimes called the "cumulative translation adjustment."

translation gain (or loss). *Foreign exchange gain (or loss)*.

transportation-in. *Freight-in*.

transposition error. An error in record keeping resulting from reversing the order of digits in a number, such as recording "32" for "23." If the only errors in a *trial balance* result from one or more transposition errors, then the difference between the sum of the *debits* and the sum of the *credits* will be divisible by nine. Not all such differences result from transposition errors. See *slide*.

treasurer. The financial officer responsible for managing cash and raising funds.

treasury bond. A bond issued by a corporation and then reacquired. Such bonds are treated as retired when reacquired, and an *extraordinary gain or loss* on reacquisition is recognized. This term also refers to a *bond* issued by the U.S. Treasury Department.

treasury shares. *Capital stock* issued and then reacquired by the corporation. Such reacquisitions result in a reduction of *shareholders' equity* and usually appear on the balance sheet as contra to shareholders' equity. Accounting recognizes neither *gain* nor *loss* on transactions involving treasury stock. The accounting debits (if positive) or credits (if negative) any difference between the amounts paid and received for treasury stock transactions to *additional paid-in capital*. See *cost method* and *par value method*.

treasury stock. *Treasury shares*.

trial balance. A two-column listing of *account balances*. The left-hand column shows all accounts with *debit* balances and their total. The right-hand column shows all accounts with *credit* balances and their total. The two totals should be equal. Accountants compute trial balances as a partial check of the arithmetic accuracy of the entries previously made. See *adjusted, preclosing, post-closing, unadjusted trial balance, plug, slide,* and *transposition error*.

troubled debt restructuring. As defined in *SFAS No. 15*, a concession (changing of the terms of a *debt*) that is granted by a *creditor* for economic or legal reasons related to the *debtor's* financial difficulty and that the creditor would not otherwise consider.

TSE. *Toronto Stock Exchange*.

t-statistic. For an estimated *regression* coefficient, the estimated coefficient divided by the *standard error* of the estimate.

turnover. The number of times that *assets,* such as *inventory* or *accounts receivable,* are replaced on average during the period. Accounts receivable turnover, for example, is total sales on account for a period divided by the average accounts receivable balance for the period. See *ratio*. In the UK, "turnover" means *sales*.

turnover of plant and equipment. See *ratio*.

t-value. In *regression analysis,* the ratio of an estimated regression coefficient divided by its *standard error.*

20-F. Form required by the *SEC* for foreign companies issuing or trading their securities in the United States. This form reconciles the foreign accounting amounts resulting from using foreign *GAAP* to amounts resulting from using U.S. GAAP.

two T-account method. A method for computing either (1) *foreign-exchange gains and losses* or (2) *monetary gains* or *losses* for *constant-dollar accounting statements.* The left-hand *T-account* shows actual net balances of *monetary items,* and the right-hand T-account shows implied (common) dollar amounts.

2/10, n(et)/30. See *terms of sale.*

U

unadjusted trial balance. *Trial balance* taken before the accountant makes *adjusting* and *closing entries* at the end of the period.

unappropriated retained earnings. *Retained earnings* not appropriated and therefore against which the *board* can declare *dividends* in the absence of retained earnings restrictions. See *restricted retained earnings.*

unavoidable cost. A *cost* that is not an *avoidable cost.*

uncertainty. See *risk* for definition and contrast.

uncollectible account. An *account receivable* that the *debtor* will not pay. If the firm uses the preferable *allowance method,* the entry on judging a specific account to be uncollectible *debits* the allowance for uncollectible accounts and *credits* the specific account receivable. See *bad debt expense* and *sales contra, estimated uncollectibles.*

unconsolidated subsidiary. A *subsidiary* not consolidated and, hence, not accounted for in the *equity method.*

uncontrollable cost. The opposite of *controllable cost.*

underapplied (underabsorbed) overhead. An excess of actual *overhead costs* for a period over costs applied, or charged, to products produced during the period; a *debit balance* remaining in an overhead account after the accounting assigns overhead to product.

underlying document. The record, memorandum, *voucher,* or other signal that is the authority for making an *entry* into a *journal.*

underwriter. One who agrees to purchase an entire *security issue* for a specified price, usually for resale to others.

undistributed earnings. *Retained earnings.* Typically, this term refers to that amount retained for a given year.

unearned income (revenue). *Advances from customers;* strictly speaking, a contradiction in terms because the terms "income" and "revenue" mean earned.

unemployment tax. See *FUTA.*

unencumbered appropriation. In governmental accounting, portion of an *appropriation* not yet spent or encumbered.

unexpired cost. An *asset.*

unfavorable variance. In *standard cost* accounting, an excess of expected revenue over actual revenue or an excess of actual cost over standard cost.

unfunded. Not *funded.* An obligation or *liability,* usually for *pension costs,* exists, but no *funds* have been set aside to discharge the obligation or liability.

Uniform Partnership Act. A model law, enacted by many states, to govern the relations between partners when the *partnership* agreement fails to specify the agreed-upon treatment.

unissued capital stock. *Stock* authorized but not yet issued.

uniting-of-interests method. The IASB's term for the *pooling-of-interests method.* The IASB allows uniting of interests only when the merging firms are roughly equal in size and the shareholders retain substantially the same, relative to each other, voting rights and interests in the combined entity after the combination as before.

units-of-production method. The *production method of depreciation.*

unlimited liability. The legal obligation of *general partners* or the sole proprietor for all debts of the *partnership* or *sole proprietorship.*

unqualified opinion. See *auditor's report.*

unrealized appreciation. An *unrealized holding gain;* frequently used in the context of *marketable securities.*

unrealized gain (loss) on marketable securities. An *income statement account* title for the amount of *gain (loss)* during the current period on the portfolio of *marketable securities* held as *trading securities. SFAS No. 115* requires the firm to recognize, in the income statement, gains and losses caused by changes in market values, even though the firm has not yet *realized* them.

unrealized gross margin (profit). A *contra account* to *installment accounts receivable* used with the *installment method* of revenue recognition; shows the amount of profit that the firm will eventually realize when it collects the receivable. Some accountants show this account as a *liability.*

unrealized holding gain. See *inventory profit* for the definition and an example.

unrecovered cost. *Book value* of an *asset.*

unused capacity. The difference between resources supplied and resources used.

usage variance. *Efficiency variance.*

use of funds. Any transaction that reduces funds (however "funds" is defined).

useful life. *Service life.*

V

valuation account. A *contra account* or *adjunct account.* When the firm reports *accounts receivable* at expected collectible amounts, it will credit any expected uncollectible amounts to the *allowance for uncollectibles,* a valuation account. In this way, the firm can show both the gross receivables amount and the amount it expects to collect. *SFAC No. 6* says a valuation account is "a separate item that reduces and increases the carrying amount" of an asset (or liability). The accounts are part of the related assets (or liabilities) and are not assets (or liabilities) in their own right.

value. Monetary worth. This term is usually so vague that you should not use it without a modifying adjective unless most people would agree on the amount. Do not confuse with cost. See *fair market price (value), entry value,* and *exit value.*

value added. *Cost* of a product or *work-in-process* minus the cost of the material purchased for the product or work-in-process.

value-added activity. Any activity that increases the usefulness to a customer of a product or service.

value chain. The set of business functions that increase the usefulness to the customer of a product or service; typically including research and development, design of products and services, production, marketing, distribution, and customer service.

value engineering. An evaluation of the activities in the value chain to reduce costs.

value variance. *Price variance.*

variable annuity. An *annuity* whose periodic payments depend on some uncertain outcome, such as stock market prices.

variable budget. *Flexible budget.*

variable costing. In allocating costs, a method that assigns only *variable manufacturing costs* to products and treats *fixed manufacturing costs* as *period expenses.* Contrast with *full absorption costing.*

variable costs. *Costs* that change as activity levels change. Strictly speaking, variable costs are zero when the activity level is zero. See *semivariable costs.* In accounting, this term most often means the sum of *direct costs* and variable *overhead.*

variable overhead variance. Difference between actual and *standard variable overhead costs.*

variable rate debt. *Debt* whose interest rate results from the periodic application of a formula, such as "three-month LIBOR [London Interbank Offered Rate] plus 1 percent [one hundred basis points] set on the 8th day of each February, May, August, and November."

variables sampling. The use of a sampling technique in which the sampler infers a particular quantitative characteristic of an entire population from a sample (e.g., mean amount of accounts receivable). See also *estimation sampling.* See *attribute(s) sampling* for contrast and further examples.

variance. Difference between actual and *standard costs* or between *budgeted* and actual *expenditures* or, sometimes, *expenses.* The word has completely different meanings in accounting and in statistics, where it means a measure of dispersion of a distribution.

variance analysis. *Variance investigation.* This term's meaning differs in statistics.

variance investigation. A step in managerial control processes. *Standard costing systems* produce *variance* numbers of various sorts. These numbers seldom exactly equal to zero. Management must decide when a variance differs sufficiently from zero to study its cause. This term refers both to the decision about when to study the cause and to the study itself.

variation analysis. Analysis of the causes of changes in financial statement items of interest such as *net income* or *gross margin.*

VAT (Value-added tax). A tax levied on the market value of a firm's outputs less the market value of its purchased inputs.

vendor. A seller; sometimes spelled "vender."

verifiable. A qualitative *objective* of financial reporting specifying that accountants can trace items in *financial*

statements back to *underlying documents*—supporting *invoices,* canceled *checks,* and other physical pieces of evidence.

verification. The auditor's act of reviewing or checking items in *financial statements* by tracing back to *underlying documents*—supporting *invoices,* canceled *checks,* and other business documents—or sending out *confirmations* to be returned. Compare with *physical verification.*

vertical analysis. Analysis of the financial statements of a single firm or across several firms for a particular time, as opposed to *horizontal* or *time-series analysis,* in which the analyst compares items over time for a single firm or across firms.

vertical integration. The extension of activity by an organization into business directly related to the production or distribution of the organization's end products. Although a firm may sell products to others at various stages, a vertically integrated firm devotes the substantial portion of the output at each stage to the production of the next stage or to end products. Compare *horizontal integration.*

vested. An employee's *pension plan* benefits that are not contingent on the employee's continuing to work for the employer.

visual curve fitting method. One crude form of cost *estimation.* Sometimes, when a firm needs only rough approximations of the amounts of *fixed* and *variable* costs, management need not perform a formal *regression analysis* but can plot the data and draw a line that seems to fit the data. Then it can use the parameters of that line for the rough approximations.

volume variance. *Production volume variance;* less often, used to mean *sales volume variance.*

voucher. A document that signals recognition of a *liability* and authorizes the disbursement of cash; sometimes used to refer to the written evidence documenting an *accounting entry,* as in the term *journal voucher.*

voucher system. In controlling *cash,* a method that requires someone in the firm to authorize each *check* with an approved *voucher.* The firm makes no *disbursements* of currency or coins except from *petty cash funds.*

vouching. The function performed by an *auditor* to ascertain that underlying data or documents support a *journal entry.*

W

wage. Compensation of employees based on time worked or output of product for manual labor. But see *take-home pay.*

warning signal. Tool used to identify quality-control problems; only signals a problem. Contrast with *diagnostic signal,* which both signals a problem and suggests its cause.

warrant. A certificate entitling the owner to buy a specified number of shares at a specified time(s) for a specified price; differs from a *stock option* only in that the firm grants options to employees and issues warrants to the public. See *right.*

warranty. A promise by a seller to correct deficiencies in products sold. When the seller gives warranties, proper accounting practice recognizes an estimate of warranty *expense* and an *estimated liability* at the time of sale. See *guarantee* for contrast in proper usage.

wash sale. The sale and purchase of the same or similar *asset* within a short time period. For *income tax* purposes, the taxpayer may not recognize *losses* on a sale of stock if the taxpayer purchases equivalent stock within 30 days before or after the date of sale.

waste. Material that is a residue from manufacturing operations and that has no sale value. Frequently, this has negative value because a firm must incur additional costs for disposal.

wasting asset. A *natural resource* that has a limited *useful life* and, hence, is subject to *amortization,* called *depletion.* Examples are timberland, oil and gas wells, and ore deposits.

watered stock. Shares issued for *assets* with *fair market price* (*value*) less than *par* or *stated value.* The firm records the assets on the books at the overstated values. In the law, for shares to be considered watered, the *board of directors* must have acted in bad faith or fraudulently in issuing the shares under these circumstances. The term originated from a former practice of cattle owners who fed cattle ("stock") large quantities of salt to make them thirsty. The cattle then drank much water before their owner took them to market. The owners did this to make the cattle appear heavier and more valuable than otherwise.

weighted average. An average computed by counting each occurrence of each value, not merely a single occurrence of each value. For example, if a firm purchases one unit for $1 and two units for $2 each, then the simple average of the purchase prices is $1.50, but the weighted average price per unit is $5/3 = $1.67. Contrast with *moving average.*

weighted-average inventory method. Valuing either *withdrawals* or *ending inventory* at the *weighted-average* purchase price of all units on hand at the time of withdrawal or of computation of ending inventory. The firm uses the *inventory equation* to calculate the other quantity. If a firm uses the *perpetual inventory* method, accountants often call it the *moving average method.*

where-got, where-gone statement. A term allegedly used in the 1920s by W. M. Cole for a statement much like the *statement of cash flows.* Noted accounting historian S. Zeff reports that Cole actually used the term "where-got-gone" statement.

wind up. To bring to an end, such as the life of a corporation. The *board* winds up the life of a corporation by following the winding-up provisions of applicable statutes, by surrendering the charter, or by following *bankruptcy* proceedings. See also *liquidation.*

window dressing. The attempt to make financial statements show *operating* results, or a *financial position,* more favorable than they would otherwise show.

with recourse. See *note receivable discounted.*

withdrawals. *Assets* distributed to an owner. *Partner's drawings.* See *inventory equation* for another context.

withholding. Deductions that are taken from *salaries* or *wages,* usually for *income taxes,* and that the employer remits, in the employee's name, to the taxing authority.

without recourse. See *note receivable discounted.*

work sheet (program). (1) A computer program designed to combine explanations and calculations. This type of program helps in preparing *financial statements* and *schedules.* (2) A tabular schedule for convenient summary of *adjusting* and *closing entries.* The work sheet usually begins with an *unadjusted trial balance.* Adjusting entries appear in the next two columns, one for *debits* and one for *credits.* The work sheet carries the horizontal sum of each line to the right into either the *income statement* or the *balance sheet* column, as appropriate. The *plug* to equate the income statement column totals is, if a debit, the income or, if a credit, a loss for the period. That income will close retained earnings on the balance sheet. The income statement credit columns are the revenues for the period, and the debit columns are the expenses (and revenue contras) that appear on the income statement. "Work sheet" also refers to *schedules* for ascertaining other items that appear on the *financial statements* and that require adjustment or compilation.

working capital. *Current assets* minus *current liabilities;* sometimes called "net working capital" or "net current assets."

work(ing) papers. The schedules and analyses prepared by the *auditor* in carrying out investigations before issuing an *opinion* on *financial statements.*

work-in-process (inventory account). Partially completed product; appears on the balance sheet as *inventory.*

worth. *Value.* See *net worth.*

worth-debt ratio. Reciprocal of the *debt-equity ratio.* See *ratio.*

write down. To *write off,* except that the firm does not charge all the *asset's* cost to *expense* or *loss;* generally used for nonrecurring items.

write off. To *charge* an *asset* to *expense* or *loss;* that is, to *debit* expense (or loss) and *credit* the asset.

write-off method. For treating *uncollectible accounts,* a method that *debits bad debt expense* and *credits* accounts receivable of specific customers as the firm identifies specific accounts as uncollectible. The firm cannot use this method when it can estimate uncollectible amounts and they are significant. See *bad debt expense, sales contra, estimated uncollectibles,* and the *allowance method* for contrast.

write up. To increase the recorded *cost* of an *asset* with no corresponding *disbursement* of *funds;* that is, to *debit* asset and *credit revenue* or, perhaps, *owners' equity;* seldom done in the United States because currently accepted accounting principles await actual transactions before recording asset increases. An exception occurs in accounting for *marketable equity securities.*

Y

yield. *Internal rate of return* of a stream of cash flows. Cash yield is cash flow divided by book value. See also *dividend yield.*

yield curve. The relation between *interest rates* and the term to maturity of loans. Ordinarily, longer-term loans have higher interest rates than shorter-term loans. This is called a "normal" yield curve. Sometimes long-term and short-term rates are approximately the same—a "flat" yield curve. Sometimes short-term loans have a higher rate than long-term ones—an "inverted" yield curve. *Term structure* of interest rates.

yield to maturity. At a given time, the *internal rate of return* of a series of cash flows; usually said of a *bond;* sometimes called the "effective rate."

yield variance. Measures the input-output relation while holding the standard mix of inputs constant: (standard price multiplied by actual amount of input used in the standard mix)—w(standard price multiplied by standard quantity allowed for the actual output). It is the part of the *efficiency variance* not called the *mix variance*.

Z

zero-base(d) budgeting (ZBB). One philosophy for setting budgets. In preparing an ordinary *budget* for the next period, a manager starts with the budget for the current period and makes adjustments as seem necessary because of changed conditions for the next period. Since most managers like to increase the scope of the activities managed and since most prices increase most of the time, amounts in budgets prepared in the ordinary, incremental way seem to increase period after period. The authority approving the budget assumes that managers will carry out operations in the same way as in the past and that next period's expenditures will have to be at least as large as those of the current period. Thus, this authority tends to study only the increments to the current period's budget. In ZBB, the authority questions the process for carrying out a program and the entire budget for the next period. The authority studies every dollar in the budget, not just the dollars incremental to the previous period's amounts. The advocates of ZBB claim that in this way, (1) management will more likely delete programs or divisions of marginal benefit to the business or governmental unit, rather than continuing with costs at least as large as the present ones, and (2) management may discover and implement alternative, more cost-effective ways of carrying out programs. ZBB implies questioning the existence of programs and the fundamental nature of the way that firms carry them out, not merely the amounts used to fund them. Experts appear to divide evenly as to whether the middle word should be "base" or "based."

Index